Benchmark Series

Levels 1 & 2

Microsoft® Excel®

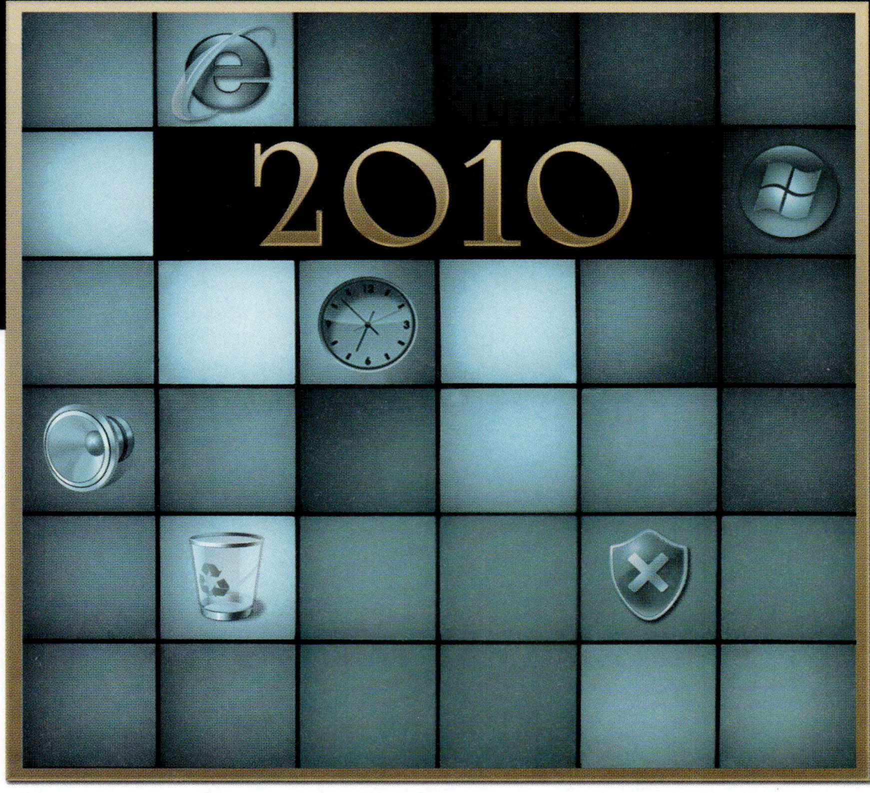

Nita Rutkosky
Pierce College at Puyallup
Puyallup, Washington

Denise Seguin
Fanshawe College
London, Ontario

Audrey Rutkosky Roggenkamp
Pierce College at Puyallup
Puyallup, Washington

St. Paul • Indianapolis

Managing Editor Sonja Brown
Senior Developmental Editor Christine Hurney
Production Editor Donna Mears
Copy Editor Susan Capecchi
Cover and Text Designer Leslie Anderson
Desktop Production Ryan Hamner, Julie Johnston, Jack Ross
Proofreader Laura Nelson
Indexer Sandi Schroeder

Acknowledgements: The authors, editors, and publisher thank the following instructors for their helpful suggestions during the planning and development of the books in the Benchmark Office 2010 Series: Somasheker Akkaladevi, Virginia State University, Petersburg, VA; Ed Baker, Community College of Philadelphia, Philadelphia, PA; Lynn Baldwin, Madison Area Technical College, Madison, WI; Letty Barnes, Lake Washington Technical College, Kirkland, WA; Richard Bell, Coastal Carolina Community College, Jacksonville, NC; Perry Callas, Clatsop Community College, Astoria, OR; Carol DesJardins, St. Clair County Community College, Port Huron, MI; Stacy Gee Hollins, St. Louis Community College--Florissant Valley, St. Louis, MO Sally Haywood, Prairie State College, Chicago Heights, IL; Dr. Penny Johnson, Madison Technical College, Madison, WI; Jan Kehm, Spartanburg Community College, Spartanburg, SC; Jacqueline Larsen, Asheville Buncombe Tech, Asheville, NC; Sherry Lenhart, Terra Community College, Fremont, OH; Andrea Robinson Hinsey, Ivy Tech Community College NE, Fort Wayne, IN; Bari Siddique, University of Texas at Brownsville, Brownsville, TX; Joan Splawski, Northeast Wisconsin Technical College, Green Bay, WI; Diane Stark, Phoenix College, Phoenix, AZ; Mary Van Haute, Northeast Wisconsin Technical College, Green Bay, WI; Rosalie Westerberg, Clover Park Technical College, Lakewood, WA.

The publishing team also thanks the following individuals for their contributions to this project: checking the accuracy of the instruction and exercises—Robertt (Rob) W. Neilly, Traci Post, and Lindsay Ryan; developing lesson plans, supplemental assessments, and supplemental case studies—Jan Davidson, Lambton College, Sarnia, Ontario; writing rubrics to support end-of-chapter and end-of-unit activities—Robertt (Rob) W. Neilly, Seneca College, Toronto, Ontario; writing test item banks—Jeff Johnson; writing online quiz item banks—Trudy Muller; and developing PowerPoint presentations—Janet Blum, Fanshawe College, London, Ontario.

ISBN 978-0-76384-310-6 (Text)
ISBN 978-0-76384-313-7 (Text + CD)

875 Montreal Way
St. Paul, MN 55102
Email: educate@emcp.com
Website: www.emcp.com

Printed in the United States of America

19 18 17 16 15 14 13 12 11 4 5 6 7 8 9 10

Contents

Microsoft Excel 2010 Level 2

Preface

Benchmark Microsoft Excel 2010 is designed for students who want to learn how to use this powerful spreadsheet program to manipulate numerical data in resolving issues related to finances or other numbers-based information. No prior knowledge of spreadsheets is required. After successfully completing a course using this textbook, students will be able to

- Create and edit spreadsheets of varying complexity
- Format cells, columns, and rows as well as entire workbooks in a uniform, attractive style
- Analyze numerical data and project outcomes to make informed decisions
- Plan, research, create, revise, and publish worksheets and workbooks to meet specific communication needs
- Given a workplace scenario requiring a numbers-based solution, assess the information requirements and then prepare the materials that achieve the goal efficiently and effectively

In addition to mastering Excel skills, students will learn the essential features and functions of computer hardware, the Windows 7 operating system, and Internet Explorer 8.0. Upon completing the text, they can expect to be proficient in using Excel to organize, analyze, and present information.

Achieving Proficiency in Excel 2010

Since its inception several Office versions ago, the Benchmark Series has served as a standard of excellence in software instruction. Elements of the book function individually and collectively to create an inviting, comprehensive learning environment that produces successful computer users. The following visual tour highlights the text's features.

UNIT OPENERS display the unit's four chapter titles. Each level has two units, which conclude with a comprehensive unit performance assessment.

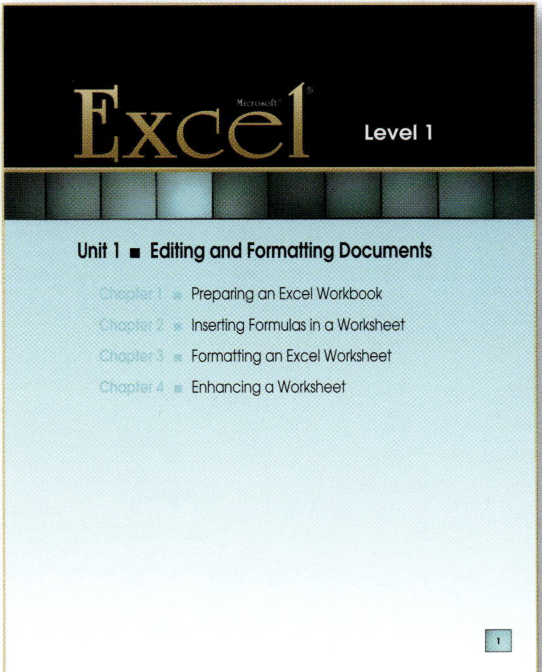

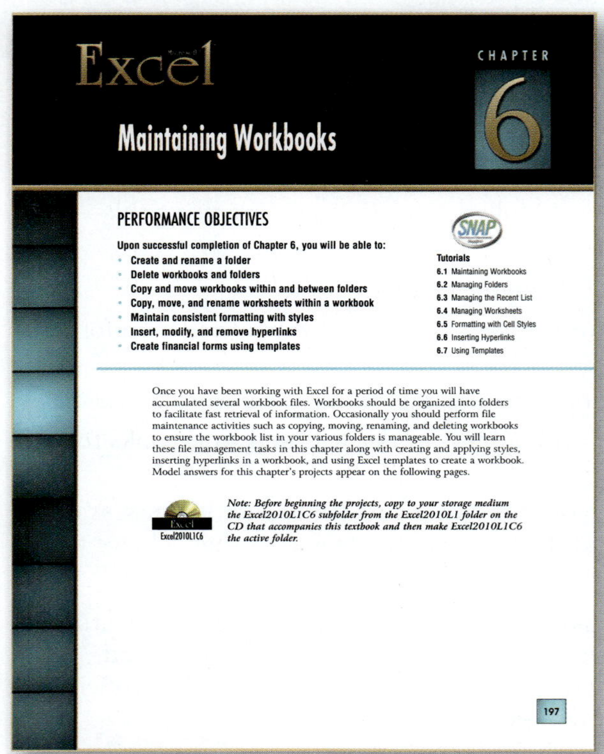

Excel

CHAPTER 6

Maintaining Workbooks

PERFORMANCE OBJECTIVES

Upon successful completion of Chapter 6, you will be able to:

- Create and rename a folder
- Delete workbooks and folders
- Copy and move workbooks within and between folders
- Copy, move, and rename worksheets within a workbook
- Maintain consistent formatting with styles
- Insert, modify, and remove hyperlinks
- Create financial forms using templates

SNAP

Tutorials

6.1 Maintaining Workbooks
6.2 Managing Folders
6.3 Managing the Recent List
6.4 Managing Worksheets
6.5 Formatting with Cell Styles
6.6 Inserting Hyperlinks
6.7 Using Templates

Once you have been working with Excel for a period of time you will have accumulated several workbook files. Workbooks should be organized into folders to facilitate fast retrieval of information. Occasionally you should perform file maintenance activities such as copying, moving, renaming, and deleting workbooks to ensure the workbook list in your various folders is manageable. You will learn these file management tasks in this chapter along with creating and applying styles, inserting hyperlinks in a workbook, and using Excel templates to create a workbook. Model answers for this chapter's projects appear on the following pages.

Excel2010L1C6

Note: Before beginning the projects, copy to your storage medium the Excel2010L1C6 subfolder from the Excel2010L1 folder on the CD that accompanies this textbook and then make Excel2010L1C6 the active folder.

197

CHAPTER OPENERS present the performance objectives and an overview of the skills taught.

SNAP interactive tutorials are available to support chapter-specific skills at www.snap2010.emcp.com.

DATA FILES are provided for each chapter. A prominent note reminds students to copy the appropriate chapter data folder and make it active.

PROJECT APPROACH: Builds Skill Mastery within Realistic Context

MODEL ANSWERS provide a preview of the finished chapter projects and allow students to confirm they have created the materials accurately.

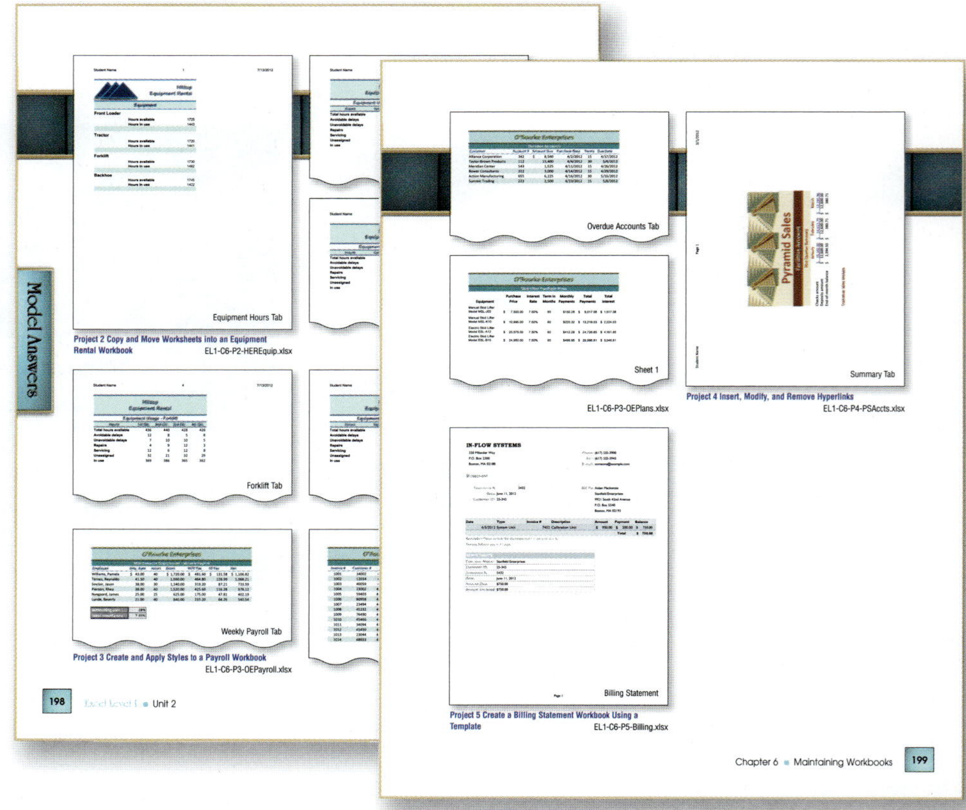

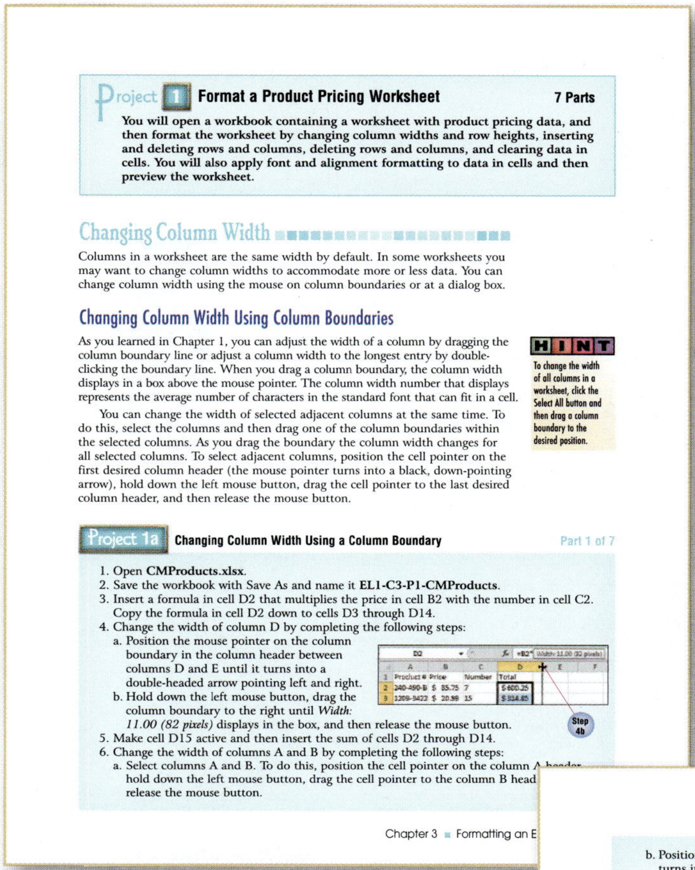

Project 1 **Format a Product Pricing Worksheet** **7 Parts**

You will open a workbook containing a worksheet with product pricing data, and then format the worksheet by changing column widths and row heights, inserting and deleting rows and columns, deleting rows and columns, and clearing data in cells. You will also apply font and alignment formatting to data in cells and then preview the worksheet.

Changing Column Width

Columns in a worksheet are the same width by default. In some worksheets you may want to change column widths to accommodate more or less data. You can change column width using the mouse on column boundaries or at a dialog box.

Changing Column Width Using Column Boundaries

As you learned in Chapter 1, you can adjust the width of a column by dragging the column boundary line or adjust a column width to the longest entry by double-clicking the boundary line. When you drag a column boundary, the column width displays in a box above the mouse pointer. The column width number that displays represents the average number of characters in the standard font that can fit in a cell.

You can change the width of selected adjacent columns at the same time. To do this, select the columns and then drag one of the column boundaries within the selected columns. As you drag the boundary the column width changes for all selected columns. To select adjacent columns, position the cell pointer on the first desired column header (the mouse pointer turns into a black, down-pointing arrow), hold down the left mouse button, drag the cell pointer to the last desired column header, and then release the mouse button.

HINT
To change the width of all columns in a worksheet, click the Select All button and then drag a column boundary to the desired position.

Project 1a **Changing Column Width Using a Column Boundary** Part 1 of 7

1. Open **CMProducts.xlsx**.
2. Save the workbook with Save As and name it **EL1-C3-P1-CMProducts**.
3. Insert a formula in cell D2 that multiplies the price in cell B2 with the number in cell C2. Copy the formula in cell D2 down to cells D3 through D14.
4. Change the width of column D by completing the following steps:
   a. Position the mouse pointer on the column boundary in the column header between columns D and E until it turns into a double-headed arrow pointing left and right.
   b. Hold down the left mouse button, drag the column boundary to the right until *Width: 11.00 (82 pixels)* displays in the box, and then release the mouse button.
5. Make cell D15 active and then insert the sum of cells D2 through D14.
6. Change the width of columns A and B by completing the following steps:
   a. Select columns A and B. To do this, position the cell pointer on the column A header, hold down the left mouse button, drag the cell pointer to the column B head... release the mouse button.

Step 4b

Chapter 3 ■ Formatting an E...

MULTIPART PROJECTS provide a framework for the instruction and practice on software features. A project overview identifies tasks to accomplish and key features to use in completing the work.

STEP-BY-STEP INSTRUCTIONS guide students to the desired outcome for each project part. Screen captures illustrate what the student's screen should look like at key points.

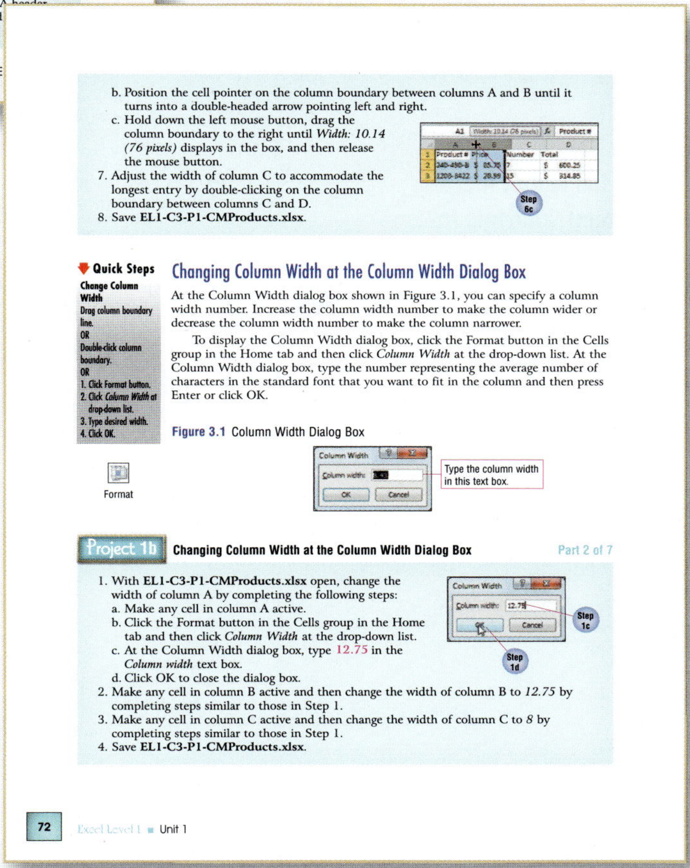

   b. Position the cell pointer on the column boundary between columns A and B until it turns into a double-headed arrow pointing left and right.
   c. Hold down the left mouse button, drag the column boundary to the right until *Width: 10.14 (76 pixels)* displays in the box, and then release the mouse button.
7. Adjust the width of column C to accommodate the longest entry by double-clicking on the column boundary between columns C and D.
8. Save **EL1-C3-P1-CMProducts.xlsx**.

Step 6c

Quick Steps
Change Column Width
Drag column boundary line.
OR
Double-click column boundary.
OR
1. Click Format button.
2. Click *Column Width* at drop-down list.
3. Type desired width.
4. Click OK.

Format

Changing Column Width at the Column Width Dialog Box

At the Column Width dialog box shown in Figure 3.1, you can specify a column width number. Increase the column width number to make the column wider or decrease the column width number to make the column narrower.

To display the Column Width dialog box, click the Format button in the Cells group in the Home tab and then click *Column Width* at the drop-down list. At the Column Width dialog box, type the number representing the average number of characters in the standard font that you want to fit in the column and then press Enter or click OK.

Figure 3.1 Column Width Dialog Box

Type the column width in this text box.

Project 1b **Changing Column Width at the Column Width Dialog Box** Part 2 of 7

1. With **EL1-C3-P1-CMProducts.xlsx** open, change the width of column A by completing the following steps:
   a. Make any cell in column A active.
   b. Click the Format button in the Cells group in the Home tab and then click *Column Width* at the drop-down list.
   c. At the Column Width dialog box, type 12.75 in the *Column width* text box.
   d. Click OK to close the dialog box.
2. Make any cell in column B active and then change the width of column B to *12.75* by completing steps similar to those in Step 1.
3. Make any cell in column C active and then change the width of column C to *8* by completing steps similar to those in Step 1.
4. Save **EL1-C3-P1-CMProducts.xlsx**.

Step 1c

Step 1d

72 Excel Level 1 ■ Unit 1

Between project parts, the text presents instruction on the features and skills necessary to accomplish the next section of the project.

Typically, a file remains open throughout all parts of the project. Students save their work incrementally.

QUICK STEPS provide feature summaries for reference and review.

HINTS provide useful tips on how to use features efficiently and effectively.

MAGENTA TEXT identifies material to type.

At the end of the project, students save, print, and then close the file.

Working with Ranges

A selected group of cells is referred to as a ***range***. A range of cells can be formatted, moved, copied, or deleted. You can also name a range of cells and then move the insertion point to the range or use a named range as part of a formula.

To name a range, select the cells and then click in the Name Box located at the left of the Formula bar. Type a name for the range (do not use a space) and then press Enter. To move the insertion point to a specific range and select the range, click the down-pointing arrow at the right side of the Name Box and then click the range name.

You can also name a range using the Define Name button in the Formulas tab. To do this, click the Formulas tab and then click the Define Name button in the Defined Names group. At the New Name dialog box, type a name for the range and then click OK.

You can use a range name in a formula. For example, if a range is named *Profit* and you want to insert the average of all cells in the *Profit* range, you would make the desired cell active and then type *=AVERAGE(Profit)*. You can use a named range in the current worksheet or in another worksheet within the workbook.

Quick Steps

Name a Range
1. Select cells.
2. Click in Name Box.
3. Type range name.
4. Press Enter.

HINT

Another method for moving to a range is to click the Find & Select button in the Editing group in the Home tab and then click *Go To*. At the Go To dialog box, double-click the range name.

Define Name

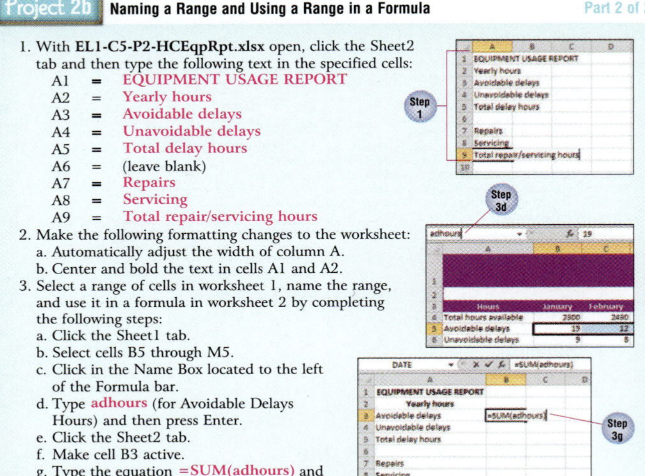

Project 2b **Naming a Range and Using a Range in a Formula** Part 2 of 2

1. With **EL1-C5-P2-HCEqpRpt.xlsx** open, click the Sheet2 tab and then type the following text in the specified cells:
   - A1 = EQUIPMENT USAGE REPORT
   - A2 = Yearly hours
   - A3 = Avoidable delays
   - A4 = Unavoidable delays
   - A5 = Total delay hours
   - A6 = (leave blank)
   - A7 = Repairs
   - A8 = Servicing
   - A9 = Total repair/servicing hours
2. Make the following formatting changes to the worksheet:
   a. Automatically adjust the width of column A.
   b. Center and bold the text in cells A1 and A2.
3. Select a range of cells in worksheet 1, name the range, and use it in a formula in worksheet 2 by completing the following steps:
   a. Click the Sheet1 tab.
   b. Select cells B5 through M5.
   c. Click in the Name Box located to the left of the Formula bar.
   d. Type adhours (for Avoidable Delays Hours) and then press Enter.
   e. Click the Sheet2 tab.
   f. Make cell B3 active.
   g. Type the equation =SUM(adhours) and then press Enter.

Chapter 5 ■ Moving Data within and between Workbooks 177

CHAPTER REVIEW ACTIVITIES: A Hierarchy of Learning Assessments

Chapter Summary

- The Page Setup group in the Page Layout tab contains buttons for changing margins, page orientation and size, and buttons for establishing a print area, inserting a page break, applying a picture background, and printing titles.
- The default left and right margins are 0.7 inch and the default top and bottom margins are 0.75 inch. Change these default margins with the Margins button in the Page Setup group in the Page Layout tab.
- Display the Page Setup dialog box with the Margins tab selected by clicking the Margins button and then clicking *Custom Margins* at the drop-down list.
- Center a worksheet on the page with the *Horizontally* and *Vertically* options at the Page Setup dialog box with the Margins tab selected.
- Click the Orientation button in the Page Setup group in the Page Layout tab to display the two orientation choices — *Portrait* and *Landscape*.
- Insert a page break by selecting the column or row, clicking the Breaks button in the Page Setup group in the Page Layout tab, and then clicking *Insert Page Break* at the drop-down list.
- To insert both a horizontal and vertical page break at the same time, make a cell active, click the Br
down list.
- Display a worksheet in
button in the view area
clicking the Page Break
- Use options at the Page
that you want column
box by clicking the Pri
Layout tab.
- Use options in the Sca
on a specific number o
- Use the Background bu
insert a worksheet back
screen but does not pri
- Use options in the She
want gridlines and hea
- Specify a print area by
in the Page Setup grou
at the drop-down list.
clicking the Print Area
down list.
- Create a header and/or
group in the Insert tab
dialog box with the He
- Customize print jobs w
- To check spelling in a
Spelling button.

CHAPTER SUMMARY captures the purpose and execution of key features.

- Click the Undo button on the Quick Access toolbar to reverse the most recent action and click the Redo button to redo a previously reversed action.
- Use options at the Find and Replace dialog box with the Find tab selected to find specific data and/or formatting in a worksheet.
- Use options at the Find and Replace dialog box with the Replace tab selected to find specific data and/or formatting and replace with other data and/or formatting.
- Sort data in a worksheet with options from the Sort & Filter button in the Editing group in the Home tab.
- Create a custom sort with options at the Sort dialog box. Display this dialog box by clicking the Sort & Filter button and then clicking *Custom Sort* at the drop-down list.
- Use the filter feature to temporarily isolate specific data. Turn on the filter feature by clicking the Sort & Filter button in the Editing group in the Home tab and then clicking *Filter* at the drop-down list. This inserts filter arrows in each column label. Click a filter arrow and then use options at the drop-down list that displays to specify the filter data.

Commands Review

FEATURE	RIBBON TAB, GROUP	BUTTON, OPTION	KEYBOARD SHORTCUT
Margins	Page Layout		
Page Setup dialog box with Margins tab selected	Page Layout		
Orientation	Page Layout		
Size	Page Layout		
Insert page break	Page Layout		
Remove page break	Page Layout		
Page Break Preview	View, Workb		
Page Setup dialog box with Sheet tab selected	Page Layout		
Scale width	Page Layout		
Scale height	Page Layout		
Scale	Page Layout		
Background picture	Page Layout		

COMMANDS REVIEW summarizes visually the major features and alternative methods of access.

FEATURE	RIBBON TAB, GROUP	BUTTON, OPTION	KEYBOARD SHORTCUT
Print Area	Page Layout, Page Setup		
Header and footer	Insert, Text		
Page Layout view	View, Workbook Views		
Spelling	Review, Proofing		F7
Find and Replace dialog box with Find tab selected	Home, Editing	Find	Ctrl + F
Find and Replace dialog box with Replace tab selected	Home, Editing	Replace	Ctrl + H
Sort data	Home, Editing		
Filter data	Home, Editing		

Concepts Check Test Your Knowledge

Completion: In the space provided at the right, indicate the correct term, symbol, or command.

1. This is the default left and right margin measurement. ____________
2. This is the default top and bottom margin measurement. ____________
3. The Margins button is located in this tab. ____________
4. By default, a worksheet prints in this orientation on a page. ____________
5. Click the Print Titles button in the Page Setup group in the Page Layout tab and the Page Setup dialog box displays with this tab selected. ____________
6. Use options in this group in the Page Layout tab to adjust the printed output by a percentage to fit the number of pages specified. ____________
7. Use this button in the Page Setup group in the Page Layout tab to select and print specific areas in a worksheet. ____________
8. Click the Header & Footer button in the Text group in the Insert tab and the worksheet displays in this view. ____________

CONCEPTS CHECK questions assess knowledge recall.

SKILLS CHECK exercises ask students to create a variety of documents using multiple features without how-to directions.

Skills Check Assess Your Performance

Assessment 1
INSERT AVERAGE, MAX, AND MIN FUNCTIONS
1. Open **DISalesAnalysis.xlsx**.
2. Save the workbook with Save As and name it **EL1-C2-A1-DISalesAnalysis**.
3. Use the AVERAGE function to determine the monthly sales (cells H4 through H9).
4. Format cell H4 with the Accounting Number Format with no decimal places.
5. Total each monthly column including the Average column (cells B10 through H10).
6. Use the MAX ... through G10) ...
7. Use the MIN ... through G10) ...
8. Save, print, ar...

Assessment 2
INSERT PMT FUNCT...
1. Open **CMRef**...
2. Save the work...
3. The manager ... either $125,0... total payment... specifications:
   a. Make cell E...
   b. Use the Ins... using the P...
      Rate = ...
      Nper = ...
      Pv = ...
   c. Copy the fo...
4. Insert a formul...
5. Copy the form...
6. Insert a formu... in F5. (The fo...
7. Copy the form...
8. Save, print, ar...

Assessment 3
INSERT FV FUNCTI...
1. Open **RPInve**...
2. Save the work...
3. Make the foll...
   a. Change the...

Assessment 5
APPLY CONDITIONAL FORMATTING TO A SALES WORKBOOK
1. Use Excel Help files or experiment with the options at the Conditional Formatting button drop-down gallery to learn about conditional formatting.
2. Open **PSSales.xlsx** and then save the workbook with Save As and name it **EL1-C6-A5-PSSales**.
3. Select cells D5 through D19 and then use conditional formatting to display the amounts as data bars.
4. Insert a header that prints your name, a page number, and the current date.
5. Save, print, and then close **EL1-C6-A5-PSSales.xlsx**.

Visual Benchmark Demonstrate Your Proficiency

FILL IN AN EXPENSE REPORT FORM
1. Display the New tab Backstage view, click the Sample templates button, and then double-click the *Expense Report* template.
2. With the expense report open, apply the Paper theme.
3. Select cells J1 through L1 and then apply the Note cell style.
4. Type the information in the cells as indicated in Figure 6.9.
5. Make cell L18 active and apply the Bad cell style.
6. Save the completed workbook and name it **EL1-C6-VB-OEExpRpt**.
7. Print and then close **EL1-C6-VB-OEExpRpt.xlsx**.

Figure 6.9 Visual Benchmark

O'Rourke Enterprises

For Office Use Only

Expense Report

PURPOSE: Advertising Media Conference

EMPLOYEE INFORMATION:

Name Sophia Constanza

Department Advertising

Date	Account	Description	Hotel
22-Oct-12	Advertising	Travel to conference	$ 210.00
23-Oct-12	Advertising	Conference/dinner with client	$ 210.00
24-Oct-12	Advertising	Conference	$ 210.00
25-Oct-12	Advertising	Conference	$ 210.00
26-Oct-12	Advertising	Conference	
Total			$ 840.00

APPROVED: Approved by Seth Morgenstern on 10/31/2012

VISUAL BENCHMARK assessments test students' problem-solving skills and mastery of program features.

Case Study Apply Your Skills

Part 1

You are a loan officer for Dollar Wise Financial Services and work in the department that specializes in home loans. You have decided to prepare a sample home mortgage worksheet to show prospective clients. This sample home mortgage worksheet will show the monthly payments on variously priced homes with varying interest rates. Open the **DWMortgages.xlsx** worksheet and then complete the home mortgage worksheet by inserting the following formulas:

- Since many homes in your area sell for at least $400,000, you decide to add that amount to the worksheet with a 5%, 10%, 15%, and 20% down payment.
- In column C, insert a formula that determines the down payment amount.
- In column D, insert a formula that determines the loan amount.
- In column G, insert a formula using the PMT function. (The monthly payment will display as a negative number.)

Save the worksheet and name it **EL1-C2-CS-DWMortgages**.

Part 2

If home buyers put down less than 20 percent of the home's purchase price, mortgage insurance is required. With **EL1-C2-CS-DWMortgages.xlsx** open, insert an IF statement in the cells in column H that inserts the word "No" if the percentage in column B is equal to or greater than 20% or inserts the word "Yes" if the percentage in column B is less than 20%. Save and then print **EL1-C2-CS-DWMortgages.xlsx**.

Part 3

Interest rates fluctuate on a regular basis. Using the resources available to you, determine a current interest rate in your area. Delete the interest rate of 7% in the Dollar Wise worksheet and insert the interest rate for your area. Save and then print **EL1-C2-CS-DWMortgages.xlsx**.

Part 4

Help

When a client is required to purchase mortgage insurance, you would like to provide information to the client concerning this insurance. Use the Help feature to learn about creating hyperlinks in Excel. Locate a helpful website that specializes in private mortgage insurance. Create a hyperlink in the worksheet that will display the website. Save, print, and then close **EL1-C2-CS-DWMortage.xlsx**.

Chapter 2 ■ Inserting Formulas in a Worksheet 67

CASE STUDY requires analyzing a workplace scenario and then planning and executing multipart projects.

Students search the Web and/or use the program's Help feature to locate additional information required to complete the Case Study.

UNIT PERFORMANCE ASSESSMENT: Cross-Disciplinary, Comprehensive Evaluation

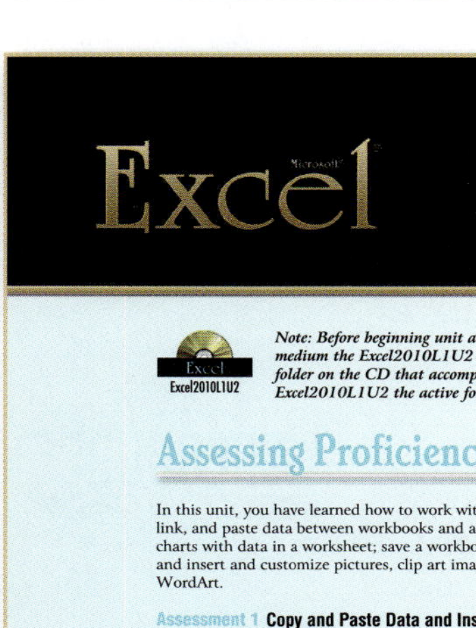

UNIT 2

Performance Assessment

Note: Before beginning unit assessments, copy to your storage medium the Excel2010L1U2 subfolder from the Excel2010L1 folder on the CD that accompanies this textbook and then make Excel2010L1U2 the active folder.

Excel2010L1U2

Assessing Proficiency

In this unit, you have learned how to work with multiple windows; move, copy, link, and paste data between workbooks and applications; create and customize charts with data in a worksheet; save a workbook as a web page; insert hyperlinks; and insert and customize pictures, clip art images, shapes, SmartArt diagrams, and WordArt.

Assessment 1 Copy and Paste Data and Insert WordArt in a Training Scores Workbook

1. Open **RLTraining.xlsx** and then save the workbook with Save As and name it **EL1-U2-A1-RLTraining**.
2. Delete row 15 (the row for *Kwieciak, Kathleen*).
3. Insert a formula in cell D4 that averages the percentages in cells B4 and C4.
4. Copy the formula in cell D4 down to cells D5 through D20.
5. Make cell A22 active, turn on bold, and then type Highest Averages.
6. Display the Clipboard task pane and make sure it is empty.
7. Select and then copy each of the following rows (individually): row 7, 10, 14, 16, and 18.
8. Make cell A23 active and then paste row 14 (the row for *Jewett, Troy*).
9. Make cell A24 active and then paste row 7 (the row for *Cumpston, Kurt*).
10. Make cell A25 active and then paste row 10 (the row for *Fisher-Edwards, Theresa*).
11. Make cell A26 active and then paste row 16 (the row for *Mathias, Caleb*).
12. Make cell A27 active and then paste row 18 (the row for *Nyegaard, Curtis*).
13. Click the Clear All button in the Clipboard task pane and then close the task pane.
14. Insert in cell A1 the text *Roseland* as WordArt. Format the WordArt text to add visual appeal to the worksheet.
15. Save, print, and then close **EL1-U2-A1-RLTraining.xlsx**.

ASSESSING PROFICIENCY checks mastery of features.

WRITING ACTIVITIES involve applying program skills in a communication context.

9	Payroll taxes	2,430.00	2,200.00	91%
10	Telephone	1,450.00	1,500.00	103%
11				

Writing Activities

The following activities give you the opportunity to practice your writing skills along with demonstrating an understanding of some of the important Excel features you have mastered in this unit. Use correct grammar, appropriate word choices, and clear sentence constructions.

Activity 1 Prepare a Projected Budget

You are the accounting assistant in the financial department of McCormack Funds and you have been asked to prepare a yearly proposed department budget. The total amount for the department is $1,450,000. You are given the percentages for the proposed budget items, which are: Salaries, 45%; Benefits, 12%; Training, 14%; Administrative Costs, 10%; Equipment, 11%; and Supplies, 8%. Create a worksheet with this information that shows the projected yearly budget, the budget items in the department, the percentage of the budget, and the amount for each item. After the worksheet is completed, save the workbook and name it **EL1-U2-Act1-MFBudget**. Print and then close the workbook.

Optional: Using Word 2010, write a memo to the McCormack Funds Finance Department explaining that the proposed annual department budget is attached for their review. Comments and suggestions are to be sent to you within one week. Save the file and name it **EL1-U2-Act1-MFMemo**. Print and then close the file.

310 Excel Level 1 ■ Unit 2 Performance Assessment

- Include the following information somewhere in the workshee
  - Book your vacation today at special discount prices.
  - Two-for-one discount at many of the local ski resorts.

Save the workbook and name it **EL1-U2-Act3-CTSkiTrips**. Print an **EL1-U2-Act3-CTSkiTrips.xlsx**.

Internet Research

Find Information on Excel Books and Present the Data in a Worksheet

Locate two companies on the Internet that sell new books. At the first new book company site, locate three books on Microsoft Excel. Record the title, author, and price for each book. At the second new book company site, locate the same three books and record the prices. Create an Excel worksheet that includes the following information:

- Name of each new book company
- Title and author of the three books
- Prices for each book from the two book company sites

Create a hyperlink for each book company to the website on the Internet. Then save the completed workbook and name it **EL1-U2-DR-Books**. Print and then close the workbook.

Excel Level 1 ■ Unit

INTERNET RESEARCH project reinforces research and spreadsheet development skills.

Job Study

Create a Customized Time Card for a Landscaping Company

You are the manager of a landscaping company and are responsible for employee time cards. Locate the time card template that is available with *Sample templates* selected at the New tab Backstage view. Use the template to create a customized time card for your company. With the template open, insert additional blank rows to increase the spacing above the Employee row. Insert a clip art image related to landscaping or gardening and position and size it attractively in the form. Include a text box with the text Lawn and Landscaping Specialists inside the box. Format, size, and position the text attractively in the form. Fill in the form for the current week with the following employee information:

Employee = Jonathan Holder
Address = 12332 South 152nd Street, Baton Rouge, LA 70804
Manager = (Your name)
Employee phone = (225) 555-3092
Employee email = None
Regular hours = 8 hours for Monday, Tuesday, Wednesday, and Thursday
Overtime = 2 hours on Wednesday
Sick hours = None
Vacation = 8 hours on Friday
Rate per hour = $20.00
Overtime pay = $30.00

Save the completed form and name it **EL1-U2-JS-TimeCard**. Print and then close **EL1-U2-JS-TimeCard.xlsx**.

JOB STUDY at the end of Unit 2 presents a capstone assessment requiring critical thinking and problem solving.

Student Courseware

Student Resources CD Each Benchmark Series textbook is packaged with a Student Resources CD containing the data files required for completing the projects and assessments. A CD icon and folder name displayed on the opening page of chapters reminds students to copy a folder of files from the CD to the desired storage medium before beginning the project exercises. Directions for copying folders are printed on the inside back cover.

Internet Resource Center Additional learning tools and reference materials are available at the book-specific website at www.emcp.net/BenchmarkExcel10. Students can access the same files that are on the Student Resources CD along with study aids, web links, and tips for using computers effectively in academic and workplace settings.

SNAP Training and Assessment SNAP is a web-based program offering an interactive venue for learning Microsoft Office 2010, Windows 7, and Internet Explorer 8.0. Along with a web-based learning management system, SNAP provides multimedia tutorials, performance skill items, document-based assessments, a concepts test bank, an online grade book, and a set of course planning tools. A CD of tutorials teaching the basics of Office, Windows, and Internet Explorer is also available if instructors wish to assign additional SNAP tutorial work without using the web-based SNAP program.

eBook For students who prefer studying with an eBook, the texts in the Benchmark Series are available in an electronic form. The web-based, password-protected eBooks feature dynamic navigation tools, including bookmarking, a linked table of contents, and the ability to jump to a specific page. The eBook format also supports helpful study tools, such as highlighting and note taking.

Instructor Resources

Instructor's Guide and Disc Instructor support for the Benchmark Series includes an *Instructor's Guide and Instructor Resources Disc* package. This resource includes planning information, such as Lesson Blueprints, teaching hints, and sample course syllabi; presentation resources, such as PowerPoint slide shows with lecture notes and audio support; and assessment resources, including an overview of available assessment venues, live model answers for chapter activities, and live and PDF model answers for end-of-chapter exercises. Contents of the *Instructor's Guide and Instructor Resources Disc* package are also available on the password-protected section of the Internet Resource Center for this title at www.emcp.net/BenchmarkExcel10.

Computerized Test Generator Instructors can use the EXAMVIEW® Assessment Suite and test banks of multiple-choice items to create customized web-based or print tests.

Blackboard Cartridge This set of files allows instructors to create a personalized Blackboard website for their course and provides course content, tests, and the mechanisms for establishing communication via e-discussions and online group conferences. Available content includes a syllabus, test banks, PowerPoint presentations with audio support, and supplementary course materials. Upon request, the files can be available within 24–48 hours. Hosting the site is the responsibility of the educational institution.

System Requirements

This text is designed for the student to complete projects and assessments on a computer running a standard installation of Microsoft Office 2010, Professional Edition, and the Microsoft Windows 7 operating system. To effectively run this suite and operating system, your computer should be outfitted with the following:

- 1 gigahertz (GHz) processor or higher; 1 gigabyte (GB) of RAM
- DVD drive
- 15 GB of available hard-disk space
- Computer mouse or compatible pointing device

Office 2010 will also operate on computers running the Windows XP Service Pack 3 or the Windows Vista operating system.

Screen captures in this book were created using a screen resolution display setting of 1280 × 800. Refer to the *Customizing Settings* section of *Getting Started in Office 2010* following this preface for instructions on changing your monitor's resolution. Figure G.10 on page 10 shows the Microsoft Office Word ribbon at three resolutions for comparison purposes. Choose the resolution that best matches your computer; however, be aware that using a resolution other than 1280 × 800 means that your screens may not match the illustrations in this book.

About the Authors

Nita Rutkosky began teaching business education courses at Pierce College in Puyallup, Washington, in 1978. Since then she has taught a variety of software applications to students in postsecondary Information Technology certificate and degree programs. In addition to *Benchmark Office 2010,* she has co-authored *Marquee Series: Microsoft Office 2010, 2007,* and *2003; Signature Series: Microsoft Word 2010, 2007,* and *2003;* and *Using Computers in the Medical Office: Microsoft Word, Excel, and PowerPoint 2007* and *2003*. She has also authored textbooks on keyboarding, WordPerfect, desktop publishing, and voice recognition for Paradigm Publishing, Inc.

Denise Seguin has been teaching at Fanshawe College in London, Ontario, since 1986. She has taught a variety of software applications to learners in postsecondary Information Technology diploma programs and in Continuing Education courses. In addition to co-authoring books in the *Benchmark Office 2010* series, she has authored *Microsoft Outlook 2010, 2007, 2003, 2002*, and *2000*. She has also co-authored *Our Digital World*; *Marquee Series: Microsoft Office 2010, 2007,* and *2003*; *Office 2003*; *Office XP*; and *Using Computers in the Medical Office 2007* and *2003* for Paradigm Publishing, Inc.

Audrey Rutkosky Roggenkamp has been teaching courses in the Business Information Technology department at Pierce College in Puyallup since 2005. Her courses have included keyboarding, skill building, and Microsoft Office programs. In addition to this title, she has co-authored *Marquee Series: Microsoft Office 2010* and *2007; Signature Series: Microsoft Word 2010* and *2007;* and *Using Computers in the Medical Office 2007* and *2003* for Paradigm Publishing, Inc.

What is the Microsoft® Office Specialist Program?

The Microsoft Office Specialist Program enables candidates to show that they have something exceptional to offer—proven expertise in certain Microsoft programs. Recognized by businesses and schools around the world, over 4 million certifications have been obtained in over 100 different countries. The Microsoft Office Specialist Program is the only Microsoft-approved certification program of its kind.

What is the Microsoft Office Specialist Certification?

The Microsoft Office Specialist certification validates through the use of exams that you have obtained specific skill sets within the applicable Microsoft Office programs and other Microsoft programs included in the Microsoft Office Specialist Program. Candidates can choose which exam(s) they want to take according to which skills they want to validate.

The available Microsoft Office Specialist Program exams* include:

- Using Windows Vista®
- Using Microsoft® Office Word 2007
- Using Microsoft® Office Word 2007 - Expert
- Using Microsoft® Office Excel® 2007
- Using Microsoft® Office Excel® 2007 - Expert
- Using Microsoft® Office PowerPoint® 2007
- Using Microsoft® Office Access® 2007
- Using Microsoft® Office Outlook® 2007
- Using Microsoft SharePoint® 2007

The Microsoft Office Specialist Program 2010 exams* include:

- Microsoft Word 2010
- Microsoft Word 2010 Expert
- Microsoft Excel® 2010
- Microsoft Excel® 2010 Expert
- Microsoft PowerPoint® 2010
- Microsoft Access® 2010
- Microsoft Outlook® 2010
- Microsoft SharePoint® 2010

What does the Microsoft Office Specialist Approved Courseware logo represent?

The logo indicates that this courseware has been approved by Microsoft to cover the course objectives that will be included in the relevant exam. It also means that after utilizing this courseware, you may be better prepared to pass the exams required to become a certified Microsoft Office Specialist.

For more information:

To learn more about Microsoft Office Specialist exams, visit www.microsoft.com/learning/msbc. To learn about other Microsoft approved courseware from Paradigm Publishing, Inc., visit www.ParadigmCollege.com.

*The availability of Microsoft Office Specialist certification exams varies by Microsoft program, program version, and language. Visit www.microsoft.com/learning for exam availability.

Getting Started in Office 2010

In this textbook, you will learn to operate several computer application programs that combine to make an application "suite." This suite of programs is called Microsoft Office 2010. The programs you will learn to operate are the software, which includes instructions telling the computer what to do. Some of the application programs in the suite include a word processing program named Word, a spreadsheet program named Excel, a database program named Access, and a presentation program named PowerPoint.

Identifying Computer Hardware

The computer equipment you will use to operate the suite of programs is referred to as hardware. You will need access to a microcomputer system that should consist of the CPU, monitor, keyboard, printer, drives, and mouse. If you are not sure what equipment you will be operating, check with your instructor. The computer system shown in Figure G.1 consists of six components. Each component is discussed separately in the material that follows.

Figure G.1 Microcomputer System

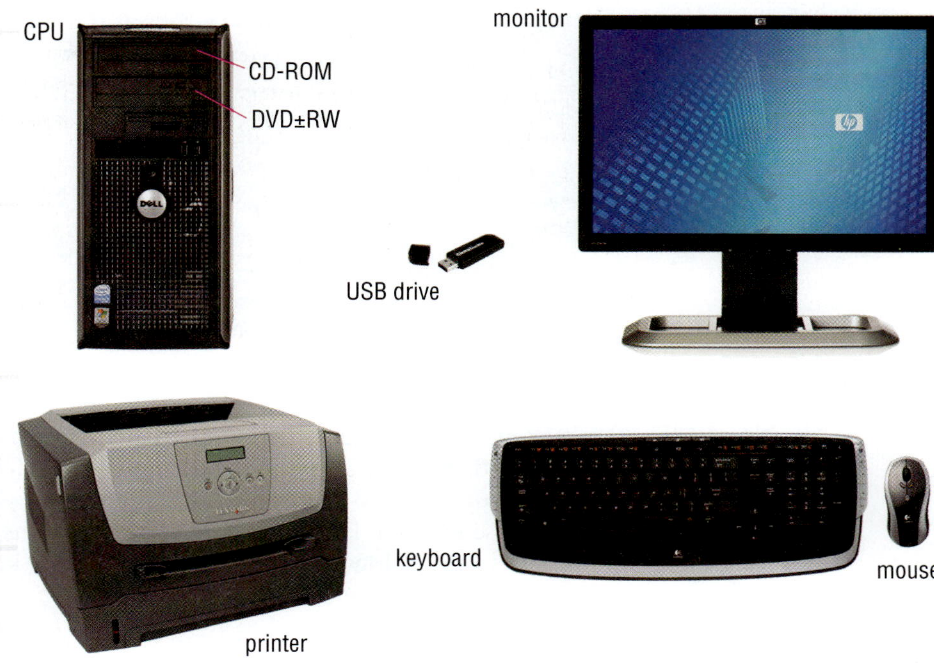

CPU

CPU stands for Central Processing Unit and it is the intelligence of the computer. All the processing occurs in the CPU. Silicon chips, which contain miniaturized circuitry, are placed on boards that are plugged into slots within the CPU. Whenever an instruction is given to the computer, that instruction is processed through circuitry in the CPU.

Monitor

The monitor is a piece of equipment that looks like a television screen. It displays the information of a program and the text being input at the keyboard. The quality of display for monitors varies depending on the type of monitor and the level of resolution. Monitors can also vary in size—generally from 15-inch size up to 26-inch size or larger.

Keyboard

The keyboard is used to input information into the computer. Keyboards for microcomputers vary in the number and location of the keys. Microcomputers have the alphabetic and numeric keys in the same location as the keys on a typewriter. The symbol keys, however, may be placed in a variety of locations, depending on the manufacturer. In addition to letters, numbers, and symbols, most microcomputer keyboards contain function keys, arrow keys, and a numeric keypad. Figure G.2 shows an enhanced keyboard.

Figure G.2 Keyboard

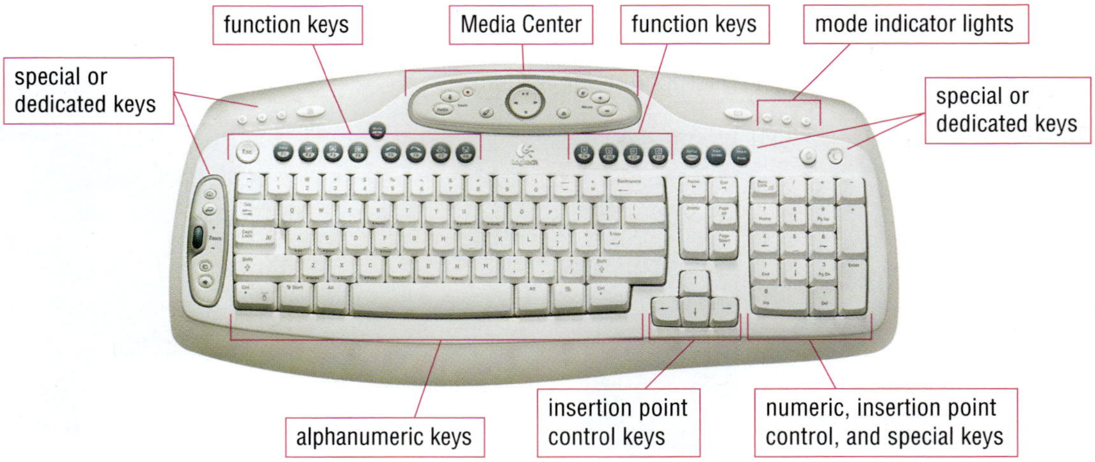

The 12 keys at the top of the keyboard, labeled with the letter F followed by a number, are called ***function keys***. Use these keys to perform functions within each of the suite programs. To the right of the regular keys is a group of ***special*** or ***dedicated keys***. These keys are labeled with specific functions that will be performed when you press the key. Below the special keys are arrow keys. Use these keys to move the insertion point in the document screen.

A keyboard generally includes three mode indicator lights. When you select certain modes, a light appears on the keyboard. For example, if you press the Caps Lock key, which disables the lowercase alphabet, a light appears next to Caps Lock. Similarly, pressing the Num Lock key will disable the special functions on the numeric keypad, which is located at the right side of the keyboard.

Disk Drives

Depending on the computer system you are using, Microsoft Office 2010 is installed on a hard drive or as part of a network system. Whether you are using Office on a hard drive or network system, you will need to have available a DVD or CD drive and a USB drive or other storage medium. You will insert the CD (compact disc) that accompanies this textbook in the DVD or CD drive and then copy folders from the CD to your storage medium. You will also save documents you complete at the computer to folders on your storage medium.

Printer

A document you create in Word is considered soft copy. If you want a hard copy of a document, you need to print it. To print documents you will need to access a printer, which will probably be either a laser printer or an ink-jet printer. A laser printer uses a laser beam combined with heat and pressure to print documents, while an ink-jet printer prints a document by spraying a fine mist of ink on the page.

Mouse

Many functions in the suite of programs are designed to operate more efficiently with a mouse. A mouse is an input device that sits on a flat surface next to the computer. You can operate a mouse with the left or the right hand. Moving the mouse on the flat surface causes a corresponding mouse pointer to move on the screen. Figure G.1 shows an illustration of a mouse.

Using the Mouse

The programs in the Microsoft Office suite can be operated with the keyboard and a mouse. The mouse may have two or three buttons on top, which are tapped to execute specific functions and commands. To use the mouse, rest it on a flat surface or a mouse pad. Put your hand over it with your palm resting on top of the mouse and your wrist resting on the table surface. As you move the mouse on the flat surface, a corresponding pointer moves on the screen.

When using the mouse, you should understand four terms — point, click, double-click, and drag. When operating the mouse, you may need to point to a specific command, button, or icon. Point means to position the mouse pointer on the desired item. With the mouse pointer positioned on the desired item, you may need to click a button on the mouse. Click means quickly tapping a button on the mouse once. To complete two steps at one time, such as choosing and then executing a function, double-click a mouse button. Double-click means to tap the left mouse button twice in quick succession. The term drag means to press and hold the left mouse button, move the mouse pointer to a specific location, and then release the button.

Using the Mouse Pointer

The mouse pointer will change appearance depending on the function being performed or where the pointer is positioned. The mouse pointer may appear as one of the following images:

- The mouse pointer appears as an I-beam (called the I-beam pointer) in the document screen and can be used to move the insertion point or select text.
- The mouse pointer appears as an arrow pointing up and to the left (called the arrow pointer) when it is moved to the Title bar, Quick Access toolbar, ribbon, or an option in a dialog box.
- 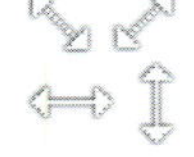The mouse pointer becomes a double-headed arrow (either pointing left and right, pointing up and down, or pointing diagonally) when performing certain functions such as changing the size of an object.
- In certain situations, such as moving an object or image, the mouse pointer displays with a four-headed arrow attached. The four-headed arrow means that you can move the object left, right, up, or down.
- When a request is being processed or when a program is being loaded, the mouse pointer may appear with a circle beside it. The moving circle means "please wait." When the process is completed, the circle is removed.
- The mouse pointer displays as a hand with a pointing index finger in certain functions such as Help and indicates that more information is available about the item. The mouse pointer also displays as a hand when you hover the mouse over a hyperlink.

Choosing Commands

Once a program is open, you can use several methods in the program to choose commands. A command is an instruction that tells the program to do something. You can choose a command using the mouse or the keyboard. When a program such as Word or PowerPoint is open, the ribbon contains buttons for completing tasks and contains tabs you click to display additional buttons. To choose a button on the Quick Access toolbar or in the ribbon, position the tip of the mouse arrow pointer on a button and then click the left mouse button.

The Office suite provides access keys you can press to use a command in a program. Press the Alt key on the keyboard to display KeyTips that identify the access key you need to press to execute a command. For example, press the Alt key in a Word document with the Home tab active and KeyTips display as shown in Figure G.3. Continue pressing access keys until you execute the desired command. For example, if you want to begin spell checking a document, you would press the Alt key, press the R key on the keyboard to display the Review tab, and then press the letter S on the keyboard.

Choosing Commands from Drop-Down Lists

To choose a command from a drop-down list with the mouse, position the mouse pointer on the desired option and then click the left mouse button. To make a selection from a drop-down list with the keyboard, type the underlined letter in the desired option.

Figure G.3 Word Home Tab KeyTips

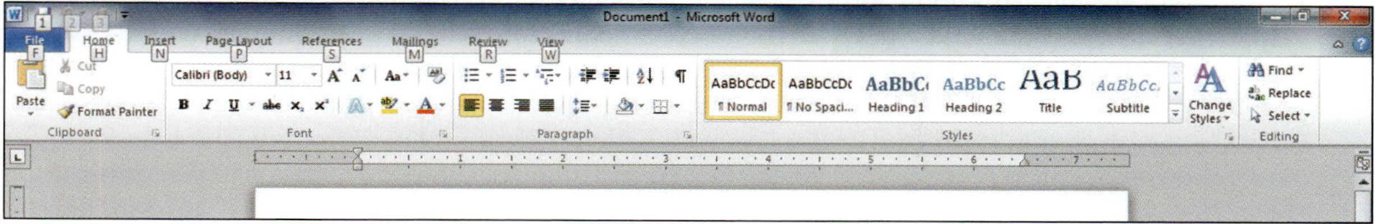

Some options at a drop-down list may be gray-shaded (dimmed), indicating that the option is currently unavailable. If an option at a drop-down list displays preceded by a check mark, that indicates that the option is currently active. If an option at a drop-down list displays followed by an ellipsis (...), a dialog box will display when that option is chosen.

Choosing Options from a Dialog Box

A dialog box contains options for applying formatting to a file or data within a file. Some dialog boxes display with tabs along the top providing additional options. For example, the Font dialog box shown in Figure G.4 contains two tabs — the Font tab and the Advanced tab. The tab that displays in the front is the active tab. To make a tab active using the mouse, position the arrow pointer on the desired tab and then click the left mouse button. If you are using the keyboard, press Ctrl + Tab or press Alt + the underlined letter on the desired tab.

Figure G.4 Word Font Dialog Box

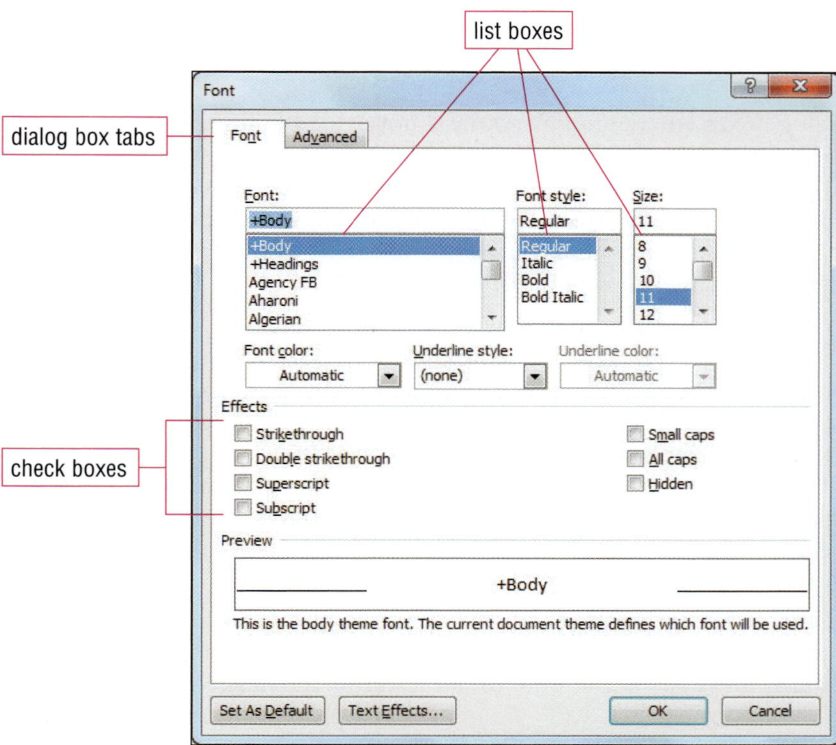

To choose options from a dialog box with the mouse, position the arrow pointer on the desired option and then click the left mouse button. If you are using the keyboard, press the Tab key to move the insertion point forward from option to option. Press Shift + Tab to move the insertion point backward from option to option. You can also hold down the Alt key and then press the underlined letter of the desired option. When an option is selected, it displays with a blue background or surrounded by a dashed box called a marquee. A dialog box contains one or more of the following elements: text boxes, list boxes, check boxes, option buttons, measurement boxes, and command buttons.

List Boxes

Some dialog boxes such as the Word Font dialog box shown in Figure G.4 may contain a list box. The list of fonts below the *Font* option is contained in a list box. To make a selection from a list box with the mouse, move the arrow pointer to the desired option and then click the left mouse button.

Some list boxes may contain a scroll bar. This scroll bar will display at the right side of the list box (a vertical scroll bar) or at the bottom of the list box (a horizontal scroll bar). You can use a vertical scroll bar or a horizontal scroll bar to move through the list if the list is longer than the box. To move down through a list on a vertical scroll bar, position the arrow pointer on the down-pointing arrow and hold down the left mouse button. To scroll up through the list in a vertical scroll bar, position the arrow pointer on the up-pointing arrow and hold down the left mouse button. You can also move the arrow pointer above the scroll box and click the left mouse button to scroll up the list or move the arrow pointer below the scroll box and click the left mouse button to move down the list. To move through a list with a horizontal scroll bar, click the left-pointing arrow to scroll to the left of the list or click the right-pointing arrow to scroll to the right of the list.

To make a selection from a list using the keyboard, move the insertion point into the box by holding down the Alt key and pressing the underlined letter of the desired option. Press the Up and/or Down Arrow keys on the keyboard to move through the list.

In some dialog boxes where enough room is not available for a list box, lists of options are inserted in a drop-down list box. Options that contain a drop-down list box display with a down-pointing arrow. For example, the *Underline style* option at the Word Font dialog box shown in Figure G.4 contains a drop-down list. To display the list, click the down-pointing arrow to the right of the *Underline style* option box. If you are using the keyboard, press Alt + U.

Check Boxes

Some dialog boxes contain options preceded by a box. A check mark may or may not appear in the box. The Word Font dialog box shown in Figure G.4 displays a variety of check boxes within the *Effects* section. If a check mark appears in the box, the option is active (turned on). If the check box does not contain a check mark, the option is inactive (turned off). Any number of check boxes can be active. For example, in the Word Font dialog box, you can insert a check mark in any or all of the boxes in the *Effects* section and these options will be active.

To make a check box active or inactive with the mouse, position the tip of the arrow pointer in the check box and then click the left mouse button. If you are using the keyboard, press Alt + the underlined letter of the desired option.

Text Boxes

Some options in a dialog box require you to enter text. For example, the boxes below the *Find what* and *Replace with* options at the Excel Find and Replace dialog box shown in Figure G.5 are text boxes. In a text box, you type text or edit existing text. Edit text in a text box in the same manner as normal text. Use the Left and Right Arrow keys on the keyboard to move the insertion point without deleting text and use the Delete key or Backspace key to delete text.

Option Buttons

The Word Insert Table dialog box shown in Figure G.6 contains options in the *AutoFit behavior* section preceded by option buttons. Only one option button can be selected at any time. When an option button is selected, a blue circle displays in the button. To select an option button with the mouse, position the tip of the arrow pointer inside the option button and then click the left mouse button. To make a selection with the keyboard, hold down the Alt key and then press the underlined letter of the desired option.

Measurement Boxes

Some options in a dialog box contain measurements or numbers you can increase or decrease. These options are generally located in a measurement box. For example, the Word Paragraph dialog box shown in Figure G.7 contains the *Left*, *Right*, *Before*, and *After* measurement boxes. To increase a number in a measurement box, position the tip of the arrow pointer on the up-pointing arrow to the right of the desired option and then click the left mouse button. To decrease the number, click the down-pointing arrow. If you are using the keyboard, press Alt + the underlined letter of the desired option and then press the Up Arrow key to increase the number or the Down Arrow key to decrease the number.

Command Buttons

In the Excel Find and Replace dialog box shown in Figure G.5, the boxes along the bottom of the dialog box are called command buttons. Use a command button to execute or cancel a command. Some command buttons display with an ellipsis (...). A command button that displays with an ellipsis will open another dialog box. To choose a command button with the mouse, position the arrow pointer on the desired button and then click the left mouse button. To choose a command button with the keyboard, press the Tab key until the desired command button contains the marquee and then press the Enter key.

Figure G.5 Excel Find and Replace Dialog Box

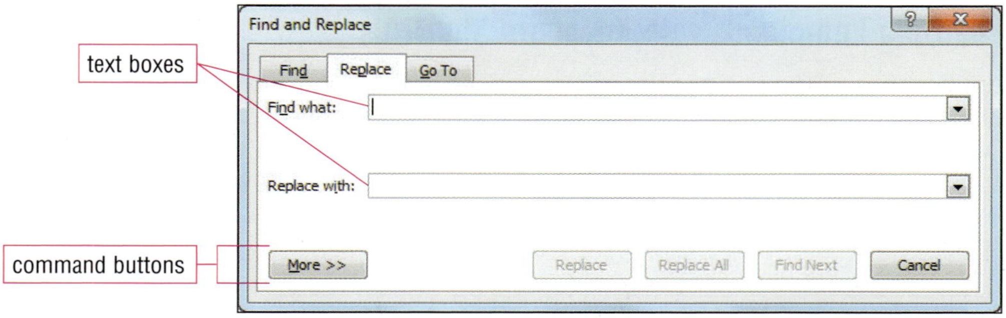

Figure G.6 Word Insert Table Dialog Box

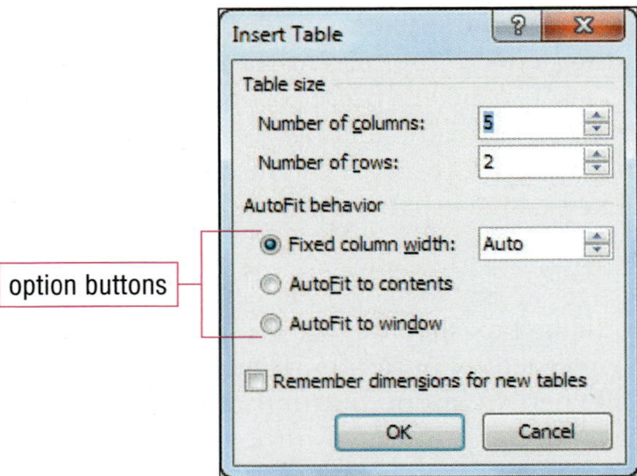

Figure G.7 Word Paragraph Dialog Box

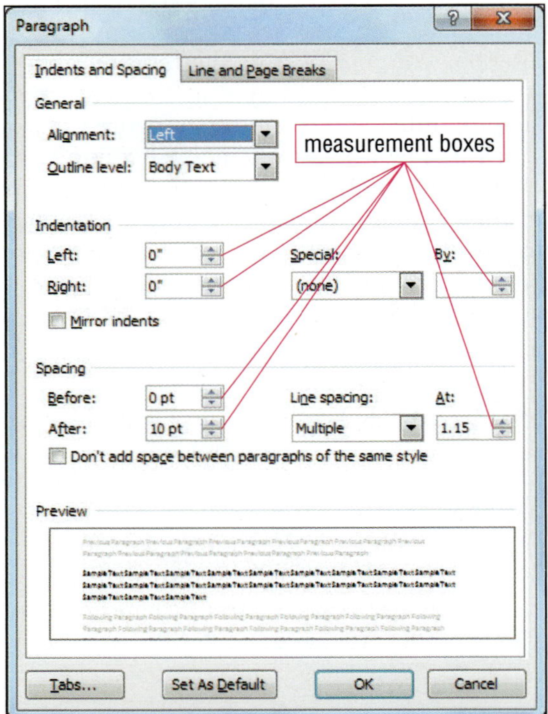

Choosing Commands with Keyboard Shortcuts

Applications in the Office suite offer a variety of keyboard shortcuts you can use to execute specific commands. Keyboard shortcuts generally require two or more keys. For example, the keyboard shortcut to display the Open dialog box in an application is Ctrl + O. To use this keyboard shortcut, hold down the Ctrl key, type the letter O on the keyboard, and then release the Ctrl key. For a list of keyboard shortcuts, refer to the Help files.

Choosing Commands with Shortcut Menus

The software programs in the suite include menus that contain commands related to the item with which you are working. A shortcut menu appears in the file in the location where you are working. To display a shortcut menu, click the right mouse button or press Shift + F10. For example, if the insertion point is positioned in a paragraph of text in a Word document, clicking the right mouse button or pressing Shift + F10 will cause the shortcut menu shown in Figure G.8 to display in the document screen (along with the Mini toolbar).

To select an option from a shortcut menu with the mouse, click the desired option. If you are using the keyboard, press the Up or Down Arrow key until the desired option is selected and then press the Enter key. To close a shortcut menu without choosing an option, click anywhere outside the shortcut menu or press the Esc key.

Working with Multiple Programs

As you learn the various programs in the Microsoft Office suite, you will notice how executing commands in each is very similar. For example, the steps to save, close, and print are virtually the same whether you are working in Word, Excel, or PowerPoint. This consistency between programs greatly enhances a user's ability to transfer knowledge learned in one program to another within the suite. Another appeal of Microsoft Office is the ability to have more than one program open at the same time. For example, you can open Word, create a document, and then open Excel, create a spreadsheet, and copy the spreadsheet into Word.

Figure G.8 Word Shortcut Menu

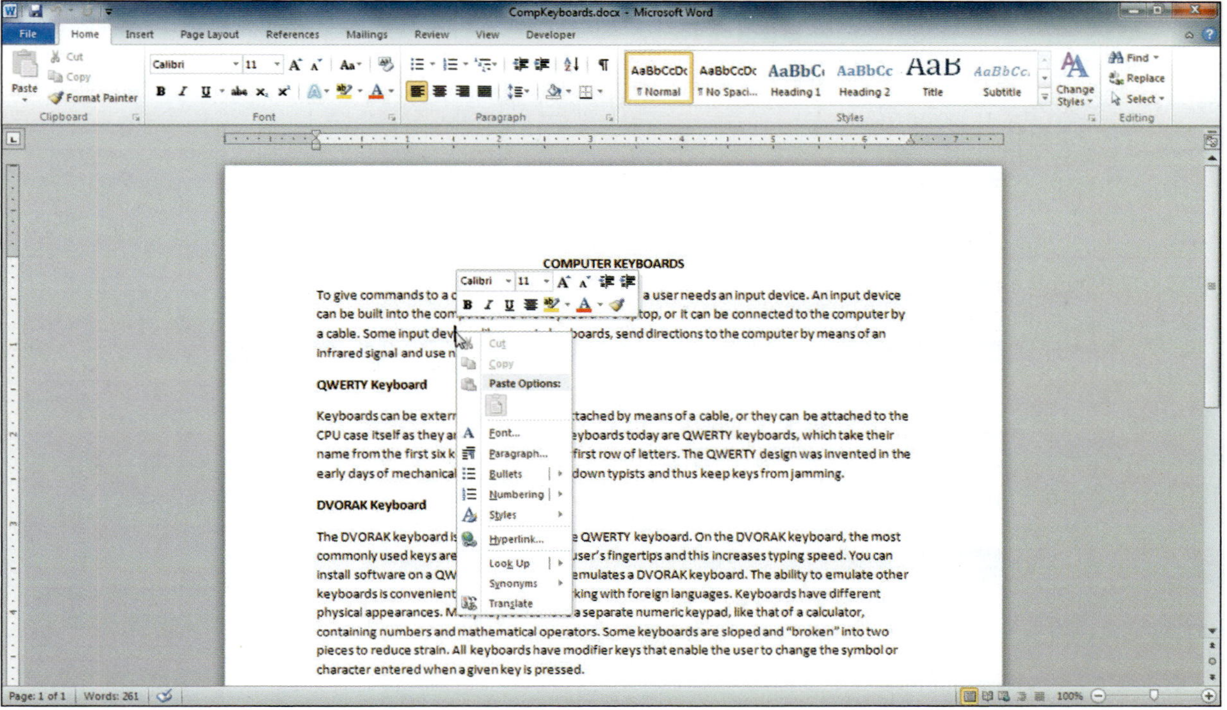

Figure G.9 Taskbar with Word, Excel, and PowerPoint Open

When you open a program, a button displays on the Taskbar containing an icon representing the program. If you open another program, a button containing an icon representing the program displays to the right of the first program button. Figure G.9 shows the Taskbar with Word, Excel, and PowerPoint open. To move from one program to another, click the button on the Taskbar representing the desired program file.

Customizing Settings

Before beginning computer projects in this textbook, you may need to customize the monitor settings and turn on the display of file extensions. Projects in the chapters in this textbook assume that the monitor display is set at 1280 by 800 pixels and that the display of file extensions is turned on.

Changing Monitor Resolutions

Before you begin learning the applications in the Microsoft Office 2010 suite, take a moment to check the display settings on the computer you are using. The ribbon in the Microsoft Office suite adjusts to the screen resolution setting of your computer monitor. Computer monitors set at a high resolution will have the ability to show more buttons in the ribbon than will a monitor set to a low resolution. The illustrations in this textbook were created with a screen resolution display set at 1280 × 800 pixels. In Figure G.10 the Word ribbon is shown three ways: at a lower screen resolution (1024 × 768 pixels), at the screen resolution featured

Figure G.10 Monitor Resolution

1024 × 768 screen resolution

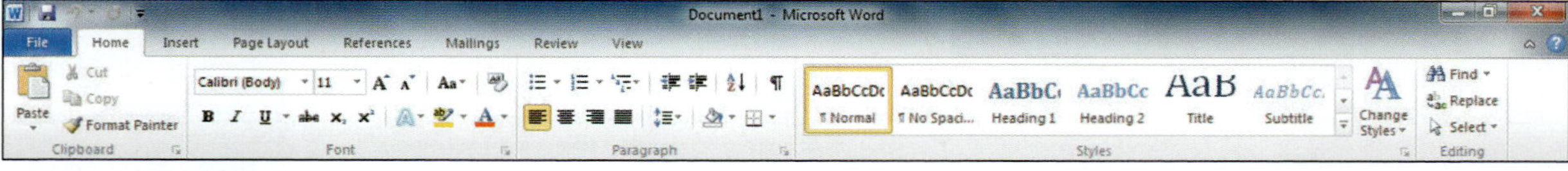

1280 × 800 screen resolution

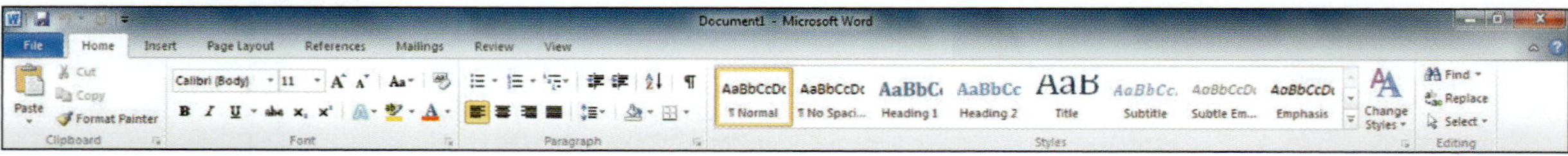

1440 × 900 screen resolution

throughout this textbook, and at a higher screen resolution (1440 × 900 pixels). Note the variances in the ribbon in all three examples. If possible, set your display to 1280 × 800 pixels to match the illustrations you will see in this textbook.

Project 1 Setting Monitor Display to 1280 by 800

1. At the Windows 7 desktop, click the Start button and then click *Control Panel*.
2. At the Control Panel dialog box, click the *Adjust screen resolution* option in the Appearance and Personalization category.
3. At the Control Panel Screen Resolution window, click the Resolution option button. (This displays a drop-down slider bar. Your drop-down slider bar may display differently than what you see in the image at the right.)
4. Drag the slider bar button on the slider bar until *1280 × 800* displays to the right of the slider button.
5. Click in the Control Panel Screen Resolution window to remove the slider bar.
6. Click the Apply button.
7. Click the Keep Changes button.
8. Click the OK button.
9. Close the Control Panel window.

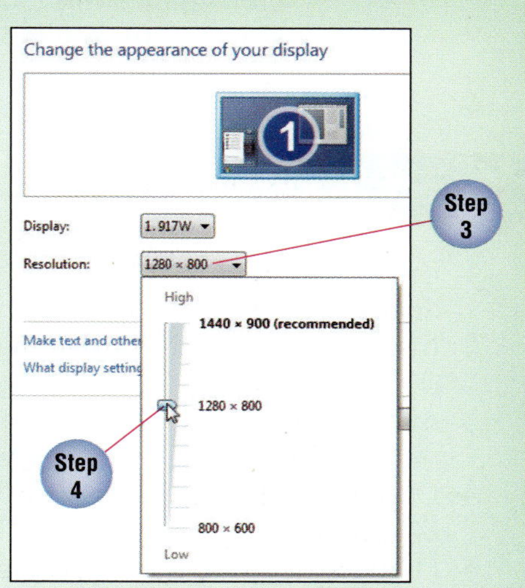

Project 2 Displaying File Extensions

1. At the Windows 7 desktop, click the Start button and then click *Computer*.
2. At the Computer window, click the Organize button on the toolbar and then click *Folder and search options* at the drop-down list.
3. At the Folder Options dialog box, click the View tab.
4. Click the *Hide extensions for known file types* check box to remove the check mark.
5. Click the Apply button.
6. Click the OK button.
7. Close the Computer window.

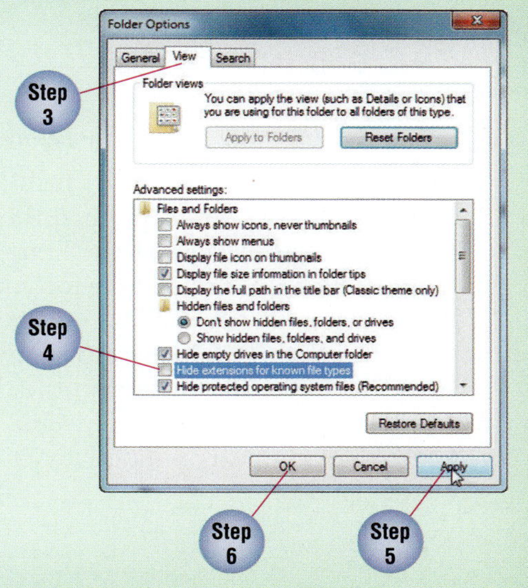

Completing Computer Projects

Some computer projects in this textbook require that you open an existing file. Project files are saved on the Student Resources CD that accompanies this textbook. The files you need for each chapter are saved in individual folders. Before beginning a chapter, copy the necessary folder from the CD to your storage medium (such as a USB flash drive) using the Computer window. If storage capacity is an issue with your storage medium, delete any previous chapter folders before copying a chapter folder onto your storage medium.

Project 3 Copying a Folder from the Student Resources CD

1. Insert the CD that accompanies this textbook in the CD drive. At the AutoPlay window that displays, click the Close button located in the upper right corner of the window.
2. Insert your USB flash drive in an available USB port. If an AutoPlay window displays, click the Close button.
3. At the Windows desktop, open the Computer window by clicking the Start button and then clicking *Computer* at the Start menu.
4. Double-click the CD drive in the Content pane (displays with the name *BM10StudentResources* preceded by the drive letter).
5. Double-click the desired program folder name in the Content pane.
6. Click once on the desired chapter subfolder name to select it.
7. Click the Organize button on the toolbar and then click *Copy* at the drop-down list.
8. In the Computer window Content pane, click the drive containing your storage medium.
9. Click the Organize button on the toolbar and then click *Paste* at the drop-down list.
10. Close the Computer window by clicking the Close button located in the upper right corner of the window.

Project 4 Deleting a Folder

Note: Check with your instructor before deleting a folder.

1. Insert your storage medium (such as a USB flash drive) in the USB port.
2. At the Windows desktop, open the Computer window by clicking the Start button and then clicking *Computer* at the Start menu.
3. Double-click the drive letter for your storage medium (drive containing your USB flash drive such as *Removable Disk (F:)*).
4. Click the chapter folder in the Content pane.
5. Click the Organize button on the toolbar and then click *Delete* at the drop-down list.
6. At the message asking if you want to delete the folder, click the Yes button.
7. Close the Computer window by clicking the Close button located in the upper right corner of the window.

Using Windows 7

A computer requires an operating system to provide necessary instructions on a multitude of processes including loading programs, managing data, directing the flow of information to peripheral equipment, and displaying information. Windows 7 is an operating system that provides functions of this type (along with much more) in a graphical environment. Windows is referred to as a ***graphical user interface*** (GUI—pronounced *gooey*) that provides a visual display of information with features such as icons (pictures) and buttons. In this introduction, you will learn these basic features of Windows 7:

- Use desktop icons and the Taskbar to launch programs and open files or folders
- Add and remove gadgets
- Organize and manage data, including copying, moving, creating, and deleting files and folders; and create a shortcut
- Explore the Control Panel and personalize the desktop
- Use the Windows Help and Support features
- Use search tools
- Customize monitor settings

Before using one of the software programs in the Microsoft Office suite, you will need to start the Windows 7 operating system. To do this, turn on the computer. Depending on your computer equipment configuration, you may also need to turn on the monitor and printer. If you are using a computer that is part of a network system or if your computer is set up for multiple users, a screen will display showing the user accounts defined for your computer system. At this screen, click your user account name and, if necessary, type your password and then press the Enter key. The Windows 7 operating system will start and, after a few moments, the desktop will display as shown in Figure W.1. (Your desktop may vary from what you see in Figure W.1.)

Exploring the Desktop

When Windows is loaded, the main portion of the screen is called the ***desktop***. Think of the desktop in Windows as the top of a desk in an office. A business person places necessary tools—such as pencils, pens, paper, files, calculator—on the desktop to perform functions. Like the tools that are located on a desk, the desktop contains tools for operating the computer. These tools are logically grouped and placed in dialog boxes or panels that you can display using icons on the desktop. The desktop contains a variety of features for using your computer and software programs installed on the computer. The features available on the desktop are represented by icons and buttons.

Figure W.1 Windows 7 Desktop

Using Icons

Icons are visual symbols that represent programs, files, or folders. Figure W.1 identifies the Recycle Bin icon located on the Windows desktop. The Windows desktop on your computer may contain additional icons. Programs that have been installed on your computer may be represented by an icon on the desktop. Also, icons may display on your desktop representing files or folders. Double-click an icon and the program, file, or folder it represents opens on the desktop.

Using the Taskbar

The bar that displays at the bottom of the desktop (see Figure W.1) is called the Taskbar. The Taskbar, shown in Figure W.2, contains the Start button, pinned items, a section that displays task buttons representing active tasks, the notification area, and the Show Desktop button.

Figure W.2 Windows 7 Taskbar

Click the Start button, located at the left side of the Taskbar, and the Start menu displays as shown in Figure W.3 (your Start menu may vary). You can also display the Start menu by pressing the Windows key on your keyboard or by pressing Ctrl + Esc. The left side of the Start menu contains links to the most recently and frequently used programs. The name of the currently logged on user displays at the top of the darker right portion of the menu followed by the user's libraries. The two sections below the personal libraries provide links to other Windows features, such as games, the Control Panel, and Windows Help and Support. Use the Shut down button to put the system in a power-conserving state or into a locked, shut down, or sleep mode.

To choose an option from the Start menu, drag the arrow pointer to the desired option (referred to as ***pointing***) and then click the left mouse button. Pointing to options at the Start menu that are followed by a right-pointing arrow will cause a side menu to display with additional options. When a program is open, a task button representing the program appears on the Taskbar. If multiple programs are open, each program will appear as a task button on the Taskbar (a few specialized tools may not).

Manipulating Windows

When you open a program, a defined work area displays on the screen, which is referred to as a ***window***. A Title bar displays at the top of a window and contains buttons at the right side for closing the window and minimizing, maximizing, and restoring the size of the window. You can open more than one window at a time and the open windows can be cascaded or stacked. Windows 7 contains a Snap feature that causes a window to "stick" to the edge of the screen when the window

Figure W.3 Start Menu

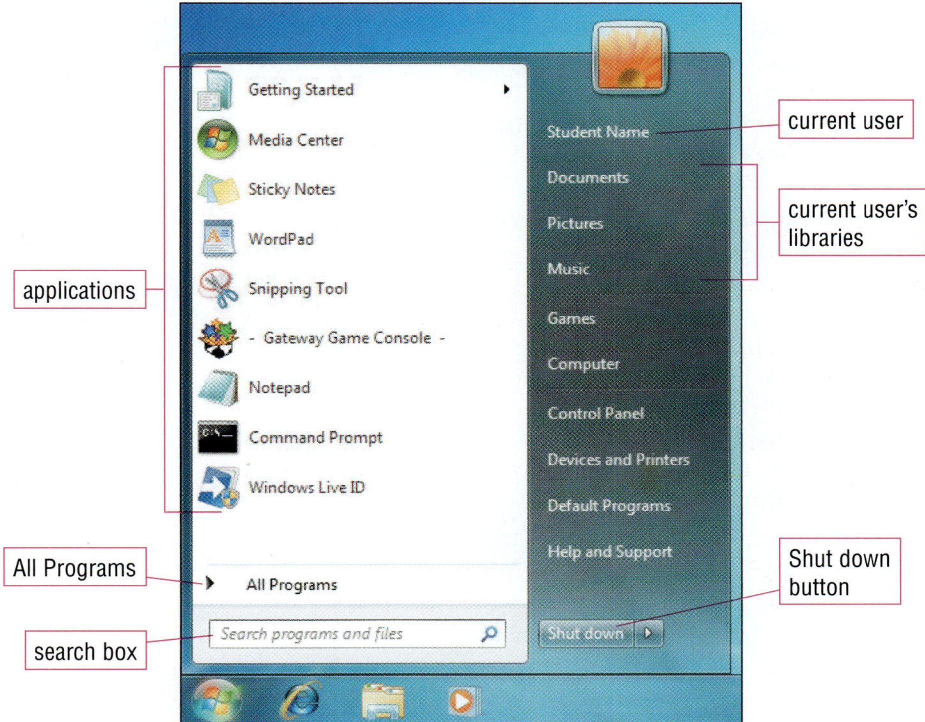

is moved to the left or right side of the screen. Move a window to the top of the screen and the window is automatically maximized. If you drag down a maximized window, the window is automatically restored down.

In addition to moving and sizing a window, you can change the display of all open windows. To do this, position the mouse pointer on the Taskbar and then click the right mouse button and a pop-up list displays with options for displaying multiple open windows. You can cascade the windows, stack the windows, and display the windows side by side.

Project 1 Opening Programs, Switching between Programs, and Manipulating Windows

1. Open Windows 7. (To do this, turn on the computer and, if necessary, turn on the monitor and/or printer. If you are using a computer that is part of a network system or if your computer is set up for multiple users, you may need to click your user account name and, if necessary, type your password and then press the Enter key. Check with your instructor to determine if you need to complete any additional steps.)
2. When the Windows 7 desktop displays, open Microsoft Word by completing the following steps:
   a. Position the arrow pointer on the Start button on the Taskbar and then click the left mouse button.
   b. At the Start menu, click *All Programs* and then click *Microsoft Office* (this displays programs in the Office suite below Microsoft Office).
   c. Drag the arrow pointer down to *Microsoft Word 2010* and then click the left mouse button.
   d. When the Microsoft Word program is open, notice that a task button representing Word displays on the Taskbar.

Step 2d

3. Open Microsoft Excel by completing the following steps:
   a. Position the arrow pointer on the Start button on the Taskbar and then click the left mouse button.
   b. At the Start menu, click *All Programs* and then click *Microsoft Office*.
   c. Drag the arrow pointer down to *Microsoft Excel 2010* and then click the left mouse button.
   d. When the Microsoft Excel program is open, notice that a task button representing Excel displays on the Taskbar to the right of the task button representing Word.
4. Switch to the Word program by clicking the task button on the Taskbar representing Word.
5. Switch to the Excel program by clicking the task button on the Taskbar representing Excel.

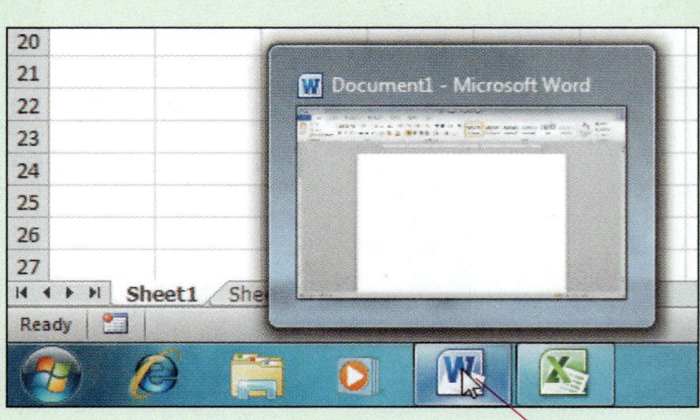

6. Restore down the Excel window by clicking the Restore Down button that displays immediately left of the Close button in the upper right corner of the screen. (This reduces the Excel window so it displays along the bottom half of the screen.)
7. Restore down the Word window by clicking the Restore Down button located immediately left of the Close button in the upper right corner of the screen.
8. Position the mouse pointer on the Word window Title bar, hold down the left mouse button, drag to the left side of the screen until an outline of the window displays in the left half of the screen, and then release the mouse button. (This "sticks" the window to the left side of the screen.)
9. Position the mouse pointer on the Excel window Title bar, hold down the left mouse button, drag to the right until an outline of the window displays in the right half of the screen, and then release the mouse button.
10. Minimize the Excel window by clicking the Minimize button that displays in the upper right corner of the Excel window Title bar.
11. Hover your mouse over the Excel button on the Taskbar and notice the Excel window thumbnail that displays above the button and then click the thumbnail. (This displays the Excel window at the right side of the screen.)
12. Cascade the Word and Excel windows by positioning the arrow pointer on an empty area on the Taskbar, clicking the right mouse button, and then clicking *Cascade windows* at the pop-up list.
13. After viewing the windows cascaded, display them stacked by right-clicking an empty area on the Taskbar and then clicking *Show windows stacked* at the pop-up list.
14. Display the desktop by right-clicking an empty area on the Taskbar and then clicking *Show the desktop* at the pop-up list.
15. Display the windows stacked by right-clicking an empty area on the Taskbar and then clicking *Show open windows* at the pop-up list.
16. Position the mouse pointer on the Word window Title bar, hold down the left mouse button, drag the window to the top of the screen, and then release the mouse button. This maximizes the Word window so it fills the screen.
17. Close the Word window by clicking the Close button located in the upper right corner of the window.
18. At the Excel window, click the Maximize button located immediately left of the Close button in the upper right corner of the Excel window.
19. Close the Excel window by clicking the Close button located in the upper right corner of the window.

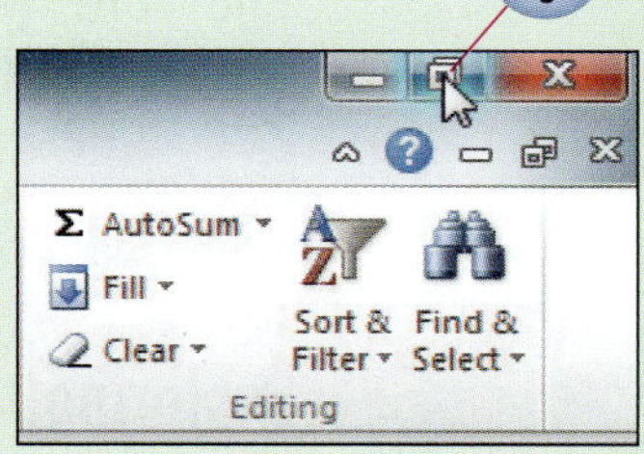

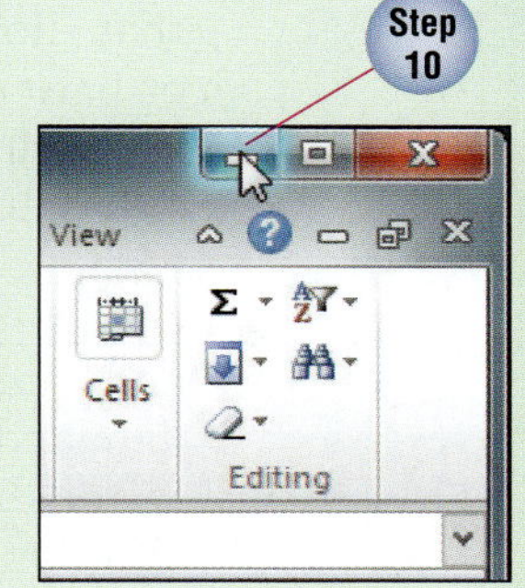

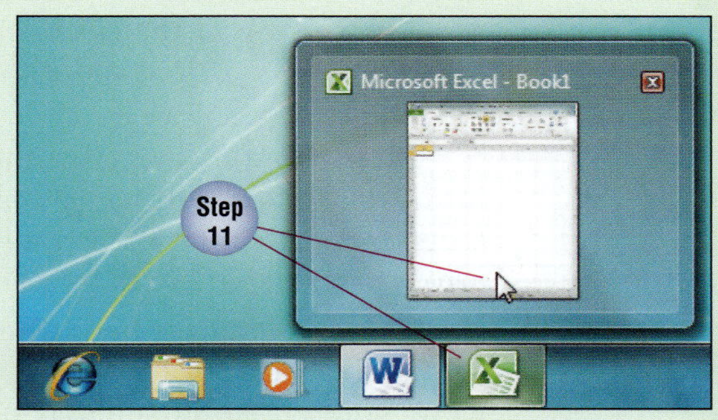

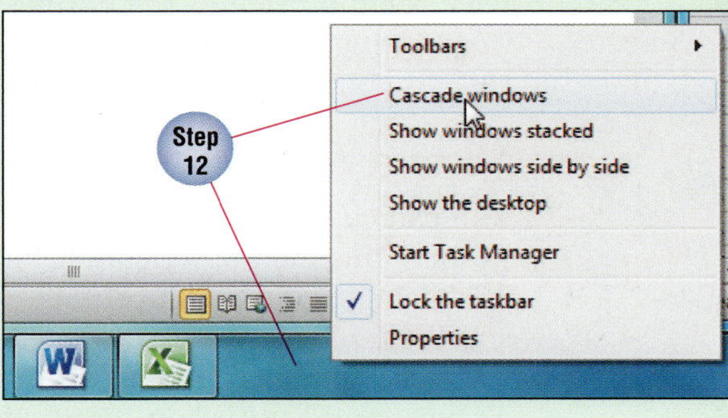

Using the Pinned Area

The icons that display immediately right of the Start button are pinned programs. Clicking an icon opens the program associated with the icon. Click the first icon to open the Internet Explorer web browser, click the second icon to open a window containing Libraries, and click the third icon to open the Windows media player window.

Exploring the Notification Area

The notification area is located at the right side of the Taskbar and contains icons that show the status of certain system functions such as a network connection or battery power. It also contains icons you can use to manage certain programs and Windows 7 features. The notification area also contains the system clock and date. Click the time or date in the notification area and a window displays with a clock and a calendar of the current month. Click the Change date and time settings hyperlink that displays at the bottom of the window and the Date and Time dialog box displays. To change the date and/or time, click the Change date and time button and the Date and Time Settings dialog box displays similar to the dialog box shown in Figure W.4. (If a dialog box displays telling you that Windows needs your permission to continue, click the Continue button.)

Change the month and year by clicking the left-pointing or right-pointing arrow at the top of the calendar in the *Date* section. Click the left-pointing arrow to display the previous month(s) and click the right-pointing arrow to display the next month(s).

To change the day, click the desired day in the monthly calendar that displays in the dialog box. To change the time, double-click either the hour, minute, or seconds and then type the appropriate time or use the up- and down-pointing arrows in the spin boxes to adjust the time.

Some programs, when installed, will add an icon to the notification area of the Taskbar. Display the name of the icon by positioning the mouse pointer on the icon and, after approximately one second, the icon label displays. If more icons have been inserted in the notification area than can be viewed at one time, an up-pointing arrow button displays at the left side of the notification area. Click this up-pointing arrow button and the remaining icons display.

Setting Taskbar Properties

You can customize the Taskbar with options from the Taskbar shortcut menu. Display this menu by right-clicking on an empty portion of the Taskbar. The Taskbar shortcut menu contains options for turning on or off the display of specific toolbars, specifying the display of multiple windows, displaying the Start Task Manager dialog box, locking or unlocking the Taskbar, and displaying the Taskbar and Start Menu Properties dialog box.

With options in the Taskbar and Start Menu Properties dialog box shown in Figure W.5, you can change settings for the Taskbar as well as the Start menu. Display this dialog box by right-clicking on an empty area on the Taskbar and then clicking *Properties* at the shortcut menu.

Each property is controlled by a check box. Property options containing a check mark are active. Click the option to remove the check mark and make the option inactive. If an option is inactive, clicking the option will insert a check mark in the check box and turn on the option (make it active).

Figure W.4 Date and Time Settings Dialog Box

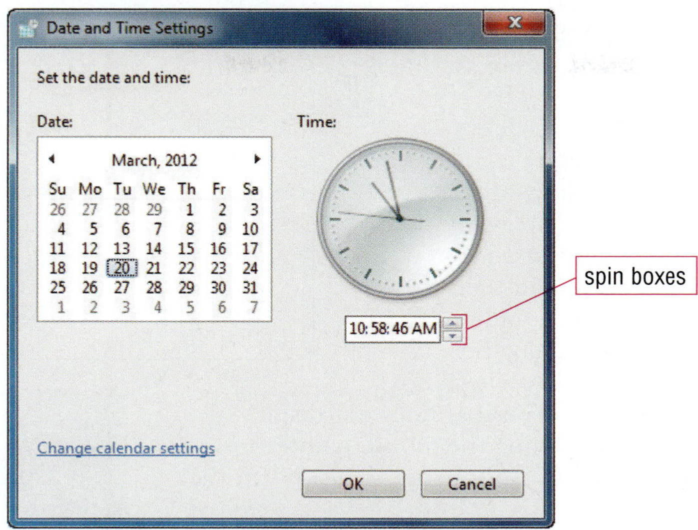

Figure W.5 Taskbar and Start Menu Properties Dialog Box

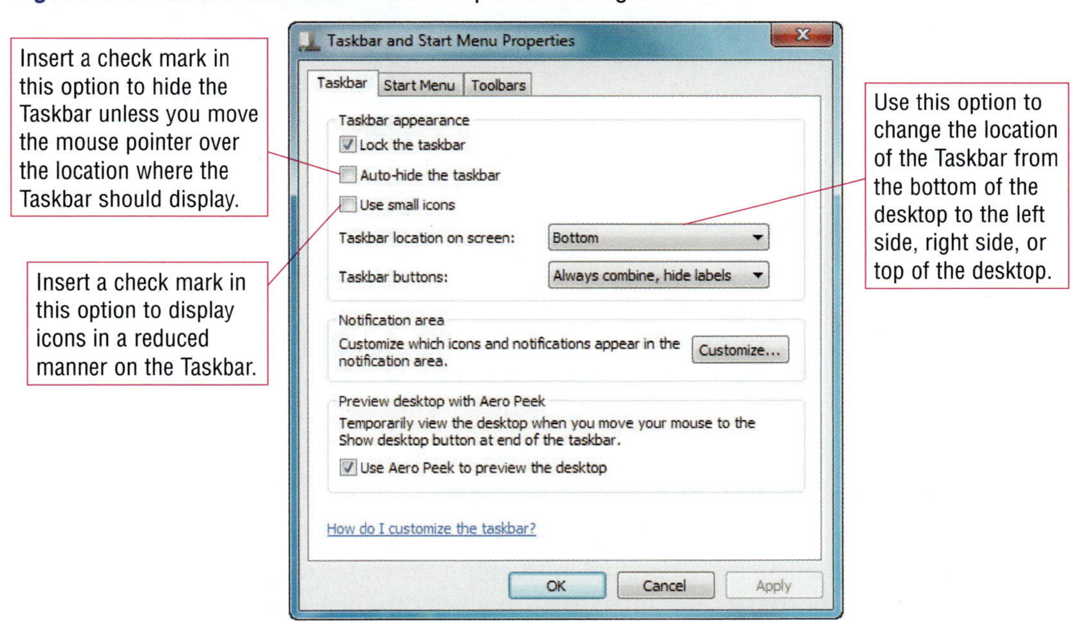

Project 2 Changing Taskbar Properties

1. Make sure the Windows 7 desktop displays.
2. Change Taskbar properties by completing the following steps:
   a. Position the arrow pointer on any empty area on the Taskbar and then click the right mouse button.
   b. At the shortcut menu that displays, click *Properties*.

c. At the Taskbar and Start Menu Properties dialog box, click the *Auto-hide the taskbar* check box to insert a check mark.
d. Click the *Use small icons* check box to insert a check mark.
e. Click the button (displays with the word *Bottom*) that displays at the right side of the *Taskbar location on screen* option and then click *Right* at the drop-down list.
f. Click OK to close the dialog box.

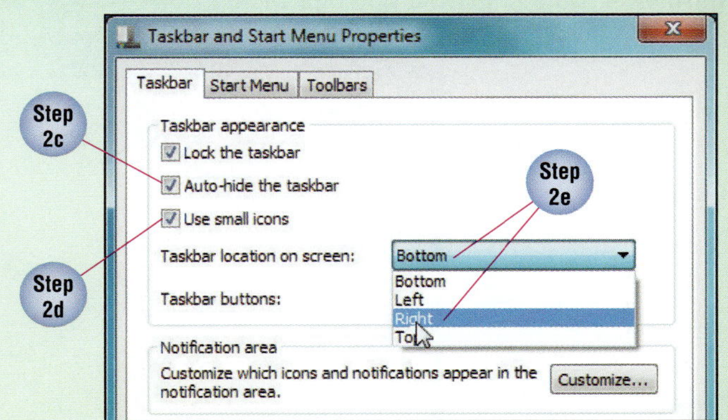

3. Since the *Auto-hide the taskbar* check box contains a check mark, the Taskbar does not display. Display the Taskbar by moving the mouse pointer to the right side of the screen. Notice that the icons on the Taskbar are smaller.
4. Return to the default settings for the Taskbar by completing the following steps:
   a. Move the mouse pointer to the right side of the screen to display the Taskbar.
   b. Right-click any empty area on the Taskbar and then click *Properties* at the shortcut menu.
   c. Click the *Auto-hide the taskbar* check box to remove the check mark.
   d. Click the *Use small icons* check box to remove the check mark.
   e. Click the button (displays with the word *Right*) that displays at the right side of the *Taskbar location on screen* option and then click *Bottom* at the drop-down list.
   f. Click OK to close the dialog box.

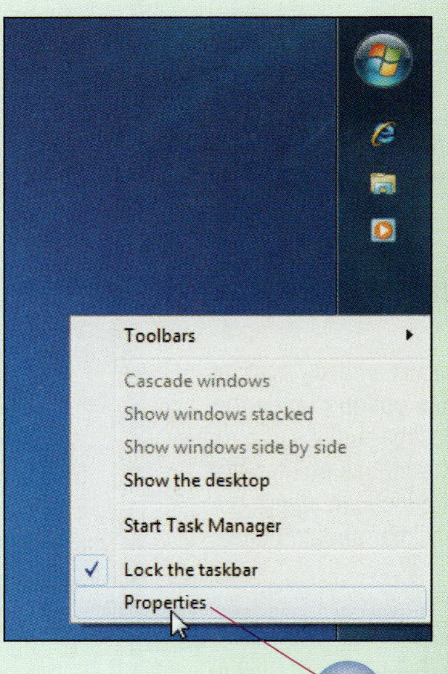

Powering Down the Computer

If you want to shut down Windows, close any open programs, click the Start button on the Taskbar, and then click the Shut down button as shown in Figure W.6. Click the button containing a right-pointing triangle that displays at the right side of the Shut down button and a drop-down list displays with options for powering down the computer.

In a multi-user environment, click the *Switch user* option to change users or click the *Log off* option to log off your computer, which shuts down your applications and files and makes system resources available to other users logged on to the system. If you need to walk away from your computer and you want to protect your work, consider locking the computer by clicking the *Lock* option. When you lock the computer, the desktop is hidden but the system is not shut down and the power is not conserved. To unlock the computer, click the icon on the desktop representing your account, type your password, and then press Enter. Click the *Restart* option to shut down and then restart the computer and click

Figure W.6 Shut Down Button and Power Options Button

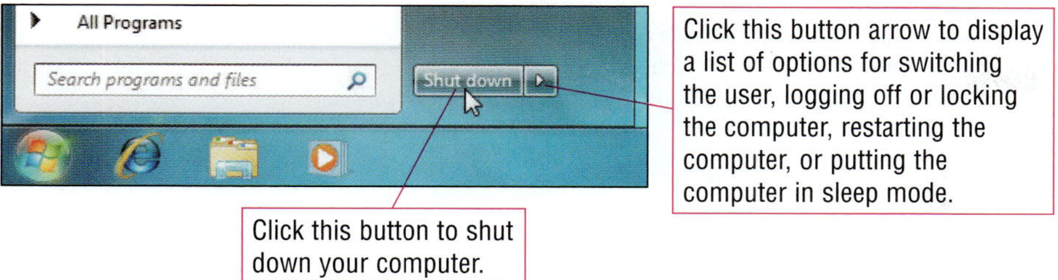
All Programs
Search programs and files
Shut down
Click this button arrow to display a list of options for switching the user, logging off or locking the computer, restarting the computer, or putting the computer in sleep mode.
Click this button to shut down your computer.

the *Sleep* option to save power without having to close all files and applications. In sleep mode, Windows saves files and information about programs and then powers down the computer to a low-power state. To "wake" the computer back up, quickly press the computer's power button.

Using Gadgets

You can add gadgets to your desktop. A gadget is a mini program providing information at a glance and easy access to frequently used tools. For example, you can add a Clock gadget to your desktop that shows the current time, a Weather gadget that displays the current temperature where you live, or a Calendar gadget that displays the current date. Gadgets are added to the Sidebar, which is a location at the right side of the Windows 7 desktop.

To view available gadgets, right-click in a blank area on the desktop and then click *Gadgets* at the shortcut menu. This displays the gadget gallery similar to what you see in Figure W.7. To add a gadget to the Sidebar, double-click the desired gadget. To remove a gadget from the Sidebar, hover the mouse pointer over the gadget and then click the Close button that displays at the upper right side of the gadget. ***Note: The Gadget option on the shortcut menu may be missing if the computer you are using is located in a school setting where customization options have been disabled. If you do not see* Gadget *on the shortcut menu, please skip Project 3.***

Figure W.7 Gadget Gallery

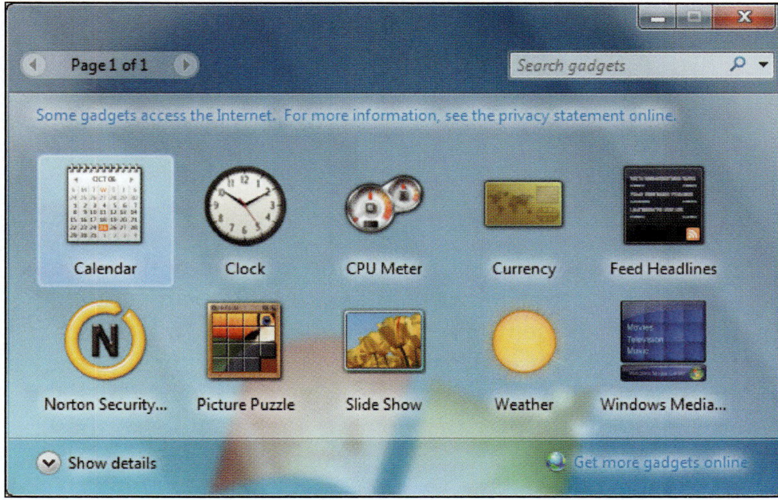
Page 1 of 1
Search gadgets
Some gadgets access the Internet. For more information, see the privacy statement online.
Calendar
Clock
CPU Meter
Currency
Feed Headlines
Norton Security...
Picture Puzzle
Slide Show
Weather
Windows Media...
Show details
Get more gadgets online

Project 3 Adding and Removing Gadgets

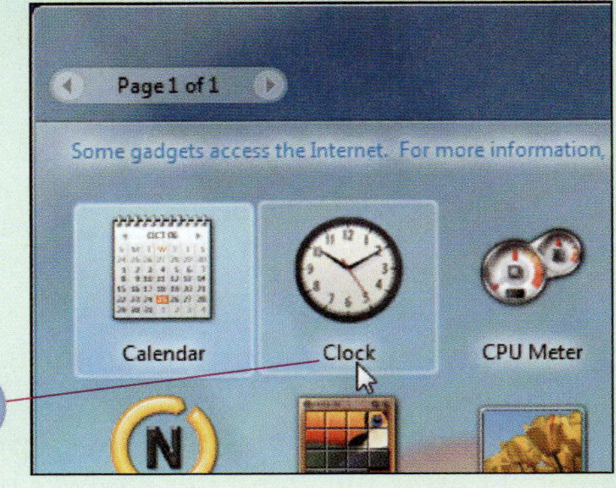

1. At the Windows 7 desktop, right-click in a blank area on the desktop and then click *Gadgets* at the shortcut menu.
2. At the Gadgets Gallery, double-click the *Clock* gadget.
3. Double-click the *Weather* gadget.
4. Double-click the *Calendar* gadget.
5. Close the Gadget Gallery by clicking the Close button located in the upper right corner of the gallery.
6. Hover your mouse over the Calendar gadget until buttons display at the right side of the gadget and then click the Larger size button. (This expands the calendar to display the days of the month.)
7. Hover your mouse over the Weather gadget and then click the Options button.
8. At the Weather dialog box that displays, type in the *Select current location* text box the name of your city followed by your state (or province) and then press Enter.
9. If a drop-down list displays with city names, scroll down the list to display your city and then click your city and state (or province).
10. Click OK to close the Weather dialog box.
11. After viewing the gadgets, remove the Clock gadget by hovering the mouse over the clock and then clicking the Close button that displays at the upper right side of the clock.
12. Close the Weather gadget by hovering the mouse over the gadget and then clicking the Close button that displays.
13. Close the Calendar gadget by hovering the mouse over the gadget and then clicking the Close button that displays.

Managing Files and Folders

As you begin working with programs in Windows 7, you will create files in which data (information) is saved. A file might contain a Word document, an Excel workbook, or a PowerPoint presentation. As you begin creating files, consider creating folders into which those files will be stored. You can complete file management tasks such as creating a folder and copying and moving files and folders at the Computer window. To display the Computer window shown in Figure W.8, click the Start button on the Taskbar and then click *Computer*. The various components of the Computer window are identified in Figure W.8.

Figure W.8 Computer Window

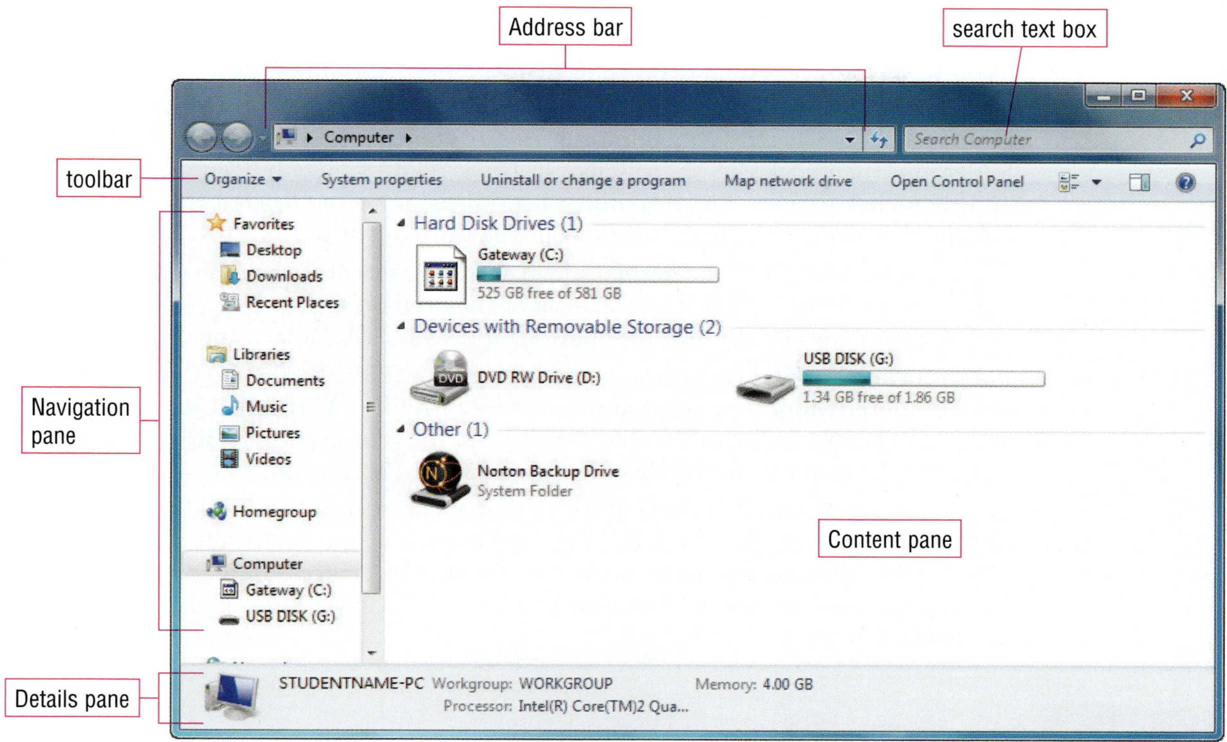

In the Content pane of the Computer window, icons display representing each hard disk drive and removable storage medium such as a CD, DVD, or USB device connected to your computer. Next to each storage device icon, Windows provides the amount of storage space available as well as a bar with the amount of used space shaded with color. This visual cue allows you to see at a glance the proportion of space available relative to the capacity of the device. Double-click a device icon in the Content pane to change the display to show the contents stored on the device. You can display contents from another device or folder using the Navigation pane or the Address bar on the Computer window.

Copying, Moving, and Deleting Files and Folders

File and folder management activities might include copying and moving files or folders from one folder or drive to another, or deleting files or folders. The Computer window offers a variety of methods for copying, moving, and deleting files and folders. This section will provide you with steps for copying, moving, and deleting files and folders using options from the Organize button on the toolbar and the shortcut menu.

To copy a file to another folder or drive, first display the file in the Content pane by identifying the location of the file. If the file is located in the Documents folder, click the *Documents* folder in the *Libraries* section in the Navigation pane and then click the file name in the Content pane that you want to copy. Click the Organize button on the toolbar and then click *Copy* at the drop-down list. In the Navigation pane, click the location where you want to copy the file. Click the Organize button and then click *Paste* at the drop-down list. You would complete similar steps to copy and paste a folder to another location.

If the desired file is located on a storage medium such as a CD, DVD, or USB device, double-click the device in the section of the Content pane labeled *Devices with Removable Storage*. (Each removable device is assigned an alphabetic drive letter by Windows, usually starting at F or G and continuing through the alphabet depending on the number of removable devices that are currently in use.) After double-clicking the storage medium in the Content pane, navigate to the desired folder and then click the file to select it. Click the Organize button on the toolbar and then click *Copy* at the drop-down list. Navigate to the desired folder, click the Organize button, and then click *Paste* at the drop-down list.

To move a file, click the desired file in the Content pane, click the Organize button on the toolbar, and then click *Cut* at the drop-down list. Navigate to the desired location, click the Organize button, and then click *Paste* at the drop-down list.

To delete a file(s) or folder(s), click the file or folder in the Content pane in the Computer window or select multiple files or folders. Click the Organize button and then click *Delete* at the drop-down list. At the message asking if you want to move the file or folder to the Recycle Bin, click the Yes button.

In Project 4, you will insert the CD that accompanies this book into the DVD or CD drive. When the CD is inserted, the drive may automatically activate and a dialog box may display telling you that the disc or device contains more than one type of content and asking what you want Windows to do. If this dialog box displays, click the Cancel button.

Project 4 Copying a File and Folder and Deleting a File

1. Insert the CD that accompanies this textbook into the appropriate drive. If a dialog box displays telling you that the disc or device contains more than one type of content and asking what you want Windows to do, click the Cancel button.
2. Insert your storage medium (such as a USB flash drive) in the USB port (or other drive). If an AutoPlay window displays, click the Close button.
3. At the Windows 7 desktop, click the Start button and then click *Computer* located at the right side of the Start menu.
4. Copy a file from the CD that accompanies this textbook to the drive containing your storage medium by completing the following steps:
   a. Double-click the CD drive in the Content pane containing the CD from the book.
   b. Double-click the *StudentDataFiles* folder in the Content pane.
   c. Double-click the *Windows7* folder in the Content pane.
   d. Click ***WordDocument01.docx*** in the Content pane.
   e. Click the Organize button on the toolbar and then click *Copy* at the drop-down list.

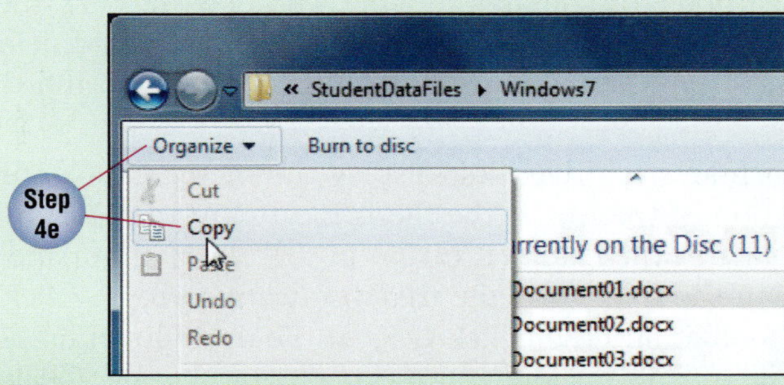

f. In the Computer section in the Navigation pane, click the drive containing your storage medium. (You may need to scroll down the Navigation pane.)
g. Click the Organize button and then click *Paste* at the drop-down list.

5. Delete ***WordDocument01.docx*** from your storage medium by completing the following steps:
   a. Make sure the contents of your storage medium display in the Content pane in the Computer window.
   b. Click ***WordDocument01.docx*** in the Content pane to select it.
   c. Click the Organize button and then click *Delete* at the drop-down list.
   d. At the message asking if you want to permanently delete the file, click the Yes button.
6. Copy the Windows7 folder from the CD to your storage medium by completing the following steps:
   a. With the Computer window open, click the drive in the *Computer* section in the Navigation pane that contains the CD that accompanies this book.
   b. Double-click *StudentDataFiles* in the Content pane.
   c. Click the *Windows7* folder in the Content pane.
   d. Click the Organize button and then click *Copy* at the drop-down list.
   e. In the *Computer* section in the Navigation pane, click the drive containing your storage medium.
   f. Click the Organize button and then click *Paste* at the drop-down list.
7. Close the Computer window by clicking the Close button located in the upper right corner of the window.

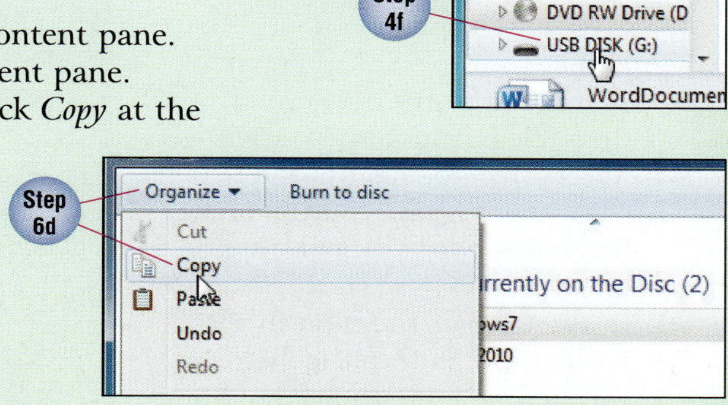

In addition to options in the Organize button drop-down list, you can use options in a shortcut menu to copy, move, and delete files or folders. To use a shortcut menu, select the desired file(s) or folder(s), position the mouse pointer on the selected item, and then click the right mouse button. At the shortcut menu that displays, click the desired option such as Copy, Cut, or Delete.

Selecting Files and Folders

You can move, copy, or delete more than one file or folder at the same time. Before moving, copying, or deleting files or folders, select the desired files or folders. To make selecting easier, consider changing the display in the Content pane to List or Details. To change the display, click the Views button arrow on the toolbar in the Computer window and then click *List* or *Details* at the drop-down list. You can also cycle through the various views by clicking the Views button. Hover your mouse over the Views button and the ScreenTip *Change your view* displays.

To select adjacent files or folders, click the first file or folder, hold down the Shift key, and then click the last file or folder. To select nonadjacent files or folders, click the first file or folder, hold down the Ctrl key, and then click any other files or folders.

Project 5 Copying and Deleting Files

1. At the Windows 7 desktop, click the Start button and then click *Computer*.
2. Copy files from the CD that accompanies this textbook to the drive containing your storage medium by completing the following steps:
   a. Make sure the CD that accompanies this textbook and your storage medium are inserted in the appropriate drives.

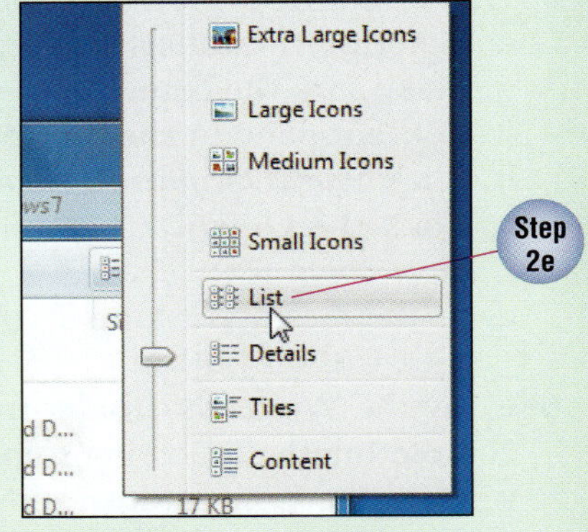

   b. Double-click the CD drive in the Content pane in the Computer window.
   c. Double-click the *StudentDataFiles* folder in the Content pane.
   d. Double-click the *Windows7* folder in the Content pane.
   e. Change the display to List by clicking the Views button arrow on the toolbar and then clicking *List* at the drop-down list.
   f. Click ***WordDocument01.docx*** in the Content pane.
   g. Hold down the Shift key, click ***WordDocument05.docx***, and then release the Shift key. (This selects five documents.)
   h. Click the Organize button and then click *Copy* at the drop-down list.
   i. In the *Computer* section in the Navigation pane, click the drive containing your storage medium.
   j. Click the Organize button and then click *Paste* at the drop-down list.
3. Delete the files from your storage medium that you just copied by completing the following steps:

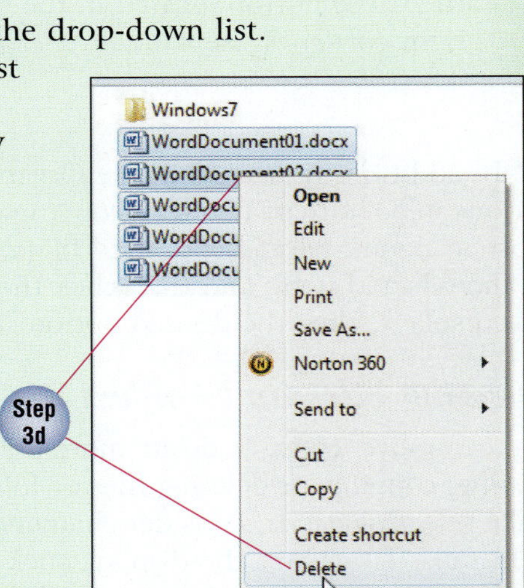

   a. Change the view by clicking the Views button arrow bar and then clicking *List* at the drop-down list.
   b. Click ***WordDocument01.docx*** in the Content pane.
   c. Hold down the Shift key, click ***WordDocument05.docx***, and then release the Shift key.
   d. Position the mouse pointer on any selected file, click the right mouse button, and then click *Delete* at the shortcut menu.
   e. At the message asking if you are sure you want to permanently delete the files, click Yes.
4. Close the Computer window by clicking the Close button located in the upper right corner of the window.

Manipulating and Creating Folders

As you begin working with and creating a number of files, consider creating folders in which you can logically group the files. To create a folder, display the Computer window and then display in the Content pane the drive or folder where you want to create the folder. Position the mouse pointer in a blank area in the Content pane, click the right mouse button, point to *New* in the shortcut menu, and then click *Folder* at the side menu. This inserts a folder icon in the Content pane and names the folder *New folder*. Type the desired name for the new folder and then press Enter.

Project 6 Creating a New Folder

1. At the Windows 7 desktop, open the Computer window.
2. Create a new folder by completing the following steps:
   a. Double-click in the Content pane the drive that contains your storage medium.
   b. Double-click the *Windows7* folder in the Content pane. (This opens the folder.)
   c. Click the Views button arrow and then click *List* at the drop-down list.
   d. Position the mouse pointer in a blank area in the Content pane and then click the right mouse button.
   e. Point to *New* in the shortcut menu and then click *Folder* at the side menu.

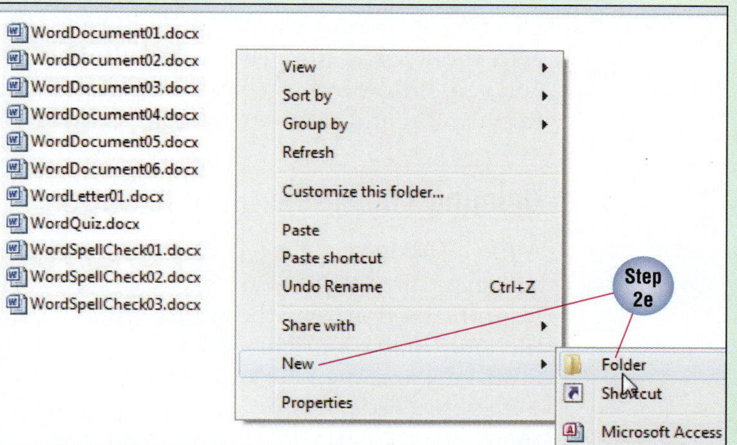

   f. Type **SpellCheckFiles** and then press Enter. (This changes the name from *New folder* to *SpellCheckFiles*.)

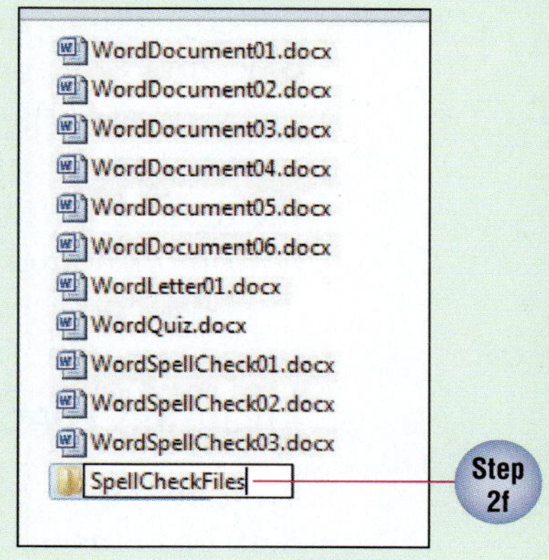

3. Copy **WordSpellCheck01.docx**, **WordSpellCheck02.docx**, and **WordSpellCheck03.docx** into the SpellCheckFiles folder you just created by completing the following steps:
   a. Click the Views button arrow and then click *List* at the drop-down list. (Skip this step if *List* is already selected.)
   b. Click once on the file named **WordSpellCheck01.docx** located in the Content pane.
   c. Hold down the Shift key, click once on the file named **WordSpellCheck03.docx**, and then release the Shift key. (This selects three documents.)
   d. Click the Organize button and then click *Copy* at the drop-down list.
   e. Double-click the *SpellCheckFiles* folder in the Content pane.
   f. Click the Organize button and then click *Paste* at the drop-down list.

4. Delete the SpellCheckFiles folder and its contents by completing the following steps:
   a. Click the Back button (contains a left-pointing arrow) located at the left side of the Address bar.
   b. With the SpellCheckFiles folder selected in the Content pane, click the Organize button and then click *Delete* at the drop-down list.
   c. At the message asking you to confirm the deletion, click Yes.

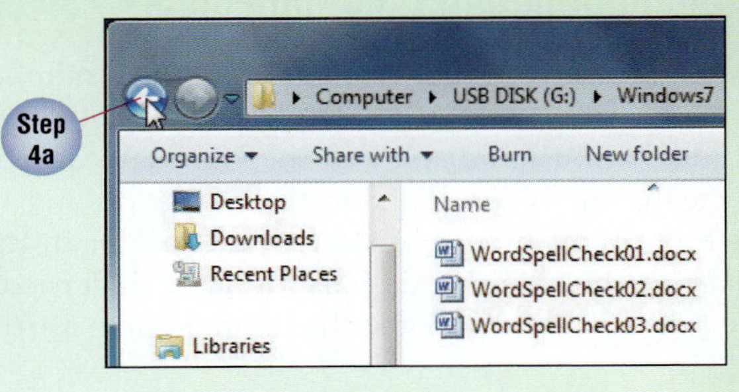

5. Close the window by clicking the Close button located in the upper right corner of the window.

Using the Recycle Bin

Deleting the wrong file can be a disaster but Windows 7 helps protect your work with the Recycle Bin. The Recycle Bin acts just like an office wastepaper basket; you can "throw away" (delete) unwanted files, but you can "reach in" to the Recycle Bin and take out (restore) a file if you threw it away by accident.

Deleting Files to the Recycle Bin

A file or folder or selected files or folders you delete from the hard drive are sent automatically to the Recycle Bin. If you want to permanently delete files or folders from the hard drive without first sending them to the Recycle Bin, select the desired file(s) or folder(s), right click on one of the selected files or folders, hold down the Shift key, and then click *Delete* at the shortcut menu.

Files and folders deleted from a USB flash drive or disc are deleted permanently. (Recovery programs are available, however, that will help you recover deleted files or folders. If you accidentally delete a file or folder from a USB flash drive or disc, do not do anything more with the USB flash drive or disc until you can run a recovery program.)

You can delete files in the manner described earlier in this section and you can also delete a file by dragging the file icon to the Recycle Bin. To do this, click the desired file in the Content pane in the Computer window, drag the file icon on top of the Recycle Bin icon on the desktop until the text *Move to Recycle Bin* displays, and then release the mouse button.

Restoring Files from the Recycle Bin

To restore a file from the Recycle Bin, double-click the Recycle Bin icon on the desktop. This opens the Recycle Bin window shown in Figure W.9. (The contents of the Recycle Bin will vary.) To restore a file, click the file you want restored and then click the Restore this item button on the toolbar. This removes the file from the Recycle Bin and returns it to its original location. You can also restore a file by positioning the mouse pointer on the file, clicking the right mouse button, and then clicking *Restore* at the shortcut menu.

Figure W.9 Recycle Bin Window

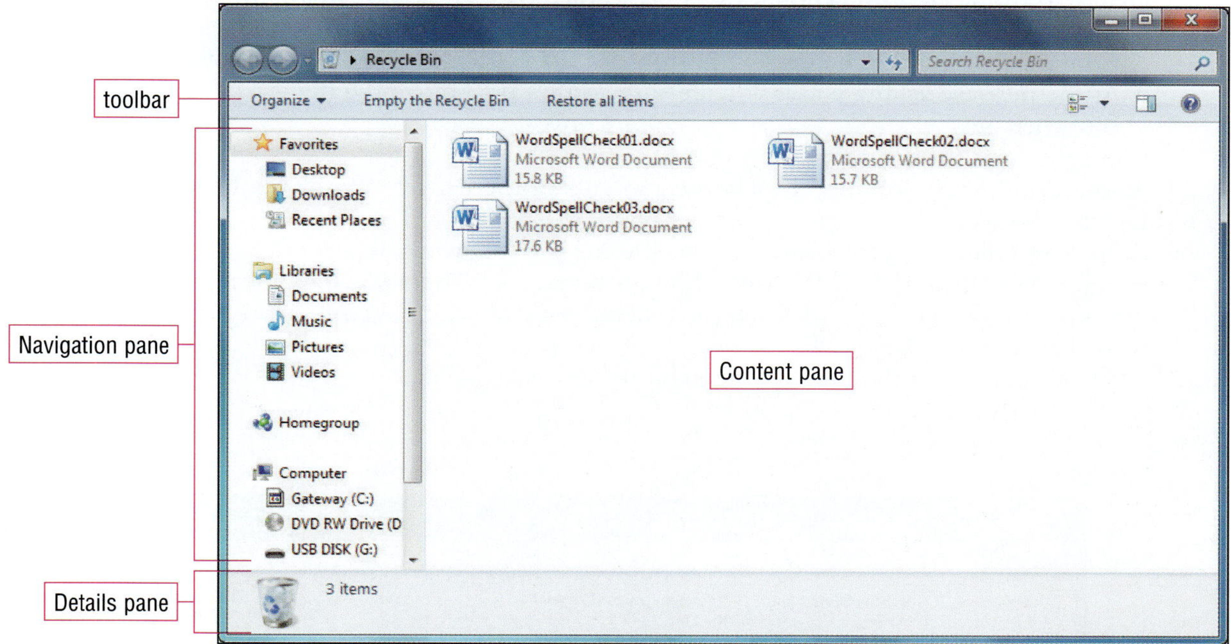

Project 7 Deleting Files to and Restoring Files from the Recycle Bin

Before beginning this project, check with your instructor to determine if you can copy files to the hard drive.

1. At the Windows 7 desktop, open the Computer window.
2. Copy files from your storage medium to the Documents folder on your hard drive by completing the following steps:
   a. Double-click in the Content pane the drive containing your storage medium.
   b. Double-click the *Windows7* folder in the Content pane.
   c. Click the Views button arrow and then click *List* at the drop-down list. (Skip this step if *List* is already selected.)
   d. Click ***WordSpellCheck01.docx*** in the Content pane.
   e. Hold down the Shift key, click ***WordSpellCheck03.docx***, and then release the Shift key.
   f. Click the Organize button and then click *Copy* at the drop-down list.
   g. Click the *Documents* folder in the *Libraries* section in the Navigation pane.
   h. Click the Organize button and then click *Paste* at the drop-down list.

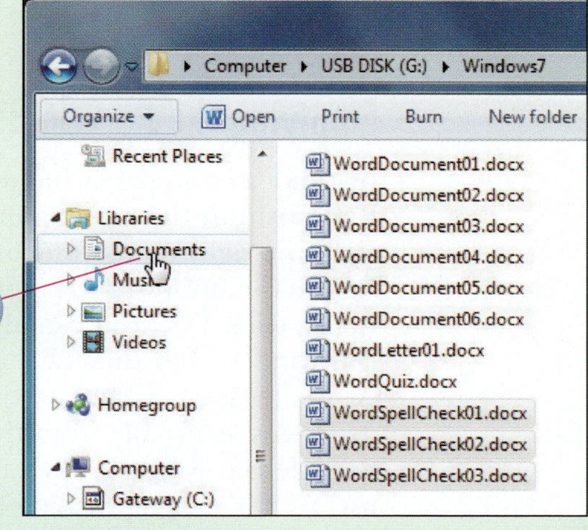

3. Delete to the Recycle Bin the files you just copied by completing the following steps:
   a. With **WordSpellCheck01.docx** through **WordSpellCheck03.docx** selected in the Content pane, click the Organize button and then click *Delete* at the drop-down list.
   b. At the message asking you if you are sure you want to move the items to the Recycle Bin, click Yes.
4. Close the Computer window.
5. At the Windows 7 desktop, display the contents of the Recycle Bin by double-clicking the Recycle Bin icon.
6. Restore the files you just deleted by completing the following steps:
   a. Select **WordSpellCheck01.docx** through **WordSpellCheck03.docx** in the Recycle Bin Content pane. (If these files are not visible, you will need to scroll down the list of files in the Content pane.)
   b. Click the Restore the selected items button on the toolbar.

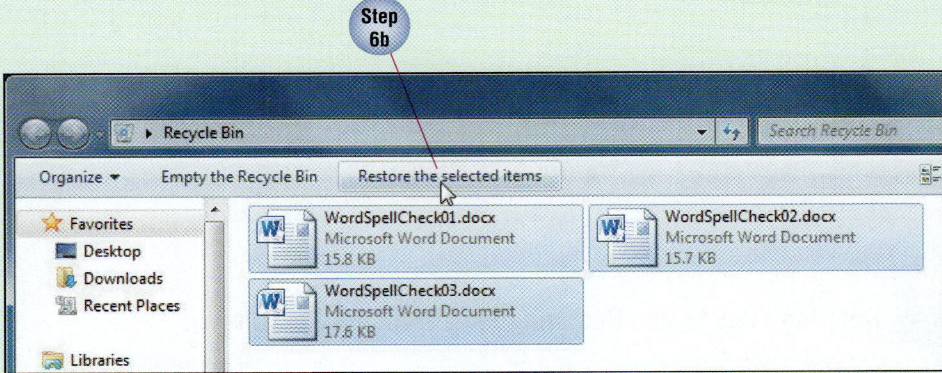

7. Close the Recycle Bin by clicking the Close button located in the upper right corner of the window.
8. Display the Computer window.
9. Click the *Documents* folder in the *Libraries* section in the Navigation pane.
10. Delete the files you restored.
11. Close the Computer window.

Emptying the Recycle Bin

Just like a wastepaper basket, the Recycle Bin can get full. To empty the Recycle Bin, position the arrow pointer on the Recycle Bin icon on the desktop and then click the right mouse button. At the shortcut menu that displays, click the *Empty Recycle Bin* option. At the message asking if you want to permanently delete the items, click Yes. You can also empty the Recycle Bin by displaying the Recycle Bin window and then clicking the Empty the Recycle Bin button on the toolbar. At the message asking if you want to permanently delete the items, click Yes. To delete a specific file from the Recycle Bin window, click the desired file in the Recycle Bin window, click the Organize button, and then *Delete* at the drop-down list. At the message asking if you want to permanently delete the file, click Yes. When you empty the Recycle Bin, the files cannot be recovered by the Recycle Bin or by Windows 7. If you have to recover a file, you will need to use a file recovery program.

Project 8 Emptying the Recycle Bin

Before beginning this project, check with your instructor to determine if you can delete files/folders from the Recycle Bin.

1. At the Windows 7 desktop, double-click the Recycle Bin icon.
2. At the Recycle Bin window, empty the contents by clicking the Empty the Recycle Bin button on the toolbar.
3. At the message asking you if you want to permanently delete the items, click Yes.
4. Close the Recycle Bin by clicking the Close button located in the upper right corner of the window.

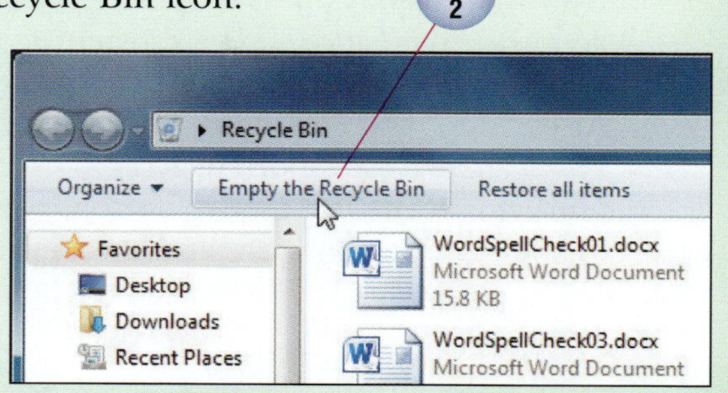

Creating a Shortcut

If you use a file or program on a consistent basis, consider creating a shortcut to the file or program. A shortcut is a specialized icon that represents very small files that point the operating system to the actual item, whether it is a file, a folder, or an application. If you create a shortcut to a Word document, the shortcut icon is not the actual document but a path to the document. Double-click the shortcut icon and Windows 7 opens the document in Word.

One method for creating a shortcut is to display the Computer window and then make active the drive or folder where the file is located. Right-click the desired file, point to *Send To*, and then click *Desktop (create shortcut)*. You can easily delete a shortcut icon from the desktop by dragging the shortcut icon to the Recycle Bin icon. This deletes the shortcut icon but does not delete the file to which the shortcut pointed.

Project 9 Creating a Shortcut

1. At the Windows 7 desktop, display the Computer window.
2. Double-click the drive containing your storage medium.
3. Double-click the *Windows7* folder in the Content pane.
4. Change the display of files to a list by clicking the Views button arrow and then clicking *List* at the drop-down list. (Skip this step if *List* is already selected.)
5. Create a shortcut to the file named **WordLetter01.docx** by right-clicking ***WordLetter01.docx***, pointing to *Send to*, and then clicking *Desktop (create shortcut)*.

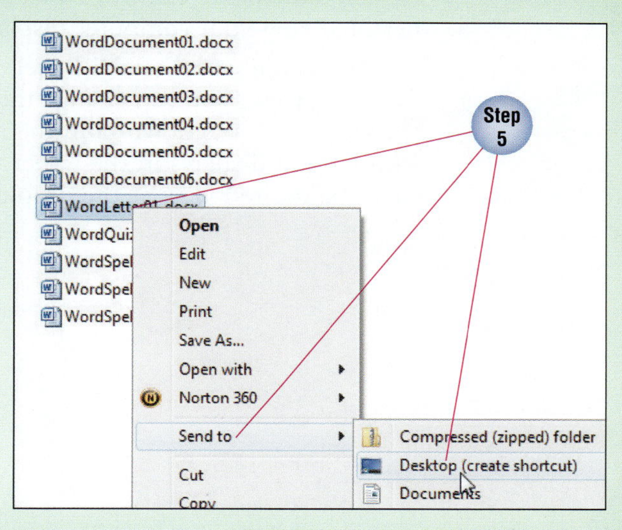

6. Close the Computer window.
7. Open Word and the file named **WordLetter01.docx** by double-clicking the *WordLetter01.docx* shortcut icon on the desktop.
8. After viewing the file in Word, exit Word by clicking the Close button that displays in the upper right corner of the window.
9. Delete the *WordLetter01.docx* shortcut icon by completing the following steps:
   a. At the desktop, position the mouse pointer on the *WordLetter01.docx* shortcut icon.
   b. Hold down the left mouse button, drag the icon on top of the Recycle Bin icon, and then release the mouse button.

Exploring the Control Panel

The Control Panel, shown in Figure W.10, contains a variety of icons you can use to customize the appearance and functionality of your computer as well as access and change system settings. Display the Control Panel by clicking the Start button on the Taskbar and then clicking *Control Panel* at the Start menu. The Control Panel organizes settings into categories to make them easier to find. Click a category icon and the Control Panel displays lower-level categories and tasks within each of them.

Hover your mouse over a category icon in the Control Panel and a ScreenTip displays with an explanation of what options are available. For example, if you hover the mouse over the Appearance and Personalization icon, a ScreenTip displays with information about the tasks available in the category such as changing the appearance of desktop items, applying a theme or screen saver to your computer, or customizing the Start menu and Taskbar.

If you click a category icon in the Control Panel, the Control Panel displays all of the available subcategories and tasks in the category. Also, the categories display in text form at the left side of the Control Panel. For example, if you click the Appearance and Personalization category icon, the Control Panel displays as shown in Figure W.11. Notice how the Control Panel categories display at the left side of the Control Panel and options for changing the appearance and personalizing your computer display in the middle of the Control Panel.

By default, the Control Panel displays categories of tasks in what is called Category view. You can change this view to *Large icons* or *Small icons*. To change the view, click the down-pointing arrow that displays at the right side of the text *View by* that displays in the upper right corner of the Control Panel, and then click the desired view at the drop-down list (see Figure W.10).

Figure W.10 The Control Panel

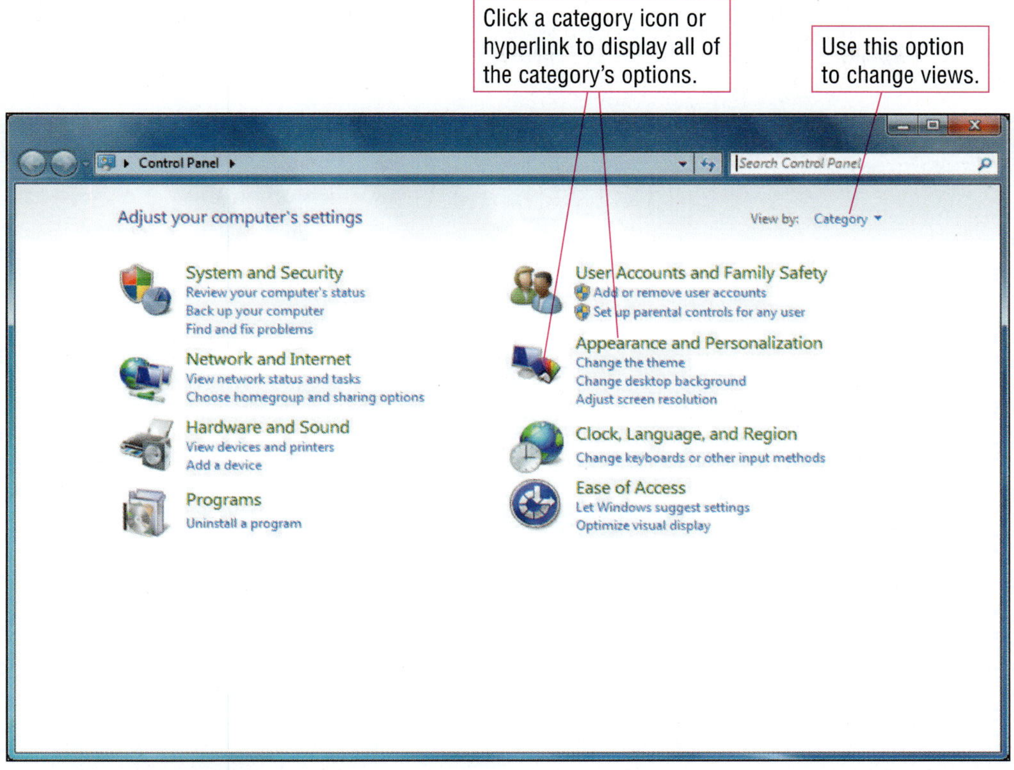

Figure W.11 Appearance and Personalization Window

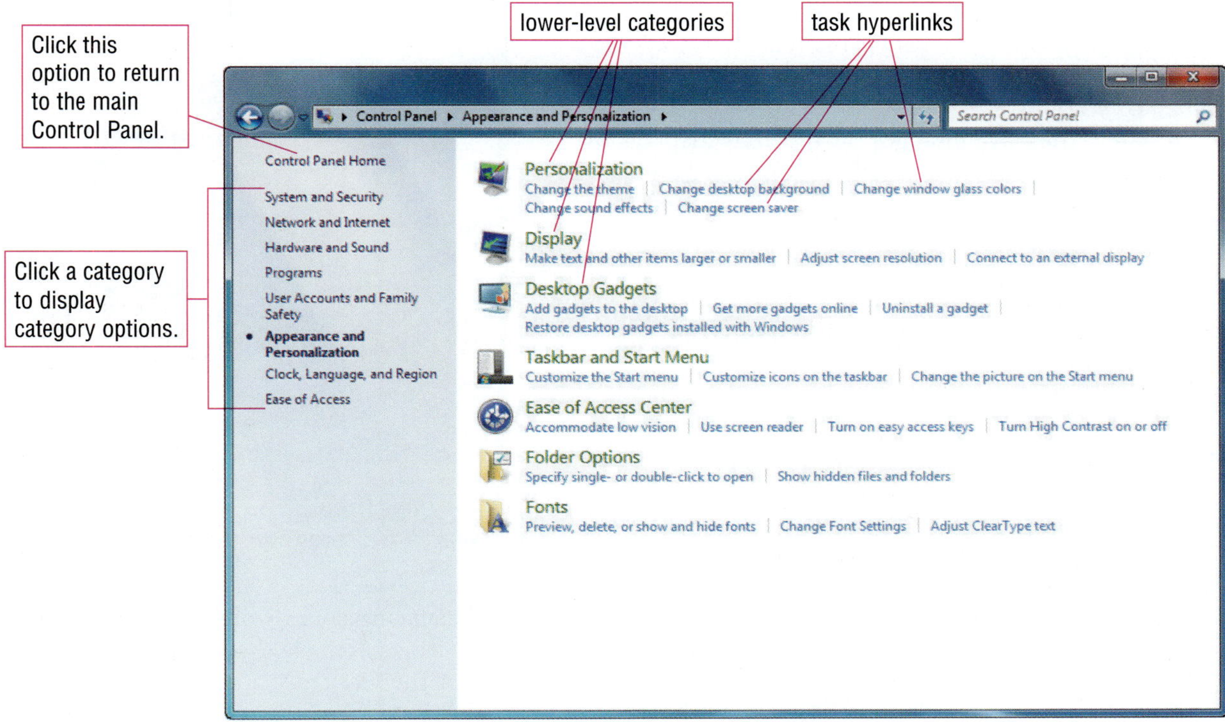

Project 10 Changing the Desktop Theme

1. At the Windows 7 desktop, click the Start button and then click *Control Panel* at the Start menu.
2. At the Control Panel, click the Appearance and Personalization category icon.

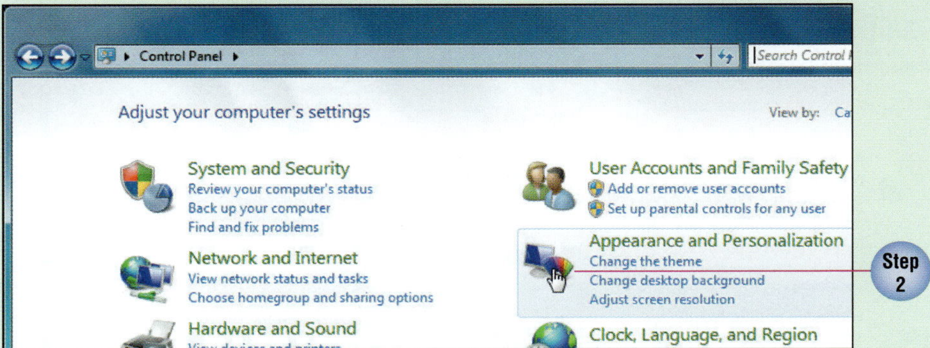

3. Click the Change the theme hyperlink that displays below the Personalization category in the panel at the right in the Control Panel.

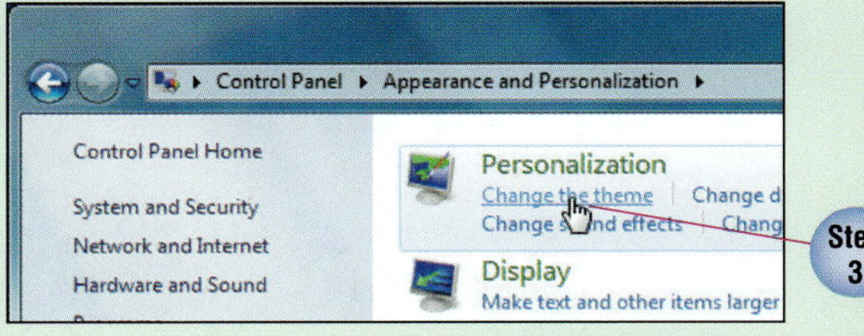

4. At the window that displays with options for changing visuals and sounds on your computer, click the *Landscapes* theme.
5. Click the Desktop Background hyperlink that displays in the lower left corner of the panel at the right.
6. Click the button that displays below the text *Change picture every* and then click *10 Seconds* at the drop-down list. (This tells Windows to change the picture on your desktop every 10 seconds.)
7. Click the Save changes button that displays in the lower right corner of the Control Panel.
8. Click the Close button located in the upper right corner to close the Control Panel.
9. Look at the picture that displays as the background at the desktop. Wait for 10 seconds and then look at the second picture that displays.
10. Click the Start button and then click *Control Panel* at the Start menu.
11. At the Control Panel, click the Appearance and Personalization category icon.
12. Click the Change the theme hyperlink that displays below the Personalization category in the panel at the right.

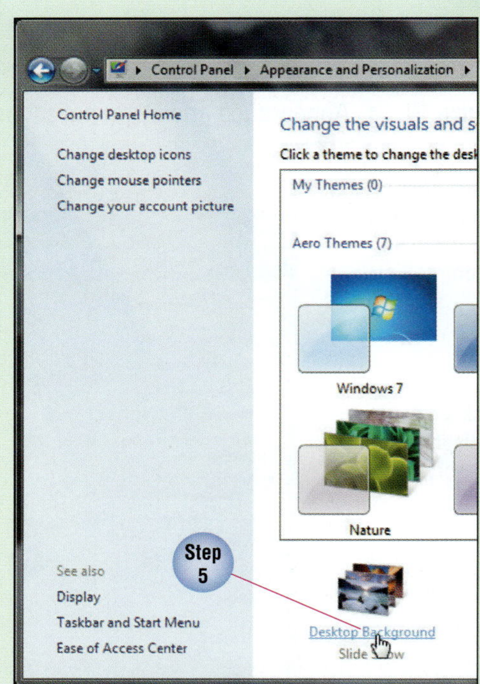

13. At the window that displays with options for changing visuals and sounds on your computer, click the *Windows 7* theme in the *Aero Themes* section. (This is the default theme.)
14. Click the Close button located in the upper right corner of the Control Panel.

Searching in the Control Panel

The Control Panel contains a large number of options for customizing the appearance and functionality of your computer. If you want to customize a feature and are not sure where the options for the feature are located, search for the feature. To do this, display the Control Panel and then type the name of the desired feature. By default, the insertion point is positioned in the *Search Control Panel* text box. When you type the feature name in the Search Control Panel, options related to the feature display in the Control Panel.

Project 11 Customizing the Mouse

1. Click the Start button and then click *Control Panel*.
2. At the Control Panel, type **mouse**. (The insertion point is automatically located in the *Search Control Panel* text box when you open the Control Panel. When you type *mouse*, features for customizing the mouse display in the Control Panel.)
3. Click the Mouse icon that displays in the Control Panel.
4. At the Mouse Properties dialog box, notice the options that display. (The *Switch primary and secondary buttons* option might be useful, for example, if you are left-handed and want to switch the buttons on the mouse.)
5. Click the Cancel button to remove the dialog box.
6. At the Control Panel, click the Change the mouse pointer display or speed hyperlink.

Step 2

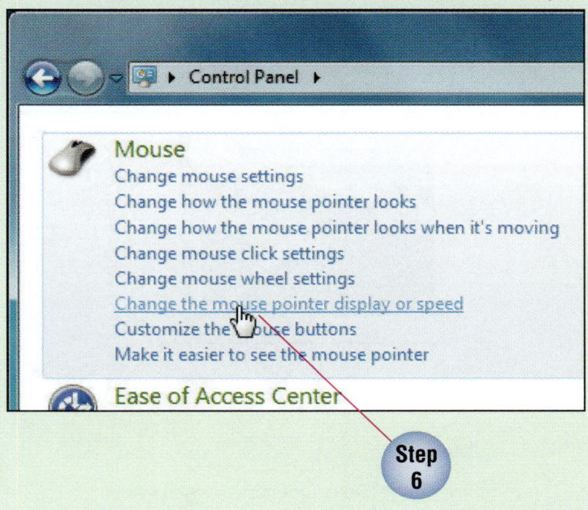

Step 6

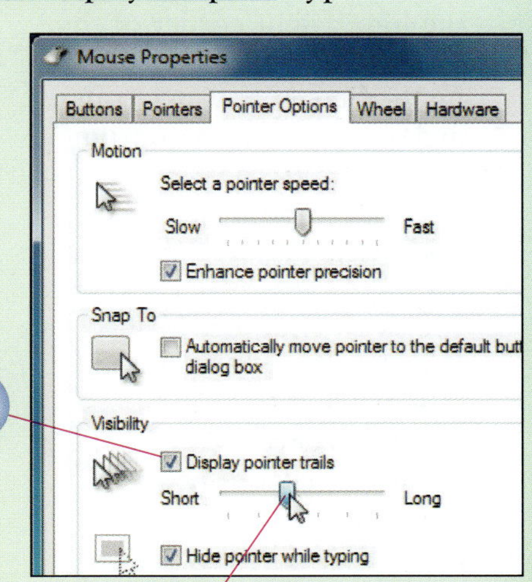

Step 7

Step 8

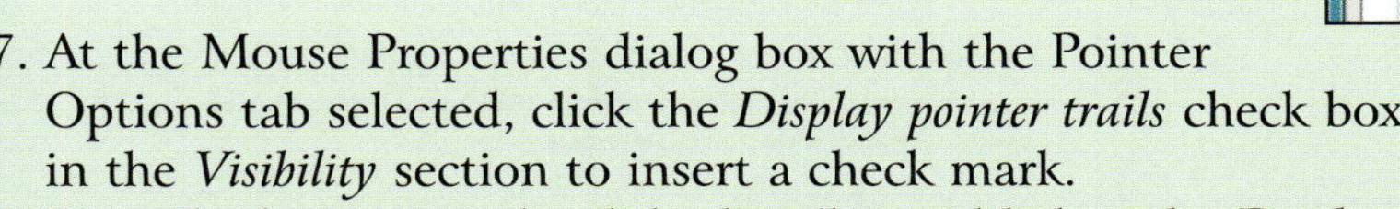

7. At the Mouse Properties dialog box with the Pointer Options tab selected, click the *Display pointer trails* check box in the *Visibility* section to insert a check mark.
8. Drag the button on the slider bar (located below the *Display pointer trails* check box) approximately to the middle of the bar.
9. Click OK to close the dialog box.
10. Close the Control Panel.
11. Move the mouse pointer around the screen to see the pointer trails as well as the speed at which the mouse moves.

Displaying Personalize Options with a Shortcut Command

In addition to the Control Panel, you can display customization options with a command from a shortcut menu. Display a shortcut menu by positioning the mouse pointer in the desired position and then clicking the right mouse button. For example, display a shortcut menu with options for customizing the desktop by positioning the mouse pointer in an empty area on the desktop and then clicking the right mouse button. At the shortcut menu that displays, click the desired shortcut command.

Project 12 Customizing with a Shortcut Command

1. At the Windows 7 desktop, position the mouse pointer in an empty area on the desktop, click the right mouse button, and then click *Personalize* at the shortcut menu.
2. At the Control Panel Appearance and Personalization window that displays, click the Change mouse pointers hyperlink that displays at the left side of the window.
3. At the Mouse Properties dialog box, click the Pointer Options tab.
4. Click in the *Display pointer trails* check box to remove the check mark.
5. Click OK to close the dialog box.
6. At the Control Panel Appearance and Personalization window, click the Screen Saver hyperlink that displays in the lower right corner of the window.
7. At the Screen Saver Settings dialog box, click the option button below the *Screen saver* option and then click *Ribbons* at the drop-down list.
8. Check the number in the *Wait* text box. If a number other than *1* displays, click the down-pointing arrow in the spin box at the right side of the text box until *1* displays. (This tells Windows to display the screen saver after one minute of inactivity.)
9. Click OK to close the dialog box.
10. Close the Control Panel by clicking the Close button located in the upper right corner of the window.

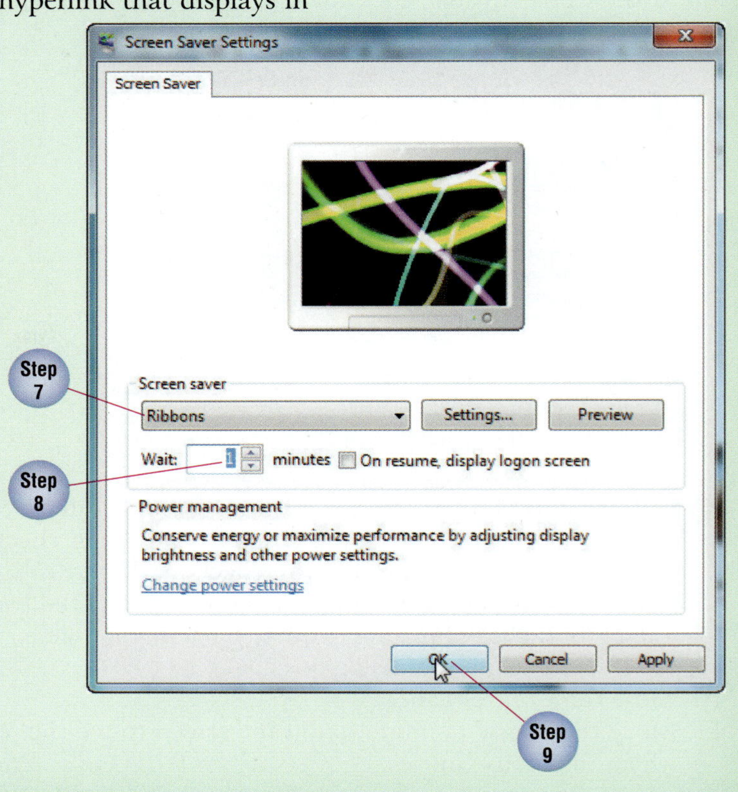

11. Do not touch the mouse or keyboard and wait over one minute for the screen saver to display. After watching the screen saver, move the mouse. (This redisplays the desktop.)
12. Right-click in an empty area on the desktop and then click *Personalize* at the shortcut menu.
13. At the Control Panel Appearance and Personalization window, click the Screen Saver hyperlink.
14. At the Screen Saver Settings dialog box, click the option button below the *Screen saver* option and then click *(None)* at the drop-down list.
15. Click OK to close the dialog box.
16. Close the Control Panel Appearance and Personalization window.

Exploring Windows Help and Support

Windows 7 includes an on-screen reference guide providing information, explanations, and interactive help on learning Windows features. Get help at the Windows Help and Support window shown in Figure W.12. Display this window by clicking the Start button and then clicking *Help and Support* at the Start menu. Use buttons in the window toolbar to display the opening Windows Help and Support window, print the current information, display a list of contents, get customer support or other types of services, and display a list of Help options.

Figure W.12 Windows Help and Support Window

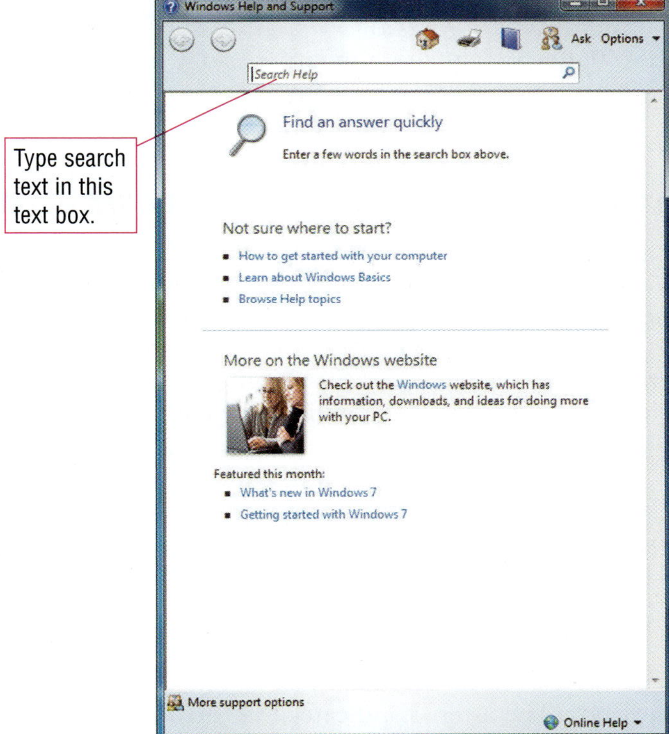

Project 13 Getting Help

1. At the Windows 7 desktop, click the Start button and then click *Help and Support* at the Start menu.
2. At the Windows Help and Support window, click the Learn about Windows Basics hyperlink.
3. Click a hyperlink that interests you, read the information, and then click the Back button on the Windows Help and Support window toolbar. (The Back button is located in the upper left corner of the window.)
4. Click another hyperlink that interests you and then read the information.
5. Click the Help and Support home button that displays on the window toolbar. (This returns you to the opening Windows Help and Support window.)
6. Click in the *Search Help* text box, type **delete files**, and then press Enter.
7. Click the Delete a file or folder hyperlink that displays in the window.
8. Read the information that displays about deleting files or folders and then click the
   Print button on the window toolbar.
9. At the Print dialog box, click the Print button.
10. Click the Close button to close the Windows Help and Support window.

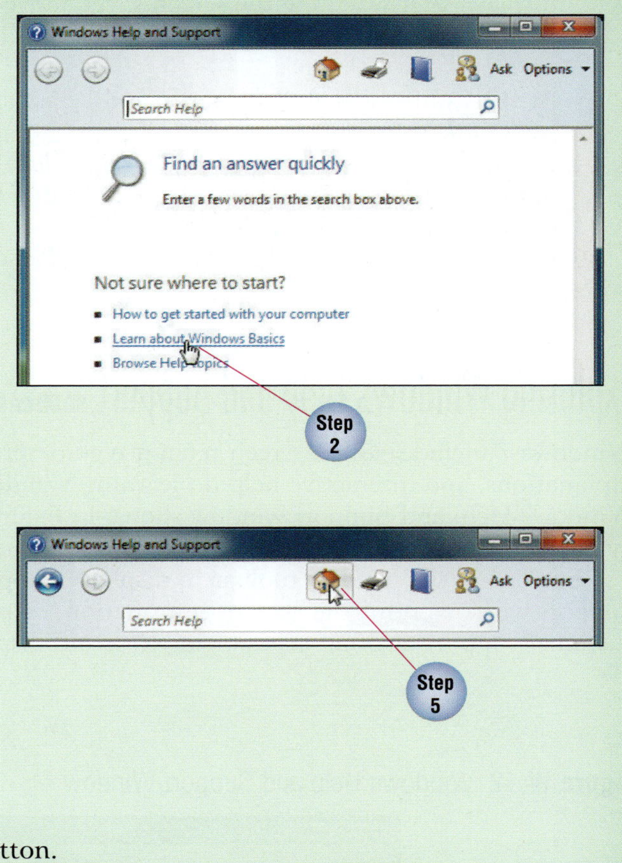

Using Search Tools

The Start menu contains a search tool you can use to quickly find a program or file on your computer. To use the search tool, click the Start button and then type the first few characters of the program or file for which you are searching in the *Search programs and files* text box. As you type characters in the text box, a pop-up list displays with program names or file names that begin with the characters. As you continue typing characters, the search tool refines the list.

You can also search for programs or files with the search text box in the Computer window. The search text box displays in the upper right corner of the Computer window at the right side of the Address bar. If you want to search a specific folder, make that folder active in the Content pane and then type the search text in the text box.

When conducting a search, you can use the asterisk (*) as a wildcard character in place of any letters, numbers, or symbols within a file name. For example, in the following project you will search for file names containing *check* by typing ***check** in the search text box. The asterisk indicates that the file name can start with any letter but it must contain the letters *check* somewhere in the file name.

Project 14 Searching for Programs and Files

1. At the Windows 7 desktop, click the Start button.
2. With the insertion point positioned in the *Search programs and files* text box, type **paint**. (Notice as you type the letters that Windows displays programs and/or files that begin with the same letters you are typing or that are associated with the same letters in a keyword. Notice that the Paint program displays below the heading *Programs* at the top of the list. Depending on the contents stored in the computer you are using, additional items may display below Paint.)

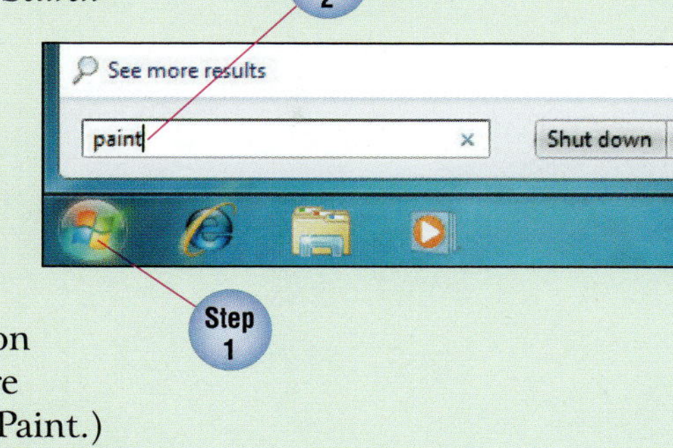

3. Click *Paint* that displays below the *Programs* heading.
4. Close the Paint window.
5. Click the Start button and then click *Computer*.
6. At the Computer window, double-click the icon representing your storage medium.
7. Double-click the *Windows7* folder.
8. Click in the search text box located at the right of the Address bar and then type **document**. (As you begin typing the letters, Windows filters the list of files in the Content pane to those that contain the letters you type. Notice that the Address bar displays *Search Results in Windows7* to indicate that the files that display matching your criteria were limited to the current folder.)

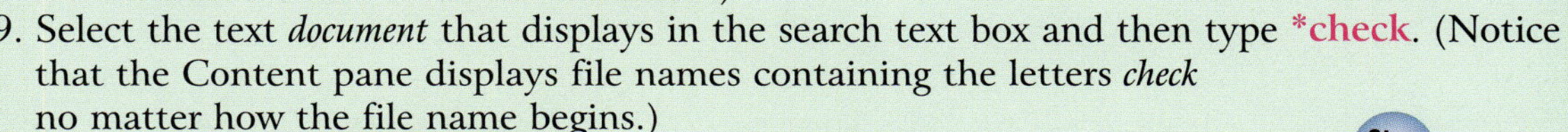

9. Select the text *document* that displays in the search text box and then type ***check**. (Notice that the Content pane displays file names containing the letters *check* no matter how the file name begins.)
10. Double-click ***WordSpellCheck02.docx*** to open the document in Word.
11. Close the document and exit Word by clicking the Close button located in the upper right corner of the window.
12. Close the Computer window.

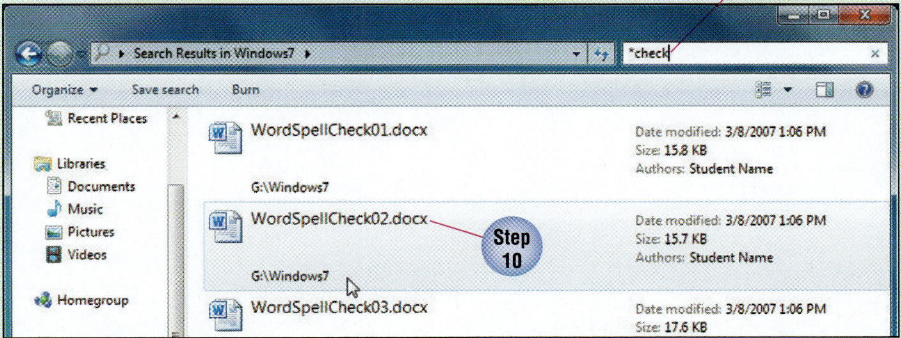

Browsing the Internet Using Internet Explorer 8.0

Microsoft Internet Explorer 8.0 is a web browser program with options and features for displaying sites as well as navigating and searching for information on the Internet. The ***Internet*** is a network of computers connected around the world. Users access the Internet for several purposes: to communicate using instant messaging and/or email, to subscribe to newsgroups, to transfer files, to socialize with other users around the globe in chat rooms, and also to access virtually any kind of information imaginable.

Using the Internet, people can find a phenomenal amount of information for private or public use. To use the Internet, three things are generally required: an Internet Service Provider (ISP), a program to browse the Web (called a ***web browser***), and a ***search engine***. In this section, you will learn how to:

- Navigate the Internet using URLs and hyperlinks
- Use search engines to locate information
- Download web pages and images

You will use the Microsoft Internet Explorer web browser to locate information on the Internet. Uniform Resource Locators, referred to as URLs, are the method used to identify locations on the Internet. The steps for browsing the Internet vary but generally include: opening Internet Explorer, typing the URL for the desired site, navigating the various pages of the site, navigating to other sites using links, and then closing Internet Explorer.

To launch Internet Explorer 8.0, click the Internet Explorer icon on the Taskbar at the Windows desktop. Figure IE.1 identifies the elements of the Internet Explorer, version 8.0, window. The web page that displays in your Internet Explorer window may vary from what you see in Figure IE.1.

If you know the URL for the desired website, click in the Address bar, type the URL, and then press Enter. The website's home page displays in a tab within the Internet Explorer window. URLs (Uniform Resource Locators) are the method used to identify locations on the Internet. The format of a URL is *http://server-name.path*. The first part of the URL, *http*, stands for HyperText Transfer Protocol, which is the protocol or language used to transfer data within the World Wide Web. The colon and slashes separate the protocol from the server name. The server name is the second component of the URL. For example, in the URL http://www.microsoft.com, the server name is *microsoft*. The last part of the URL specifies the domain to which the server belongs. For example, *.com* refers to "commercial" and establishes that the URL is a commercial company. Examples of other domains include *.edu* for "educational," *.gov* for "government," and *.mil* for "military."

Figure IE.1 Internet Explorer Window

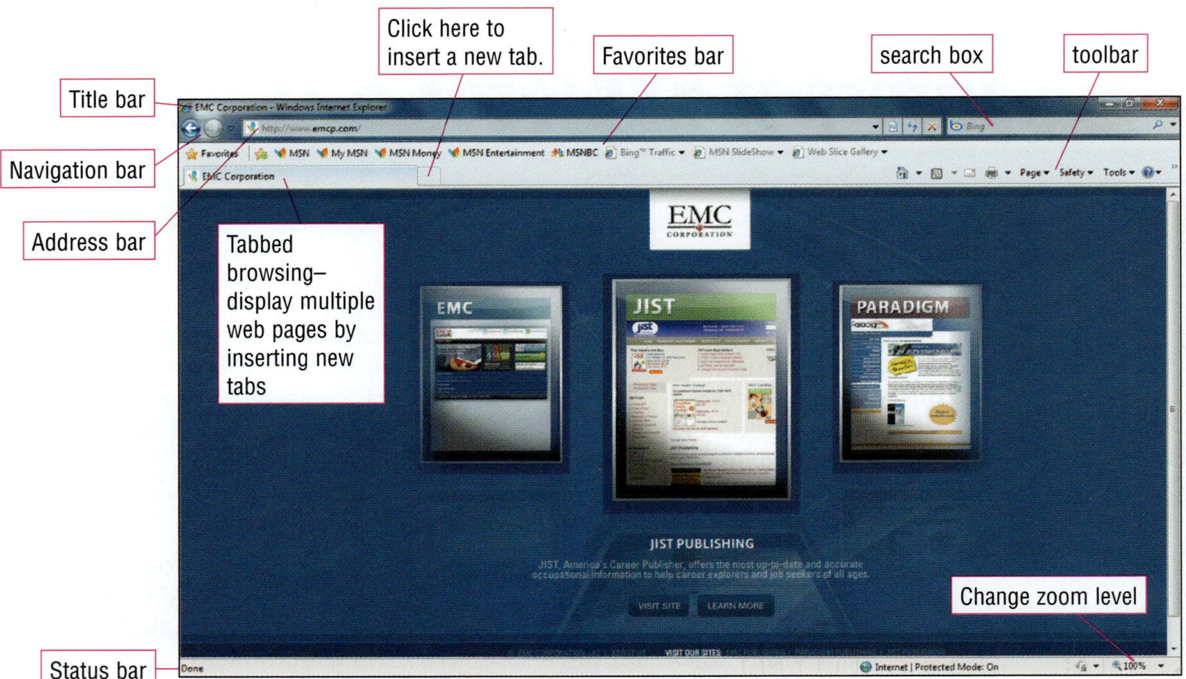

Project 1 Browsing the Internet Using URLs

1. Make sure you are connected to the Internet through an Internet Service Provider and that the Windows desktop displays. (Check with your instructor to determine if you need to complete steps for accessing the Internet such as typing a user name and password to log on.)
2. Launch Microsoft Internet Explorer by clicking the Internet Explorer icon located on the Taskbar located at the bottom of the Windows desktop.
3. At the Internet Explorer window, explore the website for Yosemite National Park by completing the following steps:
   a. Click in the Address bar, type www.nps.gov/yose, and then press Enter.
   b. Scroll down the home page for Yosemite National Park by clicking the down-pointing arrow on the vertical scroll bar located at the right side of the Internet Explorer window.
   c. Print the home page by clicking the Print button located on the Internet Explorer toolbar. (Some websites have a printer friendly button you can click to print the page.)

MSN.com - Windows Internet Explorer
www.nps.gov/yose
Go to ' www.nps.gov/yose '
Favorites
MSN.com
Step 3a

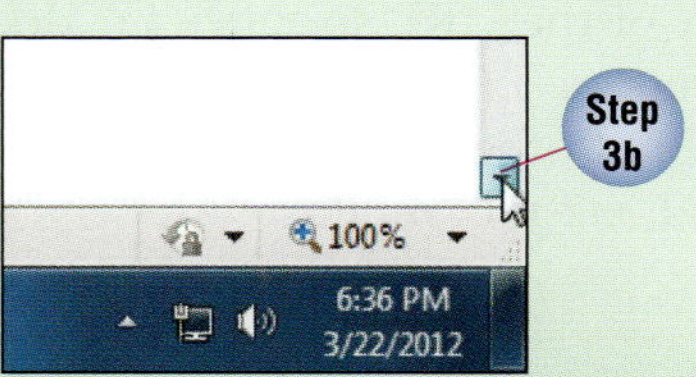

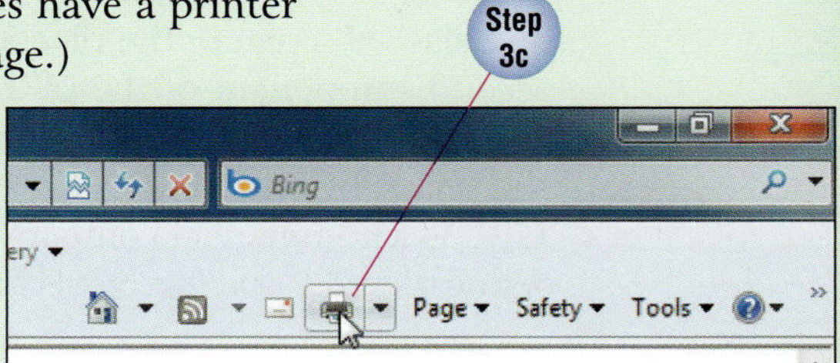

4. Explore the website for Glacier National Park by completing the following steps:
   a. Click in the Address bar, type **www.nps.gov/glac**, and then press Enter.
   b. Print the home page by clicking the Print button located on the Internet Explorer toolbar.
5. Close Internet Explorer by clicking the Close button (contains an X) located in the upper right corner of the Internet Explorer window.

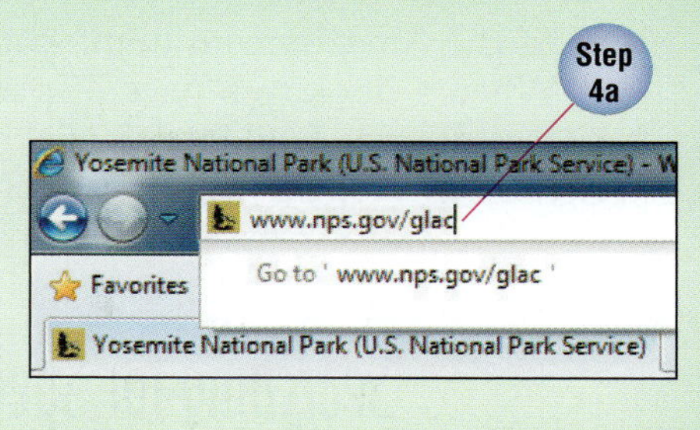

Navigating Using Hyperlinks

Most web pages contain "hyperlinks" that you click to connect to another page within the website or to another site on the Internet. Hyperlinks may display in a web page as underlined text in a specific color or as images or icons. To use a hyperlink, position the mouse pointer on the desired hyperlink until the mouse pointer turns into a hand, and then click the left mouse button. Use hyperlinks to navigate within and between sites on the Internet. The navigation bar in the Internet Explorer window contains a Back button that, when clicked, takes you to the previous web page viewed. If you click the Back button and then want to return to the previous page, click the Forward button. You can continue clicking the Back button to back your way out of several linked pages in reverse order since Internet Explorer maintains a history of the websites you visit.

Project 2 Navigating Using Hyperlinks

1. Make sure you are connected to the Internet and then click the Internet Explorer icon on the Taskbar.
2. At the Internet Explorer window, display the White House web page and navigate in the page by completing the following steps:
   a. Click in the Address bar, type **whitehouse.gov**, and then press Enter.
   b. At the White House home page, position the mouse pointer on a hyperlink that interests you until the pointer turns into a hand, and then click the left mouse button.
   c. At the linked web page, click the Back button. (This returns you to the White House home page.)
   d. At the White House home page, click the Forward button to return to the previous web page viewed.
   e. Print the web page by clicking the Print button on the Internet Explorer toolbar.
3. Display the website for Amazon.com and navigate in the site by completing the following steps:
   a. Click in the Address bar, type **www.amazon.com**, and then press Enter.

b. At the Amazon.com home page, click a hyperlink related to books.
c. When a book web page displays, click the Print button on the Internet Explorer toolbar.
4. Close Internet Explorer by clicking the Close button (contains an X) located in the upper right corner of the Internet Explorer window.

Searching for Specific Sites

If you do not know the URL for a specific site or you want to find information on the Internet but do not know what site to visit, complete a search with a search engine. A search engine is a software program created to search quickly and easily for desired information. A variety of search engines are available on the Internet, each offering the opportunity to search for specific information. One method for searching for information is to click in the search box located to the right of the Address bar, type a keyword or phrase related to your search, and then click the Search button or press Enter. Another method for completing a search is to visit the website for a search engine and use options at the site.

Bing is Microsoft's online search portal and is the default search engine used by Internet Explorer. Bing organizes search results by topic category and provides related search suggestions.

Project 3 Searching for Information by Topic

1. Start Internet Explorer.
2. At the Internet Explorer window, search for sites on bluegrass music by completing the following steps:
   a. Click in the search box (may display *Bing*) located at the right side of the Address bar.
   b. Type **bluegrass music** and then press Enter.
   c. When a list of sites displays in the Bing results window, click a site that interests you.
   d. When the page displays, click the Print button.

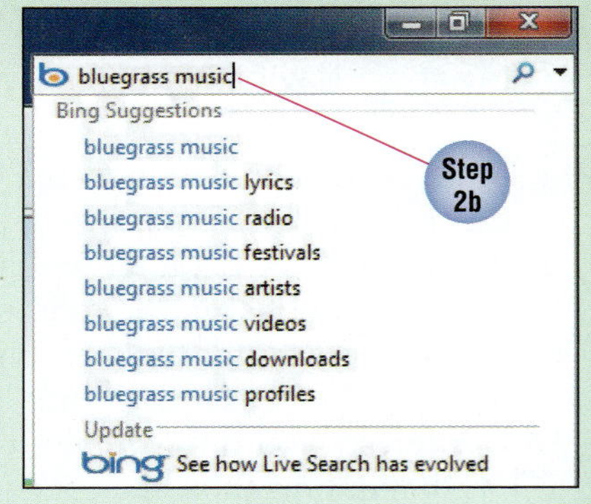

3. Use the Yahoo! search engine to find sites on bluegrass music by completing the following steps:
   a. Click in the Address bar, type **www.yahoo.com**, and then press Enter.
   b. At the Yahoo! website, with the insertion point positioned in the search text box, type **bluegrass music** and then press Enter. (Notice that the sites displayed vary from sites displayed in the earlier search.)
   c. Click hyperlinks until a website displays that interests you.
   d. Print the page.

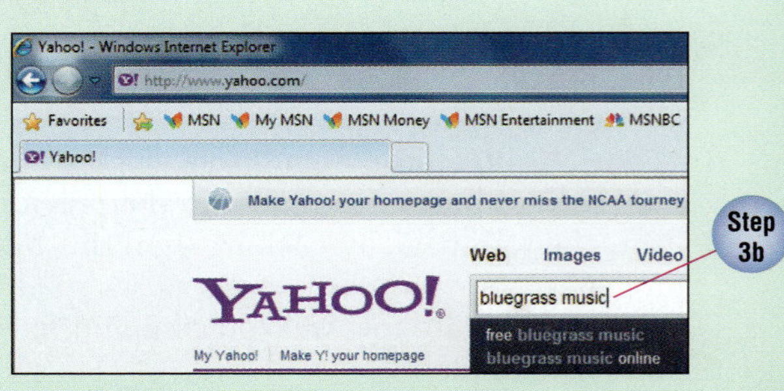

4. Use the Google search engine to find sites on jazz music by completing the following steps:
    a. Click in the Address bar, type www.google.com, and then press Enter.
    b. At the Google website, with the insertion point positioned in the search text box, type jazz music and then press Enter.
    c. Click a site that interests you.
    d. Print the page.
5. Close Internet Explorer.

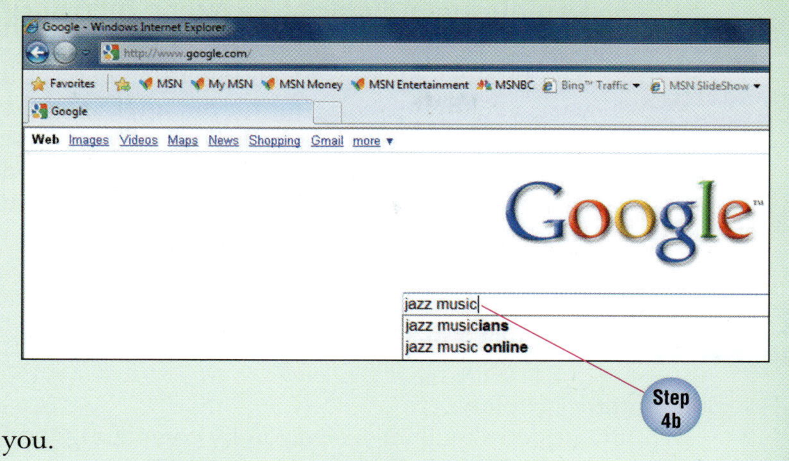

Using a Metasearch Engine

Bing, Yahoo!, and Google are search engines that search the Web for content and display search results. In addition to individual search engines, you can use a metasearch engine, such as Dogpile, that sends your search text to other search engines and then compiles the results in one list. With a metasearch engine, you type the search text once and then access results from a wider group of search engines. The Dogpile metasearch engine provides search results from Google, Yahoo!, Bing, and Ask.

Project 4 Searching with a Metasearch Search Engine

1. At the Windows desktop, click the Internet Explorer icon on the Taskbar.
2. Click in the Address bar.
3. Type www.dogpile.com and then press Enter.
4. At the Dogpile website, type jazz music in the search text box and then press Enter.
5. Click a hyperlink that interests you.
6. Close the Internet Explorer window.

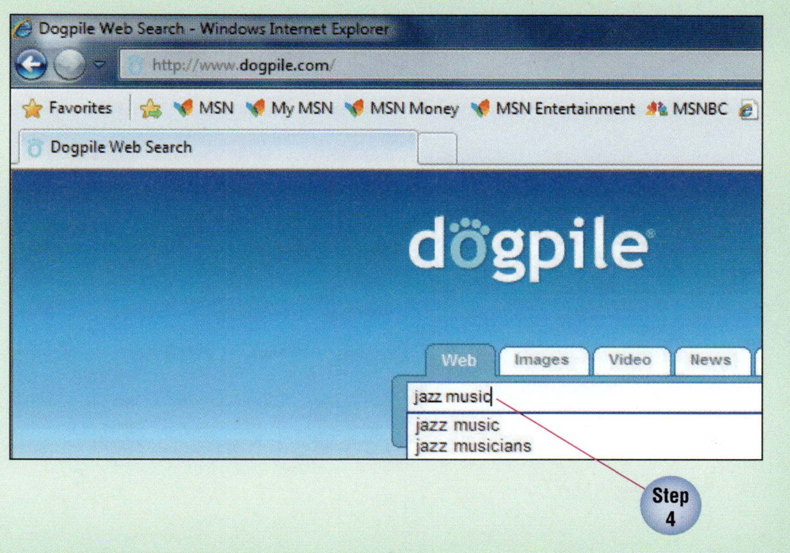

Completing Advanced Searches for Specific Sites

Web Search

The Internet contains an enormous amount of information. Depending on what you are searching for on the Internet and the search engine you use, some searches can result in several thousand "hits" (sites). Wading through a large number of sites can be very time-consuming and counterproductive. Narrowing a search to very specific criteria can greatly reduce the number of hits for a search. To narrow a search, use the advanced search options offered by the search engine.

Project 5 Narrowing a Search

1. Start Internet Explorer.
2. Search for sites on skydiving in Oregon by completing the following steps:
   a. Click in the Address bar, type **www.yahoo.com**, and then press Enter.
   b. At the Yahoo! home page, click the Web Search button next to the search text box.
   c. Click the more hyperlink located above the search text box and then click Advanced Search at the drop-down list.
   d. At the Advanced Web Search page, click in the search text box next to *all of these words*.
   e. Type **skydiving Oregon tandem static line**. (This limits the search to web pages containing all of the words typed in the search text box.)
   f. Click the Yahoo! Search button.
   g. When the list of websites displays, click a hyperlink that interests you.
   h. Click the Back button until the Yahoo! Advanced Web Search page displays.
   i. Click in the *the exact phrase* text box and then type **skydiving in Oregon**.
   j. Click the *Only .com domains* in the *Site/Domain* section.
   k. Click the Yahoo! Search button.
   l. When the list of websites displays, click a hyperlink that interests you.
   m. Print the page.
3. Close Internet Explorer.

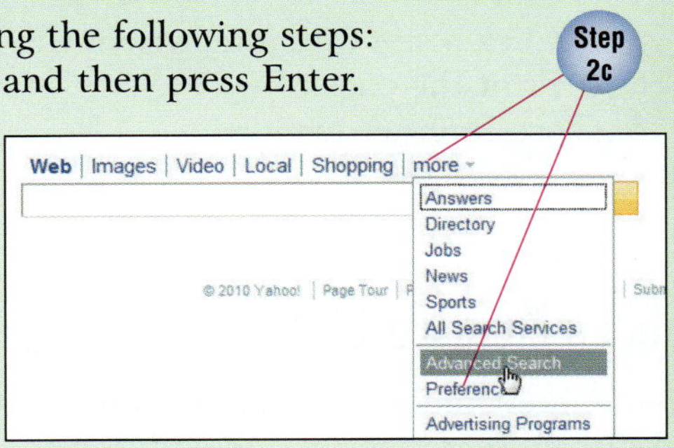

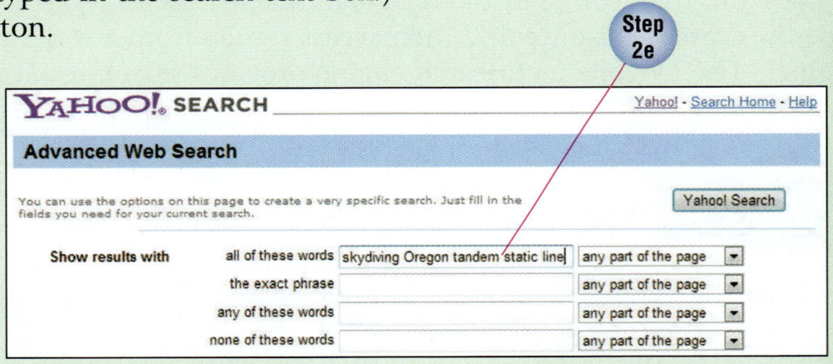

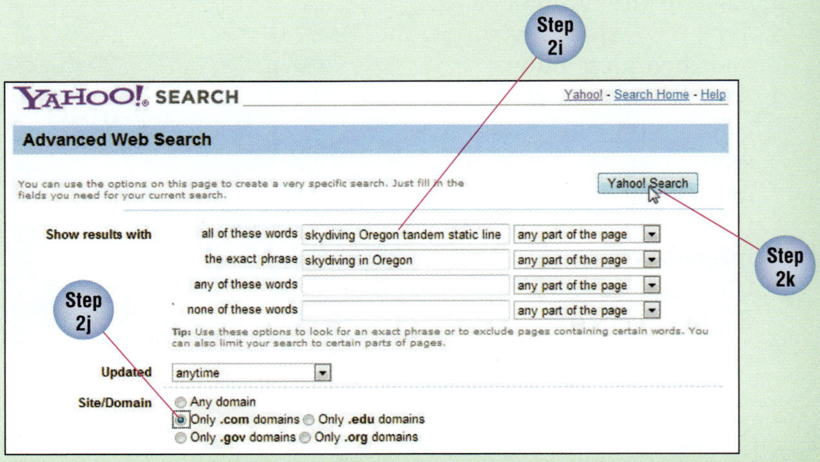

Downloading Images, Text, and Web Pages from the Internet

The image(s) and/or text that display when you open a web page as well as the web page itself can be saved as a separate file. This separate file can be viewed, printed, or inserted in another file. The information you want to save in a separate file is downloaded from the Internet by Internet Explorer and saved in a folder of your choosing with the name you specify. Copyright laws protect much of the information on the Internet. Before using information downloaded from the Internet, check the site for restrictions. If you do use information, make sure you properly cite the source.

Project 6 Downloading Images and Web Pages

1. Start Internet Explorer.
2. Download a web page and image from Banff National Park by completing the following steps:
   a. Search for sites on the Internet for Banff National Park.
   b. From the list of sites that displays, choose a site that contains information about Banff National Park and at least one image of the park.
   c. Save the web page as a separate file by clicking the Page button on the Internet Explorer toolbar and then clicking *Save As* at the drop-down list.
   d. At the Save Webpage dialog box, type **BanffWebPage**.
   e. Navigate to the drive containing your storage medium and then click the Save button.

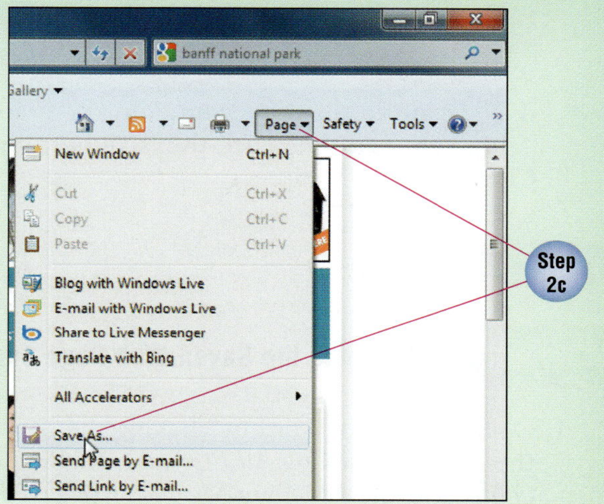

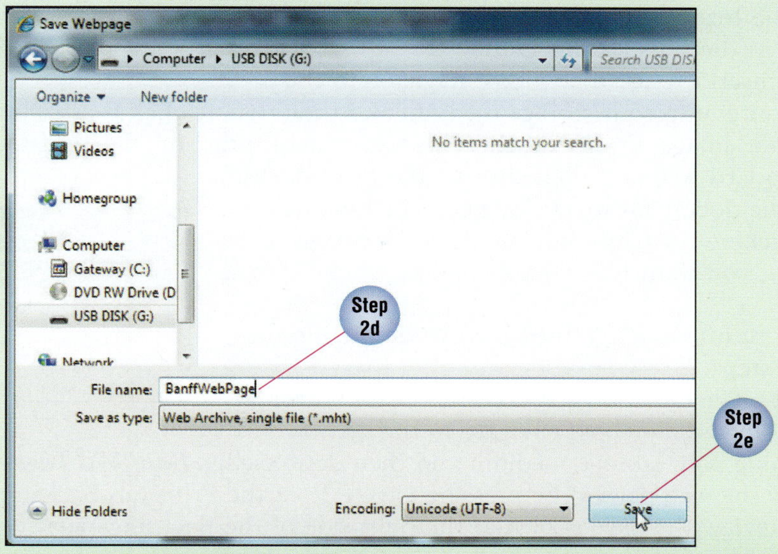

3. Save an image file by completing the following steps:
   a. Right-click an image that displays at the website. (The image that displays may vary from what you see below.)
   b. At the shortcut menu that displays, click *Save Picture As*.
   c. At the Save Picture dialog box, type **BanffImage** in the *File name* text box.

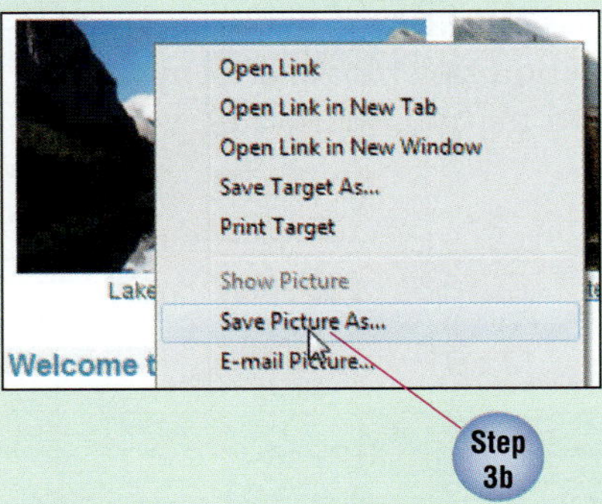

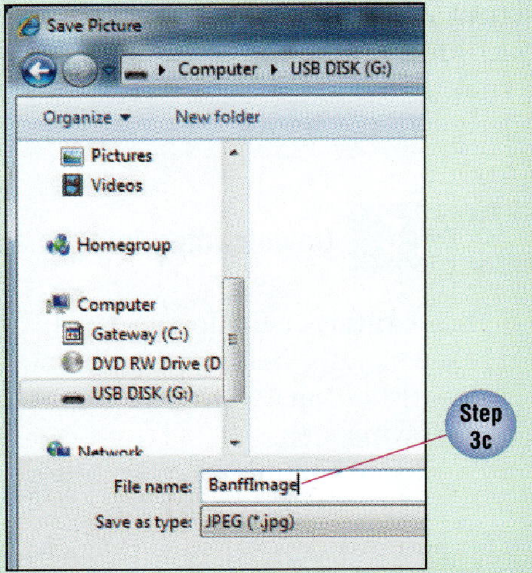

   d. Navigate to the drive containing your storage medium and then click the Save button.
4. Close Internet Explorer.

Project 7 Opening the Saved Web Page and Image in a Word Document

1. Open Microsoft Word by clicking the Start button on the Taskbar, clicking *All Programs*, clicking *Microsoft Office*, and then clicking *Microsoft Word 2010*.
2. With Microsoft Word open, insert the image in a document by completing the following steps:
   a. Click the Insert tab and then click the Picture button in the Illustrations group.
   b. At the Insert Picture dialog box, navigate to the drive containing your storage medium and then double-click ***BanffImage.jpg***.

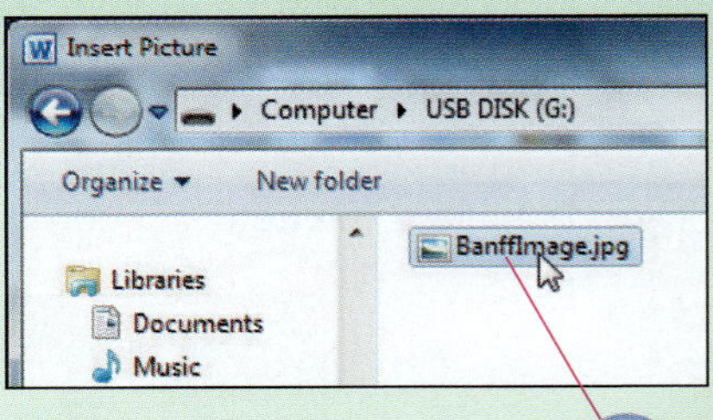

   c. When the image displays in the Word document, print the document by pressing Ctrl + P and then clicking the Print button.
   d. Close the document by clicking the File tab and then clicking the Close button. At the message asking if you want to save the changes, click *Don't Save*.
3. Open the **BanffWebPage.mht** file by completing the following steps:
   a. Click the File tab and then click the Open button.
   b. At the Open dialog box, navigate to the drive containing your storage medium and then double-click ***BanffWebPage.mht***.

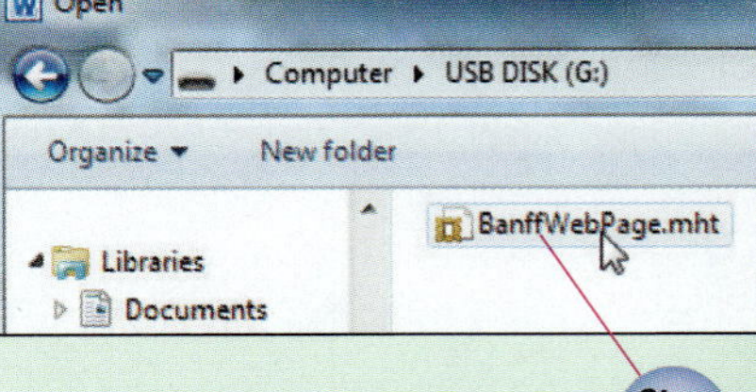

   c. Preview the web page(s) by pressing Ctrl + P. At the Print tab Backstage view, preview the page shown at the right side of the Backstage view.
4. Close Word by clicking the Close button (contains an X) that displays in the upper right corner of the screen.

Microsoft® Excel® Level 1

Unit 1 ■ Editing and Formatting Documents

Microsoft® Excel®

CHAPTER

Preparing an Excel Workbook

PERFORMANCE OBJECTIVES

Upon successful completion of Chapter 1, you will be able to:

- **Identify the various elements of an Excel workbook**
- **Create, save, and print a workbook**
- **Enter data in a workbook**
- **Edit data in a workbook**
- **Insert a formula using the AutoSum button**
- **Apply basic formatting to cells in a workbook**
- **Use the Help feature**

Tutorials

1.1 Creating and Saving a Workbook

1.2 Editing Cells and Using Proofing Tools

1.3 Displaying Formulas and Navigating a Worksheet

1.4 Applying Basic Formatting

1.5 Applying Formatting; Using Undo and Redo; Changing Alignment

Many companies use a spreadsheet for numerical and financial data and to analyze and evaluate information. An Excel spreadsheet can be used for such activities as creating financial statements, preparing budgets, managing inventory, and analyzing cash flow. In addition, numbers and values can be easily manipulated to create "what if" situations. For example, using a spreadsheet, a person in a company can ask questions such as "What if the value in this category is decreased? How would that change affect the department budget?" Questions like these can be easily answered in an Excel spreadsheet. Change the value in a category and Excel will recalculate formulas for the other values. In this way, a spreadsheet can be used not only for creating financial statements or budgets, but also as a planning tool. Model answers for this chapter's projects appear on the following page.

Excel2010L1C1

Note: Before beginning the projects, copy to your storage medium the Excel2010L1C1 subfolder from the Excel2010L1 folder on the CD that accompanies this textbook. Steps on how to copy a folder are presented on the inside of the back cover of this textbook. Do this every time you start a chapter's projects.

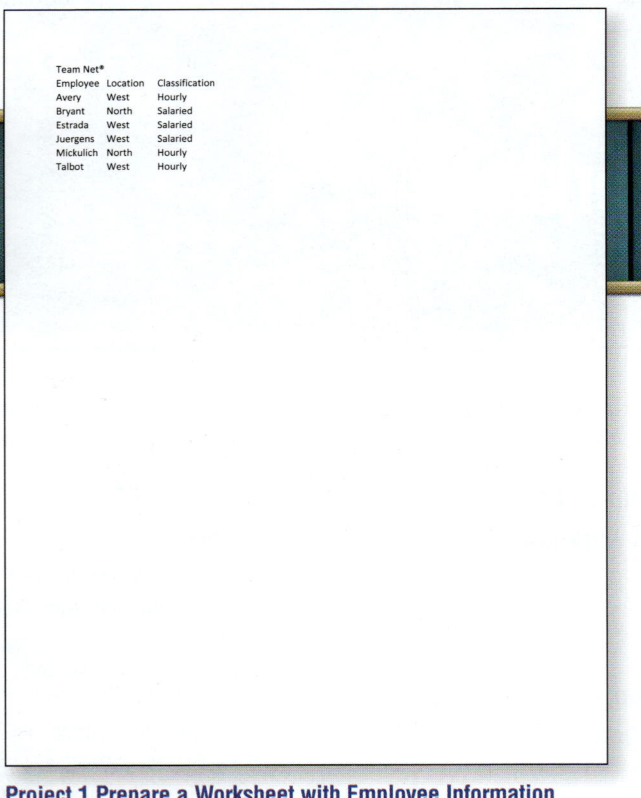

Team Net®

Employee	Location	Classification
Avery	West	Hourly
Bryant	North	Salaried
Estrada	West	Salaried
Juergens	West	Salaried
Mickulich	North	Hourly
Talbot	West	Hourly

Project 1 Prepare a Worksheet with Employee Information

EL1-C1-P1-EmpBene.xlsx

	January	February	March	April	May	June
Year 1	**100**	100	100	100	125	125
Year 3	**150**	150	150	150	175	175
Year 5	**200**	200	200	150	150	150
Year 7	**250**	250	250	250	250	250
Total	700	700	700	650	700	700

Qtr 1	$5,500	$6,250	$7,000	$8,500	$5,500	$4,500
Qtr 2	$6,000	$7,250	$6,500	$9,000	$4,000	$5,000
Qtr 3	$4,500	$8,000	$6,000	$7,500	$6,000	$5,000
Qtr 4	$6,500	$8,500	$7,000	$8,000	$5,500	$6,000
Average	$5,625	$7,500	$6,625	$8,250	$5,250	$5,125

Project 2 Open and Format a Workbook and Insert Formulas

EL1-C1-P2-FillCells.xlsx

Monthly Expenses
January, 2013

Expense	Budget	Actual
Accounting Services	$ 500	$ 423
Advertising	3,200	3,475
Utilities	2,700	3,045
Estimated Taxes	25,000	25,000
Health Insurance	9,420	9,595
Inventory Purchases	4,200	2,155
Equipment Repair	500	214
Loan Payment	5,586	5,586
Office Supplies	225	415
Total	$ 51,331	$ 49,908

Budget Percentages

Department	Percentage
Personnel	26%
Development	22%
Sales	18%
Production	13%
Maintenance	8%
Accounting	7%
Administration	6%

Project 3 Format a Worksheet

EL1-C1-P3-MoExps.xlsx

Project 1 Prepare a Worksheet with Employee Information — 3 Parts

You will create a worksheet containing employee information, edit the contents, and then save and close the workbook.

Creating a Worksheet

Start

Open Excel by clicking the Start button at the left side of the Taskbar, pointing to *All Programs*, clicking *Microsoft Office*, and then clicking *Microsoft Excel 2010*. (Depending on your operating system, these steps may vary.) When Excel is open, you are presented with a blank worksheet like the one shown in Figure 1.1. The elements of a blank Excel worksheet are described in Table 1.1.

A file created in Excel is referred to as a ***workbook***. An Excel workbook consists of individual worksheets (or *sheets*) like the sheets of paper in a notebook. Notice the tabs located toward the bottom of the Excel window that are named *Sheet1*, *Sheet2*, and so on. The area containing the gridlines in the Excel window is called the ***worksheet area***. Figure 1.2 identifies the elements of the worksheet area. Create a worksheet in the worksheet area that will be saved as part of a workbook. Columns in a worksheet are labeled with letters of the alphabet and rows are numbered.

Figure 1.1 Blank Excel Worksheet

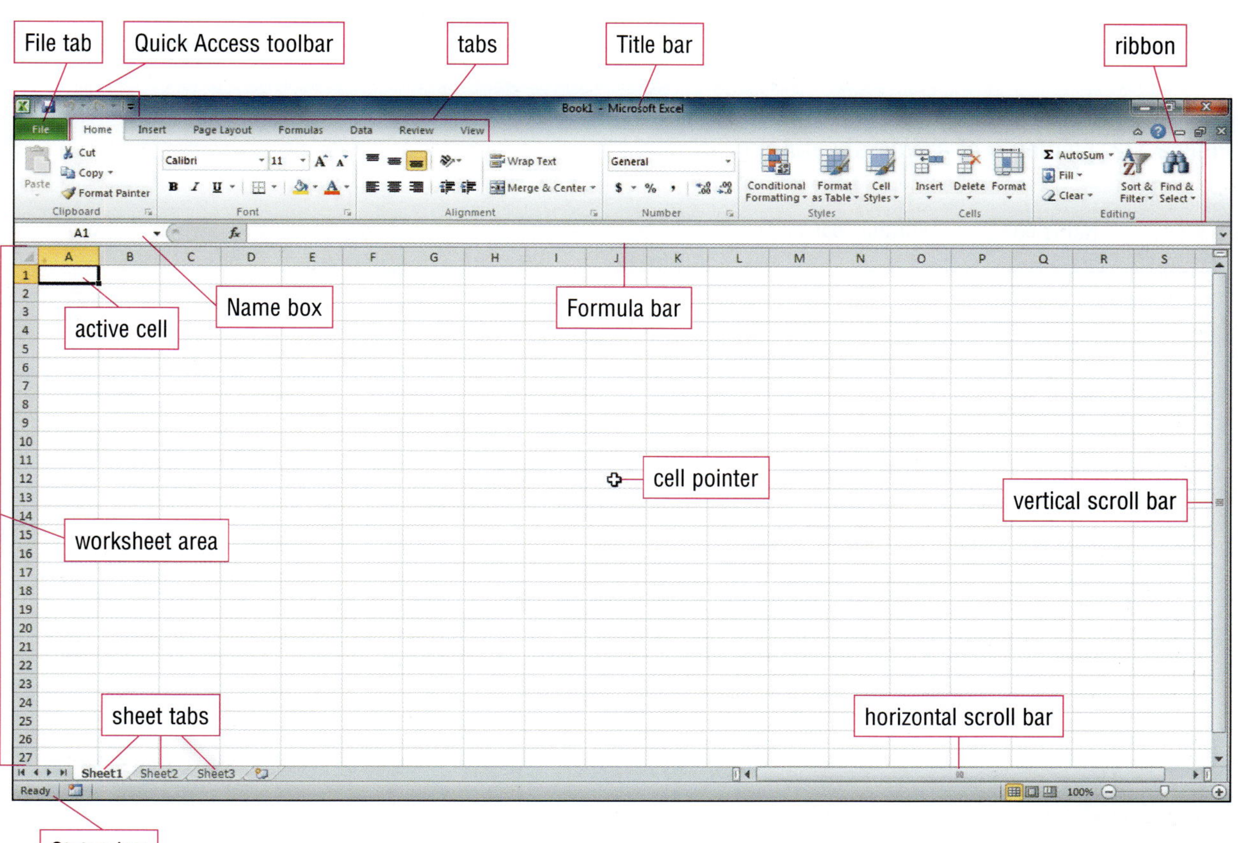

Table 1.1 Elements of an Excel Worksheet

Feature	*Description*
Quick Access toolbar	Contains buttons for commonly used commands.
File tab	Click the File tab and the Backstage view displays containing buttons and tabs for working with and managing files.
Title bar	Displays workbook name followed by program name.
Tabs	Contain commands and features organized into groups.
Ribbon	Area containing the tabs and commands divided into groups.
Name box	Displays cell address (also called the cell reference) and includes the column letter and row number.
Formula bar	Provides information about active cell; enter and edit formulas in this bar.
Scroll bars	Use vertical and horizontal scroll bars to navigate within a worksheet.
Sheet tab	Displays toward bottom of screen and identifies current worksheet.
Status bar	Displays information about worksheet and active cell, view buttons, and Zoom slider bar.

Figure 1.2 Elements of a Worksheet Area

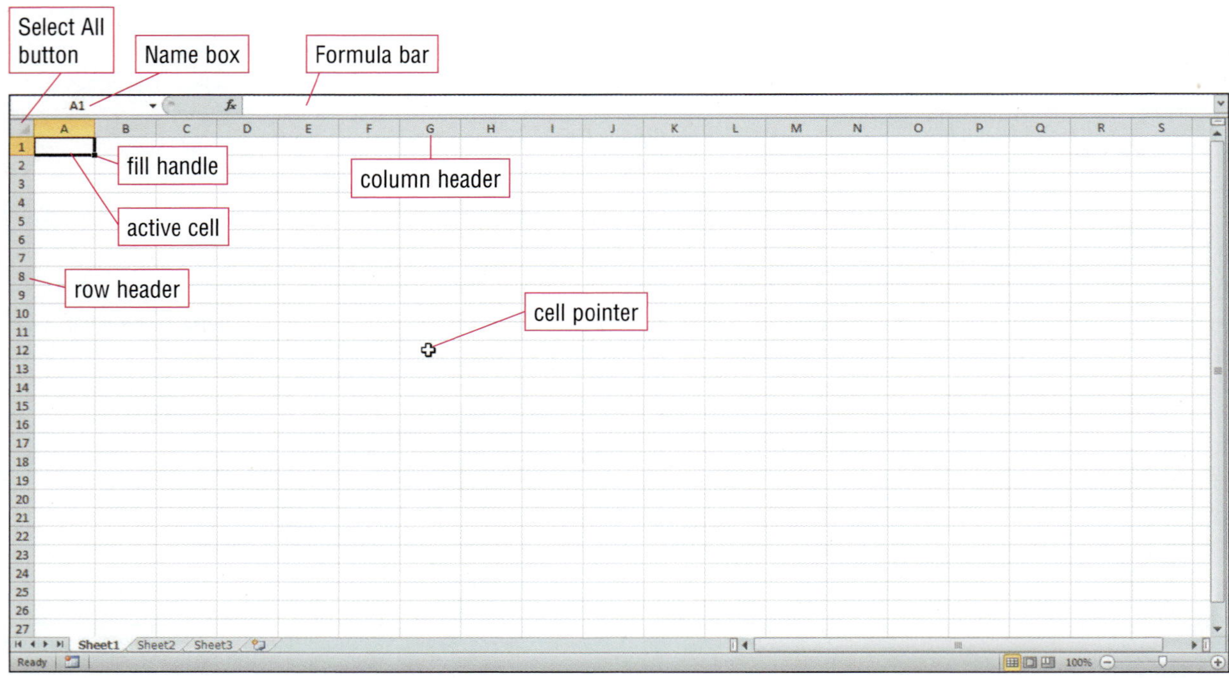

The horizontal and vertical lines that define the cells in the worksheet area are called ***gridlines***. When a cell is active (displays with a black border), the ***cell address***, also called the ***cell reference***, displays in the ***Name box***. The cell reference includes the column letter and row number. For example, if the first cell of the worksheet is active, the cell reference *A1* displays in the Name box. A thick black border surrounds the active cell.

To make a cell active, position the cell pointer in the cell and then click the left mouse button.

Enter data such as text, a number, or a value in a cell. To enter data in a cell, make the desired cell active and then type the data. To make the next cell active, press the Tab key. Table 1.2 displays additional commands for making a specific cell active.

Another method for making a specific cell active is to use the Go To feature. To use this feature, click the Find & Select button in the Editing group in the Home tab and then click Go To. At the Go To dialog box, type the cell reference in the *Reference* text box, and then click OK.

Ctrl + G is the keyboard command to display the Go To dialog box.

Find & Select

When you are ready to type data into the active cell, check the Status bar. The word *Ready* should display at the left side. As you type data, the word *Ready* changes to *Enter*. Data you type in a cell displays in the cell as well as in the Formula bar. If the data you type is longer than the cell can accommodate, the data overlaps the next cell to the right. (It does not become a part of the next cell—it simply overlaps it.) You will learn how to change column widths to accommodate data later in this chapter.

Table 1.2 Commands for Making a Specific Cell Active

To make this cell active	*Press*
Cell below current cell	Enter
Cell above current cell	Shift + Enter
Next cell	Tab
Previous cell	Shift + Tab
Cell at beginning of row	Home
Next cell in the direction of the arrow	Up, Down, Left, or Right Arrow keys
Last cell in worksheet	Ctrl + End
First cell in worksheet	Ctrl + Home
Cell in next window	Page Down
Cell in previous window	Page Up
Cell in window to right	Alt + Page Down
Cell in window to left	Alt + Page Up

If the data you enter in a cell consists of text and the text does not fit into the cell, it overlaps the next cell. If, however, you enter a number in a cell, specify it as a number (rather than text) and the number is too long to fit in the cell, Excel changes the display of the number to number symbols *(###)*. This is because Excel does not want you to be misled by a number when you see only a portion of it in the cell.

Along with the keyboard, you can use the mouse to make a specific cell active. To make a specific cell active with the mouse, position the mouse pointer, which displays as a white plus sign (called the ***cell pointer***), on the desired cell, and then click the left mouse button. The cell pointer displays as a white plus sign when positioned in a cell in the worksheet and displays as an arrow pointer when positioned on other elements of the Excel window such as options in tabs or scroll bars.

Scroll through a worksheet using the horizontal and/or vertical scroll bars. Scrolling shifts the display of cells in the worksheet area, but does not change the active cell. Scroll through a worksheet until the desired cell is visible and then click the desired cell.

Saving a Workbook

Quick Steps

Save a Workbook

1. Click Save button.
2. Type workbook name.
3. Press Enter.

HINT

Ctrl + S is the keyboard command to save a workbook.

Save

Save an Excel workbook, which may consist of a worksheet or several worksheets, by clicking the Save button on the Quick Access toolbar or by clicking the File tab and then clicking the Save button in the Quick commands area of the Backstage view. At the Save As dialog box, type a name for the workbook in the *File name* text box and then press Enter or click the Save button. A workbook file name can contain up to 255 characters, including drive letter and any folder names, and can include spaces. Note that you cannot give a workbook the same name in first uppercase and then lowercase letters. Also, some symbols cannot be used in a file name such as:

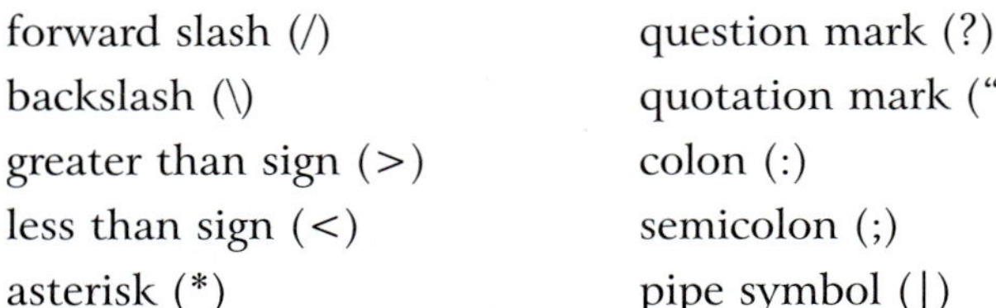

forward slash (/)	question mark (?)
backslash (\)	quotation mark (“)
greater than sign (>)	colon (:)
less than sign (<)	semicolon (;)
asterisk (*)	pipe symbol (|)

To save an Excel workbook in the Excel2010L1C1 folder on your storage medium, display the Save As dialog box, click the drive representing your storage medium in the Navigation pane, and then double-click *Excel2010L1C1* in the Content pane.

Project 1a Creating and Saving a Document

1. Open Excel by clicking the Start button on the Taskbar, pointing to *All Programs*, clicking *Microsoft Office*, and then clicking *Microsoft Excel 2010*. (Depending on your operating system, these steps may vary.)
2. At the Excel worksheet that displays, create the worksheet shown in Figure 1.3 by completing the following steps:
   a. Press the Enter key once to make cell A2 the active cell.
   b. With cell A2 active (displays with a thick black border), type **Employee**.
   c. Press the Tab key. (This makes cell B2 active.)
   d. Type **Location** and then press the Tab key. (This makes cell C2 active.)
   e. Type **Benefits** and then press the Enter key to move the insertion point to cell A3.
   f. With cell A3 active, type the name **Avery**.
   g. Continue typing the data shown in Figure 1.3. (For commands for making specific cells active, refer to Table 1.2.)

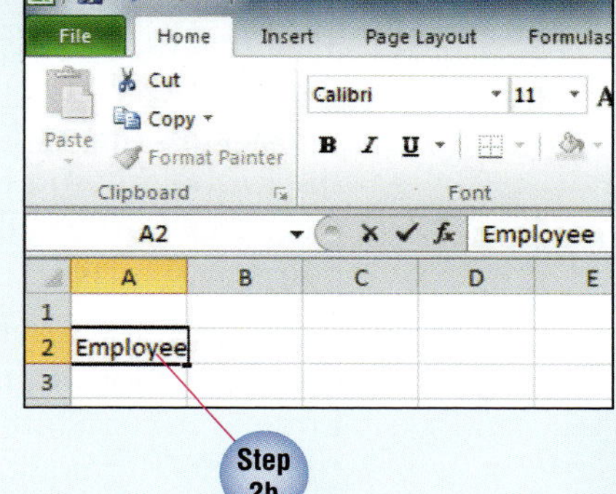

3. After typing the data shown in the cells in Figure 1.3, save the workbook by completing the following steps:
   a. Click the Save button on the Quick Access toolbar.
   b. At the Save As dialog box, click the drive representing your storage medium in the Navigation pane.
   c. Double-click the *Excel2010L1C1* folder that displays in the Content pane.
   d. Select the text in the *File name* text box and then type **EL1-C1-P1-EmpBene** (for Excel Level 1, Chapter 1, Project 1, and the workbook that contains information about employee benefits).
   e. Press the Enter key or click the Save button.

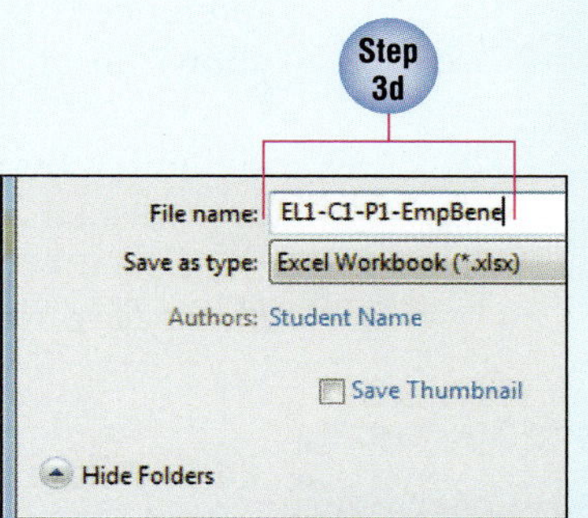

Figure 1.3 Project 1a

	A	B	C	D
1				
2	Employee	Location	Benefits	
3	Avery			
4	Connors			
5	Estrada			
6	Juergens			
7	Mikulich			
8	Talbot			
9				

Editing Data in a Cell

Edit data being typed in a cell by pressing the Backspace key to delete the character to the left of the insertion point or pressing the Delete key to delete the character to the right of the insertion point. To change the data in a cell, click the cell once to make it active and then type the new data. When a cell containing data is active, anything typed will take the place of the existing data.

If you want to edit only a portion of the data in a cell, double-click the cell. This makes the cell active, moves the insertion point inside the cell, and displays the word *Edit* at the left side of the Status bar. Move the insertion point using the arrow keys or the mouse and then make the needed corrections. If you are using the keyboard, you can press the Home key to move the insertion point to the first character in the cell or Formula bar, or press the End key to move the insertion point to the last character.

When you are finished editing the data in the cell, be sure to change out of the Edit mode. To do this, make another cell active. You can do this by pressing Enter, Tab, or Shift + Tab. You can also change out of the Edit mode and return to the Ready mode by clicking another cell or clicking the Enter button on the Formula bar.

Cancel

Enter

If the active cell does not contain data, the Formula bar displays only the cell reference (by column letter and row number). As you type data, the two buttons shown in Figure 1.4 display on the Formula bar to the right of the Name box. Click the Cancel button to delete the current cell entry. You can also delete the cell entry by pressing the Delete key. Click the Enter button to indicate that you are finished typing or editing the cell entry. When you click the Enter button on the Formula bar, the word *Enter* (or *Edit*) located at the left side of the Status bar changes to *Ready*.

Project 1b **Editing Data in a Cell** Part 2 of 3

1. With **EL1-C1-P1-EmpBene.xlsx** open, double-click cell A7 (contains *Mikulich*).
2. Move the insertion point immediately left of the *k* and then type a **c**. (This changes the spelling to *Mickulich*.)
3. Click once in cell A4 (contains *Connors*), type **Bryant**, and then press the Tab key. (Clicking only once allows you to type over the existing data.)
4. Edit cell C2 by completing the following steps:
   a. Click the Find & Select button in the Editing group in the Home tab and then click *Go To* at the drop-down list.
   b. At the Go To dialog box, type **C2** in the *Reference* text box and then click OK.
   c. Type **Classification** (over *Benefits*).
5. Click once in any other cell.
6. Click the Save button on the Quick Access toolbar to save the workbook again.

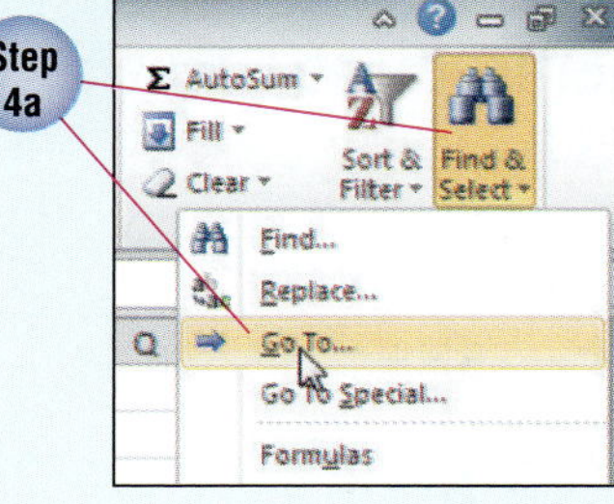

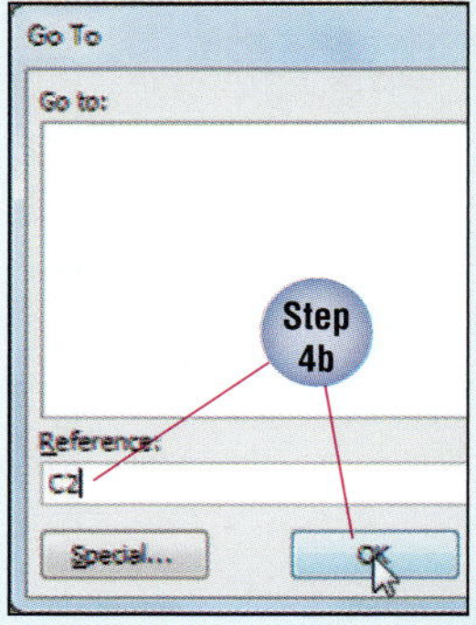

Figure 1.4 Buttons on the Formula Bar

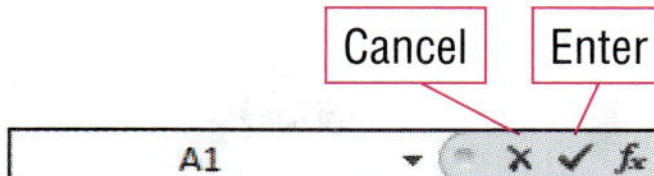

Printing a Workbook

Click the File tab and the Backstage view displays as shown in Figure 1.5. Use buttons and tabs at this view to work with and manage workbooks such as opening, closing, saving, and printing a workbook. If you want to remove the Backstage view without completing an action, click the File tab, click any other tab in the ribbon, or press the Esc key on your keyboard.

Ctrl + P is the keyboard command to display the Print dialog box.

Many of the computer projects you will be creating will need to be printed. Print a workbook from the Print tab of the Backstage view shown in Figure 1.6. To display this view, click the File tab and then click the Print tab. You can also display the Print tab Backstage view with the keyboard command Ctrl + P.

Figure 1.5 Backstage View

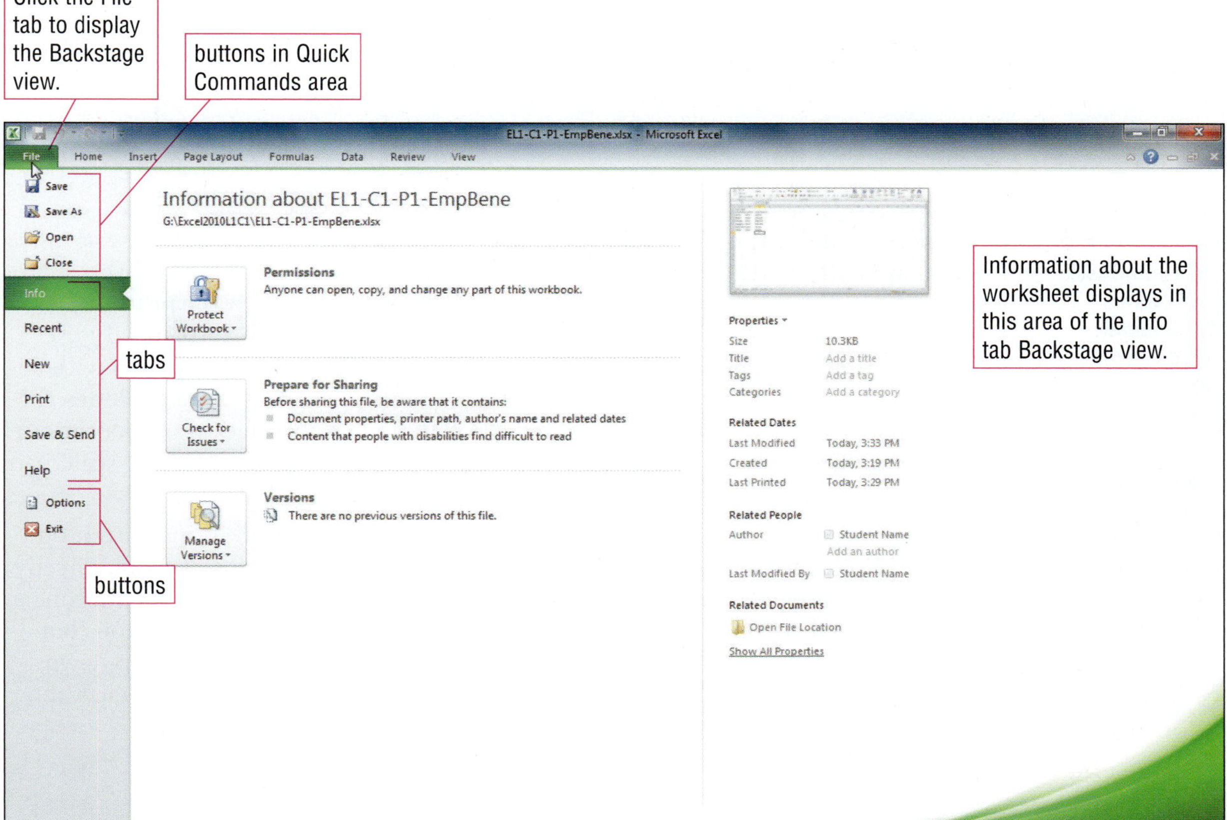

Figure 1.6 Print Tab Backstage View

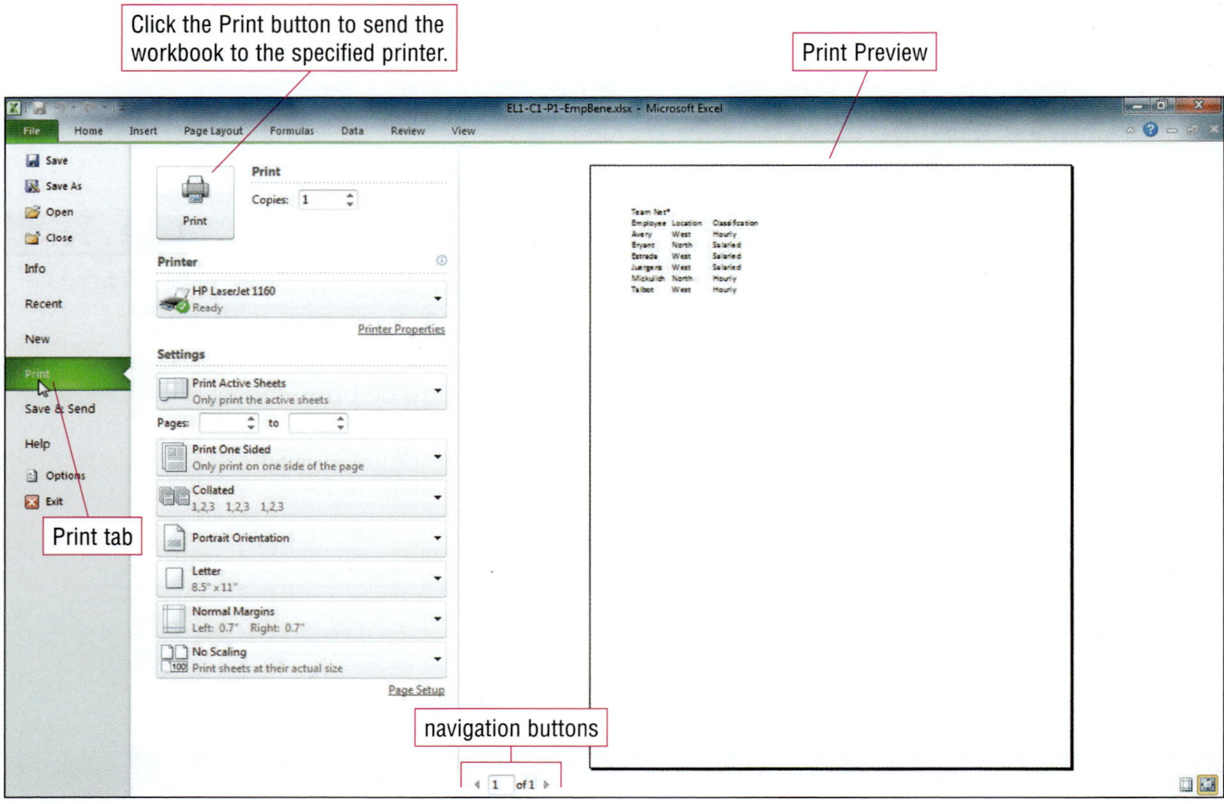

Quick Steps

Print a Workbook
1. Click File tab.
2. Click Print tab.
3. Click Print button.

OR

Click Quick Print button.

Close a Workbook
Click Close Window button.

OR

Click File tab, Close button.

Exit Excel
Click Close button.

OR

Click File tab, Exit button.

The left side of the Print tab Backstage view displays three categories—*Print, Printer*, and *Settings*. Click the Print button in the Print category to send the workbook to the printer and specify the number of copies you want printed in the *Copies* option text box. Use the gallery in the Printer category to specify the desired printer. The Settings category contains a number of galleries, each with options for specifying how you want your workbook printed. Use the galleries to specify whether or not you want the pages collated when printed; the orientation, page size, and margins of your workbook; and if you want the worksheet scaled to print all rows and columns of data on one page.

Another method for printing a workbook is to insert the Quick Print button on the Quick Access toolbar and then click the button. This sends the workbook directly to the printer without displaying the Print tab Backstage view. To insert the button on the Quick Access toolbar, click the Customize Quick Access Toolbar button that displays at the right side of the toolbar and then click *Quick Print* at the drop-down list. To remove the Quick Print button from the Quick Access toolbar, right-click the button and then click *Remove from Quick Access Toolbar* at the drop-down list.

Closing a Workbook

Close Window

To close an Excel workbook, click the File tab and then click the Close button. You can also close a workbook by clicking the Close Window button located toward the upper right corner of the screen. Position the mouse pointer on the button and a ScreenTip displays with the name *Close Window*.

Exiting Excel

To exit Excel, click the Close button that displays in the upper right corner of the screen. The Close button contains an X and if you position the mouse pointer on the button a ScreenTip displays with the name *Close*. You can also exit Excel by clicking the File tab and then clicking the Exit button.

Using Automatic Entering Features

Excel contains several features that help you enter data into cells quickly and efficiently. These features include ***AutoComplete***, which automatically inserts data in a cell that begins the same as a previous entry; ***AutoCorrect***, which automatically corrects many common typographical errors; and ***AutoFill***, which will automatically insert words, numbers, or formulas in a series.

Using AutoComplete and AutoCorrect

The AutoComplete feature will automatically insert data in a cell that begins the same as a previous entry. If the data inserted by AutoComplete is the data you want in the cell, press Enter. If it is not the desired data, simply continue typing the correct data. This feature can be very useful in a worksheet that contains repetitive data entries. For example, consider a worksheet that repeats the word *Payroll*. The second and subsequent times this word is to be inserted in a cell, simply typing the letter *P* will cause AutoComplete to insert the entire word.

The AutoCorrect feature automatically corrects many common typing errors. To see what symbols and words are in the AutoCorrect feature, click the File tab and then click the Options button located below the Help tab. At the Excel Options dialog box, click *Proofing* in the left panel and then click the AutoCorrect Options button located in the right panel. This displays the AutoCorrect dialog box with the AutoCorrect tab selected as shown in Figure 1.7 with a list box containing the replacement data.

Figure 1.7 AutoCorrect Dialog Box with AutoCorrect Tab Selected

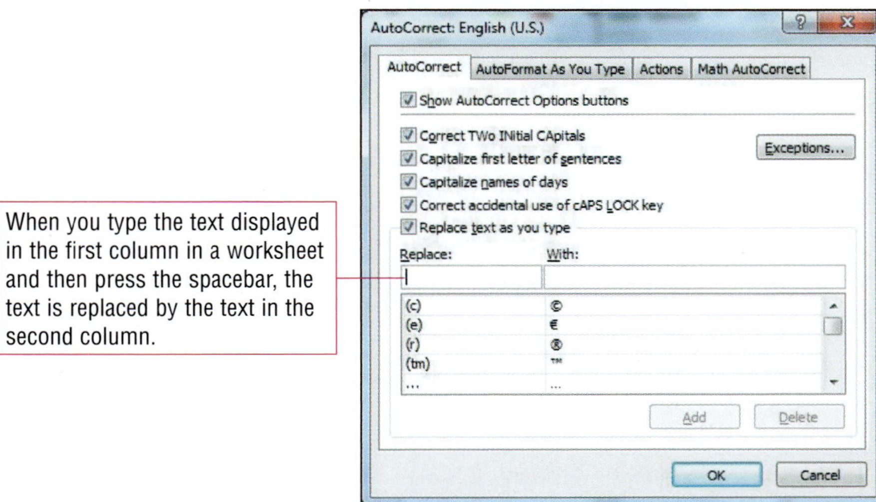

At the AutoCorrect dialog box, type the text shown in the first column in the list box and the text in the second column is inserted in the cell. Along with symbols, the AutoCorrect dialog box contains commonly misspelled words and common typographical errors.

Project 1c Inserting Data in Cells with AutoComplete

Part 3 of 3

1. With **EL1-C1-P1-EmpBene.xlsx** open make cell A1 active.
2. Type the text in cell A1 as shown in Figure 1.8. Insert the ® symbol by typing **(r)**. [AutoCorrect will change (r) to ®.]
3. Type the remaining text in the cells. When you type the **W** in *West* in cell B5, the AutoComplete feature will insert *West*. Accept this by pressing the Enter key. (Pressing the Enter key accepts *West* and also makes the cell below active.) Use the AutoComplete feature to enter *West* in B6 and B8 and *North* in cell B7. Use AutoComplete to enter the second and subsequent occurrences of *Salaried* and *Hourly*.
4. Click the Save button on the Quick Access toolbar.
5. Print **EL1-C1-P1-EmpBene.xlsx** by clicking the File tab, clicking the Print tab, and then clicking the Print button at the Print tab Backstage view. (The gridlines will not print.)

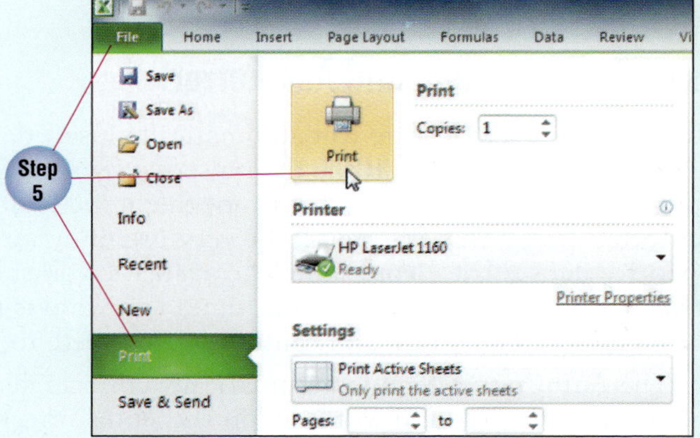

6. Close the workbook by clicking the Close Window button (contains an X) that displays in the upper right corner of the screen. (Make sure you click the Close Window button and not the Close button.)

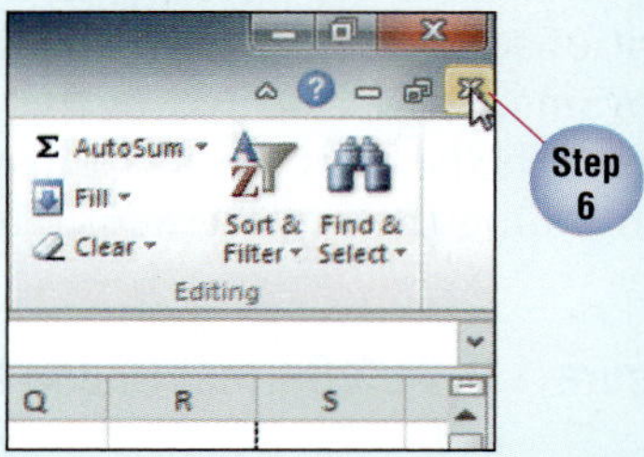

Figure 1.8 Project 1c

	A	B	C	D
1	Team Net®			
2	Employee	Location	Classification	
3	Avery	West	Hourly	
4	Bryant	North	Salaried	
5	Estrada	West	Salaried	
6	Juergens	West	Salaried	
7	Mickulich	North	Hourly	
8	Talbot	West	Hourly	
9				

Project 2 **Open and Format a Workbook and Insert Formulas** **3 Parts**

You will open an existing workbook and insert formulas to find the sum and averages of numbers.

Using AutoFill

When a cell is active, a thick black border surrounds it and a small black square displays in the bottom right corner of the border. This black square is called the AutoFill ***fill handle*** (see Figure 1.2). With the fill handle, you can quickly fill a range of cells with the same data or with consecutive data. For example, suppose you need to insert the year 2012 in a row or column of cells. To do this quickly, type **2012** in the first cell, position the mouse pointer on the fill handle, hold down the left mouse button, drag across the cells in which you want the year inserted, and then release the mouse button.

You can also use the fill handle to insert a series in a row or column of cells. For example, suppose you are creating a worksheet with data for all of the months in the year. Type **January** in the first cell, position the mouse pointer on the fill handle, hold down the left mouse button, drag down or across to 11 more cells, and then release the mouse button. Excel automatically inserts the other 11 months in the year in the proper order. When using the fill handle, the cells must be adjacent. Table 1.3 identifies the sequence inserted in cells by Excel when specific data is entered.

If you do not want a series to increment, hold down the Ctrl key while dragging the fill handle.

Certain sequences, such as *2, 4* and *Jan 12, Jan 13,* require that both cells be selected before using the fill handle. If only the cell containing *2* is active, the fill handle will insert *2*s in the selected cells. The list in Table 1.3 is only a sampling of what the fill handle can do. You may find a variety of other sequences that can be inserted in a worksheet using the fill handle.

An Auto Fill Options button displays when you fill cells with the fill handle. Click this button and a list of options displays for filling the cells. By default, data and formatting are filled in each cell. You can choose to fill only the formatting in the cells or fill only the data without the formatting.

Auto Fill Options

Table 1.3 AutoFill Fill Handle Series

Enter this data *(Commas represent data in separate cells.)*	***And the fill handle will insert this sequence in adjacent cells***
January	February, March, April, and so on . . .
Jan	Feb, Mar, Apr, and so on . . .
Jan 12, Jan 13	14-Jan, 15-Jan, 16-Jan, and so on . . .
Monday	Tuesday, Wednesday, Thursday, and so on . . .
Product 1	Product 2, Product 3, Product 4, and so on . . .
Qtr 1	Qtr 2, Qtr 3, Qtr 4
2, 4	6, 8, 10, and so on . . .

Quick Steps

Open a Workbook

1. Click File tab.
2. Click Open button.
3. Display desired folder.
4. Double-click workbook name.

Opening a Workbook

Open an Excel workbook by displaying the Open dialog box and then double-clicking the desired workbook name. Display the Open dialog box by clicking the File tab and then clicking the Open button. You can also use the keyboard command Ctrl + O to display the Open dialog box.

Project 2a Inserting Data in Cells with the Fill Handle

Part 1 of 3

1. Open **FillCells.xlsx**. (This workbook is located in the Excel2010L1C1 folder on your storage medium.)
2. Save the workbook with Save As and name it **EL1-C1-P2-FillCells**.
3. Add data to cells as shown in Figure 1.9. Begin by making cell B1 active and then typing **January**.
4. Position the mouse pointer on the fill handle for cell B1, hold down the left mouse button, drag across to cell G1, and then release the mouse button.

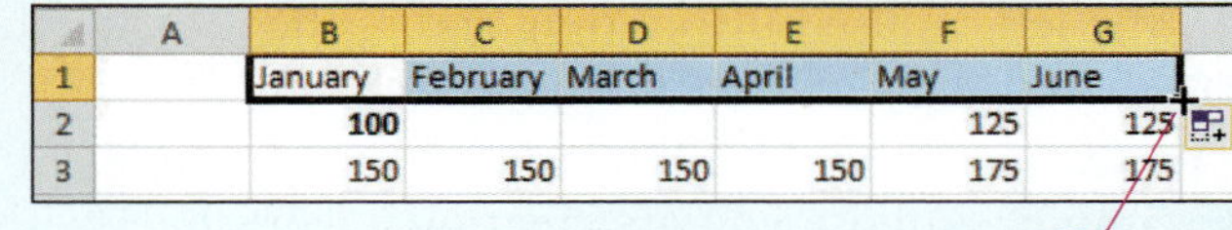

	A	B	C	D	E	F	G
1		January	February	March	April	May	June
2		100				125	125
3		150	150	150	150	175	175

Step 4

5. Type a sequence and then use the fill handle to fill the remaining cells by completing the following steps:
   a. Make cell A2 active and then type **Year 1**.
   b. Make cell A3 active and then type **Year 3**.
   c. Select cells A2 and A3 by positioning the mouse pointer in cell A2, holding down the left mouse button, dragging down to cell A3, and then releasing the mouse button.
   d. Drag the fill handle for cell A3 to cell A5. (This inserts *Year 5* in cell A4 and *Year 7* in cell A5.)
6. Use the fill handle to fill adjacent cells with a number but not the formatting by completing the following steps:
   a. Make cell B2 active. (This cell contains *100* with bold formatting.)
   b. Drag the fill handle for cell B2 to cell E2. (This inserts ***100*** in cells C2, D2, and E2.)
   c. Click the Auto Fill Options button that displays at the bottom right of the selected cells.
   d. Click the *Fill Without Formatting* option at the drop-down list.

	A	B	C	D	E	F	G	H
1		January	February	March	April	May	June	
2	Year 1	100	100	100	100	125	125	
3	Year 3	150	150	150	150	175	175	
4	Year 5	200	200	200	150			
5	Year 7	250	250	250	250			

Copy Cells
Fill Series
Fill Formatting Only
Fill Without Formatting

Step 6c

Step 6d

7. Use the fill handle to apply formatting only by completing the following steps:
   a. Make cell B2 active.
   b. Drag the fill handle to cell B5.
   c. Click the Auto Fill Options button and then click *Fill Formatting Only* at the drop-down list.
8. Make cell A10 active and then type **Qtr 1**.
9. Drag the fill handle for cell A10 to cell A13.
10. Save **EL1-C1-P2-FillCells.xlsx**.

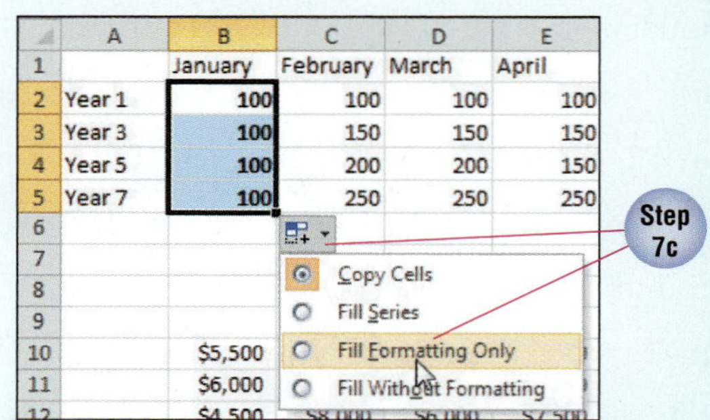

	A	B	C	D	E
1		January	February	March	April
2	Year 1	100	100	100	100
3	Year 3	100	150	150	150
4	Year 5	100	200	200	150
5	Year 7	100	250	250	250
10		$5,500			
11		$6,000			

Figure 1.9 Project 2a

	A	B	C	D	E	F	G	H
1		January	February	March	April	May	June	
2	Year 1	**100**	100	100	100	125	125	
3	Year 3	**150**	150	150	150	175	175	
4	Year 5	**200**	200	200	150	150	150	
5	Year 7	**250**	250	250	250	250	250	
6								
7								
8								
9								
10	Qtr 1	$5,500	$6,250	$7,000	$8,500	$5,500	$4,500	
11	Qtr 2	$6,000	$7,250	$6,500	$9,000	$4,000	$5,000	
12	Qtr 3	$4,500	$8,000	$6,000	$7,500	$6,000	$5,000	
13	Qtr 4	$6,500	$8,500	$7,000	$8,000	$5,500	$6,000	
14								

Inserting Formulas

Excel is a powerful decision-making tool you can use to manipulate data to answer "what if" situations. Insert a formula in a worksheet and then manipulate the data to make projections, answer specific questions, and use as a planning tool. For example, the manager of a department might use an Excel worksheet to prepare a department budget and then determine the impact on the budget of hiring a new employee or increasing the volume of production.

Insert a ***formula*** in a worksheet to perform calculations on values. A formula contains a mathematical operator, value, cell reference, cell range, and a function. Formulas can be written that add, subtract, multiply, and/or divide values. Formulas can also be written that calculate averages, percentages, minimum and maximum values, and much more. Excel includes an AutoSum button in the Editing group in the Home tab that inserts a formula to calculate the total of a range of cells.

Quick Steps

Insert Formula Using Sum Button

1. Click in desired cell.
2. Click AutoSum button.
3. Check range identified and make changes if necessary.
4. Press Enter.

HINT

You can use the keyboard command Alt + = to insert the SUM function in the cell.

Using the AutoSum Button to Add Numbers

AutoSum

You can use the AutoSum button in the Editing group in the Home tab to insert a formula. The AutoSum button adds numbers automatically with the SUM function. Make active the cell in which you want to insert the formula (this cell should be empty) and then click the AutoSum button. Excel looks for a range of cells containing numbers above the active cell. If no cell above contains numbers, then Excel looks to the left of the active cell. Excel suggests the range of cells to be added. If the suggested range is not correct, drag through the desired range of cells with the mouse, and then press Enter. You can also just double-click the AutoSum button and this will insert the SUM function with the range Excel chooses.

Adding Values with the AutoSum Button

Part 2 of 3

1. With **EL1-C1-P2-FillCells.xlsx** open, make cell A6 active and then type **Total**.
2. Make cell B6 active and then calculate the sum of cells by clicking the AutoSum button in the Editing group in the Home tab.
3. Excel inserts the formula *=SUM(B2:B5)* in cell B6. This is the correct range of cells, so press Enter.

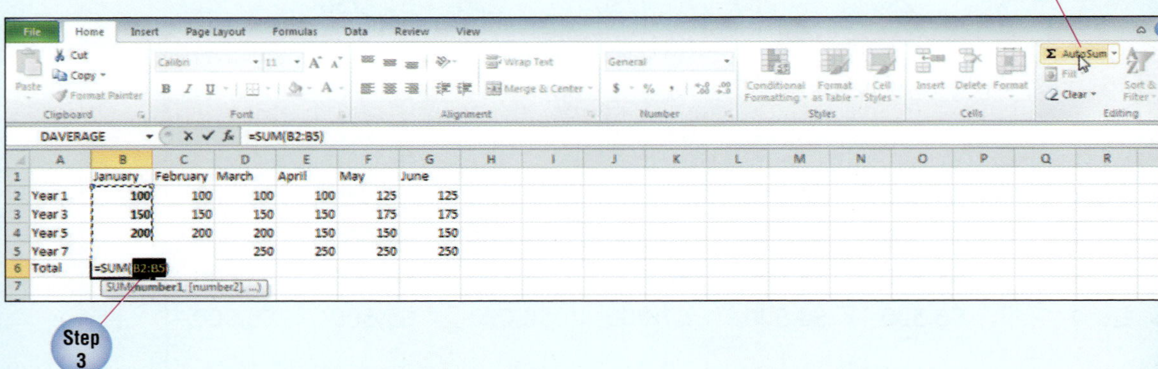

4. Make cell C6 active and then click the AutoSum button in the Editing group.
5. Excel inserts the formula *=SUM(C2:C5)* in cell C6. This is the correct range of cells, so press Enter.
6. Make cell D6 active.
7. Double-click the AutoSum button. [This inserts the formula *=SUM(D2:D5)* in cell D6 and inserts the sum *700*.]
8. Insert the sum in cells E6, F6, and G6.
9. Save **EL1-C1-P2-FillCells**.

Quick Steps

Insert Average Formula Using Sum Button
1. Click in desired cell.
2. Click AutoSum button arrow.
3. Click *Average*.
4. Specify range.
5. Press Enter.

Copy Formula Using Fill Handle
1. Insert formula in cell.
2. Make active the cell containing formula.
3. Using fill handle, drag through cells you want to contain formula.

Using the AutoSum Button to Average Numbers

A common function in a formula is the AVERAGE function. With this function, a range of cells is added together and then divided by the number of cell entries. The AVERAGE function is available on the AutoSum button. Click the AutoSum button arrow and a drop-down list displays with a number of common functions.

Using the Fill Handle to Copy a Formula

In a worksheet, you may want to insert the same basic formula in other cells. In a situation where a formula is copied to other locations in a worksheet, use a ***relative cell reference***. Copy a formula containing relative cell references and the cell references change. For example, if you enter the formula *=SUM(A2:C2)* in cell D2 and then copy it relatively to cell D3, the formula in cell D3 displays as *=SUM(A3:C3)*. You can use the fill handle to copy a formula relatively in a worksheet. To do this, position the mouse pointer on the fill handle until the mouse pointer turns into a thin black cross, hold down the left mouse button, drag and select the desired cells, and then release the mouse button.

Project 2c Inserting the AVERAGE Function and Copying a Formula Relatively — Part 3 of 3

1. With **EL1-C1-P2-FillCells.xlsx** open, make cell A14 active, and then type Average.
2. Insert the average of cells B10 through B13 by completing the following steps:
   a. Make cell B14 active.
   b. Click the AutoSum button arrow in the Editing group and then click *Average* at the drop-down list.
   c. Excel inserts the formula *=AVERAGE(B10:B13)* in cell B14. This is the correct range of cells, so press Enter.
3. Copy the formula relatively to cells C14 through G14 by completing the following steps:
   a. Make cell B14 active.
   b. Position the mouse pointer on the fill handle, hold down the left mouse button, drag across to cell G14, and then release the mouse button.

9							
10	Qtr 1	$5,500	$6,250	$7,000	$8,500	$5,500	$4,500
11	Qtr 2	$6,000	$7,250	$6,500	$9,000	$4,000	$5,000
12	Qtr 3	$4,500	$8,000	$6,000	$7,500	$6,000	$5,000
13	Qtr 4	$6,500	$8,500	$7,000	$8,000	$5,500	$6,000
14	Average	$5,625	$7,500	$6,625	$8,250	$5,250	$5,125
15							
16							

4. Save, print, and then close **EL1-C1-P2-FillCells.xlsx**.

Format a Worksheet — 2 Parts

You will open a monthly expenses workbook and then change column width, merge and center cells, and apply number formatting to numbers in cells.

Selecting Cells

You can use a variety of methods for formatting cells in a worksheet. For example, you can change the alignment of data in cells or rows or add character formatting. To identify the cells that are to be affected by the formatting, select the specific cells.

Selecting Cells Using the Mouse

Select specific cells in a worksheet using the mouse or select columns or rows. Table 1.4 displays the methods for selecting cells using the mouse.

Selected cells, except the active cell, display with a light blue background (this may vary) rather than a white background. The active cell is the first cell in the selection block and displays in the normal manner (white background with black data). Selected cells remain selected until you click a cell with the mouse or press an arrow key on the keyboard.

The first cell in a range displays with a white background and is the active cell.

Table 1.4 Selecting with the Mouse

To select this	*Do this*
Column	Position the cell pointer on the column header (a letter) and then click the left mouse button.
Row	Position the cell pointer on the row header (a number) and then click the left mouse button.
Adjacent cells	Drag with mouse to select specific cells.
Nonadjacent cells	Hold down the Ctrl key while clicking column header, row header, or specific cells.
All cells in worksheet	Click Select All button (refer to Figure 1.2).

Selecting Cells Using the Keyboard

You can use the keyboard to select specific cells within a worksheet. Table 1.5 displays the commands for selecting specific cells. If a worksheet contains data, the last entry in Table 1.5 will select the cells containing data. If the worksheet contains groups of data separated by empty cells, Ctrl + A or Ctrl + Shift + spacebar will select a group of cells rather than all of the cells.

Selecting Data within Cells

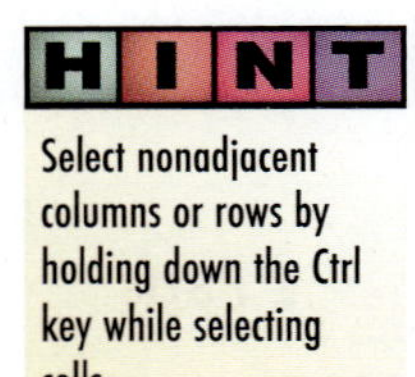

HINT
Select nonadjacent columns or rows by holding down the Ctrl key while selecting cells.

The selection commands presented select the entire cell. You can also select specific characters within a cell. To do this with the mouse, position the cell pointer in the desired cell, and then double-click the left mouse button. Drag with the I-beam pointer through the data you want selected. Data selected within a cell displays in white with a black background. If you are using the keyboard to select data in a cell, hold down the Shift key, and then press the arrow key that moves the insertion point in the desired direction. Data the insertion point passes through will be selected. You can also press F8 to turn on the Extend Selection mode, move the insertion point in the desired direction to select the data, and then press F8 to turn off the Extend Selection mode. When the Extend Selection mode is on, the words *Extend Selection* display toward the left side of the Status bar.

Table 1.5 Selecting Cells Using the Keyboard

To select	*Press*
Cells in direction of arrow key	Shift + arrow key
From active cell to beginning of row	Shift + Home
From active cell to beginning of worksheet	Shift + Ctrl + Home
From active cell to last cell in worksheet containing data	Shift + Ctrl + End
An entire column	Ctrl + spacebar
An entire row	Shift + spacebar
An entire worksheet	Ctrl + A

Applying Basic Formatting

Excel provides a wide range of formatting options you can apply to cells in a worksheet. Some basic formatting options that are helpful when creating a worksheet include changing column width, merging and centering cells, and formatting numbers.

Changing Column Width

If data such as text or numbers overlaps in a cell, you can increase the width of the column to accommodate the data. To do this, position the mouse pointer on the blue boundary line between columns in the column header (Figure 1.2 identifies the column header) until the pointer turns into a double-headed arrow pointing left and right and then drag the boundary to the desired location. If the column contains data, you can double-click the column boundary at the right side of the column and the column will increase in size to accommodate the longest entry.

Quick Steps

Change Column Width
Drag column boundary line.
OR
Double-click column boundary.

Merge and Center Cells
1. Select cells.
2. Click Merge & Center button.

Merge & Center

Merging and Centering Cells

As you learned earlier in this chapter, if text you type is longer than the cell can accommodate, the text overlaps the next cell to the right. You can merge cells to accommodate the text and also center the text within the merged cells. To merge cells and center text, select the desired cells and then click the Merge & Center button located in the Alignment group in the Home tab.

Project 3a **Changing Column Width and Merging and Centering Cells** Part 1 of 2

1. Open **MoExps.xlsx** from the Excel2010L1C1 folder on your storage medium.
2. Save the workbook with Save As and name it **EL1-C1-P3-MoExps**.
3. Change column width by completing the following steps:
   a. Position the mouse pointer in the column header on the boundary line between columns A and B until the pointer turns into a double-headed arrow pointing left and right.

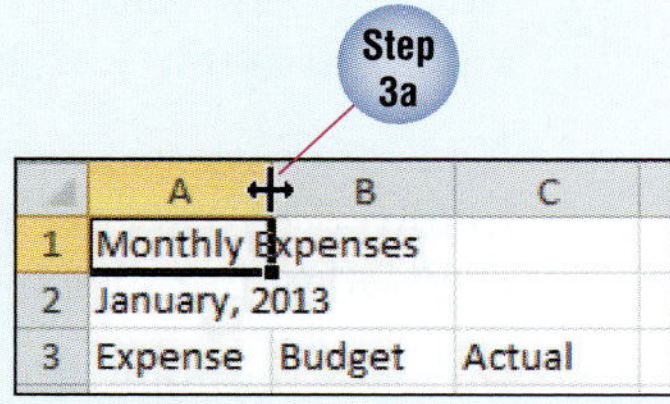

   b. Double-click the left mouse button.
   c. Position the mouse pointer in the column header on the boundary line between columns E and F and then double-click the left mouse button.
   d. Position the mouse pointer in the column header on the boundary line between columns F and G and then double-click the left mouse button.

4. Merge and center cells by completing the following steps:
   a. Select cells A1 through C1.
   b. Click the Merge & Center button in the Alignment group in the Home tab.
   c. Select cells A2 through C2.
   d. Click the Merge & Center button.
   e. Select cells E1 and F1 and then click the Merge & Center button.
5. Save **EL1-C1-P3-MoExps.xlsx**.

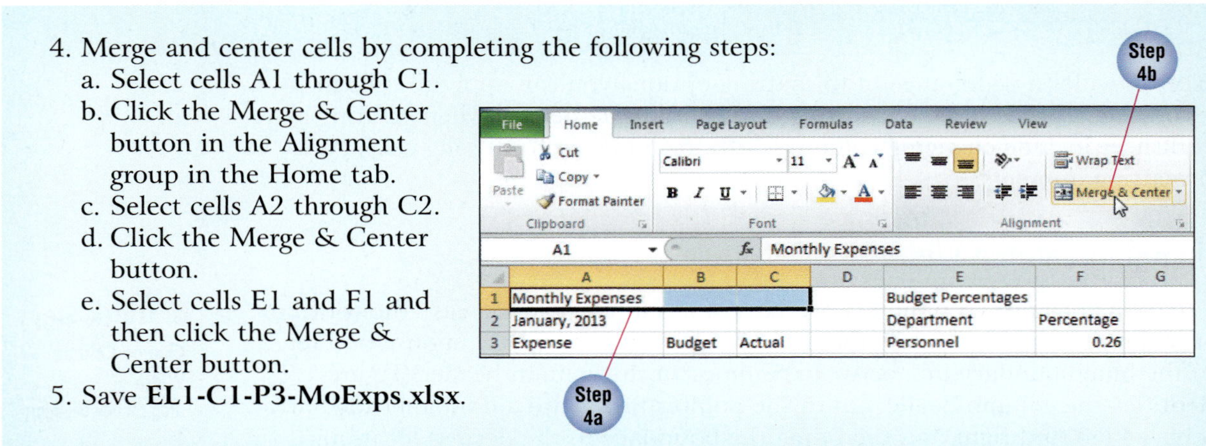

Formatting Numbers

Numbers in a cell, by default, are aligned at the right and decimals and commas do not display unless they are typed in the cell. You can change the format of numbers with buttons in the Number group in the Home tab. Symbols you can use to format numbers include a percent sign (%), a comma (,), and a dollar sign ($). For example, if you type the number *$45.50* in a cell, Excel automatically applies Currency formatting to the number. If you type *45%*, Excel automatically applies the Percent formatting to the number. The Number group in the Home tab contains five buttons you can use to format numbers in cells. The five buttons are shown and described in Table 1.6.

Table 1.6 Number Formatting Buttons

	Click this button	*To do this*
$	Accounting Number Format	Add a dollar sign, any necessary commas, and a decimal point followed by two decimal digits, if none are typed; right-align number in cell.
%	Percent Style	Multiply cell value by 100 and display result with a percent symbol; right-align number in cell.
,	Comma Style	Add any necessary commas and a decimal point followed by two decimal digits, if none are typed; right-align number in cell.
.0 .00	Increase Decimal	Increase number of decimal places displayed after decimal point in selected cell.
.00 .0	Decrease Decimal	Decrease number of decimal places displayed after decimal point in selected cell.

Specify the formatting for numbers in cells in a worksheet before typing the numbers, or format existing numbers in a worksheet. The Increase Decimal and Decrease Decimal buttons in the Number group in the Home tab will change decimal places for existing numbers only. The Number group in the Home tab also contains the Number Format button. Click the Number Format button arrow and a drop-down list displays of common number formats. Click the desired format at the drop-down list to apply the number formatting to the cell or selected cells.

A general guideline in accounting is to insert a dollar sign before the first number amount in a column and before the total number amount but not before the number amounts in between. You can format a worksheet following this guideline by applying the Accounting Number Format to the first amount and total amount and apply the Comma Style formatting to the number amounts in between.

Project 3b Formatting Numbers

Part 2 of 2

1. With **EL1-C1-P3-MoExps.xlsx** open, make cell B13 active and then double-click the AutoSum button. (This inserts the total of the numbers in cells B4 through B12.)
2. Make cell C13 active and then double-click the AutoSum button.
3. Apply Accounting Number Format to cells by completing the following steps:
   a. Select cells B4 and C4.
   b. Click the Accounting Number Format button in the Number group in the Home tab.
   c. Decrease the decimals by clicking twice on the Decrease Decimal button in the Number group.

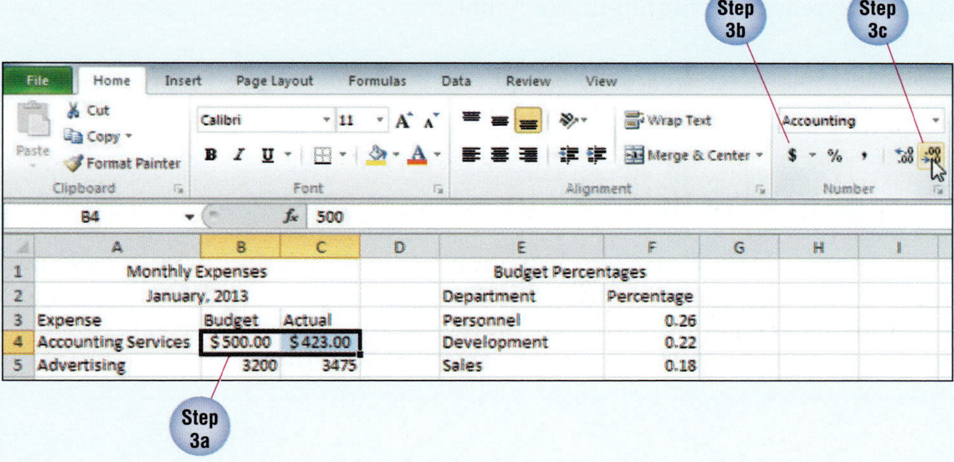

   d. Select cells B13 and C13.
   e. Click the Accounting Number Format button.
   f. Click twice on the Decrease Decimal button.

4. Apply Comma Style formatting to numbers by completing the following steps:
   a. Select cells B5 through C12.
   b. Click the Comma Style button in the Number group.
   c. Click twice on the Decrease Decimal button.

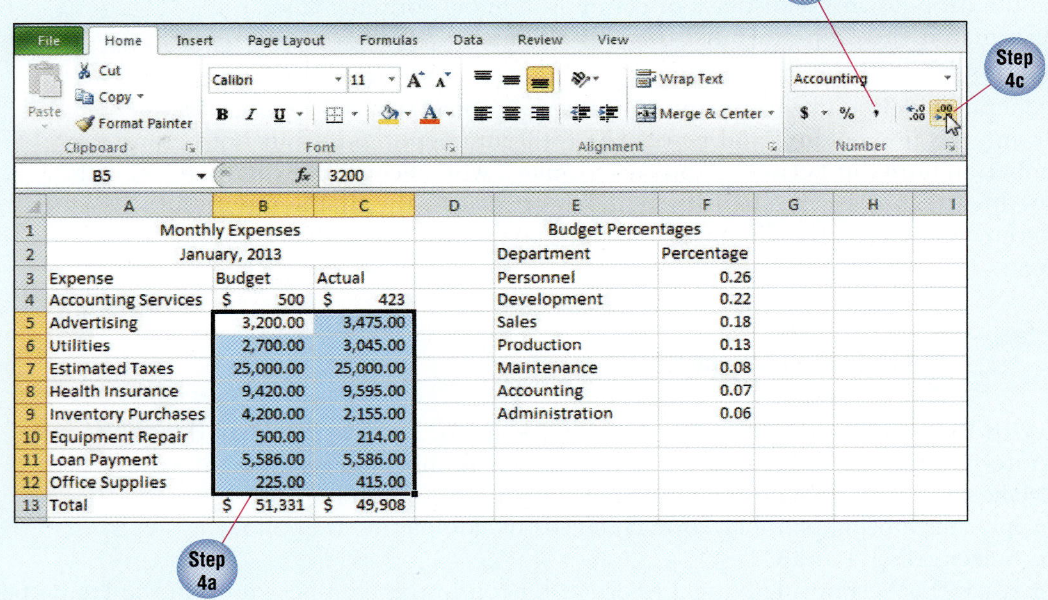

5. Apply Percent Style formatting to numbers by completing the following steps:
   a. Select cells F3 through F9.
   b. Click the Percent Style button in the Number group in the Home tab.
6. Click in cell A1.
7. Save, print, and then close **EL1-C1-P3-MoExps.xlsx**.

Project 4 Use the Help Feature — 3 Parts

You will use the Help feature to learn more about entering data in cells and saving a workbook and use the ScreenTip to display information about a specific button. You will also learn about options available at the Help tab Backstage view and how to customize Help to search for information offline.

Using Help

Quick Steps

Use the Help Feature
1. Click Microsoft Excel Help button.
2. Type topic or feature.
3. Press Enter.
4. Click desired topic.

Microsoft Excel includes a Help feature that contains information about Excel features and commands. This on-screen reference manual is similar to Windows Help and the Help features in Word, PowerPoint, and Access. Click the Microsoft Excel Help button (the circle with the question mark) located in the upper right corner of the screen or press the keyboard shortcut F1 to display the Excel Help window. In this window, type a topic, feature, or question in the search text box and then press the Enter key. Topics related to the search text display in the Excel Help window. Click a topic that interests you. If the topic window contains a

Show All hyperlink in the upper right corner, click this hyperlink and the topic options expand to show additional help information related to the topic. When you click the Show All hyperlink, it becomes the Hide All hyperlink.

Help

Getting Help at the Help Tab Backstage View

The Help tab Backstage view, shown in Figure 1.10, contains an option for displaying the Excel Help window as well as other options. Click the Microsoft Office Help button in the Support category to display the Excel Help window and click the Getting Started button to access the Microsoft website that displays information about getting started with Excel 2010. Click the Contact Us button in the Support category and the Microsoft Support website displays. Click the Options button in the Tools for Working With Office category and the Excel Options dialog box displays. You will learn about this dialog box in a later chapter. Click the Check for Updates button and the Microsoft Update website displays with information on available updates. The right side of the Help tab Backstage view displays information about Office and Excel.

Quick Steps

Display Help Tab Backstage View
1. Click File tab.
2. Click Help button.

Getting Help on a Button

When you position the mouse pointer on a button, a ScreenTip displays with information about the button. Some button ScreenTips display with the message "Press F1 for more help" that is preceded by an image of the Help button. With the ScreenTip visible, press the F1 function key on your keyboard and the Excel Help window opens and displays information about the specific button.

Figure 1.10 Help Tab Backstage View

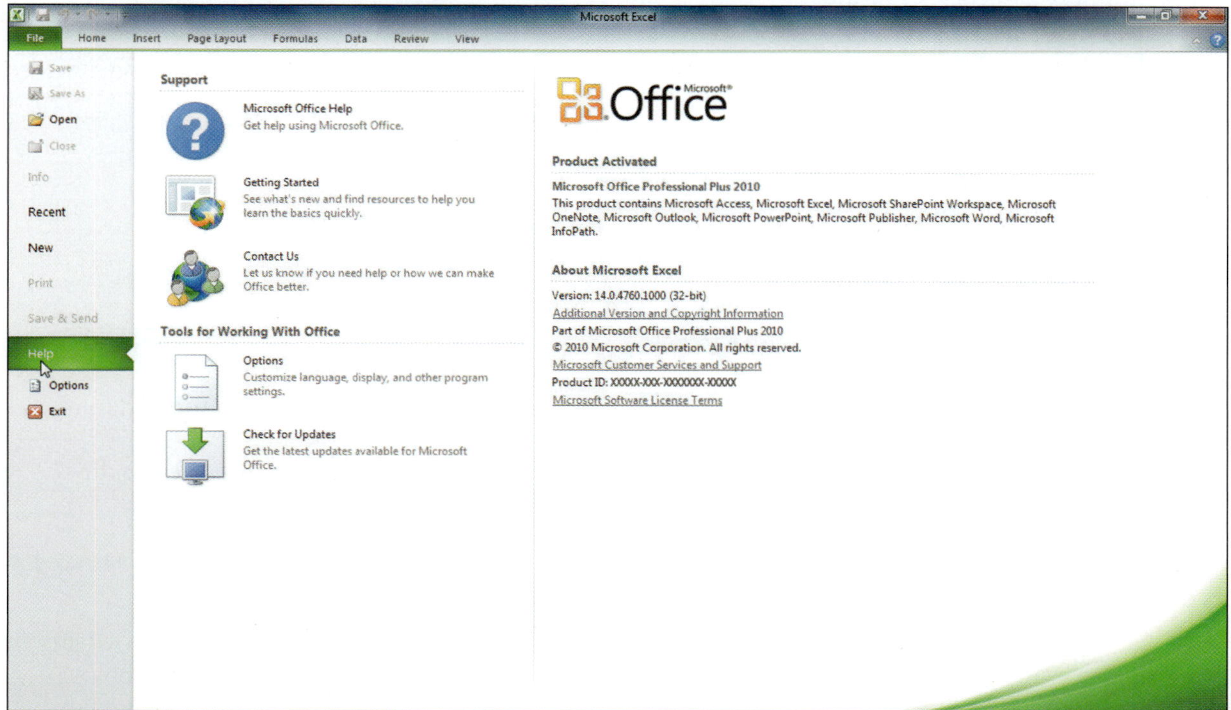

Project 4a Using the Help Feature

Part 1 of 3

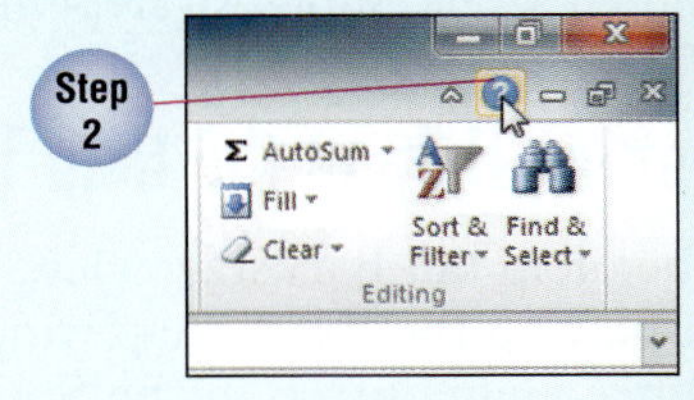

1. At the blank screen, press Ctrl + N to display a blank workbook. (Ctrl + N is the keyboard command to open a blank workbook.)
2. Click the Microsoft Excel Help button located in the upper right corner of the screen.
3. At the Excel Help window, type **enter data** in the search text box and then press the Enter key. (Make sure that *Connected to Office.com* displays in the lower right corner of the window. If not, click the Search button arrow and then click *Content from Office.com* at the drop-down list.)
4. When the list of topics displays, click the <u>Enter data manually in worksheet cells</u> hyperlink.
5. Read the information about entering data in cells. (If you want a printing of the information, you can click the Print button located toward the top of the Excel Help window and then click the Print button at the Print dialog box.)
6. Close the Excel Help window by clicking the Close button located in the upper right corner of the window.

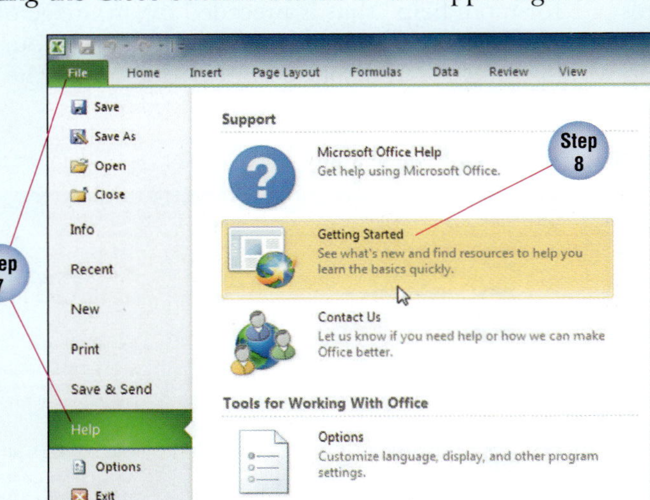

7. Click the File tab and then click the Help tab.
8. At the Help tab Backstage view, click the Getting Started button in the Support category. (You must be connected to the Internet to display the web page.)
9. Look at the information that displays at the website and then click the Close button located in the upper right corner of the web page.
10. Click the File tab and then click the Help tab.
11. Click the Contact Us button, look at the information that displays at the website, and then close the web page.
12. Hover the mouse pointer over the Wrap Text button in the Alignment group in the Home tab until the ScreenTip displays and then press F1.
13. At the Excel Help window, read the information that displays and then close the window.

Getting Help in a Dialog Box or Backstage View

Some dialog boxes, as well as the Backstage view, contain a Help button you can click to display a help window with specific information about the dialog box or Backstage view. After reading and/or printing the information, close a dialog box by clicking the Close button located in the upper right corner of the dialog box or close the Backstage view by clicking the File tab or clicking any other tab in the ribbon.

Project 4b Getting Help in a Dialog Box and Backstage View

Part 2 of 3

1. At the blank workbook, click the File tab and then click the Save As button.
2. At the Save As dialog box, click the Help button located near the upper right corner of the dialog box.
3. Read the information about saving files that displays in the Windows Help and Support window.
4. Close the window by clicking the Close button located in the upper right corner of the window.
5. Close the Save As dialog box.
6. Click the File tab.
7. At the Backstage view, click the Help button located near the upper right corner of the window.
8. At the Excel Help window, click a hyperlink that interests you.
9. Read the information and then close the Excel Help window by clicking the Close button located in the upper right corner of the window.
10. Click the File tab to return to the blank workbook.

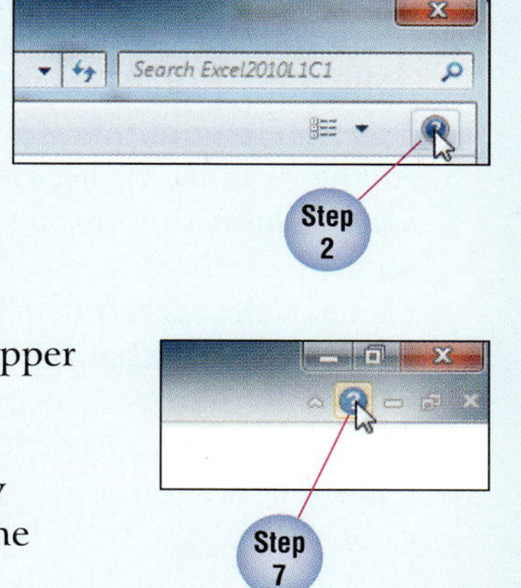

Customizing Help

By default, the Excel Help feature will search for an Internet connection and, if one is found, display help resources from Office Online. If you are connected online to help resources, the message "Connected to Office.com" displays in the lower right corner of the Excel Help window. If you are not connected to the Internet, the message displays as "Offline."

Office Online provides additional help resources such as training and templates. To view the resources, display the Excel Help window and then click the down-pointing arrow at the right side of the Search button. This displays a drop-down list similar to the one shown in Figure 1.11. Generally, the *All Excel* option in the *Content from Office.com* section is selected. If you want to search only the Help resources available with your computer (offline), click the *Excel Help* option in the *Content from this computer* section. To access Office.com training, click the *Excel Training* option in the *Content from Office.com* section, type a training topic in the search text box, and then click OK.

Figure 1.11 Excel Help Search Drop-down List

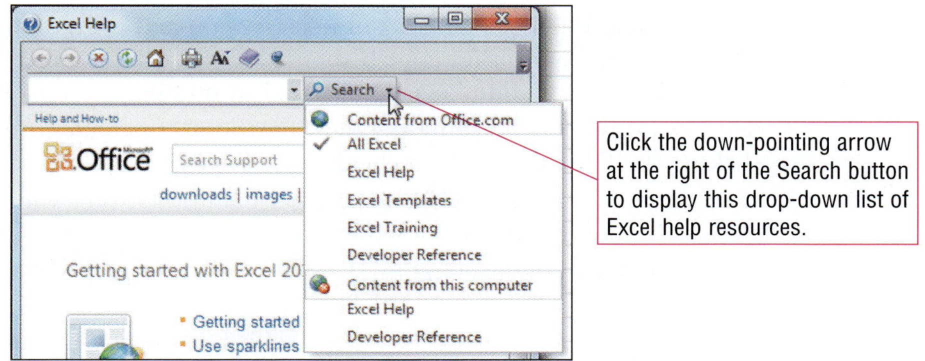

Click the down-pointing arrow at the right of the Search button to display this drop-down list of Excel help resources.

Project 4c Customizing Help

Part 3 of 3

1. At a blank worksheet, click the Microsoft Excel Help button located toward the upper right corner of the screen.
2. Click the down-pointing arrow at the right side of the Search button in the Excel Help window.
3. At the drop-down list that displays, click *Excel Help* in the *Content from this computer* section.
4. Click in the search text box, type **formulas**, and then press Enter.
5. Click a hyperlink that interests you and then read the information that displays.
6. Click the down-pointing arrow at the right side of the Search button and then click *Excel Training* in the *Content from Office.com* section.

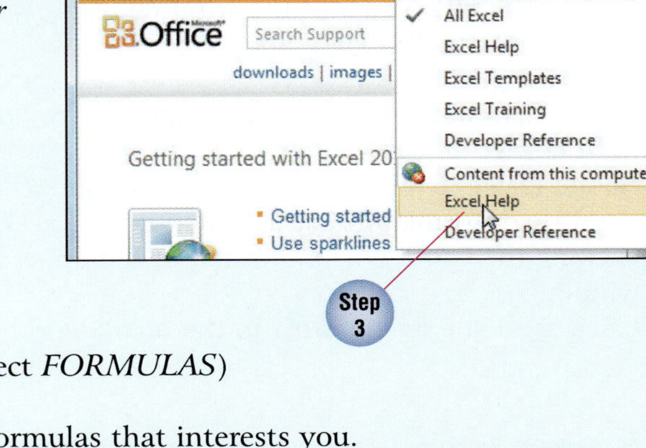

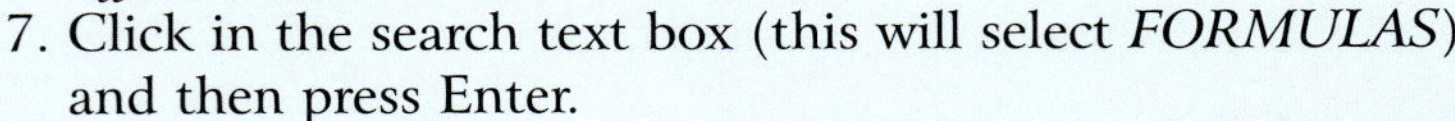

7. Click in the search text box (this will select *FORMULAS*) and then press Enter.
8. Click the hyperlink of a training about formulas that interests you.
9. After completing the training, close Internet Explorer and then close the Excel Help window.

Chapter Summary

- A file created in Excel is called a workbook, which consists of individual worksheets. The intersection of columns and rows is referred to as a cell. Gridlines are the horizontal and vertical lines that define cells.
- An Excel window contains the following elements: Quick Access toolbar, File tab, Title bar, tabs, ribbon, Name box, Formula bar, scroll bars, sheet tabs, and Status bar.
- When the insertion point is positioned in a cell, the cell name (also called the cell reference) displays in the Name box located at the left side of the Formula bar. The cell name includes the column letter and row number.
- If data entered in a cell consists of text (letters) and it does not fit into the cell, it overlaps the cell to the right. If the data consists of numbers and it does not fit into the cell, the numbers are changed to number symbols (###).
- Save a workbook by clicking the Save button on the Quick Access toolbar or by clicking the File tab and then clicking the Save button.
- To replace data in a cell, click the cell once and then type the new data. To edit data within a cell, double-click the cell and then make necessary changes.
- Print a workbook by clicking the File tab, clicking the Print tab, and then clicking the Print button.

- Close a workbook by clicking the Close Window button located in the upper right corner of the screen or by clicking the File tab and then clicking the Close button.
- Exit Excel by clicking the Close button located in the upper right corner of the screen or by clicking the File tab and then clicking the Exit button.
- The AutoComplete feature will automatically insert a previous entry if the character or characters being typed in a cell match a previous entry. The AutoCorrect feature corrects many common typographical errors. Use the AutoFill fill handle to fill a range of cells with the same or consecutive data.
- Open a workbook by clicking the File tab and then clicking the Open button. At the Open dialog box, double-click the desired workbook.
- Use the AutoSum button in the Editing group in the Home tab to find the total or average of data in columns or rows.
- Select all cells in a column by clicking the column header. Select all cells in a row by clicking the row header. Select all cells in a worksheet by clicking the Select All button located immediately to the left of the column headers.
- Change column width by dragging the column boundary or double-clicking the column boundary.
- Merge and center cells by selecting the desired cells and then clicking the Merge & Center button in the Alignment group in the Home tab.
- Format numbers in cells with buttons in the Number group in the Home tab.
- Click the Microsoft Excel Help button or press F1 to display the Excel Help window. At this window, type a topic in the search text box and then press Enter.
- Some dialog boxes as well as the Backstage view contain a Help button you can click to display information specific to the dialog box or Backstage view.
- The ScreenTip for some buttons displays with a message telling you to press F1. Press F1 and the Excel Help window opens with information about the button.

Commands Review

FEATURE	RIBBON TAB, GROUP	BUTTON	FILE TAB	KEYBOARD SHORTCUT
Close workbook			Close	Ctrl + F4
Exit Excel			Exit	
Go To dialog box	Home, Editing			Ctrl + G
Excel Help window				F1
Open workbook			Open	Ctrl + O
Print tab Backstage view			Print	
Save workbook			Save	Ctrl + S

FEATURE	RIBBON TAB, GROUP	BUTTON	FILE TAB	KEYBOARD SHORTCUT
AutoSum button	Home, Editing	Σ		Alt + =
Merge & Center	Home, Alignment			
Accounting Number Format	Home, Number	$		
Comma Style	Home, Number	,		
Percent Style	Home, Number	%		Ctrl + Shift + %
Increase Decimal	Home, Number			
Decrease Decimal	Home, Number			

Concepts Check Test Your Knowledge

Completion: In the space provided at the right, indicate the correct term, symbol, or command.

1. The horizontal and vertical lines that define the cells in a worksheet area are referred to as this. ____________
2. Columns in a worksheet are labeled with these. ____________
3. Rows in a worksheet are labeled with these. ____________
4. Press this key on the keyboard to move the insertion point to the next cell. ____________
5. Press these keys on the keyboard to move the insertion point to the previous cell. ____________
6. Data being typed in a cell displays in the cell as well as here. ____________
7. If a number entered in a cell is too long to fit inside the cell, the number is changed to this. ____________
8. This feature will automatically insert words, numbers, or formulas in a series. ____________
9. This is the name of the small black square that displays in the bottom right corner of the active cell. ____________
10. Use this button in the Editing group in the Home tab to insert a formula in a cell. ____________

11. With this function, a range of cells is added together and then divided by the number of cell entries. ____________________

12. To select nonadjacent columns using the mouse, hold down this key on the keyboard while clicking the column headers. ____________________

13. Click this button in the worksheet area to select all of the cells in the table. ____________________

14. Click this button to merge selected cells and center data within the merged cells. ____________________

15. The Accounting Number Format button is located in this group in the Home tab. ____________________

16. Press this function key to display the Excel Help window. ____________________

Skills Check Assess Your Performance

Assessment 1

CREATE A WORKSHEET USING AUTOCOMPLETE

1. Create the worksheet shown in Figure 1.12 with the following specifications:
   a. To create the © symbols in cell A1, type (c).
   b. Type the misspelled words as shown and let the AutoCorrect feature correct the spelling. Use the AutoComplete feature to insert the second occurrence of *Category, Available,* and *Balance*.
   c. Merge and center cells A1 and B1.
2. Save the workbook and name it **EL1-C1-A1-Plan**.
3. Print and then close **EL1-C1-A1-Plan.xlsx**.

Figure 1.12 Assessment 1

	A	B	C
1	Premiere Plan©		
2	Plan A	Catagory	
3		Availalbe	
4		Balence	
5	Plan B	Category	
6		Available	
7		Balance	
8			

Assessment 2

CREATE AND FORMAT A WORKSHEET

1. Create the worksheet shown in Figure 1.13 with the following specifications:
   a. Merge and center cells A1 through C1.
   b. After typing the data, automatically adjust the width of column A.
   c. Insert in cell B8 the sum of cells B3 through B7 and insert in cell C8 the sum of cells C3 through C7.
   d. Apply the Accounting Number Format style and decrease the decimal point by two positions to cells B3, C3, B8, and C8.
   e. Apply the Comma Style and decrease the decimal point two times to cells B4 through C7.
   f. If any of the number amounts displays as number symbols (###), automatically adjust the width of the appropriate columns.
2. Save the workbook and name it **EL1-C1-A2-Exp**.
3. Print and then close **EL1-C1-A2-Exp.xlsx**.

Figure 1.13 Assessment 2

	A	B	C	D
1	Construction Project			
2	Expense	Original	Current	
3	Material	$129,000	$153,000	
4	Labor	97,000	98,500	
5	Equipmental rental	14,500	11,750	
6	Permits	1,200	1,350	
7	Tax	1,950	2,145	
8	Total	$243,650	$266,745	
9				

Assessment 3

CREATE A WORKSHEET USING THE FILL HANDLE

1. Type the worksheet data shown in Figure 1.14 with the following specifications:
   a. Type **Monday** in cell B2 and then use the fill handle to fill in the remaining days of the week.
   b. Type **350** in cell B3 and then use the fill handle to fill in the remaining numbers in the row.
   c. Merge and center cells A1 through G1.
2. Insert in cell G3 the sum of cells B3 through F3 and insert in cell G4 the sum of cells B4 through F4.
3. After typing the data, select cells B3 through G4 and then change to the accounting number format with two decimal points.
4. If necessary, adjust column widths.
5. Save the workbook and name it **EL1-C1-A3-Invest**.
6. Print and then close **EL1-C1-A3-Invest.xlsx**.

Figure 1.14 Assessment 3

	A	B	C	D	E	F	G	H
1	CAPITAL INVESTMENTS							
2		Monday	Tuesday	Wednesday	Thursday	Friday	Total	
3	Budget	350	350	350	350	350		
4	Actual	310	425	290	375	400		
5								

Assessment 4

INSERT FORMULAS IN A WORKSHEET

1. Open **DIAnalysis.xlsx** and then save the workbook with Save As and name it **EL1-C1-A4-DIAnalysis**.
2. Insert a formula in cell B15 that totals the amounts in cells B4 through B14.
3. Use the fill handle to copy relatively the formula in cell B15 to cell C15.
4. Insert a formula in cell D4 that finds the average of cells B4 and C4.
5. Use the fill handle to copy relatively the formula in cell D4 down to cells D5 through D14.
6. Select cells D5 through D14 and then apply the Comma Style with zero decimals.
7. Save, print, and then close **EL1-C1-A4-DIAnalysis.xlsx**.

Visual Benchmark Demonstrate Your Proficiency

CREATE, FORMAT, AND INSERT FORMULAS IN A WORKSHEET

1. At a blank workbook, create the worksheet shown in Figure 1.15 with the following specifications:
   a. Type the data in cells as shown in the figure. Use the fill handle when appropriate, merge and center the text *Personal Expenses – July through December*, and automatically adjust column widths.
   b. Insert formulas to determine averages and totals.
   c. Apply the Accounting Number Format style with zero decimal places to the amounts in cells B4 through H4 and cells B12 through H12.
   d. Apply the Comma Style with zero decimals to the amounts in cells B5 through G11.
2. Save the workbook and name it **EL1-C1-VB-PersExps**.
3. Print and then close **EL1-C1-VB-PersExps.xlsx**.

Figure 1.15 Visual Benchmark

	A	B	C	D	E	F	G	H	I
1									
2				Personal Expenses - July through December					
3	Expense	July	August	September	October	November	December	Average	
4	Rent	$ 850	$ 850	$ 850	$ 850	$ 850	$ 850		
5	Rental Insurance	55	55	55	55	55	55		
6	Health Insurance	120	120	120	120	120	120		
7	Electricity	129	135	110	151	168	173		
8	Utilities	53	62	49	32	55	61		
9	Telephone	73	81	67	80	82	75		
10	Groceries	143	137	126	150	147	173		
11	Gasoline	89	101	86	99	76	116		
12	Total								
13									

Case Study Apply Your Skills

Part 1

You are the office manager for Deering Industries. One of your responsibilities is creating a monthly calendar containing information on staff meetings, training, and due dates for time cards. Open **DICalendar.xlsx** and then insert the following information:

- Insert the text *October, 2012* in cell A2.
- Insert the days of the week (*Sunday*, *Monday*, *Tuesday*, *Wednesday*, *Thursday*, *Friday*, and *Saturday*) in cells A3 through G3. (Use the fill handle to fill in the days of the week and fill without formatting.)
- Insert the number *1* in cell B4, number *2* in cell C4, number *3* in cell D4, number *4* in cell E4, number *5* in cell F4, and number *6* in cell G4.
- Insert in the calendar the remaining numbers of the days (numbers *7* through *13* in cells A6 through G6, numbers *14* through *20* in cells A8 through G8, numbers *21* through *27* in cells A10 through G10, and numbers *28* through *31* in cells A12 through D12). If you use the fill handle, fill without formatting.
- Excel training will be held Thursday, October 4, from 9-11 a.m. Insert this information in cell E5. (Insert the text on two lines by typing **Excel Training**, pressing Alt + Enter to move the insertion point to the next line, and then typing **9-11 a.m.**)
- A staff meeting is held the second and fourth Monday of each month from 9-10 a.m. Insert this information in cell B7 and cell B11.
- Time cards are due the first and third Fridays of the month. Insert in cells F5 and F9 information indicating that time cards are due.
- A production team meeting is scheduled for Tuesday, October 23, from 1-3 p.m. Insert this information in cell C11.

Save the workbook and name it **EL1-C1-CS-DICalendar**. Print and then close the workbook.

Part 2

The manager of the Purchasing Department has asked you to prepare a worksheet containing information on quarterly purchases. Open **DIExpenditures.xlsx** and then insert the data as shown in Figure 1.16. After typing the data, insert in the appropriate cells formulas to calculate averages and totals. Save the workbook and name it **EL1-C1-CS-DIExpenditures**. Print and then close the workbook.

Figure 1.16 Case Study, Part 2

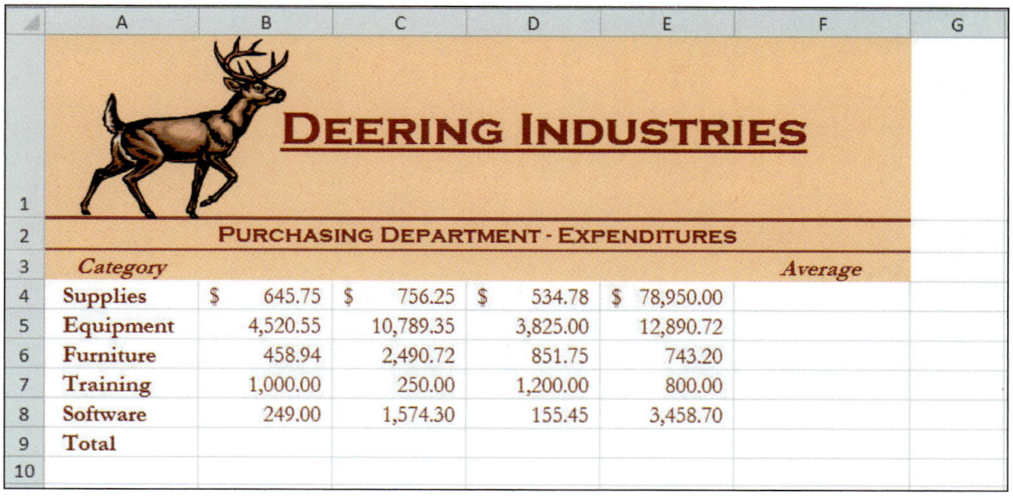

	A	B	C	D	E	F	G
1	DEERING INDUSTRIES						
2	PURCHASING DEPARTMENT - EXPENDITURES						
3	*Category*					*Average*	
4	**Supplies**	$ 645.75	$ 756.25	$ 534.78	$ 78,950.00		
5	**Equipment**	4,520.55	10,789.35	3,825.00	12,890.72		
6	**Furniture**	458.94	2,490.72	851.75	743.20		
7	**Training**	1,000.00	250.00	1,200.00	800.00		
8	**Software**	249.00	1,574.30	155.45	3,458.70		
9	**Total**						
10							

Part 3

The manager of the Purchasing Department has asked you to prepare a note to the finances coordinator, Jennifer Strauss. In Word, type a note to Jennifer Strauss explaining that you have prepared an Excel worksheet with the Purchasing Department expenditures. You are including the cells from the worksheet containing the expenditure information. In Excel, open **EL1-C1-CS-DIExpenditures.xlsx**, copy cells A3 through F9, and then paste them in the Word document. Make any corrections to the table so the information is readable. Save the document and name it **EL1-C1-CS-DINotetoJS**. Print and then close the document. Close **EL1-C1-CS-DIExpenditures.xlsx**.

Part 4

You will be ordering copy machines for several departments in the company and decide to research prices. Using the Internet, find three companies that sell copiers and write down information on different copier models. Open **DICopiers.xlsx** and then type the company, model number, and price in the designated cells. Save the completed workbook and name it **EL1-C1-CS-DICopiers**. Print and then close **EL1-C1-CS-DICopiers.xlsx**.

Microsoft® Excel®

CHAPTER 2

Inserting Formulas in a Worksheet

PERFORMANCE OBJECTIVES

Upon successful completion of Chapter 2, you will be able to:

- **Write formulas with mathematical operators**
- **Type a formula in the Formula bar**
- **Copy a formula**
- **Use the Insert Function feature to insert a formula in a cell**
- **Write formulas with the AVERAGE, MAX, MIN, COUNT, PMT, FV, DATE, NOW, and IF functions**
- **Create an absolute and mixed cell reference**

Tutorials

2.1 Performing Calculations Using Formulas

2.2 Writing Formulas in Excel

2.3 Copying and Testing Formulas

2.4 Creating Formulas with Absolute Addressing

2.5 Using Financial Functions

2.6 Writing Formulas with the FV Function

2.7 Using the Logical IF Function

Excel is a powerful decision-making tool containing data that can be manipulated to answer "what if" situations. Insert a formula in a worksheet and then manipulate the data to make projections, answer specific questions, and use as a planning tool. For example, the owner of a company might prepare a worksheet on production costs and then determine the impact on company revenues if production is increased or decreased.

Insert a formula in a worksheet to perform calculations on values. A formula contains a mathematical operator, value, cell reference, cell range, and a function. Formulas can be written that add, subtract, multiply, and/or divide values. Formulas can also be written that calculate averages, percentages, minimum and maximum values, and much more. As you learned in Chapter 1, Excel includes an AutoSum button in the Editing group in the Home tab that inserts a formula to calculate the total of a range of cells and also includes some commonly used formulas. Along with the AutoSum button, Excel includes a Formulas tab that offers a variety of functions to create formulas. Model answers for this chapter's projects appear on the following pages.

Excel2010L1C2

Note: Before beginning the projects, copy to your storage medium the Excel2010L1C2 subfolder from the Excel2010L1 folder on the CD that accompanies this textbook and make Excel2010L1C2 the active folder.

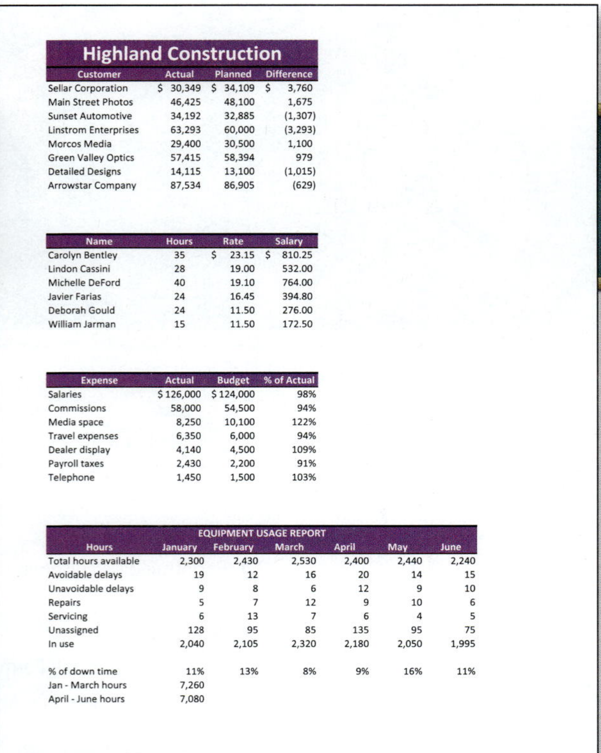

Highland Construction

Customer	Actual	Planned	Difference
Sellar Corporation	$ 30,349	$ 34,109	$ 3,760
Main Street Photos	46,425	48,100	1,675
Sunset Automotive	34,192	32,885	(1,307)
Linstrom Enterprises	63,293	60,000	(3,293)
Morcos Media	29,400	30,500	1,100
Green Valley Optics	57,415	58,394	979
Detailed Designs	14,115	13,100	(1,015)
Arrowstar Company	87,534	86,905	(629)

Name	Hours	Rate	Salary
Carolyn Bentley	35	$ 23.15	$ 810.25
Lindon Cassini	28	19.00	532.00
Michelle DeFord	40	19.10	764.00
Javier Farias	24	16.45	394.80
Deborah Gould	24	11.50	276.00
William Jarman	15	11.50	172.50

Expense	Actual	Budget	% of Actual
Salaries	$ 126,000	$ 124,000	98%
Commissions	58,000	54,500	94%
Media space	8,250	10,100	122%
Travel expenses	6,350	6,000	94%
Dealer display	4,140	4,500	109%
Payroll taxes	2,430	2,200	91%
Telephone	1,450	1,500	103%

EQUIPMENT USAGE REPORT						
Hours	January	February	March	April	May	June
Total hours available	2,300	2,430	2,530	2,400	2,440	2,240
Avoidable delays	19	12	16	20	14	15
Unavoidable delays	9	8	6	12	9	10
Repairs	5	7	12	9	10	6
Servicing	6	13	7	6	4	5
Unassigned	128	95	85	135	95	75
In use	2,040	2,105	2,320	2,180	2,050	1,995
% of down time	11%	13%	8%	9%	16%	11%
Jan - March hours	7,260					
April - June hours	7,080					

Project 1 Insert Formulas in a Worksheet

EL1-C2-P1-HCReports.xlsx

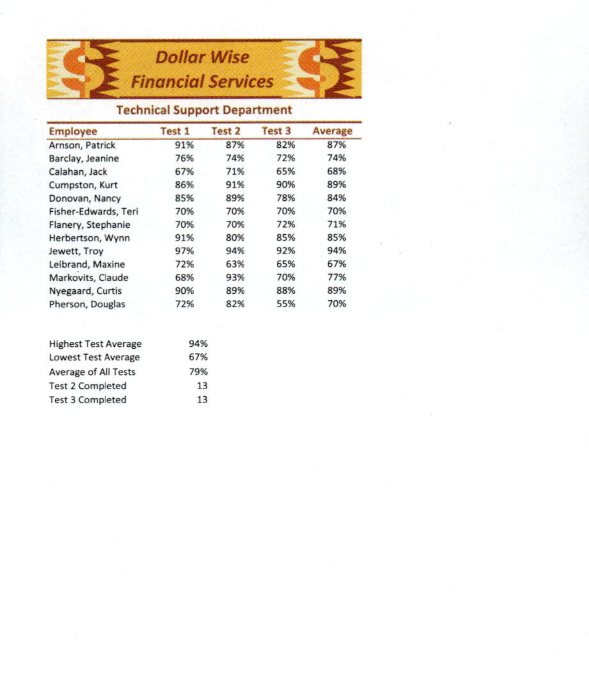

Dollar Wise
Financial Services

Technical Support Department

Employee	Test 1	Test 2	Test 3	Average
Arnson, Patrick	91%	87%	82%	87%
Barclay, Jeanine	76%	74%	72%	74%
Calahan, Jack	67%	71%	65%	68%
Cumpston, Kurt	86%	91%	90%	89%
Donovan, Nancy	85%	89%	78%	84%
Fisher-Edwards, Teri	70%	70%	70%	70%
Flanery, Stephanie	70%	70%	72%	71%
Herbertson, Wynn	91%	80%	85%	85%
Jewett, Troy	97%	94%	92%	94%
Leibrand, Maxine	72%	63%	65%	67%
Markovits, Claude	68%	93%	70%	77%
Nyegaard, Curtis	90%	89%	88%	89%
Pherson, Douglas	72%	82%	55%	70%

Highest Test Average	94%
Lowest Test Average	67%
Average of All Tests	79%
Test 2 Completed	13
Test 3 Completed	13

Project 2 Insert Formulas with Statistical Functions

EL1-C2-P2-DWTests.xlsx

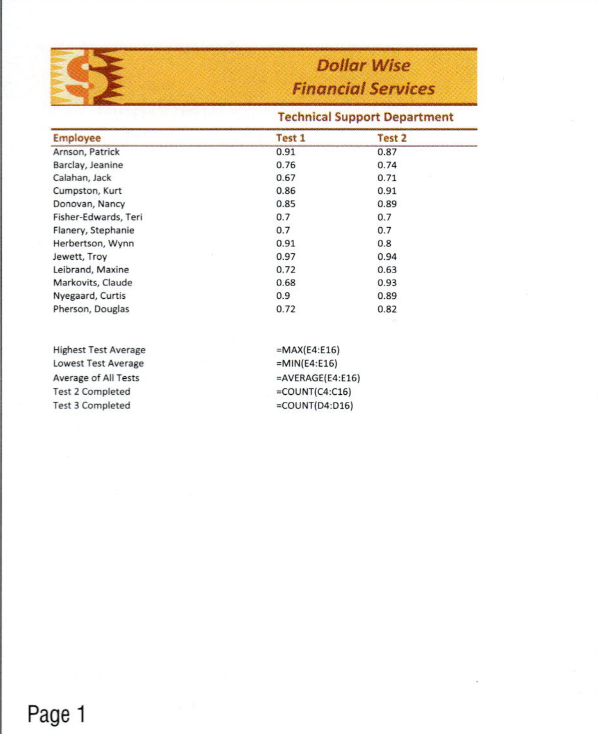

Dollar Wise
Financial Services

Technical Support Department

Employee	Test 1	Test 2
Arnson, Patrick	0.91	0.87
Barclay, Jeanine	0.76	0.74
Calahan, Jack	0.67	0.71
Cumpston, Kurt	0.86	0.91
Donovan, Nancy	0.85	0.89
Fisher-Edwards, Teri	0.7	0.7
Flanery, Stephanie	0.7	0.7
Herbertson, Wynn	0.91	0.8
Jewett, Troy	0.97	0.94
Leibrand, Maxine	0.72	0.63
Markovits, Claude	0.68	0.93
Nyegaard, Curtis	0.9	0.89
Pherson, Douglas	0.72	0.82

Highest Test Average	=MAX(E4:E16)
Lowest Test Average	=MIN(E4:E16)
Average of All Tests	=AVERAGE(E4:E16)
Test 2 Completed	=COUNT(C4:C16)
Test 3 Completed	=COUNT(D4:D16)

Page 1

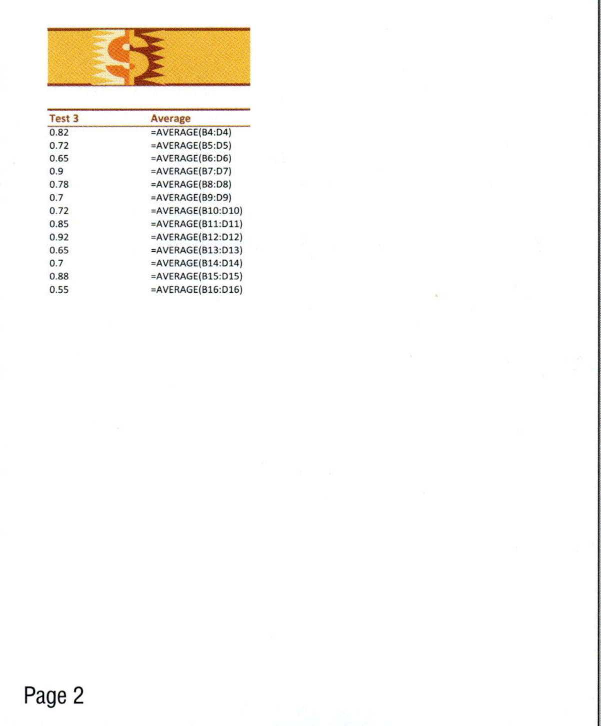

Test 3	Average
0.82	=AVERAGE(B4:D4)
0.72	=AVERAGE(B5:D5)
0.65	=AVERAGE(B6:D6)
0.9	=AVERAGE(B7:D7)
0.78	=AVERAGE(B8:D8)
0.7	=AVERAGE(B9:D9)
0.72	=AVERAGE(B10:D10)
0.85	=AVERAGE(B11:D11)
0.92	=AVERAGE(B12:D12)
0.65	=AVERAGE(B13:D13)
0.7	=AVERAGE(B14:D14)
0.88	=AVERAGE(B15:D15)
0.55	=AVERAGE(B16:D16)

Page 2

EL1-C2-P2-DWTests.xlsx, Formulas

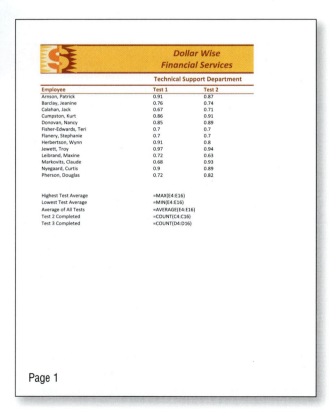

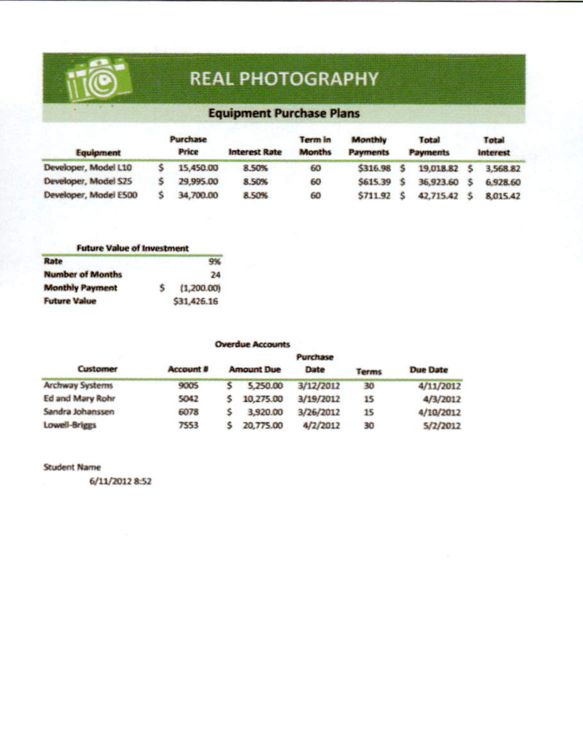

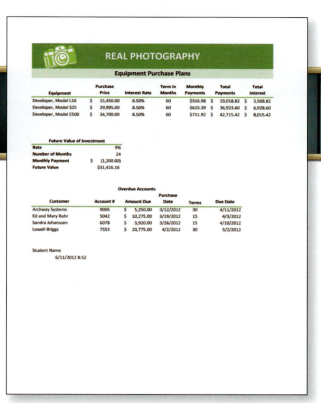

REAL PHOTOGRAPHY

Equipment Purchase Plans

Equipment	Purchase Price	Interest Rate	Term in Months	Monthly Payments	Total Payments	Total Interest
Developer, Model L10	$ 15,450.00	8.50%	60	$316.98	$ 19,018.82	$ 3,568.82
Developer, Model S25	$ 29,995.00	8.50%	60	$615.39	$ 36,923.60	$ 6,928.60
Developer, Model E500	$ 34,700.00	8.50%	60	$711.92	$ 42,715.42	$ 8,015.42

Future Value of Investment	
Rate	9%
Number of Months	24
Monthly Payment	$ (1,200.00)
Future Value	$31,426.16

Overdue Accounts

Customer	Account #	Amount Due	Purchase Date	Terms	Due Date
Archway Systems	9005	$ 5,250.00	3/12/2012	30	4/11/2012
Ed and Mary Rohr	5042	$ 10,275.00	3/19/2012	15	4/3/2012
Sandra Johanssen	6078	$ 3,920.00	3/26/2012	15	4/10/2012
Lowell-Briggs	7553	$ 20,775.00	4/2/2012	30	5/2/2012

Student Name
6/11/2012 8:52

Project 3 Insert Formulas with Financial and Date and Time Functions EL1-C2-P3-RPReports.xlsx

Capstan Marine Products

Sales Department			
Salesperson	Quota	Actual Sales	Bonus
Allejandro	$ 95,500.00	$ 103,295.00	$ 25,823.75
Crispin	137,000.00	129,890.00	-
Frankel	124,000.00	133,255.00	33,313.75
Hiesmann	85,500.00	94,350.00	23,587.50
Jarvis	159,000.00	167,410.00	41,852.50
Littleman	110,500.00	109,980.00	-

New Employee Orientation					
Name	Quiz 1	Quiz 2	Quiz 3	Average	Grade
Angelo	78	69	88	78	FAIL
Cunningham	90	95	86	90	PASS
Elliot	82	88	94	88	PASS
Kennedy	100	98	96	98	PASS
Lipscomb	64	76	62	67	FAIL

Sales Department			
Product #	Price	Discount	Discount %
C-2340	$ 1,250.00	YES	5%
C-3215	$ 695.00	YES	5%
C-4390	$ 475.00	NO	0%
E-2306	$ 225.00	NO	0%
E-3420	$ 520.00	NO	0%
G-2312	$ 2,150.00	YES	5%
G-4393	$ 2,450.00	YES	5%
J-1203	$ 755.00	YES	5%
J-3288	$ 455.00	NO	0%
J-4594	$ 1,050.00	YES	5%
M-2355	$ 890.00	YES	5%
M-3129	$ 645.00	YES	5%
M-4392	$ 475.00	NO	0%

Project 4 Insert Formulas with the IF Logical Function EL1-C2-P4-CMPReports.xlsx

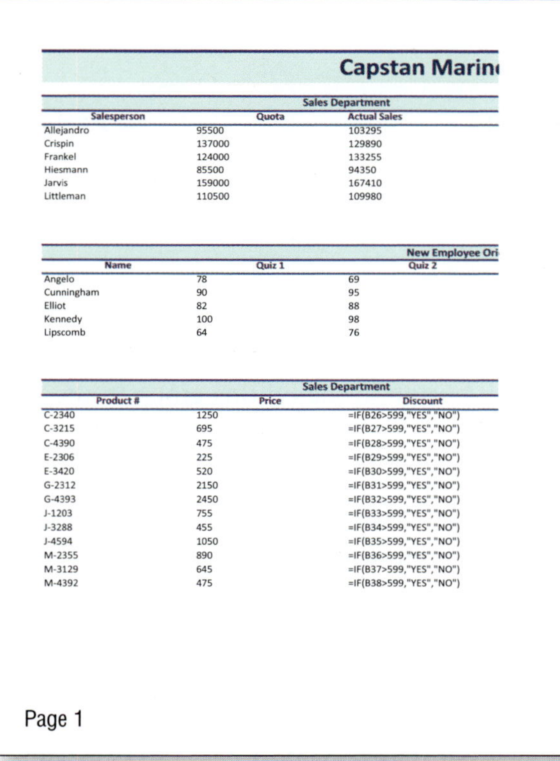

Capstan Marin

Sales Department		
Salesperson	Quota	Actual Sales
Allejandro	95500	103295
Crispin	137000	129890
Frankel	124000	133255
Hiesmann	85500	94350
Jarvis	159000	167410
Littleman	110500	109980

New Employee Ori		
Name	Quiz 1	Quiz 2
Angelo	78	69
Cunningham	90	95
Elliot	82	88
Kennedy	100	98
Lipscomb	64	76

Sales Department		
Product #	Price	Discount
C-2340	1250	=IF(B26>599,"YES","NO")
C-3215	695	=IF(B27>599,"YES","NO")
C-4390	475	=IF(B28>599,"YES","NO")
E-2306	225	=IF(B29>599,"YES","NO")
E-3420	520	=IF(B30>599,"YES","NO")
G-2312	2150	=IF(B31>599,"YES","NO")
G-4393	2450	=IF(B32>599,"YES","NO")
J-1203	755	=IF(B33>599,"YES","NO")
J-3288	455	=IF(B34>599,"YES","NO")
J-4594	1050	=IF(B35>599,"YES","NO")
M-2355	890	=IF(B36>599,"YES","NO")
M-3129	645	=IF(B37>599,"YES","NO")
M-4392	475	=IF(B38>599,"YES","NO")

Page 1

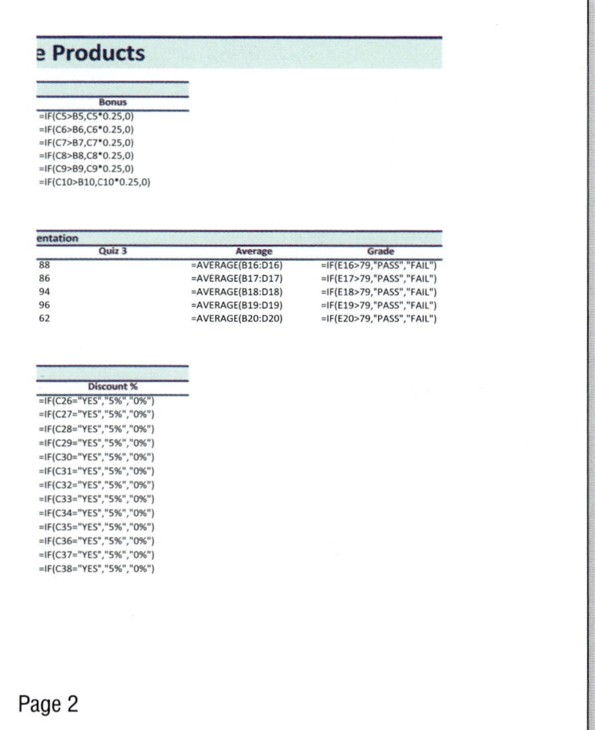

e Products

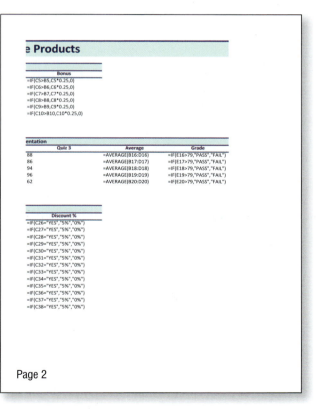

Bonus
=IF(C5>B5,C5*0.25,0)
=IF(C6>B6,C6*0.25,0)
=IF(C7>B7,C7*0.25,0)
=IF(C8>B8,C8*0.25,0)
=IF(C9>B9,C9*0.25,0)
=IF(C10>B10,C10*0.25,0)

entation		
Quiz 3	Average	Grade
88	=AVERAGE(B16:D16)	=IF(E16>79,"PASS","FAIL")
86	=AVERAGE(B17:D17)	=IF(E17>79,"PASS","FAIL")
94	=AVERAGE(B18:D18)	=IF(E18>79,"PASS","FAIL")
96	=AVERAGE(B19:D19)	=IF(E19>79,"PASS","FAIL")
62	=AVERAGE(B20:D20)	=IF(E20>79,"PASS","FAIL")

Discount %
=IF(C26="YES","5%","0%")
=IF(C27="YES","5%","0%")
=IF(C28="YES","5%","0%")
=IF(C29="YES","5%","0%")
=IF(C30="YES","5%","0%")
=IF(C31="YES","5%","0%")
=IF(C32="YES","5%","0%")
=IF(C33="YES","5%","0%")
=IF(C34="YES","5%","0%")
=IF(C35="YES","5%","0%")
=IF(C36="YES","5%","0%")
=IF(C37="YES","5%","0%")
=IF(C38="YES","5%","0%")

Page 2

EL1-C2-P4-CMPReports.xlsx, Formulas

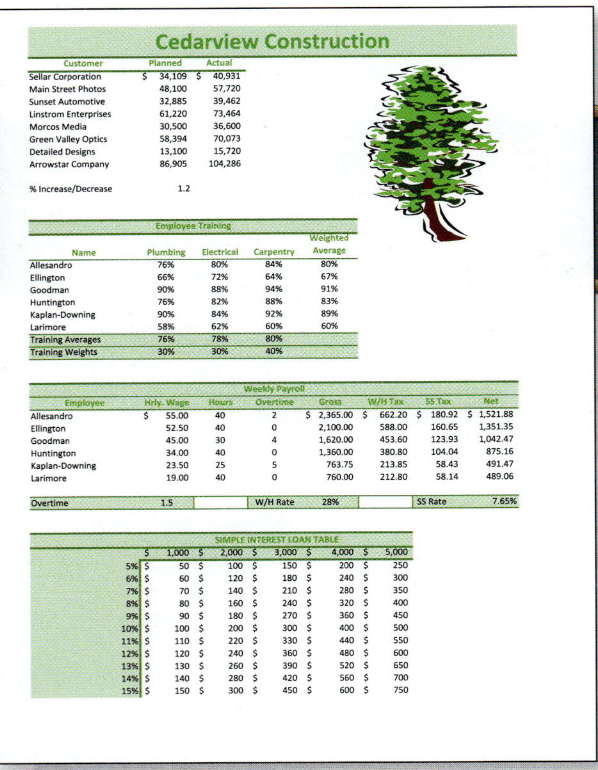

Cedarview Construction

Customer	Planned	Actual
Sellar Corporation	$ 34,109	$ 40,931
Main Street Photos	48,100	57,720
Sunset Automotive	32,885	39,462
Linstrom Enterprises	61,220	73,464
Morcos Media	30,500	36,600
Green Valley Optics	58,394	70,073
Detailed Designs	13,100	15,720
Arrowstar Company	86,905	104,286
% Increase/Decrease	1.2	

Employee Training

Name	Plumbing	Electrical	Carpentry	Weighted Average
Allesandro	76%	80%	84%	80%
Ellington	66%	72%	64%	67%
Goodman	90%	88%	94%	91%
Huntington	76%	82%	88%	83%
Kaplan-Downing	90%	84%	92%	89%
Larimore	58%	62%	60%	60%
Training Averages	76%	78%	80%	
Training Weights	30%	30%	40%	

Weekly Payroll

Employee	Hrly. Wage	Hours	Overtime	Gross	W/H Tax	SS Tax	Net
Allesandro	$ 55.00	40	2	$ 2,365.00	$ 662.20	$ 180.92	$ 1,521.88
Ellington	52.50	40	0	2,100.00	588.00	160.65	1,351.35
Goodman	45.00	30	4	1,620.00	453.60	123.93	1,042.47
Huntington	34.00	40	0	1,360.00	380.80	104.04	875.16
Kaplan-Downing	23.50	25	5	763.75	213.85	58.43	491.47
Larimore	19.00	40	0	760.00	212.80	58.14	489.06
Overtime	1.5		W/H Rate	28%		SS Rate	7.65%

SIMPLE INTEREST LOAN TABLE

	$ 1,000	$ 2,000	$ 3,000	$ 4,000	$ 5,000
5%	$ 50	$ 100	$ 150	$ 200	$ 250
6%	$ 60	$ 120	$ 180	$ 240	$ 300
7%	$ 70	$ 140	$ 210	$ 280	$ 350
8%	$ 80	$ 160	$ 240	$ 320	$ 400
9%	$ 90	$ 180	$ 270	$ 360	$ 450
10%	$ 100	$ 200	$ 300	$ 400	$ 500
11%	$ 110	$ 220	$ 330	$ 440	$ 550
12%	$ 120	$ 240	$ 360	$ 480	$ 600
13%	$ 130	$ 260	$ 390	$ 520	$ 650
14%	$ 140	$ 280	$ 420	$ 560	$ 700
15%	$ 150	$ 300	$ 450	$ 600	$ 750

Project 5 Insert Formulas Using Absolute and Mixed Cell References EL1-C2-P5-CCReports.xlsx

Model Answers

Project 1 Insert Formulas in a Worksheet — 4 Parts

You will open a worksheet containing data and then insert formulas to calculate differences, salaries, and percentages of budgets.

Writing Formulas with Mathematical Operators

HINT

After typing a formula in a cell, press the Enter key, the Tab key, Shift + Tab, or click the Enter button on the Formula bar.

As you learned in Chapter 1, the AutoSum button in the Editing group in the Home tab creates the formula for you. You can also write your own formulas using ***mathematical operators***. Commonly used mathematical operators and their functions are displayed in Table 2.1. When writing your own formula, begin the formula with the equals sign (=). For example, to create a formula that divides the contents of cell B2 by the contents of cell C2 and inserts the result in cell D2, you would make D2 the active cell and then type =B2/C2.

If a formula contains two or more operators, Excel uses the same order of operations used in algebra. From left to right in a formula, this order, called the ***order of operations***, is: negations (negative number — a number preceded by -) first, then percents (%), then exponentiations (^), followed by multiplications (*), divisions (/), additions (+), and finally subtractions (-). If you want to change the order of operations, use parentheses around the part of the formula you want calculated first.

Table 2.1 Mathematical Operators

Operator	*Function*
+	Addition
-	Subtraction
*	Multiplication
/	Division
%	Percent
^	Exponentiation

Copying a Formula with Relative Cell References

In many worksheets, the same basic formula is used repetitively. In a situation where a formula is copied to other locations in a worksheet, use a ***relative cell reference***. Copy a formula containing relative cell references and the cell references change. For example, if you enter the formula *=SUM(A2:C2)* in cell D2 and then copy it relatively to cell D3, the formula in cell D3 displays as *=SUM(A3:C3)*. (Additional information on cell references is discussed later in this chapter in the "Using an Absolute Cell Reference in a Formula" section.)

Quick Steps

Copy Relative Formula

1. Insert formula in cell.
2. Select cell containing formula and all cells you want to contain formula.
3. Click Fill button.
4. Click desired direction.

To copy a formula relatively in a worksheet, use the Fill button or the fill handle. (You used the fill handle to copy a formula in Chapter 1.) To use the Fill button, select the cell containing the formula as well as the cells to which you want the formula copied and then click the Fill button in the Editing group in the Home tab. At the Fill button drop-down list, click the desired direction. For example, if you are copying the formula down cells, click the *Down* option.

Fill

Project 1a **Finding Differences by Inserting and Copying a Formula** Part 1 of 4

1. Open **HCReports.xlsx**.
2. Save the workbook with Save As and name it **EL1-C2-P1-HCReports**.
3. Insert a formula by completing the following steps:
   a. Make cell D3 active.
   b. Type the formula **=C3-B3**.
   c. Press Enter.
4. Copy the formula to cells D4 through D10 by completing the following steps:
   a. Select cells D3 through D10.
   b. Click the Fill button in the Editing group in the Home tab and then click *Down* at the drop-down list.
5. Save **EL1-C2-P1-HCReports.xlsx**.
6. With the worksheet open, make the following changes to cell contents:
   B4: Change *48,290* to *46425*
   C6: Change *61,220* to *60000*
   B8: Change *55,309* to *57415*
   B9: Change *12,398* to *14115*

Step 4b

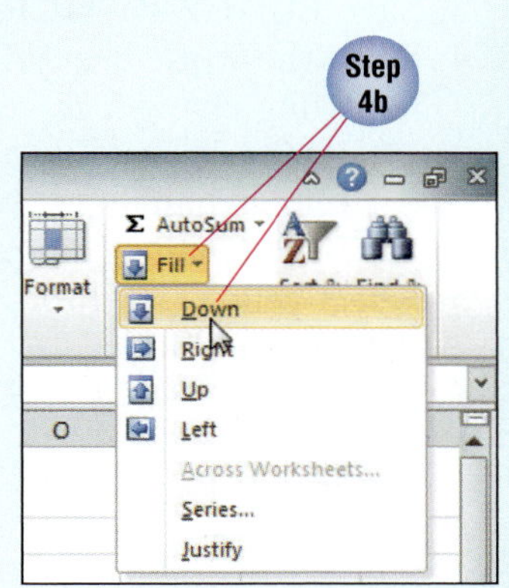

7. Make cell D3 active, apply the Accounting Number Format, and decrease the decimal point by two positions.
8. Save **EL1-C2-P1-HCReports.xlsx**.

Copying Formulas with the Fill Handle

HINT
Use the fill handle to copy a relative version of a formula.

Use the fill handle to copy a formula up, down, left, or right within a worksheet. To use the fill handle, insert the desired data in the cell (text, value, formula, etc.). With the cell active, position the mouse pointer on the fill handle until the mouse pointer turns into a thin, black cross. Hold down the left mouse button, drag and select the desired cells, and then release the mouse button. If you are dragging a cell containing a formula, a relative version of the formula is copied to the selected cells.

Project 1b **Calculating Salary by Inserting and Copying a Formula with the Fill Handle** Part 2 of 4

1. With **EL1-C2-P1-HCReports.xlsx** open, insert a formula by completing the following steps:
   a. Make cell D15 active.
   b. Click in the Formula bar text box and then type **=C15*B15**.
   c. Click the Enter button on the Formula bar.
2. Copy the formula to cells D16 through D20 by completing the following steps:
   a. Make sure cell D15 is the active cell.
   b. Position the mouse pointer on the fill handle that displays at the lower right corner of cell D15 until the pointer turns into a thin, black cross.
   c. Hold down the left mouse button, drag down to cell D20, and then release the mouse button.
3. Save **EL1-C2-P1-HCReports.xlsx**.
4. With the worksheet still open, make the following changes to cell contents:
   B16: Change *20* to *28*
   C17: Change *18.75* to *19.10*
   B19: Change *15* to *24*
5. Select cells D16 through D20 and then apply the Comma Style.
6. Save **EL1-C2-P1-HCReports.xlsx**.

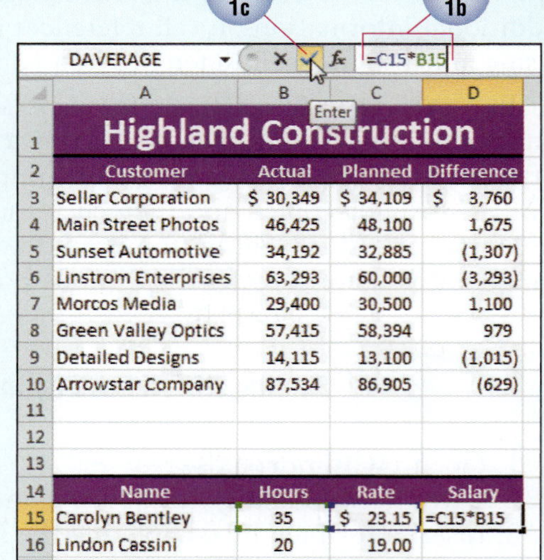

	A	B	C	D
1	Highland Construction			
2	Customer	Actual	Planned	Difference
3	Sellar Corporation	$ 30,349	$ 34,109	$ 3,760
4	Main Street Photos	46,425	48,100	1,675
5	Sunset Automotive	34,192	32,885	(1,307)
6	Linstrom Enterprises	63,293	60,000	(3,293)
7	Morcos Media	29,400	30,500	1,100
8	Green Valley Optics	57,415	58,394	979
9	Detailed Designs	14,115	13,100	(1,015)
10	Arrowstar Company	87,534	86,905	(629)
11				
12				
13				
14	Name	Hours	Rate	Salary
15	Carolyn Bentley	35	$ 23.15	=C15*B15
16	Lindon Cassini	20	19.00	

13				
14	Name	Hours	Rate	Salary
15	Carolyn Bentley	35	$ 23.15	$ 810.25
16	Lindon Cassini	20	19.00	$ 380.00
17	Michelle DeFord	40	18.75	$ 750.00
18	Javier Farias	24	16.45	$ 394.80
19	Deborah Gould	15	11.50	$ 172.50
20	William Jarman	15	11.50	$ 172.50
21				

Step 2c

Writing a Formula by Pointing

In Project 1a and Project 1b, you wrote formulas using cell references such as *=C3-B3*. Another method for writing a formula is to "point" to the specific cells that are to be part of the formula. Creating a formula by pointing is more accurate than typing the cell reference since a mistake can happen when typing the cell reference.

To write a formula by pointing, click the cell that will contain the formula, type the equals sign to begin the formula, and then click the cell you want to reference in the formula. This inserts a moving border around the cell and also changes the mode from Enter to Point. (The word *Point* displays at the left side of the Status bar.) Type the desired mathematical operator and then click the next cell reference. Continue in this manner until all cell references are specified and then press the Enter key. This ends the formula and inserts the result of the calculation of the formula in the active cell. When writing a formula by pointing, you can also select a range of cells you want included in a formula.

Quick Steps

Write Formula by Pointing

1. Click cell that will contain formula.
2. Type equals sign.
3. Click cell you want to reference in formula.
4. Type desired mathematical operator.
5. Click next cell reference.

Project 1c Writing a Formula by Pointing that Calculates Percentage of Actual Budget

Part 3 of 4

1. With **EL1-C2-P1-HCReports.xlsx** open, enter a formula by pointing that calculates the percentage of actual budget by completing the following steps:
   a. Make cell D25 active.
   b. Type the equals sign.
   c. Click cell C25. (This inserts a moving border around the cell and the mode changes from Enter to Point.)
   d. Type the forward slash symbol (/).
   e. Click cell B25.
   f. Make sure the formula in D25 is *=C25/B25* and then press Enter.
2. Make cell D25 active, position the mouse pointer on the fill handle, drag down to cell D31, and then release the mouse button.
3. Save **EL1-C2-P1-HCReports.xlsx**.

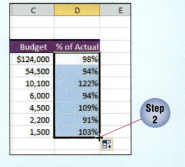

	A	B	C	D	E
22					
23					
24	Expense	Actual	Budget	% of Actual	
25	Salaries	$126,000	$124,000	=C25/B25	
26	Commissions	58,000	54,500		
27	Media space	8,250	10,100		
28	Travel expenses	6,350	6,000		
29	Dealer display	4,140	4,500		
30	Payroll taxes	2,430	2,200		
31	Telephone	1,450	1,500		

Steps 1a-1e

C	D	E
Budget	% of Actual	
$124,000	98%	
54,500	94%	
10,100	122%	
6,000	94%	
4,500	109%	
2,200	91%	
1,500	103%	

Step 2

Using the Trace Error Button

Trace Error

As you are working in a worksheet, you may occasionally notice a button pop up near the active cell. The general term for this button is ***smart tag***. The display of the smart tag button varies depending on the action performed. In Project 1d, you will insert a formula that will cause a smart tag button, named the Trace Error button, to appear. When the Trace Error button appears, a small dark green triangle also displays in the upper left corner of the cell. Click the Trace Error button and a drop-down list displays with options for updating the formula to include specific cells, getting help on the error, ignoring the error, editing the error in the Formula bar, and completing an error check. In Project 1d, two of the formulas you insert return the desired results. You will click the Trace Error button, read information on what Excel perceives as the error, and then tell Excel to ignore the error.

Project 1d Writing a Formula by Pointing that Calculates Percentage of Down Time

Part 4 of 4

1. With **EL1-C2-P1-HCReports.xlsx** open, enter a formula by pointing that computes the percentage of equipment down time by completing the following steps:
   a. Make cell B45 active.
   b. Type the equals sign followed by the left parenthesis (=().
   c. Click cell B37. (This inserts a moving border around the cell and the mode changes from Enter to Point.)
   d. Type the minus symbol (-).
   e. Click cell B43.
   f. Type the right parenthesis followed by the forward slash ()/).
   g. Click cell B37.
   h. Make sure the formula in B45 is *=(B37-B43)/B37* and then press Enter.
2. Make cell B45 active, position the mouse pointer on the fill handle, drag across to cell G45, and then release the mouse button.
3. Enter a formula by dragging through a range of cells by completing the following steps:
   a. Click in cell B46 and then click the AutoSum button in the Editing group in the Home tab.
   b. Select cells B37 through D37.
   c. Click the Enter button on the Formula bar. (This inserts *7,260* in cell B46.)
4. Click in cell B47 and then complete steps similar to those in Step 3 to create a formula that totals hours available from April through June (cells E37 through G37). (This inserts *7,080* in cell B47.)
5. Click in cell B46 and notice the Trace Error button that displays. Complete the following steps to read about the error and then tell Excel to ignore the error:
   a. Click the Trace Error button.
   b. At the drop-down list that displays, click the *Help on this error* option.
   c. Read the information that displays in the Excel Help window and then close the window.
   d. Click the Trace Error button again and then click *Ignore Error* at the drop-down list.

	A	B	C	D
33				
34				
35		EQUIPMENT USAGE REPO		
36	Hours	January	February	March
37	Total hours available	2,300	2,430	2,530
38	Avoidable delays	19	12	16
39	Unavoidable delays	9	8	6
40	Repairs	5	7	12
41	Servicing	6	13	7
42	Unassigned	128	95	85
43	In use	2,040	2,105	2,320
44				
45	% of down time	=(B37-B43)/B37		
46	Jan - March hours			
47	April - June hours			

Steps 1a-1g

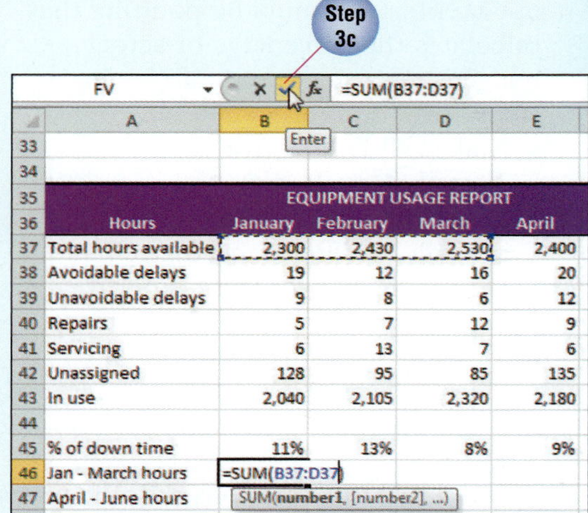

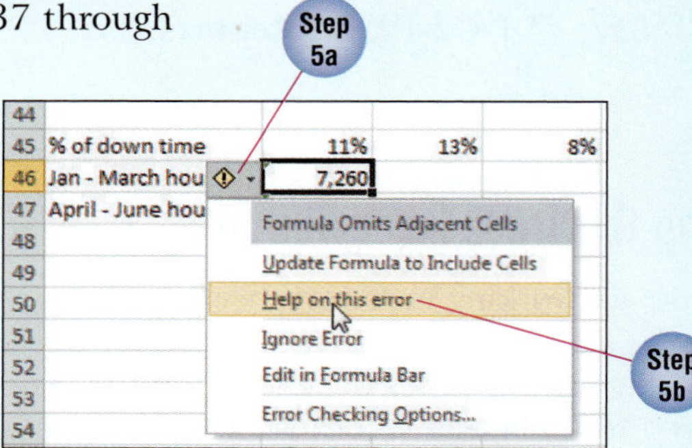

6. Remove the dark green triangle from cell B47 by completing the following steps:
   a. Click in cell B47.
   b. Click the Trace Error button and then click *Ignore Error* at the drop-down list.
7. Save, print, and then close **EL1-C2-P1-HCReports.xlsx**.

Insert Formulas with Statistical Functions — 4 Parts

You will use the AVERAGE function to determine average test scores, use the MINIMUM and MAXIMUM functions to determine lowest and highest averages, use the COUNT function to count number of students taking a test, and display formulas in a cell rather than the result of the formula.

Inserting Formulas with Functions

In Project 2a in Chapter 1, you used the AutoSum button to insert the formula *=SUM(B2:B5)* in a cell. The beginning section of the formula, *=SUM*, is called a ***function***, which is a built-in formula. Using a function takes fewer keystrokes when creating a formula. For example, the *=SUM* function saved you from having to type each cell to be included in the formula with the plus (+) symbol between cell entries.

Excel provides other functions for writing formulas. A function operates on what is referred to as an ***argument***. An argument may consist of a constant, a cell reference, or another function. In the formula *=SUM(B2:B5)*, the cell range *(B2:B5)* is an example of a cell reference argument. An argument may also contain a ***constant***. A constant is a value entered directly into the formula. For example, if you enter the formula *=SUM(B3:B9,100)*, the cell range *B3:B9* is a cell reference argument and *100* is a constant. In this formula, 100 is always added to the sum of the cells.

When a value calculated by the formula is inserted in a cell, this process is referred to as ***returning the result***. The term *returning* refers to the process of calculating the formula and the term *result* refers to inserting the value in the cell.

Insert Function

You can type a function in a cell in a worksheet or you can use the Insert Function button on the Formula bar or in the Formulas tab to help you write the formula. Figure 2.1 displays the Formulas tab. The Formulas tab provides the Insert Function button as well as other buttons for inserting functions in a worksheet. The Function Library group in the Formulas tab contains a number of buttons for inserting functions from a variety of categories such as Financial, Logical, Text, and Date & Time.

Click the Insert Function button on the Formula bar or in the Formulas tab and the Insert Function dialog box displays as shown in Figure 2.2. At the

Figure 2.1 Formulas Tab

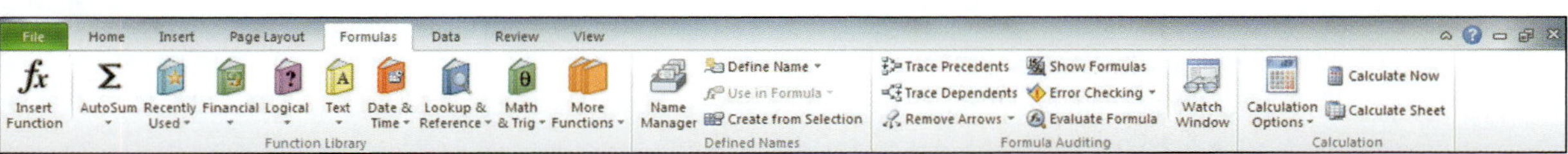

Figure 2.2 Insert Function Dialog Box

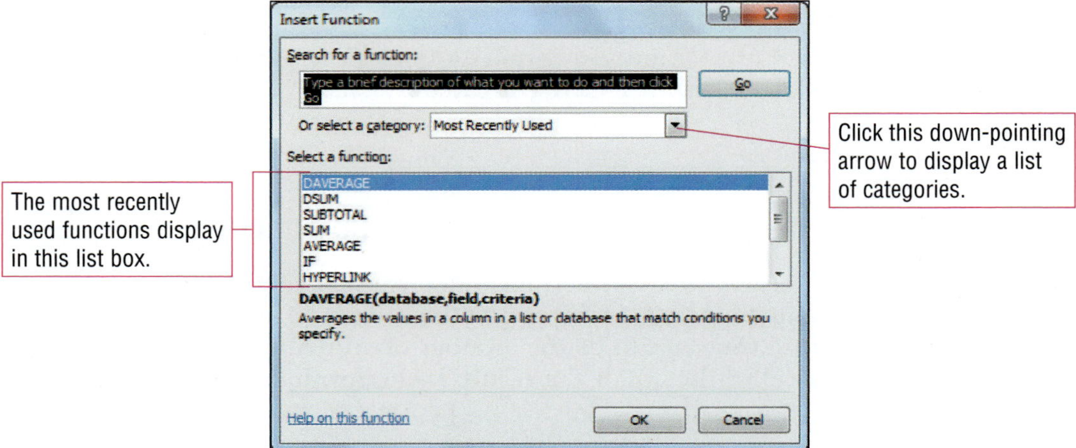

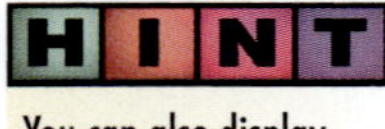

You can also display the Insert Function dialog box by clicking the down-pointing arrow at the right side of the AutoSum button and then clicking *More Functions.*

Click the AutoSum button arrow in the Formulas tab and common functions display in a drop-down list.

Insert Function dialog box, the most recently used functions display in the *Select a function* list box. You can choose a function category by clicking the down-pointing arrow at the right side of the *Or select a category* list box and then clicking the desired category at the drop-down list. Use the *Search for a function* option to locate a specific function.

With the desired function category selected, choose a function in the *Select a function* list box and then click OK. This displays a Function Arguments palette like the one shown in Figure 2.3. At this palette, enter in the *Number1* text box the range of cells you want included in the formula, enter any constants that are to be included as part of the formula, or enter another function. After entering a range of cells, a constant, or another function, click the OK button. You can include more than one argument in a function. If the function you are creating contains more than one argument, press the Tab key to move the insertion point to the *Number2* text box, and then enter the second argument. If you need to display a specific cell or cells behind the function palette, move the palette by clicking and dragging it.

Figure 2.3 Example Function Arguments Palette

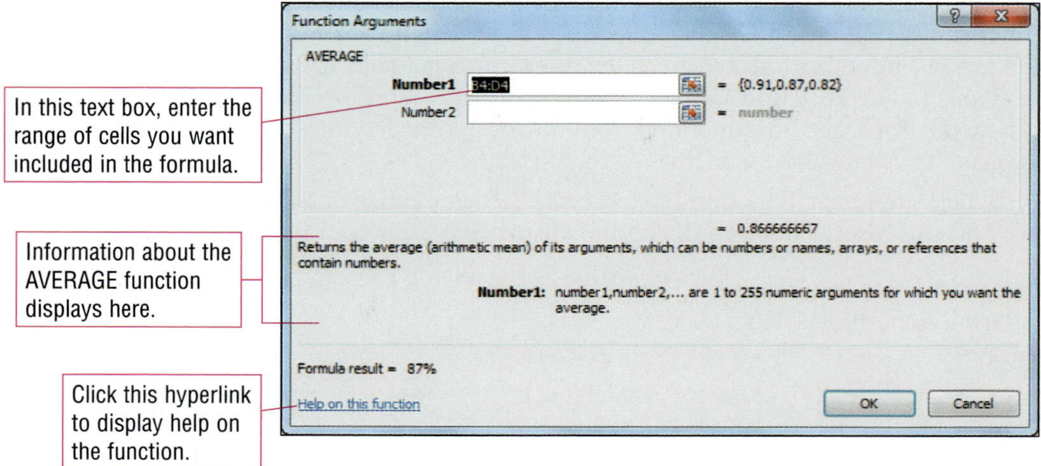

Excel includes over 200 functions that are divided into twelve different categories including *Financial*, *Date & Time*, *Math & Trig*, *Statistical*, *Lookup & Reference*, *Database*, *Text*, *Logical*, *Information*, *Engineering*, *Cube*, and *Compatibility*. Clicking the AutoSum button in the Function Library group in the Formulas tab or the Editing group in the Home tab automatically adds numbers with the SUM function. The SUM function is included in the *Math & Trig* category. In some projects in this chapter, you will write formulas with functions in other categories including *Statistical*, *Financial*, *Date & Time*, and *Logical*.

Excel includes the Formula AutoComplete feature that displays a drop-down list of functions. To use this feature, click in the desired cell or click in the Formula bar text box, type the equals sign (=), and then type the first letter of the desired function. This displays a drop-down list with functions that begin with the letter. Double-click the desired function, enter the cell references, and then press Enter.

Writing Formulas with Statistical Functions

In this section, you will learn to write formulas with the statistical functions AVERAGE, MAX, MIN, and COUNT. The AVERAGE function returns the average (arithmetic mean) of the arguments. The MAX function returns the largest value in a set of values and the MIN function returns the smallest value in a set of values. Use the COUNT function to count the number of cells that contain numbers within the list of arguments.

Finding Averages

A common function in a formula is the AVERAGE function. With this function, a range of cells is added together and then divided by the number of cell entries. In Project 2a you will use the AVERAGE function, which will add all of the test scores for a student and then divide that number by the total number of tests. You will use the Insert Function button to simplify the creation of the formula containing an AVERAGE function.

One of the advantages to using formulas in a worksheet is the ability to easily manipulate data to answer certain questions. In Project 2a you will learn the impact of retaking certain tests on the final average score.

Project 2a **Averaging Test Scores in a Worksheet** Part 1 of 4

1. Open **DWTests.xlsx**.
2. Save the workbook with Save As and name it **EL1-C2-P2-DWTests**.
3. Use the Insert Function button to find the average of test scores by completing the following steps:
   a. Make cell E4 active.
   b. Click the Insert Function button on the Formula bar.

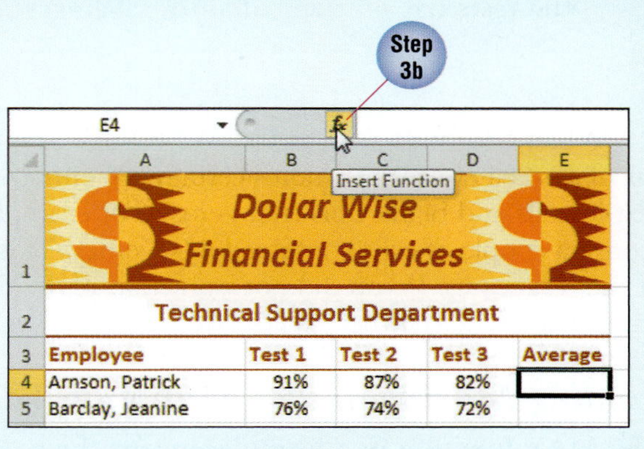

c. At the Insert Function dialog box, click the down-pointing arrow at the right side of the *Or select a category* list box and then click *Statistical* at the drop-down list.
d. Click *AVERAGE* in the *Select a function* list box.
e. Click OK.
f. At the Function Arguments palette, make sure *B4:D4* displays in the *Number1* text box. (If not, type **B4:D4** in the *Number1* text box.)
g. Click OK.

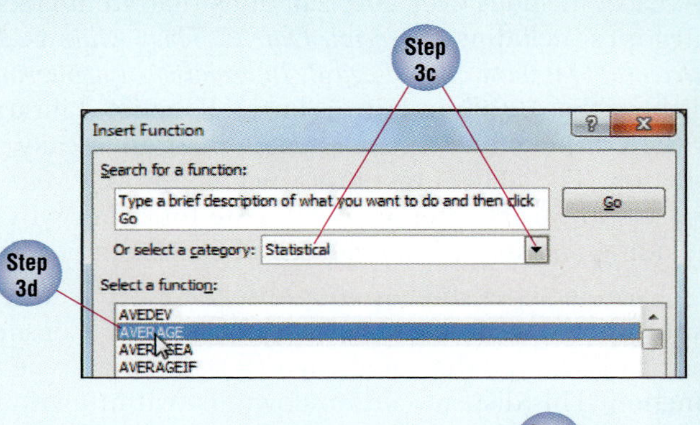

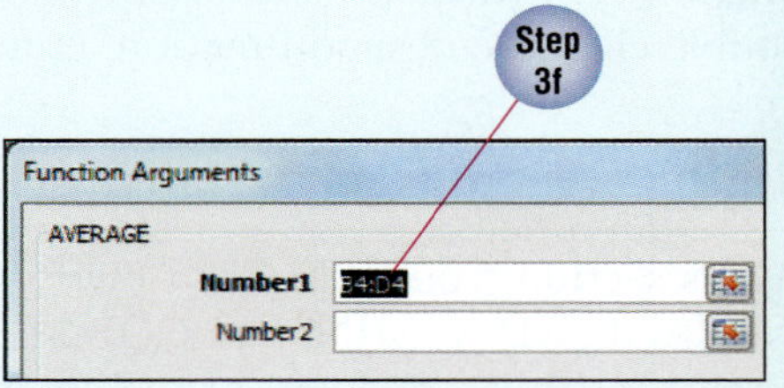

4. Copy the formula by completing the following steps:
   a. Make sure cell E4 is active.
   b. Position the mouse pointer on the fill handle until the pointer turns into a thin black cross.
   c. Hold down the left mouse button, drag down to cell E16, and then release the mouse button.
5. Save and then print **EL1-C2-P2-DWTests.xlsx**.
6. After viewing the averages of test scores, you notice that a couple of people have a low average. You decide to see what happens to the average score if students make up tests where they scored the lowest. You decide that a student can score a maximum of 70% on a retake of the test. Make the following changes to test scores to see how the changes will affect the test average.
   B9: Change *50* to *70*
   C9: Change *52* to *70*
   D9: Change *60* to *70*
   B10: Change *62* to *70*
   B14: Change *0* to *70*
   D14: Change *0* to *70*
   D16: Change *0* to *70*
7. Save and then print **EL1-C2-P2-DWTests.xlsx**. (Compare the test averages for Teri Fisher-Edwards, Stephanie Flanery, Claude Markovits, and Douglas Pherson to see what the effect of retaking the tests has on their final test averages.)

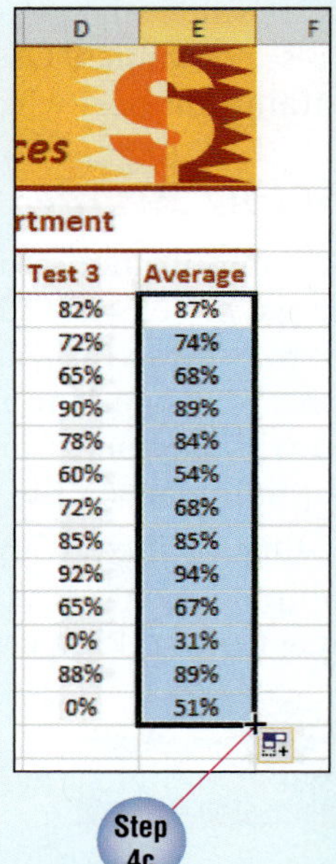

When a formula such as the AVERAGE formula you inserted in a cell in Project 2a calculates cell entries, it ignores certain cell entries. The AVERAGE function will ignore text in cells and blank cells (not zeros). For example, in the worksheet containing test scores, a couple of cells contained a *0%* entry. This entry was included in the averaging of the test scores. If you did not want that particular test to be included in the average, enter text in the cell such as *N/A* (for *not applicable*) or leave the cell blank.

Finding Maximum and Minimum Values

The MAX function in a formula returns the maximum value in a cell range and the MIN function returns the minimum value in a cell range. As an example, you could use the MAX and MIN functions in a worksheet containing employee hours to determine which employee worked the most number of hours and which worked the least. In a worksheet containing sales commissions, you could use the MAX and MIN functions to determine the salesperson who earned the most commission dollars and the one who earned the least.

Insert a MAX and MIN function into a formula in the same manner as an AVERAGE function. In Project 2b, you will use the Formula AutoComplete feature to insert the MAX function in cells to determine the highest test score average and the Insert Function button to insert the MIN function to determine the lowest test score average.

Project 2b **Finding Maximum and Minimum Values in a Worksheet** Part 2 of 4

1. With **EL1-C2-P2-DWTests.xlsx** open, type the following in the specified cells:
   A19: **Highest Test Average**
   A20: **Lowest Test Average**
   A21: **Average of All Tests**
2. Insert a formula to identify the highest test score average by completing the following steps:
   a. Make cell B19 active.
   b. Type **=M**. (This displays the Formula AutoComplete list.)
   c. Double-click *MAX* in the Formula AutoComplete list.
   d. Type **E4:E16)** and then press Enter.

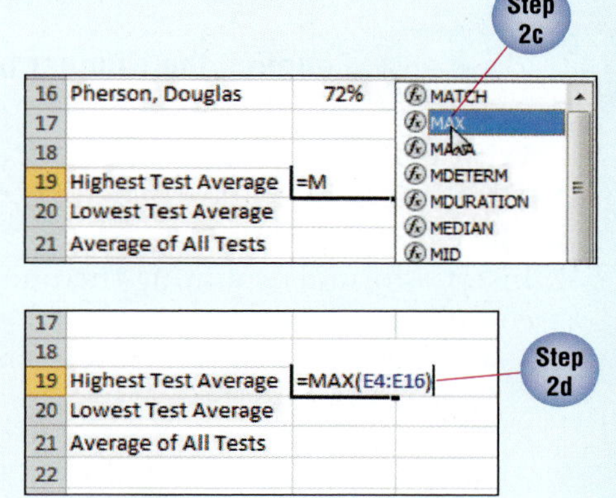

3. Insert a formula to identify the lowest test score average by completing the following steps:
   a. Make cell B20 active.
   b. Click the Insert Function button on the Formula bar.
   c. At the Insert Function dialog box, make sure *Statistical* is selected in the *Or select a category* list box, and then click *MIN* in the *Select a function* list box. (You will need to scroll down the list to display *MIN*.)
   d. Click OK.
   e. At the Function Arguments palette, type **E4:E16** in the *Number1* text box.
   f. Click OK.

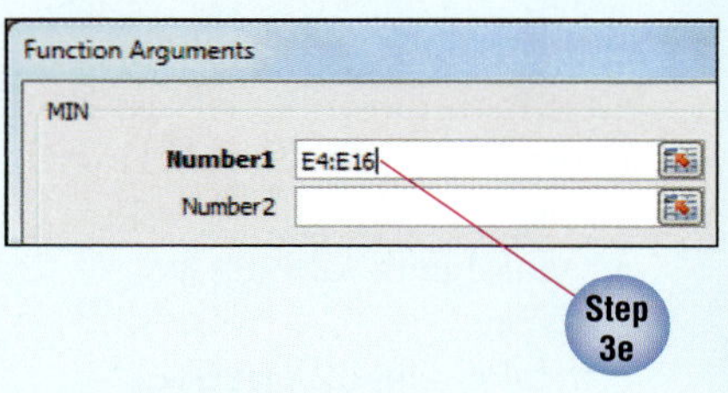

4. Insert a formula to determine the average of all test scores by completing the following steps:
   a. Make cell B21 active.
   b. Click the Formulas tab.
   c. Click the Insert Function button in the Function Library group.
   d. At the Insert Function dialog box, make sure *Statistical* is selected in the *Or select a category* list box and then click *AVERAGE* in the *Select a function* list box.
   e. Click OK.
   f. At the Function Arguments palette, type **E4:E16** in the *Number1* text box, and then click OK.

5. Save and then print **EL1-C2-P2-DWTests.xlsx**.
6. Change the *70%* values (which were previously *0%*) in cells B14, D14, and D16 to *N/A*. (This will cause the average of test scores for Claude Markovits and Douglas Pherson to increase and will change the minimum number and average of all test scores.)
7. Save and then print **EL1-C2-P2-DWTests.xlsx**.

Counting Numbers in a Range

Use the COUNT function to count the numeric values in a range. For example, in a range of cells containing cells with text and cells with numbers, you can count how many cells in the range contain numbers. In Project 2c, you will use the COUNT function to specify the number of students taking Test 2 and Test 3. In the worksheet, the cells containing the text N/A are not counted by the COUNT function.

Project 2c Counting the Number of Students Taking Tests

Part 3 of 4

1. With **EL1-C2-P2-DWTests.xlsx** open, make cell A22 active.
2. Type Test 2 Completed.
3. Make cell B22 active.
4. Insert a formula counting the number of students who have taken Test 2 by completing the following steps:
   a. With cell B22 active, click in the Formula bar text box.
   b. Type =C.
   c. At the Formula AutoComplete list that displays, scroll down the list until *COUNT* displays and then double-click *COUNT*.
   d. Type C4:C16) and then press Enter.

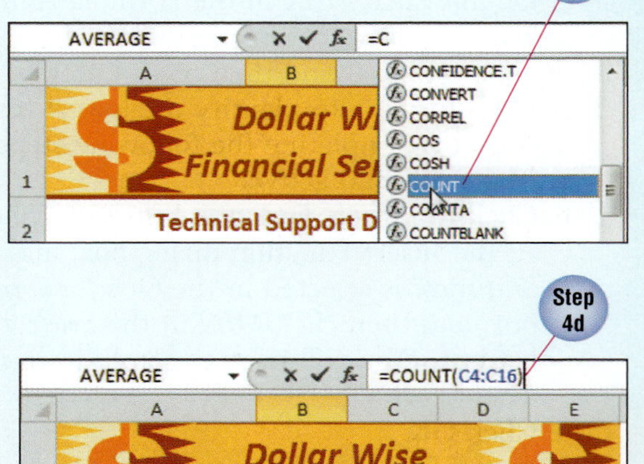

5. Count the number of students who have taken Test 3 by completing the following steps:
   a. Make cell A23 active.
   b. Type Test 3 Completed.
   c. Make cell B23 active.
   d. Click the Insert Function button on the Formula bar.
   e. At the Insert Function dialog box, make sure *Statistical* is selected in the *Or select a category* list box.
   f. Scroll down the list of functions in the *Select a function* list box until *COUNT* is visible and then double-click *COUNT*.
   g. At the formula palette, type D4:D16 in the *Value1* text box and then click OK.
6. Save and then print **EL1-C2-P2-DWTests.xlsx**.
7. Add test scores by completing the following steps:
   a. Make cell B14 active and then type 68.
   b. Make cell D14 active and then type 70.
   c. Make cell D16 active and then type 55.
   d. Press Enter.
8. Save and then print **EL1-C2-P2-DWTests.xlsx**.

Displaying Formulas

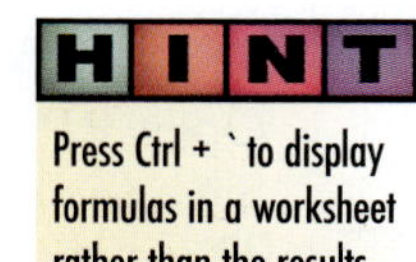

Press Ctrl + ` to display formulas in a worksheet rather than the results.

In some situations, you may need to display the formulas in a worksheet rather than the results of the formula. You may want to turn on formulas for auditing purposes or check formulas for accuracy. Display all formulas in a worksheet rather than the results by pressing Ctrl + ` (this is the grave accent, generally located to the left of the 1 key on the keyboard). Press Ctrl + ` to turn off the display of formulas.

Displaying Formulas Part 4 of 4

1. With **EL1-C2-P2-DWTests.xlsx** open, make cell A3 active.
2. Press Ctrl + ` to turn on the display of formulas.
3. Print the worksheet with the formulas. (The worksheet will print on two pages.)
4. Press Ctrl + ` to turn off the display of formulas.
5. Save and then close **EL1-C2-P2-DWTests.xlsx**.

Insert Formulas with Financial and Date and Time Functions **3 Parts**

You will use the PMT financial function to calculate payments and the FV function to find the future value of an investment. You will also use the DATE function to return the serial number for a date and the NOW function to insert the current date and time as a serial number.

Writing Formulas with Financial Functions

In this section, you will learn to write formulas with the financial functions PMT and FV. The PMT function calculates the payment for a loan based on constant payments and a constant interest rate. Use the FV function to return the future value of an investment.

Finding the Periodic Payments for a Loan

The PMT function finds the payment for a loan based on constant payments and a constant interest rate. The PMT function contains the arguments Rate, Nper, Pv, Fv, and Type. The Rate argument is the interest rate per period for a loan, the Nper is the number of payments that will be made to an investment or loan, Pv is the current value of amounts to be received or paid in the future, Fv is the value of a loan or investment at the end of all periods, and Type determines whether calculations will be based on payments made in arrears (at the end of each period) or in advance (at the beginning of each period).

Project 3a Calculating Payments

1. Open **RPReports.xlsx**.
2. Save the workbook with Save As and name it **EL1-C2-P3-RPReports**.
3. The owner of Real Photography is interested in purchasing a new developer and needs to determine monthly payments on three different models. Insert a formula that calculates monthly payments and then copy that formula by completing the following steps:
   a. Make cell E5 active.
   b. Click the Formulas tab.
   c. Click the Financial button in the Function Library group, scroll down the drop-down list until *PMT* displays, and then click *PMT*.
   d. At the Function Arguments palette, type **C5/12** in the *Rate* text box. (This tells Excel to divide the interest rate by 12 months.)
   e. Press the Tab key. (This moves the insertion point to the *Nper* text box).
   f. Type **D5**. (This is the total number of months in the payment period.)
   g. Press the Tab key. (This moves the insertion point to the *Pv* text box.)
   h. Type **-B5**. (Excel displays the result of the PMT function as a negative number since the loan represents a negative cash flow to the borrower. Insert a minus sign before *B5* to show the monthly payment as a positive number rather than a negative number.)
   i. Click OK. (This closes the palette and inserts the monthly payment of *$316.98* in cell E5.)
   j. Copy the formula in cell E5 down to cells E6 and E7.

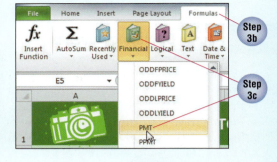

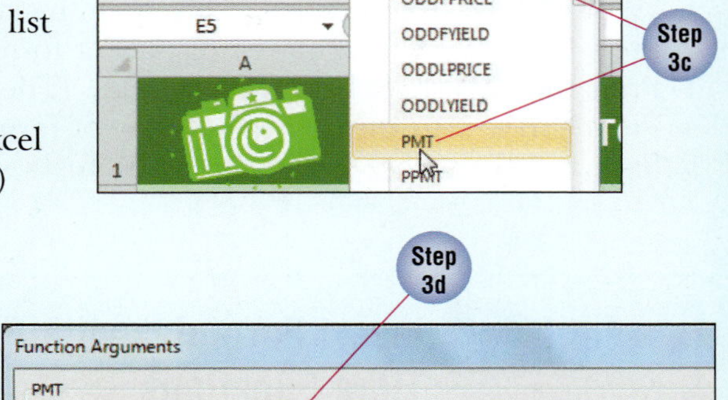

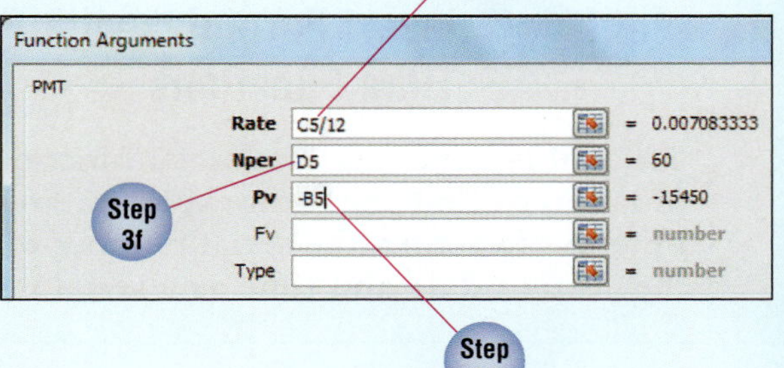

4. Insert a formula in cell F5 that calculates the total amount of the payments by completing the following steps:
   a. Make cell F5 active.
   b. Type **=E5*D5** and then press Enter.
   c. Make cell F5 active and then copy the formula down to cells F6 and F7.
5. Insert a formula in cell G5 that calculates the total amount of interest paid by completing the following steps:
   a. Make cell G5 active.
   b. Type **=F5-B5** and then press Enter.
   c. Make cell G5 active and then copy the formula down to cells G6 and G7.
6. Save **EL1-C2-P3-RPReports.xlsx**.

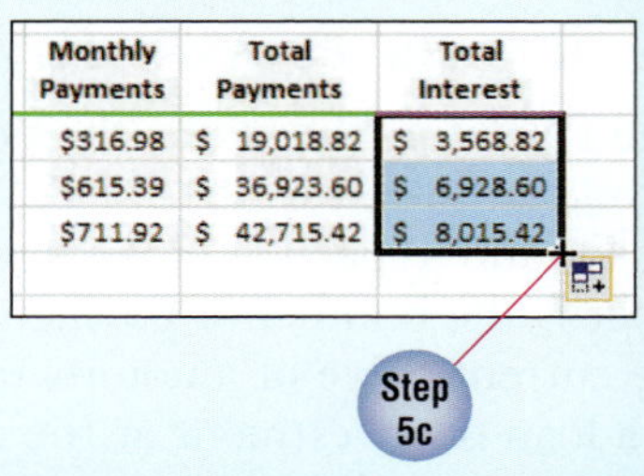

Finding the Future Value of a Series of Payments

The FV function calculates the future value of a series of equal payments or an annuity. Use this function to determine information such as how much money can be earned in an investment account with a specific interest rate and over a specific period of time.

Project 3b Finding the Future Value of an Investment

Part 2 of 3

1. Make sure **EL1-C2-P3-RPReports.xlsx** is open.
2. The owner of Real Photography has decided to save money to purchase a new developer and wants to compute how much money can be earned by investing the money in an investment account that returns 9% annual interest. The owner determines that $1,200 per month can be invested in the account for three years. Complete the following steps to determine the future value of the investment account by completing the following steps:
   a. Make cell B15 active.
   b. Click the Financial button in the Function Library group in the Formulas tab.
   c. At the drop-down list that displays, scroll down the list until *FV* is visible and then click *FV*.
   d. At the Function Arguments palette, type **B12/12** in the *Rate* text box.
   e. Press the Tab key.
   f. Type **B13** in the *Nper* text box.
   g. Press the Tab key.
   h. Type **B14** in the *Pmt* text box.
   i. Click OK. (This closes the palette and also inserts the future value of *$49,383.26* in cell B15.)
3. Save and then print **EL1-C2-P3-RPReports.xlsx**.
4. The owner decides to determine the future return after two years. To do this, change the amount in cell B13 from *36* to *24* and then press Enter. (This recalculates the future investment amount in cell B15.)
5. Save and then print **EL1-C2-P3-RPReports.xlsx**.

Function Arguments

FV

Rate	B12/12	=	0.0075
Nper	B13	=	36
Pmt	B14	=	-1200
Pv		=	number
Type		=	number

Step 2d

Step 2f

Step 2h

10		
11	Future Value of Investment	
12	Rate	9%
13	Number of Months	24
14	Monthly Payment	$ (1,200.00)
15	Future Value	$31,426.16
16		

Step 4

Writing Formulas with Date and Time Functions

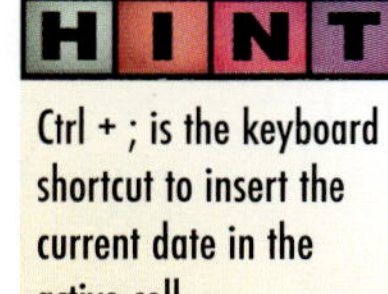

HINT
Ctrl + ; is the keyboard shortcut to insert the current date in the active cell.

In this section, you will learn to write formulas with the date and time functions NOW and DATE. The NOW function returns the serial number of the current date and time. The DATE function returns the serial number that represents a particular date. Excel can make calculations using dates because the dates are represented as serial numbers. To calculate a date's serial number, Excel counts the days since the beginning of the twentieth century. The date serial number for January 1, 1900, is 1. The date serial number for January 1, 2000, is 36,526. To access the DATE and NOW functions, click the Date & Time button in the Function Library group in the Formulas tab.

Date & Time

Project 3c Using the DATE and NOW Functions

Part 3 of 3

1. Make sure **EL1-C2-P3-RPReports.xlsx** is open.
2. Certain cells in this worksheet establish overdue dates for Real Photography accounts. Enter a formula in cell D20 that returns the serial number for the date March 12, 2012, by completing the following steps:

a. Make cell D20 active.
b. Click the Formulas tab.
c. Click the Date & Time button in the Function Library group.
d. At the drop-down list that displays, click *DATE*.
e. At the Function Arguments palette, type **2012** in the *Year* text box.
f. Press the Tab key and then type **03** in the *Month* text box.
g. Press the Tab key and then type **12** in the *Day* text box.
h. Click OK.

3. Complete steps similar to those in Step 2 to enter the following dates as serial numbers in the specified cells:
   D21 = March 19, 2012
   D22 = March 26, 2012
   D23 = April 2, 2012
4. Enter a formula in cell F20 that inserts the due date (the purchase date plus the number of days in the *Terms* column) by completing the following steps:
   a. Make cell F20 active.
   b. Type **=D20+E20** and then press Enter.
   c. Make cell F20 active and then copy the formula down to cells F21, F22, and F23.

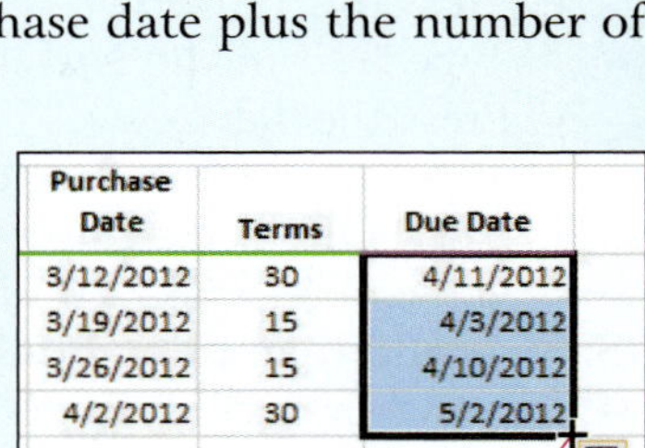

Purchase Date	Terms	Due Date
3/12/2012	30	4/11/2012
3/19/2012	15	4/3/2012
3/26/2012	15	4/10/2012
4/2/2012	30	5/2/2012

5. Make cell A26 active and then type your name.
6. Insert the current date and time as a serial number by completing the following steps:
   a. Make cell A27 active.
   b. Click the Date & Time button in the Function Library group in the Formulas tab and then click *NOW* at the drop-down list.
   c. At the Function Arguments palette telling you that the function takes no argument, click OK.
7. Save, print, and then close **EL1-C2-P3-RPReports.xlsx**.

Insert Formulas with the IF Logical Function — 2 Parts

You will use the IF logical function to calculate sales bonuses, determine letter grades based on test averages, and identify discounts and discount amounts.

Writing a Formula with the IF Logical Function

The IF function is considered a ***conditional function***. With the IF function you can perform conditional tests on values and formulas. A question that can be answered with true or false is considered a ***logical test***. The IF function makes a logical test and then performs a particular action if the answer is true and another action if the answer is false.

For example, an IF function can be used to write a formula that calculates a salesperson's bonus as 10% if the quota of $100,000 is met or exceeded, and zero if the quota is less than $100,000. That formula would look like this: *=IF(quota=>100000,quota*0.1,0)*. The formula contains three parts—the condition or logical test, *IF(quota=>100000*, action taken if the condition or logical test is true, *quota*0.1*, and the action taken if the condition or logical test is false, *0*. Commas separate the condition and the actions. In the bonus formula, if the quota is equal to or greater than $100,000, then the quota is multiplied by 10%. If the quota is less than $100,000, then the bonus is zero.

In Project 4a, you will write a formula with cell references rather than cell data. The formula in Project 4a is *=IF(C5>B5,C5*0.15,0)*. In this formula the condition or logical test is whether or not the number in cell C5 is greater than the number in cell B5. If the condition is true and the number is greater, then the number in cell C5 is multiplied by 0.15 (providing a 15% bonus). If the condition is false and the number in cell C5 is less than the number in cell B5, then nothing happens (no bonus). Notice how commas are used to separate the logical test from the actions.

Editing a Formula

Edit a formula by making active the cell containing the formula and then editing the formula in the cell or in the Formula bar text box. After editing the formula, press Enter or click the Enter button on the Formula bar and Excel will recalculate the result of the formula.

Enter

Project 4a **Writing a Formula with an IF Function and Editing the Formula** Part 1 of 2

1. Open **CMPReports.xlsx**.
2. Save the workbook with Save As and name it **EL1-C2-P4-CMPReports**.
3. Write a formula with the IF function by completing the following steps. (The formula will determine if the quota has been met and, if it has, will insert the bonus [15% of the actual sales]. If the quota has not been met, the formula will insert a zero.)
   a. Make cell D5 active.
   b. Type **=IF(C5>B5,C5*0.15,0)** and then press Enter.
   c. Make cell D5 active and then use the fill handle to copy the formula to cells D6 through D10.

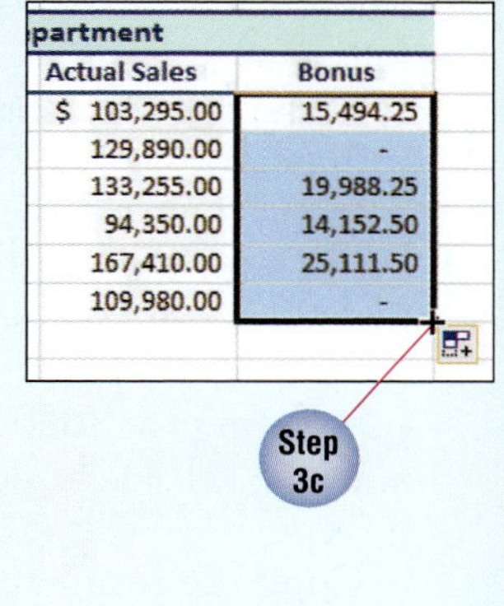

4. Print the worksheet.
5. Revise the formula so it will insert a 25% bonus if the quota has been met by completing the following steps:
   a. Make cell D5 active.
   b. Click in the Formula bar, edit the formula so it displays as *=IF(C5>B5,C5*0.25,0)*, and then click the Enter button on the Formula bar.
   c. Copy the formula down to cells D6 through D10.
   d. Apply the Accounting Number Format to cell D5.
6. Save **EL1-C2-P4-CMPReports.xlsx**.

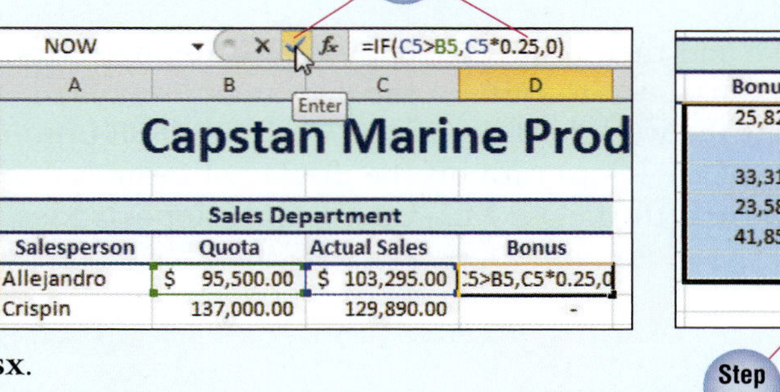

Writing IF Formulas Containing Text

If you write a formula with an IF function and you want text inserted in a cell rather than a value, you must insert quotation marks around the text. For example, in Project 4b, you will write a formula with an IF function that inserts the word *PASS* in a cell if the average of the new employee quizzes is greater than 79 and inserts the word *FAIL* if the condition is not met. To write this formula in Project 4b, you will type *=IF(E16>79,"PASS","FAIL")*. The quotation marks before and after PASS and FAIL identify the data as text rather than a value.

Project 4b **Writing IF Statements with Text** Part 2 of 2

1. With **EL1-C2-P4-CMPReports.xlsx** open, insert quiz averages by completing the following steps:
   a. Make E16 active and then insert a formula that calculates the average of the test scores in cells B16 through D16.
   b. Copy the formula in cell E16 down to cells E17 through E20.
2. Write a formula with an IF function that inserts the word *PASS* if the quiz average is greater than 79 and inserts the word *FAIL* if the quiz average is not greater than 79 by completing the following steps:
   a. Make cell F16 active.
   b. Type **=IF(E16>79,"PASS","FAIL")** and then press Enter.
   c. Copy the formula in cell F16 down to cells F17 through F20.

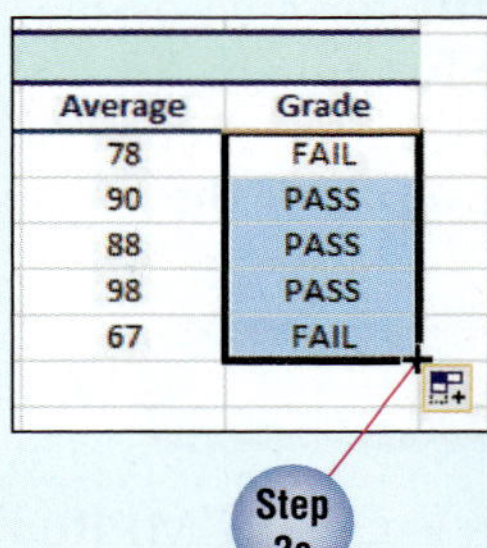

3. Write a formula with an IF function that inserts the word *YES* in the cell if the product price is greater than $599 and inserts the word *NO* if the price is not greater than $599 by completing the following steps:
   a. Make cell C26 active.
   b. Type **=IF(B26>599,"YES","NO")** and then press Enter.
   c. Copy the formula in cell C26 down to cells C27 through C38.
4. Write a formula with an IF function that inserts the text *5%* in the cell if the previous cell contains the text *YES* and inserts the text *0%* if the previous cell does not contain the text *YES* by completing the following steps:
   a. Make cell D26 active.
   b. Type **=IF(C26="YES","5%","0%")** and then press Enter.
   c. Copy the formula in cell D26 down to cells D27 through D38.

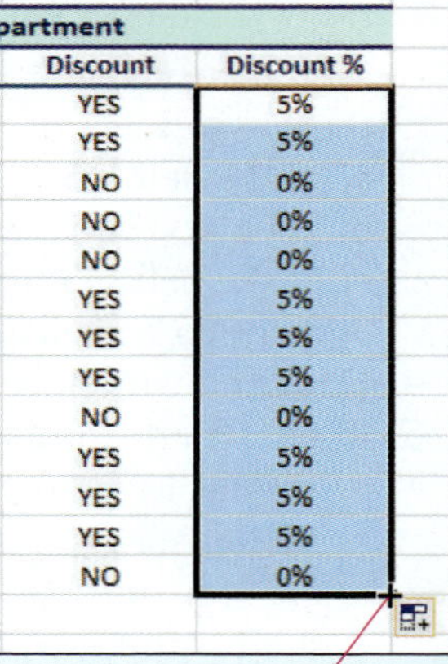

5. Save and then print **EL1-C2-P4-CMPReports.xlsx**.
6. Press Ctrl + ` to turn on the display of formulas.
7. Print the worksheet again (the worksheet will print on two pages).
8. Press Ctrl + ` to turn off the display of formulas.
9. Save and then close **EL1-C2-P4-CMPReports.xlsx**.

Project 5 Insert Formulas Using Absolute and Mixed Cell References

4 Parts

You will insert a formula containing an absolute cell reference that determines the effect on earnings with specific increases, insert a formula with multiple absolute cell references that determine the weighted average of scores, and use mixed cell references to determine simple interest.

Using Absolute and Mixed Cell References in Formulas

A reference identifies a cell or a range of cells in a worksheet and can be relative, absolute, or mixed. ***Relative cell references*** refer to cells relative to a position in a formula. ***Absolute cell references*** refer to cells in a specific location. When a formula is copied, a relative cell reference adjusts while an absolute cell reference remains constant. A ***mixed cell reference*** does both—either the column remains absolute and the row is relative or the column is relative and the row is absolute. Distinguish between relative, absolute, and mixed cell references using the dollar sign ($). Type a dollar sign before the column and/or row cell reference in a formula to specify that the column or row is an absolute cell reference.

Using an Absolute Cell Reference in a Formula

In this chapter you have learned to copy a relative formula. For example, if the formula *=SUM(A2:C2)* in cell D2 is copied relatively to cell D3, the formula changes to *=SUM(A3:C3)*. In some situations, you may want a formula to contain an absolute cell reference, which always refers to a cell in a specific location. In Project 5a, you will add a column for projected job earnings and then perform "what if" situations using a formula with an absolute cell reference. To identify an absolute cell reference, insert a $ sign before the row and the column. For example, the absolute cell reference C12 would be typed as *$C$12* in a formula.

Project 5a Inserting and Copying a Formula with an Absolute Cell Reference

Part 1 of 4

1. Open **CCReports.xlsx**.
2. Save the workbook with Save As and name it **EL1-C2-P5-CCReports**.
3. Determine the effect on actual job earnings with a 10% increase by completing the following steps:
   a. Make cell C3 active, type the formula **=B3*$B$12**, and then press Enter.
   b. Make cell C3 active and then use the fill handle to copy the formula to cells C4 through C10.

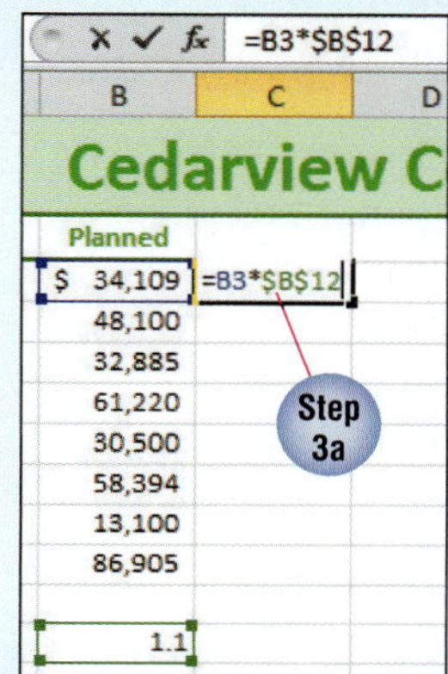

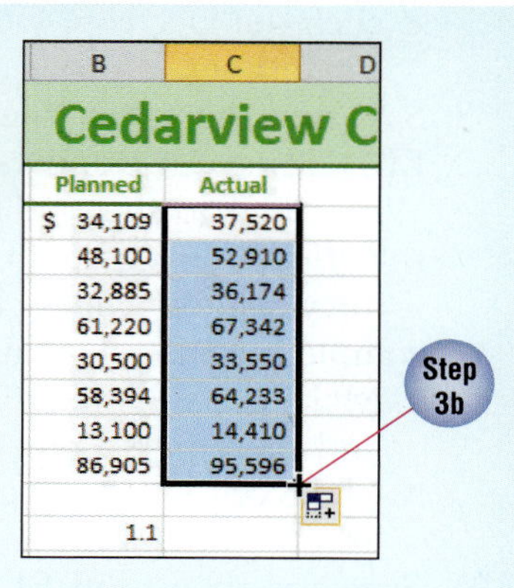

c. Make C3 active, click the Accounting Number Format button, and then click twice on the Decrease Decimal button.
4. Save and then print **EL1-C2-P5-CCReports.xlsx**.
5. With the worksheet still open, determine the effect on actual job earnings with a 10% decrease by completing the following steps:
   a. Make cell B12 active.
   b. Type 0.9 and then press Enter.
6. Save and then print the **EL1-C2-P5-CCReports.xlsx**.
7. Determine the effects on actual job earnings with a 20% increase. (To do this, type 1.2 in cell B12.)
8. Save and then print **EL1-C2-P5-CCReports.xlsx**.

B	C
Cedarview	
Planned	Actual
$ 34,109	$ 30,698
48,100	43,290
32,885	29,597
61,220	55,098
30,500	27,450
58,394	52,555
13,100	11,790
86,905	78,215
0.9	

Step 5b

In Project 5a, you created a formula with one absolute cell reference. You can also create a formula with multiple absolute cell references. For example, in Project 5b you will create a formula that contains both relative and absolute cell references to determine the average of training scores based on specific weight percentages.

Project 5b Inserting and Copying a Formula with Multiple Absolute Cell References

Part 2 of 4

1. With **EL1-C2-P5-CCReports.xlsx** open, insert the following formulas:
   a. Insert a formula in cell B23 that averages the percentages in cells B17 through B22.
   b. Copy the formula in cell B23 to the right to cells C23 and D23.
2. Insert a formula that determines the weighted average of training scores by completing the following steps:
   a. Make cell E17 active.
   b. Type the following formula:
      =$B$24*B17+$C$24*C17+$D$24*D17
   c. Press the Enter key.
   d. Copy the formula in cell E17 down to cells E18 through E22.
   e. With cells E17 through E22 selected, click the Decrease Decimal button three times.
3. Save and then print the **EL1-C2-P5-CCReports.xlsx**.
4. With the worksheet still open, determine the effect on weighted training scores if the weighted values change by completing the following steps:
   a. Make cell B24 active, type 30, and then press Enter.
   b. Make cell D24 active, type 40, and then press Enter.
5. Save and then print **EL1-C2-P5-CCReports.xlsx**.

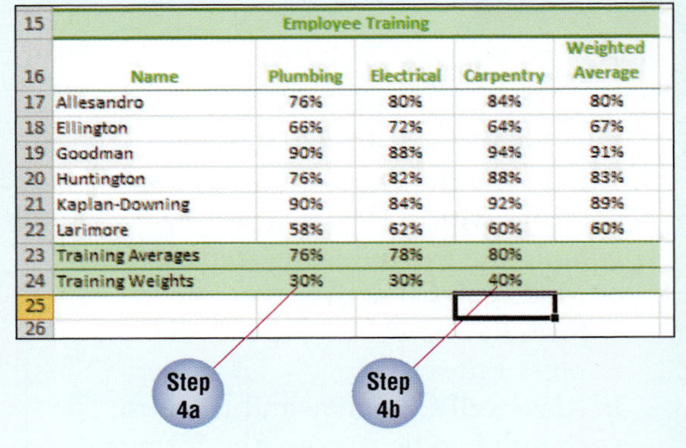

	Employee Training				
16	Name	Plumbing	Electrical	Carpentry	Weighted Average
17	Allesandro	76%	80%	84%	80%
18	Ellington	66%	72%	64%	67%
19	Goodman	90%	88%	94%	91%
20	Huntington	76%	82%	88%	83%
21	Kaplan-Downing	90%	84%	92%	89%
22	Larimore	58%	62%	60%	60%
23	Training Averages	76%	78%	80%	
24	Training Weights	30%	30%	40%	
25					
26					

Using a Mixed Cell Reference in a Formula

The formula you created in Step 3a in Project 5a contained a relative cell reference (B3) and an absolute cell reference ($B$12). A formula can also contain a mixed cell reference. In a mixed cell reference either the column remains absolute and the row is relative or the column is relative and the row is absolute. In Project 5c you will insert a number of formulas, two of which will contain mixed cell references. You will insert the formula *=E29*E$26* to calculate withholding tax and *=E29*H$36* to calculate Social Security tax. The dollar sign before the rows indicates that the row is an absolute cell reference.

Project 5c **Determining Payroll Using Formulas with Absolute and Mixed Cell References**

Part 3 of 4

1. With **EL1-C2-P5-CCReports.xlsx** open, make cell E29 active and then type the following formula containing mixed cell references:
   =(B29*C29+(B29*$B$36*D29))
2. Copy the formula in cell E29 down to cells E30 through E34.
3. Make cell F29 active and then type the following formula that calculates the amount of withholding tax:
   =E29*E$36
4. Copy the formula in cell F29 down to cells F30 through F34.
5. Make cell G29 active and then type the following formula that calculates the amount of Social Security tax:
   =E29*H$36
6. Copy the formula in cell G29 down to cells G30 through G34.
7. Make cell H29 active and then type the following formula that calculates net pay:
   =E29-(F29+G29)
8. Copy the formula in cell H29 down to cells H30 through H34.
9. Select cells E29 through H29 and then click the Accounting Number Format button.
10. Save **EL1-C2-P5-CCReports.xlsx**.

As you learned in Project 5c, a formula can contain a mixed cell reference. In a mixed cell reference either the column remains absolute and the row is relative or the column is relative and the row is absolute. In Project 5d, you will create the formula *=$A41*B$40*. In the first cell reference in the formula, *$A41*, the column is absolute and the row is relative. In the second cell reference, *B$40*, the column is relative and the row is absolute. The formula containing the mixed cell references allows you to fill in the column and row data using only one formula.

Identify an absolute or mixed cell reference by typing a dollar sign before the column and/or row reference or press the F4 function key to cycle through the various cell references. For example, type *=A41* in a cell, press F4, and the cell reference changes to *=$A$41*. Press F4 again and the cell reference changes to *=A$41*. The next time you press F4, the cell reference changes to *=$A41* and press it again to change the cell reference back to *=A41*.

Determining Simple Interest Using a Formula with Mixed Cell References

Part 4 of 4

1. With **EL1-C2-P5-CCReports.xlsx** open, make cell B41 the active cell and then insert a formula containing mixed cell references by completing the following steps:
   a. Type **=A41** and then press the F4 function key three times. (This changes the cell reference to *$A41*.)
   b. Type ***B40** and then press the F4 function key twice. (This changes the cell reference to *B$40*.)
   c. Make sure the formula displays as *=$A41*B$40* and then press Enter.
2. Copy the formula to the right by completing the following steps:
   a. Make cell B41 active and then use the fill handle to copy the formula right to cell F41.
   b. With cells B41 through F41 selected, use the fill handle to copy the formula down to cell F51.
3. Save, print, and then close **EL1-C2-P5-CCReports.xlsx**.

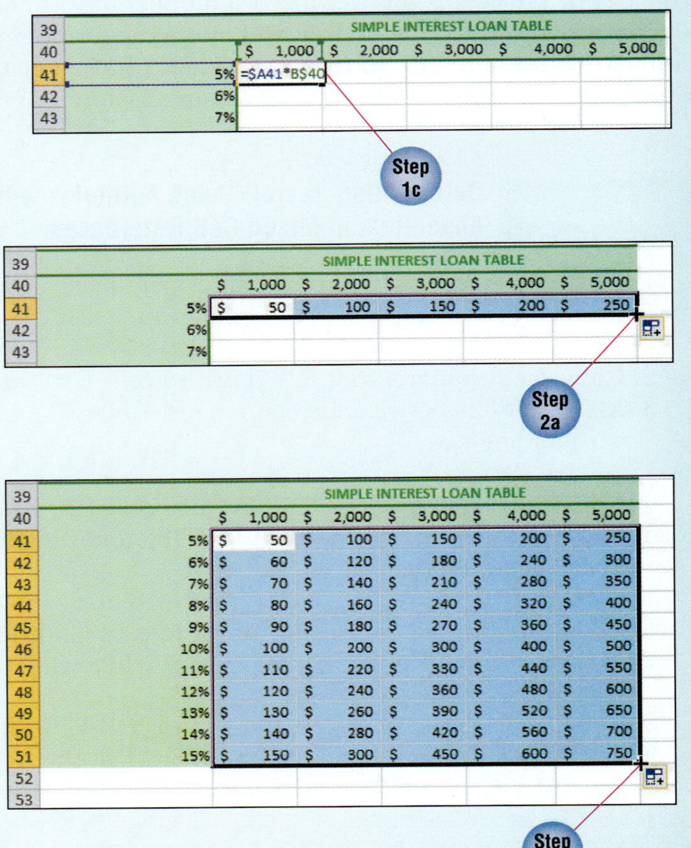

		B	C	D	E	F
39	SIMPLE INTEREST LOAN TABLE					
40		$ 1,000	$ 2,000	$ 3,000	$ 4,000	$ 5,000
41	5%	$ 50	$ 100	$ 150	$ 200	$ 250
42	6%	$ 60	$ 120	$ 180	$ 240	$ 300
43	7%	$ 70	$ 140	$ 210	$ 280	$ 350
44	8%	$ 80	$ 160	$ 240	$ 320	$ 400
45	9%	$ 90	$ 180	$ 270	$ 360	$ 450
46	10%	$ 100	$ 200	$ 300	$ 400	$ 500
47	11%	$ 110	$ 220	$ 330	$ 440	$ 550
48	12%	$ 120	$ 240	$ 360	$ 480	$ 600
49	13%	$ 130	$ 260	$ 390	$ 520	$ 650
50	14%	$ 140	$ 280	$ 420	$ 560	$ 700
51	15%	$ 150	$ 300	$ 450	$ 600	$ 750

Chapter Summary

- Type a formula in a cell and the formula displays in the cell as well as in the Formula bar. If cell entries are changed, a formula will automatically recalculate the values and insert the result in the cell.
- Create your own formula with commonly used operators such as addition (+), subtraction (-), multiplication (*), division (/), percent (%), and exponentiation (^). When writing a formula, begin with the equals sign (=).
- Copy a formula to other cells in a row or column with the Fill button in the Editing group in the Home tab or with the fill handle that displays in the bottom right corner of the active cell.

- Another method for writing a formula is to point to specific cells that are part of the formula as the formula is being built.
- If Excel detects an error in a formula, a Trace Error button appears and a dark green triangle displays in the upper left corner of the cell containing the formula.
- Excel includes over 200 functions that are divided into twelve categories. Use the Insert Function feature to create formulas using built-in functions.
- A function operates on an argument, which may consist of a cell reference, a constant, or another function. When a value calculated by a formula is inserted in a cell, this is referred to as returning the result.
- The AVERAGE function returns the average (arithmetic mean) of the arguments. The MAX function returns the largest value in a set of values, and the MIN function returns the smallest value in a set of values. The COUNT function counts the number of cells containing numbers within the list of arguments.
- Use the keyboard shortcut Ctrl + ` (grave accent) to turn on the display of formulas in a worksheet.
- The PMT function calculates the payment for a loan based on constant payments and a constant interest rate. The FV function returns the future value of an investment based on periodic, constant payments and a constant interest rate.
- The NOW function returns the serial number of the current date and time and the DATE function returns the serial number that represents a particular date.
- Use the IF function, considered a conditional function, to perform conditional tests on values and formulas. Use quotation marks around data in an IF statement to identify the data as text rather than a value.
- A reference identifies a cell or a range of cells in a worksheet and can be relative, absolute, or mixed. Identify an absolute cell reference by inserting a $ sign before the column and row. Cycle through the various cell reference options by typing the cell reference and then pressing F4.

Commands Review

FEATURE	RIBBON TAB, GROUP	BUTTON	KEYBOARD SHORTCUT
SUM function	Home, Editing OR Formulas, Function Library	Σ	Alt + =
Insert Function dialog box	Formulas, Function Library	fx	Shift + F3
Display formulas			Ctrl + `

Concepts Check Test Your Knowledge

Completion: In the space provided at the right, indicate the correct term, symbol, or command.

1. When typing a formula, begin the formula with this sign. ____________________
2. This is the operator for division that is used when writing a formula. ____________________
3. This is the operator for multiplication that is used when writing a formula. ____________________
4. As an alternative to the fill handle, use this button to copy a formula relatively in a worksheet. ____________________
5. A function operates on this, which may consist of a constant, a cell reference, or other function. ____________________
6. This function returns the largest value in a set of values. ____________________
7. This is the keyboard shortcut to display formulas in a worksheet. ____________________
8. This function finds the periodic payment for a loan based on constant payments and a constant interest rate. ____________________
9. This function returns the serial number of the current date and time. ____________________
10. This function is considered a conditional function. ____________________
11. Suppose cell B2 contains the total sales amount. Write a formula that would insert the word *BONUS* in cell C2 if the sales amount was greater than $99,999 and inserts the words *NO BONUS* if the sales amount is not greater than $99,999. ____________________
12. To identify an absolute cell reference, type this symbol before the column and row. ____________________

Skills Check Assess Your Performance

Assessment 1

INSERT AVERAGE, MAX, AND MIN FUNCTIONS

1. Open **DISalesAnalysis.xlsx**.
2. Save the workbook with Save As and name it **EL1-C2-A1-DISalesAnalysis**.
3. Use the AVERAGE function to determine the monthly sales (cells H4 through H9).
4. Format cell H4 with the Accounting Number Format with no decimal places.
5. Total each monthly column including the Average column (cells B10 through H10).
6. Use the MAX function to determine the highest monthly total (for cells B10 through G10) and insert the amount in cell B11.
7. Use the MIN function to determine the lowest monthly total (for cells B10 through G10) and insert the amount in cell B12.
8. Save, print, and then close **EL1-C2-A1-DISalesAnalysis.xlsx**.

Assessment 2

INSERT PMT FUNCTION

1. Open **CMRefiPlan.xlsx**.
2. Save the workbook with Save As and name it **EL1-C2-A2-CMRefiPlan**.
3. The manager of Clearline Manufacturing is interested in refinancing a loan for either $125,000 or $300,000 and wants to determine the monthly payments, total payments, and total interest paid. Insert a formula with the following specifications:
   a. Make cell E5 active.
   b. Use the Insert Function button on the Formula bar to insert a formula using the PMT function. At the formula palette, enter the following:
      Rate = C5/12
      Nper = D5
      Pv = -B5
   c. Copy the formula in cell E5 down to cells E6 through E8.
4. Insert a formula in cell F5 that multiplies the amount in E5 by the amount in D5.
5. Copy the formula in cell F5 down to cells F6 through F8.
6. Insert a formula in cell G5 that subtracts the amount in B5 from the amount in F5. (The formula is *=F5-B5*.)
7. Copy the formula in cell G5 down to cells G6 through G8.
8. Save, print, and then close **EL1-C2-A2-CMRefiPlan.xlsx**.

Assessment 3

INSERT FV FUNCTION

1. Open **RPInvest.xlsx**.
2. Save the workbook with Save As and name it **EL1-C2-A3-RPInvest**.
3. Make the following changes to the worksheet:
   a. Change the percentage in cell B3 from *9%* to *10%*.

   b. Change the number in cell B4 from *36* to *60*.
   c. Change the amount in cell B5 from *($1,200) to -500*.
   d. Use the FV function to insert a formula that calculates the future value of the investment. ***Hint: For help with the formula, refer to Project 3b.***
4. Save, print, and then close **EL1-C2-A3-RPInvest.xlsx**.

Assessment 4

WRITE IF STATEMENT FORMULAS

1. Open **DISalesBonuses.xlsx**.
2. Save the workbook with Save As and name it **EL1-C2-A4-DISalesBonuses**.
3. Insert a formula in cell C4 that inserts the word *YES* if the amount in B4 is greater than 99999 and inserts *NO* if the amount is not greater than 99999. Copy the formula in cell C4 down to cells C5 through C14.
4. Make cell D4 active and then insert the formula **=IF(C4="YES",B4*0.05,0)**. If sales are over $99,000, this formula will multiply the amount of sales by 5 percent and then insert the product (result) of the formula in the cell. Copy the formula in cell D4 down to cells D5 through D14.
5. Format cell D4 with the accounting number format with no decimal places.
6. Save and then print **EL1-C2-A4-DISalesBonuses.xlsx**.
7. Display the formulas in the worksheet and then print the worksheet.
8. Turn off the display of formulas.
9. Save and then close **EL1-C2-A4-DISalesBonuses.xlsx**.

Assessment 5

WRITE FORMULAS WITH ABSOLUTE CELL REFERENCES

1. Open **CCQuotas.xlsx**.
2. Save the workbook with Save As and name it **EL1-C2-A5-CCQuotas**.
3. Make the following changes to the worksheet:
   a. Insert a formula using an absolute reference to determine the projected quotas with a 10% increase from the current quotas.
   b. Save and then print **EL1-C2-A5-CCQuotas.xlsx**.
   c. Determine the projected quotas with a 15% increase from the current quota by changing cell A15 to *15% Increase* and cell B15 to *1.15*.
   d. Save and then print **EL1-C2-A5-CCQuotas.xlsx**.
   e. Determine the projected quotas with a 20% increase from the current quota.
4. Format cell C4 with the Accounting Number Format with no decimal places.
5. Save, print, and then close **EL1-C2-A5-CCQuotas.xlsx**.

Assessment

USE HELP TO LEARN ABOUT EXCEL OPTIONS

1. Learn about specific options in the Excel Options dialog box by completing the following steps:
   a. At a blank workbook, display the Excel Options dialog box by clicking the File tab and then clicking the Options button.
   b. At the Excel Options dialog box, click the *Advanced* option located in the left panel.

c. Scroll down and look for the section *Display options for this workbook* and then read the information in the section. Read the information that displays in the *Display options for this worksheet* section.

d. Write down the check box options available in the *Display options for this workbook* section and the *Display options for this worksheet* section and identify whether or not the check box contains a check mark. (Record only check box options and ignore buttons and options preceded by circles.)

2. With the information you wrote down about the options, create an Excel spreadsheet with the following information:
   a. In column C, type each option you wrote down. (Include an appropriate heading.)
   b. In column B, insert an X in the cell that precedes any option that contains a check mark in the check box. (Include an appropriate heading.)
   c. In column A, write a formula with the IF function that inserts the word ON in the cell if the cell in column B contains an X and inserts the word OFF if it does not (the cell is blank). (Include an appropriate heading.)
   d. Apply formatting to improve the visual appeal of the worksheet.
3. Save the workbook and name it **EL1-C2-A6-DisplayOptions**.
4. Turn on the display of formulas.
5. Print the worksheet.
6. Turn off the display of formulas.
7. Save, print, and then close **EL1-C2-A6-DisplayOptions.xlsx**.

Visual Benchmark Demonstrate Your Proficiency

CREATE A WORKSHEET AND INSERT FORMULAS

1. At a blank workbook, type the data in the cells indicated in Figure 2.4 but <u>do not</u> type the data in the following cells—instead insert the formulas as indicated (the results of your formulas should match the results you see in the figure):
   - Cells D3 through D9: Insert a formula that calculates the salary.
   - Cells D14 through D19: Insert a formula that calculates the differences.
   - Cells D24 through D27: Insert the dates as serial numbers.
   - Cells F24 through F27: Insert a formula that calculates the due date.
   - Cells B37 through D37: Insert a formula that calculates the averages.
   - Cells E32 through E36: Insert a formula that calculates the weighted average of test scores.
2. Apply any other formatting so your worksheet looks similar to the worksheet shown in Figure 2.4.
3. Save the workbook and name it **EL1-C2-VB-Formulas**.
4. Print **EL1-C2-VB-Formulas.xlsx**.
5. Press Ctrl + ` to turn on the display of formulas and then print the worksheet again.
6. Turn off the display of formulas and then close the workbook.

Figure 2.4 Visual Benchmark

	A	B	C	D	E	F	G
1		Weekly Payroll					
2	Employee	Hours	Rate	Salary			
3	Alvarez, Rita	40	$ 22.50	$ 900.00			
4	Campbell, Owen	15	22.50	337.50			
5	Heitmann, Luanne	25	19.00	475.00			
6	Malina, Susan	40	18.75	750.00			
7	Parker, Kenneth	40	18.75	750.00			
8	Reitz, Collette	20	15.00	300.00			
9	Shepard, Gregory	15	12.00	180.00			
10							
11							
12		Construction Projects					
13	Project	Projected	Actual	Difference			
14	South Cascade	$ 145,000	$ 141,597	$ (3,403)			
15	Rogue River Park	120,000	124,670	4,670			
16	Meridian	120,500	99,450	(21,050)			
17	Lowell Ridge	95,250	98,455	3,205			
18	Walker Canyon	70,000	68,420	(1,580)			
19	Nettleson Creek	52,000	49,517	(2,483)			
20							
21							
22			Overdue Accounts				
23	Client	Account #	Amount Due	Pur. Date	Terms	Due Date	
24	Sunrise Marketing	120	$ 9,875	12/4/2012	15	12/19/2012	
25	National Systems	398	8,525	12/7/2012	30	1/6/2013	
26	First Street Signs	188	5,000	12/12/2012	15	12/27/2012	
27	Valley Services	286	3,250	12/19/2012	30	1/18/2013	
28							
29							
30			Test Scores				
31	Employee	Test No. 1	Test No. 2	Test No. 3	Wgt. Avg.		
32	Coffey, Annette	62%	64%	76%	70%		
33	Halverson, Ted	88%	96%	90%	91%		
34	Kohler, Jeremy	80%	76%	82%	80%		
35	McKnight, Carol	68%	72%	78%	74%		
36	Parkhurst, Jody	98%	96%	98%	98%		
37	Test Averages	79%	81%	85%			
38	Test Weights	25%	25%	50%			

Case Study Apply Your Skills

Part 1

You are a loan officer for Dollar Wise Financial Services and work in the department that specializes in home loans. You have decided to prepare a sample home mortgage worksheet to show prospective clients. This sample home mortgage worksheet will show the monthly payments on variously priced homes with varying interest rates. Open the **DWMortgages.xlsx** worksheet and then complete the home mortgage worksheet by inserting the following formulas:

- Since many homes in your area sell for at least $400,000, you decide to add that amount to the worksheet with a 5%, 10%, 15%, and 20% down payment.
- In column C, insert a formula that determines the down payment amount.
- In column D, insert a formula that determines the loan amount.
- In column G, insert a formula using the PMT function. (The monthly payment will display as a negative number.)

Save the worksheet and name it **EL1-C2-CS-DWMortgages**.

Part 2

If home buyers put down less than 20 percent of the home's purchase price, mortgage insurance is required. With **EL1-C2-CS-DWMortgages.xlsx** open, insert an IF statement in the cells in column H that inserts the word "No" if the percentage in column B is equal to or greater than 20% or inserts the word "Yes" if the percentage in column B is less than 20%. Save and then print **EL1-C2-CS-DWMortgages.xlsx**.

Part 3

Interest rates fluctuate on a regular basis. Using the resources available to you, determine a current interest rate in your area. Delete the interest rate of 7% in the Dollar Wise worksheet and insert the interest rate for your area. Save and then print **EL1-C2-CS-DWMortgages.xlsx**.

When a client is required to purchase mortgage insurance, you would like to provide information to the client concerning this insurance. Use the Help feature to learn about creating hyperlinks in Excel. Locate a helpful website that specializes in private mortgage insurance. Create a hyperlink in the worksheet that will display the website. Save, print, and then close **EL1-C2-CS-DWMortage.xlsx**.

Part 5

Once a loan has been approved and finalized, a letter is sent to the client explaining the details of the loan. Use a letter template in Word to create a letter that is sent to the client. Copy and link the information in the **EL1-C2-CS-DWMortage.xlsx** worksheet to the client letter. Save the letter document and name it **DWLetter**. Print and then close **DWLetter.docx**.

CHAPTER 3

Formatting an Excel Worksheet

PERFORMANCE OBJECTIVES

Upon successful completion of Chapter 3, you will be able to:

- Change column widths
- Change row heights
- Insert rows and columns in a worksheet
- Delete cells, rows, and columns in a worksheet
- Clear data in cells
- Apply formatting to data in cells
- Apply formatting to selected data using the Mini toolbar
- Preview a worksheet
- Apply a theme and customize the theme font and color
- Format numbers
- Repeat the last action
- Automate formatting with Format Painter
- Hide and unhide rows and columns

Tutorials

3.1 Inserting, Adjusting, and Deleting Rows and Columns

3.2 Using Cell Styles and Themes

3.3 Formatting Numbers

3.4 Adding Borders and Shading; Copying Formats with Format Painter

3.5 Hiding and Unhiding Rows and Columns

The appearance of a worksheet on the screen and how it looks when printed is called the ***format***. In Chapter 1, you learned how to apply basic formatting to cells in a worksheet. Additional types of formatting you may want to apply to a worksheet include changing column width and row height; applying character formatting such as bold, italics, and underlining; specifying number formatting; inserting and deleting rows and columns; and applying borders, shading, and patterns to cells. You can also apply formatting to a worksheet with a theme. A theme is a set of formatting choices that include colors and fonts. Model answers for this chapter's projects appear on the following page.

Note: Before beginning the projects, copy to your storage medium the Excel2010L1C3 subfolder from the Excel2010L1 folder on the CD that accompanies this textbook and then make Excel2010L1C3 the active folder.

Model Answers

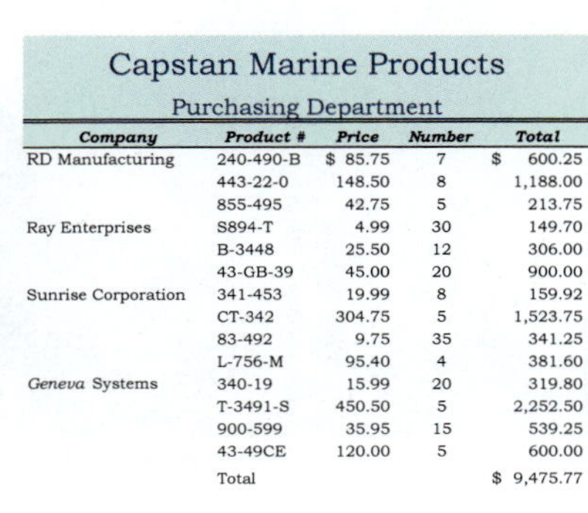

Capstan Marine Products

Purchasing Department

Company	*Product #*	*Price*	*Number*	*Total*
RD Manufacturing	240-490-B	$ 85.75	7	$ 600.25
	443-22-0	148.50	8	1,188.00
	855-495	42.75	5	213.75
Ray Enterprises	S894-T	4.99	30	149.70
	B-3448	25.50	12	306.00
	43-GB-39	45.00	20	900.00
Sunrise Corporation	341-453	19.99	8	159.92
	CT-342	304.75	5	1,523.75
	83-492	9.75	35	341.25
	L-756-M	95.40	4	381.60
Geneva Systems	340-19	15.99	20	319.80
	T-3491-S	450.50	5	2,252.50
	900-599	35.95	15	539.25
	43-49CE	120.00	5	600.00
	Total			$ 9,475.77

Project 1 Format a Product Pricing Worksheet

EL1-C3-P1-CMProducts.xlsx

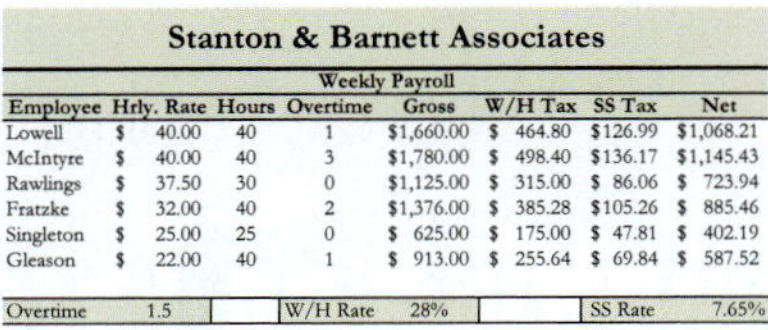

Stanton & Barnett Associates

Weekly Payroll

Employee	Hrly. Rate	Hours	Overtime	Gross	W/H Tax	SS Tax	Net
Lowell	$ 40.00	40	1	$1,660.00	$ 464.80	$126.99	$1,068.21
McIntyre	$ 40.00	40	3	$1,780.00	$ 498.40	$136.17	$1,145.43
Rawlings	$ 37.50	30	0	$1,125.00	$ 315.00	$ 86.06	$ 723.94
Fratzke	$ 32.00	40	2	$1,376.00	$ 385.28	$105.26	$ 885.46
Singleton	$ 25.00	25	0	$ 625.00	$ 175.00	$ 47.81	$ 402.19
Gleason	$ 22.00	40	1	$ 913.00	$ 255.64	$ 69.84	$ 587.52

Overtime	1.5		W/H Rate	28%		SS Rate	7.65%

Project 2 Apply a Theme to a Payroll Worksheet

EL1-C3-P2-SBAPayroll.xlsx

REAL PHOTOGRAPHY

Invoices

Invoice #	Client #	Service	Amount	Tax	Amount Due
2930	03-392	Family Portraits	$ 450.00	8.5%	$ 488.25
2942	02-498	Wedding Portraits	$ 1,075.00	8.8%	$ 1,169.60
2002	11-279	Development	$ 225.00	0.0%	$ 225.00
2007	04-325	Sports Portraits	$ 750.00	8.5%	$ 813.75
2376	03-392	Senior Portraits	$ 850.00	8.5%	$ 922.25
2129	11-279	Development	$ 350.00	0.0%	$ 350.00
2048	11-325	Wedding Portraits	$ 875.00	8.5%	$ 949.38
2054	04-325	Sports Portraits	$ 750.00	8.5%	$ 813.75
2064	05-665	Family Portraits	$ 560.00	8.8%	$ 609.28
2077	11-279	Development	$ 400.00	0.0%	$ 400.00
2079	04-325	Sports Portraits	$ 600.00	8.5%	$ 651.00
2908	55-340	Senior Portraits	$ 725.00	8.8%	$ 788.80
3001	11-279	Development	$ 310.00	8.8%	$ 337.28

Project 3 Format an Invoices Worksheet

EL1-C3-P3-RPInvoices.xlsx

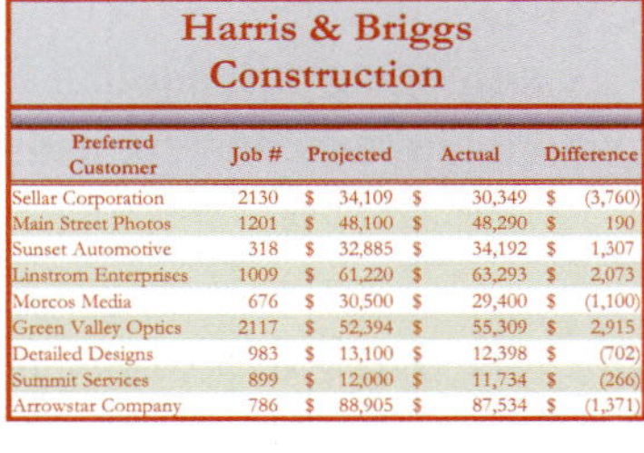

Harris & Briggs Construction

Preferred Customer	Job #	Projected	Actual	Difference
Sellar Corporation	2130	$ 34,109	$ 30,349	$ (3,760)
Main Street Photos	1201	$ 48,100	$ 48,290	$ 190
Sunset Automotive	318	$ 32,885	$ 34,192	$ 1,307
Linstrom Enterprises	1009	$ 61,220	$ 63,293	$ 2,073
Morcos Media	676	$ 30,500	$ 29,400	$ (1,100)
Green Valley Optics	2117	$ 52,394	$ 55,309	$ 2,915
Detailed Designs	983	$ 13,100	$ 12,398	$ (702)
Summit Services	899	$ 12,000	$ 11,734	$ (266)
Arrowstar Company	786	$ 88,905	$ 87,534	$ (1,371)

Project 4 Format a Company Budget Worksheet

EL1-C3-P4-HBCJobs.xlsx

Format a Product Pricing Worksheet — 7 Parts

You will open a workbook containing a worksheet with product pricing data, and then format the worksheet by changing column widths and row heights, inserting and deleting rows and columns, deleting rows and columns, and clearing data in cells. You will also apply font and alignment formatting to data in cells and then preview the worksheet.

Changing Column Width

Columns in a worksheet are the same width by default. In some worksheets you may want to change column widths to accommodate more or less data. You can change column width using the mouse on column boundaries or at a dialog box.

Changing Column Width Using Column Boundaries

As you learned in Chapter 1, you can adjust the width of a column by dragging the column boundary line or adjust a column width to the longest entry by double-clicking the boundary line. When you drag a column boundary, the column width displays in a box above the mouse pointer. The column width number that displays represents the average number of characters in the standard font that can fit in a cell.

To change the width of all columns in a worksheet, click the Select All button and then drag a column boundary to the desired position.

You can change the width of selected adjacent columns at the same time. To do this, select the columns and then drag one of the column boundaries within the selected columns. As you drag the boundary the column width changes for all selected columns. To select adjacent columns, position the cell pointer on the first desired column header (the mouse pointer turns into a black, down-pointing arrow), hold down the left mouse button, drag the cell pointer to the last desired column header, and then release the mouse button.

Project 1a — Changing Column Width Using a Column Boundary — Part 1 of 7

1. Open **CMProducts.xlsx**.
2. Save the workbook with Save As and name it **EL1-C3-P1-CMProducts**.
3. Insert a formula in cell D2 that multiplies the price in cell B2 with the number in cell C2. Copy the formula in cell D2 down to cells D3 through D14.
4. Change the width of column D by completing the following steps:
   a. Position the mouse pointer on the column boundary in the column header between columns D and E until it turns into a double-headed arrow pointing left and right.
   b. Hold down the left mouse button, drag the column boundary to the right until *Width: 11.00 (82 pixels)* displays in the box, and then release the mouse button.
5. Make cell D15 active and then insert the sum of cells D2 through D14.
6. Change the width of columns A and B by completing the following steps:
   a. Select columns A and B. To do this, position the cell pointer on the column A header, hold down the left mouse button, drag the cell pointer to the column B header, and then release the mouse button.

b. Position the cell pointer on the column boundary between columns A and B until it turns into a double-headed arrow pointing left and right.

c. Hold down the left mouse button, drag the column boundary to the right until *Width: 10.14 (76 pixels)* displays in the box, and then release the mouse button.

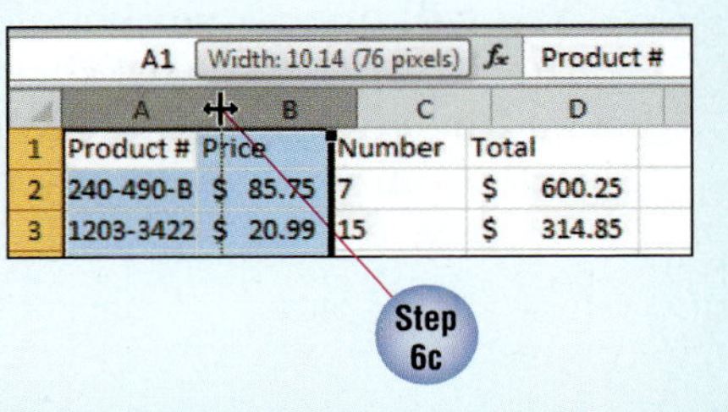

A1
Width: 10.14 (76 pixels)
Product #
Product # Price Number Total
240-490-B $ 85.75 7 $ 600.25
1203-3422 $ 20.99 15 $ 314.85
Step 6c

7. Adjust the width of column C to accommodate the longest entry by double-clicking on the column boundary between columns C and D.
8. Save **EL1-C3-P1-CMProducts.xlsx**.

Quick Steps

Change Column Width
Drag column boundary line.
OR
Double-click column boundary.
OR
1. Click Format button.
2. Click *Column Width* at drop-down list.
3. Type desired width.
4. Click OK.

Format

Changing Column Width at the Column Width Dialog Box

At the Column Width dialog box shown in Figure 3.1, you can specify a column width number. Increase the column width number to make the column wider or decrease the column width number to make the column narrower.

To display the Column Width dialog box, click the Format button in the Cells group in the Home tab and then click *Column Width* at the drop-down list. At the Column Width dialog box, type the number representing the average number of characters in the standard font that you want to fit in the column and then press Enter or click OK.

Figure 3.1 Column Width Dialog Box

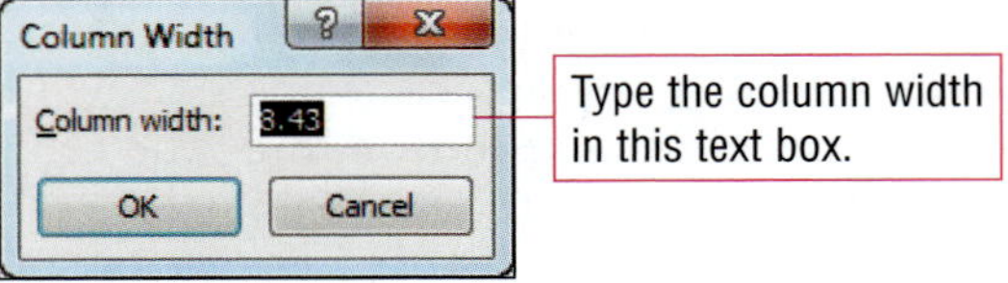

Project 1b **Changing Column Width at the Column Width Dialog Box** Part 2 of 7

1. With **EL1-C3-P1-CMProducts.xlsx** open, change the width of column A by completing the following steps:
   a. Make any cell in column A active.
   b. Click the Format button in the Cells group in the Home tab and then click *Column Width* at the drop-down list.
   c. At the Column Width dialog box, type 12.75 in the *Column width* text box.
   d. Click OK to close the dialog box.
2. Make any cell in column B active and then change the width of column B to *12.75* by completing steps similar to those in Step 1.
3. Make any cell in column C active and then change the width of column C to *8* by completing steps similar to those in Step 1.
4. Save **EL1-C3-P1-CMProducts.xlsx**.

Changing Row Height

Row height can be changed in much the same manner as column width. For example, you can change the row height using the mouse on a row boundary, or at the Row Height dialog box. Change row height using a row boundary in the same manner as you learned to change column width. To do this, position the cell pointer on the boundary between rows in the row header until it turns into a double-headed arrow pointing up and down, hold down the left mouse button, drag up or down until the row is the desired height, and then release the mouse button.

The height of selected rows that are adjacent can be changed at the same time. (The height of nonadjacent rows will not all change at the same time.) To do this, select the rows and then drag one of the row boundaries within the selected rows. As the boundary is being dragged the row height changes for all selected rows.

As a row boundary is being dragged, the row height displays in a box above the mouse pointer. The row height number that displays represents a point measurement. A vertical inch contains approximately 72 points. Increase the point size to increase the row height; decrease the point size to decrease the row height.

At the Row Height dialog box shown in Figure 3.2, you can specify a row height number. To display the Row Height dialog box, click the Format button in the Cells group in the Home tab and then click *Row Height* at the drop-down list.

Quick Steps

Change Row Height

Drag row boundary line.

OR

1. Click Format button.
2. Click *Row Height* at drop-down list.
3. Type desired height.
4. Click OK.

To change the height of all rows in a worksheet, click the Select All button and then drag a row boundary to the desired position.

Figure 3.2 Row Height Dialog Box

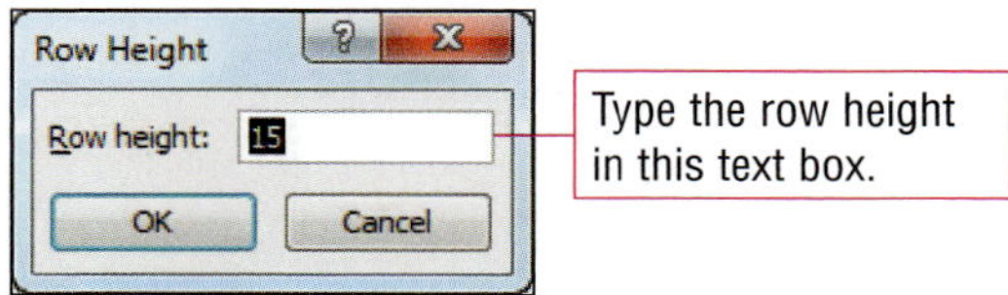

Project 1c Changing Row Height

Part 3 of 7

1. With **EL1-C3-P1-CMProducts.xlsx** open, change the height of row 1 by completing the following steps:
   a. Position the cell pointer in the row header on the row boundary between rows 1 and 2 until it turns into a double-headed arrow pointing up and down.
   b. Hold down the left mouse button, drag the row boundary down until *Height: 19.50 (26 pixels)* displays in the box, and then release the mouse button.
2. Change the height of rows 2 through 14 by completing the following steps:
   a. Select rows 2 through 14. To do this, position the cell pointer on the number 2 in the row header, hold down the left mouse button, drag the cell pointer to the number 14 in the row header, and then release the mouse button.
   b. Position the cell pointer on the row boundary between rows 2 and 3 until it turns into a double-headed arrow pointing up and down.

c. Hold down the left mouse button, drag the row boundary down until *Height: 16.50 (22 pixels)* displays in the box, and then release the mouse button.

3. Change the height of row 15 by completing the following steps:
   a. Make cell A15 active.
   b. Click the Format button in the Cells group in the Home tab and then click *Row Height* at the drop-down list.
   c. At the Row Height dialog box, type **20** in the *Row height* text box and then click OK.

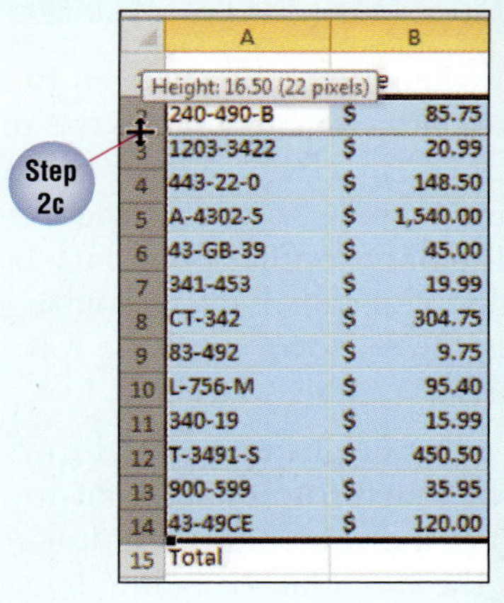

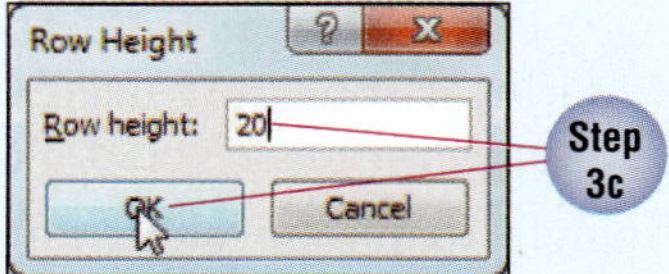

4. Save **EL1-C3-P1-CMProducts.xlsx**.

Inserting and Deleting Cells, Rows, and Columns

Quick Steps

Insert Row
Click Insert button.
OR
1. Click Insert button arrow.
2. Click *Insert Sheet Rows* at drop-down list.

OR
1. Click Insert button arrow.
2. Click *Insert Cells*.
3. Click *Entire row* in dialog box.
4. Click OK.

Insert

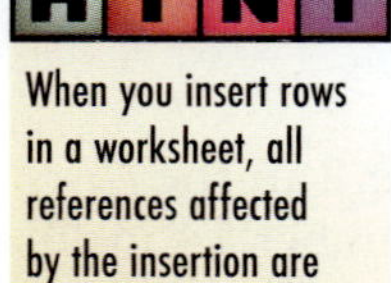

When you insert rows in a worksheet, all references affected by the insertion are automatically adjusted.

New data may need to be included in an existing worksheet. For example, a row or several rows of new data may need to be inserted into a worksheet or data may need to be removed from a worksheet.

Inserting Rows

After you create a worksheet, you can add (insert) rows to the worksheet. Insert a row with the Insert button in the Cells group in the Home tab or with options at the Insert dialog box. By default, a row is inserted above the row containing the active cell. To insert a row in a worksheet, select the row below where the row is to be inserted and then click the Insert button. If you want to insert more than one row, select the number of rows in the worksheet that you want inserted and then click the Insert button.

You can also insert a row by making a cell active in the row below where the row is to be inserted, clicking the Insert button arrow, and then clicking *Insert Sheet Rows*. Another method for inserting a row is to click the Insert button arrow and then click *Insert Cells*. This displays the Insert dialog box as shown in Figure 3.3. At the Insert dialog box, click *Entire row*. This inserts a row above the active cell.

Figure 3.3 Insert Dialog Box

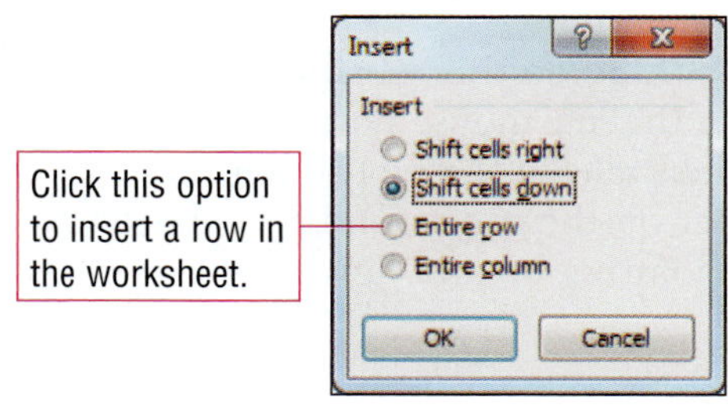

Inserting Rows Part 4 of 7

1. With **EL1-C3-P1-CMProducts.xlsx** open, insert two rows at the beginning of the worksheet by completing the following steps:
   a. Make cell A1 active.
   b. Click the Insert button arrow in the Cells group in the Home tab.
   c. At the drop-down list that displays, click *Insert Sheet Rows*.
   d. With cell A1 active, click the Insert button arrow and then click *Insert Sheet Rows* at the drop-down list.

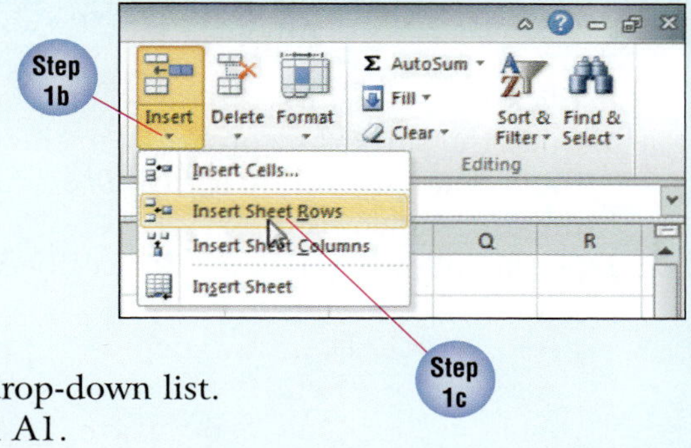

2. Type the text **Capstan Marine Products** in cell A1.
3. Make cell A2 active and then type **Purchasing Department**.
4. Change the height of row 1 to *42.00 (56 pixels)*.
5. Change the height of row 2 to *21.00 (28 pixels)*.
6. Insert two rows by completing the following steps:
   a. Select rows 7 and 8 in the worksheet.
   b. Click the Insert button in the Cells group in the Home tab.

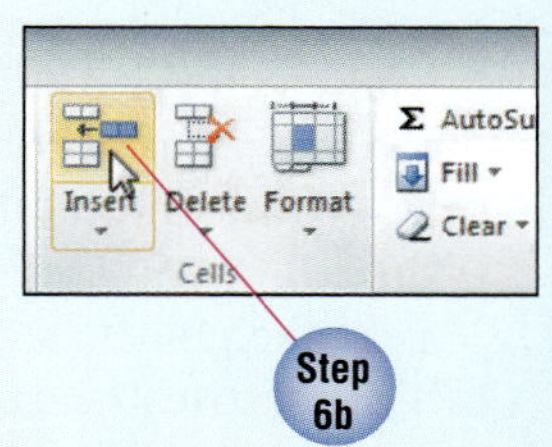

7. Type the following data in the specified cells: (You do not need to type the dollar sign in cells containing money amounts.)
   A7 = **855-495**
   B7 = **42.75**
   C7 = **5**
   A8 = **ST039**
   B8 = **12.99**
   C8 = **25**
8. Make D6 the active cell and then use the fill handle to copy the formula down to cells D7 and D8.
9. Save **EL1-C3-P1-CMProducts.xlsx**.

Inserting Columns

Insert columns in a worksheet in much the same way as rows. Insert a column with options from the Insert button drop-down list or with options at the Insert dialog box. By default, a column is inserted immediately to the left of the column containing the active cell. To insert a column in a worksheet, make a cell active in the column immediately to the right of where the new column is to be inserted, click the Insert button arrow, and then click *Insert Sheet Columns* at the drop-down list. If you want to insert more than one column, select the number of columns in the worksheet that you want inserted, click the Insert button arrow, and then click *Insert Sheet Columns*.

You also can insert a column by making a cell active in the column immediately to the right of where the new column is to be inserted, clicking the Insert button arrow, and then clicking *Insert Cells* at the drop-down list. This causes the Insert dialog box to display. At the Insert dialog box, click *Entire column*. This inserts an entire column immediately to the left of the active cell.

Excel includes an especially helpful and time-saving feature related to inserting columns. When you insert columns in a worksheet, all references affected by the insertion are automatically adjusted.

Quick Steps

Insert Column
Click Insert button.
OR
1. Click Insert button arrow.
2. Click *Insert Sheet Columns* at drop-down list.

OR
1. Click Insert button arrow.
2. Click *Insert Cells.*
3. Click *Entire column.*
4. Click OK.

Inserting a Column Part 5 of 7

1. With **EL1-C3-P1-CMProducts.xlsx** open, insert a column by completing the following steps:
   a. Click in any cell in column A.
   b. Click the Insert button arrow in the Cells group in the Home tab and then click *Insert Sheet Columns* at the drop-down list.
2. Type the following data in the specified cell:
   A3 = **Company**
   A4 = **RD Manufacturing**
   A8 = **Smithco, Inc.**
   A11 = **Sunrise Corporation**
   A15 = **Geneva Systems**
3. Make cell A1 active and then adjust the width of column A to accommodate the longest entry.
4. Insert another column by completing the following steps:
   a. Make cell B1 active.
   b. Click the Insert button arrow and then click *Insert Cells* at the drop-down list.
   c. At the Insert dialog box, click *Entire column*.
   d. Click OK.
5. Type **Date** in cell B3 and then press Enter.
6. Save **EL1-C3-P1-CMProducts.xlsx**.

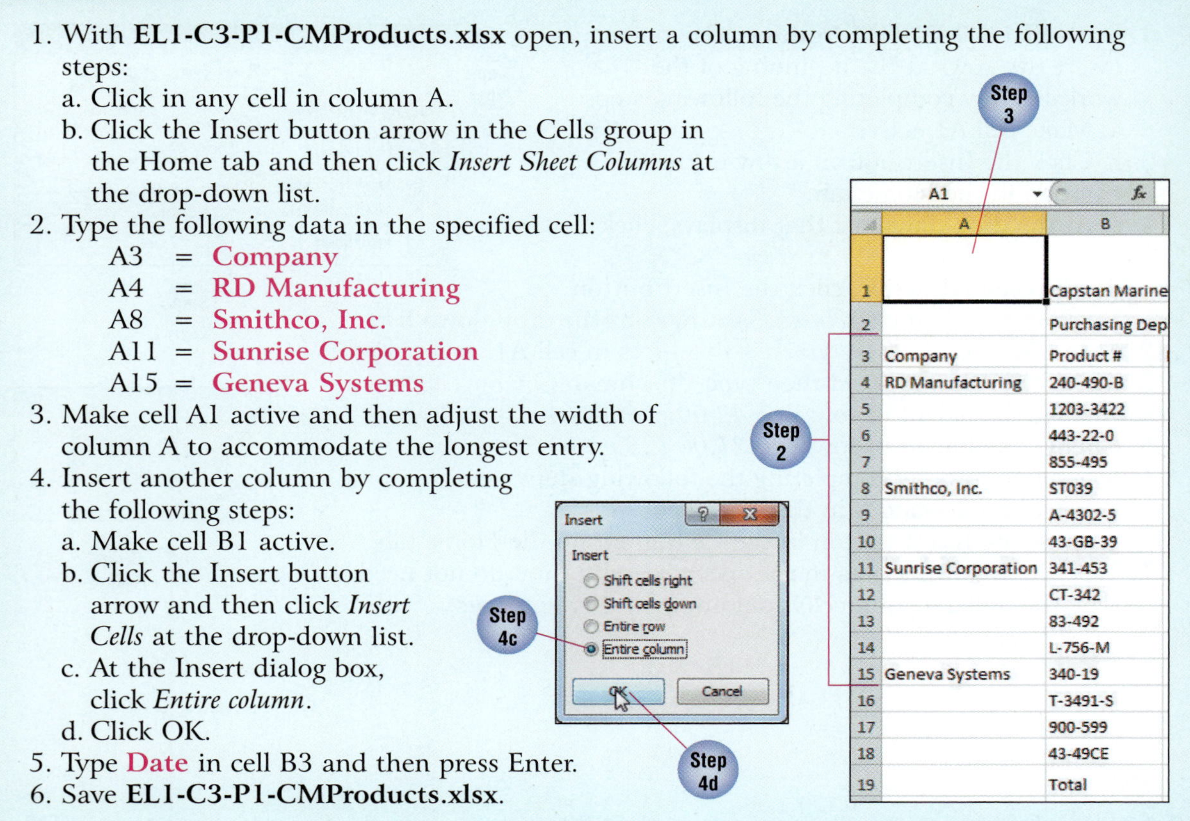

Deleting Cells, Rows, or Columns

HINT
Display the Delete dialog box by positioning the cell pointer in the worksheet, clicking the right mouse button, and then clicking *Delete* at the shortcut menu.

You can delete specific cells in a worksheet or rows or columns in a worksheet. To delete a row, select the row and then click the Delete button in the Cells group in the Home tab. To delete a column, select the column and then click the Delete button. Delete a specific cell by making the cell active, clicking the Delete button arrow, and then clicking *Delete Cells* at the drop-down list. This displays the Delete dialog box shown in Figure 3.4. At the Delete dialog box, specify what you want deleted and then click OK. You can also delete adjacent cells by selecting the cells and then displaying the Delete dialog box.

Delete

Figure 3.4 Delete Dialog Box

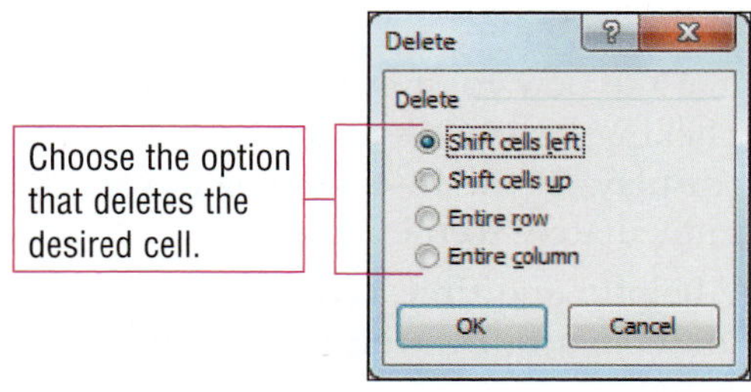

Clearing Data in Cells

> **Quick Steps**
>
> **Clear Data in Cells**
> 1. Select desired cells.
> 2. Press Delete key.
>
> OR
> 1. Select desired cells.
> 2. Click Clear button.
> 3. Click *Clear Contents* at drop-down list.

Clear

If you want to delete cell contents but not the cell, make the cell active or select desired cells and then press the Delete key. A quick method for clearing the contents of a cell is to right-click the cell and then click *Clear Contents* at the shortcut menu. Another method for deleting cell contents is to make the cell active or select desired cells, click the Clear button in the Editing group in the Home tab, and then click *Clear Contents* at the drop-down list.

With the options at the Clear button drop-down list you can clear the contents of the cell or selected cells as well as formatting and comments. Click the *Clear Formats* option to remove formatting from cells or selected cells while leaving the data. You can also click the *Clear All* option to clear the contents of the cell or selected cells as well as the formatting.

Project 1f Deleting and Clearing Rows in a Worksheet

Part 6 of 7

1. With **EL1-C3-P1-CMProducts.xlsx** open, delete column B in the worksheet by completing the following steps:
   a. Click in any cell in column B.
   b. Click the Delete button arrow in the Cells group in the Home tab and then click *Delete Sheet Columns* at the drop-down list.

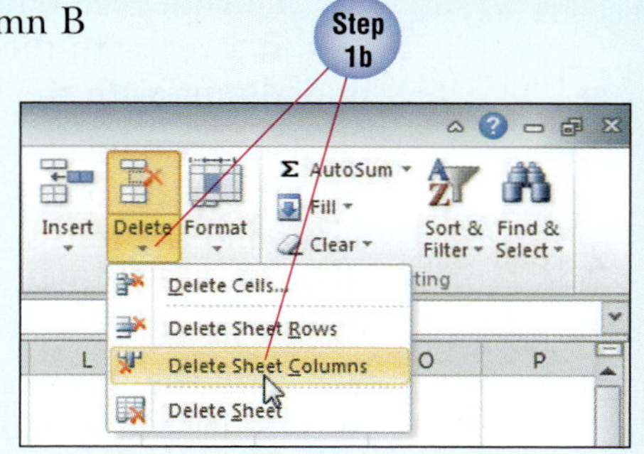

2. Delete row 5 by completing the following steps:
   a. Select row 5.
   b. Click the Delete button in the Cells group.
3. Clear row contents by completing the following steps:
   a. Select rows 7 and 8.
   b. Click the Clear button in the Editing group in the Home tab and then click *Clear Contents* at the drop-down list.

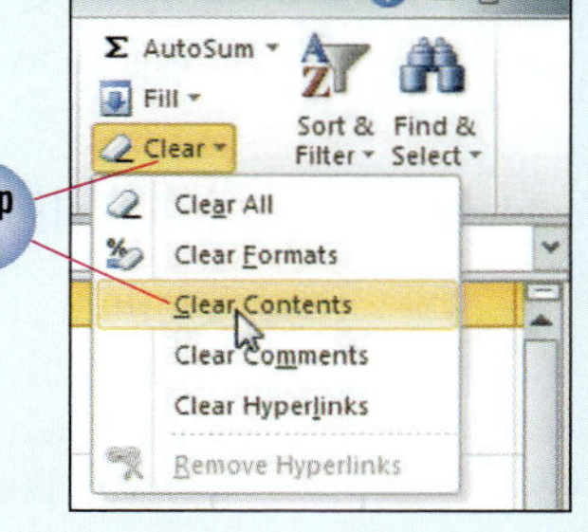

4. Type the following data in the specified cell:
   A7 = Ray Enterprises
   B7 = S894-T
   C7 = 4.99
   D7 = 30
   B8 = B-3448
   C8 = 25.50
   D8 = 12

Step 4

6		855-495	$	42.75	5	$	213.75
7	Ray Enterprises	S894-T	$	4.99	30		
8		B-3448	$	25.50	12		
9		43-GB-39	$	45.00	20	$	900.00

5. Make cell E6 active and then copy the formula down to cells E7 and E8.
6. Save **EL1-C3-P1-CMProducts.xlsx**.

Applying Formatting

With many of the groups in the Home tab you can apply formatting to text in the active cells or selected cells. Use buttons in the Font group to apply font formatting to text and use buttons in the Alignment group to apply alignment formatting to text.

Figure 3.5 Font Group

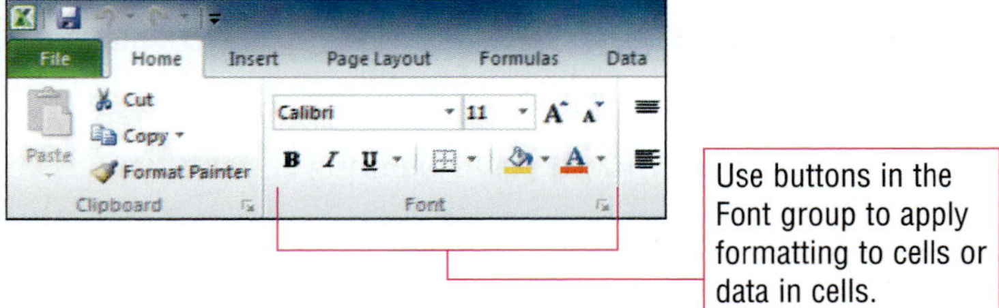

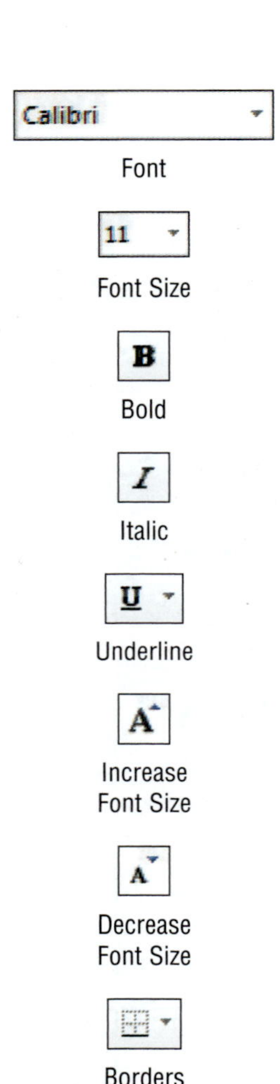

Applying Font Formatting

You can apply a variety of formatting to cells in a worksheet with buttons in the Font group in the Home tab. With buttons in the Font group shown in Figure 3.5, you can change the font, font size, and font color; bold, italicize, and underline data in cells; change the text color; and apply a border or add fill to cells.

Use the Font button in the Font group to change the font of text in a cell and use the Font Size button to specify size for the text. Apply bold formatting to text in a cell with the Bold button, italic formatting with the Italic button, and underlining with the Underline button.

Click the Increase Font Size button and the text in the active cell or selected cells increases from 11 points to 12 points. Click the Increase Font Size button again and the font size increases to 14. Each additional time you click the button, the font size increases by two points. Click the Decrease Font Size button and text in the active cell or selected cells decreases in point size.

With the Borders button in the Font group, you can insert a border on any or all sides of the active cell or any or all sides of selected cells. The name of the button changes depending on the most recent border applied to a cell or selected cells. Use the Fill Color button to insert color in the active cell or in selected cells. With the Font Color button, you can change the color of text within a cell.

Formatting with the Mini Toolbar

Double-click in a cell and then select data within the cell and the Mini toolbar displays in a dimmed fashion above the selected data. The Mini toolbar also displays when you right-click in any cell. Hover the mouse pointer over the Mini toolbar and it becomes active. The Mini toolbar contains buttons for applying font formatting such as font, font size, and font color as well as bold and italic formatting. Click a button on the Mini toolbar to apply formatting to selected text.

Applying Alignment Formatting

The alignment of data in cells depends on the type of data entered. Enter words or text combined with numbers in a cell and the text is aligned at the left edge of the cell. Enter numbers in a cell and the numbers are aligned at the right side of the cell. Use options in the Alignment group to align text at the left, center, or right side of the cell; align text at the top, center, or bottom of the cell; increase and/or decrease the indent of text; and change the orientation of text in a cell. As you learned in Chapter 1, you can merge selected cells by clicking the Merge & Center button. If you merged cells, you can split the merged cell into the original cells by selecting the cell and then clicking the Merge & Center button. If you click the Merge & Center button arrow, a drop-down list of options displays. Click the *Merge & Center* option to merge all of the selected cells and change to center cell alignment. Click the *Merge Across* to merge each row of the selected cells. For example, if you select three cells and two rows, clicking the *Merge Across* option will merge the three cells in the first row and merge the three cells in the second row so you end up with two cells. Click the *Merge Cells* option to merge all selected cells but not change to center cell alignment. Use the last option, *Unmerge Cells* to split cells that were previously merged. If you select and merge cells containing data, only the data in the upper-left cell will remain. Data in any other cells in the merged cells is deleted.

Orientation

Click the Orientation button to rotate data in a cell. Click the Orientation button and a drop-down list displays with options for rotating text in a cell. If data typed in a cell is longer than the cell, it overlaps the next cell to the right. If you want data to remain in a cell and wrap to the next line within the same cell, click the Wrap Text button in the Alignment group.

Wrap Text

Project 1g Applying Font and Alignment Formatting

Part 7 of 7

1. With **EL1-C3-P1-CMProducts.xlsx** open, make cell B1 active and then click the Wrap Text button in the Alignment group in the Home tab. (This wraps the company name within the cell.)
2. Select cells B1 through C2, click the Merge & Center button arrow in the Alignment group in the Home tab, and then click *Merge Across* at the drop-down list.
3. After looking at the merged cells, you decide to merge additional cells and horizontally and vertically center text in the cells by completing the following steps:
   a. With cells B1 through C2 selected, click the Merge & Center button and then click *Unmerge Cells* at the drop-down list.
   b. Select cells A1 through E2.
   c. Click the Merge & Center button arrow in the Alignment group in the Home tab and then click the *Merge Across* option at the drop-down list.
   d. Click the Middle Align button in the Alignment group and then click the Center button.

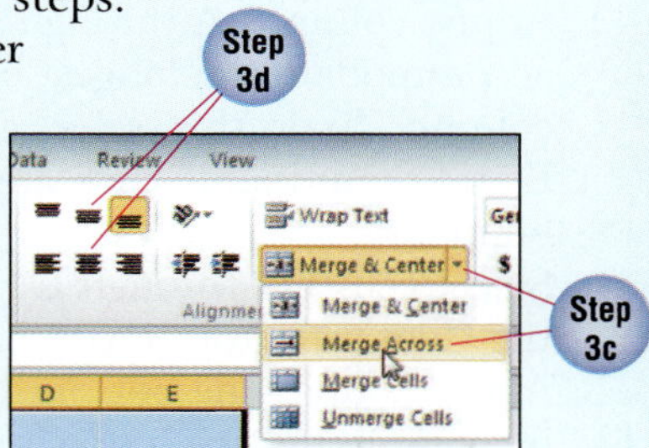

4. Rotate text in the third row by completing the following steps:
   a. Select cells A3 through E3.
   b. Click the Orientation button in the Alignment group in the Home tab and then click *Angle Counterclockwise* at the drop-down list.
   c. After looking at the rotated text, you decide to return the orientation back to the horizontal by clicking the Undo button on the Quick Access toolbar.

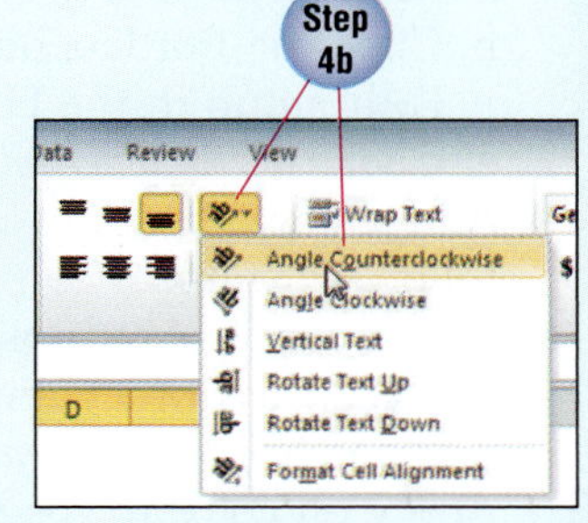

5. Change the font, font size, and font color for text in specific cells by completing the following steps:
   a. Make cell A1 active.
   b. Click the Font button arrow in the Font group in the Home tab, scroll down the drop-down gallery, and then click *Bookman Old Style*.
   c. Click the Font Size button arrow in the Font group and then click *22* at the drop-down gallery.

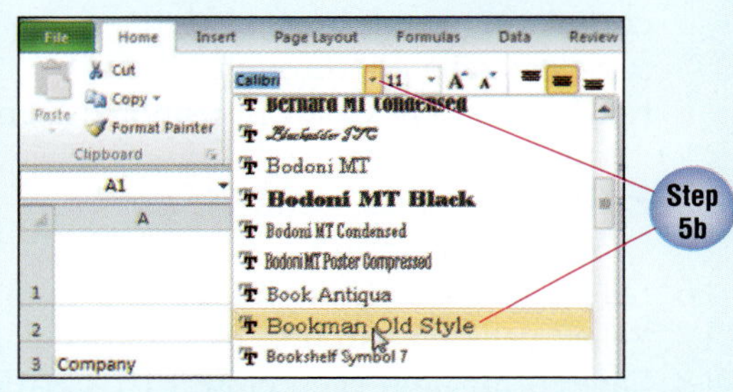

d. Click the Font Color button arrow and then click *Dark Blue* in the *Standard Colors* section of the drop-down color palette.

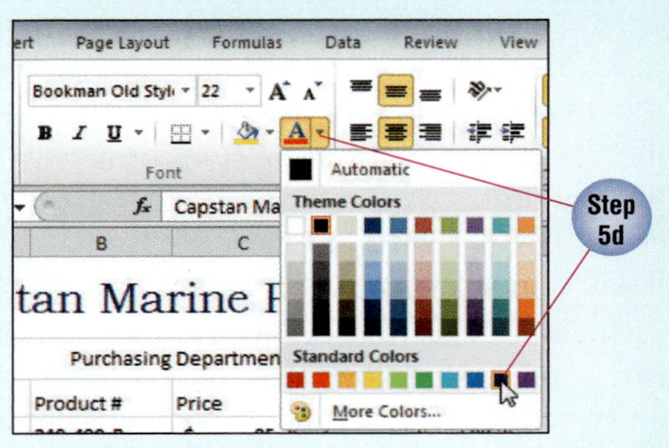

6. Make cell A2 active and then complete steps similar to those in Step 5 to change the font to Bookman Old Style, the font size to 16, and the font color to Dark Blue.
7. Select cells A3 through E3 and then click the Center button in the Alignment group.
8. With cells A3 through E3 still selected, click the Bold button in the Font group and then click the Italic button.
9. Select cells A3 through E18 and then change the font to Bookman Old Style.

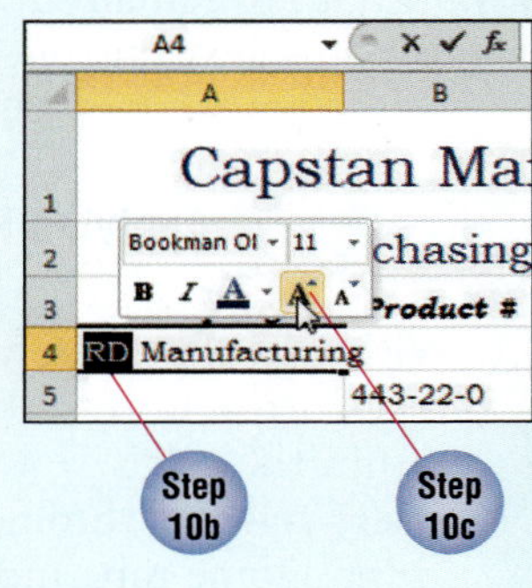

10. Apply formatting to selected data using the Mini toolbar by completing the following steps:
    a. Double-click cell A4.
    b. Select the letters *RD*. (This displays the dimmed Mini toolbar above the selected word.)
    c. Click the Increase Font Size button on the Mini toolbar.
    d. Double-click cell A14.
    e. Select the word *Geneva* and then click the Italic button on the Mini toolbar.

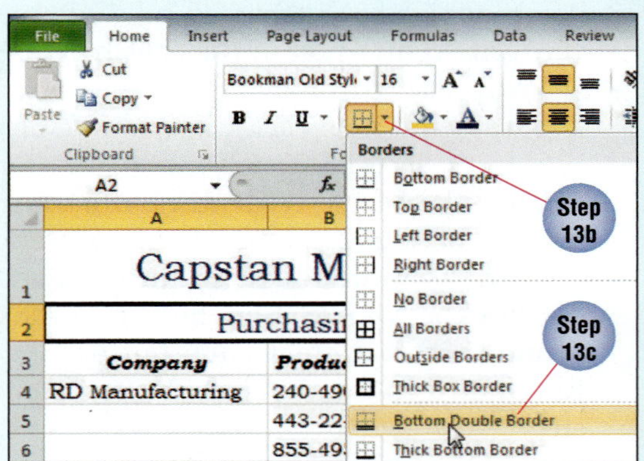

11. Adjust columns A through E to accommodate the longest entry in each column. To do this, select columns A through E and then double-click any selected column boundary.
12. Select cells D4 through D17 and then click the Center button in the Alignment group.
13. Add a double-line bottom border to cell A2 by completing the following steps:
    a. Make cell A2 active.
    b. Click the Borders button arrow in the Font group in the Home tab.
    c. Click the *Bottom Double Border* option at the drop-down list.
14. Add a single-line bottom border to cells A3 through E3 by completing the following steps:
    a. Select cells A3 through E3.
    b. Click the Borders button arrow and then click the *Bottom Border* option.
15. Apply fill color to specific cells by completing the following steps:
    a. Select cells A1 through E3.
    b. Click the Fill Color button arrow in the Font group.
    c. Click the *Aqua, Accent 5, Lighter 80%* color option.
16. Select cells C5 through C17 and then click the Comma Style button.
17. Select cells E5 through E17 and then click the Comma Style button.
18. Save, print, and then close **EL1-C3-P1-CMProducts.xlsx**.

Project 2 Apply a Theme to a Payroll Worksheet — 1 Part

You will open a workbook containing a worksheet with payroll information and then insert text, apply formatting to cells and cell contents, apply a theme, and then change the theme font and colors.

Applying a Theme

Excel provides a number of themes you can use to format text and cells in a worksheet. A theme is a set of formatting choices that include a color theme (a set of colors), a font theme (a set of heading and body text fonts), and an effects theme (a set of lines and fill effects). To apply a theme, click the Page Layout tab and then click the Themes button in the Themes group. At the drop-down gallery that displays, click the desired theme. Position the mouse pointer over a theme and the ***live preview*** feature will display the worksheet with the theme formatting applied. With the live preview feature you can see how the theme formatting affects your worksheet before you make your final choice.

HINT
Apply a theme to give your worksheet a professional look.

Themes

Project 2 Applying a Theme — Part 1 of 1

1. Open **SBAPayroll.xlsx** and then save it with Save As and name it **EL1-C3-P2-SBAPayroll**.
2. Make G4 the active cell and then insert a formula that calculates the amount of Social Security tax. (Multiply the gross pay amount in E4 with the Social Security rate in cell H11; you will need to use the mixed cell reference H$11 when writing the formula.)
3. Copy the formula in cell G4 down to cells G5 through G9.
4. Make H4 the active cell and then insert a formula that calculates the net pay (gross pay minus withholding and Social Security tax).
5. Copy the formula in H4 down to cells H5 through H9.
6. Increase the height of row 1 to 36.00.
7. Make A1 the active cell, click the Middle Align button in the Alignment group, click the Font Size button arrow, click *18* at the drop-down list, and then click the Bold button.
8. Type **Stanton & Barnett Associates** in cell A1.
9. Select cells A2 through H3 and then click the Bold button in the Font group.
10. Apply a theme and customize the font and colors by completing the following steps:
    a. Click the Page Layout tab.
    b. Click the Themes button in the Themes group and then click *Apothecary* at the drop-down gallery. (You might want to point the mouse to various themes to see how each theme's formatting affects the worksheet.)

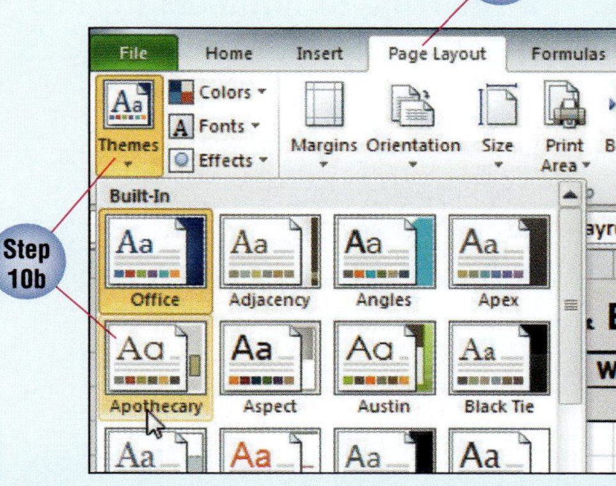

c. Click the Colors button in the Themes group and then click *Flow* at the drop-down gallery.

d. Click the Fonts button in the Themes group, scroll down the drop-down gallery, and then click *Black Tie*.

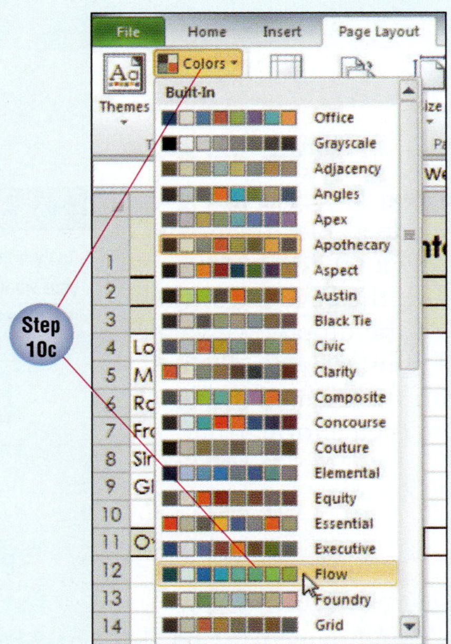

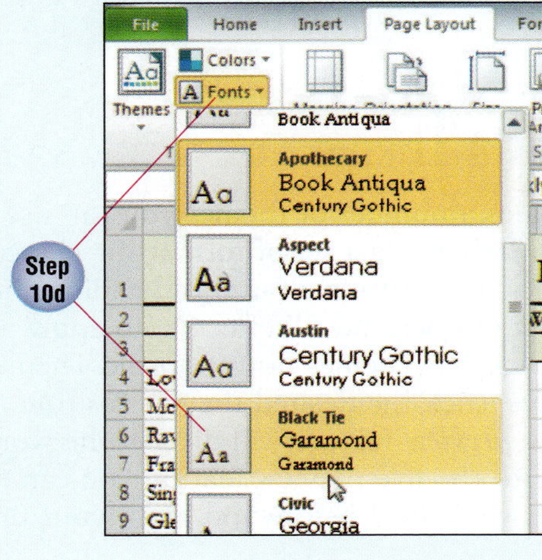

11. Select columns A through H and then adjust the width of the columns to accommodate the longest entries.
12. Save, print, and then close **EL1-C3-P2-SBAPayroll.xlsx**.

Project 3 Format an Invoices Worksheet — 2 Parts

You will open a workbook containing an invoice worksheet and apply number formatting to numbers in cells.

Formatting Numbers

Numbers in a cell, by default, are aligned at the right and decimals and commas do not display unless they are typed in the cell. Change the format of numbers with buttons in the Number group in the Home tab or with options at the Format Cells dialog box with the Number tab selected.

Formatting Numbers Using Number Group Buttons

Format symbols you can use to format numbers include a percent sign (%), a comma (,), and a dollar sign ($). For example, if you type the number *$45.50* in a cell, Excel automatically applies Currency formatting to the number. If you type *45%*, Excel automatically applies the Percent formatting to the number.

The Number group in the Home tab contains five buttons you can use to format numbers in cells. You learned about these buttons in Chapter 1.

Specify the formatting for numbers in cells in a worksheet before typing the numbers, or format existing numbers in a worksheet. The Increase Decimal and Decrease Decimal buttons in the Number group in the Home tab will change decimal places for existing numbers only.

The Number group in the Home tab also contains the Number Format button. Click the Number Format button arrow and a drop-down list displays of common number formats. Click the desired format at the drop-down list to apply the number formatting to the cell or selected cells.

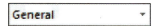

Number Format

Project 3a **Formatting Numbers with Buttons in the Number Group** Part 1 of 2

1. Open **RPInvoices.xlsx**.
2. Save the workbook with Save As and name it **EL1-C3-P3-RPInvoices**.
3. Make the following changes to column widths:
   a. Change the width of column C to 17.00.
   b. Change the width of column D to 10.00.
   c. Change the width of column E to 7.00.
   d. Change the width of column F to 12.00.
4. Select row 1 and then click the Insert button in the Cells group.
5. Change the height of row 1 to 42.00.
6. Select cells A1 through F1 and then make the following changes:
   a. Click the Merge & Center button in the Alignment group in the Home tab.
   b. With cell A1 active, change the font size to 24 points.
   c. Click the Fill Color button arrow in the Font group and then click *Olive Green, Accent 3, Lighter 80%*.
   d. Click the Borders button arrow in the Font group and then click the *Top and Thick Bottom Border* option.
   e. With cell A1 active, type **REAL PHOTOGRAPHY** and then press Enter.
7. Change the height of row 2 to 24.00.
8. Select cells A2 through F2 and then make the following changes:
   a. Click the Merge & Center button in the Alignment group.
   b. With cell A2 active, change the font size to 18.
   c. Click the Fill Color button in the Font group. (This will fill the cell with light green color.)
   d. Click the Borders button arrow in the Font group and then click the *Bottom Border* option.
9. Make the following changes to row 3:
   a. Change the height of row 3 to 18.00.
   b. Select cells A3 through F3, click the Bold button in the Font group, and then click the Center button in the Alignment group.

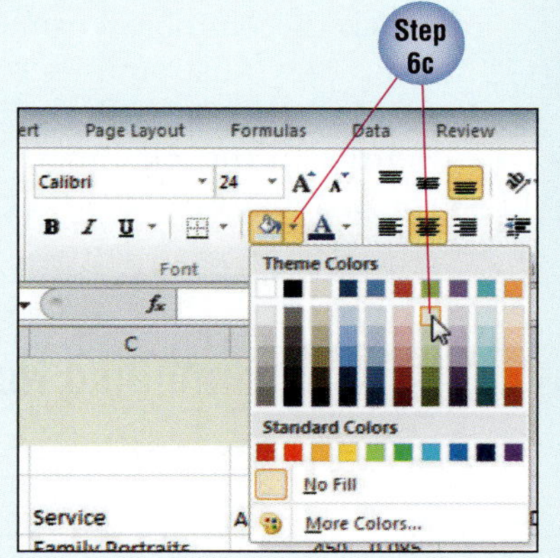

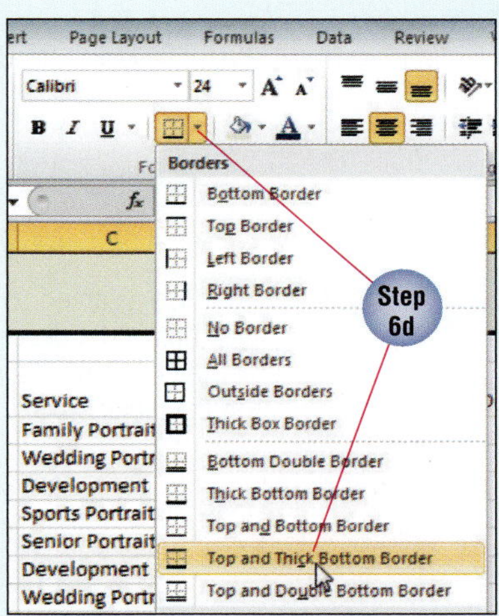

c. With the cells still selected, click the Borders button arrow and then click the *Bottom Border* option.

10. Make the following number formatting changes:
    a. Select cells E4 through E16 and then click the *Percent Style* button in the Number group in the Home tab.
    b. With the cells still selected, click once on the Increase Decimal button in the Number group. (The percent numbers should contain one decimal place.)

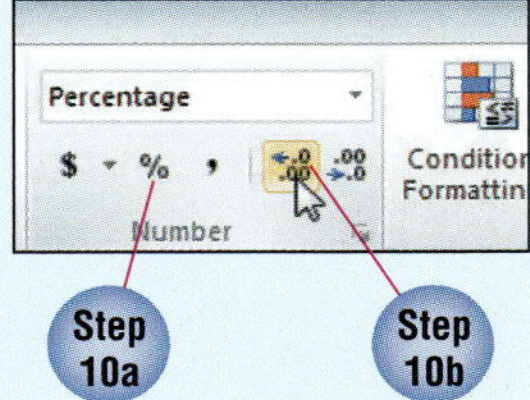

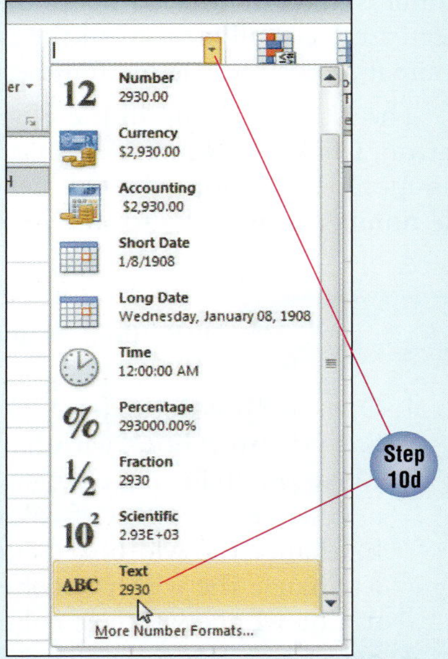

    c. Select cells A4 through B16.
    d. Click the Number Format button arrow, scroll down the drop-down list, and then click *Text*.
    e. With A4 through B16 still selected, click the Center button in the Alignment group.

11. Save **EL1-C3-P3-RPInvoices.xlsx**.

Formatting Numbers Using the Format Cells Dialog Box

Along with buttons in the Number group, you can format numbers with options at the Format Cells dialog box with the Number tab selected as shown in Figure 3.6. Display this dialog box by clicking the Number group dialog box

Figure 3.6 Format Cells Dialog Box with Number Tab Selected

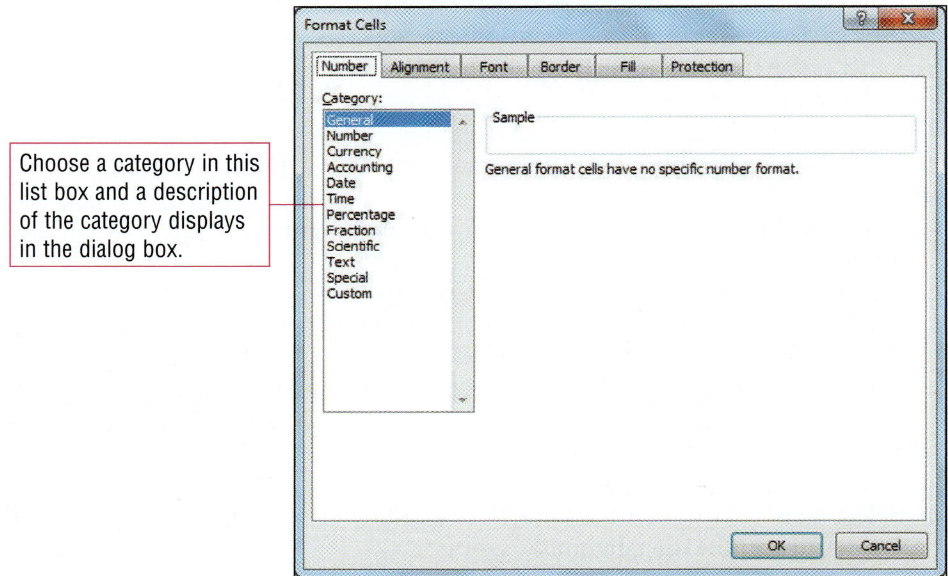

launcher or by clicking the Number Format button arrow and then clicking *More Number Formats* at the drop-down list. The left side of the dialog box displays number categories with a default category of *General*. At this setting no specific formatting is applied to numbers except right-aligning numbers in cells. The other number categories are described in Table 3.1.

Table 3.1 Number Categories at the Format Cells Dialog Box

Click this category	*To apply this number formatting*
Number	Specify number of decimal places and whether or not a thousand separator should be used; choose the display of negative numbers; right-align numbers in cell.
Currency	Apply general monetary values; dollar sign is added as well as commas and decimal points, if needed; right-align numbers in cell.
Accounting	Line up the currency symbol and decimal points in a column; add dollar sign and two digits after a decimal point; right-align numbers in cell.
Date	Display date as date value; specify the type of formatting desired by clicking an option in the *Type* list box; right-align date in cell.
Time	Display time as time value; specify the type of formatting desired by clicking an option in the *Type* list box; right-align time in cell.
Percentage	Multiply cell value by 100 and display result with a percent symbol; add decimal point followed by two digits by default; number of digits can be changed with the *Decimal places* option; right-align number in cell.
Fraction	Specify how fraction displays in cell by clicking an option in the *Type* list box; right-align fraction in cell.
Scientific	Use for very large or very small numbers. Use the letter *E* to tell Excel to move a decimal point a specified number of positions.
Text	Treat number in cell as text; number is displayed in cell exactly as typed.
Special	Choose a number type, such as *Zip Code*, *Phone Number*, or *Social Security Number* in the *Type* option list box; useful for tracking list and database values.
Custom	Specify a numbering type by choosing an option in the *Type* list box.

Project 3b Formatting Numbers at the Format Cells Dialog Box

Part 2 of 2

1. With **EL1-C3-P3-PRInvoices.xlsx** open, make cell F4 active, insert the following formula: **=(D4*E4)+D4**, and then press Enter.
2. Make cell F4 active and then copy the formula down to cells F5 through F16.
3. Change number formatting by completing the following steps:
   a. Select cells D4 through D16.
   b. Click the Number group dialog box launcher.

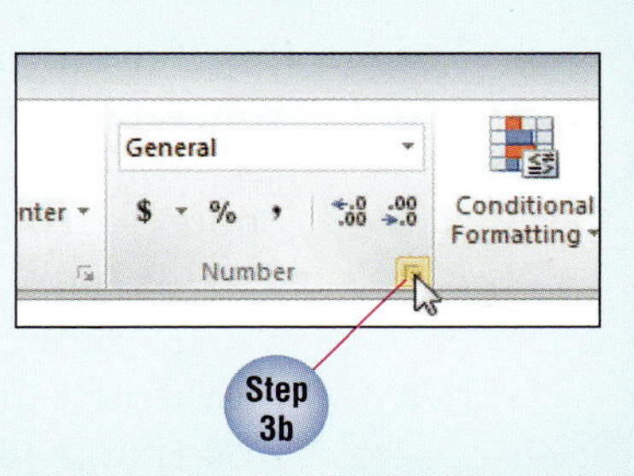

c. At the Format Cells dialog box with the Number tab selected, click *Accounting* in the *Category* section.
d. Make sure a *2* displays in the *Decimal places* option box and a dollar sign *$* displays in the *Symbol* option box.
e. Click OK.

4. Apply Accounting formatting to cells F4 through F16 by completing steps similar to those in Step 3.
5. Save, print, and then close **EL1-C3-P3-RPInvoices.xlsx**.

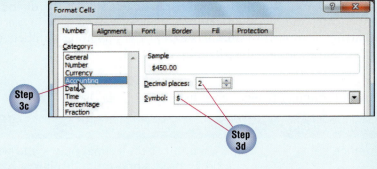

Format a Company Budget Worksheet — 6 Parts

You will open a workbook containing a company budget worksheet and then apply formatting to cells with options at the Format Cells dialog box, use the Format Painter to apply formatting, and hide and unhide rows and columns in the worksheet.

Formatting Cells Using the Format Cells Dialog Box

In the previous section, you learned how to format numbers with options at the Format Cells dialog box with the Number tab selected. This dialog box contains a number of other tabs you can select to format cells.

Aligning and Indenting Data

You can align and indent data in cells using buttons in the Alignment group in the Home tab or with options at the Format Cells dialog box with the Alignment tab selected as shown in Figure 3.7. Display this dialog box by clicking the Alignment group dialog box launcher.

In the *Orientation* section, you can choose to rotate data. A portion of the *Orientation* section shows points on an arc. Click a point on the arc to rotate the text along that point. You can also type a rotation degree in the *Degrees* text box. Type a positive number to rotate selected text from the lower left to the upper right of the cell. Type a negative number to rotate selected text from the upper left to the lower right of the cell.

If data typed in a cell is longer than the cell, it overlaps the next cell to the right. If you want data to remain in a cell and wrap to the next line within the same cell, click the *Wrap text* option in the *Text control* section of the dialog box. Click the *Shrink to fit* option to reduce the size of the text font so all selected data fits within the column. Use the *Merge cells* option to combine two or more selected cells into a single cell.

If you want to enter data on more than one line within a cell, enter the data on the first line and then press Alt + Enter. Pressing Alt + Enter moves the insertion point to the next line within the same cell.

Figure 3.7 Format Cells Dialog Box with Alignment Tab Selected

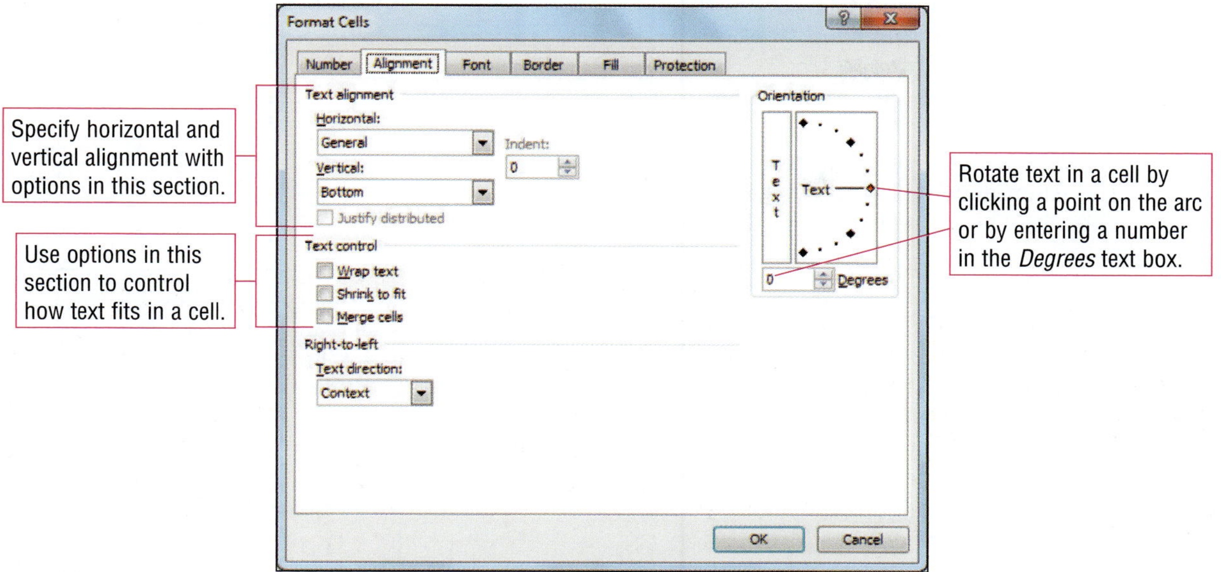

Project 4a Aligning and Rotating Data in Cells

Part 1 of 6

1. Open **HBCJobs.xlsx**.
2. Save the workbook with Save As and name it **EL1-C3-P4-HBCJobs**.
3. Make the following changes to the worksheet:
   a. Insert a new row at the beginning of the worksheet.
   b. Change the height of row 1 to 66.00.
   c. Merge and center cells A1 through E1.
   d. Type **Harris & Briggs** in cell A1 and then press Alt + Enter. (This moves the insertion point down to the next line in the same cell.)
   e. Type **Construction** and then press Enter.
   f. With cell A2 active, type **Preferred**, press Alt + Enter, type **Customer**, and then press Enter.
   g. Change the width of column A to 20.00.
   h. Change the width of column B to 7.00.
   i. Change the width of columns C, D, and E to 10.00.
4. Change number formatting for specific cells by completing the following steps:
   a. Select cells C3 through E11.
   b. Click the Number group dialog box launcher.
   c. At the Format Cells dialog box with the Number tab selected, click *Accounting* in the *Category* section.
   d. Click the down-pointing arrow at the right side of the *Decimal places* option until *0* displays.
   e. Make sure a dollar sign *$* displays in the *Symbol* option box.
   f. Click OK.

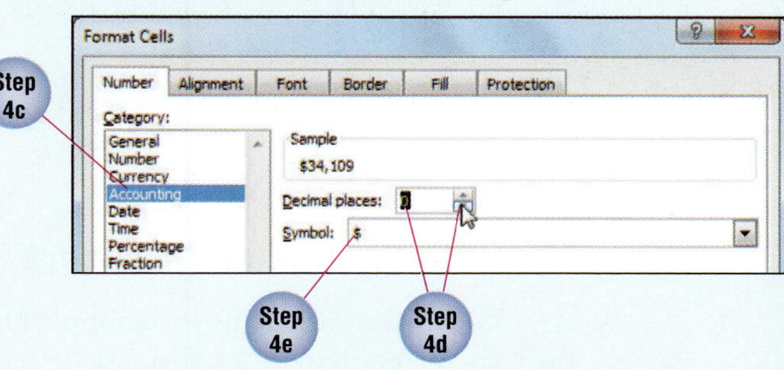

5. Make cell E3 active and then insert the formula **=D3-C3**. Copy this formula down to cells E4 through E11.

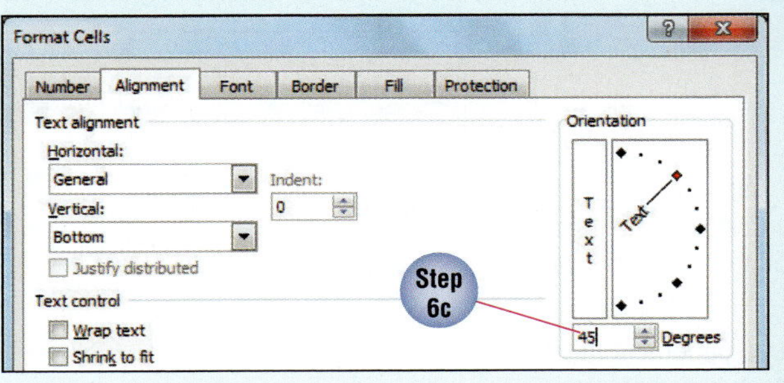

6. Change the orientation of data in cells by completing the following steps:
   a. Select cells B2 through E2.
   b. Click the Alignment group dialog box launcher.
   c. At the Format Cells dialog box with the Alignment tab selected, select *0* in the *Degrees* text box and then type **45**.
   d. Click OK.

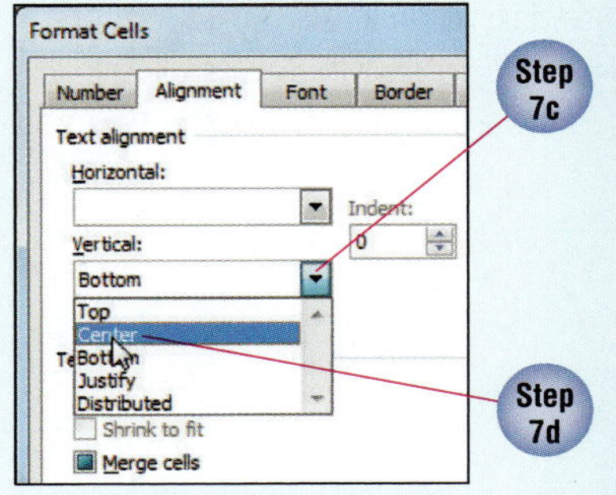

7. Change the vertical alignment of text in cells by completing the following steps:
   a. Select cells A1 through E2.
   b. Click the Alignment group dialog box launcher.
   c. At the Format Cells dialog box with the Alignment tab selected, click the down-pointing arrow at the right side of the *Vertical* alignment option.
   d. Click *Center* at the drop-down list.
   e. Click OK.

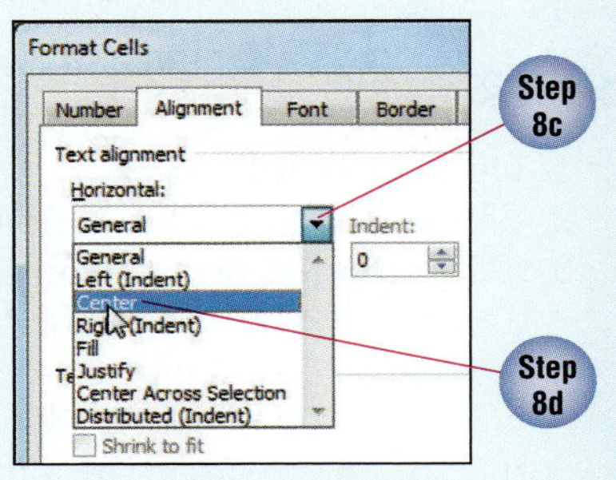

8. Change the horizontal alignment of text in cells by completing the following steps:
   a. Select cells A2 through E2.
   b. Click the Alignment group dialog box launcher.
   c. At the Format Cells dialog box with the Alignment tab selected, click the down-pointing arrow at the right side of the *Horizontal* alignment option.
   d. Click *Center* at the drop-down list.
   e. Click OK.

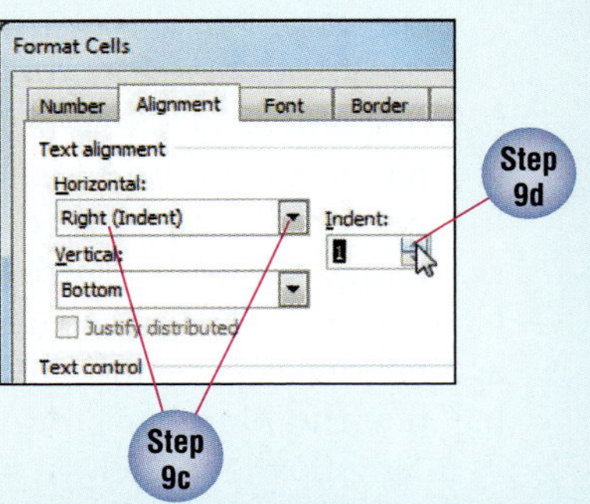

9. Change the horizontal alignment and indent of text in cells by completing the following steps:
   a. Select cells B3 through B11.
   b. Click the Alignment group dialog box launcher.
   c. At the Format Cells dialog box with the Alignment tab selected, click the down-pointing arrow at the right side of the *Horizontal* alignment option and then click *Right (Indent)* at the drop-down list.
   d. Click once on the up-pointing arrow at the right side of the *Indent* option box. (This displays *1* in the box.)
   e. Click OK.
10. Save **EL1-C3-P4-HBCJobs.xlsx**.

Changing the Font at the Format Cells Dialog Box

As you learned earlier in this chapter, the Font group in the Home tab contains buttons for applying font formatting to data in cells. You can also change the font for data in cells with options at the Format Cells dialog box with the Font tab selected as shown in Figure 3.8. At the Format Cells dialog box with the Font tab selected, you can change the font, font style, font size, and font color. You can also change the underlining method and add effects such as superscript and subscript. Click the Font group dialog box launcher to display this dialog box.

Figure 3.8 Format Cells Dialog Box with Font Tab Selected

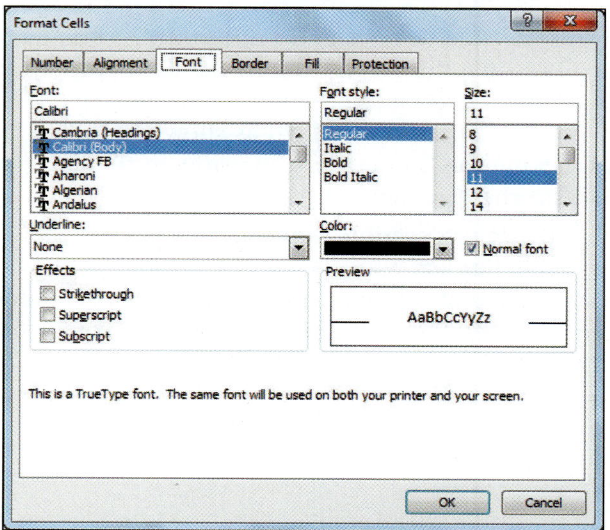

Project 4b Applying Font Formatting at the Format Cells Dialog Box

Part 2 of 6

1. With **EL1-C3-P4-HBCJobs.xlsx** open, change the font and font color by completing the following steps:
   a. Select cells A1 through E11.
   b. Click the Font group dialog box launcher.
   c. At the Format Cells dialog box with the Font tab selected, click *Garamond* in the *Font* list box. (You will need to scroll down the list to make this font visible.)
   d. Click *12* in the *Size* list box.
   e. Click the down-pointing arrow at the right of the *Color* option box.
   f. At the palette of color choices that displays, click the *Dark Red* color (first color option from the left in the *Standard Colors* section).
   g. Click OK to close the dialog box.
2. Make cell A1 active and then change the font to 24-point Garamond bold.
3. Select cells A2 through E2 and then apply bold formatting.
4. Save and then print **EL1-C3-P4-HBCJobs.xlsx**.

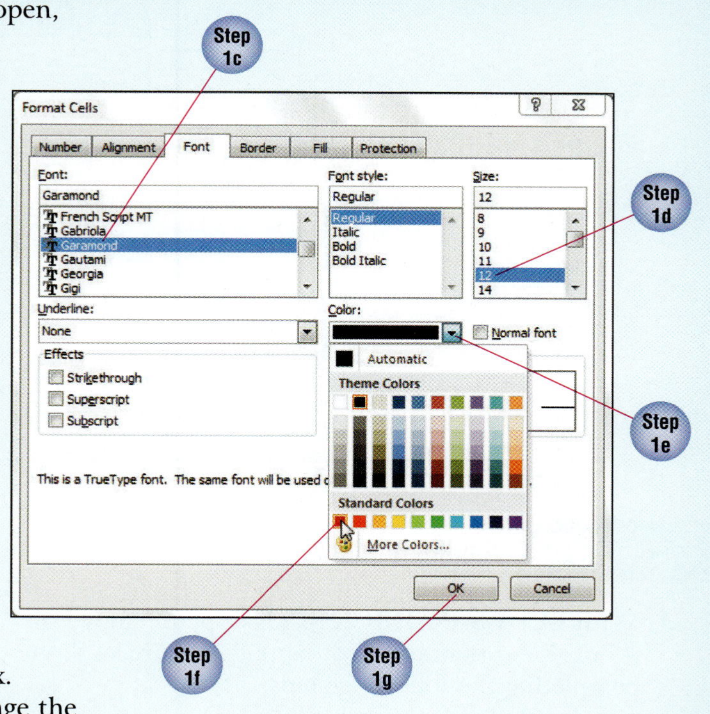

Adding Borders to Cells

Quick Steps

Add Borders to Cells
1. Select cells.
2. Click Borders button arrow.
3. Click desired border.

OR
1. Select cells.
2. Click Borders button arrow.
3. Click *More Borders*.
4. Use options in dialog box to apply desired border.
5. Click OK.

The gridlines that display in a worksheet do not print. As you learned earlier in this chapter, you can use the Borders button in the Font group to add borders to cells that will print. You can also add borders to cells with options at the Format Cells dialog box with the Border tab selected as shown in Figure 3.9. Display this dialog box by clicking the Borders button arrow in the Font group and then clicking *More Borders* at the drop-down list.

With options in the *Presets* section, you can remove borders with the *None* option, add only outside borders with the *Outline* option, or click the *Inside* option to add borders to the inside of selected cells. In the *Border* section of the dialog box, specify the side of the cell or selected cells to which you want to apply a border. Choose the style of line desired for the border with the options that display in the *Style* list box. Add color to border lines with choices from the color palette that displays when you click the down-pointing arrow located at the right side of the *Color* option box.

Figure 3.9 Format Cells Dialog Box with Border Tab Selected

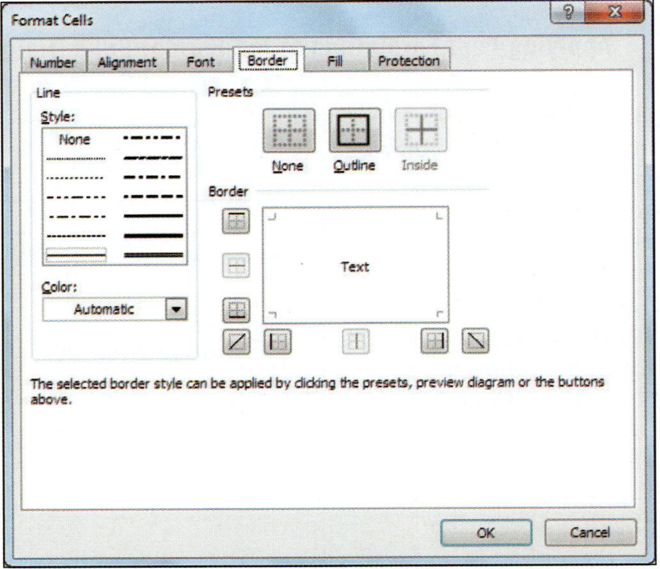

Project 4c **Adding Borders to Cells** Part 3 of 6

1. With **EL1-C3-P4-HBCJobs.xlsx** open, remove the 45 degrees orientation you applied in Project 4a by completing the following steps:
   a. Select cells B2 through E2.
   b. Click the Alignment group dialog box launcher.
   c. At the Format Cells dialog box with the Alignment tab selected, select *45* in the *Degrees* text box and then type **0**.
   d. Click OK.

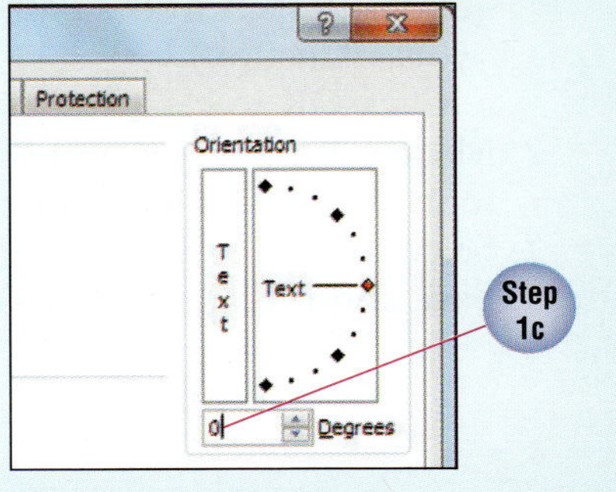

2. Change the height of row 2 to 33.00.
3. Add a thick, dark red border line to cells by completing the following steps:
   a. Select cells A1 through E11 (cells containing data).
   b. Click the Border button arrow in the Font group and then click the *More Borders* option at the drop-down list.
   c. At the Format Cells dialog box with the Border tab selected, click the down-pointing arrow at the right side of the *Color* option and then click *Dark Red* at the color palette (first color option from the left in the *Standard Colors* section).
   d. Click the thick single line option located in the second column (sixth option from the top) in the *Style* option box in the *Line* section.
   e. Click the *Outline* option in the *Presets* section.
   f. Click OK.
4. Add a border above and below cells by completing the following steps:
   a. Select cells A2 through E2.

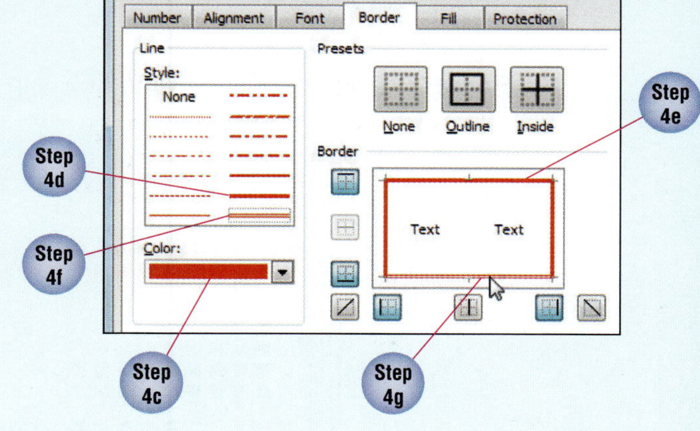

   b. Click the Border button arrow in the Font group and then click *More Borders* at the drop-down list.
   c. At the Format Cells dialog box with the Border tab selected, make sure the color is Dark Red.
   d. Make sure the thick single line option (sixth option from the top in the second column) is selected in the *Style* option box in the *Line* section.
   e. Click the top border of the sample cell in the *Border* section of the dialog box.
   f. Click the double-line option (bottom option in the second column) in the *Style* option box.
   g. Click the bottom border of the sample cell in the *Border* section of the dialog box.
   h. Click OK.
5. Save **EL1-C3-P4-HBCJobs.xlsx**.

Adding Fill and Shading to Cells

Quick Steps

Add Shading to Cells
1. Select cells.
2. Click Fill Color button arrow.
3. Click desired color.

OR

1. Select cells.
2. Click Format button.
3. Click *Format Cells* at drop-down list.
4. Click Fill tab.
5. Use options in dialog box to apply desired shading.
6. Click OK.

Repeat Last Action
1. Apply formatting.
2. Move to desired location.
3. Press F4 or Ctrl + Y.

To enhance the visual display of cells and data within cells, consider adding fill and/or shading to cells. As you learned earlier in this chapter, you can add fill color to cells with the Fill Color button in the Font group. You can also add fill color and/or shading to cells in a worksheet with options at the Format Cells dialog box with the Fill tab selected as shown in Figure 3.10. Display the Format Cells dialog box by clicking the Format button in the Cells group and then clicking *Format Cells* at the drop-down list. You can also display the dialog box by clicking the Font group, Alignment group, or Number group dialog box launcher. At the Format Cells dialog box, click the Fill tab or right-click in a cell and then click Format Cells at the shortcut menu.

Choose a fill color for a cell or selected cells by clicking a color choice in the Color palette. To add shading to a cell or selected cells, click the Fill Effects button and then click the desired shading style at the Fill Effects dialog box.

Repeating the Last Action

If you want to apply other types of formatting, such as number, border, or shading formatting to other cells in a worksheet, use the Repeat command by pressing F4 or Ctrl + Y. The Repeat command repeats the last action performed.

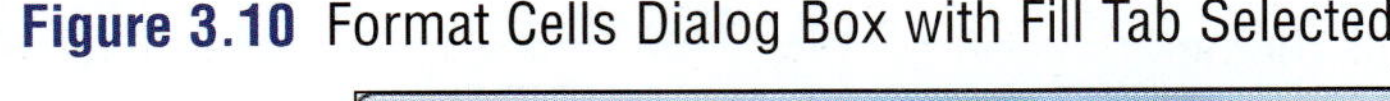

Figure 3.10 Format Cells Dialog Box with Fill Tab Selected

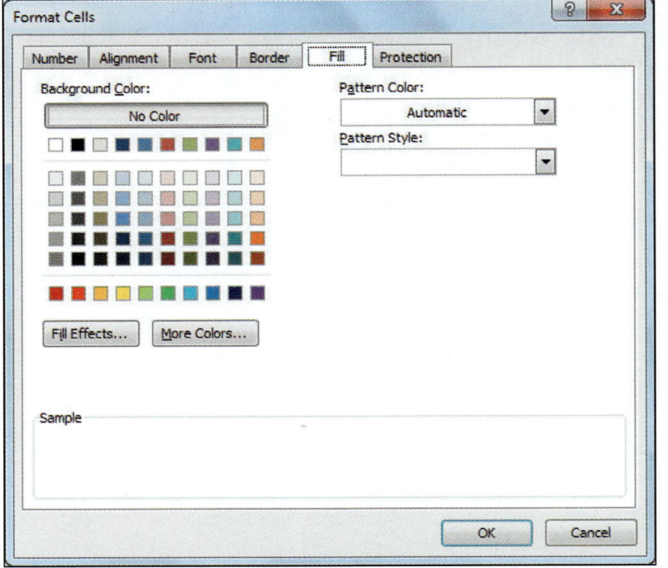

Adding Fill Color and Shading to Cells

Part 4 of 6

1. With **EL1-C3-P4-HBCJobs.xlsx** open, add fill color to cell A1 and repeat the formatting by completing the following steps:
   a. Make cell A1 active.
   b. Click the Format button in the Cells group and then click *Format Cells* at the drop-down list.
   c. At the Format Cells dialog box, click the Fill tab.
   d. Click a light purple color in the *Background Color* section. (Click the eighth color from the left in the second row.)

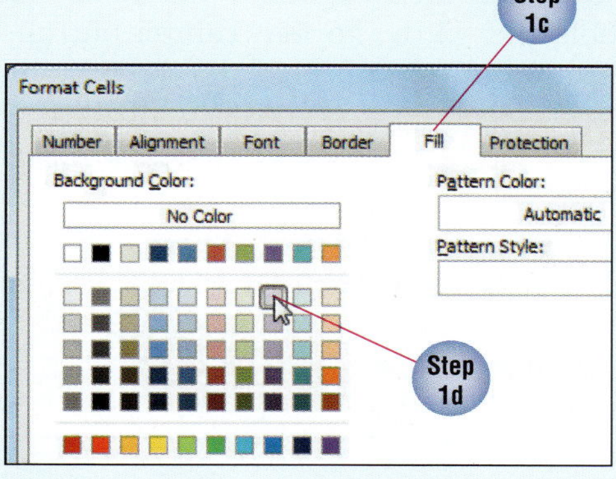

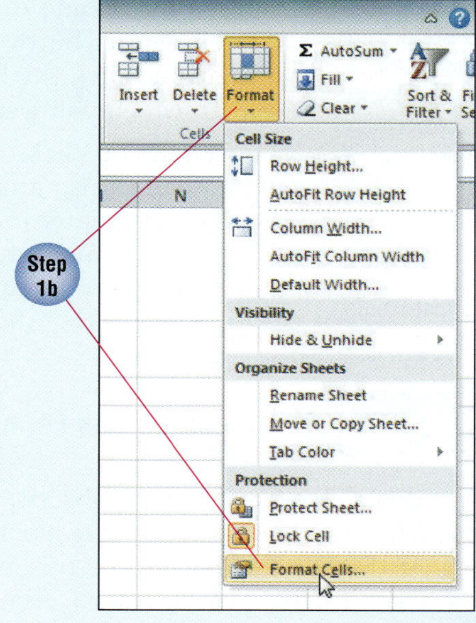

   e. Click OK.
   f. Select cells A2 through E2 and then press the F4 function key. (This repeats the light purple fill.)
2. Select row 2, insert a new row, and then change the height of the new row to 12.00.
3. Add shading to cells by completing the following steps:
   a. Select cells A2 through E2.
   b. Click the Format button in the Cells group and then click *Format Cells* at the drop-down list.
   c. At the Format Cells dialog box, if necessary, click the Fill tab.
   d. Click the Fill Effects button.
   e. At the Fill Effects dialog box, click the down-pointing arrow at the right side of the *Color 2* option box and then click *Purple, Accent 4* (eighth color from the left in the top row).
   f. Click OK to close the Fill Effects dialog box.
   g. Click OK to close the Format Cells dialog box.
4. Save **EL1-C3-P4-HBCJobs.xlsx**.

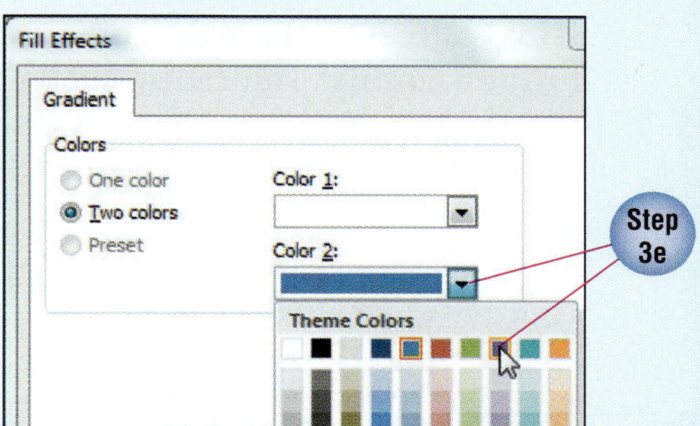

Quick Steps

Format with Format Painter
1. Select cells with desired formatting.
2. Double-click Format Painter button.
3. Select cells.
4. Click Format Painter button.

Format Painter

Formatting with Format Painter

The Clipboard group in the Home tab contains a button you can use to copy formatting to different locations in the worksheet. This button is the Format Painter button and displays in the Clipboard group as a paintbrush. To use the Format Painter button, make a cell or selected cells active that contain the desired formatting, click the Format Painter button, and then click the cell or selected cells to which you want the formatting applied.

When you click the Format Painter button, the mouse pointer displays with a paintbrush attached. If you want to apply formatting a single time, click the Format Painter button once. If, however, you want to apply the character formatting in more than one location in the worksheet, double-click the Format Painter button. If you have double-clicked the Format Painter button, turn off the feature by clicking the Format Painter button once.

Project 4e **Formatting with Format Painter** Part 5 of 6

1. With **EL1-C3-P4-HBCJobs.xlsx** open, select cells A5 through E5.
2. Click the Font group dialog box launcher.
3. At the Format Cells dialog box, click the Fill tab.
4. Click the light green color (seventh color from the left in the second row).
5. Click OK to close the dialog box.
6. Use Format Painter to "paint" formatting to rows by completing the following steps:
   a. With A5 through E5 selected, double-click the Format Painter button in the Clipboard group.
   b. Select cells A7 through E7.
   c. Select cells A9 through E9.
   d. Select cells A11 through E11.
   e. Turn off Format Painter by clicking the Format Painter button in the Clipboard group.
7. Save and then print **EL1-C3-P4-HBCJobs.xlsx**.

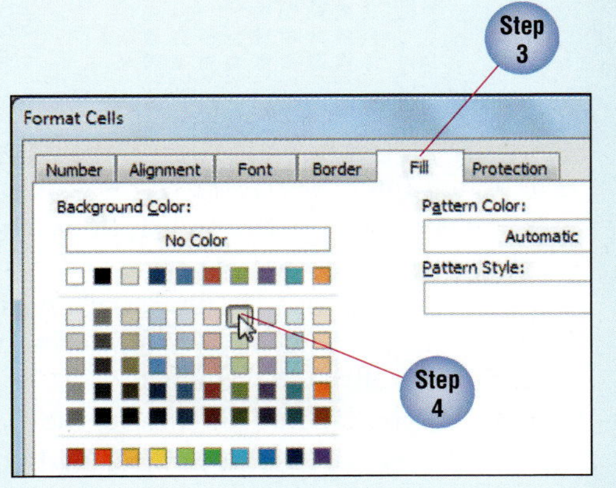

Hiding and Unhiding Columns and/or Rows

Set the column width to zero and the column is hidden. Set the row height to zero and the row is hidden.

If a worksheet contains columns and/or rows of sensitive data or data that you are not using or do not want to view, consider hiding the columns and/or rows. To hide columns in a worksheet, select the columns to be hidden, click the Format button in the Cells group in the Home tab, point to *Hide & Unhide*, and then click *Hide Columns*. To hide selected rows, click the Format button in the Cells group, point to *Hide & Unhide*, and then click *Hide Rows*. To make a hidden column visible, select the column to the left and the column to the right of the hidden column, click the Format button in the Cells group, point to *Hide & Unhide*, and then click *Unhide Columns*. To make a hidden row visible, select the row above and the row below the hidden row, click the Format button in the Cells group, point to *Hide & Unhide*, and then click *Unhide Rows*.

If the first row or column is hidden, use the Go To feature to make the row or column visible. To do this, click the Find & Select button in the Editing group in the Home tab and then click *Go To* at the drop-down list. At the Go To dialog box, type *A1* in the *Reference* text box and then click OK. At the worksheet, click the Format button in the Cells group, point to *Hide & Unhide*, and then click *Unhide Columns* or click *Unhide Rows*.

You can also unhide columns or rows using the mouse. If a column or row is hidden, the light blue boundary line in the column or row header displays as a slightly thicker blue line. To unhide a column, position the mouse pointer on the slightly thicker blue line that displays in the column header until the mouse pointer changes to left- and right-pointing arrows with a double line between. (Make sure the mouse pointer displays with two lines between the arrows. If a single line displays, you will simply change the size of the visible column.) Hold down the left mouse button, drag to the right until the column displays at the desired width, and then release the mouse button. Unhide a row in a similar manner. Position the mouse pointer on the slightly thicker blue line in the row header until the mouse pointer changes to up- and down-pointing arrows with a double line between. Drag down to display the row and then release the mouse button. If two or more adjacent columns or rows are hidden, you will need to unhide each column or row separately.

Quick Steps

Hide Columns
1. Select columns.
2. Click Format button.
3. Point to *Hide & Unhide*.
4. Click *Hide Columns*.

Hide Rows
1. Select rows.
2. Click Format button.
3. Point to *Hide & Unhide*.
4. Click *Hide Rows*.

Project 4f Hiding and Unhiding Columns and Rows

Part 6 of 6

1. With **EL1-C3-P4-HBCJobs.xlsx** open, hide the row for Linstrom Enterprises and the row for Summit Services by completing the following steps:
   a. Click the row 7 header to select the entire row.
   b. Hold down the Ctrl key and then click the row 11 header to select the entire row.
   c. Click the Format button in the Cells group in the Home tab, point to *Hide & Unhide*, and then click *Hide Rows*.

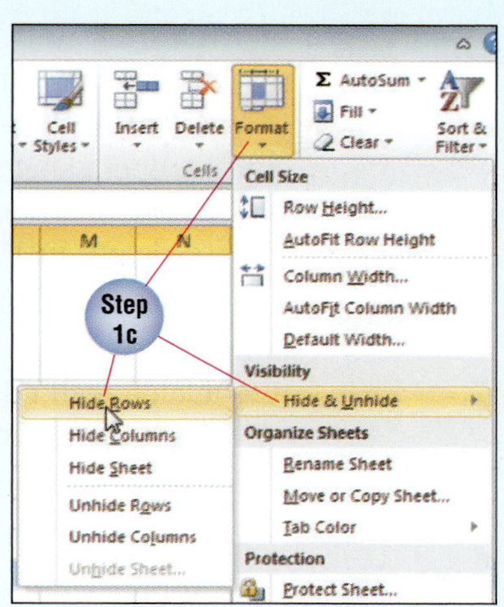

2. Hide the column containing the actual amounts by completing the following steps:
   a. Click cell D3 to make it the active cell.
   b. Click the Format button in the Cells group, point to *Hide & Unhide*, and then click *Hide Columns*.
3. Save and then print **EL1-C3-P4-HBCJobs.xlsx**.
4. Unhide the rows by completing the following steps:
   a. Select rows 6 through 12.
   b. Click the Format button in the Cells group, point to *Hide & Unhide*, and then click *Unhide Rows*.
   c. Click in cell A4.

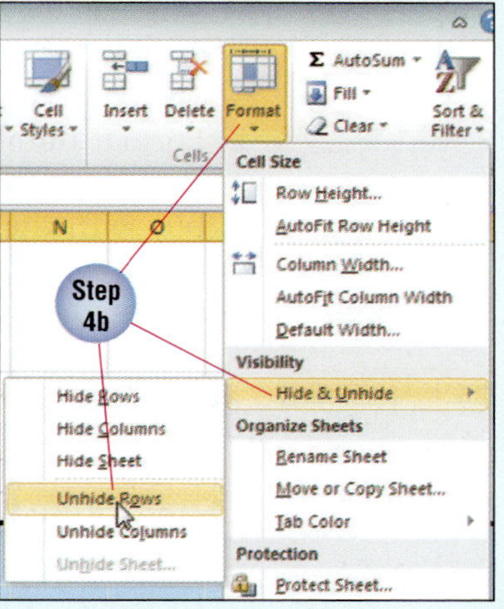

5. Unhide column D by completing the following steps:
   a. Position the mouse pointer on the thicker gray line that displays between columns C and E in the column header until the pointer turns into arrows pointing left and right with a double line between.

b. Hold down the left mouse button, drag to the right until *Width: 12.57 (93 pixels)* displays in a box above the mouse pointer, and then release the mouse button.

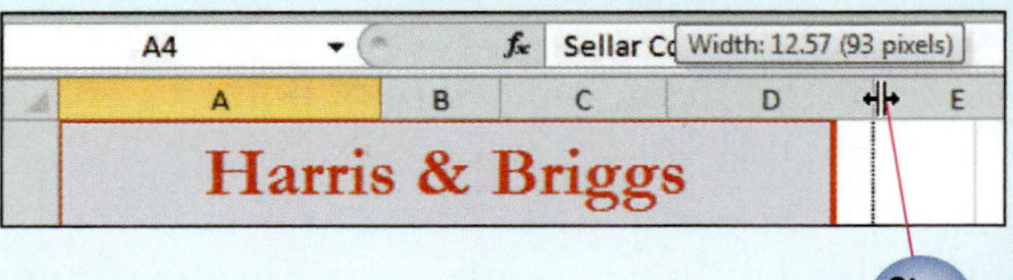

6. Save, print, and then close **EL1-C3-P4-HBCJobs.xlsx**.

Chapter Summary

- Change column width using the mouse on column boundaries or with options at the Column Width dialog box.
- Change row height using the mouse on row boundaries or with options at the Row Height dialog box.
- Insert a row in a worksheet with the Insert button in the Cells group in the Home tab or with options at the Insert dialog box.
- Insert a column in a worksheet with the Insert button in the Cells group or with options at the Insert dialog box.
- Delete a specific cell by clicking the Delete button arrow and then clicking *Delete Cells* at the drop-down list. At the Delete dialog box, specify if you want to delete just the cell or an entire row or column.
- Delete a selected row(s) or column(s) by clicking the Delete button in the Cells group.
- Delete cell contents by pressing the Delete key or clicking the Clear button in the Editing group and then clicking *Clear Contents* at the drop-down list.
- Apply font formatting with buttons in the Font group in the Home tab.
- Use the Mini toolbar to apply font formatting to selected data in a cell.
- Apply alignment formatting with buttons in the Alignment group in the Home tab.
- Use the Themes button in the Themes group in the Page Layout tab to apply a theme to cells in a worksheet that applies formatting such as color, font, and effects. Use the other buttons in the Themes group to customize the theme.
- Format numbers in cells with buttons in the Number group in the Home tab. You can also apply number formatting with options at the Format Cells dialog box with the Number tab selected.
- Apply formatting to cells in a worksheet with options at the Format Cells dialog box. This dialog box includes the following tabs for formatting cells: Number, Alignment, Font, Border, and Fill.
- Press F4 or Ctrl + Y to repeat the last action performed.
- Use the Format Painter button in the Clipboard group in the Home tab to apply formatting to different locations in a worksheet.
- Hide selected columns or rows in a worksheet by clicking the Format button in the Cells group in the Home tab, pointing to *Hide & Unhide*, and then clicking *Hide Columns* or *Hide Rows*.

- To make a hidden column visible, select the column to the left and right, click the Format button in the Cells group, point to *Hide & Unhide,* and then click *Unhide Columns*.
- To make a hidden row visible, select the row above and below, click the Format button in the Cells group, point to *Hide & Unhide*, and then click *Unhide Rows*.

Commands Review

FEATURE	RIBBON TAB, GROUP	BUTTON	KEYBOARD SHORTCUT
Format	Home, Cells		
Insert cells, rows, columns	Home, Cells		
Delete cells, rows, columns	Home, Cells		
Clear cell or cell contents	Home, Editing	Clear	
Font	Home, Font	Calibri	
Font size	Home, Font	11	
Increase font size	Home, Font		
Decrease font size	Home, Font		
Bold	Home, Font	B	Ctrl + B
Italic	Home, Font	I	Ctrl + I
Underline	Home, Font	U	Ctrl + U
Borders	Home, Font		
Fill color	Home, Font		
Font color	Home, Font	A	
Top align	Home, Alignment		
Middle align	Home, Alignment		
Bottom align	Home, Alignment		
Orientation	Home, Alignment		

FEATURE	RIBBON TAB, GROUP	BUTTON	KEYBOARD SHORTCUT
Align text left	Home, Alignment		
Center	Home, Alignment		
Align text right	Home, Alignment		
Decrease indent	Home, Alignment		Ctrl + Alt + Shift + Tab
Increase indent	Home, Alignment		Ctrl + Alt + Tab
Wrap text	Home, Alignment		
Merge & Center	Home, Alignment		
Themes	Page Layout, Themes		
Number Format	Home, Number	General	
Format Painter	Home, Clipboard		
Repeat			F4 or Ctrl + Y

Concepts Check Test Your Knowledge

Completion: In the space provided at the right, indicate the correct term, symbol, or command.

1. By default, a column is inserted in this direction from the column containing the active cell. ________________
2. To delete a row, select the row and then click the Delete button in this group in the Home tab. ________________
3. With the options at this button's drop-down list, you can clear the contents of the cell or selected cells. ________________
4. Use this button to insert color in the active cell or selected cells. ________________
5. Select data in a cell and this displays in a dimmed fashion above the selected text. ________________
6. By default, numbers are aligned at this side of a cell. ________________
7. Click this button in the Alignment group in the Home tab to rotate data in a cell. ________________

8. The Themes button is located in this tab. ________________

9. If you type a number with a dollar sign, such as $50.25, Excel automatically applies this formatting to the number. ________________

10. If you type a number with a percent sign, such as 25%, Excel automatically applies this formatting to the number. ________________

11. Align and indent data in cells using buttons in the Alignment group in the Home tab or with options at this dialog box with the Alignment tab selected. ________________

12. You can repeat the last action performed with the command Ctrl + Y or by pressing this function key. ________________

13. The Format Painter button is located in this group in the Home tab. ________________

14. To hide a column, select the column, click this button in the Cells group in the Home tab, point to *Hide & Unhide*, and then click *Hide Columns*. ________________

Skills Check Assess Your Performance

Assessment 1

FORMAT A SALES AND BONUSES WORKSHEET

1. Open **NSPSales.xlsx**.
2. Save the workbook with Save As and name it **EL1-C3-A1-NSPSales**.
3. Change the width of columns as follows:
   Column A = 14.00
   Columns B – E = 10.00
   Column F = 6.00
4. Select row 2 and then insert a new row.
5. Merge and center cells A2 through F2.
6. Type Sales Department in cell A2 and then press Enter.
7. Increase the height of row 1 to 33.00.
8. Increase the height of row 2 to 21.00.
9. Increase the height of row 3 to 18.00.
10. Make the following formatting changes to the worksheet:
    a. Make cell A1 active, change the font size to 18 points, and turn on bold.
    b. Make cell A2 active, change the font size to 14 points, and turn on bold.
    c. Select cells A3 through F3, click the Bold button in the Font group, and then click the Center button in the Alignment group.
    d. Select cells A1 through F3, change the vertical alignment to Middle Align.
11. Insert the following formulas in the worksheet:
    a. Insert a formula in D4 that adds the amounts in B4 and C4. Copy the formula down to cells D5 through D11.

b. Insert a formula in E4 that averages the amounts in B4 and C4. Copy the formula down to cells E5 through E11.
c. Insert an IF statement in cell F4 that says that if the amount in cell E4 is greater than 74999, then insert the word "Yes" and if the amount is not greater than 74999, then insert the word "No." Copy this formula down to cells F5 through F11.

12. Make the following changes to the worksheet:
    a. Select cells F4 through F11 and then click the Center button in the Alignment group.
    b. Select cells B4 through E4 and then change the number formatting to Accounting with 0 decimal places and a dollar sign.
    c. Select cells B5 through E11, click the Comma Style button, and then click twice on the Decrease Decimal button.
    d. Add a double-line border around cells A1 through F11.
    e. Select cells A1 and A2 and then apply a light orange fill color.
    f. Select cells A3 through F3 and then apply an orange fill color.
13. Save and then print the worksheet.
14. Apply the Verve theme to the worksheet.
15. Save, print, and then close **EL1-C3-A1-NSPSales.xlsx**.

Assessment 2

FORMAT AN OVERDUE ACCOUNTS WORKSHEET

1. Open **CCorpAccts.xlsx**.
2. Save the workbook with Save As and name it **EL1-C3-A2-CCorpAccts**.
3. Change the width of columns as follows:

   Column A = 21.00
   Column B = 10.00
   Column C = 10.00
   Column D = 12.00
   Column E = 7.00
   Column F = 12.00
4. Make cell A1 active and then insert a new row.
5. Merge and center cells A1 through F1.
6. Type **Compass Corporation** in cell A1 and then press Enter.
7. Increase the height of row 1 to 42.00.
8. Increase the height of row 2 to 24.00.
9. Make the following formatting changes to the worksheet:
    a. Select cells A1 through F11 and then change the font to 10-point Cambria.
    b. Make cell A1 active, change the font size to 24 points, and turn on bold.
    c. Make cell A2 active, change the font size to 18 points, and turn on bold.
    d. Select cells A3 through F3, click the Bold button in the Font group and then click the Center button in the Alignment group.
    e. Select cells A1 through F3, click the Middle Align button in the Alignment group.
    f. Select cells B4 through B11 and then click the Center button in the Alignment group.
    g. Select cells E4 through E11 and then click the Center button in the Alignment group.

10. Use the DATE function in the following cells to enter a formula that returns the serial number for the following dates:

    D4 = October 1, 2012
    D5 = October 3, 2012
    D6 = October 8, 2012
    D7 = October 10, 2012
    D8 = October 15, 2012
    D9 = October 30, 2012
    D10 = November 6, 2012
    D11 = November 13, 2012
11. Enter a formula in cell F4 that inserts the due date (the purchase date plus the number of days in the Terms column). Copy the formula down to cells F5 through F11.
12. Apply the following borders and fill color:
    a. Add a thick line border around cells A1 through F11.
    b. Make cell A2 active and then add a double-line border at the top and bottom of the cell.
    c. Select cells A3 through F3 and then add a single line border to the bottom of the cells.
    d. Select cells A1 and A2 and then apply a light blue fill color.
13. Save, print, and then close **EL1-C3-A2-CCorpAccts.xlsx**.

Assessment 3

FORMAT A SUPPLIES AND EQUIPMENT WORKSHEET

1. Open **OEBudget.xlsx**.
2. Save the workbook with Save As and name it **EL1-C3-A3-OEBudget**.
3. Select and then merge across cells A1 through D2. ***Hint: Use the* Merge Across *option at the Merge & Center button drop-down list.***
4. With cells A1 and A2 selected, click the Middle Align button in the Alignment group and then click the Center button.
5. Make cell A1 active and then change the font size to 22 points and turn on bold.
6. Make cell A2 active and then change the font size to 12 points and turn on bold.
7. Change the height of row 1 to 36.00.
8. Change the height of row 2 to 21.00.
9. Change the width of column A to 15.00.
10. Select cells A3 through A17, turn on bold, and then click the Wrap Text button in the Alignment group.
11. Make cell B3 active and then change the number formatting to Currency with no decimal places.
12. Select cells C6 through C19 and then change the number formatting to Percentage with one decimal place.
13. Automatically adjust the width of column B.
14. Make cell D6 active and then type a formula that multiplies the absolute cell reference $B$3 with the percentage in cell C6. Copy the formula down to cells D7 through D19.
15. With cells D6 through D19 selected, change the number formatting to Currency with no decimal places.
16. Make cell D8 active and then clear the cell contents. Use the Repeat command, F4, to clear the contents from cells D11, D14, and D17.
17. Select cells A1 through D19, change the font to Constantia, and then change the font color to dark blue.

18. Add light green fill color to the following cells: A1, A2, A5–D5, A8–D8, A11–D11, A14–D14, and A17–D17.
19. Add borders and/or additional shading of your choosing to enhance the visual appeal of the worksheet.
20. Save, print, and then close **EL1-C3-A3-OEBudget.xlsx**.

Assessment 4

FORMAT A FINANCIAL ANALYSIS WORKSHEET

1. At a blank workbook, display the Format Cells dialog box with the Alignment tab selected and then experiment with the options in the *Text control* section.
2. Open **FinAnalysis.xlsx**.
3. Save the workbook with Save As and name it **EL1-C3-A4-FinAnalysis**.
4. Make cell B9 active and then insert a formula that averages the percentages in cells B3 through B8. Copy the formula to the right to cells C9 and D9.
5. Select cells B3 through D9, display the Format Cells dialog box with the Alignment tab selected, change the horizontal alignment to *Right (Indent)* and the indent to *2*, and then close the dialog box.
6. Select cells A1 through D9 and then change the font size to 14.
7. Select cells B2 through D2 and then change the orientation to 45 degrees.
8. With cells B2 through D2 still selected, shrink the font size to show all data in the cells.
9. Save, print, and then close **EL1-C3-A4-FinAnalysis.xlsx**.

Visual Benchmark Demonstrate Your Proficiency

CREATE A WORKSHEET AND INSERT FORMULAS

1. At a blank workbook, type the data in the cells indicated in Figure 3.11 but **do not** type the data in the following cells—instead insert the formulas as indicated (the results of your formulas should match the results you see in the figure):
   - Cells C4 through C14: Insert a formula with an IF statement that inserts the word *Yes* if the sales amount is greater than $114,999 and inserts the word *No* if the sales amount is not greater than $114,999.
   - Cells D4 through D14: Insert a formula with an IF statement that if the content of the previous cell is *Yes*, then multiply the amount in the cell in column B by 0.05 and if the previous cell does not contain the word *Yes*, then insert a zero.
2. Apply formatting so your worksheet looks similar to the worksheet shown in Figure 3.11.
3. Save the workbook and name it **EL1-C3-VB-BonusAmounts**.
4. Print **EL1-C3-VB-BonusAmounts.xlsx**.
5. Press Ctrl + ` to turn on the display of formulas and then print the worksheet again.
6. Turn off the display of formulas and then close the workbook.

Figure 3.11 Visual Benchmark

	A	B	C	D	E
1	Capstan Marine Products				
2	Sales Department Bonuses				
3	Salesperson	Sales	Bonus	Amount	
4	Abrams, Warner	$ 130,490.00	Yes	$ 6,524.50	
5	Allejandro, Elaine	95,500.00	No	-	
6	Crispin, Nicolaus	137,000.00	Yes	6,850.00	
7	Frankel, Maria	124,000.00	Yes	6,200.00	
8	Hiesmann, Thomas	85,500.00	No	-	
9	Jarvis, Lawrence	159,000.00	Yes	7,950.00	
10	Littleman, Shirley	110,500.00	No	-	
11	McBride, Leah	78,420.00	No	-	
12	Ostlund, Sonya	101,435.00	No	-	
13	Ryckman, Graham	83,255.00	No	-	
14	Sharma, Anja	121,488.00	Yes	6,074.40	
15					

Case Study Apply Your Skills

Part 1

You are the office manager for HealthWise Fitness Center and you decide to prepare an Excel worksheet that displays the various plans offered by the health club. In this worksheet, you want to include yearly dues for each plan as well as quarterly and monthly payments. Open the **HFCDues.xlsx** workbook and then save it with Save As and name it **EL1-C3-CS-HFCDues-1**. Make the following changes to the worksheet:

- Select cells B3 through D8 and then change the number formatting to Accounting with two decimal places and a dollar sign.
- Make cell B3 active and then insert *500.00*.
- Make cell B4 active and then insert a formula that adds the amount in B3 with the product (multiplication) of B3 multiplied by 10%. (The formula should look like this: **=B3+(B3*10%)**. The Economy plan is the base plan and each additional plan costs 10% more than the previous plan.)
- Copy the formula in cell B4 down to cells B5 through B8.
- Insert a formula in cell C3 that divides the amount in cell B3 by 4 and then copy the formula down to cells C4 through C8.
- Insert a formula in cell D3 that divides the amount in cell B3 by 12 and then copy the formula down to cells D4 through D8.
- Apply formatting to enhance the visual display of the worksheet.

Save and print the completed worksheet.

With **EL1-C3-CS-HFCDues-1.xlsx** open, save the workbook with Save As and name it **EL1-C3-CS-HFCDues-2**, and then make the following changes:

- You have been informed that the base rate for yearly dues has increased from $500.00 to $600.00. Change this amount in cell B3 of the worksheet.
- If clients are late with their quarterly or monthly dues payments, a late fee is charged. You decide to add the late fee information to the worksheet. Insert a new column to the right of Column C. Type **Late Fees** in cell D2 and also in cell F2.
- Insert a formula in cell D3 that multiplies the amount in C3 by 5%. Copy this formula down to cells D4 through D8.
- Insert a formula in cell F3 that multiplies the amount in E3 by 7%. Copy this formula down to cells F4 through F8. If necessary, change the number formatting for cells F3 through F8 to Accounting with two decimal places and a dollar sign.
- Apply any additional formatting to enhance the visual display of the worksheet.

Save, print, and then close **EL1-C3-CS-HFCDues-2.xlsx**.

Part 2

Prepare a payroll sheet for the employees of the fitness center and include the following information:

HealthWise Fitness Center

Weekly Payroll

Employee	Hourly Wage	Hours	Weekly Salary	Benefits
Heaton, Kelly	$26.50	40		
Severson, Joel	$25.00	40		
Turney, Amanda	$20.00	15		
Walters, Leslie	$19.65	30		
Overmeyer, Jean	$18.00	20		
Haddon, Bonnie	$16.00	20		
Baker, Grant	$15.00	40		
Calveri, Shannon	$12.00	15		
Dugan, Emily	$10.50	10		
Joyner, Daniel	$10.50	10		
Lee, Alexander	$10.50	10		

Insert a formula in the *Weekly Salary* column that multiplies the hourly wage by the number of hours. Insert an IF statement in the *Benefits* column that states that if the number in the *Hours* column is greater than 19, then insert "Yes" and if not, then insert "No." Apply formatting to enhance the visual display of the worksheet. Save the workbook and name it **EL1-C3-CS-HFCPayroll**. Print **EL1-C3-CS-HFCPayroll.xlsx**. Press Ctrl + ` to turn on the display of formulas, print the worksheet, and then press Ctrl + ` to turn off the display of formulas.

Make the following changes to the worksheet:

- Change the hourly wage for Amanda Turney to *$22.00*.
- Increase the hours for Emily Dugan to *20*.
- Remove the row for Grant Baker.
- Insert a row between Jean Overmeyer and Bonnie Haddon and then type the following information in the cells in the new row: Employee: **Tonya McGuire**; Hourly Wage: **$17.50**; Hours: **15**.

Save and then print **EL1-C3-CS-HFCPayroll.xlsx**. Press Ctrl + ` to turn on the display of formulas and then print the worksheet. Press Ctrl + ` to turn off the display of formulas and then save and close **EL1-C3-CS-HFCPayroll.xlsx**.

Part 3

Your boss is interested in ordering new equipment for the health club. She is interested in ordering three elliptical machines, three recumbent bikes, and three upright bikes. She has asked you to use the Internet to research models and prices for this new equipment. She then wants you to prepare a worksheet with the information. Using the Internet, search for the following equipment:

- Search for elliptical machines for sale. Locate two different models and, if possible, find at least two companies that sell each model. Make a note of the company names, model numbers, and prices.
- Search for recumbent bikes for sale. Locate two different models and, if possible, find at least two companies that sell each model. Make a note of the company names, model numbers, and prices.
- Search for upright bikes for sale. Locate two different models and, if possible, find at least two companies that sell each model. Make a note of the company names, model numbers, and prices.

Using the information you found on the Internet, prepare an Excel worksheet with the following information:

- Equipment name
- Equipment model
- Price
- A column that multiplies the price by the number required (which is 3).

Include the fitness center name, HealthWise Fitness Center, and any other information you determine is necessary to the worksheet. Apply formatting to enhance the visual display of the worksheet. Save the workbook and name it **EL1-C3-CS-HFCEquip**. Print and then close **EL1-C3-CS-HFCEquip.xlsx**.

Part 4

When a prospective client contacts HealthWise about joining, you send a letter containing information about the fitness center, the plans offered, and the dues amounts. Use a letter template in Word to create a letter to send to a prospective client (you determine the client's name and address). Copy the cells in **EL1-C3-CS-HFCDues-02.xlsx** containing data and paste them into the body of the letter. Make any formatting changes to make the data readable. Save the document and name it **HFCLetter**. Print and then close **HFCLetter.docx**.

CHAPTER 4

Enhancing a Worksheet

PERFORMANCE OBJECTIVES

Upon successful completion of Chapter 4, you will be able to:

- **Change worksheet margins**
- **Center a worksheet horizontally and vertically on the page**
- **Insert a page break in a worksheet**
- **Print gridlines and row and column headings**
- **Set and clear a print area**
- **Insert headers and footers**
- **Customize print jobs**
- **Complete a spelling check on a worksheet**
- **Find and replace data and cell formatting in a worksheet**
- **Sort data in cells in ascending and descending order**
- **Filter a list using AutoFilter**

Tutorials

4.1 Changing Page Margins and Layout Options
4.2 Formatting and Printing Options
4.3 Inserting a Page Break
4.4 Formatting a Worksheet Page
4.5 Adding Headers and Footers
4.6 Using Undo and Redo
4.7 Using Find and Replace
4.8 Sorting Data and Using Help

Excel contains features you can use to enhance and control the formatting of a worksheet. In this chapter, you will learn how to change worksheet margins, orientation, size, and scale; print column and row titles; print gridlines; and center a worksheet horizontally and vertically on the page. You will also learn how to complete a spell check on text in a worksheet, find and replace specific data and formatting in a worksheet, sort and filter data, and plan and create a worksheet. Model answers for this chapter's projects appear on the following pages.

Excel2010L1C4

Note: Before beginning the projects, copy to your storage medium the Excel2010L1C4 subfolder from the Excel2010L1 folder on the CD that accompanies this textbook and make Excel2010L1C4 the active folder.

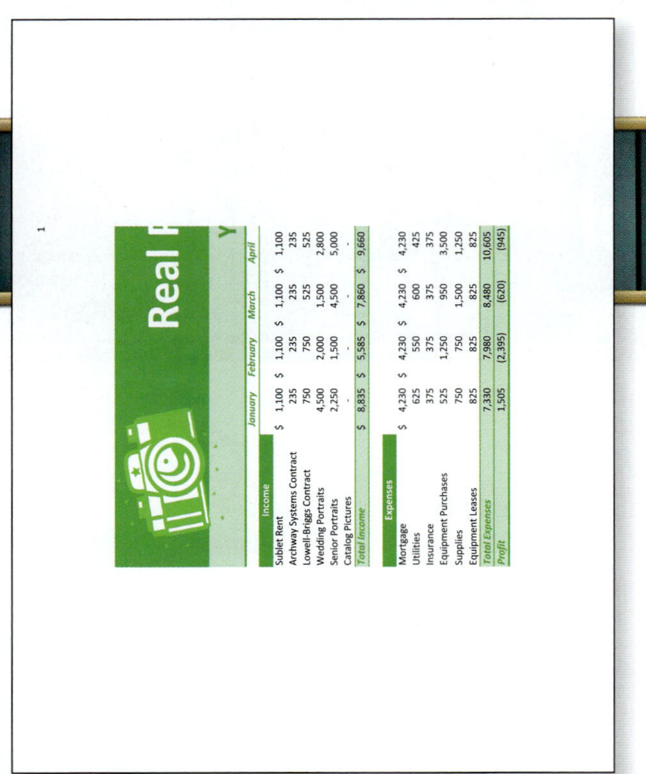

1

Real P

Y

Income	January	February	March	April
Sublet Rent	$ 1,100	$ 1,100	$ 1,100	$ 1,100
Archway Systems Contract	235	235	235	235
Lowell-Briggs Contract	750	750	525	525
Wedding Portraits	4,500	2,000	1,500	2,800
Senior Portraits	2,250	1,500	4,500	5,000
Catalog Pictures	-	-	-	-
Total Income	$ 8,835	$ 5,585	$ 7,860	$ 9,660
Expenses				
Mortgage	$ 4,230	$ 4,230	$ 4,230	$ 4,230
Utilities	625	550	600	425
Insurance	375	375	375	375
Equipment Purchases	525	1,250	950	3,500
Supplies	750	750	1,500	1,250
Equipment Leases	825	825	825	825
Total Expenses	7,330	7,980	8,480	10,605
Profit	1,505	(2,395)	(620)	(945)

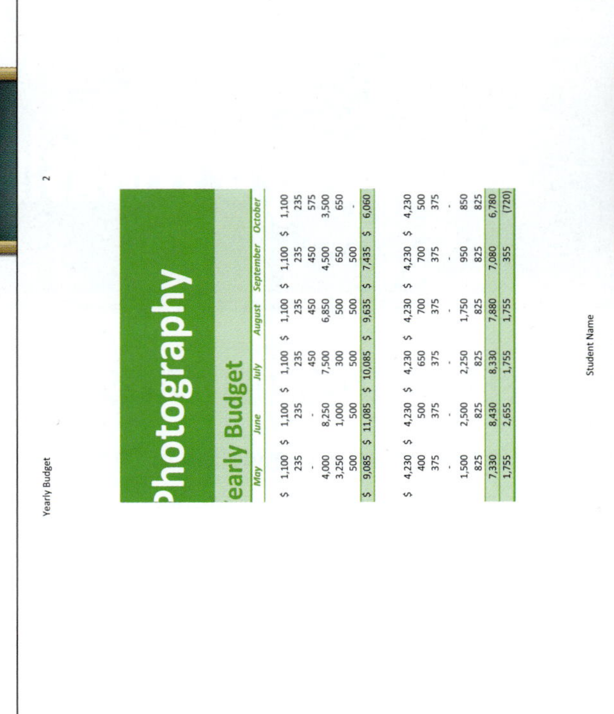

Yearly Budget

2

hotography

early Budget

May	June	July	August	September	October
$ 1,100	$ 1,100	$ 1,100	$ 1,100	$ 1,100	$ 1,100
235	235	235	235	235	235
-	-	450	450	450	575
4,000	8,250	7,500	6,850	4,500	3,500
3,250	1,000	300	500	650	650
500	500	500	500	500	-
$ 9,085	$ 11,085	$ 10,085	$ 9,635	$ 7,435	$ 6,060
$ 4,230	$ 4,230	$ 4,230	$ 4,230	$ 4,230	$ 4,230
400	500	650	700	700	500
375	375	375	375	375	375
-	-	-	-	-	-
1,500	2,500	2,250	1,750	950	850
825	825	825	825	825	825
7,330	8,430	8,330	7,880	7,080	6,780
1,755	2,655	1,755	1,755	355	(720)

Student Name

Project 1 Format a Yearly Budget Worksheet

EL1-C4-P1-RPBudget.xlsx

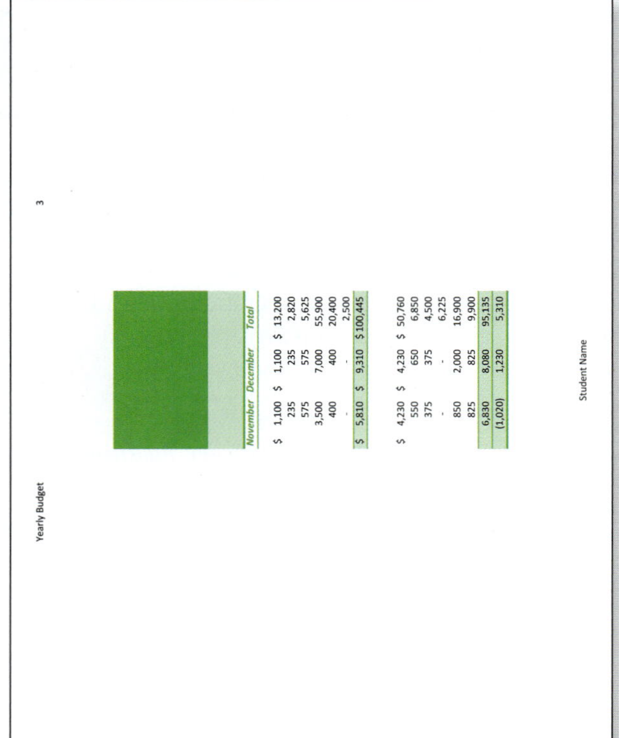

Yearly Budget

3

November	December	Total
$ 1,100	$ 1,100	$ 13,200
235	235	2,820
575	575	5,625
3,500	7,000	55,900
400	400	20,400
-	-	2,500
$ 5,810	$ 9,310	$ 100,445
$ 4,230	$ 4,230	$ 50,760
550	650	6,850
375	375	4,500
-	-	6,225
850	2,000	16,900
825	825	9,900
6,830	8,080	95,135
(1,020)	1,230	5,310

Student Name

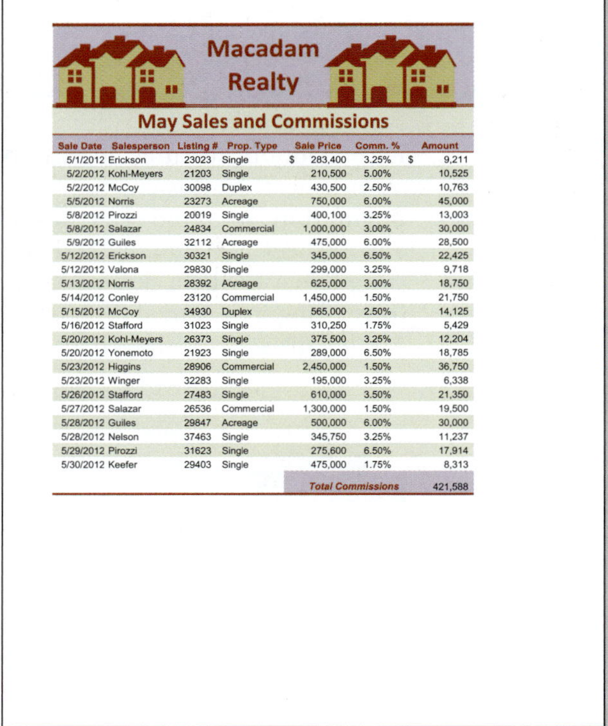

Macadam Realty

May Sales and Commissions

Sale Date	Salesperson	Listing #	Prop. Type	Sale Price	Comm. %	Amount
5/1/2012	Erickson	23023	Single	$ 283,400	3.25%	$ 9,211
5/2/2012	Kohl-Meyers	21203	Single	210,500	5.00%	10,525
5/2/2012	McCoy	30098	Duplex	430,500	2.50%	10,763
5/5/2012	Norris	23273	Acreage	750,000	6.00%	45,000
5/8/2012	Pirozzi	20019	Single	400,100	3.25%	13,003
5/8/2012	Salazar	24834	Commercial	1,000,000	3.00%	30,000
5/9/2012	Guiles	32112	Acreage	475,000	6.00%	28,500
5/12/2012	Erickson	30321	Single	345,000	6.50%	22,425
5/12/2012	Valona	29830	Single	299,000	3.25%	9,718
5/13/2012	Norris	28392	Acreage	625,000	3.00%	18,750
5/14/2012	Conley	23120	Commercial	1,450,000	1.50%	21,750
5/15/2012	McCoy	34930	Duplex	565,000	2.50%	14,125
5/16/2012	Stafford	31023	Single	310,250	1.75%	5,429
5/20/2012	Kohl-Meyers	26373	Single	375,500	3.25%	12,204
5/20/2012	Yonemoto	21923	Single	289,000	6.50%	18,785
5/23/2012	Higgins	28906	Commercial	2,450,000	1.50%	36,750
5/23/2012	Winger	32283	Single	195,000	3.25%	6,338
5/26/2012	Stafford	27483	Single	610,000	3.50%	21,350
5/27/2012	Salazar	26536	Commercial	1,300,000	1.50%	19,500
5/28/2012	Guiles	29847	Acreage	500,000	6.00%	30,000
5/28/2012	Nelson	37463	Single	345,750	3.25%	11,237
5/29/2012	Pirozzi	31623	Single	275,600	6.50%	17,914
5/30/2012	Keefer	29403	Single	475,000	1.75%	8,313
				Total Commissions		421,588

Project 2 Format a May Sales and Commissions Worksheet

EL1-C4-P2-MRSales.xlsx

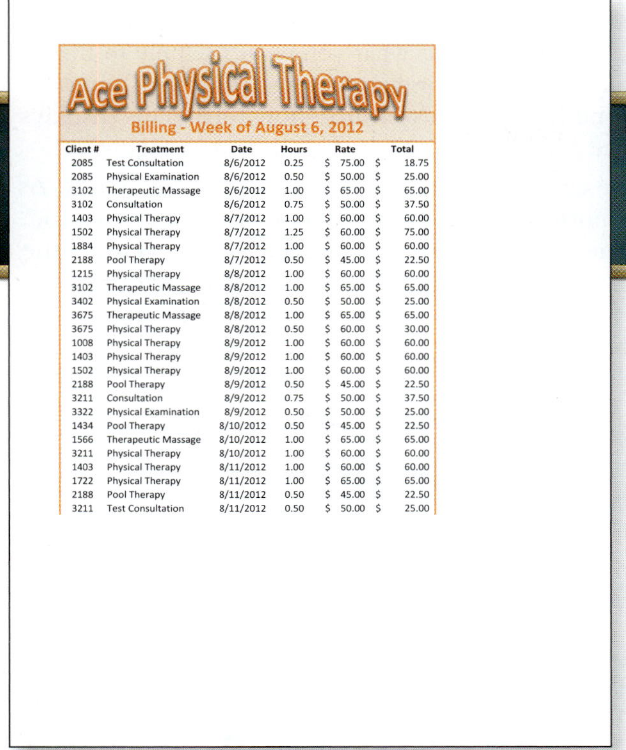

Ace Physical Therapy

Billing - Week of August 6, 2012

Client #	Treatment	Date	Hours	Rate	Total
2085	Test Consultation	8/6/2012	0.25	$ 75.00	$ 18.75
2085	Physical Examination	8/6/2012	0.50	$ 50.00	$ 25.00
3102	Therapeutic Massage	8/6/2012	1.00	$ 65.00	$ 65.00
3102	Consultation	8/6/2012	0.75	$ 50.00	$ 37.50
1403	Physical Therapy	8/7/2012	1.00	$ 60.00	$ 60.00
1502	Physical Therapy	8/7/2012	1.25	$ 60.00	$ 75.00
1884	Physical Therapy	8/7/2012	1.00	$ 60.00	$ 60.00
2188	Pool Therapy	8/7/2012	0.50	$ 45.00	$ 22.50
1215	Physical Therapy	8/8/2012	1.00	$ 60.00	$ 60.00
3102	Therapeutic Massage	8/8/2012	1.00	$ 65.00	$ 65.00
3402	Physical Examination	8/8/2012	0.50	$ 50.00	$ 25.00
3675	Therapeutic Massage	8/8/2012	1.00	$ 65.00	$ 65.00
3675	Physical Therapy	8/8/2012	0.50	$ 60.00	$ 30.00
1008	Physical Therapy	8/9/2012	1.00	$ 60.00	$ 60.00
1403	Physical Therapy	8/9/2012	1.00	$ 60.00	$ 60.00
1502	Physical Therapy	8/9/2012	1.00	$ 60.00	$ 60.00
2188	Pool Therapy	8/9/2012	0.50	$ 45.00	$ 22.50
3211	Consultation	8/9/2012	0.75	$ 50.00	$ 37.50
3322	Physical Examination	8/9/2012	0.50	$ 50.00	$ 25.00
1434	Pool Therapy	8/10/2012	0.50	$ 45.00	$ 22.50
1566	Therapeutic Massage	8/10/2012	1.00	$ 65.00	$ 65.00
3211	Physical Therapy	8/10/2012	1.00	$ 60.00	$ 60.00
1403	Physical Therapy	8/11/2012	1.00	$ 60.00	$ 60.00
1722	Physical Therapy	8/11/2012	1.00	$ 65.00	$ 65.00
2188	Pool Therapy	8/11/2012	0.50	$ 45.00	$ 22.50
3211	Test Consultation	8/11/2012	0.50	$ 50.00	$ 25.00

Project 3 Format a Billing Worksheet

EL1-C4-P3-APTBilling.xlsx

Project 1 Format a Yearly Budget Worksheet — **12 Parts**

You will format a yearly budget worksheet by inserting formulas; changing margins, page orientation, and page size; inserting a page break; printing column headings on multiple pages; scaling data to print on one page; inserting a background picture; inserting headers and footers; and identifying a print area and customizing print jobs.

Formatting a Worksheet Page

An Excel worksheet contains default page formatting. For example, a worksheet contains left and right margins of 0.7 inch and top and bottom margins of 0.75 inch, a worksheet prints in portrait orientation, and the worksheet page size is 8.5 inches by 11 inches. These default settings as well as additional options can be changed and/or controlled with options in the Page Layout tab.

Quick Steps

Change Worksheet Margins

1. Click Page Layout tab.
2. Click Margins button.
3. Click desired predesigned margin.

OR

1. Click Page Layout tab.
2. Click Margins button.
3. Click *Custom Margins* at drop-down list.
4. Change the top, left, right, and/or bottom measurements.
5. Click OK.

Changing Margins

The Page Setup group in the Page Layout tab contains buttons for changing margins, the page orientation and size, as well as buttons for establishing a print area, inserting a page break, applying a picture background, and printing titles.

Change the worksheet margins by clicking the Margins button in the Page Setup group in the Page Layout tab. This displays a drop-down list of predesigned

Margins

margin choices. If one of the predesigned choices is what you want to apply to the worksheet, click the option. If you want to customize margins, click the *Custom Margins* option at the bottom of the Margins button drop-down list. This displays the Page Setup dialog box with the Margins tab selected as shown in Figure 4.1.

A worksheet page showing the cells and margins displays in the dialog box. As you increase or decrease the top, bottom, left, or right margin measurements, the sample worksheet page reflects the change. You can also increase or decrease the measurement from the top of the page to the header with the *Header* option or the measurement from the footer to the bottom of the page with the *Footer* option. (You will learn about headers and footers later in this chapter.)

Figure 4.1 Page Setup Dialog Box with Margins Tab Selected

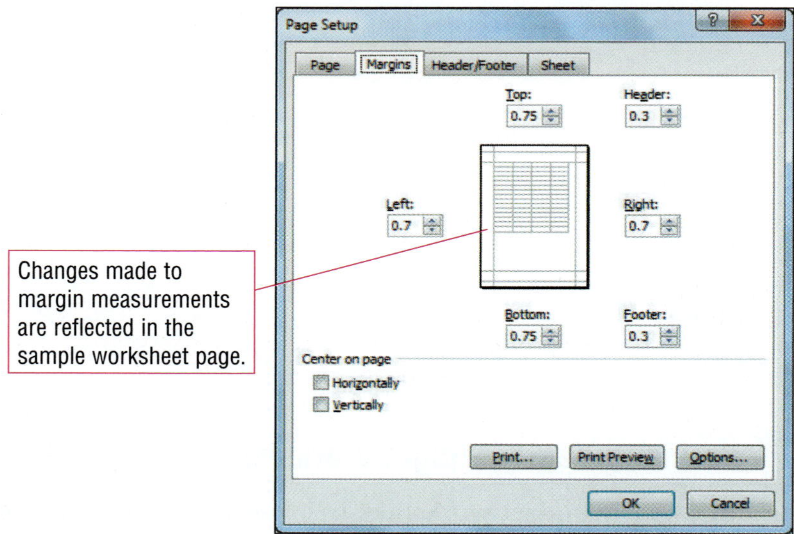

Quick Steps

Center Worksheet Horizontally/ Vertically

1. Click Page Layout tab.
2. Click Margins button.
3. Click *Custom Margins* at drop-down list.
4. Click *Horizontally* option and/or click *Vertically* option.
5. Click OK.

Centering a Worksheet Horizontally and/or Vertically

By default, worksheets print in the upper left corner of the page. You can center a worksheet on the page by changing the margins; however, an easier method for centering a worksheet is to use the *Horizontally* and/or *Vertically* options that display in the Page Setup dialog box with the Margins tab selected. If you choose one or both of these options, the worksheet page in the preview section displays how the worksheet will print on the page.

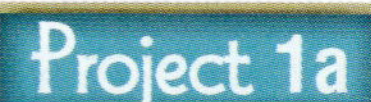

Project 1a

Changing Margins and Horizontally and Vertically Centering a Worksheet

Part 1 of 12

1. Open **RPBudget.xlsx**.
2. Save the workbook with Save As and name it **EL1-C4-P1-RPBudget**.
3. Insert the following formulas in the worksheet:
   a. Insert formulas in column N, rows 5 through 10 that sum the totals for each income item.
   b. Insert formulas in row 11, columns B through N that sum the income as well as the total for all income items.

c. Insert formulas in column N, rows 14 through 19 that sum the totals for each expense item.
d. Insert formulas in row 20, columns B through N that sum the expenses as well as the total of expenses.
e. Insert formulas in row 21, columns B through N that subtract the total expenses from the income. (To begin the formula, make cell B21 active and then type the formula **=B11-B20**. Copy this formula to columns C through N.)
f. Apply the Accounting Number Format style with no decimal places to cells N5 and N14.

4. Click the Page Layout tab.
5. Click the Margins button in the Page Setup group and then click *Custom Margins* at the drop-down list.
6. At the Page Setup dialog box with the Margins tab selected, click the up-pointing arrow at the right side of the *Top* text box until *3.5* displays.
7. Click the up-pointing arrow at the right side of the *Bottom* text box until *1.5* displays.
8. Preview the worksheet by clicking the Print Preview button located toward the bottom of the Page Setup dialog box. The worksheet appears to be a little low on the page so you decide to horizontally and vertically center it by completing the following steps:
   a. Click the Page Setup hyperlink that displays below the categories in the Print tab Backstage view.
   b. Click the Margins tab at the Page Setup dialog box.
   c. Change the *Top* and *Bottom* measurements to *1*.
   d. Click the *Horizontally* option. (This inserts a check mark.)
   e. Click the *Vertically* option. (This inserts a check mark.)
   f. Click OK to close the dialog box.
   g. Look at the preview of the worksheet and then click the File tab to return to the worksheet.
9. Save **EL1-C4-P1-RPBudget.xlsx**.

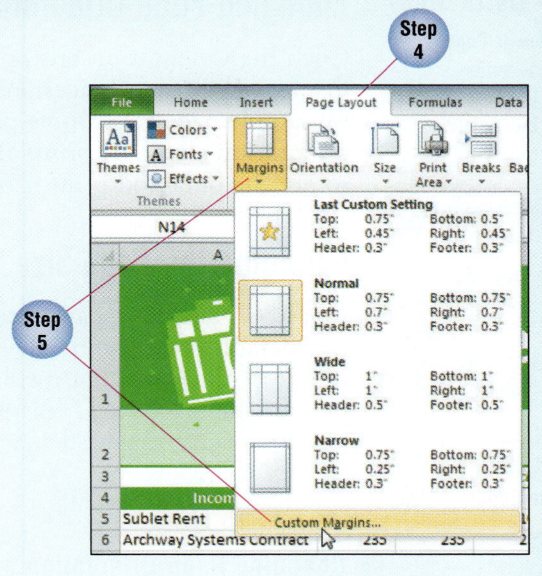

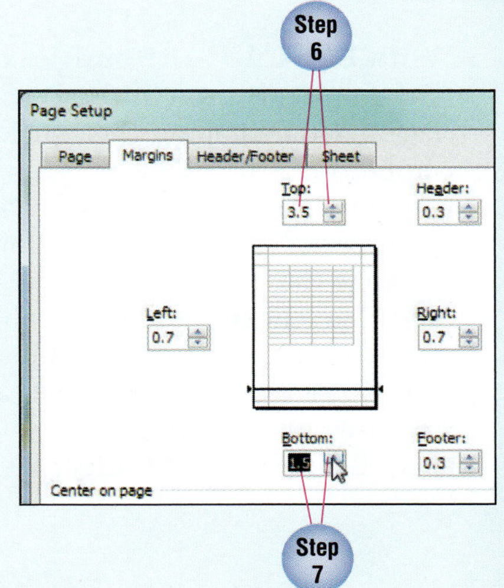

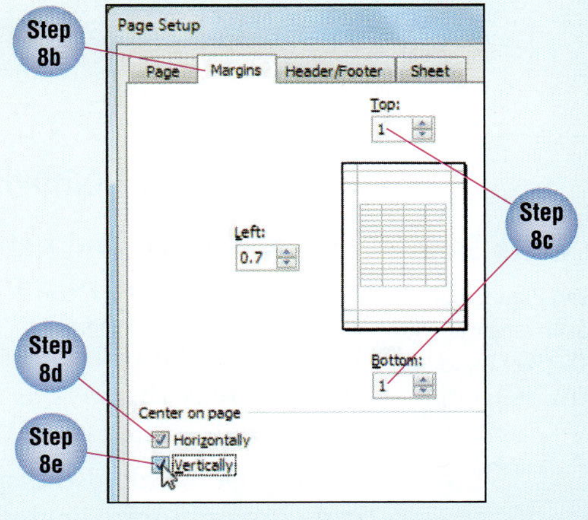

Quick Steps

Change Page Orientation
1. Click Page Layout tab.
2. Click Orientation button.
3. Click desired orientation at drop-down list.

Change Page Size
1. Click Page Layout tab.
2. Click Size button.
3. Click desired size at drop-down list.

Orientation

Size

Changing Page Orientation

Click the Orientation button in the Page Setup group and a drop-down list displays with two choices, *Portrait* and *Landscape*. The two choices are represented by sample pages. A sample page that is taller than it is wide shows how the default orientation (*Portrait*) prints data on the page. The other choice, *Landscape*, will rotate the data and print it on a page that is wider than it is tall.

Changing the Page Size

An Excel worksheet page size, by default, is set at 8.5 × 11 inches. You can change this default page size by clicking the Size button in the Page Setup group. At the drop-down list that displays, notice that the default setting is *Letter* and the measurement *8.5" × 11"* displays below *Letter*. This drop-down list also contains a number of page sizes such as *Executive*, *Legal*, and a number of envelope sizes.

Project 1b Changing Page Orientation and Size

Part 2 of 12

1. With **EL1-C4-P1-RPBudget.xlsx** open, click the Orientation button in the Page Setup group in the Page Layout tab and then click *Landscape* at the drop-down list.
2. Click the Size button in the Page Setup group and then click *Legal* at the drop-down list.
3. Preview the worksheet by clicking the File tab and then clicking the Print tab. After viewing the worksheet in the Print tab Backstage view, click the File tab to return to the worksheet.
4. Save **EL1-C4-P1-RPBudget.xlsx**.

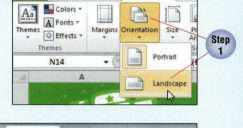

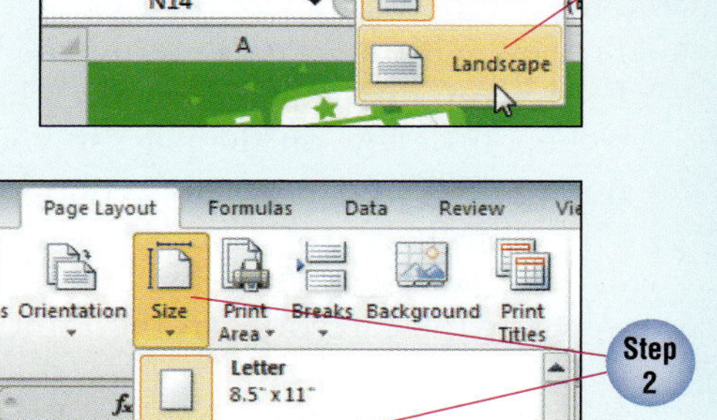

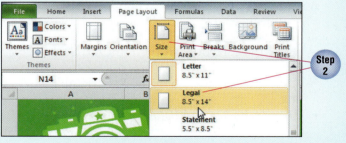

Inserting and Removing Page Breaks

Quick Steps

Insert Page Break
1. Select column or row.
2. Click Page Layout tab.
3. Click Breaks button.
4. Click *Insert Page Break* at drop-down list.

The default left and right margins of 0.7 inch allow approximately 7 inches of cells across the page (8.5 inches minus 1.4 inches equals 7.1 inches). If a worksheet contains more than 7 inches of cells across the page, a page break is inserted in the worksheet and the remaining columns are moved to the next page. A page break displays as a broken line along cell borders. Figure 4.2 shows the page break in **EL1-C4-P1-RPBudget.xlsx**.

A page break also displays horizontally in a worksheet. By default, a worksheet can contain approximately 9.5 inches of cells vertically down the page. This is because the paper size is set by default at 11 inches. With the default top and bottom margins of 0.75 inch, this allows 9.5 inches of cells to print on one page.

Figure 4.2 Page Break

	A	B	C	D	E	F	G	H	I	J	K	L	M	N
1	Real Photography											page break		
2	Yearly Budget													
3		January	February	March	April	May	June	July	August	September	October	November	December	Total
4	Income													
5	Sublet Rent	$ 1,100	$ 1,100	$ 1,100	$ 1,100	$ 1,100	$ 1,100	$ 1,100	$ 1,100	$ 1,100	$ 1,100	$ 1,100	$ 1,100	$ 13,200
6	Archway Systems Contract	235	235	235	235	235	235	235	235	235	235	235	235	2,820
7	Lowell-Briggs Contract	750	750	525	525	-	-	450	450	450	575	575	575	5,625
8	Wedding Portraits	4,500	2,000	1,500	2,800	4,000	8,250	7,500	6,850	4,500	3,500	3,500	7,000	55,900
9	Senior Portraits	2,250	1,500	4,500	5,000	3,250	1,000	300	500	650	650	400	400	20,400
10	Catalog Pictures	-	-	-	-	500	500	500	500	500	-	-	-	2,500
11	*Total Income*	$ 8,835	$ 5,585	$ 7,860	$ 9,660	$ 9,085	$ 11,085	$ 10,085	$ 9,635	$ 7,435	$ 6,060	$ 5,810	$ 9,310	$100,445
12														
13	Expenses													
14	Mortgage	$ 4,230	$ 4,230	$ 4,230	$ 4,230	$ 4,230	$ 4,230	$ 4,230	$ 4,230	$ 4,230	$ 4,230	$ 4,230	$ 4,230	$ 50,760
15	Utilities	625	550	600	425	400	500	650	700	700	500	550	650	6,850
16	Insurance	375	375	375	375	375	375	375	375	375	375	375	375	4,500
17	Equipment Purchases	525	1,250	950	3,500	-	-	-	-	-	-	-	-	6,225
18	Supplies	750	750	1,500	1,250	1,500	2,500	2,250	1,750	950	850	850	2,000	16,900
19	Equipment Leases	825	825	825	825	825	825	825	825	825	825	825	825	9,900
20	*Total Expenses*	7,330	7,980	8,480	10,605	7,330	8,430	8,330	7,880	7,080	6,780	6,830	8,080	95,135
21	*Profit*	1,505	(2,395)	(620)	(945)	1,755	2,655	1,755	1,755	355	(720)	(1,020)	1,230	5,310

Sheet1 Sheet2 Sheet3

Excel automatically inserts a page break in a worksheet. You can insert your own if you would like more control over what cells print on a page. To insert your own page break, select the column or row, click the Breaks button in the Page Setup group in the Page Layout tab, and then click *Insert Page Break* at the drop-down list. A page break is inserted immediately left of the selected column or immediately above the selected row.

Breaks

If you want to insert both a horizontal and vertical page break at the same time, make a cell active, click the Breaks button in the Page Setup group and then click *Insert Page Break*. This causes a horizontal page break to be inserted immediately above the active cell, and a vertical page break to be inserted at the left side of the active cell. To remove a page break, select the column or row or make the desired cell active, click the Breaks button in the Page Setup group, and then click *Remove Page Break* at the drop-down list.

The page break automatically inserted by Excel may not be visible initially in a worksheet. One way to display the page break is to display the worksheet in the Print tab Backstage view. When you return to the worksheet, the page break will display in the worksheet.

Excel provides a page break view that displays worksheet pages and page breaks. To display this view, click the Page Break Preview button located in the view area at the right side of the Status bar or click the View tab and then click the Page Break Preview button in the Workbook Views group. This causes the worksheet to display similar to the worksheet shown in Figure 4.3. The word *Page* along with the page number is displayed in gray behind the cells in the worksheet. A solid blue line indicates a page break inserted by Excel and a dashed blue line indicates a page break inserted manually.

HINT
You can edit a worksheet in Page Break Preview.

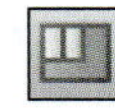

Page Break Preview

You can move the page break by positioning the arrow pointer on the blue line, holding down the left mouse button, dragging the line to the desired location, and then releasing the mouse button. To return to the Normal view, click the Normal button in the view area on the Status bar or click the View tab and then click the Normal button in the Workbook Views group.

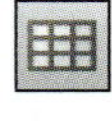

Normal

Figure 4.3 Worksheet in Page Break Preview

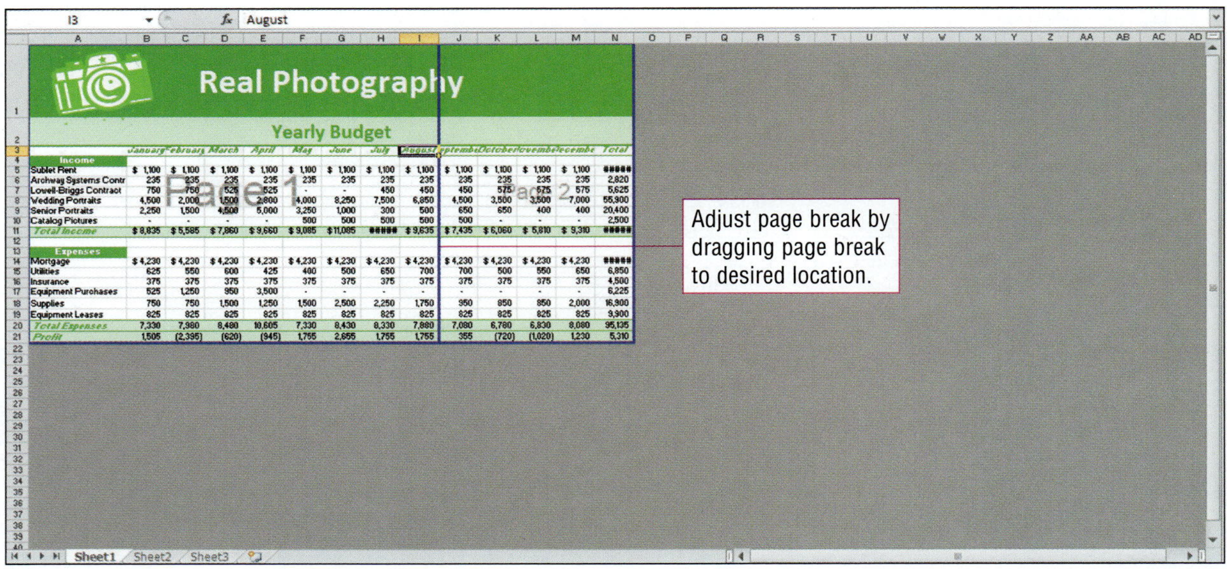

Project 1c Inserting a Page Break in a Worksheet

Part 3 of 12

1. With **EL1-C4-P1-RPBudget.xlsx** open, click the Size button in the Page Setup group in the Page Layout tab and then click *Letter* at the drop-down list.
2. Click the Margins button and then click *Custom Margins* at the drop-down list.
3. At the Page Setup dialog box with the Margins tab selected, click *Horizontally* to remove the check mark, click *Vertically* to remove the check mark, and then click OK to close the dialog box.
4. Insert a page break between columns I and J by completing the following steps:
   a. Select column J.
   b. Click the Breaks button in the Page Setup group and then click *Insert Page Break* at the drop-down list. Click in any cell in column I.

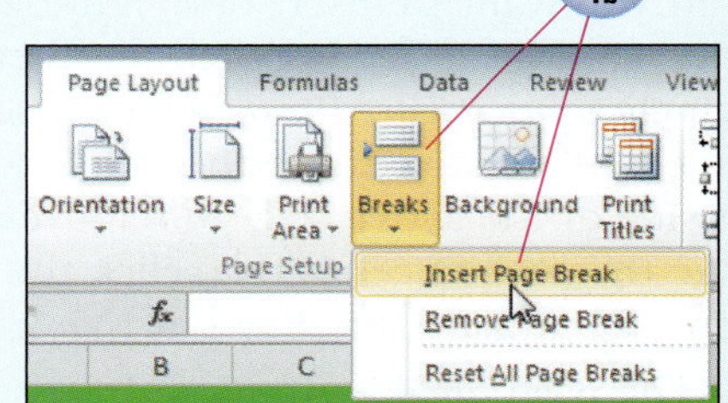

5. View the worksheet in Page Break Preview by completing the following steps:
   a. Click the Page Break Preview button located in the view area on the Status bar. (If a welcome message displays, click OK.)
   b. View the pages and page breaks in the worksheet.
   c. You decide to include the first six months of the year on one page. To do this, position the arrow pointer on the vertical blue line, hold down the left mouse button, drag the line to the left so it is positioned between columns G and H, and then release the mouse button.

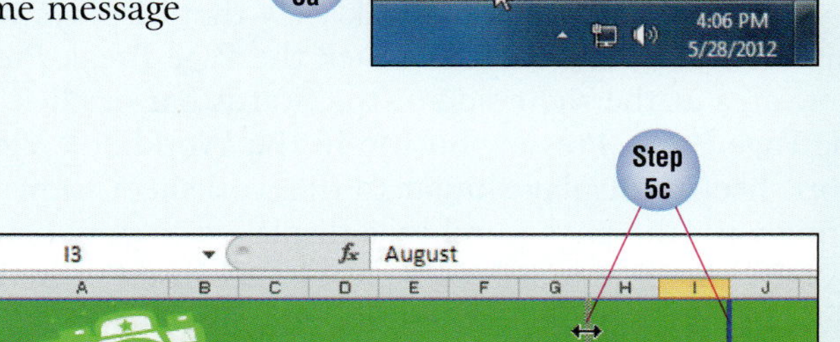

d. Click the Normal button located in the view area on the Status bar.

6. Save **EL1-C4-P1-RPBudget.xlsx**.

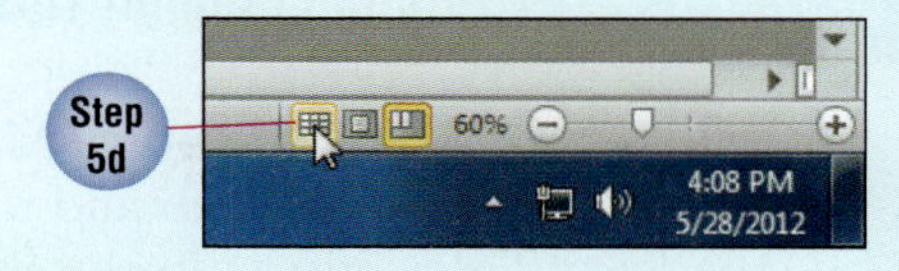

Printing Column and Row Titles on Multiple Pages

Columns and rows in a worksheet are usually titled. For example, in **EL1-C4-P1-RPBudget.xlsx**, column titles include *Income*, *Expenses*, *January*, *February*, *March*, and so on. Row titles include the income and expenses categories. If a worksheet prints on more than one page, having column and/or row titles printing on each page can be useful. To do this, click the Print Titles button in the Page Setup group in the Page Layout tab. This displays the Page Setup dialog box with the Sheet tab selected as shown in Figure 4.4.

At the Page Setup dialog box with the Sheet tab selected, specify the range of row cells you want to print on every page in the *Rows to repeat at top* text box. Type a cell range using a colon. For example, if you want cells A1 through J1 to print on every page, you would type *A1:J1* in the *Rows to repeat at top* text box. Type the range of column cells you want to print on every page in the *Columns to repeat at left* text box. To make rows and columns easier to identify on the printed page, specify that row and/or column headings print on each page.

Quick Steps

Print Column and Row Titles

1. Click Page Layout tab.
2. Click Print Titles button.
3. Type row range in *Rows to repeat at top* option.
4. Type column range in *Columns to repeat at left* option.
5. Click OK.

Print Titles

Figure 4.4 Page Setup Dialog Box with Sheet Tab Selected

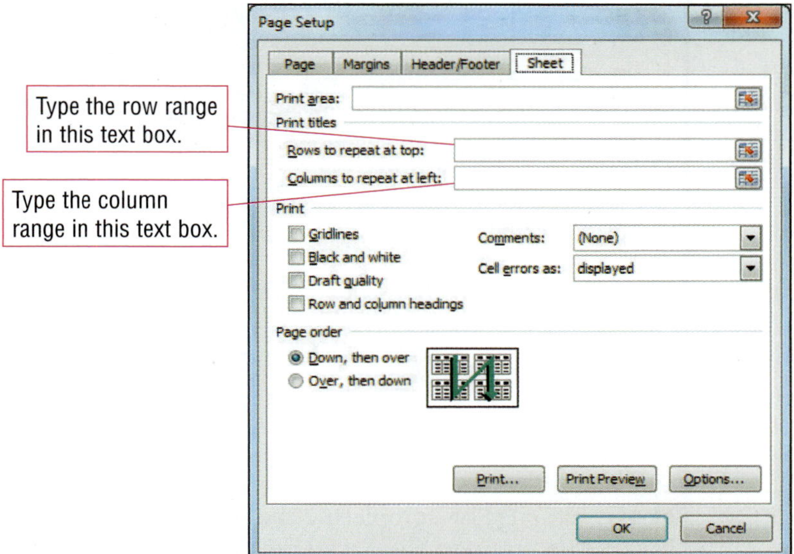

Project 1d Printing Column Titles on Each Page of a Worksheet

Part 4 of 12

1. With **EL1-C4-P1-RPBudget.xlsx** open, click the Page Layout tab and then click the Print Titles button in the Page Setup group.
2. At the Page Setup dialog box with the Sheet tab selected, click in the *Columns to repeat at left* text box.
3. Type A1:A21.
4. Click OK to close the dialog box.
5. Save and then print **EL1-C4-P1-RPBudget.xlsx**.

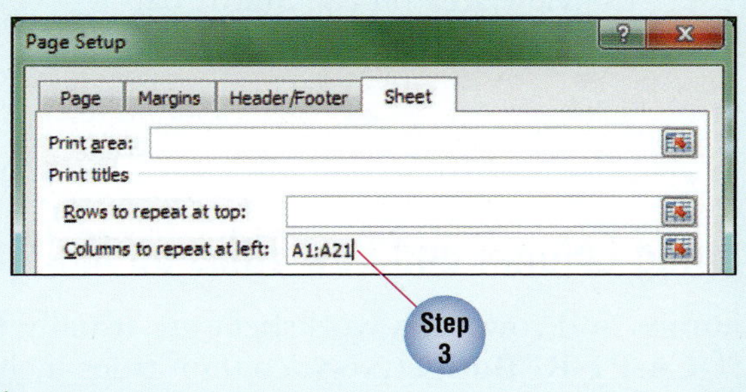

Scaling Data

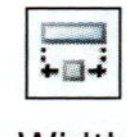

Width

With buttons in the Scale to Fit group in the Page Layout tab, you can adjust the printed output by a percentage to fit the number of pages specified. For example, if a worksheet contains too many columns to print on one page, click the down-pointing arrow at the right side of the *Width* box in the Scale to Fit group in the Page Layout tab and then click *1 page*. This causes the data to shrink so all columns display and print on one page.

Project 1e Scaling Data to Fit on One Page and Printing Row Titles on Each Page

Part 5 of 12

1. With **EL1-C4-P1-RPBudget.xlsx** open, click the down-pointing arrow at the right side of the *Width* box in the Scale to Fit group in the Page Layout tab.
2. At the drop-down list that displays, click the *1 page* option.
3. Display the Print tab Backstage view, notice that all cells containing data display on one page in the worksheet, and then return to the worksheet.
4. Change margins by completing the following steps:
   a. Click the Page Layout tab.
   b. Click the Margins button in the Page Setup group and then click *Custom Margins* at the drop-down list.
   c. At the Page Setup dialog box with the Margins tab selected, select the current number in the *Top* text box and then type 3.5.
   d. Select the current number in the *Left* text box and then type 0.3.
   e. Select the current number in the *Right* text box and then type 0.3.
   f. Click OK to close the Page Setup dialog box.
5. Specify that you want row titles to print on each page by completing the following steps:
   a. Click the Print Titles button in the Page Setup group in the Page Layout tab.
   b. At the Page Setup dialog box with the Sheet tab selected, select and then delete the text that displays in the *Columns to repeat at left* text box.

c. Click in the *Rows to repeat at top* text box and then type A3:N3.
d. Click OK to close the dialog box.

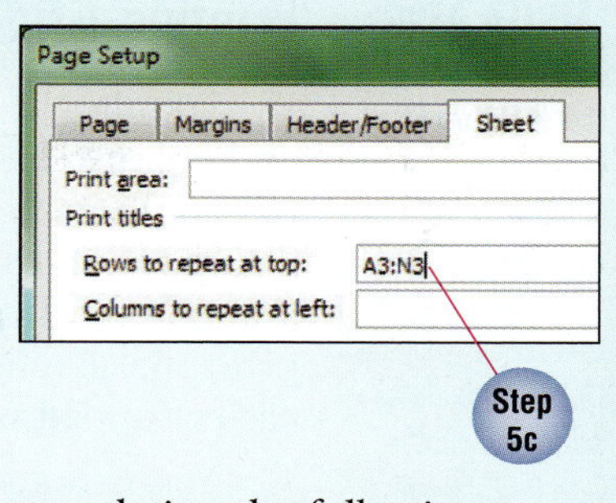

6. Save and then print **EL1-C4-P1-RPBudget.xlsx**. (The worksheet will print on two pages with the row titles repeated on the second page.)
7. At the worksheet, return to the default margins by clicking the Page Layout tab, clicking the Margins button, and then clicking the *Normal* option at the drop-down list.
8. Remove titles from printing on second and subsequent pages by completing the following steps:
   a. Click the Print Titles button in the Page Setup group.
   b. At the Page Setup dialog box with the Sheet tab selected, select and then delete the text that displays in the *Rows to repeat at top* text box.
   c. Click OK to close the dialog box.
9. Change the scaling back to the default by completing the following steps:
   a. Click the down-pointing arrow at the right side of the *Width* box in the Scale to Fit group and then click *Automatic* at the drop-down list.
   b. Click the up-pointing arrow at the right side of the *Scale* measurement box until *100%* displays in the box.

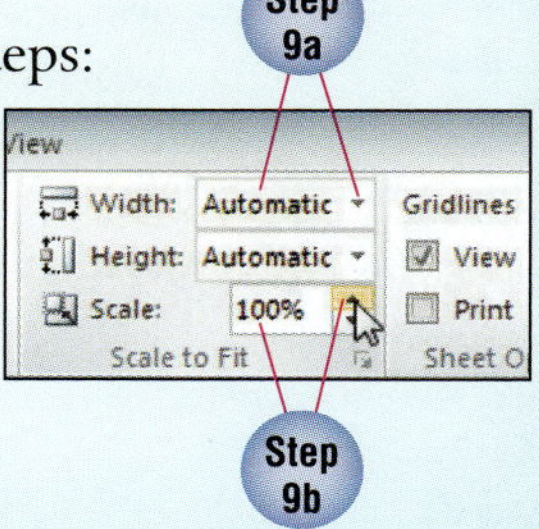

10. Save **EL1-C4-P1-RPBudget.xlsx**.

Inserting a Background Picture

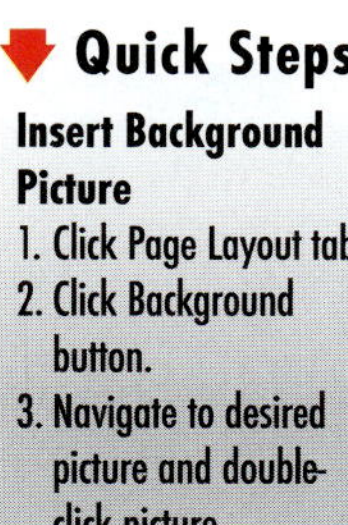

Quick Steps

Insert Background Picture
1. Click Page Layout tab.
2. Click Background button.
3. Navigate to desired picture and double-click picture.

Background

With the Background button in the Page Setup group in the Page Layout tab you can insert a picture as a background to the worksheet. The picture displays only on the screen and does not print. To insert a picture, click the Background button in the Page Setup group. At the Sheet Background dialog box navigate to the folder containing the desired picture and then double-click the picture. To remove the picture from the worksheet, click the Delete Background button.

Project 1f **Inserting a Background Picture** Part 6 of 12

1. With **EL1-C4-P1-RPBudget.xlsx** open, insert a background picture by completing the following steps:
   a. Click the Background button in the Page Setup group in the Page Layout tab.
   b. At the Sheet Background dialog box, navigate to the Excel2010L1C4 folder, and then double-click ***Ship.jpg***.
   c. Scroll down the worksheet to display the ship.

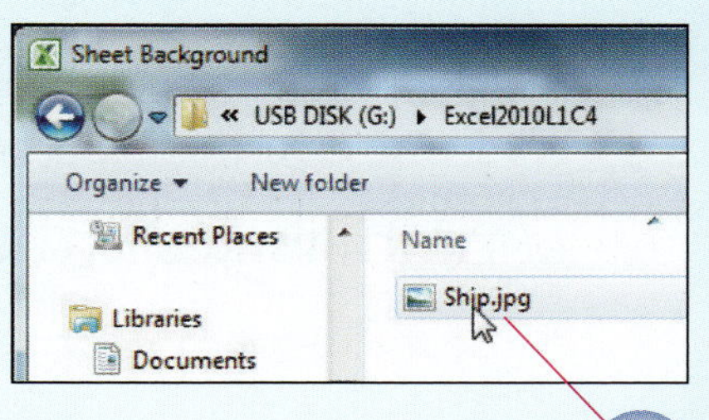

2. Display the Print tab Backstage view, notice that the picture does not display in the preview worksheet, and then return to the worksheet.
3. Remove the picture by clicking the Delete Background button in the Page Setup group in the Page Layout tab.
4. Save **EL1-C4-P1-RPBudget.xlsx**.

Quick Steps

Print Gridlines
1. Click Page Layout tab.
2. Click *Print* check box in *Gridlines* section in Sheet Options group.

OR

1. Click Page Layout tab.
2. Click Sheet Options dialog box launcher.
3. Click *Gridlines* option.
4. Click OK.

Print Row and Column Headings
1. Click Page Layout tab.
2. Click *Print* check box in *Headings* section in Sheet Options group.

OR

1. Click Page Layout tab.
2. Click Sheet Options dialog box launcher.
3. Click *Row and column headings* option.
4. Click OK.

Printing Gridlines and Row and Column Headings

By default, the gridlines that create the cells in a worksheet and the row numbers and column letters do not print. The Sheet Options group in the Page Layout tab contain check boxes for gridlines and headings. The *View* check boxes for Gridlines and Headings contain check marks. At these settings, gridlines and row and column headings display on the screen but do not print. If you want them to print, insert check marks in the *Print* check boxes. Complex worksheets may be easier to read with the gridlines printed.

You can also control the display and printing of gridlines and headings with options at the Page Setup dialog box with the Sheet tab selected. Display this dialog box by clicking the Sheet Options dialog box launcher. To print gridlines and headings, insert check marks in the check boxes located in the *Print* section of the dialog box. The *Print* section contains two additional options — *Black and white* and *Draft quality*. If you are printing with a color printer, you can print the worksheet in black and white by inserting a check mark in the *Black and white* check box. Insert a check mark in the *Draft* option if you want to print a draft of the worksheet. With this option checked, some formatting such as shading and fill do not print.

Project 1g **Printing Gridlines and Row and Column Headings** Part 7 of 12

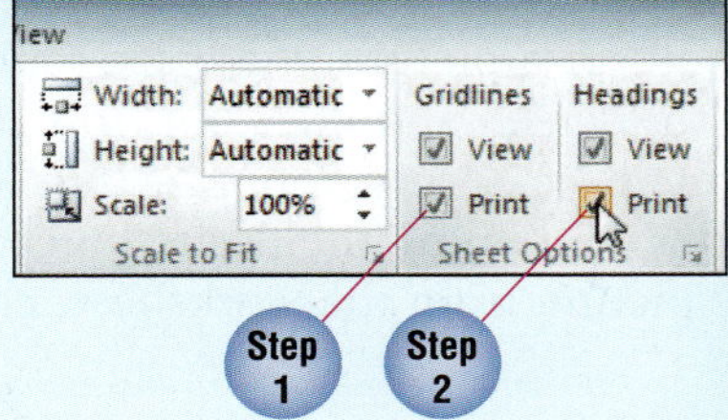

1. With **EL1-C4-P1-RPBudget.xlsx** open, click in the *Print* check box below Gridlines in the Sheet Options group in the Page Layout tab to insert a check mark.
2. Click in the *Print* check box below Headings in the Sheet Options group to insert a check mark.
3. Click the Margins button in the Page Setup group and then click *Custom Margins* at the drop-down list.
4. At the Page Setup dialog box with the Margins tab selected, click in the *Horizontally* check box to insert a check mark.
5. Click in the *Vertically* check box to insert a check mark.
6. Click OK to close the dialog box.
7. Save and then print **EL1-C4-P1-RPBudget.xlsx**.
8. Click in the *Print* check box below Headings in the Sheet Options group to remove the check mark.
9. Click in the *Print* check box below Gridlines in the Sheet Options group to remove the check mark.
10. Save **EL1-C4-P1-RPBudget.xlsx**.

Printing a Specific Area of a Worksheet

Print Area

With the Print Area button in the Page Setup group in the Page Layout tab you can select and print specific areas in a worksheet. To do this, select the cells you want to print, click the Print Area button in the Page Setup group in the Page Layout tab, and then click *Set Print Area* at the drop-down list. This inserts a border around the selected cells. Display the Print tab Backstage view, click the Print button, and the cells within the border are printed.

You can specify more than one print area in a worksheet. To do this, select the first group of cells, click the Print Area button in the Page Setup group, and then click *Set Print Area*. Select the next group of cells, click the Print Area button, and then click *Add to Print Area*. Clear a print area by clicking the Print Area button in the Page Setup group and then clicking *Clear Print Area* at the drop-down list.

Each area specified as a print area will print on a separate page. If you want nonadjacent print areas to print on the same page, consider hiding columns and/or rows in the worksheet to bring the areas together.

Project 1h Printing Specific Areas

Part 8 of 12

1. With **EL1-C4-P1-RPBudget.xlsx** open, print the first half of the year's income and expenses by completing the following steps:
   a. Select cells A3 through G21.
   b. Click the Print Area button in the Page Setup group in the Page Layout tab and then click *Set Print Area* at the drop-down list.
   c. With the border surrounding the cells A3 through G21, click the File tab, click the Print tab, and then click the Print button at the Print tab Backstage view.
   d. Clear the print area by clicking the Print Area button in the Page Setup group and then clicking *Clear Print Area* at the drop-down list.

Step 1b

Page Layout | Formulas | Data | Revie

Orientation | Size | Print Area | Breaks | Background

Set Print Area

Clear Print Area

2. Suppose you want to print the income and expenses information as well as the totals for the month of April. To do this, hide columns and select a print area by completing the following steps:
   a. Select columns B through D.
   b. Click the Home tab.
   c. Click the Format button in the Cells group, point to *Hide & Unhide*, and then click *Hide Columns*.
   d. Click the Page Layout tab.
   e. Select cells A3 through E21. (Columns A and E are now adjacent.)
   f. Click the Print Area button in the Page Setup group and then click *Set Print Area* at the drop-down list.
3. Click the File tab, click the Print tab, and then click the Print button.
4. Clear the print area by making sure cells A3 through E21 are selected, clicking the Print Area button in the Page Setup group, and then clicking *Clear Print Area* at the drop-down list.
5. Unhide the columns by completing the following steps:
   a. Click the Home tab.
   b. Select columns A and E. (These columns are adjacent.)
   c. Click the Format button in the Cells group, point to *Hide & Unhide*, and then click *Unhide Columns*.
   d. Deselect the text by clicking in any cell containing data in the worksheet.
6. Save **EL1-C4-P1-RPBudget.xlsx**.

Figure 4.5 Header & Footer Tools Design Tab

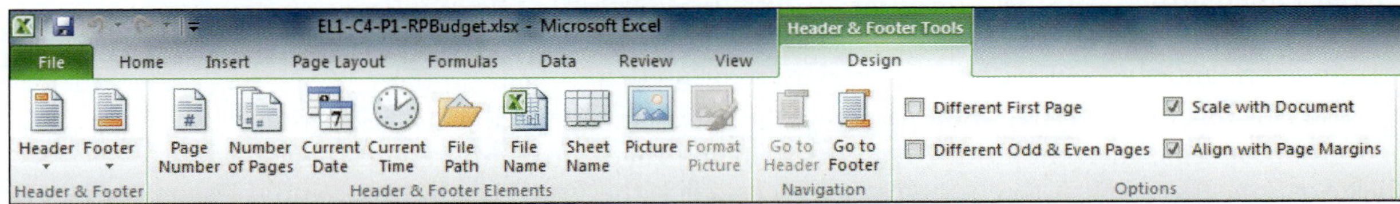

Quick Steps

Insert a Header or Footer

1. Click Insert tab.
2. Click Header & Footer button.
3. Click Header button and then click predesigned header or click Footer button and then click predesigned footer.

OR

1. Click Insert tab.
2. Click Header & Footer button.
3. Click desired header or footer elements.

Close the header or footer pane by clicking in the worksheet or pressing Esc.

Header & Footer

Inserting Headers and Footers

Text that prints at the top of each worksheet page is called a ***header*** and text that prints at the bottom of each worksheet page is called a ***footer***. You can create a header and/or footer with the Header & Footer button in the Text group in the Insert tab, in Page Layout View, or with options at the Page Setup dialog box with the Header/Footer tab selected.

To create a header with the Header & Footer button, click the Insert tab and then click the Header & Footer button in the Text group. This displays the worksheet in Page Layout view and displays the Header & Footer Tools Design tab. Use buttons in this tab, shown in Figure 4.5, to insert predesigned headers and/or footers or insert header and footer elements such as the page number, date, time, path name, and file name. You can also create a different header or footer on the first page of the worksheet or create a header or footer for even pages and another for odd pages.

At the Print tab Backstage view, you can preview your headers and footers before printing. Click the File tab and then the Print tab to display the Print tab Backstage view. A preview of the worksheet displays at the right side of the Backstage view. If your worksheet will print on more than one page, you can view different pages by clicking the Next Page button or the Previous Page button. These buttons are located below and to the left of the preview worksheet at the Print tab Backstage view. Two buttons display in the bottom right corner of the Print tab Backstage view. Click the Show Margins button and margin guidelines display in the preview of the worksheet. Click the Zoom to Page button to zoom in or out of the preview of the worksheet.

Project 1i Inserting a Header in a Worksheet

Part 9 of 12

1. With **EL1-C4-P1-RPBudget.xlsx** open, create a header by completing the following steps:
   a. Click the Insert tab.
   b. Click the Header & Footer button in the Text group.

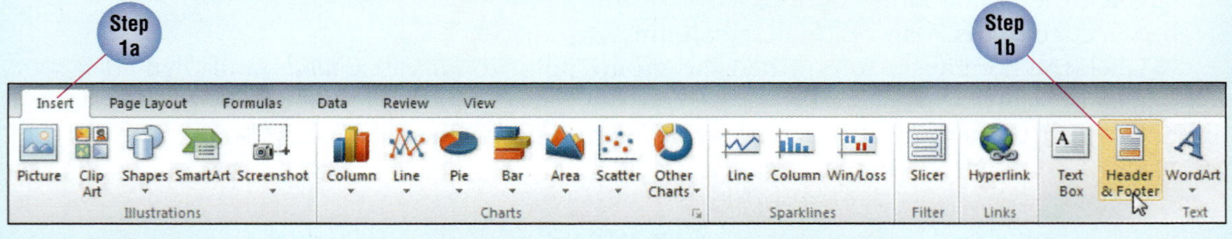

c. Click the Header button located at the left side of the Header & Footer Tools Design tab and then click *Page 1, EL1-C4-P1-RPBudget.xlsx* at the drop-down list. (This inserts the page number in the middle header box and the workbook name in the right header box.)

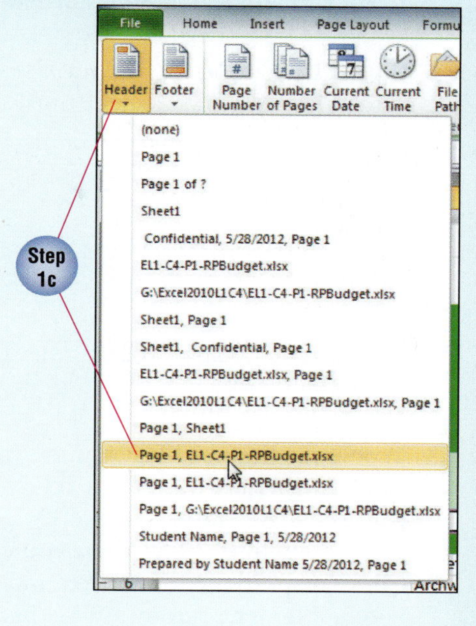

2. Preview the worksheet by completing the following steps:
   a. Click the File tab and then click the Print tab.
   b. At the Print tab Backstage view look at the preview worksheet that displays at the right.
   c. View the next page of the worksheet by clicking the Next Page button that displays below and to the left of the preview worksheet.

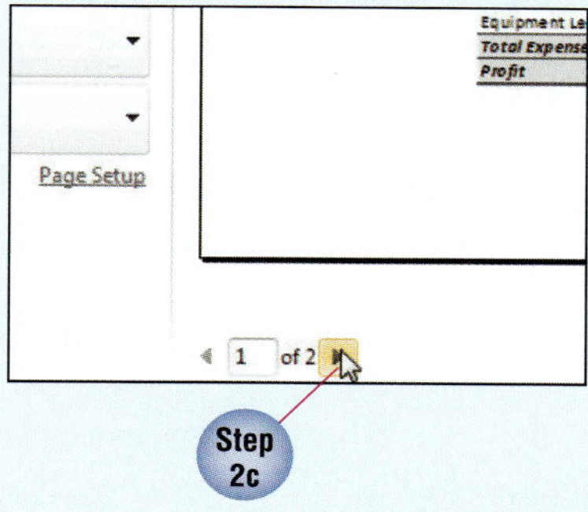

   d. View the first page by clicking the Previous Page button that displays left of the Next Page button.
   e. Click the File tab to return to the workbook.
3. Save **EL1-C4-P1-RPBudget.xlsx**.

You also can insert a header and/or footer by switching to Page Layout view. In Page Layout view, the top of the worksheet page displays with the text *Click to add header*. Click this text and the insertion point is positioned in the middle header box. Type the desired header in this box or click in the left box or the right box and then type the header. Create a footer in a similar manner. Scroll down the worksheet until the bottom of the page displays and then click the text *Click to add footer*. Type the footer in the center footer box or click the left or right box and then type the footer.

Inserting a Footer and Modifying a Header in a Worksheet Part 10 of 12

1. With **EL1-C4-P1-RPBudget.xlsx** open, make sure the workbook displays in Page Layout view.
2. Scroll down the worksheet until the text *Click to add footer* displays and then click the text.

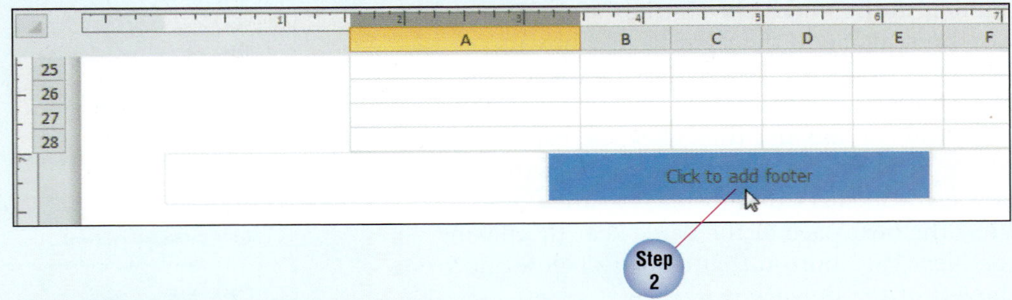

3. Type your first and last names.
4. Click in the left footer box, click the Header & Footer Tools Design tab, and then click the Current Date button in the Header & Footer Elements group. (This inserts a date code. The date will display when you click outside the footer box.)
5. Click in the right footer box and then click the Current Time button in the Header & Footer Elements group. (This inserts the time as a code. The time will display when you click outside the footer box.)
6. View the headers and footers at the Print tab Backstage view and then return to the worksheet.
7. Modify the header by completing the following steps:
   a. Scroll to the beginning of the worksheet and display the header text.
   b. Click the page number in the middle header box. (This displays the Header & Footer Tools Design tab, changes the header to a field, and selects the field.)
   c. Press the Delete key to delete the header.
   d. Click the header text that displays in the right header box and then press the Delete key.
   e. With the insertion point positioned in the right header box, insert the page number by clicking the Header & Footer Tools Design tab and then clicking the Page Number button in the Header & Footer Elements group.
   f. Click in the left header box and then click the File Name button in the Header & Footer Elements group.

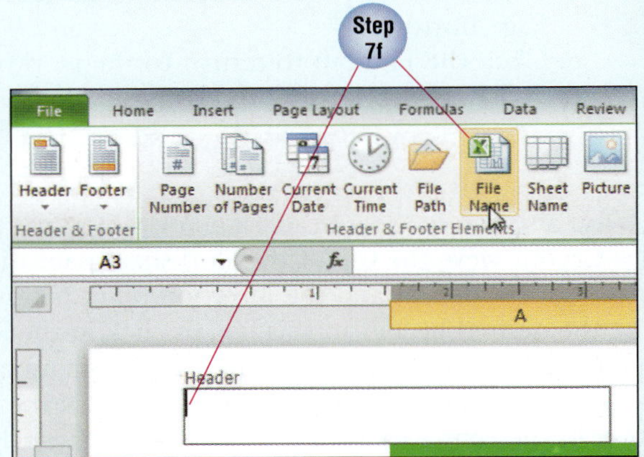

8. Click in any cell in the worksheet containing data.
9. View the headers and footers at the Print tab Backstage view and then return to the worksheet.
10. Save **EL1-C4-P1-RPBudget.xlsx**.

In addition to options in the Header & Footer Tools Design tab, you can insert and customize headers and footers with options at the Page Setup dialog box with the Header/Footer tab selected that displays in Figure 4.6. Display this dialog box by clicking the Page Layout tab and then clicking the Page Setup group dialog box launcher. At the Page Setup dialog box, click the Header/Footer tab. If your worksheet contains headers or footers, they will display in the dialog box.

Figure 4.6 Page Setup Dialog Box with Header/Footer Tab Selected

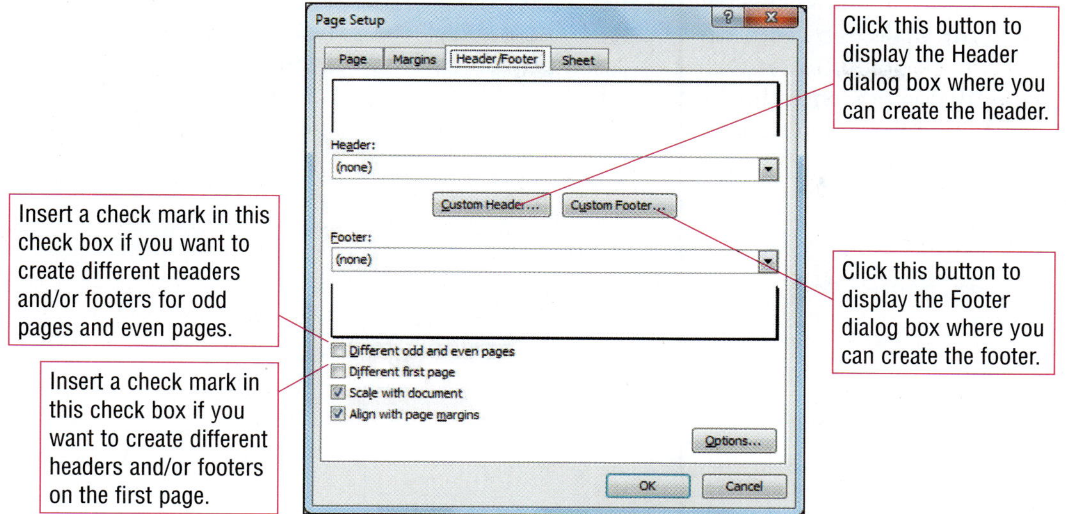
Page Setup
Page
Margins
Header/Footer
Sheet
Header:
(none)
Custom Header...
Custom Footer...
Footer:
(none)
Different odd and even pages
Different first page
Scale with document
Align with page margins
Options...
OK
Cancel
Click this button to display the Header dialog box where you can create the header.
Insert a check mark in this check box if you want to create different headers and/or footers for odd pages and even pages.
Click this button to display the Footer dialog box where you can create the footer.
Insert a check mark in this check box if you want to create different headers and/or footers on the first page.

With the check box options that display in the lower left corner of the dialog box, you can specify that you want to insert a different odd and even page header or footer or insert a different first page header or footer. The bottom two check box options are active by default. These defaults scale the header and footer text with the worksheet text and align the header and footer with the page margins.

To create different odd and even page headers, click the *Different odd and even pages* check box to insert a check mark and then click the Custom Header button. This displays the Header dialog box with the Odd Page Header tab selected. Type or insert the desired odd page header data in the left, center, or right section boxes and then click the Even Page Header tab. Type or insert the desired even page header data in the section boxes and then click OK. Use the buttons that display above the section boxes to format the header text and insert information such as the page number, current date, current time, file name, worksheet name, and so on. Complete similar steps to create different odd and even page footers and different first page headers or footers.

Project 1k Creating Different Odd and Even Page Headers and Footers and a Different First Page Header and Footer

Part 11 of 12

1. With **EL1-C4-P1-RPBudget.xlsx** open, remove the page break by clicking the Page Layout tab, clicking the Breaks button in the Page Setup group, and then clicking *Reset All Page Breaks* at the drop-down list.
2. Change the margins by completing the following steps:
   a. Click the Margins button in the Page Setup group in the Page Layout tab and then click *Custom Margins* at the drop-down list.
   b. At the Page Setup dialog box with the Margins tab selected, select the current number in the *Left* text box and then type 3.
   c. Select the current number in the *Right* text box and then type 3.
   d. Click OK to close the dialog box.
3. Click the Page Layout tab and then click the Page Setup group dialog box launcher.

4. At the Page Setup dialog box, click the Header/Footer tab.
5. At the Page Setup dialog box with the Header/Footer tab selected, click the *Different odd and even pages* check box to insert a check mark and then click the Custom Header button.
6. At the Header dialog box with the Odd Page Header tab selected, click the Format Text button (located above the left section box). At the Font dialog box, click *12* in the *Size* text box and then click OK.
7. At the Header dialog box, type **Yearly Budget**.

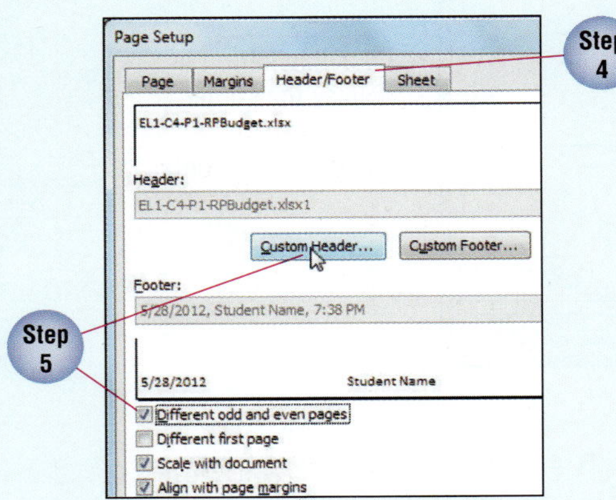

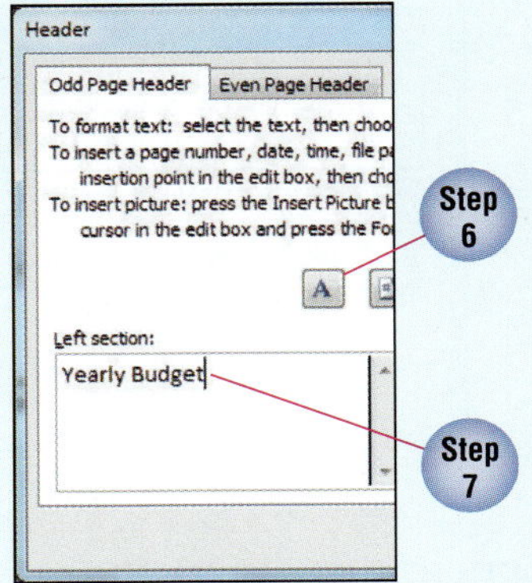

8. Click the Even Page Header tab, click in the left section box, and then click the Insert Page Number button.
9. Click in the right section box and then type **Yearly Budget**.
10. Select *Yearly Budget*, click the Format Text button, click *12* in the *Size* text box, and then click OK.
11. Click OK to close the Header dialog box.
12. Click the Custom Footer button and, at the Footer dialog box with the Odd Page Footer tab selected, delete the data in the left section box and select and delete the data in the right section box. (The footer should only contain your name.)
13. Select your name, click the Format Text button, click *12* in the *Size* text box, and then click OK.
14. Click the Even Page Footer tab, type your name in the center section box, select your name, and then change the font size to *12*.
15. Click OK to close the Footer dialog box and then click OK to close the Page Setup dialog box. (View the headers and footers in Print tab Backstage view and then return to the worksheet.)
16. Click the Page Setup group dialog box launcher in the Page Layout tab.
17. At the Page Setup dialog box, click the Header/Footer tab.
18. At the Page Setup dialog box with the Header/Footer tab selected, click the *Different odd and even pages* check box to remove the check mark.
19. Click the *Different first page* check box to insert a check mark and then click the Custom Header button.
20. At the Header dialog box with the Header tab selected, click the First Page Header tab.
21. Click in the right section box and then click the Insert Page Number button located above the section boxes.

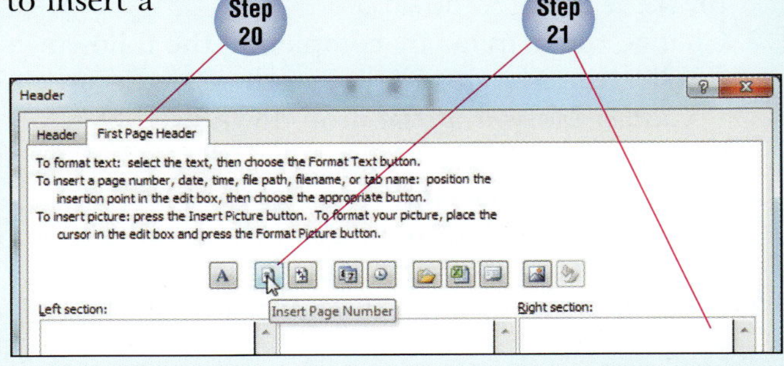

22. Click OK to close the Header dialog box and then click OK to close the Page Setup dialog box.
23. View the headers and footers in the Print tab Backstage view and then return to the worksheet.
24. Save **EL1-C4-P1-RPBudget.xlsx**.

Customizing Print Jobs

As you learned in this chapter, you can preview worksheets in the Print tab Backstage view. With options in the Settings category at the Print tab Backstage view, you can also specify what you want printed. By default, the active worksheet prints. You can change this by clicking the first gallery that displays in the Settings category. At the drop-down list that displays, you can specify that you want the entire workbook to print (this is useful when a workbook contains more than one worksheet) or print the selected cells. With the other galleries in the Settings category, you can specify if you want pages printed on one side or both sides (this is dependent on your printer) and collated. You can also specify the worksheet orientation, size, and margins as well as specify if you want the worksheet scaled to fit all columns or rows on one page.

With the *Pages* text boxes in the Settings category, you can specify the pages you want printed of your worksheet. For example, if you wanted to print pages 2 and 3 of your active worksheet, you would type 2 in the text box immediately right of the word *Pages* in the Settings category and then type 3 in the text box immediately right of the word *to*. You can also use the up- and down-pointing arrows to insert page numbers.

Project 1l **Printing Specific Pages of a Worksheet** Part 12 of 12

1. With **EL1-C4-P1-RPBudget.xlsx** open, print the first two pages of the worksheet by completing the following steps:
   a. Click the File tab and then click the Print tab.
   b. At the Print tab Backstage view, click in the text box immediately right of *Pages* located below the first gallery in the Settings category and then type 1.
   c. Click in the text box immediately right of *to* in the Settings category and then type 2.
   d. Click the Print button.

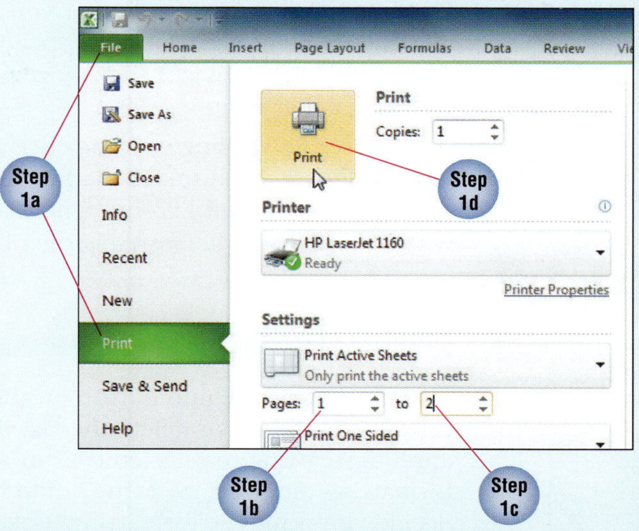

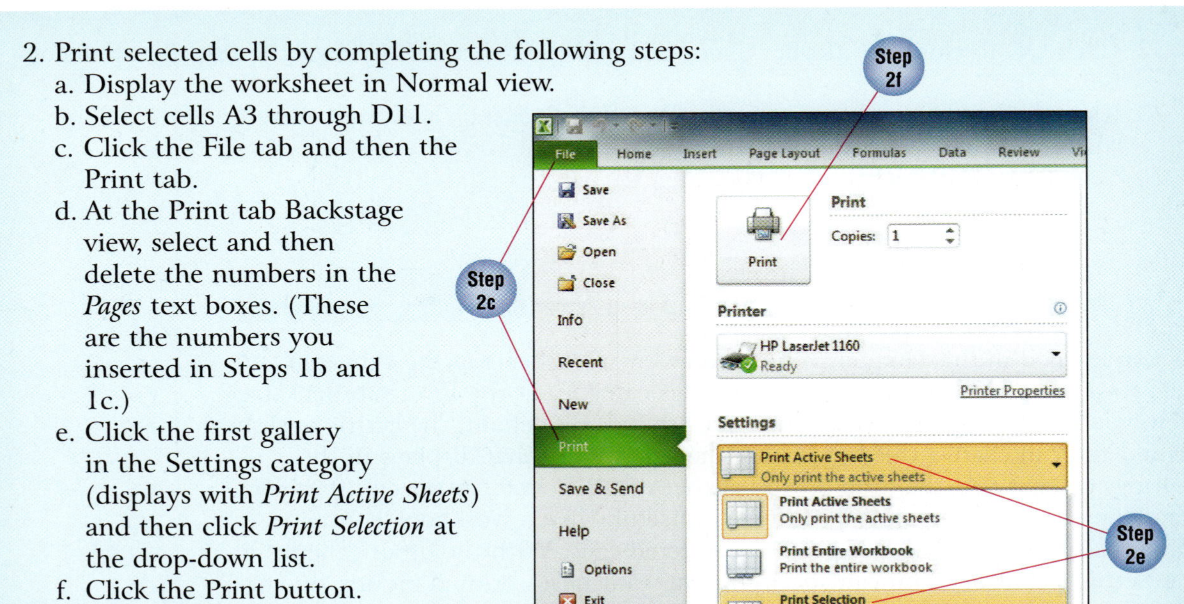

2. Print selected cells by completing the following steps:
   a. Display the worksheet in Normal view.
   b. Select cells A3 through D11.
   c. Click the File tab and then the Print tab.
   d. At the Print tab Backstage view, select and then delete the numbers in the *Pages* text boxes. (These are the numbers you inserted in Steps 1b and 1c.)
   e. Click the first gallery in the Settings category (displays with *Print Active Sheets*) and then click *Print Selection* at the drop-down list.
   f. Click the Print button.
3. Save and then close **EL1-C4-P1-RPBudget.xlsx**.

Project 2 Format a May Sales and Commissions Worksheet 3 Parts

You will format a sales commission worksheet by inserting a formula, completing a spelling check, and finding and replacing data and cell formatting.

Completing a Spelling Check

Quick Steps

Complete a Spelling Check
1. Click Review tab.
2. Click Spelling button.
3. Replace or ignore selected words.

Customize spell checking options at the Excel Options dialog box with *Proofing* selected.

Spelling

Excel includes a spelling checker you can use to check the spelling of text in a worksheet. Before checking the spelling in a worksheet, make the first cell active. The spell checker checks the worksheet from the active cell to the last cell in the worksheet that contains data.

To use the spelling checker, click the Review tab and then click the Spelling button. Figure 4.7 displays the Spelling dialog box. At this dialog box, you can click a button to tell Excel to ignore a word or you can replace a misspelled word with a word from the *Suggestions* list box.

Using Undo and Redo

Excel includes an Undo button on the Quick Access toolbar that will reverse certain commands or delete the last data typed in a cell. For example, if you apply formatting to selected cells in a worksheet and then decide you want the formatting removed, click the Undo button on the Quick Access toolbar. If you decide you want the formatting back again, click the Redo button on the Quick Access toolbar.

Figure 4.7 Excel Spelling Dialog Box

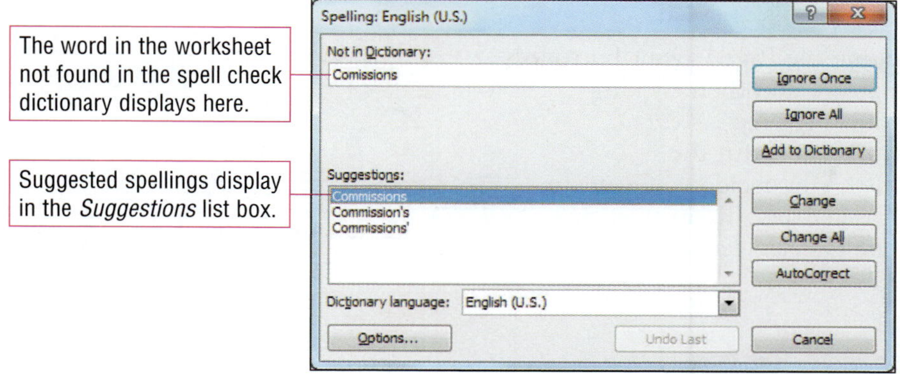

HINT

Ctrl + Z is the keyboard shortcut to undo a command.

Excel maintains actions in temporary memory. If you want to undo an action performed earlier, click the down-pointing arrow at the right side of the Undo button and a drop-down list displays containing the actions performed on the worksheet. Click the desired action at the drop-down list. Any actions preceding a chosen action are also undone. You can do the same with the Redo drop-down list. Multiple actions must be undone or redone in sequence.

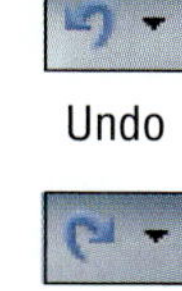

Project 2a Spell Checking and Formatting a Worksheet

Part 1 of 3

1. Open **MRSales.xlsx**.
2. Save the workbook with Save As and name it **EL1-C4-P2-MRSales**.
3. Complete a spelling check on the worksheet by completing the following steps:
   a. Make cell A1 active.
   b. Click the Review tab.
   c. Click the Spelling button in the Proofing group.
   d. Click the Change button as needed to correct misspelled words in the worksheet. (When the spell checker stops at proper names *Pirozzi* and *Yonemoto*, click the Ignore All button.)
   e. At the message telling you the spelling check is completed, click OK.

Step 3c Step 3b

File Home Insert Page Layout Formulas Data Review View
Spelling Research Thesaurus Translate New Comment Delete Previous Next Show/Hide Show All Comments Show Ink
Proofing Language Comments

4. Insert a formula and then copy the formula without the formatting by completing the following steps:
   a. Make cell G4 active and then insert a formula that multiplies the sale price by the commission percentage.
   b. Copy the formula down to cells G5 through G26.
   c. Some of the cells contain shading that you do not want removed, so click the Auto Fill Options button that displays at the bottom right of the selected cells and then click the *Fill Without Formatting* option at the drop-down list.
5. Apply the Accounting Number Format style with no decimal places to cell G4.

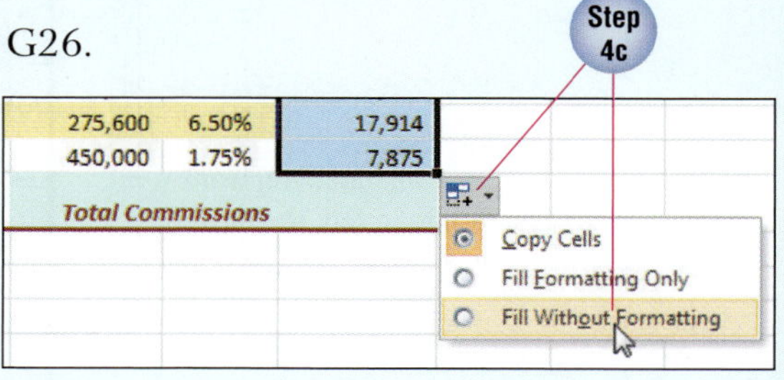

6. Make cell G27 active and then insert the sum of cells G4 through G26.
7. Apply a theme by clicking the Page Layout button, clicking the Themes button, and then clicking *Elemental* at the drop-down gallery.
8. After looking at the worksheet with the Elemental theme applied, you decide you want to return to the original formatting. To do this, click the Undo button on the Quick Access toolbar.

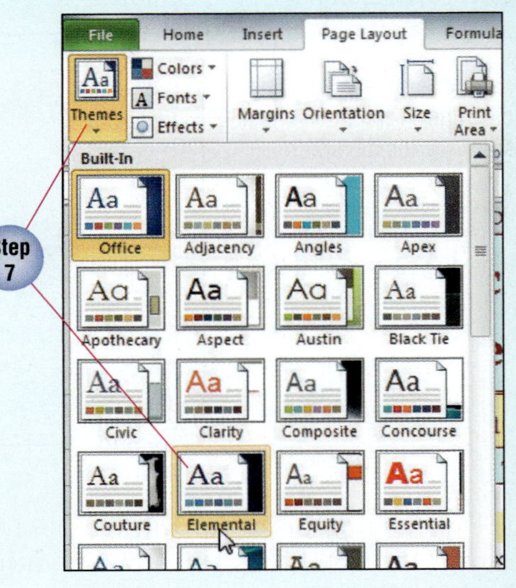

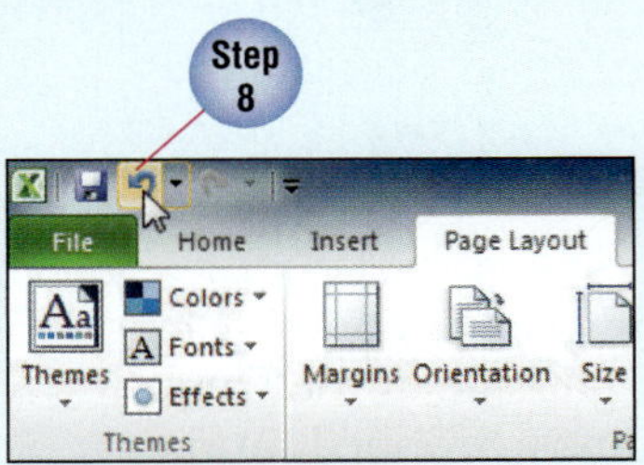

9. Save **EL1-C4-P2-MRSales.xlsx**.

Finding and Replacing Data and Cell Formatting in a Worksheet

Quick Steps

Find Data

1. Click Find & Select button.
2. Click *Find* at drop-down list.
3. Type data in *Find what* text box.
4. Click Find Next button.

Find & Select

Excel provides a Find feature you can use to look for specific data and either replace it with nothing or replace it with other data. This feature is particularly helpful in a large worksheet with data you want to find quickly. Excel also includes a find and replace feature. Use this to look for specific data in a worksheet and replace it with other data.

To find specific data in a worksheet, click the Find & Select button located in the Editing group in the Home tab and then click *Find* at the drop-down list. This displays the Find and Replace dialog box with the Find tab selected as shown in Figure 4.8. Type the data you want to find in the *Find what* text box and then click the Find Next button. Continue clicking the Find Next button to move to the next occurrence of the data. If the Find and Replace dialog box obstructs your view of the worksheet, use the mouse pointer on the title bar to drag the box to a different location.

Figure 4.8 Find and Replace Dialog Box with Find Tab Selected

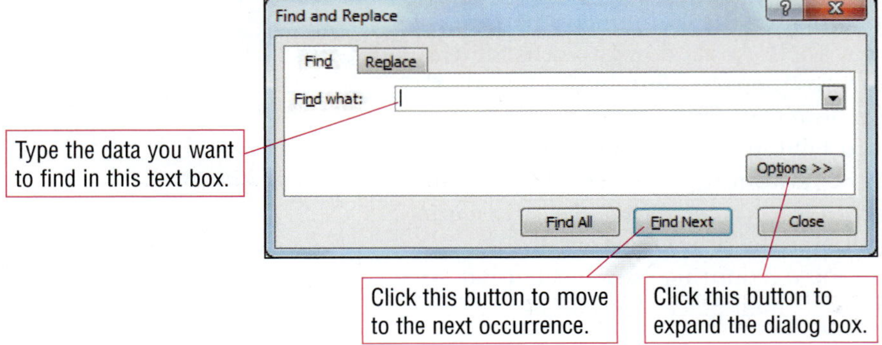

To find specific data in a worksheet and replace it with other data, click the Find & Select button in the Editing group in the Home tab and then click *Replace* at the drop-down list. This displays the Find and Replace dialog box with the Replace tab selected as shown in Figure 4.9. Enter the data for which you are looking in the *Find what* text box. Press the Tab key or click in the *Replace with* text box and then enter the data that is to replace the data in the *Find what* text box.

Click the Find Next button to tell Excel to find the next occurrence of the data. Click the Replace button to replace the data and find the next occurrence. If you know that you want all occurrences of the data in the *Find what* text box replaced with the data in the *Replace with* text box, click the Replace All button. Click the Close button to close the Replace dialog box.

Display additional find and replace options by clicking the Options button. This expands the dialog box as shown in Figure 4.10. By default, Excel will look for any data that contains the same characters as the data in the *Find what* text box, without concern for the characters before or after the entered data. For example, in Project 2b, you will be looking for sale prices of $450,000 and replacing with $475,000. If you do not specify to Excel that you want to find cells that contain only *450000,* Excel will stop at any cell containing *450000.* In this example, Excel would stop at a cell containing *$1,450,000* or a cell containing *$2,450,000.* To specify that the only data that should be contained in the cell is what is entered in the *Find what* text box, click the Options button to expand the dialog box and then insert a check mark in the *Match entire cell contents* check box.

Quick Steps

Find and Replace Data

1. Click Find & Select button.
2. Click *Replace* at drop-down list.
3. Type data in *Find what* text box.
4. Type data in *Replace with* text box.
5. Click Replace button or Replace All button.

Figure 4.9 Find and Replace Dialog Box with Replace Tab Selected

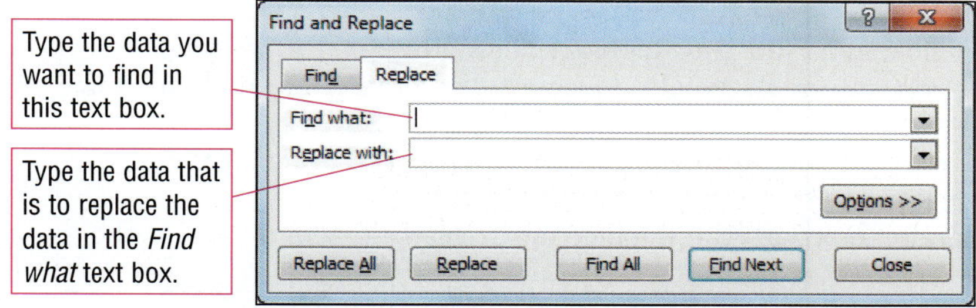
Type the data you want to find in this text box.
Type the data that is to replace the data in the *Find what* text box.
Find and Replace
Find
Replace
Find what:
Replace with:
Options >>
Replace All
Replace
Find All
Find Next
Close

Figure 4.10 Expanded Find and Replace Dialog Box

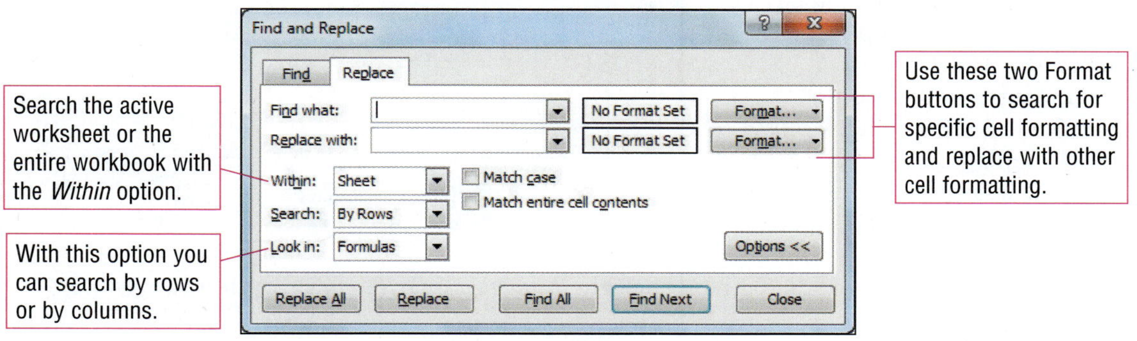
Search the active worksheet or the entire workbook with the *Within* option.
With this option you can search by rows or by columns.
Use these two Format buttons to search for specific cell formatting and replace with other cell formatting.
Find and Replace
Find
Replace
Find what:
Replace with:
No Format Set
No Format Set
Format...
Format...
Within:
Sheet
Search:
By Rows
Look in:
Formulas
Match case
Match entire cell contents
Options <<
Replace All
Replace
Find All
Find Next
Close

If the *Match case* option is active (contains a check mark), Excel will look for only that data that exactly matches the case of the data entered in the *Find what* text box. Remove the check mark from this check box if you do not want Excel to find exact case matches. Excel will search in the current worksheet. If you want Excel to search an entire workbook, change the *Within* option to *Workbook*. Excel, by default, searches by rows in a worksheet. You can change this to *By Columns* with the *Search* option.

Project 2b Finding and Replacing Data

Part 2 of 3

1. With **EL1-C4-P2-MRSales.xlsx** open, find all occurrences of *Land* in the worksheet and replace with *Acreage* by completing the following steps:
   a. Click the Find & Select button in the Editing group in the Home tab and then click *Replace* at the drop-down list.
   b. At the Find and Replace dialog box with the Replace tab selected, type **Land** in the *Find what* text box.
   c. Press the Tab key. (This moves the insertion point to the *Replace with* text box.)
   d. Type **Acreage**.
   e. Click the Replace All button.
   f. At the message telling you that four replacements were made, click OK.
   g. Click the Close button to close the Find and Replace dialog box.
2. Find all occurrences of *$450,000* and replace with *$475,000* by completing the following steps:
   a. Click the Find & Select button in the Editing group and then click *Replace* at the drop-down list.
   b. At the Find and Replace dialog box with the Replace tab selected, type **450000** in the *Find what* text box.
   c. Press the Tab key.
   d. Type **475000**.
   e. Click the Options button to display additional options. (If additional options already display, skip this step.)
   f. Click the *Match entire cell contents* option to insert a check mark in the check box.
   g. Click Replace All.
   h. At the message telling you that two replacements were made, click OK.
   i. At the Find and Replace dialog box, click the *Match entire cell contents* option to remove the check mark.
   j. Click the Close button to close the Find and Replace dialog box.
3. Save **EL1-C4-P2-MRSales.xlsx**.

Use the Format buttons at the expanded Find and Replace dialog box (see Figure 4.10) to search for specific cell formatting and replace with other formatting. Click the down-pointing arrow at the right side of the Format button and a drop-down list displays. Click the *Format* option and the Find Format dialog box displays with the Number, Alignment, Font, Border, Fill, and Protection tabs. Specify formatting at this dialog box. Click the *Choose Format From Cell* option and the mouse pointer displays with a pointer tool attached. Click in the cell containing the desired formatting and the formatting displays in the *Preview* box to the left of the Format button. Click the *Clear Find Format* option and any formatting in the *Preview* box is removed.

Project 2c **Finding and Replacing Cell Formatting** Part 3 of 3

1. With **EL1-C4-P2-MRSales.xlsx** open, search for light turquoise fill color and replace with a purple fill color by completing the following steps:
   a. Click the Find & Select button in the Editing group in the Home tab and then click *Replace* at the drop-down list.
   b. At the Find and Replace dialog box with the Replace tab selected, make sure the dialog box is expanded. (If not, click the Options button.)
   c. Select and then delete any text that displays in the *Find what* text box.
   d. Select and then delete any text that displays in the *Replace with* text box.
   e. Make sure the boxes immediately preceding the two Format buttons display with the text *No Format Set*. (If not, click the down-pointing arrow at the right of the Format button, and then click the *Clear Find Format* option at the drop-down list. Do this for each Format button.)
   f. Click the top Format button.
   g. At the Find Format dialog box, click the Fill tab.
   h. Click the More Colors button.
   i. At the Colors dialog box with the Standard tab selected, click the light turquoise color shown at the right.
   j. Click OK to close the Colors dialog box.
   k. Click OK to close the Find Format dialog box.
   l. Click the bottom Format button.
   m. At the Replace Format dialog box with the Fill tab selected, click the purple color shown at the right.
   n. Click OK to close the dialog box.
   o. At the Find and Replace dialog box, click the Replace All button.
   p. At the message telling you that 10 replacements were made, click OK.

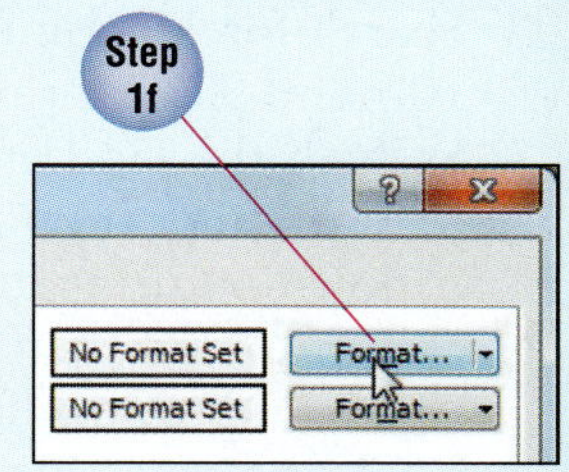

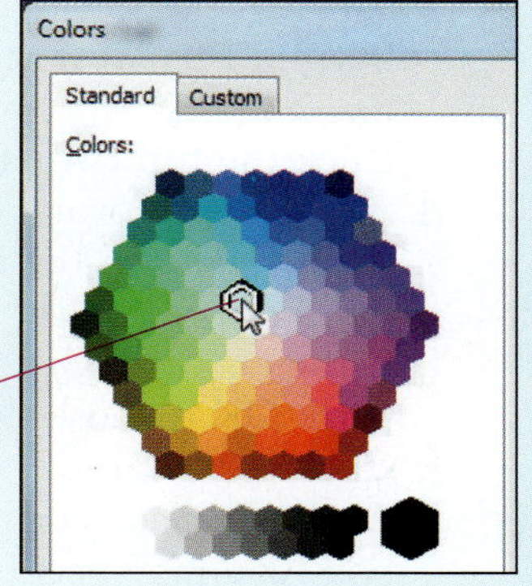

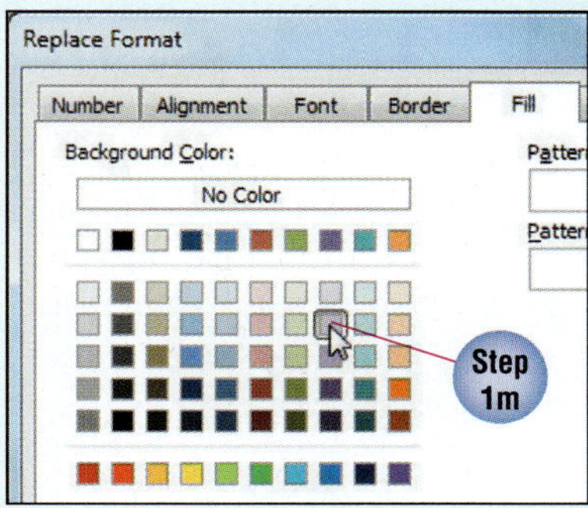

2. Search for yellow fill color and replace with a green fill color by completing the following steps:
   a. At the Find and Replace dialog box, click the top Format button.
   b. At the Find Format dialog box with the Fill tab selected, click the More Colors button.

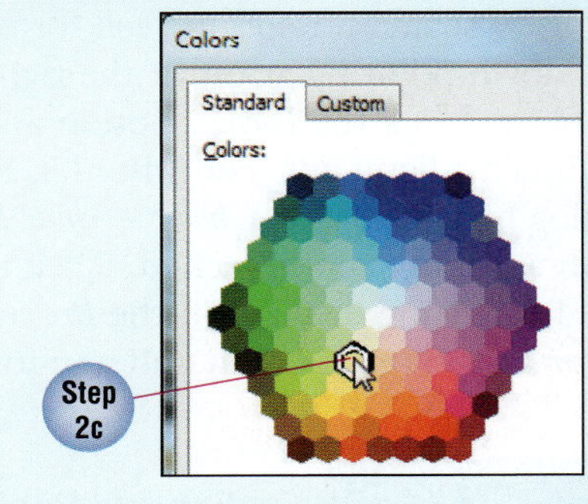

c. At the Colors dialog box with the Standard tab selected, click the yellow color as shown at the right.
d. Click OK to close the Colors dialog box.
e. Click OK to close the Find Format dialog box.
f. Click the bottom Format button.
g. At the Replace Format dialog box with the Fill tab selected, click the green color shown below and to the right.
h. Click OK to close the dialog box.
i. At the Find and Replace dialog box, click the Replace All button.
j. At the message telling you that 78 replacements were made, click OK.

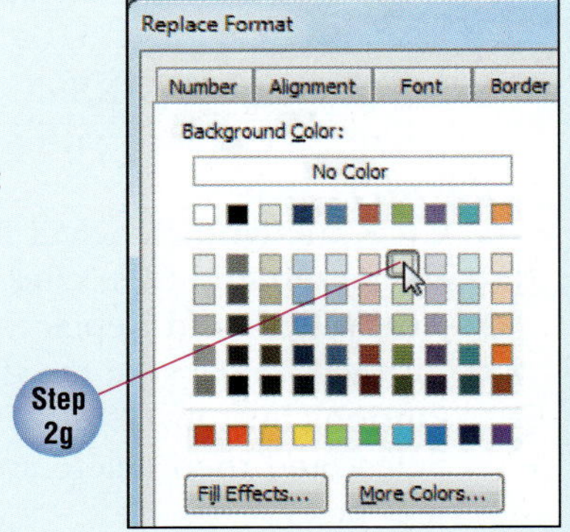

3. Search for 11-point Calibri formatting and replace with 10-point Arial formatting by completing the following steps:
   a. With the Find and Replace dialog box open, clear formatting from the top Format button by clicking the down-pointing arrow at the right side of the top Format button and then clicking the *Clear Find Format* option at the drop-down list.
   b. Clear formatting from the bottom Format button by clicking the down-pointing arrow at the right side of the bottom Format button and then clicking *Clear Replace Format.*

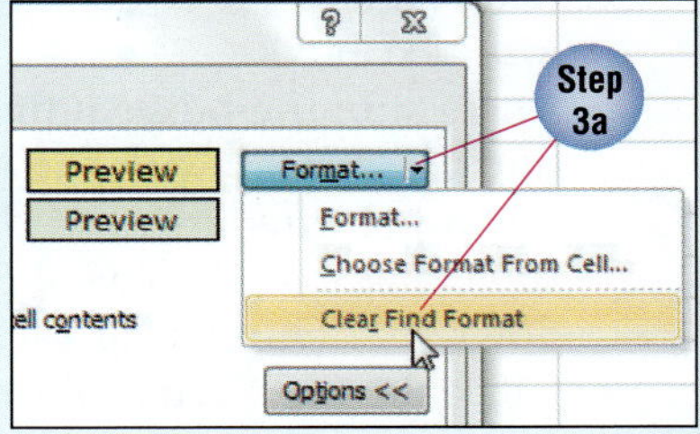

   c. Click the top Format button.
   d. At the Find Format dialog box, click the Font tab.
   e. Click *Calibri* in the *Font* list box. (You may need to scroll down the list to display this typeface.)
   f. Click *11* in the *Size* text box.
   g. Click OK to close the dialog box.
   h. Click the bottom Format button.
   i. At the Replace Format dialog box with the Font tab selected, click *Arial* in the *Font* list box (you may need to scroll down the list to display this typeface).
   j. Click *10* in the *Size* list box.
   k. Click OK to close the dialog box.
   l. At the Find and Replace dialog box, click the Replace All button.
   m. At the message telling you that 174 replacements were made, click OK.
   n. At the Find and Replace dialog box, remove formatting from both Format buttons.
   o. Click the Close button to close the Find and Replace dialog box.
4. Save, print, and then close **EL1-C4-P2-MRSales.xlsx**.

Project 3 Format a Billing Worksheet 4 Parts

You will insert a formula in a weekly billing worksheet and then sort and filter specific data in the worksheet.

Sorting Data

Excel is primarily a spreadsheet program, but it also includes some basic database functions. With a database program, you can alphabetize information or arrange numbers numerically. Data can be sorted by columns in a worksheet. Sort data in a worksheet with the Sort & Filter button in the Editing group in the Home tab.

To sort data in a worksheet, select the cells containing data you want to sort, click the Sort & Filter button in the Editing group and then click the option representing the desired sort. The sort option names vary depending on the data in selected cells. For example, if the first column of selected cells contains text, the sort options in the drop-down list display as *Sort A to Z* and *Sort Z to A*. If the selected cells contain dates, the sort options in the drop-down list display as *Sort Oldest to Newest* and *Sort Newest to Oldest* and if the cells contain numbers or values, the sort options display as *Sort Smallest to Largest* and *Sort Largest to Smallest*. If you select more than one column in a worksheet, Excel will sort the data in the first selected column.

Quick Steps

Sort Data
1. Select cells.
2. Click Sort & Filter button.
3. Click desired sort option at drop-down list.

If you are not satisfied with the results of the sort, immediately click the Undo button.

Sort & Filter

Project 3a **Sorting Data** Part 1 of 4

1. Open **APTBilling.xlsx** and save it with Save As and name it **EL1-C4-P3-APTBilling**.
2. Insert a formula in cell F4 that multiplies the rate by the hours. Copy the formula down to cells F5 through F29.
3. Sort the data in the first column in descending order by completing the following steps:
   a. Make cell A4 active.
   b. Click the Sort & Filter button in the Editing group in the Home tab.
   c. Click the *Sort Largest to Smallest* option at the drop-down list.
4. Sort in ascending order by clicking the Sort & Filter button and then clicking *Sort Smallest to Largest* at the drop-down list.
5. Save **EL1-C4-P3-APTBilling.xlsx**.

Step 3b

Step 3c

Completing a Custom Sort

If you want to sort data in a column other than the first column, use the Sort dialog box. If you select just one column in a worksheet, click the Sort & Filter button, and then click the desired sort option, only the data in that column is sorted. If this data is related to data to the left or right of the data in the sorted column, that relationship is broken. For example, if you sort cells C4 through C29 in EL1-C4-P3-APTBilling.xlsx, the client number, treatment, hours, and total would no longer match the date.

Use the Sort dialog box to sort data and maintain the relationship of all cells. To sort using the Sort dialog box, select the cells you want sorted, click the Sort & Filter button, and then click *Custom Sort*. This displays the Sort dialog box shown in Figure 4.11.

The data displayed in the *Sort by* option box will vary depending on what you have selected. Generally, the data that displays is the title of the first column

Quick Steps

Complete Custom Sort
1. Select cells.
2. Click Sort & Filter button.
3. Click *Custom Sort* at drop-down list.
4. Specify options at Sort dialog box.
5. Click OK.

Figure 4.11 Sort Dialog Box

Click this down-pointing arrow to specify if you are sorting on values, cell color, font color, or cell icon.

Click this button to specify a second column for sorting.

Click this down-pointing arrow and then specify the sort order.

Click this down-pointing arrow and then click the desired column in the drop-down list.

Sort

Add Level | Delete Level | Copy Level | Options... | My data has headers

Column: Sort by: Client # | Sort On: Values | Order: Smallest to Largest

OK | Cancel

of selected cells. If the selected cells do not have a title, the data may display as *Column A*. Use this option to specify what column you want sorted. Using the Sort dialog box to sort data in a column maintains the relationship of the data.

Project 3b Sorting Data Using the Sort Dialog Box

Part 2 of 4

1. With **EL1-C4-P3-APTBilling.xlsx** open, sort the rates in cells E4 through E29 in descending order and maintain the relationship to the other data by completing the following steps:
   a. Select cells A3 through F29.
   b. Click the Sort & Filter button and then click *Custom Sort*.
   c. At the Sort dialog box, click the down-pointing arrow at the right of the *Sort by* option box, and then click *Rate* at the drop-down list.
   d. Click the down-pointing arrow at the right of the *Order* option box and then click *Largest to Smallest* at the drop-down list.
   e. Click OK to close the Sort dialog box.
   f. Deselect the cells.

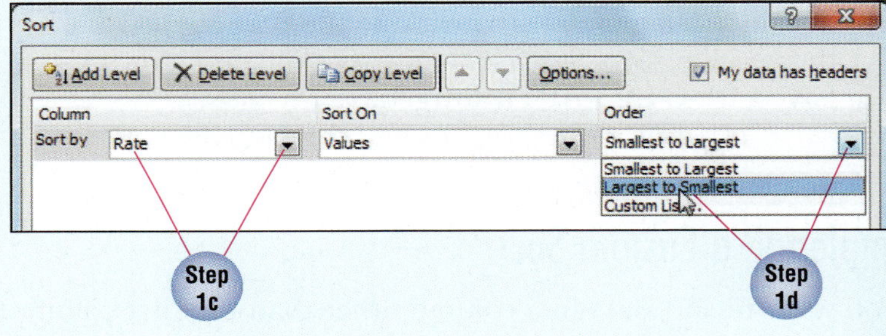

2. Sort the dates in ascending order (oldest to newest) by completing steps similar to those in Step 1.
3. Save and then print **EL1-C4-P3-APTBilling.xlsx**.

Sorting More Than One Column

When sorting data in cells, you can sort in more than one column. For example, in Project 3c you will be sorting the date from oldest to newest and then sorting client numbers from lowest to highest. In this sort, the dates are sorted first and then client numbers are sorted in ascending order within the same date.

To sort in more than one column, select all columns in the worksheet that need to remain relative and then display the Sort dialog box. At the Sort dialog box, specify the first column you want sorted in the *Sort by* option box, click the *Add Level* button, and then specify the second column in the first *Then by* option box. In Excel, you can sort on multiple columns. Add additional *Then by* option boxes by clicking the *Add Level* button.

Project 3c **Sorting Data in Two Columns** Part 3 of 4

1. With **EL1-C4-P3-APTBilling.xlsx** open, select cells A3 through F29.
2. Click the Sort & Filter button and then click *Custom Sort*.
3. At the Sort dialog box, click the down-pointing arrow at the right side of the *Sort by* option box, and then click *Date* in the drop-down list. (Skip this step if Date already displays in the Sort by option box.)
4. Make sure *Oldest to Newest* displays in the *Order* option box.
5. Click the *Add Level* button.
6. Click the down-pointing arrow at the right of the *Then by* option box and then click *Client #* in the drop-down list.
7. Click OK to close the dialog box.
8. Deselect the cells.
9. Save and then print **EL1-C4-P3-APTBilling.xlsx**.

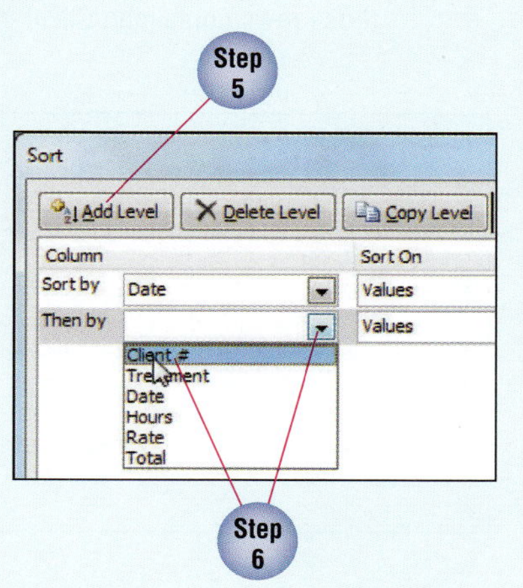

Filtering Data

You can place a restriction, called a *filter*, on data in a worksheet to temporarily isolate specific data. To turn on filtering, make a cell containing data active, click the Sort & Filter button in the Editing group in the Home tab, and then click *Filter* at the drop-down list. This turns on filtering and causes a filter arrow to appear in each column label in the worksheet as shown in Figure 4.12. You do not need to select before turning on filtering because Excel automatically searches for column labels in a worksheet.

Quick Steps

Filter a List

1. Select cells.
2. Click Sort & Filter button.
3. Click *Filter* at drop-down list.
4. Click down-pointing arrow of heading to filter.
5. Click desired option at drop-down list.

To filter data in a worksheet, click the filter arrow in the heading you want to filter. This causes a drop-down list to display with options to filter all records, create a custom filter, or select an entry that appears in one or more of the cells in the column. When you filter data, the filter arrow changes to a funnel icon. The funnel icon indicates that rows in the worksheet have been filtered. To turn off filtering, click the Sort & Filter button and then click *Filter*.

If a column contains numbers, click the filter arrow, point to *Number Filters*, and a side menu displays with options for filtering numbers. For example, you can filter numbers that are equal to, greater than, or less than a number you specify; filter the top ten numbers; and filter numbers that are above or below a specified number.

Figure 4.12 Filtering Data

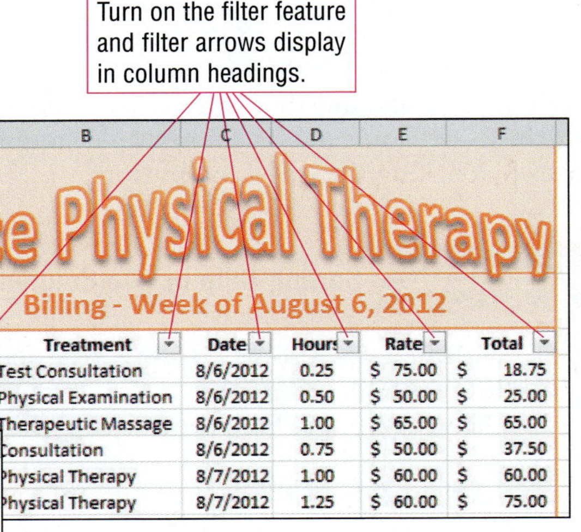

Click the filter in the Client # heading, click the *(Select All)* check box to remove the check mark, and then click the *3102* check box to display only those rows containing Client # 3102.

Ace Physical Therapy

Billing - Week of August 6, 2012

	Client #	Treatment	Date	Hours	Rate	Total
6	3102	Therapeutic Massage	8/6/2012	1.00	$ 65.00	$ 65.00
7	3102	Consultation	8/6/2012	0.75	$ 50.00	$ 37.50
13	3102	Therapeutic Massage	8/8/2012	1.00	$ 65.00	$ 65.00
30						

Project 3d Filtering Data

Part 4 of 4

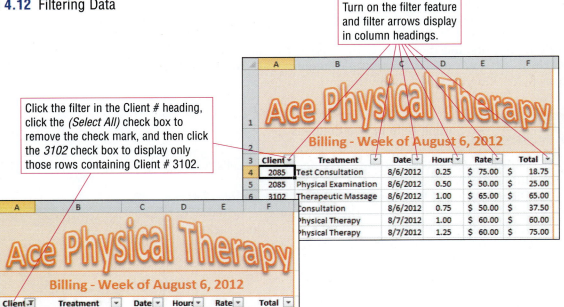

1. With **EL1-C4-P3-APTBilling.xlsx** open, click in cell A4.
2. Turn on filtering by clicking the Sort & Filter button in the Editing group in the Home tab and then clicking *Filter* at the drop-down list.
3. Filter rows for client number 3102 by completing the following steps:
   a. Click the filter arrow in the *Client #* heading.
   b. Click the *(Select All)* check box to remove the check mark.
   c. Scroll down the list box and then click *3102* to insert a check mark in the check box.
   d. Click OK.

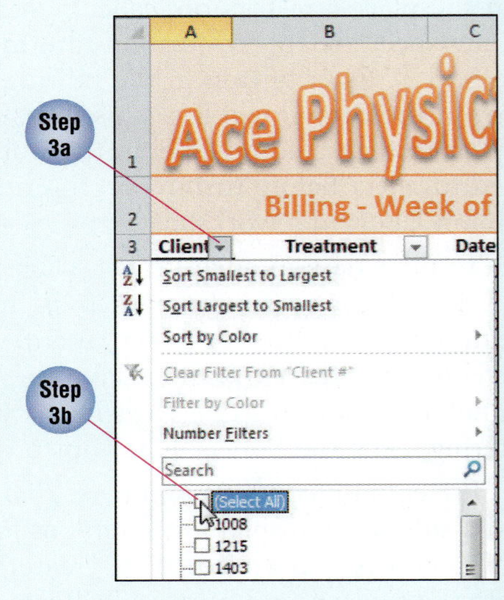

4. Redisplay all rows containing data by completing the following steps:
   a. Click the funnel icon in the *Client #* heading.
   b. Click the *(Select All)* check box to insert a check mark. (This also inserts a check mark for all items in the list.)
   c. Click OK.
5. Filter a list of clients receiving physical therapy by completing the following steps:
   a. Click the filter arrow in the *Treatment* heading.
   b. Click the *(Select All)* check box.
   c. Click the *Physical Therapy* check box.
   d. Click OK.

6. Redisplay all rows containing data by completing the following steps:
   a. Click the funnel icon in the *Treatment* heading.
   b. Click the *(Select All)* check box to insert a check mark. (This also inserts a check mark for all items in the list.)
   c. Click OK.
7. Display the top two highest rates by completing the following steps:
   a. Click the filter arrow in the *Rate* heading.
   b. Point to *Number Filters* and then click *Top 10* at the side menu.
   c. At the Top 10 AutoFilter dialog box, select the *10* that displays in the middle text box and then type **2**.
   d. Click OK to close the dialog box.

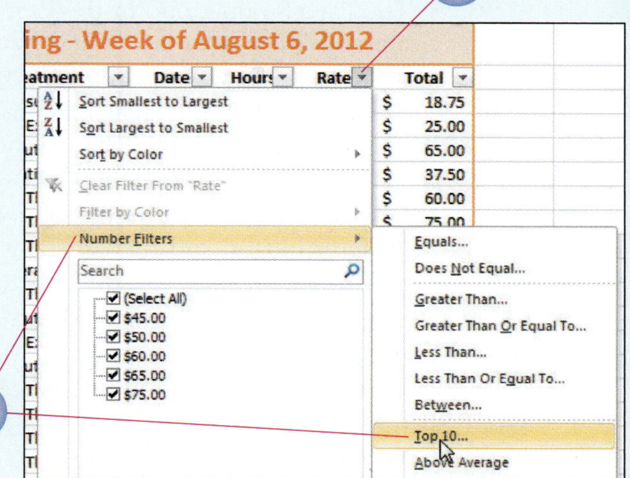

8. Redisplay all rows containing data by completing the following steps:
   a. Click the funnel icon in the *Rate* heading.
   b. Click the *(Select All)* check box to insert a check mark. (This also inserts a check mark for all items in the list.)
   c. Click OK.

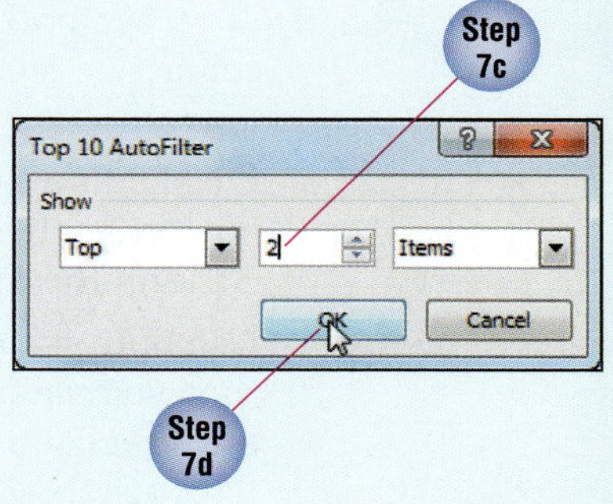

9. Display totals greater than $60 by completing the following steps:
   a. Click the filter arrow in the *Total* heading.
   b. Point to *Number Filters* and then click *Greater Than*.
   c. At the Custom AutoFilter dialog box, type **60** and then click OK.
   d. Print the worksheet by clicking the File tab, clicking the Print tab, and then clicking the Print button.

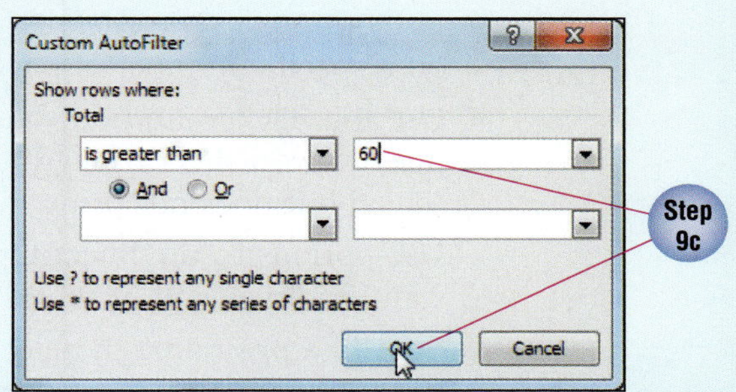

10. Turn off the filtering feature by clicking the Sort & Filter button and then clicking *Filter* at the drop-down list.
11. Save, print, and then close **EL1-C4-P3-APTBilling.xlsx**.

Chapter Summary

- The Page Setup group in the Page Layout tab contains buttons for changing margins, page orientation and size, and buttons for establishing a print area, inserting a page break, applying a picture background, and printing titles.
- The default left and right margins are 0.7 inch and the default top and bottom margins are 0.75 inch. Change these default margins with the Margins button in the Page Setup group in the Page Layout tab.
- Display the Page Setup dialog box with the Margins tab selected by clicking the Margins button and then clicking *Custom Margins* at the drop-down list.
- Center a worksheet on the page with the *Horizontally* and *Vertically* options at the Page Setup dialog box with the Margins tab selected.
- Click the Orientation button in the Page Setup group in the Page Layout tab to display the two orientation choices — *Portrait* and *Landscape*.
- Insert a page break by selecting the column or row, clicking the Breaks button in the Page Setup group in the Page Layout tab, and then clicking *Insert Page Break* at the drop-down list.
- To insert both a horizontal and vertical page break at the same time, make a cell active, click the Breaks button, and then click *Insert Page Break* at the drop-down list.
- Display a worksheet in page break preview by clicking the Page Break Preview button in the view area on the Status bar or clicking the View tab and then clicking the Page Break Preview button.
- Use options at the Page Setup dialog box with the Sheet tab selected to specify that you want column or row titles to print on each page. Display this dialog box by clicking the Print Titles button in the Page Setup group in the Page Layout tab.
- Use options in the Scale to Fit group in the Page Layout tab to scale data to fit on a specific number of pages.
- Use the Background button in the Page Setup group in the Page Layout tab to insert a worksheet background picture. A background picture displays on the screen but does not print.
- Use options in the Sheet Options group in the Page Layout tab to specify if you want gridlines and headings to view and/or print.
- Specify a print area by selecting the desired cells, clicking the Print Area button in the Page Setup group in the Page Layout tab, and then clicking *Set Print Area* at the drop-down list. Add another print area by selecting the desired cells, clicking the Print Area button, and then clicking *Add to Print Area* at the drop-down list.
- Create a header and/or footer with the Header & Footer button in the Text group in the Insert tab, in Page Layout view, or with options at the Page Setup dialog box with the Header/Footer tab selected.
- Customize print jobs with options at the Print tab Backstage view.
- To check spelling in a worksheet, click the Review tab and then click the Spelling button.

- Click the Undo button on the Quick Access toolbar to reverse the most recent action and click the Redo button to redo a previously reversed action.
- Use options at the Find and Replace dialog box with the Find tab selected to find specific data and/or formatting in a worksheet.
- Use options at the Find and Replace dialog box with the Replace tab selected to find specific data and/or formatting and replace with other data and/or formatting.
- Sort data in a worksheet with options from the Sort & Filter button in the Editing group in the Home tab.
- Create a custom sort with options at the Sort dialog box. Display this dialog box by clicking the Sort & Filter button and then clicking *Custom Sort* at the drop-down list.
- Use the filter feature to temporarily isolate specific data. Turn on the filter feature by clicking the Sort & Filter button in the Editing group in the Home tab and then clicking *Filter* at the drop-down list. This inserts filter arrows in each column label. Click a filter arrow and then use options at the drop-down list that displays to specify the filter data.

Commands Review

FEATURE	RIBBON TAB, GROUP	BUTTON, OPTION	KEYBOARD SHORTCUT
Margins	Page Layout, Page Setup		
Page Setup dialog box with Margins tab selected	Page Layout, Page Setup	, Custom Margins	
Orientation	Page Layout, Page Setup		
Size	Page Layout, Page Setup		
Insert page break	Page Layout, Page Setup	, Insert Page Break	
Remove page break	Page Layout, Page Setup	, Remove Page Break	
Page Break Preview	View, Workbook Views		
Page Setup dialog box with Sheet tab selected	Page Layout, Page Setup		
Scale width	Page Layout, Scale to Fit		
Scale height	Page Layout, Scale to Fit		
Scale	Page Layout, Scale to Fit		
Background picture	Page Layout, Page Setup		

FEATURE	RIBBON TAB, GROUP	BUTTON, OPTION	KEYBOARD SHORTCUT
Print Area	Page Layout, Page Setup		
Header and footer	Insert, Text		
Page Layout view	View, Workbook Views		
Spelling	Review, Proofing		F7
Find and Replace dialog box with Find tab selected	Home, Editing	, Find	Ctrl + F
Find and Replace dialog box with Replace tab selected	Home, Editing	, Replace	Ctrl + H
Sort data	Home, Editing		
Filter data	Home, Editing		

Concepts Check Test Your Knowledge

Completion: In the space provided at the right, indicate the correct term, symbol, or command.

1. This is the default left and right margin measurement. ____________________
2. This is the default top and bottom margin measurement. ____________________
3. The Margins button is located in this tab. ____________________
4. By default, a worksheet prints in this orientation on a page. ____________________
5. Click the Print Titles button in the Page Setup group in the Page Layout tab and the Page Setup dialog box displays with this tab selected. ____________________
6. Use options in this group in the Page Layout tab to adjust the printed output by a percentage to fit the number of pages specified. ____________________
7. Use this button in the Page Setup group in the Page Layout tab to select and print specific areas in a worksheet. ____________________
8. Click the Header & Footer button in the Text group in the Insert tab and the worksheet displays in this view. ____________________

9. This tab contains options for formatting and customizing a header and/or footer. ____________________

10. Click this tab to display the Spelling button. ____________________

11. The Undo and Redo buttons are located on this toolbar. ____________________

12. Click this button in the Find and Replace dialog box to expand the dialog box. ____________________

13. Use these two buttons at the expanded Find and Replace dialog box to search for specific cell formatting and replace with other formatting. ____________________

14. Use this button in the Editing group in the Home tab to sort data in a worksheet. ____________________

15. Use this feature to temporarily isolate specific data in a worksheet. ____________________

Skills Check Assess Your Performance

Assessment

1 FORMAT A DATA ANALYSIS WORKSHEET

1. Open **DISemiSales.xlsx**.
2. Save the workbook with Save As and name it **EL1-C4-A1-DISemiSales**.
3. Make the following changes to the worksheet:
   a. Insert a formula in cell H4 that averages the amounts in cells B4 through G4.
   b. Copy the formula in cell H4 down to cells H5 through H9.
   c. Insert a formula in cell B10 that adds the amounts in cells B4 through B9.
   d. Copy the formula in cell B10 over to cells C10 through H10. (Click the Auto Fill Options button and then click *Fill Without Formatting* at the drop-down list.)
   e. Apply the Accounting Number Format style to cell H4.
   f. Change the orientation of the worksheet to landscape.
   g. Change the top margin to 3 inches and the left margin to 1.5 inches.
4. Save and then print **EL1-C4-A1-DISemiSales.xlsx**.
5. Make the following changes to the worksheet:
   a. Change the orientation back to portrait.
   b. Change the top margin to 1 inch and the left margin to 0.7 inch.
   c. Horizontally and vertically center the worksheet on the page.
   d. Scale the worksheet so it fits on one page.
6. Save, print, and then close **EL1-C4-A1-DISemiSales.xlsx**.

Assessment

2 FORMAT A TEST RESULTS WORKSHEET

1. Open **CMTests.xlsx**.
2. Save the workbook with Save As and name it **EL1-C4-A2-CMTests**.
3. Make the following changes to the worksheet.
   a. Insert a formula in cell N4 that averages the test scores in cells B4 through M4.
   b. Copy the formula in cell N4 down to cells N5 through N21.
   c. Type Average in cell A22.
   d. Insert a formula in cell B22 that averages the test scores in cells B4 through B21.
   e. Copy the formula in cell B22 across to cells C22 through N22.
   f. Insert a page break between columns G and H.
4. View the worksheet in Page Break Preview.
5. Change back to the Normal view.
6. Specify that the column titles (A3 through A22) are to print on each page.
7. Create a header that prints the page number at the right side of the page.
8. Create a footer that prints your name at the left side of the page and the workbook file name at the right side of the page.
9. Save and then print the worksheet.
10. Set a print area for cells N3 through N22 and then print the cells.
11. Clear the print area.
12. Save and then close **EL1-C4-A2-CMTests.xlsx**.

Assessment

3 FORMAT AN EQUIPMENT RENTAL WORKSHEET

1. Open **HERInvoices.xlsx**.
2. Save the workbook with Save As and name it **EL1-C4-A3-HERInvoices**.
3. Insert a formula in cell H3 that multiplies the rate in cell G3 by the hours in cell F3. Copy the formula in cell H3 down to cells H4 through H16.
4. Insert a formula in cell H17 that sums the amounts in cells H3 through H16.
5. Complete the following find and replaces:
   a. Find all occurrences of cells containing *75* and replace with *90*.
   b. Find all occurrences of cells containing *55* and replace with *60*.
   c. Find all occurrences of *Barrier Concrete* and replace with *Lee Sand and Gravel*.
   d. Find all occurrences of 11-point Calibri and replace with 10-point Cambria.
   e. After completing the find and replace, clear all formatting from the Format buttons.
6. Insert a header that prints the date at the left side of the page and the time at the right side of the page.
7. Insert a footer that prints your name at the left side of the page and the workbook file name at the right side of the page.
8. Print the worksheet horizontally and vertically centered on the page.
9. Save and then close **EL1-C4-A3-HERInvoices.xlsx**.

Assessment 4

FORMAT AN INVOICES WORKSHEET

1. Open **RPInvoices.xlsx**.
2. Save the workbook with Save As and name it **EL1-C4-A4-RPInvoices**.
3. Insert a formula in G4 that multiplies the amount in E4 with the percentage in F4 and then adds the product to cell E4. (If you write the formula correctly, the result in G4 will display as *$488.25*.)
4. Copy the formula in cell G4 down to cells G5 through G17, click the Auto Fill Options button, and then click the *Fill Without Formatting* option.
5. Complete a spelling check on the worksheet.
6. Find all occurrences of *Picture* and replace with *Portrait*. (Do not type a space after *Picture* or *Portrait* because you want to find occurrences that end with an "s." Make sure the *Match entire cell contents* check box does not contain a check mark.)
7. Sort the records by invoice number in ascending order (smallest to largest).
8. Complete a new sort that sorts the records by client number in ascending order (A to Z).
9. Complete a new sort that sorts the date in ascending order (oldest to newest).
10. Insert a footer in the worksheet that prints your name at the left side of the page and the current date at the right side of the page.
11. Center the worksheet horizontally and vertically on the page.
12. Save and then print **EL1-C4-A4-RPInvoices.xlsx**.
13. Select cells A3 through G3 and then turn on the filter feature and complete the following filters:
    a. Filter and then print a list of rows containing client number 11-279 and then clear the filter.
    b. Filter and then print a list of rows containing the top three highest amounts due and then clear the filter.
    c. Filter and then print a list of rows containing amounts due that are less than $500 and then clear the filter.
14. Save and then close **EL1-C4-A4-RPInvoices.xlsx**.

Assessment 5

CREATE A WORKSHEET CONTAINING KEYBOARD SHORTCUTS

1. Use Excel's Help feature and learn about keyboard shortcuts in Excel. After reading the information presented, create a worksheet with the following feature:
    - Create a title for the worksheet.
    - Include at least 10 keyboard shortcuts along with an explanation of the keyboard shortcut.
    - Set the data in cells in a typeface other than Calibri and change the data color.
    - Add borders to the cells. (You determine the border style.)
    - Add a color shading to cells. (You determine the color—make it complementary to the data color.)
    - Create a header that prints the date at the right margin and create a footer that prints your name at the left margin and the file name at the right margin.
2. Save the workbook and name it **EL1-C4-A5-KeyboardShortcuts**.
3. Print and then close **EL1-C4-A5-KeyboardShortcuts.xlsx**.

Visual Benchmark Demonstrate Your Proficiency

CREATE AND FORMAT AN EXPENSE WORKSHEET

1. At a blank workbook, type the data in the cells indicated in Figure 4.13 but **do not** type the data in the following cells—instead insert the formulas as indicated (the results of your formulas should match the results you see in the figure):
   - Cells N3 through N8: Insert a formula that sums the monthly expenses for the year.
   - Cells B9 through N9: Insert a formula that sums the monthly expenses for each month and the entire year.
2. Change the left and right margins to *0.45* and change the top margin to *1.5*.
3. Apply formatting so your worksheet looks similar to the worksheet shown in Figure 4.13. (Set the heading in 26-point Cambria and set the remaining data in 10-point Cambria. Apply bold formatting as shown in the figure.)
4. Save the workbook and name it **EL1-C4-VB-HERExpenses**.
5. Look at the printing of the worksheet shown in Figure 4.14 and then make the following changes:
   - Insert a page break between columns G and H.
   - Insert the headers and footer as shown.
   - Specify that the column titles print on the second page as shown in Figure 4.14.
6. Save and then print **EL1-C4-VB-HERExpenses.xlsx**. (Your worksheet should print on two pages and appear as shown in Figure 4.14.)
7. Close **EL1-C4-VB-HERExpenses.xlsx**.

Figure 4.13 Visual Benchmark Data

	A	B	C	D	E	F	G	H	I	J	K	L	M	N
1	**Hilltop Equipment Rental**													
2	**Expenses**	**January**	**February**	**March**	**April**	**May**	**June**	**July**	**August**	**September**	**October**	**November**	**December**	***Total***
3	Lease	$ 3,250	$ 3,250	$ 3,250	$ 3,250	$ 3,250	$ 3,250	$ 3,250	$ 3,250	$ 3,250	$ 3,250	$ 3,250	$ 3,250	$ 39,000
4	Utilities	3,209	2,994	2,987	2,500	2,057	1,988	1,845	1,555	1,890	2,451	2,899	3,005	29,380
5	Payroll	10,545	9,533	11,542	10,548	11,499	12,675	13,503	13,258	12,475	10,548	10,122	9,359	135,607
6	Insurance	895	895	895	895	895	895	895	895	895	895	895	895	10,740
7	Maintenance	2,439	1,856	2,455	5,410	3,498	3,110	2,479	3,100	1,870	6,105	4,220	3,544	40,086
8	Supplies	341	580	457	330	675	319	451	550	211	580	433	601	5,528
9	***Total Expenses***	$ 20,679	$ 19,108	$ 21,586	$ 22,933	$ 21,874	$ 22,237	$ 22,423	$ 22,608	$ 20,591	$ 23,829	$ 21,819	$ 20,654	$ 260,341
10														

Figure 4.14 Visual Benchmark Printed Pages

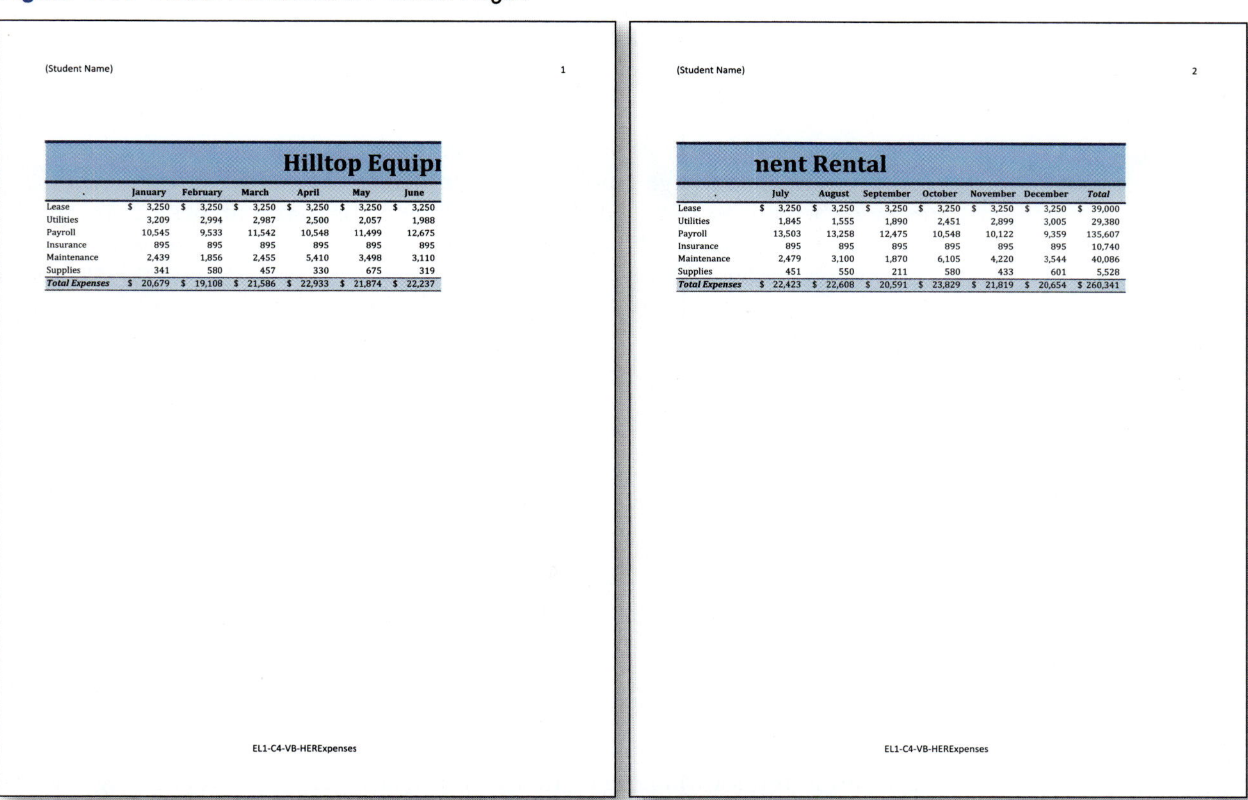

(Student Name) 1

Hilltop Equipı

	January	February	March	April	May	June
Lease	$ 3,250	$ 3,250	$ 3,250	$ 3,250	$ 3,250	$ 3,250
Utilities	3,209	2,994	2,987	2,500	2,057	1,988
Payroll	10,545	9,533	11,542	10,548	11,499	12,675
Insurance	895	895	895	895	895	895
Maintenance	2,439	1,856	2,455	5,410	3,498	3,110
Supplies	341	580	457	330	675	319
Total Expenses	$ 20,679	$ 19,108	$ 21,586	$ 22,933	$ 21,874	$ 22,237

EL1-C4-VB-HERExpenses

(Student Name) 2

nent Rental

	July	August	September	October	November	December	*Total*
Lease	$ 3,250	$ 3,250	$ 3,250	$ 3,250	$ 3,250	$ 3,250	$ 39,000
Utilities	1,845	1,555	1,890	2,451	2,899	3,005	29,380
Payroll	13,503	13,258	12,475	10,548	10,122	9,359	135,607
Insurance	895	895	895	895	895	895	10,740
Maintenance	2,479	3,100	1,870	6,105	4,220	3,544	40,086
Supplies	451	550	211	580	433	601	5,528
Total Expenses	$ 22,423	$ 22,608	$ 20,591	$ 23,829	$ 21,819	$ 20,654	$ 260,341

EL1-C4-VB-HERExpenses

Case Study Apply Your Skills

Part 1

You are the sales manager for Macadam Realty. You decide that you want to display sample mortgage worksheets in the reception area display rack. Open the **MRMortgages.xlsx** workbook, save it with Save As and name it **EL1-C4-CS-MRMortgages-01**, and then add the following information and make the following changes:

- In column C, insert a formula that determines the down payment amount.
- In column D, insert a formula that determines the loan amount.
- In column G, insert a formula using the PMT function. (Enter the *Pv* as a negative.)
- Insert the date and time as a header and your name and the workbook name (**EL1-C4-CS-MRMortgages-01.xlsx**) as a footer.
- Find 11-point Calibri formatting and replace with 11-point Candara formatting.
- Scale the worksheet so it prints on one page.

Save and then print **EL1-C4-CS-MRMortgages-01.xlsx**. After looking at the printed worksheet, you decide that you need to make the following changes:

- Sort the *Price of Home* column from smallest to largest.
- Change the percentage amount in column E from 6% to 7%.
- Shade the cells in row 4 in the light yellow color that matches the fill in cell A2. Copy this shading to every other row of cells in the worksheet (stopping at row 46).

Save the edited worksheet with Save As and name it **EL1-C4-CS-MRMortgages-02**. Edit the footer to reflect the workbook name change. Save, print, and then close **EL1-C4-CS-MRMortgages-02.xlsx**. (Make sure the worksheet prints on one page.)

Part 2

You are preparing for a quarterly sales meeting during which you will discuss retirement issues with the sales officers. You want to encourage them to consider opening an Individual Retirement Account (IRA) to supplement the retirement contributions made by Macadam Realty. You have begun an IRA worksheet but need to complete it. Open **MRIRA.xlsx** and then save it with Save As and name it **EL1-C4-CS-MRIRA-01**. Make the following changes to the worksheet:

- Insert in cell C6 a formula that calculates the future value of an investment. Use the FV function to write the formula. You must use absolute and mixed cell references for the formula. When entering the *Rate* (percentage), the column letter is variable but the row number is fixed; when entering the *Nper* (years), the column letter is fixed but the row number is variable; and when entering the *Pmt* (the contribution amount), both the column letter and row number are absolute.
- Copy the formula in cell C6 down to cells C7 through C19. Copy the formula in cell C6 across to cells D6 through K6. Continue in this manner until the amounts are entered in all the appropriate cells.

- Select and then merge and center cells A6 through A19. Type the text **Number of Years** and then rotate the text up. Make sure the text is centered in the merged cell. Apply 12-point Calibri bold formatting to the text.
- Adjust the column widths so all text is visible in the cells.
- Change the page orientation to landscape.
- Vertically and horizontally center the worksheet.
- Include a header that prints the page number and insert a footer that prints your name.

Save the worksheet and then print it so that the row titles print on both pages. After looking at the worksheet, you decide to make the following changes:

- Remove the header containing the page number.
- Edit the footer so the date prints at the left margin and your name prints at the right margin.
- Scale the worksheet so it prints on one page.

Save the workbook with Save As and name it **EL1-C4-CS-MRIRA-02** and then print the worksheet. Change the amount in cell D3 to *$3,000* and then print the worksheet again. Save and then close **EL1-C4-CS-MRIRA-02.xlsx**.

Part 3

You have clients living in Canada that are interested in purchasing real estate in the United States. For those clients, you like to keep a conversion worksheet available. Using the Internet, search for the MS MoneyCentral Investor Currency Rates site. Determine the current currency exchange rate for Canada and then create a worksheet with the following specifications:

- Apply formatting that is similar to the formatting in the worksheets you worked with in the first two parts of the case study.
- Create the following columns:
  - Column for home price in American dollars.
  - Column for home price in Canadian dollars.
  - Column for amount of down payment.
  - Column for loan total.
  - Column for monthly payment.
- In the column for home prices, insert home amounts beginning with $100,000, incrementing every $50,000, and ending with $1,000,000.
- Insert a formula in the home price in the Canadian dollars column that displays the home price in Canadian dollars.
- Insert a formula in the down payment column that multiplies the Canadian home price by 20%.
- Insert a formula in the loan total column that subtracts the down payment from the Canadian home price.
- Insert a formula in the monthly payment column that determines the monthly payment using the PMT function. Use 6% as the rate (be sure to divide by 12 months), 360 as the number of payments, and the loan amount as a negative as the present value.
- Apply any other formatting you feel necessary to improve the worksheet.

Save the completed workbook and name it **EL1-C4-CS-CanadaPrices**. Display formulas and then print the worksheet. Turn off the display of formulas and then save and close the workbook.

UNIT 1

Performance Assessment

Note: Before beginning unit assessments, copy to your storage medium the Excel2010L1U1 subfolder from the Excel2010L1 folder on the CD that accompanies this textbook and then make Excel2010L1U1 the active folder.

Assessing Proficiency

In this unit, you have learned to create, save, print, edit, and format Excel worksheets; create and insert formulas; and enhance worksheets with features such as headers and footers, page numbering, sorting, and filtering.

Assessment 1 Create Sales Bonuses Workbook

1. Create the Excel worksheet shown in Figure U1.1. Format the cells as you see them in the figure.
2. Insert an IF statement in cell C4 that inserts *7%* if B4 is greater than 99999 and inserts *3%* if B4 is not greater than 99999.
3. Format the number in cell C4 so it displays as a percentage with no decimal places. Copy the formula in cell C4 down to cells C5 through C11. Center the percents in cells C4 through C11.
4. Insert a formula in cell D4 that multiplies the amount in B4 with the percentage in cell C4. Copy the formula in D4 down to cells D5 through D11.
5. Insert the sum of cells B4 through B11 in B12 and insert the sum of cells D4 through D11 in cell D12.
6. Apply the Accounting Number Format style with two decimal places to cells B4, B12, D4, and D12. Apply the Comma style with two decimal places to cells B5 through B11 and cells D5 through D11.
7. Insert a footer that contains your first and last names and the current date.
8. Print the worksheet horizontally and vertically centered on the page.
9. Save the workbook and name it **EL1-U1-A1-SBASales**.
10. Close **EL1-U1-A1-SBASales.xlsx**.

Figure U1.1 Assessment 1

	A	B	C	D	E
1	Stanton & Barnet Associates				
2	Sales Department				
3	Associate	Sales	Bonus	Bonus Amount	
4	Conway, Edward	$ 101,450.00			
5	Eckhart, Geneva	94,375.00			
6	Farris, Amanda	73,270.00			
7	Greenwood, Wayne	110,459.00			
8	Hagen, Chandra	120,485.00			
9	Logan, Courtney	97,520.00			
10	Pena, Geraldo	115,850.00			
11	Rubin, Alice	76,422.00			
12	Total				
13					

Assessment 2 Format Equipment Purchase Plan Workbook

1. Open **HERPurPlans.xlsx** and then save the workbook with Save As and name it **EL1-U1-A2-HERPurPlans**.
2. The owner of Hilltop Equipment Rental is interested in purchasing a new tractor and needs to determine monthly payments on three different models. Insert a formula in cell E4 that uses the PMT function to calculate monthly payments. Copy the formula down to cells E5 and E6.
3. Insert a formula in cell F4 that multiplies the amount in E4 by the amount in D4.
4. Copy the formula in cell F4 down to cells F5 and F6.
5. Insert a formula in cell G4 that subtracts the amount in B4 from the amount in F4. ***Hint: The formula should return a positive number, not a negative number (a number surrounded by parentheses)***.
6. Copy the formula in cell G4 down to cells G5 and G6.
7. Change the vertical alignment of cell A2 to Middle Align.
8. Change the vertical alignment of cells A3 through G3 to Bottom Align.
9. Save, print, and then close **EL1-U1-A2-HERPurPlans.xlsx**.

Assessment 3 Format Accounts Due Workbook

1. Open **RPAccts.xlsx** and then save the workbook with Save As and name it **EL1-U1-A3-RPAccts**.
2. Using the DATE function, enter a formula in each of the specified cells that returns the serial number for the specified date:

C4	=	October 29, 2012
C5	=	October 30, 2012
C6	=	October 30, 2012
C7	=	November 1, 2012
C8	=	November 5, 2012
C9	=	November 7, 2012
C10	=	November 7, 2012
C11	=	November 14, 2012
C12	=	November 14, 2012

3. Enter a formula in cell E4 that inserts the due date (date of service plus the number of days in the *Terms* column).
4. Copy the formula in cell E4 down to cells E5 through E12.
5. Make cell A14 active and then type your name.
6. Make cell A15 active and then use the NOW function to insert the current date and time as a serial number.
7. Save, print, and then close **EL1-U1-A3-RPAccts.xlsx**.

Assessment 4 Format First Quarter Sales Workbook

1. Open **PSQtrlySales.xlsx** and then save the workbook with Save As and name it **EL1-U1-A4-PSQtrlySales**.
2. Insert a formula in cell E4 that totals the amounts in B4, C4, and D4. Copy the formula in cell E4 down to cells E5 through E18. Apply the Accounting Number Format style with no decimal places to cell E4.
3. Insert an IF statement in cell F4 that inserts *5%* if E4 is greater than 74999 and inserts *0%* if E4 is not greater than 74999.
4. Make sure the result of the IF formula displays in cell F4 as a percentage with no decimal points and then copy the formula down to cells F5 through F18. Center the percent amounts in cells F4 through F18.
5. Select cells A5 through F5 and then insert the same yellow fill as cell A2. Apply the same yellow fill to cells A7 through F7, A9 through F9, A11 through F11, A13 through F13, A15 through F15, and cells A17 through F17.
6. Insert a footer that prints your name at the left, the current date at the middle, and the current time at the right.
7. Print the worksheet horizontally and vertically centered on the page.
8. Save, print, and then close **EL1-U1-A4-PSQtrlySales.xlsx**.

Assessment 5 Format Weekly Payroll Workbook

1. Open **CCPayroll.xlsx** and then save the workbook with Save As and name it **EL1-U1-A5-CCPayroll**.
2. Insert a formula in cell E3 that multiplies the hourly rate by the hours and then adds that to the multiplication of the hourly rate by the overtime pay rate (1.5) and then overtime hours. (Use parentheses in the formula and use an absolute cell reference for the overtime pay rate (1.5). Refer to Chapter 2, Project 5c.) Copy the formula down to cells E4 through E16.

3. Insert a formula in cell F3 that multiplies the gross pay by the withholding tax rate (W/H Rate). (Use an absolute cell reference for the cell containing the withholding rate. Refer to Chapter 2, Project 5c.) Copy the formula down to cells F4 through F16.
4. Insert a formula in cell G3 that multiplies the gross pay by the Social Security rate (SS Rate). Use an absolute cell reference for the cell containing the Social Security rate. (Refer to Chapter 2, Project 5c.) Copy the formula down to cells G4 through G16.
5. Insert a formula in cell H4 that adds together the Social Security tax and the withholding tax and subtracts that from the gross pay. (Refer to Chapter 2, Project 5c.) Copy the formula down to cells H4 through H16.
6. Sort the employee last names alphabetically in ascending order (A to Z).
7. Center the worksheet horizontally and vertically on the page.
8. Insert a footer that prints your name at the left side of the page and the file name at the right side of the page.
9. Save, print, and then close **EL1-U1-A5-CCPayroll.xlsx**.

Assessment 6 Format Customer Sales Analysis Workbook

1. Open **DIAnnualSales.xlsx** and then save the workbook with Save As and name it **EL1-U1-A6-DIAnnualSales**.
2. Insert formulas and drag formulas to complete the worksheet. After dragging the total formula in row 10, specify that you want to fill without formatting. (This retains the right border in cell N10.) Do this with the AutoFill Options button.
3. Insert in cell B11 the highest total from cells B10 through M10. Insert in cell B12 the lowest total from cells B10 through M10.
4. Change the orientation to landscape.
5. Insert a header that prints the page number at the right side of the page.
6. Insert a footer that prints your name at the right side of the page.
7. Horizontally and vertically center the worksheet on the page.
8. Specify that the column headings in cells A3 through A12 print on both pages.
9. Save, print, and then close **EL1-U1-A6-DIAnnualSales.xlsx**.

Assessment 7 Format Invoices Workbook

1. Open **RPInvoices.xlsx** and then save the workbook with Save As and name it **EL1-U1-A7-RPInvoices**.
2. Insert a formula in cell G4 that multiplies the amount in E4 by the percentage in F4 and then adds that total to the amount in E4. (Use parentheses in this formula.)
3. Copy the formula in cell G4 down to cells G5 through G18.
4. Find all occurrences of cells containing *11-279* and replace with *10-005*.
5. Find all occurrences of cells containing *8.5* and replace with *9.0*.
6. Search for the Calibri font and replace with the Candara font. (Do not specify a type size so that Excel replaces all sizes of Calibri with Candara.)
7. Print **EL1-U1-A7-RPInvoices.xlsx**.
8. Filter and then print a list of rows containing only the client number *04-325*. (After printing, return the list to *(Select All)*.)
9. Filter and then print a list of rows containing only the service *Development*. (After printing, return the list to *(Select All)*.)
10. Filter and then print a list of rows containing the top three highest totals in the *Amount Due* column. (After printing, turn off the filter feature.)
11. Save and then close **EL1-U1-A7-RPInvoices.xlsx**.

Writing Activities

The following activities give you the opportunity to practice your writing skills along with demonstrating an understanding of some of the important Excel features you have mastered in this unit. Use correct grammar, appropriate word choices, and clear sentence construction.

Activity 1 Plan and Prepare Orders Summary Workbook

Plan and prepare a worksheet with the information shown in Figure U1.2. Apply formatting of your choosing to the worksheet. Save the completed worksheet and name it **EL1-U1-Act1-OrdersSumm**. Print and then close **EL1-U1-Act1-OrdersSumm.xlsx**.

Figure U1.2 Activity 1

Prepare a weekly summary of orders taken that itemizes the products coming into the company and the average order size.
The products and average order size include:

Black and gold wall clock: $2,450 worth of orders, average order size of $125
Traveling alarm clock: $l,358 worth of orders, average order size of $195
Waterproof watch: $890 worth of orders, average order size of $90
Dashboard clock: $2,135 worth of orders, average order size of $230
Pyramid clock: $3,050 worth of orders, average order size of $375
Gold chain watch: $755 worth of orders, average order size of $80

In the worksheet, total the amount ordered and also calculate the average weekly order size. Sort the data in the worksheet by the order amount in descending order.

Activity 2 Prepare Depreciation Workbook

Assets within a company, such as equipment, can be depreciated over time. Several methods are available for determining the amount of depreciation such as the straight-line depreciation method, fixed-declining balance method, and the double-declining method. Use Excel's Help feature to learn about two depreciation methods — straight-line and double-declining depreciation. (The straight-line depreciation function, SNL, and the double-declining depreciation function, DDB, are located in the Financial category.) After reading about the two methods, create an Excel worksheet with the following information:

- An appropriate title
- A heading for straight-line depreciation
- The straight-line depreciation function
- The name and a description for each straight-line depreciation function argument category
- A heading for double-declining depreciation

- The double-declining depreciation function
- The name and a description for each double-declining depreciation function argument category

Apply formatting of your choosing to the worksheet. Save the completed workbook and name it **EL1-U1-Act2-DepMethods**. Print the worksheet horizontally and vertically centered on the page. Close **EL1-U1-Act2-DepMethods.xlsx**.

Activity 3 Insert Straight-Line Depreciation Formula

Open **RPDepreciation.xlsx** and then save the workbook and name it **EL1-U1-Act3-RPDepreciation**. Insert the function to determine straight-line depreciation in cell E3. Copy the formula down to cells E4 through E10. Apply formatting of your choosing to the worksheet. Print the worksheet horizontally and vertically centered on the page. Save and then close **EL1-U1-Act3-RPDepreciation.xlsx**.

Optional: Briefly research the topic of straight-line and double-declining depreciation to find out why businesses depreciate their assets. What purpose does it serve? Locate information about the topic on the Internet or in your school library. Then use Word 2010 to write a half-page, single-spaced report explaining the financial reasons for using depreciation methods. Save the document and name it **EL1-U1-Act3-DepReport**. Print and then close the document.

Internet Research

Activity 4 Create a Travel Planning Worksheet

Make sure you are connected to the Internet. Use a search engine of your choosing to look for information on traveling to a specific country that interests you. Find sites that provide cost information for airlines, hotels, meals, entertainment, and car rentals. Create a travel planning worksheet for the country that includes the following:

- appropriate title
- appropriate headings
- airline costs
- hotel costs (off-season and in-season rates if available)
- estimated meal costs
- entertainment costs
- car rental costs

Save the completed workbook and name it **EL1-U1-Act4-TrvlWksht**. Print and then close the workbook.

Microsoft® Excel® Level 1

Unit 2 ■ Enhancing the Display of Workbooks

Microsoft® Excel®

Moving Data within and between Workbooks

PERFORMANCE OBJECTIVES

Upon successful completion of Chapter 5, you will be able to:

- **Create a workbook with multiple worksheets**
- **Move, copy, and paste cells within a worksheet**
- **Split a worksheet into windows and freeze panes**
- **Name a range of cells and use a range in a formula**
- **Open multiple workbooks**
- **Arrange, size, and move workbooks**
- **Copy and paste data between workbooks**
- **Link data between worksheets**

Tutorials

5.1 Moving and Copying Cells
5.2 Inserting, Moving, Renaming, and Hiding a Worksheet
5.3 Formatting Multiple Worksheets
5.4 Setting a Print Area and Printing Multiple Worksheets
5.5 Splitting a Worksheet into Windows
5.6 Freezing Panes and Changing the Zoom
5.7 Naming and Using a Range
5.8 Working with Windows
5.9 Linking Data and Using 3-D References
5.10 Copying and Pasting Data between Programs

Up to this point, the workbooks in which you have been working have consisted of only one worksheet. In this chapter, you will learn to create a workbook with several worksheets and complete tasks such as copying and pasting data within and between worksheets. Moving and pasting or copying and pasting selected cells in and between worksheets is useful for rearranging data or for saving time. You will also work with multiple workbooks and complete tasks such as arranging, sizing, and moving workbooks, and opening and closing multiple workbooks. Model answers for this chapter's projects appear on the following pages.

Excel2010L1C5

Note: Before beginning the projects, copy to your storage medium the Excel2010L1C5 subfolder from the Excel2010L1 folder on the CD that accompanies this textbook and then make Excel2010L1C5 the active folder.

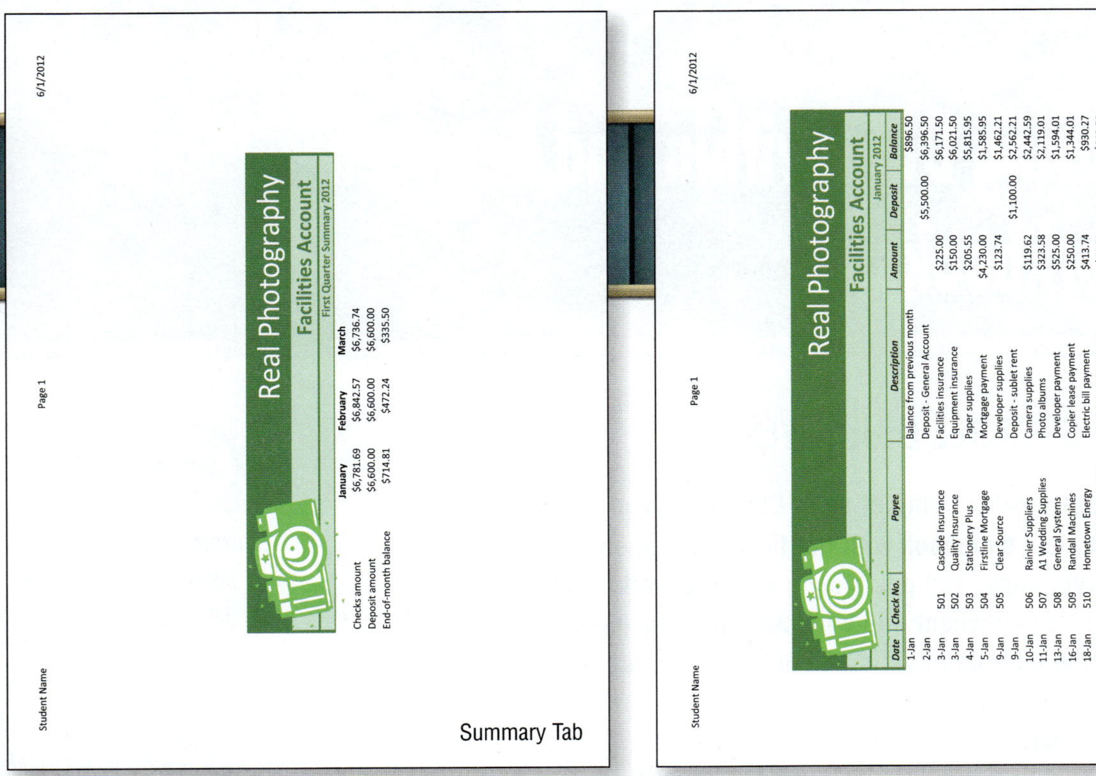

Student Name | Page 1 | 6/1/2012

Real Photography
Facilities Account
First Quarter Summary 2012

	January	February	March
Checks amount	$6,781.69	$6,842.57	$6,736.74
Deposit amount	$6,600.00	$6,600.00	$6,600.00
End-of-month balance	$714.81	$472.24	$335.50

Summary Tab

Student Name | Page 1 | 6/1/2012

Real Photography
Facilities Account
January 2012

Date	Check No.	Payee	Description	Amount	Deposit	Balance
1-Jan			Balance from previous month			$896.50
2-Jan			Deposit - General Account		$5,500.00	$6,396.50
3-Jan	501	Cascade Insurance	Facilities insurance	$225.00		$6,171.50
3-Jan	502	Quality Insurance	Equipment insurance	$150.00		$6,021.50
4-Jan	503	Stationery Plus	Paper supplies	$205.55		$5,815.95
5-Jan	504	Firstline Mortgage	Mortgage payment	$4,230.00		$1,585.95
9-Jan	505	Clear Source	Developer supplies	$123.74		$1,462.21
9-Jan			Deposit - sublet rent		$1,100.00	$2,562.21
10-Jan	506	Rainier Suppliers	Camera supplies	$119.62		$2,442.59
11-Jan	507	A1 Wedding Supplies	Photo albums	$323.58		$2,119.01
13-Jan	508	General Systems	Developer payment	$525.00		$1,594.01
16-Jan	509	Randall Machines	Copier lease payment	$250.00		$1,344.01
18-Jan	510	Hometown Energy	Electric bill payment	$413.74		$930.27
19-Jan	511	Steward-Holmes Energy	Natural gas bill payment	$86.51		$843.76
24-Jan	512	Parkland City Services	Water/sewer payment	$45.70		$798.06
26-Jan	513	New Century Telephones	Telephone bill payment	$83.25		$714.81
			Total	$6,781.69	$6,600.00	

January Tab

Project 1 Manage Data in a Multiple-Worksheet Account Workbook

EL1-C5-P1-RPFacAccts.xlsx

Student Name | Page 1 | 6/1/2012

Real Photography
Facilities Account
February 2012

Date	Check No.	Payee	Description	Amount	Deposit	Balance
1-Feb			Balance from previous month			$714.81
1-Feb			Deposit - General Account		$5,500.00	$6,214.81
6-Feb	514	Firstline Mortgage	Mortgage payment	$4,230.00		$1,984.81
6-Feb	515	Cascade Insurance	Facilities insurance	$225.00		$1,759.81
10-Feb	516	Quality Insurance	Equipment insurance	$150.00		$1,609.81
11-Feb	517	Stationery Plus	Paper supplies	$266.43		$1,343.38
12-Feb	518	Clear Source	Developer supplies	$123.74		$1,219.64
12-Feb			Deposit - sublet rent		$1,100.00	$2,319.64
16-Feb	519	Rainier Suppliers	Camera supplies	$119.62		$2,200.02
17-Feb	520	A1 Wedding Supplies	Photo albums	$323.58		$1,876.44
17-Feb	521	General Systems	Developer payment	$525.00		$1,351.44
20-Feb	522	Randall Machines	Copier lease payment	$250.00		$1,101.44
20-Feb	523	Hometown Energy	Electric bill payment	$413.74		$687.70
21-Feb	524	Steward-Holmes Energy	Natural gas bill payment	$86.51		$601.19
23-Feb	525	Parkland City Services	Water/sewer payment	$45.70		$555.49
26-Feb	526	New Century Telephones	Telephone bill payment	$83.25		$472.24
			Total	$6,842.57	$6,600.00	

February Tab

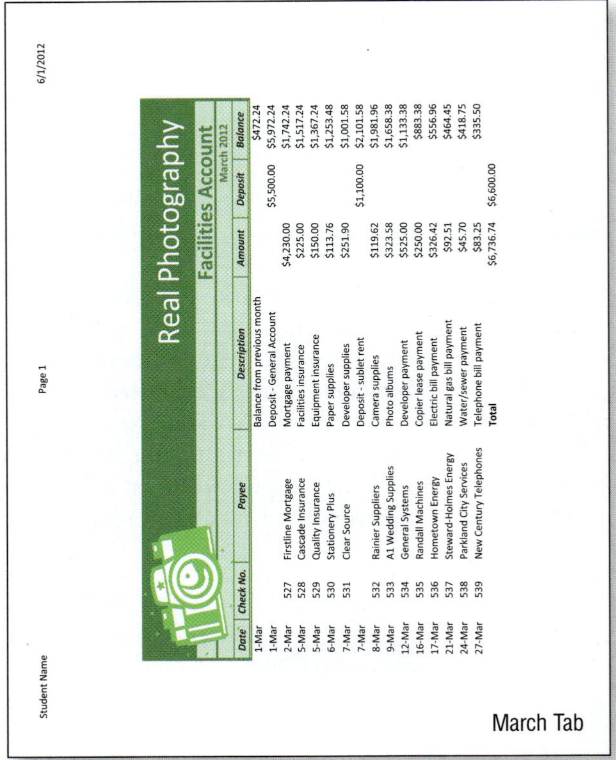

Student Name | Page 1 | 6/1/2012

Real Photography
Facilities Account
March 2012

Date	Check No.	Payee	Description	Amount	Deposit	Balance
1-Mar			Balance from previous month			$472.24
1-Mar			Deposit - General Account		$5,500.00	$5,972.24
2-Mar	527	Firstline Mortgage	Mortgage payment	$4,230.00		$1,742.24
5-Mar	528	Cascade Insurance	Facilities insurance	$225.00		$1,517.24
5-Mar	529	Quality Insurance	Equipment insurance	$150.00		$1,367.24
6-Mar	530	Stationery Plus	Paper supplies	$113.76		$1,253.48
7-Mar	531	Clear Source	Developer supplies	$251.90		$1,001.58
7-Mar			Deposit - sublet rent		$1,100.00	$2,101.58
8-Mar	532	Rainier Suppliers	Camera supplies	$119.62		$1,981.96
9-Mar	533	A1 Wedding Supplies	Photo albums	$323.58		$1,658.38
12-Mar	534	General Systems	Developer payment	$525.00		$1,133.38
16-Mar	535	Randall Machines	Copier lease payment	$250.00		$883.38
17-Mar	536	Hometown Energy	Electric bill payment	$326.42		$556.96
21-Mar	537	Steward-Holmes Energy	Natural gas bill payment	$92.51		$464.45
24-Mar	538	Parkland City Services	Water/sewer payment	$45.70		$418.75
27-Mar	539	New Century Telephones	Telephone bill payment	$83.25		$335.50
			Total	$6,736.74	$6,600.00	

March Tab

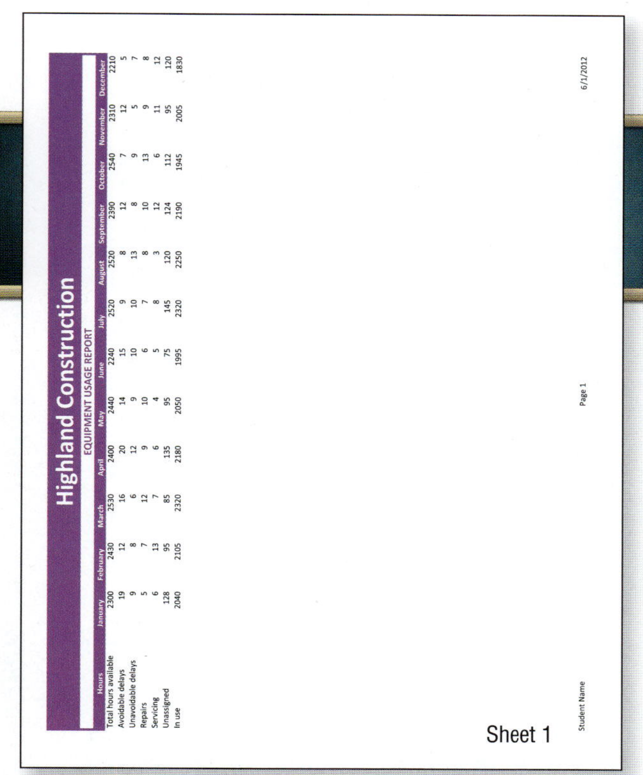

Highland Construction

EQUIPMENT USAGE REPORT

Hours	January	February	March	April	May	June	July	August	September	October	November	December
Total hours available	2300	2430	2530	2400	2440	2240	2520	2520	2390	2540	2310	2210
Avoidable delays	19	12	16	20	14	15	9	8	12	7	12	5
Unavoidable delays	9	8	6	12	9	10	10	13	8	9	5	7
Repairs	5	7	12	9	10	6	7	8	10	13	9	8
Servicing	6	13	7	6	4	5	8	3	12	6	11	12
Unassigned	128	95	85	135	95	75	145	120	124	112	95	120
In use	2040	2105	2320	2180	2050	1995	2320	2250	2190	1945	2005	1830

Student Name Page 1 6/1/2012

Sheet 1

EQUIPMENT USAGE REPORT

Yearly hours	
Avoidable delays	149
Unavoidable delays	106
Total delay hours	255
Repairs	104
Servicing	93
Total repair/servicing hours	197

Student Name Page 2 6/1/2012

Sheet 2

Project 2 Write Formulas Using Ranges in an Equipment Usage Workbook EL1-C5-P2-HCEqpRpt.xlsx

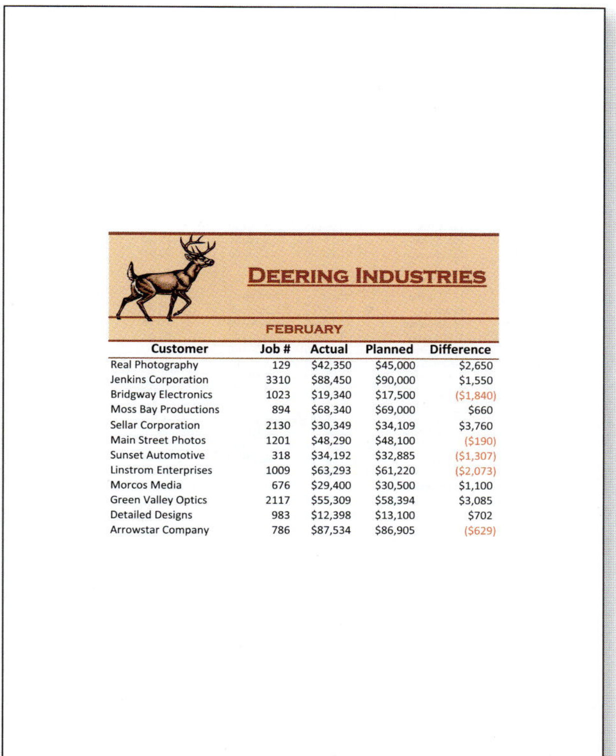

DEERING INDUSTRIES

FEBRUARY

Customer	Job #	Actual	Planned	Difference
Real Photography	129	$42,350	$45,000	$2,650
Jenkins Corporation	3310	$88,450	$90,000	$1,550
Bridgway Electronics	1023	$19,340	$17,500	($1,840)
Moss Bay Productions	894	$68,340	$69,000	$660
Sellar Corporation	2130	$30,349	$34,109	$3,760
Main Street Photos	1201	$48,290	$48,100	($190)
Sunset Automotive	318	$34,192	$32,885	($1,307)
Linstrom Enterprises	1009	$63,293	$61,220	($2,073)
Morcos Media	676	$29,400	$30,500	$1,100
Green Valley Optics	2117	$55,309	$58,394	$3,085
Detailed Designs	983	$12,398	$13,100	$702
Arrowstar Company	786	$87,534	$86,905	($629)

Project 3 Arrange, Size, and Copy Data between Workbooks EL1-C5-P3-DIFebJobs.xlsx

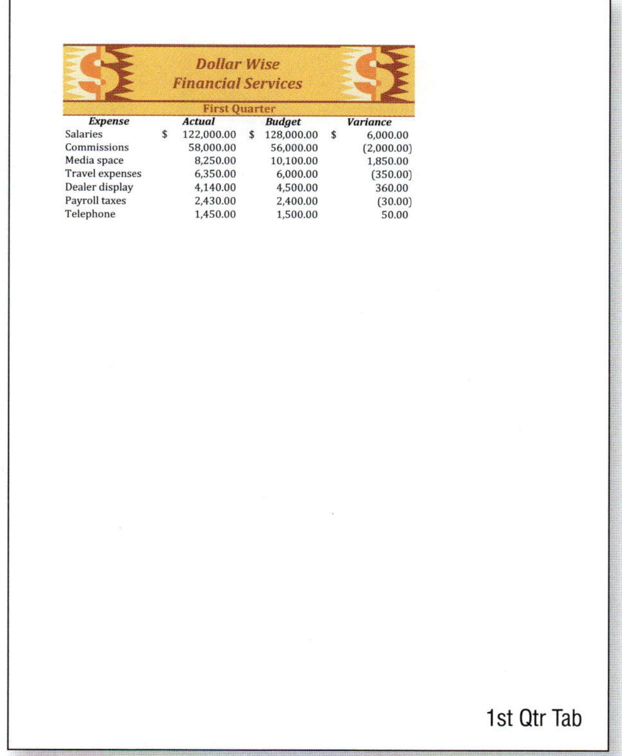

Dollar Wise Financial Services

First Quarter

Expense	*Actual*	*Budget*	*Variance*
Salaries	$ 122,000.00	$ 128,000.00	$ 6,000.00
Commissions	58,000.00	56,000.00	(2,000.00)
Media space	8,250.00	10,100.00	1,850.00
Travel expenses	6,350.00	6,000.00	(350.00)
Dealer display	4,140.00	4,500.00	360.00
Payroll taxes	2,430.00	2,400.00	(30.00)
Telephone	1,450.00	1,500.00	50.00

1st Qtr Tab

Project 4 Linking and Copying Data within and between Worksheets and Word EL1-C5-P4-DWQtrlyExp.xlsx

Model Answers

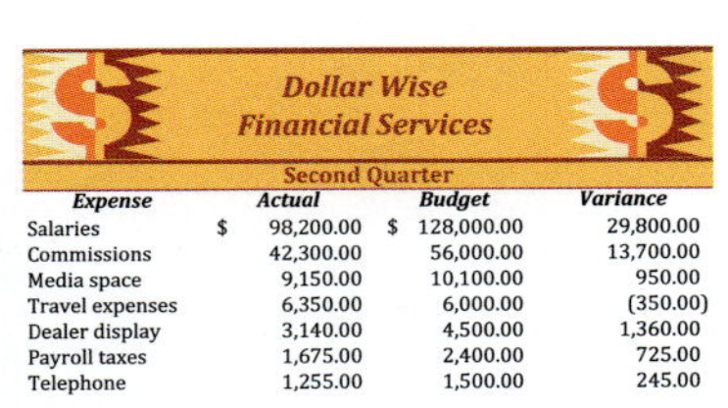

Second Quarter			
Expense	Actual	Budget	Variance
Salaries	$ 98,200.00	$ 128,000.00	29,800.00
Commissions	42,300.00	56,000.00	13,700.00
Media space	9,150.00	10,100.00	950.00
Travel expenses	6,350.00	6,000.00	(350.00)
Dealer display	3,140.00	4,500.00	1,360.00
Payroll taxes	1,675.00	2,400.00	725.00
Telephone	1,255.00	1,500.00	245.00

2nd Qtr Tab

Dollar Wise
Financial Services

Third Quarter			
Expense	Actual	Budget	Variance
Salaries	$ 129,000.00	$ 128,000.00	(1,000.00)
Commissions	48,000.00	56,000.00	8,000.00
Media space	9,000.00	10,100.00	1,100.00
Travel expenses	5,250.00	6,000.00	750.00
Dealer display	5,140.00	4,500.00	(640.00)
Payroll taxes	2,150.00	2,400.00	250.00
Telephone	1,250.00	1,500.00	250.00

3rd Qtr Tab

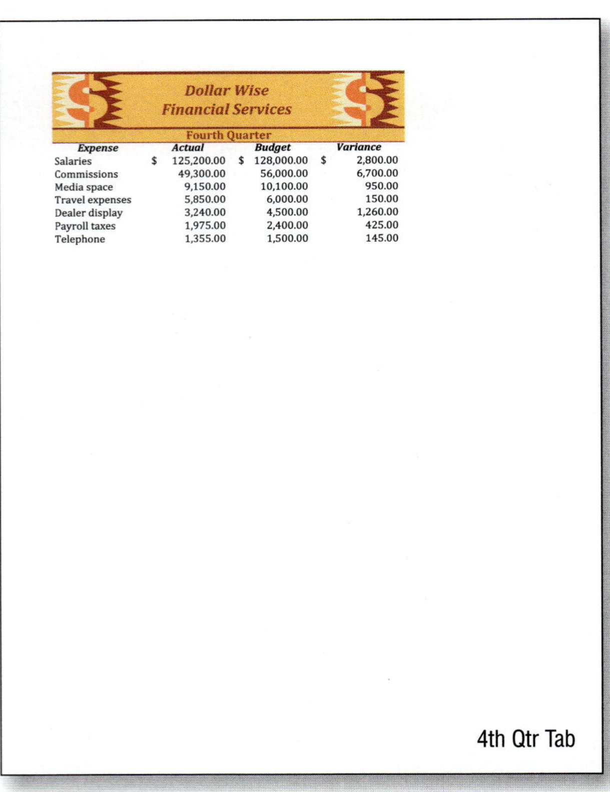

Dollar Wise
Financial Services

Fourth Quarter			
Expense	Actual	Budget	Variance
Salaries	$ 125,200.00	$ 128,000.00	$ 2,800.00
Commissions	49,300.00	56,000.00	6,700.00
Media space	9,150.00	10,100.00	950.00
Travel expenses	5,850.00	6,000.00	150.00
Dealer display	3,240.00	4,500.00	1,260.00
Payroll taxes	1,975.00	2,400.00	425.00
Telephone	1,355.00	1,500.00	145.00

4th Qtr Tab

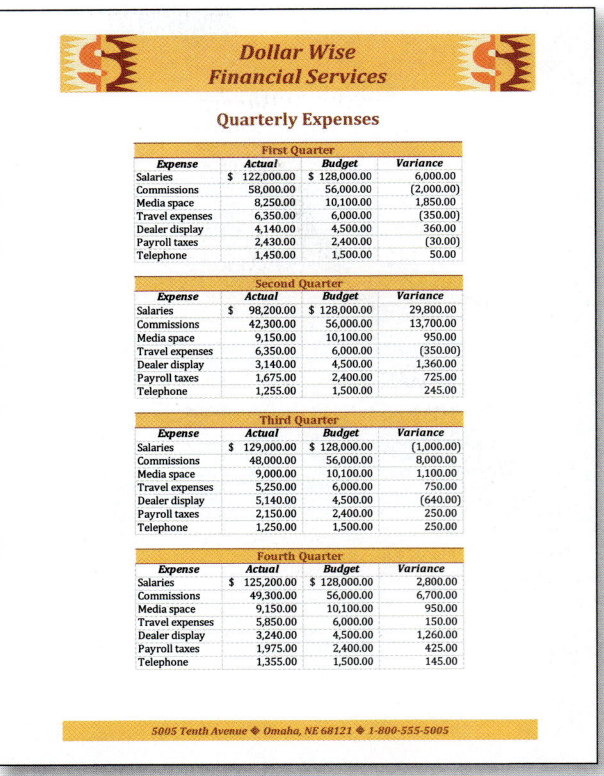

Dollar Wise
Financial Services

Quarterly Expenses

First Quarter			
Expense	Actual	Budget	Variance
Salaries	$ 122,000.00	$ 128,000.00	6,000.00
Commissions	58,000.00	56,000.00	(2,000.00)
Media space	8,250.00	10,100.00	1,850.00
Travel expenses	6,350.00	6,000.00	(350.00)
Dealer display	4,140.00	4,500.00	360.00
Payroll taxes	2,430.00	2,400.00	(30.00)
Telephone	1,450.00	1,500.00	50.00

Second Quarter			
Expense	Actual	Budget	Variance
Salaries	$ 98,200.00	$ 128,000.00	29,800.00
Commissions	42,300.00	56,000.00	13,700.00
Media space	9,150.00	10,100.00	950.00
Travel expenses	6,350.00	6,000.00	(350.00)
Dealer display	3,140.00	4,500.00	1,360.00
Payroll taxes	1,675.00	2,400.00	725.00
Telephone	1,255.00	1,500.00	245.00

Third Quarter			
Expense	Actual	Budget	Variance
Salaries	$ 129,000.00	$ 128,000.00	(1,000.00)
Commissions	48,000.00	56,000.00	8,000.00
Media space	9,000.00	10,100.00	1,100.00
Travel expenses	5,250.00	6,000.00	750.00
Dealer display	5,140.00	4,500.00	(640.00)
Payroll taxes	2,150.00	2,400.00	250.00
Telephone	1,250.00	1,500.00	250.00

Fourth Quarter			
Expense	Actual	Budget	Variance
Salaries	$ 125,200.00	$ 128,000.00	2,800.00
Commissions	49,300.00	56,000.00	6,700.00
Media space	9,150.00	10,100.00	950.00
Travel expenses	5,850.00	6,000.00	150.00
Dealer display	3,240.00	4,500.00	1,260.00
Payroll taxes	1,975.00	2,400.00	425.00
Telephone	1,355.00	1,500.00	145.00

5005 Tenth Avenue ◆ Omaha, NE 68121 ◆ 1-800-555-5005

EL1-C5-P4-DWQtrlyRpt.docx

Project 1 Manage Data in a Multiple-Worksheet Account Workbook

9 Parts

You will open an account workbook containing three worksheets and then move, copy, and paste data between the worksheets. You will also hide and unhide worksheets, and format and print multiple worksheets in the workbook.

Creating a Workbook with Multiple Worksheets

An Excel workbook can contain multiple worksheets. You can create a variety of worksheets within a workbook for related data. For example, a workbook may contain a worksheet for the expenses for each salesperson in a company and another worksheet for the monthly payroll for each department within the company. Another example is recording sales statistics for each quarter in individual worksheets within a workbook.

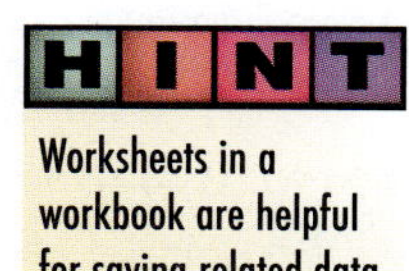

HINT
Worksheets in a workbook are helpful for saving related data.

By default, a workbook contains three worksheets named *Sheet1*, *Sheet2*, and *Sheet3*. (Later in this chapter, you will learn how to change these default names.) Display various worksheets in the workbook by clicking the desired tab.

Project 1a Displaying Worksheets in a Workbook

Part 1 of 9

1. Open **RPFacAccts.xlsx** and then save the workbook with Save As and name it **EL1-C5-P1-RPFacAccts**.
2. This workbook contains three worksheets. Display the various worksheets by completing the following steps:
   a. Display the second worksheet by clicking the Sheet2 tab that displays immediately above the Status bar.
   b. Display the third worksheet by clicking the Sheet3 tab that displays immediately above the Status bar.
   c. Return to the first worksheet by clicking the Sheet1 tab.
3. Make the following changes to worksheets in the workbook:
   a. Click the Sheet2 tab and then change the column width for columns E, F, and G to 10.00.
   b. Click the Sheet3 tab and then change the column width for columns E, F, and G to 10.00.
   c. Click the Sheet1 tab to display the first worksheet.
4. Save **EL1-C5-P1-RPFacAccts.xlsx**.

Step 2a

Cutting, Copying, and Pasting Selected Cells

Situations may arise where you need to move cells to a different location within a worksheet, or you may need to copy repetitive data in a worksheet. You can perform these actions by selecting cells and then using the Cut, Copy, and/or Paste buttons in the Clipboard group in the Home tab. You can also perform these actions with the mouse.

Quick Steps

Move and Paste Cells
1. Select cells.
2. Click Cut button.
3. Click desired cell.
4. Click Paste button.

Ctrl + X is the keyboard shortcut to cut selected data. Ctrl + V is the keyboard shortcut to paste data.

Cut

Paste

Moving Selected Cells

You can move selected cells and cell contents in a worksheet and between worksheets. Move selected cells with the Cut and Paste buttons in the Clipboard group in the Home tab or by dragging with the mouse.

To move selected cells with buttons in the Home tab, select the cells and then click the Cut button in the Clipboard group. This causes a moving dashed line border (called a ***marquee***) to display around the selected cells. Click the cell where you want the first selected cell inserted and then click the Paste button in the Clipboard group. If you change your mind and do not want to move the selected cells, press the Esc key to remove the moving dashed line border or double-click in any cell.

To move selected cells with the mouse, select the cells and then position the mouse pointer on any border of the selected cells until the pointer turns into an arrow pointer with a four-headed arrow attached. Hold down the left mouse button, drag the outline of the selected cells to the desired location, and then release the mouse button.

Project 1b **Moving Selected Cells** Part 2 of 9

1. With **EL1-C5-P1-RPFacAccts.xlsx** open, you realize that the sublet rent deposit was recorded on the wrong day. The correct day is January 9. To move the cells containing information on the deposit, complete the following steps:
   a. Make cell A13 active and then insert a row. (The new row should display above the row containing information on *Rainer Suppliers*.)
   b. Select cells A7 through F7.
   c. Click the Cut button in the Clipboard group in the Home tab.

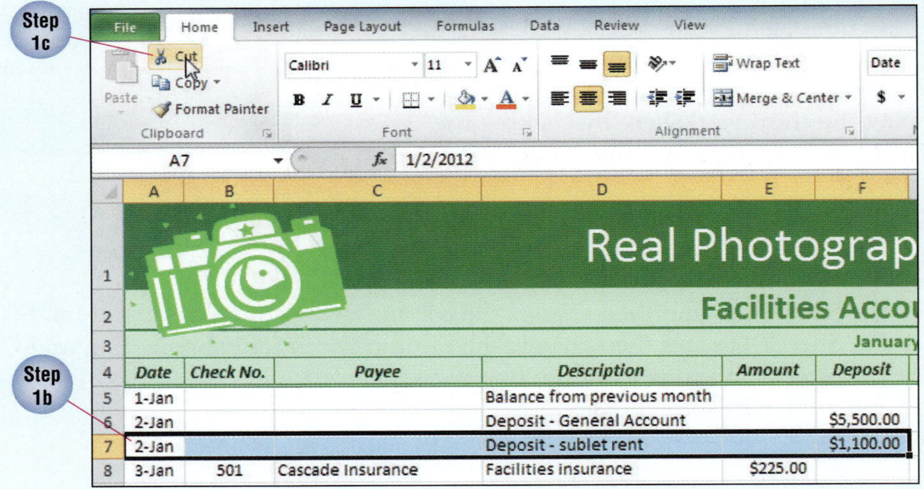

   d. Click cell A13 to make it active.
   e. Click the Paste button in the Clipboard group.
   f. Change the date of the deposit from January 2 to January 9.
   g. Select row 7 and then delete it.

2. Click the Sheet2 tab and then complete steps similar to those in Step 1 to move the sublet deposit row so it is positioned above the *Rainier Suppliers* row and below the *Clear Source* row. Change the date of the deposit to February 12 and make sure you delete row 7.
3. Move cells using the mouse by completing the following steps:
   a. Click the Sheet3 tab.
   b. Make cell A13 active and then insert a new row.
   c. Using the mouse, select cells A7 through F7.
   d. Position the mouse pointer on any boundary of the selected cells until it turns into an arrow pointer with a four-headed arrow attached.
   e. Hold down the left mouse button, drag the outline of the selected cells to row 13, and then release the mouse button.

Step 3c

4	Date	Check No.	Payee	Description	Amount	Deposit
5	1-Mar			Balance from previous month		
6	1-Mar			Deposit - General Account		$5,500.00
7	1-Mar			Deposit - sublet rent		$1,100.00
8	2-Mar	527				
9	5-Mar	528				
10	5-Mar	529				
11	6-Mar	530	Stationery Plus	Paper supplies	$113.76	
12	7-Mar	531	Clear Source	Developer supplies	$251.90	
13						
14	8-Mar	53 A13:F13	inier Suppliers	Camera supplies	$119.62	
15	9-Mar	533	A1 Wedding Supplies	Photo albums	$323.58	

Step 3e

   f. Change the date of the deposit to March 7.
   g. Delete row 7.
4. Save **EL1-C5-P1-RPFacAccts.xlsx**.

Copying Selected Cells

Quick Steps

Copy and Paste Cells
1. Select cells.
2. Click Copy button.
3. Click desired cell.
4. Click Paste button.

Ctrl + C is the keyboard shortcut to copy selected data.

Copying selected cells can be useful in worksheets that contain repetitive data. To copy cells, select the cells and then click the Copy button in the Clipboard group in the Home tab. Click the cell where you want the first selected cell copied and then click the Paste button in the Clipboard group.

You can also copy selected cells using the mouse and the Ctrl key. To do this, select the cells you want to copy and then position the mouse pointer on any border around the selected cells until it turns into an arrow pointer. Hold down the Ctrl key and the left mouse button, drag the outline of the selected cells to the desired location, release the left mouse button, and then release the Ctrl key.

Using the Paste Options Button

Copy

Paste Options

The Paste Options button displays in the lower right corner of the pasted cell(s) when you paste a cell or cells. Display a list of paste options by hovering the mouse pointer over the button and then clicking the button or by pressing the Ctrl key. This causes a drop-down list to display as shown in Figure 5.1. Hover your mouse over a button in the drop-down list and the descriptive name of the button displays along with the keyboard shortcut. With buttons in this drop-down list, you can specify what you want pasted.

Figure 5.1 Paste Options Button Drop-down List

Click the button that specifies the formatting you desire for the pasted data.

Copying Selected Cells in a Worksheet

Part 3 of 9

1. With **EL1-C5-P1-RPFacAccts.xlsx** open, make Sheet2 active.
2. Select cells C7 through E9.
3. Click the Copy button in the Clipboard group in the Home tab.

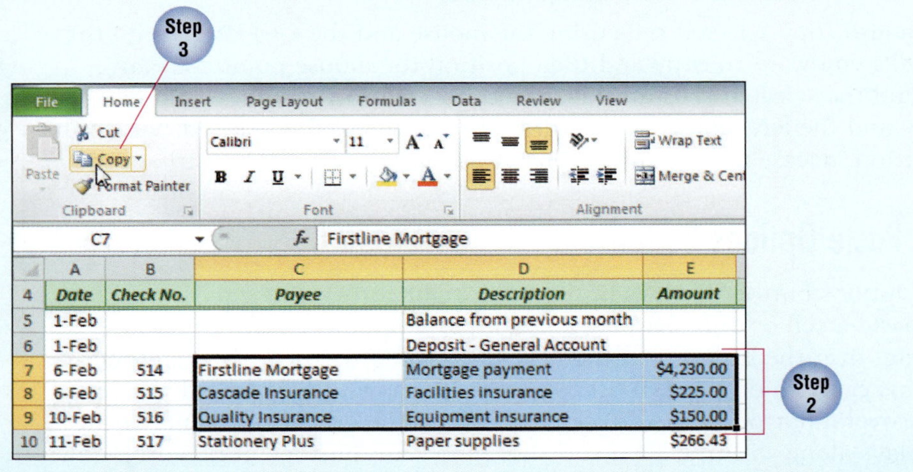

4. Make Sheet3 active.
5. Make cell C7 active.
6. Click the Paste button in the Clipboard group.
7. Click the Paste Options button that displays in the lower right corner of the pasted cells and then click the Keep Source Column Widths button at the drop-down list.
8. Make Sheet2 active and then press the Esc key to remove the moving marquee.
9. Save **EL1-C5-P1-RPFacAccts.xlsx**.

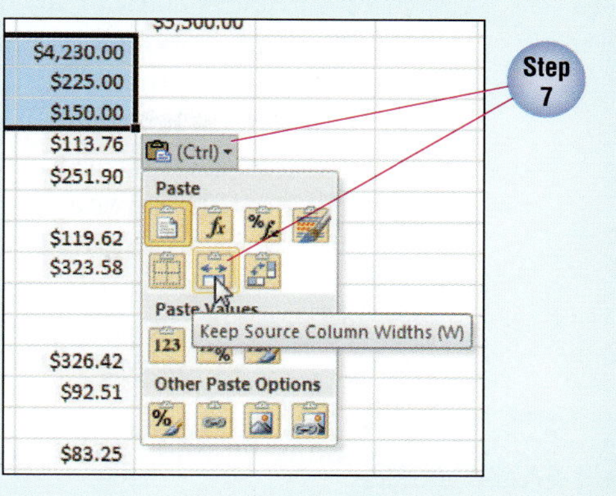

Using the Office Clipboard

Use the Office Clipboard feature to collect and paste multiple items. To use the Office Clipboard, display the Clipboard task pane by clicking the Clipboard group dialog box launcher. This button is located in the lower right corner of the Clipboard group in the Home tab. The Clipboard task pane displays at the left side of the screen in a manner similar to what you see in Figure 5.2.

Quick Steps

Copy and Paste Multiple Items

1. Click Clipboard group dialog box launcher.
2. Select desired cells.
3. Click Copy button.
4. Continue selecting desired cells and then clicking the Copy button.
5. Make desired cell active.
6. Click item in Clipboard task pane that you want inserted in the worksheet.
7. Continue pasting desired items from the Clipboard task pane.

Figure 5.2 Clipboard Task Pane

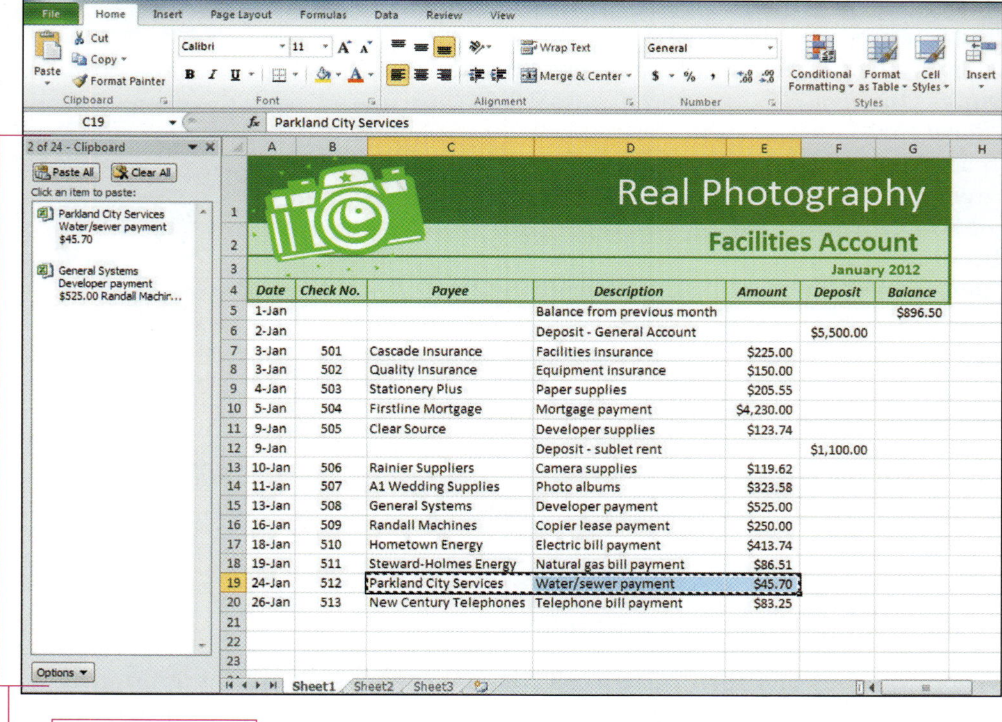

Select data or an object you want to copy and then click the Copy button in the Clipboard group. Continue selecting text or items and clicking the Copy button. To insert an item, position the insertion point in the desired location and then click the item in the Clipboard task pane. If the copied item is text, the first 50 characters display. When all desired items are inserted, click the Clear All button to remove any remaining items. Sometimes, you may have a situation in which you want to copy all of the selected items to a single location. If so, position the insertion point in the desired location and then click the Paste All button in the Clipboard task pane.

Project 1d Copying and Pasting Cells Using the Office Clipboard

Part 4 of 9

1. With **EL1-C5-P1-RPFacAccts.xlsx** open, select cells for copying by completing the following steps:
   a. Display the Clipboard task pane by clicking the Clipboard group dialog box launcher. (If the Clipboard contains any copied data, click the Clear All button.)
   b. Click the Sheet1 tab.
   c. Select cells C15 through E16.
   d. Click the Copy button in the Clipboard group.
   e. Select cells C19 through E19.
   f. Click the Copy button in the Clipboard group.
2. Paste the copied cells by completing the following steps:
   a. Click the Sheet2 tab.
   b. Make cell C15 active.
   c. Click the item in the Clipboard task pane representing *General Systems Developer*.
   d. Click the Sheet3 tab.
   e. Make C15 active.
   f. Click the item in the Clipboard task pane representing *General Systems Developer*.
   g. Make cell C19 active.
   h. Click the item in the Clipboard task pane representing *Parkland City Services*.
3. Click the Clear All button located toward the top of the Clipboard task pane.
4. Close the Clipboard task pane by clicking the Close button (contains an X) located in the upper right corner of the task pane.
5. Save **EL1-C5-P1-RPFacAccts.xlsx**.

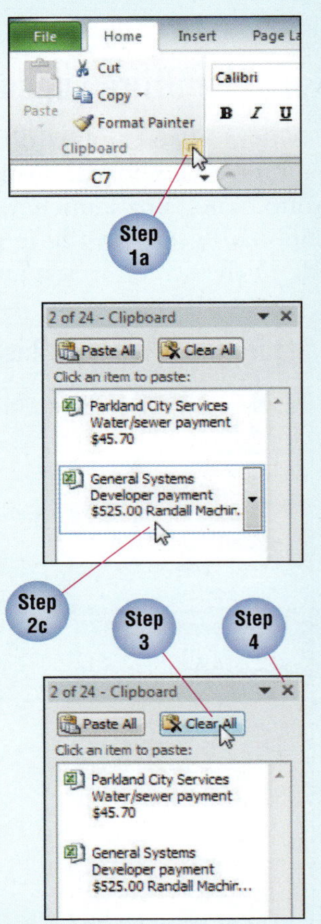

Pasting Values Only and Formulas

When you copy and then paste a cell containing a value as well as a formula, you can use buttons in the Paste Options button drop-down list to specify what you want pasted. For example, you can paste all data and formatting, only the formula, or only the value. Click the Paste Options button and a drop-down list of buttons displays in three sections—*Paste*, *Paste Values*, and *Other Paste Options*. To paste only the formula, click the Formulas button in the *Paste* section and to paste only the value, click the Values button in the *Paste Values* section.

Project 1e Copying and Pasting Values

Part 5 of 9

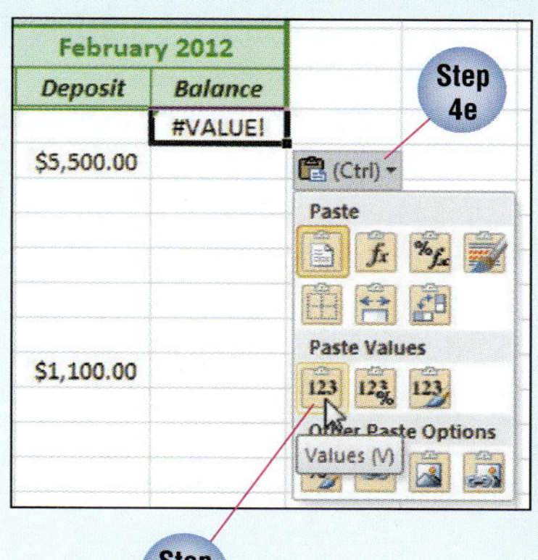

1. With **EL1-C5-P1-RPFacAccts.xlsx** open, make Sheet1 active.
2. Make cell G6 active, insert the formula =(F6-E6)+G5, and then press Enter.
3. Copy the formula in cell G6 down to cells G7 through G20.
4. Copy the final balance amount from Sheet1 to Sheet2 by completing the following steps:
   a. Make cell G20 active.
   b. Click the Copy button in the Clipboard group.
   c. Click the Sheet2 tab.
   d. Make cell G5 active and then click the Paste button in the Clipboard group.
   e. Click the Paste Options button.
   f. At the drop-down list, click the Values button in the *Paste Values* section of the drop-down list. (This inserts the value and not the formula.)
5. Make Sheet1 active, make cell G6 active, click the Bold button, and then click the Copy button.
6. Make Sheet2 active, make cell G6 active, and then click the Paste button.
7. Click the Paste Options button and then click the Formulas button in the *Paste* section.
8. Copy the formula in G6 down to cells G7 through G20.
9. Copy the amount in cell G20 and then paste the value only into cell G5 in Sheet3.
10. Make Sheet2 active, make cell G6 active, and then click the Copy button.
11. Make Sheet3 active, make cell G6 active, and then click the Paste button. Copy the formula in cell G6 down to cells G7 through G20.
12. Make Sheet1 active, make cell G6 active, and then click the Bold button to remove bold formatting.
13. Save **EL1-C5-P1-RPFacAccts.xlsx**.

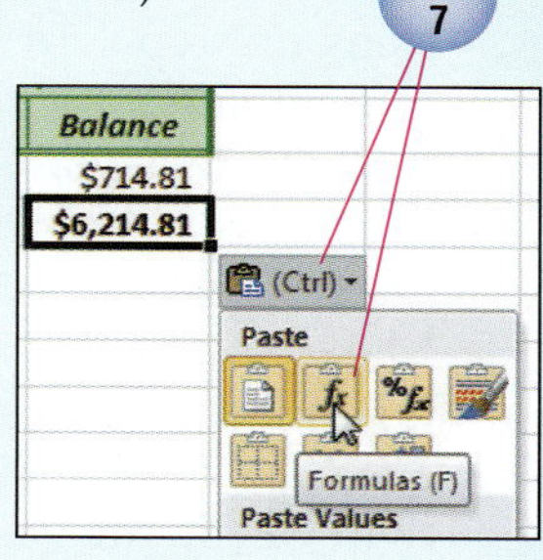

Inserting and Deleting Worksheets

A workbook, by default, contains three worksheets. You can insert additional worksheets in a workbook by clicking the Insert Worksheet tab located to the right of the Sheet3 tab. You can also press Shift + F11 to insert a worksheet or click the Insert button arrow in the Cells group in the Home tab and then click *Insert Sheet*. Insert multiple worksheets by selecting the desired number of worksheet tabs in the current workbook, clicking the Insert button in the Home tab, and then clicking *Insert Sheet* at the drop-down list.

Delete an individual worksheet from a workbook by clicking the desired worksheet tab, clicking the Delete button arrow in the Cells group in the Home tab, and then clicking *Delete Sheet* at the drop-down list. You can also delete a worksheet by right-clicking the desired tab and then clicking *Delete* at the shortcut menu. Delete multiple worksheets by selecting the desired worksheet tabs, clicking the Delete button arrow, and then clicking *Delete Sheet*. You can delete multiple worksheets by selecting the worksheet tabs, right-clicking one of the tabs, and then clicking *Delete* at the shortcut menu.

Quick Steps

Insert Worksheet
Click Insert Worksheet tab.
OR
Press Shift + F11.

Delete a Worksheet
1. Click worksheet tab.
2. Click Delete button arrow.
3. Click *Delete Sheet*.

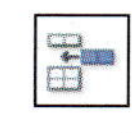

Insert

Project 1f Inserting a Worksheet

1. With **EL1-C5-P1-RPFacAccts.xlsx** open, make the following changes:
   a. Make Sheet1 active.
   b. Make cell D21 active, turn on bold, and then type **Total**.
   c. Make cell E21 active and then click once on the AutoSum button located in the Editing group in the Home tab. (This inserts the formula *=SUM(E13:E20)*.)
   d. Change the formula to *=SUM(E7:E20)* and then press Enter.
   e. Make cell F21 active and then click once on the AutoSum button in the Editing group. (This inserts the formula *=SUM(F12:F20)*.)
   f. Change the formula to *=SUM(F6:F20)* and then press Enter.

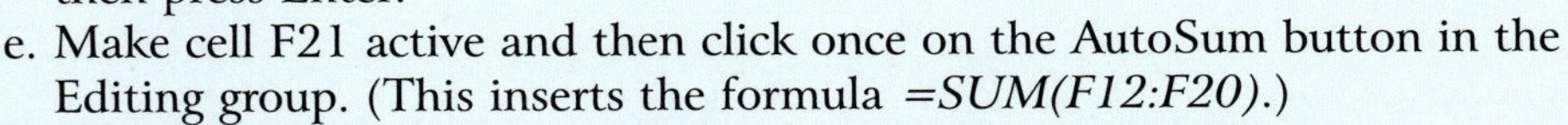

2. Make Sheet2 active and then complete the steps in Step 1 to insert the totals of the *Amount* and *Deposit* columns.
3. Make Sheet3 active and then complete the steps in Step 1 to insert the totals of the *Amount* and *Deposit* columns.
4. Insert a new worksheet by clicking the Insert Worksheet tab located to the right of the Sheet3 tab.
5. Make Sheet1 active, copy cells A1 through G3, make Sheet4 active (with cell A1 active), and then paste the cells. (When copying the cells, position the cell pointer to the right of the image, make sure the pointer displays as a white plus symbol, and then drag to select the cells.)
6. Make the following changes to the worksheet:
   a. Make cell A3 active and then type **First Quarter Summary 2012**.
   b. Change the width of column A to 20.00.
   c. Change the width of columns B, C, and D to 12.00.
   d. Select cells B4 through D4, click the Bold button in the Font group in the Home tab, and then click the Center button in the Alignment group.
   e. Select cells B5 through D7 and then change the number formatting to Currency with two decimal places and include the dollar sign symbol.
   f. Type the following text in the specified cells:

B4	=	**January**
C4	=	**February**
D4	=	**March**
A5	=	**Checks amount**
A6	=	**Deposit amount**
A7	=	**End-of-month balance**

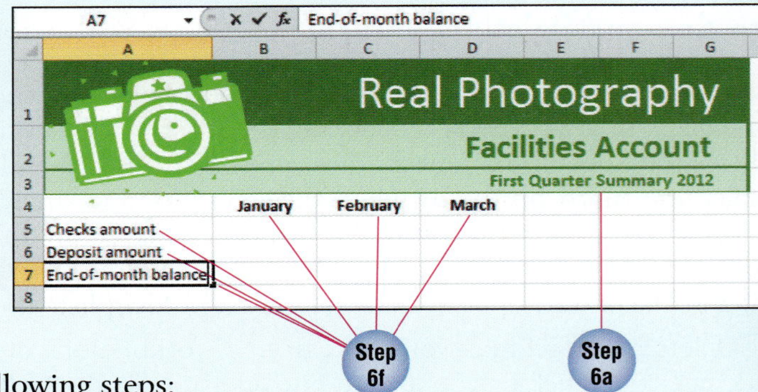

7. Copy a value by completing the following steps:
   a. Make Sheet1 active.
   b. Make cell E21 active and then click the Copy button in the Clipboard group in the Home tab.
   c. Make Sheet4 active.
   d. Make cell B5 active and then click the Paste button in the Clipboard group.

e. Click the Paste Options button and then click the Values button in the *Paste Values* section of the drop-down list.
f. Make Sheet1 active.
g. Press the Esc key to remove the moving marquee.
h. Make cell F21 active and then click the Copy button.
i. Make Sheet4 active.
j. Make cell B6 active and then click the Paste button.
k. Click the Paste Options button and then click the Values button at the drop-down list.
l. Make Sheet1 active.
m. Press the Esc key to remove the moving marquee.
n. Make cell G20 active and then click the Copy button.
o. Make Sheet4 active.
p. Make cell B7 active and then click the Paste button.
q. Click the Paste Options button and then click the Values button at the drop-down list.

8. Complete steps like those in Step 7 to insert amounts and balances for February and March.
9. Insert two new worksheets by completing the following steps:
   a. Click the Sheet1 tab, hold down the Shift key, and then click the Sheet2 tab. (This selects both tabs.)
   b. Make sure the Home tab is active, click the Insert button arrow in the Cells group, and then click *Insert Sheet* at the drop-down list. (This inserts a new Sheet5 and Sheet6.)
10. Click each of the sheet tabs in the workbook.
11. Remove the two worksheets you inserted by completing the following steps:
   a. Click the Sheet5 tab, hold down the Shift key, and then click the Sheet6 tab.
   b. Click the Delete button arrow in the Cells group in the Home tab and then click *Delete Sheet* at the drop-down list.
12. Save **EL1-C5-P1-RPFacAccts.xlsx**.

Managing Worksheets

Right-click a sheet tab and a shortcut menu displays as shown in Figure 5.3 with the options for managing worksheets. For example, remove a worksheet by clicking the *Delete* option. Move or copy a worksheet by clicking the *Move or Copy* option. Clicking this option causes a Move or Copy dialog box to display where

Quick Steps

Move or Copy a Worksheet
1. Right-click sheet tab.
2. Click *Move or Copy*.
3. At Move or Copy dialog box, click desired worksheet name in *Before sheet* list box.
4. Click OK.

OR

Drag worksheet tab to the desired position. (To copy, hold down Ctrl key while dragging.)

Figure 5.3 Sheet Tab Shortcut Menu

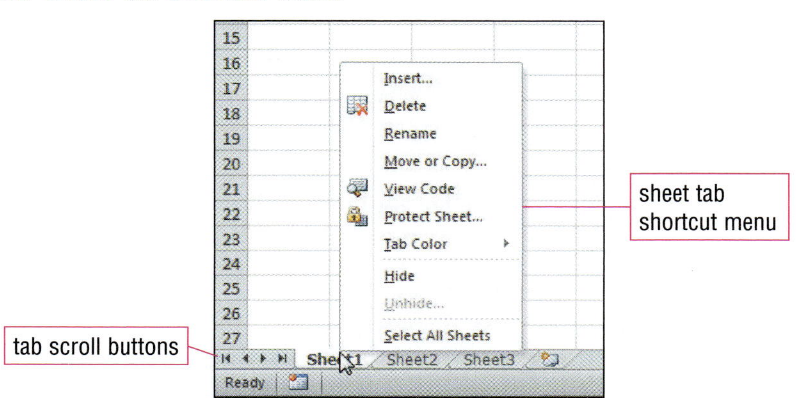

Use the tab scroll button to bring into view any worksheet tabs not currently visible.

Quick Steps

Recolor Sheet Tab

1. Right-click sheet tab.
2. Point to *Tab Color*.
3. Click desired color at color palette.

you specify before what sheet you want to move or copy the selected sheet. By default, Excel names worksheets in a workbook *Sheet1, Sheet2, Sheet3,* and so on. To rename a worksheet, click the *Rename* option (this selects the default sheet name) and then type the desired name.

In addition to the shortcut menu options, you can use the mouse to move or copy worksheets. To move a worksheet, position the mouse pointer on the worksheet tab, hold down the left mouse button (a page icon displays next to the mouse pointer), drag the page icon to the desired position, and then release the mouse button. For example, to move the Sheet2 tab after the Sheet3 tab you would position the mouse pointer on the Sheet2 tab, hold down the left mouse button, drag the page icon so it is positioned after the Sheet3 tab, and then release the mouse button. To copy a worksheet, hold down the Ctrl key while dragging the sheet tab.

Use the *Tab Color* option at the shortcut menu to apply a color to a worksheet tab. Right-click a worksheet tab, point to *Tab Color* at the shortcut menu, and then click the desired color at the color palette.

Project 1g Selecting, Moving, Renaming, and Changing the Color of Worksheet Tabs Part 7 of 9

1. With **EL1-C5-P1-RPFacAccts.xlsx** open, move Sheet4 by completing the following steps:
   a. Right-click Sheet4 and then click *Move or Copy* at the shortcut menu.
   b. At the Move or Copy dialog box, make sure *Sheet1* is selected in the *Before sheet* section, and then click OK.

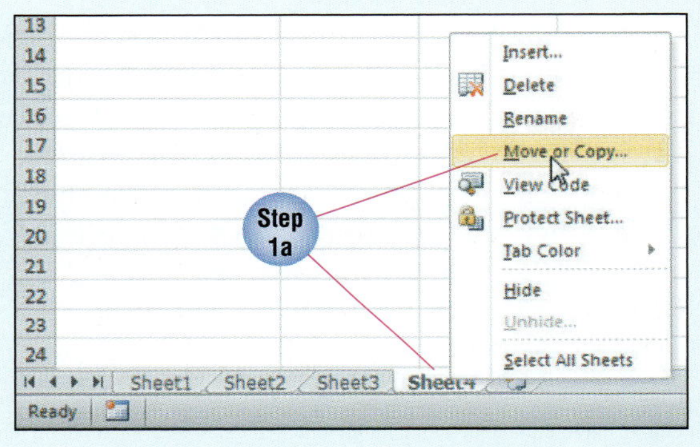

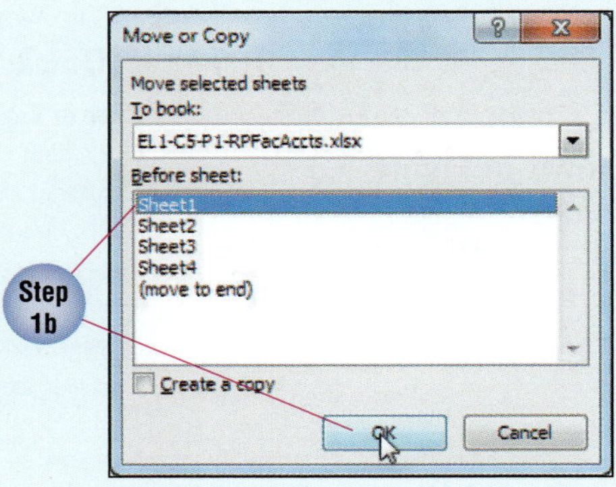

2. Rename Sheet4 by completing the following steps:
   a. Right-click the Sheet4 tab and then click *Rename*.
   b. Type **Summary** and then press Enter.

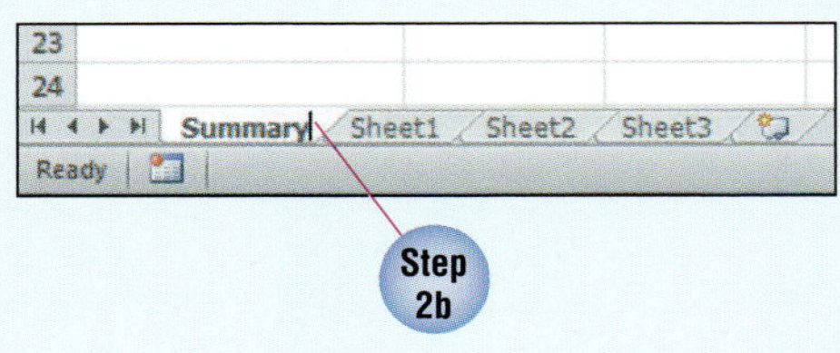

3. Complete steps similar to those in Step 2 to rename Sheet1 to January, Sheet2 to February, and Sheet3 to March.
4. Change the color of the Summary sheet tab by completing the following steps:
   a. Right-click the Summary sheet tab.
   b. Point to *Tab Color* at the shortcut menu.
   c. Click a red color of your choosing at the color palette.
5. Follow steps similar to those in Step 4 to change the January sheet tab to a blue color, the February sheet tab to a purple color, and the March sheet tab to a green color.
6. Save **EL1-C5-P1-RPFacAccts.xlsx**.

Hiding a Worksheet in a Workbook

In a workbook containing multiple worksheets, you can hide a worksheet that may contain sensitive data or data you do not want to display or print with the workbook. To hide a worksheet in a workbook, click the Format button in the Cells group in the Home tab, point to *Hide & Unhide*, and then click *Hide Sheet*. You can also hide a worksheet by right-clicking a worksheet tab and then clicking the *Hide* option at the shortcut menu. To make a hidden worksheet visible, click the Format button in the Cells group, point to *Hide & Unhide*, and then click *Unhide Sheet*, or right-click a worksheet tab and then click *Unhide* at the shortcut menu. At the Unhide dialog box shown in Figure 5.4, double-click the name of the hidden worksheet you want to display.

Quick Steps

Hide a Worksheet
1. Click Format button.
2. Point to *Hide & Unhide*.
3. Click *Hide Sheet*.

OR

1. Right-click worksheet tab.
2. Click *Hide* at shortcut menu.

Unhide a Worksheet
1. Click Format button.
2. Point to *Hide & Unhide*.
3. Click *Unhide Sheet*.
4. Double-click desired hidden worksheet in Unhide dialog box.

OR

1. Right-click worksheet tab.
2. Click *Unhide* at shortcut menu.
3. Double-click desired hidden worksheet in Unhide dialog box.

If the *Hide* option is unavailable, the workbook is protected from change.

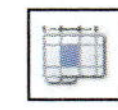

Format

Formatting Multiple Worksheets

When you apply formatting to a worksheet, such as changing margins, orientation, or inserting a header or footer, and so on, the formatting is applied only to the active worksheet. If you want formatting to apply to multiple worksheets in a workbook, select the tabs of the desired worksheets and then apply the formatting. For example, if a workbook contains three worksheets and you want to apply formatting to the first and second worksheets only, select the tabs for the first and second worksheets and then apply the formatting.

To select adjacent worksheet tabs, click the first tab, hold down the Shift key, and then click the last tab. To select nonadjacent worksheet tabs, click the first tab, hold down the Ctrl key, and then click any other tabs you want selected.

Figure 5.4 Unhide Dialog Box

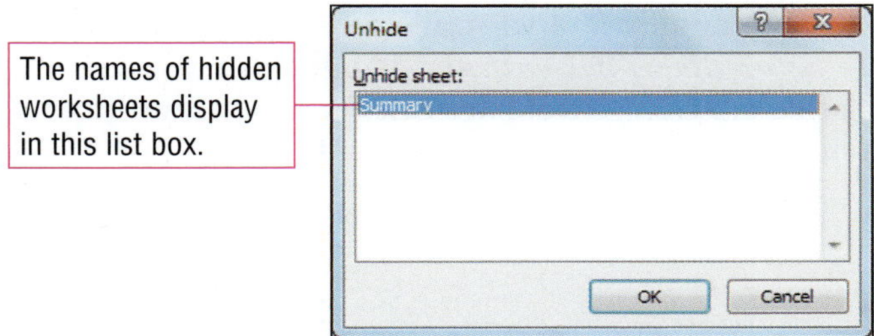

Hiding a Worksheet and Formatting Multiple Worksheets

1. With **EL1-C5-P1-RPFacAccts.xlsx** open, hide the Summary worksheet by completing the following steps:
   a. Click the Summary tab.
   b. Click the Format button in the Cells group in the Home tab, point to *Hide & Unhide*, and then click *Hide Sheet*.

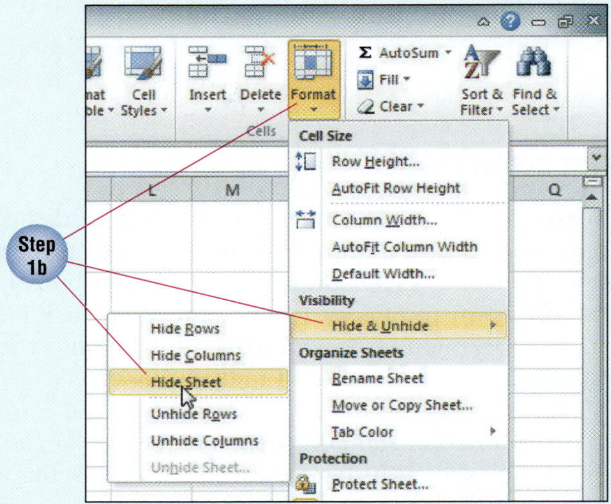

2. Unhide the worksheet by completing the following steps:
   a. Click the Format button in the Cells group, point to *Hide & Unhide*, and then click *Unhide Sheet*.
   b. At the Unhide dialog box, make sure *Summary* is selected and then click OK.
3. Insert a header for each worksheet by completing the following steps:
   a. Click the Summary tab.
   b. Hold down the Shift key and then click the March tab. (This selects all four tabs.)
   c. Click the Insert tab.
   d. Click the Header & Footer button in the Text group.
   e. Click the Header button in the Header & Footer group in the Header & Footer Tools Design tab and then click the option at the drop-down list that prints your name at the left side of the page, the page number in the middle, and the date at the right side of the page.
4. With all the sheet tabs selected, horizontally and vertically center each worksheet on the page. ***Hint: Do this at the Page Setup dialog box with the Margins tab selected.***
5. With all of the sheet tabs still selected, change the page orientation to landscape. ***Hint: Do this with the Orientation button in the Page Layout tab.***
6. Save **EL1-C5-P1-RPFacAccts.xlsx**.

Printing a Workbook Containing Multiple Worksheets

By default, Excel prints the currently displayed worksheet. If you want to print all worksheets in a workbook, display the Print tab Backstage view, click the first gallery in the Settings category, click *Print Entire Workbook* at the drop-down list, and then click the Print button. You can also print specific worksheets in a workbook by selecting the tabs of the worksheets you want printed. With the desired worksheet tabs selected, display the Print tab Backstage view and then click the Print button.

Quick Steps

Print All Worksheets in Workbook

1. Click File tab.
2. Click Print tab.
3. Click first gallery in Settings category.
4. Click *Print Entire Workbook.*
5. Click Print button.

Project 1i **Printing All Worksheets in a Workbook** Part 9 of 9

1. With **EL1-C5-P1-RPFacAccts.xlsx** open, click the File tab and then click the Print tab.
2. At the Print tab Backstage view, click the first gallery in the Settings category and then click *Print Entire Workbook* at the drop-down list.
3. Click the Print button.

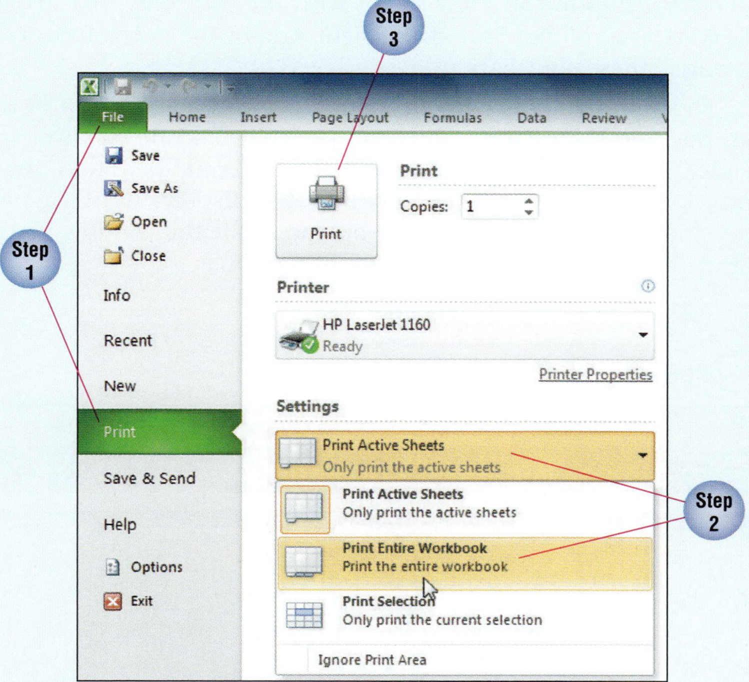

4. Save and then close **EL1-C5-P1-RPFacAccts.xlsx**.

Project 2 Write Formulas Using Ranges in an Equipment Usage Workbook

2 Parts

You will open an equipment usage workbook and then split the window and edit cells. You will also name ranges and then use the range names to write formulas in the workbook.

Quick Steps

Split a Worksheet
1. Click View tab.
2. Click Split button.
OR
Drag horizontal and/or vertical split bars.

HINT

Restore a split window by double-clicking anywhere on the split bar that divides the panes.

Split

Splitting a Worksheet into Windows and Freezing and Unfreezing Panes

In some worksheets, not all cells display at one time in the worksheet area (such as EL1-C5-P2-HCEqpRpt.xlsx). When working in worksheets with more cells than can display at one time, you may find splitting the worksheet window into panes helpful. Split the worksheet window into panes with the Split button in the Window group in the View tab or with the split bars that display at the top of the vertical scroll bar and at the right side of the horizontal scroll bar. Figure 5.5 identifies these split bars.

To split a window with the split bar located at the top of the vertical scroll bar, position the mouse pointer on the split bar until it turns into a double-headed arrow with a short double line in the middle. Hold down the left mouse button, drag down the thick gray line that displays until the pane is the desired size, and then release the mouse button. Split the window vertically with the split bar at the right side of the horizontal scroll bar.

Figure 5.5 Split Bars

horizontal split bar

A1 | Highland Construction

Highland Construction

EQUIPMENT USAGE REPORT

Hours	January	February	March	April	May	June	July	August	September	October	November	December
Total hours available	2300	2430	2530	2400	2440	2240	2520	2520	2390	2540		
Avoidable delays	19	12	16	20	14	15	9	8	12	7		
Unavoidable delays	9	8	6	12	9	10	10	13	8	9		
Repairs	5	7	12	9	10	6	7	8	10	13		
Servicing	6	13	7	6	4	5	8	3	12	6		
Unassigned	128	95	85	135	95	75	145	120	124	112		
In use	2040	2105	2320	2180	2050	1995	2320	2250	2190	1945		

Sheet1 Sheet2 Sheet3

Ready 100%

vertical split bar

Figure 5.6 Split Window

Highland Construction

EQUIPMENT USAGE REPORT

Hours	January	February	March	April	May	June	July	August	September	October	November	December
Total hours available	2300	2430	2530	2400	2440	2240	2520	2520	2390	2540		
Avoidable delays	19	12	16	20	14	15	9	8	12	7		
Unavoidable delays	9	8	6	12	9	10	10	13	8	9		
Repairs	5	7	12	9	10	6	7	8	10	13		
Servicing	6	13	7	6	4	5	8	3	12	6		
Unassigned	128	95	85	135	95	75	145	120	124	112		
In use	2040	2105	2320	2180	2050	1995	2320	2250	2190	1945		

To split a worksheet window with the Split button, click the View tab and then click the Split button. This causes the worksheet to split into four window panes as shown in Figure 5.6. The windows are split by thick, light blue lines (with a three-dimensional look). To remove a split from a worksheet click the Split button to deactivate it or drag the split bars to the upper left corner of the worksheet.

A window pane will display the active cell. As the insertion point is moved through the pane, another active cell with a blue background may display. This additional active cell displays when the insertion point passes over one of the light blue lines that creates the pane. As you move through a worksheet, you may see both active cells — one with a normal background and one with a blue background. If you make a change to the active cell, the change is made in both. If you want only one active cell to display, freeze the window panes by clicking the Freeze Panes button in the Window group in the View tab and then clicking *Freeze Panes* at the drop-down list. You can maintain the display of column headings while editing or typing text in cells by clicking the Freeze Panes button and then clicking *Freeze Top Row*. Maintain the display of row headings by clicking the Freeze Panes button and then clicking *Freeze First Column*. Unfreeze window panes by clicking the Freeze Panes button and then clicking *Unfreeze Panes* at the drop-down list.

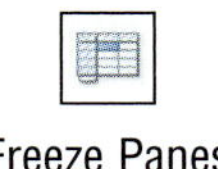
Freeze Panes

Using the mouse, you can move the thick, light blue lines that divide the window into panes. To do this, position the mouse pointer on the line until the pointer turns into a double-headed arrow with a double line in the middle. Hold down the left mouse button, drag the outline of the light blue line to the desired location, and then release the mouse button. If you want to move both the horizontal and vertical lines at the same time, position the mouse pointer on the intersection of the thick, light blue lines until it turns into a four-headed arrow. Hold down the left mouse button, drag the thick, light blue lines in the desired direction, and then release the mouse button.

Splitting Windows and Editing Cells

Part 1 of 2

1. Open **HCEqpRpt.xlsx** and then save the workbook with Save As and name it **EL1-C5-P2-HCEqpRpt**.
2. Make sure cell A1 is active and then split the window by clicking the View tab and then clicking the Split button in the Window group. (This splits the window into four panes.)
3. Drag the vertical light gray line by completing the following steps:
   a. Position the mouse pointer on the vertical split line until the pointer turns into a double-headed arrow pointing left and right with a double-line between.
   b. Hold down the left mouse button, drag to the left until the vertical light gray line is immediately to the right of the first column, and then release the mouse button.

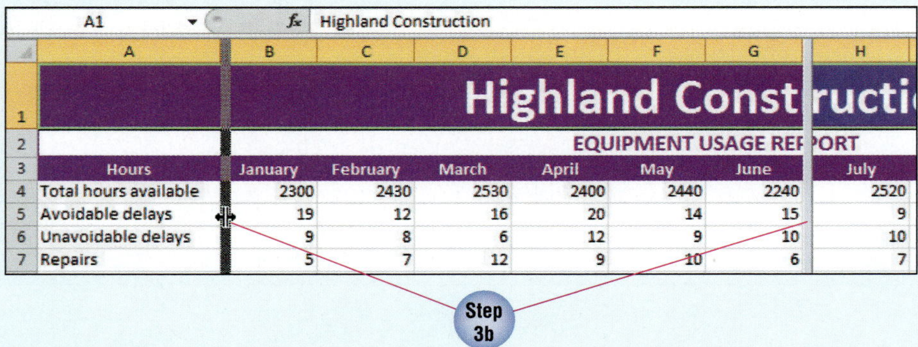

4. Freeze the window panes by clicking the Freeze Panes button in the Window group in the View tab and then clicking *Freeze Panes* at the drop-down list.

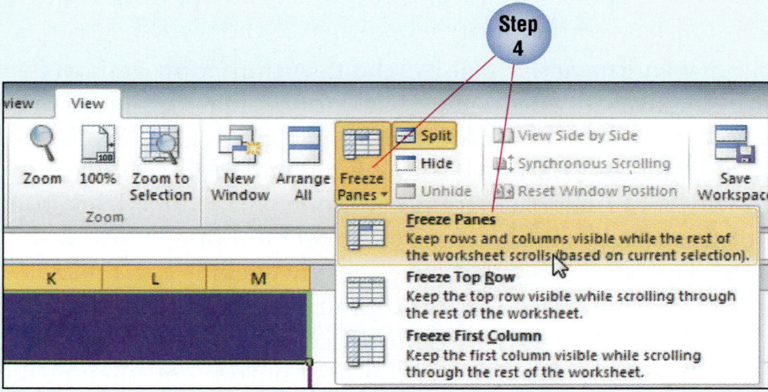

5. Make cell L4 active and then type the following data in the specified cells:

L4	=	2310	M4	=	2210
L5	=	12	M5	=	5
L6	=	5	M6	=	7
L7	=	9	M7	=	8
L8	=	11	M8	=	12
L9	=	95	M9	=	120
L10	=	2005	M10	=	1830

6. Unfreeze the window panes by clicking the Freeze Panes button and then clicking *Unfreeze Panes* at the drop-down list.
7. Remove the panes by clicking the Split button in the Window group to deactivate it.
8. Save **EL1-C5-P2-HCEqpRpt.xlsx**.

Working with Ranges

A selected group of cells is referred to as a ***range***. A range of cells can be formatted, moved, copied, or deleted. You can also name a range of cells and then move the insertion point to the range or use a named range as part of a formula.

To name a range, select the cells and then click in the Name Box located at the left of the Formula bar. Type a name for the range (do not use a space) and then press Enter. To move the insertion point to a specific range and select the range, click the down-pointing arrow at the right side of the Name Box and then click the range name.

You can also name a range using the Define Name button in the Formulas tab. To do this, click the Formulas tab and then click the Define Name button in the Defined Names group. At the New Name dialog box, type a name for the range and then click OK.

You can use a range name in a formula. For example, if a range is named *Profit* and you want to insert the average of all cells in the *Profit* range, you would make the desired cell active and then type *=AVERAGE(Profit)*. You can use a named range in the current worksheet or in another worksheet within the workbook.

Quick Steps

Name a Range
1. Select cells.
2. Click in Name Box.
3. Type range name.
4. Press Enter.

Another method for moving to a range is to click the Find & Select button in the Editing group in the Home tab and then click *Go To*. At the Go To dialog box, double-click the range name.

Define Name

Project 2b Naming a Range and Using a Range in a Formula

Part 2 of 2

1. With **EL1-C5-P2-HCEqpRpt.xlsx** open, click the Sheet2 tab and then type the following text in the specified cells:
   A1 = EQUIPMENT USAGE REPORT
   A2 = Yearly hours
   A3 = Avoidable delays
   A4 = Unavoidable delays
   A5 = Total delay hours
   A6 = (leave blank)
   A7 = Repairs
   A8 = Servicing
   A9 = Total repair/servicing hours
2. Make the following formatting changes to the worksheet:
   a. Automatically adjust the width of column A.
   b. Center and bold the text in cells A1 and A2.
3. Select a range of cells in worksheet 1, name the range, and use it in a formula in worksheet 2 by completing the following steps:
   a. Click the Sheet1 tab.
   b. Select cells B5 through M5.
   c. Click in the Name Box located to the left of the Formula bar.
   d. Type adhours (for Avoidable Delays Hours) and then press Enter.
   e. Click the Sheet2 tab.
   f. Make cell B3 active.
   g. Type the equation =SUM(adhours) and then press Enter.

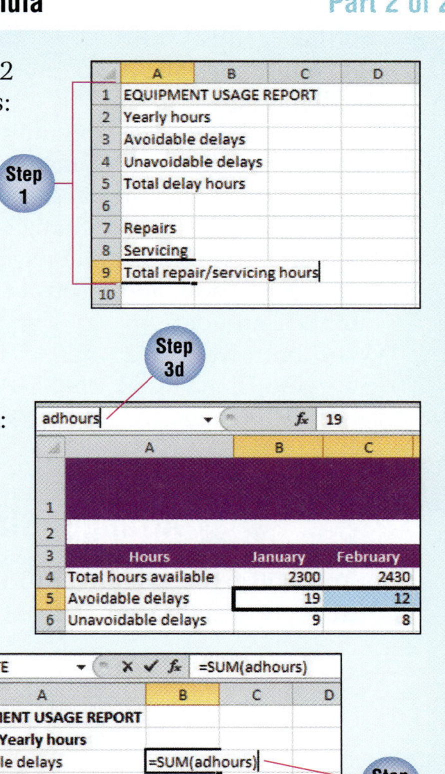

4. Click the Sheet1 tab and then complete the following steps:
   a. Select cells B6 through M6.
   b. Click the Formulas tab.
   c. Click the Define Name button in the Defined Names group.
   d. At the New Name dialog box, type **udhours** and then click OK.
   e. Make worksheet 2 active, make cell B4 active, and then type the equation **=SUM(udhours)**.

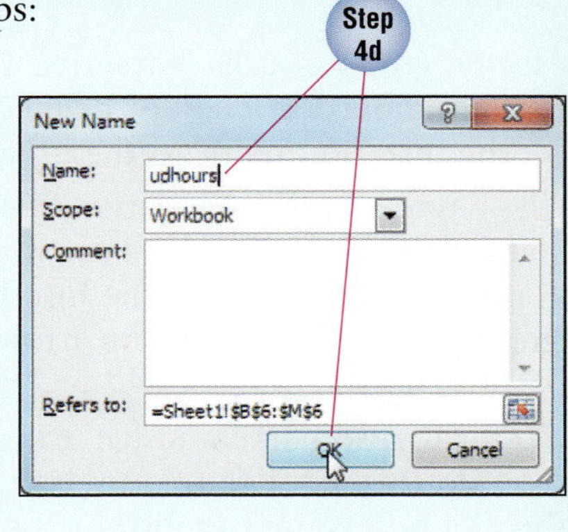

5. Make worksheet 1 active and then complete the following steps:
   a. Select cells B7 through M7 and then name the range *rhours*.
   b. Make worksheet 2 active, make cell B7 active, and then type the equation **=SUM(rhours)**.
   c. Make worksheet 1 active.
   d. Select cells B8 through M8 and then name the range *shours*.
   e. Make worksheet 2 active, make cell B8 active, and then type the equation **=SUM(shours)**.
6. With worksheet 2 still active, make the following changes:
   a. Make cell B5 active.
   b. Double-click the AutoSum button in the Editing group in the Home tab.
   c. Make cell B9 active.
   d. Double-click the AutoSum button in the Editing group in the Home tab.
7. Make worksheet 1 active and then move to the range *adhours* by clicking the down-pointing arrow at the right side of the Name Box and then clicking *adhours* at the drop-down list.
8. Select both sheet tabs, change the orientation to landscape, scale the contents to fit on one page (in Page Layout tab, change width to *1 page*), and insert a custom footer with your name, page number, and date.
9. With both worksheet tabs selected, print both worksheets in the workbook.
10. Save and then close **EL1-C5-P2-HCEqpRpt.xlsx**.

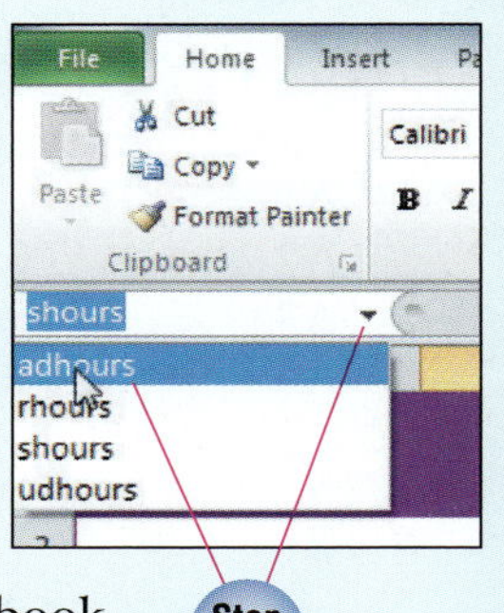

Project 3 Arrange, Size, and Copy Data between Workbooks 3 Parts

You will open, arrange, hide, unhide, size, and move multiple workbooks. You will also copy cells from one workbook and paste in another workbook.

Working with Windows

You can open multiple workbooks in Excel, open a new window with the current workbook, and arrange the open workbooks in the Excel window. With multiple workbooks open, you can cut and paste or copy and paste cell entries from one workbook to another using the same techniques discussed earlier in this chapter with the exception that you activate the destination workbook before executing the Paste command.

Opening Multiple Workbooks

New Window

With multiple workbooks open, or more than one version of the current workbook open, you can move or copy information between workbooks and compare the contents of several workbooks. When you open a new workbook or a new window of the current workbook, it is placed on top of the original workbook. Open a new window of the current workbook by clicking the View tab and then clicking the New Window button in the Window group. Excel adds a colon followed by the number *2* to the end of the workbook title and adds a colon followed by the number *1* to the end of the originating workbook name. Open multiple workbooks at one time at the Open dialog box. Select adjacent workbooks by clicking the name of the first workbook to be opened, holding down the Shift key, clicking the name of the last workbook to be opened, and then clicking the Open button. If workbooks are nonadjacent, click the name of the first workbook to be opened, hold down the Ctrl key, and then click the names of any other workbooks you want to open.

Switch Windows

To see what workbooks are currently open, click the View tab and then click the Switch Windows button in the Window group. The names of the open workbooks display in a drop-down list and the workbook name preceded by a check mark is the active workbook. To make one of the other workbooks active, click the desired workbook name at the drop-down list.

Another method for determining which workbooks are open is to hover your mouse over the Excel icon button that displays on the Taskbar. This causes a thumbnail to display of each open workbook. If you have more than one workbook open, the Excel button on the Taskbar displays another layer in a cascaded manner. The layer behind the Excel button displays only a portion of the edge at the right side of the button. If you have multiple workbooks open, hovering the mouse over the Excel button on the Taskbar will cause thumbnails of all of the workbooks to display above the button. (This is dependent on your monitor size.) To change to the desired workbook, click the thumbnail that represents the workbook.

Arranging Workbooks

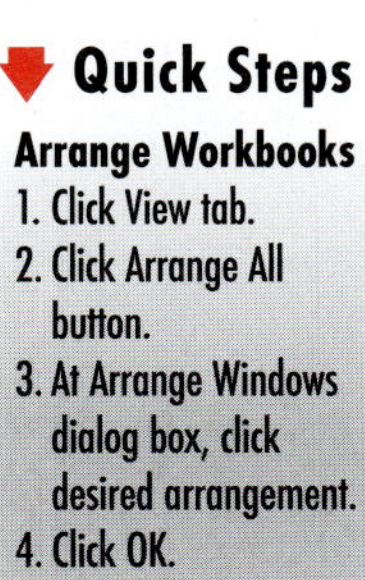

Quick Steps

Arrange Workbooks

1. Click View tab.
2. Click Arrange All button.
3. At Arrange Windows dialog box, click desired arrangement.
4. Click OK.

Arrange All

If you have more than one workbook open, you can arrange the workbooks at the Arrange Windows dialog box shown in Figure 5.7. To display this dialog box, open several workbooks and then click the Arrange All button in the Window group in the View tab. At the Arrange Windows dialog box, click *Tiled* to display a portion of each open workbook. Figure 5.8 displays four tiled workbooks.

Figure 5.7 Arrange Windows Dialog Box

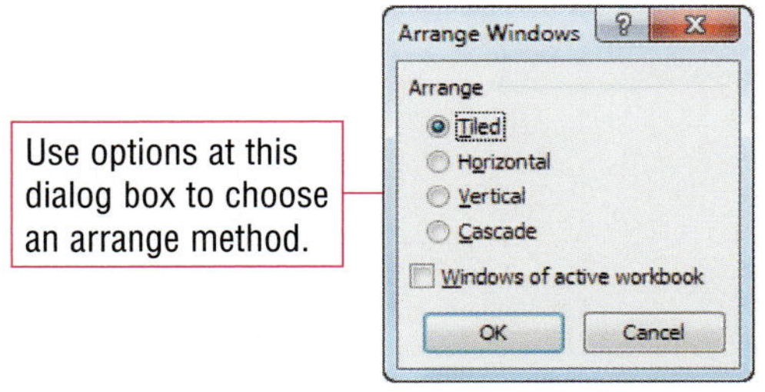

Figure 5.8 Tiled Workbooks

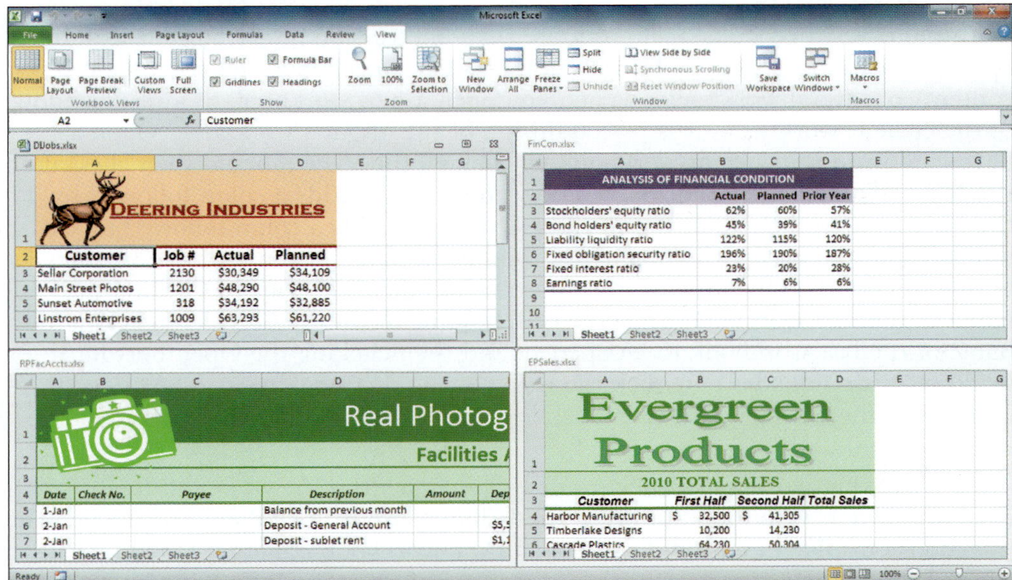

Choose the *Horizontal* option at the Arrange Windows dialog box and the open workbooks display across the screen. The *Vertical* option displays the open workbooks up and down the screen. The last option, *Cascade*, displays the Title bar of each open workbook. Figure 5.9 shows four cascaded workbooks.

The option you select for displaying multiple workbooks depends on which part of the workbooks is most important to view simultaneously. For example, the tiled workbooks in Figure 5.8 allow you to view the company logos and the first few rows and columns of each workbook.

Figure 5.9 Cascaded Workbooks

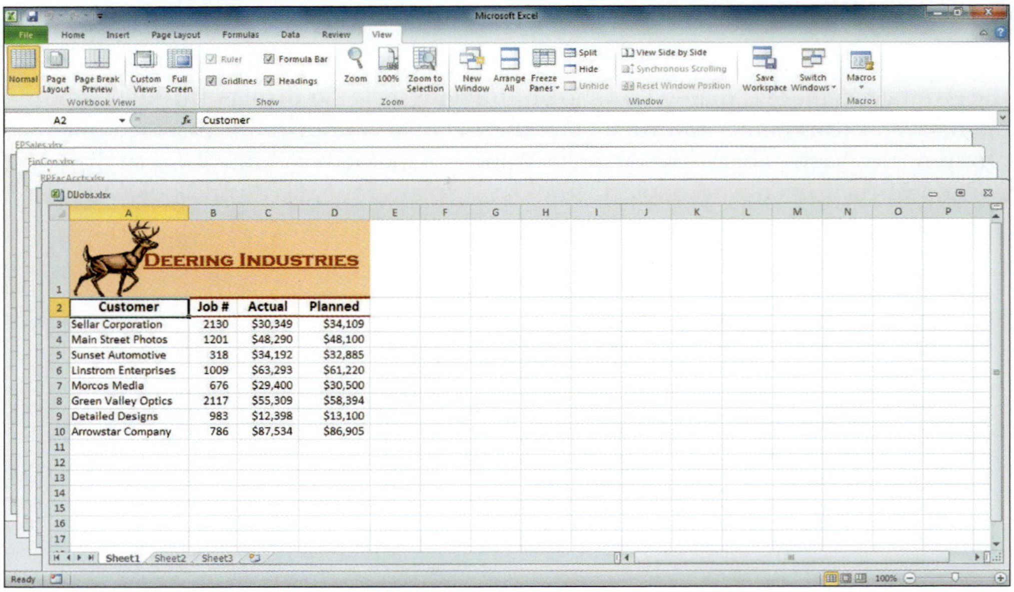

Hiding/Unhiding Workbooks

Hide

Unhide

With the Hide button in the Window group in the View tab, you can hide the active workbook. If a workbook has been hidden, redisplay the workbook by clicking the Unhide button in the Window group in the View tab. At the Unhide dialog box, make sure the desired workbook is selected in the list box and then click OK.

Project 3a Opening, Arranging, and Hiding/Unhiding Workbooks

Part 1 of 3

1. Open several workbooks at the same time by completing the following steps:
   a. Display the Open dialog box.
   b. Click the workbook named ***DIJobs.xlsx***.
   c. Hold down the Ctrl key, click ***EPSales.xlsx***, click ***FinCon.xlsx***, and click ***RPFacAccts.xlsx***.
   d. Release the Ctrl key and then click the Open button in the dialog box.
2. Make **DIJobs.xlsx** the active workbook by clicking the View tab, clicking the Switch Windows button, and then clicking ***DIJobs.xlsx*** at the drop-down list.

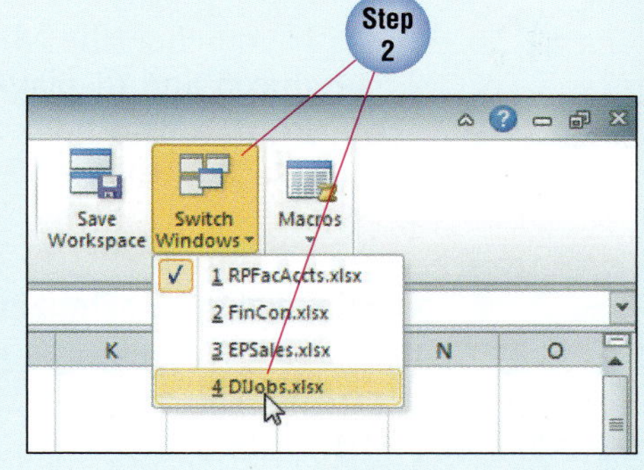

3. Tile the workbooks by completing the following steps:
   a. Click the Arrange All button in the Window group in the View tab.
   b. At the Arrange Windows dialog box, make sure *Tiled* is selected and then click OK.

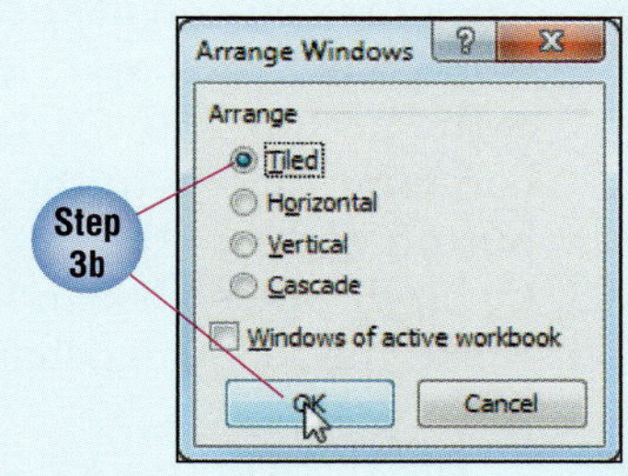

4. Tile the workbooks horizontally by completing the following steps:
   a. Click the Arrange All button.
   b. At the Arrange Windows dialog box, click *Horizontal*.
   c. Click OK.
5. Cascade the workbooks by completing the following steps:
   a. Click the Arrange All button.
   b. At the Arrange Windows dialog box, click *Cascade*.
   c. Click OK.
6. Hide and unhide workbooks by completing the following steps:
   a. Make sure **DIJobs.xlsx** is the active workbook (displays on top of the other workbooks).
   b. Click the Hide button in the Window group in the View tab.
   c. Make sure **RPFacAccts.xlsx** is the active workbook (displays on top of the other workbooks).
   d. Click the Hide button.
   e. Click the Unhide button.
   f. At the Unhide dialog box, click ***RPFacAccts.xlsx*** in the list box, and then click OK.
   g. Click the Unhide button.
   h. At the Unhide dialog box, make sure **DIJobs.xlsx** is selected in the list box and then click OK.

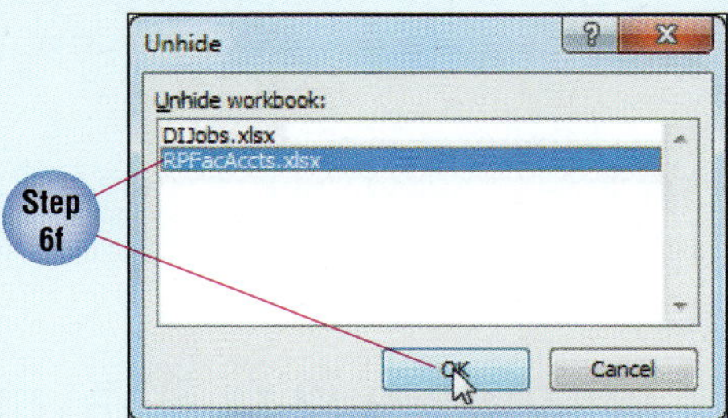

7. Close all of the open workbooks (without saving changes) except **DIJobs.xlsx**.
8. Open a new window with the current workbook by clicking the View tab and then clicking the New Window button in the Window group. (Notice that the new window contains the workbook name followed by a colon and the number 2.)
9. Switch back and forth between the two versions of the workbook.
10. Make **DIJobs.xlsx:2** the active window and then close the workbook.

Sizing and Moving Workbooks

Maximize

Minimize

Close

Restore Down

You can use the Maximize and Minimize buttons located in the upper right corner of the active workbook to change the size of the window. The Maximize button is the button in the upper right corner of the active workbook immediately to the left of the Close button. (The Close button is the button containing the *X*.) The Minimize button is located immediately to the left of the Maximize button.

If you arrange all open workbooks and then click the Maximize button in the active workbook, the active workbook expands to fill the screen. In addition, the Maximize button changes to the Restore Down button. To return the active workbook back to its size before it was maximized, click the Restore Down button.

If you click the Minimize button in the active workbook, the workbook is reduced and displays as a layer behind the Excel button on the Taskbar. To maximize a workbook that has been minimized, click the Excel button on the Taskbar and then click the thumbnail representing the workbook.

Project 3b Minimizing, Maximizing, and Restoring Workbooks

Part 2 of 3

1. Make sure **DIJobs.xlsx** is open.
2. Maximize **DIJobs.xlsx** by clicking the Maximize button at the right side of the workbook Title bar. (The Maximize button is the button at the right side of the Title bar, immediately to the left of the Close button.)
3. Open **EPSales.xlsx** and **FinCon.xlsx**.
4. Make the following changes to the open workbooks:
   a. Tile the workbooks.
   b. Make **DIJobs.xlsx** the active workbook. (Title bar displays with a light gray background [the background color may vary depending on how Windows is customized]).
   c. Minimize **DIJobs.xlsx** by clicking the Minimize button that displays at the right side of the Title bar.
   d. Make **EPSales.xlsx** the active workbook and then minimize it.
   e. Minimize **FinCon.xlsx**.
5. Close all workbooks.

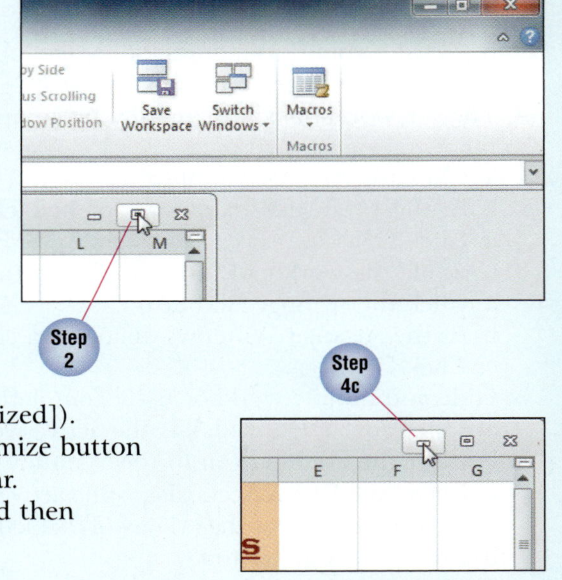

Moving, Copying, and Pasting Data

With more than one workbook open, you can move, copy, and/or paste data from one workbook to another. To move, copy, and/or paste data between workbooks, use the cutting and pasting options you learned earlier in this chapter, together with the information about windows in this chapter.

Project 3c Copying Selected Cells from One Open Worksheet to Another

Part 3 of 3

1. Open **DIFebJobs.xlsx**.
2. If you just completed Project 3b, click the Maximize button so the worksheet fills the entire worksheet window.
3. Save the workbook with Save As and name it **EL1-C5-P3-DIFebJobs**.
4. With **EL1-C5-P3-DIFebJobs.xlsx** open, open **DIJobs.xlsx**.
5. Select and then copy text from **DIJobs.xlsx** to **EL1-C5-P3-DIFebJobs.xlsx** by completing the following steps:
   a. With **DIJobs.xlsx** the active workbook, select cells A3 through D10.
   b. Click the Copy button in the Clipboard group in the Home tab.
   c. Click the Excel button on the Taskbar and then click the **EL1-C5-P3-DIFebJobs.xlsx** thumbnail.

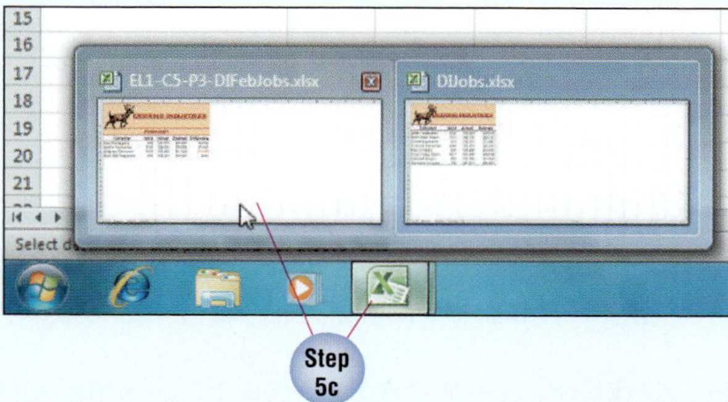

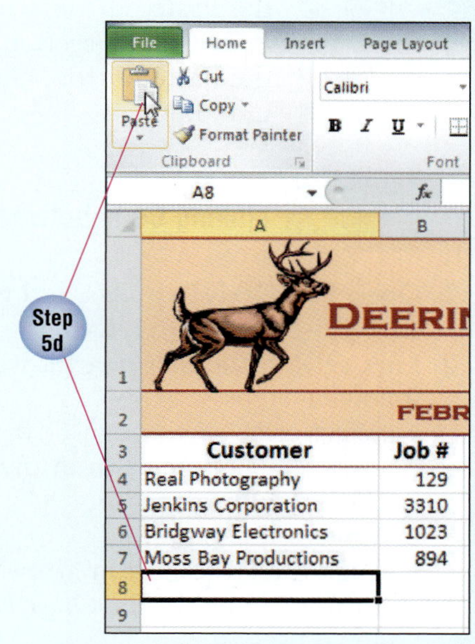

   d. Make cell A8 the active cell and then click the Paste button in the Clipboard group in the Home tab.
   e. Make cell E7 active and then drag the fill handle down to cell E15.
6. Print **EL1-C5-P3-DIFebJobs.xlsx** horizontally and vertically centered on the page.
7. Save and then close **EL1-C5-P3-DIFebJobs.xlsx**.
8. Close **DIJobs.xlsx**.

Project 4 Linking and Copying Data within and between Worksheets and Word

2 Parts

You will open a workbook containing four worksheets with quarterly expenses data, copy and then link cells between the worksheets, and then copy and paste the worksheets into Word as picture objects.

Moving Data

You can move or copy data within a worksheet, between worksheets, and also between workbooks and other programs such as Word, PowerPoint, or Access. The Paste Options button provides a variety of options for pasting data in a worksheet, another workbook, or another program. In addition to pasting data, you can also link data and paste data as an object or a picture object.

Linking Data

In some situations, you may want to copy and link data within or between worksheets or workbooks rather than copy and paste data. Linking data is useful in worksheets or workbooks where you need to maintain consistency and control over critical data. When data is linked, a change made in a linked cell is automatically made to the other cells in the link. You can make links with individual cells or with a range of cells. When linking data, the worksheet that contains the original data is called the ***source worksheet*** and the worksheet relying on the source worksheet for the data in the link is called the ***dependent worksheet***.

Quick Steps

Link Data between Worksheets

1. Select cells.
2. Click Copy button.
3. Click desired worksheet tab.
4. Click in desired cell.
5. Click Paste button arrow.
6. Click *Paste Link* at drop-down list.

To create a link, make active the cell containing the data to be linked (or select the cells) and then click the Copy button in the Clipboard group in the Home tab. Make active the worksheet where you want to paste the cells, click the Paste button arrow, and then click the Paste Link button located in the *Other Paste Options* section in the drop-down list. You can also create a link by clicking the Paste button, clicking the Paste Options button, and then clicking the Paste Link button.

Project 4a Linking Cells between Worksheets

Part 1 of 2

1. Open **DWQtrlyExp.xlsx** and then save the workbook with Save As and name it **EL1-C5-P4-DWQtrlyExp**.
2. Link cells in the first quarter worksheet to the other three worksheets by completing the following steps:
   a. Select cells C4 through C10.
   b. Click the Copy button in the Clipboard group in the Home tab.
   c. Click the 2nd Qtr tab.
   d. Make cell C4 active.
   e. Click the Paste button arrow and then click the Paste Link button located in the *Other Paste Options* section in the drop-down list.
   f. Click the 3rd Qtr tab and then make cell C4 active.
   g. Click the Paste button arrow and then click the Paste Link button.
   h. Click the 4th Qtr tab and then make cell C4 active.
   i. Click the Paste button.
   j. Click the Paste Options button and then click the Paste Link button in the *Other Paste Options* section in the drop-down list.

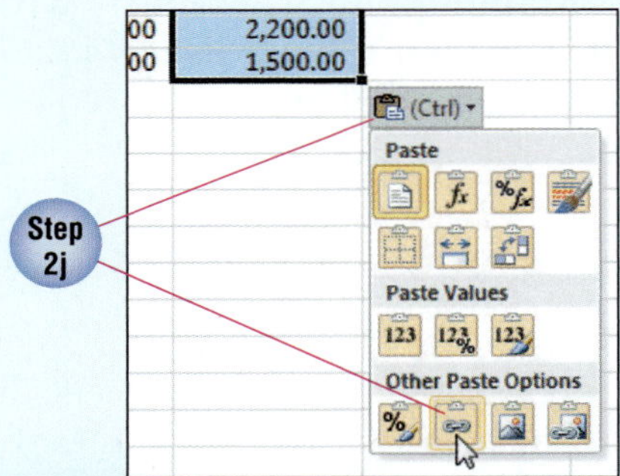

3. Click the 1st Qtr tab and then press the Esc key to remove the moving marquee.
4. Insert a formula in all worksheets that subtracts the Budget amount from the Variance amount by completing the following steps:
   a. Make sure the first quarter worksheet displays.
   b. Hold down the Shift key and then click the 4th Qtr tab. (This selects all four tabs.)
   c. Make cell D4 active and then type the formula =C4-B4 and press Enter.
   d. Copy the formula in cell D4 down to cells D5 through D10.
   e. Make cell D4 active and then click the Accounting Number Format button.
   f. Click the 2nd Qtr tab and notice that the formula was inserted and copied in this worksheet.
   g. Click the other worksheet tabs and notice the amounts in column D.
   h. Click the 1st Qtr tab.
5. With the first quarter worksheet active, make the following changes to some of the linked cells:

   C4: Change *$126,000* to *$128,000*

   C5: Change *54,500* to *56,000*

   C9: Change *2,200* to *2,400*
6. Click the 2nd Qtr tab and notice that the values in cells C4, C5, and C9 automatically changed (because they were linked to the first quarter worksheet).
7. Click the other tabs and notice that the values changed.
8. Save **EL1-C5-P4-DWQtrlyExp.xlsx** and then print all four worksheets in the workbook.

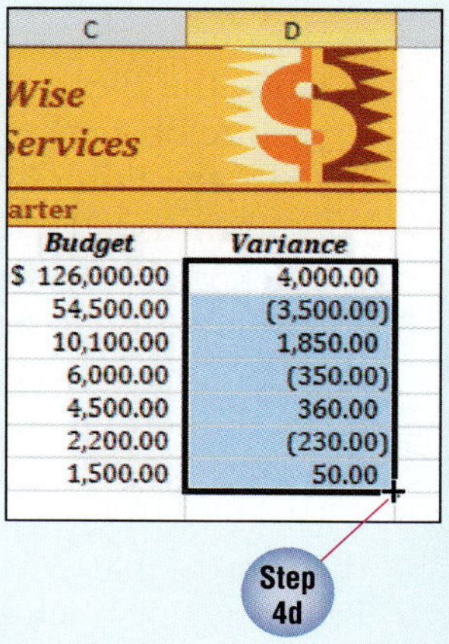

Copying and Pasting Data between Programs

Microsoft Office is a suite that allows integration, which is the combining of data from two or more programs into one file. Integration can occur by copying and pasting data between programs. For example, you can create a worksheet in Excel, select specific data in the worksheet, and then copy it to a Word document. When pasting Excel data in a Word document, you can choose to keep the source formatting, use destination styles, link the data, insert the data as a picture, or keep the text only.

Project 4b Copying and Pasting Excel Data into a Word Document Part 2 of 2

1. With **EL1-C5-P4-DWQtrlyExp.xlsx** open, open the Word program.
2. In Word, open the document named **DWQtrlyRpt.docx** located in the Excel2010L1C5 folder on your storage medium.
3. Save the Word document with Save As and name it **EL1-C5-P4-DWQtrlyRpt**.
4. Click the Excel button on the Taskbar.
5. Copy the first quarter data into the Word document by completing the following steps:
   a. Click the 1st Qtr tab.
   b. Select cells A2 through D10.
   c. Click the Copy button in the Clipboard group in the Home tab.
   d. Click the Word button on the Taskbar.

e. In the **EL1-C5-P4-DWQtrlyRpt.docx** document, press Ctrl + End to move the insertion point below the heading.
f. Click the Paste button arrow. (This displays a drop-down list of paste option buttons.)
g. Move your mouse over the various buttons in the drop-down list to see how each option will insert the data in the document.
h. Click the Picture button. (This inserts the data as a picture object.)
i. Press the Enter key twice. (This moves the insertion point below the data.)
j. Click the Excel button on the Taskbar.

6. Click the 2nd Qtr tab and then complete steps similar to those in Step 5 to copy and paste the second quarter data to the Word document.
7. Click the 3rd Qtr tab and then complete steps similar to those in Step 5 to copy and paste the third quarter data to the Word document.
8. Click the 4th Qtr tab and then complete steps similar to those in Step 5 to copy and paste the fourth quarter data to the Word document. (The data should fit on one page.)
9. Print the document by clicking the File tab, clicking the Print tab, and then clicking the Print button at the Print tab Backstage view.
10. Save and then close **EL1-C5-P4-DWQtrlyRpt.docx** and then exit Word.
11. In Excel, press the Esc key to remove the moving marquee and then make cell A1 active.
12. Save and then close **EL1-C5-P4-DWQtrlyExp.xlsx**.

Chapter Summary

- An Excel workbook, by default, contains three worksheets. Click a worksheet tab to display the worksheet.
- Move selected cells and cell contents in and between worksheets using the Cut, Copy, and Paste buttons in the Clipboard group in the Home tab or by dragging with the mouse.
- Move selected cells with the mouse by dragging the outline of the selected cells to the desired position.
- Copy selected cells with the mouse by holding down the Ctrl key and the left mouse button, dragging the outline of the selected cells to the desired location, releasing the left mouse button, and then releasing the Ctrl key.
- When pasting data, use the Paste Options button to specify what you want pasted. Click the Paste Options button and a drop-down list of buttons displays with options to specify how you want the data posted.
- Use the Clipboard task pane to collect and paste data within and between worksheets and workbooks. Display the Clipboard task pane by clicking the Clipboard group dialog box launcher.
- Insert a worksheet in a workbook by clicking the Insert Worksheet tab located to the right of the Sheet3 tab or pressing Shift + F11.

- Perform maintenance activities, such as deleting and renaming, on worksheets within a workbook by clicking the right mouse button on a sheet tab and then clicking the desired option at the shortcut menu.
- You can use the mouse to move or copy worksheets. To move a worksheet, drag the worksheet tab with the mouse. To copy a worksheet hold down the Ctrl key and then drag the worksheet tab with the mouse.
- Use the *Tab Color* option at the sheet tab shortcut menu to apply a color to a worksheet tab.
- Hide and unhide a worksheet by clicking the Format button in the Cells group and then clicking the desired option at the drop-down list or by right-clicking the worksheet tab and then clicking the desired option at the shortcut menu.
- Manage more than one worksheet at a time by first selecting the worksheets. Use the mouse together with the Shift key to select adjacent worksheet tabs and use the mouse together with the Ctrl key to select nonadjacent worksheet tabs.
- If you want formatting to apply to multiple worksheets in a workbook, select the tabs of the desired worksheets and then apply the formatting.
- To print all worksheets in a workbook, display the Print tab Backstage view, click the first gallery in the Settings category, and then click *Print Entire Workbook* at the drop-down list. You can also print specific worksheets by selecting the tabs of the worksheets you want to print.
- Split the worksheet window into panes with the Split button in the Window group in the View tab or with the split bars on the horizontal and vertical scroll bars.
- To remove a split from a worksheet, click the Split button to deactivate it or drag the split bars to the upper left corner of the worksheet.
- Freeze window panes by clicking the Freeze Panes button in the Window group in the View tab and then clicking *Freeze Panes* at the drop-down list. Unfreeze window panes by clicking the Freeze Panes button and then clicking *Unfreeze Panes* at the drop-down list.
- A selected group of cells is referred to as a range. A range can be named and used in a formula. Name a range by typing the name in the Name Box located to the left of the Formula bar or at the New Name dialog box.
- To open multiple workbooks that are adjacent, display the Open dialog box, click the first workbook, hold down the Shift key, click the last workbook, and then click the Open button. If workbooks are nonadjacent, click the first workbook, hold down the Ctrl key, click the desired workbooks, and then click the Open button.
- To see a list of open workbooks, click the View tab and then click the Switch Windows button in the Window group.
- Arrange multiple workbooks in a window with options at the Arrange Windows dialog box.
- Hide the active workbook by clicking the Hide button and unhide a workbook by clicking the Unhide button in the Window group in the View tab.
- Click the Maximize button located in the upper right corner of the active workbook to make the workbook fill the entire window area. Click the Minimize button to shrink the active workbook to a button on the Taskbar. Click the Restore Down button to return the workbook to its previous size.
- You can move, copy, and/or paste data between workbooks.

Commands Review

FEATURE	RIBBON TAB, GROUP	BUTTON, OPTION	KEYBOARD SHORTCUT
Cut selected cells	Home, Clipboard		Ctrl + X
Copy selected cells	Home, Clipboard		Ctrl + C
Paste selected cells	Home, Clipboard		Ctrl + V
Clipboard task pane	Home, Clipboard		
Insert worksheet			Shift + F11
Hide worksheet	Home, Cells	, Hide & Unhide, Hide Sheet	
Unhide worksheet	Home, Cells	, Hide & Unhide, Unhide Sheet	
Split window into pane	View, Window		
Freeze window panes	View, Window	, Freeze Panes	
Unfreeze window panes	View, Window	, Unfreeze Panes	
New Name dialog box	Formulas, Defined Names		
Arrange Windows dialog box	View, Window		
Maximize window			
Restore Down			
Minimize window			

Concepts Check Test Your Knowledge

Completion: In the space provided at the right, indicate the correct term, symbol, or command.

1. By default, a workbook contains this number of worksheets. ____________________
2. The Cut, Copy, and Paste buttons are located in this group in the Home tab. ____________________
3. To copy selected cells with the mouse, hold down this key while dragging the outline of the selected cells to the desired location. ____________________

4. This button displays in the lower right corner of pasted cells. ________________

5. Use this task pane to collect and paste multiple items. ________________

6. Click this tab to insert a new worksheet. ________________

7. Click this option at the sheet tab shortcut menu to apply a color to a worksheet tab. ________________

8. To select adjacent worksheet tabs, click the first tab, hold down this key, and then click the last tab. ________________

9. To select nonadjacent worksheet tabs, click the first tab, hold down this key, and then click any other tabs you want selected. ________________

10. To print all worksheets in a workbook, display the Print tab Backstage view, click the first gallery in the Settings category, and then click this option at the drop-down list. ________________

11. The Split button is located in this tab. ________________

12. Display the Arrange Windows dialog box by clicking this button in the Window group in the View tab. ________________

13. Click this button to make the active workbook expand to fill the screen. ________________

14. Click this button to reduce the active workbook to a layer behind the Excel button on the Taskbar. ________________

15. When linking data between worksheets, the worksheet containing the original data is called this. ________________

Skills Check Assess Your Performance

Assessment 1

COPY AND PASTE DATA BETWEEN WORKSHEETS IN A SALES WORKBOOK

1. Open **EPSales.xlsx** and then save the workbook with Save As and name it **EL1-C5-A1-EPSales**.
2. Turn on the display of the Clipboard task pane, click the Clear All button to clear any content, and then complete the following steps:
   a. Select and copy cells A7 through C7.
   b. Select and copy cells A10 through C10.
   c. Select and copy cells A13 through C13.
   d. Display the second worksheet, make cell A7 active, and then paste the *Avalon Clinic* cells.
   e. Make cell A10 active and then paste the *Stealth Media* cells.

f. Make A13 active and then paste the *Danmark Contracting* cells.
g. Make the third worksheet active and then complete similar steps to paste the cells in the same location as the second worksheet.
h. Clear the contents of the Clipboard task pane and then close the task pane.

3. Change the name of the Sheet1 tab to *2010 Sales*, the name of the Sheet2 tab to *2011 Sales*, and the name of the Sheet3 tab to *2012 Sales*.
4. Change the color of the 2010 Sales tab to blue, the color of the 2011 Sales tab to green, and the color of the 2012 Sales tab to yellow.
5. Display the 2010 Sales worksheet, select all three tabs, and then insert a formula in cell D4 that sums the amounts in cells B4 and C4. Copy the formula in cell D4 down to cells D5 through D14.
6. Make cell D15 active and then insert a formula that sums the amounts in cells D4 through D14.
7. Apply the Accounting Number Format style with no decimal places to cell D4 (on all three worksheets).
8. Insert a footer on all three worksheets that prints your name at the left side and the current date at the right.
9. Save **EL1-C5-A1-EPSales.xlsx**.
10. Print all three worksheets and then close **EL1-C5-A1-EPSales.xlsx**.

Assessment 2

COPY, PASTE, AND FORMAT WORKSHEETS IN AN INCOME STATEMENT WORKBOOK

1. Open **CMJanIncome.xlsx** and then save the workbook with Save As and name it **EL1-C5-A2-CMJanIncome**.
2. Copy cells A1 through B17 in Sheet1 and paste them into Sheet2. (Click the Paste Options button and then click the Keep Source Column Widths button at the drop-down list.)
3. Make the following changes to the Sheet2 worksheet:
   a. Adjust the row heights so they match the heights in the Sheet1 worksheet.
   b. Change the month from *January* to *February*.
   c. Change the amount in B4 to *97,655*.
   d. Change the amount in B5 to *39,558*.
   e. Change the amount in B11 to *1,105*.
4. Select both sheet tabs and then insert the following formulas:
   a. Insert a formula in B6 that subtracts the *Cost of Sales* from the *Sales Revenue* (*=B4-B5*).
   b. Insert a formula in B16 that sums the amounts in B8 through B15.
   c. Insert a formula in B17 that subtracts the *Total Expenses* from the *Gross Profit* (*=B6-B16*).
5. Change the name of the Sheet1 tab to *January* and the name of the Sheet2 tab to *February*.
6. Change the color of the January tab to blue and the color of the February tab to red.
7. Insert a custom header on both worksheets that prints your name at the left side, the date in the middle, and the file name at the right side.
8. Save, print, and then close **EL1-C5-A2-CMJanIncome.xlsx**.

Assessment 3

FREEZE AND UNFREEZE WINDOW PANES IN A TEST SCORES WORKBOOK

1. Open **CMCertTests.xlsx** and then save the workbook with Save As and name it **EL1-C5-A3-CertTests**.
2. Make cell A1 active and then split the window by clicking the View tab and then clicking the Split button in the Window group. (This causes the window to split into four panes.)
3. Drag both the horizontal and vertical gray lines up and to the left until the horizontal gray line is immediately below the second row and the vertical gray line is immediately to the right of the first column.
4. Freeze the window panes.
5. Add two rows immediately above row 18 and then type the following text in the specified cells:

A18	=	Nauer, Sheryl	A19	=	Nunez, James
B18	=	75	B19	=	98
C18	=	83	C19	=	96
D18	=	85	D19	=	100
E18	=	78	E19	=	90
F18	=	82	F19	=	95
G18	=	80	G19	=	93
H18	=	79	H19	=	88
I18	=	82	I19	=	91
J18	=	92	J19	=	89
K18	=	90	K19	=	100
L18	=	86	L19	=	96
M18	=	84	M19	=	98

6. Insert a formula in cell N3 that averages the percentages in cells B3 through M3 and then copy the formula down to cells N4 through N22.
7. Unfreeze the window panes.
8. Remove the split.
9. Change the orientation to *Landscape* and then scale the worksheet to print on one page. ***Hint: Do this with the* Width *option in the Scale to Fit group in the Page Layout tab.***
10. Save, print, and then close **EL1-C5-A3-CertTests.xlsx**.

Assessment 4

CREATE, COPY, PASTE, AND FORMAT CELLS IN AN EQUIPMENT USAGE WORKBOOK

1. Create the worksheet shown in Figure 5.10. (Change the width of column A to 21.00.)
2. Save the workbook and name it **EL1-C5-A4-HCMachRpt**.
3. With **EL1-C5-A4-HCMachRpt.xlsx** open, open **HCEqpRpt.xlsx**.
4. Select and copy the following cells from **HCEqpRpt.xlsx** to **EL1-C5-A4-HCMachRpt.xlsx**:
   a. Copy cells A4 through G4 in **HCEqpRpt.xlsx** and paste them into **EL1-C5-A4-HCMachRpt.xlsx** beginning with cell A12.

b. Copy cells A10 through G10 in **HCEqpRpt.xlsx** and paste them into **EL1-C5-A4-HCMachRpt.xlsx** beginning with cell A13.

5. With **EL1-C5-A4-HCMachRpt.xlsx** the active workbook, make cell A1 active and then apply the following formatting:
   a. Change the height of row 1 to 25.50.
   b. Change the font size of the text in cell A1 to 14 points.
   c. Insert Olive Green, Accent 3, Lighter 60% fill color to cell A1.
6. Select cells A2 through G2 and then insert Olive Green, Accent 3, Darker 50% fill color.
7. Select cells B2 through G2, change the text color to white, and turn on italics. (Make sure the text in the cells is right aligned.)
8. Select cells A3 through G3 and then insert Olive Green, Accent 3, Lighter 80% fill color.
9. Select cells A7 through G7 and then insert Olive Green, Accent 3, Lighter 80% fill color.
10. Select cells A11 through G11 and then insert Olive Green, Accent 3, Lighter 80% fill color.
11. Print the worksheet centered horizontally and vertically on the page.
12. Save and then close **EL1-C5-A4-HCMachRpt.xlsx**.
13. Close **HCEqpRpt.xlsx** without saving the changes.

Figure 5.10 Assessment 4

	A	B	C	D	E	F	G	H
1				EQUIPMENT USAGE REPORT				
2		January	February	March	April	May	June	
3	Machine #12							
4	Total hours available	2300	2430	2530	2400	2440	2240	
5	In use	2040	2105	2320	2180	2050	1995	
6								
7	Machine #25							
8	Total hours available	2100	2240	2450	2105	2390	1950	
9	In use	1800	1935	2110	1750	2215	1645	
10								
11	Machine #30							
12								

Assessment 5

COPYING AND LINKING DATA IN A WORD DOCUMENT

1. In this chapter you learned how to link data in cells between worksheets. You can also copy data in an Excel worksheet and then paste and link the data in a file in another program such as Word. Use buttons in the Paste Options button drop-down list to link data or use options at the Paste Special dialog box. Open Word and then open the document named **DWLtr.docx** located in the Excel2010L1C5 folder on your storage medium. Save the document with Save As and name it **EL1-C5-A5-DWLtr**.
2. Click the Excel button on the Taskbar, open **DWMortgages.xlsx** and then save the workbook with Save As and name it **EL1-C5-A5-DWMortgages**.
3. In column G, insert a formula using the PMT function. Automatically adjust the width of column G.

4. Select cells A2 through G10 and then click the Copy button.
5. Click the Word button on the Taskbar. (This displays **EL1-C5-A5-DWLtr.docx**.)
6. Move the insertion point between the two paragraphs of text.
7. Click the Paste button arrow and then click *Paste Special* at the drop-down list.
8. At the Paste Special dialog box, look at the options available and then click the *Paste link* option, click *Microsoft Excel Worksheet Object* in the *As* list box, and then click OK.
9. Click the Center button in the Paragraph group in the Home tab. (This enters the cells between the left and right margins.)
10. Save, print, and then close **EL1-C5-A5-DWLtr.docx**.
11. Click the Excel button on the Taskbar.
12. Make cell A3 active and then change the number from $300,000 to $400,000. Copy the number in cell A3 down to cells A4 through A10. (Cells A3 through A10 should now contain the amount $400,000.)
13. Save, print, and then close **EL1-C5-A5-DWMortgages.xlsx**.
14. Click the Word button on the Taskbar.
15. Open **EL1-C5-A5-DWLtr.docx**. At the message that displays asking if you want to update the data from the linked files, click Yes.
16. Save, print, and then close **EL1-C5-A5-DWLtr.docx**.
17. Exit Word.

Visual Benchmark Demonstrate Your Proficiency

CREATE AND FORMAT A SALES WORKSHEET USING FORMULAS

1. At a blank workbook, create the worksheet shown in Figure 5.11 with the following specifications:
   - Do not type the data in cells D4 through D9; instead enter a formula that totals the first-half and second-half yearly sales.
   - Apply the formatting shown in the figure including changing font sizes, column widths, and row heights; and inserting shading and border lines.
   - Rename the sheet tab and change the tab color as shown in the figure.
2. Copy cells A1 through D9 and then paste the cells in Sheet2.
3. Edit the cells and apply formatting so your worksheet matches the worksheet shown in Figure 5.12. Rename the sheet tab and change the tab color as shown in the figure.
4. Save the completed workbook and name it **EL1-C5-VB-CMSemiSales**.
5. Print both worksheets.
6. Close **EL1-C5-VB-CMSemiSales.xlsx**.

Figure 5.11 Sales 2011 Worksheet

	A	B	C	D
1	Clearline Manufacturing			
2	SEMIANNUAL SALES - 2011			
3	Customer	1st Half	2nd Half	Total
4	Lakeside Trucking	$ 84,300	$ 73,500	$ 157,800
5	Gresham Machines	33,000	40,500	73,500
6	Real Photography	30,890	35,465	66,355
7	Genesis Productions	72,190	75,390	147,580
8	Landower Company	22,000	15,000	37,000
9	Jewell Enterprises	19,764	50,801	70,565

Sales 2011 | Sales 2012

Figure 5.12 Sales 2012 Worksheet

	A	B	C	D
1	Clearline Manufacturing			
2	SEMIANNUAL SALES - 2012			
3	Customer	1st Half	2nd Half	Total
4	Lakeside Trucking	$ 84,300	$ 73,500	$ 157,800
5	Gresham Machines	33,000	40,500	73,500
6	Real Photography	20,750	15,790	36,540
7	Genesis Productions	51,270	68,195	119,465
8	Landower Company	22,000	15,000	37,000
9	Jewell Enterprises	14,470	33,770	48,240

Sales 2011 | Sales 2012

Case Study Apply Your Skills

Part 1

You are an administrator for Gateway Global, an electronics manufacturing corporation. You are gathering information on money spent on supplies and equipment purchases. You have gathered information for the first quarter of the year and decide to create a workbook containing worksheets for monthly information. To do this, create a worksheet that contains the following information:

- Company name is Gateway Global.
- Create the title *January Expenditures*.
- Create the following columns:

Department	**Supplies**	**Equipment**	**Total**
Production	$25,425	$135,500	
Research and Development	$50,000	$125,000	
Technical Support	$14,500	$65,000	
Finance	$5,790	$22,000	
Sales and Marketing	$35,425	$8,525	
Facilities	$6,000	$1,200	
Total			

- Insert a formula in the *Total* column that sums the amounts in the *supplies* and *equipment* columns and insert a formula in the *total* row that sums the supplies amounts, equipment amounts, and total amounts.
- Apply formatting such as fill color, borders, font color, and shading to enhance the visual appeal of the worksheet.

After creating and formatting the worksheet, complete the following:

- Copy the worksheet data to Sheet2 and then to Sheet3.
- Make the following changes to data in Sheet2:
    - Change *January Expenditures* to *February Expenditures*.
    - Change the Production department supplies amount to *$38,550* and the equipment amount to *$88,500*.
    - Change the Technical Support department equipment amount to *$44,250*.
    - Change the Finance department supplies amount to *$7,500*.
- Make the following changes to data in Sheet3:
    - Change *January Expenditures* to *March Expenditures*.
    - Change the Research and Development department supplies amount to *$65,000* and the equipment amount to *$150,000*.
    - Change the Technical Support department supplies amount to *$21,750* and the equipment amount to *$43,525*.
    - Change the Facilities department equipment amount to *$18,450*.

Create a new worksheet that summarizes the supplies and equipment totals for January, February, and March. Apply the same formatting to the worksheet as applied to the other three. Change the tab name for Sheet1 to *Jan. Expenditures*, the tab name for Sheet2 to *Feb. Expenditures*, the tab name for Sheet3 to *Mar. Expenditures*, and the tab name for Sheet4 to *Qtr. Summary*. Change the color of each tab. (You determine the colors.)

Insert a header that prints your name at the left side of each worksheet and the current date at the right side of each worksheet. Save the workbook and name it **EL1-C5-CS-GGExp**. Print all the worksheets in the workbook and then close the workbook.

Part 2

Employees of Gateway Global have formed two intramural co-ed softball teams and you have volunteered to keep statistics for the players. Open **GGStats.xlsx** and then make the following changes to both worksheets in the workbook:

- Insert a formula that calculates a player's batting average (Hits ÷ At Bats).
- Insert a formula that calculates a player's on-base percentage: (Walks + Hits) ÷ (At Bats + Walks). Select E5 through F15 and then specify that you want three decimal places displayed.
- Insert the company name.
- Apply formatting to enhance the visual appeal of the worksheets.
- Horizontally and vertically center the worksheets.
- Insert a footer that prints on both worksheets and prints your name at the left side of the worksheet and the date at the right of the worksheet.

Use the Help feature to learn about applying cell styles or click the Cells Styles button in the Styles group in the Home tab and then experiment with applying different styles. Apply the *Good* cell style to any cell in the *Batting Average* column with an average over .400. Apply this style to cells in both worksheets. Save the workbook and name it **EL1-C5-CS-GGStats**. Print both worksheets and then close **EL1-C5-CS-GGStats.xlsx**.

Part 3

Many of the suppliers for Gateway Global are international and use different length, weight, and volume measurements. The purchasing manager has asked you to prepare a conversion chart in Excel that displays conversion tables for length, weight, volume, and temperature. Use the Internet to locate conversion tables for length, weight, and volume. When preparing the workbook, create a worksheet with the following information:

- Include the following length conversions:
  - 1 inch to centimeters
  - 1 foot to centimeters
  - 1 yard to meters
  - 1 mile to kilometers
- Include the following weight conversions:
  - 1 ounce to grams
  - 1 pound to kilograms
  - 1 ton to metric tons
- Include the following volume conversions:
  - 1 fluid ounce to milliliters
  - 1 pint to liters
  - 1 quart to liters
  - 1 gallon to liters

Locate a site on the Internet that provides the formula for converting Fahrenheit temperatures to Celsius temperatures and then create another worksheet in the workbook with the following information:

- Insert Fahrenheit temperatures beginning with zero, continuing to 100, and incrementing by 5 (for example, 0, 5, 10, 15, and so on).
- Insert a formula that converts the Fahrenheit temperature to a Celsius temperature.

Include the company name, Gateway Global, in both worksheets. Apply additional formatting to improve the visual appeal of both worksheets. Rename both sheet names and apply a color to each tab (you determine the names and colors). Save the workbook and name it **EL1-C5-CS-GGConv**. Print both worksheets centered horizontally and vertically on the page and then close **EL1-C5-CS-GGConv.xlsx**.

Part 4

Open Microsoft Word and then create a letterhead document that contains the company name *Gateway Global*, the address (you decide the address including street address, city, state, and ZIP code or street address, city, province, and postal code), and the telephone number (you determine the telephone number). Apply formatting to improve the visual appeal of the letterhead. Save the document and name it **EL1-C5-CS-GGLtrhd**. Save the document again and name it **EL1-C5-CS-GGConvLtr**.

In Excel, open **EL1-C5-CS-GGConv.xlsx** (the workbook you created in Part 3). In the first worksheet, copy the cells containing data and then paste the cells in **EL1-C5-CS-GGConvLtr.docx** as a picture object. Center the cells (picture object) between the left and right margins. Save, print, and then close **EL1-C5-CS-GGConvLtr.docx**. Exit Microsoft Word and then, in Excel, close **EL1-C5-CS-GGConv.xlsx**.

Microsoft® Excel®

CHAPTER 6

Maintaining Workbooks

PERFORMANCE OBJECTIVES

Upon successful completion of Chapter 6, you will be able to:

- **Create and rename a folder**
- **Delete workbooks and folders**
- **Copy and move workbooks within and between folders**
- **Copy and move worksheets between workbooks**
- **Maintain consistent formatting with styles**
- **Insert, modify, and remove hyperlinks**
- **Create financial forms using templates**

Tutorials

6.1 Maintaining Workbooks
6.2 Managing Folders
6.3 Managing the Recent List
6.4 Managing Worksheets
6.5 Formatting with Cell Styles
6.6 Inserting Hyperlinks
6.7 Using Templates

Once you have been working with Excel for a period of time you will have accumulated several workbook files. Workbooks should be organized into folders to facilitate fast retrieval of information. Occasionally you should perform file maintenance activities such as copying, moving, renaming, and deleting workbooks to ensure the workbook list in your various folders is manageable. You will learn these file management tasks in this chapter along with creating and applying styles, inserting hyperlinks in a workbook, and using Excel templates to create a workbook. Model answers for this chapter's projects appear on the following pages.

Excel2010L1C6

Note: Before beginning the projects, copy to your storage medium the Excel2010L1C6 subfolder from the Excel2010L1 folder on the CD that accompanies this textbook and then make Excel2010L1C6 the active folder.

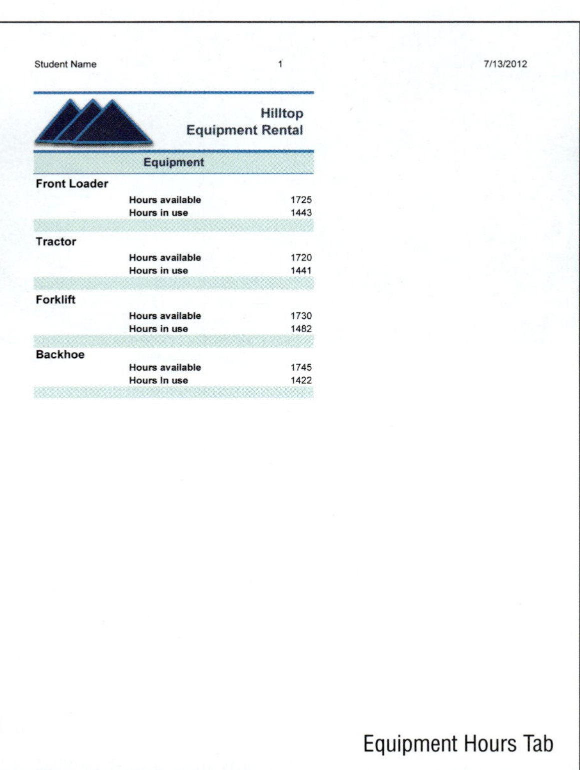

Student Name 1 7/13/2012

Hilltop
Equipment Rental

Equipment		
Front Loader		
	Hours available	1725
	Hours in use	1443
Tractor		
	Hours available	1720
	Hours in use	1441
Forklift		
	Hours available	1730
	Hours in use	1482
Backhoe		
	Hours available	1745
	Hours In use	1422

Equipment Hours Tab

Student Name 2 7/13/2012

Hilltop
Equipment Rental

Equipment Usage - Front Loader

Hours	1st Qtr.	2nd Qtr.	3rd Qtr.	4th Qtr.
Total hours available	434	425	440	426
Avoidable delays	11	9	11	9
Unavoidable delays	8	14	7	11
Repairs	10	4	12	7
Servicing	5	10	8	11
Unassigned	32	24	36	40
In use	368	372	366	337

Front Loader Tab

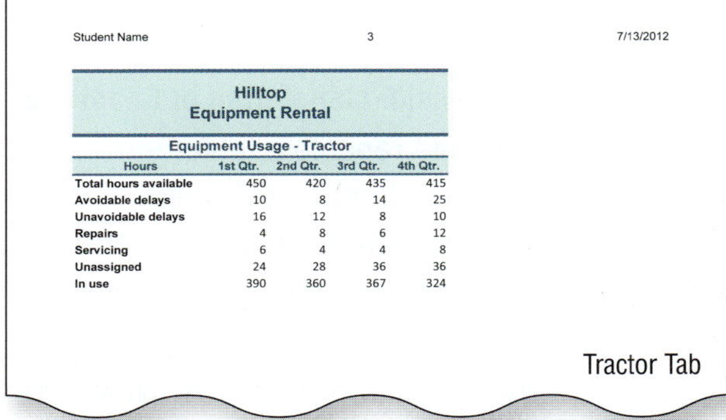

Student Name 3 7/13/2012

Hilltop
Equipment Rental

Equipment Usage - Tractor

Hours	1st Qtr.	2nd Qtr.	3rd Qtr.	4th Qtr.
Total hours available	450	420	435	415
Avoidable delays	10	8	14	25
Unavoidable delays	16	12	8	10
Repairs	4	8	6	12
Servicing	6	4	4	8
Unassigned	24	28	36	36
In use	390	360	367	324

Tractor Tab

Project 2 Copy and Move Worksheets into an Equipment Rental Workbook EL1-C6-P2-HEREquip.xlsx

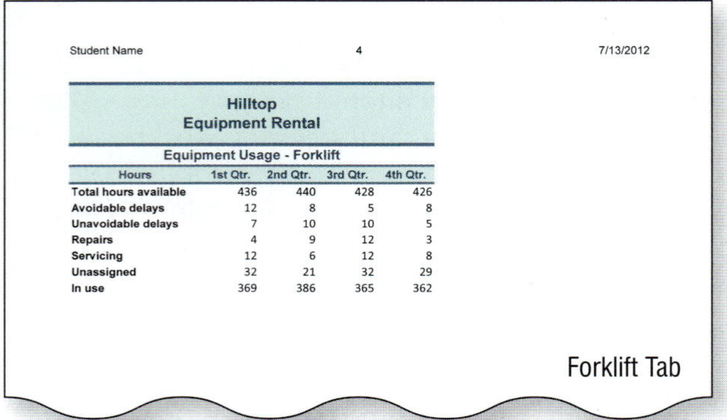

Student Name 4 7/13/2012

Hilltop
Equipment Rental

Equipment Usage - Forklift

Hours	1st Qtr.	2nd Qtr.	3rd Qtr.	4th Qtr.
Total hours available	436	440	428	426
Avoidable delays	12	8	5	8
Unavoidable delays	7	10	10	5
Repairs	4	9	12	3
Servicing	12	6	12	8
Unassigned	32	21	32	29
In use	369	386	365	362

Forklift Tab

Student Name 5 7/13/2012

Hilltop
Equipment Rental

Equipment Usage - Backhoe

Hours	1st Qtr.	2nd Qtr.	3rd Qtr.	4th Qtr.
Total hours available	450	435	440	420
Avoidable delays	14	10	8	15
Unavoidable delays	12	8	12	12
Repairs	8	5	14	8
Servicing	10	8	10	4
Unassigned	62	32	26	45
In use	344	372	370	336

Backhoe Tab

O'Rourke Enterprises

Maintenance Department - Weekly Payroll

Employee	Hrly. Rate	Hours	Gross	W/H Tax	SS Tax	Net
Williams, Pamela	$ 43.00	40	$ 1,720.00	$ 481.60	$ 131.58	$ 1,106.82
Ternes, Reynaldo	41.50	40	1,660.00	464.80	126.99	1,068.21
Sinclair, Jason	38.00	30	1,140.00	319.20	87.21	733.59
Pierson, Rhea	38.00	40	1,520.00	425.60	116.28	978.12
Nyegaard, James	25.00	25	625.00	175.00	47.81	402.19
Lunde, Beverly	21.00	40	840.00	235.20	64.26	540.54

Withholding rate	28%
Social Security rate	7.65%

Weekly Payroll Tab

O'Rourke Enterprises

Invoices

Invoice #	Customer #	Date	Amount	Tax	Amount Due
1001	34002	4/2/2012	$ 450.00	8.50%	$ 488.25
1002	12034	4/4/2012	1,075.00	8.80%	1,169.60
1003	40059	4/6/2012	225.00	0.00%	225.00
1004	23002	4/10/2012	750.00	8.50%	813.75
1005	59403	4/10/2012	350.00	0.00%	350.00
1006	80958	4/11/2012	875.00	8.50%	949.38
1007	23494	4/13/2012	750.00	8.50%	813.75
1008	45232	4/17/2012	560.00	8.80%	609.28
1009	76490	4/18/2012	400.00	0.00%	400.00
1010	45466	4/19/2012	600.00	8.50%	651.00
1011	34094	4/23/2012	95.00	0.00%	95.00
1012	45450	4/25/2012	2,250.00	8.50%	2,441.25
1013	23044	4/26/2012	225.00	8.80%	244.80
1014	48933	4/30/2012	140.00	0.00%	140.00

Invoices Tab

Project 3 Create and Apply Styles to a Payroll Workbook EL1-C6-P3-OEPayroll.xlsx

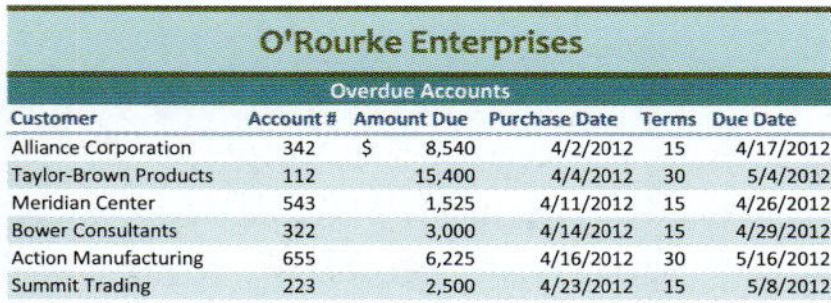

O'Rourke Enterprises

Overdue Accounts

Customer	Account #	Amount Due	Purchase Date	Terms	Due Date
Alliance Corporation	342	$ 8,540	4/2/2012	15	4/17/2012
Taylor-Brown Products	112	15,400	4/4/2012	30	5/4/2012
Meridian Center	543	1,525	4/11/2012	15	4/26/2012
Bower Consultants	322	3,000	4/14/2012	15	4/29/2012
Action Manufacturing	655	6,225	4/16/2012	30	5/16/2012
Summit Trading	223	2,500	4/23/2012	15	5/8/2012

Overdue Accounts Tab

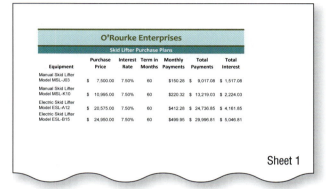

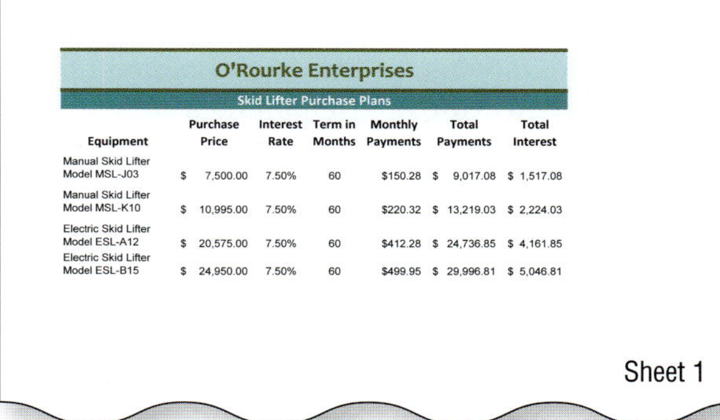

O'Rourke Enterprises

Skid Lifter Purchase Plans

Equipment	Purchase Price	Interest Rate	Term in Months	Monthly Payments	Total Payments	Total Interest
Manual Skid Lifter Model MSL-J03	$ 7,500.00	7.50%	60	$150.28	$ 9,017.08	$ 1,517.08
Manual Skid Lifter Model MSL-K10	$ 10,995.00	7.50%	60	$220.32	$ 13,219.03	$ 2,224.03
Electric Skid Lifter Model ESL-A12	$ 20,575.00	7.50%	60	$412.28	$ 24,736.85	$ 4,161.85
Electric Skid Lifter Model ESL-B15	$ 24,950.00	7.50%	60	$499.95	$ 29,996.81	$ 5,046.81

Sheet 1

EL1-C6-P3-OEPlans.xlsx

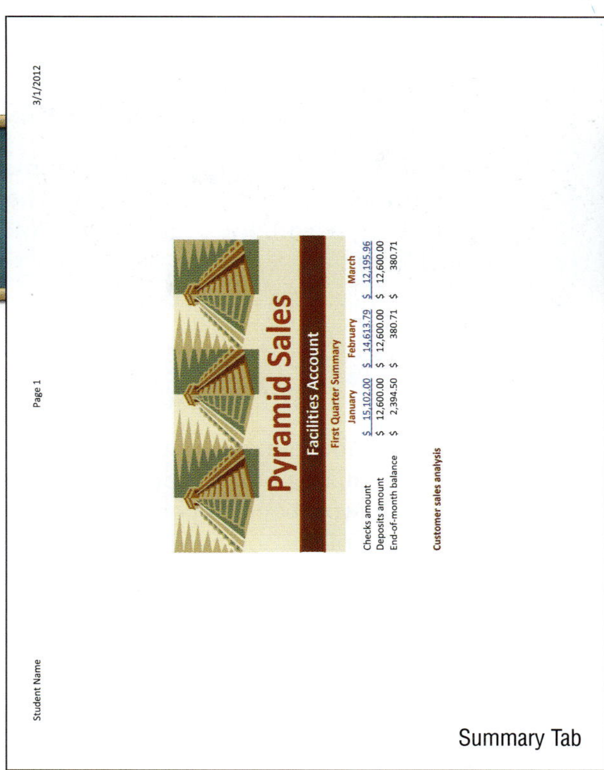

3/1/2012

Pyramid Sales

Facilities Account

First Quarter Summary

	January	February	March
Checks amount	$ 15,102.00	$ 14,613.79	$ 12,195.96
Deposits amount	$ 12,600.00	$ 12,600.00	$ 12,600.00
End-of-month balance	$ 2,394.50	$ 380.71	$ 380.71

Customer sales analysis

Page 1

Student Name

Summary Tab

Project 4 Insert, Modify, and Remove Hyperlinks

EL1-C6-P4-PSAccts.xlsx

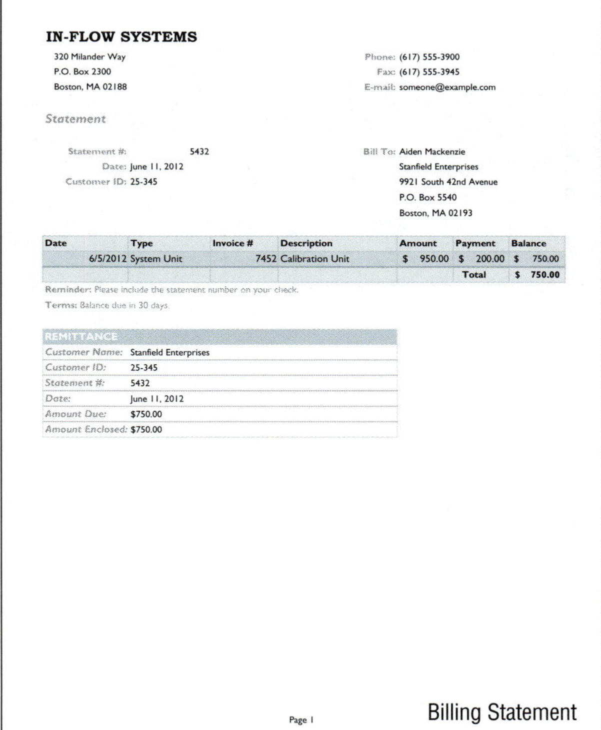

IN-FLOW SYSTEMS

320 Milander Way
P.O. Box 2300
Boston, MA 02188

Phone: (617) 555-3900
Fax: (617) 555-3945
E-mail: someone@example.com

Statement

Statement #: 5432
Date: June 11, 2012
Customer ID: 25-345

Bill To: Aiden Mackenzie
Stanfield Enterprises
9921 South 42nd Avenue
P.O. Box 5540
Boston, MA 02193

Date	Type	Invoice #	Description	Amount	Payment	Balance
6/5/2012	System Unit	7452	Calibration Unit	$ 950.00	$ 200.00	$ 750.00
					Total	$ 750.00

Reminder: Please include the statement number on your check.
Terms: Balance due in 30 days.

REMITTANCE	
Customer Name:	Stanfield Enterprises
Customer ID:	25-345
Statement #:	5432
Date:	June 11, 2012
Amount Due:	$750.00
Amount Enclosed:	$750.00

Page 1

Billing Statement

Project 5 Create a Billing Statement Workbook Using a Template

EL1-C6-P5-Billing.xlsx

Project 1 Manage Workbooks — 8 Parts

You will perform a variety of file management tasks including creating and renaming a folder; selecting and then deleting, copying, cutting, pasting, and renaming workbooks; deleting a folder; and opening, printing, and closing a workbook.

Maintaining Workbooks

You can complete many workbook management tasks at the Open and Save As dialog boxes. These tasks can include copying, moving, printing, and renaming workbooks; opening multiple workbooks; and creating and renaming a new folder. You can perform some file maintenance tasks such as creating a folder and deleting files with options from the Organize button drop-down list or a shortcut menu and navigate to folders using the Address bar. The elements of the Open dialog box are identified in Figure 6.1.

Figure 6.1 Open Dialog Box

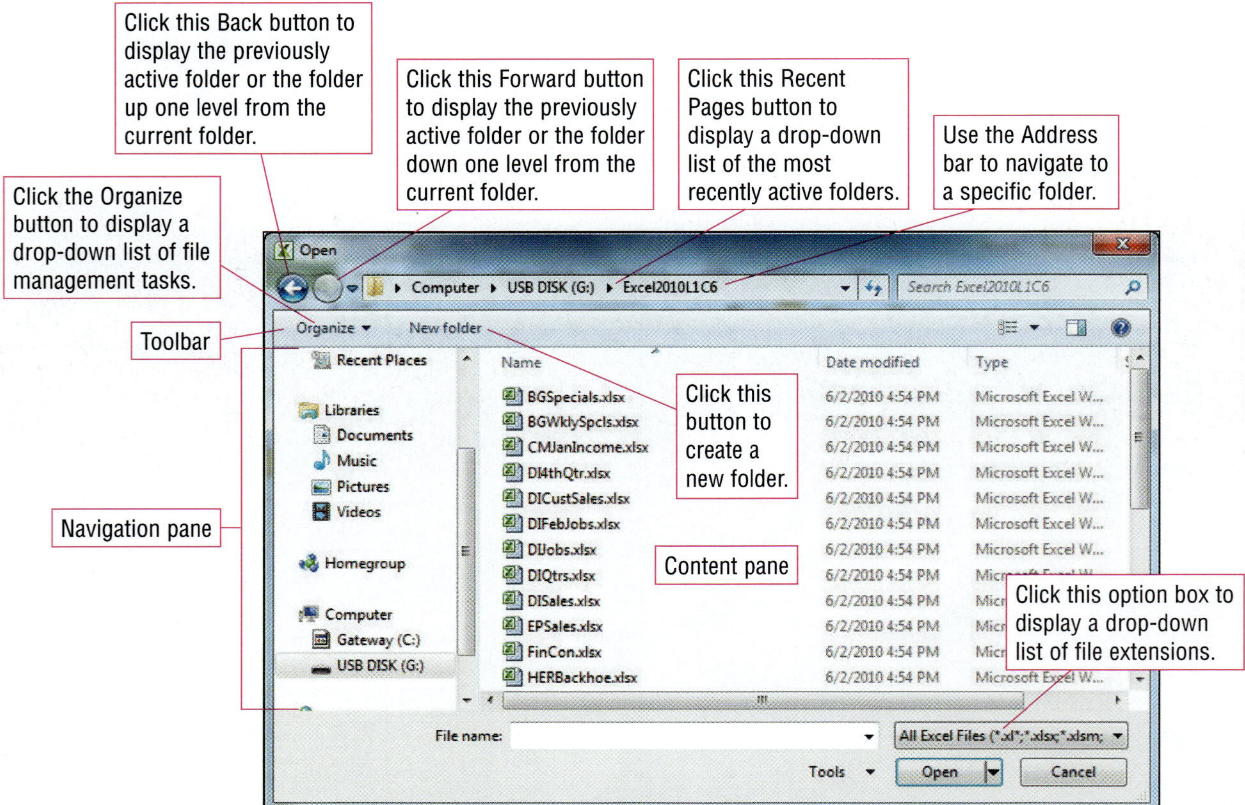

Click this Back button to display the previously active folder or the folder up one level from the current folder.
Click this Forward button to display the previously active folder or the folder down one level from the current folder.
Click this Recent Pages button to display a drop-down list of the most recently active folders.
Use the Address bar to navigate to a specific folder.
Click the Organize button to display a drop-down list of file management tasks.
Toolbar
Click this button to create a new folder.
Navigation pane
Content pane
Click this option box to display a drop-down list of file extensions.
Open
Computer
USB DISK (G:)
Excel2010L1C6
Search Excel2010L1C6
Organize
New folder
Recent Places
Libraries
Documents
Music
Pictures
Videos
Homegroup
Computer
Gateway (C:)
USB DISK (G:)
Name
Date modified
Type
BGSpecials.xlsx
BGWklySpcls.xlsx
CMJanIncome.xlsx
DI4thQtr.xlsx
DICustSales.xlsx
DIFebJobs.xlsx
DIJobs.xlsx
DIQtrs.xlsx
DISales.xlsx
EPSales.xlsx
FinCon.xlsx
HERBackhoe.xlsx
File name:
Tools
Open
Cancel

Creating a Folder

In Excel, you should logically group and store workbooks in folders. For example, you could store all of the workbooks related to one department in one folder with the department name being the folder name. You can create a folder within a folder (called a ***subfolder***). If you create workbooks for a department by individuals, each individual name could have a subfolder within the department folder. The main folder on a disk or drive is called the root folder. You create additional folders as branches of this root folder.

At the Open or Save As dialog boxes, workbook file names display in the Content pane preceded by a workbook icon and a folder name displays preceded by a folder icon. Create a new folder by clicking the New folder button located in the toolbar at the Open dialog box or Save As dialog box. This inserts a new folder in the Content pane. Type the name for the folder and then press Enter.

A folder name can contain a maximum of 255 characters. Numbers, spaces, and symbols can be used in the folder name, except those symbols explained in Chapter 1 in the "Saving a Workbook" section.

Quick Steps

Create a Folder

1. Click File tab, Open button.
2. Click New folder button.
3. Type folder name.
4. Press Enter.

HINT

Change the default folder with the *Default file location* option at the Excel Options dialog box with *Save* selected.

New Folder

Project 1a **Creating a Folder** Part 1 of 8

1. Create a folder named *Payroll* on your storage medium. To begin, display the Open dialog box.
2. Double-click the *Excel2010L1C6* folder name to make it the active folder.
3. Click the New folder button on the toolbar.
4. Type **Payroll** and then press Enter.
5. Close the Open dialog box.

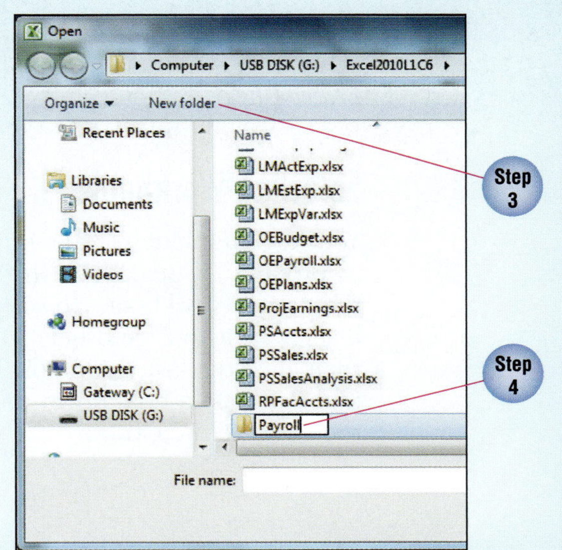

Quick Steps

Rename a Folder
1. Click File tab, Open button.
2. Click desired folder.
3. Click Organize button, *Rename*.
4. Type new name.
5. Press Enter.

OR

1. Click File tab, Open button.
2. Right-click folder name.
3. Click *Rename*.
4. Type new name.
5. Press Enter.

Renaming a Folder

As you organize your files and folders, you may decide to rename a folder. Rename a folder using the Organize button in the Open dialog box or using a shortcut menu. To rename a folder using the Organize button, display the Open dialog box, click in the Content pane the folder you want to rename, click the Organize button located on the toolbar, and then click *Rename* at the drop-down list. This selects the folder name and inserts a border around the name. Type the new name for the folder and then press Enter. To rename a folder using a shortcut menu, display the Open dialog box, right-click the folder name in the Content pane, and then click *Rename* at the shortcut menu. Type a new name for the folder and then press Enter.

A tip to remember when you are organizing files and folders is to be sure that your system is set up to display all of the files in a particular folder and not just the Excel files, for example. You can display all files in a folder by clicking the button to the right of the *File name* text box and then clicking *All Files (*.*)* at the drop-down list.

Project 1b **Renaming a Folder** Part 2 of 8

1. Display the Open dialog box.
2. Right-click the *Payroll* folder name in the Content pane.
3. Click *Rename* at the shortcut menu.
4. Type **Finances** and then press Enter.

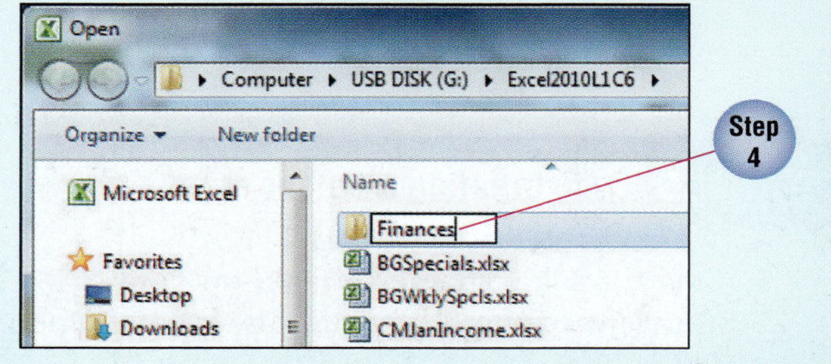

Selecting Workbooks

You can complete workbook management tasks on one workbook or selected workbooks. To select one workbook, display the Open dialog box and then click the desired workbook. To select several adjacent workbooks (workbooks that display next to each other), click the first workbook, hold down the Shift key, and then click the last workbook. To select workbooks that are not adjacent, click the first workbook, hold down the Ctrl key, click any other desired workbooks, and then release the Ctrl key.

Deleting Workbooks and Folders

At some point, you may want to delete certain workbooks from your storage medium or any other drive or folder in which you may be working. To delete a workbook, display the Open or Save As dialog box, click the workbook in the Content pane, click the Organize button, and then click *Delete* at the drop-down list. At the dialog box asking you to confirm the deletion, click Yes. To delete a workbook using a shortcut menu, display the Open dialog box, right-click the workbook name in the Content pane, and then click *Delete* at the shortcut menu. Click Yes at the confirmation dialog box.

Quick Steps

Delete Workbook/Folder

1. Click File tab, Open button.
2. Right-click workbook or folder name.
3. Click *Delete*.
4. Click Yes.

Deleting to the Recycle Bin

Workbooks deleted from the hard drive are automatically sent to the Windows Recycle Bin. You can easily restore a deleted workbook from the Recycle Bin. To free space on the drive, empty the Recycle Bin on a periodic basis. Restoring a workbook from or emptying the contents of the Recycle Bin is completed at the Windows desktop (not in Excel). To display the Recycle Bin, minimize the Excel window and then double-click the Recycle Bin icon located on the Windows desktop. At the Recycle Bin, you can restore file(s) and empty the Recycle Bin.

Project 1c **Selecting and Deleting Workbooks** Part 3 of 8

1. At the Open dialog box, open **RPFacAccts.xlsx** (located in the Excel2010L1C6 folder).
2. Save the workbook with Save As and name it **EL1-C6-P1-RPFacAccts**.
3. Close **EL1-C6-P1-RPFacAccts.xlsx**.
4. Delete **EL1-C6-P1-RPFacAccts.xlsx** by completing the following steps:
   a. Display the Open dialog box with Excel2010L1C6 the active folder.
   b. Click ***EL1-C6-P1-RPFacAccts.xlsx*** to select it.
   c. Click the Organize button and then click *Delete* at the drop-down list.
   d. At the question asking if you are sure you want to delete the worksheet, click Yes.

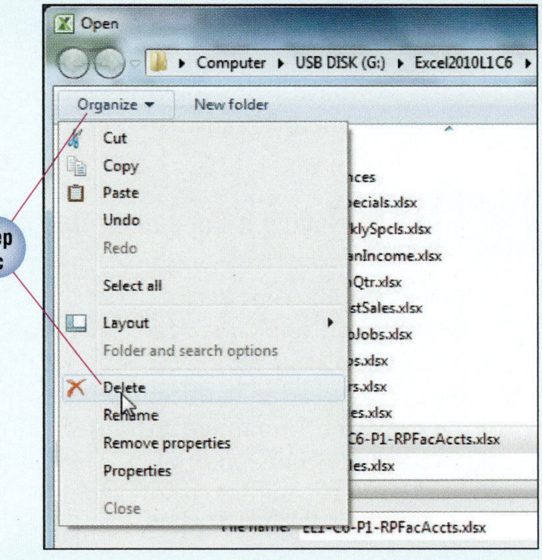

5. Delete selected workbooks by completing the following steps:
   a. Click ***DICustSales.xlsx*** in the Content pane.
   b. Hold down the Shift key and then click ***DIJobs.xlsx***.
   c. Position the mouse pointer on one of the selected workbooks and then click the right mouse button.
   d. At the shortcut menu that displays, click *Delete*.
   e. At the question asking if you are sure you want to delete the items, click Yes.
6. Close the Open dialog box.

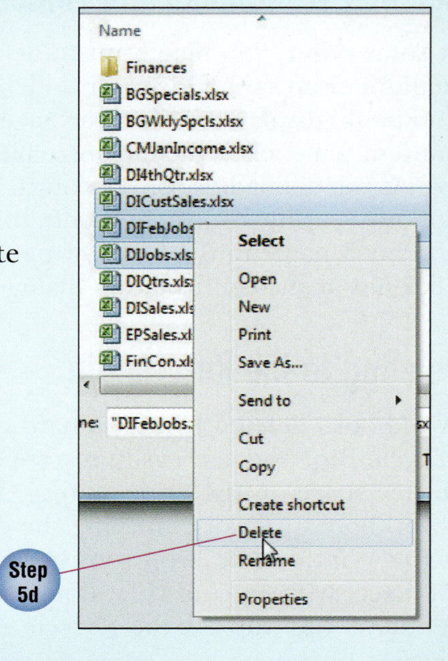

Copying Workbooks

In previous chapters, you have been opening a workbook from your storage medium and saving it with a new name in the same location. This process makes an exact copy of the workbook, leaving the original on your storage medium. You have been copying workbooks and saving the new workbook in the same folder as the original workbook. You can also copy a workbook into another folder.

Project 1d **Saving a Copy of an Open Workbook** Part 4 of 8

1. Open **EPSales.xlsx**.
2. Save the workbook with Save As and name it **TotalSales**. (Make sure Excel2010L1C6 is the active folder.)
3. Save a copy of the **TotalSales.xlsx** workbook in the Finances folder you created in Project 1a (and renamed in Project 1b) by completing the following steps:
   a. With **TotalSales.xlsx** open, display the Save As dialog box.
   b. At the Save As dialog box, change to the Finances folder. To do this, double-click *Finances* at the beginning of the Content pane. (Folders are listed before workbooks.)
   c. Click the Save button located in the lower right corner of the dialog box.
4. Close **TotalSales.xlsx**.
5. Change back to the Excel2010L1C6 folder by completing the following steps:
   a. Display the Open dialog box.
   b. Click *Excel2010L1C6* that displays in the Address bar.
6. Close the Open dialog box.

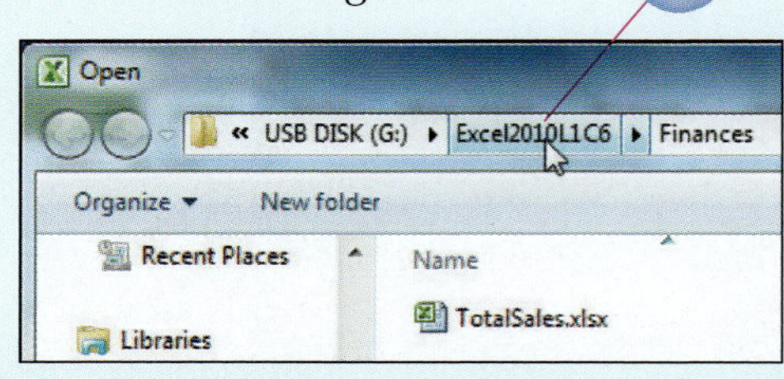

You can copy a workbook to another folder without opening the workbook first. To do this, use the *Copy* and *Paste* options from a shortcut menu at the Open (or Save As) dialog box. You can also copy a workbook or selected workbooks into the same folder. When you do this, Excel adds a hyphen followed by the word *Copy* to the end of the document name. You can copy one workbook or selected workbooks into the same folder.

Quick Steps

Copy a Workbook

1. Click File tab, Open button.
2. Right-click workbook name.
3. Click *Copy*.
4. Navigate to desired folder.
5. Right-click blank area in Content pane.
6. Click *Paste*.

Project 1e **Copying a Workbook at the Open Dialog Box** Part 5 of 8

1. Copy **CMJanIncome.xlsx** to the Finances folder. To begin, display the Open dialog box with the Excel2010L1C6 folder active.
2. Position the arrow pointer on **CMJanIncome.xlsx**, click the right mouse button, and then click *Copy* at the shortcut menu.
3. Change to the Finances folder by double-clicking *Finances* at the beginning of the Content pane.
4. Position the arrow pointer in any blank area in the Content pane, click the right mouse button, and then click *Paste* at the shortcut menu.
5. Change back to the Excel2010L1C6 folder by clicking *Excel2010L1C6* that displays in the Address bar.
6. Close the Open dialog box.

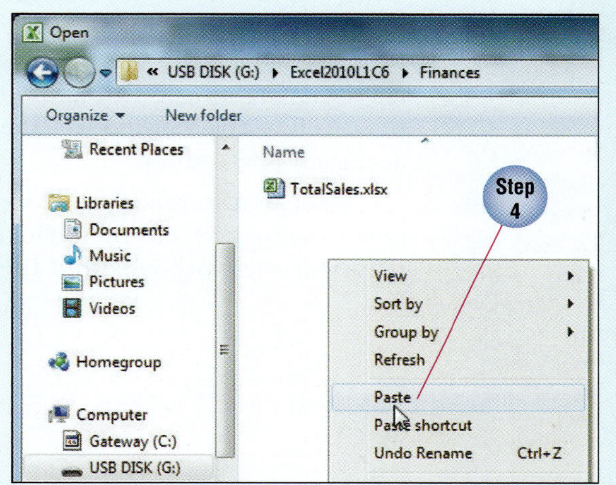

Sending Workbooks to a Different Drive or Folder

Copy workbooks to another folder or drive with the *Copy* and *Paste* options from the shortcut menu at the Open or Save As dialog box. With the *Send To* option, you can send a copy of a workbook to another drive or folder. To use this option, position the arrow pointer on the workbook you want copied, click the right mouse button, point to *Send To* (this causes a side menu to display), and then click the desired drive or folder.

Quick Steps

Move a Workbook

1. Click File tab, Open button.
2. Right-click workbook name.
3. Click *Cut*.
4. Navigate to desired folder.
5. Right-click blank area in Content pane.
6. Click *Paste*.

Cutting and Pasting a Workbook

You can remove a workbook from one folder and insert it in another folder using the *Cut* and *Paste* options from the shortcut menu at the Open dialog box. To do this, display the Open dialog box, position the arrow pointer on the workbook to be removed (cut), click the right mouse button, and then click *Cut* at the shortcut menu. Change to the desired folder or drive, position the arrow pointer in any blank area in the Content pane, click the right mouse button, and then click *Paste* at the shortcut menu.

Project 1f Cutting and Pasting a Workbook

Part 6 of 8

1. Move a workbook to a different folder. To begin, display the Open dialog box with the Excel2010L1C6 folder active.
2. Position the arrow pointer on **FinCon.xlsx**, click the right mouse button, and then click *Cut* at the shortcut menu.
3. Double-click *Finances* to make it the active folder.
4. Position the arrow pointer in any blank area in the Content pane, click the right mouse button, and then click *Paste* at the shortcut menu.
5. Click *Excel2010L1C6* that displays in the Address bar.

Quick Steps

Rename Workbook

1. Click File tab, Open button.
2. Click desired workbook.
3. Click Organize button, *Rename*.
4. Type new name.
5. Press Enter.

OR

1. Click File tab, Open button.
2. Right-click workbook name.
3. Click *Rename*.
4. Type new name.
5. Press Enter.

Renaming Workbooks

At the Open dialog box, use the *Rename* option from the Organize button drop-down list or the shortcut menu to give a workbook a different name. The *Rename* option changes the name of the workbook and keeps it in the same folder. To use *Rename*, display the Open dialog box, click once on the workbook to be renamed, click the Organize button, and then click *Rename*. This causes a thin black border to surround the workbook name and the name to be selected. Type the new name and then press Enter.

You can also rename a workbook by right-clicking the workbook name at the Open dialog box and then clicking *Rename* at the shortcut menu. Type the new name for the workbook and then press the Enter key.

Project 1g Renaming a Workbook

Part 7 of 8

1. Rename a workbook located in the Finances folder. To begin, make sure the Open dialog box displays with Excel2010L1C6 the active folder.
2. Double-click *Finances* to make it the active folder.
3. Click once on ***FinCon.xlsx*** to select it.
4. Click the Organize button on the toolbar.
5. Click *Rename* at the drop-down list.
6. Type Analysis and then press the Enter key.
7. Complete steps similar to those in Steps 3 through 6 to rename **CMJanIncome.xlsx** to *CMJanProfits*.

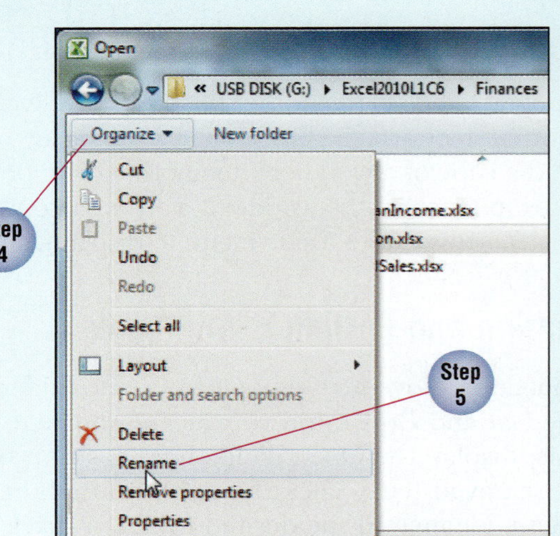

8. Click the Back button (displays as *Back to Excel2010L1C6*) at the left side of the Address bar.

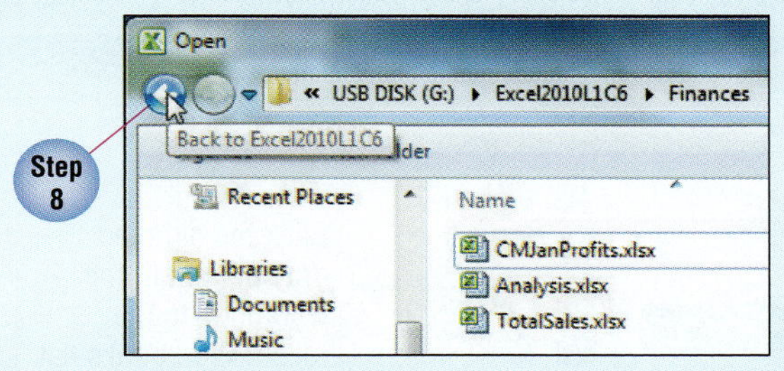

Deleting a Folder and Its Contents

As you learned earlier in this chapter, you can delete a workbook or selected workbooks. In addition to workbooks, you can delete a folder and all of its contents. Delete a folder in the same manner as you delete a workbook.

Deleting a Folder and Its Contents Part 8 of 8

1. Delete the Finances folder and its contents. To begin, make sure the Open dialog box displays with the Excel2010L1C6 folder active.
2. Right-click on the *Finances* folder.
3. Click *Delete* at the shortcut menu.
4. At the Delete Folder dialog box, click Yes.
5. Close the Open dialog box.

Copy and Move Worksheets into an Equipment Rental Workbook — 3 Parts

You will manage workbooks at the Recent tab Backstage view and then open multiple workbooks and copy and move worksheets between the workbooks.

Managing the Recent List

When you open and close workbooks, Excel keeps a list of the most recently opened workbooks. To view this list, click the File tab and then click the Recent tab. This displays the Recent tab Backstage view similar to what you see in Figure 6.2. (Your workbook names and recent places may vary from what you see in the figure.) The most recently opened workbook names display in the *Recent Workbooks* list and the most recently accessed folder names display in the *Recent Places* list. Generally, the 20 most recently opened workbook names display in the *Recent Workbooks* list. To open a workbook, scroll down the list and then click the desired workbook name.

Figure 6.2 Recent Tab Backstage View

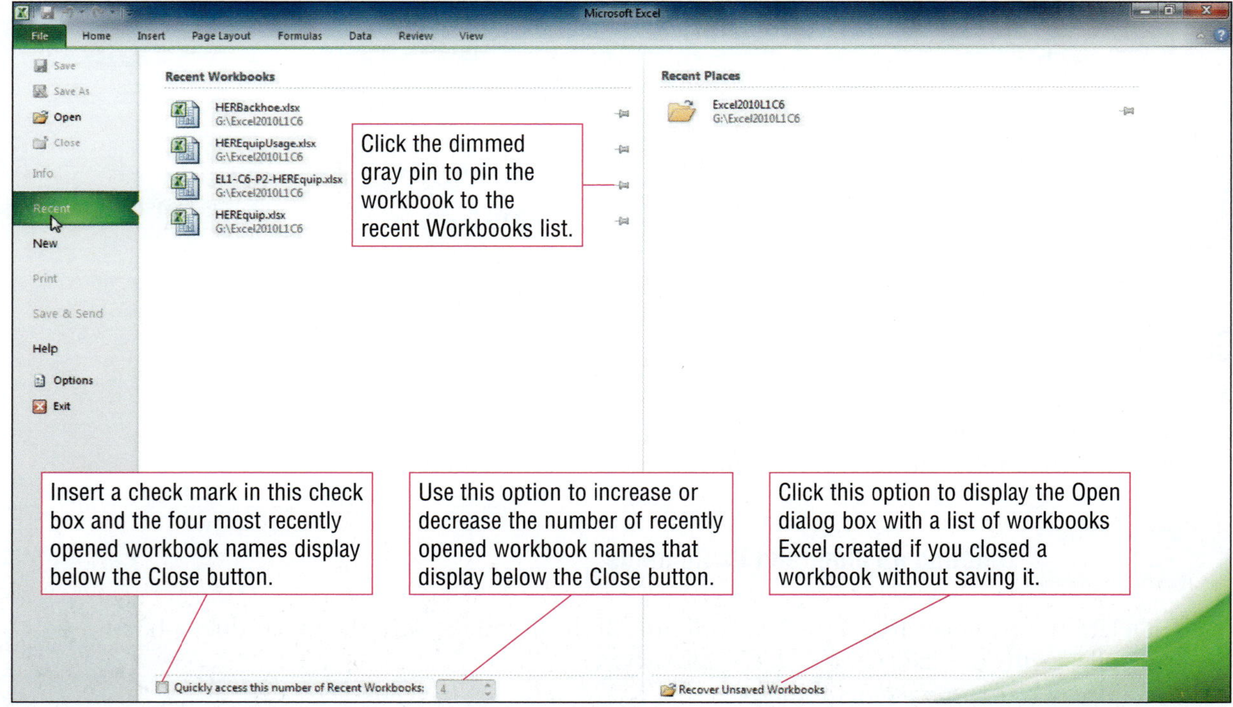

Microsoft Excel
File
Home
Insert
Page Layout
Formulas
Data
Review
View
Save
Save As
Open
Close
Info
Recent
New
Print
Save & Send
Help
Options
Exit
Recent Workbooks
HERBackhoe.xlsx
G:\Excel2010L1C6
HEREquipUsage.xlsx
G:\Excel2010L1C6
EL1-C6-P2-HEREquip.xlsx
G:\Excel2010L1C6
HEREquip.xlsx
G:\Excel2010L1C6
Recent Places
Excel2010L1C6
G:\Excel2010L1C6
Click the dimmed gray pin to pin the workbook to the recent Workbooks list.
Insert a check mark in this check box and the four most recently opened workbook names display below the Close button.
Use this option to increase or decrease the number of recently opened workbook names that display below the Close button.
Click this option to display the Open dialog box with a list of workbooks Excel created if you closed a workbook without saving it.
Quickly access this number of Recent Workbooks:
4
Recover Unsaved Workbooks

Displaying a Quick List

The Recent tab Backstage view contains the option *Quickly access this number of Recent Workbooks* located below the *Recent Workbooks* list. Insert a check mark in this option and the names of the four most recently opened workbooks display in the Backstage navigation bar (the panel at the left) below the Close button. You can increase or decrease the number of displayed workbook names by increasing or decreasing the number that displays at the right side of the *Quickly access this number of Recent Workbooks* option. To remove the list of most recently opened workbooks from the navigation bar, click the *Quickly access this number of Recent Workbooks* option to remove the check mark.

Pinning a Workbook

If you want a workbook name to remain at the top of the *Recent Workbooks* list, pin the workbook name. To do this, click the dimmed, gray pin that displays at the right side of the workbook name. This changes the dimmed, gray pin to a blue pin. The next time you display the Recent tab Backstage view, the workbook name you pinned displays at the top of the list. To unpin a workbook name, click the blue pin to change it to a dimmed, gray pin. You can also pin a workbook name to the Recent Workbooks list by right-clicking the workbook name and then clicking *Pin to list* at the shortcut menu. To unpin the workbook name, right-click the workbook name and then click *Unpin from list* at the shortcut menu.

Recovering an Unsaved Workbook

If you close a workbook without saving it, you can recover it with the *Recover Unsaved Workbooks* option located below the *Recent Places* list. Click this option and the Open dialog box displays with workbook names that Excel automatically saved. At this dialog box, double-click the desired workbook name to open the workbook.

Clearing the Recent Workbooks List

You can clear the contents (except pinned workbooks) of the *Recent Workbooks* list by right-clicking a workbook name in the list and then clicking *Clear unpinned Workbooks* at the shortcut menu. At the message asking if you are sure you want to remove the items, click the Yes button. To clear the *Recent Places* list, right-click a folder in the list and then click *Clear unpinned Places* at the shortcut menu. Click Yes at the message asking if you are sure you want to remove the items.

Project 2a **Managing Workbooks at the Recent Tab Backstage View** Part 1 of 3

1. Close any open workbooks.
2. Click the File tab. (This displays the Recent tab Backstage view.)
3. Notice the workbook names that display in the *Recent Workbooks* list and the folders that display in the *Recent Places* list.
4. Open **HEREquip.xlsx** and then save the workbook with Save As and name it **EL1-C6-P2-HEREquip**.
5. Close **EL1-C6-P2-HEREquip.xlsx**.
6. Open **HEREquipUsage.xlsx** and then close it.
7. Open **HERBackhoe.xlsx** and then close it.
8. You will use the three workbooks you just opened in Project 2b, so you decide to pin them to the *Recent Workbooks* list and display the three most recently opened workbook names below the Close button. To do this, complete the following steps:
   a. Click the File tab. (This should display the Recent tab Backstage view. If it does not display, click the Recent tab.)
   b. Click the dimmed gray pin that displays at the right side of **EL1-C6-P2-HEREquip.xlsx**. (This changes the gray pin to a blue pin.)

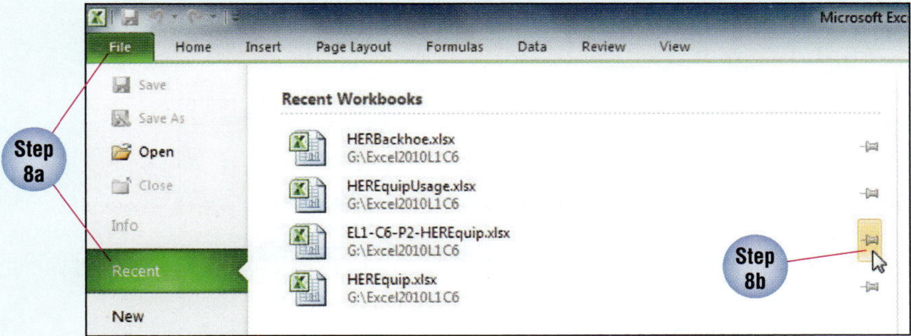

   c. Click the dimmed gray pin that displays at the right side of **HEREquipUsage.xlsx**.

d. Right-click **HERBackhoe.xlsx** and then click *Pin to list* at the shortcut menu.
e. Click the *Quickly access this number of Recent Workbooks* option located at the bottom of the Recent tab Backstage view to insert a check mark.
f. Click the down-pointing arrow at the right side of the number *4*. (This changes *4* to *3*.)
g. Click the File tab to remove the Recent tab Backstage view.

9. Open **EL1-C6-P2-HEREquip.xlsx** by clicking the File tab (this displays the Recent tab Backstage view) and then clicking ***EL1-C6-P2-HEREquip.xlsx*** in the *Recent Workbooks* list.

Managing Worksheets

You can move or copy individual worksheets within the same workbook or to another existing workbook. Exercise caution when moving sheets since calculations or charts based on data on a worksheet might become inaccurate if you move the worksheet. To make a duplicate of a worksheet in the same workbook, hold down the Ctrl key and then drag the worksheet tab to the desired position.

Quick Steps

Copy a Worksheet to Another Workbook

1. Right-click desired sheet tab.
2. Click *Move or Copy*.
3. Select desired destination workbook.
4. Select desired worksheet location.
5. Click *Create a copy* check box.
6. Click OK.

Copying a Worksheet to Another Workbook

To copy a worksheet to another existing workbook, open both the source and the destination workbooks. Right-click the sheet tab and then click *Move or Copy* at the shortcut menu. At the Move or Copy dialog box shown in Figure 6.3, select the destination workbook name from the *To book* drop-down list, select the worksheet that you want the copied worksheet placed before in the *Before sheet* list box, click the *Create a copy* check box, and then click OK.

Figure 6.3 Move or Copy Dialog Box

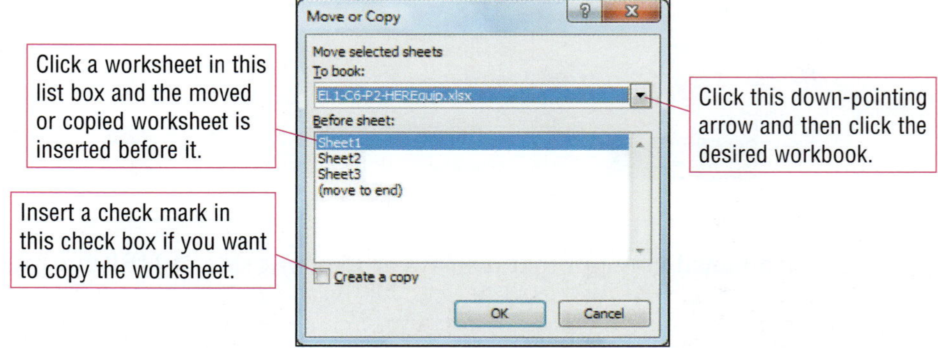

Move or Copy
Move selected sheets
To book:
EL1-C6-P2-HEREquip.xlsx
Before sheet:
Sheet1
Sheet2
Sheet3
(move to end)
Create a copy
OK
Cancel
Click a worksheet in this list box and the moved or copied worksheet is inserted before it.
Insert a check mark in this check box if you want to copy the worksheet.
Click this down-pointing arrow and then click the desired workbook.

Copying a Worksheet to Another Workbook

Part 2 of 3

1. With **EL1-C6-P2-HEREquip.xlsx** open, open **HEREquipUsage.xlsx**.
2. Copy the Front Loader worksheet by completing the following steps:
   a. With **HEREquipUsage.xlsx** the active workbook, right-click the Front Loader tab and then click *Move or Copy* at the shortcut menu.
   b. Click the down-pointing arrow next to the *To book* option box and then click ***EL1-C6-P2-HEREqip.xlsx*** at the drop-down list.
   c. Click *Sheet2* in the *Before sheet* list box.
   d. Click the *Create a copy* check box to insert a check mark.
   e. Click OK. (Excel switches to the **EL1-C6-P2-HEREquip.xlsx** workbook and inserts the copied Front Loader worksheet between Sheet1 and Sheet2.)
3. Complete steps similar to those in Step 2 to copy the Tractor worksheet to the **EL1-C6-P2-HEREquip.xlsx** workbook. (Insert the Tractor worksheet between Front Loader and Sheet2.)
4. Complete steps similar to those in Step 2 to copy the Forklift worksheet to the **EL1-C6-P2-HEREquip.xlsx** workbook. (Insert the Forklift worksheet between Tractor and Sheet2.)
5. Save **EL1-C6-P2-HEREquip.xlsx**.
6. Make **HEREquipUsage.xlsx** the active workbook and then close it.

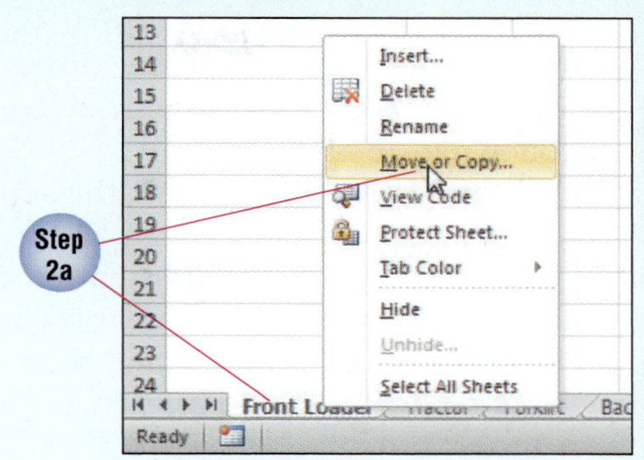

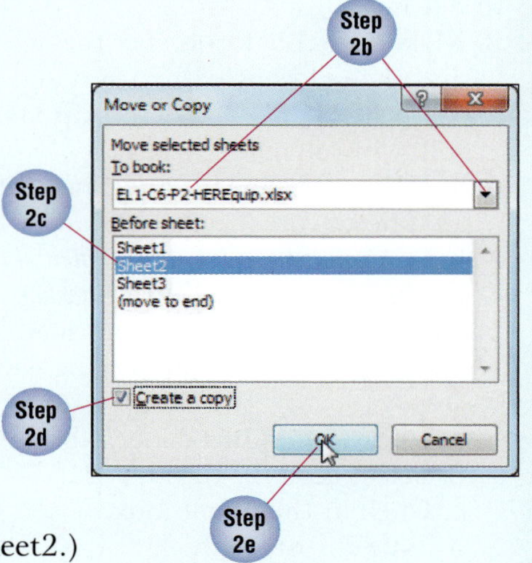

Moving a Worksheet to Another Workbook

To move a worksheet to another existing workbook, open both the source and the destination workbooks. Make active the sheet you want to move in the source workbook, right-click the sheet tab and then click *Move or Copy* at the shortcut menu. At the Move or Copy dialog box shown in Figure 6.3, select the destination workbook name from the *To book* drop-down list, select the worksheet that you want the worksheet placed before in the *Before sheet* list box, and then click OK. If you need to reposition a worksheet tab, drag the tab to the desired position.

Be careful when moving a worksheet to another workbook file. If formulas exist in the workbook that depend on the contents of the cells in the worksheet that is moved, they will no longer calculate properly.

Quick Steps

Move a Worksheet to Another Workbook

1. Right-click desired sheet tab.
2. Click *Move or Copy*.
3. Select desired destination workbook.
4. Select desired worksheet location.
5. Click OK.

Moving a Worksheet to Another Workbook

1. With **EL1-C6-P2-HEREquip.xlsx** open, open **HERBackhoe.xlsx**.
2. Move Sheet1 from **HERBackhoe.xlsx** to **EL1-C6-P2-HEREquip.xlsx** by completing the following steps:
   a. With **HERBackhoe.xlsx** the active workbook, right-click the Sheet1 tab and then click *Move or Copy* at the shortcut menu.
   b. Click the down-pointing arrow next to the *To book* option box and then click ***EL1-C6-P2-HEREquip.xlsx*** at the drop-down list.
   c. Click *Sheet2* in the *Before sheet* list box.
   d. Click OK.

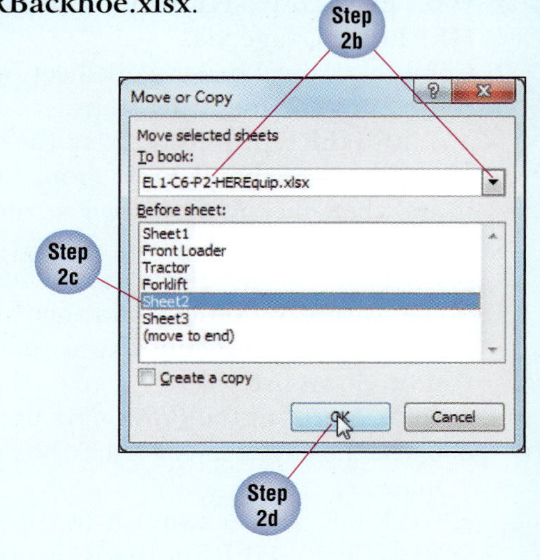

3. Make **HERBackhoe.xlsx** the active workbook and then close it without saving the changes.
4. With **EL1-C6-P2-HEREquip.xlsx** open, make the following changes:
   a. Delete the Sheet2 and Sheet3 tabs. (These worksheets are blank.)
   b. Rename Sheet1 to *Equipment Hours*.
   c. Rename Sheet1 (2) to *Backhoe*.
5. Create a range for the front loader total hours available by completing the following steps:
   a. Click the Front Loader tab.
   b. Select cells B4 through E4.
   c. Click in the Name Box.
   d. Type **FrontLoaderHours**.
   e. Press Enter.

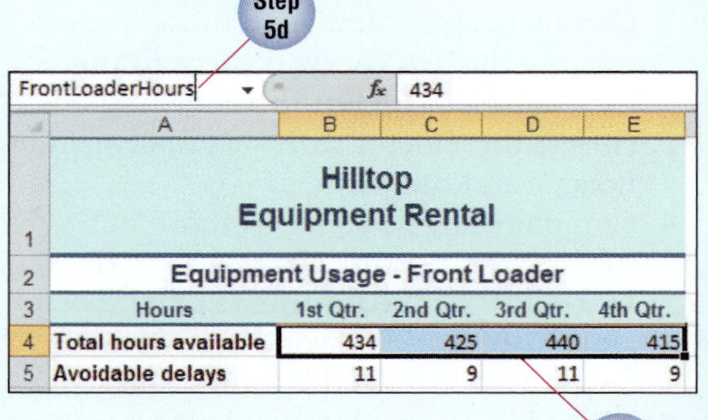

6. Complete steps similar to those in Step 5 to create the following ranges:
   a. In the Front Loader worksheet, create a range with cells B10 through E10 and name it *FrontLoaderHoursInUse*.
   b. Click the Tractor tab and then create a range with cells B4 through E4 and name it *TractorHours* and create a range with cells B10 through E10 and name it *TractorHoursInUse*.
   c. Click the Forklift tab and then create a range with cells B4 through E4 and name it *ForkliftHours* and create a range with cells B10 through E10 and name it *ForkliftHoursInUse*.
   d. Click the Backhoe tab and then create a range with cells B4 through E4 and name it *BackhoeHours* and create a range with cells B10 through E10 and name it *BackhoeHoursInUse*.
7. Click the EquipmentHours tab to make it the active worksheet and then insert a formula that inserts the total hours for the front loader by completing the following steps:
   a. Make cell C4 active.
   b. Type **=SUM(Fr**.
   c. When you type *Fr* a drop-down list displays with the front loader ranges. Double-click *FrontLoaderHours*.

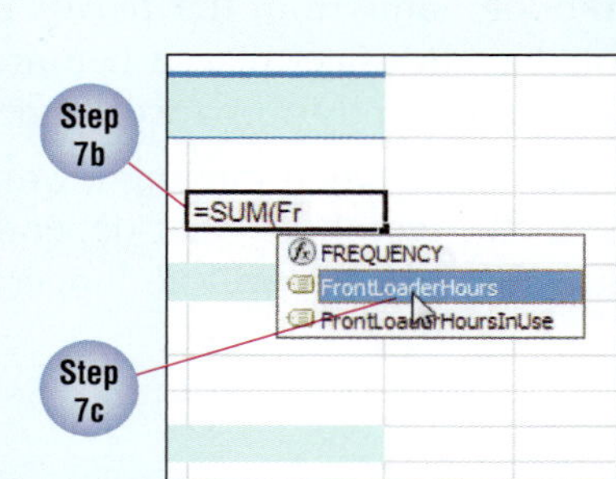

d. Type) (the closing parenthesis).
e. Press Enter.

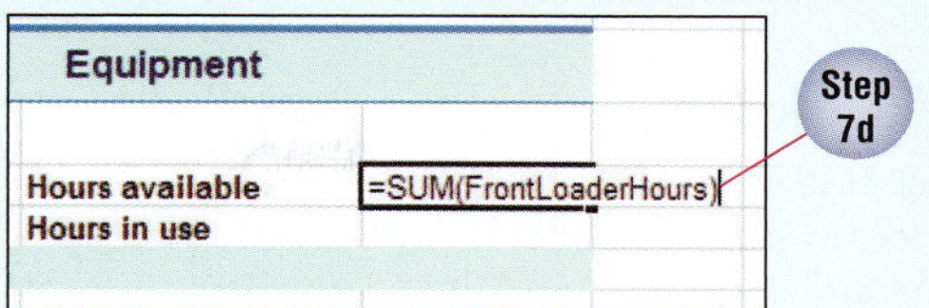

8. Complete steps similar to those in Step 7 to insert ranges in the following cells:
   a. Make cell C5 active and then insert a formula that inserts the total in-use hours for the front loader.
   b. Make cell C8 active and then insert a formula that inserts the total hours available for the tractor.
   c. Make cell C9 active and then insert a formula that inserts the total in-use hours for the tractor.
   d. Make cell C12 active and then insert a formula that inserts the total hours available for the forklift.
   e. Make cell C13 active and then insert a formula that inserts the total in-use hours for the forklift.
   f. Make cell C16 active and then insert a formula that inserts the total hours available for the backhoe.
   g. Make cell C17 active and then insert a formula that inserts the total in-use hours for the backhoe.
9. Make the following changes to specific worksheets:
   a. Click the Front Loader tab and then change the number in cell E4 from *415* to *426* and change the number in cell C6 from *6* to *14*.
   b. Click the Forklift tab and then change the number in cells E4 from *415* to *426* and change the number in cell D8 from *4* to *12*.
10. Select all of the worksheet tabs and then create a header that prints your name at the left side of each worksheet, the page number in the middle, and the current date at the right side of each worksheet.
11. Save and then print all of the worksheets in **EL1-C6-P2-HEREquip.xlsx**.
12. Close the workbook.
13. Make the following changes to the Recent tab Backstage view.
   a. Click the File tab.
   b. Change the number to the right of *Quickly access this number of Recent Workbooks* from *3* to *4*.
   c. Click the *Quickly access this number of Recent Workbooks* option to remove the check mark.
   d. Unpin the **EL1-C6-P2-HEREquip.xlsx** workbook name from the *Recent Workbooks* list by clicking the blue pin that displays at the right side of **EL1-C6-P2-HEREquip.xlsx**. (This changes the blue pin to a dimmed, gray pin and moves the file down the list.)
   e. Unpin the **HERBackhoe.xlsx** workbook and the **HEREquip.xlsx** workbook.
   f. Click the File tab to remove the Recent tab Backstage view.

Project  Create and Apply Styles to a Payroll Workbook — 5 Parts

You will open a payroll workbook, define and apply styles, and then modify the styles. You will also copy the styles to another workbook and then apply the styles in the new workbook.

Formatting with Cell Styles

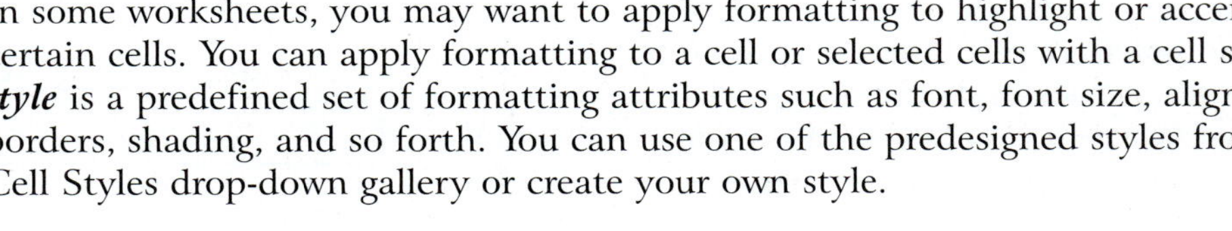

Quick Steps

Apply Cell Style
1. Select desired cell(s).
2. Click Cell Styles button.
3. Click desired style option.

Cell Styles

In some worksheets, you may want to apply formatting to highlight or accentuate certain cells. You can apply formatting to a cell or selected cells with a cell style. A ***style*** is a predefined set of formatting attributes such as font, font size, alignment, borders, shading, and so forth. You can use one of the predesigned styles from the Cell Styles drop-down gallery or create your own style.

Applying a Style

To apply a style, select the desired cell(s), click the Cell Styles button in the Styles group in the Home tab and then click the desired option at the drop-down gallery shown in Figure 6.4. If you hover your mouse pointer over a style option in the drop-down gallery, the cell or selected cells display with the formatting applied.

Figure 6.4 Cell Styles Drop-Down Gallery

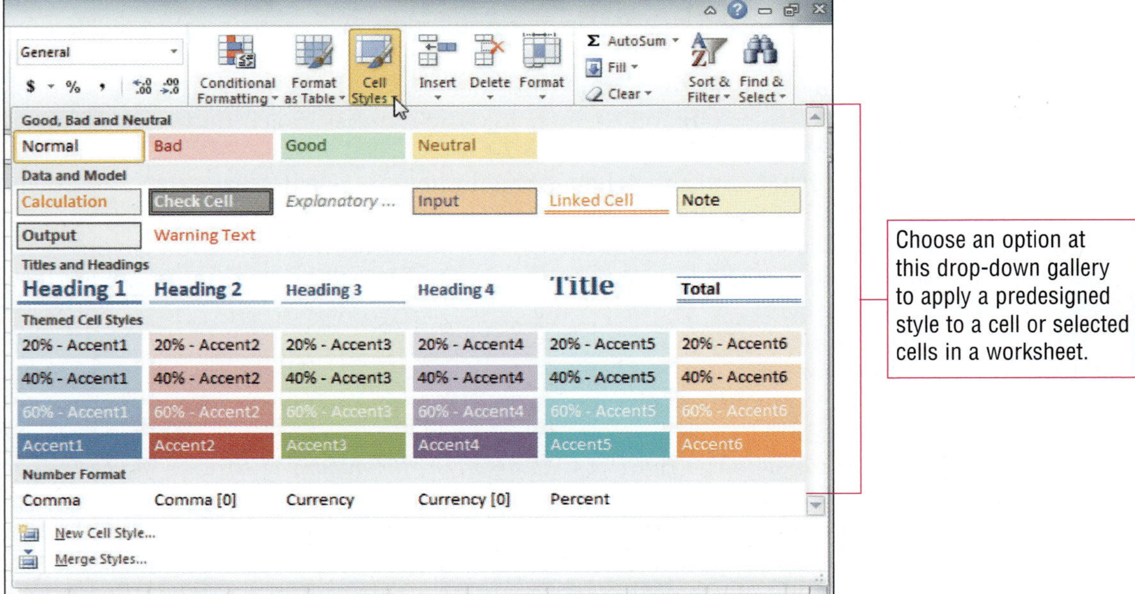

Project 3a Formatting with Cell Styles

Part 1 of 5

1. Open **OEPayroll.xlsx** and then save the workbook with Save As and name it **EL1-C6-P3-OEPayroll**.
2. With Sheet1 the active worksheet, insert the necessary formulas to calculate gross pay, withholding tax amount, Social Security tax amount, and net pay. ***Hint: Refer to Project 5c in Chapter 2 for assistance***. Apply the Accounting Number Format style to cells D4 through G4.
3. Make Sheet2 active and then insert a formula that calculates the amount due. Apply the Accounting Number Format style to cell F4.

4. Make Sheet3 active and then insert a formula in the *Due Date* column that calculates the purchase date plus the number of days in the *Terms* column. ***Hint: Refer to Project 3c in Chapter 2 for assistance***.
5. Apply cell styles to cells by completing the following steps:
   a. Make Sheet1 active and then select cells A11 and A12.
   b. Click the Cell Styles button in the Styles group in the Home tab.
   c. At the drop-down gallery, hover your mouse over style options to see how the style formatting affects the selected cells.
   d. Click the *Check Cell* option in the *Data and Model* section.
6. Select cells B11 and B12, click the Cell Styles button, and then click the *Output* option in the *Data and Model* section (first option from the left in the second row in the *Data and Model* section).

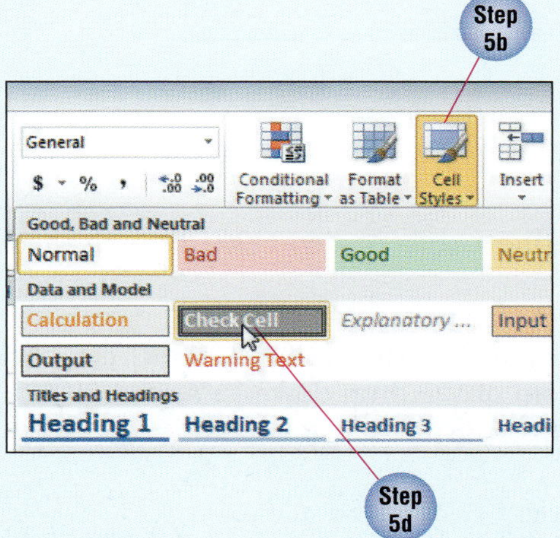

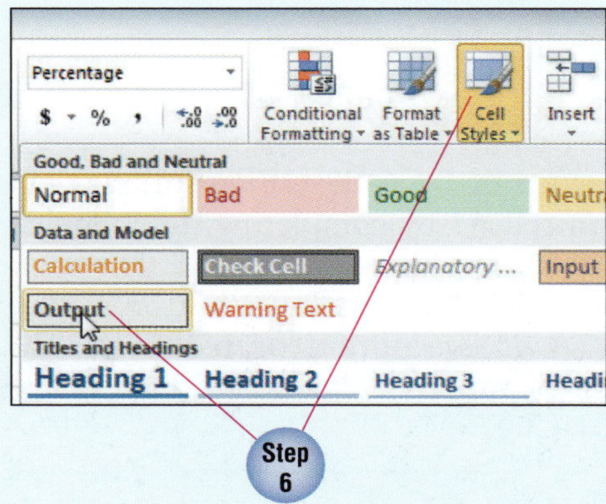

7. Save **EL1-C6-P3-OEPayroll.xlsx**.

Defining a Cell Style

You can apply styles from the Cell Styles drop-down gallery or you can create your own style. Using a style to apply formatting has several advantages. A style helps to ensure consistent formatting from one worksheet to another. Once you define all attributes for a particular style, you do not have to redefine them again. If you need to change the formatting, change the style and all cells formatted with that style automatically reflect the change.

Two basic methods are available for defining your own cell style. You can define a style with formats already applied to a cell or you can display the Style dialog box, click the Format button, and then choose formatting options at the Format Cells dialog box. Styles you create are only available in the workbook in which they are created. To define a style with existing formatting, select the cell or cells containing the desired formatting, click the Cell Styles button in the Styles group in the Home tab, and then click the *New Cell Style* option located toward the bottom of the drop-down gallery. At the Style dialog box, shown in Figure 6.5, type a name for the new style in the *Style name* text box and then click OK to close the dialog box. The styles you create display at the top of the drop-down gallery in the *Custom* section when you click the Cell Styles button.

Quick Steps

Define a Cell Style with Existing Formatting
1. Select cell containing formatting.
2. Click Cell Styles button.
3. Click *New Cell Style*.
4. Type name for new style.
5. Click OK.

Cell styles are based on the workbook theme.

Quick Steps

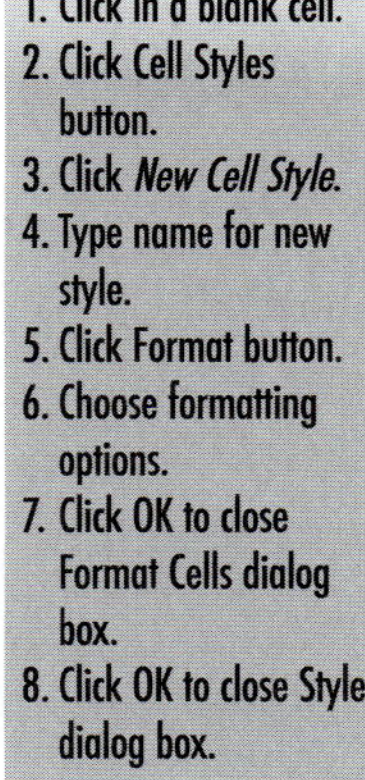

Define a Style

1. Click in a blank cell.
2. Click Cell Styles button.
3. Click *New Cell Style.*
4. Type name for new style.
5. Click Format button.
6. Choose formatting options.
7. Click OK to close Format Cells dialog box.
8. Click OK to close Style dialog box.

Figure 6.5 Style Dialog Box

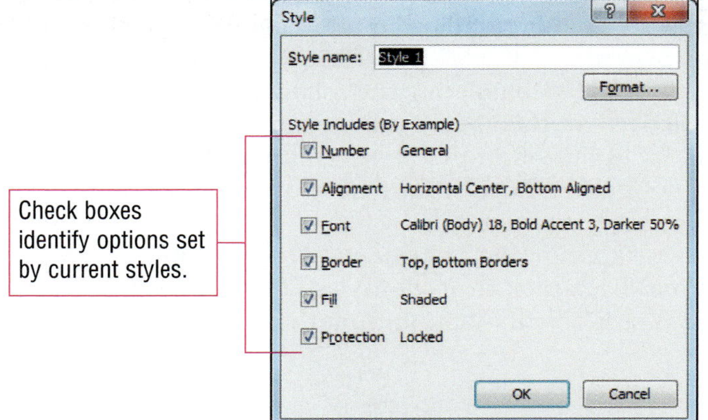

Project 3b Defining and Applying a Style

Part 2 of 5

1. With **EL1-C6-P3-OEPayroll.xlsx** open, define a style named *C06Title* with the formatting in cell A1 by completing the following steps:
   a. Make Sheet 1 active and then make cell A1 active.
   b. Click the Cell Styles button in the Styles group in the Home tab and then click the *New Cell Style* option located toward the bottom of the drop-down gallery.
   c. At the Style dialog box, type **C06Title** in the *Style name* text box.
   d. Click OK.

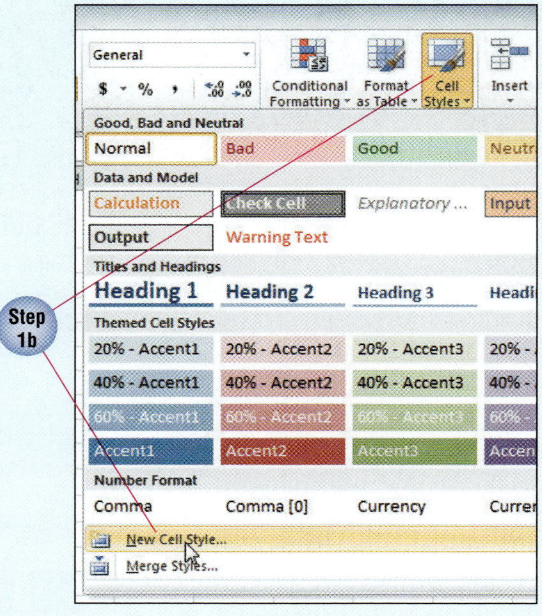

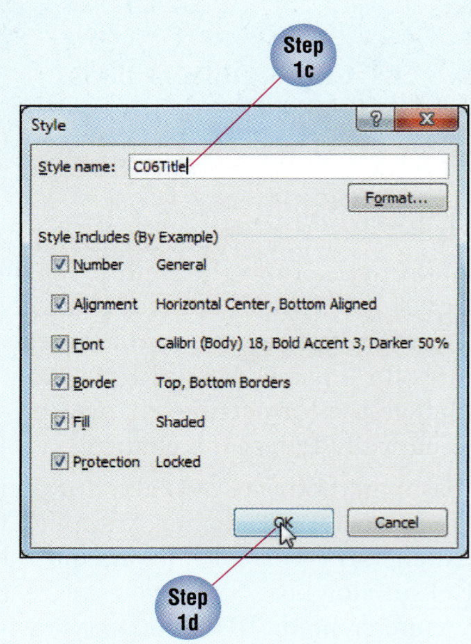

2. Even though cell A1 is already formatted, the style has not been applied to it. Later, you will modify the style and the style must be applied to the cell for the change to affect it. Apply the C06Title style to cell A1 by completing the following steps:
   a. Make sure cell A1 is the active cell.

b. Click the Cell Styles button in the Styles group in the Home tab.
c. Click the *C06Title* style in the *Custom* section located toward the top of the drop-down gallery.

3. Apply the C06Title style to other cells by completing the following steps:
   a. Click the Sheet2 tab.
   b. Make cell A1 active.
   c. Click the Cell Styles button in the Styles group and then click the *C06Title* style at the drop-down gallery. (Notice that the style did not apply the row height formatting. The style applies only cell formatting.)
   d. Click the Sheet3 tab.
   e. Make cell A1 active.
   f. Click the Cell Styles button and then click the *C06Title* style at the drop-down gallery.
   g. Click the Sheet1 tab.
4. Save **EL1-C6-P3-OEPayroll.xlsx**.

In addition to defining a style based on cell formatting, you can also define a new style without first applying the formatting. To do this, you would display the Style dialog box, type a name for the new style, and then click the Format button. At the Format Cells dialog box, apply any desired formatting and then click OK to close the dialog box. At the Style dialog box, remove the check mark from any formatting that you do not want included in the style and then click OK to close the Style dialog box.

Project 3c **Defining a Style without First Applying Formatting** Part 3 of 5

1. With **EL1-C6-P3-OEPayroll.xlsx** open, define a new style named *C06Subtitle* without first applying the formatting by completing the following steps:
   a. With Sheet1 active, click in any empty cell.
   b. Click the Cell Styles button in the Styles group and then click *New Cell Style* at the drop-down gallery.
   c. At the Style dialog box, type **C06Subtitle** in the *Style name* text box.
   d. Click the Format button in the Style dialog box.
   e. At the Format Cells dialog box, click the Font tab.
   f. At the Format Cells dialog box with the Font tab selected, change the font to Candara, the font style to bold, the size to 12, and the color to white.

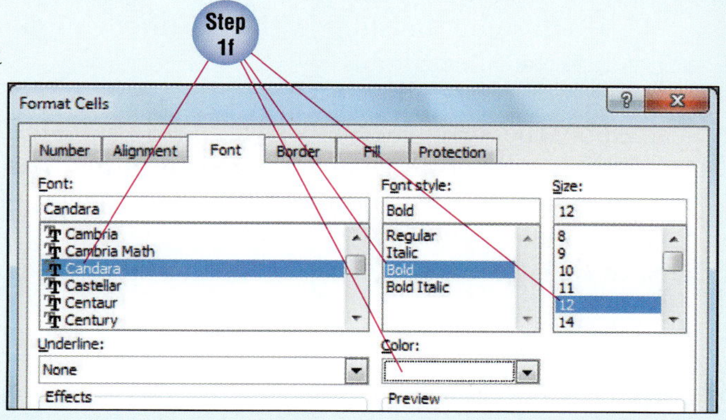

g. Click the Fill tab.
h. Click the bottom color in the green column as shown at the right.
i. Click the Alignment tab.
j. Change the Horizontal alignment to Center.
k. Click OK to close the Format Cells dialog box.
l. Click OK to close the Style dialog box.

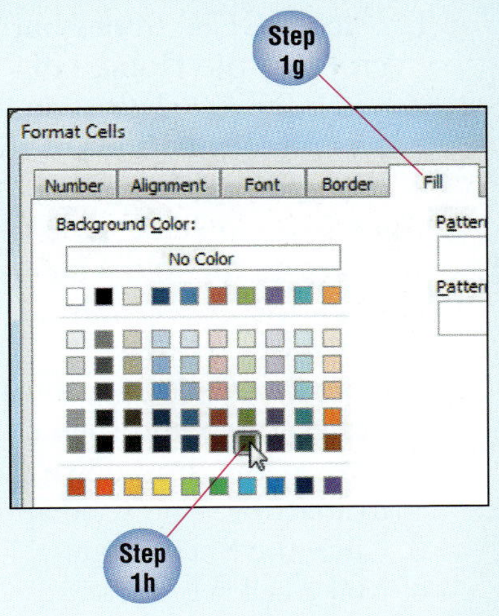

2. Apply the C06Subtitle style by completing the following steps:
   a. Make cell A2 active.
   b. Click the Cell Styles button and then click the C06Subtitle style located toward the top of the drop-down gallery in the *Custom* section.
   c. Click the Sheet2 tab.
   d. Make cell A2 active.
   e. Click the Cell Styles button and then click the C06Subtitle style.
   f. Click the Sheet3 tab.
   g. Make cell A2 active.
   h. Click the Cell Styles button and then click the C06Subtitle style.
   i. Click the Sheet1 tab.
3. Apply the following predesigned cell styles:
   a. Select cells A3 through G3.
   b. Click the Cell Styles button and then click the Heading 3 style at the drop-down gallery.
   c. Select cells A5 through G5.
   d. Click the Cell Styles button and then click the 20% - Accent3 style.
   e. Apply the 20% - Accent3 style to cells A7 through G7 and cells A9 through G9.
   f. Click the Sheet2 tab.
   g. Select cells A3 through F3 and then apply the Heading 3 style.
   h. Select cells A5 through F5 and then apply the 20% - Accent3 style.
   i. Apply the 20% - Accent3 style to every other row of cells (A7 through F7, A9 through F9, and so on, finishing with A17 through F17).
   j. Click the Sheet3 tab.
   k. Select cells A3 through F3 and then apply the Heading 3 style.
   l. Apply the 20% - Accent3 style to A5 through F5, A7 through F7, and A9 through F9.
4. With Sheet3 active, change the height of row 1 to 36.00 (48 pixels).
5. Make Sheet2 active and then change the height of row 1 to 36.00 (48 pixels).
6. Make Sheet1 active.
7. Save **EL1-C6-P3-OEPayroll.xlsx** and then print only the first worksheet.

Modifying a Style

One of the advantages to formatting with a style is that you can modify the formatting of the style and all cells formatted with that style automatically reflect the change. You can modify a style you create or one of the predesigned styles provided by Word. When you modify a predesigned style, only the style in the current workbook is affected. If you open a blank workbook, the cell styles available are the default styles.

To modify a style, click the Cell Styles button in the Styles group in the Home tab and then right-click the desired style at the drop-down gallery. At the shortcut menu that displays, click *Modify*. At the Style dialog box, click the Format button. Make the desired formatting changes at the Format Cells dialog box and then click OK. Click OK to close the Style dialog box and any cells formatted with the specific style are automatically updated.

Quick Steps

Modify a Style
1. Click Cell Styles button.
2. Right-click desired style at drop-down gallery.
3. Click *Modify*.
4. Click Format button.
5. Make desired formatting changes.
6. Click OK to close Format Cells dialog box.
7. Click OK to close Style dialog box.

Project 3d **Modifying Styles** Part 4 of 5

1. With **EL1-C6-P3-OEPayroll.xlsx** open, modify the C06Title style by completing the following steps:
   a. Click in any empty cell.
   b. Click the Cell Styles button in the Styles group.
   c. At the drop-down gallery, right-click on the C06Title style located toward the top of the gallery in the *Custom* section, and then click *Modify*.
   d. At the Style dialog box, click the Format button.
   e. At the Format Cells dialog box, click the Font tab, and then change the font to Candara.
   f. Click the Alignment tab.
   g. Click the down-pointing arrow to the right of the *Vertical* option box, and then click *Center* at the drop-down list.
   h. Click the Fill tab.
   i. Click the light turquoise fill color as shown at the right.
   j. Click OK to close the Format Cells dialog box.
   k. Click OK to close the Style dialog box.

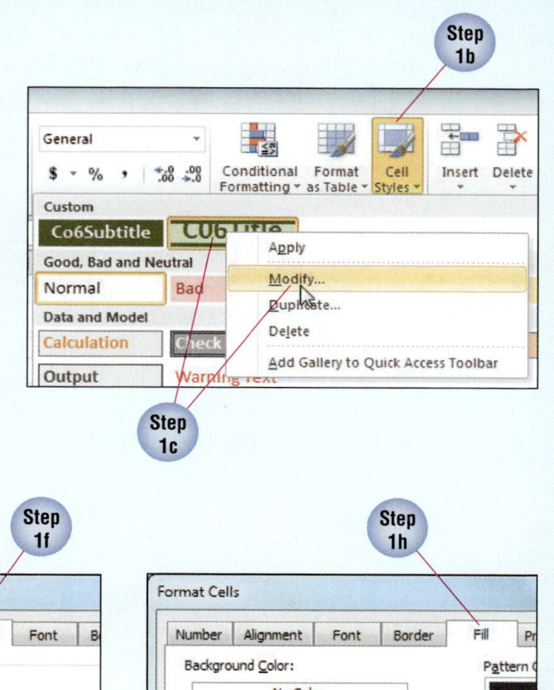

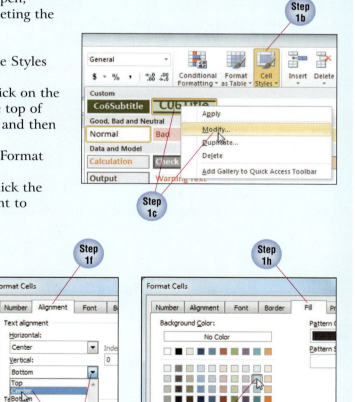

2. Modify the C06Subtitle style by completing the following steps:
   a. Click in any empty cell.
   b. Click the Cell Styles button in the Styles group.
   c. At the drop-down gallery, right-click on the C06Subtitle style located toward the top of the gallery in the *Custom* section, and then click *Modify*.
   d. At the Style dialog box, click the Format button.
   e. At the Format Cells dialog box, click the Font tab, and then change the font to Calibri.
   f. Click the Fill tab.
   g. Click the dark turquoise fill color as shown at the right.
   h. Click OK to close the Format Cells dialog box.
   i. Click OK to close the Style dialog box.

Step 2f

Format Cells
Number | Alignment | Font | Border | Fill
Background Color:
No Color
Pattern
Pattern

Step 2g

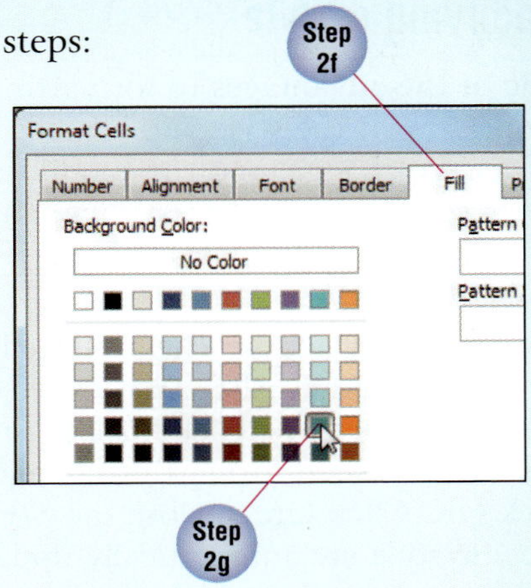

3. Modify the predefined 20% - Accent3 style by completing the following steps:
   a. Click the Cell Styles button in the Styles group.
   b. At the drop-down gallery, right-click on the 20% - Accent3 style and then click *Modify*.
   c. At the Style dialog box, click the Format button.
   d. At the Format Cells dialog box, make sure the Fill tab is active.
   e. Click the light turquoise fill color as shown at the right.
   f. Click OK to close the Format Cells dialog box.
   g. Click OK to close the Style dialog box.

Step 3d

Format Cells
Number | Alignment | Font | Border | Fill
Background Color:
No Color
Pattern
Pattern

Step 3e

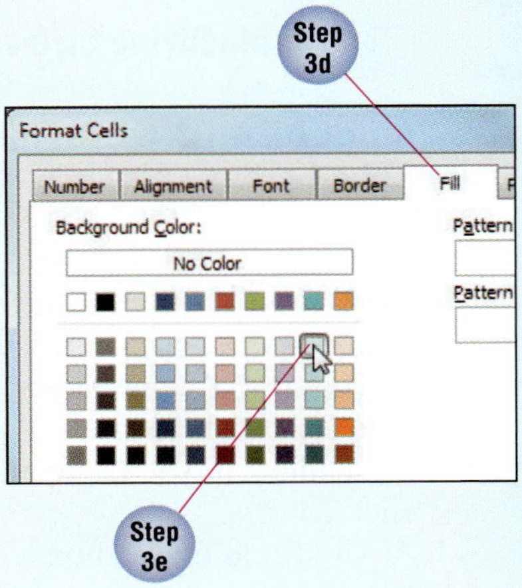

4. Click each sheet tab and notice the formatting changes made by the modified styles.
5. Change the name of Sheet1 to *Weekly Payroll*, the name of Sheet2 to *Invoices*, and the name of Sheet3 to *Overdue Accounts*.
6. Apply a different color to each of the three worksheet tabs.
7. Save and then print all the worksheets in **EL1-C6-P3-OEPayroll.xlsx**.

Copying Styles to Another Workbook

Styles you define are saved with the workbook in which they are created. You can, however, copy styles from one workbook to another. To do this, open the workbook containing the styles you want to copy and open the workbook into which you want to copy the styles. Click the Cell Styles button in the Styles group in the Home tab and then click the *Merge Styles* option located at the bottom of the drop-down gallery. At the Merge Styles dialog box shown in Figure 6.6, double-click the name of the workbook that contains the styles you want to copy and then click OK.

Quick Steps

Copy Styles to Another Workbook
1. Open workbook containing desired styles.
2. Open workbook you want to modify.
3. Click Cell Styles button.
4. Click *Merge Styles* option.
5. Double-click name of workbook that contains styles you want to copy.

Removing a Style

If you apply a style to text and then decide you do not want the formatting applied, return the formatting to Normal, which is the default formatting. To do this, select the cells formatted with the style you want to remove, click the Cell Styles button, and then click *Normal* at the drop-down gallery.

Figure 6.6 Merge Styles Dialog Box

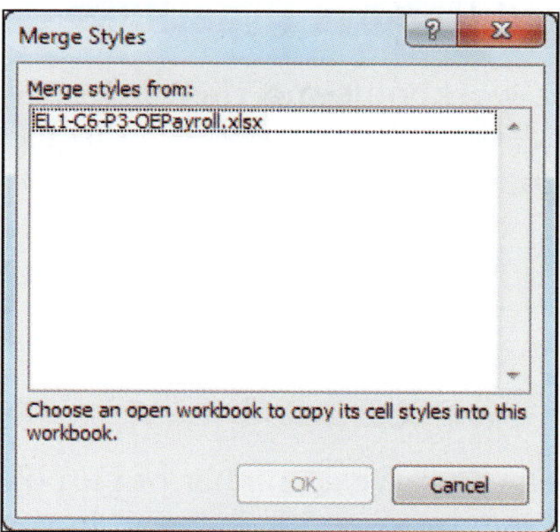

Quick Steps

Remove a Style
1. Select cells formatted with style you want removed.
2. Click Cell Styles button.
3. Click *Normal* at drop-down gallery.

Delete a Style
1. Click Cell Styles button.
2. Right-click desired style to delete.
3. Click *Delete* at shortcut menu.

You cannot delete the Normal style.

The Undo command will not reverse the effects of the Merge Styles dialog box.

Deleting a Style

To delete a style, click the Cell Styles button in the Styles group in the Home tab. At the drop-down gallery that displays, right-click the style you want to delete and then click *Delete* at the shortcut menu. Formatting applied by the deleted style is removed from cells in the workbook.

Project 3e **Copying Styles** Part 5 of 5

1. With **EL1-C6-P3-OEPayroll.xlsx** open, open **OEPlans.xlsx**.
2. Save the workbook with Save As and name it **EL1-C6-P3-OEPlans**.
3. Copy the styles in **EL1-C6-P3-Payroll.xlsx** into **EL1-C6-P3-OEPlans.xlsx** by completing the following steps:
   a. Click the Cell Styles button in the Styles group in the Home tab.
   b. Click the *Merge Styles* option located toward the bottom of the drop-down gallery.
   c. At the Merge Styles dialog box, double-click ***EL1-C6-P3-OEPayroll.xlsx*** in the *Merge styles from* list box.
   d. At the message that displays asking if you want to merge styles that have the same names, click Yes.
4. Apply the C06Title style to cell A1 and the C06Subtitle style to cell A2.
5. Increase the height of row 1 to 36.00 (48 pixels).
6. Insert the required formulas in the workbook. ***Hint: Refer to Project 3a in Chapter 2 for assistance.***
7. If neccessary, adjust column widths so all text is visible in cells.
8. Save, print, and then close **EL1-C6-P3-OEPlans.xlsx**.
9. Close **EL1-C6-P3-OEPayroll.xlsx**.

Project 4 Insert, Modify, and Remove Hyperlinks — 3 Parts

You will open a facilities account workbook and then insert hyperlinks to a website, to cells in other worksheets in the workbook, and to another workbook. You will modify and edit hyperlinks and then remove a hyperlink from the workbook.

Inserting Hyperlinks

Quick Steps

Insert Hyperlink
1. Click Insert tab.
2. Click Hyperlink button.
3. Make desired changes at Insert Hyperlink dialog box.
4. Click OK.

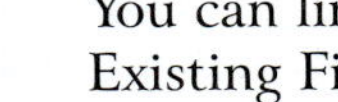

Hyperlink

A hyperlink in a workbook can serve a number of purposes: Click it to navigate to a web page on the Internet or a specific location in the workbook, to display a different workbook, to open a file in a different program, to create a new document, or to link to an email address. You can create a customized hyperlink by clicking the desired cell in a workbook, clicking the Insert tab, and then clicking the Hyperlink button in the Links group. This displays the Insert Hyperlink dialog box, shown in Figure 6.7. At this dialog box, identify what you want to link to and the location of the link. Click the ScreenTip button to customize the hyperlink ScreenTip.

Linking to an Existing Web Page or File

You can link to a web page on the Internet by typing a web address or with the Existing File or Web Page button in the *Link to* group. To link to an existing web page, type the address of the web page such as *www.emcp.com*. By default, the automatic formatting of hyperlinks is turned on and the web address is formatted as a hyperlink (text is underlined and the color changes to blue). You can turn off the automatic formatting of hyperlinks at the AutoCorrect dialog box. Display this dialog box by clicking the File tab, clicking the Options button, and then clicking *Proofing* in the left panel of the Excel Options dialog box. Click the AutoCorrect Options button to display the AutoCorrect dialog box. At this dialog

Figure 6.7 Insert Hyperlink Dialog Box

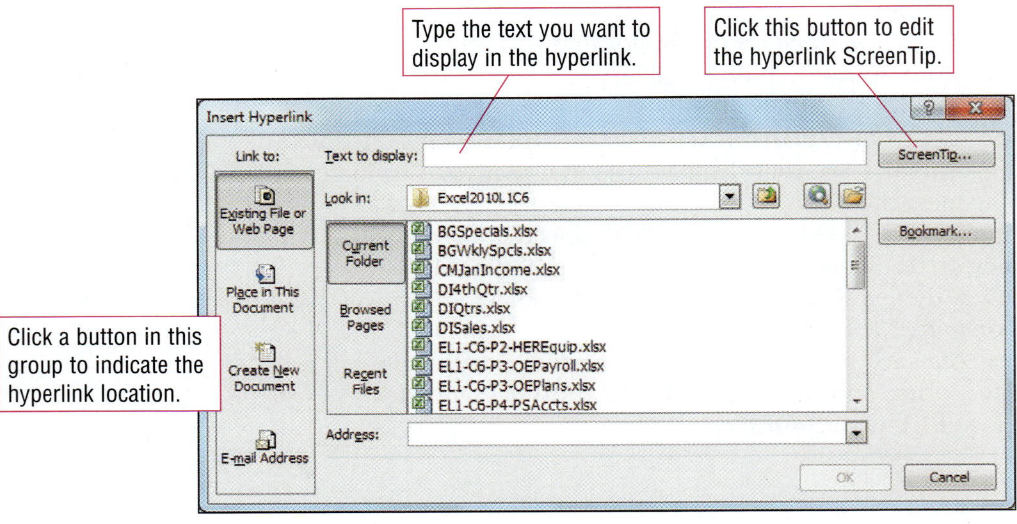

box, click the AutoFormat As You Type tab and then remove the check mark from the *Internet and network paths with hyperlinks* check box. To link to a web page at the Insert Hyperlink dialog box, display the dialog box, click the Existing File or Web Page button in the *Link to* group and then type the web address in the *Address* text box.

In some situations, you may want to provide information to your readers from a variety of sources. You may want to provide additional information in an Excel workbook, a Word document, or a PowerPoint presentation. To link an Excel workbook to a workbook or a file in another application, display the Insert Hyperlink dialog box and then click the Existing File or Web Page button in the *Link to* group. Use the *Look in* option to navigate to the folder containing the desired file and then click the file. Make other changes in the Insert Hyperlink dialog box as needed and then click OK.

Navigating Using Hyperlinks

Navigate to a hyperlink by clicking the hyperlink in the worksheet. Hover the mouse over the hyperlink and a ScreenTip displays with the hyperlink. If you want specific information to display in the ScreenTip, click the ScreenTip button in the Insert Hyperlink dialog box, type the desired text in the Set Hyperlink ScreenTip dialog box, and then click OK.

Project 4a Linking to a Website and Another Workbook

Part 1 of 3

1. Open **PSAccts.xlsx** and then save the workbook with Save As and name it **EL1-C6-P4-PSAccts**.
2. Insert a hyperlink to company information (since Pyramid Sales is a fictitious company, you will hyperlink to the publishing company website) by completing the following steps:
   a. Make cell A13 active.
   b. Click the Insert tab and then click the Hyperlink button in the Links group.
   c. At the Insert Hyperlink dialog box, if necessary, click the Existing File or Web Page button in the *Link to* group.
   d. Type **www.emcp.com** in the *Address* text box.
   e. Select the text that displays in the *Text to display* text box and then type **Company information**.
   f. Click the ScreenTip button located in the upper right corner of the dialog box.

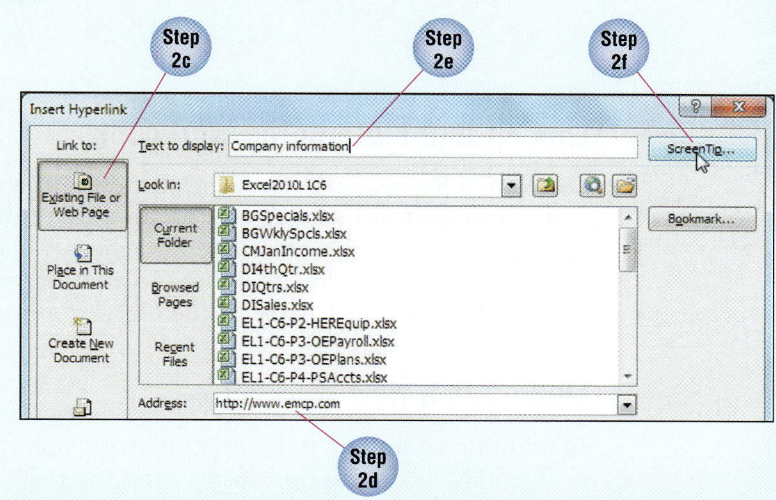

g. At the Set Hyperlink ScreenTip dialog box, type **View the company website.** and then click OK.
h. Click OK to close the Insert Hyperlink dialog box.

3. Navigate to the company website (in this case, the publishing company website) by clicking the Company information hyperlink in cell A13.
4. Close the Web browser.
5. Create a link to another workbook by completing the following steps:
   a. Make cell A11 active, type **Semiannual sales**, and then press the Enter key.
   b. Make cell A11 active and then click the Hyperlink button in the Links group in the Insert tab.
   c. At the Insert Hyperlink dialog box, make sure the Existing File or Web Page button is selected.
   d. If necessary, click the down-pointing arrow at the right side of the *Look in* option and then navigate to the Excel2010L1C6 folder on your storage medium.
   e. Double-click ***PSSalesAnalysis.xlsx***.
6. Click the Semiannual sales hyperlink to open the **PSSalesAnalysis.xlsx** workbook.
7. Look at the information in the workbook and then close the workbook.
8. Save **EL1-C6-P4-PSAccts.xlsx**.

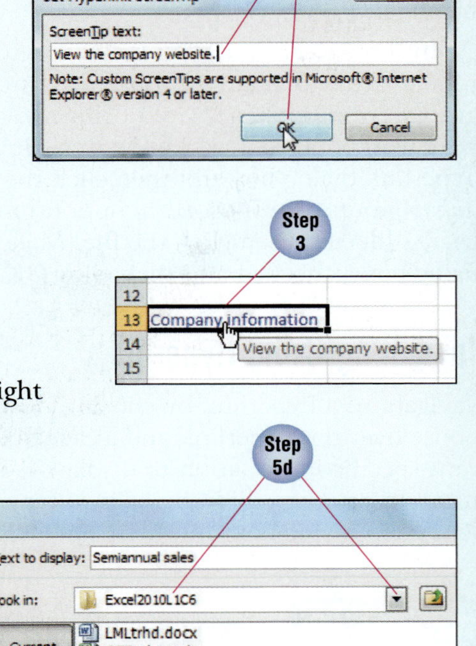

Linking to a Place in the Workbook

To create a hyperlink to another location in the workbook, click the Place in This Document button in the *Link to* group in the Edit Hyperlink dialog box. If you are linking to a cell within the same worksheet, type the cell name in the *Type the cell reference* text box. If you are linking to another worksheet in the workbook, click the desired worksheet name in the *Or select a place in this document* list box.

Linking to a New Workbook

In addition to linking to an existing workbook, you can create a hyperlink to a new workbook. To do this, display the Insert Hyperlink dialog box and then click the Create New Document button in the *Link to* group. Type a name for the new workbook in the *Name of new document* text box and then specify if you want to edit the workbook now or later.

Linking Using a Graphic

You can use a graphic such as a clip art image, picture, or text box to hyperlink to a file or website. To hyperlink with a graphic, select the graphic, click the Insert tab, and then click the Hyperlink button. You can also right-click the graphic and then click *Hyperlink* at the shortcut menu. At the Insert Hyperlink dialog box, specify where you want to link to and text you want to display in the hyperlink.

Linking to an Email Address

You can insert a hyperlink to an email address at the Insert Hyperlink dialog box. To do this, click the E-Mail Address button in the *Link to* group, type the desired address in the *E-mail address* text box, and type a subject for the email in the *Subject* text box. Click in the *Text to display* text box and then type the text you want to display in the document. To use this feature, the email address you use must be set up in Outlook 2010.

Project 4b Linking to Place in a Workbook, to Another Workbook, and Using a Graphic

Part 2 of 3

1. With **EL1-C6-P4-PSAccts.xlsx** open, create a link from the checks amount in cell B6 to the check amount in cell G20 in the January worksheet by completing the following steps:
   a. Make cell B6 active.
   b. Click the Insert tab and then click the Hyperlink button in the Links group.
   c. At the Insert Hyperlink dialog box, click the Place in This Document button in the *Link to* group.
   d. Select the text in the *Type the cell reference* text box and then type G20.
   e. Click *January* in the *Or select a place in this document* list box.
   f. Click OK to close the Insert Hyperlink dialog box.

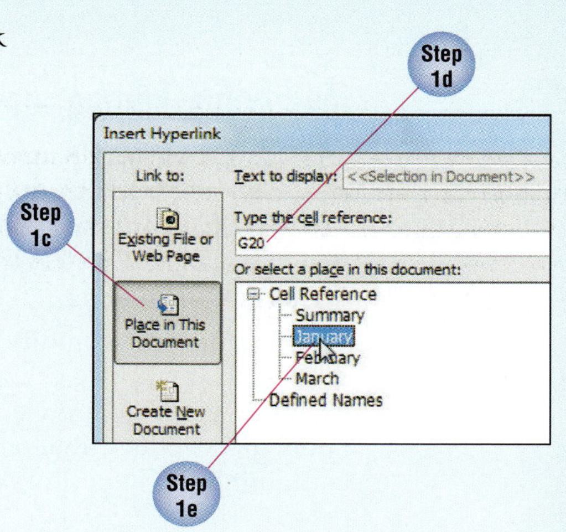

2. Make cell C6 active and then complete steps similar to those in Steps 1b through 1f except click *February* in the *Or select a place in this document* list box.
3. Make cell D6 active and then complete steps similar to those in Steps 1b through 1f except click *March* in the *Or select a place in this document* list box.
4. Click the hyperlinked amount in cell B6. (This makes cell G20 active in the January worksheet.)
5. Click the Summary worksheet tab.
6. Click the hyperlinked amount in cell C6. (This makes cell G20 active in the February worksheet.)
7. Click the Summary worksheet tab.
8. Click the hyperlinked amount in cell D6. (This makes cell G20 active in the March worksheet.)
9. Click the Summary worksheet tab.

10. Use the first pyramid graphic image in cell A1 to create a link to the company web page by completing the following steps:
    a. Right-click the first pyramid graphic image in cell A1 and then click *Hyperlink* at the shortcut menu.
    b. At the Insert Hyperlink dialog box, if necessary, click the Existing File or Web Page button in the *Link to* group.
    c. Type **www.emcp.com** in the *Address* text box.
    d. Click the ScreenTip button located in the upper right corner of the dialog box.
    e. At the Set Hyperlink ScreenTip dialog box, type **View the company website.** and then click OK.
    f. Click OK to close the Insert Hyperlink dialog box.

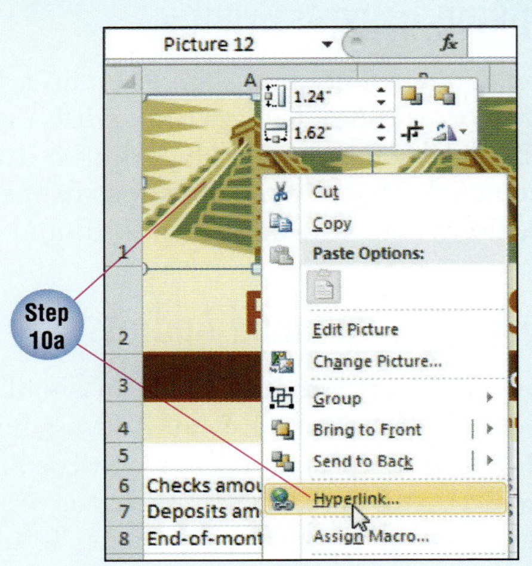

11. Make cell A5 active.
12. Navigate to the company website (the publishing company website) by clicking the first pyramid graphic image.
13. Close the Web browser.
14. Save **EL1-C6-P4-PSAccts.xlsx**.

Modifying, Editing, and Removing a Hyperlink

You can modify or change hyperlink text or the hyperlink destination. To do this, right-click the hyperlink and then click *Edit Hyperlink* at the shortcut menu. At the Edit Hyperlink dialog box, make any desired changes and then close the dialog box. The Edit Hyperlink dialog box contains the same options as the Insert Hyperlink dialog box.

In addition to modifying the hyperlink, you can edit hyperlink text in a cell. To do this, make the cell active and then make the desired editing changes. For example, you can apply a different font or font size, change the text color, and apply a text effect. Remove a hyperlink from a workbook by right-clicking the cell containing the hyperlink and then clicking *Remove Hyperlink* at the shortcut menu.

Project 4c Modifying, Editing, and Removing a Hyperlink Part 3 of 3

1. With **EL1-C6-P4-PSAccts.xlsx** open, modify the Semiannual sales hyperlink by completing the following steps:
    a. Position the mouse pointer on the Semiannual sales hyperlink in cell A11, click the right mouse button, and then click *Edit Hyperlink* at the shortcut menu.
    b. At the Edit Hyperlink dialog box, select the text *Semiannual sales* in the *Text to display* text box and then type **Customer sales analysis**.
    c. Click the ScreenTip button located in the upper right corner of the dialog box.
    d. At the Set Hyperlink ScreenTip dialog box, type **Click this hyperlink to display workbook containing customer sales analysis.**

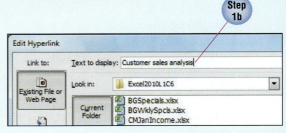

e. Click OK to close the Set Hyperlink ScreenTip dialog box.
f. Click OK to close the Edit Hyperlink dialog box.
2. Click the Customer sales analysis hyperlink.
3. After looking at the **PSSalesAnalysis.xlsx** workbook, close the workbook.
4. With cell A11 active, edit the Customer sales analysis hyperlink text by completing the following steps:
   a. Click the Home tab.
   b. Click the Font Color button arrow in the Font group and then click the *Red, Accent 2, Darker 50%* color (located toward the bottom of the sixth column).
   c. Click the Bold button.
   d. Click the Underline button. (This removes underlining from the text.)
5. Remove the Company information hyperlink by right-clicking in cell A13 and then clicking *Remove Hyperlink* at the shortcut menu.
6. Press the Delete key to remove the contents of cell A13.
7. Save, print only the first worksheet (the Summary worksheet), and then close **EL1-C6-P4-PSAccts.xlsx**.

Create a Billing Statement Workbook Using a Template

1 Part

You will open a Billing Statement template provided by Excel, add data, save it as an Excel workbook, and then print the workbook.

Using Excel Templates

Excel includes a number of template worksheet forms formatted for specific uses. With Excel templates you can create a variety of worksheets with specialized formatting such as balance sheets, billing statements, loan amortizations, sales invoices, and time cards. Display installed templates by clicking the File tab and then clicking the New tab. This displays the New tab Backstage view as shown in Figure 6.8.

Quick Steps
Use an Excel Template
1. Click File tab.
2. Click New tab.
3. Click Sample templates button.
4. Double-click desired template.

Click the Sample templates button in the *Available Templates* category and installed templates display. Click the desired template in the Sample templates list box and a preview of the template displays at the right side of the screen. Click the Create button that displays below the template preview and the template opens and displays on the screen. Locations for personalized text display in placeholders in the template worksheet. To enter information in the worksheet, position the mouse pointer (white plus sign) in the location where you want to type data and then click the left mouse button. After typing the data, click the next location. You can also move the insertion point to another cell using the commands learned in Chapter 1. For example, press the Tab key to make the next cell active or press Shift + Tab to make the previous cell active.

If you are connected to the Internet, you can download a number of predesigned templates that Microsoft offers. Templates are grouped into categories and the category names display in the *Office.com Templates* section of the New tab Backstage view. Click the desired template category and available templates display. Click the desired template and then click the Download button.

Figure 6.8 New Tab Backstage View

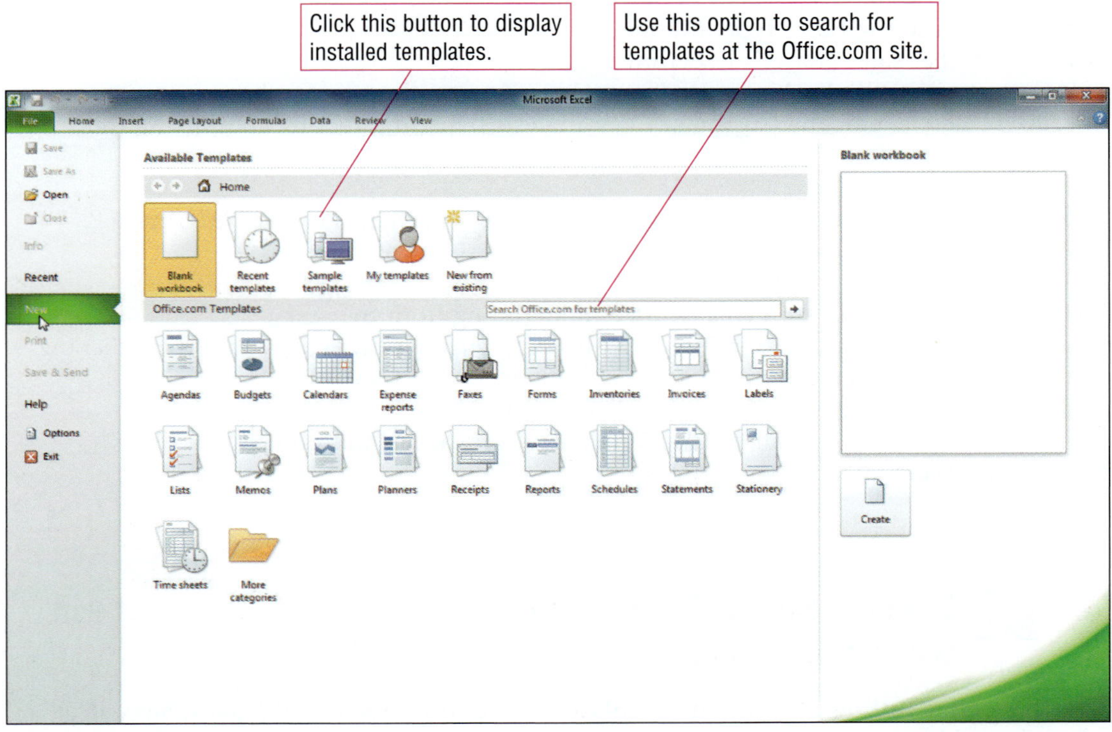

Project 5 Preparing a Billing Statement Using a Template

1 Part

1. Click the File tab and then click the New tab.
2. At the New tab Backstage view, click the Sample templates button in the *Available Templates* category.
3. Double-click the *Billing Statement* template in the *Available Templates* category of the dialog box.
4. Click the Normal button in the view area on the Status bar.
5. With cell B1 active, type **IN-FLOW SYSTEMS**.
6. Click the text *Street Address* (cell B2) and then type **320 Milander Way**.

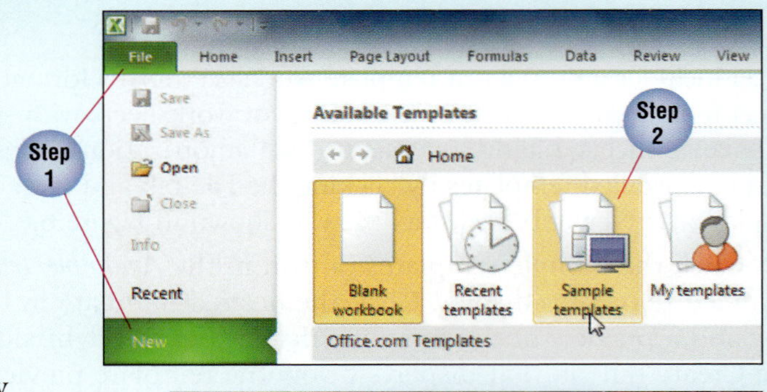

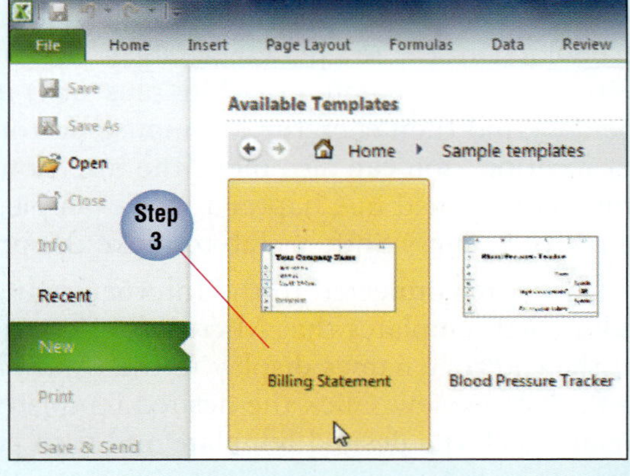

7. Click in the specified location (cell) and then type the text indicated:
   Address 2 (cell B3) = **P.O. Box 2300**
   City, ST ZIP Code (cell B4) = **Boston, MA 02188**
   Phone (cell F2) = **(617) 555-3900**
   Fax (cell F3) = **(617) 555-3945**
   Statement # (cell C8) = **5432**
   Customer ID (cell C10) = **25-345**
   Name (cell F8) = **Aidan Mackenzie**
   Company Name (cell F9) = **Stanfield Enterprises**
   Street Address (cell F10) = **9921 South 42nd Avenue**
   Address 2 (cell F11) = **P.O. Box 5540**
   City, ST ZIP Code (cell F12) = **Boston, MA 02193**
   Date (cell B15) = (insert current date in numbers as ##/##/####)
   Type (cell C15) = **System Unit**
   Invoice # (cell D15) = **7452**
   Description (cell E15) = **Calibration Unit**
   Amount (cell F15) = **950**
   Payment (cell G15) = **200**
   Customer Name (cell C21) = **Stanfield Enterprises**
   Amount Enclosed (C26) = **750**

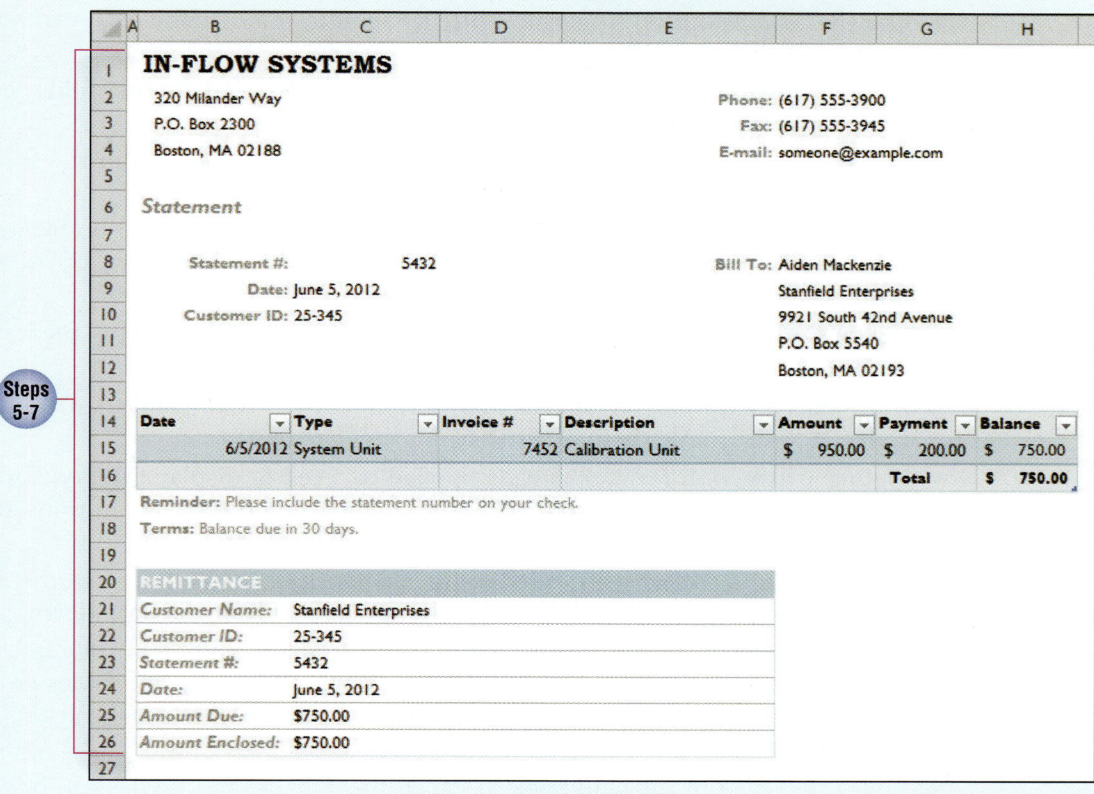

8. Save the completed invoice and name it **EL1-C6-P5-Billing**.
9. Print and then close **EL1-C6-P5-Billing.xlsx**.

Chapter Summary

- Perform file management tasks such as copying, moving, printing, and renaming workbooks and creating a new folder and renaming a folder at the Open or Save As dialog boxes.
- Create a new folder by clicking the New folder button located on the toolbar at the Open dialog box or Save As dialog box.
- Rename a folder with the *Rename* option from the Organize button drop-down list or with a shortcut menu.
- Use the Shift key to select adjacent workbooks in the Open dialog box and use the Ctrl key to select nonadjacent workbooks.
- To delete a workbook, use the *Delete* option from the Organize button drop-down list or with a shortcut menu option. Workbooks deleted from the hard drive are automatically sent to the Windows Recycle Bin where they can be restored or permanently deleted.
- Use the *Copy* and *Paste* options from the shortcut menu at the Open (or Save As) dialog box to copy a workbook from one folder to another folder or drive.
- Use the *Send To* option from the shortcut menu to send a copy of a workbook to another drive or folder.
- Remove a workbook from a folder or drive and insert it in another folder or drive using the *Cut* and *Paste* options from the shortcut menu.
- Use the *Rename* option from the Organize button drop-down list or the shortcut menu to give a workbook a different name.
- To move or copy a worksheet to another existing workbook, open both the source and the destination workbook and then open the Move or Copy dialog box.
- Use options from the Cell Styles button drop-down gallery to apply predesigned styles to a cell or selected cells.
- Automate the formatting of cells in a workbook by defining and then applying styles. A style is a predefined set of formatting attributes.
- Define a style with formats already applied to a cell or display the Style dialog box by clicking the Format button and then choosing formatting options at the Format Cells dialog box.
- To apply a style, select the desired cells, click the Cell Styles button in the Styles group in the Home tab, and then click the desired style at the drop-down gallery.
- Modify a style and all cells to which the style is applied automatically reflect the change. To modify a style, click the Cell Styles button in the Styles group in the Home tab, right-click the desired style, and then click *Modify* at the shortcut menu.
- Styles are saved in the workbook in which they are created. Styles can be copied, however, to another workbook. Do this with options at the Merge Styles dialog box.
- With options at the Insert Hyperlink dialog box, you can create a hyperlink to a web page, another workbook, a location within a workbook, a new workbook, or to an email. You can also create a hyperlink using a graphic.

- You can modify, edit, and remove hyperlinks.
- Excel provides preformatted templates for creating forms. Display the available templates by clicking the Sample templates button in the New tab Backstage view.
- Templates contain unique areas where information is entered at the keyboard. These areas vary depending on the template.

Commands Review

FEATURE	RIBBON TAB, GROUP	BUTTON, OPTION	KEYBOARD SHORTCUT
Open dialog box	File	Open	Ctrl + O
Save As dialog box	File	Save As	Ctrl + S
Cell Styles drop-down gallery	Home, Styles		
Style dialog box	Home, Styles	, New Cell Style	
Merge Styles dialog box	Home, Styles	, Merge Styles	
Insert Hyperlink dialog box	Insert, Links		
New tab Backstage view	File	New	
New folder	File	Open, New folder	

Concepts Check Test Your Knowledge

Completion: In the space provided at the right, indicate the correct term, symbol, or command.

1. Perform file management tasks such as copying, moving, or deleting workbooks with options at the Open dialog box or this dialog box. ____________
2. At the Open dialog box, a list of folders and files displays in this pane. ____________
3. Rename a folder or file at the Open dialog box using a shortcut menu or this button. ____________
4. At the Open dialog box, hold down this key while selecting nonadjacent workbooks. ____________

5. Workbooks deleted from the hard drive are automatically sent to this location. ____________

6. Insert a check mark in this check box at the Recent tab Backstage view and the four most recently opened workbook names display in the Backstage navigation bar. ____________

7. Do this to a workbook name you want to remain at the top of the *Recent Workbooks* list at the Recent tab Backstage view. ____________

8. If you close a workbook without saving it, you can recover it with this option at the Recent tab Backstage view. ____________

9. The Cell Styles button is located in this group in the Home tab. ____________

10. Click the *New Cell Style* option at the Cell Styles button drop-down gallery and this dialog box displays. ____________

11. A style you create displays in this section of the Cell Styles button drop-down gallery. ____________

12. Copy styles from one workbook to another with options at this dialog box. ____________

13. To link a workbook to another workbook, click this button in the *Link to* group in the Insert Hyperlink dialog box. ____________

14. Display installed templates by clicking this button in the *Available Templates* category at the New tab Backstage view. ____________

Skills Check Assess Your Performance

Assessment 1

MANAGE WORKBOOKS

1. Display the Open dialog box with Excel2010L1C6 the active folder.
2. Create a new folder named *O'Rourke* in the Excel2010L1C6 folder.
3. Copy **OEBudget.xlsx**, **OEPayroll.xlsx**, and **OEPlans.xlsx** to the O'Rourke folder.
4. Display the contents of the O'Rourke folder and then rename **OEBudget.xlsx** to **OEEquipBudget.xlsx**.
5. Rename **OEPlans.xlsx** to **OEPurchasePlans.xlsx** in the O'Rourke folder.
6. Change the active folder back to Excel2010L1C6.
7. Close the Open dialog box.

Assessment 2

MOVE AND COPY WORKSHEETS BETWEEN SALES ANALYSIS WORKBOOKS

1. Open **DISales.xlsx** and then save the workbook with Save As and name it **EL1-C6-A2-DISales**.
2. Rename Sheet1 to *1st Qtr*.
3. Open **DIQtrs.xlsx**.
4. Rename Sheet1 to *2nd Qtr* and then copy it to **EL1-C6-A2-DISales.xlsx** following the 1st Qtr worksheet. (When copying the worksheet, make sure you insert a check mark in the *Create a copy* check box in the Move or Copy dialog box.)
5. Make **DIQtrs.xlsx** active, rename Sheet 2 to *3rd Qtr* and then copy it to **EL1-C6-A2-DISales.xlsx** following the 2nd Qtr tab. (Make sure you insert a check mark in the *Create a copy* check box.)
6. Make **DIQtrs.xlsx** active and then close it without saving the changes.
7. Open **DI4thQtr.xlsx**.
8. Rename Sheet1 to *4th Qtr* and then move it to **EL1-C6-A2-DISales.xlsx** following the 3rd Qtr worksheet.
9. Make **DI4thQtr.xlsx** active and then close it without saving the changes.
10. With **EL1-C6-A2-DISales.xlsx** open, make the following changes to all four quarterly worksheets at the same time:
    a. Make 1st Qtr the active worksheet.
    b. Hold down the Shift key and then click the 4th Qtr tab. (This selects the four quarterly worksheet tabs.)
    c. Insert in cell E4 a formula to calculate average of cells B4 through D4 and then copy the formula down to cells E5 through E9.
    d. Insert in cell B10 a formula to calculate the sum of cells B4 through B9 and then copy the formula across to cells C10 through E10.
    e. Make cell E4 active and apply the Accounting Number Format with no decimal places.
11. Insert a footer on all worksheets that prints your name at the left, the page number in the middle, and the current date at the right.
12. Horizontally and vertically center all of the worksheets.
13. Click the Sheet2 tab and then delete it. Click the Sheet3 tab and then delete it.
14. Save and then print all four worksheets.
15. Close **EL1-C6-A2-DISales.xlsx**.

Assessment 3

DEFINE AND APPLY STYLES TO A PROJECTED EARNINGS WORKBOOK

1. At a blank worksheet, define a style named *C06Heading* that contains the following formatting:
    a. 14-point Cambria bold in dark blue color
    b. Horizontal alignment of Center
    c. Top and bottom border in a dark red color
    d. Light purple fill
2. Define a style named *C06Subheading* that contains the following formatting:
    a. 12-point Cambria bold in dark blue color
    b. Horizontal alignment of Center
    c. Top and bottom border in dark red color
    d. Light purple fill

3. Define a style named *C06Column* that contains the following formatting:
   a. At the Style dialog box, click the *Number* check box to remove the check mark.
   b. 12-point Cambria in dark blue color
   c. Light purple fill
4. Save the workbook and name it **EL1-C6-A3-Styles**.
5. With **EL1-C6-A3-Styles.xlsx** open, open **ProjEarnings.xlsx**.
6. Save the workbook with Save As and name it **EL1-C6-A3-ProjEarnings**.
7. Make cell C6 active and then insert a formula that multiplies the content of cell B6 with the amount in cell B3. (When writing the formula, identify cell B3 as an absolute reference.) Copy the formula down to cells C7 through C17.
8. Make cell C6 active and then click the Accounting Number Format button.
9. Copy the styles from **EL1-C6-A3-Styles.xlsx** into **EL1-C6-A3-ProjEarnings.xlsx**. ***Hint: Do this at the Merge Styles dialog box.***
10. Apply the following styles:
    a. Select cells A1 and A2 and then apply the C06Heading style.
    b. Select cells A5 through C5 and then apply the C06Subheading style.
    c. Select cells A6 through A17 and then apply the C06Column style.
11. Save the workbook again and then print **EL1-C6-A3-ProjEarnings.xlsx**.
12. With **EL1-C6-A3-ProjEarnings.xlsx** open, modify the following styles:
    a. Modify the C06Heading style so it changes the font color to dark purple (instead of dark blue), changes the vertical alignment to Center, and inserts a top and bottom border in dark purple (instead of dark red).
    b. Modify the C06Subheading style so it changes the font color to dark purple (instead of dark blue) and inserts a top and bottom border in dark purple (instead of dark red).
    c. Modify the C06Column style so it changes the font color to dark purple (instead of dark blue). Leave all of the other formatting attributes.
13. Save and then print the workbook.
14. Close **EL1-C6-A3-ProjEarnings.xlsx** and then close **EL1-C6-A3-Styles.xlsx** without saving the changes.

Assessment 4

INSERT HYPERLINKS IN A BOOK STORE WORKBOOK

1. Open **BGSpecials.xlsx** and then save the workbook with Save As and name it **EL1-C6-A4-BGSpecials.xlsx**.
2. Make cell E3 active and then hyperlink it to the www.microsoft.com website.
3. Make cell E4 active and then hyperlink it to the www.symantec.com website.
4. Make cell E5 active and then hyperlink it to the www.nasa.gov website.
5. Make cell E6 active and then hyperlink it to the www.cnn.com website.
6. Make cell A8 active, type **Weekly specials!**, and then create a hyperlink to the workbook named **BGWklySpcls.xlsx**.
7. Click the hyperlink to the Microsoft website, explore the site, and then close the web browser.
8. Click the hyperlink to the NASA website, explore the site, and then close the web browser.
9. Click the Weekly specials! hyperlink, view the workbook, and then close the workbook.
10. Save, print, and then close **EL1-C6-A4-BGSpecials.xlsx**.

Assessment 5

APPLY CONDITIONAL FORMATTING TO A SALES WORKBOOK

1. Use Excel Help files or experiment with the options at the Conditional Formatting button drop-down gallery to learn about conditional formatting.
2. Open **PSSales.xlsx** and then save the workbook with Save As and name it **EL1-C6-A5-PSSales**.
3. Select cells D5 through D19 and then use conditional formatting to display the amounts as data bars.
4. Insert a header that prints your name, a page number, and the current date.
5. Save, print, and then close **EL1-C6-A5-PSSales.xlsx**.

Visual Benchmark Demonstrate Your Proficiency

FILL IN AN EXPENSE REPORT FORM

1. Display the New tab Backstage view, click the Sample templates button, and then double-click the *Expense Report* template.
2. With the expense report open, apply the Paper theme.
3. Select cells J1 through L1 and then apply the Note cell style.
4. Type the information in the cells as indicated in Figure 6.9.
5. Make cell L18 active and apply the Bad cell style.
6. Save the completed workbook and name it **EL1-C6-VB-OEExpRpt**.
7. Print and then close **EL1-C6-VB-OEExpRpt.xlsx**.

Figure 6.9 Visual Benchmark

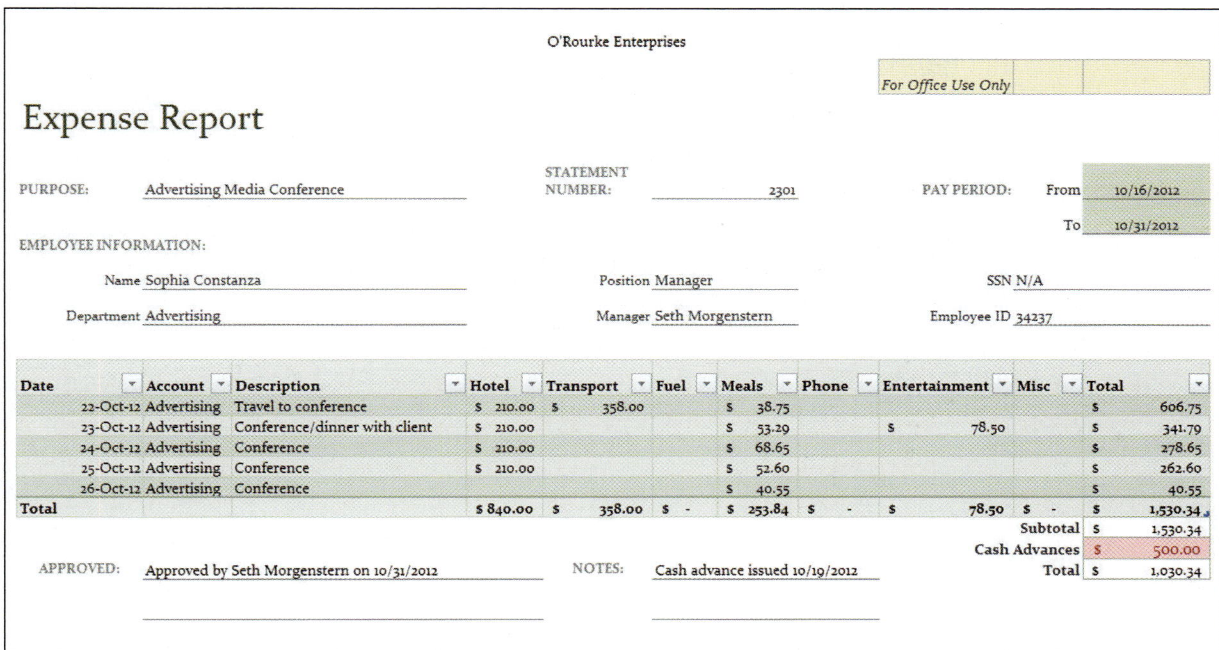

O'Rourke Enterprises

For Office Use Only

Expense Report

PURPOSE: Advertising Media Conference   STATEMENT NUMBER: 2301   PAY PERIOD: From 10/16/2012 To 10/31/2012

EMPLOYEE INFORMATION:

Name Sophia Constanza   Position Manager   SSN N/A

Department Advertising   Manager Seth Morgenstern   Employee ID 34237

Date	Account	Description	Hotel	Transport	Fuel	Meals	Phone	Entertainment	Misc	Total
22-Oct-12	Advertising	Travel to conference	$ 210.00	$ 358.00		$ 38.75				$ 606.75
23-Oct-12	Advertising	Conference/dinner with client	$ 210.00			$ 53.29		$ 78.50		$ 341.79
24-Oct-12	Advertising	Conference	$ 210.00			$ 68.65				$ 278.65
25-Oct-12	Advertising	Conference	$ 210.00			$ 52.60				$ 262.60
26-Oct-12	Advertising	Conference				$ 40.55				$ 40.55
Total			**$ 840.00**	**$ 358.00**	**$ -**	**$ 253.84**	**$ -**	**$ 78.50**	**$ -**	**$ 1,530.34**
									Subtotal	$ 1,530.34
									Cash Advances	$ 500.00
									Total	$ 1,030.34

APPROVED: Approved by Seth Morgenstern on 10/31/2012   NOTES: Cash advance issued 10/19/2012

Case Study Apply Your Skills

Part 1

You are the office manager for Leeward Marine and you decide to consolidate into one workbook worksheets containing information on expenses. Open **LMEstExp.xlsx** and then save the workbook and name it **EL1-C6-CS-LMExpSummary**. Open **LMActExp.xlsx**, copy the worksheet into **EL1-C6-CS-LMExpSummary.xlsx**, make **LMActExp.xlsx** the active workbook, and then close it. Apply appropriate formatting to numbers and insert necessary formulas in each worksheet. (Use the Clear button in the Home tab to clear the contents of cells N8, N9, M13, and M14 in both worksheets.) Include the company name, Leeward Marine, in each worksheet. Create styles and apply the styles to cells in each worksheet to maintain consistent formatting. Automatically adjust the widths of the columns to accommodate the longest entry. Save **EL1-C6-CS-LMExpSummary.xlsx**.

Part 2

You decide that you want to include another worksheet that displays the yearly estimated expenses, the actual expenses, and the variances (differences) between the expenses. With **EL1-C6-CS-LMExpSummary.xlsx** open, open **LMExpVar.xlsx**. Copy the worksheet into **EL1-C6-CS-LMExpSummary.xlsx**, make **LMExpVar.xlsx** the active workbook, and then close it. Rename the sheet tab containing the estimated expenses to *Estimated Exp*, rename the sheet tab containing the actual expenses to *Actual Exp*, and rename the sheet tab containing the variances to *Summary*. Recolor the three sheet tabs you just renamed.

Select the yearly estimated expense amounts (column N) in the Estimated Exp worksheet and then paste the amounts in the appropriate cells in the Summary worksheet. Click the Paste Options button and then click the Values & Number Formatting button in the *Paste Values* section of the drop-down list. (This pastes the value and the cell formatting rather than the formula.) Select the yearly actual expense amounts (column N) in the Actual Exp worksheet and then paste the amounts in the appropriate cells in the Summary worksheet. Click the Paste Options button and then click the Values & Number Formatting button in the *Paste Values* section of the drop-down list. Apply appropriate formatting to numbers and insert a formula to insert the variances (differences) of estimated and actual expenses. Clear the contents of cells D8, D9, D13, and D14. Apply styles to the Summary worksheet so it appears with formatting similar to the Estimated Exp and Actual Exp worksheets.

Insert an appropriate header or footer in each worksheet. Scale the worksheets so each prints on one page. Save, print all of the worksheets, and then close **EL1-C6-CS-LMExpSummary.xlsx**.

Part 3

You are not happy with the current product list form, so you decide to look at template forms available at Office.com. Display the New tab Backstage view, click the *Lists* option in the *Office.com Templates* section, click the *Business* folder, and then double-click the *Product price list* template. (These steps may vary.) Use the information below to fill in the form in the appropriate locations:

Leeward Marine
4500 Shoreline Drive
Ketchikan, AK 99901
(907) 555-2200
(907) 555-2595 (fax)
www.emcp.com/lmarine

Insert the following information in the appropriate columns:

Product Number	Name	Description	Retail Price Per Unit	Bulk Price Per Unit*
210-19	Ring Buoy	19-inch, white, solid plastic	$49.95	$42.00
210-20	Ring Buoy	20-inch, white, solid plastic	$52.95	$49.50
210-24	Ring Buoy	24-inch, white, solid plastic	$59.95	$52.00
320-05	Horseshoe Buoy	Vinyl fabric over plastic core	$83.95	$78.50
225-01	Ring Buoy Holder	Aluminum holder	$6.50	$5.75
234-24	Ring Buoy Bracket	Stainless steel bracket	$7.25	$6.50

Save the completed products list form and name it **EL1-C6-CS-LMProdList**. Print and then close the workbook.

Part 4

You need to print a number of copies of the product list and you want the company letterhead to print at the top of the page. You decide to use the letterhead you created in Word and copy the product list information from Excel into the Word letterhead document. To do this, open Word and then open the document named **LMLtrd.docx**. Press the Enter key four times. Make Excel the active program and then open **EL1-C6-CS-LMProdList.xlsx**. Copy cells A2 through E11 and then paste them into the **LMLtrhd.docx** Word document as a picture object (click the Paste Options button and then click the Picture button). Save the document with Save As and name it **EL1-C6-CS-LMProducts**. Print and then close **EL1-C6-CS-LMProducts.docx** and then exit Word. In Excel, close **EL1-C6-CS-ProdList.xlsx**.

Microsoft® Excel®

Creating a Chart in Excel

CHAPTER

PERFORMANCE OBJECTIVES

Upon successful completion of Chapter 7, you will be able to:

- **Create a chart with data in an Excel worksheet**
- **Size, move, and delete charts**
- **Print a selected chart and print a worksheet containing a chart**
- **Choose a chart style, layout, and formatting**
- **Change chart location**
- **Insert, move, size, and delete chart labels, shapes, and pictures**

Tutorials

7.1 Creating Charts in Excel
7.2 Editing Chart Data
7.3 Changing the Chart Design
7.4 Changing a Chart Type
7.5 Inserting Shapes and Images
7.6 Changing the Chart Formatting

In the previous Excel chapters, you learned to create data in worksheets. While a worksheet does an adequate job of representing data, you can present some data more visually by charting the data. A ***chart*** is sometimes referred to as a ***graph*** and is a picture of numeric data. In this chapter, you will learn to create and customize charts in Excel. Model answers for this chapter's projects appear on the following pages.

Excel2010L1C7

Note: Before beginning the projects, copy to your storage medium the Excel2010L1C7 subfolder from the Excel2010L1 folder on the CD that accompanies this textbook and then make Excel2010L1C7 the active folder.

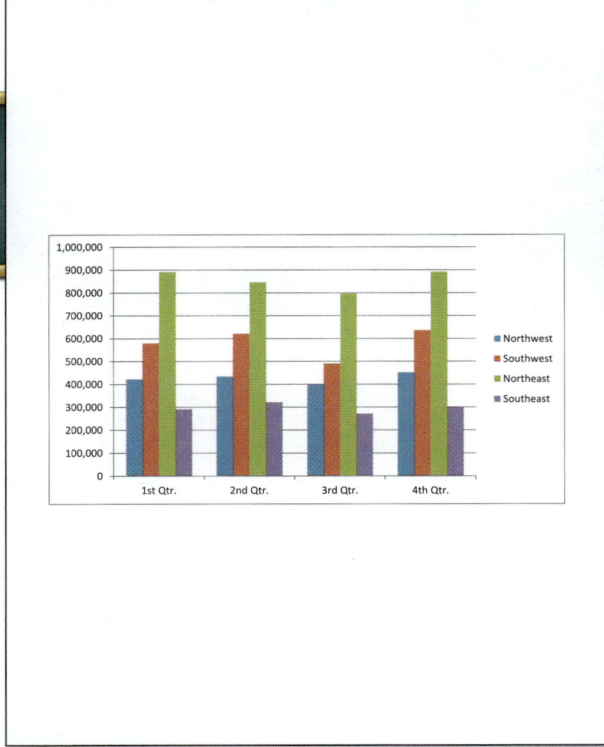

Project 1 Create a Quarterly Sales Column Chart
EL1-C7-P1-SalesChart.xlsx

DEERING INDUSTRIES

Technology Purchases

Department	Amount
Administration	$12,750
Finance	$15,700
Training	$51,350
Purchasing	$12,450
Research	$60,570
Marketing	$5,600

Sheet 1 Tab

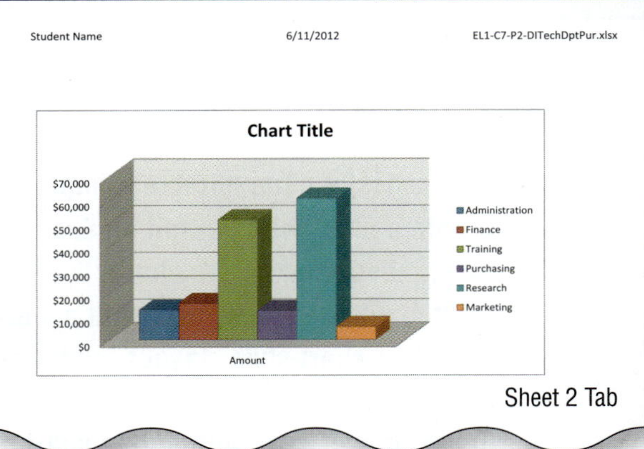

Project 2 Create a Technology Purchases Bar Chart and Column Chart
EL1-C7-P2-DITechDptPur.xlsx

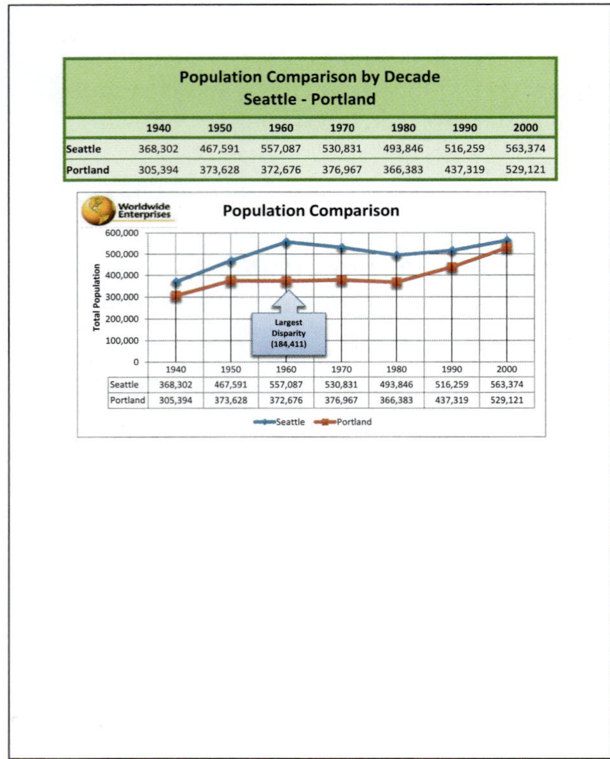

Population Comparison by Decade
Seattle - Portland

	1940	1950	1960	1970	1980	1990	2000
Seattle	368,302	467,591	557,087	530,831	493,846	516,259	563,374
Portland	305,394	373,628	372,676	376,967	366,383	437,319	529,121

	1940	1950	1960	1970	1980	1990	2000
Seattle	368,302	467,591	557,087	530,831	493,846	516,259	563,374
Portland	305,394	373,628	372,676	376,967	366,383	437,319	529,121

Project 3 Create a Population Comparison Bar Chart
EL1-C7-P3-PopComp.xlsx

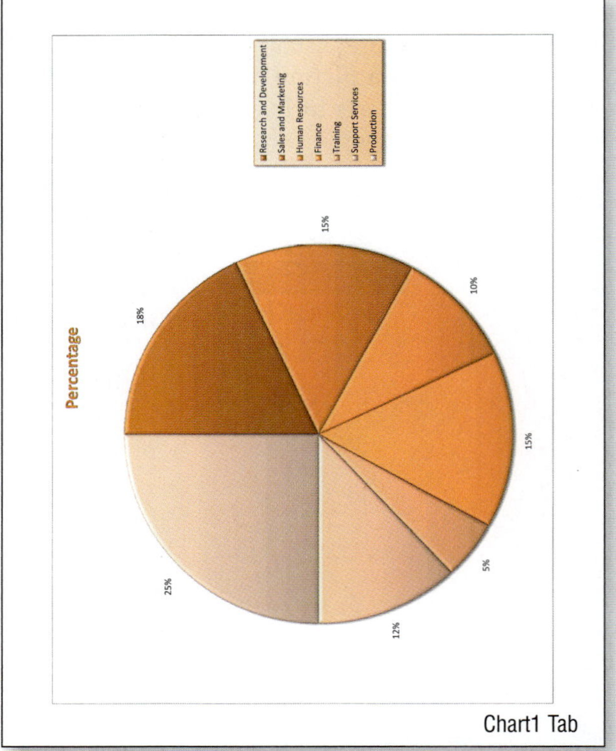

Project 4 Create a Costs Percentage Pie Chart
EL1-C7-P4-DIDptCosts.xlsx

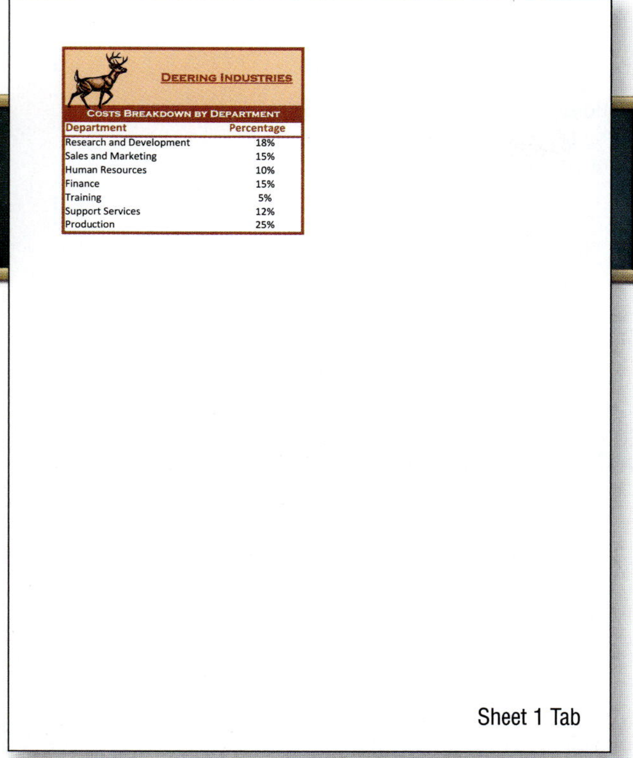

DEERING INDUSTRIES	
COSTS BREAKDOWN BY DEPARTMENT	
Department	Percentage
Research and Development	18%
Sales and Marketing	15%
Human Resources	10%
Finance	15%
Training	5%
Support Services	12%
Production	25%

Sheet 1 Tab

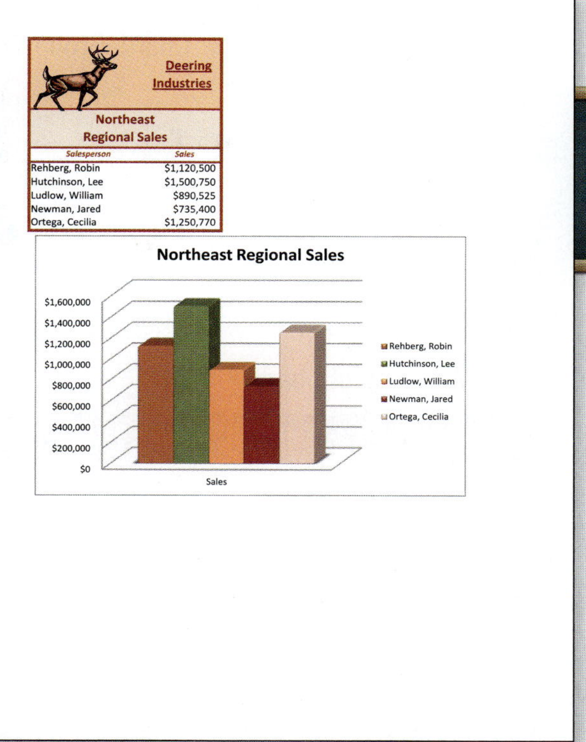

Deering Industries	
Northeast Regional Sales	
Salesperson	Sales
Rehberg, Robin	$1,120,500
Hutchinson, Lee	$1,500,750
Ludlow, William	$890,525
Newman, Jared	$735,400
Ortega, Cecilia	$1,250,770

Project 5 Create a Regional Sales Column Chart

EL1-C7-P5-DIRegSales.xlsx

Project 1 Create a Quarterly Sales Column Chart — 2 Parts

You will open a workbook containing quarterly sales data and then use the data to create a column chart. You will decrease the size of the chart, move it to a different location in the worksheet, and then make changes to sales numbers.

Creating a Chart

In Excel, create a chart with buttons in the Charts group in the Insert tab as shown in Figure 7.1. With buttons in the Charts group you can create a variety of charts such as a column chart, line chart, pie chart, and much more. Excel provides 11 basic chart types as described in Table 7.1. To create a chart, select cells in a worksheet that you want to chart, click the Insert tab, and then click the desired chart button in the Charts group. At the drop-down gallery that displays, click the desired chart style. You can also create a chart by selecting the desired cells and then pressing Alt + F1. This keyboard shortcut, by default, inserts the data in a 2-D column chart (unless the default chart type has been changed).

Quick Steps

Create a Chart
1. Select cells.
2. Click Insert tab.
3. Click desired chart button.
4. Click desired chart style at drop-down list.

Create Chart as Default Chart Type
1. Select cells.
2. Press Alt + F1.

Figure 7.1 Charts Group Buttons

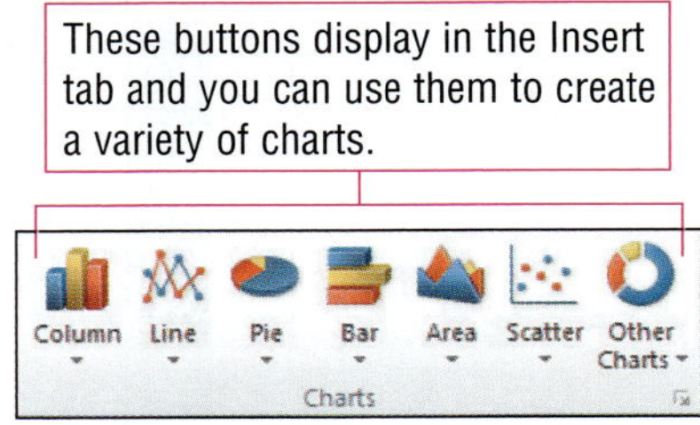

Table 7.1 Type of Charts

Chart	*Description*
Area	Emphasizes the magnitude of change, rather than time and the rate of change. It also shows the relationship of parts to a whole by displaying the sum of the plotted values.
Bar	Shows individual figures at a specific time, or shows variations between components but not in relationship to the whole.
Bubble	Compares sets of three values in a manner similar to a scatter chart, with the third value displayed as the size of the bubble marker.
Column	Compares separate (noncontinuous) items as they vary over time.
Doughnut	Shows the relationship of parts of the whole.
Line	Shows trends and change over time at even intervals. It emphasizes the rate of change over time rather than the magnitude of change.
Pie	Shows proportions and relationships of parts to the whole.
Radar	Emphasizes differences and amounts of change over time and variations and trends. Each category has its own value axis radiating from the center point. Lines connect all values in the same series.
Stock	Shows four values for a stock—open, high, low, and close.
Surface	Shows trends in values across two dimensions in a continuous curve.
XY (Scatter)	Shows the relationships among numeric values in several data series or plots the interception points between *x* and *y* values. It shows uneven intervals of data and is commonly used in scientific data.

Sizing, Moving, and Deleting a Chart

When you create a chart, the chart is inserted in the same worksheet as the selected cells. Figure 7.2 displays the worksheet and chart you will create in Project 1a. The chart is inserted in a box which you can size and/or move in the worksheet.

To size the worksheet, position the mouse pointer on the four dots located in the middle of the border you want to size until the pointer turns into a two-headed arrow, hold down the left mouse button, and then drag to increase or decrease the size of the chart. To increase or decrease the height and width of

Figure 7.2 Project 1a Chart

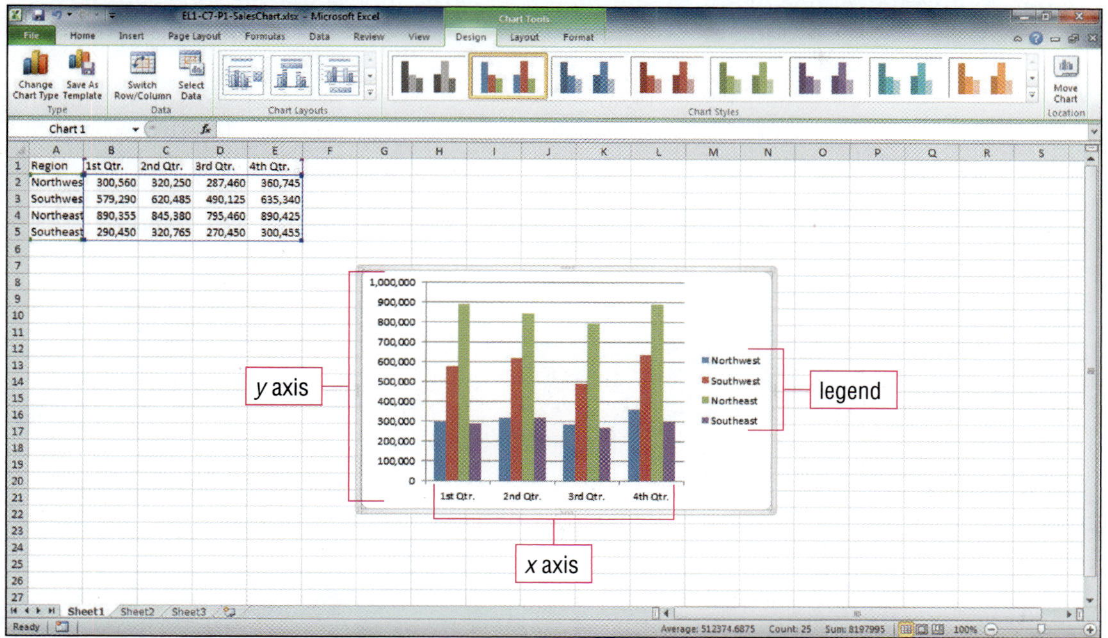

the chart at the same time, position the mouse pointer on the three dots that display in a chart border corner until the pointer displays as a two-headed arrow, hold down the left mouse button, and then drag to the desired size. To increase or decrease the size of the chart and maintain the proportions of the chart, hold down the Shift key while dragging a chart corner border.

To move the chart, make sure the chart is selected (light gray border displays around the chart), position the mouse pointer on a border until it turns into a four-headed arrow, hold down the left mouse button, and then drag to the desired position.

Editing Data

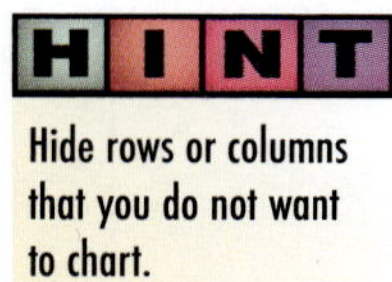

HINT
Hide rows or columns that you do not want to chart.

The cells you select to create the chart are linked to the chart. If you need to change data for a chart, edit the data in the desired cell and the corresponding section of the chart is automatically updated.

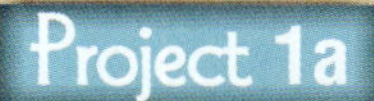

Creating a Chart Part 1 of 2

1. Open **SalesChart.xlsx** and then save the workbook with Save As and name it **EL1-C7-P1-SalesChart**.
2. Select cells A1 through E5.
3. Press Alt + F1.
4. Slightly increase the size of the chart and maintain the proportions of the chart by completing the following steps:
   a. Position the mouse pointer on the bottom right corner of the chart border until the pointer turns into a two-headed arrow pointing diagonally.
   b. Hold down the Shift key and then hold down the left mouse button.

c. Drag out approximately one-half inch and then release the mouse button and then the Shift key.

5. Move the chart below the cells containing data by completing the following steps:
   a. Make sure the chart is selected (light gray border surrounds the chart).
   b. Position the mouse pointer on the chart border until the pointer turns into a four-headed arrow.
   c. Hold down the left mouse button, drag the chart so it is positioned below the cells containing data, and then release the mouse button.

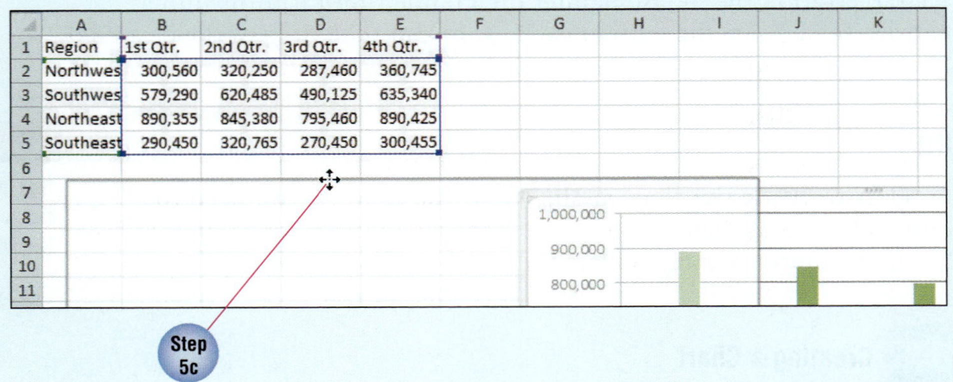

	A	B	C	D	E
1	Region	1st Qtr.	2nd Qtr.	3rd Qtr.	4th Qtr.
2	Northwes	300,560	320,250	287,460	360,745
3	Southwes	579,290	620,485	490,125	635,340
4	Northeast	890,355	845,380	795,460	890,425
5	Southeast	290,450	320,765	270,450	300,455

6. Make the following changes to the specified cells:
   a. Make cell B2 active and then change *300,560* to *421,720*.
   b. Make cell C2 active and then change *320,250* to *433,050*.
   c. Make cell D2 active and then change *287,460* to *397,460*.
   d. Make cell E2 active and then change *360,745* to *451,390*.
7. Save **EL1-C7-P1-SalesChart.xlsx**.

Printing a Chart

In a worksheet containing data in cells as well as a chart, you can print only the chart. To do this, select the chart, display the Print tab Backstage view, and then click the Print button. With a chart selected, the first gallery in the *Settings* category is automatically changed to *Print Selected Chart*. A preview of the chart displays at the right side of the Print tab Backstage view.

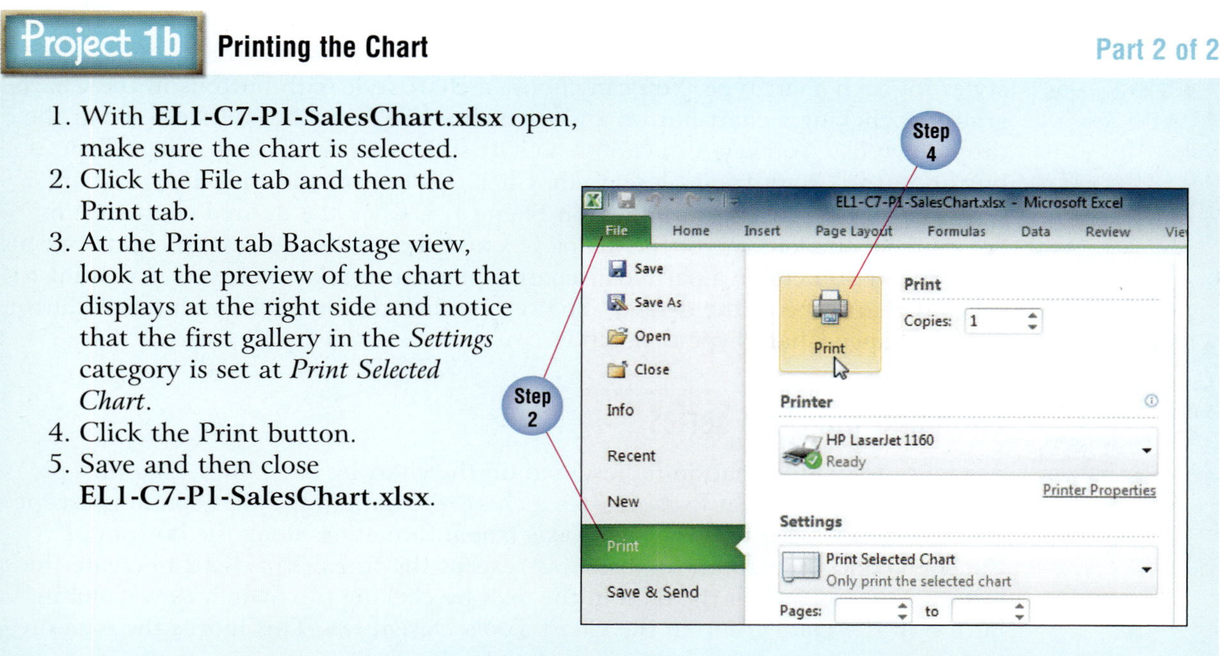

Project 1b Printing the Chart

Part 2 of 2

1. With **EL1-C7-P1-SalesChart.xlsx** open, make sure the chart is selected.
2. Click the File tab and then the Print tab.
3. At the Print tab Backstage view, look at the preview of the chart that displays at the right side and notice that the first gallery in the *Settings* category is set at *Print Selected Chart*.
4. Click the Print button.
5. Save and then close **EL1-C7-P1-SalesChart.xlsx**.

Project 2 Create a Technology Purchases Bar Chart and Column Chart

2 Parts

You will open a workbook containing technology purchases data by department and then create a bar chart with the data. You will then change the chart type, layout, and style and move the chart to a new sheet.

Changing the Chart Design

When you insert a chart in a worksheet, the Chart Tools Design tab displays as shown in Figure 7.3. With options in this tab, you can change the chart type, specify a different layout or style for the chart, and change the location of the chart so it displays in a separate worksheet.

Figure 7.3 Chart Tools Design Tab

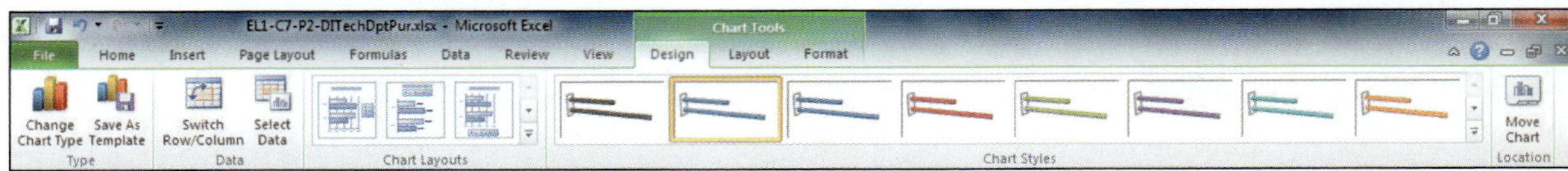

Quick Steps

Change Chart Type and Style

1. Make the chart active.
2. Click Chart Tools Design tab.
3. Click Change Chart Type button.
4. Click desired chart type.
5. Click desired chart style.
6. Click OK.

Change Chart Data Series

1. Make the chart active.
2. Click Chart Tools Design tab.
3. Click Switch Row/Column button.

Change Chart Type

Switch Row/Column

Choosing a Custom Chart Style

The chart feature offers a variety of preformatted custom charts and offers varying styles for each chart type. You can choose a chart style with buttons in the Charts group by clicking a chart button and then choosing from the styles offered at the drop-down list. You can also choose a chart style with the Change Chart Type button in the Chart Tools Design tab. Click this button and the Change Chart Type dialog box displays as shown in Figure 7.4. Click the desired chart type in the panel at the left side of the dialog box and then click the desired chart style at the right. If you create a particular chart type on a regular basis, you may want to set that chart type as the default. To do this, click the Set as Default Chart button in the Change Chart Type dialog box.

Changing the Data Series

A data series is information represented on the chart by bars, lines, columns, pie slices, and so on. When Excel creates a chart, the data in the first column (except the first cell) is used to create the *x* axis (the information along the bottom of the chart) and the data in the first row (except the first cell) is used to create the legend. You can switch the data in the axes by clicking the Switch Row/Column button in the Data group in the Chart Tools Design tab. This moves the data on the *x* axis to the *y* axis and the *y* axis data to the *x* axis.

Figure 7.4 Change Chart Type Dialog Box

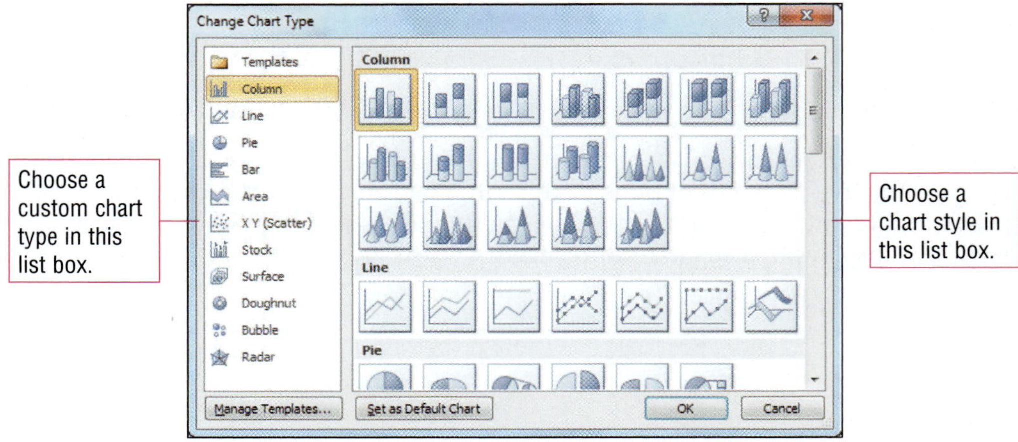

Project 2a Creating a Chart and Changing the Design

Part 1 of 2

1. Open **DITechDptPur.xlsx** and then save the workbook with Save As and name it **EL1-C7-P2-DITechDptPur**.
2. Create a bar chart by completing the following steps:
   a. Select cells A3 through B9.
   b. Click the Insert tab.
   c. Click the Bar button in the Charts group.
   d. Click the first option from the left in the *Cylinder* section (*Clustered Horizontal Cylinder*).
3. With the chart selected and the Chart Tools Design tab displayed, change the data series by clicking the Switch Row/Column button located in the Data group.

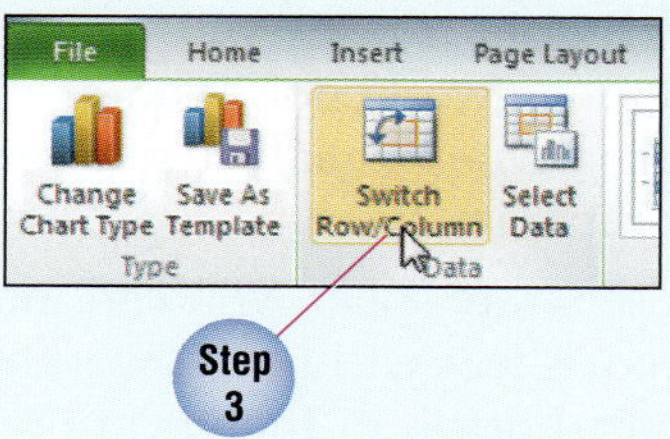

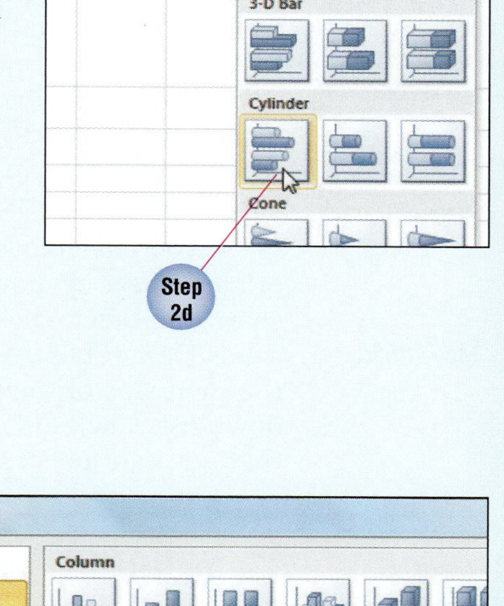

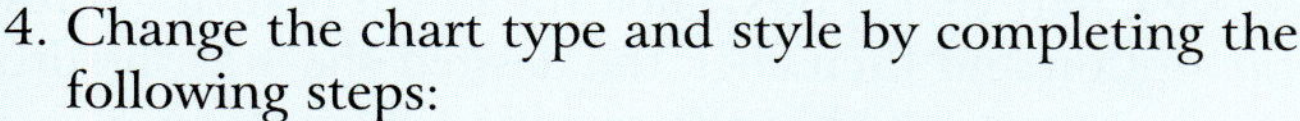

4. Change the chart type and style by completing the following steps:
   a. Click the Change Chart Type button located in the Type group.
   b. At the Change Chart Type dialog box, click the *Column* option in the left panel.
   c. Click the *3-D Cylinder* option in the *Column* section (fourth chart style from the left in the second row of the *Column* section).
   d. Click OK to close the Change Chart Type dialog box.
5. Save **EL1-C7-P2-DITechDptPur.xlsx**.

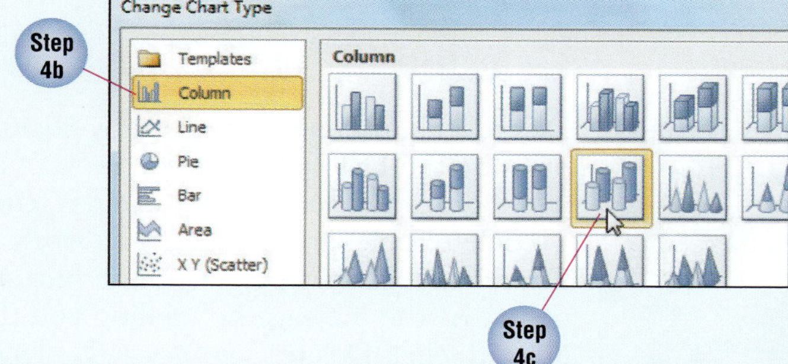

Changing Chart Layout and Style

The Chart Tools Design tab contains options for changing the chart layout and style. The Chart Layouts group in the tab contains preformatted chart layout options. Click the More button (contains an underline and a down-pointing arrow) to display a drop-down list of layout options. Hover the mouse pointer over an option and a ScreenTip displays with the option name. You can also scroll through layout options by clicking the up-pointing arrow or the down-pointing arrow located at the right side of the Chart Layouts group.

Click the Save As Template button in the Type group in the Chart Tools Design tab to save the formatting and layout of the current chart as a template you can use to create future charts.

Use options in the Chart Styles group to apply a particular style of formatting to a chart. Click the More button located at the right side of the Chart Styles group to display a drop-down list with all the style options or click the up-pointing or down-pointing arrow at the right of the group to scroll through the options.

Changing Chart Location

Quick Steps

Change Chart Location
1. Make the chart active.
2. Click Chart Tools Design tab.
3. Click Move Chart button.
4. Click *New Sheet* option.
5. Click OK.

Move Chart

Create a chart and the chart is inserted in the currently open worksheet as an embedded object. You can change the location of a chart with the Move Chart button in the Location group. Click this button and the Move Chart dialog box displays as shown in Figure 7.5. Click the *New sheet* option to move the chart to a new sheet within the workbook. Excel automatically names the sheet *Chart1*. Click the down-pointing arrow at the right side of the *Object in* option box and then click the desired location. The drop-down list will generally display the names of the worksheets within the open workbook. You can use the keyboard shortcut, F11, to create a default chart type (usually a column chart) and Excel automatically inserts the chart in a separate sheet.

If you have moved a chart to a separate sheet, you can move it back to the original sheet or move it to a different sheet within the workbook. To move a chart to a sheet, click the Move Chart button in the Location group in the Chart Tools Design tab. At the Move Chart dialog box, click the down-pointing arrow at the right side of the *Object in* option and then click the desired sheet at the drop-down list. Click OK and the chart is inserted in the specified sheet as an object that you can move, size, and format.

Deleting a Chart

Quick Steps

Delete a Chart
1. Click once in chart.
2. Press Delete key.

OR
1. Right-click chart tab.
2. Click Cut.

Delete a chart created in Excel by clicking once in the chart to select it and then pressing the Delete key. If you move a chart to a different worksheet in the workbook and then delete the chart, the chart is deleted but not the worksheet. To delete the chart as well as the worksheet, position the mouse pointer on the Chart1 tab, click the right mouse button, and then click *Delete* at the shortcut menu. At the message box telling you that selected sheets will be permanently deleted, click Delete.

Figure 7.5 Move Chart Dialog Box

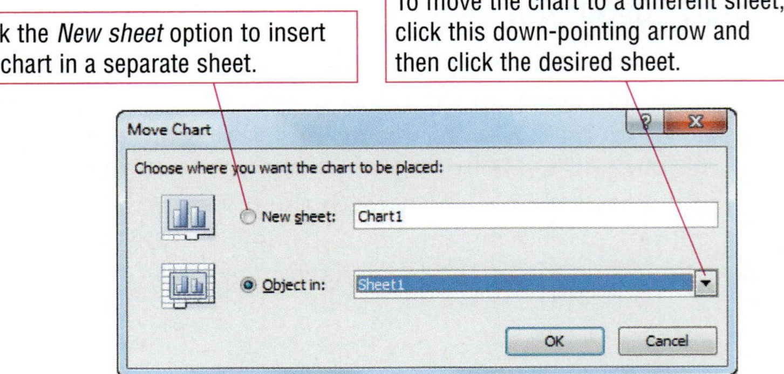
Click the New sheet option to insert the chart in a separate sheet.
To move the chart to a different sheet, click this down-pointing arrow and then click the desired sheet.
Move Chart
Choose where you want the chart to be placed:
New sheet:
Chart1
Object in:
Sheet1
OK
Cancel

Project 2b Changing Chart Layout, Style, and Location

Part 2 of 2

1. With **EL1-C7-P2-DITechDeptPur.xlsx** open, make sure the Chart Tools Design tab displays. (If it does not, make sure the chart is selected and then click the Chart Tools Design tab.)
2. Change the chart type by completing the following steps:
   a. Click the Change Chart Type button in the Type tab.
   b. Click *3-D Clustered Column* (fourth column style from the left in the top row).
   c. Click OK to close the dialog box.

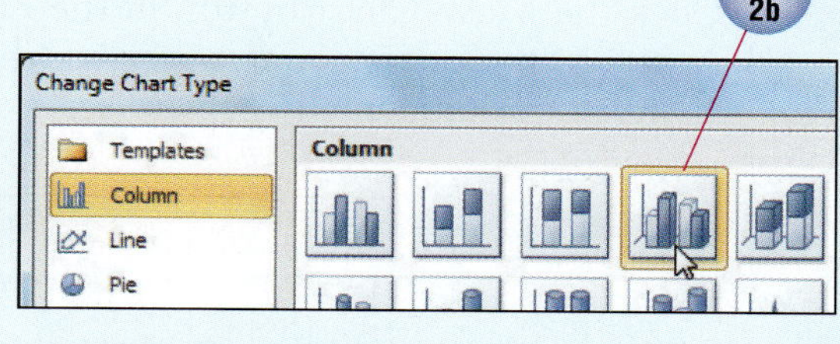

3. Change the chart layout by clicking the *Layout 1* option in the Chart Layouts group (first option from the left). This layout inserts the words *Chart Title* at the top of the chart.

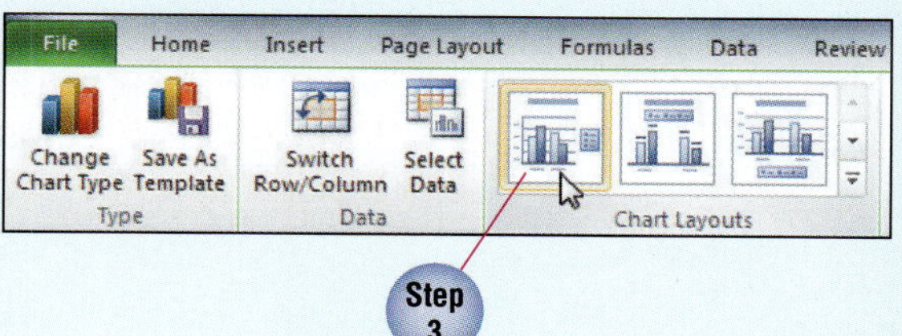

4. Change the chart style by clicking the More button located at the right side of the Chart Styles group and then clicking *Style 34* (second option from the left in the fifth row).

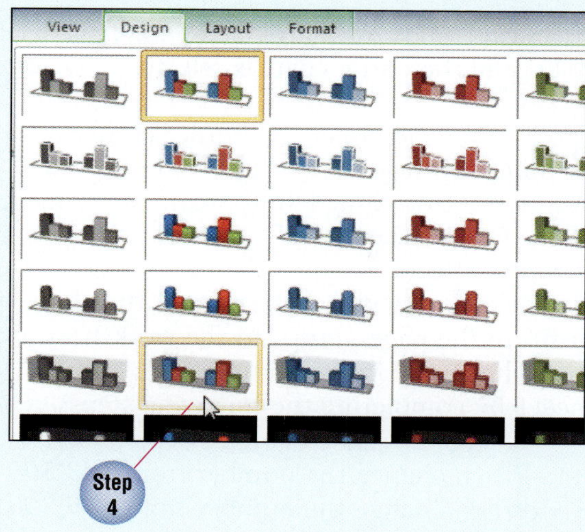

5. Move the chart to a new location by completing the following steps:
   a. Click the Move Chart button in the Location group.
   b. At the Move Chart dialog box, click the *New sheet* option and then click OK. (The chart is inserted in a worksheet named *Chart1*.)

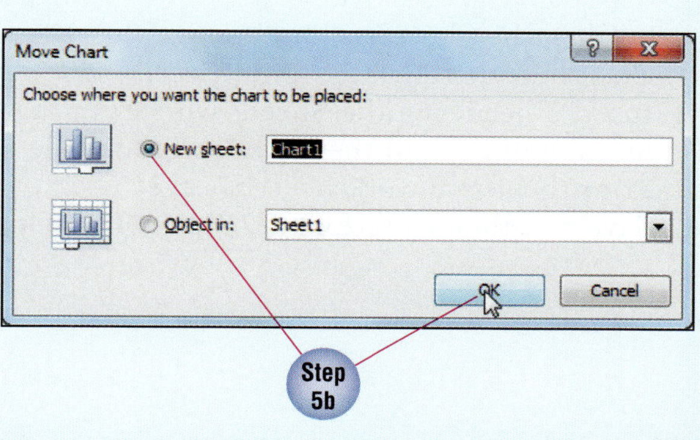

6. Save **EL1-C7-P2-DITechDptPur.xlsx**.
7. Print the Chart1 worksheet containing the chart.

8. Move the chart from Chart1 to Sheet2 by completing the following steps:
   a. Make sure Chart1 is the active sheet and that the chart is selected (not an element in the chart).
   b. Make sure the Chart Tools Design tab is active.
   c. Click the Move Chart button in the Location group.
   d. At the Move Chart dialog box, click the down-pointing arrow at the right side of the *Object in* option and then click *Sheet2* at the drop-down list.

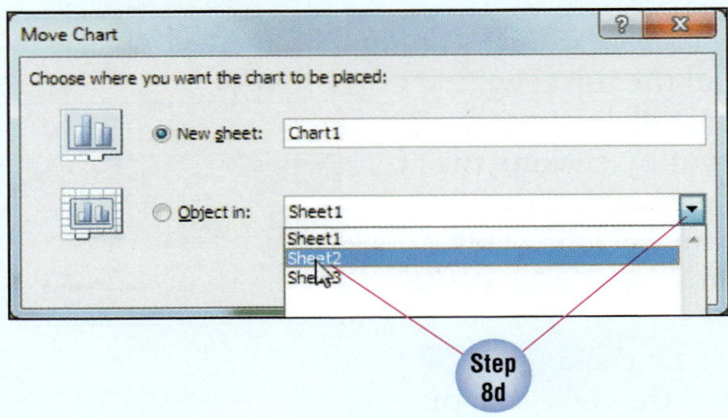

   e. Click OK.
9. Increase the size of the chart and maintain the proportions by completing the following steps:
   a. Click inside the chart but outside any chart elements. (This displays a light gray border around the chart. Make sure the entire chart is selected and not a specific chart element.)
   b. Hold down the Shift key.
   c. Position the mouse pointer on the upper left border corner until the pointer turns into a double-headed arrow pointing diagonally.
   d. Hold down the left mouse button, drag left approximately one inch and then release the mouse button and then the Shift key.
   e. Click outside the chart to deslect it.
   f. Display the Print tab Backstage view to determine if the chart will print on one page. If the chart does not fit on the page, return to the worksheet and then move and/or decrease the size of the chart until it fits on one page.
10. Change amounts in Sheet1 by completing the following steps:
    a. Click Sheet1.
    b. Make cell B4 active and then change the number from *$33,500* to *$12,750*.
    c. Make cell B9 active and then change the number from *$19,200* to *$5,600*.
    d. Make cell A2 active.
    e. Click the Sheet2 tab and notice that the chart displays the updated amounts.
11. Click outside the chart to deselect it.
12. Insert a header in the Sheet2 worksheet that prints your name at the left, the current date in the middle, and the workbook file name at the right.
13. Print the active worksheet (Sheet2).
14. Save and then close **EL1-C7-P2-DITechDptPur.xlsx**.

Project 3 Create a Population Comparison Bar Chart 3 Parts

You will open a workbook containing population comparison data for Seattle and Portland and then create a bar chart with the data. You will also add chart labels and shapes and move, size, and delete labels and shapes.

Changing the Chart Layout

Customize the layout of labels in a chart with options in the Chart Tools Layout tab as shown in Figure 7.6. With buttons in this tab, you can change the layout and/or insert additional chart labels. Certain chart labels are automatically inserted in a chart including a chart legend and labels for the *x* axis and *y* axis. Add chart labels to an existing chart with options in the Labels group in the Chart Tools Layout tab. In addition to chart labels, you can also insert shapes, pictures, and/or clip art and change the layout of 3-D chart labels.

Inserting, Moving, and Deleting Chart Labels

Certain chart labels are automatically inserted in a chart, including a chart legend and labels for the *x* axis and *y* axis. The legend identifies which data series is represented by which data marker. Insert additional chart labels with options in the Labels group in the Chart Tools Layout tab. For example, click the Chart Title button in the Labels group and a drop-down list displays with options for inserting a chart title in a specific location in the chart.

You can move and/or size a chart label. To move a chart label, click the label to select it and then move the mouse pointer over the border line until the pointer turns into a four-headed arrow. Hold down the left mouse button, drag the label to the desired location, and then release the mouse button. To size a chart label, use the sizing handles that display around the selected label to increase or decrease the size. To delete a chart label, click the label to select it and then press the Delete key. You can also delete a label by right-clicking the label and then clicking *Delete* at the shortcut menu.

Quick Steps

Add Chart Labels

1. Make the chart active.
2. Click Chart Tools Layout tab.
3. Click desired chart labels button.
4. Choose desired option at drop-down list.

Chart Title

Figure 7.6 Chart Tools Layout Tab

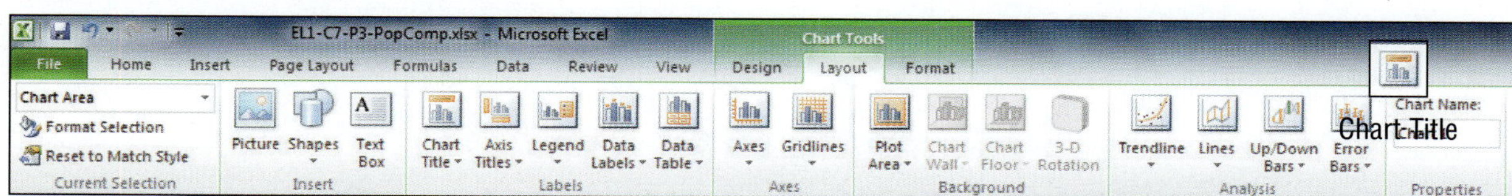

Project 3a Creating a Chart and Changing Layout of Chart Labels

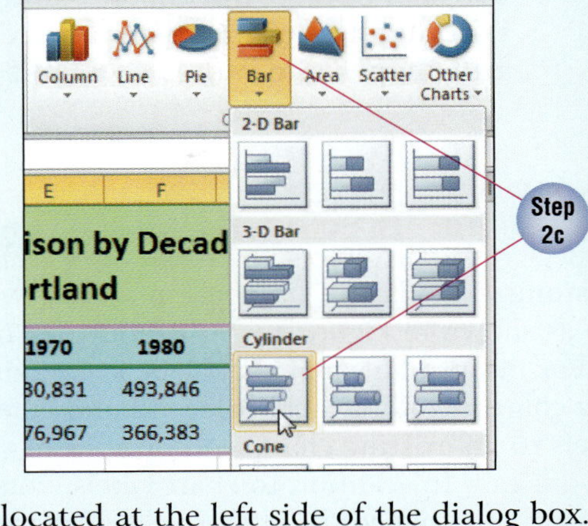

1. Open **PopComp.xlsx** and then save the workbook with Save As and name it **EL1-C7-P3-PopComp**.
2. Create a Bar chart by completing the following steps:
   a. Select cells A2 through H4.
   b. Click the Insert tab.
   c. Click the Bar button in the Charts group and then click the *Clustered Horizontal Cylinder* option in the *Cylinder* section.
3. Change to a Line chart by completing the following steps:
   a. Click the Change Chart Type button in the Type group.
   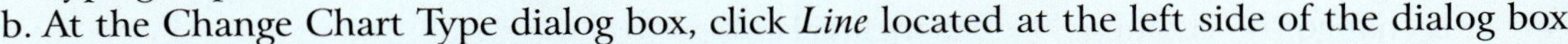
   b. At the Change Chart Type dialog box, click *Line* located at the left side of the dialog box.
   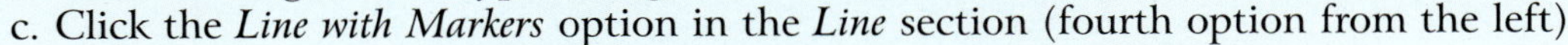
   c. Click the *Line with Markers* option in the *Line* section (fourth option from the left).

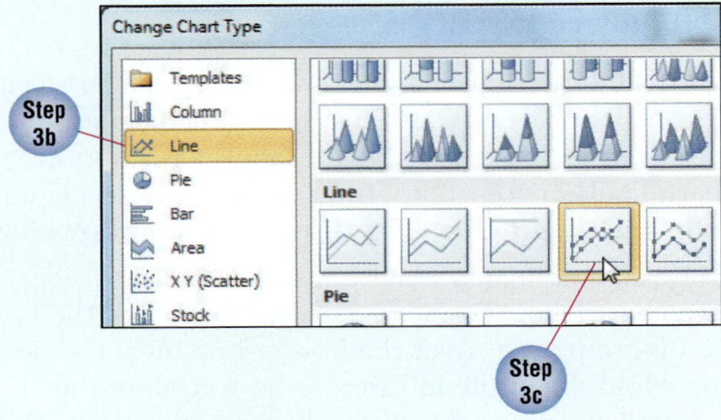

   d. Click OK to close the Change Chart Type dialog box.
4. Click the More button in the Chart Styles group in the Chart Tools Design tab and then click *Style 18* at the drop-down gallery (second option from left in the third row).

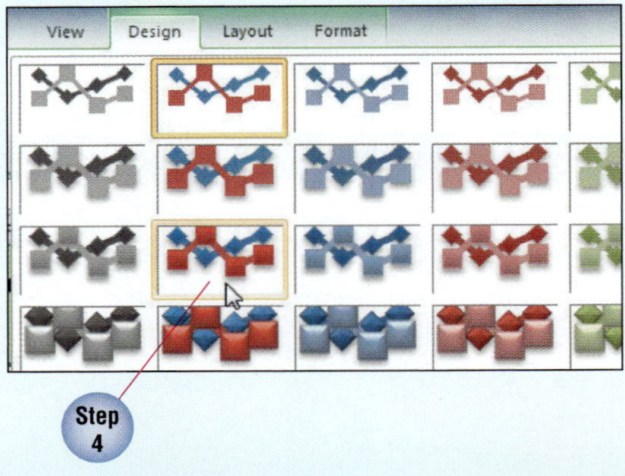

5. Change the layout of the chart by completing the following steps:
   a. Click the Chart Tools Layout tab.
   b. Click the Legend button in the Labels group.
   c. At the drop-down list, click the *Show Legend at Bottom* option.
   d. Click the Chart Title button in the Labels group.
   e. At the drop-down list, click the *Above Chart* option.

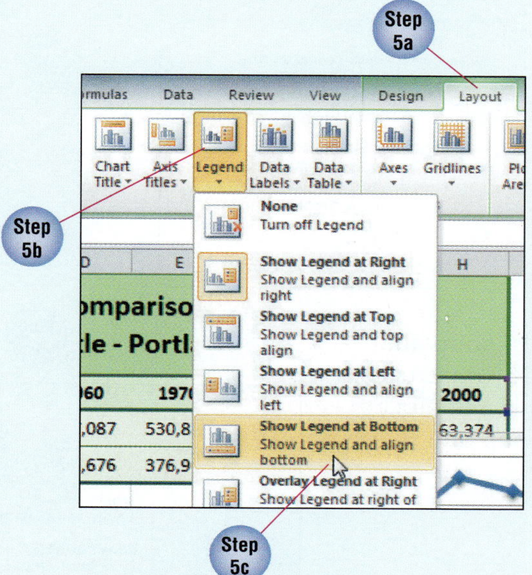

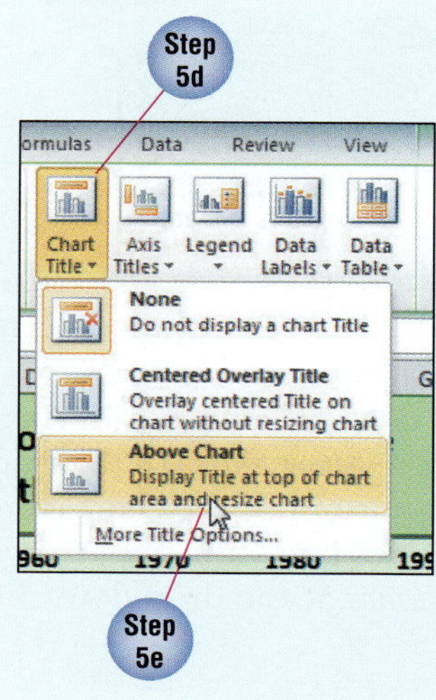

   f. Select the text *Chart Title* located in the chart title text box and then type **Population Comparison**.
6. Insert an *x*-axis title by completing the following steps:
   a. Click the Axis Titles button, point to the *Primary Horizontal Axis Title* option at the drop-down list, and then click *Title Below Axis* at the side menu.
   b. Select the text *Axis Title* located in the title text box and then type **Decades**.

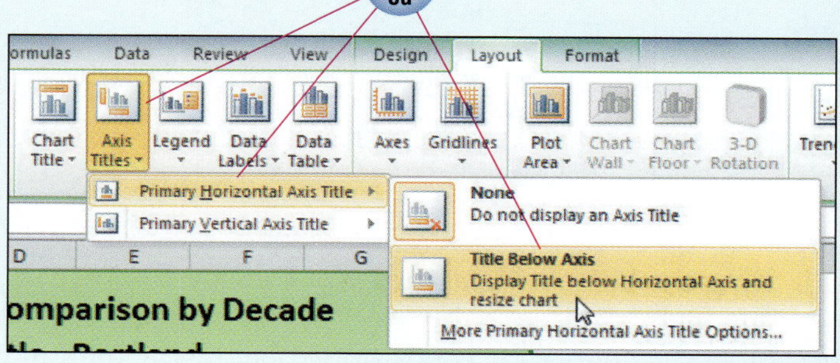

7. Insert a *y*-axis title by completing the following steps:
   a. Click the Axis Titles button, point to the *Primary Vertical Axis Title* option at the drop-down list, and then click *Rotated Title* at the side menu. (This inserts a rotated title at the left side of the chart containing the text *Axis Title*).
   b. Select the text *Axis Title* located in the axis title text box and then type **Total Population**.

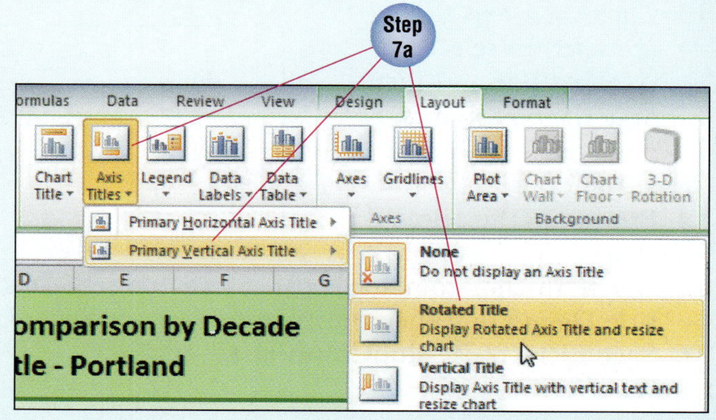

8. Click the Gridlines button in the Axes group, point to *Primary Vertical Gridlines*, and then click the *Major & Minor Gridlines* option at the side menu.

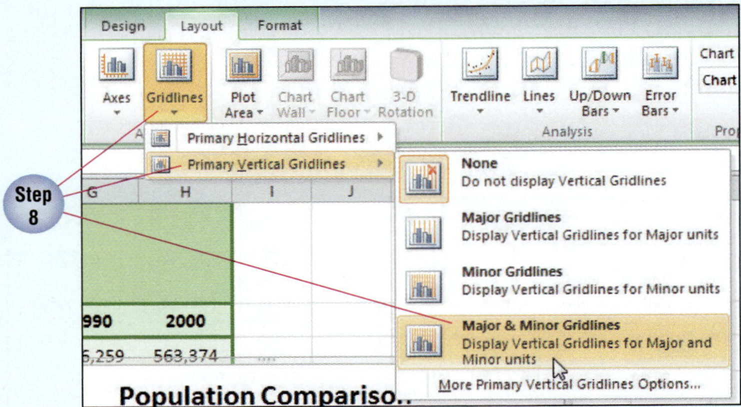

9. Click the Data Table button in the Labels group and then click the *Show Data Table* option. (This inserts cells toward the bottom of the chart containing cell data.)
10. Click the Lines button in the Analysis group and then click *Drop Lines* at the drop-down list.

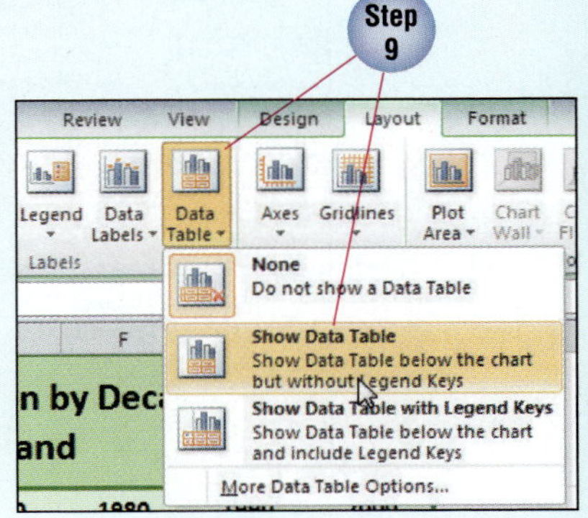

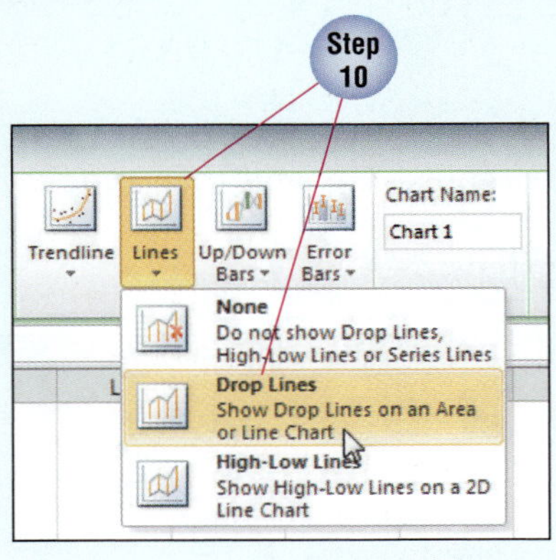

11. Drag the bottom right corner of the chart border to increase the size by approximately one inch.
12. Drag the chart so it is positioned below the data in cells but not overlapping the data.
13. Click the *x*-axis title (*Decades*) to select the title text box and then drag the box so it is positioned as shown at right.
14. Print only the selected chart.
15. Delete the horizontal axis title by clicking the axis title *Decades* and then pressing the Delete key.
16. Save **EL1-C7-P3-PopComp.xlsx**.

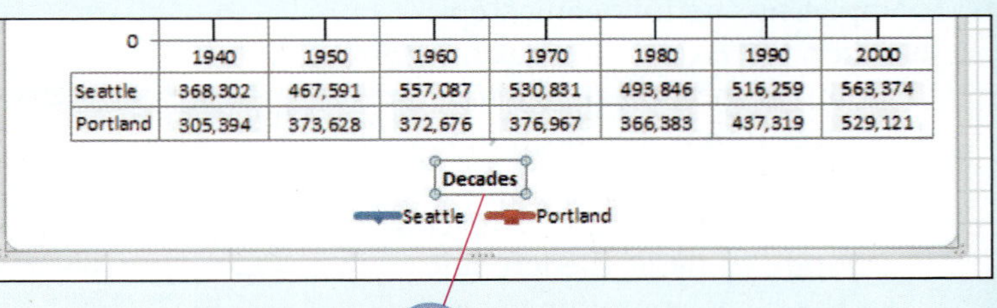

	1940	1950	1960	1970	1980	1990	2000
Seattle	368,302	467,591	557,087	530,831	493,846	516,259	563,374
Portland	305,394	373,628	372,676	376,967	366,383	437,319	529,121

Inserting Shapes

The Insert group in the Chart Tools Layout tab contains three buttons with options for inserting shapes or images in a chart. Click the Shapes button in the Insert group and a drop-down list displays with a variety of shape options as shown in Figure 7.7. Click the desired shape at the drop-down list and the mouse pointer turns into a thin, black plus symbol. Drag with this pointer symbol to create the shape in the chart. The shape is inserted in the chart with default formatting. You can change this formatting with options in the Drawing Tools Format tab. This tab contains many of the same options as the Chart Tools Format tab. For example, you can insert a shape, apply a shape or WordArt style, and arrange and size the shape.

Quick Steps

Insert Shape

1. Make the chart active.
2. Click Chart Tools Layout tab.
3. Click Shapes button.
4. Click desired shape at drop-down list.
5. Drag pointer symbol to create shape in chart.

Shapes

Chart elements can be repositioned for easier viewing.

Moving, Sizing, and Deleting Shapes

Move, size, and delete shapes in the same manner as moving, sizing, and deleting chart elements. To move a shape, select the shape, position the mouse pointer over the border line until the pointer turns into a four-headed arrow. Hold down the left mouse button, drag the shape to the desired location, and then release the mouse button. To size a shape, select the shape and then use the sizing handles that display around the shape to increase or decrease the size. Delete a selected shape by clicking the Delete key or right-clicking the shape and then clicking *Cut* at the shortcut menu.

Figure 7.7 Shapes Button Drop-down List

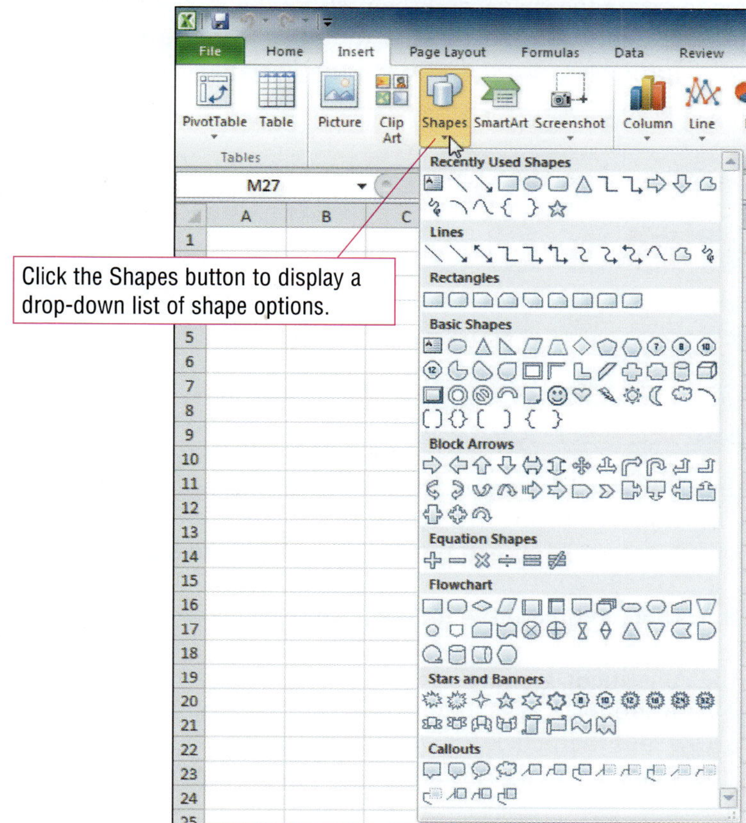

Project 3b Inserting and Customizing a Shape

Part 2 of 3

1. With **EL1-C7-P3-PopComp.xlsx** open, make sure the Chart Tools Layout tab displays.
2. Create a shape similar to the shape shown in Figure 7.8. Begin by clicking the Shapes button in the Insert group.
3. Click the *Up Arrow Callout* shape in the *Block Arrows* section (last shape in the second row).

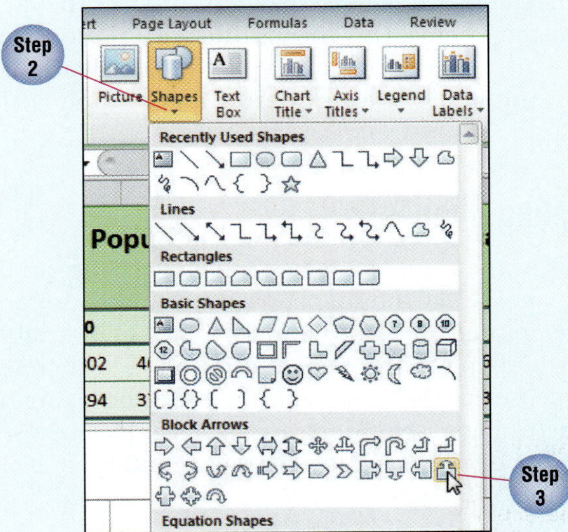

4. Drag in the chart to create the shape. To do this, position the mouse pointer in the chart, hold down the left mouse button, drag to create the shape, and then release the mouse button.
5. Click the More button located to the right of the shape style thumbnails in the Shapes Styles group and then click *Subtle Effect - Blue, Accent 1* at the drop-down gallery.

6. With the shape selected, use the sizing handles around the shape to increase and/or decrease the size so it displays as shown in Figure 7.8.
7. With the shape still selected, type **Largest Disparity** in the shape box, press Enter, and then type **(184,411)**.
8. Select the text you just typed and then complete the following steps:
   a. Click the Home tab.
   b. Click the Center button in the Alignment group.
   c. Click the Bold button in the Font group.
   d. Click the Font Size button arrow and then click *9*.
9. With the shape selected, drag the shape so it is positioned as shown in Figure 7.8.
10. Save **EL1-C7-P3-PopComp.xlsx**.

Figure 7.8 Project 3b Chart

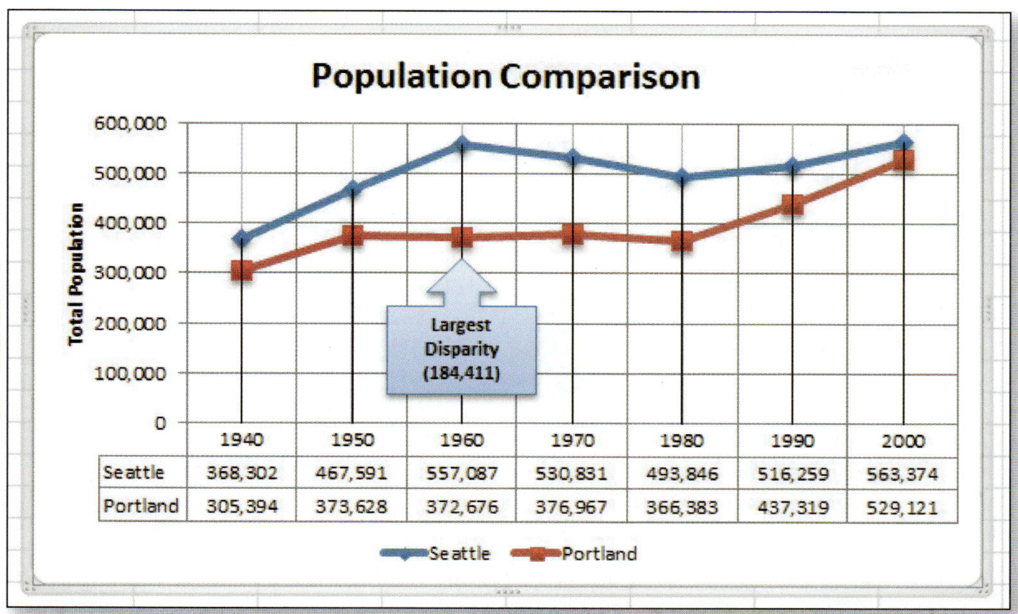

	1940	1950	1960	1970	1980	1990	2000
Seattle	368,302	467,591	557,087	530,831	493,846	516,259	563,374
Portland	305,394	373,628	372,676	376,967	366,383	437,319	529,121

Inserting Images

Click the Picture button in the Insert group in the Chart Tools Layout tab and the Insert Picture dialog box displays. If you have a picture or image file saved in a folder, navigate to the desired folder and then double-click the file name. This inserts the picture or image in the chart. Drag the picture or image to the desired position in the chart and use the sizing handles to change the size.

Quick Steps

Insert Image
1. Make the chart active.
2. Click Chart Tools Layout tab.
3. Click Picture button.
4. Double-click desired file name.

Project 3c Inserting a Picture in a Chart

Part 3 of 3

1. With **EL1-C7-P3-PopComp.xlsx** open, make sure the chart is selected and then click the Chart Tools Layout tab.
2. Insert the company logo by completing the following steps:
   a. Click the Picture button in the Insert group.
   b. At the Insert Picture dialog box, navigate to the Excel2010L1C7 folder on your storage medium and then double-click ***WELogo.jpg*** in the list box.
3. With the logo image inserted in the chart, use the sizing handles to decrease the size of the image and then move the image so it displays in the upper left corner of the chart area as shown in Figure 7.9.
4. Print only the selected chart.
5. Save and then close **EL1-C7-P3-PopComp.xlsx**.

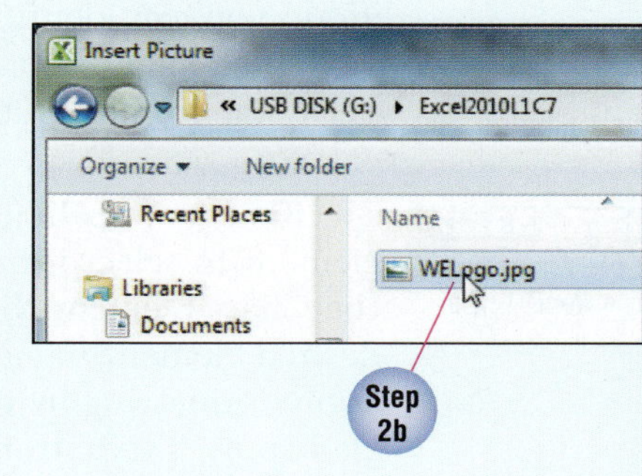

Figure 7.9 Project 3c Chart

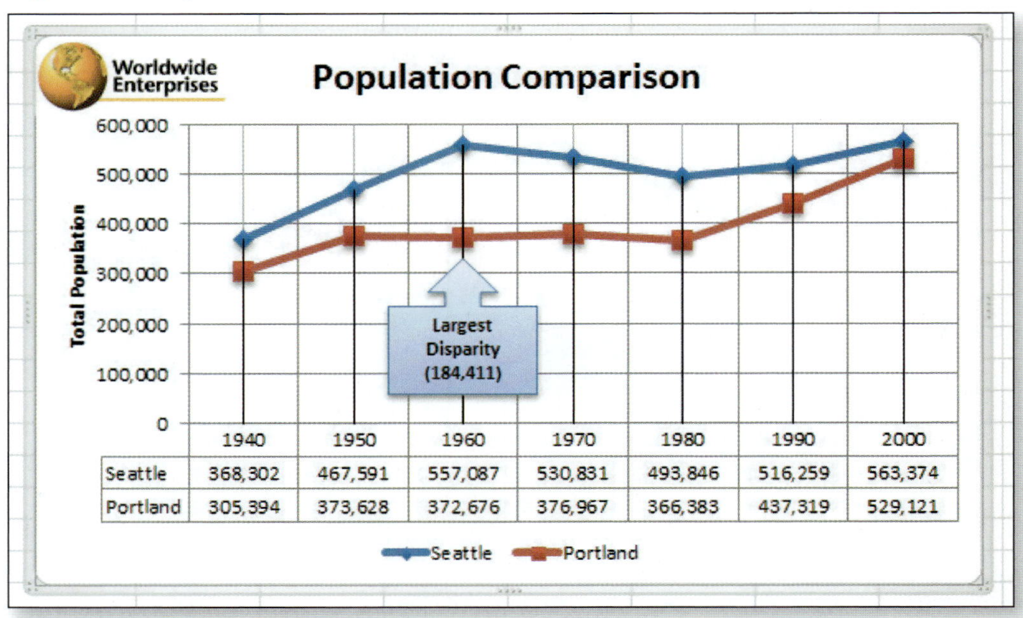

Project 4 Create a Costs Percentage Pie Chart — 1 Part

You will open a workbook containing percentage of costs for company departments and then create a pie chart with the data. You will apply formatting to the chart and then move the chart to a new worksheet.

Reset to Match Style

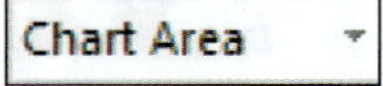

Chart Elements

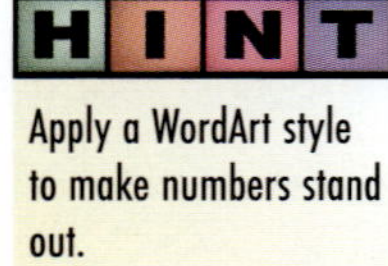

Apply a WordArt style to make numbers stand out.

Changing the Chart Formatting

Customize the format of the chart and chart elements with options in the Chart Tools Format tab as shown in Figure 7.10. With buttons in the Current Selection group you can identify a specific element in the chart and then apply formatting to that element. You can also click the Reset to Match Style button in the Current Selection group to return the formatting of the chart back to the original layout.

With options in the Shape Styles group, you can apply formatting styles to specific elements in a chart. Identify the desired element either by clicking the element to select it or by clicking the down-pointing arrow at the right side of the Chart Elements button in the Current Selection group and then clicking the desired element name at the drop-down list. With the chart element specified, apply formatting by clicking a style button in the Shape Styles group. You can also apply a style from a drop-down gallery. Display this gallery by clicking the

Figure 7.10 Chart Tools Format Tab

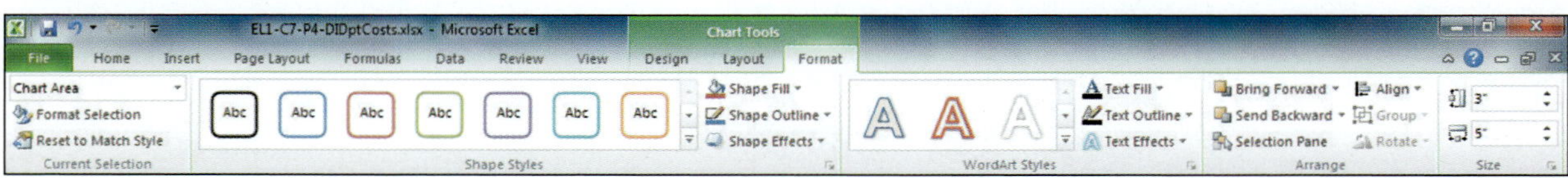

More button located at the right side of the shape styles. Click the up-pointing or the down-pointing arrow at the right of the shape styles to cycle through the available style options.

Project 4 Creating and Formatting a Pie Chart

Part 1 of 1

1. Open **DIDptCosts.xlsx** and then save the workbook with Save As and name it **EL1-C7-P4-DIDptCosts**.
2. Create the pie chart as shown in Figure 7.11 by completing the following steps:
   a. Select cells A3 through B10.
   b. Click the Insert tab.
   c. Click the Pie button in the Charts group and then click the first pie option in the *2-D Pie* section.
3. Click the More button located at the right side of the Chart Styles group.
4. At the drop-down gallery, click the *Style 32* option (last option in the fourth row).

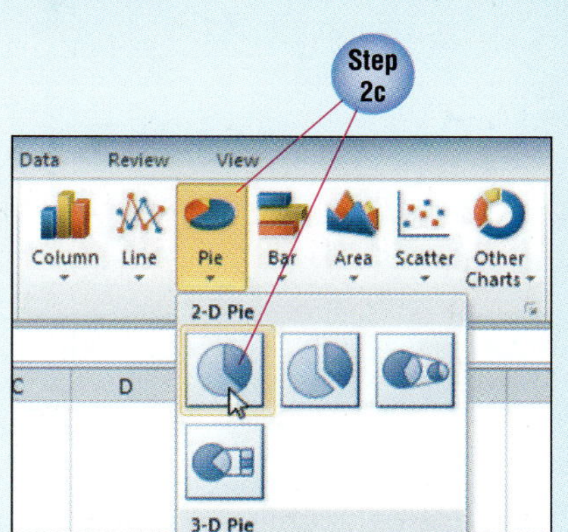

5. Click the Chart Tools Layout tab.
6. Insert data labels by clicking the Data Labels button in the Labels group and then clicking *Outside End* at the drop-down list.
7. Format chart elements by completing the following steps:
   a. Click the Chart Tools Format tab.
   b. Click the down-pointing arrow at the right side of the Chart Elements button in the Current Selection group and then click *Legend* at the drop-down list.
   c. Click the More button at the right of the shape style thumbnails in the Shape Styles group and then click the last option in the fourth row (*Subtle Effect - Orange, Accent 6*).
   d. Click the down-pointing arrow at the right side of the Chart Elements button in the Current Selection group and then click *Chart Title*.

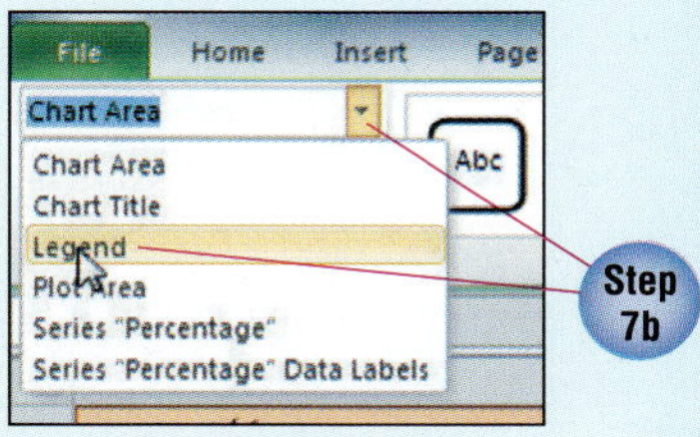

e. Click the More button at the right side of the WordArt style thumbnails in the WordArt Styles group and then click the *Gradient Fill - Orange, Accent 6, Inner Shadow* (second option from the left in the fourth row).

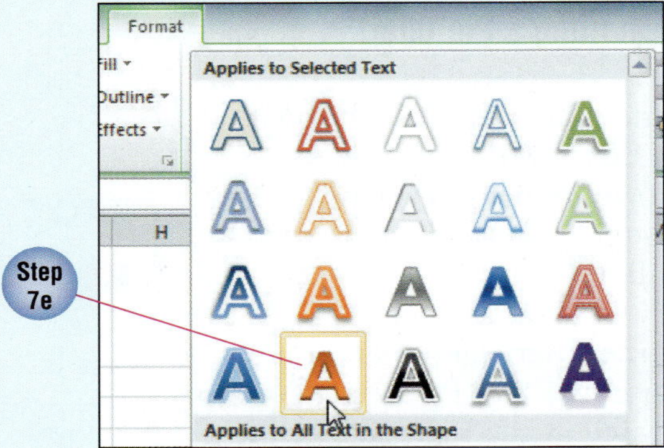

f. Deselect the chart title.

8. Insert the chart in a new sheet by completing the following steps:
   a. With the chart selected, click the Chart Tools Design tab.
   b. Click the Move Chart button in the Location group.
   c. At the Move Chart dialog box, click the *New sheet* option.
   d. Click OK.
9. Print only the worksheet containing the chart.
10. Save and then close **EL1-C7-P4-DIDptCosts.xlsx**.

Figure 7.11 Project 4

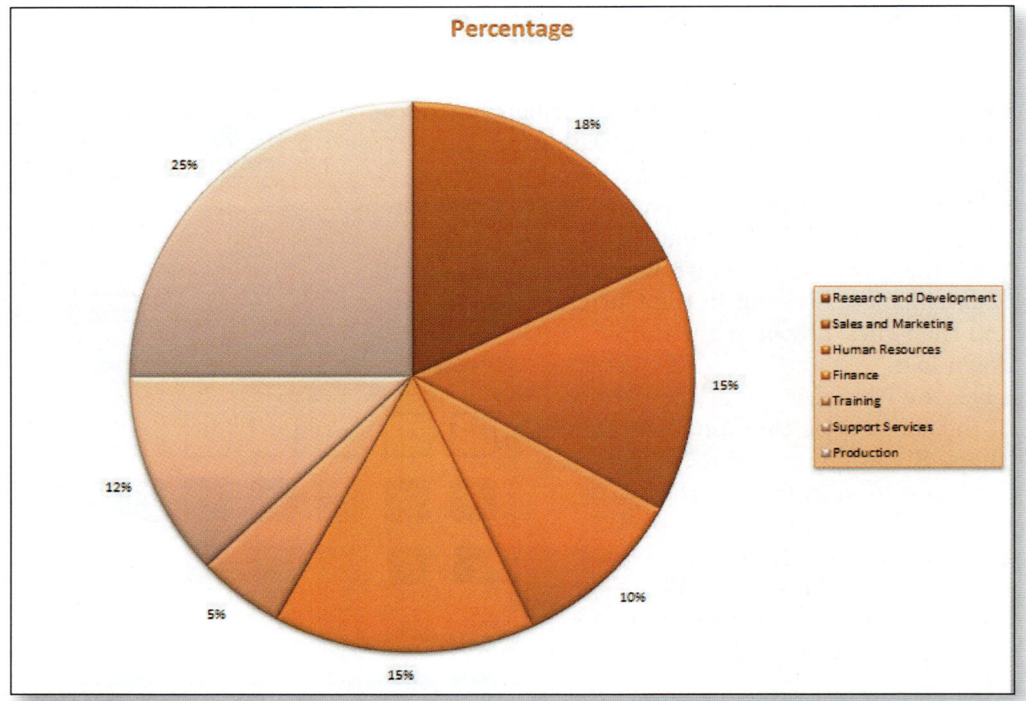

Project 5 Create a Regional Sales Column Chart

1 Part

You will create a column chart using regional sales data, change the layout of the chart, apply formatting, and change the height and width of the chart.

You can size a chart by selecting the chart and then dragging a sizing handle. You can also size a chart to specific measurements with the *Shape Height* and *Shape Width* measurement boxes in the Size group in the Chart Tools Format tab. Change the height or width by clicking the up- or down-pointing arrows that display at the right side of the button or select the current measurement in the measurement box and then type a specific measurement.

Quick Steps

Change Chart Height and/or Width

1. Make the chart active.
2. Click Chart Tools Format tab.
3. Insert desired height and/or width with *Shape Height* and/ or *Shape Width* text boxes.

Project 5 Changing the Height and Width of a Chart

Part 1 of 1

1. Open **DIRegSales.xlsx**.
2. Save the workbook with Save As and name it **EL1-C7-P5-DIRegSales**.
3. Create a Column chart by completing the following steps:
   a. Select cells A3 through B8.
   b. Click the Insert tab.
   c. Click the Column button in the Charts group.
   d. Click the *3-D Clustered Column* option (first option in the *3-D Column* section).
   e. Click the Switch Row/Column button located in the Data group to change the data series.
   f. Click the *Layout 1* option in the Chart Layouts group (first option from the left in the group).
   g. Select the text *Chart Title* and then type **Northeast Regional Sales**.
   h. Click the More button located at the right side of the thumbnails in the Chart Styles group and then click *Style 32* at the drop-down gallery (last option in fourth row).

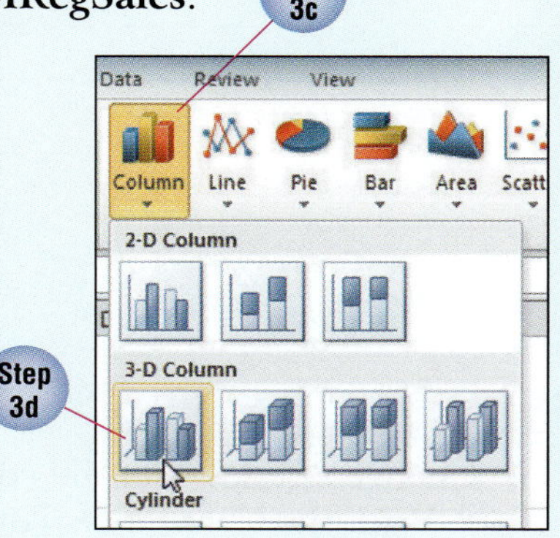

4. Change a series color by completing the following steps:
   a. Click the Chart Tools Format tab.
   b. Click the down-pointing arrow at the right side of the Chart Elements button in the Current Selection group and then click *Series "Newman, Jared"* at the drop-down list.

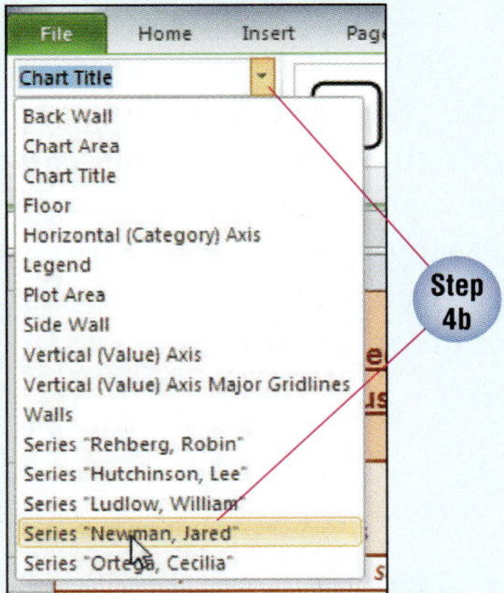

   c. Click the Shape Fill button arrow in the Shape Styles group and then click the dark red color *Red, Accent 2, Darker 25%*.

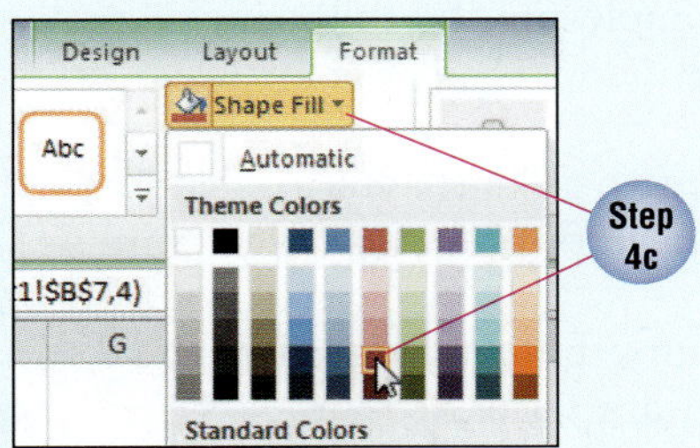

5. Change a series color by completing the following steps:
   a. With the Chart Tools Format tab active, click the down-pointing arrow at the right side of the Chart Elements button and then click *Series "Hutchinson, Lee"* at the drop-down list.
   b. Click the Shape Fill button arrow in the Shape Styles group and then click the dark green color *Olive Green, Accent 3, Darker 25%*.
6. Drag the chart down below the cells containing data.
7. Make sure the Chart Tools Format tab is selected.
8. Click in the *Shape Height* measurement box in the Size group and then type 3.8.
9. Click the up-pointing arrow at the right side of the *Shape Width* measurement box in the Size group until *5.5* displays in the text box.
10. Click outside the chart to deselect it.
11. Make sure the chart fits on one page and then print the worksheet (cells containing data and the chart).
12. Save and then close **EL1-C7-P5-DIRegSales.xlsx**.

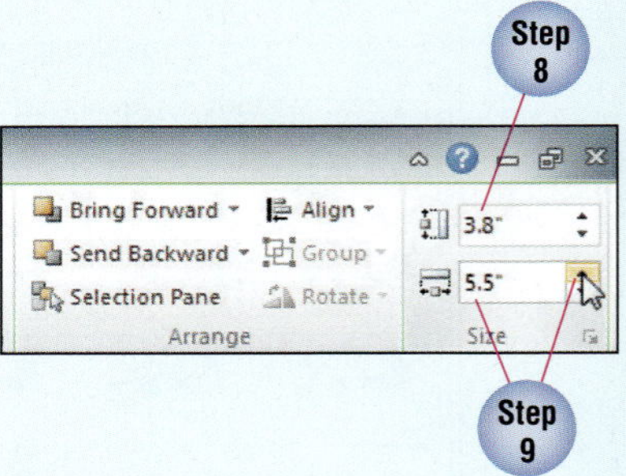

Chapter Summary

- A chart is a visual presentation of data. Excel provides 11 basic chart types: Area, Bar, Bubble, Column, Doughnut, Line, Pyramid, Radar, Stock, Surface, and XY (Scatter).
- To create a chart, select cells containing data you want to chart, click the Insert tab, and then click the desired chart button in the Charts group.
- A chart you create is inserted in the same worksheet as the selected cells.
- You can increase or decrease the size of a chart by positioning the mouse pointer on the four dots located in the middle of each border line or the three dots at each corner, and then dragging to the desired size.
- Move a chart by positioning the mouse pointer on the chart border until it turns into a four-headed arrow and then dragging with the mouse.
- Data in cells used to create the chart are linked to the chart. If you change the data in cells, the chart reflects the changes.
- Print by selecting the chart, displaying the Print tab Backstage view, and then clicking the Print button.
- When you insert a chart in a worksheet, the Chart Tools Design tab is active. Use options in this tab to change the chart type, specify a different layout or style, and change the location of the chart.
- Choose a chart style with buttons in the Charts group in the Insert tab or at the Change Chart Type dialog box.
- The Chart Layouts group in the Chart Tools Design tab contains preformatted chart layout options. Use options in the Chart Styles group to apply a particular style of formatting to a chart.
- By default, a chart is inserted in the active worksheet. You can move the chart to a new sheet within the workbook with the *New sheet* option at the Move Chart dialog box.
- To delete a chart in a worksheet, click the chart to select it, and then press the Delete key. To delete a chart created in a separate sheet, position the mouse pointer on the chart tab, click the right mouse button, and then click Delete.
- Use options in the Chart Tools Layout tab to change the layout and/or insert additional chart labels, shapes, pictures, or clip art images.
- Insert additional chart labels with options in the Labels group in the Chart Tools Layout tab.
- Use buttons in the Insert group in the Chart Tools Layout tab to insert shapes, pictures, or text boxes.
- To move a chart label, click the label to select it and then drag the label with the mouse. To delete a label, click the label and then press the Delete key.
- Use options in the Chart Tools Format tab to customize the format of the chart and chart elements.
- Change the chart size by dragging the chart sizing handles or by entering a measurement in the *Shape Height* and *Shape Width* measurement boxes in the Size group in the Chart Tools Format tab.

Commands Review

FEATURE	RIBBON TAB, GROUP	BUTTON, OPTION	KEYBOARD SHORTCUT
Default chart in worksheet			Alt + F1
Default chart in separate sheet			F11
Change Chart Type dialog box	Chart Tools Design, Type		
Move Chart dialog box	Chart Tools Design, Location		
Shapes button drop-down list	Chart Tools Layout, Insert		
Insert Picture dialog box	Chart Tools Layout, Insert		

Concepts Check Test Your Knowledge

Completion: In the space provided at the right, indicate the correct term, symbol, or command.

1. This is the keyboard shortcut to create a chart with the default chart type in the active worksheet. ____________________
2. The Charts group contains buttons for creating charts and is located in this tab. ____________________
3. This type of chart shows proportions and relationships of parts to the whole. ____________________
4. When you create a chart, the chart is inserted in this location by default. ____________________
5. Select a chart in a worksheet, display the Print tab Backstage view, and the first gallery in the Settings category is automatically changed to this option. ____________________
6. Use buttons in the Insert group in this tab to insert shapes or pictures. ____________________
7. When Excel creates a chart, the data in the first row (except the first cell) is used to create this. ____________________
8. Click this option at the Move Chart dialog box to move the chart to a separate sheet. ____________________

9. Click the Picture button in the Chart Tools Layout tab and this dialog box displays. ____________________

10. Change the chart size by entering measurements in these measurement boxes in the Size group in the Chart Tools Format tab. ____________________

Skills Check Assess Your Performance

Assessment 1

CREATE A COMPANY SALES COLUMN CHART

1. Open **CMSales.xlsx** and then save the workbook with Save As and name it **EL1-C7-A1-CMSales**.
2. Select cells A3 through C15 and then create a Column chart with the following specifications:
   a. Choose the *3-D Clustered Column* chart at the Chart button drop-down list.
   b. At the Chart Tools Design tab, click the *Layout 3* option in the Chart Layouts group.
   c. Change the chart style to *Style 26*.
   d. Select the text *Chart Title* and then type **Company Sales**.
   e. Move the location of the chart to a new sheet.
3. Print only the worksheet containing the chart.
4. Save and then close **EL1-C7-A1-CMSales.xlsx**.

Assessment 2

CREATE QUARTERLY DOMESTIC AND FOREIGN SALES BAR CHART

1. Open **CMPQtrlySales.xlsx** and then save the workbook with Save As and name it **EL1-C7-A2-CMPQtrlySales**.
2. Select cells A3 through E5 and then create a Bar chart with the following specifications:
   a. Click the *Clustered Bar in 3-D* option at the Bar button drop-down list.
   b. At the Chart Tools Design tab choose the *Layout 2* option in the Chart Layouts group.
   c. Choose the *Style 23* option in the Chart Styles group.
   d. Select the text *Chart Title*, type **Quarterly Sales**, and then click in the chart but outside any chart elements.
   e. Display the Chart Tools Layout tab and then insert primary vertical minor gridlines. (Do this with the Gridlines button.)
   f. Display the Chart Tools Format tab and then apply to the chart the *Subtle Effect - Olive Green, Accent 3* option in the Shape Styles group.
   g. Select the *Domestic* series (using the Chart Elements button) and then apply a purple fill (*Purple, Accent 4, Darker 25%*) using the Shape Fill button in the Shape Styles group.
   h. Select the Foreign series and then apply a dark aqua fill (*Aqua, Accent 5, Darker 25%*) using the Shape Fill button in the Shape Styles group.

i. Select the chart title and then apply the *Gradient Fill - Purple, Accent 4, Reflection* option with the WordArt Styles button.
j. Increase the height of the chart to 4 inches and the width to 6 inches.
k. Move the chart below the cells containing data and make sure the chart fits on the page with the data.

3. Print only the worksheet.
4. Save and then close **EL1-C7-A2-CMPQtrlySales.xlsx**.

Assessment 3

CREATE AND FORMAT A CORPORATE SALES COLUMN CHART

1. Open **CorpSales.xlsx** and then save the workbook with Save As and name it **EL1-C7-A3-CorpSales**.
2. Create a column chart and format the chart so it displays as shown in Figure 7.12.
3. Save, print, and then close **EL1-C7-A3-CorpSales.xlsx**.

Figure 7.12 Assessment 3

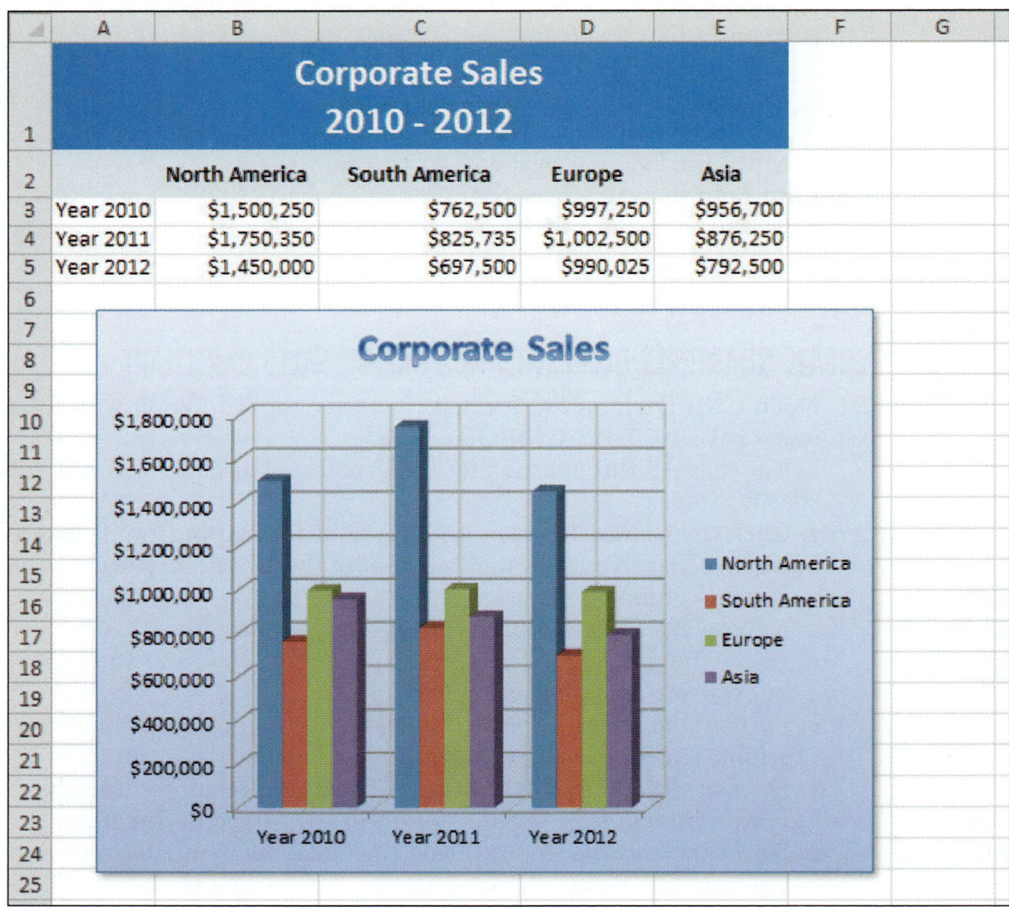

Corporate Sales 2010 - 2012

	North America	South America	Europe	Asia
Year 2010	$1,500,250	$762,500	$997,250	$956,700
Year 2011	$1,750,350	$825,735	$1,002,500	$876,250
Year 2012	$1,450,000	$697,500	$990,025	$792,500

Assessment 4

CREATE A FUND ALLOCATIONS PIE CHART

1. At a blank worksheet, create a worksheet with the following data:

Fund Allocations	
Fund	Percentage
Annuities	23%
Stocks	42%
Bonds	15%
Money Market	20%

2. Using the data above, create a pie chart as a separate worksheet with the following specifications:
   a. Create a title for the pie chart.
   b. Add data labels to the chart.
   c. Add any other enhancements that will improve the visual presentation of the data.
3. Save the workbook and name it **EL1-C7-A4-Funds**.
4. Print only the worksheet containing the chart.
5. Close **EL1-C7-A4-Funds.xlsx**.

Assessment 5

CREATE AN ACTUAL AND PROJECTED SALES CHART

1. Open **StateSales.xlsx** and then save the workbook with Save As and name it **EL1-C7-A5-StateSales**.
2. Look at the data in the worksheet and then create a chart to represent the data. Add a title to the chart and add any other enhancements to improve the visual display of the chart.
3. Save the workbook and then print the chart.
4. Close **EL1-C7-A5-StateSales.xlsx**.

Assessment 6

CREATE A STACKED CYLINDER CHART

1. Use Excel's help feature to learn more about chart types and specifically about stacked 3-D column charts and then create a worksheet with the data shown in Figure 7.13. Create with the data a 100% stacked cylinder chart in a separate sheet. Create an appropriate title for the chart and apply any other formatting to enhance the appearance of the chart.
2. Save the completed workbook and name it **EL1-C7-A6-CMPerSales**.
3. Print both sheets of the workbook (the sheet containing the data in cells and the sheet containing the chart).
4. Close **EL1-C7-A6-CMPerSales.xlsx**.

Figure 7.13 Assessment 6

Clearline Manufacturing Regional Sales Percentages				
	Region 1	Region 2	Region 3	Region 4
Jan-June	12%	20%	41%	27%
July-Dec	16%	27%	35%	22%

Visual Benchmark Demonstrate Your Proficiency

CREATE AND FORMAT A PIE CHART

1. At a blank workbook, enter data and then create a pie chart in a separate sheet as shown in Figure 7.14. Use the information shown in the pie chart to create the data. Format the pie chart so it appears similar to what you see in Figure 7.14.
2. Save the completed workbook and name it **EL1-C7-VB-CMFebExp**.
3. Print both worksheets in the workbook.
4. Close **EL1-C7-VB-CMFebExp.xlsx**

Figure 7.14 Visual Benchmark

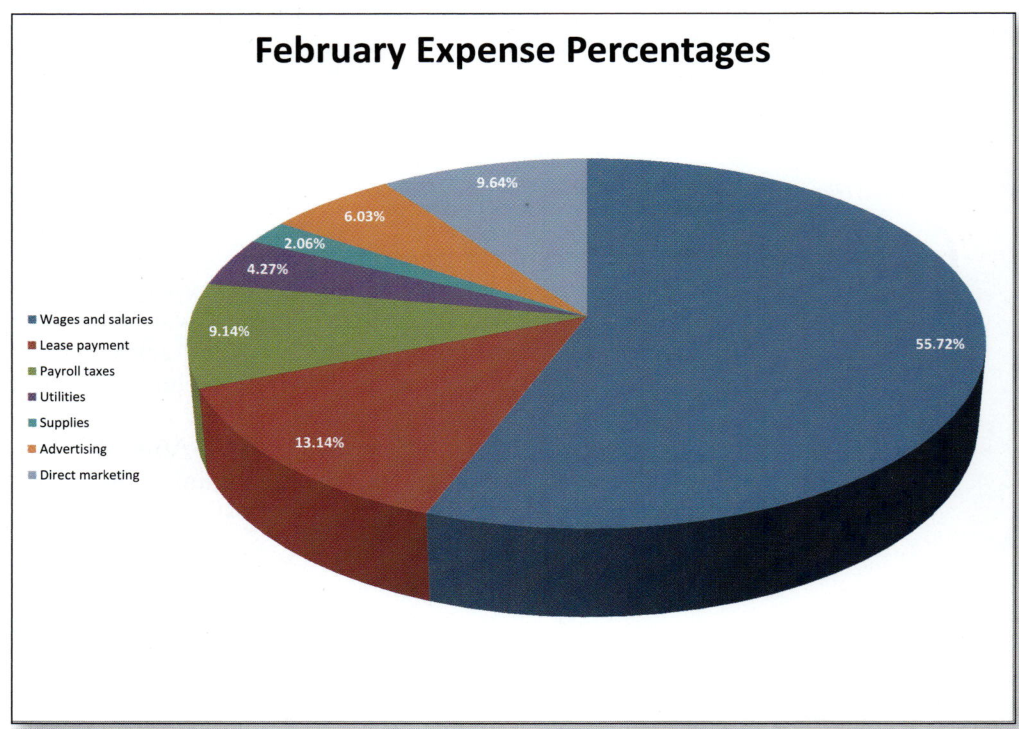

Case Study Apply Your Skills

Part 1

You are an administrator for Dollar Wise Financial Services and you need to prepare charts indicating home loan and commercial loan amounts for the past year. Use the information below to prepare a chart in Excel. You determine the type and style of chart and the layout and formatting of the chart. Insert a shape in the Commercial Loans chart that contains the text *All-time High* and points to the second quarter amount (*$6,785,250*).

Home Loans
1st Qtr. = $2,675,025
2nd Qtr. = $3,125,750
3rd Qtr. = $1,975,425
4th Qtr. = $875,650

Commercial Loans
1st Qtr. = $5,750,980
2nd Qtr. = $6,785,250
3rd Qtr. = $4,890,625
4th Qtr. = $2,975,900

Save the workbook and name it **EL1-C7-CS-DWQtrSales**. Print only the chart and then close **EL1-C7-CS-DWQtrSales.xlsx**.

Part 2

You need to present information on the budget for the company. You have the dollar amounts and need to convert the amounts to a percentage of the entire budget. Use the information below to calculate the percentage of the budget for each item and then create a pie chart with the information. You determine the chart style, layout, and formatting.

Total Budget: $6,000,000

Building Costs	=	$720,000
Salaries	=	$2,340,000
Benefits	=	$480,000
Advertising	=	$840,000
Marketing	=	$600,000
Client Expenses	=	$480,000
Equipment	=	$420,000
Supplies	=	$120,000

Save the workbook containing the pie chart and name it **EL1-C7-CS-DWBudgetPercentages**. Print only the chart and then close **EL1-C7-CS-DWBudgetPercentages.xlsx**.

Part 3

One of your clients owns a number of stocks and you would like to prepare a daily chart of the stocks' high, low, and close price. Use the Help feature to learn about stock charts and then create a stock chart with the following information (the company stock symbols are fictitious):

	IDE	POE	QRR
High	$23.75	$18.55	$34.30
Low	$18.45	$15.00	$31.70
Close	$19.65	$17.30	$33.50

Save the workbook containing the stock chart and name it **EL1-C7-CS-DWStocks**. Print only the chart and then close **EL1-C7-CS-DWStocks.xlsx**.

Part 4

You need to prepare information on mortgage rates for a community presentation. You decide to include the information on mortgage rates in a chart for easy viewing. Use the Internet to search for historical data on the national average for mortgage rates. Determine the average mortgage rate for a 30-year FRM (fixed-rate mortgage) for each January and July beginning with the year 2008 and continuing to the current year. Also include the current average rate. Use this information to create the chart. Save the workbook and name it **EL1-C7-CS-DWRates**. Print only the chart and then close **EL1-C7-CS-DWRates.xlsx**.

Microsoft® Excel®

Adding Visual Interest to Workbooks

PERFORMANCE OBJECTIVES

Upon successful completion of Chapter 8, you will be able to:

- **Insert symbols and special characters**
- **Insert, size, move, and format a clip art image**
- **Insert a screenshot**
- **Draw, format, and copy shapes**
- **Insert, size, move, and format a picture image**
- **Insert, format, and type text in a text box**
- **Insert a picture image as a watermark**
- **Insert and format SmartArt diagrams**
- **Insert and format WordArt**

Tutorials

8.1 Inserting Symbols and Special Characters
8.2 Inserting Pictures and Clip Art
8.3 Creating Screenshots
8.4 Inserting a Picture as a Watermark
8.5 Inserting and Formatting a SmartArt Diagram
8.6 Creating WordArt

Microsoft Excel includes a variety of features that you can use to enhance the visual appeal of a workbook. Some methods for adding visual appeal that you will learn in this chapter include inserting and modifying clip art images, screenshots, shapes, pictures, text boxes, SmartArt, and WordArt. Model answers for this chapter's projects appear on the following pages.

Excel2010L1C8

Note: Before beginning the projects, copy to your storage medium the Excel2010L1C8 subfolder from the Excel2010L1 folder on the CD that accompanies this textbook and make Excel2010L1C8 the active folder.

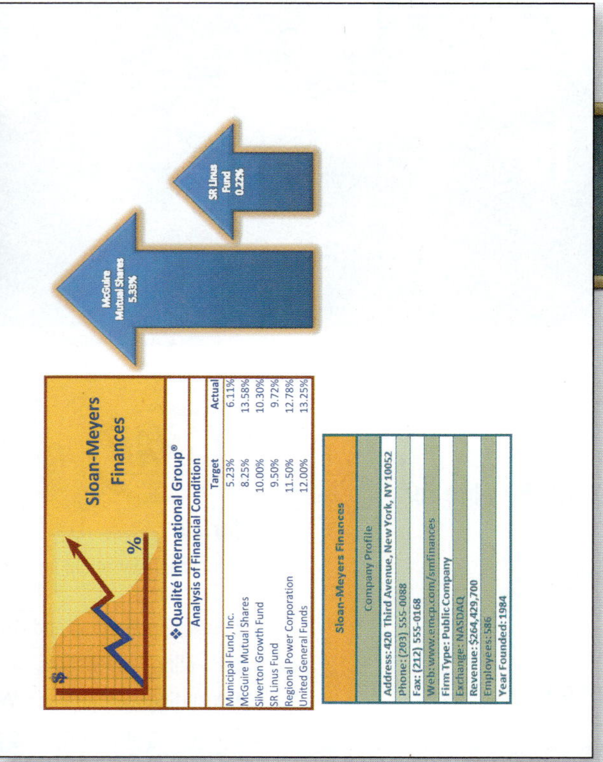

Sloan-Meyers Finances

❖Qualité International Group®

Analysis of Financial Condition

	Target	Actual
Municipal Fund, Inc.	5.23%	6.11%
McGuire Mutual Shares	8.25%	13.58%
Silverton Growth Fund	10.00%	10.30%
SR Linus Fund	9.50%	9.72%
Regional Power Corporation	11.50%	12.78%
United General Funds	12.00%	13.25%

Sloan-Meyers Finances

Company Profile

Address: 420 Third Avenue, New York, NY 10052

Phone: (203) 555-0088

Fax: (212) 555-0168

Web: www.emcp.com/smfinances

Firm Type: Public Company

Exchange: NASDAQ

Revenue: $264,429,700

Employees: 586

Year Founded: 1984

Project 1 Insert a Clip Art Image and Shapes in a Financial Analysis Workbook EL1-C8-P1-SFFinCon.xlsx

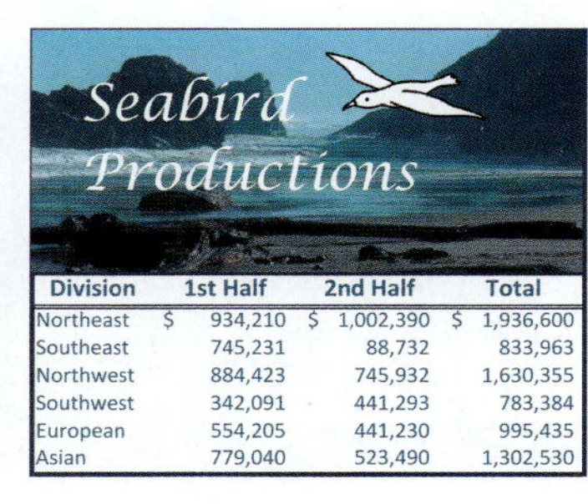

Division	1st Half	2nd Half	Total
Northeast	$ 934,210	$ 1,002,390	$ 1,936,600
Southeast	745,231	88,732	833,963
Northwest	884,423	745,932	1,630,355
Southwest	342,091	441,293	783,384
European	554,205	441,230	995,435
Asian	779,040	523,490	1,302,530

Project 2 Insert a Picture and Text Box in a Division Sales Workbook EL1-C8-P2-SPDivSales.xlsx

Highland Constr

EQUIPMENT USAGE REP

Hours	January	February	March	April	May	June
Total hours available	2300	2430	2530	2400	2440	2240
Avoidable delays	19	12	16	20	14	15
Unavoidable delays	9	8	6	12	9	10
Repairs	5	7	12	9	10	6
Servicing	6	13	7	6	4	5
Unassigned	128	95	85	135	95	75
In use	2040	2105	2320	2180	2050	1995

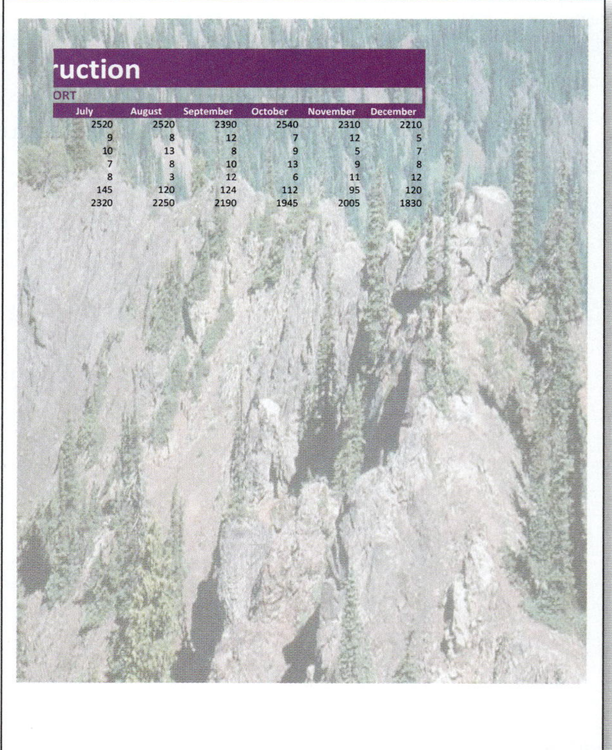

uction

ORT

July	August	September	October	November	December
2520	2520	2390	2540	2310	2210
9	8	12	7	12	5
10	13	8	9	5	7
7	8	10	13	9	8
8	3	12	6	11	12
145	120	124	112	95	120
2320	2250	2190	1945	2005	1830

Project 3 Insert a Watermark in an Equipment Usage Workbook EL1-C8-P3-HCEqpRpt.xlsx

Model Answers

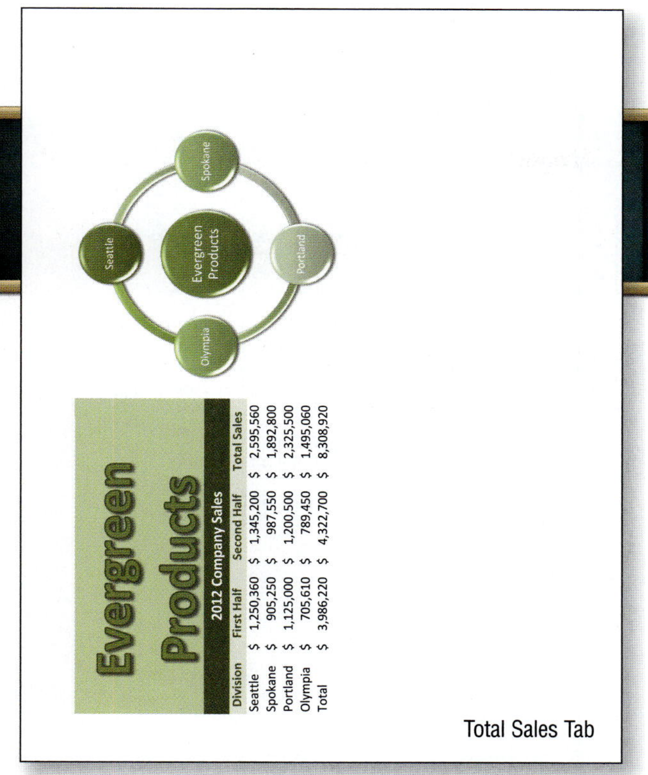

2012 Company Sales

Division	First Half	Second Half	Total Sales
Seattle	$ 1,250,360	$ 1,345,200	$ 2,595,560
Spokane	$ 905,250	$ 987,550	$ 1,892,800
Portland	$ 1,125,000	$ 1,200,500	$ 2,325,500
Olympia	$ 705,610	$ 789,450	$ 1,495,060
Total	$ 3,986,220	$ 4,322,700	$ 8,308,920

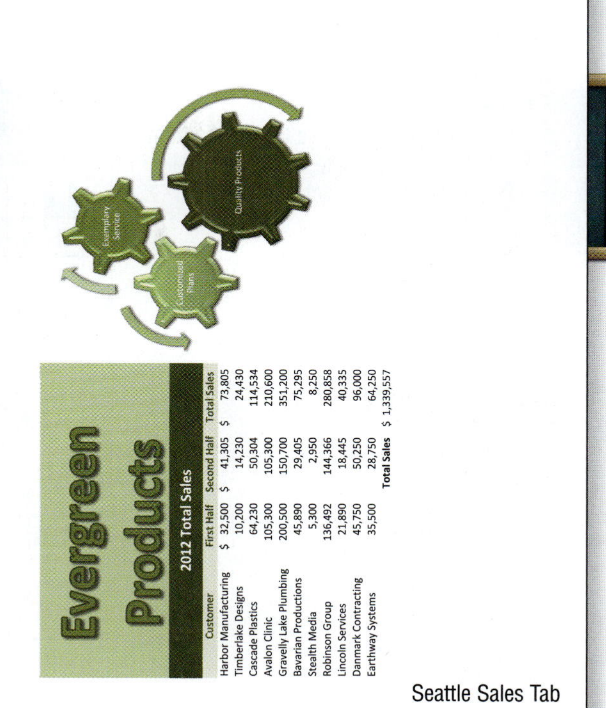

2012 Total Sales

Customer	First Half	Second Half	Total Sales
Harbor Manufacturing	$ 32,500	$ 41,305	$ 73,805
Timberlake Designs	10,200	14,230	24,430
Cascade Plastics	64,230	50,304	114,534
Avalon Clinic	105,300	105,300	210,600
Gravelly Lake Plumbing	200,500	150,700	351,200
Bavarian Productions	45,890	29,405	75,295
Stealth Media	5,300	2,950	8,250
Robinson Group	136,492	144,366	280,858
Lincoln Services	21,890	18,445	40,335
Danmark Contracting	45,750	50,250	96,000
Earthway Systems	35,500	28,750	64,250
		Total Sales	$ 1,339,557

Project 4 Insert and Format Diagrams in a Company Sales Workbook EL1-C8-P4-EPSales.xlsx

Project 1 Insert a Clip Art Image and Shapes in a Financial Analysis Workbook — 5 Parts

You will open a financial analysis workbook and then insert, move, size, and format a clip art image in the workbook. You will also insert an arrow shape, type and format text in the shape, and then copy the shape.

Inserting Symbols and Special Characters

You can use the Symbol button in the Insert tab to insert special symbols in a worksheet. Click the Symbol button in the Symbols group in the Insert tab and the Symbol dialog box displays as shown in Figure 8.1. At the Symbol dialog box, double-click the desired symbol and then click Close; or click the desired symbol, click the Insert button, and then click Close. At the Symbol dialog box with the Symbols tab selected, you can change the font with the *Font* option. When you change the font, different symbols display in the dialog box. Click the Special Characters tab at the Symbol dialog box and a list of special characters displays along with keyboard shortcuts to create the special character.

Quick Steps

Insert Symbol
1. Click in desired cell.
2. Click the Insert tab.
3. Click Symbol button.
4. Double-click desired symbol.
5. Click Close.

Symbol

Quick Steps

Insert Special Character
1. Click in desired cell.
2. Click Insert tab.
3. Click Symbol button.
4. Click Special Characters tab.
5. Double-click desired special character.
6. Click Close.

HINT

You can increase or decrease the size of the Symbol dialog box by positioning the mouse pointer on the lower right corner until the pointer displays as a two-headed arrow and then dragging with the mouse.

Figure 8.1 Symbol Dialog Box with Symbols Tab Selected

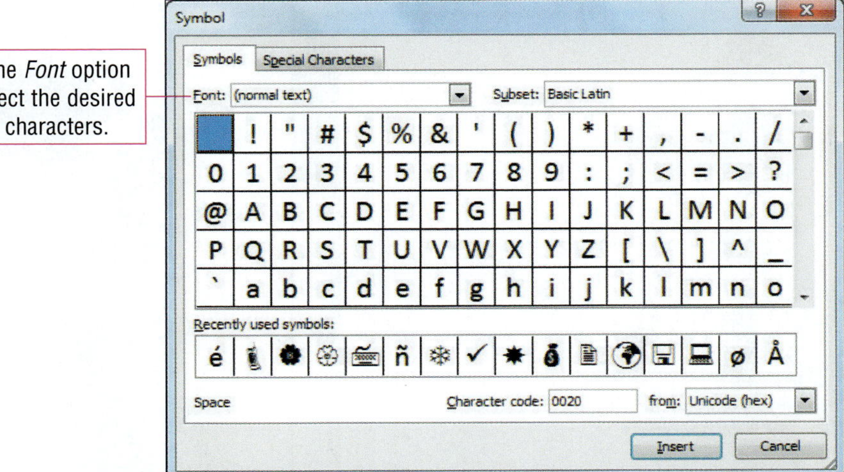

Project 1a Inserting Symbols and Special Characters

Part 1 of 5

1. Open **SFFinCon.xlsx** and then save the workbook with Save As and name it **EL1-C8-P1-SFFinCon**.
2. Insert a symbol by completing the following steps:
   a. Double-click cell A2.
   b. Delete the *e* that displays at the end of *Qualite*.
   c. With the insertion point positioned immediately right of the *t* in *Qualit*, click the Insert tab.
   d. Click the Symbol button in the Symbols group.
   e. At the Symbol dialog box, scroll down the list box and then click the *é* symbol (located in approximately the tenth or eleventh row).
   f. Click the Insert button and then click the Close button.

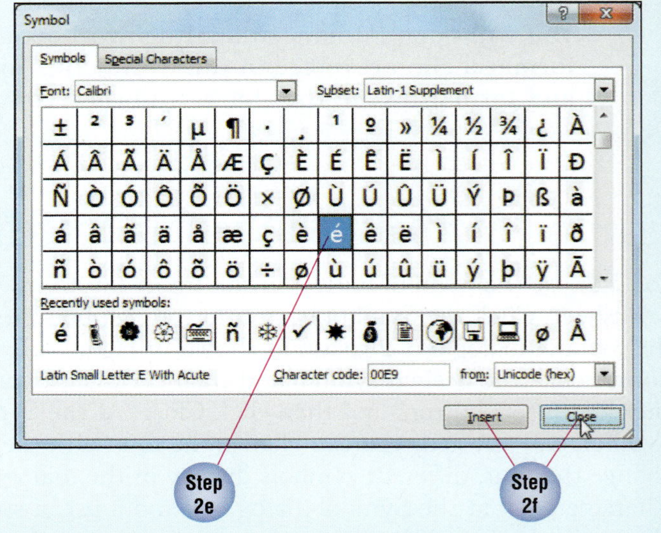

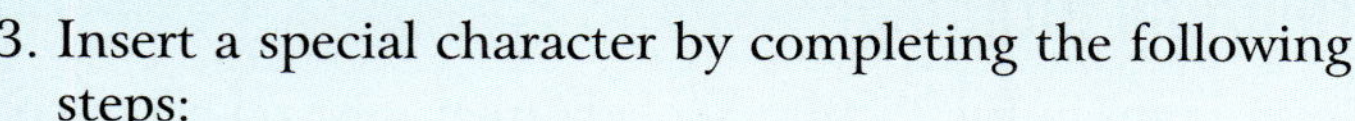

3. Insert a special character by completing the following steps:
   a. With cell A2 selected and in Edit mode, move the insertion point so it is positioned immediately right of *Group*.
   b. Click the Symbol button in the Symbols group.
   c. At the Symbol dialog box, click the Special Characters tab.
   d. Double-click the ® symbol (tenth option from the top).
   e. Click the Close button.
4. Insert a symbol by completing the following steps:
   a. With cell A2 selected and in Edit mode, move the insertion point so it is positioned immediately left of the *Q* in *Qualité*.
   b. Click the Symbol button in the Symbols group.
   c. At the Symbol dialog box, click the down-pointing arrow at the right side of the *Font* option box and then click *Wingdings* at the drop-down list. (You will need to scroll down the list to display this option.)
   d. Click the ❖ symbol (located in approximately the sixth row).
   e. Click the Insert button and then click the Close button.
5. Click in cell A3.
6. Save **EL1-C8-P1-SFFinCon.xlsx**.

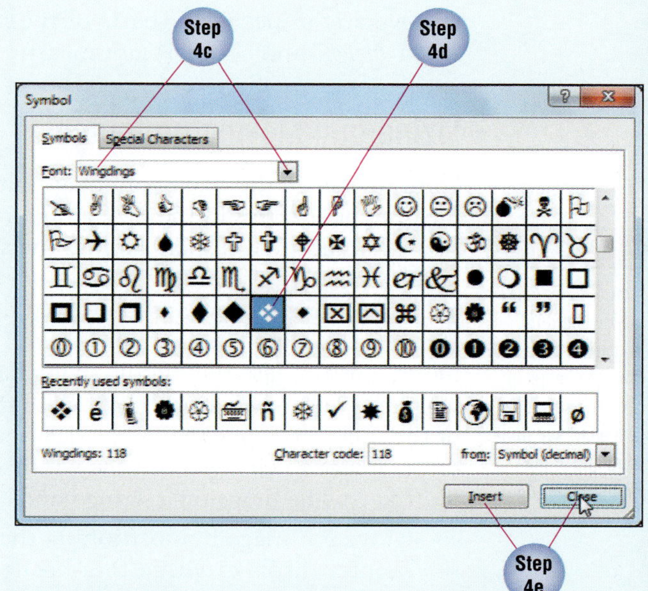

Inserting an Image

You can insert an image such as a picture or clip art in an Excel workbook with buttons in the Illustrations group in the Insert tab. Click the Picture button to display the Insert Picture dialog box where you can specify the desired picture file, or click the Clip Art button and then choose from a variety of images available at the Clip Art task pane. When you insert a picture or a clip art image in a worksheet, the Picture Tools Format tab displays as shown in Figure 8.2.

Picture

Figure 8.2 Picture Tools Format Tab

Customizing and Formatting an Image

Compress Pictures

Crop

With buttons in the Adjust group in the Picture Tools Format tab you can recolor the picture or clip art image, correct its brightness and contrast, and apply artistic effects. Use the Remove Background button to remove unwanted portions of the image. You can reset the picture or clip art back to its original color or change to a different image. You can also compress the size of the image file with the Compress Pictures button. Compressing the size of an image is a good idea because it reduces the amount of space the image requires on your storage medium.

With buttons in the Picture Styles group, you can apply a predesigned style to your image, change the image border, or apply other effects to the image. With options in the Arrange group, you can position the image in the worksheet, specify how text will wrap around it, align the image with other elements in the worksheet, and rotate the image. With the Crop button in the Size group, you can remove any unnecessary parts of the image and specify the image size with the *Shape Height* and *Shape Width* measurement boxes.

Sizing and Moving an Image

HINT

You can use arrow keys on the keyboard to move a selected object. To move the image in small increments, hold down the Ctrl key while pressing one of the arrow keys.

You can change the size of an image with the *Shape Height* and *Shape Width* measurement boxes in the Size group in the Picture Tools Format tab or with the sizing handles that display around the selected image. To change size with a sizing handle, position the mouse pointer on a sizing handle until the pointer turns into a double-headed arrow and then hold down the left mouse button. Drag the sizing handle in or out to decrease or increase the size of the image and then release the mouse button. Use the middle sizing handles at the left or right side of the image to make the image wider or thinner. Use the middle sizing handles at the top or bottom of the image to make the image taller or shorter. Use the sizing handles at the corners of the image to change both the width and height at the same time. Hold down the Shift key while dragging a sizing handle to maintain the proportions of the image.

Move an image by positioning the mouse pointer on the image border until the pointer displays with a four-headed arrow attached. Hold down the left mouse button, drag the image to the desired position, and then release the mouse button. Rotate the image by positioning the mouse pointer on the green, round rotation handle until the pointer displays as a circular arrow. Hold down the left mouse button, drag in the desired direction, and then release the mouse button.

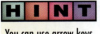

Project 1b Formatting an Image — Part 2 of 5

1. With **EL1-C8-P1-SFFinCon.xlsx** open, scroll down the worksheet and then click the Wall Street image to select it. (This image is located below the cells containing data.)
2. Remove the yellow background from the image by completing the following steps:
   a. Click the Picture Tools Format tab.
   b. Click the Remove Background button in the Adjust group in the Picture Tools Format tab.

Step 2b — Step 2a

c. Position the mouse pointer on the middle sizing handle at the top of the image until the pointer displays as a two-headed arrow pointing up and down.

d. Hold down the left mouse button, drag the border up to the top of the image, and then release the mouse.

e. Position the mouse pointer on the middle sizing handle at the bottom of the image until the pointer displays as a two-headed arrow pointing up and down.

f. Hold down the left mouse button, drag the border down to the bottom of the image, and then release the mouse button.

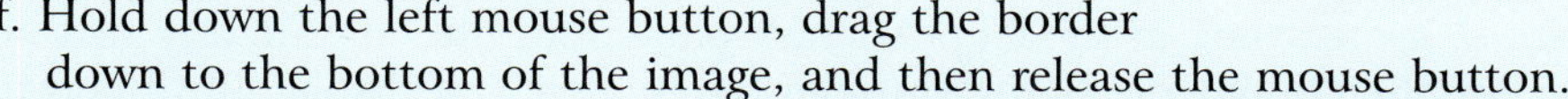

g. Click the Keep Changes button in the Close group in the Background Removal tab.

3. Change the color by clicking the Color button in the Adjust group and then clicking the *Blue, Accent color 1 Light* color (second color from the left in the third row of the *Recolor* section).
4. Apply a correction by clicking the Corrections button and then clicking the *Brightness: +20% Contrast: +20%* option (fourth option from the left in the fourth row in the *Brightness and Contrast* section).

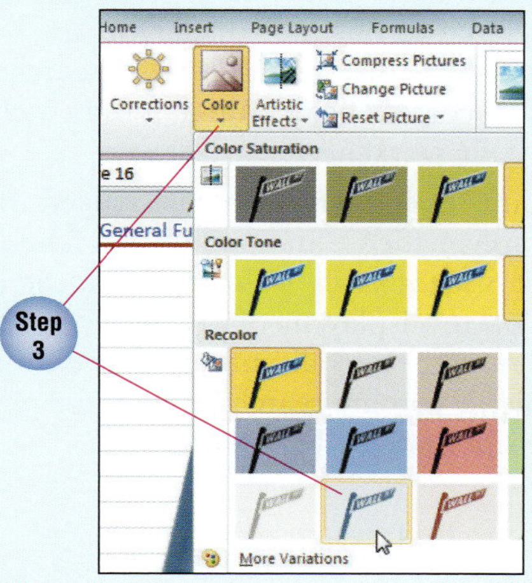

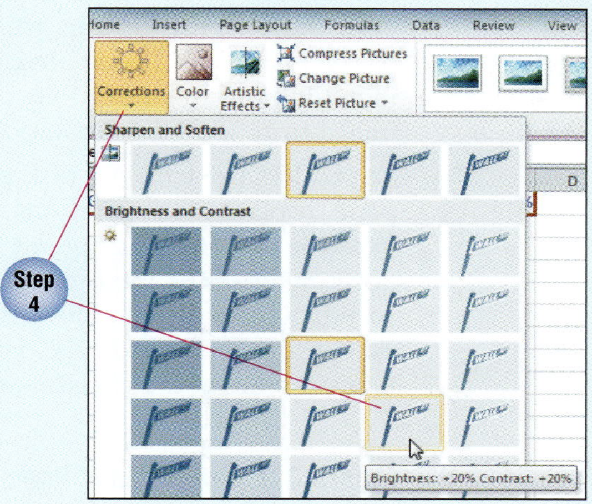

5. Apply an artistic effect by clicking the Artistic Effects button and then clicking the Glow Edges option (last option in the drop-down gallery).
6. Click in the *Height* measurement box in the Size group, type 2, and then press Enter.
7. Move the image by completing the following steps:
   a. Position the mouse pointer on the image (displays with a four-headed arrow attached).
   b. Hold down the left mouse button, drag the image to the upper left corner of the worksheet, and then release the mouse button.

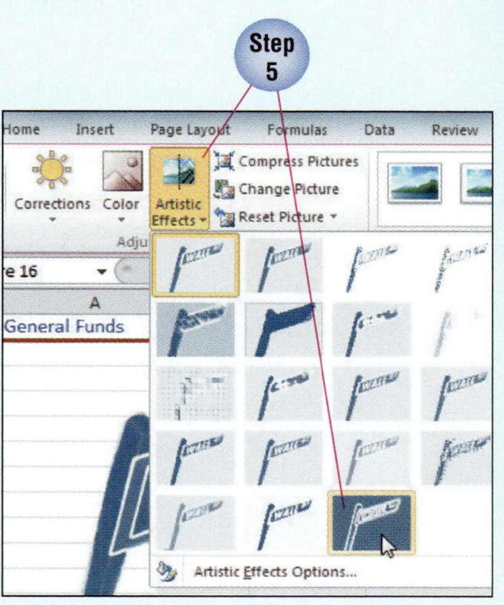

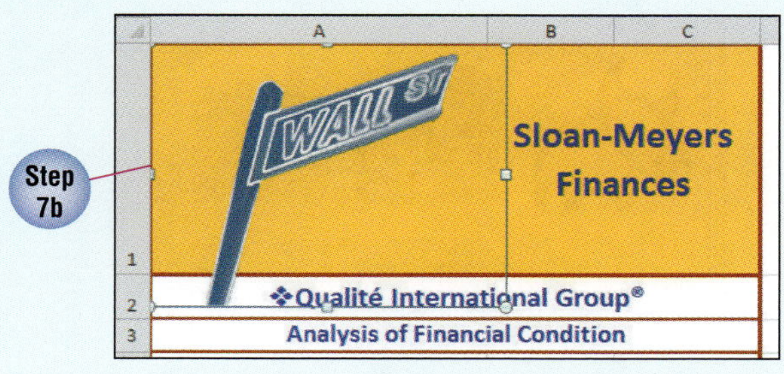
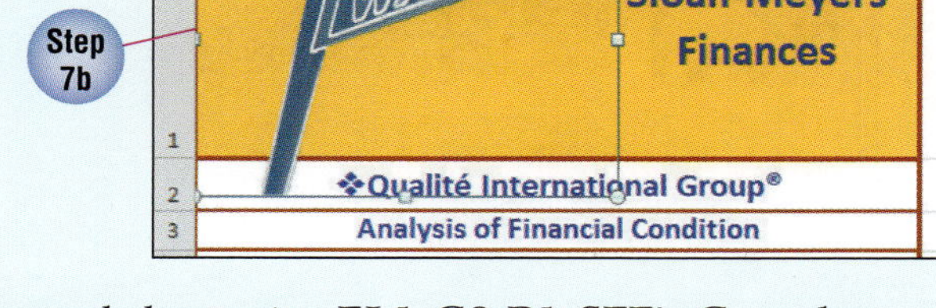
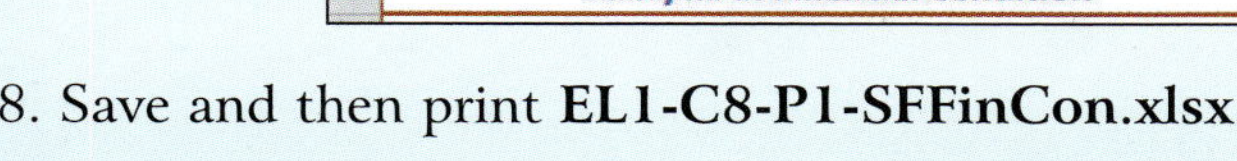

8. Save and then print **EL1-C8-P1-SFFinCon.xlsx**.

Inserting a Clip Art Image

Quick Steps

Insert Clip Art Image
1. Click Insert tab.
2. Click Clip Art button.
3. Type desired word or topic in *Search for* text box.
4. Click Go button or press Enter.
5. Click desired image.

Clip Art

Microsoft Office includes a gallery of media images you can insert in a worksheet. The gallery includes clip art, photographs, and movie images, as well as sound clips. To insert an image, click the Insert tab and then click the Clip Art button in the Illustrations group. This displays the Clip Art task pane at the right side of the screen, as shown in Figure 8.3.

To view all picture, sound, and motion files available in the gallery, make sure the *Search for* text box in the Clip Art task pane does not contain any text and then click the Go button. Scroll through the images that display until you find one you want to use and then click the image to insert it in the worksheet. Use buttons in the Picture Tools Format tab (see Figure 8.2 on page 275) to format and customize the clip art image.

If you are searching for a specific type of image, click in the *Search for* text box, type a category and then click the Go button. For example, if you want to find images related to business, click in the *Search for* text box, type *business*, and then click the Go button. Clip art images related to business display in the viewing area of the task pane. If you are connected to the Internet, Word will search for images matching the word or topic at the Office.com website. You can drag a clip art image from the Clip Art task pane to your worksheet.

Unless the Clip Art task pane default setting has been customized, the task pane displays all illustrations, photographs, videos, and audio files. The *Results should be* option has a default setting of *Selected media file types*. Click the down-pointing arrow at the right of this option to display media types. To search for a specific media type, remove the check mark before all options at the drop-down list except for the desired type. For example, if you are searching only for photograph images, remove the check mark before *Illustrations*, *Videos*, and *Audio*.

Figure 8.3 Clip Art Task Pane

Project 1c Inserting and Formatting a Clip Art Image

Part 3 of 5

1. With **EL1-C8-P1-SFFinCon.xlsx** open, delete the Wall Street sign image by clicking the image and then pressing the Delete key.
2. Insert a clip art image by completing the following steps:
   a. Make cell A1 active.
   b. Click the Insert tab and then click the Clip Art button in the Illustrations group.
   c. At the Clip Art task pane, click the down-pointing arrow at the right of the *Results should be* option box and then click in the *Photographs*, *Videos*, and *Audio* check boxes to remove the check marks. (The *Illustrations* check box should be the only one with a check mark.)
   d. Select any text that displays in the *Search for* text box, type **stock market**, and then press the Enter key.
   e. Click the image in the list box as shown at the right. (You will need to scroll down the list box to display the image. If this image is not available, click a similar image.)
   f. Click the down-pointing arrow at the right of the *Results should be* option box and then click in the *All media types* check box to insert check marks in all of the check boxes.
   g. Close the Clip Art task pane by clicking the Close button (contains an X) located in the upper right corner of the task pane.

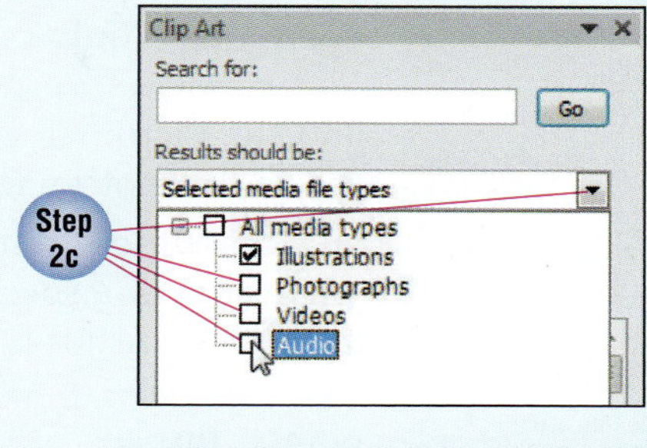

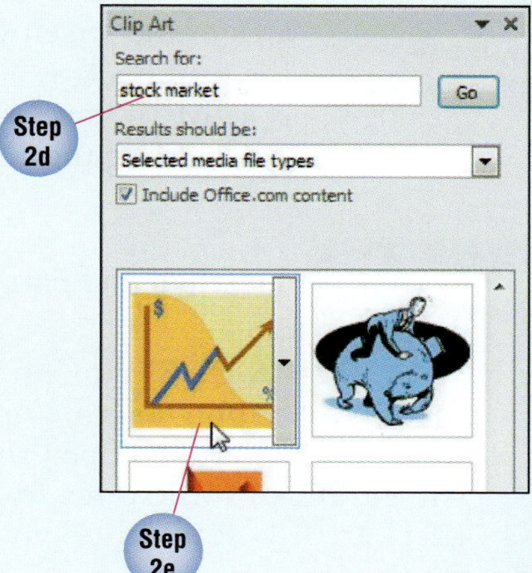

3. Apply a correction by clicking the Corrections button in the Adjust group in the Picture Tools Format tab and then clicking the *Brightness: -20% Contrast: +40%* option (second option from the left in the bottom row of the drop-down gallery).
4. Apply a picture style by clicking the More button that displays at the right side of the thumbnails in the Picture Styles group and then clicking the *Soft Edge Rectangle* option.

5. Increase the width of the image by completing the following steps:
   a. Position the mouse pointer on the middle sizing handle at the right side of the image until the pointer displays as a two-headed arrow pointing left and right.
   b. Hold down the left mouse button, drag to the right until the right edge of the image border aligns with the right edge of column A, and then release the mouse button.
6. Click outside the clip art image to deselect it.
7. Save **EL1-C8-P1-SFFinCon.xlsx**.

Creating Screenshots

Screenshot

The Illustrations group in the Insert tab contains a Screenshot button you can use to capture the contents of a screen as an image or capture a portion of a screen. This is useful for capturing information from a web page or from a file in

Quick Steps

Insert Screenshot
1. Open workbook.
2. Open another file.
3. Display desired information.
4. Make workbook active.
5. Click Insert tab.
6. Click Screenshot button.
7. Click desired window at drop-down list.

OR

6. Click Screenshot button, Screen Clipping.
7. Drag to specify capture area.

another program. If you want to capture the entire screen, display the desired web page or open the desired file from a program, make Excel active, and then open a workbook or a blank workbook. Click the Insert tab, click the Screenshot button, and then click the desired screen thumbnail at the drop-down list. The currently active worksheet does not display as a thumbnail at the drop-down list, only any other file or program you have open. If you do not have another file or program open, the Windows desktop displays. When you click the desired thumbnail, the screenshot is inserted as an image in the open workbook, the image is selected, and the Picture Tools Format tab is active. Use buttons in this tab to customize the screenshot image.

In addition to making a screenshot of an entire screen, you can make a screenshot of a specific portion of the screen by clicking the *Screen Clipping* option at the Screenshot button drop-down list. When you click this option, the open web page, file, or Windows desktop displays in a dimmed manner and the mouse pointer displays as crosshairs. Using the mouse, draw a border around the specific area of the screen you want to capture. The specific area you identify is inserted in the workbook as an image, the image is selected, and the Picture Tools Format tab is active. If you have only one workbook or file open when you click the Screenshot tab, clicking the *Screen Clipping* option will cause the Windows desktop to display.

Project 1d Inserting and Formatting a Screenshot

Part 4 of 5

1. With **EL1-C8-P1-SFFinCon.xlsx** open, make sure that no other programs are open.
2. Open Word and then open the document named **SFCoProfile.docx** from the Excel2010L1C8 folder on your storage medium.
3. Click the Excel button on the Taskbar.
4. Insert a screenshot of the table in the Word document by completing the following steps:
   a. Click the Insert tab.
   b. Click the Screenshot button in the Illustrations group and then click *Screen Clipping* at the drop-down list.
   c. When the **SFCoProfile.docx** document displays in a dimmed manner, position the mouse crosshairs in the upper left corner of the table, hold down the left mouse button, drag down to the lower right corner of the table, and then release the mouse button. (See image at the right.)
5. With the screenshot image inserted in the **EL1-C8-P1-SFFinCon.xlsx** workbook, make the following changes:
   a. Click in the *Width* measurement box in the Size group in the Picture Tools Format tab, type 3.7, and then press Enter.

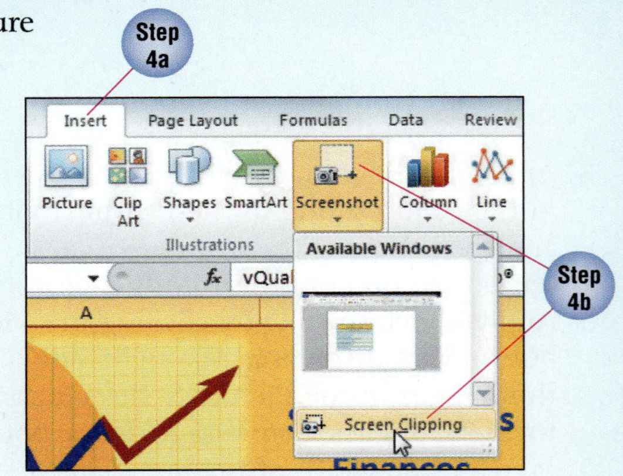

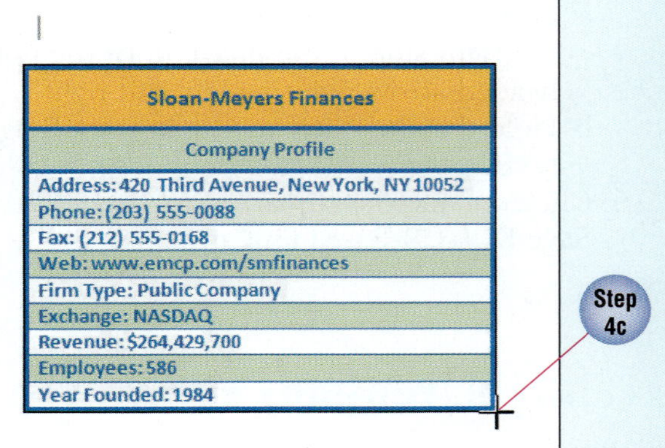

b. Click the Corrections button and then click the *Sharpen 25%* option (fourth option from the left in the *Sharpen and Soften* section).
c. Click the Corrections button and then click the *Brightness: 0% (Normal) Contrast: -40%* (third option from the left in the top row in the *Brightness and Contrast* section).
d. Using the mouse, drag the screenshot image one row below the data in row 10.

6. Make cell A4 active.
7. Save **EL1-C8-P1-SFFinCon.xlsx**.
8. Click the Word button, close **SFCoProfile.docx**, and then exit Word.

Inserting and Copying Shapes

In Chapter 7, you learned how to insert shapes in a chart. With the Shapes button in the Illustrations group in the Insert tab, you can also insert shapes in a worksheet. Use the Shapes button in the Insert tab to draw shapes in a worksheet including lines, basic shapes, block arrows, flow chart shapes, callouts, stars, and banners. Click a shape and the mouse pointer displays as crosshairs (plus sign). Position the crosshairs where you want the shape to begin, hold down the left mouse button, drag to create the shape, and then release the mouse button. This inserts the shape in the worksheet and also displays the Drawing Tools Format tab shown in Figure 8.4. Use buttons in this tab to change the shape, apply a style to the shape, arrange the shape, and change the size of the shape.

If you choose a shape in the *Lines* section of the Shapes button drop-down list, the shape you draw is considered a line drawing. If you choose an option in the other sections of the drop-down list, the shape you draw is considered an enclosed object. When drawing an enclosed object, you can maintain the proportions of the shape by holding down the Shift key while dragging with the mouse to create the shape. You can type text in an enclosed object and then use buttons in the WordArt Styles group to format the text.

If you have drawn or inserted a shape, you may want to copy it to other locations in the worksheet. To copy a shape, select the shape and then click the Copy button in the Clipboard group in the Home tab. Position the insertion point at the location where you want the copied image and then click the Paste button. You can also copy a selected shape by holding down the Ctrl key while dragging the shape to the desired location.

Quick Steps

Insert Shape
1. Click Insert tab.
2. Click Shapes button.
3. Click desired shape at drop-down list.
4. Drag in worksheet to create shape.

Copy Shape
1. Select shape.
2. Click Copy button.
3. Position insertion point in desired location.
4. Click Paste button.

OR
1. Select shape.
2. Hold down Ctrl key.
3. Drag shape to desired location.

Shapes

Figure 8.4 Drawing Tools Format Tab

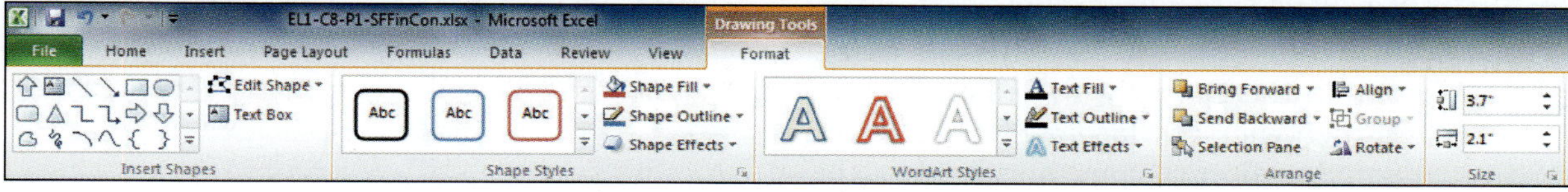

Project 1e Drawing Arrow Shapes

1. With **EL1-C8-P1-SFFinCon.xlsx** open, create the tallest arrow shown in Figure 8.5 on page 284 by completing the following steps:
   a. Click the Insert tab.
   b. Click the Shapes button and then click the *Up Arrow* shape (third option from the left in the top row of the *Block Arrows* section).

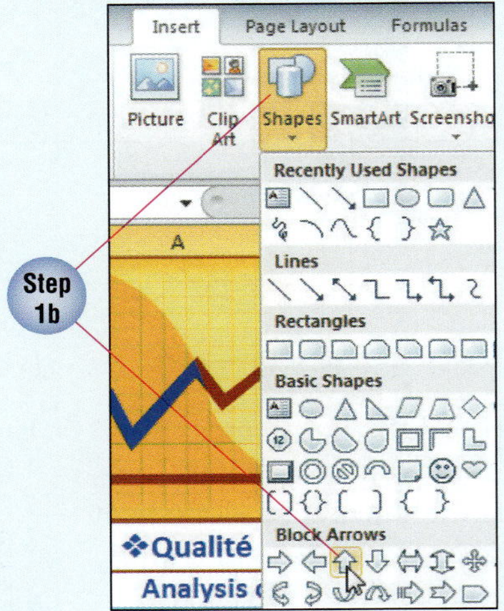

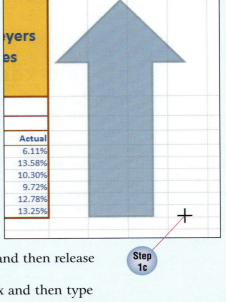

   c. Position the mouse pointer (displays as a thin, black cross) near the upper left corner of cell D1, hold down the left mouse button, drag down and to the right to create the shape as shown below, and then release the mouse button.

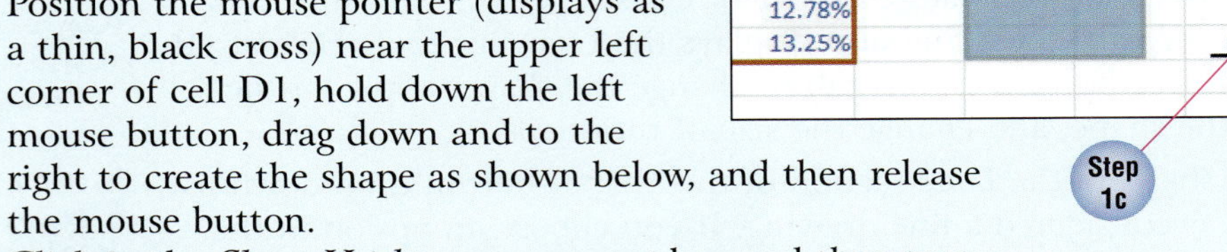

   d. Click in the *Shape Height* measurement box and then type 3.7.
   e. Click in the *Shape Width* measurement box, type 2.1, and then press Enter.
   f. If necessary, drag the arrow so it is positioned as shown in Figure 8.5. (To drag the arrow, position the mouse pointer on the border of the selected arrow until the pointer turns into a four-headed arrow, hold down the left mouse button, drag the arrow to the desired position, and then release the mouse button.)
   g. Click the More button at the right side of the thumbnails in the Shape Styles group in the Drawing Tools Format tab and then click the *Intense Effect - Blue, Accent 1* option (second option from the left in the bottom row).

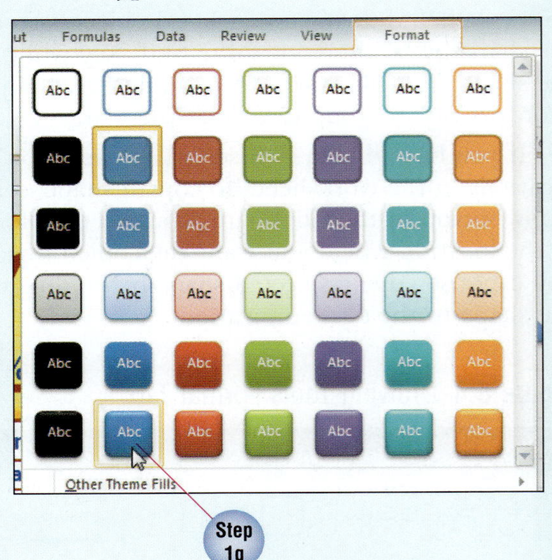

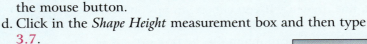

h. Click the Shape Effects button in the Shape Styles group, point to *Glow*, and then click the last option in the third row in the *Glow Variations* section (*Orange, 11 pt glow, Accent color 6*).

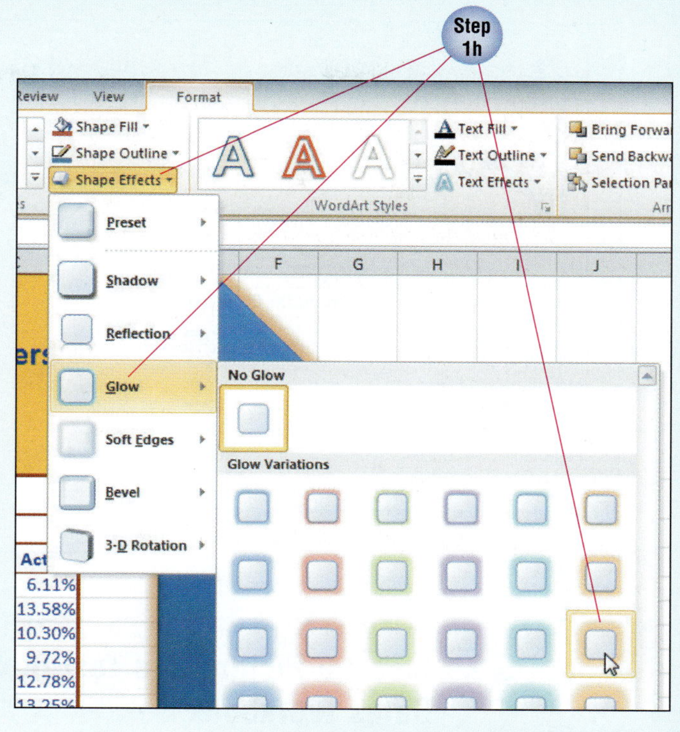

2. Insert text in the arrow shape by completing the following steps:
   a. With the arrow shape selected, type **McGuire Mutual Shares 5.33%**.
   b. Select the text you just typed (*McGuire Mutual Shares 5.33%*).
   c. Click the More button at the right side of the thumbnails in the WordArt Styles group and then click the third option from the left in the top row (*Fill - White, Drop Shadow*).
   d. Click the Home tab.
   e. Click the Center button in the Alignment group.

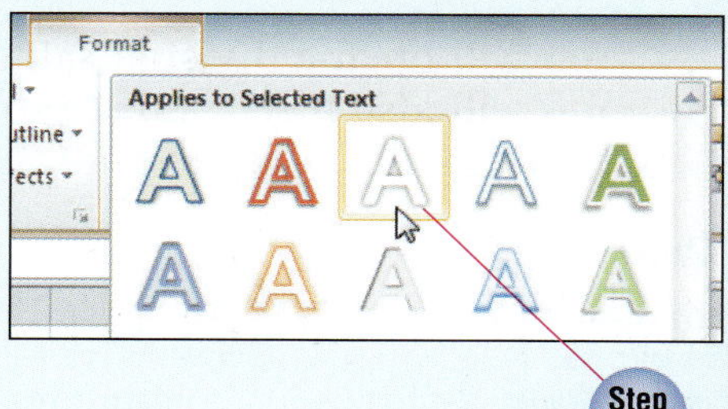

3. With the arrow selected, copy the arrow by completing the following steps:
   a. Hold down the Ctrl key.
   b. Position the mouse pointer on the arrow border until the pointer displays with a square box and plus symbol attached.
   c. Hold down the left mouse button and drag to the right so the outline of the arrow is positioned at the right side of the existing arrow.
   d. Release the mouse button and then release the Ctrl key.
4. Format the second arrow by completing the following steps:
   a. With the second arrow selected, click the Drawing Tools Format tab.
   b. Click in the *Shape Height* measurement box and then type **2**.
   c. Click in the *Shape Width* measurement box, type **1.6**, and then press Enter
   d. Select the text *McGuire Mutual Shares 5.33%* and then type **SR Linus Fund 0.22%**.
   e. Drag the arrow so it is positioned as shown in Figure 8.5.
5. Change the orientation to landscape. (Make sure the cells containing data, the screenshot image, and the arrows will print on the same page.)
6. Save, print, and then close **EL1-C8-P1-SFFinCon.xlsx**.

Figure 8.5 Project 1e

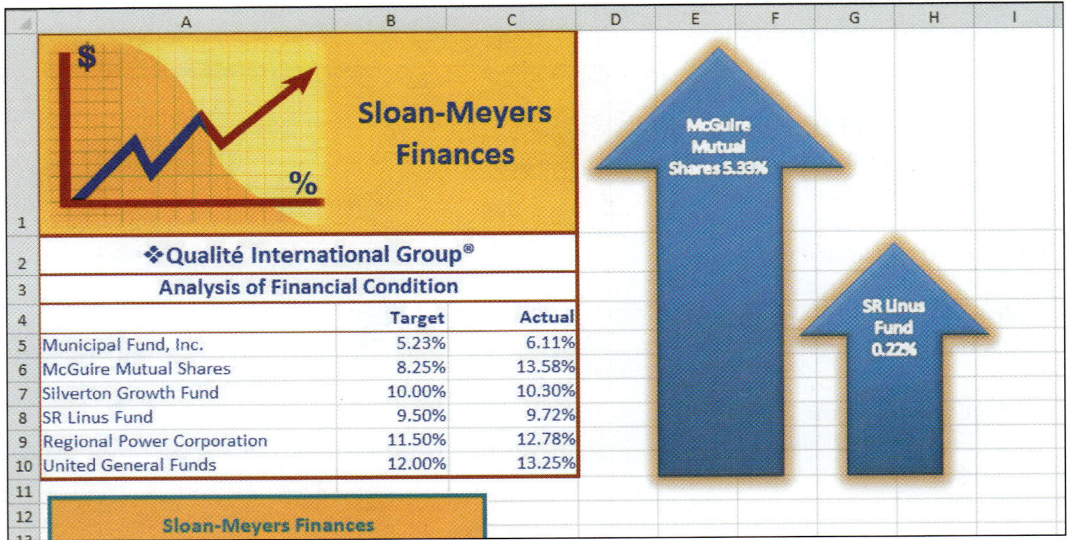

Insert a Picture and Text Box in a Division Sales Workbook

2 Parts

You will open a division sales workbook and then insert, move, and size a picture. You will also insert a text box and then format the text.

Quick Steps

Insert Picture

1. Click Insert tab.
2. Click Picture button.
3. Navigate to desired folder.
4. Double-click desired picture.

Pictures

Inserting a Picture

To insert a picture in a worksheet, click the Insert tab and then click the Picture button in the Illustrations group. At the Insert Picture dialog box, navigate to the folder containing the desired picture and then double-click the picture. Use buttons in the Picture Tools Format tab to format and customize the picture.

Project 2a Inserting and Customizing a Picture

Part 1 of 2

1. Open **SPDivSales.xlsx** and then save the workbook with Save As and name it **EL1-C8-P2-SPDivSales**.
2. Make the following changes to the bird clip art image:
   a. Click the bird clip art image to select it.
   b. Click the Picture Tools Format tab.
   c. Click the Rotate button in the Arrange group and then click *Flip Horizontal* at the drop-down list.

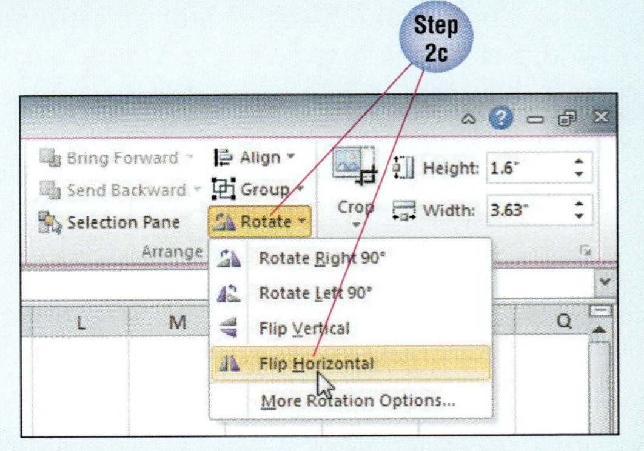

d. Click the Color button in the Adjust group and then click the *Black and White: 75%* option in the *Recolor* section (last option in the top row).
e. Click in the *Shape Height* measurement box, type **0.6**, and then press Enter.

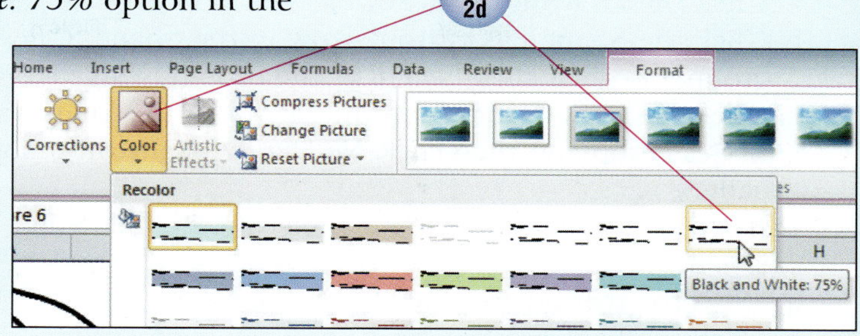

3. Insert and format a picture by completing the following steps:
   a. Click in cell A1 outside of the bird image.
   b. Click the Insert tab.
   c. Click the Picture button in the Illustrations group.
   d. At the Insert Picture dialog box, navigate to the Excel2010L1C8 folder on your storage medium and then double-click ***Ocean.jpg***.
   e. With the picture selected, click the Send Backward button in the Arrange group in the Picture Tools Format tab.
   f. Use the sizing handles that display around the picture image to move and size it so it fills cell A1 as shown in Figure 8.6.
   g. Click the bird clip art image and then drag the image so it is positioned as shown in Figure 8.6.
4. Save **EL1-C8-P2-SPDivSales.xlsx**.

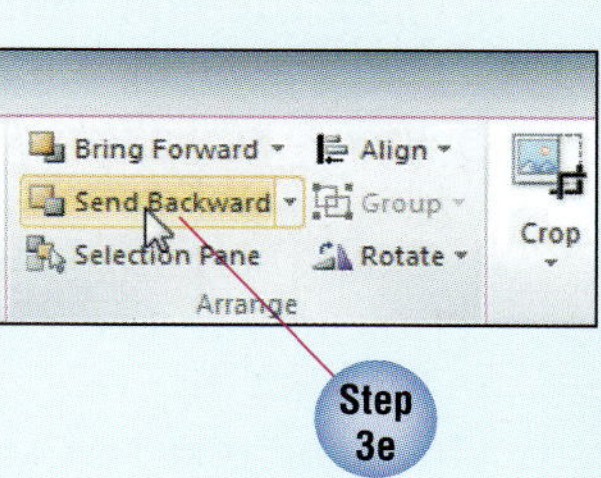

Drawing and Formatting a Text Box

Use the Text Box button in the Insert tab to draw a text box in a worksheet. To draw a text box, click the Insert tab and then click the Text Box button in the Text group. This causes the mouse pointer to display as a long, thin, cross-like pointer. Position the pointer in the worksheet and then drag to create the text box. When a text box is selected, the Drawing Tools Format tab displays with options for customizing the text box.

Quick Steps

Draw Text Box
1. Click Insert tab.
2. Click Text Box button.
3. Drag in worksheet to create text box.

Click a text box to select it and a dashed border and sizing handles display around the text box. If you want to delete the text box, click the text box border again to change the dashed border lines to solid border lines and then press the Delete key.

Text Box

Project 2b **Inserting and Formatting a Text Box** Part 2 of 2

1. With **EL1-C8-P2-SPDivSales.xlsx** open, draw a text box by completing the following steps:
   a. Click the Insert tab.
   b. Click the Text Box button in the Text group.
   c. Drag in cell A1 to draw a text box the approximate size and shape shown at the right.

2. Format the text box by completing the following steps:
   a. Click the Drawing Tools Format tab.
   b. Click the Shape Fill button arrow in the Shape Styles group and then click *No Fill* at the drop-down gallery.
   c. Click the Shape Outline button arrow in the Shape Styles group and then click *No Outline* at the drop-down gallery.
3. Insert text in the text box by completing the following steps:
   a. With the text box selected, click the Home tab.
   b. Click the Font button arrow and then click *Lucida Calligraphy* at the drop-down gallery. (You will need to scroll down the gallery to display this font.)
   c. Click the Font Size button arrow and then click *32* at the drop-down gallery.
   d. Click the Font Color button arrow and then click *White, Background 1* (first option in the first row in the *Theme Colors* section).
   e. Type **Seabird Productions**.
4. Move the text box so the text is positioned in cell A1 as shown in Figure 8.6. If necessary, move the bird clip art image. (To move the bird image, you may need to move the text box so you can select the image. Move the text box back to the desired location after moving the bird image.)
5. Save, print, and then close **EL1-C8-P2-SPDivSales.xlsx**.

Figure 8.6 Projects 2a and 2b

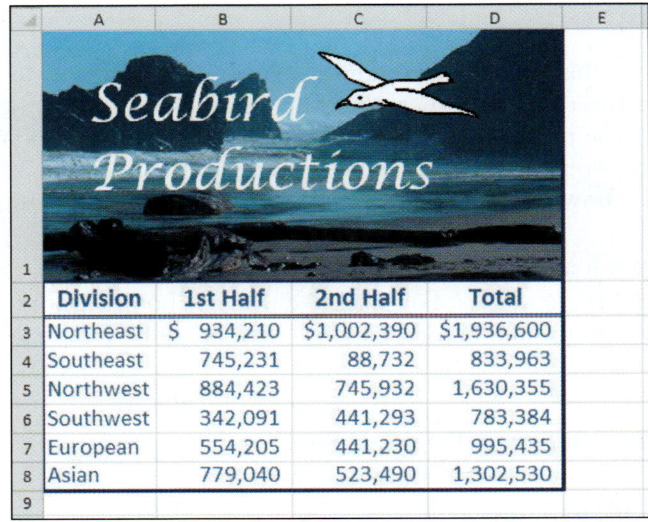

Division	1st Half	2nd Half	Total
Northeast	$ 934,210	$1,002,390	$1,936,600
Southeast	745,231	88,732	833,963
Northwest	884,423	745,932	1,630,355
Southwest	342,091	441,293	783,384
European	554,205	441,230	995,435
Asian	779,040	523,490	1,302,530

Project 3 Insert a Watermark in an Equipment Usage Workbook

1 Part

You will open an equipment usage report workbook and then insert a picture as a watermark that prints on both pages of the worksheet.

Inserting a Picture as a Watermark

A ***watermark*** is a lightened image that displays behind data in a file. You can create a watermark in a Word document but the watermark functionality is not available in Excel. You can, however, insert a picture in a header or footer and then resize and format the picture to display behind each page of the worksheet.

To create a picture watermark in a worksheet, click the Insert tab and then click the Header & Footer button in the Text group. With the worksheet in Print Layout view, click the Picture button in the Header & Footer Elements group in the Header & Footer Tools Design tab. At the Insert Picture dialog box, navigate to the desired folder and then double-click the desired picture. This inserts *&[Picture]* in the header. Resize and format the picture by clicking the Format Picture button in the Header & Footer Elements group. Use options at the Format Picture dialog box with the Size tab selected to specify the size of the picture and use options in the dialog box with the Picture tab selected to specify brightness and contrast.

Quick Steps

Insert Picture as Watermark
1. Click Insert tab.
2. Click Header & Footer button.
3. Click Picture button.
4. Navigate to desired folder.
5. Double-click desired picture.

Format Picture

Project 3 **Inserting a Picture as a Watermark** Part 1 of 1

1. Open **HCEqpRpt.xlsx** and then save the workbook with Save As and name it **EL1-C8-P3-HCEqpRpt**.
2. Insert a picture as a watermark by completing the following steps:
   a. Click the Insert tab.
   b. Click the Header & Footer button in the Text group.
   c. Click the Picture button in the Header & Footer Elements group in the Header & Footer Tools Design tab.
   d. At the Insert Picture dialog box, navigate to the Excel2010L1C8 folder on your storage medium and then double-click ***Olympics.jpg***.
   e. Click the Format Picture button in the Header & Footer Elements group.
   f. At the Format Picture dialog box with the Size tab selected, click the *Lock aspect ratio* check box in the *Scale* section to remove the check mark.
   g. Select the current measurement in the *Height* measurement box in the *Size and rotate* section and then type 10.
   h. Select the current measurement in the *Width* measurement box in the *Size and rotate* section and then type 7.5.
   i. Click the Picture tab.
   j. At the Format Picture dialog box with the Picture tab selected, select the current percentage number in the *Brightness* option box in the *Image control* section and then type 75.
   k. Select the current percentage number in the *Contrast* option box and then type 25.
   l. Click OK to close the Format Picture dialog box.

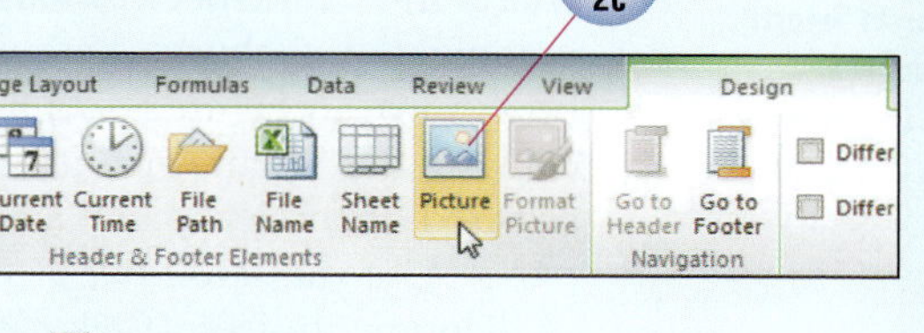

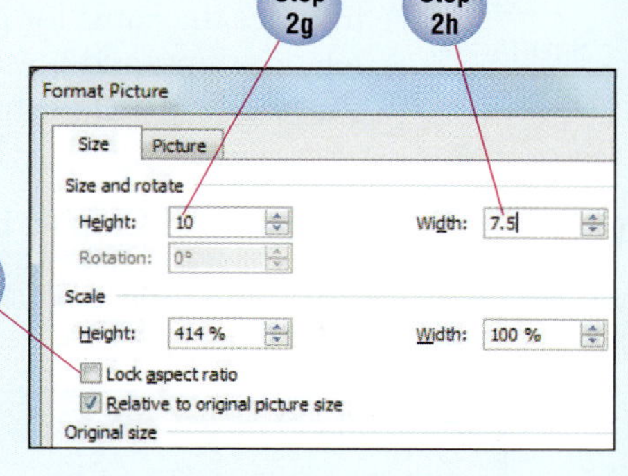

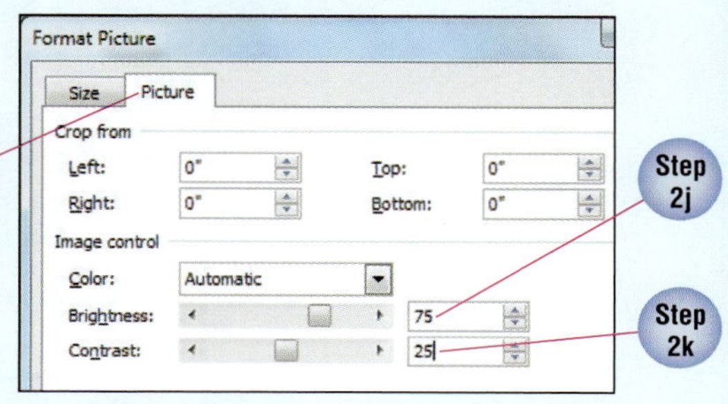

3. Click in the worksheet.
4. Display the worksheet in the Print tab Backstage view to view how the image will print on page 1 and page 2 and then print the worksheet.
5. Save and then close **EL1-C8-P3-HCEqpRpt.xlsx**.

Insert and Format Diagrams in a Company Sales Workbook — 4 Parts

You will open a workbook that contains two company sales worksheets. You will insert and format a cycle diagram in one worksheet and insert and format a relationship diagram in the other. You will also create and format WordArt text.

Inserting a SmartArt Diagram

Quick Steps

Insert SmartArt Diagram
1. Click Insert tab.
2. Click SmartArt button.
3. Double-click desired diagram.

SmartArt

Excel includes the SmartArt feature you can use to insert diagrams and organizational charts in a worksheet. SmartArt offers a variety of predesigned diagrams and organizational charts that are available at the Choose a SmartArt Graphic dialog box shown in Figure 8.7. Display this dialog box by clicking the Insert tab and then clicking the SmartArt button in the Illustrations group. At the dialog box, *All* is selected in the left panel and all available predesigned diagrams display in the middle panel. Use the scroll bar at the right side of the middle panel to scroll down the list of diagram choices. Click a diagram in the middle panel and the name of the diagram displays in the right panel along with a description of the diagram type. SmartArt includes diagrams for presenting a list of data; showing data processes, cycles, and relationships; and presenting data in a matrix or pyramid. Double-click a diagram in the middle panel of the dialog box and the diagram is inserted in the worksheet.

Figure 8.7 Choose a SmartArt Graphic Dialog Box

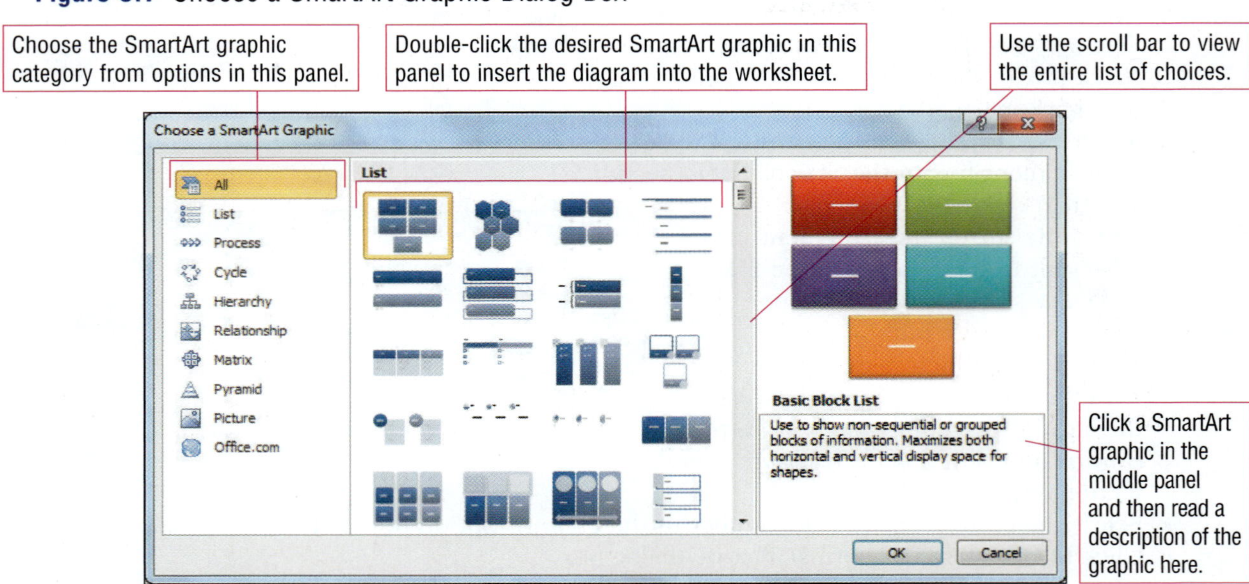
Choose the SmartArt graphic category from options in this panel.
Double-click the desired SmartArt graphic in this panel to insert the diagram into the worksheet.
Use the scroll bar to view the entire list of choices.
Choose a SmartArt Graphic
All
List
Process
Cycle
Hierarchy
Relationship
Matrix
Pyramid
Picture
Office.com
List
Basic Block List
Use to show non-sequential or grouped blocks of information. Maximizes both horizontal and vertical display space for shapes.
OK
Cancel
Click a SmartArt graphic in the middle panel and then read a description of the graphic here.

Entering Data in a Diagram

Some diagrams are designed to include text. You can type text in a diagram by selecting the shape and then typing text in the shape or you can display a text pane and then type text in the pane. Display the text pane by clicking the Text Pane button in the Create Graphic group in the SmartArt Tools Design tab. Turn off the display of the pane by clicking the Text Pane button or by clicking the Close button that displays in the upper right corner of the text pane.

HINT

Generally, you would use a SmartArt diagram to represent text and a chart to represent numbers.

Text Pane

Sizing, Moving, and Deleting a Diagram

Increase or decrease the size of a diagram by dragging the diagram border. Increase or decrease the width of the diagram by positioning the mouse pointer on the set of four dots that displays in the middle of the left and right borders until the pointer turns into a left- and right-pointing arrow, hold down the left mouse button and then drag the border to the desired size. Increase or decrease the height of the diagram in a similar manner using the set of four dots that displays in the middle of the top and bottom borders. To increase or decrease both the height and the width of the diagram, drag one of the sets of three dots that displays in each corner of the border.

To move a diagram, select the diagram and then position the mouse pointer on the diagram border until the pointer turns into a four-headed arrow. Hold down the left mouse button, drag the diagram to the desired position, and then release the mouse button. Delete a diagram by selecting the diagram and then pressing the Delete key.

Project 4a Inserting a Diagram in a Worksheet

Part 1 of 4

1. Open **EPSales.xlsx** and then save the workbook with Save As and name it **EL1-C8-P4-EPSales**.
2. Create the diagram shown in Figure 8.8 on page 291. To begin, click the Insert tab.
3. Click the SmartArt button in the Illustrations group.
4. At the Choose a SmartArt Graphic dialog box, click *Cycle* in the left panel.
5. Double-click *Radial Cycle* as shown at the right.
6. If the text pane is not open, click the Text Pane button in the Create Graphic group. (The text pane will display at the left side of the diagram.)
7. With the insertion point positioned after the top bullet in the text pane, type **Evergreen Products**.
8. Click the *[Text]* box below *Evergreen Products* and then type **Seattle**.
9. Click the next *[Text]* box and then type **Olympia**.

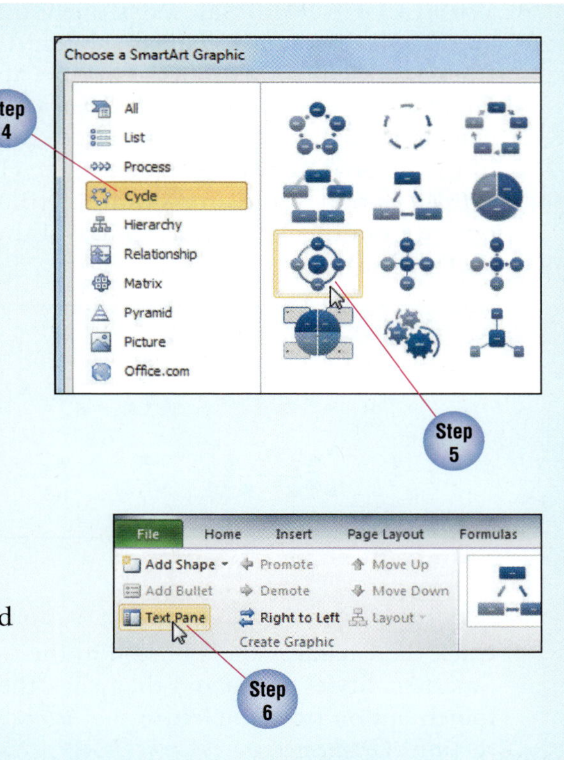

10. Click the next *[Text]* box and then type **Portland**.
11. Click the next *[Text]* box and then type **Spokane**.
12. Click the Text Pane button to turn off the display of the text pane.
13. Drag the diagram so it is positioned as shown in Figure 8.8. To drag the diagram, position the mouse pointer on the diagram border until the pointer turns into a four-headed arrow. Hold down the left mouse button, drag the diagram to the desired position, and then release the mouse button.
14. Increase or decrease the size of the diagram so it displays as shown in Figure 8.8. Use the sets of dots on the diagram border to drag the border to the desired size.
15. Save **EL1-C8-P4-EPSales.xlsx**.

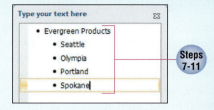

Type your text here
- Evergreen Products
  - Seattle
  - Olympia
  - Portland
  - Spokane

Steps 7-11

To restore the SmartArt default layout and color, click the Reset Graphic button in the Reset group in the SmartArt Tools Design tab.

Changing the Diagram Design

When you double-click a diagram at the dialog box, the diagram is inserted in the worksheet and the SmartArt Tools Design tab is active. With options and buttons in this tab, you can add objects, change the diagram layout, apply a style to the diagram, and reset the diagram back to the original formatting.

Project 4b Changing the Diagram Design

Part 2 of 4

1. With **EL1-C8-P4-EPSales.xlsx** open, make sure the SmartArt Tools Design tab is active and the *Spokane* circle shape is selected.
2. Click the Right to Left button in the Create Graphic group. (This switches *Olympia* and *Spokane*.)
3. Click the More button located at the right side of the SmartArt Styles group and then click the *Polished* option at the drop-down list (first option from the left in the top row of the *3-D* section).

File Home Insert Page Layout
Add Shape Promote Move Up
Add Bullet Demote Move Down
Text Pane Right to Left Layout
Create Graphic

Step 2

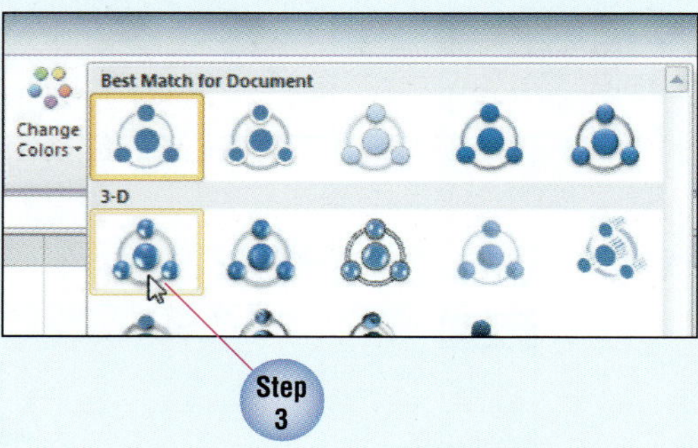

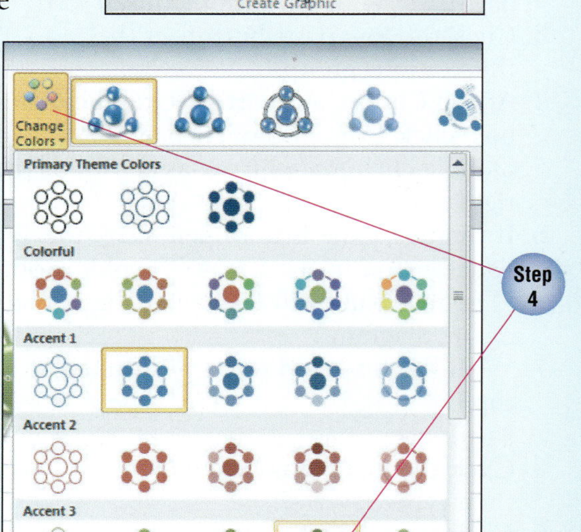

4. Click the Change Colors button in the SmartArt Styles group and then click the fourth option from the left in the *Accent 3* section (*Gradient Loop - Accent 3*).

5. Click outside the diagram to deselect it.
6. Change the orientation to landscape. (Make sure the diagram fits on the first page.)
7. Save **EL1-C8-P4-EPSales.xlsx** and then print the Total Sales worksheet.

Figure 8.8 Projects 4a and 4b

	A	B	C	D
1	**Evergreen Products**			
2	2012 Company Sales			
3	Division	First Half	Second Half	Total Sales
4	Seattle	$ 1,250,360	$ 1,345,200	$ 2,595,560
5	Spokane	$ 905,250	$ 987,550	$ 1,892,800
6	Portland	$ 1,125,000	$ 1,200,500	$ 2,325,500
7	Olympia	$ 705,610	$ 789,450	$ 1,495,060
8	Total	$ 3,986,220	$ 4,322,700	$ 8,308,920
9				

Diagram (columns E–I): Seattle, Olympia, Evergreen Products, Spokane, Portland

Changing the Diagram Formatting

Click the SmartArt Tools Format tab and options display for formatting a diagram. Use buttons in this tab to insert and customize shapes; apply a shape quick style; customize shapes; insert WordArt quick styles; and specify the position, alignment, rotation, wrapping style, height, and width of the diagram.

Project 4c Changing the Diagram Formatting — Part 3 of 4

1. With **EL1-C8-P4-EPSales.xlsx** open, click the Seattle Sales worksheet tab.
2. Create the diagram shown in Figure 8.9. To begin, click the Insert tab and then click the SmartArt button in the Illustrations group.
3. At the Choose a SmartArt Graphic dialog box, click *Relationship* in the left panel and then double-click *Gear* in the middle panel.
4. Click *[Text]* that appears in the bottom gear and then type Quality Products.
5. Click *[Text]* that appears in the left gear and then type Customized Plans.
6. Click *[Text]* that appears in the top gear and then type Exemplary Service.
7. Click inside the diagram border but outside any diagram element.
8. Click the More button that displays at the right side of the SmartArt Styles group and then click the *Inset* option (second option from the left in the top row of the *3-D* section).

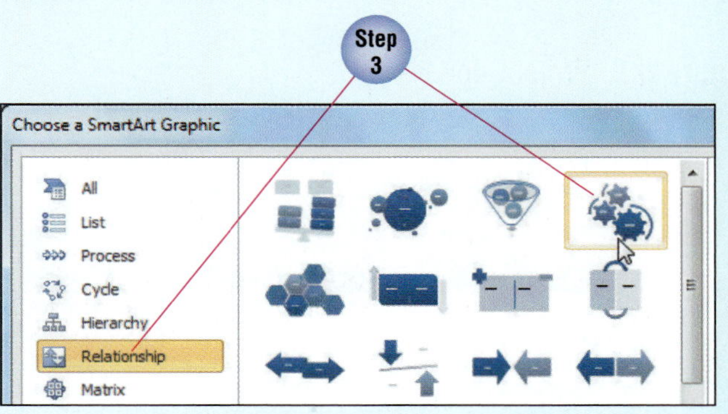

9. Click the Change Colors button in the SmartArt Styles group and then click the third option from the left in the *Accent 3* section (*Gradient Range - Accent 3*).
10. Click the SmartArt Tools Format tab.
11. Click in the *Height* text box in the Size group and then type 3.75.
12. Click in the *Width* text box, type 5.25, and then press Enter.

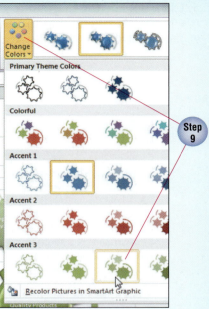

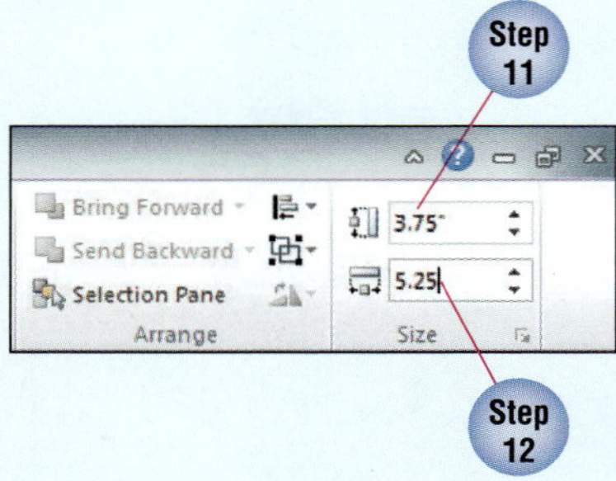

13. Click the bottom gear to select it.
14. Click the Shape Fill button arrow in the Shape Styles group and then click the bottom dark green color (*Olive Green, Accent 3, Darker 50%*) that displays in the *Theme Colors* section.
15. Click the top gear to select it.
16. Click the Shape Fill button arrow and then click the dark green color (*Olive Green, Accent 3, Darker 25%*) that displays in the *Theme Colors* section.

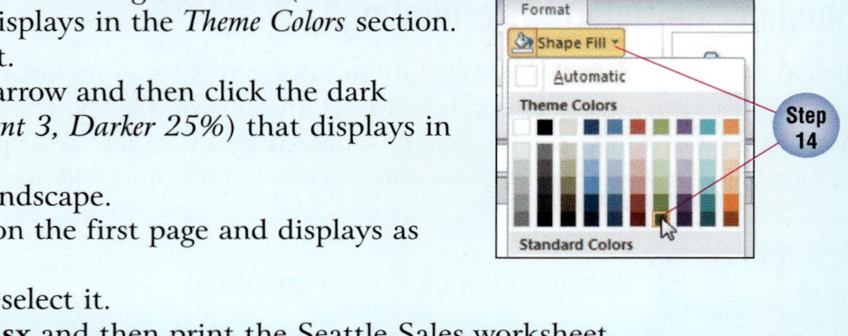

17. Change the orientation to landscape.
18. Move the diagram so it fits on the first page and displays as shown in Figure 8.9.
19. Click outside the chart to deselect it.
20. Save **EL1-C8-P4-EPSales.xlsx** and then print the Seattle Sales worksheet.

Figure 8.9 Project 4c

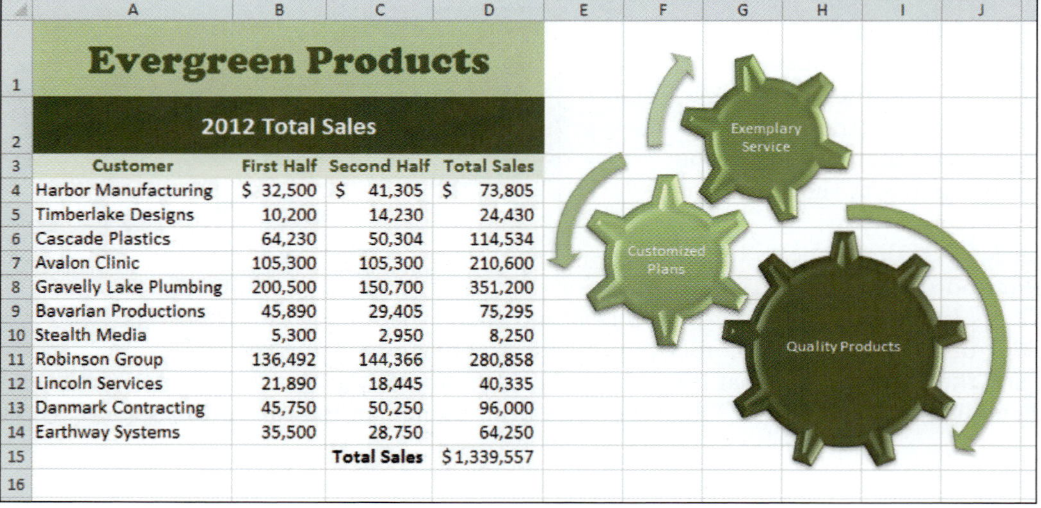

	A	B	C	D
1	Evergreen Products			
2	2012 Total Sales			
3	Customer	First Half	Second Half	Total Sales
4	Harbor Manufacturing	$ 32,500	$ 41,305	$ 73,805
5	Timberlake Designs	10,200	14,230	24,430
6	Cascade Plastics	64,230	50,304	114,534
7	Avalon Clinic	105,300	105,300	210,600
8	Gravelly Lake Plumbing	200,500	150,700	351,200
9	Bavarian Productions	45,890	29,405	75,295
10	Stealth Media	5,300	2,950	8,250
11	Robinson Group	136,492	144,366	280,858
12	Lincoln Services	21,890	18,445	40,335
13	Danmark Contracting	45,750	50,250	96,000
14	Earthway Systems	35,500	28,750	64,250
15			Total Sales	$1,339,557
16				

Creating WordArt

With the WordArt application, you can distort or modify text to conform to a variety of shapes. This is useful for creating company logos and headings. With WordArt, you can change the font, style, and alignment of text. You can also use different fill patterns and colors, customize border lines, and add shadow and three-dimensional effects.

To insert WordArt in an Excel worksheet, click the Insert tab, click the WordArt button in the Text group, and then click the desired option at the drop-down list. This displays *Your Text Here* inserted in the worksheet in the WordArt option you selected at the gallery. Type the desired text and then use the buttons on the Drawing Tools Format tab to format the WordArt.

Quick Steps

Create WordArt
1. Click Insert tab.
2. Click WordArt button.
3. Click desired WordArt style at drop-down list.
4. Type desired text.

To remove WordArt style from text and retain the text, click the More button in the WordArt Styles group in the Drawing Tools Format tab and then click *Clear WordArt*.

WordArt

Sizing and Moving WordArt

WordArt text inserted in a worksheet is surrounded by white sizing handles. Use the white sizing handles to change the height and width of the WordArt text. To move WordArt text, position the arrow pointer on the border of the WordArt until the pointer displays with a four-headed arrow attached. Hold down the left mouse button, drag the outline of the WordArt text box to the desired position, and then release the mouse button. When you change the shape of the WordArt text, the WordArt border displays with a purple diamond shape. Use this shape to change the slant of the WordArt text.

Project 4d **Inserting and Formatting WordArt** Part 4 of 4

1. With **EL1-C8-P4-EPSales.xlsx** open, click the Total Sales worksheet tab.
2. Make cell A1 active and then press the Delete key. (This removes the text from the cell.)
3. Increase the height of row 1 to 136.50.
4. Click the Insert tab.
5. Click the WordArt button in the Text group and then click the last option in the top row (*Fill - Olive Green, Accent 3, Outline - Text 2*).
6. Type **Evergreen**, press the Enter key, and then type **Products**.
7. Position the mouse pointer on the WordArt border until the pointer displays with a four-headed arrow attached and then drag the WordArt inside cell A1.

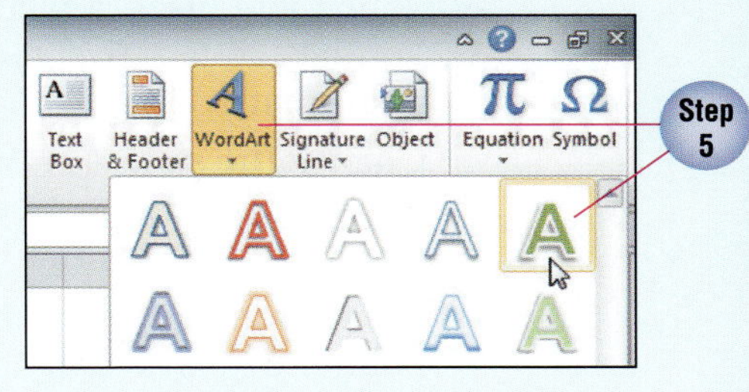

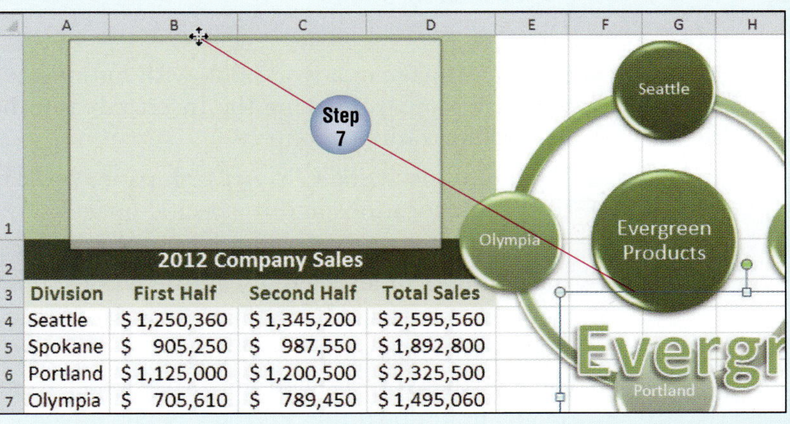

Step 7
2012 Company Sales
Division
First Half
Second Half
Total Sales
Seattle $ 1,250,360 $ 1,345,200 $ 2,595,560
Spokane $ 905,250 $ 987,550 $ 1,892,800
Portland $ 1,125,000 $ 1,200,500 $ 2,325,500
Olympia $ 705,610 $ 789,450 $ 1,495,060
Seattle
Olympia
Evergreen Products
Portland
Evergr

8. Click the Text Fill button arrow in the WordArt Styles group and then click the dark green color (*Olive Green, Accent 3, Darker 25%*).
9. Click the Text Outline button arrow in the WordArt Styles group and then click the dark green color (*Olive Green, Accent 3, Darker 50%*).
10. If necessary, resize the diagram and position it so it prints on one page with the data.
11. Click the Seattle Sales worksheet tab and then complete steps similar to those in Steps 2 through 9 to insert *Evergreen Products* as WordArt.
12. Make sure the SmartArt diagram fits on the page with the data. If necessary, decrease the size of the diagram.
13. Save **EL1-C8-P4-EPSales.xlsx** and then print both worksheets.
14. Close **EL1-C8-P4-EPSales.xlsx**.

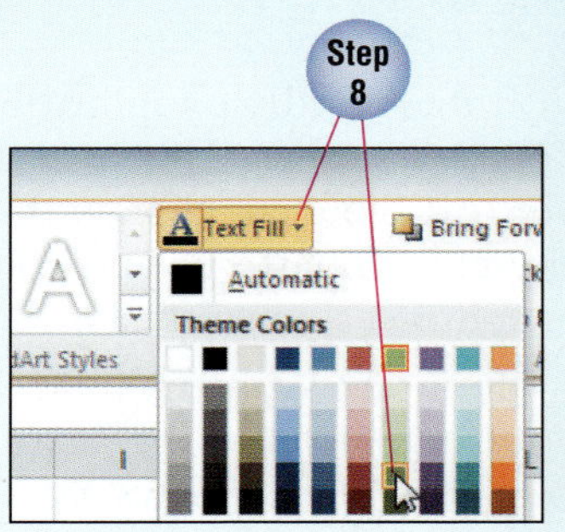

Chapter Summary

- Insert symbols with options at the Symbol dialog box with the Symbols tab or the Special Characters tab selected.
- With buttons in the Illustrations group in the Insert tab, you can insert a picture, clip art image, shape, or a SmartArt diagram.
- When you insert a picture or clip art image in a worksheet, the Picture Tools Format tab is active and includes options for adjusting the image, applying preformatted styles, and arranging and sizing the image.
- Change the size of an image with the *Shape Height* and *Shape Width* measurement boxes in the Size group in the Picture Tools Format tab or with the sizing handles that display around the selected image.
- Move an image by positioning the mouse pointer on the image border until the pointer displays with a four-headed arrow attached and then drag the image to the desired location.
- Delete a selected image by pressing the Delete key.
- Insert an image in a workbook with options at the Clip Art task pane. Display this task pane by clicking the Insert tab and then clicking the Clip Art button in the Illustrations group.
- With options at the Clip Art task pane, you can narrow the search for images to specific locations and to specific images.
- Use the Screenshot button in the Illustrations group in the Insert tab to capture the contents of a screen or capture a portion of a screen.
- To draw shapes in a workbook, click the Insert tab, click the Shapes button in the Illustrations group, and then click the desired shape at the drop-down list. Drag in the worksheet to draw the shape. To maintain the proportions of the shape, hold down the Shift key while dragging in the worksheet.

- Copy a shape with the Copy and Paste buttons in the Clipboard group in the Home tab or by holding down the Ctrl key while dragging the shape.
- You can type text in an enclosed drawn object.
- To insert a picture in a worksheet, click the Insert tab and then click the Picture button in the Illustrations group. At the Insert Picture dialog box, navigate to the desired folder and then double-click the file name.
- Draw a text box in a worksheet by clicking the Insert tab, clicking the Text Box button in the Text group and then dragging in the worksheet. Use options at the Drawing Tools Format tab to format and customize the text box.
- A watermark is a lightened image that displays behind data in a file. You can create a picture watermark in a worksheet by inserting a picture in a header or footer and then changing the size and formatting of the picture.
- Insert a SmartArt diagram in a worksheet by clicking the Insert tab, clicking the SmartArt button in the Illustrations group, and then double-clicking the desired diagram at the Choose a SmartArt Graphic dialog box. Customize a diagram with options in the SmartArt Tools Design tab or the SmartArt Tools Format tab.
- Use WordArt to create, distort, modify, and/or conform text to a variety of shapes. Insert WordArt in a worksheet with the WordArt button in the Text group in the Insert tab. Customize WordArt text with options in the Drawing Tools Format tab.

Commands Review

FEATURE	RIBBON TAB, GROUP	BUTTON
Symbol dialog box	Insert, Symbols	Ω
Clip Art task pane	Insert, Illustrations	
Screenshot	Insert, Illustrations	
Shapes drop-down list	Insert, Illustrations	
Insert Picture dialog box	Insert, Illustrations	
Text box	Insert, Text	
Choose a SmartArt Graphic dialog box	Insert, Illustrations	
WordArt drop-down list	Insert, Text	

Concepts Check Test Your Knowledge

Completion: In the space provided at the right, indicate the correct term, symbol, or command.

1. The Symbol button is located in this tab. ____________________
2. The *Font* option is available at the Symbol dialog box with this tab selected. ____________________
3. Insert a picture, clip art image, screenshot, shape, or SmartArt diagram with buttons in this group in the Insert tab. ____________________
4. When you insert a picture or clip art image in a worksheet, this tab is active. ____________________
5. Maintain the proportions of the image by holding down this key while dragging a sizing handle. ____________________
6. To move an image, position the mouse pointer on the image border until the mouse pointer displays with this attached and then drag the image to the desired location. ____________________
7. To capture a portion of a screen, click the Screenshot button and then click this option at the drop-down list. ____________________
8. To copy a shape, hold down this key while dragging the shape. ____________________
9. When you draw a text box in a worksheet and then release the mouse button, this tab is active. ____________________
10. This term refers to a lightened image that displays behind data in a file. ____________________
11. Click the SmartArt button in the Illustrations group in the Insert tab and this dialog box displays. ____________________

Skills Check Assess Your Performance

Assessment 1

INSERT A CLIP ART IMAGE AND WORDART IN AN EQUIPMENT PURCHASE WORKBOOK

1. Open **ASPurPlans.xlsx** and then save the workbook with Save As and name it **EL1-C8-A1-ASPurPlans**.
2. Insert a formula in cell E4 using the PMT function that calculates monthly payments. ***Hint: Refer to Chapter 2, Project 3a.***
3. Copy the formula in cell E4 down to cells E5 and E6.
4. Insert a formula in cell F4 that calculates the total amount of the payments. ***Hint: Refer to Chapter 2, Project 3a.***
5. Copy the formula in cell F4 down to cells F5 and F6.
6. Insert a formula in cell G4 that calculates the total amount of interest paid. ***Hint: Refer to Chapter 2, Project 3a.***
7. Copy the formula in cell G4 down to cells G5 and G6.
8. Insert the clip art image shown in Figure 8.10 with the following specifications:
   - Search for the clip art image using the search word *movies*. (The colors of the original clip art image are yellow and black.)
   - Change the clip art image color to *Blue, Accent color 1 Light*.
   - Apply the *Brightness: 0% (normal) Contrast: +40%* correction.
   - Apply the *Reflected Rounded Rectangle* picture style.
   - Size and move the image so it is positioned as shown in Figure 8.10.
9. Insert the company name *Azure Studios* in cell A1 as WordArt. Use the *Fill - Blue, Accent 1, Metal Bevel, Reflection* option to create the WordArt.
10. Change the worksheet orientation to landscape.
11. Save, print, and then close **EL1-C8-A1-ASPurPlans.xlsx**.

Figure 8.10 Assessment 1

	A	B	C	D	E	F	G	H
1	AZURE STUDIOS							
2	Equipment Purchase Plans							
3	Equipment	Purchase Price	Interest Rate	Term in Months	Monthly Payments	Total Payments	Total Interest	
4	Photocopier, Model C120	$8,500.00	8.80%	60				
5	Photocopier, Model C150	$12,750.00	8.80%	60				
6	Photocopier, Model C280	$19,250.00	8.80%	60				
7								

Assessment 2

INSERT FORMULAS AND FORMAT A TRAVEL COMPANY WORKBOOK

1. Open **TSGEVacs.xlsx** and then save the workbook with Save As and name it **EL1-C8-A2-TSGEVacs**.
2. Apply the shading to data in cells as shown in Figure 8.11. (Use shading options in the Aqua column.)
3. Insert appropriate formulas to calculate the prices based on a 10 percent and 20 percent discount and apply the appropriate number formatting. ***Hint: For the 10% discount column, multiply the price per person by .90 (this determines 90 percent of the price) and multiply the price per person by .80 for the 20% discount column.***
4. Format the image of the airplane and position as shown in Figure 8.11 with the following specifications:
   a. Use the Remove Background button in the Picture Tools Format tab to remove a portion of the yellow background so your image displays similar to what you see in the figure.
   b. Rotate the image.
   c. Apply the *Brightness: +20% Contrast: +20%* correction.
   d. Position the image as shown in the figure.
5. Open Word and then open the document named **TSAirfare.docx** located in the Excel2010L1C8 folder on your storage medium. Click the Excel button on the Taskbar and then use the Screenshot button (use the *Screen Clipping* option) to select and then insert the airfare information in **EL1-C8-A2-TSGEVacs.xlsx**. Position the information at the right side of the data in the worksheet.
6. Change the orientation to landscape.
7. Make sure the data and the airfare information display on one page and then print the worksheet.
8. Save and then close **EL1-C8-A2-TSGEVacs.xslx**.
9. Click the Word button on the Taskbar and then exit Word.

Figure 8.11 Assessment 2

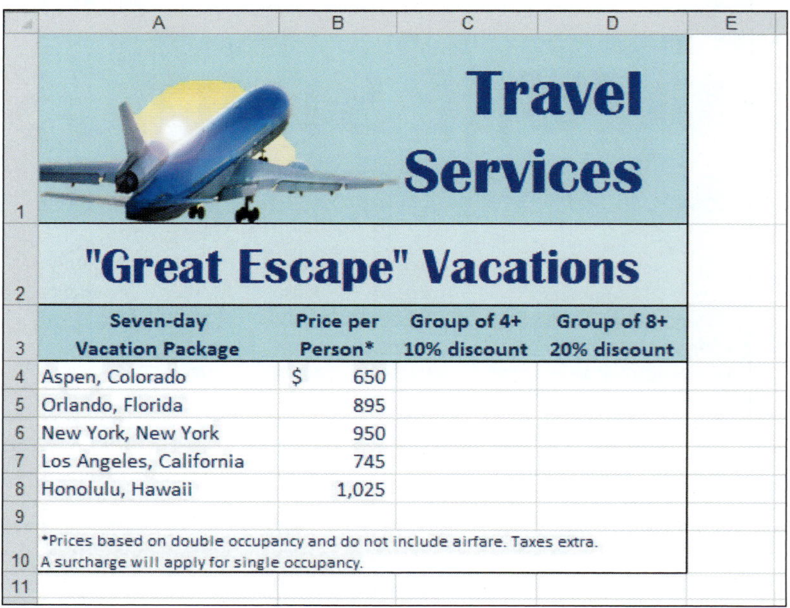

	A	B	C	D	E
1	Travel Services				
2	"Great Escape" Vacations				
3	Seven-day Vacation Package	Price per Person*	Group of 4+ 10% discount	Group of 8+ 20% discount	
4	Aspen, Colorado	$ 650			
5	Orlando, Florida	895			
6	New York, New York	950			
7	Los Angeles, California	745			
8	Honolulu, Hawaii	1,025			
9					
10	*Prices based on double occupancy and do not include airfare. Taxes extra. A surcharge will apply for single occupancy.				
11					

Assessment 3

INSERT AND FORMAT SHAPES IN A COMPANY SALES WORKBOOK

1. Open **MSSales.xlsx** and then save the workbook with Save As and name it **EL1-C8-A3-MSSales**.
2. In cell A1, type Mountain, press Alt + Enter, and then type Systems.
3. Select *Mountain Systems* and then change the font to 26-point Calibri bold.
4. Change the horizontal alignment of cell A1 to left and the vertical alignment to middle.
5. Display the Format Cells dialog box with the Alignment tab selected and then change the *Indent* measurement to *2*. ***Hint: Display the Format Cells dialog box by clicking the Alignment group dialog box launcher in the Home tab.***
6. Click outside cell A1.
7. Use the *Isosceles Triangle* shape located in the *Basic Shapes* section of the Shapes drop-down palette to draw a triangle as shown in Figure 8.12.
8. Copy the triangle three times. Add olive green fill and dark olive green outline color of your choosing to the triangles so they appear in a similar manner to the triangles in Figure 8.12. Position the triangles as shown in the figure.
9. Apply shading to cells as shown in the figure (use colors in the Olive Green column).
10. Insert the total amounts in cells B10 through D10.
11. Insert the arrow pointing to $97,549 using the left arrow shape. Apply olive green fill to the shape and remove the shape outline. Set the text in 10-point Calibri bold. Position the arrow as shown in the figure.
12. Save, print, and then close **EL1-C8-A3-MSSales.xlsx**.

Figure 8.12 Assessment 3

	A	B	C	D	E	F
1	**Mountain Systems**					
2	**FIRST QUARTER SALES - 2012**					
3	**Customer**	**January**	**February**	**March**		
4	Lakeside Trucking	$ 84,231	$ 73,455	$ 97,549	**Largest Order**	
5	Gresham Machines	33,199	40,390	50,112		
6	Real Photography	30,891	35,489	36,400		
7	Genesis Productions	72,190	75,390	83,219		
8	Landower Company	22,188	14,228	38,766		
9	Jewell Enterprises	19,764	50,801	32,188		
10	***Total***					
11						

Assessment

4 INSERT AND FORMAT A SMARTART DIAGRAM IN A SALES WORKBOOK

1. Open **PS2ndQtrSales.xlsx** and then save the workbook with Save As and name it **EL1-C8-A4-PS2ndQtrSales**.
2. Change the orientation to landscape.
3. Insert a pyramid shape at the right side of the worksheet data using the *Pyramid List* diagram with the following specifications:
   a. Change the color to *Gradient Loop - Accent 3*.
   b. Apply the *Cartoon* SmartArt style.
   c. In the bottom text box, type **Red Level**, press Enter, and then type **$25,000 to $49,999**.
   d. In the middle text box, type **Blue Level**, press Enter, and then type **$50,000 to $99,999**.
   e. In the top text box, type **Gold Level**, press Enter, and then type **$100,000+**.
   f. Apply fill to each of the text boxes to match the level color.
4. Size and/or move the diagram so it displays attractively at the right side of the worksheet data. (Make sure the entire diagram will print on the same page as the worksheet data.)
5. Save, print, and then close **EL1-C8-A4-PS2ndQtrSales.xlsx**.

Assessment

5 CREATE AND INSERT A SCREENSHOT

1. Open **RPRefiPlan.xlsx** and then display formulas by pressing Ctrl + `.
2. Insert the arrow shape shown in Figure 8.13. Add fill to the shape, remove the shape outline, bold the text in the shape, and then figure out how to rotate the shape using the rotation handle (green circle). Rotate, size, and position the arrow as shown in the figure.
3. Open Word.
4. At a blank document, press Ctrl + E to center the insertion point, press Ctrl + B to turn on bold, type **Excel Worksheet with PMT Formula**, and then press the Enter key twice.
5. Click the Insert tab, click the Screenshot button, and then click the thumbnail of the Excel worksheet.
6. Save the Word document and name it **EL1-C8-A5-PMTFormula**.
7. Print and then close the document and then exit Word.
8. In Excel, close **RPRefiPlan.xlsx** without saving the changes.

Figure 8.13 Assessment 5

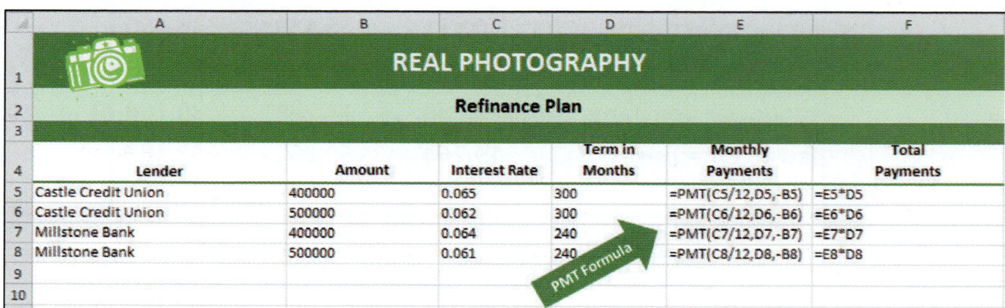

	A	B	C	D	E	F
1	REAL PHOTOGRAPHY					
2	Refinance Plan					
3						
4	Lender	Amount	Interest Rate	Term in Months	Monthly Payments	Total Payments
5	Castle Credit Union	400000	0.065	300	=PMT(C5/12,D5,-B5)	=E5*D5
6	Castle Credit Union	500000	0.062	300	=PMT(C6/12,D6,-B6)	=E6*D6
7	Millstone Bank	400000	0.064	240	=PMT(C7/12,D7,-B7)	=E7*D7
8	Millstone Bank	500000	0.061	240	=PMT(C8/12,D8,-B8)	=E8*D8
9						
10						
11						

Visual Benchmark Demonstrate Your Proficiency

INSERT FORMULAS, WORDART, AND CLIP ART IN A WORKSHEET

1. Open **TSYrlySales.xlsx** and then save the workbook with Save As and name it **EL1-C8-VB-TSYrlySales**.
2. Insert the following formulas in the worksheet shown in Figure 8.14: (***Do not*** type the data in the following cells—instead insert the formulas as indicated. The results of your formulas should match the results you see in the figure.)
    - Cells C4 through C14: Insert a formula with an IF function that inserts *5%* if the amount in the cell in column B is greater than $249,999 and inserts *2%* if the amount is not greater than $249,999.
    - Cells D4 through D14: Insert a formula that multiplies the amount in column B with the amount in column C.
3. Insert the company name *Target Supplies* as WordArt with the following specifications:
    - Use the *Gradient Fill - Black, Outline - White, Outer Shadow* WordArt option.
    - To type the WordArt text, press Ctrl + L (this changes to left text alignment), type **Target**, press Enter, and then type **Supplies**.
    - Change the text outline color to *Orange, Accent 6, Darker 25%*.
    - Move the WordArt so it is positioned as shown in Figure 8.14.
4. Insert the target clip art image (use the word *target* to search for this clip art image) with the following specifications:
    - Change the color to *Red, Accent color 2 Dark*.
    - Change the correction to *Brightness: 0% (Normal) Contrast: +40%*.
    - Apply the *Drop Shadow Rectangle* picture style.
    - Size and position the clip art image as shown in the figure.
5. Draw the shape that displays below the data with the following specifications:
    - Use the *Bevel* shape (located in the *Basic Shapes* section).
    - Type the text in the shape, apply bold formatting, and change to center and middle alignment.
    - Change the shape fill color to *Red, Accent 2, Darker 50%*.
    - Change the shape outline color to *Orange, Accent 6, Darker 25%*.
6. Save and then print the worksheet.
7. Press Ctrl + ` to turn on the display of formulas and then print the worksheet again.
8. Turn off the display of formulas and then close the workbook.

Figure 8.14 Visual Benchmark

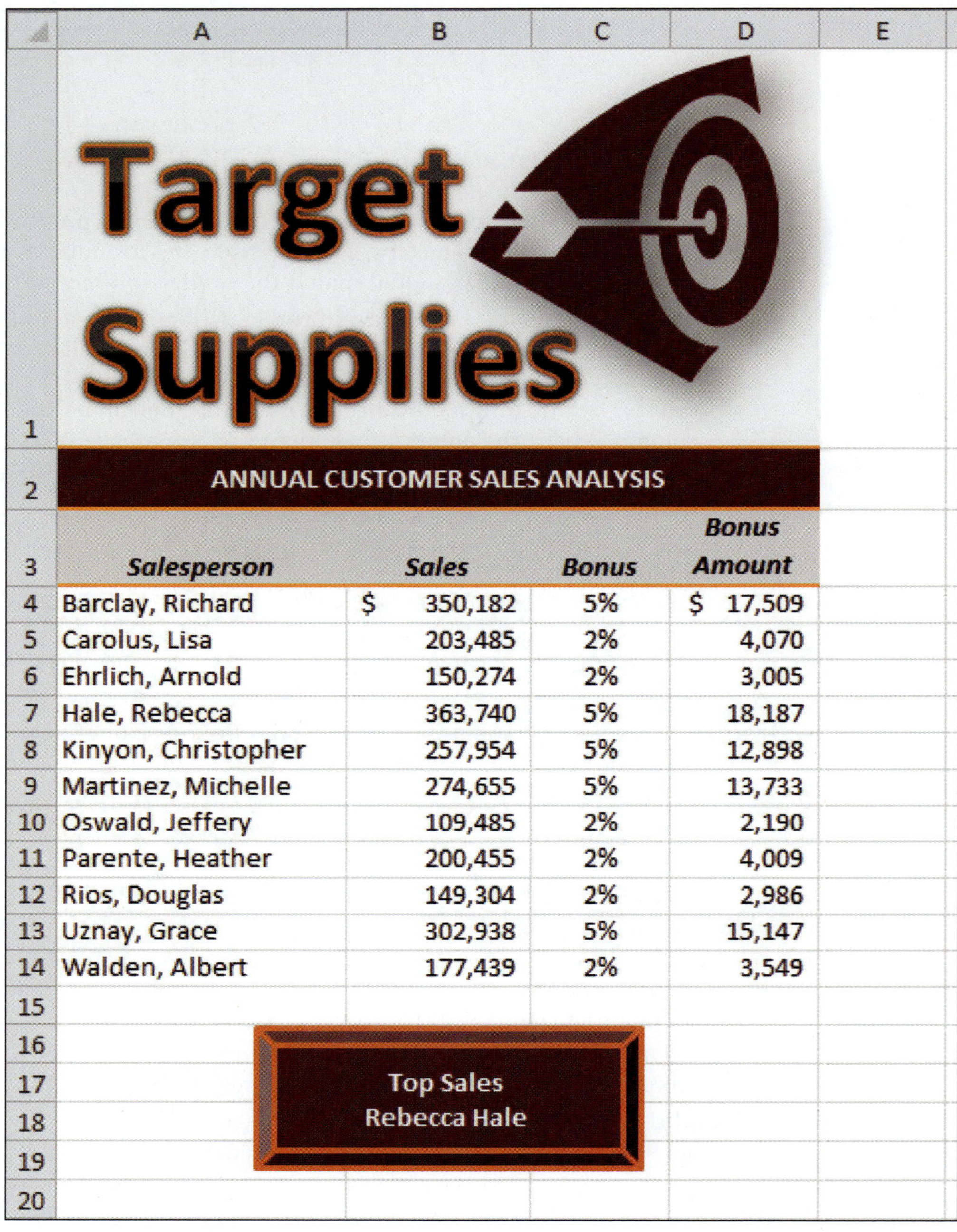

	A	B	C	D	E
1	Target Supplies				
2	ANNUAL CUSTOMER SALES ANALYSIS				
3	*Salesperson*	*Sales*	*Bonus*	*Bonus Amount*	
4	Barclay, Richard	$ 350,182	5%	$ 17,509	
5	Carolus, Lisa	203,485	2%	4,070	
6	Ehrlich, Arnold	150,274	2%	3,005	
7	Hale, Rebecca	363,740	5%	18,187	
8	Kinyon, Christopher	257,954	5%	12,898	
9	Martinez, Michelle	274,655	5%	13,733	
10	Oswald, Jeffery	109,485	2%	2,190	
11	Parente, Heather	200,455	2%	4,009	
12	Rios, Douglas	149,304	2%	2,986	
13	Uznay, Grace	302,938	5%	15,147	
14	Walden, Albert	177,439	2%	3,549	
15					
16					
17		Top Sales			
18		Rebecca Hale			
19					
20					

Case Study Apply Your Skills

Part 1

You are the office manager for Ocean Truck Sales and are responsible for maintaining a spreadsheet of the truck and SUV inventory. Open **OTSales.xlsx** and then save the workbook and name it **EL1-C8-CS-OTSales**. Apply formatting to improve the appearance of the worksheet and insert at least one clip art image (related to "truck" or "ocean"). Save **EL1-C8-CS-OTSales.xlsx** and then print the worksheet.

Part 2

With **EL1-C8-CS-OTSales.xlsx** open, save the workbook with Save As and name it **EL1-C8-CS-OTSalesF&C**. You make the inventory workbook available to each salesperson at the beginning of the week. For easier viewing, you decide to divide the workbook into two worksheets with one worksheet containing all Ford vehicles and the other worksheet containing all Chevrolet vehicles. Rename the worksheet tabs to reflect the contents. Sort each worksheet by price from the most expensive to the least expensive. The owner offers incentives each week to help motivate the sales force. Insert in the first worksheet a SmartArt diagram of your choosing that contains the following information:

Small-sized truck = $100

2WD Regular Cab = $75

SUV 4x4 = $50

Copy the diagram in the first worksheet and then paste it into the second worksheet. Change the orientation to landscape and then save, print, and close **EL1-C8-CS-OTSalesF&C.xlsx**.

Part 3

You have been asked to save the inventory worksheet as a web page for viewing online. Open **EL1-C8-CS-OTSales.xlsx**, display the Save As dialog box, click the *Save as type* option, and then determine how to save the workbook as a single file web page (*.mht, *.mhtml). Save the workbook as a single file web page with the name **EL1-CS-OTSales-WebPage**. Open your Internet browser and then open the web page. Look at the information in the file and then close the Internet browser.

Part 4

As part of your weekly duties, you need to post the incentive diagram in various locations throughout the company. You decide to insert the diagram in PowerPoint for easy printing. Open **EL1-C8-CS-OTSalesF&C.xlsx** and then open PowerPoint. Change the slide layout in PowerPoint to Blank. Copy the diagram in the first worksheet and paste it into the PowerPoint blank slide. Increase and/or move the diagram so it better fills the slide. Print the slide and then close PowerPoint without saving the presentation. Close **EL1-C8-CS-OTSalesF&C.xlsx**.

UNIT 2

Performance Assessment

Note: Before beginning unit assessments, copy to your storage medium the Excel2010L1U2 subfolder from the Excel2010L1 folder on the CD that accompanies this textbook and then make Excel2010L1U2 the active folder.

Assessing Proficiency

In this unit, you have learned how to work with multiple windows; move, copy, link, and paste data between workbooks and applications; create and customize charts with data in a worksheet; save a workbook as a web page; insert hyperlinks; and insert and customize pictures, clip art images, shapes, SmartArt diagrams, and WordArt.

Assessment 1 Copy and Paste Data and Insert WordArt in a Training Scores Workbook

1. Open **RLTraining.xlsx** and then save the workbook with Save As and name it **EL1-U2-A1-RLTraining**.
2. Delete row 15 (the row for *Kwieciak, Kathleen*).
3. Insert a formula in cell D4 that averages the percentages in cells B4 and C4.
4. Copy the formula in cell D4 down to cells D5 through D20.
5. Make cell A22 active, turn on bold, and then type Highest Averages.
6. Display the Clipboard task pane and make sure it is empty.
7. Select and then copy each of the following rows (individually): row 7, 10, 14, 16, and 18.
8. Make cell A23 active and then paste row 14 (the row for *Jewett, Troy*).
9. Make cell A24 active and then paste row 7 (the row for *Cumpston, Kurt*).
10. Make cell A25 active and then paste row 10 (the row for *Fisher-Edwards, Theresa*).
11. Make cell A26 active and then paste row 16 (the row for *Mathias, Caleb*).
12. Make cell A27 active and then paste row 18 (the row for *Nyegaard, Curtis*).
13. Click the Clear All button in the Clipboard task pane and then close the task pane.
14. Insert in cell A1 the text *Roseland* as WordArt. Format the WordArt text to add visual appeal to the worksheet.
15. Save, print, and then close **EL1-U2-A1-RLTraining.xlsx**.

Assessment 2 Manage Multiple Worksheets in a Projected Earnings Workbook

1. Open **RLProjEarnings.xlsx** and then save the workbook with Save As and name it **EL1-U2-A2-RLProjEarnings**.
2. Delete *Roseland* in cell A1. Open **EL1-U2-A1-RLTraining.xlsx** and then copy the *Roseland* WordArt text and paste it into cell A1 in **EL1-U2-A2-RLProjEarnings.xlsx**. If necessary, increase the height of row 1 to accommodate the WordArt text.
3. Notice the fill color in cells in **EL1-U2-A1-RLTraining.xlsx** and then apply the same fill color to cells of data in **EL1-U2-A2-RLProjEarnings.xlsx**. Close **EL1-U2-A1-RLTraining.xlsx**.
4. Select cells A1 through C11 and then copy and paste the cells to Sheet2 keeping the source column widths.
5. With Sheet2 displayed, make the following changes:
   a. Increase the height of row 1 to accommodate the WordArt text.
   b. Delete the contents of cell B2.
   c. Change the contents of the following cells:
      A6: Change *January* to *July*
      A7: Change *February* to *August*
      A8: Change *March* to *September*
      A9: Change *April* to *October*
      A10: Change *May* to *November*
      A11: Change *June* to *December*
      B6: Change *8.30%* to *8.10%*
      B8: Change *9.30%* to *8.70%*
6. Make Sheet1 active and then copy cell B2 and paste link it to cell B2 in Sheet2.
7. Rename Sheet1 to *First Half* and rename Sheet2 to *Second Half*.
8. Make the First Half worksheet active and then determine the effect on projected monthly earnings if the projected yearly income is increased by 10% by changing the number in cell B2 to *$1,480,380*.
9. Horizontally and vertically center both worksheets in the workbook and insert a custom header that prints your name at the left, the current date in the center, and the sheet name (click the Sheet Name button in the Header & Footer Elements group in the Header & Footer Tools Design tab) at the right.
10. Print both worksheets.
11. Determine the effect on projected monthly earnings if the projected yearly income is increased by 20% by changing the number in cell B2 to *$1,614,960*.
12. Save the workbook again and then print both worksheets.
13. Close **EL1-U2-A2-RLProjEarnings.xlsx**.

Assessment 3 Create Charts in Worksheets in a Sales Totals Workbook

1. Open **EPYrlySales.xlsx** and then save the workbook with Save As and name it **EL1-U2-A3-EPYrlySales**.
2. Rename Sheet1 to *2010 Sales*, rename Sheet2 to *2011 Sales*, and rename Sheet3 to *2012 Sales*.
3. Select all three sheet tabs, make cell A12 active, click the Bold button, and then type Total. Make cell B12 active and then insert a formula to total the amounts in cells B4 through B11. Make cell C12 active and then insert a formula to total the amounts in cells C4 through C11.
4. Make the 2010 Sales worksheet active, select cells A3 through C11 (make sure you do not select the totals in row 12) and create a column chart. Click the Switch Row/Column button at the Chart Tools Design tab. Apply formatting to increase the visual appeal of the chart. Drag the chart below the worksheet data. (Make sure the chart fits on the page.)
5. Make the 2011 Sales worksheet active and then create the same type of chart you created in Step 4.
6. Make the 2012 Sales worksheet active and then create the same type of chart you created in Step 4.
7. Save the workbook and then print the entire workbook.
8. Close **EL1-U2-A3-EPYrlySales.xlsx**.

Assessment 4 Create and Format a Line Chart

1. Type the following information in a worksheet:

Country	**Total Sales**
Denmark	$85,345
Finland	$71,450
Norway	$135,230
Sweden	$118,895

2. Using the data just entered in the worksheet, create a line chart with the following specifications:
   a. Apply a chart style of your choosing.
   b. Insert major and minor primary vertical gridlines.
   c. Insert drop lines. (Do this with the Lines button in the Analysis group in the Chart Tools Layout tab.)
   d. Apply any other formatting to improve the visual appeal of the chart.
   e. Move the chart to a new sheet.
3. Save the workbook and name it **EL1-U2-A4-CtrySales**.
4. Print only the sheet containing the chart.
5. Change the line chart to a bar chart of your choosing.
6. Save the workbook and then print only the sheet containing the chart.
7. Close **EL1-U2-A4-CtrySales.xlsx**.

Assessment 5 Create and Format a Pie Chart

1. Open **EPProdDept.xlsx** and then save the workbook with Save As and name it **EL1-U2-A5-EPProdDept**.
2. Create a pie chart as a separate sheet with the data in cells A3 through B10. You determine the type of pie. Include an appropriate title for the chart and include percentage labels.
3. Print only the sheet containing the chart.
4. Save and then close **EL1-U2-A5-EPProdDept.xlsx**.

Assessment 6 Insert a Text Box in and Save a Travel Workbook as a Web Page

1. Open **TravDest.xlsx** and then save the workbook with Save As and name it **EL1-U2-A6-TravDest**.
2. Insert a text box in the workbook with the following specifications:
   a. Draw the text box at the right side of the clip art image.
   b. Remove the fill in the text box and the outline around the text box.
   c. Type **Call 1-888-555-1288 for last-minute vacation specials!**
   d. Select the text and then change the font to 24-point Forte in a blue color.
   e. Size and position the text box so it appears visually balanced with the travel clip art image.
3. Make sure you are connected to the Internet and then search for sites that might be of interest to tourists for each of the cities in the worksheet. Write down the web address for the best web page you find for each city.
4. Create a hyperlink for each city to the web address you wrote down in Step 3. (Select the hyperlink text in each cell and change the font size to 18 points.)
5. Test the hyperlinks to make sure you entered the web addresses correctly by clicking each hyperlink and then closing the web browser.
6. Save, print, and then close **EL1-U2-A6-TravDest.xlsx**.

Assessment 7 Insert Clip Art Image and SmartArt Diagram in a Projected Quotas Workbook

1. Open **SalesQuotas.xlsx** and then save the workbook with Save As and name it **EL1-U2-A7-SalesQuotas**.
2. Insert a formula in cell C3 using an absolute reference to determine the projected quotas at a 10% increase of the current quotas.
3. Copy the formula in cell C3 down to cells C4 through C12. Apply the Accounting Number Format style to cell C3.
4. Insert a clip art image in row 1 related to money. You determine the size and position of the clip art image. If necessary, increase the height of the row.
5. Insert a SmartArt diagram at the right side of the data that contains three shapes. Insert the following quota ranges in the shapes and apply the specified fill color:
   $50,000 to $99,999 (apply green color)
   $100,000 to $149,999 (apply blue color)
   $150,000 to $200,000 (apply red color)
6. Apply formatting to the SmartArt diagram to improve the visual appeal.
7. Insert a custom header that prints your name at the left, the current date in the middle, and the file name at the right.
8. Change the orientation to landscape and make sure the diagram fits on the page.
9. Save, print, and then close **EL1-U2-A7-SalesQuotas.xlsx**.

Assessment 8 Insert Symbol, Clip Art, and Comments in a Sales Workbook

1. Open **CISales.xlsx** and then save the workbook with Save As and name it **EL1-U2-A8-CISales**.
2. Delete the text *Landower Company* in cell A7 and then type **Económico** in the cell. (Use the Symbol dialog box to insert *ó*.)
3. Insert a new row at the beginning of the worksheet.
4. Select and then merge cells A1 through D1.
5. Increase the height of row 1 to approximately 141.00.
6. Insert the text *Custom Interiors* as WordArt in cell A1. You determine the formatting of the WordArt. Move and size the WordArt so it fits in cell A1.
7. Open Word and then open **CICustomers.docx** located in the Excel2010L1U2 folder on your storage medium. Click the Excel button and with **EL1-U2-A8-CISales.xlsx** open, make a screenshot (use the *Screen Clipping* option) of the customer information in the Word document. Position the screenshot image below the data in the cells.
8. Insert a custom footer that prints your name at the left and the file name at the right.
9. Make sure the data in cells and the screenshot display on the same page and then print the worksheet.
10. Save and then close **EL1-U2-A8-CISales.xlsx**.

Assessment 9 Insert and Format a Shape in a Budget Workbook

1. Open **SEExpenses.xlsx** and then save the workbook with Save As and name it **EL1-U2-A9-SEExpenses**.
2. Make the following changes to the worksheet so it displays as shown in Figure U2.1:
   a. Select and then merge cells A1 through D1.
   b. Add fill to the cells as shown in Figure U2.1.
   c. Increase the height of row 1 to the approximate size shown in Figure U2.1.
   d. Type the text **SOLAR ENTERPRISES** in cell A1 set in 20-point Calibri bold, center and middle aligned, and set in aqua (*Aqua, Accent 5, Darker 25%*).
   e. Insert the sun shape (located in the *Basic Shapes* section of the Shapes button drop-down list). Apply orange shape fill and change the shape outline to aqua (*Aqua, Accent 5, Darker 25%*)
3. Save, print, and then close **EL1-U2-A9-SEExpenses.xlsx**.

Figure U2.1 Assessment 9

	A	B	C	D	E
1	SOLAR ENTERPRISES				
2	***Expense***	***Actual***	***Budget***	***% of Actual***	
3	Salaries	$ 126,000.00	$ 124,000.00	98%	
4	Benefits	25,345.00	28,000.00	110%	
5	Commissions	58,000.00	54,500.00	94%	
6	Media space	8,250.00	10,100.00	122%	
7	Travel expenses	6,350.00	6,000.00	94%	
8	Dealer display	4,140.00	4,500.00	109%	
9	Payroll taxes	2,430.00	2,200.00	91%	
10	Telephone	1,450.00	1,500.00	103%	
11					

Writing Activities

The following activities give you the opportunity to practice your writing skills along with demonstrating an understanding of some of the important Excel features you have mastered in this unit. Use correct grammar, appropriate word choices, and clear sentence constructions.

Activity 1 Prepare a Projected Budget

You are the accounting assistant in the financial department of McCormack Funds and you have been asked to prepare a yearly proposed department budget. The total amount for the department is $1,450,000. You are given the percentages for the proposed budget items, which are: Salaries, 45%; Benefits, 12%; Training, 14%; Administrative Costs, 10%; Equipment, 11%; and Supplies, 8%. Create a worksheet with this information that shows the projected yearly budget, the budget items in the department, the percentage of the budget, and the amount for each item. After the worksheet is completed, save the workbook and name it **EL1-U2-Act1-MFBudget**. Print and then close the workbook.

Optional: Using Word 2010, write a memo to the McCormack Funds Finance Department explaining that the proposed annual department budget is attached for their review. Comments and suggestions are to be sent to you within one week. Save the file and name it **EL1-U2-Act1-MFMemo**. Print and then close the file.

Activity 2 Create a Travel Tours Bar Chart

Prepare a worksheet in Excel for Carefree Travels that includes the following information:

Scandinavian Tours	
Country	**Tours Booked**
Norway	52
Sweden	62
Finland	29
Denmark	38

Use the information in the worksheet to create and format a bar chart as a separate sheet. Save the workbook and name it **EL1-U2-Act2-CTTours**. Print only the sheet containing the chart and then close **EL1-U2-Act2-CTTours.xlsx**.

Activity 3 Prepare a Ski Vacation Worksheet

Prepare a worksheet for Carefree Travels that advertises a snow skiing trip. Include the following information in the announcement:

- At the beginning of the worksheet, create a company logo that includes the company name *Carefree Travels* and a clip art image related to travel.
- Include the heading *Whistler Ski Vacation Package* in the worksheet.
- Include the following below the heading:
    - Round-trip air transportation: $395
    - Seven nights' hotel accommodations: $1,550
    - Four all-day ski passes: $425
    - Compact rental car with unlimited mileage: $250
    - Total price of the ski package: (calculate the total price)
- Include the following information somewhere in the worksheet:
    - Book your vacation today at special discount prices.
    - Two-for-one discount at many of the local ski resorts.

Save the workbook and name it **EL1-U2-Act3-CTSkiTrips**. Print and then close **EL1-U2-Act3-CTSkiTrips.xlsx**.

Internet Research

Find Information on Excel Books and Present the Data in a Worksheet

Locate two companies on the Internet that sell new books. At the first new book company site, locate three books on Microsoft Excel. Record the title, author, and price for each book. At the second new book company site, locate the same three books and record the prices. Create an Excel worksheet that includes the following information:

- Name of each new book company
- Title and author of the three books
- Prices for each book from the two book company sites

Create a hyperlink for each book company to the website on the Internet. Then save the completed workbook and name it **EL1-U2-DR-Books**. Print and then close the workbook.

Job Study

Create a Customized Time Card for a Landscaping Company

You are the manager of a landscaping company and are responsible for employee time cards. Locate the time card template that is available with *Sample templates* selected at the New tab Backstage view. Use the template to create a customized time card for your company. With the template open, insert additional blank rows to increase the spacing above the Employee row. Insert a clip art image related to landscaping or gardening and position and size it attractively in the form. Include a text box with the text Lawn and Landscaping Specialists inside the box. Format, size, and position the text attractively in the form. Fill in the form for the current week with the following employee information:

Employee = Jonathan Holder
Address = 12332 South 152nd Street, Baton Rouge, LA 70804
Manager = (Your name)
Employee phone = (225) 555-3092
Employee email = None
Regular hours = 8 hours for Monday, Tuesday, Wednesday, and Thursday
Overtime = 2 hours on Wednesday
Sick hours = None
Vacation = 8 hours on Friday
Rate per hour = $20.00
Overtime pay = $30.00

Save the completed form and name it **EL1-U2-JS-TimeCard**. Print and then close **EL1-U2-JS-TimeCard.xlsx**.

D

I

K

L

M

N

O

X

Y

Level 2

Unit 1 ■ Advanced Formatting, Formulas, and Data Management

CHAPTER 1

Advanced Formatting Techniques

PERFORMANCE OBJECTIVES

Upon successful completion of Chapter 1, you will be able to:

- **Apply conditional formatting by entering parameters for a rule**
- **Apply conditional formatting using a predefined rule**
- **Create and apply a new rule for conditional formatting**
- **Edit, delete, and clear conditional formatting rules**
- **Apply conditional formatting using an icon set, data bars, and color scale**
- **Apply conditional formatting using a formula**
- **Apply fraction and scientific formatting**
- **Apply a special format for a number**
- **Create a custom number format**
- **Apply wrap text and shrink to fit text control options**
- **Filter a worksheet using a custom AutoFilter**
- **Filter and sort a worksheet using conditional formatting or cell attributes**

Tutorials

1.1 Applying Conditional Formatting

1.2 Applying Conditional Formatting Using Icon Sets

1.3 Applying Conditional Formatting Using Data Bars and Color Scales

1.4 Applying Conditional Formatting Using a Formula

1.5 Using Fraction, Scientific, and Special Numbers Formatting

1.6 Creating a Custom Number Format

1.7 Wrapping and Shrinking Text to Fit within a Cell

1.8 Filtering a Worksheet Using a Custom AutoFilter

1.9 Filtering and Sorting Data Using Conditional Formatting and Cell Attributes

Although many worksheets can be formatted using buttons available in the Font, Alignment, and Number groups in the Home tab of the ribbon or in the Mini toolbar, some situations require format categories that are not represented with a button. In other worksheets you may want to make use of Excel's advanced formatting techniques to format based on a condition. In this chapter you will learn how to create, edit, and apply advanced formatting and filtering techniques. Model answers for this chapter's projects appear on the following pages.

Excel2010L2C1

Note: Before beginning the projects, copy to your storage medium the Excel2010L2C1 subfolder from the Excel2010L2 folder on the CD that accompanies this textbook and make Excel2010L2C1 the active folder. Steps on how to copy a folder are presented on the inside of the back cover of this textbook. Do this every time you start a chapter's projects.

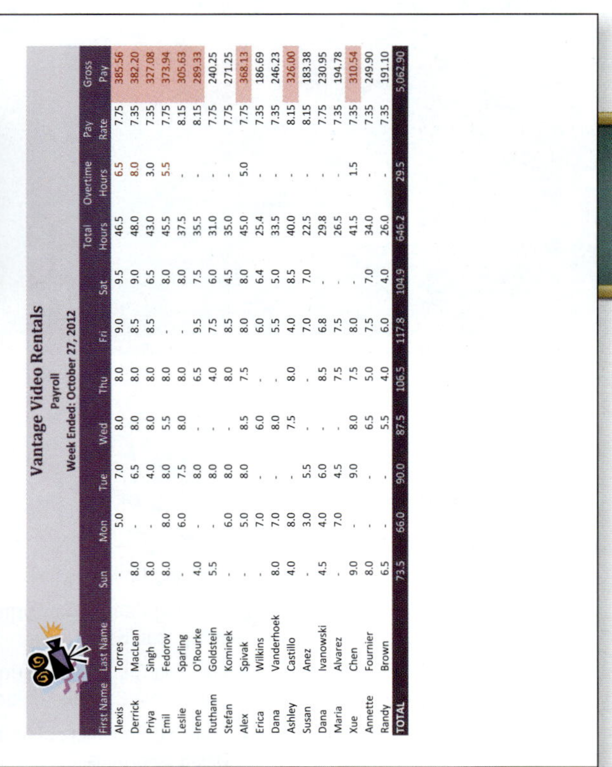

Vantage Video Rentals
Payroll
Week Ended: October 27, 2012

First Name	Last Name	Sun	Mon	Tue	Wed	Thu	Fri	Sat	Total Hours	Overtime Hours	Pay Rate	Gross Pay
Alexis	Torres	-	5.0	7.0	8.0	8.0	9.0	9.5	46.5	6.5	7.75	385.56
Derrick	MacLean	8.0	-	6.5	8.0	8.0	8.5	9.0	48.0	8.0	7.35	382.20
Priya	Singh	8.0	-	4.0	8.0	8.0	8.5	6.5	43.0	3.0	7.35	327.08
Emil	Fedorov	8.0	8.0	8.0	5.5	8.0	-	8.0	45.5	5.5	7.75	373.94
Leslie	Sparling	-	6.0	7.5	8.0	8.0	-	8.0	37.5	-	8.15	305.63
Irene	O'Rourke	4.0	-	8.0	-	6.5	9.5	7.5	35.5	-	8.15	289.33
Ruthann	Goldstein	5.5	-	8.0	-	4.0	7.5	6.0	31.0	-	7.75	240.25
Stefan	Kominek	-	6.0	8.0	-	8.0	8.5	4.5	35.0	-	7.75	271.25
Alex	Spivak	-	5.0	8.0	8.5	7.5	8.0	8.0	45.0	5.0	7.75	368.13
Erica	Wilkins	-	7.0	-	6.0	-	6.0	6.4	25.4	-	7.35	186.69
Dana	Vanderhoek	8.0	7.0	-	8.0	-	5.5	5.0	33.5	-	7.35	246.23
Ashley	Castillo	4.0	8.0	-	7.5	8.0	4.0	8.5	40.0	-	8.15	326.00
Susan	Anez	-	3.0	5.5	-	-	7.0	7.0	22.5	-	8.15	183.38
Dana	Ivanowski	4.5	4.0	6.0	-	8.5	6.8	-	29.8	-	7.75	230.95
Maria	Alvarez	-	7.0	4.5	-	7.5	7.5	-	26.5	-	7.35	194.78
Xue	Chen	9.0	-	9.0	8.0	7.5	8.0	-	41.5	1.5	7.35	310.54
Annette	Fournier	8.0	-	-	6.5	5.0	7.5	7.0	34.0	-	7.35	249.90
Randy	Brown	6.5	-	-	5.5	4.0	6.0	4.0	26.0	-	7.35	191.10
TOTAL		73.5	66.0	90.0	87.5	106.5	117.8	104.9	646.2	29.5		5,062.90

Project 1 Format Cells Based on Values
EL2-C1-P1-VantagePay-Oct27.xlsx

AllClaims Insurance Brokers
Policy Information

Customer ID	Policy ID	No. of Autos	All Perils Deductible	Liability Limit	No. of Drivers	Rating	Claims	Premium
C-025	6512485	2	500	500,000	3	1	0	1,875.00
C-055	6123584	1	250	500,000	2	1	0	995.00
C-072	6583157	2	775	1,000,000	2	2	1	1,575.00
C-085	6124893	3	1,000	500,000	4	2	1	2,250.00
C-094	3481274	1	500	2,000,000	1	5	3	2,150.00
C-114	4956875	2	250	750,000	2	4	2	2,345.00
C-124	3354867	1	250	1,000,000	2	2	1	1,168.00
C-131	6598642	3	775	500,000	4	5	2	3,247.00
C-148	4668457	3	1,000	1,000,000	3	5	2	2,948.00
C-155	8512475	4	500	2,000,000	6	8	4	4,177.00
C-168	6984563	2	250	675,000	2	5	3	2,110.00
C-171	4856972	1	500	500,000	2	6	3	1,845.00
C-184	5124876	1	500	500,000	2	1	0	995.00
C-190	6845962	1	775	900,000	1	3	2	1,550.00
C-199	8457326	1	1,000	2,000,000	1	5	3	2,150.00
C-201	4968532	2	500	500,000	3	2	1	2,025.00
C-212	2698715	2	500	500,000	2	1	0	1,140.00
				Total Policy Premiums:				$ 34,545.00
				Average Number of Claims:			1.6	

Project 2 Apply Conditional Formatting to Insurance Policy Data
EL2-C1-P2-AllClaimsInsce-Autos2+.xlsx

AllClaims Insurance Brokers
Policy Information

Customer ID	Policy ID	No. of Autos	All Perils Deductible	Liability Limit	No. of Drivers	Rating	Claims	Premium
C-025	6512485	2	500	500,000	3	1	0	1,875.00
C-055	6123584	1	250	500,000	2	1	0	995.00
C-072	6583157	2	775	1,000,000	2	2	1	1,575.00
C-085	6124893	3	1,000	500,000	4	2	1	2,250.00
C-094	3481274	1	500	2,000,000	1	5	3	2,150.00
C-114	4956875	2	250	750,000	2	4	2	2,345.00
C-124	3354867	1	250	1,000,000	2	2	1	1,168.00
C-131	6598642	3	775	500,000	4	5	2	3,247.00
C-148	4668457	3	1,000	1,000,000	3	5	2	2,948.00
C-155	8512475	4	500	2,000,000	6	8	4	4,177.00
C-168	6984563	2	250	675,000	2	5	3	2,110.00
C-171	4856972	1	500	500,000	2	6	3	1,845.00
C-184	5124876	1	500	500,000	2	1	0	995.00
C-190	6845962	1	775	900,000	1	3	2	1,550.00
C-199	8457326	1	1,000	2,000,000	1	5	3	2,150.00
C-201	4968532	2	500	500,000	3	2	1	2,025.00
C-212	2698715	2	500	500,000	2	1	0	1,140.00
				Total Policy Premiums:				$ 34,545.00
				Average Number of Claims:			1.6	

EL2-C1-P2-AllClaimsInsce.xlsx

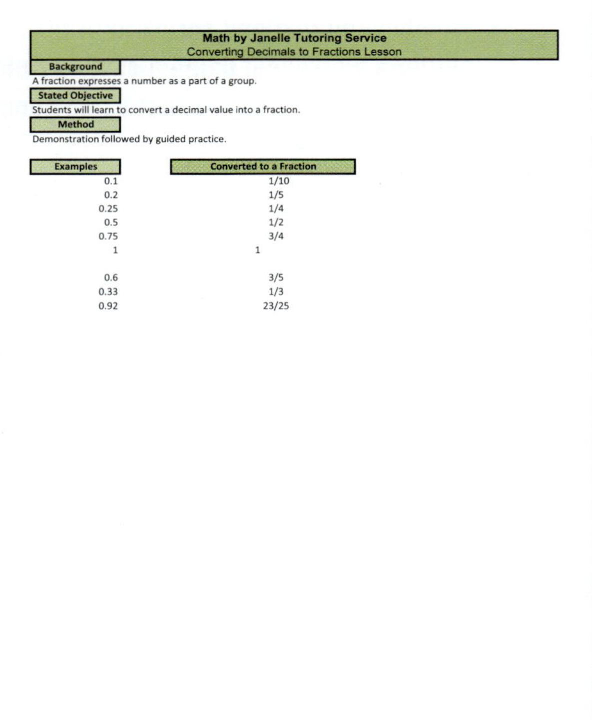

Math by Janelle Tutoring Service
Converting Decimals to Fractions Lesson

Background
A fraction expresses a number as a part of a group.

Stated Objective
Students will learn to convert a decimal value into a fraction.

Method
Demonstration followed by guided practice.

Examples	Converted to a Fraction
0.1	1/10
0.2	1/5
0.25	1/4
0.5	1/2
0.75	3/4
1	1
0.6	3/5
0.33	1/3
0.92	23/25

Project 3 Use Fraction and Scientific Formatting Options
EL2-C1-P3-JanelleTutorMathLsn.xlsx

Model Answers

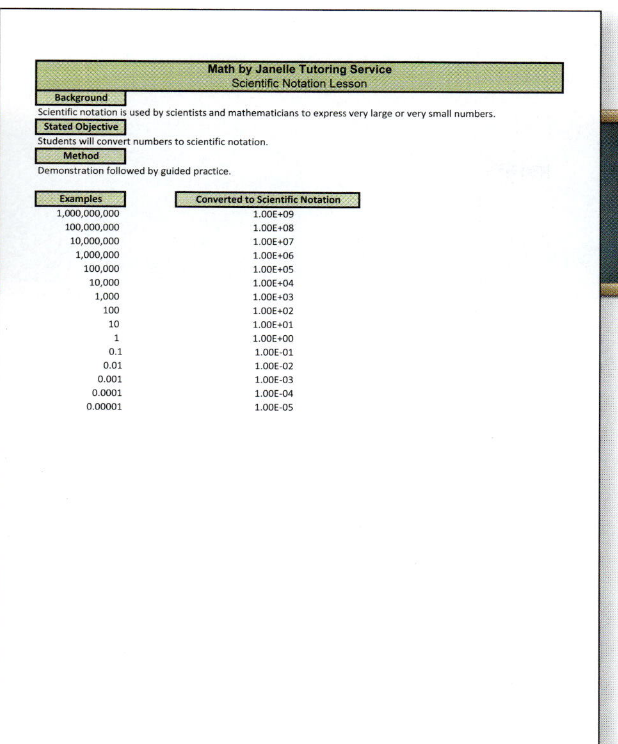

Math by Janelle Tutoring Service Scientific Notation Lesson

Background
Scientific notation is used by scientists and mathematicians to express very large or very small numbers.

Stated Objective
Students will convert numbers to scientific notation.

Method
Demonstration followed by guided practice.

Examples	Converted to Scientific Notation
1,000,000,000	1.00E+09
100,000,000	1.00E+08
10,000,000	1.00E+07
1,000,000	1.00E+06
100,000	1.00E+05
10,000	1.00E+04
1,000	1.00E+03
100	1.00E+02
10	1.00E+01
1	1.00E+00
0.1	1.00E-01
0.01	1.00E-02
0.001	1.00E-03
0.0001	1.00E-04
0.00001	1.00E-05

EL2-C1-P3-JanelleTutorMathLsn.xlsx

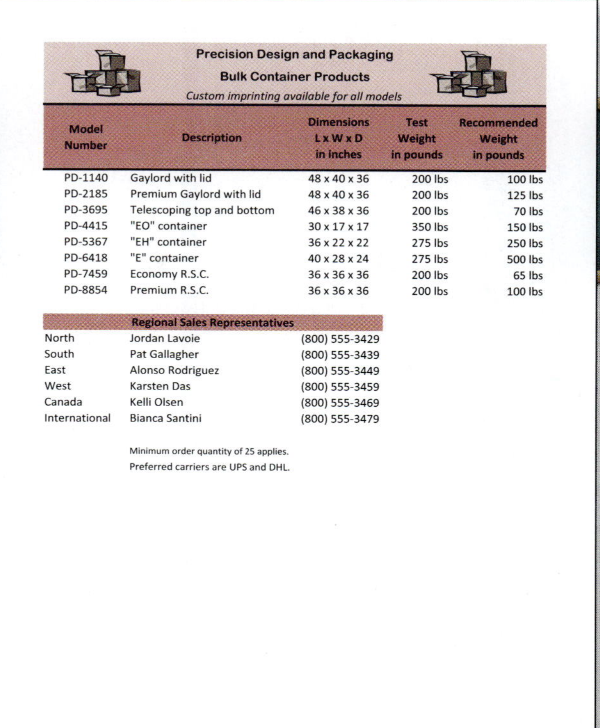

Precision Design and Packaging
Bulk Container Products
Custom imprinting available for all models

Model Number	Description	Dimensions L x W x D in inches	Test Weight in pounds	Recommended Weight in pounds
PD-1140	Gaylord with lid	48 x 40 x 36	200 lbs	100 lbs
PD-2185	Premium Gaylord with lid	48 x 40 x 36	200 lbs	125 lbs
PD-3695	Telescoping top and bottom	46 x 38 x 36	200 lbs	70 lbs
PD-4415	"EO" container	30 x 17 x 17	350 lbs	150 lbs
PD-5367	"EH" container	36 x 22 x 22	275 lbs	250 lbs
PD-6418	"E" container	40 x 28 x 24	275 lbs	500 lbs
PD-7459	Economy R.S.C.	36 x 36 x 36	200 lbs	65 lbs
PD-8854	Premium R.S.C.	36 x 36 x 36	200 lbs	100 lbs

Regional Sales Representatives		
North	Jordan Lavoie	(800) 555-3429
South	Pat Gallagher	(800) 555-3439
East	Alonso Rodriguez	(800) 555-3449
West	Karsten Das	(800) 555-3459
Canada	Kelli Olsen	(800) 555-3469
International	Bianca Santini	(800) 555-3479

Minimum order quantity of 25 applies.
Preferred carriers are UPS and DHL.

Project 4 Apply Advanced Formatting Options

EL2-C1-P4-PrecisionProducts.xlsx

AllClaims Insurance Brokers Policy Information								
Customer ID	Policy ID	No. of Autos	All Perils Deductible	Liability Limit	No. of Drivers	Rating	Claims	Premium
C-114	4956875	2	250	750,000	2	4	2	2,345.00
C-131	6598642	3	775	500,000	4	5	2	3,247.00
C-148	4668457	3	1,000	1,000,000	3	5	2	2,948.00
C-168	6984563	2	250	675,000	2	5	3	2,110.00
C-171	4856972	1	500	500,000	2	6	3	1,845.00
C-190	6845962	1	775	900,000	1	3	2	1,550.00

Project 5 Filter and Sort Data Based on Values, Icon Set, and Font Color

EL2-C1-P5-AllClaimsInsce.xlsx

AllClaims Insurance Brokers Policy Information								
Customer ID	Policy ID	No. of Autos	All Perils Deductible	Liability Limit	No. of Drivers	Rating	Claims	Premium
C-055	6123584	● 1	250	500,000	2	1	0	995.00
C-094	3481274	● 1	500	2,000,000	1	5	3	2,150.00
C-124	3354867	● 1	250	1,000,000	2	2	1	1,168.00
C-171	4856972	● 1	500	500,000	2	6	3	1,845.00
C-184	5124876	● 1	500	500,000	2	1	0	995.00
C-190	6845962	● 1	775	900,000	1	3	2	1,550.00
C-199	8457326	● 1	1,000	2,000,000	1	5	3	2,150.00

EL2-C1-P5-AllClaimsInsce-1Auto.xlsx

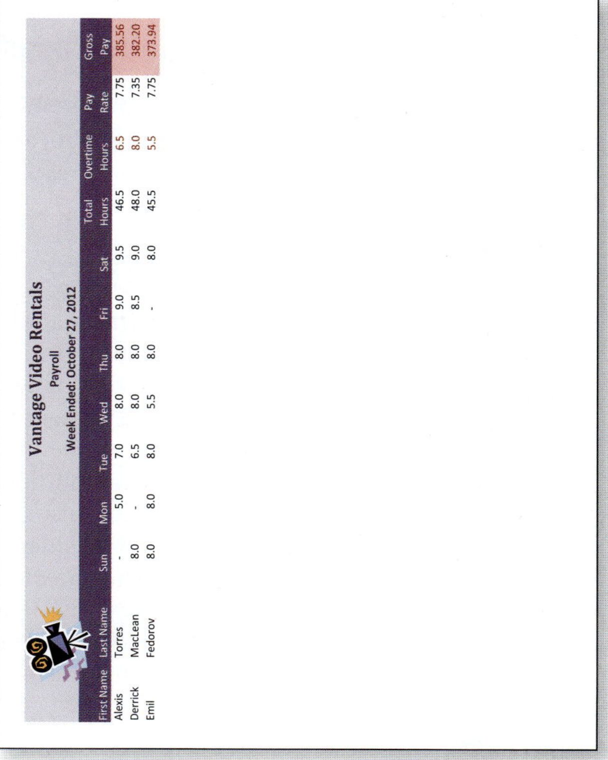

Vantage Video Rentals
Payroll
Week Ended: October 27, 2012

First Name	Last Name	Sun	Mon	Tue	Wed	Thu	Fri	Sat	Total Hours	Overtime Hours	Pay Rate	Gross Pay
Alexis	Torres	-	5.0	7.0	8.0	8.0	9.0	9.5	46.5	6.5	7.75	385.56
Derrick	MacLean	8.0	-	6.5	8.0	8.0	8.5	9.0	48.0	8.0	7.35	382.20
Emil	Fedorov	8.0	8.0	8.0	5.5	8.0	-	8.0	45.5	5.5	7.75	373.94

EL2-C1-P5-VantagePay-Oct27-HighOT.xlsx

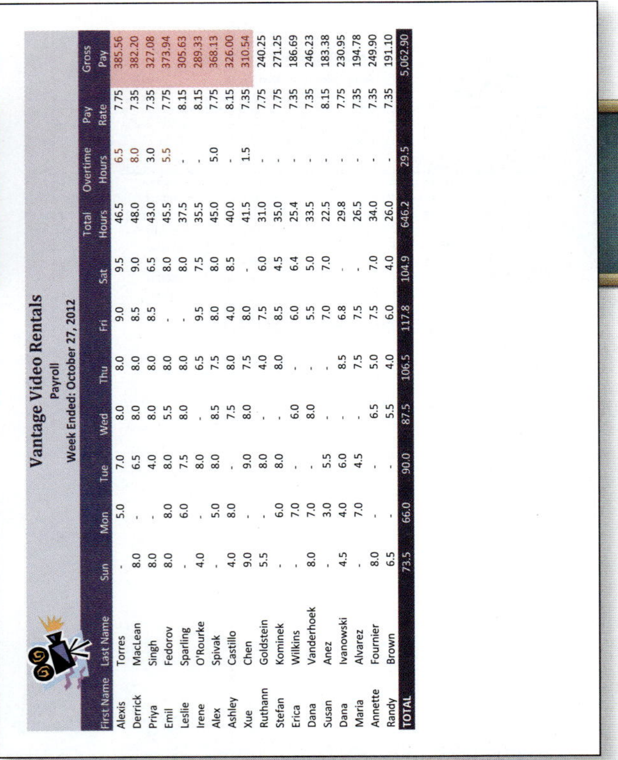

Vantage Video Rentals
Payroll
Week Ended: October 27, 2012

First Name	Last Name	Sun	Mon	Tue	Wed	Thu	Fri	Sat	Total Hours	Overtime Hours	Pay Rate	Gross Pay
Alexis	Torres	-	5.0	7.0	8.0	8.0	9.0	9.5	46.5	6.5	7.75	385.56
Derrick	MacLean	8.0	-	6.5	8.0	8.0	8.5	9.0	48.0	8.0	7.35	382.20
Priya	Singh	8.0	-	4.0	8.0	8.0	8.5	6.5	43.0	3.0	7.35	327.08
Emil	Fedorov	8.0	8.0	8.0	5.5	8.0	-	8.0	45.5	5.5	7.75	373.94
Leslie	Sparling	-	6.0	7.5	8.0	8.0	-	8.0	37.5	-	8.15	305.63
Irene	O'Rourke	4.0	-	8.0	-	6.5	9.5	7.5	35.5	-	8.15	289.33
Alex	Spivak	-	5.0	8.0	8.5	7.5	8.0	8.0	45.0	5.0	7.75	368.13
Ashley	Castillo	4.0	8.0	-	7.5	8.0	4.0	8.5	40.0	-	8.15	326.00
Xue	Chen	9.0	-	9.0	8.0	7.5	8.0	-	41.5	1.5	7.35	310.54
Ruthann	Goldstein	5.5	-	8.0	-	4.0	7.5	6.0	31.0	-	7.75	240.25
Stefan	Kominek	-	6.0	8.0	-	8.0	8.5	4.5	35.0	-	7.75	271.25
Erica	Wilkins	-	7.0	-	6.0	-	6.0	6.4	25.4	-	7.35	186.69
Dana	Vanderhoek	8.0	7.0	-	8.0	-	5.5	5.0	33.5	-	7.35	246.23
Susan	Anez	-	3.0	5.5	-	-	7.0	7.0	22.5	-	8.15	183.38
Dana	Ivanowski	4.5	4.0	6.0	-	8.5	6.8	-	29.8	-	7.75	230.95
Maria	Alvarez	-	7.0	4.5	-	7.5	7.5	-	26.5	-	7.35	194.78
Annette	Fournier	8.0	-	-	6.5	5.0	7.5	7.0	34.0	-	7.35	249.90
Randy	Brown	6.5	-	-	5.5	4.0	6.0	4.0	26.0	-	7.35	191.10
TOTAL		73.5	66.0	90.0	87.5	106.5	117.8	104.9	646.2	29.5		5,062.90

EL2-C1-P5-VantagePay-Oct27-Sorted.xlsx

Model Answers

Project 1 Format Cells Based on Values — 2 Parts

Working with a payroll worksheet, you will change the appearance of cells based on criteria related to overtime hours and gross pay.

Quick Steps

Apply Conditional Formatting Using Predefined Rule

1. Select desired range.
2. Click Conditional Formatting button.
3. Point to desired rule category.
4. Click desired rule.
5. If necessary, enter parameter value.
6. If necessary, change format options.
7. Click OK.

Conditional Formatting

Conditional Formatting

Conditional formatting applies format changes to a range of cells for those cells within the selection that meet a condition. Cells that do not meet the condition remain unformatted. Changing the appearance of a cell based on a condition allows you to quickly identify values that are high, low, or that represent a trend. Formatting can be applied based on a specific value, a value that falls within a range, or by using a comparison operator such as equals (=), greater than (>), or less than (<). Conditional formats can also be based on date, text entries, or duplicated values. Consider using conditional formatting to analyze a question such as *Which store locations earned sales above their target?* Using a different color and/or shading the cells that exceeded a sales target easily identifies the top performers. Excel 2010 provides predefined conditional formatting rules accessed from the Conditional Formatting button drop-down list shown in Figure 1.1. You can also create your own conditional formatting rules.

Figure 1.1 Conditional Formatting Button Drop-down List

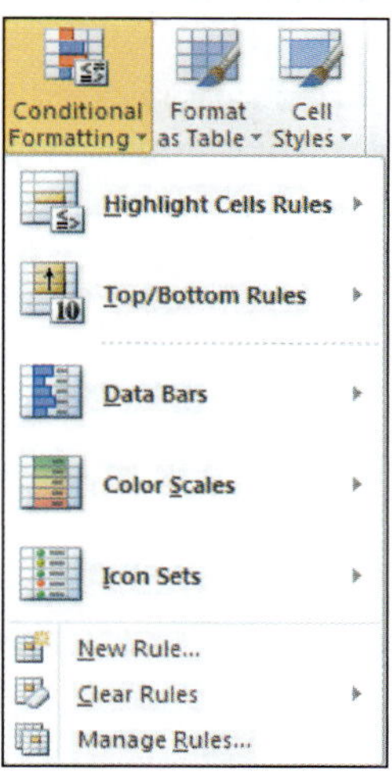

Project 1a Formatting Cells Based on a Value Comparison

Part 1 of 2

1. Start Excel.
2. Open **VantagePay-Oct27.xlsx**. (This workbook is located in the Excel2010L2C1 folder you copied to your storage medium.)
3. Save the workbook with Save As and name it **EL2-C1-P1-VantagePay-Oct27**.
4. Apply conditional formatting to highlight overtime hours that exceeded 5 for the week by completing the following steps:
   a. Select K6:K23.
   b. Click the Conditional Formatting button in the Styles group of the Home tab.
   c. Point to *Highlight Cells Rules* and then click *Greater Than* at the drop-down list.
   d. At the Greater Than dialog box, with the text already selected in the *Format cells that are GREATER THAN* text box, type 5.
   e. Click the down-pointing arrow next to the list box to the right of *with* (currently displays *Light Red Fill with Dark Red Text*) and then click *Red Text* at the drop-down list.
   f. Click OK to close the Greater Than dialog box and apply the conditional format.
   g. Click in any cell to deselect the range.
   h. Review the cells that have been conditionally formatted. Notice that cells with overtime hours greater than 5 are formatted with red text.
5. Save **EL2-C1-P1-VantagePay-Oct27.xlsx**.

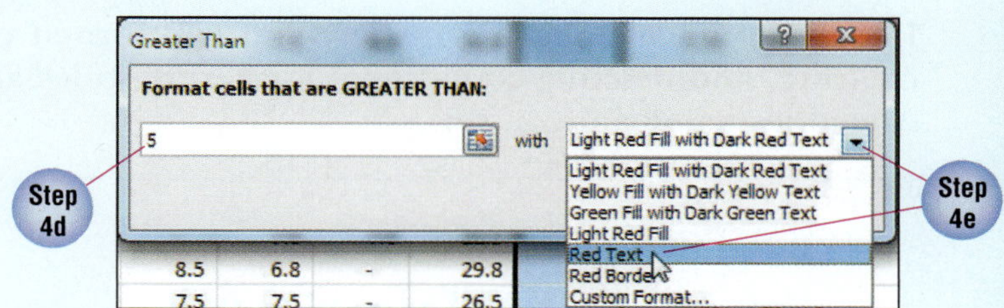

Using the Top/Bottom Rules list you can elect to highlight cells based on a top ten or bottom ten value or percent, or by above average or below average values.

Formatting Cells Based on Top/Bottom Rules Part 2 of 2

1. With **EL2-C1-P1-VantagePay-Oct27.xlsx** open, apply conditional formatting to the Gross Pay values to identify employees who earned above average wages for the week by completing the following steps:
   a. Select M6:M23.
   b. Click the Conditional Formatting button in the Styles group of the Home tab.
   c. Point to *Top/Bottom Rules* and then click *Above Average* at the drop-down list.
   d. At the Above Average dialog box, with *Light Red Fill with Dark Red Text* selected in the *Format cells that are ABOVE AVERAGE* list box, click OK.

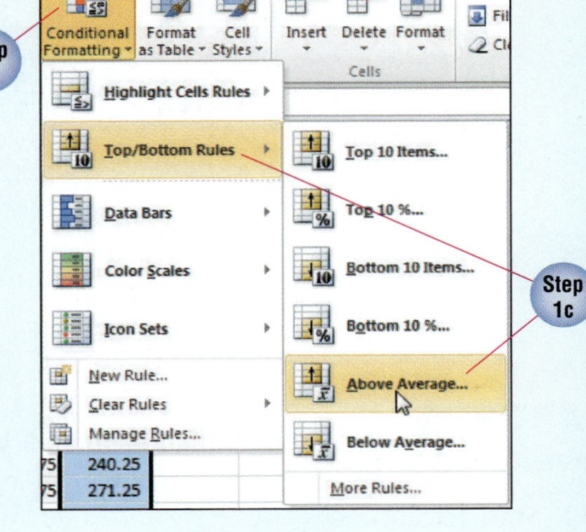

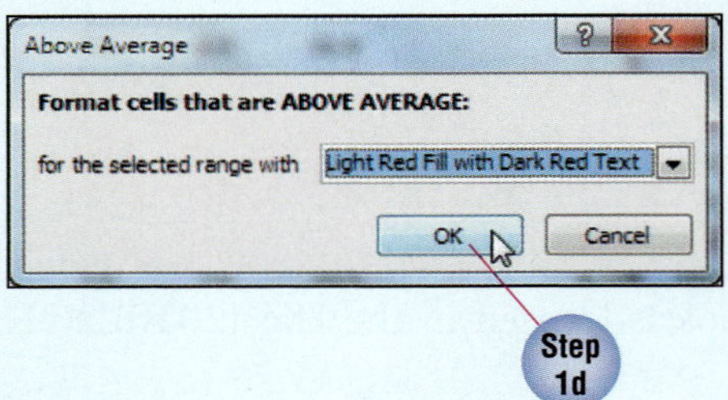

   e. Click in any cell to deselect the range.
   f. Review the cells that have been conditionally formatted.
2. Print the worksheet.
3. Save and then close **EL2-C1-P1-VantagePay-Oct27.xlsx**.

Project 2 Apply Conditional Formatting to Insurance Policy Data

4 Parts

In an insurance claims worksheet you will format cells by creating, editing, clearing, and deleting conditional formatting rules and by classifying data into categories using an icon set.

Creating a New Formatting Rule

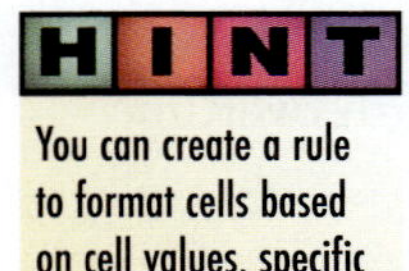

You can create a rule to format cells based on cell values, specific text, dates, blank, or error values.

Cells are conditionally formatted based on a rule. A rule defines the criterion by which the cell is selected for formatting and includes the formatting attributes that are applied to cells that meet the criterion. The predefined rules that you used in Project 1a and Project 1b allowed you to use the feature without having to specify each component in the rule's parameters. At the New Formatting Rule dialog box shown in Figure 1.2, you can create your own custom conditional formatting rule in which you define all parts of the criterion and the formatting. The *Edit the Rule Description* section of the dialog box varies depending on the active option in the *Select a Rule Type* section.

Figure 1.2 New Formatting Rule Dialog Box

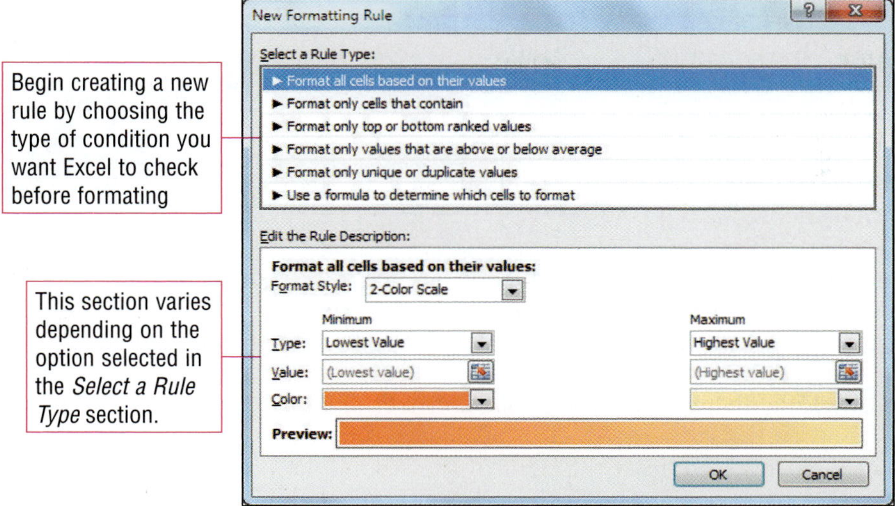

Quick Steps

Create and Apply New Formatting Rule

1. Select desired range.
2. Click Conditional Formatting button.
3. Click *New Rule*.
4. Click desired rule type.
5. Add criteria as required.
6. Click Format button.
7. Select desired formatting attributes.
8. Click OK to close Format Cells dialog box.
9. Click OK to close New Formatting Rule dialog box.

Project 2a Creating and Applying New Formatting Rules

Part 1 of 4

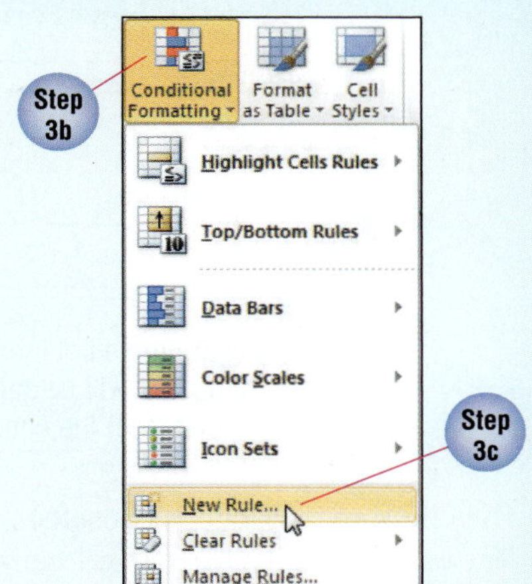

1. Open **AllClaimsInsce.xlsx**.
2. Save the workbook with Save As and name it **EL2-C1-P2-AllClaimsInsce**.
3. The owner of AllClaims Insurance Brokers is considering changing the discount plan for those customers with no claims or with only one claim. The owner would like to see the two claim criteria formatted in color to provide a reference for how many customers this discount would affect. Create a formatting rule that will change the appearance of cells in the claims columns for those values that equal 0 by completing the following steps:
   a. Select H4:H20.
   b. Click the Conditional Formatting button in the Styles group in the Home tab.
   c. Click *New Rule* at the drop-down list.
   d. At the New Formatting Rule dialog box, click *Format only cells that contain* in the *Select a Rule Type* section.
   e. Click the down-pointing arrow located at the right of the second list box from the left in the *Format only cells with* section (currently displays *between*) and then click *equal to* at the drop-down list.

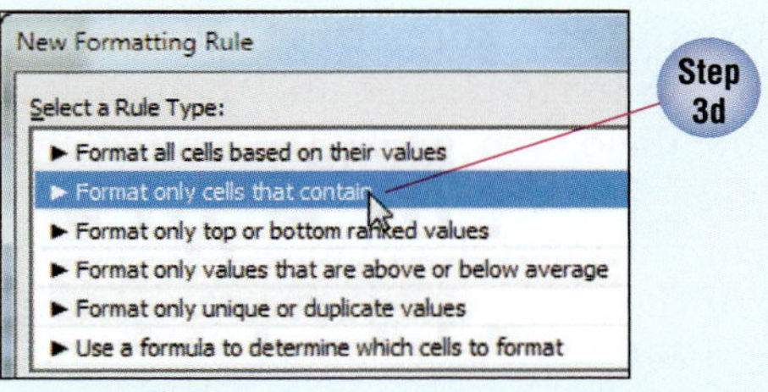

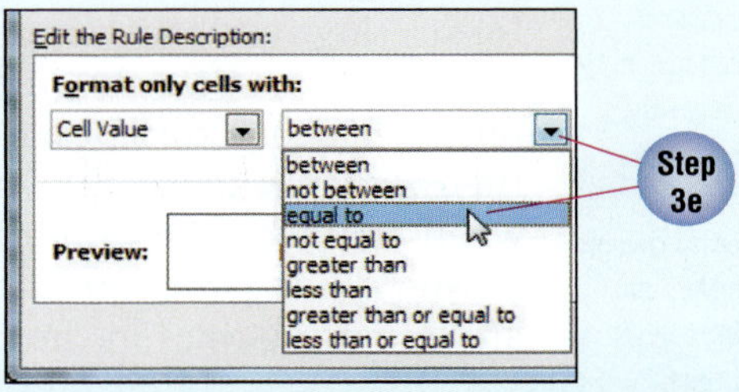

f. Click in the blank text box next to *equal to* and then type 0.
g. Click the Format button in the *Preview* section.
h. At the Format Cells dialog box with the Font tab selected, change the *Color* to *Dark Red* (in the *Standard Colors* section), turn on bold, and then click OK.
i. Click OK at the New Formatting Rule dialog box.

4. Create a second formatting rule that will change the appearance of cells in the claims columns for those values that equal 1 by completing the following steps:
   a. With H4:H20 still selected, click the Conditional Formatting button and then click *New Rule*.
   b. At the New Formatting Rule dialog box, click *Format only cells that contain* in the *Select a Rule Type* section.
   c. Click the down-pointing arrow located at the right of the second list box from the left in the *Format only cells with* section (currently displays *between*) and then click *equal to* at the drop-down list.
   d. Click in the blank text box next to *equal to* and then type 1.
   e. Click the Format button.
   f. At the Format Cells dialog box with the Font tab selected, change the *Color* to *Purple* (in the *Standard Colors* section), turn on bold, and then click OK.
   g. Click OK at the New Formatting Rule dialog box.

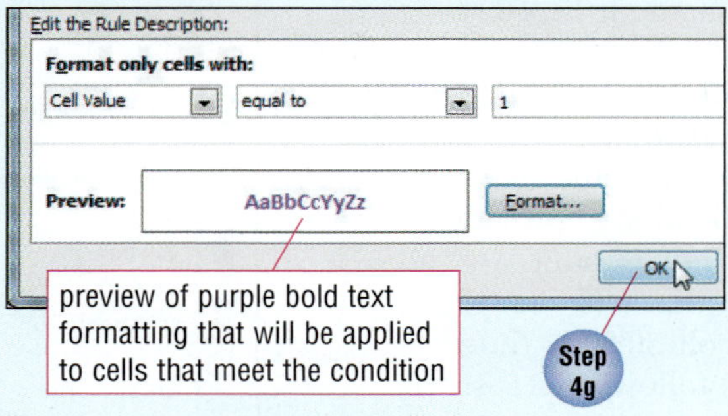

Rating	Claims
1	0
1	0
2	1
2	1
5	3
4	2
2	1
5	2
5	2
8	4
5	3
6	3
1	0
3	2
5	3
2	1
1	0

dark red bold formatting applied to cells containing 0 and purple bold formatting applied to cells containing 1

5. Click in any cell to deselect the range and review the conditionally formatted cells in column H.
6. Save **EL2-C1-P2-AllClaimsInsce.xlsx**.

Quick Steps

Edit Formatting Rule
1. Select range.
2. Click Conditional Formatting button.
3. Click *Manage Rules*.
4. Click desired rule.
5. Click Edit Rule button.
6. Make desired changes to parameters and/or formatting options.
7. Click OK twice.

Editing and Deleting Conditional Formatting Rules

Edit the comparison rule criteria and/or formatting options for a conditional formatting rule by opening the Conditional Formatting Rules Manager dialog box. Click to select the rule that you want to change and then click the Edit Rule button. At the Edit Formatting Rule dialog box, make the desired changes and then click OK twice. By default, *Show formatting rules for* is set to *Current Selection* when you open the Conditional Formatting Rules Manager. If necessary, click the down-pointing arrow to the right of the list box and select *This Worksheet* to show all formatting rules in the current sheet.

To remove conditional formatting from a range, select the range, click the Conditional Formatting button, point to *Clear Rules* at the drop-down list, and then click either *Clear Rules from Selected Cells* or *Clear Rules from Entire Sheet*. You can also delete a custom rule at the Conditional Formatting Rules Manager dialog box. Formatting options applied to the cells by the rule that was deleted are removed.

Quick Steps

Delete Formatting Rule
1. Click Conditional Formatting button.
2. Click *Manage Rules.*
3. Change *Show formatting rules for* to *This Worksheet.*
4. Click desired rule.
5. Click Delete Rule button.
6. Click OK.

Project 2b **Creating, Editing, and Deleting a Formatting Rule** Part 2 of 4

1. With **EL2-C1-P2-AllClaimsInsce.xlsx** open, create a new formatting rule to add a fill color to the cells in the *No. of Autos* column for those policies that have more than two cars by completing the following steps:
   a. Select C4:C20.
   b. Click the Conditional Formatting button and then click *New Rule* at the drop-down list.
   c. Click *Format only cells that contain* in the *Select a Rule Type* section of the New Formatting Rule dialog box.
   d. In the *Edit the Rule Description* section, change the rule's parameters to format only cells with a *Cell Value greater than 2*. (If necessary, refer to Project 2a, Steps 3e to 3f for assistance.)

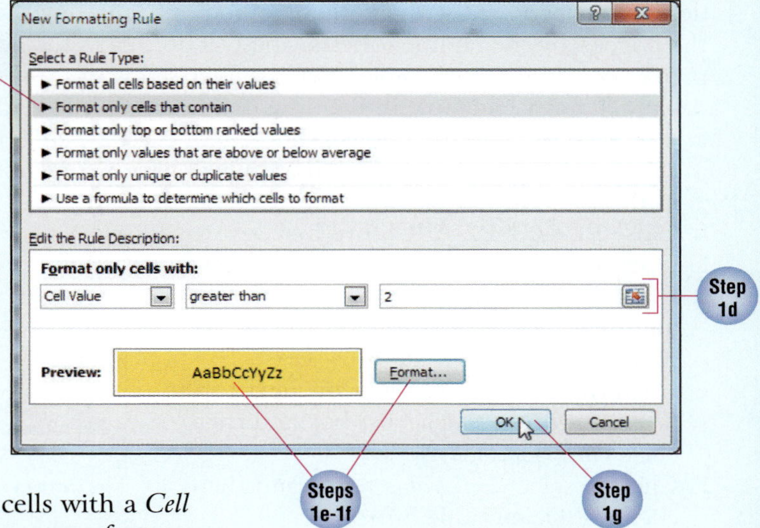

   e. Click the Format button and then click the Fill tab at the Format Cells dialog box.
   f. Click the *Yellow* color square (fourth from left in last row) in the *Background Color* palette and then click OK.
   g. Click OK to close the New Formatting Rule dialog box and apply the rule to the selected cells.
   h. Deselect the range by clicking any cell.
2. After reviewing the formatted cells, you decide that cells should be formatted for all policies with 2 or more cars. Edit the formatting rule by completing the following steps:
   a. Select C4:C20.
   b. Click the Conditional Formatting button and then click *Manage Rules* at the drop-down list.

Customer ID	Policy ID	No. of Autos
C-025	6512485	2
C-055	6123584	1
C-072	6583157	2
C-085	6124893	3
C-094	3481274	1
C-114	4956875	2
C-124	3354867	1
C-131	6598642	3
C-148	4668457	3
C-155	8512475	4
C-168	6984563	2
C-171	4856972	1
C-184	5124876	1
C-190	6845962	1
C-199	8457326	1
C-201	4968532	2
C-212	2698715	2

formatting applied to cell values greater than 2

c. Click to select *Cell Value > 2* in the Conditional Formatting Rules Manager dialog box and then click the Edit Rule button.
d. Click the down-pointing arrow next to the second list box (currently displays *greater than*) and then click *greater than or equal to* at the drop-down list.
e. Click OK.
f. Click OK to close the Conditional Formatting Rules Manager dialog box and apply the revised rule to the selected cells.
g. Deselect the range by clicking any cell.

3. Save and print the worksheet.
4. After reviewing the printed copy of the formatted worksheet, you decide to experiment with another method of formatting the data that classifies the policies by the number of cars. You will do this in the next project. In preparation for the next project, save the revised worksheet under a new name and then delete the formatting rule in the original worksheet by completing the following steps:
   a. Use Save As to name the workbook **EL2-C1-P2-AllClaimsInsce-Autos2+**. By saving the workbook under a new name you will have a copy of the conditional formatting applied in this project.
   b. Close **EL2-C1-P2-AllClaimsInsce-Autos2+.xlsx**.
   c. Open **EL2-C1-P2-AllClaimsInsce.xlsx**.
   d. Click the Conditional Formatting button and then click *Manage Rules* at the drop-down list.
   e. Click the down-pointing arrow next to the *Show formatting rules for* list box and then click *This Worksheet*.
   f. Click to select *Cell Value >= 2* and then click the Delete Rule button.
   g. Click OK to close the Conditional Formatting Rules Manager dialog box. Notice the formatting has been removed from the cells in column C.

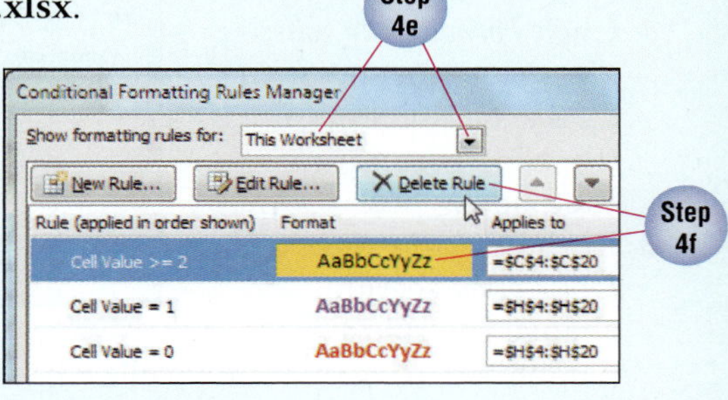

5. Save **EL2-C1-P2-AllClaimsInsce.xlsx**.

Conditional Formatting Using Icon Sets

Quick Steps

Apply Conditional Formatting Using Icon Set
1. Select desired range.
2. Click Conditional Formatting button.
3. Point to *Icon Sets*.
4. Click desired icon set.
5. Deselect range.

Format a range of values using an icon set to classify data into three to five categories. Excel places an icon in a cell to visually portray the cell's value relative to the other cell values within the selected range. Using an icon set, you can group similar data to easily spot high points, low points, or other trends. Icons are assigned to cells based on default threshold values for the selected range. For example, if you choose the *3 Arrows (Colored)* icon set, icons are assigned as follows:

- Green up arrow for values greater than or equal to 67 percent
- Red down arrow for values less than 33 percent
- Yellow sideways arrow for values between 33 and 67 percent

The available icon sets are shown in Figure 1.3 grouped into four sections: *Directional*, *Shapes*, *Indicators*, and *Ratings*. Choose the icon set that best represents the number of different categories within the range and the desired symbol type such as directional colored arrows, traffic light shapes, flag indicators, star ratings, and so on. You can modify the default threshold values or create your own icon set by opening the Manage Rules dialog box and editing an existing rule or creating a new rule.

Green Up Arrow

Red Down Arrow

Yellow Sideways Arrow

Figure 1.3 Conditional Formatting Icon Sets Gallery

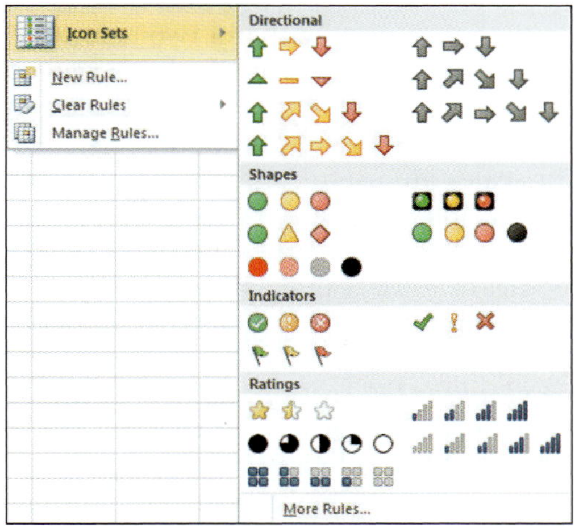

Project 2c Applying Conditional Formatting Using an Icon Set

Part 3 of 4

1. With **EL2-C1-P2-AllClaimsInsce.xlsx** open, select C4:C20.
2. Classify the number of automobiles into categories using an icon set by completing the following steps:
   a. Click the Conditional Formatting button.
   b. Point to *Icon Sets*.
   c. Click *Red To Black* at the Icon Sets drop-down gallery (third icon set in the left column of the Shapes section).
   d. Click in any cell to deselect the range. Notice that Excel assigns an icon to each cell that correlates to the icon with the value group. For example, all cells containing the value 1 have the same icon, all cells containing the value 2 have the same icon, and so on.

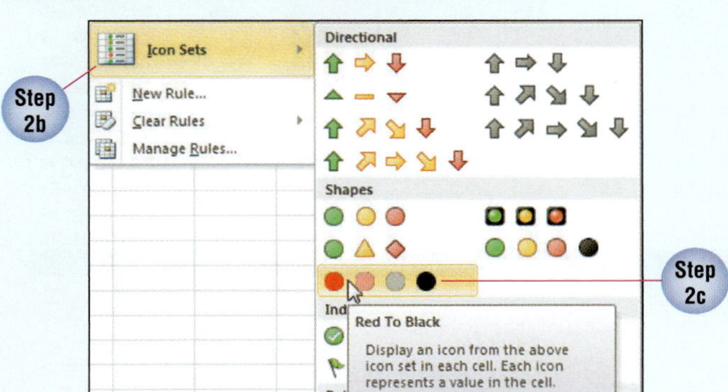

No. of Autos
2
1
2
3
1
2
1
3
3
4
2
1
1
1
1
2
2

Step 2d

3. Save **EL2-C1-P2-AllClaimsInsce.xlsx**.

Conditional Formatting Using Data Bars and Color Scales

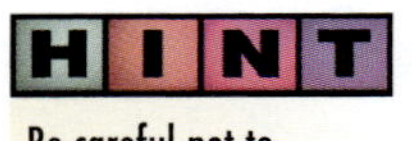

Be careful not to overdo icon sets, color scales, and data bars. A reader can quickly lose focus with too many items competing for one's attention.

Excel 2010 also provides the ability to conditionally format cells using two-color scales, three-color scales, or data bars to provide visual guides to identify distributions or variations within a range. Use a data bar to easily see the higher and lower values within the range. A bar is added to the background of the cell with the length of the bar dependent on the value within the cell. A cell with a higher value within the range displays a longer bar than a cell with a lower value within the range. Excel offers six colors for bars, available in either a gradient fill or a solid fill.

Color scales format the range using either a two-color or three-color palette. Excel provides 12 color scale options, half of which are two-color combinations and half of which are three-color combinations. The gradation of color applied to a cell illustrates the cell's value in comparison to higher or lower values within the range. Color scales are useful to view the distribution of the data. In a two-color scale, the shade applied to a cell represents either a higher or lower value within the range. In a three-color scale, the shade of color applied to a cell represents a higher, middle, or lower value within the range. Figure 1.4 displays the payroll worksheet for Vantage Video Rentals with data bar and color scale conditional formatting applied. In column M, gross pay is shown with the Red Data Bar from the *Gradient Fill* section applied to the column. Notice the length of the colored bars in the background of the cells for various gross pay amounts. In column J, the *Red-White* two-color scale has been applied to show the distribution of total hours. Cells with higher values are displayed in gradations of red, while the lowest cell in the range is displayed in white and then white is mixed with red to achieve increasingly darker shades of pink in cells as the values increase.

Figure 1.4 Data Bar and Color Scale Conditional Formatting Applied to Payroll Worksheet

	A	B	C	D	E	F	G	H	I	J	K	L	M
1						Vantage Video Rentals							
2						Payroll							
3						Week Ended: October 27, 2012							
4										Total	Overtime	Pay	Gross
5	First Name	Last Name	Sun	Mon	Tue	Wed	Thu	Fri	Sat	Hours	Hours	Rate	Pay
6	Alexis	Torres	-	5.0	7.0	8.0	8.0	9.0	9.5	46.5	6.5	7.75	385.56
7	Derrick	MacLean	8.0	-	6.5	8.0	8.0	8.5	9.0	48.0	8.0	7.35	382.20
8	Priya	Singh	8.0	-	4.0	8.0	8.0	8.5	6.5	43.0	3.0	7.35	327.08
9	Emil	Fedorov	8.0	8.0	8.0	5.5	8.0	-	8.0	45.5	5.5	7.75	373.94
10	Leslie	Sparling	-	6.0	7.5	8.0	8.0	-	8.0	37.5	-	8.15	305.63
11	Irene	O'Rourke	4.0	-	8.0	-	6.5	9.5	7.5	35.5	-	8.15	289.33
12	Ruthann	Goldstein	5.5	-	8.0	-	4.0	7.5	6.0	31.0	-	7.75	240.25
13	Stefan	Kominek	-	6.0	8.0	-	8.0	8.5	4.5	35.0	-	7.75	271.25
14	Alex	Spivak	-	5.0	8.0	8.5	7.5	8.0	8.0	45.0	5.0	7.75	368.13
15	Erica	Wilkins	-	7.0	-	6.0	-	6.0	6.4	25.4	-	7.35	186.69
16	Dana	Vanderhoek	8.0	7.0	-	8.0	-	5.5	5.0	33.5	-	7.35	246.23
17	Ashley	Castillo	4.0	8.0	-	7.5	8.0	4.0	8.5	40.0	-	8.15	326.00
18	Susan	Anez	-	3.0	5.5	-	-	7.0	7.0	22.5	-	8.15	183.38
19	Dana	Ivanowski	4.5	4.0	6.0	-	8.5	6.8	-	29.8	-	7.75	230.95
20	Maria	Alvarez	-	7.0	4.5	-	7.5	7.5	-	26.5	-	7.35	194.78
21	Xue	Chen	9.0	-	9.0	8.0	7.5	8.0	-	41.5	1.5	7.35	310.54
22	Annette	Fournier	8.0	-	-	6.5	5.0	7.5	7.0	34.0	-	7.35	249.90
23	Randy	Brown	6.5	-	-	5.5	4.0	6.0	4.0	26.0	-	7.35	191.10
24	TOTAL		73.5	66.0	90.0	87.5	106.5	117.8	104.9	646.2	29.5		5,062.90

Gross Pay column with data bar conditional formatting applied

Total Hours column with *Red-White* color scale conditional formatting applied

Conditional Formatting Using a Formula

Sometimes you may want to format a cell based upon the value in another cell or by some other logical test. At the New Formatting Rule dialog box, choose *Use a formula to determine which cells to format* in the *Select a Rule Type* section. You can enter a formula, such as an IF statement, that is used to determine if a cell is formatted. For example, in Project 2d, you will format the premium values in the insurance worksheet in column I based on the rating value for each policy that is stored in column G. In this project, an IF statement allows you to conditionally format the premiums if the rating value for the policy is greater than 3. The IF function's logical test returns only a true or false result. The value in the rating cell is either greater than 3 (true), or it is not greater than 3 (false). Excel conditionally formats only those cells for which the conditional test returns a true result.

The formula that you will enter into the New Formatting Rule dialog box in Project 2d is: *=if(g4:g20>3,true,false)*. In the first cell in the selected range (I4), Excel will perform the following test: *is the value in G4 greater than 3?* In the first row, this test returns a false result so Excel will not conditionally format the value in I4. For those cells in which the test returns a true result, Excel will apply bold red font color to the cell.

Project 2d Applying Conditional Formatting Using a Formula

Part 4 of 4

1. With **EL2-C1-P2-AllClaimsInsce.xlsx** open, clear the conditional formatting applied in the *Claims* column by completing the following steps:
   a. Select H4:H20.
   b. Click the Conditional Formatting button, point to *Clear Rules*, and then click *Clear Rules from Selected Cells*.
   c. Click in any cell to deselect the range.

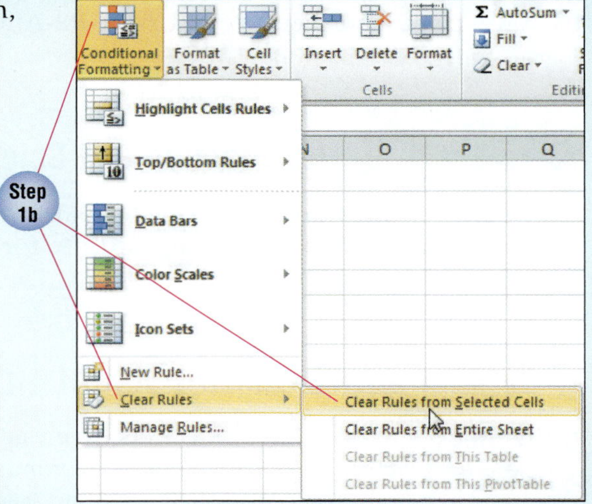

2. The owner of AllClaims Insurance Brokers would like the premiums for those clients who have a rating higher than 3 to stand out from the other cells. You decide to conditionally format the premiums using a formula that checks the value in the rating column by completing the following steps:
   a. Select I4:I20 and then click the Conditional Formatting button.
   b. Click *New Rule* at the drop-down list.
   c. At the New Formatting Rule dialog box, click *Use a formula to determine which cells to format* in the *Select a Rule Type* section.
   d. Click in the *Format values where this formula is true* text box in the *Edit the Rule Description* section of the New Formatting Rule dialog box and then type **=if(g4:g20>3,true,false)**.
   e. Click the Format button.
   f. At the Format Cells dialog box, click the Font tab and change the font color to *Red* (in the *Standard Colors* section), apply bold, and then click OK.
   g. Click OK to close the New Formatting Rule dialog box and apply the rule to the selected cells.
   h. Click in any cell to deselect the range. Notice that the cells that have bold red font color applied in column I are those for which the corresponding rating value in column G is greater than 3.
3. Save, print, and then close **EL2-C1-P2-AllClaimsInsce.xlsx**.

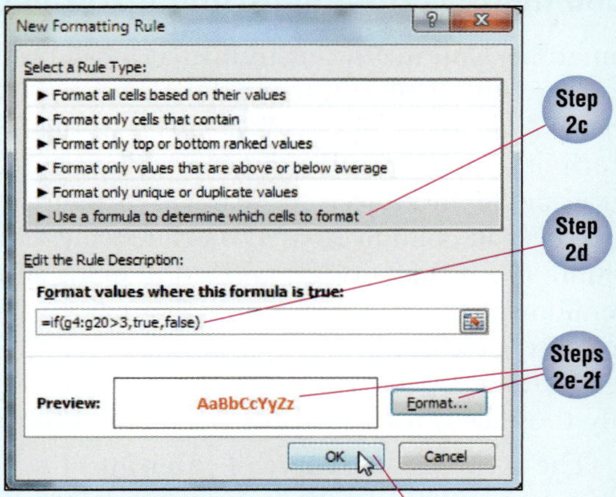

New Formatting Rule

Select a Rule Type:
- Format all cells based on their values
- Format only cells that contain
- Format only top or bottom ranked values
- Format only values that are above or below average
- Format only unique or duplicate values
- Use a formula to determine which cells to format

Edit the Rule Description:

Format values where this formula is true:

=if(g4:g20>3,true,false)

Preview: AaBbCcYyZz Format...

OK Cancel

Step 2c

Step 2d

Steps 2e-2f

Step 2g

Project 3 Use Fraction and Scientific Formatting Options 1 Part

Using two lesson plan worksheets for a math tutor, you will format cells in a solution column to the appropriate format to display the answers for the tutor.

Fraction and Scientific Formatting

Quick Steps

Apply Fraction Formatting
1. Select desired range.
2. Click *Number Format* list arrow.
3. Click *More Number Formats.*
4. Click *Fraction* in *Category* list box.
5. Click desired option in *Type* list box.
6. Click OK.
7. Deselect range.

While most worksheets have values that are formatted using the Accounting Number Format, Percent Style, or Comma Style buttons in the Number group of the Home tab, some worksheets contain values that require other number formats. The *Number Format* list box in the Number group of the Home tab displays a drop-down list with additional format options including date, time, fraction, scientific, and text options. Click *More Number Formats* at the Number Format drop-down list to open the Format Cells dialog box with the Number tab selected shown in Figure 1.5. At this dialog box you can specify additional parameters for the number format categories. For example, with the *Fraction* category you can choose the type of fraction you want displayed.

Scientific formatting converts a number to exponential notation. Part of the number is replaced with E + *n* where E means exponent and *n* represents the power. For example, the number *1,500,000.00* formatted in scientific number format displays as *1.50E+06*. In this example, *+06* means add 6 zeros to the right of the number left of E and then move the decimal point 6 positions to the right. Scientists, mathematicians, engineers, and statisticians often use exponential notation to write very large numbers or very small numbers in a more manageable way.

Figure 1.5 Format Cells Dialog Box with Number Tab Selected and Fraction Category Active

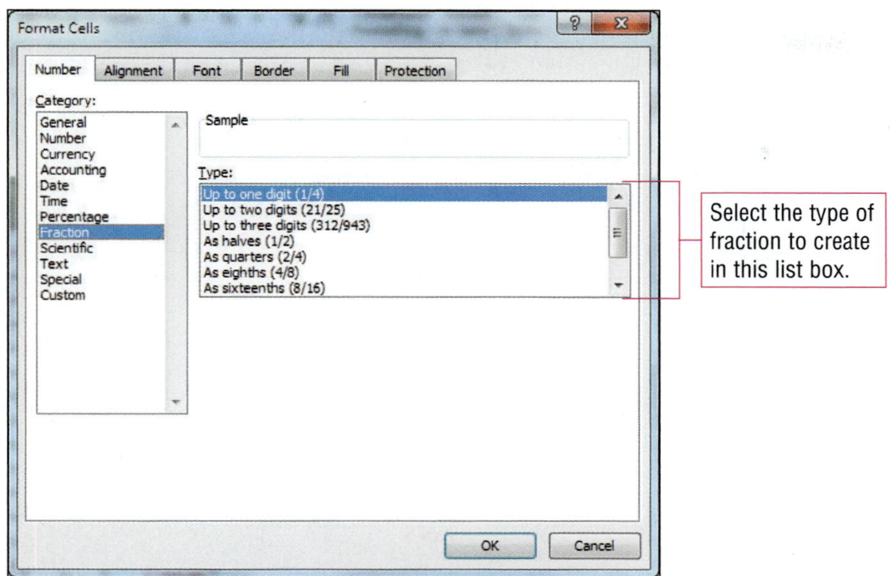

Quick Steps

Apply Scientific Notation Formatting

1. Select desired range.
2. Click *Number Format* list box arrow.
3. Click *Scientific*.
4. Deselect range.

Project 3 Applying Fraction and Scientific Formatting

Part 1 of 1

1. Open **JanelleTutorMathLsn.xlsx**.
2. Save the workbook with Save As and name it **EL2-C1-P3-JanelleTutorMathLsn**.
3. Make Fractions the active worksheet by clicking the Fractions sheet tab located at the bottom of the worksheet area just above the Status bar.
4. Apply fraction formatting to the values in column D in a fractions lesson to create the solution column for Janelle by completing the following steps:
   a. Select D11:D20.
   b. Click the down-pointing arrow at the right side of the *Number Format* list box (currently displays *General*) in the Number group of the Home tab.
   c. Click *More Number Formats* at the drop-down list.
   d. At the Format Cells dialog box with the Number tab selected, click *Fraction* in the *Category* list box.
   e. Click *Up to two digits (21/25)* in the *Type* list box.

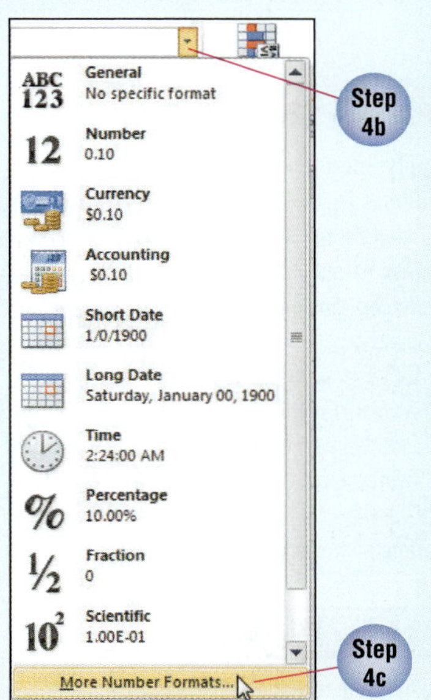

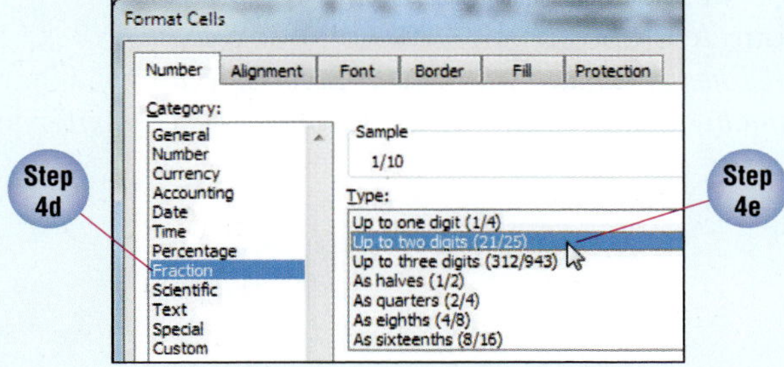

   f. Click OK.
   g. Click in any cell to deselect the range.

5. Save **EL2-C1-P3-JanelleTutorMathLsn**.
6. Print the worksheet.
7. Apply scientific notation formatting to the values in column D in a scientific notation lesson to create the solution column for Janelle by completing the following steps:
   a. Click the Exponents sheet tab located at the bottom of the worksheet area just above the Status bar.
   b. Select D11:D25.
   c. Click the down-pointing arrow at the right side of the *Number Format* list box (currently displays *Custom*) in the Number group of the Home tab and then click *Scientific* at the drop-down list.
   d. Click in any cell to deselect the range.
8. Print the worksheet.
9. Save and then close **EL2-C1-P3-JanelleTutorMathLsn.xlsx**.

10	Examples	Converted to Scientific Notation
11	1,000,000,000	1.00E+09
12	100,000,000	1.00E+08
13	10,000,000	1.00E+07
14	1,000,000	1.00E+06
15	100,000	1.00E+05
16	10,000	1.00E+04
17	1,000	1.00E+03
18	100	1.00E+02
19	10	1.00E+01
20	1	1.00E+00
21	0.1	1.00E-01
22	0.01	1.00E-02
23	0.001	1.00E-03
24	0.0001	1.00E-04
25	0.00001	1.00E-05

scientific formatting applied to D11:D25 in Steps 7a-7d

Project 4 Apply Advanced Formatting Options — 3 Parts

You will update a product worksheet by formatting telephone numbers, creating a custom number format to add descriptive characters before and after a value, and applying text alignment options for long labels.

Quick Steps

Apply Special Number Format
1. Select desired range.
2. Click Format Cells: Number dialog box launcher.
3. Click *Special* in *Category* list box.
4. Click desired option in *Type* list box.
5. Click OK.
6. Deselect range.

By applying a special number format you save typing keystrokes and ensure consistency in the data.

Special Number Formats

At the Format Cells dialog box with the Number tab active, Excel provides special number formats that are specific to a country and language. For example, in a worksheet with social security numbers you can format the range that will contain the numbers and then type the data without the hyphens. Typing *000223456* converts the entry to *000-22-3456* in the cell with special formatting applied. As shown in Figure 1.6, four *Type* options are available for the *English (U.S.)* location: *Zip Code, Zip Code + 4, Phone Number,* and *Social Security Number*. Changing the location to *English (Canada)* displays two *Type* options: *Phone Number* and *Social Insurance Number*.

Figure 1.6 Format Cells Dialog Box with Number Tab Selected and Special Category Active

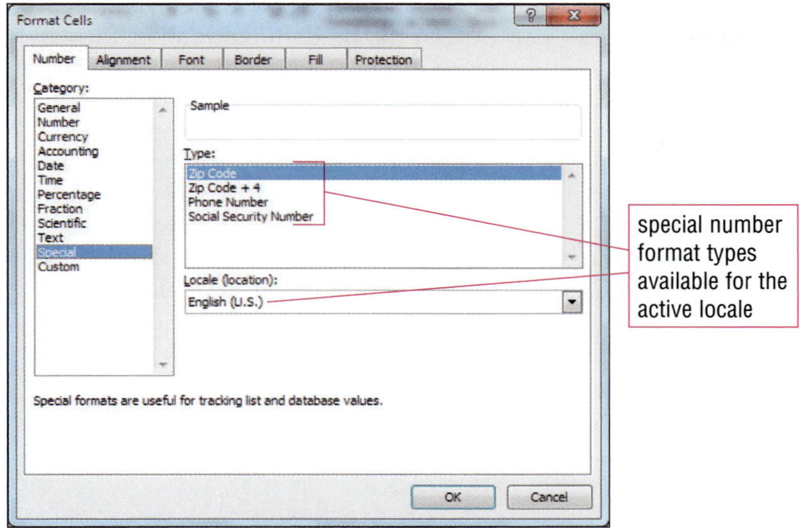

Project 4a Applying Special Formatting

Part 1 of 3

1. Open **PrecisionProducts.xlsx**.
2. Save the workbook with Save As and name it **EL2-C1-P4-PrecisionProducts**.
3. Format the range that will contain telephone numbers to include brackets around the area code and a hyphen between the first three and last four digits of the number by completing the following steps:
   a. Select C15:C20.
   b. Click the Format Cells: Number dialog box launcher located at the bottom right of the Number group in the Home tab.
   c. At the Format Cells dialog box with the Number tab selected, click *Special* in the *Category* list box.
   d. Click *Phone Number* in the *Type* list box with *Locale (location)* set to *English (U.S.)*.
   e. Click OK.
   f. Click C15 to deselect the range and make the first cell to contain a telephone number active.
4. Type the telephone numbers for the sales representatives as follows:

   C15 8005553429
   C16 8005553439
   C17 8005553449
   C18 8005553459
   C19 8005553469
   C20 8005553479

5. Save **EL2-C1-P4-PrecisionProducts.xlsx**.

14	Regional Sales Representatives		
15	North	Jordan Lavoie	(800) 555-3429
16	South	Pat Gallagher	(800) 555-3439
17	East	Alonso Rodriguez	(800) 555-3449
18	West	Karsten Das	(800) 555-3459
19	Canada	Kelli Olsen	(800) 555-3469
20	International	Bianca Santini	(800) 555-3479

Quick Steps

Create Custom Number Format

1. Select desired range.
2. Click Format Cells: Number dialog box launcher.
3. Click *Custom* in *Category* list box.
4. Select *General* in *Type* text box.
5. Press Delete.
6. Type desired custom format codes.
7. Click OK.
8. Deselect range.

Custom number formats are stored in the workbook in which they are created.

Creating a Custom Number Format

You can create a custom number format for a worksheet in which you want to enter values that do not conform to the predefined number formats or values for which you want to add punctuation or text to the number. For example, in Project 4b you will create a custom number format to add a product category letter preceding all of the model numbers. By creating the custom number format, Excel adds the letter automatically. You can also specify a font color in a custom number format. Formatting codes are used in custom formats to specify the type of formatting to apply. You can type a custom number format code from scratch or select from a list of custom formats and modify the codes as necessary. Table 1.1 displays commonly used format codes along with examples of their usage.

Once the custom format is created you can apply the format elsewhere within the workbook by opening the Format Cells dialog box with the Number tab selected, selecting the *Custom* category, scrolling down to the bottom of the *Type* list box, clicking to select the custom format code, and then clicking OK.

Table 1.1 Custom Number Format Code Examples

Format Code	*Description*	*Custom Number Format Example*	*Display Result*
#	Represents a digit; type one for each digit. Excel will round if necessary to fit the number of decimals.	####.###	Typing *145.0068* displays *145.007*
0	Also used for digits. Excel rounds numbers to fit the number of decimals but also fills in leading zeros.	000.00	Typing *50.45* displays *050.45*
?	Rounds numbers to fit the number of decimals but also aligns the numbers vertically on the decimal point by adding spaces.	???.???	Typing *123.5, .8,* and *55.356* one below each other in a column aligns the numbers vertically on the decimal point.
"text"	Adds the characters between quotation symbols to the entry.	"Model No." ###	Typing *587* displays *Model No. 587*
[color]	Applies the font color specified in square brackets to the cell entry.	[Blue]##.##	Typing *55.346* displays **55.35**
;	Separates the positive value format from the negative value format.	[Blue];[Red]	Positive numbers are displayed in blue while negative numbers are displayed in red.

Project 4b Creating a Custom Number Format

Part 2 of 3

1. With **EL2-C1-P4-PrecisionProducts.xlsx** open, select A5:A12.
2. Create a custom number format to insert the characters *PD-* in front of each model number by completing the following steps:
   a. Click the Format Cells: Number dialog box launcher located at the bottom right of the Number group of the Home tab.
   b. Click *Custom* in the *Category* list box at the Format Cells dialog box with the Number tab selected.
   c. Scroll down the list of custom formats in the *Type* list box noting the various combinations of format codes for numbers, dates, and times.
   d. Select *General* in the *Type* text box, press Delete, and then type **"PD-"####**.
   e. Click OK.
   f. With the range A5:A12 still selected, click the Center button in the Alignment group of the Home tab.
   g. Deselect the range.

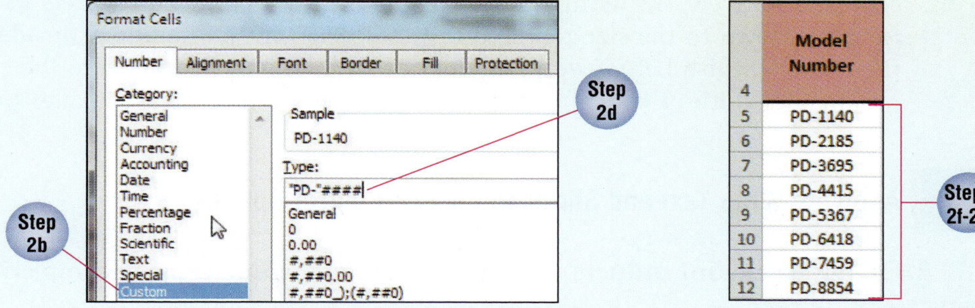

3. Create a custom number format to insert the characters *lbs* after the weights in columns D and E by completing the following steps:
   a. Select D5:E12.
   b. Click the Format Cells: Number dialog box launcher.
   c. Click *Custom* in the *Category* list box.
   d. Select *General* in the *Type* text box, press Delete, and then type **### "lbs"**. Make sure to include one space after ###.
   e. Click OK.
   f. Deselect the range.

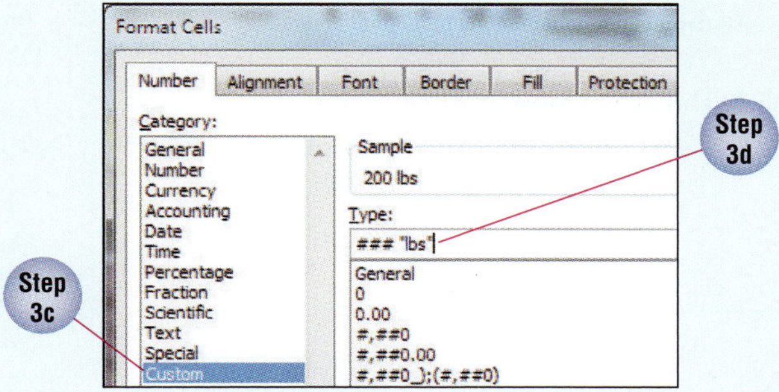

Test Weight in pounds	Recommended Weight in pounds
200 lbs	100 lbs
200 lbs	125 lbs
200 lbs	70 lbs
350 lbs	150 lbs
275 lbs	250 lbs
275 lbs	500 lbs
200 lbs	65 lbs
200 lbs	100 lbs

Step 3f

4. Save **EL2-C1-P4-PrecisionProducts.xlsx**.

Quick Steps

Wrap Text in a Cell
1. Select desired cell(s).
2. Click Wrap Text button.
3. Deselect cell(s).

Shrink Text to Fit within a Cell
1. Select desired cell(s).
2. Click Format Cells: Alignment dialog box launcher.
3. Click *Shrink to fit* in *Text control* section.
4. Click OK.
5. Deselect cell(s).

Wrap Text

To delete a custom number format, open the workbook in which you created the custom format code, open the Format Cells dialog box with the Number tab selected, click *Custom* in the *Category* list box, scroll down the list of custom formats in the *Type* list box to the bottom of the list, click the custom format code that you created, and then click the Delete button. Cells within the workbook that had the format code applied have the custom formatting removed when the format is deleted.

Wrapping and Shrinking Text to Fit within a Cell

Several options exist for formatting long labels that do not fit within the column width. The column width can be expanded, the font can be reduced to a smaller size, a group of cells can be merged, or you can allow the text to spill over into adjacent unused columns. Additional options available in the Format Cells dialog box with the Alignment tab selected include *Wrap text* and *Shrink to Fit* in the *Text control* section. Text wrapped within a cell causes the row height to automatically increase to accommodate the number of lines needed to display the text within the cell. Alternatively, shrinking the text to fit within the cell causes Excel to scale the font size down to the size required to fit all text within one line. Consider widening the column width before wrapping text or shrinking to fit to ensure the column is a reasonable width in which to display multiple lines of text or a smaller font size.

Project 4c Applying Wrap Text and Shrink to Fit Text Control Options — Part 3 of 3

1. With **EL2-C1-P4-PrecisionProducts.xlsx** open, wrap text within cells by completing the following steps:
   a. Select B22:B23.
   b. Click the Wrap Text button in the Alignment group of the Home tab.
   c. Print the worksheet.

Step 1b

Step 3a

2. You decide to try the Shrink to Fit option on the same cells to see if a better result is produced. Press Ctrl + Z or click the Undo button on the Quick Access toolbar to restore the cells back to their original state.
3. Shrink the text to fit within the cells by completing the following steps:
   a. With B22:B23 still selected, click the Format Cells: Alignment dialog box launcher button located at the bottom right of the Alignment group in the Home tab.
   b. At the Format Cells dialog box with the Alignment tab selected, click the *Shrink to fit* check box in the *Text control* section to insert a check mark.
   c. Click OK.
   d. Deselect the range.

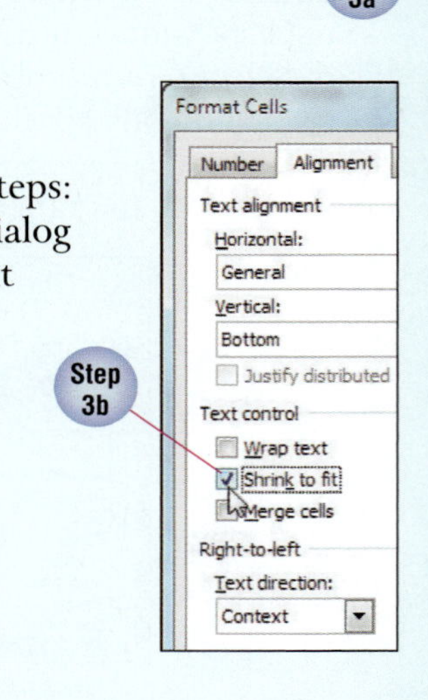

Step 3b

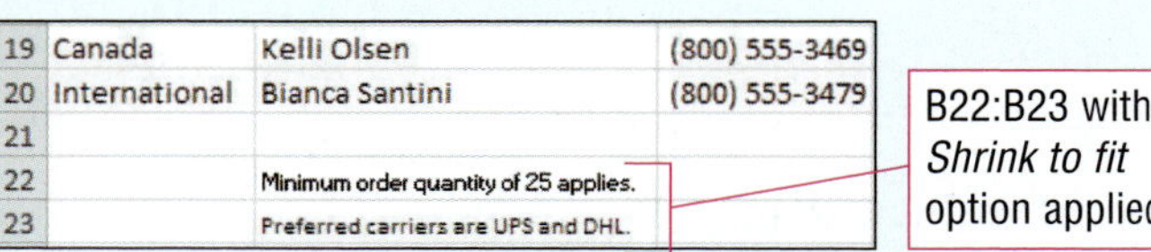

19	Canada	Kelli Olsen	(800) 555-3469
20	International	Bianca Santini	(800) 555-3479
21			
22		Minimum order quantity of 25 applies.	
23		Preferred carriers are UPS and DHL.	

B22:B23 with *Shrink to fit* option applied

4. Save, print, and then close **EL2-C1-P4-PrecisionProducts.xlsx**.

Filter and Sort Data Based on Values, Icon Set, and Font Color

4 Parts

You will filter an insurance policy worksheet to show policies based on a range of liability limits and by number of claims, filter policies based on the number of automobiles, and filter and sort a payroll worksheet by font and cell colors.

Filtering a Worksheet Using a Custom AutoFilter

The AutoFilter feature is used to display only the rows that meet specified criteria defined using the filter arrow at the top of each column. Rows that do not meet the criteria are temporarily hidden from view. For each column in the selected range or table, the filter arrow button includes in the drop-down list each unique field value that exists within the column. Display the Custom AutoFilter dialog box shown in Figure 1.7 in a worksheet where you want to filter values by more than one criterion using a comparison operator. You can use the ? and * wildcard characters in a custom filter. For example, you could filter a list of products by a product number beginning with P using P* as the criteria.

Quick Steps

Filter Using a Custom AutoFilter
1. Select range.
2. Click Sort & Filter button.
3. Click *Filter*.
4. Deselect range.
5. Click filter arrow button in desired column.
6. Point to *Number Filters*.
7. Click desired filter category.
8. Enter criteria at Custom AutoFilter dialog box.
9. Click OK.

Sort & Filter

Figure 1.7 Custom AutoFilter Dialog Box

Create a Custom AutoFilter to specify two criteria by which to filter that use either an *And* or *Or* statement.

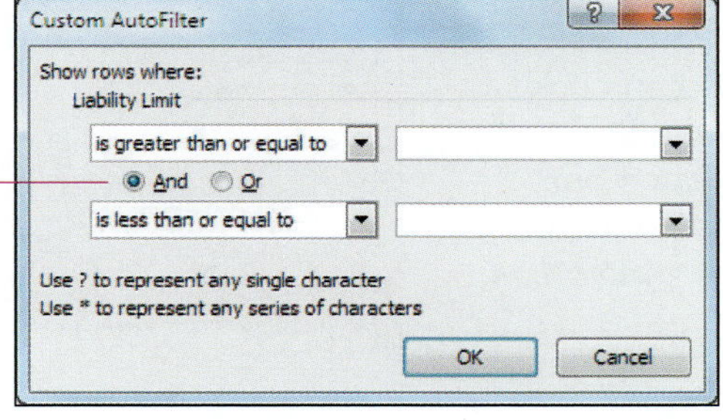

Project 5a **Filtering Policy Information** Part 1 of 4

1. Open **AllClaimsInsce.xlsx**.
2. Save the workbook with Save As and name it **EL2-C1-P5-AllClaimsInsce**.
3. The owner of AllClaims Insurance Brokers wants to review policies with liability limits from $500,000 to $1 million and with claims greater than 1 to determine if customers should increase their coverage. Filter the policy information to produce the list of policies that meet the owner's request by completing the following steps:
   a. Select A3:I20.
   b. Click the Sort & Filter button in the Editing group of the Home tab.
   c. Click *Filter* at the drop-down list to display a filter arrow button at the top of each column.
   d. Deselect the range.

Step 3b

Step 3c

e. Click the filter arrow button next to *Liability Limit* in E3.

f. Point to *Number Filters* and then click *Between* at the drop-down list.

g. At the Custom AutoFilter dialog box with the insertion point positioned in the blank text box next to *is greater than or equal to*, type **500000**.

h. Notice *And* is the option selected between criteria. This is correct since the owner wants a list of policies with the liability limit greater than or equal to 500,000 *and* less than or equal to 1,000,000.

i. Click in the blank text box next to *is less than or equal to* and type **1000000**.

j. Click OK to close the Custom AutoFilter dialog box. The range is filtered to display the rows with liability limits from $500,000 to $1 million.

k. Click the filter arrow button next to *Claims* in H3.

l. Point to *Number Filters* and then click *Greater Than* at the drop-down list.

m. At the Custom AutoFilter dialog box with the insertion point positioned in the blank text box next to *is greater than*, type **1** and then click OK.

4. Print the filtered worksheet.
5. Save and then close **EL2-C1-P5-AllClaimsInsce.xlsx**.

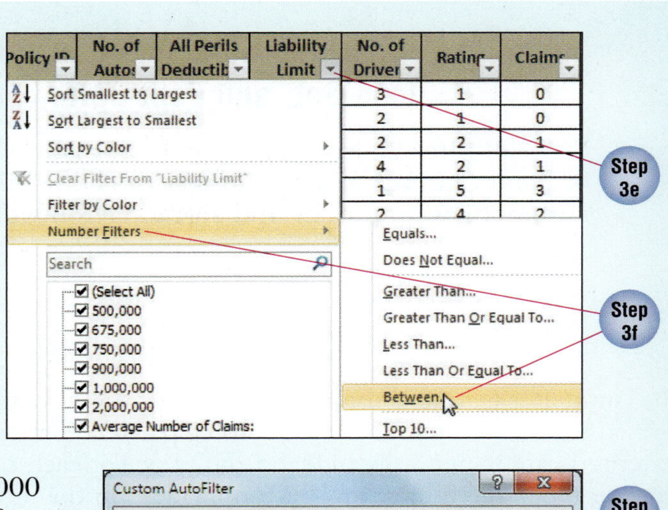

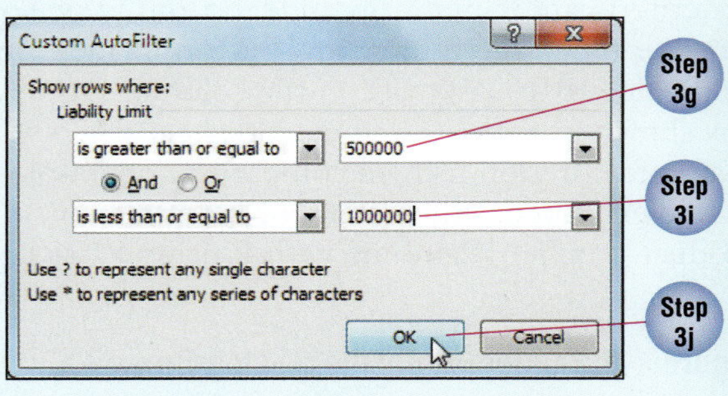

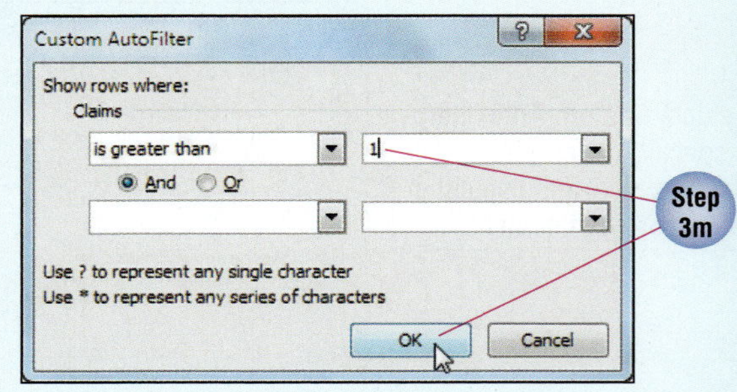

Filtering and Sorting Data Using Conditional Formatting or Cell Attributes

Quick Steps

Filter by Icon Set
1. Select range.
2. Click Sort & Filter button.
3. Click *Filter*.
4. Deselect range.
5. Click filter arrow button in desired column.
6. Point to *Filter by Color*.
7. Click desired icon.

A worksheet with cells that have been formatted manually or by conditional formatting to change the cell or font color can be filtered by the colors. As well, a worksheet conditionally formatted by icon sets can be filtered by a cell icon. Click the filter arrow button in the column by which you want to filter and then point to *Filter by Color* at the drop-down list. Depending on the formatting that has been applied, the list contains the cell colors, font colors, or icon sets that have been applied to cells within the column. Click the desired color or icon option to filter the column.

The filter drop-down list also contains a *Sort by Color* option with which you can choose to sort rows within the range or table by a specified cell color, font color, or cell icon. Follow similar steps to sort by color as you would to filter by color. For example, to sort a column by a font color, point to *Sort by Color* from the column's filter drop-down list and then click the desired font color. Excel sorts the column placing cells with the specified font color at the top.

You can also sort or filter using the shortcut menu. For example, to filter by color or icon using the shortcut menu, right-click a cell that contains the color or icon you wish to filter by, point to *Filter*, and then click *Filter by Selected Cell's Color*, *Filter by Selected Cell's Font Color*, or *Filter by Selected Cell's Icon*.

Quick Steps

Filter or Sort by Color

1. Select range.
2. Click Sort & Filter button.
3. Click *Filter*.
4. Deselect range.
5. Click filter arrow button in desired column.
6. Point to *Filter by Color* or *Sort by Color*.
7. Click desired color.

OR

1. Right-click a cell with desired color or icon.
2. Point to *Filter* or *Sort*.
3. Click desired filter or sort option.

Project 5b Filtering by Icon Set

Part 2 of 4

1. Open **EL2-C1-P2-AllClaimsInsce.xlsx**.
2. Save the workbook with Save As and name it **EL2-C1-P5-AllClaimsInsce-1Auto**.
3. Filter the worksheet to display the policies that have coverage for only one automobile by completing the following steps:
   a. Select A3:I20.
   b. Click the Sort & Filter button in the Editing group of the Home tab.
   c. Click *Filter* at the drop-down list to display a filter arrow button at the top of each column.
   d. Deselect the range. Note that the black circle icon in column C represents the *1* data set.
   e. Click the filter arrow button next to *No. of Autos* in C3.
   f. Point to *Filter by Color* at the drop-down list.
   g. Click the black circle icon in the *Filter by Cell Icon* list.
4. Print the filtered worksheet and then close **EL2-C1-P5-AllClaimsInsce-1Auto.xlsx**.

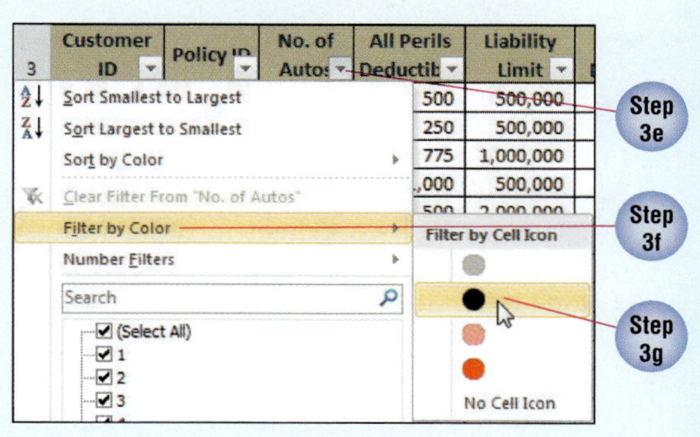

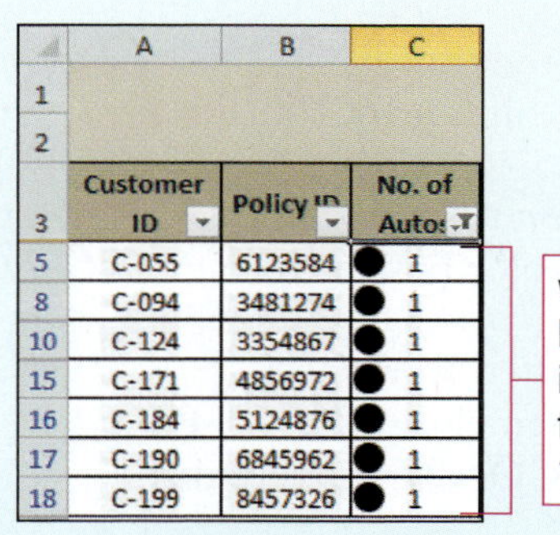

Project 5c Filtering by Font Color

Part 3 of 4

1. Open **EL2-C1-P1-VantagePay-Oct27.xlsx**.
2. Save the workbook with Save As and name it **EL2-C1-P5-VantagePay-Oct27-HighOT**.
3. The store manager wants a list of employees who worked more than five overtime hours during the pay period. You recall conditionally formatting the overtime hours by applying red font color to cells greater than 5. Filter the worksheet by the conditional formatting by completing the following steps:
   a. Select K6:K23.
   b. Right-click within the selected range.
   c. Point to *Filter* and then click *Filter by Selected Cell's Font Color* at the shortcut menu.

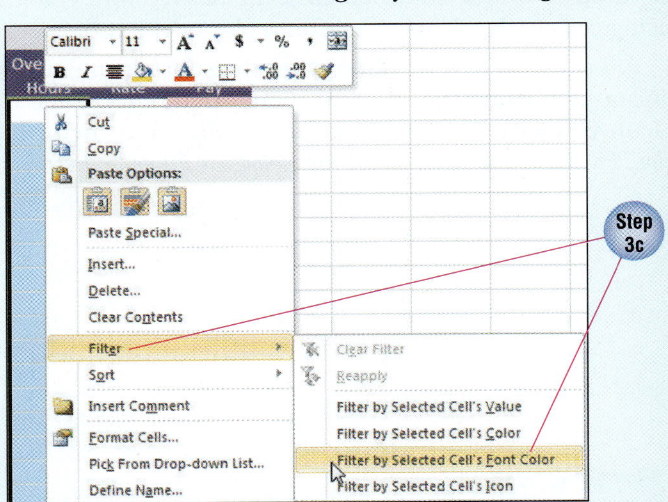

4. Print the filtered worksheet.
5. Save and then close **EL2-C1-P5-VantagePay-Oct27-HighOT.xlsx**.

Project 5d Sorting by Cell Color

Part 4 of 4

1. Open **EL2-C1-P1-VantagePay-Oct27.xlsx**.
2. Save the workbook with Save As and name it **EL2-C1-P5-VantagePay-Oct27-Sorted**.
3. Sort the payroll worksheet in descending order by cell color by completing the following steps:
   a. Select A5:M23, click the Sort & Filter button in the Editing group of the Home tab, and then click *Filter* at the drop-down list.
   b. Deselect the range.
   c. Click the filter arrow button next to Gross Pay in M5.
   d. Point to *Sort by Color* and then click the pink fill color box in the *Sort by Cell Color* section.

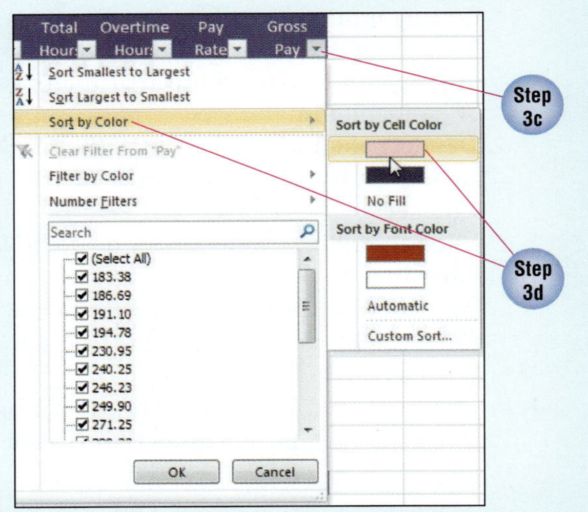

4. Print the sorted worksheet.
5. Save and then close **EL2-C1-P5-VantagePay-Oct27-Sorted.xlsx**.

In a worksheet with more than one cell or font color applied to a column, you would have to define a custom sort. Click the Sort & Filter button in the Editing group of the Home tab and then click *Custom Sort* at the drop-down list.

At the Sort dialog box, define the color to sort first and then add a level for each other color in the order in which you want sorting by color to occur. The *Sort On* drop-down list at the Sort dialog box allows you to sort by *Values*, *Cell Color*, *Font Color*, or *Cell Icon*. Figure 1.8 shows an example of a sort definition for a column in which four cell icons have been used.

Figure 1.8 Sort Dialog Box with Four-Color Sort Defined

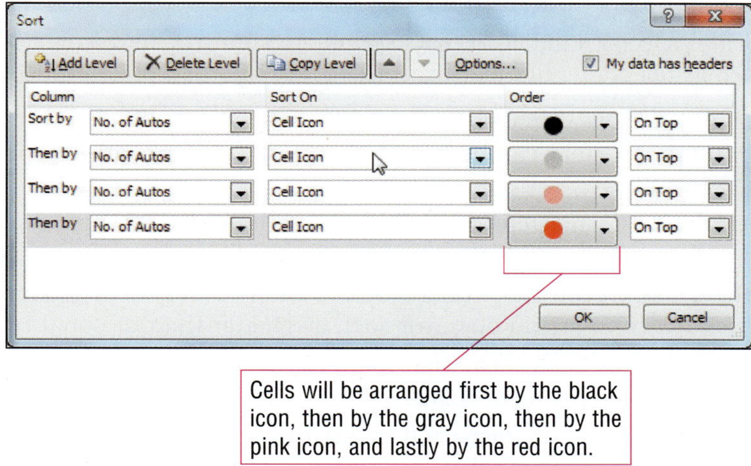

Cells will be arranged first by the black icon, then by the gray icon, then by the pink icon, and lastly by the red icon.

Chapter Summary

- Conditional formatting applies format changes to cells based on a condition; cells that meet the condition have the formatting applied whereas cells that do not meet the condition remain unformatted.
- Conditional formats can be based on values, dates, text entries, or duplicated values.
- Use the *Highlight Cells Rules* option at the Conditional Formatting button drop-down list to conditionally format based on a value comparison.
- Use the *Top/Bottom Rules* option at the Conditional Formatting button drop-down list to conditionally format based on the top ten or bottom ten percent values or on average values.
- Conditional formats are based on rules which specify the criterion by which the cells are tested and the formatting attributes to apply to cells that meet the condition.
- Create your own conditional formatting rules by selecting *New Rule* at the Conditional Formatting button drop-down list.
- Edit or delete a rule at the Conditional Formatting Rules Manager dialog box.
- Conditionally format using data bars, color scales, or icon sets to add small bar charts, gradations of color, or icons to cells to draw attention to data.
- Conditionally format using a formula to apply desired formatting to the selected range of cells based on values in other cells.

- An IF statement can be used to conditionally format those cells that calculate to a true result for the logical test.
- Fraction formatting converts decimal values to fractions.
- To choose the type of fraction you want to convert, open the Format Cells dialog box with the Number tab selected.
- Scientific formatting displays numbers in exponential notation where part of the number that is formatted is replaced with E + *n* where E stands for exponent and *n* represents the power.
- Excel provides special number formats specific to countries and language to format entries such as telephone numbers, social security numbers, or postal codes.
- Custom number formats use formatting codes to create the format definition.
- A custom number format can be used to add text or punctuation to a value entered into a cell.
- Long labels can be formatted to fit within a cell by either wrapping the text within the cell or shrinking the font size to fit the cell.
- Display the Custom AutoFilter dialog box to filter values by more than one criterion using a comparison operator such as greater than or equal to.
- A worksheet that has been formatted manually or by conditional formatting can be filtered by the colors or icons.
- A worksheet that has been formatted manually or by conditional formatting can also be sorted by the colors.
- Define a custom sort if the worksheet contains more than one cell color, font color, or cell icon and you want to specify the order of the colors to sort.

Commands Review

FEATURE	RIBBON TAB, GROUP	BUTTON	KEYBOARD SHORTCUT
Conditional formatting	Home, Styles		
Custom AutoFilter	Home, Editing		Ctrl + Shift + L
Custom number format	Home, Number		Ctrl + 1
Fraction number format	Home, Number		Ctrl + 1
Scientific number format	Home, Number		Ctrl + 1
Shrink to Fit	Home, Alignment		
Special number format	Home, Number		Ctrl + 1
Wrap text	Home, Alignment		

Concepts Check Test Your Knowledge

Completion: In the space provided at the right, indicate the correct term, command, or number.

1. Point to this option from the Conditional Formatting button drop-down list to format cells based on a comparison operator such as *Greater Than*. ____________________
2. To conditionally format a range using the *Above Average* condition, click this option from the Conditional Formatting button drop-down list. ____________________
3. Open this dialog box to create, edit, or delete a conditional formatting rule. ____________________
4. Excel uses threshold values to classify data into three to five categories when conditionally formatting by this option. ____________________
5. Select this option in the *Select a Rule Type* section of the New Formatting Rule dialog box to create a rule that conditionally formats cells based on the value(s) in another cell. ____________________
6. Open this dialog box to format a selected range using a fraction and select the type of fraction to display. ____________________
7. Scientific formatting is used by scientists or others who need to write very large numbers using this notation. ____________________
8. The special number format options displayed in the *Type* list box are dependent on this other setting. ____________________
9. What would display in a cell in which you typed *156.3568* for which the custom number format code ###.## is applied? ____________________
10. Use either of these two text control options to format a long label within the existing column width. ____________________
11. Open this dialog box to filter by more than one criterion using a comparison operator. ____________________
12. A worksheet can be filtered by a cell color that has been applied manually or by this feature. ____________________
13. Open this dialog box to arrange cells in a worksheet by more than one color. ____________________

Skills Check Assess Your Performance

Assessment 1

USE CONDITIONAL AND FRACTION FORMATTING

1. Open **RSRServRpt.xlsx**.
2. Save the workbook with Save As and name it **EL2-C1-A1-RSRServRpt**.
3. Apply the following formatting changes to the worksheet:
   a. Format C6:C23 to fractions using the type *As quarters (2/4)*.
   b. Format the rate codes in D6:D22 with icon set *3 Traffic Lights (Rimmed)*. This is the first option in the right column of the Shapes section.
   c. Format the parts values in F6:F22 to color the cell with *Light Red Fill* for those cells that are equal to zero.
   d. Bold the values in G6:G22.
   e. Format the total invoice values in G6:G22 using the *Red Data Bar* option in the *Gradient Fill* section of the Data Bars side menu.
4. Save, print, and then close **EL2-C1-A1-RSRServRpt.xlsx**.

Assessment 2

APPLY CUSTOM NUMBER FORMATTING

1. Open **EL2-C1-A1-RSRServRpt.xlsx**.
2. Save the workbook with Save As and name it **EL2-C1-A2-RSRServRpt**.
3. Create and apply the following custom number formats:
   a. Create a custom number format that displays *hrs* one space after the values in C6:C23. ***Hint: After selecting Custom in the* Category *list box, click after the existing format codes in the* Type *text box and then add the required entry after the existing codes (do not delete what is already in the* Type *text box).***
   b. Create a custom number format that displays *RSR-* in front of each work order number in B6:B22.
4. Save, print, and then close **EL2-C1-A2-RSRServRpt.xlsx**.

Assessment 3

USE CUSTOM AUTOFILTER; FILTER AND SORT BY COLOR

1. Open **EL2-C1-A2-RSRServRpt.xlsx**.
2. Save the workbook with Save As and name it **EL2-C1-A3-RSRServRpt**.
3. Select A5:G22 and turn on the Filter feature.
4. Filter the worksheet as follows:
   a. Using the filter arrow button in the *Hours Billed* column, display those invoices where the hours billed is between 1.75 and 3.75 hours.
   b. Print the filtered worksheet.
   c. Clear the filter from the *Hours Billed* column.
   d. Filter the *Parts* column by color to show only those invoices for which no parts were billed.
   e. Print the filtered worksheet.
   f. Clear the filter from the *Parts* column.
   g. Filter the worksheet by the icon associated with rate code 3.
   h. Print the filtered worksheet.

i. Clear the filter from the *Rate Code* column.

5. Remove the filter arrow buttons from the worksheet.
6. Define a custom sort to sort the invoices by the rate code icon set as follows:
   a. Make any cell active within the invoice list.
   b. Open the Sort dialog box.
   c. Define three sort levels as follows:

Sort by	*Sort On*	*Order*
Rate Code	Cell Icon	Red Traffic Light (On Top)
Rate Code	Cell Icon	Yellow Traffic Light (On Top)
Rate Code	Cell Icon	Green Traffic Light (On Top)

7. Print the sorted worksheet.
8. Save and then close **EL2-C1-A3-RSRServRpt.xlsx**.

Assessment

4 CREATE, EDIT, AND DELETE FORMATTING RULES

1. Open **VantagePay-Oct27.xlsx**.
2. Save the workbook with Save As and name it **EL2-C1-A4-VantagePay-Oct27**.
3. Create and apply two formatting rules for the values in the *Pay Rate* column as follows:
   a. Apply a light purple fill color to the values from 7.50 to 8.00.
   b. Apply a light green fill color to the values greater than 8.00.
4. Create a formatting rule for the *Gross Pay* column that will format the values in red bold font color if the employee has worked overtime hours.
5. Print the worksheet.
6. Edit the formatting rule for *Cell Value > 8* by changing the fill color to orange and applying bold to the font.
7. Delete the formatting rule for *Cell Value between 7.50 and 8.00*.
8. Print the revised worksheet.
9. Save and then close **EL2-C1-A4-VantagePay-Oct27.xlsx**.

Visual Benchmark Demonstrate Your Proficiency

FORMAT A BILLING SUMMARY

1. Open **BillingsOct8to12.xlsx**.
2. Save the workbook with Save As and name it **EL2-C1-VB-BillingsOct8to12**.
3. Format the worksheet to match the one shown in Figure 1.9 using the following information:
   - The data in the *Billing Code* column is custom formatted to add the text *Amicus#-* in front of the code number in blue font color.
   - Icon sets are used in the *Attorney Code* column and the same icon set should be applied in the Attorney Code Table section of the worksheet.
   - The Data bars added to the values in the *Legal Fees* column have been edited to change the bar appearance to *Turquoise, Accent 3* gradient fill. ***Hint: Select* More Rules *in the Data Bars side menu.***
   - Values below 1500.00 in the *Total Due* column have been conditionally formatted and then the worksheet is sorted by the font color used for the conditional format.
4. Save, print, and then close **EL2-C1-VB-BillingsOct8to12.xlsx**.

Figure 1.9 Visual Benchmark

	A	B	C	D	E	F	G	H	I	J
1					O'DONOVAN & SULLIVAN LAW ASSOCIATES					
2					BILLING SUMMARY					
3					OCTOBER 8 TO 12, 2012					
4	File	Client	Date	Billing Code	Attorney Code	Legal Fees	Disbursements	Total Due	Billing Code Table	
5	EP-652	10106	10/8/2012	Amicus#-3	1	1,028.50	23.75	1,052.25	Code	Area of Practice
6	EL-632	10225	10/9/2012	Amicus#-5	3	1,211.00	37.85	1,248.85	1	Corporate
7	CL-501	10341	10/10/2012	Amicus#-1	2	1,143.75	55.24	1,198.99	2	Divorce & Separation
8	IN-745	10210	10/11/2012	Amicus#-6	3	1,450.00	24.25	1,474.25	3	Wills & Estates
9	CL-412	10125	10/12/2012	Amicus#-1	2	1,143.75	38.12	1,181.87	4	Real Estate
10	IN-801	10346	10/12/2012	Amicus#-6	3	1,425.00	62.18	1,487.18	5	Employment Litigation
11	RE-501	10384	10/12/2012	Amicus#-4	4	1,237.50	34.28	1,271.78	6	Insurance Personal Injury
12	FL-325	10104	10/8/2012	Amicus#-2	1	2,273.75	95.10	2,368.85	7	Other
13	CL-412	10125	10/8/2012	Amicus#-1	2	2,493.75	55.40	2,549.15		
14	IN-745	10210	10/9/2012	Amicus#-6	3	2,425.00	65.20	2,490.20	Attorney Code Table	
15	RE-475	10285	10/9/2012	Amicus#-4	4	3,807.00	48.96	3,855.96	Code	Attorney
16	CL-521	10334	10/10/2012	Amicus#-1	2	1,518.75	27.85	1,546.60	1	Marty O'Donovan
17	PL-348	10420	10/10/2012	Amicus#-7	3	2,500.00	34.95	2,534.95	2	Toni Sullivan
18	RE-492	10425	10/10/2012	Amicus#-4	4	2,043.00	38.75	2,081.75	3	Rosa Martinez
19	EL-632	10225	10/11/2012	Amicus#-5	3	2,300.00	42.15	2,342.15	4	Kyle Williams
20	PL-512	10290	10/11/2012	Amicus#-7	3	1,620.00	65.15	1,685.15		
21	FL-385	10278	10/11/2012	Amicus#-2	1	2,040.00	85.47	2,125.47		
22	CL-450	10358	10/12/2012	Amicus#-1	2	1,762.50	55.24	1,817.74		
23	EP-685	10495	10/12/2012	Amicus#-3	3	2,375.00	94.55	2,469.55		

Case Study Apply Your Skills

Part 1

You work as a market research assistant at NuTrends Market Research. Yolanda Robertson has provided you with a workbook named **USIncomeStats.xlsx**. This workbook contains data she obtained from the U.S. Census Bureau with the two-year average median household income by state for 2008. Open the workbook and use Save As to name it **EL2-C1-CS-P1-USIncomeStats**. Yolanda wants you to format the data using color to differentiate income levels. She has proposed the following categories for which she would like you to apply color formatting.

Average Median Income Range

Less than 45,000

Between 45,000 and 55,000

Greater than 55,000

Apply color formatting using Conditional Formatting for this request since Yolanda may change these salary ranges later after she reviews the data, and you want the ability to edit the formatting rule if that happens. Choose color formats that will be easy to distinguish from each other. Create a reference table starting in E3 that provides Yolanda with a legend to read the colors. For example, in E3 type **Less than 45,000** and in H3 type a sample value (such as 35,000) and format the cell to the color that represents the formatting you applied to the rule category. Save and then print the worksheet. ***Note: If you submit your work in hard copy and do not have access to a color printer, write on the printout the color format options you applied to each category.***

Part 2

Yolanda has reviewed the worksheet from Part 1 and has requested some further work. Before you begin modifying the file, you decide to keep the original file intact in case this data can be used for another purpose. Use Save As to save the workbook using the name **EL2-C1-CS-P2-USIncomeStats**. Yolanda would like the worksheet sorted in descending order from the highest income level to the lowest. Do not include the entries in row 3 for the United States average in the sort operation. After sorting the worksheet, filter the median incomes to display the top 20 states. ***Hint: You can customize the value in the Top 10 AutoFilter.*** Yolanda wants to add a contact telephone list next to the Top 20 state data. Create the list using the telephone numbers provided below in a suitable location. Apply the special number format for phone numbers to ensure the data is displayed consistently. Save and then print the worksheet.

Yolanda (cell)	800 555 3117
Yolanda (office)	800 555 4629
Yolanda (home)	800 555 2169
Yolanda (fax)	800 555 6744

Part 3

Continuing with the worksheet formatted in Part 2 of this Case Study, you decide to experiment with the filtered census data worksheet to see if formatting using color scales will highlight the spread between the highest and lowest median incomes more distinctly. Apply conditional formatting using either a two-color or a three-color scale to the filtered cells in column C (exclude the United States median income at the top of the column). Use Save As to name the workbook **EL2-C1-CS-P3-USIncomeStats**. Print the worksheet. ***Note: If you submit your work in hard copy and do not have access to a color printer, write on the printout the two- or three-color scale conditional formatting option you applied to the filtered values in column C.***

Part 4

Yolanda is preparing a seminar for new market researchers hired at NuTrends Market Research. For background material for the training section on U.S. Census Bureau statistics, Yolanda has asked you to research the history of the bureau. Using the Internet, go to the URL www.census.gov/ and find the page that describes the history of the Census Bureau. ***Hint: Explore the tabbed pages at the About the Bureau link from the home page.*** In a new sheet in the same file as the median income data, type in column A five to seven interesting facts you learned about the bureau from their website. Adjust the width of column A and apply wrap text or shrink to fit formatting to improve the appearance. Save the revised workbook and name it **EL2-C1-CS-P4-USIncomeStats**. Print the worksheet and then close the workbook.

Microsoft® Excel®

CHAPTER

Advanced Functions and Formulas

PERFORMANCE OBJECTIVES

Upon successful completion of Chapter 2, you will be able to:

- **Create and use named ranges in formulas**
- **Use functions COUNTA, COUNTIF, COUNTIFS**
- **Use functions AVERAGEIF, AVERAGEIFS**
- **Use functions SUMIF, SUMIFS**
- **Edit a named range**
- **Rename and delete a named range**
- **Look up data using the lookup functions VLOOKUP and HLOOKUP**
- **Analyze loan payments using PPMT**
- **Use conditional logic functions IF, AND, and OR**
- **Modify text using the text functions PROPER, UPPER, LOWER, and SUBSTITUTE**

Tutorials

2.1 Creating and Managing Range Names

2.2 Using Statistical Functions: Count Functions

2.3 Using Statistical Functions: AVERAGEIF and AVERAGEIFS

2.4 Using Math and Trigonometry Functions

2.5 Using Lookup Functions

2.6 Using the PPMT Function

2.7 Using Logical Functions

2.8 Using Text Functions

Excel includes numerous built-in functions grouped by function category. Eleven categories contain preprogrammed formulas to facilitate complex calculations for worksheets containing statistical, financial, scientific, database, and other data. The Insert function dialog box assists with locating and building function formulas. The structure of a function formula begins with the equals sign (=), followed by the name of the function, and then the function argument. Argument is the term given to the values to be included in the calculation. The structure of the argument is dependent on the type of function being used and can include a single cell, a range, multiple ranges, or any combination of the preceding. Model answers for this chapter's projects appear on the following pages.

Excel2010L2C2

Note: Before beginning the projects, copy to your storage medium the Excel2010L2C2 subfolder from the Excel2010L2 folder on the CD that accompanies this textbook and then make Excel2010L2C2 the active folder.

Model Answers

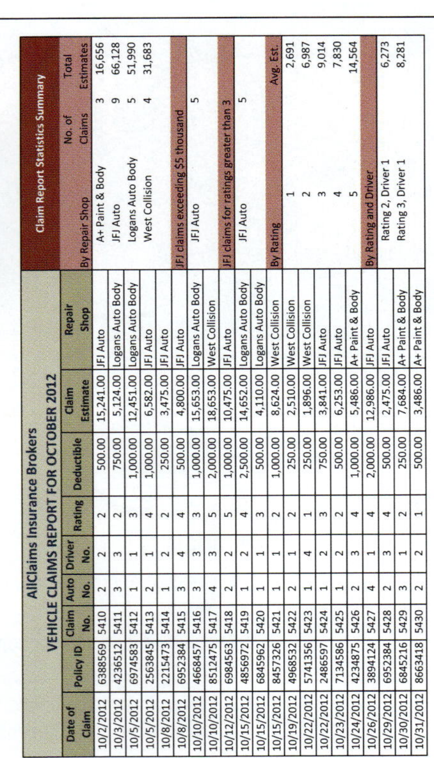

AllClaims Insurance Brokers
VEHICLE CLAIMS REPORT FOR OCTOBER 2012

Date of Claim	Policy ID	Claim No.	Auto No.	Driver No.	Rating	Deductible	Claim Estimate	Repair Shop
10/2/2012	6388569	5410	2	2	2	500.00	15,241.00	JFJ Auto
10/3/2012	4236512	5411	3	3	2	750.00	5,124.00	Logans Auto Body
10/5/2012	6974583	5412	1	1	3	1,000.00	12,451.00	Logans Auto Body
10/5/2012	2563845	5413	2	1	4	1,000.00	6,582.00	JFJ Auto
10/8/2012	2215473	5414	1	2	2	250.00	3,475.00	JFJ Auto
10/8/2012	6952384	5415	3	4	4	500.00	4,800.00	JFJ Auto
10/10/2012	4668457	5416	3	3	3	1,000.00	15,653.00	Logans Auto Body
10/10/2012	8512475	5417	4	3	5	2,000.00	18,653.00	West Collision
10/12/2012	6984563	5418	2	2	5	1,000.00	10,475.00	JFJ Auto
10/15/2012	4856972	5419	1	2	4	2,500.00	14,652.00	Logans Auto Body
10/15/2012	6845962	5420	1	1	3	500.00	4,110.00	Logans Auto Body
10/15/2012	8457326	5421	1	1	2	1,000.00	8,624.00	West Collision
10/19/2012	4968532	5422	2	1	2	250.00	2,510.00	West Collision
10/22/2012	5741356	5423	1	4	1	250.00	1,896.00	West Collision
10/22/2012	2486597	5424	1	2	3	750.00	3,841.00	JFJ Auto
10/23/2012	7134586	5425	1	2	2	500.00	6,253.00	JFJ Auto
10/24/2012	4234875	5426	2	3	4	1,000.00	5,486.00	A+ Paint & Body
10/26/2012	3894124	5427	4	1	4	2,000.00	12,986.00	JFJ Auto
10/29/2012	6952384	5428	2	3	4	500.00	2,475.00	JFJ Auto
10/30/2012	6845216	5429	3	1	2	250.00	7,684.00	A+ Paint & Body
10/31/2012	8663418	5430	2	2	1	500.00	3,486.00	A+ Paint & Body

Claim Report Statistics Summary

By Repair Shop	No. of Claims	Total Estimates
A+ Paint & Body	3	16,656
JFJ Auto	9	66,128
Logans Auto Body	5	51,990
West Collision	4	31,683
JFJ claims exceeding $5 thousand		
JFJ Auto	5	
JFJ claims for ratings greater than 3		
JFJ Auto	5	

By Rating	Avg. Est.
1	2,691
2	6,987
3	9,014
4	7,830
5	14,564
By Rating and Driver	
Rating 2, Driver 1	6,273
Rating 3, Driver 1	8,281

Project 1 Calculate Statistics and Sums Using Conditional Formulas
EL2-C2-P1-AllClaimsOct12VehRpt.xlsx

Precision Design and Packaging
Bulk Container Products Price List

Model Number	Description	Discount Category	List Price	Discount	Net Price
PD-1140	Gaylord with lid	A	18.67	10%	16.80
PD-2185	Premium Gaylord with lid	C	22.50	14%	19.35
PD-1150	Gaylord bottom	B	14.53	12%	12.79
PD-1155	Gaylord lid	D	5.25	16%	4.41
PD-3695	Telescoping top and bottom	A	18.54	10%	16.69
PD-3698	Telescoping bottom	A	17.65	10%	15.89
PD-3699	Telescoping top	A	17.65	10%	15.89
PD-4100	Additional lids for telescoping containers	D	9.88	16%	8.30
PD-4200	"D" 4 piece container	A	7.75	10%	6.98
PD-4415	"EO" container	A	8.25	10%	7.43
PD-5367	"EH" container	A	12.75	10%	11.48
PD-6418	"E" container	A	17.54	10%	15.79
PD-7459	Economy R.S.C.	E	8.56	20%	6.85
PD-8854	Premium R.S.C.	C	18.17	14%	15.63
PD-9101	Corrugated pads 15 x 15	E	1.10	20%	0.88
PD-9105	Corrugated pads 20 x 12	E	1.14	20%	0.91
PD-9110	Corrugated pads 24 x 18	E	1.17	20%	0.94
PD-9115	Corrugated pads 30 x 30	E	1.09	20%	0.87

Discount Table

Discount Category	Discount Percent
A	10%
B	12%
C	14%
D	16%
E	20%

NOTE: Use this price list for U.S. and Canadian orders only. Refer international customers to Bianca Santini for price quotations.

Project 2 Populate Cells by Looking Up Data
EL2-C2-P2-PrecisionPrices.xlsx

DEERING INDUSTRIES

BUILDING LOAN EXPANSION

	Victory Trust	Dominion Trust	
Interest Rate	8.15%	9.50%	annual rate
Amortization	20	15	years for repayment
Loan Amount	$ 775,000	$ 775,000	principal amount borrowed
Monthly Payment	($6,554.95)	($8,092.74)	includes principal and interest
Monthly Principal Payment (1st payment)	($1,291.40)	($1,957.32)	payment on principal for the first month of the loan
Total Loan Payments	($1,573,187.00)	($1,456,693.43)	

NOTE: Both payments are calculated based on a constant interest rate and a constant payment.

Project 3 Analyze an Expansion Project Loan
EL2-C2-P3-DeeringExpansion.xlsx

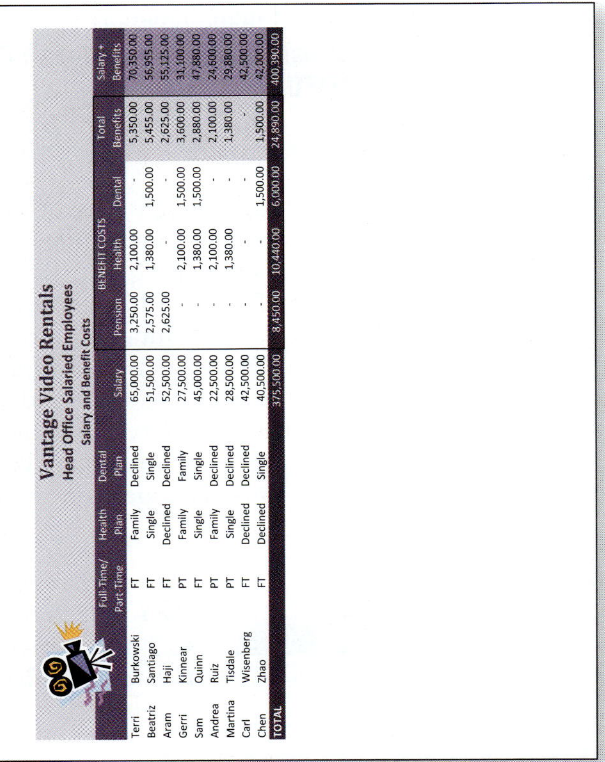

Vantage Video Rentals
Head Office Salaried Employees
Salary and Benefit Costs

		Full-Time/ Part-Time	Health Plan	Dental Plan	Salary	BENEFIT COSTS Pension	Health	Dental	Total Benefits	Salary + Benefits
Terri	Burkowski	FT	Family	Declined	65,000.00	3,250.00	2,100.00	-	5,350.00	70,350.00
Beatriz	Santiago	FT	Single	Single	51,500.00	2,575.00	1,380.00	1,500.00	5,455.00	56,955.00
Aram	Haji	FT	Declined	Declined	52,500.00	2,625.00	-	-	2,625.00	55,125.00
Gerri	Kinnear	PT	Family	Family	27,500.00	-	2,100.00	1,500.00	3,600.00	31,100.00
Sam	Quinn	FT	Single	Single	45,000.00	-	1,380.00	1,500.00	2,880.00	47,880.00
Andrea	Ruiz	PT	Family	Declined	22,500.00	-	2,100.00	-	2,100.00	24,600.00
Martina	Tisdale	PT	Single	Declined	28,500.00	-	1,380.00	-	1,380.00	29,880.00
Carl	Wisenberg	FT	Declined	Declined	42,500.00	-	-	-	-	42,500.00
Chen	Zhao	FT	Declined	Single	40,500.00	-	-	1,500.00	1,500.00	42,000.00
TOTAL					375,500.00	8,450.00	10,440.00	6,000.00	24,890.00	400,390.00

Project 4 Calculate Benefit Costs Using Conditional Logic
EL2-C2-P4-VantageHOSalaryCosts.xlsx

Two-Year Average Median Household Income by State
Median Income for 2008

United States	51,233
Alabama	44,155
Alaska	64,701
Arizona	47,972
Arkansas	40,974
California	57,445
Colorado	62,217
Connecticut	65,644
Delaware	53,695
District of Columbia	54,162
Florida	46,206
Georgia	48,369
Hawaii	64,002
Idaho	49,247
Illinois	53,889
Indiana	47,898
Iowa	50,465
Kansas	49,119
Kentucky	41,058
Louisiana	41,232
Maine	48,481
Maryland	65,932
Massachusetts	60,515
Michigan	50,528
Minnesota	57,607
Mississippi	37,579
Missouri	46,906
Montana	44,116
Nebraska	50,896
Nevada	55,440
New Hampshire	68,175
New Jersey	64,070
New Mexico	44,081
New York	50,643
North Carolina	44,058
North Dakota	49,325
Ohio	48,960
Oklahoma	45,494
Oregon	51,947
Pennsylvania	50,850
Rhode Island	54,767
South Carolina	44,034
South Dakota	49,901
Tennessee	41,240
Texas	47,157
Utah	59,062
Vermont	49,959
Virginia	61,710
Washington	58,472
West Virginia	40,851
Wisconsin	52,224
Wyoming	51,977

Two-Year Average Median Household Income by State
Median Income for 2012

UNITED STATES	54,973
ALABAMA	47,378
ALASKA	69,424
ARIZONA	51,474
ARKANSAS	43,965
CALIFORNIA	61,638
COLORADO	66,759
CONNECTICUT	70,436
DELAWARE	57,615
DISTRICT OF COLUMBIA	58,116
FLORIDA	49,579
GEORGIA	51,900
HAWAII	68,674
IDAHO	52,842
ILLINOIS	57,823
INDIANA	51,395
IOWA	54,149
KANSAS	52,705
KENTUCKY	44,055
LOUISIANA	44,242
MAINE	52,020
MARYLAND	70,745
MASSACHUSETTS	64,933
MICHIGAN	54,217
MINNESOTA	61,812
MISSISSIPPI	40,322
MISSOURI	50,330
MONTANA	47,336
NEBRASKA	54,611
NEVADA	59,487
NEW HAMPSHIRE	73,152
NEW JERSEY	68,747
NEW MEXICO	47,299
NEW YORK	54,340
NORTH CAROLINA	47,274
NORTH DAKOTA	52,926
OHIO	52,534
OKLAHOMA	48,815
OREGON	55,739
PENNSYLVANIA	54,562
RHODE ISLAND	58,765
SOUTH CAROLINA	47,248
SOUTH DAKOTA	53,544
TENNESSEE	44,251
TEXAS	50,599
UTAH	63,374
VERMONT	53,606
VIRGINIA	66,215
WASHINGTON	62,740
WEST VIRGINIA	43,833
WISCONSIN	56,036
WYOMING	55,771

Data shown above is the two-year average median for 2007 to 2008. Two-year average median is the sum of two inflation-adjusted single-year medians divided by 2.

Source: U.S. Census Bureau
http://www.census.gov/hhes/www/income/statemedfaminc08.html

Project 5 Convert Text Using Text Functions

EL2-C2-P5-USIncomeStats.xlsx

Calculate Statistics and Sums Using Conditional Formulas

7 Parts

You will create and manage range names in an insurance claims worksheet and use the range names in statistical formulas that count, find averages, and sum based on single and multiple criteria.

Naming Ranges

Assigning a name to a cell or a range of cells allows you to reference the source by a descriptive label rather than the cell address or range address when creating formulas, printing, or navigating a worksheet. Referencing by name makes the task of managing a complex formula easier. Another person editing the worksheet experiences clarity more quickly as to the formula's purpose. To demonstrate the use of names for clarity, read the formula examples in Table 2.1. Each row provides two formulas that reference the same source cells; however, the formula on the right is meaningful to you more quickly than the formula on the left. The formulas in the left column might require that you locate the source cell in the worksheet to figure out the calculation steps while the formula on the right provides comprehension almost immediately.

By default, the range to which a range name applies is referenced using absolute references. Later in this chapter when you create a lookup formula, you

Quick Steps

Create Range Name
1. Select cell(s).
2. Click in Name box.
3. Type desired range name.
4. Press Enter.

Table 2.1 Standard Formulas and Formulas with Named Ranges

Standard Formula	*Same Formula Using Named Ranges*
=D3-D13	=Sales-Expenses
=J5*K5	=Hours*PayRate
=G10/J10	=ThisYear/LastYear
=IF(E4-B2>0,E4*D2,0)	=IF(Sales-Target>0,Sales*Bonus,0)

will take advantage of a range name's absolute referencing when you need to include a group of cells in the formula that stay fixed when the formula is copied.

> **HINT**
> The Formulas tab contains a Create from Selection button in the Defined Names group that can be used to automatically create range names for a list or table. Select the list or table and click the button. Excel uses the names in the top row or leftmost column as the range names.

Create a range name by selecting a single cell or range, clicking in the Name box located at the left end of the Formula bar, typing the name, and then pressing Enter. The Name box displays the active cell address or the cell name when one has been defined. When creating a name for a cell or a range of cells, the following naming rules apply:

- Names can be a combination of letters, numbers, underscore characters, or periods up to 255 characters.
- The first character must be a letter, an underscore, or a backslash (\).
- Spaces are not valid within a range name. Use underscore characters or periods to separate words.
- A valid cell address cannot become a range name.
- Range names are not case sensitive.

Project 1a Creating Range Names

Part 1 of 7

1. Open **AllClaimsOct12VehRpt.xlsx**.
2. Save the workbook with Save As and name it **EL2-C2-P1-AllClaimsOct12VehRpt**.
3. Assign names to ranges by completing the following steps:
   a. Select D4:D24.
   b. Click in the Name box located at the left end of the Formula bar, type **AutoNo**, and then press Enter.
   c. Select E4:E24, click in the Name box, type **DriverNo**, and then press Enter.
   d. Select F4:F24, click in the Name box, type **Rating**, and then press Enter.
   e. Select H4:H24, click in the Name box, type **ClaimEst**, and then press Enter.
   f. Select I4:I24, click in the Name box, type **RepShop**, and then press Enter.

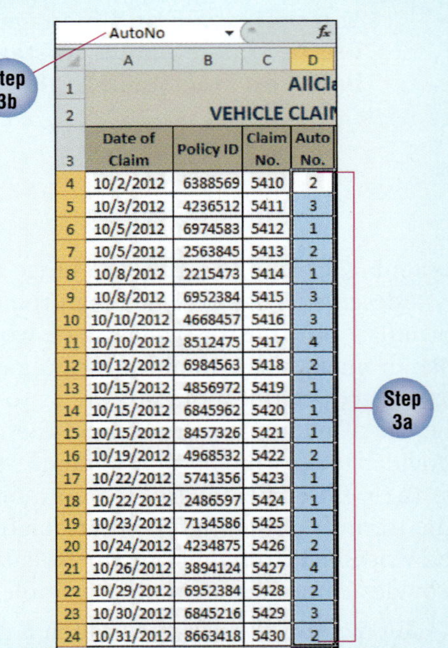

	A	B	C	D
3	Date of Claim	Policy ID	Claim No.	Auto No.
4	10/2/2012	6388569	5410	2
5	10/3/2012	4236512	5411	3
6	10/5/2012	6974583	5412	1
7	10/5/2012	2563845	5413	2
8	10/8/2012	2215473	5414	1
9	10/8/2012	6952384	5415	3
10	10/10/2012	4668457	5416	3
11	10/10/2012	8512475	5417	4
12	10/12/2012	6984563	5418	2
13	10/15/2012	4856972	5419	1
14	10/15/2012	6845962	5420	1
15	10/15/2012	8457326	5421	1
16	10/19/2012	4968532	5422	2
17	10/22/2012	5741356	5423	1
18	10/22/2012	2486597	5424	1
19	10/23/2012	7134586	5425	1
20	10/24/2012	4234875	5426	2
21	10/26/2012	3894124	5427	4
22	10/29/2012	6952384	5428	2
23	10/30/2012	6845216	5429	3
24	10/31/2012	8663418	5430	2

4. View the range names by clicking the down-pointing arrow to the right of the Name box.
5. Click *AutoNo* at the drop-down list to move the selected range to column D. One reason for creating a range name is to quickly move the active cell to navigate a large worksheet.
6. Deselect the range.
7. Save **EL2-C2-P1-AllClaimsOct12VehRpt.xlsx**.

RepShop
AutoNo
ClaimEst
DriverNo
Rating
RepShop
Step 5
Step 4

Statistical Functions

Commonly used statistical functions include AVERAGE, MAX, and MIN, where AVERAGE returns the arithmetic mean, MAX returns the largest value, and MIN returns the smallest value in the range. Another function used often is COUNT, which returns the number of cells that contain numbers or dates. Empty cells, text labels, or error values in the range are ignored. Excel provides additional AVERAGE and COUNT functions that are used to count text entries and count and find averages for a range based on a criterion.

COUNTA

In a worksheet that requires cells containing text, or cells containing a combination of text and numbers (such as *Model-2146*) to be counted, Excel provides the COUNTA function. COUNTA returns the number of cells that are not empty; therefore, this formula can be used to count a range of cells other than values. As shown in the worksheet in Figure 2.1, when the regular COUNT function is used in E8 to count parts in the range A2:A6, Excel returns a value of 0. However, in E9, when the same range is counted using COUNTA, Excel returns the value of 5.

COUNTIF and COUNTIFS

Use the COUNTIF function to count cells within a range that meet a single criterion. For example, in a grades worksheet you might use a COUNTIF function to count the number of students who achieved greater than 75 percent. This

Figure 2.1 COUNTA Example

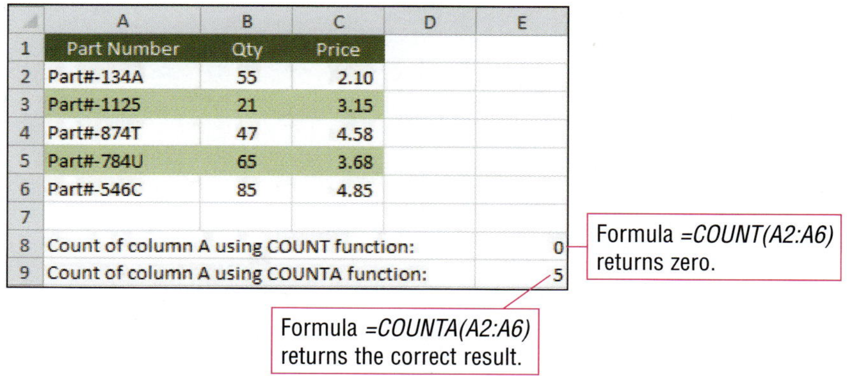

	A	B	C	D	E
1	Part Number	Qty	Price		
2	Part#-134A	55	2.10		
3	Part#-1125	21	3.15		
4	Part#-874T	47	4.58		
5	Part#-784U	65	3.68		
6	Part#-546C	85	4.85		
7					
8	Count of column A using COUNT function:				0
9	Count of column A using COUNTA function:				5

Formula *=COUNT(A2:A6)* returns zero.
Formula *=COUNTA(A2:A6)* returns the correct result.

function uses conditional logic where the criterion defines a conditional test so that only those cells that meet the test are selected for action. The structure of a COUNTIF function is *=COUNTIF(range,criteria)*. For the grades worksheet example, the function to count the cells of students who achieved greater than 75 percent would be *=COUNTIF(grades,">75")* assuming the range name *grades* has been defined. Notice the syntax of the argument requires criteria to be enclosed in quotation symbols. If you use the Insert Function dialog box to create formulas, Excel adds the required syntax automatically.

COUNTIFS is used to count cells that meet multiple criteria. The formula uses the same structure as COUNTIF with additional ranges and criteria within the argument. The structure of a COUNTIFS function is *=COUNTIFS(range1, criteria1,range2,criteria2. . .)*. Figure 2.2 illustrates a nursing education worksheet with a single criterion COUNTIF to count the number of RNs and a multiple criteria COUNTIFS to count the number of RNs who are current with their Professional Development activities. The formulas shown in Figure 2.2 include range names where *Title* references the entries in column D and *PDCurrent* references the entries in column H.

Quick Steps

Create COUNTIF Formula

1. Make desired cell active.
2. Click Insert Function button.
3. Change category to *Statistical*.
4. Select *COUNTIF*.
5. Click OK.
6. Enter range address or range name to select by in *Range* text box.
7. Enter condition expression or text in *Criteria* text box.
8. Click OK.

Create COUNTIFS Formula

1. Make desired cell active.
2. Click Insert Function button.
3. Change category to *Statistical*.
4. Select *COUNTIFS*.
5. Click OK.
6. Enter range address or range name to select by in *Criteria_range1* text box.
7. Enter condition expression or text in *Criteria1* text box.
8. Enter range address or range name to select by in *Criteria_range2* text box.
9. Enter condition expression or text in *Criteria2* text box.
10. Continue adding criteria range expressions and criteria as needed.
11. Click OK.

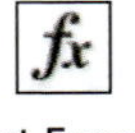

Insert Function

Figure 2.2 COUNTIF and COUNTIFS Formulas

	A	B	C	D	E	F	G	H	I	J	K
1	Department of Human Resources, Professional Development										
2	Full-Time Nursing Education Worksheet										
3	Employee Number	Employee LastName	Employee FirstName	Title	Unit	Extension	Years Experience	PD Current?		Nursing Education Statistical Summary	
4	FT02001	Santos	Susan	RN	Med/Surg	36415	30	Yes		Number of RNs	12
5	FT02002	Daniels	Jasmine	RN	Med/Surg	36415	27	No		Number of LPNs	7
6	FT02003	Walden	Virgina	RN	ICU	34211	22	No			
7	FT02004	Jaffe	Paul	LPN	CSRU	36418	24	Yes		RNs who are current with PD	7
8	FT02005	Salvatore	Terry	LPN	ICU	34211	22	Yes		LPNs who are current with PD	4
9	FT02006	Mander	Kaitlynn	RN	ICU	34211	24	Yes			
10	FT02007	Lavigne	Gisele	RN	CSRU	36418	20	No			
11	FT02008	Williamson	Forman	RN	CSRU	36418	19	Yes			
12	FT02009	Orlowski	William	RN	Ortho	31198	22	No			
13	FT02010	El-Hamid	Lianna	LPN	Med/Surg	36415	20	No			
14	FT02011	Vezina	Ursula	LPN	Ortho	31198	20	No			
15	FT02012	Jorgensen	Macy	RN	Med/Surg	36415	10	Yes			
16	FT02013	Pieterson	Eric	RN	ICU	34211	8	Yes			
17	FT02014	Costa	Michael	RN	Ortho	31198	10	No			
18	FT02015	Besterd	Mary	RN	PreOp	32881	7	Yes			
19	FT02016	Oste	Frank	LPN	Med/Surg	36415	7	Yes			
20	FT02017	Hillman	John	LPN	PreOp	32881	5	No			
21	FT02018	Cano	Rodney	RN	ICU	34211	4	Yes			
22	FT02019	Rivere	Waylan	LPN	CSRU	36418	2	Yes			

Formula
=COUNTIF(Title,"RN")

Formula
=COUNTIFS(Title,"RN",PDCurrent,"Yes")

Project 1b Creating COUNTIF Functions

Part 2 of 7

1. With **EL2-C2-P1-AllClaimsOct12VehRpt.xlsx** open, make L4 the active cell.
2. Create a COUNTIF function to count the number of claims where A+ Paint & Body is the repair shop by completing the following steps:
   a. Click the Insert Function button in the Formula bar.
   b. At the Insert Function dialog box, click the down-pointing arrow to the right of the *Or select a category* list box and then click *Statistical* at the drop-down list. ***Note: Skip this step if Statistical is already selected as the category.***
   c. Scroll down the *Select a function* list box and then click *COUNTIF*.
   d. Read the formula description below the function list box and then click OK.
   e. At the Function Arguments dialog box with the insertion point positioned in the *Range* text box, type **RepShop** and then press Tab. Recall from Project 1a that you defined a range name for the entries in column I. ***Note: If necessary, drag the Function Arguments dialog box title bar left or right if the dialog box is obscuring your view of the worksheet.***
   f. With the insertion point positioned in the *Criteria* text box, type **A+ Paint & Body** and then press Tab. When you press Tab, Excel adds the quotation symbols to the criteria text.
   g. Click OK. Excel returns the value *3* in L4.
   h. Look at the formula in the Formula bar created by the Function Arguments dialog box: *=COUNTIF(RepShop,"A+ Paint & Body")*.
3. Make L5 the active cell, type the formula **=countif(repshop,"JFJ Auto")**, and then press Enter.
4. Enter the following COUNTIF formulas in the cells indicated using either the Insert Function dialog box or by typing the formula directly into the cell.

   L6 **=COUNTIF(RepShop,"Logans Auto Body")**
   L7 **=COUNTIF(RepShop,"West Collision")**
5. Save **EL2-C2-P1-AllClaimsOct12VehRpt.xlsx**.

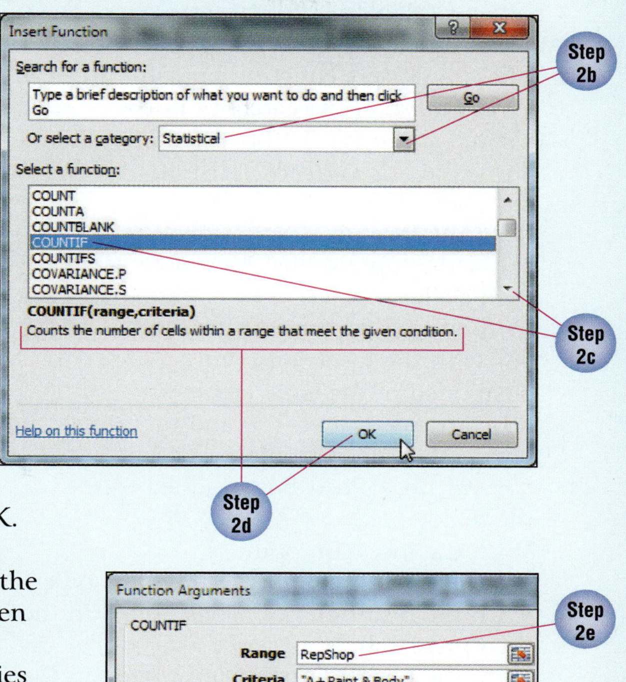

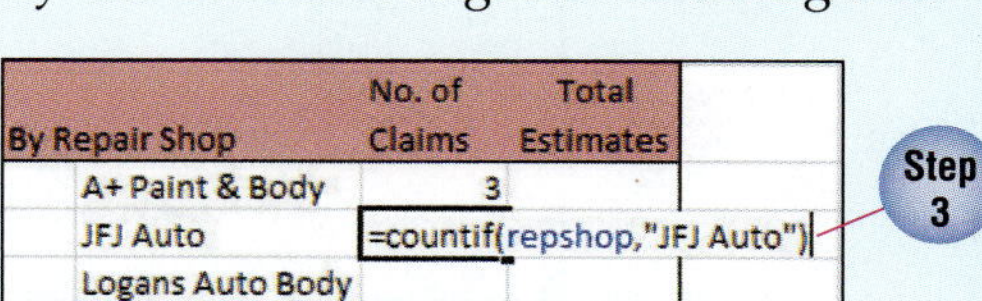

By Repair Shop	No. of Claims	Total Estimates
A+ Paint & Body	3	
JFJ Auto	=countif(repshop,"JFJ Auto")	
Logans Auto Body		

Step 3

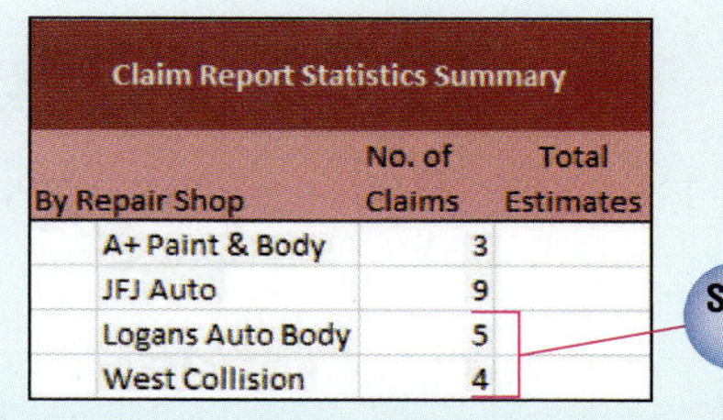

Claim Report Statistics Summary		
By Repair Shop	No. of Claims	Total Estimates
A+ Paint & Body	3	
JFJ Auto	9	
Logans Auto Body	5	
West Collision	4	

Step 4

Creating COUNTIFS Functions

1. With **EL2-C2-P1-AllClaimsOct12VehRpt.xlsx** open, make L10 the active cell.
2. Create a COUNTIFS function to count the number of claims where the repair shop is JFJ Auto and the claims estimate is greater than $5,000 by completing the following steps:
   a. Click the Insert Function button in the Formula bar.
   b. With *Statistical* the category in the *Or select a category* list box, scroll down the *Select a function* list box and then click *COUNTIFS*.
   c. Read the formula description below the function list box and then click OK.
   d. At the Function Arguments dialog box with the insertion point positioned in the *Criteria_range1* text box, type **RepShop** and then press Tab. After you press Tab, a *Criteria_range2* text box is added to the dialog box.
   e. With the insertion point positioned in the *Criteria1* text box, type **JFJ Auto** and then press Tab.
   f. With the insertion point positioned in the *Criteria_range2* text box, type **ClaimEst** and then press Tab.
   g. With the insertion point positioned in the *Criteria2* text box, type **>5000** and then press Tab.
   h. Click OK. Excel returns the value *5* in L10.

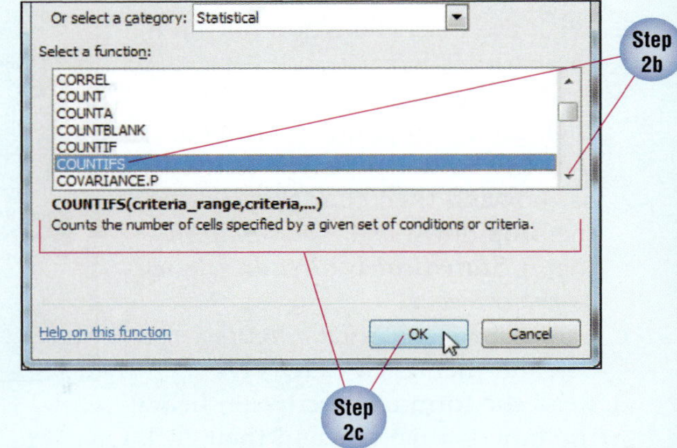

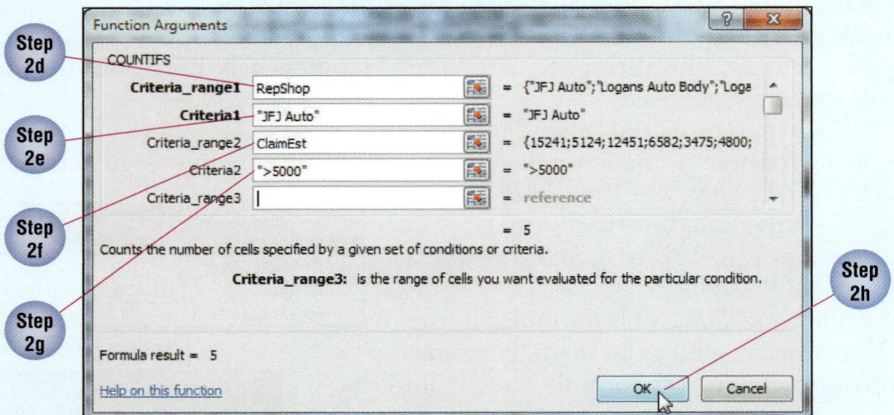

3. Look at the formula in the Formula bar created by the Function Arguments dialog box: *=COUNTIFS(RepShop,"JFJ Auto",ClaimEst,">5000")*.
4. Enter the following COUNTIFS formula in L13 using either the Insert Function dialog box or by typing the formula directly into the cell:

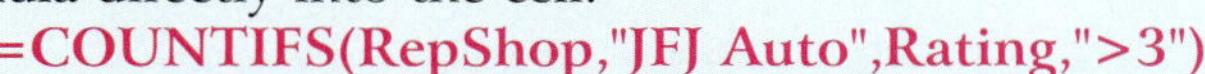

=COUNTIFS(RepShop,"JFJ Auto",Rating,">3")

5. Save **EL2-C2-P1-AllClaimsOct12VehRpt.xlsx**.

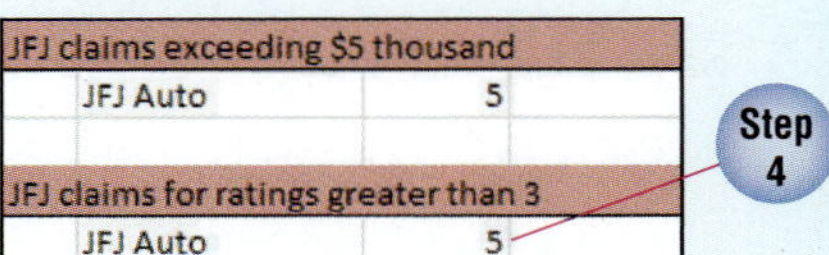

AVERAGEIF and AVERAGEIFS

The AVERAGEIF function is used to find the arithmetic mean of the cells within the specified range that meet a single criterion. The structure of an AVERAGEIF function is *=AVERAGEIF(range,criteria,average_range)* where *range* is the cells to be tested for the criterion, *criteria* is the conditional statement used to select cells, and *average_range* is the range containing the values you want to average.

AVERAGEIFS is used to average cells that meet multiple criteria using the formula *=AVERAGEIFS(average_range,criteria_range1,criteria1,criteria_range2,criteria2. . .)*. Figure 2.3 illustrates an executive management salary report for a hospital. Below the salary data, average salary statistics are shown. In the first two rows of salary statistics, the average total salary is calculated for each of two hospital campuses. In the second two rows of salary statistics, average total salary is calculated for each campus for those executives hired before 2010. The formulas shown in Figure 2.3 include range names where *Year* references the values in column E, *Campus* references the entries in column F, and *Total* references the values in column I.

Figure 2.3 AVERAGEIF and AVERAGEIFS Formulas

	A	B	C	D	E	F	G	H	I
1	Columbia River General Hospital								
2	Executive Management Salary Report								
3	For the fiscal year 2012 to 2013								
4				Job Title	Year Hired	Campus	Salary	Benefits	Total
5	Ms.	Michelle	Tan	Chief Executive Officer	2001	Sunnyside	$ 155,000	$ 18,400	$ 173,400
6	Mr.	Douglas	Brown	Legal Counsel	2011	Sunnyside	90,500	17,500	108,000
7	Mrs.	Lauren	Quandt	Chief Financial Officer	2011	Portland	110,750	18,400	129,150
8	Dr.	Dana	Pembroke	Medical Director	2005	Portland	101,500	14,650	116,150
9	Mrs.	Gina	Wright	Director of Nursing	2010	Portland	95,475	14,650	110,125
10	Mr.	Fernando	Ortega	Director of Patient Care Services	2011	Sunnyside	87,750	12,675	100,425
11	Mr.	Joshua	Vitello	Director of Facilities	2008	Sunnyside	85,000	9,275	94,275
12	Miss	Carin	Ledicke	Director of Human Resources	2006	Portland	85,000	9,275	94,275
13	Mr.	William	Formet	Director of Planning	2004	Portland	85,000	9,275	94,275
14	Mr.	Paul	Kosovic	Director, Community Relations	1998	Sunnyside	72,500	8,975	81,475
15									
16							$ 968,475	$133,075	$1,101,550
17									
18	Salary Statistics								
19		Average executive total salary at Portland campus					$ 108,795		
20		Average executive total salary at Sunnyside campus					$ 111,515		
21									
22		Average executive total salary at Portland campus hired before 2010					$ 101,567		
23		Average executive total salary at Sunnyside campus hired before 2010					$ 116,383		

Formula
=AVERAGEIF(Campus,"Portland",Total)

Formula
=AVERAGEIFS(Total,Campus,"Sunnyside",Year,"<2010")

Quick Steps

Create AVERAGEIF Formula

1. Make desired cell active.
2. Click Insert Function button.
3. Change category to *Statistical*.
4. Select *AVERAGEIF*.
5. Click OK.
6. Enter range address or range name to select by in *Range* text box.
7. Enter condition expression or text in *Criteria* text box.
8. Enter range address or range name to average in *Average_range* text box.
9. Click OK.

Create AVERAGEIFS Formula

1. Make desired cell active.
2. Click Insert Function button.
3. Change category to *Statistical*.
4. Select *AVERAGEIFS*.
5. Click OK.
6. Enter range address or range name to average in *Average_range* text box.
7. Enter range address or range name to select by in *Criteria_range1* text box.
8. Enter condition expression or text in *Criteria1* text box.
9. Enter range address or range name to select by in *Criteria_range2* text box.
10. Enter condition expression or text in *Criteria2* text box.
11. Continue adding criteria range expressions and criteria as needed.
12. Click OK.

Creating AVERAGEIF Functions

Part 4 of 7

1. With **EL2-C2-P1-AllClaimsOct12VehRpt.xlsx** open, make M16 the active cell.
2. Create an AVERAGEIF function to calculate the average claim estimate for those claims with a rating of 1 by completing the following steps:
   a. Click the Insert Function button in the Formula bar.
   b. With *Statistical* the category in the *Or select a category* list box, click *AVERAGEIF* in the *Select a function* list box.
   c. Read the formula description below the function list box and then click OK.
   d. At the Function Arguments dialog box with the insertion point positioned in the *Range* text box, type **Rating** and then press Tab.
   e. With the insertion point positioned in the *Criteria* text box, type **1** and then press Tab.
   f. With the insertion point positioned in the *Average_range* text box, type **ClaimEst** and then press Tab.
   g. Click OK. Excel returns the value *2691* in M16.

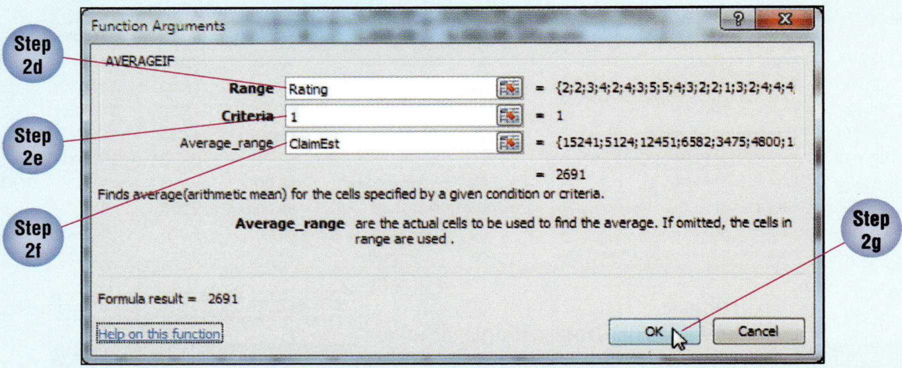

   h. Look at the formula in the Formula bar created by the Function Arguments dialog box: *=AVERAGEIF(Rating,1,ClaimEst)*.
3. Format M16 to Comma Style number format with zero decimals.
4. Make M17 the active cell, type the formula **=averageif(rating,2,claimest)**, and then press Enter.
5. Format M17 to Comma Style number format with zero decimals.
6. Make M17 the active cell and then drag the fill handle down to M18:M20.
7. Edit the formulas in M18, M19, and M20 by changing the rating criterion value from *2* to *3*, *4*, and *5*, respectively. When completed, the AVERAGEIF formulas will be as follows:
   M18 *=AVERAGEIF(Rating,3,ClaimEst)*
   M19 *=AVERAGEIF(Rating,4,ClaimEst)*
   M20 *=AVERAGEIF(Rating,5,ClaimEst)*

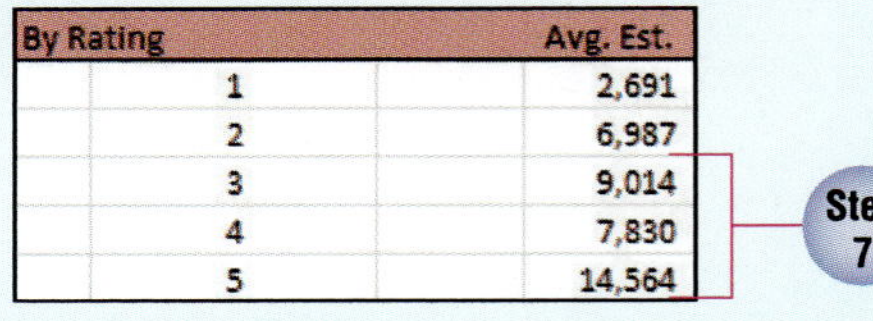

By Rating			Avg. Est.
	1		2,691
	2		6,987
	3		9,014
	4		7,830
	5		14,564

Step 7

8. Save **EL2-C2-P1-AllClaimsOct12VehRpt.xlsx**.

Creating AVERAGEIFS Functions

1. With **EL2-C2-P1-AllClaimsOct12VehRpt.xlsx** open, make M22 the active cell.
2. Create an AVERAGEIFS function to calculate the average claim estimate for those claims with a rating of 2 and driver number 1 by completing the following steps:
   a. Click the Insert Function button in the Formula bar.
   b. With *Statistical* the category in the *Or select a category* list box, click *AVERAGEIFS* in the *Select a function* list box.
   c. Read the formula description below the function list box and then click OK.
   d. At the Function Arguments dialog box with the insertion point positioned in the *Average_range* text box, type **ClaimEst** and then press Tab.
   e. Type **Rating** in the *Criteria_range1* text box and then press Tab.
   f. Type **2** in the *Criteria1* text box and then press Tab.
   g. Type **DriverNo** in the *Criteria_range2* text box and then press Tab.
   h. Type **1** in the *Criteria2* text box and then click OK. Excel returns the value *6272.666667* in the cell.

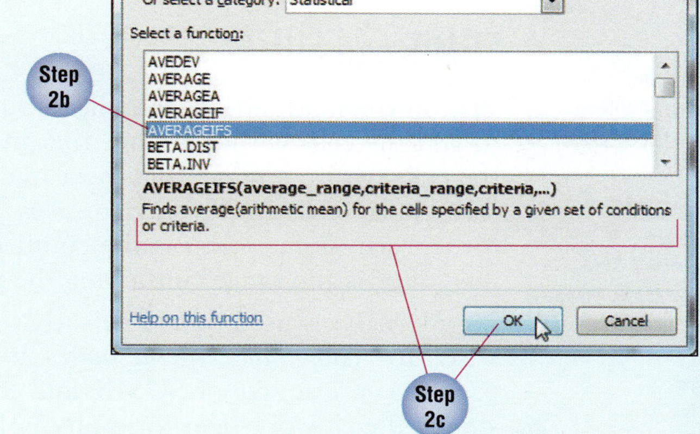

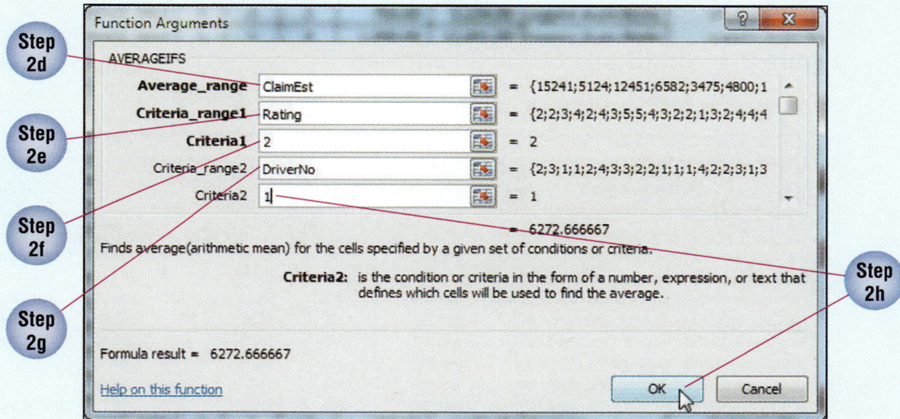

   i. Format M22 to Comma Style number format with zero decimals.
3. Copy the AVERAGEIFS formula in M22 and paste to M23.
4. Edit the formula in M23 to change the rating criterion from *2* to *3*. When completed, the AVERAGEIFS formula will be: *=AVERAGEIFS(ClaimEst,Rating,3,DriverNo,1)*.
5. If necessary, format M23 to Comma Style number format with zero decimals.
6. Save **EL2-C2-P1-AllClaimsOct12VehRpt.xlsx**.

Quick Steps

Create SUMIF Formula

1. Make desired cell active.
2. Click Formulas tab.
3. Click Math & Trig button.
4. Scroll down and click *SUMIF.*
5. Enter range address or range name to select by in *Range* text box.
6. Enter condition expression or text in *Criteria* text box.
7. Enter range address or range name to add in *Sum_range* text box.
8. Click OK.

Math & Trig Functions

Math and Trigonometry Functions

Excel includes several math and trigonometry functions such as ABS to return the absolute value of a number, SQRT to find the square root of a number, and RAND to return a random number between 0 and 1, to name a few. At the Insert Function dialog box change the *Or select a category* option to *Math & Trig* to scroll the list of available functions in the category.

SUMIF and SUMIFS

Within the math and trigonometry function category, Excel includes SUMIF to add the cells within a range that meet a single criterion and SUMIFS to add the cells within a range that meet multiple criteria. The structure of the SUMIF formula is *=SUMIF(range,criteria,sum_range)* where *range* is the cells to be tested for the criterion, *criteria* is the conditional statement used to select cells, and *sum_range* is the range containing the values to add.

SUMIFS is used to add cells that meet multiple criteria using the formula *=SUMIFS(sum_range,criteria_range1,criteria1,criteria_range2,criteria2. . .).* Figure 2.4 provides an example of SUMIF and SUMIFS formulas used in a medical clinic's standard cost worksheet for examination room supplies. At the right of the clinic supplies inventory, a SUMIF formula sums the cost for items by supplier number. A SUMIFS formula sums the cost for items by supplier number for items that require a minimum stock quantity over 4 items. The formulas shown in Figure 2.4 include range names where *Supplier* references the entries in column C, *MinQty* references the values in column E, and *StdCost* references the values in column F.

Figure 2.4 SUMIF and SUMIFS Formulas

Formula
=SUMIF(Supplier,"101",StdCost)

	A	B	C	D	E	F	G	H	I
1	North Shore Medical Clinic								
2	Clinic Supplies Inventory Units and Price								
3	Item	Unit	Supplier Number	Price	Minimum Stock Qty	Standard Cost		Exam Room Cost Analysis	
4	Sterile powder-free synthetic gloves, size Small	per 100	101	35.95	4	143.80	Cost by Supplier		
5	Sterile powder-free synthetic gloves, size Medium	per 100	101	35.95	8	287.60		Supplier Number 101	1,401.40
6	Sterile powder-free synthetic gloves, size Large	per 100	101	35.95	10	359.50		Supplier Number 155	364.33
7	Sterile powder-free latex gloves, size Small	per 100	101	16.25	4	65.00		Supplier Number 201	1,918.00
8	Sterile powder-free latex gloves, size Medium	per 100	101	16.25	8	130.00		Supplier Number 350	790.80
9	Sterile powder-free latex gloves, size Large	per 100	101	16.25	10	162.50			
10	Sterile powder-free vinyl gloves, size Small	per 100	101	11.50	4	46.00			
11	Sterile powder-free vinyl gloves, size Medium	per 100	101	11.50	8	92.00	Cost by Supplier with		
12	Sterile powder-free vinyl gloves, size Large	per 100	101	11.50	10	115.00	Minimum Qty over 4		
13	Disposable earloop mask	per 50	155	5.61	8	44.88		Supplier Number 101	1,146.60
14	Disposable patient gown	per dozen	155	7.90	16	126.40		Supplier Number 155	310.80
15	Disposable patient slippers	per dozen	155	4.27	16	68.32		Supplier Number 201	1,330.00
16	Cotton patient gown	per dozen	201	133.00	10	1,330.00		Supplier Number 350	659.00
17	Cotton patient robe	per dozen	201	147.00	4	588.00			
18	Disposable examination table paper	per roll	155	8.90	8	71.20			
19	Lab coat, size Small	each	350	32.95	4	131.80			
20	Lab coat, size Medium	each	350	32.95	8	263.60			
21	Lab coat, size Large	each	350	32.95	12	395.40			
22	Disposable shoe cover	per 300	155	37.75	1	37.75			
23	Disposable bouffant cap	per 100	155	7.89	2	15.78			
24	TOTAL STANDARD EXAM ROOM SUPPLIES COST:					4,474.53			

Formula
=SUMIFS(StdCost,Supplier,"350",MinQty,">4")

Project 1f Creating SUMIF Functions

Note: At Step 5 you will print the worksheet. Check with your instructor before printing to see if you need to print two copies of the worksheets for all projects in this chapter: one as displayed and another displaying cell formulas. Save the worksheet before displaying formulas (Ctrl + ~) so that you can adjust column widths as necessary and then close without saving the changes.

1. With **EL2-C2-P1-AllClaimsOct12VehRpt.xlsx** open, make M4 the active cell.
2. Create a SUMIF function to sum the claim estimates for those claims being repaired at A+ Paint & Body by completing the following steps:
   a. Click the Formulas tab.
   b. Click the Math & Trig button in the Function Library group.
   c. Scroll down the drop-down list and click *SUMIF*.
   d. At the Function Arguments dialog box with the insertion point positioned in the *Range* text box, type **RepShop** and then press Tab.
   e. Type **A+ Paint & Body** in the *Criteria* text box and then press Tab.
   f. Type **ClaimEst** in the *Sum_range* text box and then click OK. Excel returns the value *16656* in M4.

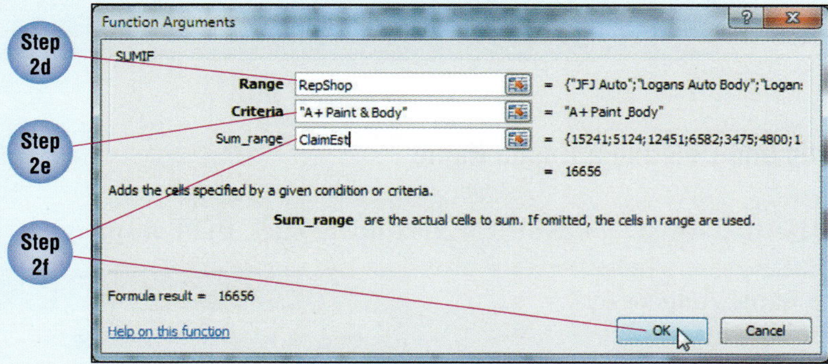

   g. Format M4 to Comma Style number format with zero decimals.
3. Enter the following SUMIF formulas in the cells indicated using either the Function Arguments dialog box or by typing the formula directly into the cell.
   M5 **=SUMIF(RepShop,"JFJ Auto",ClaimEst)**
   M6 **=SUMIF(RepShop,"Logans Auto Body",ClaimEst)**
   M7 **=SUMIF(RepShop,"West Collision",ClaimEst)**
4. Format M5:M7 to Comma Style number format with zero decimals.
5. Save and then print **EL2-C2-P1-AllClaimsOct12VehRpt.xlsx**.

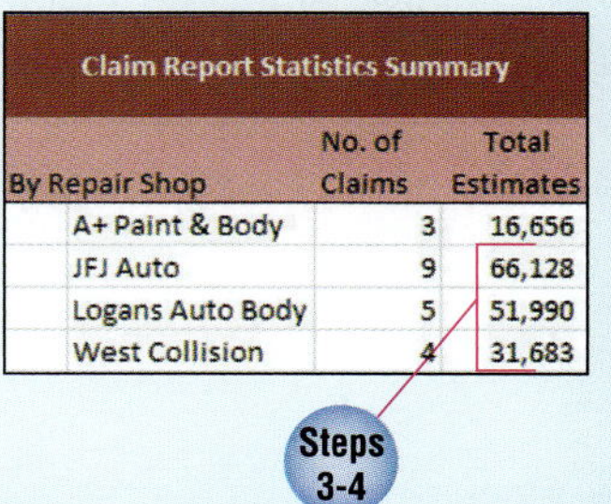

Claim Report Statistics Summary		
By Repair Shop	No. of Claims	Total Estimates
A+ Paint & Body	3	16,656
JFJ Auto	9	66,128
Logans Auto Body	5	51,990
West Collision	4	31,683

Quick Steps

Delete Range Name
1. Click Formulas tab.
2. Click Name Manager button.
3. Click desired range name.
4. Click Delete button.
5. Click OK.
6. Click Close.

Edit Range Name
1. Click Formulas tab.
2. Click Name Manager button.
3. Click desired range name.
4. Click Edit button.
5. Type new range name in *Name* text box.
6. Click OK.
7. Click Close.

Name Manager

Managing Range Names

The Name Manager dialog box can be used to create, edit, or delete range names. A range name can be edited by changing the name or modifying the range address associated with the name. A range name can also be deleted if the name is not being used. Exercise caution when deleting a range name. If a range name used in a formula is deleted, cells that used the range name display the error #NAME? New range names can also be added to the workbook using the Name Manager dialog box shown in Figure 2.5.

Figure 2.5 Name Manager Dialog Box

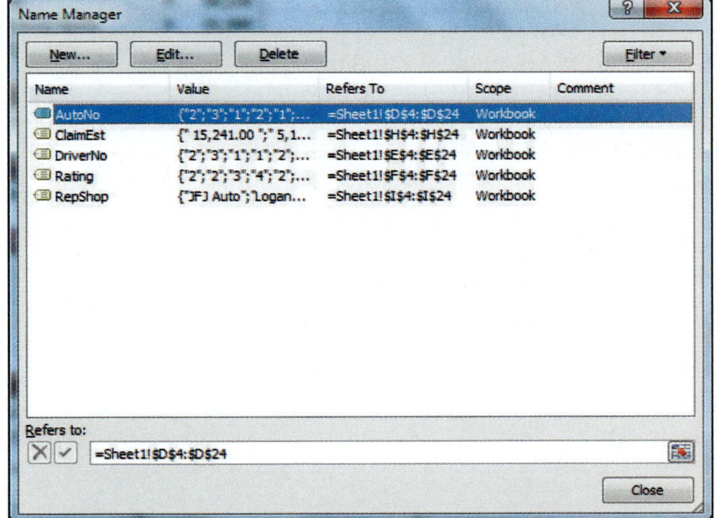

Project 1g Editing and Deleting a Range Name

Part 7 of 7

1. With **EL2-C2-P1-AllClaimsOct12VehRpt.xlsx** open, click the Formulas tab if it is not currently active.
2. Delete the range name *AutoNo* by completing the following steps:
   a. Click the Name Manager button in the Defined Names group.
   b. At the Name Manager dialog box, with *AutoNo* already selected in the *Name* list box, click the Delete button.
   c. At the Microsoft Excel message box asking you to confirm the deletion of the name *AutoNo*, click OK.

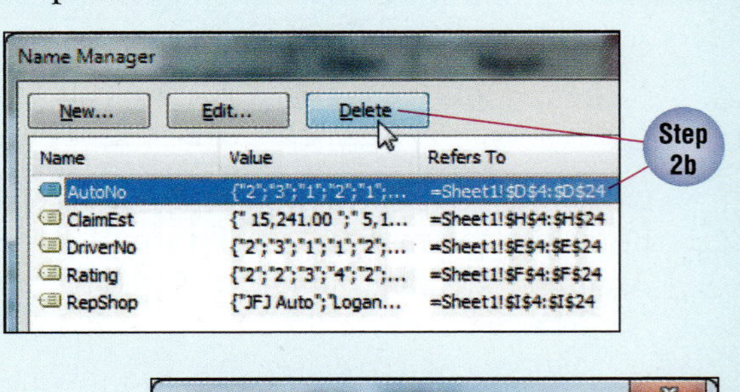

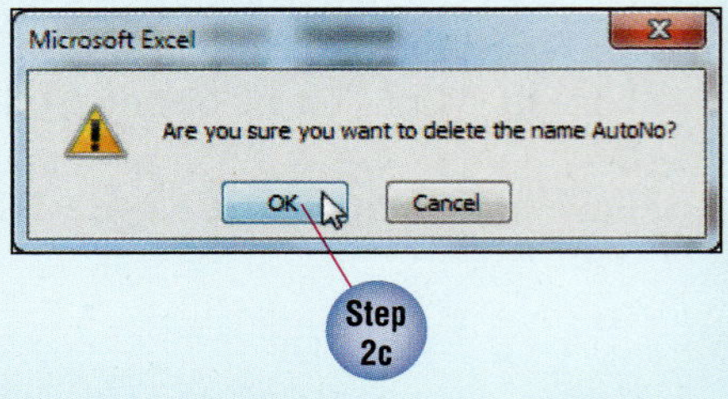

3. Edit the range name for the range named *ClaimEst* by completing the following steps:
   a. Click *ClaimEst* in the *Name* list box and then click the Edit button.
   b. At the Edit Name dialog box with *ClaimEst* already selected in the *Name* text box, type **ClaimEstimate** and then click OK. Notice the new range name is now displayed in the *Name* list box.
   c. Click the Close button located at the bottom right of the Name Manager dialog box.
4. Click in cell M4 and look at the formula in the Formula bar. Notice Excel automatically changed the range name in the formula from *ClaimEst* to *ClaimEstimate*.
5. Save and then close **EL2-C2-P1-AllClaimsOct12VehRpt.xlsx**.

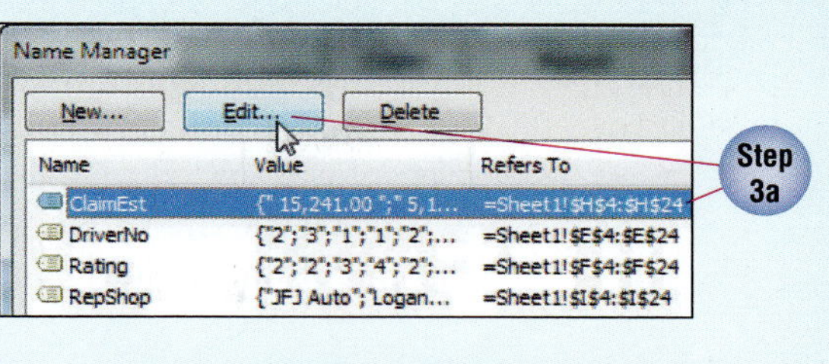

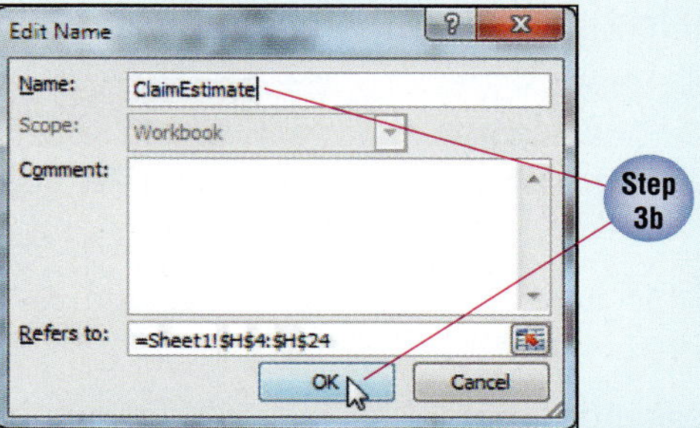

Project 2 Populate Cells by Looking Up Data — 1 Part

You will use a lookup formula to automatically enter discounts for containers and then calculate net prices.

Lookup Functions

The Lookup & Reference category of functions provides formulas that can be used to look up values in a range. For example, in a grades worksheet, the final numerical score for a student can be looked up in a range of cells that contain the letter grades with corresponding numerical scores for each grade. The letter grade can be returned in the formula cell by looking up the student's score. The ability to look up a value automates data entry in large worksheets and when used properly can avoid inaccuracies from data entry errors. Excel provides two lookup functions: VLOOKUP and HLOOKUP, which refer to a vertical or horizontal lookup, respectively. The layout of the lookup range (referred to as a lookup table) determines whether to use VLOOKUP or HLOOKUP. VLOOKUP is more commonly used since most lookup tables are arranged with comparison data in columns, which means Excel searches for the lookup value in a vertical order. HLOOKUP is used when the lookup range has placed comparison data in rows and Excel searches for the lookup value in a horizontal pattern.

Quick Steps

Create VLOOKUP Formula
1. Make desired cell active.
2. Click Formulas tab.
3. Click Lookup & Reference button.
4. Click *VLOOKUP*.
5. Enter cell address, range name, or value in *Lookup_value* text box.
6. Enter range or range name in *Table_array* text box.
7. Type column number to return values from in *Col_index_num* text box.
8. Type **FALSE** or leave blank for *TRUE* in *Range_lookup* text box.
9. Click OK.

VLOOKUP

The structure of a VLOOKUP formula is =*VLOOKUP(lookup_value,table_array,col_index_num,range_lookup)*. Table 2.2 explains each section of the VLOOKUP argument.

VLOOKUP is easier to understand using an example. In the worksheet shown in Figure 2.6, VLOOKUP is used to return the starting salary for new hires at a

medical center. Each new hire is assigned a salary grid number that places his or her starting salary depending on their education and years of work experience. The lookup table contains the grid numbers with the corresponding starting salary. VLOOKUP formulas in column E automatically insert the starting salary for each new employee based on the employee's grid number in column D. In the formula shown in Figure 2.6 range names have been included where *Rating* references the values in column D and *grid* represents the lookup table in G2:H8.

Table 2.2 VLOOKUP Argument Parameters

Argument Parameter	*Description*
Lookup_value	The value that you want Excel to search for in the lookup table. You can enter a value or a cell reference to a value.
Table_array	The range address or range name for the lookup table that you want Excel to search.
Col_index_num	The column number from the lookup table that contains the data you want placed in the formula cell.
Range_lookup	Enter TRUE or FALSE to instruct Excel to find an exact match for the lookup value or an approximate match. If this parameter is left out of the formula, Excel assumes TRUE, which means if an exact match is not found, Excel returns the value for the next largest number that is less than the lookup value. For the formula to work properly, the first column of the lookup table must be sorted in ascending order. Enter FALSE to instruct Excel to return only exact matches to the lookup value.

Figure 2.6 VLOOKUP Example

	A	B	C	D	E	F	G	H
1	HealthPlus Medical Center							
2	New Hires for 2012						Reference Table	
3	Date of Hire	First name	Last name	Salary Grid Rating	Starting Salary		Salary Grid Rating	Starting Salary
4	10/5/2012	Joel	Adams	3	34,875		1	$ 31,175
5	10/8/2012	David	Bannerman	4	35,750		2	$ 32,250
6	10/15/2012	Jill	Williams	2	32,250		3	$ 34,875
7	10/15/2012	Kendall	Borman	1	31,175		4	$ 35,750
8	10/22/2012	Leigh	Wilcox	1	31,175		5	$ 38,675
9	10/23/2012	Vanessa	Lopez	4	35,750			
10	10/25/2012	Cory	Campbell	5	38,675			
11	10/26/2012	George	Sorrenti	2	32,250			
12	10/30/2012	Paula	Gorski	1	31,175			
13	10/31/2012	Kyla	Vanwyst	3	34,875			

Lookup table is named *grid*.

VLOOKUP formula populates E4:E13 by matching the salary grid rating number in column D with the corresponding salary grid rating number in the lookup table named *grid*.

Formula in E4 is *=VLOOKUP(Rating,grid,2)*.

Project 2 Creating a VLOOKUP Function

Part 1 of 1

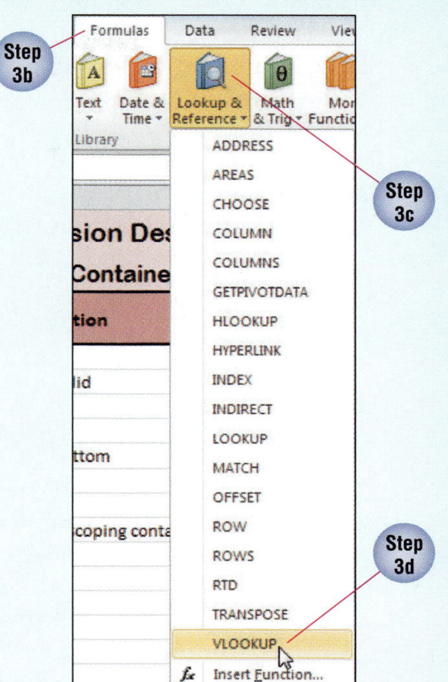

1. Open **PrecisionPrices.xlsx**.
2. Save the workbook with Save As and name it **EL2-C2-P2-PrecisionPrices**.
3. Create a VLOOKUP formula to find the correct discount values for each product by completing the following steps:
   a. Select H4:I8 and name the range *DiscTable*.
   b. Make E4 the active cell and then click the Formulas tab.
   c. Click the Lookup & Reference button in the Function Library group.
   d. Click *VLOOKUP* at the drop-down list.
   e. If necessary, drag the Function Arguments dialog box out of the way so that you can see the first few rows of the products price list and the Discount Table data.
   f. With the insertion point positioned in the *Lookup_value* text box, type **c4** and then press Tab. Product discounts are categorized by letter codes. To find the correct discount, you need Excel to look for the matching category letter code for the product within the first column of the Discount Table.
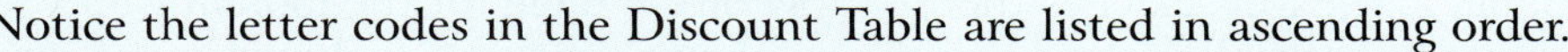
      Notice the letter codes in the Discount Table are listed in ascending order.
   g. Type **DiscTable** in the *Table_array* text box and then press Tab. Using a range name for a reference table is a good idea since the formula will be copied and absolute references are needed for the cells in the lookup table.
   h. Type **2** in the *Col_index_num* text box and then press Tab.
   i. Type **false** in the *Range_lookup* text box and then click OK. By typing *false*, you are instructing Excel to return a value for exact matches only. Should a discount category be typed into a cell in column C for which no entry exists in the Discount Table, Excel will return *#N/A* in the formula cell, which will alert you that an error has occurred in the data entry.

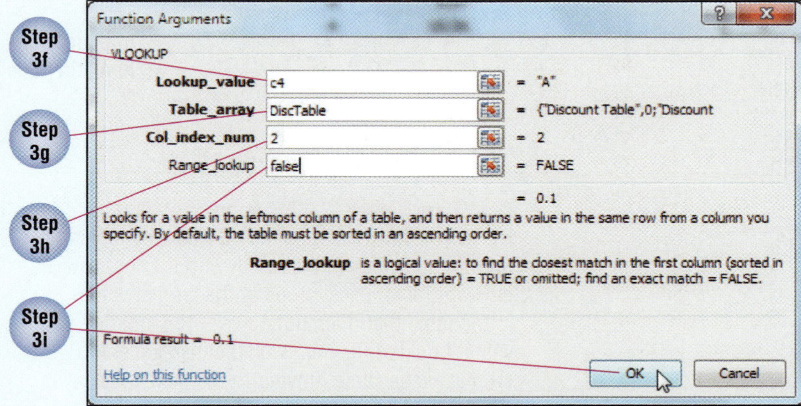

4. Look at the formula in the Formula bar *=VLOOKUP(C4,DiscTable,2,FALSE)*.
5. Format E4 to Percent Style.

6. Make F4 the active cell, type the formula =d4-(d4*e4), and then press Enter.
7. Select E4:F4 and then drag the fill handle down to row 21.
8. Deselect the range.
9. Print the worksheet.
10. Save and then close **EL2-C2-P2-PrecisionPrices.xlsx**.

C	D	E	F	G	H	I
and Packaging						
ducts Price List					Discount Table	
Discount Category	List Price	Discount	Net Price		Discount Category	Discount Percent
A	18.67	10%	=d4-(d4*e4)		A	10%
C	22.50				B	12%
B	14.53				C	14%
D	5.25				D	16%
A	18.54				E	20%

Step 6

HLOOKUP

The HLOOKUP function uses the same argument parameters as VLOOKUP. Use HLOOKUP when the table in which you want to search for a comparison value is arranged in a horizontal arrangement similar to the one shown in Figure 2.7. Excel searches across the table in the first row for a matching value and then returns to the formula cell the value from the same column. The structure of an HLOOKUP formula is *=HLOOKUP(lookup_value,table_array,row_index_num,range_lookup)*. The argument parameters are similar to VLOOKUP's parameters described in Table 2.2. Excel searches the first row of the table for the lookup value. When a match is found, Excel returns the value from the same column in the row number specified in the *row_index_num* argument.

Figure 2.7 HLOOKUP Example

	A	B	C	D	E	F	G	H	I	J	K	L	M	N	O
1	Math by Janelle Tutoring Service														
2	Student Progress Report														
3	Student Name	Test 1	Test 2	Test 3	Test 4	Total	Grade		Score	0	50	60	70	80	90
4	Dana Rosenthal	51	48	55	50	51.0	D		Grade	F	D	C	B	A	A+
5	Kelsey Williams	75	82	66	72	73.8	B								
6	Hilary Corbet	81	88	79	83	82.8	A								
7	Jose Alvarez	67	72	65	78	70.5	B								
8	Linden Porter	42	51	40	55	47.0	F								
9	Carl Quenneville	65	44	72	61	60.5	C								
10	Andrea Desmond	55	48	60	50	53.3	D								
11	Kylie Winters	78	82	67	71	74.5	B								
12	Lindsay Cortez	82	78	85	88	83.3	A								

Lookup table is named *GradeTable*.

HLOOKUP formula populates G4:G12 by looking up the total value in column F with the first row in GradeTable. Excel stops at the largest value in the table that does not go over the lookup value. Looking for *62.3* would cause Excel to stop at *60* because moving to the next value, *70*, would be over the lookup value. Formula in G4 is *=HLOOKUP(F4,GradeTable,2)*.

Project 3 Analyze an Expansion Project Loan — 1 Part

You will use a financial function to calculate the principal portion of an expansion loan payment for two lenders.

Financial Functions

Financial functions can be used for a variety of financial analyses including loan amortizations, annuity payments, investment planning, depreciation, and so on. The PMT function is used to calculate a payment for a loan based on a constant interest rate and constant payments for a set period of time. Excel provides two related financial functions: PPMT, to calculate the principal portion of the loan payment; and IPMT, to calculate the interest portion.

Quick Steps

Create PPMT Formula

1. Make desired cell active.
2. Click Formulas tab.
3. Click Financial button.
4. Click *PPMT*.
5. Enter value, cell address, or range name for interest rate in *Rate* text box.
6. Enter number representing payment to find principal for in *Per* text box.
7. Enter value, cell address, or range name for total number of payments in *Nper* text box.
8. Enter value, cell address, or range name for amount borrowed in *Pv* text box.
9. Click OK.

Financial Functions

PPMT

Knowing the principal portion of a loan payment is useful to determine the amount of the payment that is being used to reduce the principal balance owing. The difference between the loan payment and the PPMT value represents the interest cost. The function returns the principal portion of a specific payment for a loan. For example, you can calculate the principal on the first payment, the last payment, or any payment in between. The structure of a PPMT function is *=PPMT(rate,per,nper,pv,fv,type)* where:

- *rate* is the interest rate per period,
- *per* is the period for which you want to find the principal portion of the payment,
- *nper* is the number of payment periods,
- *pv* is the amount of money borrowed,
- *fv* is the balance at the end of the loan (if left blank, zero is assumed), and
- *type* is either 0 (payment at end of period) or 1 (payment at beginning of period).

Be careful to be consistent with the units for the interest rate and payment periods. If you divide the interest rate by 12 for a monthly rate, make sure the payment periods are also expressed monthly—for example, multiply the term by 12 if the amortization is entered in the worksheet in years.

Project 3 Calculating Principal Portion of Loan Payments — Part 1 of 1

1. Open **DeeringExpansion.xlsx**.
2. Save the workbook with Save As and name it **EL2-C2-P3-DeeringExpansion.xlsx**.
3. Calculate the principal portion of loan payments for two loan proposals to fund a building loan expansion project by completing the following steps:
   a. Make C10 the active cell.

b. If necessary, click the Formulas tab.
c. Click the Financial button in the Function Library group.
d. Scroll down the Financial functions drop-down list and then click *PPMT*.
e. If necessary, move the Function Arguments dialog box to the right side of the screen so that you can see all of the values in column C.
f. With the insertion point positioned in the *Rate* text box, type **c4/12** and then press Tab. Since the interest rate is stated per annum, dividing the rate by 12 calculates the monthly rate.
g. Type **1** in the *Per* text box to calculate principal for the first loan payment and then press Tab.
h. Type **c5*12** in the *Nper* text box and then press Tab. Since loan payments are made each month, the number of payments is 12 times the amortization period.
i. Type **c6** in the *Pv* text box and then click OK. Pv refers to present value and in this example means the loan amount for which the payments are being calculated. Excel returns the value *-1,291.40* in C10. Payments are shown as negative numbers since they represent cash that would be paid out. In this worksheet, negative numbers have been formatted to display in red and enclosed in brackets.

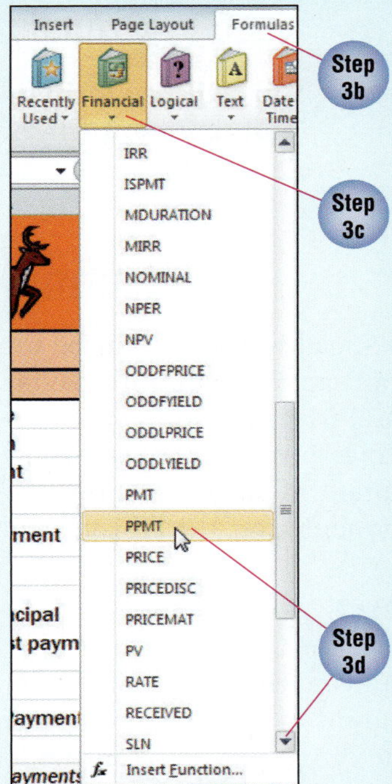

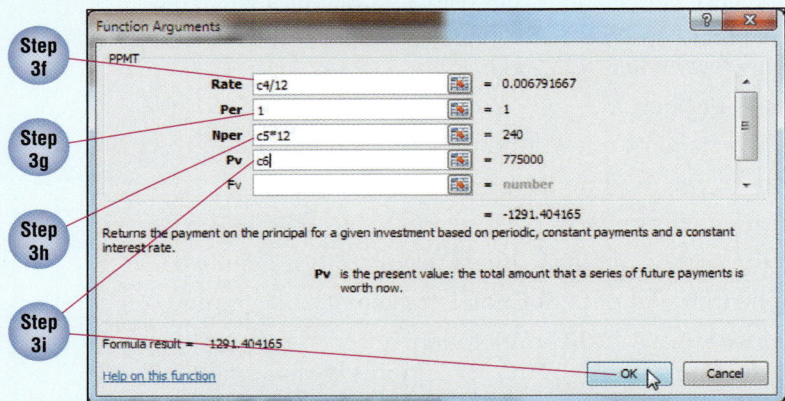

4. Copy and paste the formula from C10 to E10 and then press Esc to remove the moving marquee from C10.
5. Make C12 the active cell, type **=c8*12*c5**, and then press Enter.
6. Copy and paste the formula from C12 to E12. Press Esc to remove the moving marquee from C12 and then AutoFit the width of column E. Notice the loan from Dominion Trust is a better choice for Deering Industries provided the company can afford the higher monthly payments. Although the interest rate is higher than Victory Trust's loan, the shorter term means the loan is repaid faster at a lesser total cost.
7. Print the worksheet.
8. Save **EL2-C2-P3-DeeringExpansion.xlsx**.

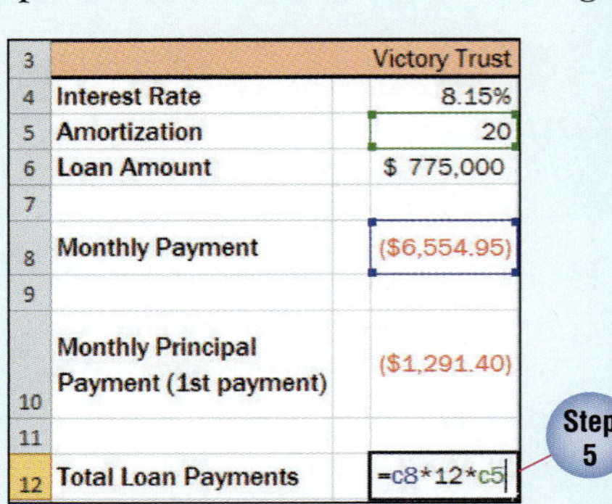

Project 4 Calculate Benefit Costs Using Conditional Logic — 2 Parts

You will create formulas to calculate the employee benefit costs for Vantage Video Rentals using logical functions to test multiple conditions.

Logical Functions

Conditional logic in formulas requires Excel to perform a calculation based on the outcome of a conditional test where one calculation is performed if the test proves true and another calculation is performed if the test proves false. For example, an IF statement to calculate a sales bonus if sales exceed a target could be created similar to the following: *=IF(Sales>Target,Bonus,0)*. Excel first tests the value in the cell named Sales to see if the value is greater than the value in the cell named Target. If the condition proves true, Excel returns the value in the cell named *Bonus;* if Sales are not greater than Target, the condition proves false and Excel places a *0* in the cell. The structure of the IF statement is *=IF(condition,value_if_true,value_if_false)*.

Quick Steps

Create IF Formula

1. Make desired cell active.
2. Click Formulas tab.
3. Click Logical button.
4. Click *IF.*
5. Type conditional test argument in *Logical_test* text box.
6. Press Tab.
7. Type argument in *Value_if_true* text box.
8. Press Tab.
9. Type argument in *Value_if_false* text box.
10. Click OK.

Nested Functions

If you need Excel to perform more than two actions, create a nested IF function. A nested IF function is an IF function inside of another IF function. For example, assume that a company has three sales commission rates based on the level of sales achieved by the salesperson. If sales are less than $40 thousand, the salesperson earns 5% commission; if sales are over $40 thousand but less than $80 thousand, the salesperson earns 7% commission; for sales over $80 thousand, the salesperson earns 9% commission. Since there are three possible sales commission rates, a single IF function will not work. To correctly calculate the sales commission rate, one would need to do two conditional tests.

HINT

If you type a nested IF function directly into a cell, Excel color-codes the brackets for each IF function so that you can keep track of each IF function separately.

Consider the following formula: *=IF(Sales<40000,Sales*5%,IF(Sales<80000,Sales*7%,Sales*9%))*. This formula includes two IF functions. In the first IF function, the conditional test is to determine if the sales value is less than $40 thousand (*Sales<40000*). If the test proves true (for example, sales are $25,000), then Excel calculates the sales times 5% and returns the result in the active cell. If the test proves false, then Excel reads the next section of the argument which is the next IF function that includes the conditional test to determine if sales are less than $80 thousand (*Sales<80000*). If this second conditional test proves true, then Excel calculates the sales times 7%. If the test proves false, Excel calculates the sales times 9%. Since these are the only three possible actions, the formula ends.

HINT

The number of right brackets needed to end a nested IF statement equals the number of times IF appears in the formula.

You can nest any function inside of another function. For example, in the PPMT formula you learned in the previous section, Excel returns a negative value for the principal portion of the payment. You can nest the PPMT formula inside of the ABS formula to have the principal payment displayed without a negative symbol. ABS is the function used to return the absolute value of a number (the number without its sign). For example, *=ABS(PPMT(C4/12,1,C5*12,C6))* would display the payment calculated in Project 3 as $1,291.40 instead of -$1,291.40.

Logical Functions

Quick Steps

Create AND Formula

1. Make desired cell active OR nest formula in IF statement *Logical_test* text box.
2. Type **=AND(** or **AND(** if nesting in IF statement.
3. Type first conditional test argument.
4. Type **,**.
5. Type second conditional test argument.
6. Repeat Steps 4–5 for remaining conditions.
7. Type **)**.

Create OR Formula

1. Make desired cell active OR nest formula in IF statement *Logical_test* text box.
2. Type **=OR(** or **OR(** if nesting in IF statement.
3. Type first conditional test argument.
4. Type **,**.
5. Type second conditional test argument.
6. Repeat Steps 4–5 for remaining conditions.
7. Type **)**.

HINT

You can nest an AND or OR function with an IF function to test multiple conditions.

AND and OR

Other logic functions offered in Excel include AND and OR. These functions use Boolean logic to construct a conditional test in a formula. Table 2.3 describes how the functions work to test a statement and provides an example for each.

Table 2.3 AND and OR Logical Functions

Logical Function	*Description*	*Example*
AND	Excel returns *True* if all conditions test true. Excel returns *False* if any one of the conditions tests false.	=AND(Sales>Target,NewClients>5) Returns *True* if both test true. If Sales>Target but NewClients<5, returns *False*. If Sales<Target but NewClients>5, returns *False*.
OR	Excel returns *True* if any condition tests true. Excel returns *False* if all conditions test false.	=OR(Sales>Target,NewClients>5) Returns *True* if either Sales>Target or NewClients>5. Returns *False* only if both Sales is not greater than Target and NewClients is not greater than 5.

Project 4a **Calculating Pension Cost Using Nested IF and AND Functions** Part 1 of 2

1. Open **VantageHOSalaryCosts.xlsx**.
2. Save the workbook with Save As and name it **EL2-C2-P4-VantageHOSalaryCosts**.
3. Vantage Video Rentals contributes 5% of an employee's salary into a privately managed company retirement account if the employee is full-time and earns more than $45 thousand in salary. Calculate the pension benefit cost for eligible employees by completing the following steps:
   a. Make H6 the active cell.
   b. Click the Formulas tab.

c. Click the Logical button in the Function Library group and then click *IF* at the drop-down list.
d. If necessary, drag the Function Arguments dialog box down until you can see all of row 6 in the worksheet.
e. With the insertion point positioned in the *Logical_test* text box, type **and(c6="FT",g6>45000)** and then press Tab. An AND function is required since both conditions must be true for the company to contribute to the pension plan. ***Note: Excel requires quotation symbols around text when used in a conditional test formula.***
f. Type **g6*5%** in the *Value_if_true* text box and then press Tab.
g. Type **0** in the *Value_if_false* text box and then click OK.

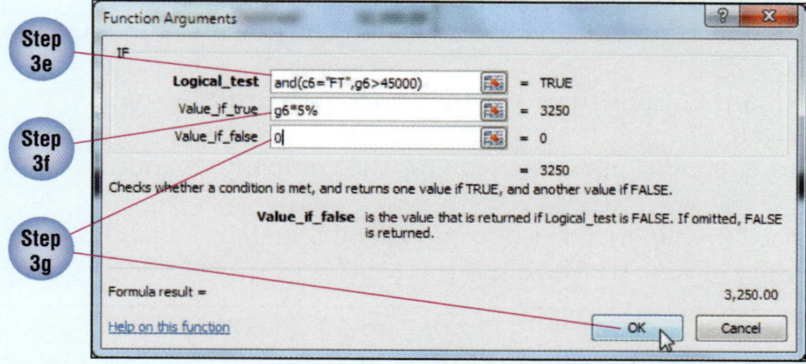

h. Look at the formula *=IF(AND(C6="FT",G6>45000),G6*5%,0)* in the Formula bar. Notice the AND function is nested within the IF function. Since both conditions for the first employee tested true, the pension cost is calculated.
i. Copy the formula in H6 to H7:H14. Notice that only the first three employees have a pension benefit value. The first three employees are the only ones who are both full-time and earn over $45 thousand.

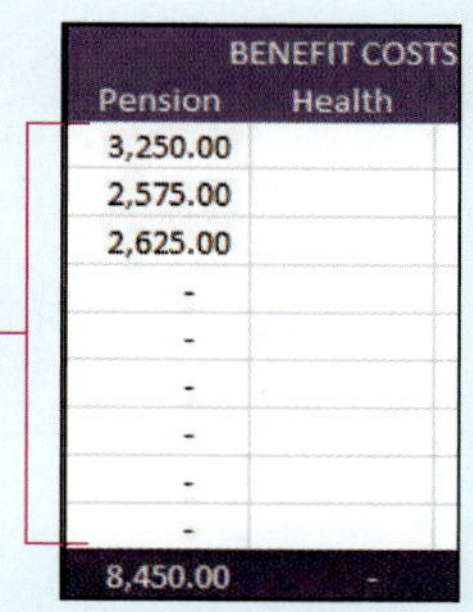

Step 3i
BENEFIT COSTS
Pension
Health
3,250.00
2,575.00
2,625.00
-
-
-
-
-
-
8,450.00
-

4. Save **EL2-C2-P4-VantageHOSalaryCosts.xlsx**.

Project 4b Calculating Health and Dental Costs Using Nested IF and OR Functions Part 2 of 2

1. With **EL2-C2-P4-VantageHOSalaryCosts.xlsx** open, make I6 the active cell.
2. Vantage Video Rentals offers to pay the annual health premiums for employees who are not covered by any other medical plan. The company pays $2,100 per year per employee for family coverage and $1,380 per year for single coverage. Calculate the cost of the health benefit for those employees who opted into the plan by completing the following steps:
   a. This formula requires a nested IF statement since the result will be either *$2,180* or *$1,380* depending on the contents in cell D6. (An OR statement will not work for this formula since two different values are used.) Type the formula shown below in I6 and then press Enter. ***Note: Recall that Excel requires quotation symbols around text entries within an IF function.***
   =if(d6="Family",2100,if(d6="Single",1380,0))

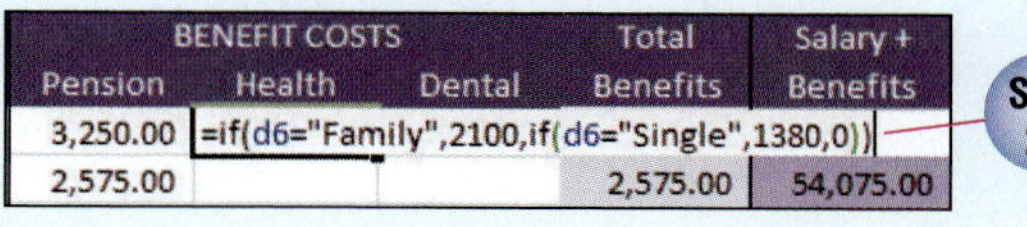

BENEFIT COSTS
Pension
Health
Dental
Total Benefits
Salary + Benefits
3,250.00
=if(d6="Family",2100,if(d6="Single",1380,0))
2,575.00
2,575.00
54,075.00

b. Copy the formula in I6 to I7:I14. Notice the cells for which no value is entered. In column D, these employees show the text *Declined*. Excel returned zero since both conditions *D6="Family"* and *D6="Single"* proved false.

3. Vantage Video Rentals negotiated a flat fee with their dental benefit service provider. The company pays the same rate of $1,500 per year for all employees regardless of the type of coverage. The service provider requires Vantage to report each person's coverage as *Family* or *Single* for audit purposes. The dental plan is optional and some employees have declined the coverage. Calculate the dental plan cost by completing the following steps:
   a. Make J6 the active cell.
   b. If necessary, click the Formulas tab.
   c. Click the Logical button and then click *IF* at the drop-down list.
   d. If necessary, drag the Function Arguments dialog box down until you can see all of row 6 in the worksheet.
   e. With the insertion point positioned in the *Logical_test* text box, type **or(e6="Family",e6="Single")** and then press Tab. An OR function is suited to this benefit since either condition can be true for the company to contribute to the dental plan.
   f. Type **1500** in the *Value_if_true* text box and then press Tab.
   g. Type **0** in the *Value_if_false* text box and then click OK.

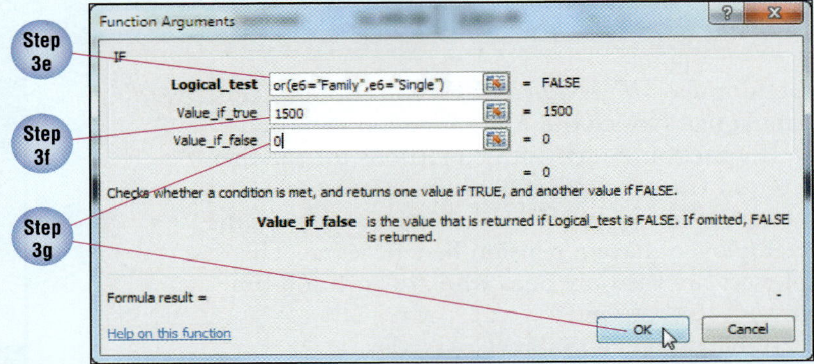

   h. Look at the formula *=IF(OR(E6="Family",E6="Single"),1500,0)* in the Formula bar. Notice the OR function is nested within the IF function. Since E6 contained neither *Family* nor *Single*, the OR statement tested false and the result of *0* is returned in J6.

Step 3i

BENEFIT COSTS			Total	Salary +
Pension	Health	Dental	Benefits	Benefits
3,250.00	2,100.00	-	5,350.00	70,350.00
2,575.00	1,380.00	1,500.00	5,455.00	56,955.00
2,625.00	-	-	2,625.00	55,125.00
-	2,100.00	1,500.00	3,600.00	31,100.00
-	1,380.00	1,500.00	2,880.00	47,880.00
-	2,100.00	-	2,100.00	24,600.00
-	1,380.00	-	1,380.00	29,880.00
-	-	-	-	42,500.00
-	-	1,500.00	1,500.00	42,000.00
8,450.00	10,440.00	6,000.00	24,890.00	400,390.00

   i. Copy the formula in J6 to J7:J14.

4. Save **EL2-C2-P4-VantageHOSalaryCosts.xlsx**.
5. Print and then close **EL2-C2-P4-VantageHOSalaryCosts.xlsx**.

Convert Text Using Text Functions

1 Part

You will open a worksheet with data downloaded from the U.S. Census Bureau and use text functions to modify a heading and convert state names to uppercase.

Text Functions

Text can be formatted or modified using a text function formula. For example, text can be converted from uppercase to lowercase or vice versa using the LOWER and UPPER functions. Text that has incorrect capitalization can be changed to initial case using the PROPER function. Substitute existing text with new text using the SUBSTITUTE function. Table 2.4 provides the structure of each of these functions, with a description and examples.

Quick Steps

Substitute Text Formula
1. Make desired cell active.
2. Type **=SUBSTITUTE(**.
3. Type source text cell address.
4. Type **,**.
5. Type text to be changed in quotation symbols.
6. Type **,**.
7. Type replacement text in quotation symbols.
8. Type **)**.
9. Press Enter.

Convert Text to Uppercase
1. Make desired cell active.
2. Type **=UPPER(**.
3. Type source cell address.
   OR
   Type text to convert in quotation symbols.
4. Type **)**.
5. Press Enter.

Text Functions

Table 2.4 Text Function Examples

Text Function	*Description*	*Example*
=PROPER(text)	Capitalizes the first letter of each word.	=PROPER("annual budget") returns *Annual Budget* in formula cell OR A3 holds the text *annual budget*; =PROPER(A3) entered in C3 causes C3 to display *Annual Budget*
=UPPER(text)	Converts text to uppercase.	=UPPER("annual budget") returns *ANNUAL BUDGET* in formula cell OR A3 holds the text *annual budget*; =UPPER(A3) entered in C3 causes C3 to display *ANNUAL BUDGET*
=LOWER(text)	Converts text to lowercase.	=LOWER("ANNUAL BUDGET") returns *annual budget* in formula cell OR A3 holds the text *ANNUAL BUDGET*; =LOWER(A3) entered in C3 causes C3 to display *annual budget*
=SUBSTITUTE(text)	New text is inserted in place of old text.	A3 holds the text *Annual Budget*; =SUBSTITUTE(A3,"Annual","2010") entered in C3 causes C3 to display *2010 Budget*

Converting Text Using SUBSTITUTE and UPPER Text Functions

Part 1 of 1

1. Open **USIncomeStats.xlsx**.
2. Save the workbook with Save As and name it **EL2-C2-P5-USIncomeStats**.
3. The worksheet contains 2008 median income data downloaded from the U.S. Census Bureau. You want to estimate 2012 median income using a formula based on 2008 statistics. To begin, copy and substitute text at the top of the worksheet to create the layout for 2012 data by completing the following steps:
   a. Copy A1 and paste to F1. Click the Paste Options button and then click the *Keep Source Column Widths* button in the *Paste* section of the drop-down gallery.

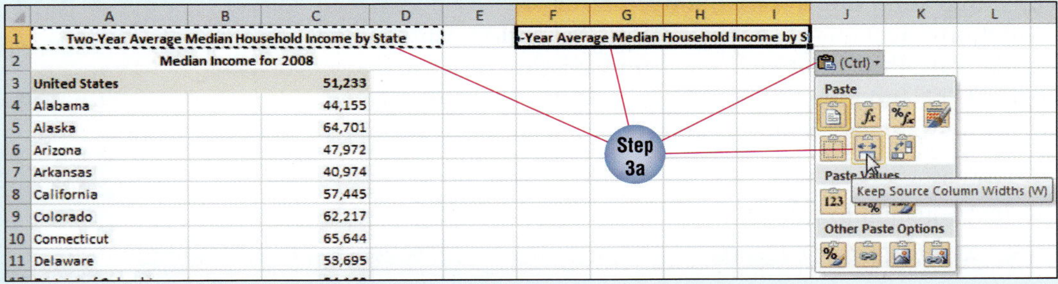

   b. Press the ESC key to remove the moving marquee from A1.
   c. Make F2 the active cell, type **=substitute(a2,"2008","2012")** and then press Enter.

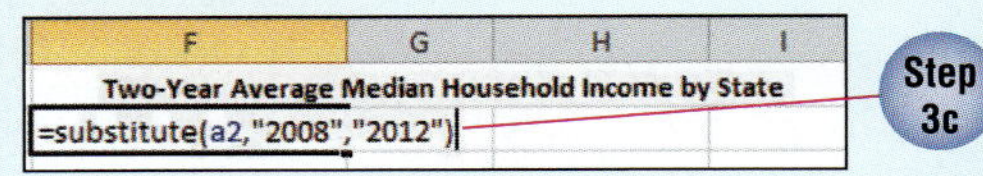

   d. Merge and center F2 across F2:I2.
4. Copy A3 and the state names below A3 from column A to column F and convert the text to uppercase by completing the following steps:
   a. Make F3 the active cell.
   b. Type **=upper(a3)** and then press Enter. Excel returns the text *UNITED STATES* in F3.
   c. Press the Up Arrow key to move the active cell back to F3 and then drag the fill handle down to F54.

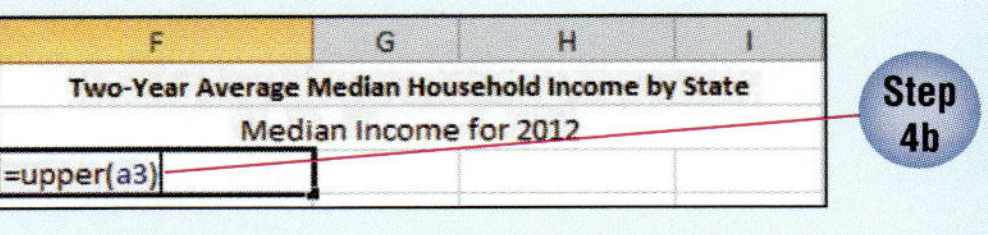

5. Enter the formula to estimate 2012 median income based on 2008 data plus 7.3 percent by completing the following steps:
   a. Make H3 the active cell.
   b. Type **=(c3*7.3%)+c3** and then press Enter.
   c. Press the Up Arrow key to move the active cell back to H3 and then format the cell to Comma Style number format with no decimals.
   d. Drag the fill handle in H3 down to H54.
   e. Deselect the range.

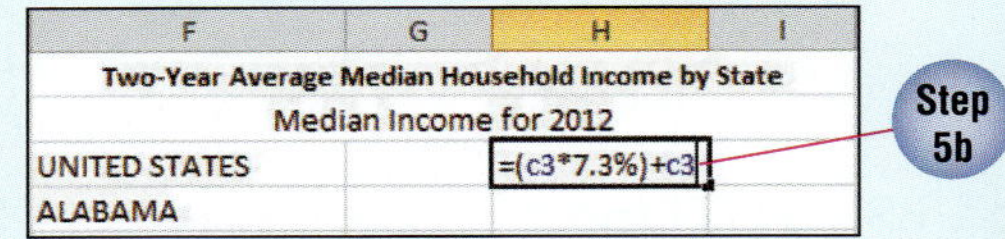

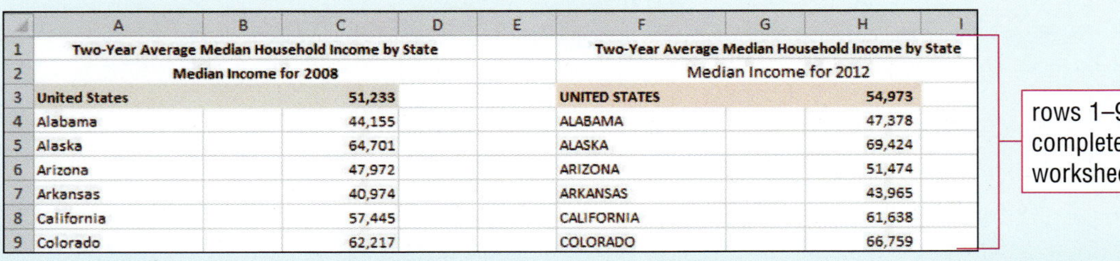

	A	B	C	D	E	F	G	H	I
1	Two-Year Average Median Household Income by State					Two-Year Average Median Household Income by State			
2	Median Income for 2008					Median Income for 2012			
3	United States		51,233			UNITED STATES		54,973	
4	Alabama		44,155			ALABAMA		47,378	
5	Alaska		64,701			ALASKA		69,424	
6	Arizona		47,972			ARIZONA		51,474	
7	Arkansas		40,974			ARKANSAS		43,965	
8	California		57,445			CALIFORNIA		61,638	
9	Colorado		62,217			COLORADO		66,759	

rows 1–9 of completed worksheet

6. Select F3:H54 and change the font size to 10.
7. Select F3:H3, apply Bold, and change the Fill Color to *Orange, Accent 6, Lighter 80%* (last option in second row of *Theme Colors* section).
8. Save, print, and then close **EL2-C2-P5-USIncomeStats.xlsx**.

In this chapter you learned how to use a small sampling of functions from the statistical, math and trigonometry, lookup, financial, logical, and text function lists. Excel includes over 300 functions in eleven categories. When you need to enter a complex formula and are not sure if Excel includes a preprogrammed function, open the Insert Function dialog box, type a description of the function in the *Search for a function* text box, and then click the Go button.

Chapter Summary

- Assign names to cells or ranges to reference by name in formulas or navigation.
- Using range names in formulas make formulas easier to comprehend.
- Create range names by selecting the source range and then typing a name in the Name box.
- COUNTA is a statistical function that counts nonblank cells. Use the function to count cells containing text and a combination of text and numbers.
- The COUNTIF statistical function counts cells within a range based on a single criterion.
- Use COUNTIFS to count cells within a range based on multiple criteria.
- Find the arithmetic mean of a range of cells based on a single criterion using the statistical AVERAGEIF function.
- AVERAGEIFS finds the arithmetic mean for a range based on multiple criteria.
- The math function SUMIF adds cells within a range based on a single criterion.
- To add cells within a range based on multiple criteria, use the SUMIFS function.
- Open the Name Manager dialog box to create, edit, or delete a range name, or edit the cells a range name references.
- Lookup & Reference functions VLOOKUP and HLOOKUP look up data in a reference table and return in the formula cell a value from a column or row in the lookup table.
- The PPMT financial function returns the principal portion of a specified loan payment within the term based on an interest rate, total number of payments, and loan amount.
- Conditional logic in a formula performs a calculation based on the outcome of a conditional test where one action is performed if the test proves true, or another action is performed if the test proves false.
- A nested function is a function inside of another function.

- Use the AND logical function to test multiple conditions. Excel returns *TRUE* if all conditions test true and returns *FALSE* if any one of the conditions tests false.
- The OR logical function also tests multiple conditions. The function returns *TRUE* if any one of the conditions tests true and *FALSE* only if all of the conditions test false.
- The text function =PROPER capitalizes the first letter of each word in the text source.
- Convert the case of text from lowercase to uppercase, or uppercase to lowercase, using the =UPPER and =LOWER text functions.
- Replace a text string with new text using the SUBSTITUTE text function.

Commands Review

FEATURE	RIBBON TAB, GROUP	BUTTON	KEYBOARD SHORTCUT
Financial functions	Formulas, Function Library		
Insert Function dialog box	Formulas, Function Library		Shift + 3
Logical functions	Formulas, Function Library		
Lookup & Reference functions	Formulas, Function Library		
Math & Trigonometry functions	Formulas, Function Library		
Name Manager dialog box	Formulas, Defined Names		Ctrl + 3
Statistical functions accessed from More Functions button	Formulas, Function Library		
Text functions	Formulas, Function Library		

Concepts Check Test Your Knowledge

Completion: In the space provided at the right, indicate the correct term, command, or number.

1. Assign a name to a selected range by typing the desired name in this text box. ____________________
2. A range name can be a combination of letters, numbers, underscore characters, and this punctuation character. ____________________
3. This COUNTIF function would count the number of cells in a range named *sales* where the values are greater than $50 thousand. ____________________
4. Use this statistical function to find the mean of a range based on two criteria. ____________________
5. SUMIF is found in this function category. ____________________
6. Open this dialog box to delete a range name. ____________________
7. Use this lookup function to look up a value in a reference table where the comparison data in the table is arranged in rows. ____________________
8. This financial function returns the principal portion of a specified loan payment. ____________________
9. The IF function is accessed from this button in the Function Library group of the Formulas tab. ____________________
10. This term refers to a formula where one function is created inside of another function. ____________________
11. Excel's AND and OR functions use this type of logic to construct a conditional test. ____________________
12. When would Excel return False for an OR function? ____________________
13. This text function can be used to capitalize the first letter of each word in a cell. ____________________
14. This formula converts text typed in lowercase within a cell to all uppercase characters. ____________________
15. Use this text function to change a text string in the source cell to new text in the formula cell. ____________________

Skills Check Assess Your Performance

Assessment 1

CREATE RANGE NAMES AND USE THE LOOKUP FUNCTION

Note: If you submit your work in hard copy, check with your instructor before printing assessments to see if you need to print two copies of each assessment—one as displayed and another with cell formulas displayed.

1. Open **RSROctLaborCost.xlsx**.
2. Save the workbook with Save As and name it **EL2-C2-A1-RSROctLaborCost**.
3. Create the following range names:

C7:C22	*Hours*
D7:D22	*TechCode*
F7:F22	*LaborCost*
I3:J5	*RateChart*

4. In E7 create the VLOOKUP formula to return the correct hourly rate based on the technician code in D7. Use the range name *RateChart* within the formula to reference the hourly rate chart. Make sure Excel will return values for exact matches only.
5. Copy the VLOOKUP formula in E7 and paste to E8:E22.
6. In F7 create the formula to extend the labor cost by multiplying the hours in C7 times the hourly rate in E7.
7. Copy the formula in F7 and paste to F8:F22.
8. Create the formula in F23 to sum the column.
9. Preview and then print the worksheet.
10. Save and then close **EL2-C2-A1-RSROctLaborCost.xlsx**.

Assessment 2

USE CONDITIONAL STATISTICAL AND MATH FUNCTIONS

Note: For all functions in Assessment 2 with the exception of Step 3, use range names in the formulas to reference sources.

1. Open **EL2-C2-A1-RSROctLaborCost.xlsx**.
2. Save the workbook with Save As and name it **EL2-C2-A2-RSROctLaborCost**.
3. In I23 create a COUNTA formula to count the number of calls made in October using the dates in column A as the source range.
4. Create the COUNTIF formulas in the cells indicated below.

I9	Count the number of calls made by Technician 1
I10	Count the number of calls made by Technician 2
I11	Count the number of calls made by Technician 3

5. In I14 create a COUNTIFS formula to count the number of calls made by Technician 3 where the hours logged were greater than 3.
6. Create the SUMIF formulas in the cells indicated below.

J9	Add the labor cost for calls made by Technician 1
J10	Add the labor cost for calls made by Technician 2
J11	Add the labor cost for calls made by Technician 3

7. Format J9:J11 to Comma Style number format.
8. In J14 create a SUMIFS formula to add the labor cost for calls made by Technician 3 where the hours logged were greater than 3.
9. Format J14 to Comma Style number format.
10. Create the AVERAGEIF formulas in the cells indicated below.

    J18 Average the labor cost for calls made by Technician 1
    J19 Average the labor cost for calls made by Technician 2
    J20 Average the labor cost for calls made by Technician 3
11. Format J18:J20 to Comma Style number format.
12. Save, print, and then close **EL2-C2-A2-RSROctLaborCost.xlsx**.

Assessment 3

USE FINANCIAL FUNCTIONS PMT AND PPMT

1. Open **PrecisionWarehouse.xlsx**.
2. Save the workbook with Save As and name it **EL2-C2-A3-PrecisionWarehouse.xlsx**.
3. Create the PMT formula in D8 to calculate the monthly loan payment for the proposed loan from NewVentures Capital Inc. ***Note: The PMT payment uses the same arguments as PPMT with the exception that there is no* Per *criterion.***
4. Find the principal portion of the loan payment for the first loan payment in D10 and the last loan payment in D11 using PPMT formulas.
5. In D13 create the formula to calculate the total cost of the loan by multiplying the monthly loan payment times 12 times the amortization period in years.
6. In D14 create the formula to calculate the interest cost of the loan by entering the formula **=d13+d6**. ***Note: Normally, you would calculate interest cost on a loan by subtracting the amount borrowed from the total payments made; however, in this worksheet you have to add the two cells because the total cost of the loan is a negative number. Subtracting D6 from D13 would cause Excel to add the two values because two negative values create a positive.***
7. Print the worksheet.
8. Save and then close **EL2-C2-A3-PrecisionWarehouse.xlsx**.

Assessment 4

USE LOGICAL FUNCTIONS

1. Open **AllClaimsPremiumReview.xlsx**.
2. Save the workbook with Save As and name it **EL2-C2-A4-AllClaimsPremiumReview.xlsx**.
3. Create the following range names:

    B4:B23 *Claims*
    C4:C23 *AtFault*
    D4:D23 *Rating*
    E4:E23 *Deductible*
4. Create the formula in G4 to display the text *Yes* if the number of At Fault Claims is greater than 1 and the Current Rating is greater than 2. Both conditions must test true to display *Yes*; otherwise display *No* in the cell. ***Hint: Use a nested IF and AND formula.***
5. Center the result in G4 and then copy the formula to G5:G23.

6. Create the formula in H4 to display the text *Yes* in the cell if either the number of claims is greater than 2 or the current deductible is less than $1,000.00; otherwise display *No* in the cell. ***Hint: Use a nested IF and OR formula.***
7. Center the result in H4 and then copy the formula to H5:H23. Deselect the range after copying.
8. Save, print, and then close **EL2-C2-A4-AllClaimsPremiumReview.xlsx**.

Assessment 5

USE THE HLOOKUP FUNCTION

1. Open **JanelleTutoringProgressRpt.xlsx**.
2. Save the workbook with Save As and name it **EL2-C2-A5-JanelleTutoringProgressRpt**.
3. Click the sheet tab labeled ProgressComments and review the layout of the lookup table. Notice that the data is organized in rows with the score in row 1 and the grade comment in row 2.
4. Select A1:G2 and create the range name *GradeTable*.
5. Deselect the range and then make StudentProgress the active sheet.
6. Create a formula in G4 that will look up the student's total score in the range named *GradeTable* and return the appropriate progress comment.
7. Copy the formula in G4 and paste it to G5:G12.
8. Save, print, and then close **EL2-C2-A5-JanelleTutoringProgressRpt.xlsx**.

Visual Benchmark Demonstrate Your Proficiency

1 USE LOOKUP, STATISTICAL, AND MATH FUNCTIONS IN A BILLING SUMMARY

1. Open **BillableHrsOct8to12.xlsx**.
2. Save the workbook with Save As and name it **EL2-C2-VB1-BillableHrsOct8to12**.
3. Review the worksheet shown in Figure 2.8. The gray shaded cells require formulas to complete the worksheet. Use the following information to create the required formulas. Create range names to use in all of the formulas so that the reader can easily interpret the formula.
   - In column F, create a formula to look up the attorney's hourly rate from the table located at the bottom right of the worksheet.
   - In column G, calculate the legal fees billed by multiplying the billable hours times the hourly rate.
   - In J6:J9 calculate the total legal fees billed by attorney.
   - In J13:J16 calculate the average hours billed by attorney.
4. Save, print, and then close **EL2-C2-VB1-BillableHrsOct8to12.xlsx**.

Figure 2.8 Visual Benchmark 1

	A	B	C	D	E	F	G	H	I	J
1					O'DONOVAN & SULLIVAN LAW ASSOCIATES					
2					BILLING SUMMARY					
3					OCTOBER 8 TO 12, 2012					
4	File	Client	Date	Attorney Code	Billable Hours	Hourly Rate	Legal Fees		Billing Statistics	
5	FL-325	10104	10/8/2012	1	26.75			Total Legal Fees Billed by Attorney		
6	EP-652	10106	10/8/2012	1	12.10			1	Marty O'Donovan	
7	CL-412	10125	10/8/2012	2	33.25			2	Toni Sullivan	
8	IN-745	10210	10/9/2012	3	24.25			3	Rosa Martinez	
9	EL-632	10225	10/9/2012	3	12.11			4	Kyle Williams	
10	RE-475	10285	10/9/2012	4	42.30				TOTAL	$ -
11	CL-501	10341	10/10/2012	2	15.25					
12	CL-521	10334	10/10/2012	2	20.25			Average Billable Hours by Attorney		
13	PL-348	10420	10/10/2012	3	25.00			1	Marty O'Donovan	
14	RE-492	10425	10/10/2012	4	22.70			2	Toni Sullivan	
15	EL-632	10225	10/11/2012	3	23.00			3	Rosa Martinez	
16	PL-512	10290	10/11/2012	3	16.20			4	Kyle Williams	
17	IN-745	10210	10/11/2012	3	14.50					
18	FL-385	10278	10/11/2012	1	24.00				Attorney Code Table	
19	CL-412	10125	10/12/2012	2	15.25			Code	Attorney	Hourly Rate
20	CL-450	10358	10/12/2012	2	23.50			1	Marty O'Donovan	85.00
21	IN-801	10346	10/12/2012	3	14.25			2	Toni Sullivan	75.00
22	EP-685	10495	10/12/2012	3	23.75			3	Rosa Martinez	100.00
23	RE-501	10384	10/12/2012	4	13.75			4	Kyle Williams	90.00
24				TOTAL	402.16	TOTAL	$ -			

2 USE LOOKUP AND LOGICAL FUNCTIONS TO CALCULATE CARDIOLOGY COSTS

1. Open **WPMCCardiologyCosts.xlsx**.
2. Save the workbook with Save As and name it **EL2-C2-VB2-WPMCCardiologyCosts**.
3. This worksheet already has range names created for you. Spend a few moments reviewing the range names and the cells each name references to become familiar with the worksheet.
4. Review the worksheet shown in Figure 2.9 and complete the worksheet to match the one shown by creating formulas using the following information:
   - In column G, create a formula to look up the surgery fee in the table located at the bottom of the worksheet. Specify in the formula to return a result for exact matches only.
   - In column H insert the aortic or mitral valve cost if the cardiac surgery required a replacement valve; otherwise place a zero into the cell. ***Hint: The surgery codes for surgeries that include a replacement valve are*** **ART** ***and*** **MRT**.
   - In column I, calculate the postoperative hospital cost by multiplying the number of days the patient was in hospital by the postoperative cost per day.
   - In column J, calculate the total cost as the sum of the surgery fee, valve cost, and postoperative hospital cost.
   - Calculate the total cost for each column in row 22.
5. Save, print, and then close **EL2-C2-VB2-WPMCCardiologyCosts.xlsx**.

Figure 2.9 Visual Benchmark 2

	A	B	C	D	E	F	G	H	I	J
1				Wellington Park Medical Center						
2				Division of Cardiology						
3				Adult Cardiac Surgery Costs						
4	Month:	October	Surgeon:	Novak						
5	Patient No	Patient Last Name	Patient First Name	Surgery Code	Days in hospital		Surgery Fee	Valve Cost	Postoperative Hospital Cost	Total Cost
6	60334124	Wagner	Sara	MRP	7		$ 5,325.00	$ -	$ 6,317.50	$ 11,642.50
7	60334567	Gonzalez	Hector	ARP	10		$ 4,876.00	$ -	$ 9,025.00	$ 13,901.00
8	60398754	Vezina	Paula	ABP	5		$ 4,820.00	$ -	$ 4,512.50	$ 9,332.50
9	60347821	Dowling	Jager	MRT	11		$ 6,240.00	$ 775.00	$ 9,927.50	$ 16,942.50
10	60328192	Ashman	Carl	ARP	4		$ 4,876.00	$ -	$ 3,610.00	$ 8,486.00
11	60321349	Kaiser	Lana	ART	12		$ 6,190.00	$ 775.00	$ 10,830.00	$ 17,795.00
12	60398545	Van Bomm	Emile	ABP	7		$ 4,820.00	$ -	$ 6,317.50	$ 11,137.50
13	60342548	Youngblood	Frank	ABP	6		$ 4,820.00	$ -	$ 5,415.00	$ 10,235.00
14	60331569	Lorimar	Hannah	MRT	8		$ 6,240.00	$ 775.00	$ 7,220.00	$ 14,235.00
15	60247859	Peterson	Mark	ART	9		$ 6,190.00	$ 775.00	$ 8,122.50	$ 15,087.50
16	60158642	O'Connor	Terry	ABP	7		$ 4,820.00	$ -	$ 6,317.50	$ 11,137.50
17	60458962	Jenkins	Esther	MRP	9		$ 5,325.00	$ -	$ 8,122.50	$ 13,447.50
18	68521245	Norfolk	Leslie	ABP	8		$ 4,820.00	$ -	$ 7,220.00	$ 12,040.00
19	63552158	Adams-Wiley	Susan	MRT	6		$ 6,240.00	$ 775.00	$ 5,415.00	$ 12,430.00
20	68451278	Estevez	Stefan	ARP	6		$ 4,876.00	$ -	$ 5,415.00	$ 10,291.00
21										
22	Postoperative hosptial cost per day:			$ 902.50	Total Cost:		$ 80,478.00	$ 3,875.00	$ 103,787.50	$ 188,140.50
23		Aortic or Mitral valve cost:		$ 775.00						
24										
25		Surgery Code	Surgery Fee	Surgery Procedure						
26		ABP	4,820	Artery Bypass						
27		ARP	4,876	Aortic Valve Repair						
28		ART	6,190	Aortic Valve Replacement						
29		MRP	5,325	Mitral Valve Repair						
30		MRT	6,240	Mitral Valve Replacement						

Case Study Apply Your Skills

Part 1

Yolanda Robertson of NuTrends Market Research was pleased with your previous work and has requested that you be assigned to assist her with a new client. Yolanda is preparing a marketing plan for a franchise expansion for the owners of Pizza By Mario. The franchise was started in Michigan and has stores in Ohio, Wisconsin, and Iowa. The owners plan to double their locations within the next two years by expanding into neighboring states. The owners have provided a confidential franchise sales report to Yolanda in an Excel file named **PizzaByMarioSales.xlsx**. Yolanda needs your help with Excel to extract some statistics and calculate franchise royalty payments. With this information, Yolanda can develop a franchise communication package for prospective franchisees. Open the workbook and name it **EL2-C2-CS-P1-PizzaByMarioSales**. Yolanda has asked for the following statistics:

- A count of the number of stores with gross sales greater than $500 thousand
- A count of the number of stores located in Michigan with sales greater than $500 thousand
- Average sales for the Detroit, Michigan stores
- Average sales for the Michigan stores established prior to 2004
- Total sales for stores established prior to 2010
- Total sales for the Michigan stores established prior to 2010

Create the formulas for Yolanda in rows 3 to 16 of columns H and I. Create range names for the data so that Yolanda will be able to easily understand the formula when she reviews the worksheet. You determine the layout, labels, and other formats for the statistics section. Save and print the worksheet.

Part 2

In the marketing package for new prospects, Yolanda plans to include sample sales figures and related franchise royalty payments. Pizza By Mario charges stores a royalty percentage based on the store's annual sales. As sales increase, the royalty percentage increases. For example, a store that earns gross sales of $430 thousand pays a royalty of 2% on sales, while a store that earns gross sales of $765 thousand pays a royalty of 5% of gross sales. A royalty rate table is included in the worksheet. Create a range name for the table and then create a lookup formula to insert the correct royalty percentage for each store in column F. Next, create a formula to calculate the dollar amount of the royalty payment based on the store's sales times the percent value in column F. Format the royalty percent and royalty fee columns appropriately. Save the revised workbook and name it **EL2-C2-CS-P2-PizzaByMarioSales**. Print the worksheet.

Part 3

Help

Use the Help feature to learn about the MEDIAN and STDEV functions. Yolanda would like to calculate further statistics in a separate worksheet. Copy A2:E29 to Sheet2 keeping the source column widths. Using the sales data in column E, calculate the following statistics. You determine the layout, labels, and other formats.

- Average sales
- Maximum store sales
- Minimum store sales
- Median store sales
- Standard deviation of the sales data

Create a text box below the statistics and write an explanation in each box to explain to the reader what the median and standard deviation numbers mean based on what you learned in Help. Print the worksheet making sure the printout fits on one page. Save the revised workbook and name it **EL2-C2-CS-P3-PizzaByMarioSales**.

Part 4

Choose two states that are in close proximity to Michigan, Ohio, Wisconsin, and Iowa and research statistics on the Internet that Yolanda can use to prepare a marketing plan. Within each state find population and income statistics for two cities. In a new worksheet within the Pizza By Mario franchise workbook, prepare a summary of your research findings. Include the URLs of the sites from which you obtained your data in the worksheet in case Yolanda wants to explore the links for further details. Print the worksheet making sure the printout fits on one page. Save the revised workbook and name it **EL2-C2-CS-P4-PizzaByMarioSales**. Close the workbook.

Microsoft® Excel®

CHAPTER 3

Working with Tables and Data Features

PERFORMANCE OBJECTIVES

Upon successful completion of Chapter 3, you will be able to:

- **Create a table in a worksheet**
- **Expand a table to include new rows and columns**
- **Add a calculated column in a table**
- **Format a table by applying table styles and table style options**
- **Add a total row to a table and add formulas to total cells**
- **Sort and filter a table**
- **Split contents of a cell into separate columns**
- **Remove duplicate records**
- **Restrict data entry by creating validation criteria**
- **Convert a table to a normal range**
- **Create subtotals in groups of related data**
- **Group and ungroup data**

Tutorials

3.1 Creating and Modifying Tables
3.2 Adding Rows to a Table
3.3 Formatting Data as a Table
3.4 Using the Sort Feature in Tables
3.5 Filtering a Table
3.6 Using Data Tools
3.7 Removing Duplicate Records
3.8 Validating and Restricting Data Entry
3.9 Converting a Table to a Normal Range; Subtotalling Related Data
3.10 Grouping and Ungrouping Data

A ***table*** is a range that can be managed separately from other rows and columns in the worksheet. Data in a table can be sorted, filtered, and totaled as a separate unit. A worksheet can contain more than one table so that multiple groups of data can be managed separately within the same workbook. In this chapter you will learn how to use the table feature to manage a range. You will use data tools such as validation, duplicate records, and converting text to a table. You will also convert a table back to a normal range and use data tools such as grouping related records and calculating subtotals. Model answers for this chapter's projects appear on the following pages.

Excel2010L2C3

Note: Before beginning the projects, copy to your storage medium the Excel2010L2C3 subfolder from the Excel2010L2 folder on the CD that accompanies this textbook and then make Excel2010L2C3 the active folder.

O'DONOVAN & SULLIVAN LAW ASSOCIATES
ASSOCIATE BILLING SUMMARY
OCTOBER 8 TO 12, 2012

File	Client	Date	Last Name	First Name	Attorney	Area	Billable Hours	Rate	Fees Due
FL-325	10104	10/8/2012	Ferreira	Joseph	Marty O'Donovan	Divorce	6.75	85.00	573.75
EP-652	10106	10/8/2012	Kolcz	Robert	Marty O'Donovan	Wills	3.25	85.00	276.25
CL-412	10125	10/8/2012	Schmidt	Hilary	Toni Sullivan	Corporate	5.25	75.00	393.75
IN-745	10210	10/9/2012	Boscovic	Victor	Rosa Martinez	Insurance	4.25	100.00	425.00
EL-632	10225	10/9/2012	Armstrong	Daniel	Rosa Martinez	Employment	3.25	100.00	325.00
RE-475	10285	10/9/2012	Cooke	Penny	Kyle Williams	Real Estate	2.75	90.00	247.50
CL-501	10341	10/10/2012	Fletcher	Dana	Toni Sullivan	Corporate	5.25	75.00	393.75
CL-521	10334	10/10/2012	Marsales	Gene	Toni Sullivan	Corporate	4.25	75.00	318.75
PL-348	10420	10/10/2012	Torrez	Alexander	Rosa Martinez	Patent	5.00	100.00	500.00
RE-492	10425	10/10/2012	Sauve	Jean	Kyle Williams	Real Estate	3.25	90.00	292.50
EL-632	10225	10/11/2012	Armstrong	Daniel	Rosa Martinez	Employment	4.50	100.00	450.00
PL-512	10290	10/11/2012	Tonini	Sam	Rosa Martinez	Pension	3.75	100.00	375.00
IN-745	10210	10/11/2012	Boscovic	Victor	Rosa Martinez	Insurance	4.50	100.00	450.00
FL-385	10278	10/11/2012	Moore	Lana	Marty O'Donovan	Separation	5.25	85.00	446.25
CL-412	10125	10/8/2012	Schmidt	Hilary	Toni Sullivan	Corporate	5.25	75.00	393.75
CL-412	10125	10/12/2012	Schmidt	Hilary	Toni Sullivan	Corporate	5.25	75.00	393.75
CL-450	10358	10/12/2012	Poissant	Henri	Toni Sullivan	Corporate	3.50	75.00	262.50
IN-801	10346	10/12/2012	Sebastian	Paul	Rosa Martinez	Insurance	4.25	100.00	425.00
EP-685	10495	10/12/2012	Kinsela	Frank	Rosa Martinez	Estate	3.75	100.00	375.00
RE-501	10384	10/12/2012	Eckler	Jade	Kyle Williams	Real Estate	4.50	90.00	405.00
RE-522	10512	10/12/2012	Melanson	Connie	Kyle Williams	Real Estate	2.50	75.00	187.50
Total	21						90.25		7,910.00

Project 1 Create and Modify a Table

Project 1c, EL2-C3-P1-BillingSummaryOctWk1.xlsx

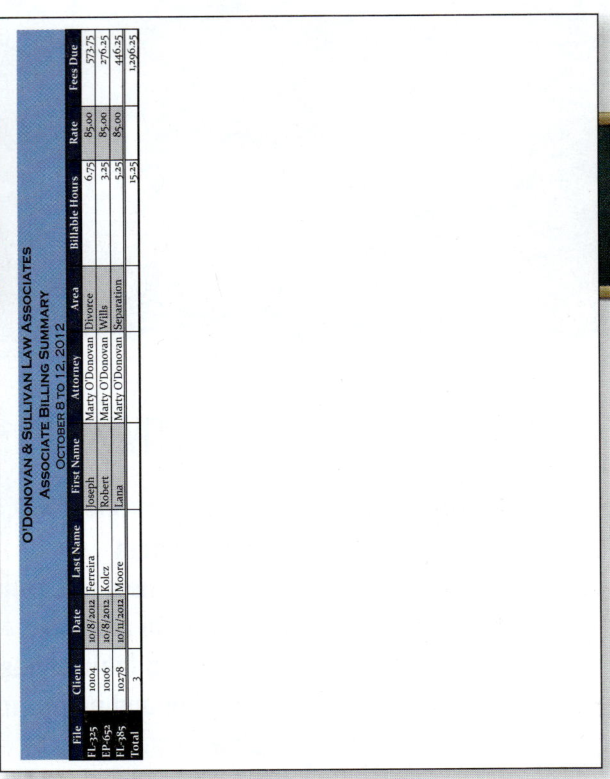

O'DONOVAN & SULLIVAN LAW ASSOCIATES
ASSOCIATE BILLING SUMMARY
OCTOBER 8 TO 12, 2012

File	Client	Date	Last Name	First Name	Attorney	Area	Billable Hours	Rate	Fees Due
FL-325	10104	10/8/2012	Ferreira	Joseph	Marty O'Donovan	Divorce	6.75	85.00	573.75
EP-652	10106	10/8/2012	Kolcz	Robert	Marty O'Donovan	Wills	3.25	85.00	276.25
FL-385	10278	10/11/2012	Moore	Lana	Marty O'Donovan	Separation	5.25	85.00	446.25
Total	3						15.25		1,296.25

Project 1d, EL2-C3-P1-BillingSummaryOctWk1.xlsx

O'DONOVAN & SULLIVAN LAW ASSOCIATES
ASSOCIATE BILLING SUMMARY
OCTOBER 8 TO 12, 2012

File	Client	Date	Last Name	First Name	Attorney	Area	Billable Hours	Rate	Fees Due
RE-475	10285	10/9/2012	Cooke	Penny	Kyle Williams	Real Estate	2.75	90.00	247.50
RE-501	10384	10/12/2012	Eckler	Jade	Kyle Williams	Real Estate	4.50	90.00	405.00
RE-522	10512	10/12/2012	Melanson	Connie	Kyle Williams	Real Estate	2.50	75.00	187.50
RE-492	10425	10/10/2012	Sauve	Jean	Kyle Williams	Real Estate	3.25	90.00	292.50
FL-325	10104	10/8/2012	Ferreira	Joseph	Marty O'Donovan	Divorce	6.75	85.00	573.75
FL-385	10278	10/11/2012	Moore	Lana	Marty O'Donovan	Separation	5.25	85.00	446.25
EP-652	10106	10/8/2012	Kolcz	Robert	Marty O'Donovan	Wills	3.25	85.00	276.25
EL-632	10225	10/9/2012	Armstrong	Daniel	Rosa Martinez	Employment	3.25	100.00	325.00
EL-632	10225	10/11/2012	Armstrong	Daniel	Rosa Martinez	Employment	4.50	100.00	450.00
EP-685	10495	10/12/2012	Kinsela	Frank	Rosa Martinez	Estate	3.75	100.00	375.00
IN-745	10210	10/9/2012	Boscovic	Victor	Rosa Martinez	Insurance	4.25	100.00	425.00
IN-745	10210	10/11/2012	Boscovic	Victor	Rosa Martinez	Insurance	4.50	100.00	450.00
IN-801	10346	10/12/2012	Sebastian	Paul	Rosa Martinez	Insurance	4.25	100.00	425.00
PL-348	10420	10/10/2012	Torrez	Alexander	Rosa Martinez	Patent	5.00	100.00	500.00
PL-512	10290	10/11/2012	Tonini	Sam	Rosa Martinez	Pension	3.75	100.00	375.00
CL-501	10341	10/10/2012	Fletcher	Dana	Toni Sullivan	Corporate	5.25	75.00	393.75
CL-521	10334	10/10/2012	Marsales	Gene	Toni Sullivan	Corporate	4.25	75.00	318.75
CL-450	10358	10/12/2012	Poissant	Henri	Toni Sullivan	Corporate	3.50	75.00	262.50
CL-412	10125	10/8/2012	Schmidt	Hilary	Toni Sullivan	Corporate	5.25	75.00	393.75
CL-412	10125	10/8/2012	Schmidt	Hilary	Toni Sullivan	Corporate	5.25	75.00	393.75
CL-412	10125	10/12/2012	Schmidt	Hilary	Toni Sullivan	Corporate	5.25	75.00	393.75
Total	21						90.25		7,910.00

Project 1d, EL2-C3-P1-BillingSummaryOctWk1.xlsx

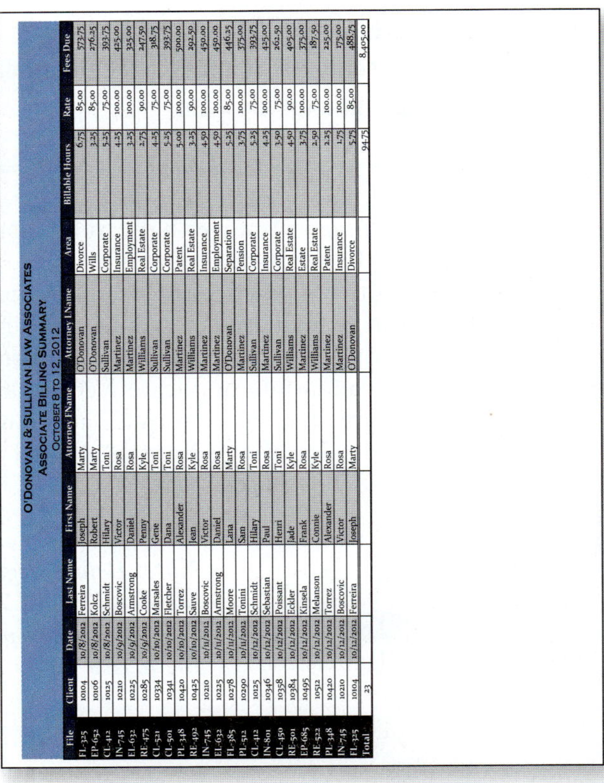

O'DONOVAN & SULLIVAN LAW ASSOCIATES
ASSOCIATE BILLING SUMMARY
OCTOBER 8 TO 12, 2012

File	Client	Date	Last Name	First Name	Attorney FName	Attorney LName	Area	Billable Hours	Rate	Fees Due
FL-325	10104	10/8/2012	Ferreira	Joseph	Marty	O'Donovan	Divorce	6.75	85.00	573.75
EP-652	10106	10/8/2012	Kolcz	Robert	Marty	O'Donovan	Wills	3.25	85.00	276.25
CL-412	10125	10/8/2012	Schmidt	Hilary	Toni	Sullivan	Corporate	5.25	75.00	393.75
IN-745	10210	10/9/2012	Boscovic	Victor	Rosa	Martinez	Insurance	4.25	100.00	425.00
EL-632	10225	10/9/2012	Armstrong	Daniel	Rosa	Martinez	Employment	3.25	100.00	325.00
RE-475	10285	10/9/2012	Cooke	Penny	Kyle	Williams	Real Estate	2.75	90.00	247.50
CL-521	10334	10/10/2012	Marsales	Gene	Toni	Sullivan	Corporate	4.25	75.00	318.75
CL-501	10341	10/10/2012	Fletcher	Dana	Toni	Sullivan	Corporate	5.25	75.00	393.75
PL-348	10420	10/10/2012	Torrez	Alexander	Rosa	Martinez	Patent	5.00	100.00	500.00
RE-492	10425	10/10/2012	Sauve	Jean	Kyle	Williams	Real Estate	3.25	90.00	292.50
IN-745	10210	10/11/2012	Boscovic	Victor	Rosa	Martinez	Insurance	4.50	100.00	450.00
EL-632	10225	10/11/2012	Armstrong	Daniel	Rosa	Martinez	Employment	4.50	100.00	450.00
FL-385	10278	10/11/2012	Moore	Lana	Marty	O'Donovan	Separation	5.25	85.00	446.25
PL-512	10290	10/11/2012	Tonini	Sam	Rosa	Martinez	Pension	3.75	100.00	375.00
CL-412	10125	10/12/2012	Schmidt	Hilary	Toni	Sullivan	Corporate	5.25	75.00	393.75
IN-801	10346	10/12/2012	Sebastian	Paul	Rosa	Martinez	Insurance	4.25	100.00	425.00
CL-450	10358	10/12/2012	Poissant	Henri	Toni	Sullivan	Corporate	3.50	75.00	262.50
RE-501	10384	10/12/2012	Eckler	Jade	Kyle	Williams	Real Estate	4.50	90.00	405.00
EP-685	10495	10/12/2012	Kinsela	Frank	Rosa	Martinez	Estate	3.75	100.00	375.00
RE-522	10512	10/12/2012	Melanson	Connie	Kyle	Williams	Real Estate	2.50	75.00	187.50
PL-348	10420	10/12/2012	Torrez	Alexander	Rosa	Martinez	Patent	2.25	100.00	225.00
IN-745	10210	10/12/2012	Boscovic	Victor	Rosa	Martinez	Insurance	1.75	100.00	175.00
FL-325	10104	10/12/2012	Ferreira	Joseph	Marty	O'Donovan	Divorce	5.75	85.00	488.75
Total	23							94.75		8,405.00

Project 2 Use Data Tools to Split Data and Ensure Data Integrity

Project 2e, EL2-C3-P2-BillingSummaryOctWk1.xlsx

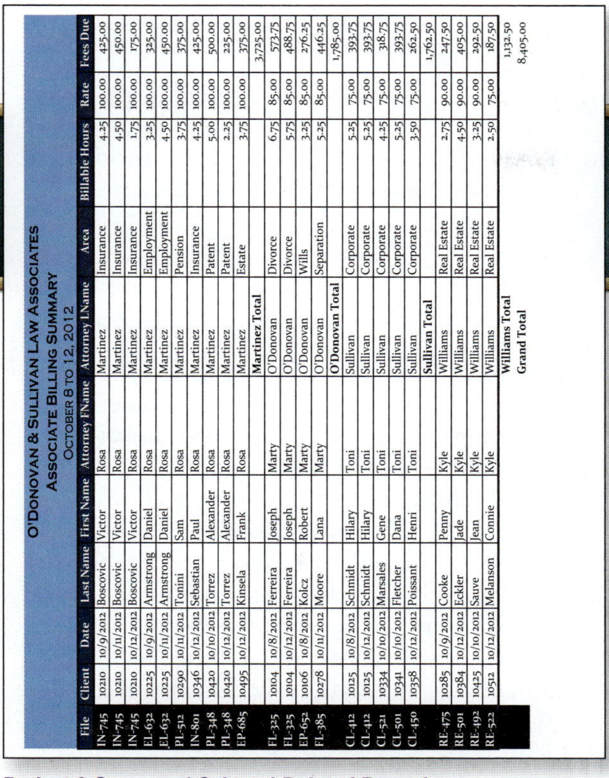

Project 3 Group and Subtotal Related Records

O'DONOVAN & SULLIVAN LAW ASSOCIATES
ASSOCIATE BILLING SUMMARY
OCTOBER 8 TO 12, 2012

File	Client	Date	Last Name	First Name	Attorney FName	Attorney LName	Area	Billable Hours	Rate	Fees Due
IN-745	10210	10/9/2012	Boscovic	Victor	Rosa	Martinez	Insurance	4.25	100.00	425.00
IN-745	10210	10/11/2012	Boscovic	Victor	Rosa	Martinez	Insurance	4.50	100.00	450.00
IN-745	10210	10/12/2012	Boscovic	Victor	Rosa	Martinez	Insurance	1.75	100.00	175.00
EL-632	10225	10/9/2012	Armstrong	Daniel	Rosa	Martinez	Employment	3.25	100.00	325.00
EL-632	10225	10/11/2012	Armstrong	Daniel	Rosa	Martinez	Employment	4.50	100.00	450.00
PL-512	10290	10/11/2012	Tonini	Sam	Rosa	Martinez	Pension	3.75	100.00	375.00
IN-801	10346	10/12/2012	Sebastian	Paul	Rosa	Martinez	Insurance	4.25	100.00	425.00
PL-348	10420	10/10/2012	Torrez	Alexander	Rosa	Martinez	Patent	5.00	100.00	500.00
PL-348	10420	10/12/2012	Torrez	Alexander	Rosa	Martinez	Patent	2.25	100.00	225.00
EP-685	10495	10/12/2012	Kinsela	Frank	Rosa	Martinez	Estate	3.75	100.00	375.00
						Martinez Total				3,725.00
FL-325	10104	10/8/2012	Ferreira	Joseph	Marty	O'Donovan	Divorce	6.75	85.00	573.75
FL-325	10104	10/12/2012	Ferreira	Joseph	Marty	O'Donovan	Divorce	5.75	85.00	488.75
EP-652	10106	10/8/2012	Kolcz	Robert	Marty	O'Donovan	Wills	3.25	85.00	276.25
FL-385	10278	10/11/2012	Moore	Lana	Marty	O'Donovan	Separation	5.25	85.00	446.25
						O'Donovan Total				1,785.00
CL-412	10125	10/8/2012	Schmidt	Hilary	Toni	Sullivan	Corporate	5.25	75.00	393.75
CL-412	10125	10/12/2012	Schmidt	Hilary	Toni	Sullivan	Corporate	5.25	75.00	393.75
CL-521	10334	10/10/2012	Marsales	Gene	Toni	Sullivan	Corporate	4.25	75.00	318.75
CL-501	10341	10/10/2012	Fletcher	Dana	Toni	Sullivan	Corporate	5.25	75.00	393.75
CL-450	10358	10/12/2012	Poissant	Henri	Toni	Sullivan	Corporate	3.50	75.00	262.50
						Sullivan Total				1,762.50
RE-475	10285	10/9/2012	Cooke	Penny	Kyle	Williams	Real Estate	2.75	90.00	247.50
RE-501	10384	10/12/2012	Eckler	Jade	Kyle	Williams	Real Estate	4.50	90.00	405.00
RE-492	10425	10/10/2012	Sauve	Jean	Kyle	Williams	Real Estate	3.25	90.00	292.50
RE-522	10512	10/12/2012	Melanson	Connie	Kyle	Williams	Real Estate	2.50	75.00	187.50
						Williams Total				1,132.50
						Grand Total				8,405.00

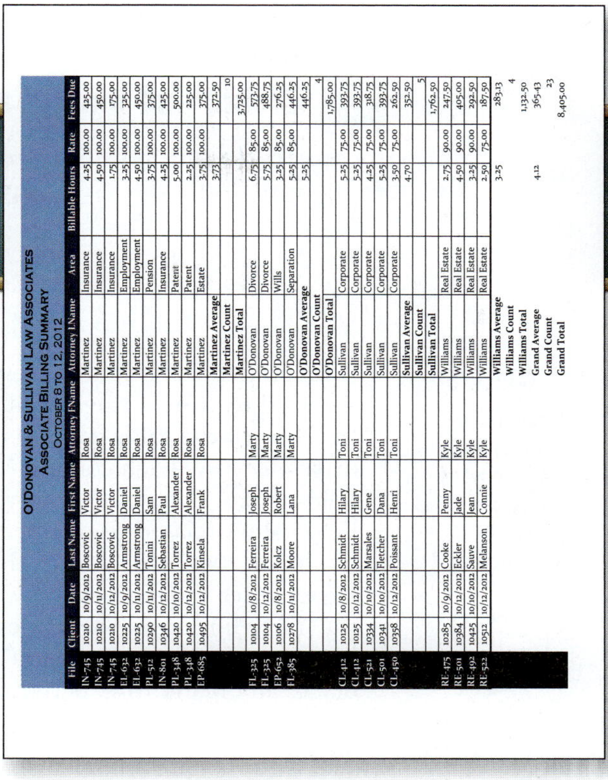

Project 3a, EL2-C3-P3-BillingSummaryOctWk1.xlsx

O'DONOVAN & SULLIVAN LAW ASSOCIATES
ASSOCIATE BILLING SUMMARY
OCTOBER 8 TO 12, 2012

File	Client	Date	Last Name	First Name	Attorney FName	Attorney LName	Area	Billable Hours	Rate	Fees Due
IN-745	10210	10/9/2012	Boscovic	Victor	Rosa	Martinez	Insurance	4.25	100.00	425.00
IN-745	10210	10/11/2012	Boscovic	Victor	Rosa	Martinez	Insurance	4.50	100.00	450.00
IN-745	10210	10/12/2012	Boscovic	Victor	Rosa	Martinez	Insurance	1.75	100.00	175.00
EL-632	10225	10/9/2012	Armstrong	Daniel	Rosa	Martinez	Employment	3.25	100.00	325.00
EL-632	10225	10/11/2012	Armstrong	Daniel	Rosa	Martinez	Employment	4.50	100.00	450.00
PL-512	10290	10/11/2012	Tonini	Sam	Rosa	Martinez	Pension	3.75	100.00	375.00
IN-801	10346	10/12/2012	Sebastian	Paul	Rosa	Martinez	Insurance	4.25	100.00	425.00
PL-348	10420	10/10/2012	Torrez	Alexander	Rosa	Martinez	Patent	5.00	100.00	500.00
PL-348	10420	10/12/2012	Torrez	Alexander	Rosa	Martinez	Patent	2.25	100.00	225.00
EP-685	10495	10/12/2012	Kinsela	Frank	Rosa	Martinez	Estate	3.75	100.00	375.00
						Martinez Average		3.73		372.50
						Martinez Count				10
						Martinez Total				3,725.00
FL-325	10104	10/8/2012	Ferreira	Joseph	Marty	O'Donovan	Divorce	6.75	85.00	573.75
FL-325	10104	10/12/2012	Ferreira	Joseph	Marty	O'Donovan	Divorce	5.75	85.00	488.75
EP-652	10106	10/8/2012	Kolcz	Robert	Marty	O'Donovan	Wills	3.25	85.00	276.25
FL-385	10278	10/11/2012	Moore	Lana	Marty	O'Donovan	Separation	5.25	85.00	446.25
						O'Donovan Average		5.25		446.25
						O'Donovan Count				4
						O'Donovan Total				1,785.00
CL-412	10125	10/8/2012	Schmidt	Hilary	Toni	Sullivan	Corporate	5.25	75.00	393.75
CL-412	10125	10/12/2012	Schmidt	Hilary	Toni	Sullivan	Corporate	5.25	75.00	393.75
CL-521	10334	10/10/2012	Marsales	Gene	Toni	Sullivan	Corporate	4.25	75.00	318.75
CL-501	10341	10/10/2012	Fletcher	Dana	Toni	Sullivan	Corporate	5.25	75.00	393.75
CL-450	10358	10/12/2012	Poissant	Henri	Toni	Sullivan	Corporate	3.50	75.00	262.50
						Sullivan Average		4.70		352.50
						Sullivan Count				5
						Sullivan Total				1,762.50
RE-475	10285	10/9/2012	Cooke	Penny	Kyle	Williams	Real Estate	2.75	90.00	247.50
RE-501	10384	10/12/2012	Eckler	Jade	Kyle	Williams	Real Estate	4.50	90.00	405.00
RE-492	10425	10/10/2012	Sauve	Jean	Kyle	Williams	Real Estate	3.25	90.00	292.50
RE-522	10512	10/12/2012	Melanson	Connie	Kyle	Williams	Real Estate	2.50	75.00	187.50
						Williams Average		3.25		283.13
						Williams Count				4
						Williams Total				1,132.50
						Grand Average		4.12		365.43
						Grand Count				23
						Grand Total				8,405.00

Project 3b, EL2-C3-P3-BillingSummaryOctWk1-Prj3b.xlsx

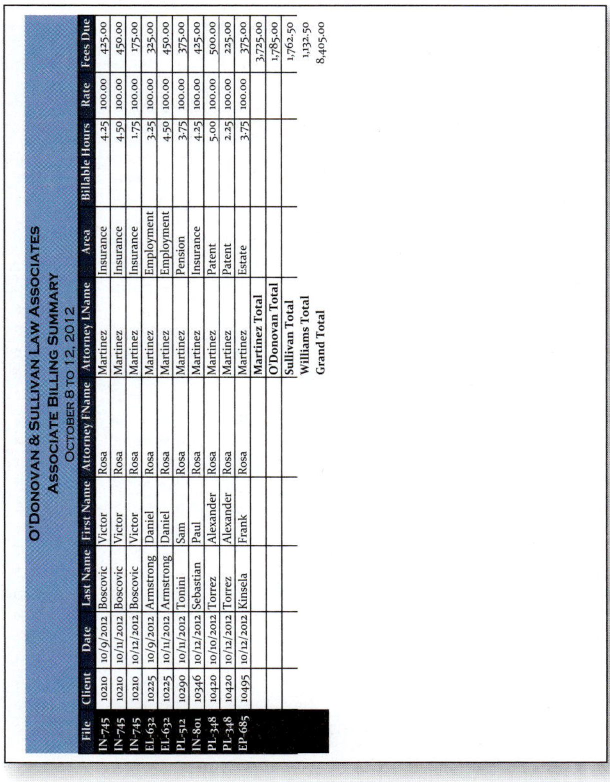

O'DONOVAN & SULLIVAN LAW ASSOCIATES
ASSOCIATE BILLING SUMMARY
OCTOBER 8 TO 12, 2012

File	Client	Date	Last Name	First Name	Attorney FName	Attorney LName	Area	Billable Hours	Rate	Fees Due
IN-745	10210	10/9/2012	Boscovic	Victor	Rosa	Martinez	Insurance	4.25	100.00	425.00
IN-745	10210	10/11/2012	Boscovic	Victor	Rosa	Martinez	Insurance	4.50	100.00	450.00
IN-745	10210	10/12/2012	Boscovic	Victor	Rosa	Martinez	Insurance	1.75	100.00	175.00
EL-632	10225	10/9/2012	Armstrong	Daniel	Rosa	Martinez	Employment	3.25	100.00	325.00
EL-632	10225	10/11/2012	Armstrong	Daniel	Rosa	Martinez	Employment	4.50	100.00	450.00
PL-512	10290	10/11/2012	Tonini	Sam	Rosa	Martinez	Pension	3.75	100.00	375.00
IN-801	10346	10/12/2012	Sebastian	Paul	Rosa	Martinez	Insurance	4.25	100.00	425.00
PL-348	10420	10/10/2012	Torrez	Alexander	Rosa	Martinez	Patent	5.00	100.00	500.00
PL-348	10420	10/12/2012	Torrez	Alexander	Rosa	Martinez	Patent	2.25	100.00	225.00
EP-685	10495	10/12/2012	Kinsela	Frank	Rosa	Martinez	Estate	3.75	100.00	375.00
						Martinez Total				3,725.00
						O'Donovan Total				1,785.00
						Sullivan Total				1,762.50
						Williams Total				1,132.50
						Grand Total				8,405.00

Project 3c, EL2-C3-P3-BillingSummaryOctWk1-Prj3c.xlsx

Project 1 Create and Modify a Table — 4 Parts

You will convert data in a billing summary worksheet to a table and then modify the table by applying Table Style options and sorting and filtering the data.

Creating Tables

Quick Steps

Create Table
1. Select range.
2. Click Insert tab.
3. Click Table button.
4. Click OK.
5. Deselect range.

Table

A table in Excel is similar in structure to a database. Columns are called ***fields*** and are used to store a single unit of information about a person, place, or object. The first row of the table contains column headings and is called the ***field names row*** or ***header row***. Each column heading in the table should be unique. Below the field names, data entered in rows are called ***records***. A record contains all of the field values related to one person, place, or object that is the topic of the table. No blank rows exist within the table as shown in Figure 3.1. To create a table in Excel, enter the data in the worksheet and then define the range as a table using the Table button in the Tables group of the Insert tab or using the Format as Table button in the Styles group of the Home tab. Before converting a range to a table, delete any blank rows between column headings and data or within the data range.

Figure 3.1 Worksheet with Range Formatted as a Table

The first row of a table contains field names and is called a header row.

	A	B	C	D	E	F	G	H	I	J	K	L
1						Vantage Video Rentals						
2						Classic Video Collection						
3												
4	Stock No.	Title	Year	Genre	Stock Dat	Director	Copie	VHS	DVD	Blu-ra	Category	Cost Pric
5	CV-1001	Abbott & Costello Go to Mars	1953	Comedy	9/5/2006	Charles Lamont	2	Yes	No	No	7-day rental	5.87
6	CV-1002	Miracle on 34th Street	1947	Family	9/15/2006	George Seaton	8	Yes	No	Yes	2-day rental	7.55
7	CV-1003	Moby Dick	1956	Action	10/4/2006	John Huston	3	No	Yes	No	7-day rental	8.10
8	CV-1004	Dial M for Murder	1954	Thriller	10/12/2006	Alfred Hitchcock	5	No	Yes	No	7-day rental	6.54
9	CV-1005	Breakfast at Tiffany's	1961	Comedy	11/1/2006	Blake Edwards	1	Yes	No	Yes	7-day rental	4.88
10	CV-1006	Gone with the Wind	1939	Drama	11/29/2006	Victor Fleming	4	Yes	No	Yes	7-day rental	8.22
11	CV-1007	Doctor Zhivago	1965	Drama	12/8/2006	David Lean	4	Yes	No	Yes	7-day rental	5.63
12	CV-1008	The Great Escape	1963	War	1/15/2007	John Sturges	3	Yes	No	No	2-day rental	6.15
13	CV-1009	The Odd Couple	1968	Comedy	2/15/2007	Gene Saks	4	Yes	Yes	No	2-day rental	4.95
14	CV-1010	The Sound of Music	1965	Musical	3/9/2007	Robert Wise	5	Yes	Yes	Yes	2-day rental	5.12
15	CV-1011	A Christmas Carol	1951	Family	7/18/2007	Brian Hurst	4	Yes	Yes	Yes	2-day rental	5.88
16	CV-1012	The Bridge on the River Kwai	1957	War	8/15/2007	David Lean	2	Yes	No	No	2-day rental	6.32
17	CV-1013	Cool Hand Luke	1967	Drama	10/23/2007	Stuart Rosenberg	5	Yes	Yes	Yes	2-day rental	5.42
18	CV-1014	Patton	1970	War	12/18/2007	Franklin Schaffner	3	Yes	Yes	Yes	7-day rental	6.84
19	CV-1015	Blue Hawaii	1961	Musical	1/25/2008	Norman Taurog	1	Yes	No	No	7-day rental	4.52
20	CV-1016	Psycho	1960	Horror	1/31/2008	Alfred Hitchcock	2	Yes	No	Yes	2-day rental	7.54
21	CV-1017	The Longest Day	1962	War	2/5/2008	Ken Annakin	5	Yes	Yes	No	7-day rental	6.51
22	CV-1018	To Kill a Mockingbird	1962	Drama	2/12/2008	Robert Mulligan	2	Yes	No	Yes	2-day rental	8.40
23	CV-1019	Bonnie and Clyde	1967	Drama	3/15/2009	Arthur Penn	3	Yes	Yes	Yes	2-day rental	8.95
24	CV-1020	The Maltese Falcon	1941	Drama	11/10/2009	John Huston	1	No	No	Yes	2-day rental	12.15
25	CV-1007	Doctor Zhivago	1965	Drama	12/8/2006	David Lean	4	Yes	No	Yes	7-day rental	5.63
26	CV-1022	The Wizard of Oz	1939	Musical	5/3/2010	Victor Fleming	5	Yes	Yes	Yes	7-day rental	9.56
27	CV-1023	Rear Window	1954	Thriller	8/15/2010	Alfred Hitchcock	3	Yes	Yes	Yes	7-day rental	8.55
28	CV-1004	Dial M for Murder	1954	Thriller	10/12/2006	Alfred Hitchcock	5	No	Yes	No	7-day rental	6.54
29	CV-1024	Citizen Kane	1941	Drama	6/10/2011	Orson Welles	2	No	Yes	Yes	2-day rental	9.85
30	CV-1025	Ben-Hur	1959	History	10/15/2011	William Wyler	1	No	No	Yes	7-day rental	9.85

A row in a table is called a record.

A column in a table contains a single unit of information and is called a field.

Project 1a Converting a Range to a Table

Part 1 of 4

1. Open **BillingSummaryOctWk1.xlsx**.
2. Save the workbook with Save As and name it **EL2-C3-P1-BillingSummaryOctWk1**.
3. Convert the billing summary data to a table by completing the following steps:
   a. Select A4:I24.
   b. Click the Insert tab.
   c. Click the Table button in the Tables group.
   d. At the Create Table dialog box with *=$A$4:$I$24* selected in the *Where is the data for your table?* text box and the *My table has headers* check box selected, click OK.
   e. Deselect the range.
4. Double-click each column boundary to AutoFit each column's width.
5. Save **EL2-C3-P1-BillingSummaryOctWk1.xlsx**.

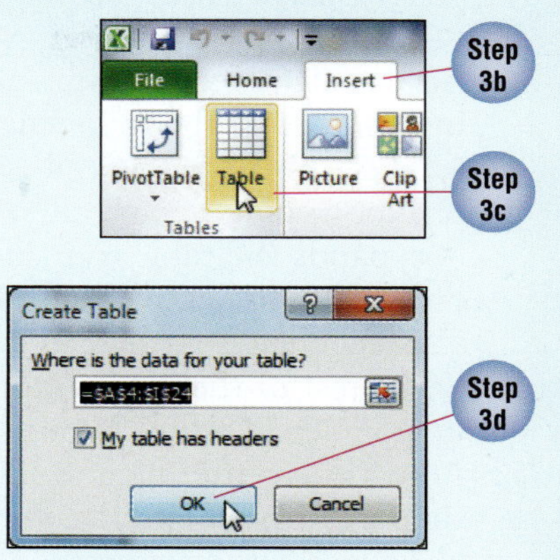

Modifying a Table

Once a table has been defined, typing new data in the row immediately below the last row of the table or in the column immediately right of the last column causes the table to automatically expand to include the new entries. Excel displays the AutoCorrect Options button when the table is expanded. Click the button to display a drop-down list with the options *Undo Table AutoExpansion* and *Stop Automatically Expanding Tables*. If you need to add data near a table without having the table expand, leave a blank column or row between the table and the new data.

Typing a formula in the first row of a new table column automatically creates a calculated column. In a calculated column, Excel copies the formula from the first cell to the remaining cells in the column as soon as you enter the formula. The AutoCorrect Options button appears when Excel converts a column to a calculated column with the options *Undo Calculated Column* and *Stop Automatically Creating Calculated Columns* available in the drop-down list.

Quick Steps

Add Rows or Columns to Table
Type data in first row below table or first column to right of table.

Add Calculated Column
1. Type formula in first record in column.
2. Press Enter.

Project 1b Adding a Row and a Calculated Column to a Table

Part 2 of 4

1. With **EL2-C3-P1-BillingSummaryOctWk1.xlsx** open, add a new record to the table by completing the following steps:
   a. Make A25 the active cell, type RE-522, and then press Enter. Excel automatically expands the table to include the new row and displays the AutoCorrect Options button.
   b. Make B25 the active cell and then type the remainder of the record as follows:

Client	10512
Date	10/12/2012
Last Name	Melanson
First Name	Connie
Attorney	Kyle Williams

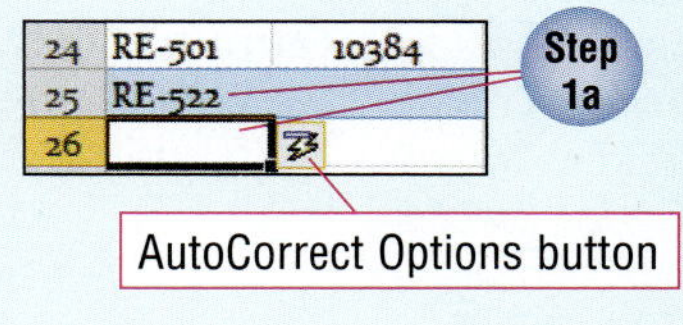

Area	**Real Estate**
Billable Hours	**2.5**
Rate	**75.00**

2. Add a calculated column to multiply Billable Hours times Rate by completing the following steps:
   a. Make J4 the active cell.
   b. Type **Fees Due** and then press Enter. Excel automatically expands the table to include the new column.
   c. With J5 the active cell, type **=h5*i5** and then press Enter. Excel creates a calculated column and copies the formula to the rest of the rows in the table.
   d. Double-click the column J boundary to AutoFit the column.
3. Adjust the centering and fill color of the titles across the top of the table by completing the following steps:
   a. Make A1 the active cell.
   b. Click the Merge & Center button in the Alignment group in the Home tab to unmerge A1:I1.
   c. Select A1:J1 and then click the Merge & Center button.
   d. Make A2 the active cell and then repeat Steps 3b and 3c to merge and center row 2 across columns A through J.
   e. Make A3 the active cell and then repeat Steps 3b and 3c to merge and center row 3 across columns A through J.
4. Save **EL2-C3-P1-BillingSummaryOctWk1.xlsx**.

Rate	Fees Du
85.00	573.75
85.00	276.25
75.00	393.75
100.00	425.00
100.00	325.00
90.00	247.50
75.00	393.75
75.00	318.75
100.00	500.00
90.00	292.50
100.00	450.00
100.00	375.00
100.00	450.00
85.00	446.25
75.00	393.75
75.00	393.75
75.00	262.50
100.00	425.00
100.00	375.00
90.00	405.00
75.00	187.50

Steps 2a & 2b

Step 2c

Quick Steps

Change Table Style
1. Make cell active within table.
2. If necessary, click Table Tools Design tab.
3. Click desired style in Table Styles gallery.
   OR
   Click More button in Table Styles gallery and click desired style at drop-down gallery.

Add Total Row
1. Make cell active within table.
2. If necessary, click Table Tools Design tab.
3. Click *Total Row* check box.
4. Click in total row in column to add function.
5. Click down-pointing arrow.
6. Click desired function.

Table Styles and Table Style Options

The contextual Table Tools Design tab shown in Figure 3.2 contains options for formatting the table. Apply a different visual style to the table using the Table Styles gallery. Excel provides several table styles categorized by Light, Medium, and Dark color themes. By default, Excel bands the rows within the table, which means that even rows are formatted differently from odd rows. ***Banding*** rows or columns makes the task of reading data across a row or down a column in a large table easier. You can remove the banding from the rows and/or add banding to the columns. Use the *First Column* and *Last Column* check boxes in the Table Style Options group to add emphasis to the first or last column in the table by formatting the column separately from the rest of the table. The *Header Row* check box is used to show or hide the column headings row in the table.

Adding a total row to the table causes Excel to add the word *Total* in a new row at the bottom of the table in the leftmost cell. A Sum function is added automatically to the last numeric column in the table. Click in a cell in the total row to display a down-pointing arrow from which you can select a function formula in a pop-up list.

More

Figure 3.2 Table Tools Design Tab

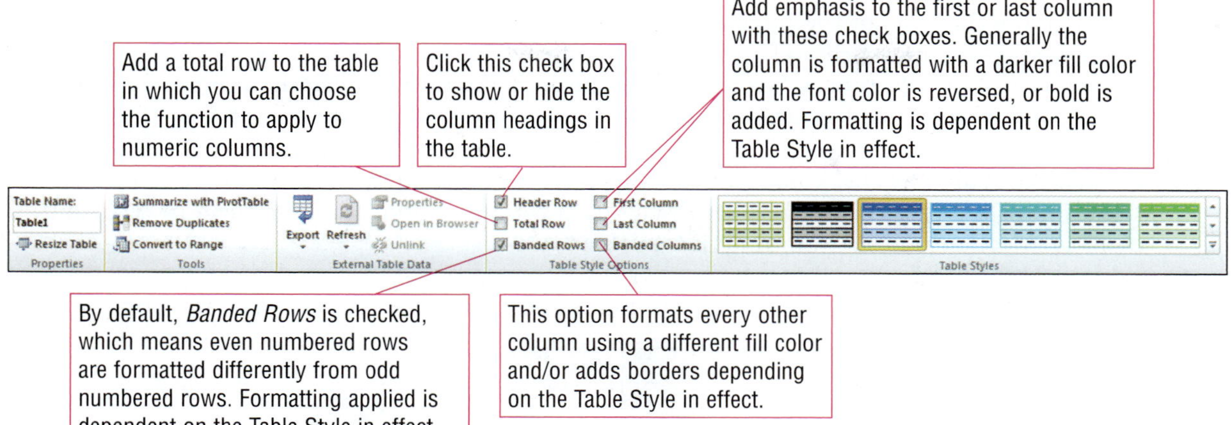
Add a total row to the table in which you can choose the function to apply to numeric columns.
Click this check box to show or hide the column headings in the table.
Add emphasis to the first or last column with these check boxes. Generally the column is formatted with a darker fill color and the font color is reversed, or bold is added. Formatting is dependent on the Table Style in effect.
Table Name:
Table1
Resize Table
Properties
Summarize with PivotTable
Remove Duplicates
Convert to Range
Tools
Export
Refresh
Properties
Open in Browser
Unlink
External Table Data
Header Row
Total Row
Banded Rows
First Column
Last Column
Banded Columns
Table Style Options
Table Styles
By default, *Banded Rows* is checked, which means even numbered rows are formatted differently from odd numbered rows. Formatting applied is dependent on the Table Style in effect.
This option formats every other column using a different fill color and/or adds borders depending on the Table Style in effect.

Project 1c Formatting a Table and Adding a Total Row

Part 3 of 4

1. With **EL2-C3-P1-BillingSummaryOctWk1.xlsx** open, change the table style by completing the following steps:
   a. Click any cell within the table to activate the table and the contextual Table Tools Design tab.
   b. Click the Table Tools Design tab.
   c. Click the More button located at the bottom of the vertical scroll bar in the Table Styles gallery.
   d. Click *Table Style Medium 15* at the drop-down gallery (first option in third row in *Medium* section).

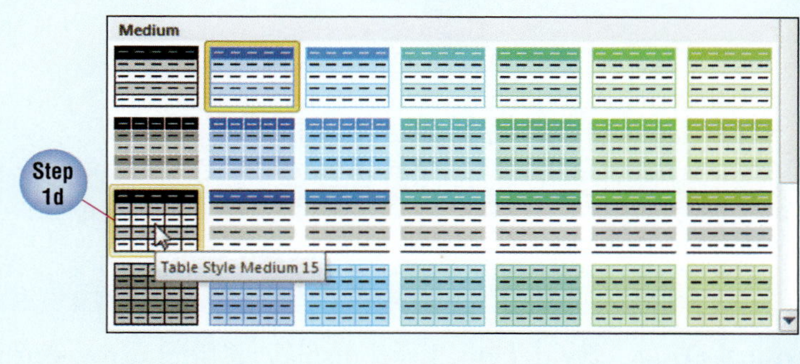
Medium
Step 1d
Table Style Medium 15

2. Change the Table Style options to remove the row banding, insert column banding, and emphasize the first column in the table by completing the following steps:
   a. Click the *Banded Rows* check box in the Table Style Options group in the Table Tools Design tab to clear the box. All of the rows in the table are now formatted the same.
   b. Click the *Banded Columns* check box in the Table Style Options group to insert a check mark. Every other column in the table is now formatted differently.
   c. Click the *First Column* check box in the Table Style Options group. Notice the first column has a darker fill color and reverse font color applied.

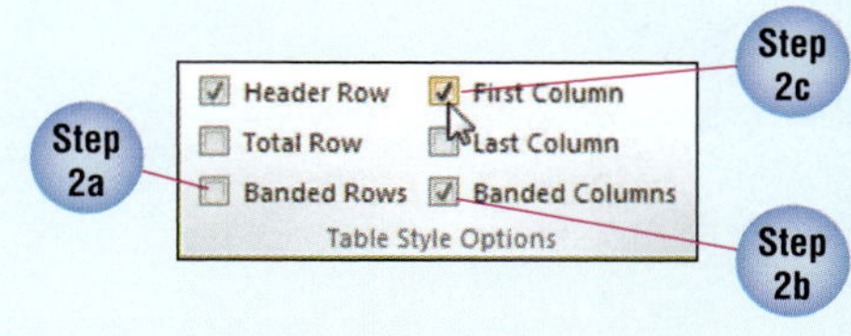
Header Row
First Column
Total Row
Last Column
Banded Rows
Banded Columns
Table Style Options
Step 2a
Step 2b
Step 2c

d. Click the *Header Row* check box in the Table Style Options group to clear the box. Notice the first row of the table containing the column headings disappears and is replaced with empty cells. The row is also removed from the table range definition.
e. Click the *Header Row* check box to insert a check mark and redisplay the column headings.

3. Add a total row and add function formulas to numeric columns by completing the following steps:
   a. Click the *Total Row* check box in the Table Style Options group to add a total row to the bottom of the table. Excel formats row 26 as a total row, adds the label *Total* in A26, and automatically creates a Sum function in J26.
   b. Make H26 the active cell.
   c. Click the down-pointing arrow that appears in H26 and then click *Sum* at the pop-up list.

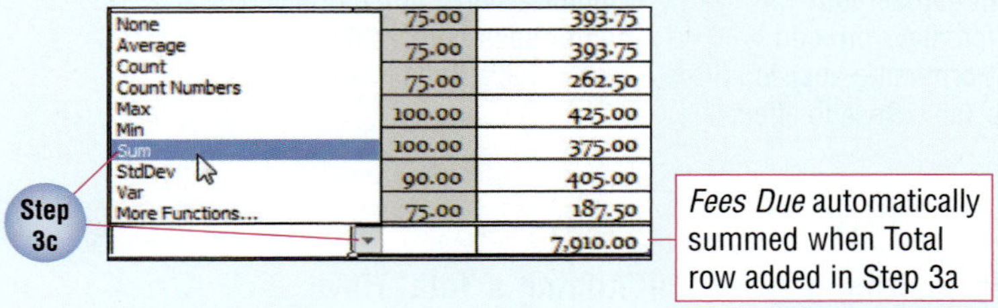

   d. Make B26 the active cell, click the down-pointing arrow that appears, and then click *Count* at the pop-up list.

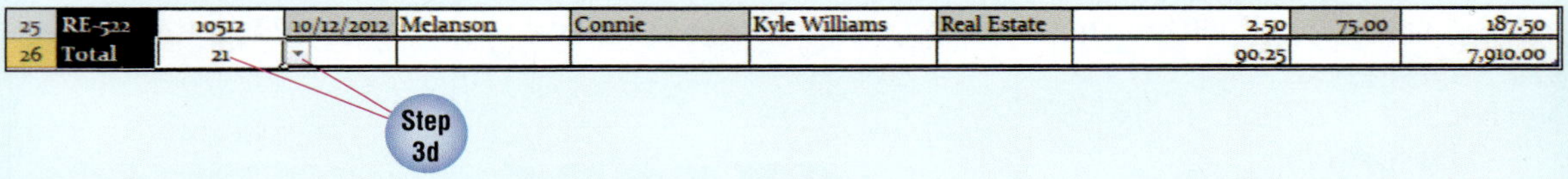

4. Click the Page Layout tab and change *Width* to *1 page* in the Scale to Fit group.
5. Preview and then print the worksheet.
6. Save **EL2-C3-P1-BillingSummaryOctWk1.xlsx**.

Sorting and Filtering a Table

Quick Steps

Filter Table
1. Click desired filter arrow button.
2. Click desired filter options.
3. Click OK.

Sort Table
1. Click desired filter arrow button.
2. Click desired sort order.

OR
1. Click Sort & Filter button.
2. Click *Custom Sort*.
3. Define sort levels.
4. Click OK.

By default, Excel displays a filter arrow button next to each label in the table header row. Click the filter arrow button to display a drop-down list with the same sort and filter options you used in Chapter 1.

Sorting and Filtering a Table

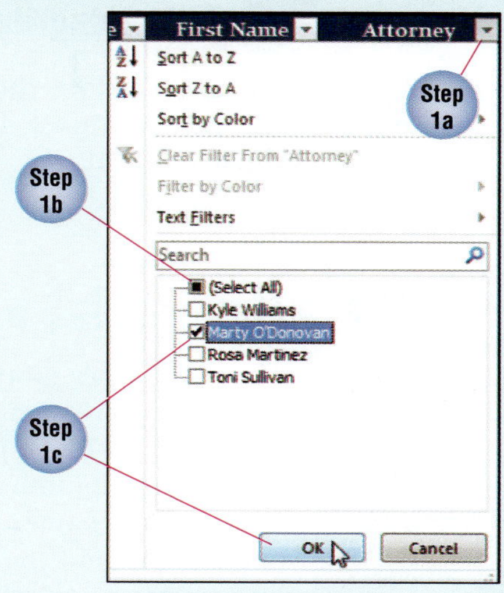

1. With **EL2-C3-P1-BillingSummaryOctWk1.xlsx** open, filter the table by attorney name to print a list of billable hours for Marty O'Donovan by completing the following steps:
   a. Click the filter arrow button located next to *Attorney* in F4.
   b. Click the *(Select All)* check box to clear the check mark from the check box.
   c. Click the *Marty O'Donovan* check box to insert a check mark and then click OK. The table is filtered to display only those records with *Marty O'Donovan* in the *Attorney* field. The Sum functions in columns H and J reflect the totals for the filtered records only.
   d. Print the filtered worksheet.
2. Redisplay all records by clicking the Attorney filter arrow button and then clicking *Clear Filter From "Attorney"* at the drop-down list.
3. Sort the table first by the attorney name, then by the area of law, and then by the client last name using the Sort dialog box by completing the following steps:
   a. With the active cell positioned anywhere within the table, click the Home tab.
   b. Click the Sort & Filter button in the Editing group and then click *Custom Sort* at the drop-down list.
   c. At the Sort dialog box, click the down-pointing arrow next to the *Sort by* list box in the *Column* section and then click *Attorney* at the drop-down list. The default options for *Sort On* and *Order* are correct since you want to sort by the column values in ascending order.
   d. Click the Add Level button.
   e. Click the down-pointing arrow next to the *Then by* list box and then click *Area* at the drop-down list.
   f. Click the Add Level button.
   g. Click the down-pointing arrow next to the second *Then by* list box and then click *Last Name* at the drop-down list.
   h. Click OK.
4. Print the sorted table.
5. Save and then close **EL2-C3-P1-BillingSummaryOctWk1.xlsx**.

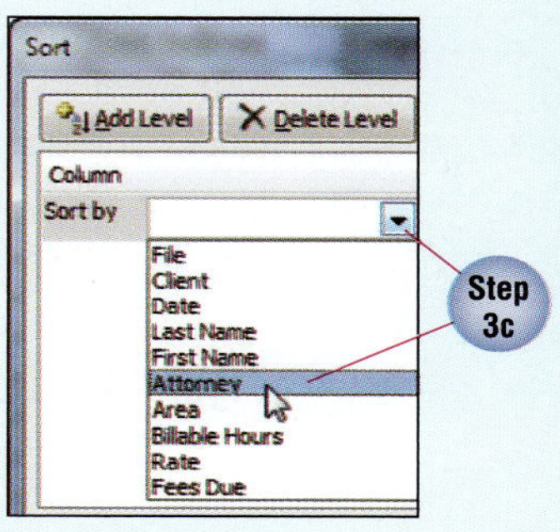

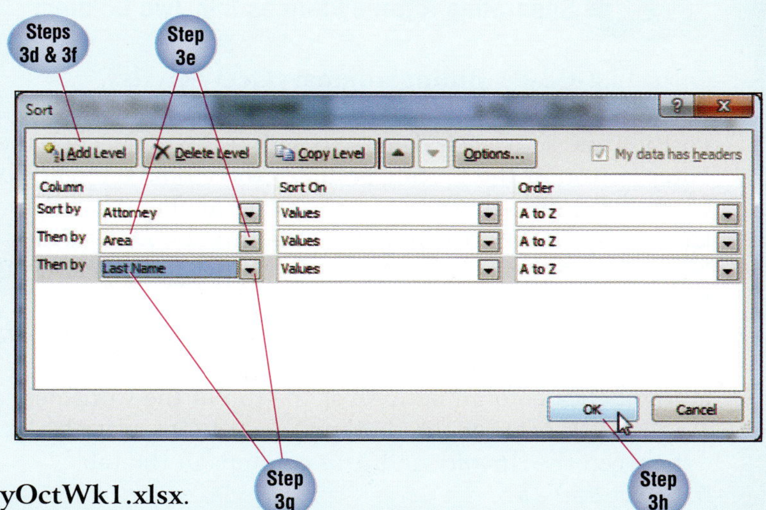

Project 2 Use Data Tools to Split Data and Ensure Data Integrity

5 Parts

You will use Excel's data tools to split the attorney first and last names into two separate columns, remove duplicate records, and restrict the type of data that can be entered into a field.

Quick Steps

Split Text into Multiple Columns
1. Insert blank column(s) next to source data.
2. Select data to be split.
3. Click Data tab.
4. Click Text to Columns button.
5. Click Next at first dialog box.
6. Select delimiter check box for character that separates data.
7. Click Next.
8. Click Finish.
9. Deselect range.

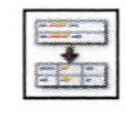

Text to Columns

Data Tools

The Data Tools group in the Data tab shown in Figure 3.3 includes features useful for working with data in tables. A worksheet in which more than one field has been entered into the same column can be separated into multiple columns using the Text to Columns feature. For example, a worksheet with a column that has first and last names entered into the same cell can have the first name split into one column and the last name split into a separate column. Breaking up the data into separate columns facilitates sorting and other data management functions. Before using the Text to Columns feature, insert the number of blank columns you will need to separate the data immediately right of the column to be split. Next, select the column containing multiple data and then click the Text to Columns button to start the Convert Text to Columns Wizard. The wizard contains three dialog boxes to guide you through the steps of separating the data.

Figure 3.3 Data Tools Group in Data Tab

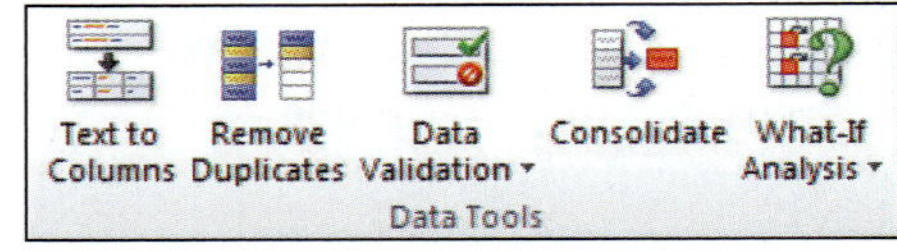

Project 2a Separating Attorney Names into Two Columns

Part 1 of 5

1. Open **EL2-C3-P1-BillingSummaryOctWk1.xlsx**.
2. Save the workbook with Save As and name it **EL2-C3-P2-BillingSummaryOctWk1**.
3. Position the active cell anywhere within the table, click the Sort & Filter button in the Editing group of the Home tab, and then click *Clear* at the drop-down list to clear the existing sort criteria.
4. Create a custom sort to sort the table first by *Date* (Oldest to Newest) and then by *Client* (Smallest to Largest). Refer to Project 1d, Step 3 if you need assistance with this step.
5. Split the attorney first and last names in column F into two columns by completing the following steps:
   a. Right-click column letter G at the top of the worksheet area and then click *Insert* at the shortcut menu to insert a blank column between the *Attorney* and *Area* columns in the table.
   b. Select F5:F25.
   c. Click the Data tab.
   d. Click the Text to Columns button in the Data Tools group.

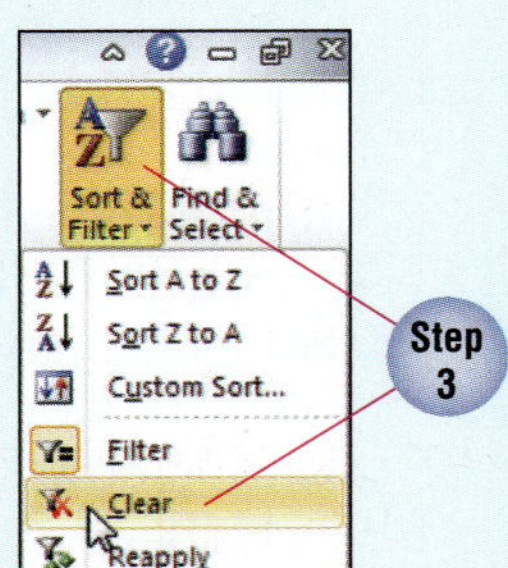

e. At the Convert Text to Columns Wizard - Step 1 of 3 dialog box, with *Delimited* selected in the *Choose the file type that best describes your data* section, click Next.

f. At the Convert Text to Columns Wizard - Step 2 of 3 dialog box, click the *Space* check box in the *Delimiters* section and then click Next. The *Data preview* section of the dialog box updates after you click the *Space* check box to show the names split into two columns.

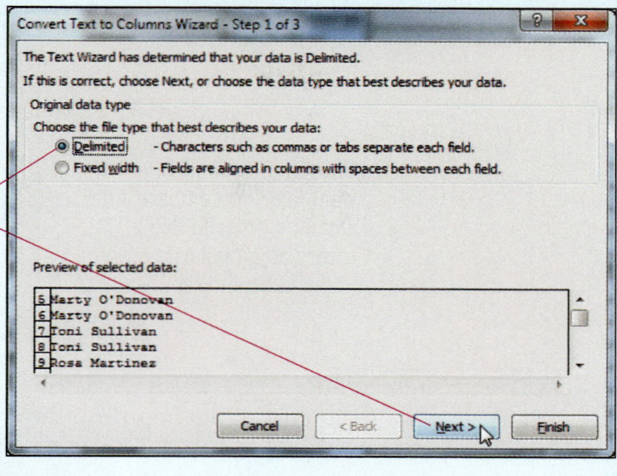

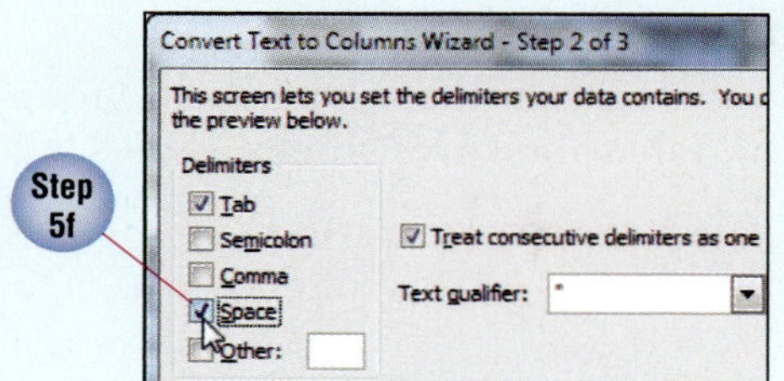

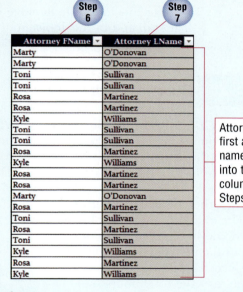

g. Click Finish at the last Convert Text to Columns Wizard dialog box to accept the default *General* data format for both columns.

h. Deselect the range.

6. Make F4 the active cell, edit the label to *Attorney FName*, and then AutoFit the column width.

7. Make G4 the active cell, edit the label to *Attorney LName*, and then AutoFit the column width.

8. Save **EL2-C3-P2-BillingSummaryOctWk1.xlsx**.

Step 6   Step 7

Attorney FName	Attorney LName
Marty	O'Donovan
Marty	O'Donovan
Toni	Sullivan
Toni	Sullivan
Rosa	Martinez
Rosa	Martinez
Kyle	Williams
Toni	Sullivan
Toni	Sullivan
Rosa	Martinez
Kyle	Williams
Rosa	Martinez
Rosa	Martinez
Marty	O'Donovan
Rosa	Martinez
Toni	Sullivan
Rosa	Martinez
Toni	Sullivan
Kyle	Williams
Rosa	Martinez
Kyle	Williams

Attorney first and last names split into two columns at Steps 5a–5g.

Removing Duplicate Records

Excel can compare records within a worksheet and automatically delete duplicate rows based on the columns you select that might contain duplicate values. At the Remove Duplicates dialog box shown in Figure 3.4, by default all columns are selected when the dialog box is opened. Click the Unselect All button to remove the check marks from each column and then click the individual columns you want to compare if you do not want Excel to check for duplicates in every column. When you click OK, Excel performs an automatic deletion of rows containing duplicate values and displays a message box when the operation is completed informing you of the number of rows that were removed from the worksheet or table and the number of unique values that remain. Consider conditionally formatting duplicate values first to view the records that will be deleted. Use the *Duplicate Values* option in *Highlight Cells Rules* from the

Quick Steps

Remove Duplicate Rows

1. Select range or make cell active in table.
2. Click Data tab.
3. Click Remove Duplicates button.
4. Select columns to compare.
5. Click OK.
6. Click OK.

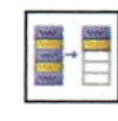

Remove Duplicates

Figure 3.4 Remove Duplicates Dialog Box

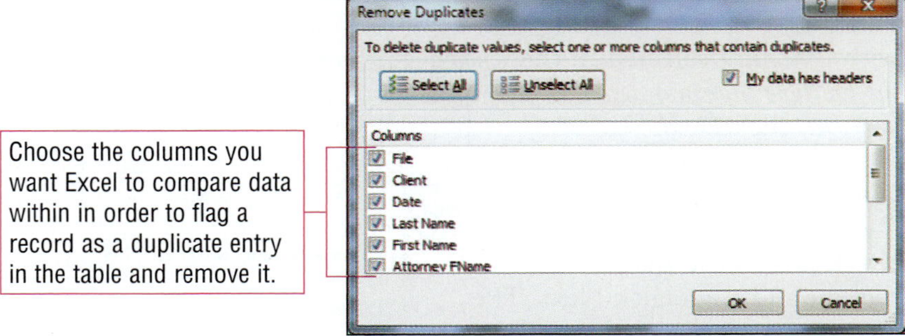

Conditional Formatting drop-down list. (Recall from Chapter 1 that you can display the Conditional Formatting drop-down list by clicking the Conditional Formatting button in the Styles group in the Home tab.)

Excel includes the Remove Duplicates button in the Data Tools group in the Data tab and in the Tools group in the Table Tools Design tab. Click Undo if you remove duplicate rows by mistake.

Project 2b Removing Duplicate Rows

Part 2 of 5

1. With **EL2-C3-P2-BillingSummaryOctWk1.xlsx** open, remove duplicate rows in the billing summary table by completing the following steps:
   a. With the active cell positioned anywhere within the table, click the Remove Duplicates button in the Data Tools group in the Data tab.
   b. At the Remove Duplicates dialog box with all columns selected in the *Columns* list box, click the Unselect All button.
   c. The billing summary table should have only one record per file per client per date since attorneys record once per day the total hours spent on each file. A record is a duplicate if the same values exist in the three columns that store the file number, client number, and date. Click the *File* check box to insert a check mark.
   d. Click the *Client* check box to insert a check mark.
   e. Click the *Date* check box to insert a check mark and then click OK.
   f. Click OK at the Microsoft Excel message box that says 1 duplicate value was found and removed and 20 unique values remain.

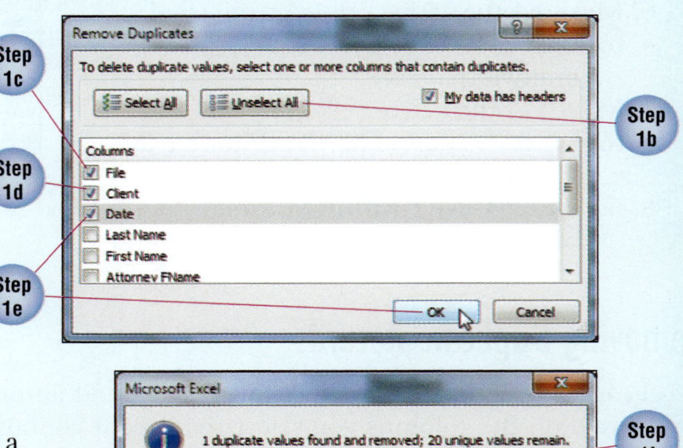

2. Scroll the worksheet to view the total in K25. Compare the total with your printout from Project 1d, Step 4. Notice the total in *Fees Due* is now *7,516.25* compared to *7,910.00* in the printout.
3. Save **EL2-C3-P2-BillingSummaryOctWk1.xlsx**.

Validating and Restricting Data Entry

Excel's data validation feature allows you to control the type of data that is accepted for entry in a cell. You can specify the type of data that is allowed as well as parameters that validate whether the entry is within a certain range of acceptable values, dates, times, or text length. You can also set up a list of values that display in a drop-down list when the cell is made active. At the Data Validation dialog box shown in Figure 3.5, begin by choosing the type of data you want to validate in the *Allow* list box in the Settings tab. Additional list or text boxes appear in the dialog box depending on the option chosen in the *Allow* list.

As well as defining acceptable data entry parameters, you have the option of adding an input message and an error alert message to the range. You define the text that appears in these messages. The input message displays when the cell is made active for which data validation rules apply. These messages are informational in nature. Error alerts are messages that appear if incorrect data is entered in the cell. Three styles of error alerts are available. A description and example for each type of alert are described in Table 3.1.

If an error alert message has not been defined, Excel displays the Stop error alert with a default error message of *The value you entered is not valid. A user has restricted values that can be entered into this cell.*

Quick Steps

Create Data Validation Rule

1. Select desired range.
2. Click Data tab.
3. Click Data Validation button.
4. Specify validation criteria in Settings tab.
5. Click Input Message tab.
6. Type input message title and text.
7. Click Error Alert tab.
8. Select error style.
9. Type error alert title and message text.
10. Click OK.

Data Validation

Figure 3.5 Data Validation Dialog Box with Settings Tab Selected

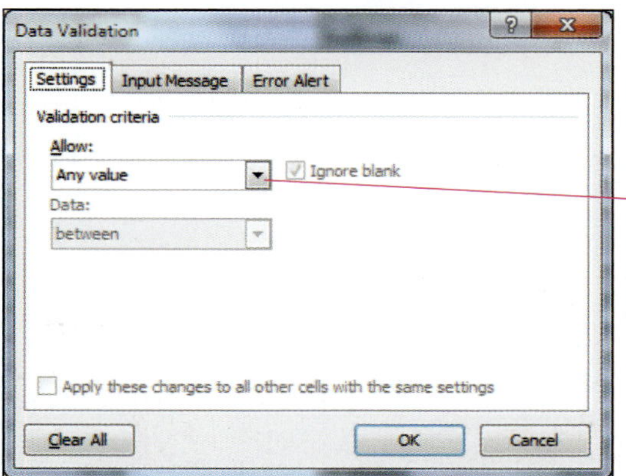

Specify the type of data you will allow to be entered into the cells within the range by specifying one of the following options: *Whole number, Decimal, List, Date, Time, Text length, Custom.* Other parameter boxes appear depending on the selection made in *Allow.*

Table 3.1 Data Validation Error Alert Message Styles

Error Alert Icon	*Error Alert Style*	*Description*
	Stop	Prevent the data from being entered into the cell. The error alert message box provides three buttons to ensure new data is entered.
	Warning	Do not prevent the data from being entered into the cell. The error alert message box provides four buttons displayed below the prompt *Continue?*
	Information	Do not prevent the data from being entered into the cell. The error alert message box provides three buttons displayed below the error message.

Project 2c Restricting Data Entry to Dates Within a Range

Part 3 of 5

1. With **EL2-C3-P2-BillingSummaryOctWk1.xlsx** open, create a validation rule, input message, and error alert for dates in the billing summary worksheet by completing the following steps:
   a. Select C5:C24.
   b. Click the Data Validation button in the Data Tools group in the Data tab.
   c. With Settings the active tab at the Data Validation dialog box, click the down-pointing arrow next to the *Allow* list box (currently displays *Any value*) and then click *Date* at the drop-down list. Validation options are dependent on the *Allow* setting. When you choose *Date*, Excel adds *Start date* and *End date* text boxes to the *Validation criteria* section.
   d. With *between* automatically selected in the *Data* list box, click in the *Start date* text box and then type 10/08/2012.
   e. Click in the *End date* text box and then type 10/12/2012. Since the billing summary worksheet is for the week of October 8 to 12, 2012, entering this validation criteria will ensure that only dates between the start date and end date are accepted.
   f. Click the Input Message tab.

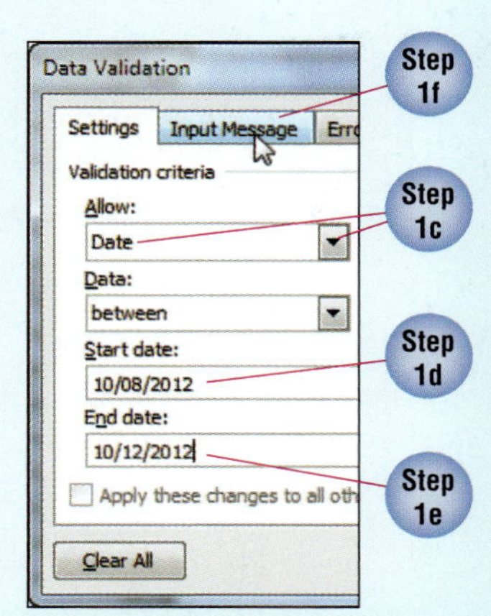

g. Click in the *Title* text box and then type **Billing Date**.
h. Click in the *Input message* text box and then type **This worksheet is for the week of October 8 to October 12 only**.
i. Click the Error Alert tab.
j. With *Stop* selected in the *Style* list box, click in the *Title* text box and then type **Date is outside accepted range**.
k. Click in the *Error message* text box and then type **Please enter a date from October 8 to October 12, 2012**.
l. Click OK. Since the range is active for which the data validation rules apply, the input message box appears.
m. Deselect the range.

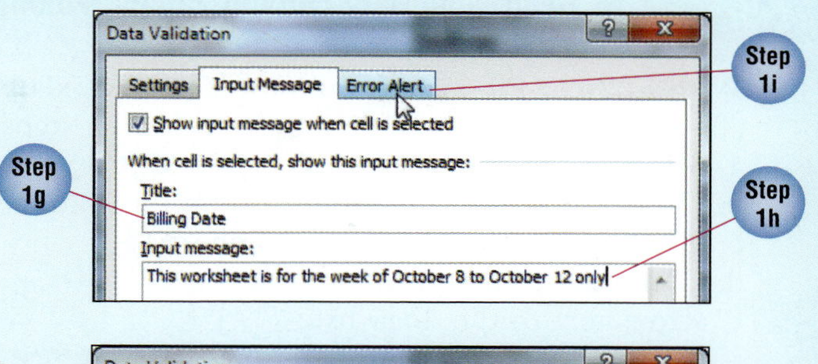

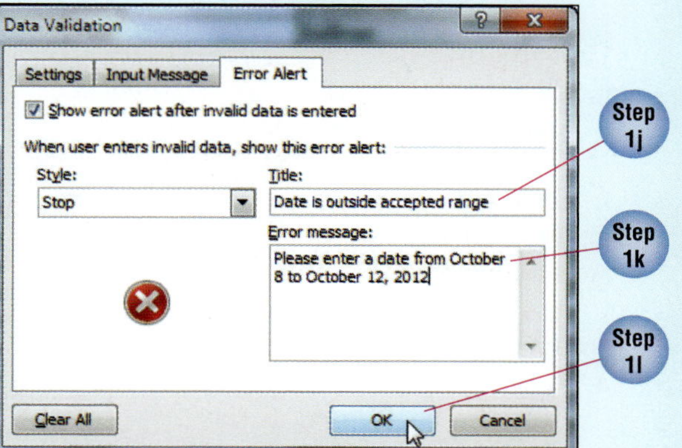

2. Add a new record to the table to test the date validation rule by completing the following steps:
   a. Right-click row number 25 and then click *Insert* at the shortcut menu to insert a new row into the table.
   b. Make A25 the active cell, type **PL-348**, and then press Tab.
   c. Type **10420** in the *Client* column and then press Tab. The input message title and text appear when the *Date* column is made active.
   d. Type **10/15/2012** and then press Enter. Since the date entered is invalid, the error alert message box appears.
   e. Click the Retry button.
   f. Type **10/12/2012** and then press Tab.
   g. Enter the data in the remaining fields as follows. Press Tab to move from column to column in the table.

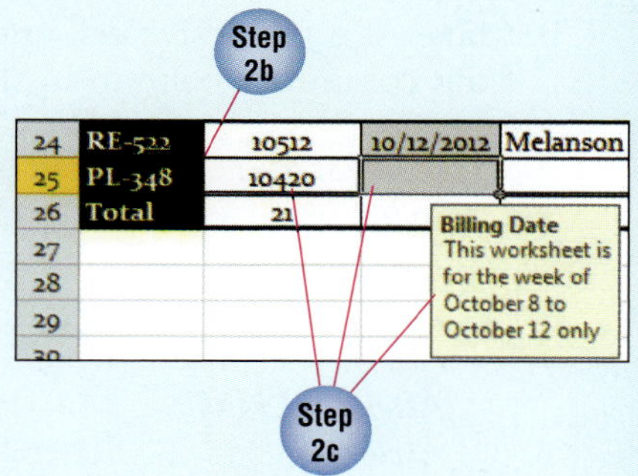

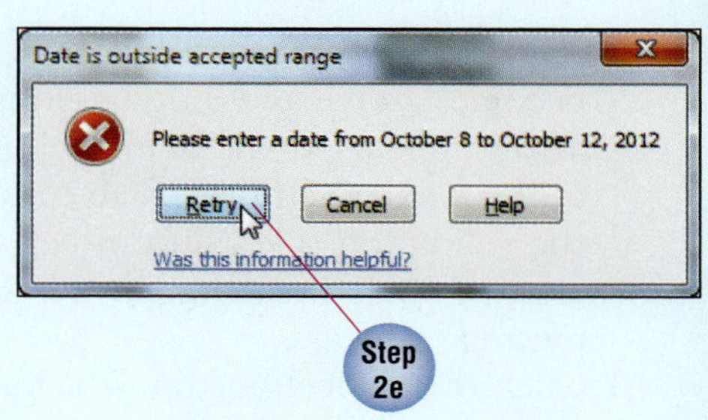

Last Name	**Torrez**
First Name	**Alexander**
Attorney FName	**Rosa**
Attorney LName	**Martinez**
Area	**Patent**
Billable Hours	**2.25**
Rate	**100.00**

3. Save **EL2-C3-P2-BillingSummaryOctWk1.xlsx**.

Project 2d **Restricting Data Entry to Values Within a List** Part 4 of 5

1. With **EL2-C3-P2-BillingSummaryOctWk1.xlsx** open, create a list of values that are allowed in a cell by completing the following steps:
   a. Select J5:J25.
   b. Click the Data Validation button in the Data Tools group.
   c. If necessary, click the Settings tab.
   d. Click the down-pointing arrow next to the *Allow* list box and then click *List* at the drop-down list.
   e. Click in the *Source* text box and then type **75.00,85.00,90.00,100.00**.
   f. Click OK.
   g. Deselect the range.

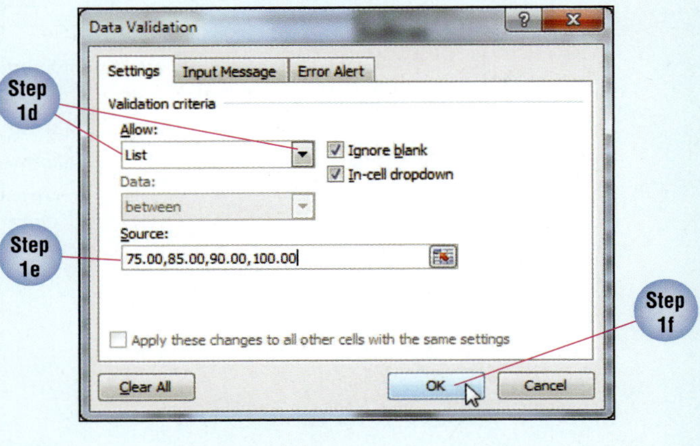

2. Add a new record to the table to test the rate validation list by completing the following steps:
   a. Right-click row number 26 and then click *Insert* at the shortcut menu to insert a new row into the table.

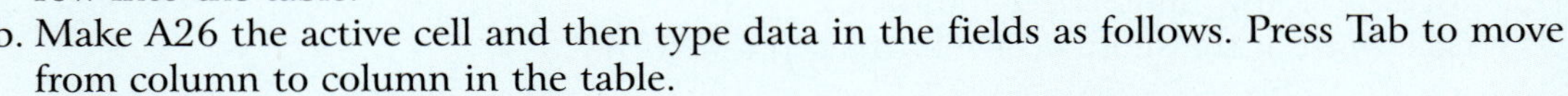

   b. Make A26 the active cell and then type data in the fields as follows. Press Tab to move from column to column in the table.

File	**IN-745**
Client	**10210**
Date	**10/12/2012**
Last Name	**Boscovic**
First Name	**Victor**
Attorney FName	**Rosa**
Attorney LName	**Martinez**
Area	**Insurance**
Billable Hours	**1.75**

   c. At the *Rate* field, the validation list becomes active and a down-pointing arrow appears at the field. Type **125.00** and then press Tab to test the validation rule. Since no error alert message was entered, the default message appears.

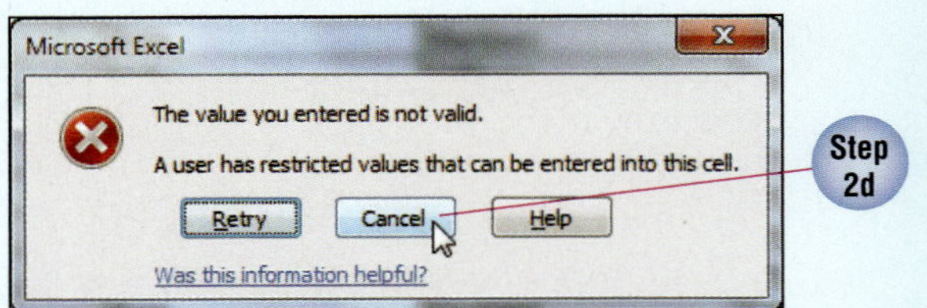

   d. Click the Cancel button. The value is cleared from the field.
   e. Click the down-pointing arrow at the end of the field, click *100.00* at the drop-down list, and then press Tab.

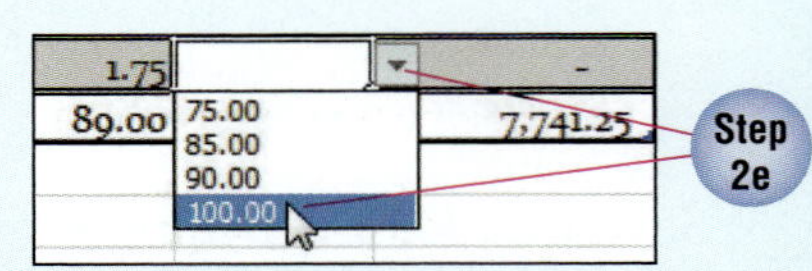

3. Save **EL2-C3-P2-BillingSummaryOctWk1.xlsx**.

Project 2e Ensuring Data Entered Is a Specified Text Length

Part 5 of 5

1. With **EL2-C3-P2-BillingSummaryOctWk1.xlsx** open, create a validation rule to ensure that all client identification numbers are five characters in length to coincide with the firm's accounting system by completing the following steps:
   a. Select B5:B26 and click the Data Validation button in the Data Tools group in the Data tab.
   b. Click the down-pointing arrow next to the *Allow* list box and then click *Text length* at the drop-down list.
   c. Click the down-pointing arrow next to *Data* and then click *equal to* at the drop-down list.
   d. Click in the *Length* text box, type 5, and then click OK.
   e. Deselect the range.

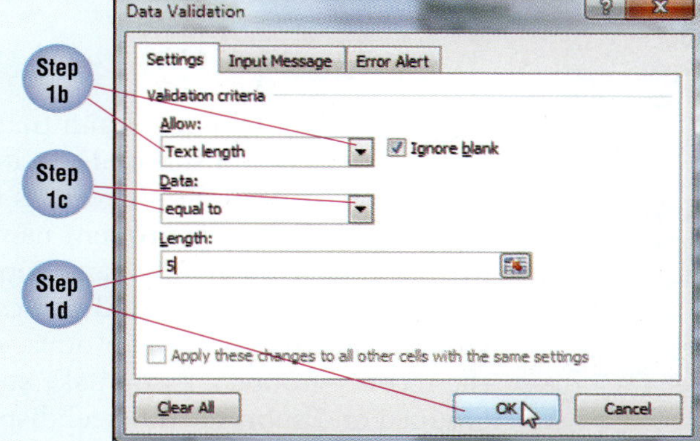

2. Add a new record to the table to test the client identification validation rule by completing the following steps:
   a. Right-click row number 27 and then click *Insert* at the shortcut menu.
   b. Make A27 the active cell, type FL-325, and then press Tab.
   c. Type 1010411 in B27 and then press Tab. Since this value is greater than the specified number of characters allowed in the cell, the default error message appears.
   d. Click the Retry button.
   e. Delete the selected text, type 1010, and then press Tab. Since this value is less than the specified text length, the default error message appears again. Using a Text Length validation rule ensures that all entries in the range have the same number of characters. This rule is useful to validate customer numbers, employee numbers, inventory numbers, or any other data that requires a consistent number of characters.
   f. Click the Cancel button, type 10104, and then press Tab. Since this entry is five characters in length, Excel moves to the next field.
   g. Enter the remaining fields as follows:

Date	10/12/2012
Last Name	Ferreira
First Name	Joseph
Attorney FName	Marty
Attorney LName	O'Donovan
Area	Divorce
Billable Hours	5.75
Rate	85.00

3. Save, print, and then close **EL2-C3-P2-BillingSummaryOctWk1.xlsx**.

Project 3 Group and Subtotal Related Records

3 Parts

You will convert the billing summary table to a normal range, sort the rows by the attorney names, and then add subtotals to display total fees due, a count of fees, and the average billable hours and fees due for each attorney.

Quick Steps

Convert Table to Range
1. Make cell active within the table.
2. Click Table Tools Design tab.
3. Click Convert to Range button.
4. Click Yes.

Create Subtotals
1. Select range.
2. Click Data tab.
3. Click Subtotals button.
4. Select field to group by in *At each change in* list box.
5. Select desired function in *Use function* list box.
6. Select field(s) to subtotal in *Add subtotal to* list box.
7. Click OK.
8. Deselect range.

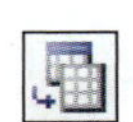
Convert to Range

Converting a Table to a Normal Range

A table can be converted to a normal range using the Convert to Range button in the Tools group of the Table Tools Design tab. Convert a table to a range in order to use the Subtotal feature or if you no longer need to treat the table data as a range independent of data in the rest of the worksheet.

Subtotaling Related Data

A range of data with a column that has multiple rows with the same field value can be grouped and subtotals created for each group automatically. For example, a worksheet with multiple records with the same department name in a field can be grouped by the department names and a subtotal of a numeric field calculated for each department. You can choose from a list of functions for the subtotal such as Average or Sum and you can also create multiple subtotal values for each group. Prior to creating subtotals, sort the data by the fields in which you want the records grouped. Also, make sure no blank rows exist within the range to be grouped and subtotaled. Excel displays a new row with a summary total when the field value for the specified subtotal column changes content. A grand total is also automatically included at the bottom of the range. Excel displays the subtotals with buttons along the left side of the worksheet area used to show or hide the details for each group using Excel's Outline feature. Excel can create an outline with up to eight levels. Figure 3.6 illustrates the data you will group and subtotal in Project 3a displayed with the worksheet at level 2 of the outline. In Figure 3.7, the same worksheet is shown with two attorney groups expanded to show the detail records.

Figure 3.6 Worksheet with Subtotals by Attorney Last Name Displaying Level 2 of the Outline

Outline level buttons

1 2 3

O'DONOVAN & SULLIVAN LAW ASSOCIATES
ASSOCIATE BILLING SUMMARY
OCTOBER 8 TO 12, 2012

	A	B	C	D	E	F	G	H	I	J	K
4	File	Client	Date	Last Name	First Name	Attorney FName	Attorney LName	Area	Billable Hours	Rate	Fees Due
15							Martinez Total				3,725.00
20							O'Donovan Total				1,785.00
26							Sullivan Total				1,762.50
31							Williams Total				1,132.50
32							Grand Total				8,405.00

Hide Detail button

Show Detail button

Figure 3.7 Worksheet with Subtotals by Attorney Last Name with Martinez and Sullivan Groups Expanded

	A	B	C	D	E	F	G	H	I	J	K
1	O'DONOVAN & SULLIVAN LAW ASSOCIATES										
2	ASSOCIATE BILLING SUMMARY										
3	OCTOBER 8 TO 12, 2012										
4	File	Client	Date	Last Name	First Name	Attorney FName	Attorney LName	Area	Billable Hours	Rate	Fees Due
5	IN-745	10210	10/9/2012	Boscovic	Victor	Rosa	Martinez	Insurance	4.25	100.00	425.00
6	IN-745	10210	10/11/2012	Boscovic	Victor	Rosa	Martinez	Insurance	4.50	100.00	450.00
7	IN-745	10210	10/12/2012	Boscovic	Victor	Rosa	Martinez	Insurance	1.75	100.00	175.00
8	EL-632	10225	10/9/2012	Armstrong	Daniel	Rosa	Martinez	Employment	3.25	100.00	325.00
9	EL-632	10225	10/11/2012	Armstrong	Daniel	Rosa	Martinez	Employment	4.50	100.00	450.00
10	PL-512	10290	10/11/2012	Tonini	Sam	Rosa	Martinez	Pension	3.75	100.00	375.00
11	IN-801	10346	10/12/2012	Sebastian	Paul	Rosa	Martinez	Insurance	4.25	100.00	425.00
12	PL-348	10420	10/10/2012	Torrez	Alexander	Rosa	Martinez	Patent	5.00	100.00	500.00
13	PL-348	10420	10/12/2012	Torrez	Alexander	Rosa	Martinez	Patent	2.25	100.00	225.00
14	EP-685	10495	10/12/2012	Kinsela	Frank	Rosa	Martinez	Estate	3.75	100.00	375.00
15							Martinez Total				3,725.00
20							O'Donovan Total				1,785.00
21	CL-412	10125	10/8/2012	Schmidt	Hilary	Toni	Sullivan	Corporate	5.25	75.00	393.75
22	CL-412	10125	10/12/2012	Schmidt	Hilary	Toni	Sullivan	Corporate	5.25	75.00	393.75
23	CL-521	10334	10/10/2012	Marsales	Gene	Toni	Sullivan	Corporate	4.25	75.00	318.75
24	CL-501	10341	10/10/2012	Fletcher	Dana	Toni	Sullivan	Corporate	5.25	75.00	393.75
25	CL-450	10358	10/12/2012	Poissant	Henri	Toni	Sullivan	Corporate	3.50	75.00	262.50
26							Sullivan Total				1,762.50
31							Williams Total				1,132.50
32							Grand Total				8,405.00

Project 3a Converting a Table to a Range and Creating Subtotals

Part 1 of 3

1. Open **EL2-C3-P2-BillingSummaryOctWk1.xlsx**.
2. Save the workbook with Save As and name it **EL2-C3-P3-BillingSummaryOctWk1.xlsx**.
3. Convert the table to a normal range in order to group and subtotal the records by completing the following steps:
   a. Position the active cell anywhere within the table and click the Table Tools Design tab.
   b. Click the *Total Row* check box in the Table Style Options group to remove the total row from the table. The Subtotal feature includes a grand total automatically so the total row is no longer needed.
   c. Click the *Banded Columns* check box in the Table Style Options to remove the banded formatting.
   d. Click the Convert to Range button in the Tools group.
   e. Click Yes at the Microsoft Excel message box asking if you want to convert the table to a normal range.

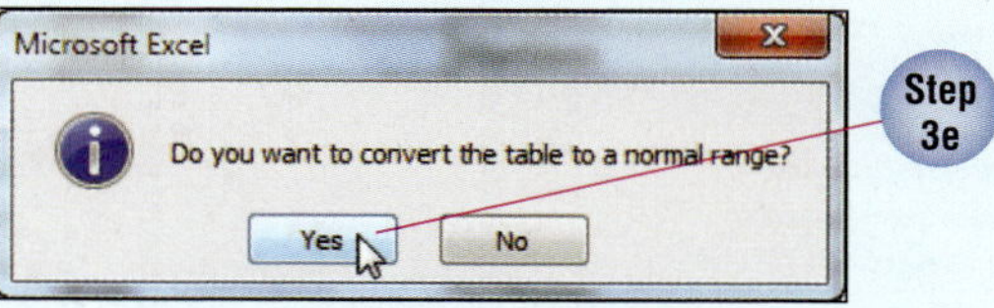

   f. Select columns A–K and adjust the column width to AutoFit.
   g. Deselect the columns.
4. Sort the data by the fields you want to subtotal and group by completing the following steps:
   a. Select A4:K27.
   b. Click the Sort & Filter button in the Editing group in the Home tab and then click *Custom Sort* at the drop-down list.

c. At the Sort dialog box, define three levels to group and sort records as follows:

Column	*Sort On*	*Order*
Attorney LName	Values	A to Z
Client	Values	Smallest to Largest
Date	Values	Oldest to Newest

d. Click OK.

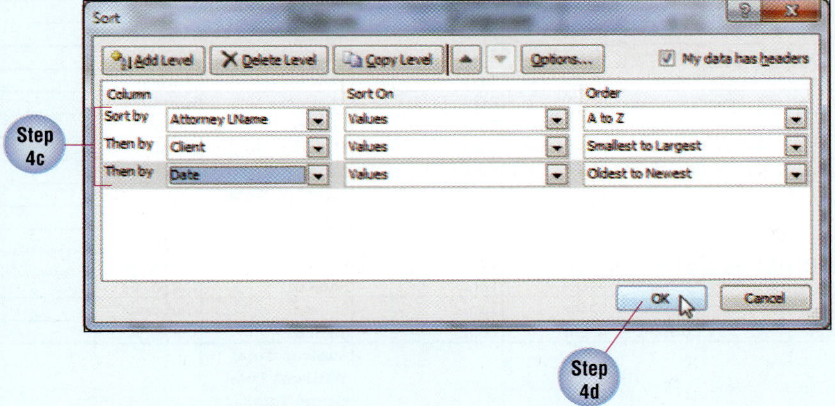

5. Create subtotals at each change in attorney last name by completing the following steps:
   a. With A4:K27 still selected, click the Data tab.
   b. Click the Subtotal button in the Outline group.
   c. At the Subtotal dialog box, click the down-pointing arrow to the right of the *At each change in* list box (current displays *File*), scroll down the list, and then click *Attorney LName*.

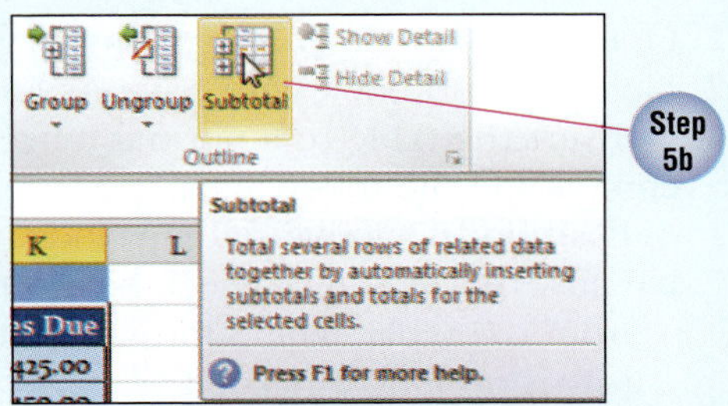

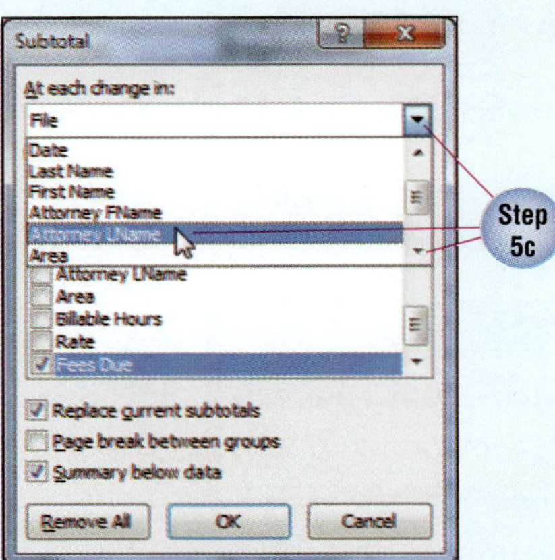

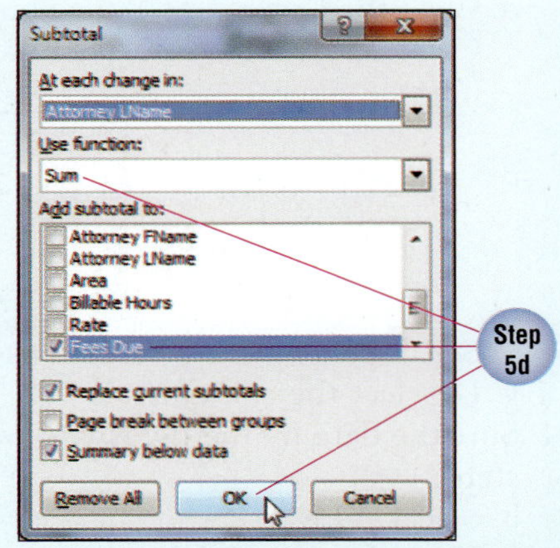

   d. With *Use function* set to *Sum* and *Fees Due* selected in the *Add subtotal to* list box, click OK.
   e. Deselect the range.
6. Print the worksheet.

7. Show and hide levels in the outlined worksheet by completing the following steps:
   a. Click the level 1 button located at the top left of the worksheet area below the Name text box. Excel collapses the worksheet to display only the grand total of the *Fees Due* column.
   b. Click the level 2 button to display the subtotals by attorney last name. Notice a button with a plus symbol displays next to each subtotal in the Outline section at the left side of the worksheet area. The button with the plus symbol is the Show Detail button and the button with the minus symbol is the Hide Detail button. Compare your worksheet with the one shown in Figure 3.6 on page 88.
   c. Click the Show Detail button (displays as a plus symbol) next to the row with the Martinez subtotal. The detail rows for the group of records for Martinez are displayed.
   d. Click the Show Detail button next to the row with the Sullivan subtotal.
   e. Compare your worksheet with the one shown in Figure 3.7 on page 89.
   f. Click the level 3 button to display all detail rows.
8. Save **EL2-C3-P3-BillingSummaryOctWk1.xlsx**.

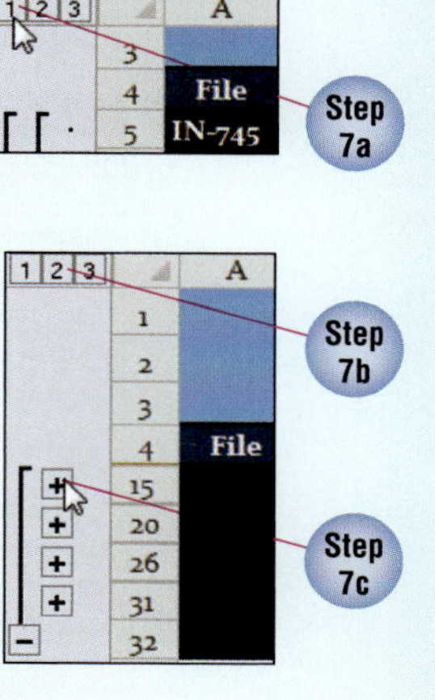

Project 3b Modifying Subtotals

Part 2 of 3

1. With **EL2-C3-P3-BillingSummaryOctWk1.xlsx** open, add a subtotal to count the number of billable records for each attorney for the week by completing the following steps:
   a. Select A4:K32 and click the Subtotal button in the Outline group in the Data tab. The Subtotal dialog box opens with the settings used for the subtotals created in Project 3a.
   b. Click the *Replace current subtotals* check box to clear the check mark. By clearing the check box you are instructing Excel to add another subtotal row to each group.
   c. Click the down-pointing arrow next to the *Use function* list box and then click *Count* at the drop-down list.
   d. With *Fees Due* still selected in the *Add subtotal to* list box, click OK. Excel adds a new subtotal row to each group with the count of records displayed.
2. Add a subtotal to calculate the average billable hours and average fees due for each attorney by completing the following steps:
   a. With the data range still selected, click the Subtotal button.
   b. Click the down-pointing arrow next to the *Use function* list box and then click *Average* at the drop-down list.

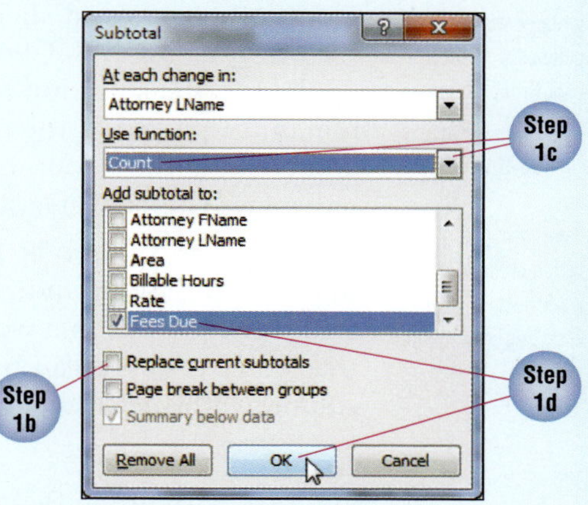

c. Click the *Billable Hours* check box in the *Add subtotal to* list box and then click OK. Excel adds a new subtotal row to each group with the average billable hours and average fees due for each attorney.

Attorney LName	Area	Billable Hours	Rate	Fees Due
Martinez	Insurance	4.25	100.00	425.00
Martinez	Insurance	4.50	100.00	450.00
Martinez	Insurance	1.75	100.00	175.00
Martinez	Employment	3.25	100.00	325.00
Martinez	Employment	4.50	100.00	450.00
Martinez	Pension	3.75	100.00	375.00
Martinez	Insurance	4.25	100.00	425.00
Martinez	Patent	5.00	100.00	500.00
Martinez	Patent	2.25	100.00	225.00
Martinez	Estate	3.75	100.00	375.00
Martinez Average		3.73		372.50
Martinez Count				10
Martinez Total				3,725.00

average row shown for Martinez group; average of *Billable Hours* and *Fees Due* columns added to subtotals for all attorneys in Steps 2a–2d

d. Deselect the range.

3. Use Save As to save the revised workbook and name it **EL2-C3-P3-BillingSummaryOctWk1-Prj3b**.
4. Click the Page Layout tab and scale the height of the worksheet to 1 page.
5. Print the worksheet.
6. Save and then close **EL2-C3-P3-BillingSummaryOctWk1-Prj3b.xlsx**.

Grouping and Ungrouping Data

Quick Steps

Group Data by Rows
1. Select range to be grouped within outlined worksheet.
2. Click Group button.
3. Click OK.

Ungroup Data by Rows
1. Select grouped range within outlined worksheet.
2. Click Ungroup button.
3. Click OK.

Use the Group and Ungroup buttons when a worksheet is outlined to individually manage collapsing and expanding groups of records at the various levels. For example, in an outlined worksheet with detailed rows displayed, selecting a group of records and clicking the Ungroup button opens the Ungroup dialog box shown in Figure 3.8. Clicking OK with *Rows* selected removes the group feature applied to the selection and the Hide Detail button is removed so the records remain displayed at the outline level. Selecting records that have been ungrouped and clicking the Group button reattaches the group feature to the selection and redisplays the Hide Detail button.

Columns can also be grouped and ungrouped. The outline section with the level numbers and Show and Hide Detail buttons displays across the top of the worksheet area. For example, in a worksheet where two columns are used to arrive at a formula, the source columns can be grouped and the details hidden so that only the formula column with the calculated results is displayed in an outlined worksheet.

Figure 3.8 Ungroup Dialog Box

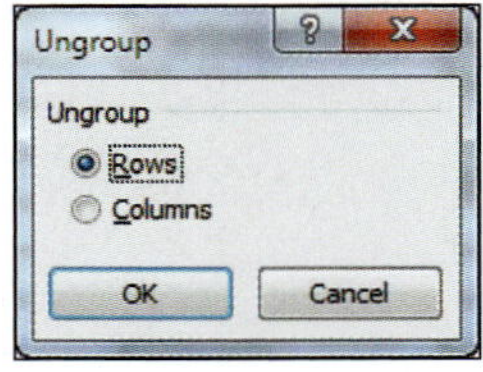

Grouping and Ungrouping Data

Part 3 of 3

1. Open **EL2-C3-P3-BillingSummaryOctWk1.xlsx.** Group client data within the Martinez attorney group by completing the following steps:
   a. Select A5:K7. These three rows contain billing information for Client 10210.
   b. Click the Group button in the Outline group in the Data tab. (Do not click the down-pointing arrow on the button.)
   c. At the Group dialog box with *Rows* selected, click OK. Excel adds a fourth outline level to the worksheet and a Hide Detail button is added below the last row of the grouped records in the Outline section.
   d. Select A12:K13, click the Group button, and then click OK at the Group dialog box.
   e. Deselect the range.

Group Ungroup Subtotal
Outline
Step 1b

Group
Group
Rows
Columns
OK Cancel
Step 1c

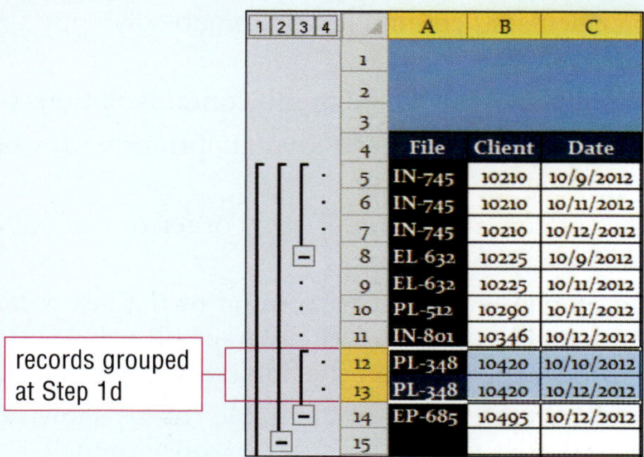

2. Experiment with the Hide Detail buttons in the Martinez group by hiding the detail for Client 10210 and then hiding the detail for Client 10420.
3. Redisplay the detail rows by clicking the Show Detail button for each client.
4. Select A5:K7, click the Ungroup button (do not click the down-pointing arrow on the button), and then click OK at the Ungroup dialog box.
5. Select A12:K13, click the Ungroup button, and then click OK at the Ungroup dialog box.
6. Select A5:K14, click the Ungroup button, and then click OK at the Ungroup dialog box. Notice the Hide Detail button is removed for the entire Martinez group.
7. Deselect the range and then click the level 2 button at the top of the outline section. Notice the Martinez records do not collapse like the others since they are no longer grouped.
8. Use Save As to save the revised workbook and name it **EL2-C3-P3-BillingSummaryOctWk1-Prj3c**.
9. Print and then close **EL2-C3-P3-BillingSummaryOctWk1-Prj3c.xlsx**.

Chapter Summary

- A table in Excel is a range of cells similar in structure to a database in which no blank rows exist and the first row of the range contains column headings.
- Define a range as a table using the Table button in the Tables group of the Insert tab.
- Columns in a table are called fields and rows are called records.
- The first row of a table contains column headings and is called the field names row or header row.
- A table automatically expands to include data typed in a row or column immediately adjacent to a range that has been defined as a table.
- Typing a formula in the first row of a new column causes Excel to define the column as a calculated column and automatically copy the formula to the remaining rows in the table.
- The contextual Table Tools Design tab contains options for formatting tables.
- The Table Styles gallery contains several options with which you can change the visual appearance of a table.
- Banding rows or columns formats every other row or column differently to make reading a large table easier.
- You can add emphasis to the first column or the last column in a table. Excel generally formats the column with a darker fill color and reverse font or bold font and borders depending on the Table Style in effect.
- The row containing field names in a table can be shown or hidden using the *Header Row* option in the Table Style Options group.
- Adding a Total row to a table causes Excel to add the word *Total* in the leftmost column and create a Sum function in the last numeric column in the table. You can add additional functions by clicking in the desired column in the Total row and selecting a function from the pop-up list.
- Excel includes a filter arrow button automatically at the top of each column in a table with which you can filter and sort the table.
- A column containing text that you want to split can be separated into multiple columns using the Text to Columns button in the Data Tools group of the Data tab. The Convert Text to Columns wizard contains three dialog boxes to define how to split the data.
- Using the Remove Duplicates dialog box, you can instruct Excel to compare records within a worksheet and automatically delete rows that are duplicated.
- Data can be validated as it is being entered into a worksheet and either invalid data can be prevented from being stored or a warning can be issued to inform that data has been entered that does not conform to the restrictions.
- At the Settings tab in the Data Validation dialog box you define the validation criteria for the cell entry. You can allow data based on values, dates, times, text length, or restrict the entries to values within a drop-down list.
- At the Input Message tab in the Data Validation dialog box you can define a message that pops up when a cell for which data is restricted becomes active.

- At the Error Alert tab in the Data Validation dialog box you define the type of error alert to display and the content of the error message.
- Convert a table to a normal range to use the Subtotal feature or when you no longer need to treat a range of cells independently from the rest of the worksheet.
- Sort a worksheet by the column(s) for which you want to group data for subtotals before opening the Subtotals dialog box.
- The Subtotals button is located in the Outline group of the Data tab.
- Excel adds a subtotal automatically at each change in content for the column you specify as the subtotal field. A grand total is also automatically added to the bottom of the range.
- You can display more than one subtotal row for a group to calculate multiple functions such as Sum and Average.
- A subtotaled range is outlined and detail records can be collapsed or expanded using level number, Hide Detail, and Show Detail buttons.
- Use the Group and Ungroup buttons when a worksheet is outlined to manage the display of individual groups.

Commands Review

FEATURE	RIBBON TAB, GROUP	BUTTON	KEYBOARD SHORTCUT
Convert Text to Columns	Data, Data Tools		
Convert to Range	Table Tools Design, Tools		
Create Table	Insert,Tables		Ctrl + T
Data Validation	Data, Data Tools		
Group Data	Data, Outline		Shift + Alt + Right arrow key
Remove Duplicates	Data, Data Tools OR Table Tools Design, Tools		
Table Styles	Table Tools Design, Table Styles		
Sort & Filter table	Home, Editing		
Subtotals	Data, Outline		
Total row	Table Tools Design, Table Style Options		Ctrl + Shift + T
Ungroup	Data, Outline		Shift + Alt + Left arrow key

Concepts Check Test Your Knowledge

Completion: In the space provided at the right, indicate the correct term, command, or number.

1. The first row of a table that contains the column headings is called the field names row or this row. __________________
2. Typing a formula in the first row of a column in a table causes Excel to define the field as this type of column. __________________
3. This is the term that describes the formatting feature in a table in which even rows are formatted differently than odd rows. __________________
4. Change the visual appearance of a table using this gallery in the Table Tools Design tab. __________________
5. Clicking this button causes the Convert Text to Columns wizard to appear. __________________
6. Open this dialog box to instruct Excel to compare the entries in the columns you specify and automatically delete rows that contain repeated data. __________________
7. Open this dialog box to restrict entries in a cell to those that you set up in a drop-down list. __________________
8. This option in the *Allow* list box is used to force data entered into a cell to be a specific number of characters. __________________
9. This is the default error alert style that prevents invalid data from being entered into a cell. __________________
10. The Convert to Range button is found in this tab. __________________
11. Prior to creating subtotals using the Subtotal button in the Outline group of the Data tab, arrange the data in this order. __________________
12. In a worksheet with subtotal rows only displayed, click this button next to a subtotal row in order to view the grouped rows. __________________
13. Click this button in an outlined worksheet to collapse the rows for a group. __________________
14. In an outlined worksheet, this button collapses all records and displays only the Grand Total row. __________________
15. Clicking this button in an outlined worksheet will cause the Hide Detail button for the selected rows to be removed. __________________

Skills Check Assess Your Performance

Assessment 1

CREATE AND FORMAT A TABLE

1. Open **VantageClassics.xlsx**.
2. Save the workbook with Save As and name it **EL2-C3-A1-VantageClassics**.
3. Select A4:L30 and create a table using *Table Style Medium 12* (fifth option in second row in *Medium* section).
4. Add a calculated column to the table in column M. Type the label **Total Cost** as the column heading and create a formula in the first record that multiplies the number of copies in column G times the cost price in column L.
5. Adjust the three rows above the table to merge and center across columns A through M.
6. Adjust all column widths to AutoFit.
7. Band the columns instead of the rows and emphasize the last column in the table.
8. Add a Total row to the table. Add Average functions that calculate the average number of copies and the average cost price of a classic video.
9. Format the average value in the *Copies* column of the Total row to zero decimals.
10. The video *Blue Hawaii* cannot be located and the manager of Vantage Videos would like to remove the record from the table. Delete the row in the table for the record with Stock No. CV-1015.
11. Format the *Total Cost* column to display two decimals.
12. Save, print, and then close **EL2-C3-A1-VantageClassics.xlsx**.

Assessment 2

USE DATA TOOLS

1. Open **EL2-C3-A1-VantageClassics.xlsx**.
2. Save the workbook with Save As and name it **EL2-C3-A2-VantageClassics**.
3. Remove the banding on the columns and band the rows.
4. Insert a new blank column to the right of the column containing the director names.
5. Split the director names into two columns. Edit the column headings to **Director FName** and **Director LName**, respectively.
6. Use the Remove Duplicates feature to find and remove any duplicate rows using *Title* as the comparison column.
7. Create the following validation rules:
   a. Create a validation rule for the *Stock No.* column that ensures all new entries are seven characters in length. Add an input message to the column to advise the user that stock numbers need to be seven characters. You determine the title and message text. Use the default error alert options.
   b. The manager would like to ensure that five copies is the maximum inventory of any individual classic video in the collection. Create a validation rule that restricts entries in the copies column to a number less than six. Add an appropriate input and error message. Use the default Stop error alert.

c. Create a drop-down list for the *Genre* column with the entries provided. Do not enter an input message and use the default error alert settings.
   Action,Comedy,Drama,Family,History,Horror,Musical,Thriller,War

8. Add the following record to the table to test the data validation rules. Initially enter incorrect values in the *Stock No.*, *Genre*, and *Copies* columns to make sure the rule and the messages work correctly.

Stock No.	**CV-1026**
Title	**The Philadelphia Story**
Year	**1940**
Genre	**Comedy**
Stock Date	**12/12/2011**
Director FName	**George**
Director LName	**Cukor**
Copies	**3**
VHS	**No**
DVD	**Yes**
Blu-ray	**Yes**
Category	**7-day rental**
Cost Price	**10.15**

9. Save, print, and then close **EL2-C3-A2-VantageClassics.xlsx**.

Assessment 3

SUBTOTAL RECORDS

1. Open **EL2-C3-A2-VantageClassics.xlsx**.
2. Save the workbook with Save As and name it **EL2-C3-A3-VantageClassics**.
3. Remove the Total row, remove the row banding, and remove the emphasis from the last column in the table.
4. Convert the table to a normal range.
5. Adjust all column widths to AutoFit.
6. Sort the list first by the genre, then by the director's last name, and then by the title of the video. Use the default sort values and sort order for each level.
7. Add subtotals using the Subtotal button in the Outline group of the Data tab to the *Total Cost* column to calculate the sum and average total costs of videos by genre.
8. Display the worksheet at Level 2 of the outline.
9. Show the details for the Comedy, Drama, and Family genres.
10. Print the worksheet.
11. Save and then close **EL2-C3-A3-VantageClassics.xlsx**.

Visual Benchmark Demonstrate Your Proficiency

1 USING TABLE AND DATA TOOLS IN A CALL LIST

1. Open **WPMCNurseCallList.xlsx**.
2. Save the workbook with Save As and name it **EL2-C3-VB1-WPMCNurseCallList**.
3. Format and apply data tools as required to duplicate the worksheet in Figure 3.9 using the following information:
   - The worksheet has *Table Style Medium 5* applied to the table range.
   - Look closely at the sorted order. The table is sorted by three levels using the fields *Designation*, *Hourly Rate*, and *Hire Date*.
   - Shift cost multiplies the hourly rate times 8 hours.
   - Split the names into two columns.
   - Include the Total row and apply the appropriate banded options.
4. Save, print, and then close **EL2-C3-VB1-WPMCNurseCallList.xlsx**.

Figure 3.9 Visual Benchmark 1

	A	B	C	D	E	F	G	H	I	J	K	L
1	Wellington Park Medical Center											
2	Nursing Division Casual Relief Call List											
3	Payroll No	First Name	Last Name	Designation	Hire Date	Telephone	OR Exp?	Day Shift Only?	Night Shift Only?	Either Shift?	Hourly Rate	Shift Cost
4	78452	Terry	Mason	RN	5/3/1998	555-1279	Yes	No	Yes	No	38.50	**308.00**
5	19658	Paula	Sanderson	RN	4/28/2000	555-3485	No	No	No	Yes	38.50	**308.00**
6	38642	Tania	Ravi	RN	6/22/2002	555-6969	Yes	Yes	No	Weekends only	38.50	**308.00**
7	96523	Lynn	Pietre	RN	10/22/1998	555-2548	Yes	Yes	No	Weekends only	35.00	**280.00**
8	45968	David	Featherstone	RN	9/9/2001	555-5961	No	No	No	Yes	35.00	**280.00**
9	46956	Orlando	Zambian	RN	11/10/2001	555-1186	No	Yes	No	No	35.00	**280.00**
10	56983	Amanda	Sanchez	RN	4/27/1999	555-4896	Yes	No	Yes	No	33.00	**264.00**
11	68429	Rene	Quenneville	RN	8/15/2003	555-4663	Yes	Yes	No	Weekends only	22.50	**180.00**
12	69417	Denis	LaPierre	RN	8/23/2003	555-8643	No	No	Yes	No	22.50	**180.00**
13	37944	Fernando	Este	RN	7/18/2005	555-4545	No	No	No	Yes	22.50	**180.00**
14	78647	Jay	Bjorg	RN	5/14/2007	555-6598	No	No	No	Yes	22.50	**180.00**
15	95558	Sam	Vargas	RN	3/2/2009	555-4571	No	No	No	Yes	22.50	**180.00**
16	98731	Zail	Singh	RN	5/6/2011	555-3561	Yes	Yes	No	No	22.50	**180.00**
17	58612	Savana	Ruiz	RN	4/15/2012	555-8457	Yes	No	Yes	Weekends only	22.50	**180.00**
18	96721	Noreen	Kalir	RN	4/3/2009	555-1876	Yes	Yes	No	No	21.50	**172.00**
19	89367	Xiu	Zheng	LPN	4/23/2006	555-7383	Yes	Yes	No	No	18.75	**150.00**
20	14586	Alma	Fernandez	LPN	8/3/1997	555-7412	Yes	No	No	Yes	16.75	**134.00**
21	48652	Dana	Casselman	LPN	10/15/1997	555-6325	Yes	No	No	Yes	16.75	**134.00**
22	85412	Kelly	Lund	LPN	11/19/1998	555-3684	No	Yes	No	Weekends only	15.75	**126.00**
23	98364	Lana	Bourne	LPN	7/15/2008	555-9012	Yes	Yes	No	No	15.50	**124.00**
24	90467	Nadir	Abouzeen	LPN	8/12/2008	555-9023	No	No	No	Yes	14.50	**116.00**
25	68475	Kelly	O'Brien	LPN	1/20/2012	555-6344	No	Yes	No	Weekends only	13.75	**110.00**
26								**Average Hourly Rate and Shift Cost:**			**24.74**	**197.91**

2 USING SUBTOTALS IN A CALL LIST

1. Open **EL2-C3-VB1-WPMCNurseCallList.xlsx**.
2. Save the workbook with Save As and name it **EL2-C3-VB2-WPMCNurseCallList**.
3. Create subtotals and view the revised worksheet at the appropriate level to display as shown in Figure 3.10
4. Save, print, and then close **EL2-C3-VB2-WPMCNurseCallList.xlsx**.

Figure 3.10 Visual Benchmark 2

	A	B	C	D	E	F	G	H	I	J	K	L
1	Wellington Park Medical Center											
2	Nursing Division Casual Relief Call List											
3	Payroll No	Firstname	Lastname	Designation	Hire Date	Telephone	OR Exp?	Day Shift Only?	Night Shift Only?	Either Shift?	Hourly Rate	Shift Cost
19				**RN Average**							**28.83**	**230.67**
27				**LPN Average**							**15.96**	**127.71**
28				**Grand Average**							**24.74**	**197.91**

Case Study Apply Your Skills

Part 1

Rajiv Patel, Vice-President of NuTrends Market Research, has sent you a file named **NuTrendsMktPlans.xlsx**. The workbook contains client information for the company's first quarter marketing plans for three marketing consultants. Rajiv would like you to improve the reporting in the file by completing the following tasks:

- Set up the data as a table sorted first by the consultant's last name and then by the marketing campaign's start date, both in ascending order. Rajiv would prefer that the consultant names be split into two columns.
- Improve the formatting of the dollar values.
- Add a Total row to sum the columns containing dollar amounts.
- Add formatting to the titles above the table that are suited to the colors in the table style you selected.
- Make any other formatting changes you think would improve the worksheet's appearance.

Save the revised workbook and name it **EL2-C3-CS-P1-NuTrendsMktPlans**. Print the worksheet in landscape orientation with the width scaled to 1 page.

Part 2

Rajiv would like statistics for each consultant added to the workbook. Specifically, Rajiv would like to see the following information:

- The total marketing plan budget values being managed by each consultant as well as the total planned expenditures by month.
- The average marketing plan budget being managed by each consultant as well as the average planned expenditures by month.

Rajiv would like a printout that displays only the total and average values for each consultant as well as the grand average and grand total. Save the revised workbook and name it **EL2-C3-CS-P2-NuTrendsMktPlans**. Print and then close the worksheet.

Part 3

Rajiv has asked that you provide another report from the file named **NuTrendsMktPlans.xlsx**. Specifically, Rajiv would like a printout of the worksheet that shows the original data at the top of the worksheet and a few blank rows below the worksheet, Rajiv would like to see the marketing plan details for Yolanda Robertson's clients that have a campaign starting after January 31, 2012.

Research in Help how to filter a range of cells using the Advanced Filter button in the Sort & Filter group of the Data tab. Make sure you read how to copy rows that meet your filter criteria to another area of the worksheet. Using the information you learned in Help, open **NuTrendsMktPlans.xlsx**, insert three new rows above the worksheet and use these rows to create the criteria range. Filter the list as per Rajiv's specifications. Rows that meet the criteria should be copied below the worksheet starting in A22. Add an appropriate title to describe the copied data in A21. Make any formatting changes you think would improve the appearance of the worksheet. Save the revised workbook and name it **EL2-C3-CS-P3-NutrendsMktPlans**. Print the worksheet and then close the workbook.

Part 4

Rajiv is looking for information on current salary ranges for a market researcher in the United States. Use the Internet to find the information for Rajiv. If possible, find salary information that is regional to your state for a minimum of three cities. Find a low salary and a high salary for a market researcher in each city. Create a workbook that summarizes the results of your research. Include in the workbook the Web site addresses as hyperlinked cells next to the salary range information. Organize the data in the workbook as a table. Apply table formatting options so that the data is attractively presented and easy to read. Add a Total row to the table and include an Average function to find the average salary from the three cities. Find a minimum of three resources and a maximum of five. Save the workbook and name it **EL2-C3-CS-P4-NuTrendsSalaryAnalysis**. Print the worksheet and then close the workbook.

Microsoft® Excel®

Summarizing and Consolidating Data

CHAPTER

PERFORMANCE OBJECTIVES

Upon successful completion of Chapter 4, you will be able to:

- **Summarize data by creating formulas with range names that reference other worksheets**
- **Modify the range assigned to a range name**
- **Summarize data by creating 3-D formulas**
- **Create formulas that link to cells in other worksheets or workbooks**
- **Edit a link to a source workbook**
- **Break a link to an external reference**
- **Use the Consolidate feature to summarize data in multiple worksheets**
- **Create, edit, and format a PivotTable**
- **Filter a PivotTable using Slicers**
- **Create and format a PivotChart**
- **Create and format Sparklines**

Tutorials

4.1 Summarizing Data in Multiple Worksheets Using Range Names and 3-D References
4.2 Summarizing Data by Linking Ranges in Other Worksheets or Workbooks
4.3 Summarizing Data Using the Consolidate Feature
4.4 Creating a PivotTable Report
4.5 Filtering a PivotTable Using Slicers
4.6 Creating a PivotChart
4.7 Summarizing Data with Sparklines

You can summarize data by creating formulas that reference cells in other areas of the active worksheet, in other worksheets within the same workbook, or by linking to cells in other worksheets or workbooks. The Consolidate feature can also be used to summarize data from other worksheets or other workbooks into a master worksheet. Once the data has been summarized, consider presenting or analyzing the data by creating and formatting a PivotTable or a PivotChart. Sparklines are miniature charts inserted into a cell that allow you to see at a glance a trend or other pattern in the data. In this chapter you will learn how to summarize data using a variety of methods and present visually summarized data for analysis. Model answers for this chapter's projects appear on the following pages.

Excel2010L2C4

Note: Before beginning the projects, copy to your storage medium the Excel2010L2C4 subfolder from the Excel2010L2 folder on the CD that accompanies this textbook and then make Excel2010L2C4 the active folder.

Model Answers

National Park Service
U.S. Department of the Interior
May 2012
Attendance Summary
Southwest Region, Zone C

Private Vehicle and Individual Entrances Only	10,460
Commercial Tour Vehicles Only	15,069
Total Attendance	25,529

National Park Service
U.S. Department of the Interior
May 2012
Attendance Summary
Southwest Region, Zone C

Private Vehicle and Individual Entrances Only	10,460
Commercial Tour Vehicles Only	15,434
Total Attendance	25,894

Project 1 Calculate Park Attendance Totals

Project 1c, EL2-C4-P1-MayParkEntries.xlsx

Project 1d, EL2-C4-P1-MayParkEntries.xlsx

NewAge Dental Services

Fee Revenue Summary

	January	February	March	Total
General Examination	3,374.47	3,386.41	3,510.45	10,271.33
Cleanings and Fillings	9,634.98	9,016.37	7,107.42	25,758.77
Teeth Whitening	2,743.90	5,993.69	4,431.19	13,168.78
Bonding	5,835.61	7,262.00	7,420.33	20,517.94
Porcelain Veneers	5,674.21	3,685.67	3,671.52	13,031.40
Crowns and Bridges	4,977.27	10,636.33	7,119.07	22,732.67
Full and Partial Dentures	7,608.05	8,926.64	11,886.13	28,420.82
Emergency Extractions	1,301.24	1,291.32	1,515.69	4,108.25
Root Canals	3,157.20	2,488.20	6,034.21	11,679.61
Total	44,306.93	52,686.63	52,696.01	149,689.57

Project 2 Calculate Total Fees Billed by Three Dentists

EL2-C4-P2-NewAgeDentalQ1Fees.xlsx

Model (Multiple Items)

Sum of Sale Price	Column Labels			
Row Labels	Clarke	Fernandez	Kazmarek	Grand Total
Central	4,470		5,224	9,694
North	1,150		8,099	9,249
South	2,499	1,150		3,649
West			1,575	1,575
Grand Total	**8,119**	**1,150**	**14,898**	**24,167**

Project 3 Analyze Fitness Equipment Sales Data in a PivotTable and PivotChart

Project 3b, EL2-C4-P3-PremiumFitnessJanSales.xlsx

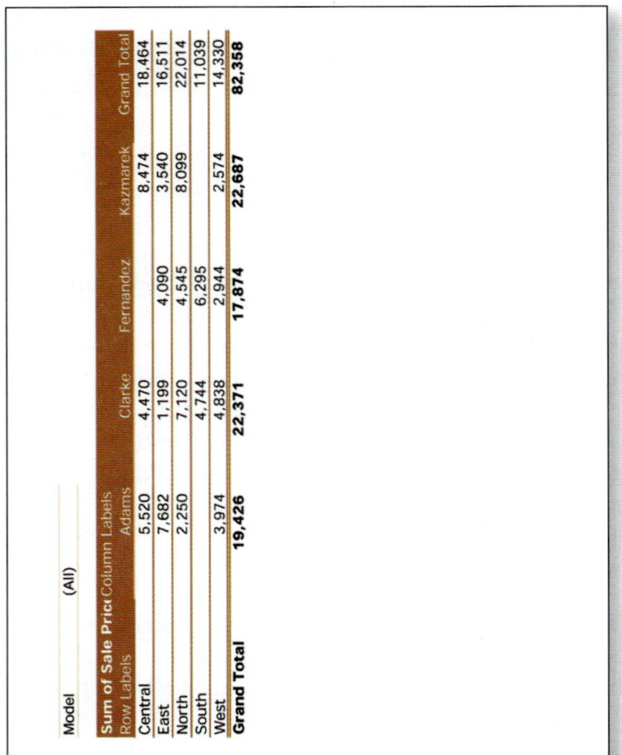

Model (All)

Sum of Sale Price	Column Labels				
Row Labels	Adams	Clarke	Fernandez	Kazmarek	Grand Total
Central	5,520	4,470		8,474	18,464
East	7,682	1,199	4,090	3,540	16,511
North	2,250	7,120	4,545	8,099	22,014
South		4,744	6,295		11,039
West	3,974	4,838	2,944	2,574	14,330
Grand Total	**19,426**	**22,371**	**17,874**	**22,687**	**82,358**

Project 3b, EL2-C4-P3-PremiumFitnessJanSales.xlsx

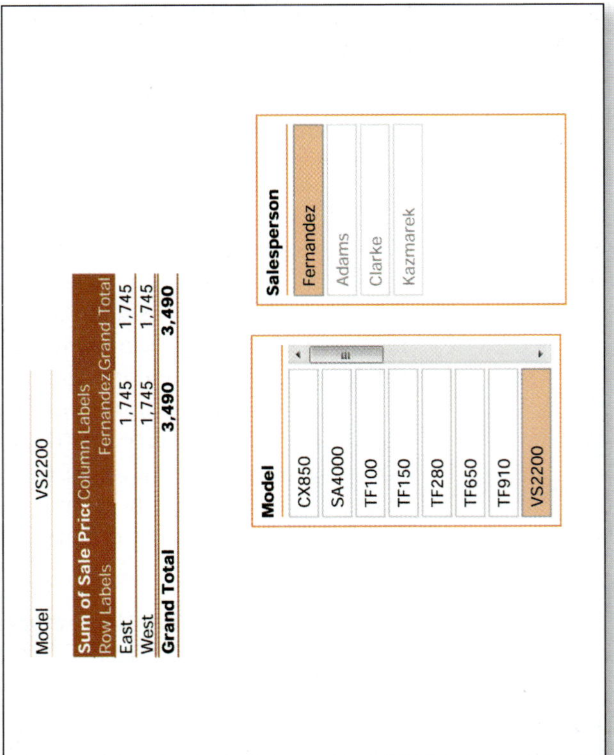

Model VS2200

Sum of Sale Price	Column Labels	
Row Labels	Fernandez	Grand Total
East	1,745	1,745
West	1,745	1,745
Grand Total	**3,490**	**3,490**

Project 3c, EL2-C4-P3-PremiumFitnessJanSales.xlsx

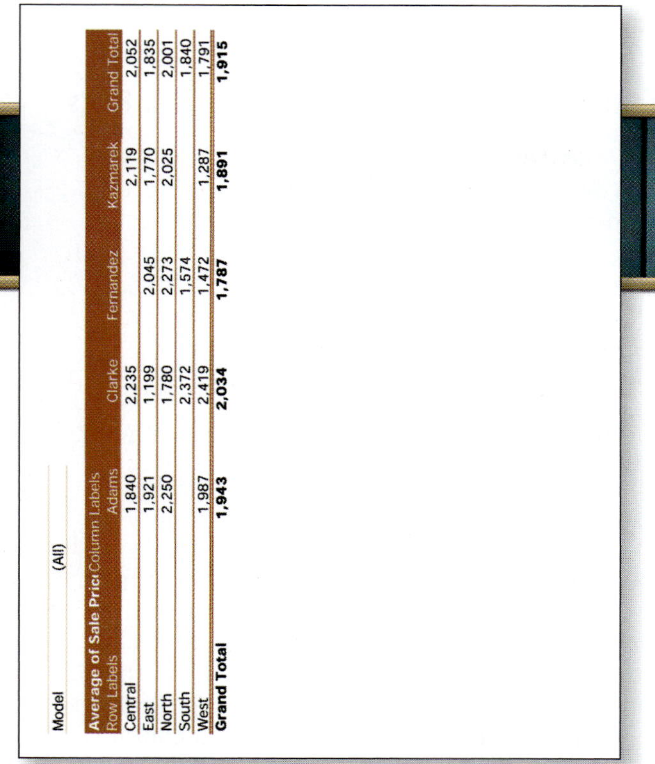

Model	(All)				
Average of Sale Price	Column Labels				
Row Labels	Adams	Clarke	Fernandez	Kazmarek	Grand Total
Central	1,840	2,235		2,119	2,052
East	1,921	1,199	2,045	1,770	1,835
North	2,250	1,780	2,273	2,025	2,001
South		2,372	1,574		1,840
West	1,987	2,419	1,472	1,287	1,791
Grand Total	**1,943**	**2,034**	**1,787**	**1,891**	**1,915**

Project 3d, EL2-C4-P3-PremiumFitnessAvgJanSales.xlsx

Project 3e, EL2-C4-P3-PremiumFitnessJanSales.xlsx

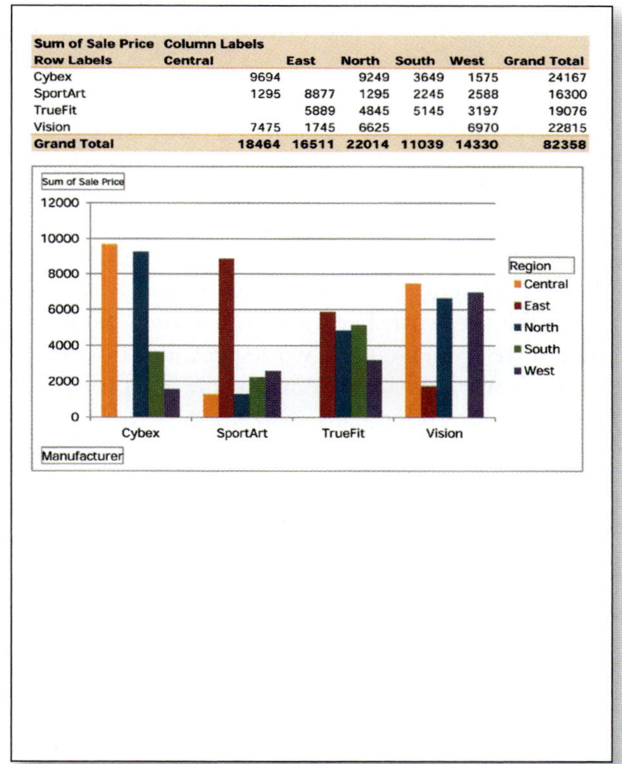

Sum of Sale Price	**Column Labels**					
Row Labels	**Central**	**East**	**North**	**South**	**West**	**Grand Total**
Cybex	9694		9249	3649	1575	24167
SportArt	1295	8877	1295	2245	2588	16300
TrueFit		5889	4845	5145	3197	19076
Vision	7475	1745	6625		6970	22815
Grand Total	**18464**	**16511**	**22014**	**11039**	**14330**	**82358**

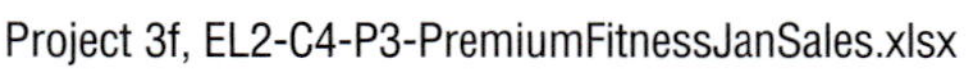
Project 3f, EL2-C4-P3-PremiumFitnessJanSales.xlsx

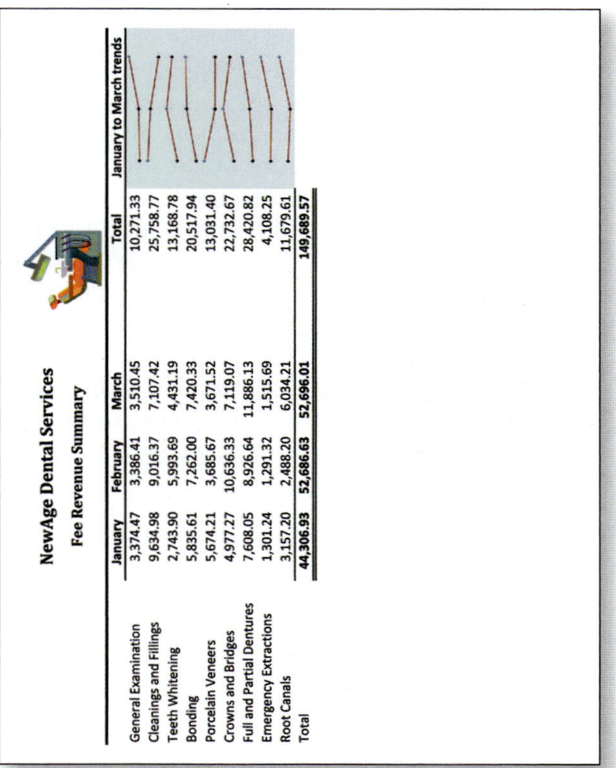

NewAge Dental Services

Fee Revenue Summary

	January	February	March	Total	January to March trends
General Examination	3,374.47	3,386.41	3,510.45	10,271.33	
Cleanings and Fillings	9,634.98	9,016.37	7,107.42	25,758.77	
Teeth Whitening	2,743.90	5,993.69	4,431.19	13,168.78	
Bonding	5,835.61	7,262.00	7,420.33	20,517.94	
Porcelain Veneers	5,674.21	3,685.67	3,671.52	13,031.40	
Crowns and Bridges	4,977.27	10,636.33	7,119.07	22,732.67	
Full and Partial Dentures	7,608.05	8,926.64	11,886.13	28,420.82	
Emergency Extractions	1,301.24	1,291.32	1,515.69	4,108.25	
Root Canals	3,157.20	2,488.20	6,034.21	11,679.61	
Total	44,306.93	52,686.63	52,696.01	149,689.57	

Project 4 Add Sparklines in a Worksheet to Show Trends
EL2-C4-P4-NewAgeDentalQ1Fees.xlsx

Project 1 Calculate Park Attendance Totals **5 Parts**

You will create and modify range names and calculate total park attendance at three national parks from data stored in separate worksheets and by linking to a cell in another workbook. You will also edit a linked workbook and update the link in the destination file.

Quick Steps

Sum Multiple Worksheets Using Range Names
1. Make formula cell active.
2. Type =sum(.
3. Type first range name.
4. Type comma ,.
5. Type second range name.
6. Type comma ,.
7. Continue typing range names separated by commas until finished.
8. Type).
9. Press Enter.

Modify a Named Range Reference
1. Click Formulas tab.
2. Click Name Manager button.
3. Click range name to be modified.
4. Click Edit button.
5. Click in *Refers to* text box or click collapse button.
6. Modify range address(es) as required.
7. Click OK.
8. Click Close.

Name Manager

Expand Dialog

Summarizing Data in Multiple Worksheets Using Range Names and 3-D References

A workbook that has been organized with data in separate worksheets can be summarized by creating formulas that reference cells in other worksheets. When you create a formula that references a cell in the same worksheet, you do not need to include the sheet name in the reference. For example, the formula *=A3+A4* causes Excel to add the value in A3 in the active worksheet to the value in A4 in the active worksheet. Assume you want Excel to add the value in A3 that resides in Sheet2 to the value in A3 that resides in Sheet3 in the workbook. To do this you need to include the worksheet name in the formula by typing *=Sheet2!A3+Sheet3!A3* into the formula cell. This formula contains worksheet references as well as cell references. A worksheet reference precedes the cell reference and is separated from the cell reference with an exclamation point. Absent a worksheet reference, Excel assumes the active worksheet. A formula that references the same cell in a range that extends over two or more worksheets is often called a ***3-D reference***. 3-D formulas can be typed directly in the cell or entered using a point and click approach.

As an alternative, consider using range names to simplify formulas that summarize data in multiple worksheets. A range name includes the worksheet reference by default; therefore typing the range name in the formula automatically references the correct worksheet. For example, assume A3 in Sheet2 has been named *ProductA* and A3 in Sheet3 has been named *ProductB*. To add the two values you would type the formula *=ProductA+ProductB* in the formula cell. Notice you do not need to remember worksheet references. Another advantage to using range names is that the name can describe the worksheet with the source data. By using range names you also do not have to make each worksheet identical in organizational structure. Recall from your work with range names in Chapter 2 that cell references in range names are absolute references.

Project 1a — Summarizing Data in Multiple Worksheets by Creating and Modifying Range Names

Part 1 of 5

1. Open **MayParkEntries.xlsx**.
2. Save the workbook with Save As and name it **EL2-C4-P1-MayParkEntries**.
3. Click each sheet tab and review the data. Each park has attendance data entered as a separate worksheet. In the workbook, range names have already been created for two of the three parks. Create the third range name needed for the data in the MesaVerde sheet by completing the following steps:
   a. Click the MesaVerde sheet tab to activate the worksheet.
   b. Select B7:B22.
   c. Hold down the Ctrl key and then select E7:E21.
   d. Click in the Name text box, type **Mesa**, and then press Enter.

Step 3d — Name box: Mesa; formula bar: 71

Step 3b, Step 3c

	A	B	C	D	E	F
1				Mesa Verde National Park		
2				Colorado		
3				http://www.nps.gov/meve		
4				May 2012		
5				Private Vehicle and Individual Entrances Only		
6	Day	Entries		Day	Entries	
7	1	68		17	71	
8	2	90		18	75	
9	3	75		19	55	
10	4	102		20	61	
11	5	112		21	62	
12	6	92		22	55	
13	7	58		23	68	
14	8	62		24	78	
15	9	65		25	90	
16	10	58		26	85	
17	11	52		27	101	
18	12	68		28	125	
19	13	31		29	112	
20	14	38		30	125	
21	15	47		31	128	
22	16	60				

4. Check each range name to make sure the cell references are correct before creating the summary formula by completing the following steps:
   a. Click the down-pointing arrow next to the Name text box and then click *Bryce* at the drop-down list. Notice the BryceCanyon sheet is active and the ranges B7:B22 and E7:E21 are selected.

Step 4a — E7 / Bryce / Grand / Mesa

   b. Click the down-pointing arrow next to the Name text box and then click *Grand* at the drop-down list. Notice the GrandCanyon sheet is active and the range B7:B22 is selected. This range is missing the entries for days 17 through 31. You will correct this range in Step 5.
   c. Click the down-pointing arrow next to the Name text box and then click *Mesa* at the drop-down list. The MesaVerde sheet is active and the ranges B7:B22 and E7:E21 are selected.
5. Modify the references in a range name by adding the data in column E of the GrandCanyon worksheet to the range named *Grand* by completing the following steps:
   a. Click in any cell to deselect the *Mesa* range.
   b. Click the Formulas tab.
   c. Click the Name Manager button in the Defined Names group.
   d. Click *Grand* in the *Name* list at the Name Manager dialog box.
   e. Click the Edit button.

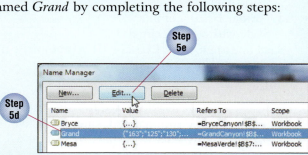

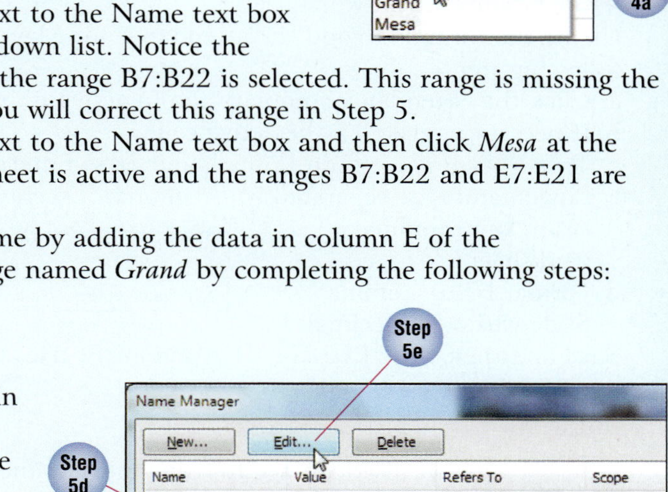

f. At the Edit Name dialog box, click the Collapse Dialog button located at the end of the *Refers to* text box (currently displays *=GrandCanyon!$B$7:$B$22*).

g. With GrandCanyon the active worksheet and with the range B7:B22 selected, hold down the Ctrl key and then select E7:E21.

h. Click the Expand Dialog button to restore the Edit Name dialog box. Notice that a comma separates nonadjacent ranges in the range name and that the cell addresses are absolute references.

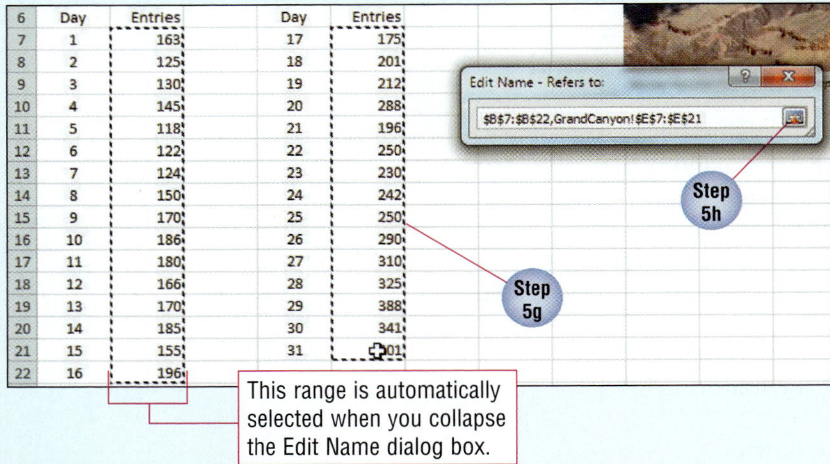

6	Day	Entries		Day	Entries
7	1	163		17	175
8	2	125		18	201
9	3	130		19	212
10	4	145		20	288
11	5	118		21	196
12	6	122		22	250
13	7	124		23	230
14	8	150		24	242
15	9	170		25	250
16	10	186		26	290
17	11	180		27	310
18	12	166		28	325
19	13	170		29	388
20	14	185		30	341
21	15	155		31	[illegible]01
22	16	196			

Edit Name - Refers to:
$B$7:$B$22,GrandCanyon!$E$7:$E$21
Step 5h
Step 5g
This range is automatically selected when you collapse the Edit Name dialog box.

i. Click OK to close the Edit Name dialog box.

j. Click Close to close the Name Manager dialog box.

k. Click the down-pointing arrow next to the Name text box and then click *Grand* at the drop-down list to make sure the revised range name is referencing B7:B22 and E7:E21 in the GrandCanyon worksheet.

6. Create the formula to add the attendance for May at all three parks by completing the following steps:

   a. Click the AttendanceSummary tab to activate the worksheet.

   b. If necessary, make F7 the active cell.

   c. Type **=sum(bryce,grand,mesa)** and press Enter. Notice that in a Sum formula, multiple range names are separated with commas. Excel returns the result *10460* in F7 of the AttendanceSummary worksheet.

   d. Format F7 to Comma Style with zero decimals.

7. Save and then close **EL2-C4-P1-MayParkEntries.xlsx**.

A disadvantage to using range names applies when several worksheets need to be summarized, since you have to create the range name reference in each individual worksheet. If several worksheets need to be summed, a more efficient method is to use a 3-D reference. Generally, when using a 3-D reference, setting up the data in each worksheet in identical cells is a good idea. In Project 1b, you will calculate the same attendance total for the three parks using a 3-D reference instead of range names.

Project 1b Summarizing Data in Multiple Worksheets Using a 3-D Reference Formula

Part 2 of 5

1. Open **MayParkEntries.xlsx**.
2. Save the workbook with Save As and name it **EL2-C4-P1-3D-MayParkEntries**.
3. Calculate the attendance total for the three parks using a point-and-click approach to creating a 3-D reference by completing the following steps:
   a. Make F7 in the AttendanceSummary worksheet the active cell, and then type **=sum(**.
   b. Click the BryceCanyon sheet tab.
   c. Hold down the Shift key and then click the MesaVerde sheet tab. Using the Shift key while clicking a sheet tab selects all worksheets from the first sheet tab through to the last sheet tab clicked. Notice in the Formula bar the formula reads *=sum('BryceCanyon:MesaVerde'!*
   d. With BryceCanyon the active worksheet, select B7:B22, hold down the Ctrl key, and select E7:E21.
   e. Type **)** and press Enter. Excel returns the value *10460* in F7 in the AttendanceSummary worksheet.
   f. Format F7 to Comma Style with zero decimals.
4. Press the Up Arrow key to move the active cell back to F7 and compare your formula with the one shown in Figure 4.1.
5. Save and then close **EL2-C4-P1-3D-MayParkEntries.xlsx**.

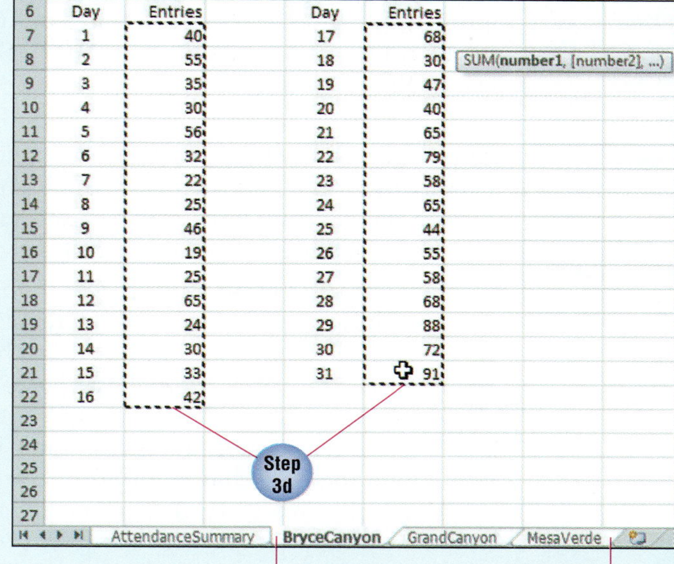

Figure 4.1 3-D Formula Created in Project 1b

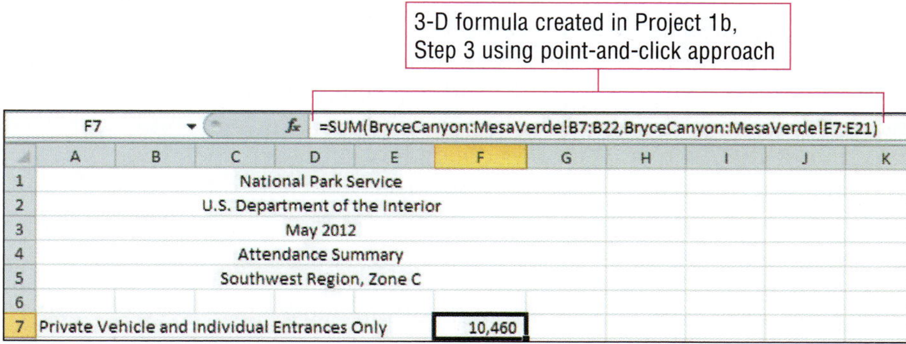

Summarizing Data by Linking to Ranges in Other Worksheets or Workbooks

Quick Steps

Create Link to External Reference

1. Open source workbook.
2. Open destination workbook.
3. Arrange windows as desired.
4. Make formula cell active in destination workbook.
5. Type =.
6. Click to activate source workbook.
7. Click source cell.
8. Press Enter.

Using a similar method as that used in Project 1a or Project 1b, you can summarize data in one workbook by linking to a cell, range, or range name in another worksheet or workbook. When data is linked, a change made in the source cell (the cell in which the original data is stored) is updated in any other cell to which the source cell has been linked. A link is established by creating a formula that references the source data. For example, the formula *=Sheet1!B10* entered into a cell in Sheet2 creates a link. The cell in Sheet2 displays the value in the source cell. If the data in B10 in Sheet1 is changed, the value in the linked cell in Sheet2 is also changed.

As an alternative to creating a formula yourself, copy the source cell to the Clipboard. Make the destination cell active, click the Paste button arrow in the Clipboard group, and then click the Paste Link button in the *Other Paste Options* section of the drop-down gallery. Excel creates the link formula for you using an absolute reference to the source cell.

Linking to a cell in another workbook incorporates external references and requires that a workbook name reference be added to a formula. For example, linking to cell A3 in a sheet named ProductA in a workbook named Sales would require that you enter *=[Sales.xlsx]ProductA!A3* in the formula cell. Notice the workbook reference is entered first in square brackets. The workbook in which the external reference is added becomes the destination workbook. The workbook containing the data that is linked to the destination workbook is called the source workbook. In Project 1c you will create a link to an external cell containing the attendance total for the tour group entrances for the three parks. The point-and-click approach to creating a linked external reference creates an absolute reference to the source cell. Delete the dollar symbols in the cell reference if you plan to copy the formula and need the source cell to be relative. Note that workbook and worksheet references remain absolute regardless.

Project 1c **Summarizing Data by Linking to Another Workbook** Part 3 of 5

1. Open **EL2-C4-P1-MayParkEntries.xlsx**.
2. Open **MayParkGroupSales.xlsx**. This workbook contains tour group attendance data for the three national parks. Tour groups are charged a flat rate entrance fee and their attendance values represent bus capacity and not actual counts of patrons on each bus.
3. Click the View tab, click the Arrange All button in the Window group, click *Vertical* in the *Arrange* section of the Arrange Windows dialog box, and then click OK.
4. Create a linked external reference in the worksheet you created in Project 1a to the total attendance in the worksheet with the commercial tour vehicle attendance data by completing the following steps:
   a. Click in the **EL2-C4-P1-MayParkEntries.xlsx** worksheet to make the worksheet active. Make sure the active worksheet is AttendanceSummary.
   b. Make A9 the active cell, type **Commercial Tour Vehicles Only**, and then press Enter.
   c. Make F9 the active cell.
   d. Type =.

e. Click the **MayParkGroupSales.xlsx** title bar to activate the worksheet and then click F7. Notice the formula that is being entered into the formula cell contains a workbook reference and a worksheet reference in front of the cell reference.
f. Press Enter.
g. Format F9 to Comma Style with zero decimals.
h. With F9 the active cell, compare your worksheet with the one shown below.

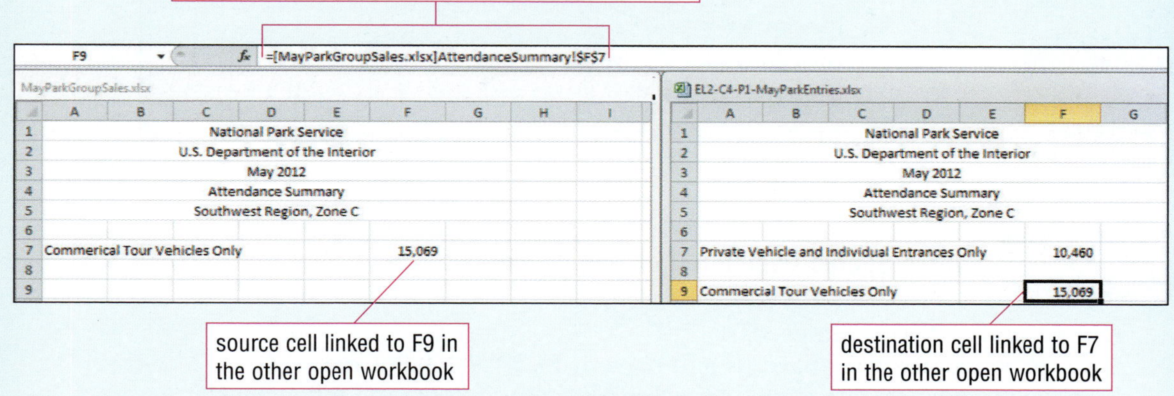

5. Click the Maximize button in the **EL2-C4-P1-MayParkEntries.xlsx** title bar.
6. Make A11 the active cell, type Total Attendance, and then press Enter.
7. Make F11 the active cell and then create a formula to add the values in F7 and F9.
8. Print the AttendanceSummary worksheet in **EL2-C4-P1-MayParkEntries.xlsx**. ***Note: Check with your instructor if you submit your work in hard copy and need to print two copies of the worksheet with one copy displaying cell formulas.***
9. Save and then close **EL2-C4-P1-MayParkEntries.xlsx**.
10. Close **MayParkGroupSales.xlsx**. Click Don't Save when prompted to save changes.

Maintaining External References

When you link to an external reference, Excel includes the drive and folder names in the path to the source workbook. If you move the source workbook or change the workbook name, the link will no longer work. By default, when you open a workbook with a linked external reference, automatic updates is disabled and Excel displays a security warning message in the Message bar area located above the worksheet. From the message bar you can enable the content so that links can be updated. Links can be edited or broken at the Edit Links dialog box shown in Figure 4.2. If more than one link is present in the workbook, begin by clicking the link to be changed in the Source list. Click the Change Source button to open the Change Source dialog box in which you can navigate to the drive and/or folder in which the source workbook was moved or renamed. Click the Break Link button to permanently remove the linked reference and convert the linked cells to their existing values. The Undo feature does not operate to restore a link. If you break a link that you decide you want to restore, you will have to recreate the linked formula.

Quick Steps

Edit Link to External Reference
1. Open destination workbook.
2. Click Data tab.
3. Click Edit Links button.
4. Click link.
5. Click Change Source button.
6. Navigate to drive and/or folder.
7. Double-click source workbook file name.
8. Click Close button.
9. Save and close destination workbook.

Edit Links

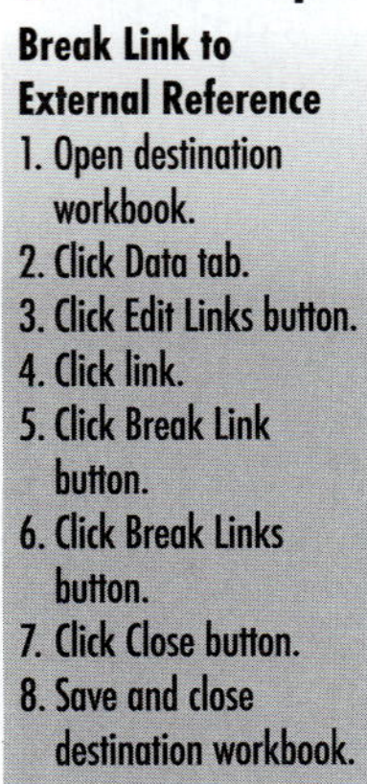

Figure 4.2 Edit Links Dialog Box

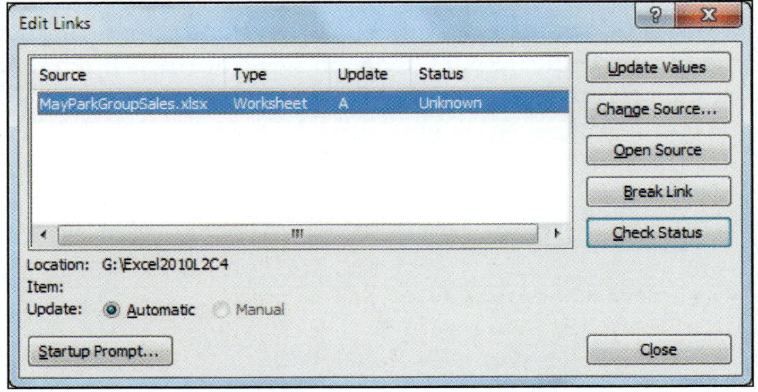

Project 1d Editing Source Data and Updating an External Link

Part 4 of 5

1. Open **MayParkGroupSales.xlsx**.
2. Save the workbook with Save As and name it **EL2-C4-P1-Source**.
3. Edit the attendance data values at each park by completing the following steps:
   a. Click the BryceCanyon tab.
   b. Make B8 the active cell and then change the value from *55* to *361*.
   c. Click the GrandCanyon tab.
   d. Make B20 the active cell and then change the value from *275* to *240*.
   e. Click the MesaVerde tab.
   f. Make E21 the active cell and then change the value from *312* to *406*.
4. Click the AttendanceSummary tab. Note the updated value in F7 is *15,434*.
5. Save and then close **EL2-C4-P1-Source.xlsx**.
6. Open **EL2-C4-P1-MayParkEntries.xlsx**. Notice the security warning that appears in the Message bar above the worksheet area with the message that automatic update of links has been disabled. Instruct Excel to allow automatic updates for this workbook since you are sure the content is from a trusted source by clicking the Enable Content button in the Message bar located between the ribbon and the worksheet area. ***Note: If a Security Warning dialog box appears asking if you want to make the file a Trusted Document, click No.***

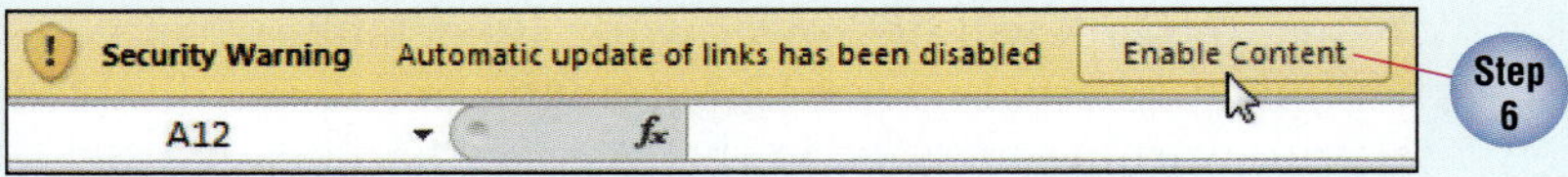

7. Edit the link to retrieve the data from the workbook revised in Steps 2–5 by completing the following steps:
   a. Click the Data tab.
   b. Click the Edit Links button in the Connections group.

c. At the Edit Links dialog box click the Change Source button.
d. At the Change Source: MayParkGroupSales.xlsx dialog box, double-click ***EL2-C4-P1-Source.xlsx*** in the file list box. Excel returns to the Edit Links dialog box and updates the source workbook file name and path.
e. Click the Close button.

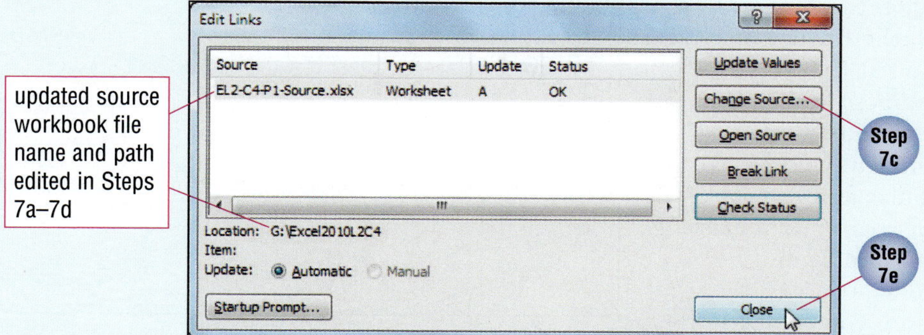

8. Click F9 in the AttendanceSummary worksheet to view the updated linked formula. Notice the workbook reference in the formula is [EL2-C4-P1-Source.xlsx] and the drive and path are included in the formula. (Your drive and/or path may vary from the one shown.)

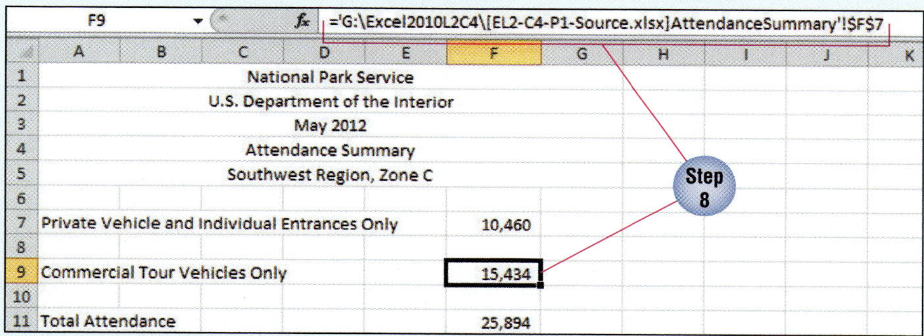

9. Print the AttendanceSummary worksheet.
10. Save and then close **EL2-C4-P1-MayParkEntries.xlsx**.

Project 1e Removing a Linked External Reference

Part 5 of 5

1. Open **EL2-C4-P1-MayParkEntries.xlsx**.
2. At the Microsoft Excel message box that appears stating that the workbook contains links to other sources, read the message text and then click the Update button to update the links. ***Note: Depending on the system settings on the computer you are using, this message may not appear. Proceed to Step 3.***

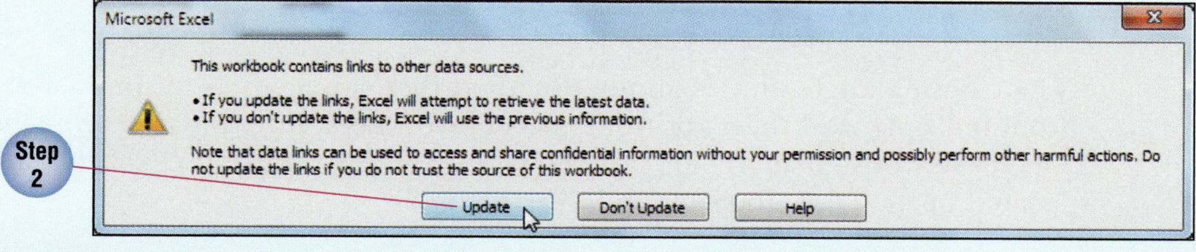

3. Remove the linked external reference to attendance values for commercial tour vehicles by completing the following steps:
   a. With Data the active tab, click the Edit Links button in the Connections group.
   b. Click the Break Link button at the Edit Links dialog box.
   c. Click the Break Links button at the Microsoft Excel message box that says breaking links permanently converts formulas and external references to their existing values and cannot be undone and asks if you are sure you want to break the links.

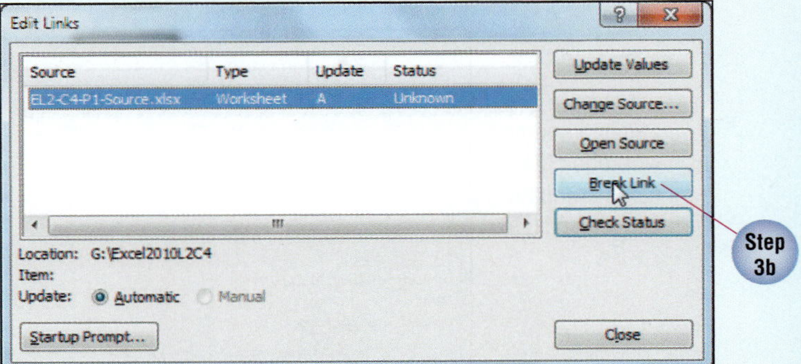

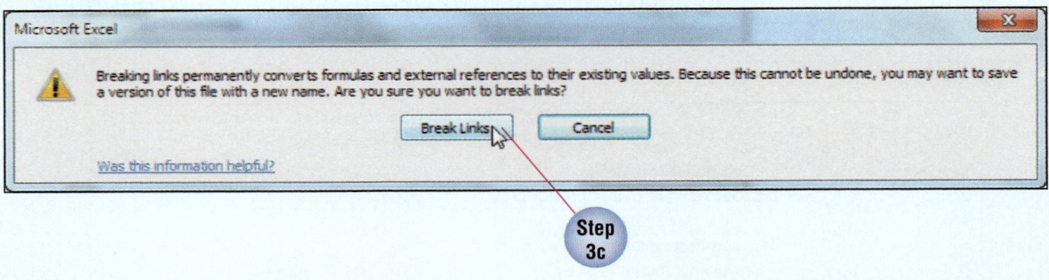

   d. Click the Close button at the Edit Links dialog box with no links displayed.
4. With F9 in the AttendanceSummary worksheet the active cell, look in the Formula bar. Notice the linked formula has been replaced with the latest cell value, *15434*.
5. Save and then close **EL2-C4-P1-MayParkEntries.xlsx**.
6. Reopen **EL2-C4-P1-MayParkEntries.xlsx**. Notice that since the workbook no longer contains a link to an external reference, the security warning message no longer appears in the Message bar.
7. Close **EL2-C4-P1-MayParkEntries.xlsx**. Click Don't Save if prompted to save changes.

Project 2 Calculate Total Fees Billed by Three Dentists — 1 Part

You will use the Consolidate feature to summarize the total dental fees billed by treatment category for three dentists.

Summarizing Data Using the Consolidate Feature

The Consolidate feature is another method that can be used to summarize data from multiple worksheets or from another workbook into a master worksheet. Open the Consolidate dialog box shown in Figure 4.3 from the Consolidate button located in the Data Tools group in the Data tab.

Figure 4.3 Consolidate Dialog Box

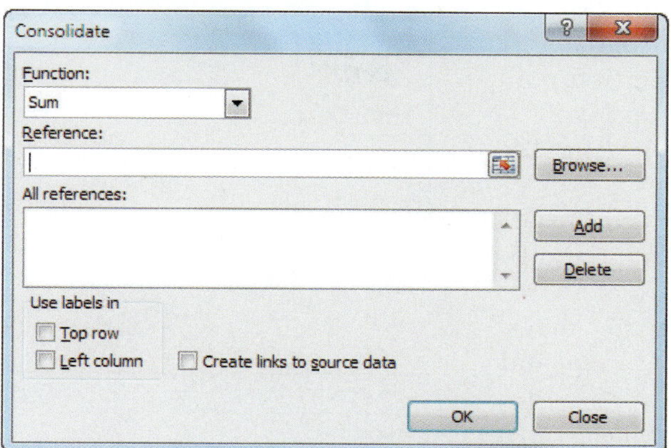

Quick Steps

Consolidate Data

1. Make starting cell active.
2. Click Data tab.
3. Click Consolidate button.
4. If necessary, change *Function*.
5. Enter first range in *Reference* text box.
6. Click Add button.
7. Enter next range in *Reference* text box.
8. Click Add button.
9. Repeat Steps 7–8 until all ranges have been added.
10. If necessary, select *Top row* and/or *Left column* check boxes.
11. If necessary, click *Create links to source data* check box.
12. Click OK.

Consolidate

By default, the Sum function is active. Change to a different function such as Count or Average using the *Function* drop-down list. In the *Reference* text box, type the range name or use the Collapse Dialog button to navigate to the cells to be consolidated. If the cells are located in another workbook, use the Browse button to navigate to the drive and/or folder and locate the file name. Once the correct reference is inserted in the *Reference* text box, click the Add button. Continue adding references for each unit of data to be summarized. Click *Top row* or *Left column* in the *Use labels in* section to indicate where the labels are located in the source ranges. Click the *Create links to source data* to instruct Excel to update the data automatically when the source ranges change. Make sure enough empty cells are available to the right and below the active cell when you open the Consolidate dialog box since Excel populates the rows and columns based on the size of the source data.

Project 2 Summarizing Data Using Consolidate Feature

Part 1 of 1

1. Open **NewAgeDentalQ1Fees.xlsx**.
2. Save the workbook using Save As and name it **EL2-C4-P2-NewAgeDentalQ1Fees**.
3. The workbook is organized with the first quarter's fees for each of three dentists entered in a separate worksheet. Range names have been defined for each dentist's first quarter earnings. Review the workbook structure by completing the following steps:
   a. Click the down-pointing arrow in the Name text box and then click *Popovich* at the drop-down list. Excel makes the Popovich worksheet active and selects the range A2:F13. Deselect the range.
   b. Display the defined range for the range name *Vanket* and then deselect the range.
   c. Display the defined range for the range name *Jovanovic* and then deselect the range.
4. Use the Consolidate feature to total the fees billed by treatment category for each month by completing the following steps:
   a. Make FeeSummary the active worksheet.
   b. With A5 the active cell, click the Data tab.
   c. Click the Consolidate button in the Data Tools group.

d. With *Sum* already selected in the *Function* list box at the Consolidate dialog box and with the insertion point positioned in the *Reference* text box, type **Popovich** and then click the Add button.
e. With the text *Popovich* selected in the *Reference* text box, type **Vanket** and then click the Add button.
f. With the text *Vanket* selected in the *Reference* text box, type **Jovanovic** and then click the Add button.
g. Click the *Top row* and *Left column* check boxes in the *Use labels in* section to insert a check mark in each check box.
h. Click OK.

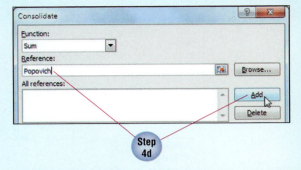

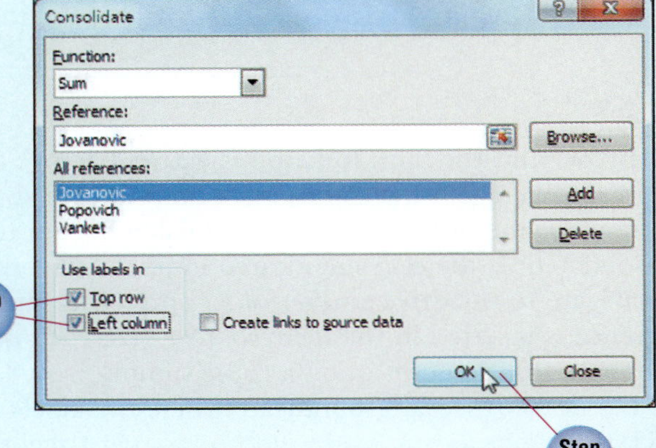

5. Deselect the consolidated range in the FeeSummary worksheet.
6. Adjust the width of each column in the FeeSummary worksheet to AutoFit.
7. Move the data in E5:E15 to F5:F15 and then AutoFit the column width.
8. Use Format Painter to apply the formatting options for the column headings and the total row from any of the three dentist worksheets to the FeeSummary worksheet.
9. Print the FeeSummary worksheet.
10. Save and then close **EL2-C4-P2-NewAgeDentalQ1Fees.xlsx**.

Project 3 Analyze Fitness Equipment Sales Data in a PivotTable and PivotChart

6 Parts

You will create and edit a PivotTable and a PivotChart to analyze fitness equipment sales by region and by salesperson.

Creating a PivotTable Report

A ***PivotTable*** is an interactive table that organizes and summarizes data based on category labels you designate from row headings and column headings. A numeric column you select is then grouped by the row and column category and the data summarized using a function such as Sum, Average, or Count. PivotTables are useful management tools since you can analyze data in a variety of scenarios by filtering a row or column category and instantly seeing the change in results. The interactivity of a PivotTable allows one to examine a variety of scenarios with just a few mouse clicks.

Before creating a PivotTable, examine the source data and determine the following elements before you begin:

- Which row and column headings will define how to group the data?
- Which numeric field contains the values that should be grouped?
- Which summary function will be applied to the values? For example, do you want to sum, average, or count?
- How do you want the layout of the table to be structured? For example, which label do you want used as a row heading and which do you want to use as a column heading?
- Do you want the ability to filter the report as a whole as well as by columns or rows?
- Do you want the PivotTable to be beside the source data or in a new sheet?
- How many reports do you want to extract from the PivotTable by filtering fields?

To begin a PivotTable, select the source range or make sure the active cell is positioned within the list range, click the Insert tab, and then click the PivotTable button in the Tables group. At the Create PivotTable dialog box, confirm the source range is correct and select whether to place the PivotTable in the existing worksheet or in a new worksheet. Figure 4.4 presents the initial PivotTable report and PivotTable Field List pane in which you define the report layout. Each column or row heading in the source range becomes a field in the PivotTable Field List.

Build a PivotTable by selecting fields in the PivotTable Field List pane. Click the check box next to a field to add it to the PivotTable. By default, non-numeric fields are added to the *Row Labels* box and numeric fields are added to the *Values* box in the layout section of the pane. You can move a field to a different box by dragging the field header or by clicking the field header to display a pop-up menu. As you add each field, the PivotTable report updates to show the results. If you do not like the results, uncheck the field's check box to remove it from the report. Figure 4.5 displays the PivotTable you will build in Project 3a.

Quick Steps

Create PivotTable

1. Select source range.
2. Click Insert tab.
3. Click PivotTable button.
4. Click OK.
5. Add fields as needed using PivotTable Field List pane.
6. Modify and/or format as required.

Make sure the source data contains no blank rows or columns and that the data is structured in such a way that repeated data in columns or rows can be grouped.

PivotTable

Figure 4.4 PivotTable Report and PivotTable Field List Pane Used to Define Report Layout

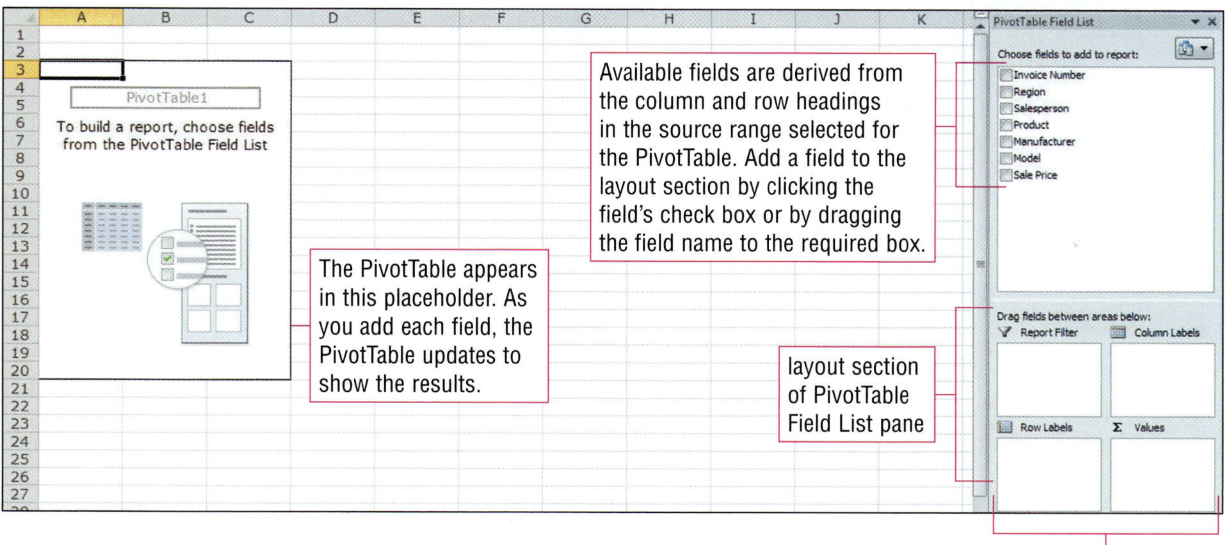

Figure 4.5 PivotTable for Project 3a

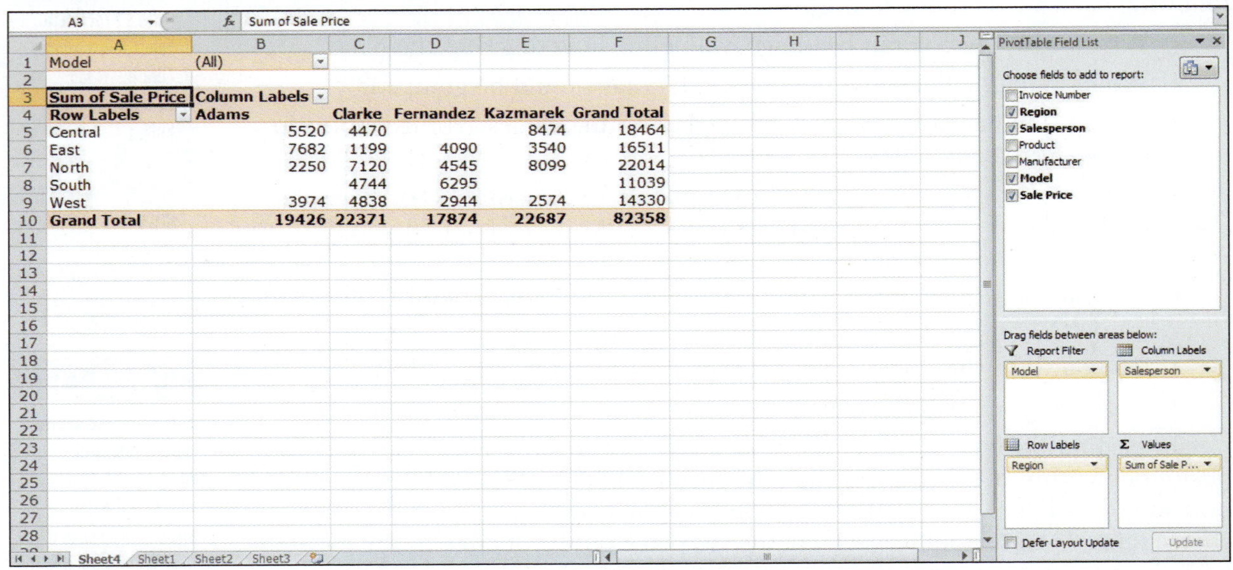

Project 3a Creating a PivotTable Report

Part 1 of 6

1. Open **PremiumFitnessJanSales.xlsx**.
2. Save the workbook with Save As and name it **EL2-C4-P3-PremiumFitnessJanSales**.
3. Create a PivotTable report to summarize the fitness equipment sales by region and by salesperson as shown in Figure 4.5 by completing the following steps:
   a. A range name has been defined to select the list data. Click the down-pointing arrow in the Name text box and then click *JanSales* at the drop-down list.
   b. Click the Insert tab.
   c. Click the PivotTable button in the Tables group. (Do not click the down-pointing arrow on the button.)
   d. At the Create PivotTable dialog box, with *Sheet1!$A$4:$G$47* entered in the *Table/Range* text box and *New Worksheet* selected for *Choose where you want the PivotTable report to be placed*, click OK.

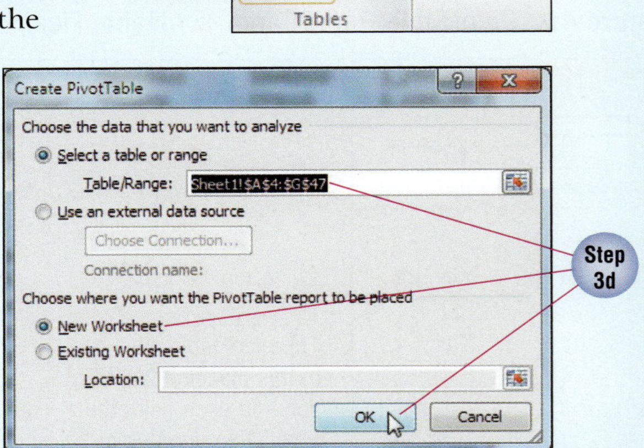

e. Click the *Region* check box in the PivotTable Field List pane. *Region* is added to the *Row Labels* list box in the layout section of the pane and the report updates to show one row per region with a filter arrow button at the top of the column and a *Grand Total* row automatically added to the bottom of the table. Since *Region* is a non-numeric field, Excel automatically placed it as a row label.

f. Click the *Salesperson* check box in the PivotTable Field List pane. Excel automatically adds *Salesperson* to the *Row Labels* list box in the layout section. In the next step you will correct the placement of the field to move it to the *Column Labels* list box.

g. Click the *Salesperson* field header in the *Row Labels* list box in the layout section and then click *Move to Column Labels* at the pop-up list. Notice the layout of the report now displays one row per region and one column per salesperson. In the next step you will drag a field from the PivotTable Field List to the desired list box in the layout section.

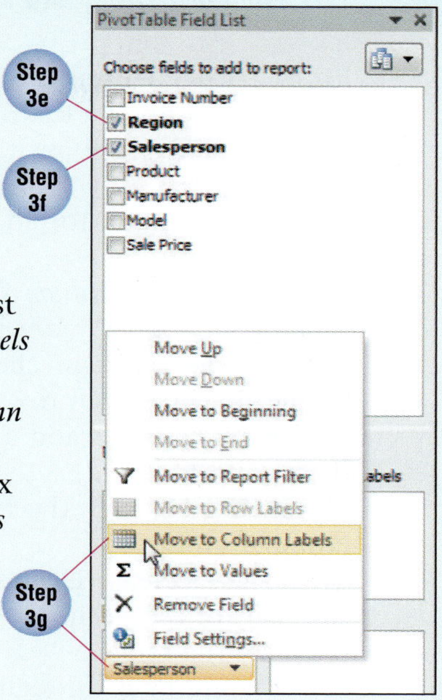

h. Position the mouse pointer over *Model* in the PivotTable Field List, hold down the left mouse button, drag the field to the *Report Filter* list box in the layout section, and then release the mouse. Notice *Model* is added as a filter at the top left of the PivotTable report in A1:B1.

i. Click the *Sale Price* check box in the PivotTable Field List pane. Since the field is a numeric field, Excel adds it automatically to the *Values* list box in the layout section and the report updates to show the Sum function applied to the grouped values in the PivotTable report. Compare your results with the PivotTable shown in Figure 4.5.

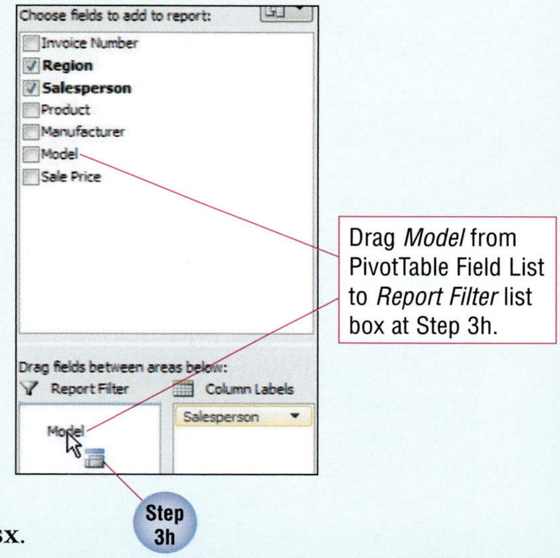

4. Save **EL2-C4-P3-PremiumFitnessJanSales.xlsx**.

Drag *Model* from PivotTable Field List to *Report Filter* list box at Step 3h.

When the active cell is positioned inside a PivotTable, the contextual PivotTable Tools Options tab and PivotTable Tools Design tab become available. Features in the PivotTable Tools Design tab shown in Figure 4.6 are similar to those learned in Chapter 3 for tables.

Figure 4.6 Contextual PivotTable Tools Design Tab

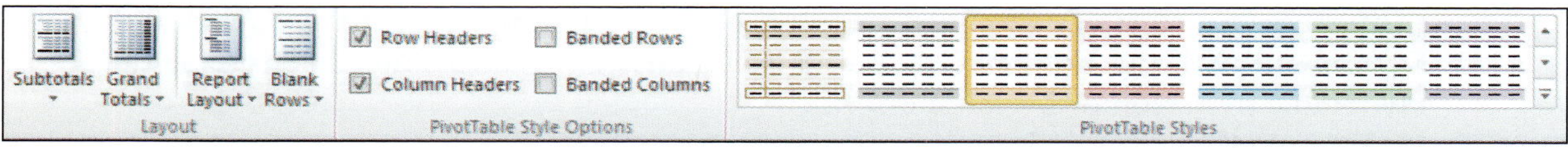

Formatting and Filtering a PivotTable

Part 2 of 6

1. With **EL2-C4-P3-PremiumFitnessJanSales.xlsx** open, apply formatting options to the PivotTable to improve the report's appearance by completing the following steps:
   a. With the active cell positioned in the PivotTable report, click the PivotTable Tools Design tab.
   b. Click the More button located at the bottom of the vertical scroll bar in the PivotTable Styles gallery.
   c. Click *Pivot Style Medium 2* at the drop-down gallery (second option in first row of *Medium* section).
   d. Click the *Banded Rows* check box in the PivotTable Style Options group. Excel adds border lines between rows in the PivotTable. Recall from Chapter 3 that banded rows or banded columns add a fill color or border style depending on the style in effect when the option is added.
   e. Select B5:F10, click the Home tab, and then click the Comma Style button in the Number group.
   f. Click the Decrease Decimal button in the Number group twice to remove the zeros to the right of the decimal.
   g. Deselect the range.
   h. Select columns B through F and change the column width to 12.
   i. Right-align the labels in B4:F4.

	A	B	C	D	E	F
1	Model	(All)				
2						
3	Sum of Sale Price	Column Labels				
4	Row Labels	Adams	Clarke	Fernandez	Kazmarek	Grand Total
5	Central	5,520	4,470		8,474	18,464
6	East	7,682	1,199	4,090	3,540	16,511
7	North	2,250	7,120	4,545	8,099	22,014
8	South		4,744	6,295		11,039
9	West	3,974	4,838	2,944	2,574	14,330
10	**Grand Total**	**19,426**	**22,371**	**17,874**	**22,687**	**82,358**

Steps 1a-1i

2. Filter the PivotTable report to view sales for a group of model numbers by completing the following steps:
   a. Click the filter arrow button next to *(All)* in B1.
   b. Click the *Select Multiple Items* check box to turn on the display of check boxes next to each model number in the drop-down list.
   c. Click the *(All)* check box to clear the check marks for all of the model numbers.
   d. Click the six check boxes for those model numbers that begin with *CX* to select all of the models from Cybex.
   e. Click OK.
   f. Select columns B through E and change the column width to 12.
   g. Print the filtered PivotTable.
   h. Click the filter arrow button next to *(Multiple Items)* in B1, click the *(All)* check box to select all model numbers in the drop-down list, and then click OK.
   i. Experiment with the Column Labels and Row Labels filter arrow buttons to filter the PivotTable by region or by salesperson.
   j. Make sure all filters are cleared.

3. Select columns B through F and change the column width to 12.
4. Print the PivotTable in landscape orientation.
5. Save **EL2-C4-P3-PremiumFitnessJanSales.xlsx**.

Filtering a PivotTable Using Slicers

Slicers are a new feature added to Excel 2010 that allow you to filter a PivotTable report or PivotChart without opening the Filter drop-down list. When Slicers are added to a PivotTable or PivotChart, a Slicer pane containing all of the unique values for the specified field is added to the window. Click the desired option in the Slicer pane to immediately filter the PivotTable or PivotChart. You can add several Slicer panes to the PivotTable or PivotChart to filter by more than one field as needed.

To insert a Slicer pane, make any cell within the PivotTable report active, click the PivotTable Tools Options tab, and then click the Insert Slicer button in the Sort & Filter group. Excel opens the Insert Slicers dialog box, which contains a list of the fields in the PivotTable with a check box next to each field. Click the check box for each field for which you wish to add a Slicer pane and then click OK.

Quick Steps

Add Slicer to PivotTable Report

1. Make any cell within PivotTable active.
2. Click PivotTable Tools Options tab.
3. Click Insert Slicer button.
4. Click check box for desired field.
5. Click OK.

Insert Slicer

Project 3c **Using a Slicer to Filter a PivotTable** Part 3 of 6

1. With **EL2-C4-P3-PremiumFitnessJanSales.xlsx** open, display a Slicer pane for the Model field by completing the following steps:
   a. Make any cell active within the PivotTable.
   b. Click the PivotTable Tools Options tab.
   c. Click the Insert Slicer button in the Sort & Filter group.
   d. At the Insert Slicers dialog box, click the *Model* check box to insert a check mark and then click OK. Excel inserts a Slicer pane in the worksheet with all of the model numbers.
2. If necessary, position the mouse pointer at the top of the Model Slicer pane until the pointer changes to the four-headed arrow move icon and then drag the pane to an empty location below the PivotTable.

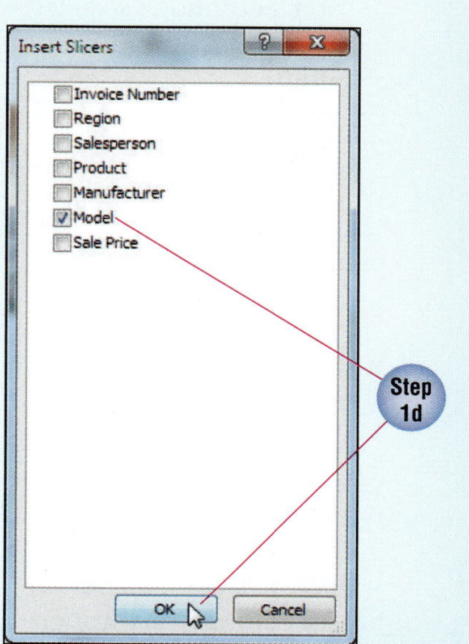

3. Click *CX700* in the Model Slicer pane to filter the PivotTable. Excel filters the PivotTable by the CX700 model number. Notice that the *Model* filter arrow button in B1 displays *CX700*.
4. Click the Clear Filter button at the top right of Model Slicer pane to redisplay all data.
5. Add a second Slicer pane and filter by two fields by completing the following steps:
   a. Make any cell active within the PivotTable.
   b. Click the PivotTable Tools Options tab and then click the Insert Slicer button.
   c. Click the *Salesperson* check box in the Insert Slicers dialog box and then click OK.
   d. Drag the Salesperson Slicer pane below the PivotTable next to the Model Slicer pane.
   e. Click *Fernandez* in the Salesperson Slicer pane to filter the PivotTable.
   f. Click *VS2200* in the Model Slicer pane to filter Fernandez's sales by the VS2200 model number.
6. Print the filtered PivotTable.
7. Redisplay all data and remove the two Slicer panes by completing the following steps:
   a. Click the Clear Filter button at the top right of the Salesperson Slicer pane.
   b. Click the Clear Filter button at the top right of the Model Slicer pane.
   c. Right-click the top of the Model Slicer pane and then click *Remove "Model"* at the shortcut menu.
   d. Right-click the top of the Salesperson Slicer pane and then click *Remove "Salesperson"* at the shortcut menu.
8. Select columns B through F and change the column width to 12.
9. Save **EL2-C4-P3-PremiumFitnessJanSales.xlsx**.

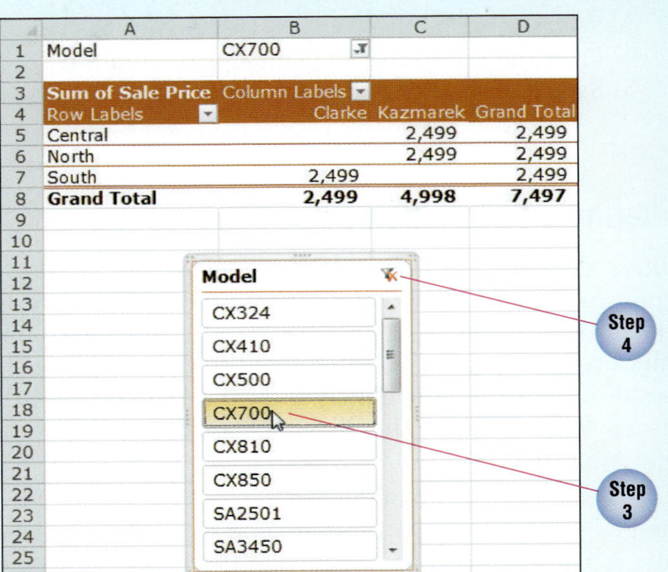

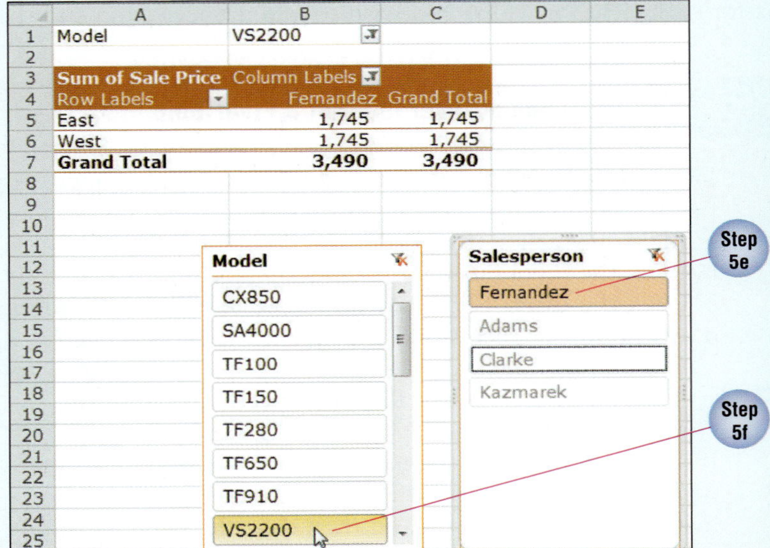

A Slicer pane can be customized with buttons in the Slicer Tools Options tab. Click a Slicer pane to activate the Slicer Tools Options tab. Click the tab to display customization options such as Slicer Styles. You can also change the height and width of the buttons in the Slicer pane and/or the height and width of the pane.

Quick Steps

Change PivotTable Summary Function

1. Make values field cell active.
2. Click PivotTable Tools Options tab.
3. Click Field Settings button.
4. Click desired function.
5. Click OK.

Field Settings

Changing the Summary Function

By default Excel uses the Sum function to summarize the numeric value added to a PivotTable. To change Sum to another function, click any numeric value within the PivotTable or click the cell containing *Sum of [Fieldname]* at the top left of the PivotTable. Click the PivotTable Tools Options tab and then click the Field Settings button in the Active Field group. This opens the Value Field Settings dialog box in which you can choose a function other than Sum. Alternatively, you can right-click any numeric value within the PivotTable, point to *Summarize Values By* at the shortcut menu, and then click the desired function name.

Project 3d Changing the Values Function in a PivotTable

Part 4 of 6

1. With **EL2-C4-P3-PremiumFitnessJanSales.xlsx** open, use Save As and name the workbook **EL2-C4-P3-PremiumFitnessAvgJanSales.**
2. Change the function for the *SalePrice* field from Sum to Average by completing the following steps:
   a. Make A3 the active cell in the PivotTable. This cell contains the label *Sum of Sale Price*.
   b. Click the PivotTable Tools Options tab.
   c. Click the Field Settings button in the Active Field group.
   d. At the Value Field Settings dialog box with the Summarize Values By tab active, click *Average* in the *Summarize value field by* list box and then click OK.
3. Select columns B through F, change the column width to 12 and then print the revised PivotTable.
4. Save and then close **EL2-C4-P3-PremiumFitnessAvgJanSales.xlsx**.

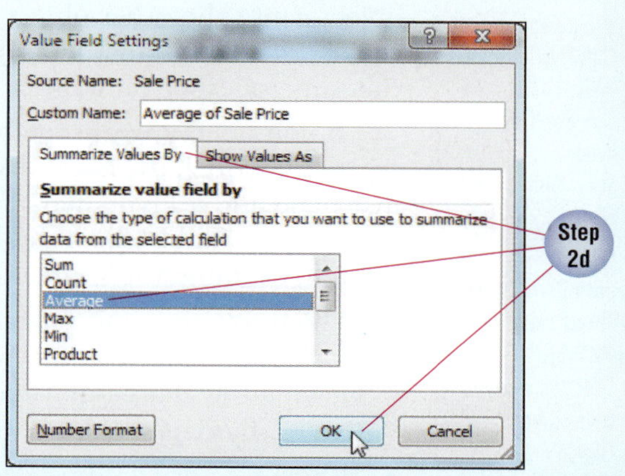

Creating a PivotChart

A ***PivotChart*** visually displays the data from a PivotTable in chart form. As with a PivotTable, you can filter the data to examine various scenarios between categories. Excel displays the PivotChart Filter pane when a PivotChart is active so that you can filter the data as needed. As you make changes to the PivotChart, the PivotTable that is associated with the PivotChart is also updated. Figure 4.7 displays the PivotChart you will create in Project 3e.

PivotChart

In a worksheet that already contains a PivotTable, position the active cell anywhere within the PivotTable, click the PivotTable Tools Options tab, and then

Figure 4.7 PivotChart for Project 3e

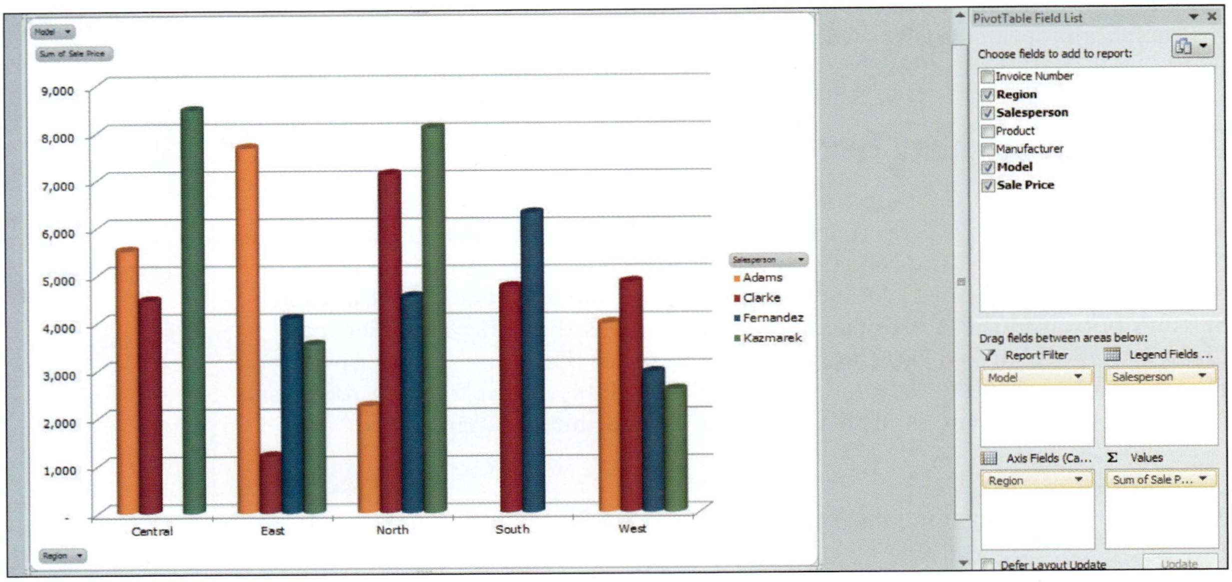

> **Quick Steps**
>
> **Create PivotChart from PivotTable**
> 1. Make cell active within PivotTable.
> 2. Click PivotTable Tools Options tab.
> 3. Click PivotChart button.
> 4. Select desired chart type.
> 5. Click OK.
>
> **Create PivotChart without Existing PivotTable**
> 1. Select range containing data for chart.
> 2. Click Insert tab.
> 3. Click down-pointing arrow on PivotTable button.
> 4. Click *PivotChart*.
> 5. Click OK.
> 6. Add fields as needed in PivotTable Field List pane to build chart.
> 7. Modify and/or format as required.

Move Chart

click the PivotChart button in the Tools group to create a chart from the existing summary data. Excel displays the Insert Chart dialog box in which you choose the type of chart to create. Once the PivotChart has been generated, the PivotTable and PivotChart become connected. Changes made to the data by filtering in one object cause the other object to update with the same filter. For example, filtering the chart by an individual salesperson name causes the PivotTable to also filter by the same salesperson name.

If you open a worksheet that does not contain a pre-existing PivotTable and create a PivotChart, Excel displays a blank chart window with the PivotTable Field List pane and a PivotChart Filter pane. Build the chart using the same techniques you used to build a PivotTable. Before you begin creating a PivotChart from scratch, examine the source data and determine the following elements:

- Which row or column heading contains the labels that you want to display along the *x* axis? In other words, how do you want to compare data when viewing the chart—by time period such as months or years, by salesperson names, by department name, or by some other category?
- Which row or column heading contains the labels that you want to display as legend fields? In other words, how many data series (bars in a column chart) do you want to view in the chart—one for each region, product, salesperson, department, or some other category?
- Which numeric field contains the values you want to graph in the chart?

As you build a PivotChart from scratch, Excel will also build a PivotTable in the background that is connected to the PivotChart.

Creating a PivotChart

Part 5 of 6

1. Open **EL2-C4-P3-PremiumFitnessJanSales.xlsx**.
2. Create a PivotChart to visually present the data in the PivotTable by completing the following steps:
   a. If necessary, click any cell within the PivotTable to activate the PivotTable contextual tabs.
   b. Click the PivotTable Tools Options tab.
   c. Click the PivotChart button in the Tools group.
   d. At the Insert Chart dialog box, with *Column* selected in the left pane, click *Clustered Cylinder* (first option in second row in *Column* section) and then click OK.

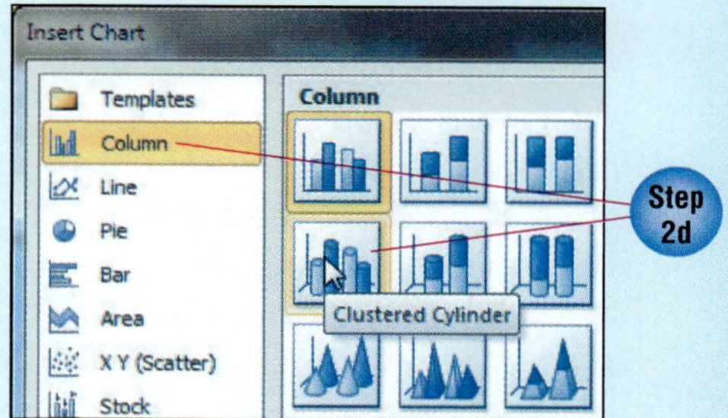

3. Filter the PivotChart to display sales for only one salesperson by completing the following steps:
   a. Click the Salesperson field button in the PivotChart. This is the button above the salesperson names in the PivotChart legend.
   b. Click the *(Select All)* check box to clear all of the check boxes.
   c. Click the *Kazmarek* check box and then click OK.
   d. Notice the PivotTable behind the chart is also filtered to reflect the chart's display. ***Note: If necessary, drag the PivotChart border to move the chart out of the way if the chart is obscuring your view of the PivotTable.***
   e. Click the Salesperson field button in the PivotChart and then click *Clear Filter From "Salesperson"*.

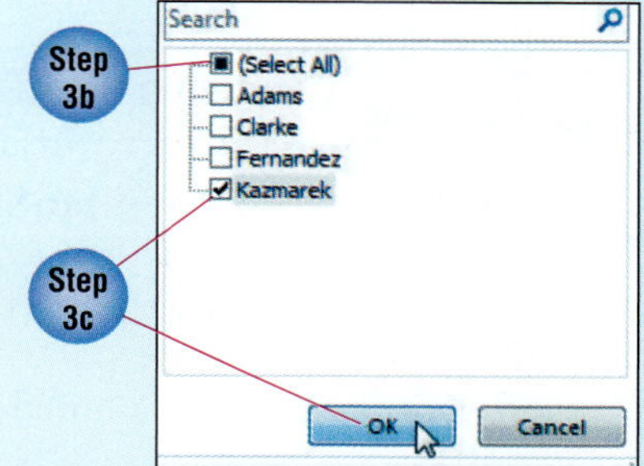

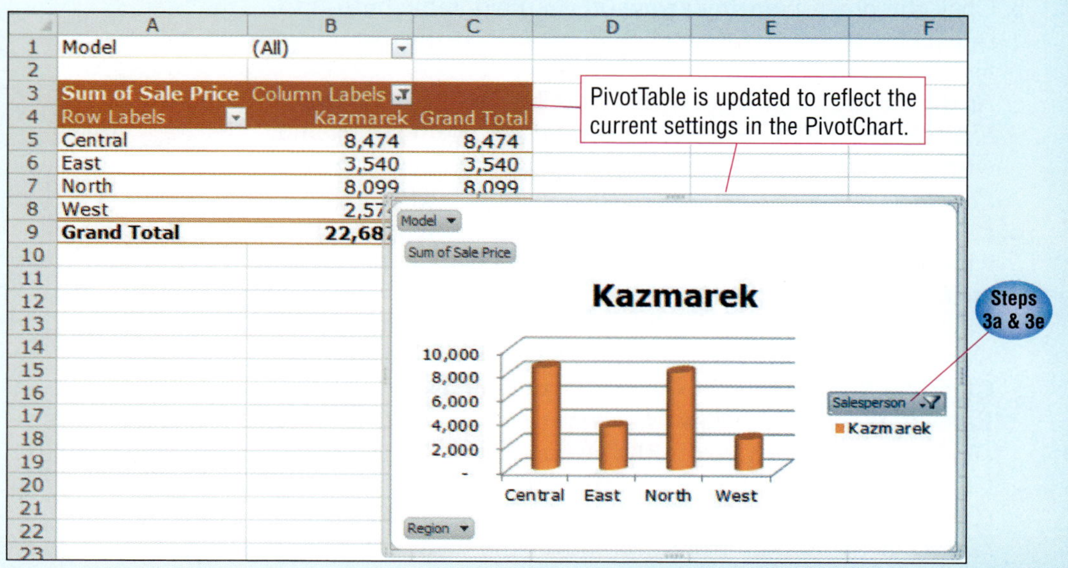

4. Move the PivotChart to a separate worksheet by completing the following steps:
   a. Click the Move Chart button in the Location group of the PivotChart Tools Design tab.
   b. At the Move Chart dialog box, click *New sheet*, type **PivotChart** in the *New sheet* text box, and then click OK. Excel moves the PivotChart to a separate worksheet. Compare your PivotChart with the one shown in Figure 4.7 on page 124.
5. Print the PivotChart.
6. Rename the sheet tab for the worksheet containing the PivotTable (Sheet4) to *PivotTable*.
7. Save and then close **EL2-C4-P3-PremiumFitnessJanSales.xlsx**.

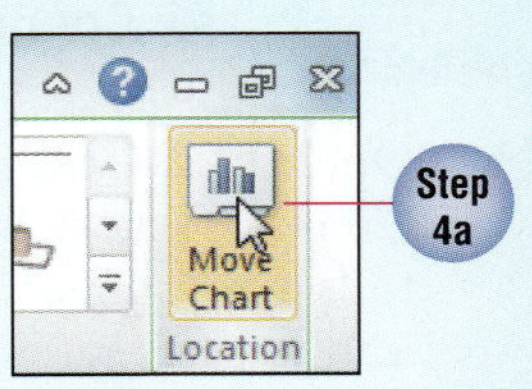

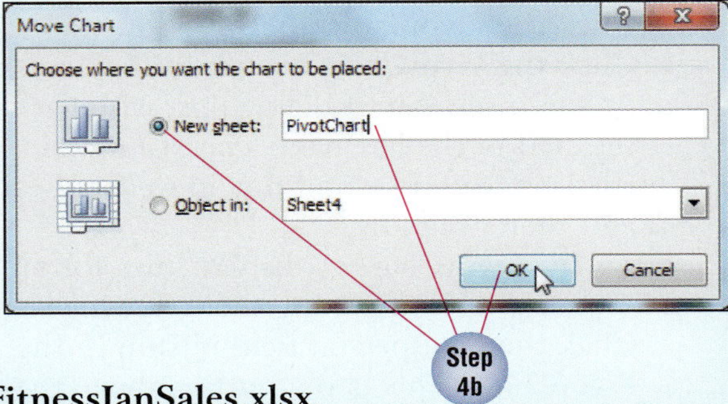

Project 3f Creating a PivotChart from Scratch

Part 6 of 6

1. Open **PremiumFitnessJanSales.xlsx**.
2. Save the workbook with Save As and name it **EL2-C4-P3-PremiumFitnessChart**.
3. Create a PivotChart to chart the sales by manufacturer by region by completing the following steps:
   a. Select the *JanSales* named range and then click the Insert tab.
   b. Click the down-pointing arrow on the PivotTable button in the Tables group and then click *PivotChart* at the drop-down list.
   c. At the Create PivotTable with PivotChart dialog box, with *Sheet1!$A$4:$G$47* entered in the *Table/Range* text box and with *New Worksheet* selected in the *Choose where you want the PivotTable and PivotChart to be placed* section, click OK.
   d. Excel displays a blank sheet with the PivotTable Field List pane at the right side of the window. A PivotTable placeholder and a PivotChart placeholder appear in the worksheet area. As you build the PivotChart, notice that a PivotTable is created automatically.
   e. Click the *Manufacturer* check box in the PivotTable Field List. Excel adds the field to the *Axis Fields (Categories)* list box in the layout section.
   f. Click the *Region* check box in the PivotTable Field List. Excel adds the field below *Manufacturer* in the *Axis Fields (Categories)* list box in the layout section.
   g. Click the *Region* field header in the *Axis Fields (Categories)* list box and then click *Move to Legend Fields (Series)* at the pop-up list. Excel moves the field and updates the chart and the PivotTable.
   h. Click the *Sale Price* check box in the PivotTable Field List. Excel graphs the sum of the Sale Price values in the PivotChart and updates the PivotTable.

Step 3a
Step 3b

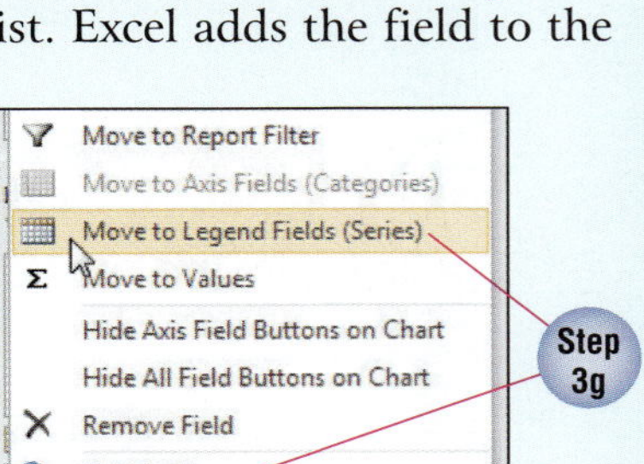

4. Point to the border of the PivotChart and then drag the PivotChart below the PivotTable.
5. Resize the chart to the approximate height and width shown.

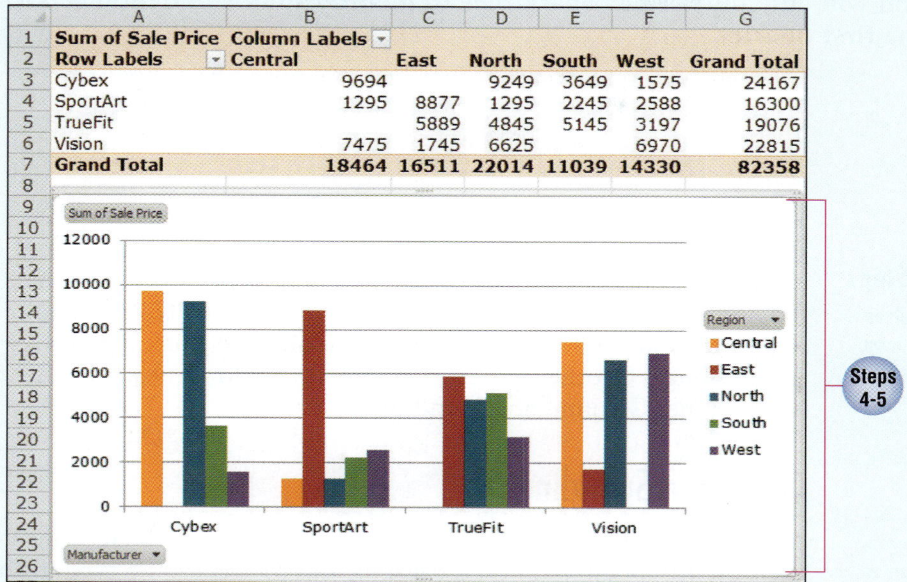

Sum of Sale Price	Column Labels					
Row Labels	Central	East	North	South	West	Grand Total
Cybex	9694		9249	3649	1575	24167
SportArt	1295	8877	1295	2245	2588	16300
TrueFit		5889	4845	5145	3197	19076
Vision	7475	1745	6625		6970	22815
Grand Total	18464	16511	22014	11039	14330	82358

6. Select A1:G7 and then change the font size to 10.
7. Print the PivotTable and PivotChart worksheet.
8. Rename the sheet containing the PivotTable and PivotChart (Sheet4) to *SummaryData*.
9. Save and then close **EL2-C4-P3-PremiumFitnessJanSales.xlsx**.

Table 4.1 provides a summary of the functions of a PivotTable and PivotChart for reporting and summarizing large amounts of data.

Table 4.1 Functions of a PivotTable and PivotChart

Type of Report	*Description*
PivotTable Report	Summarizes large amounts of data by grouping the data on a column or row label. The report presents the results in a tabular format. By default Excel uses a Sum function to aggregate the values. Once tabulated, the PivotTable report can be filtered or sliced by a field to show various results.
PivotChart Report	Graphically presents data from a PivotTable report. A PivotChart is like any other Excel chart with data series and axes. A PivotChart can also be filtered or sliced to present various comparisons.

Project 4 Add Sparklines in a Worksheet to Show Trends — 2 Parts

You will add and format Sparklines to identify trends in dental services fees over the first quarter.

Summarizing Data with Sparklines

Quick Steps

Create Sparklines
1. Select empty range in which to insert Sparklines.
2. Click Insert tab.
3. Click Line, Column, or Win/Loss in Sparklines group.
4. Type data range address or drag to select data range in *Data Range* text box.
5. Click OK.

Sparklines are a new feature added to Excel 2010. ***Sparklines*** are miniature charts that are embedded into the background of a cell. The entire chart exists in a single cell. Since Sparklines can be placed directly next to the data which is being represented, the reader can quickly determine visually if a trend or pattern exists within the data set. Consider using Sparklines to show high or low values within a range, trends, or other patterns. Figure 4.8 illustrates each of the three Sparklines charts: Line, Column, and Win/Loss.

Creating a Sparkline

To create a Sparkline, select the empty cell range in which to insert Sparklines, click the Insert tab, and then click the desired Sparkline type in the Sparklines group shown in Figure 4.9. At the Create Sparklines dialog box, type or click the range for the cells that contain the data that you wish to graph in the *Data Range* text box and then click OK.

Figure 4.8 Line, Column, and Win/Loss Sparklines Added to a Worksheet

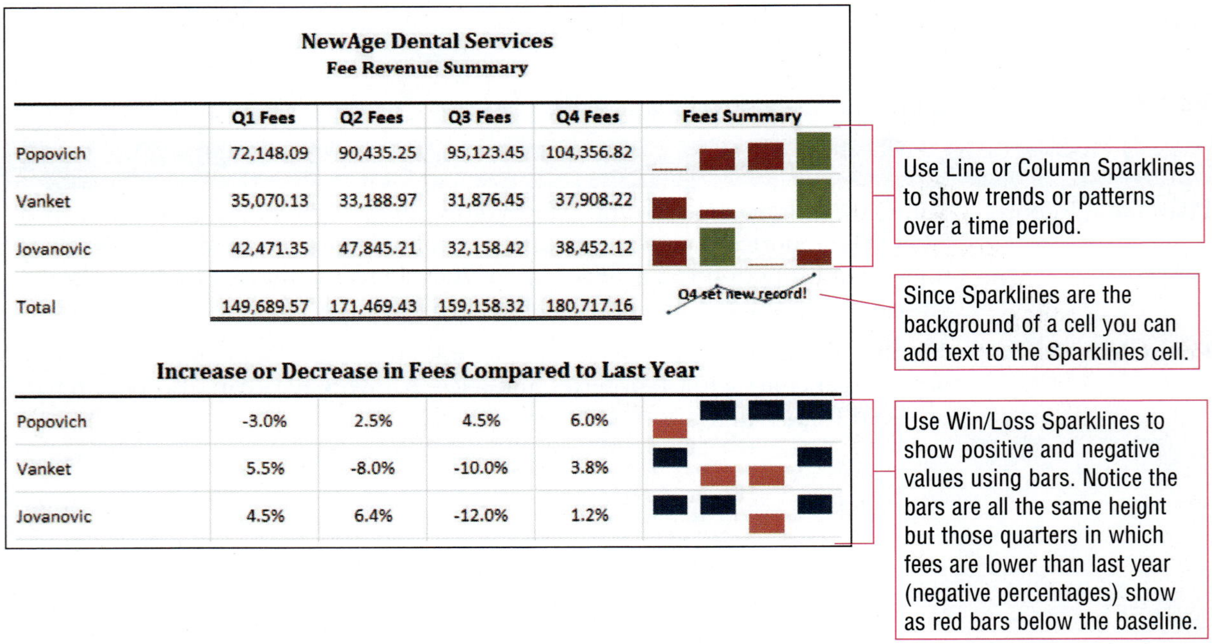

NewAge Dental Services
Fee Revenue Summary

	Q1 Fees	Q2 Fees	Q3 Fees	Q4 Fees	Fees Summary
Popovich	72,148.09	90,435.25	95,123.45	104,356.82	
Vanket	35,070.13	33,188.97	31,876.45	37,908.22	
Jovanovic	42,471.35	47,845.21	32,158.42	38,452.12	
Total	149,689.57	171,469.43	159,158.32	180,717.16	Q4 set new record!

Increase or Decrease in Fees Compared to Last Year

Popovich	-3.0%	2.5%	4.5%	6.0%	
Vanket	5.5%	-8.0%	-10.0%	3.8%	
Jovanovic	4.5%	6.4%	-12.0%	1.2%	

Use Line or Column Sparklines to show trends or patterns over a time period.

Since Sparklines are the background of a cell you can add text to the Sparklines cell.

Use Win/Loss Sparklines to show positive and negative values using bars. Notice the bars are all the same height but those quarters in which fees are lower than last year (negative percentages) show as red bars below the baseline.

Figure 4.9 Sparklines Group

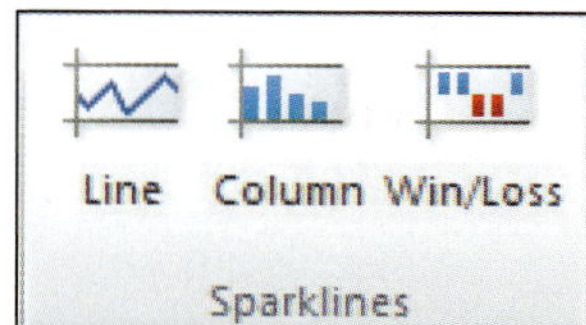

Project 4a **Creating Sparklines** Part 1 of 2

1. Open **EL2-C4-P2-NewAgeDentalQ1Fees.xlsx**.
2. Save the workbook with Save As and name it **EL2-C4-P4-NewAgeDentalQ1Fees**.
3. Create a Sparkline to illustrate the trends in each dental service fee category during the first quarter by completing the following steps:
   a. Select G6:G14.
   b. Click the Insert tab.
   c. Click the Line button in the Sparklines group.
   d. At the Create Sparklines dialog box, with the insertion point positioned in the *Data Range* text box, type **b6:d14** and then click OK. Excel inserts miniature line charts within the cells.
4. Spend a few moments reviewing the Sparklines to determine what the charts are indicating. Notice that the lines in G7 (Cleanings and Fillings) and G10 (Porcelain Veneers) have a downward slope. The lines in G8 (Teeth Whitening) and G11 (Crowns and Bridges) have a similar shape that shows these dental services peaked in February and are on a decline.
5. Save **EL2-C4-P4-NewAgeDentalQ1Fees.xlsx**.

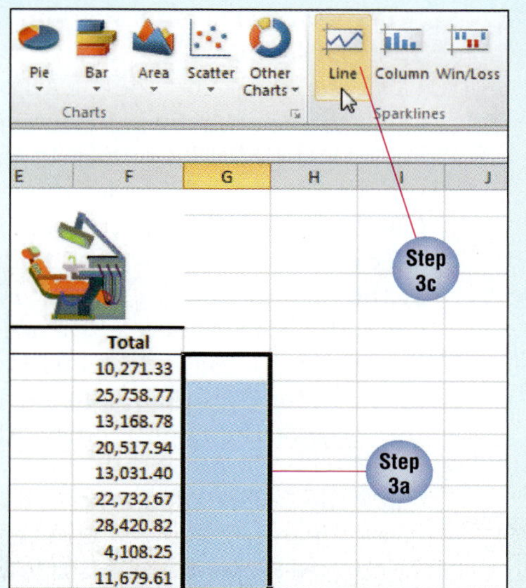

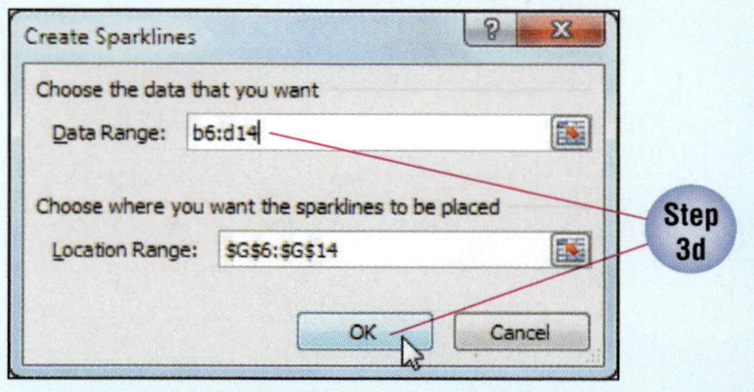

Customizing Sparklines

Activate any Sparkline cell and the Sparkline Tools Design tab shown in Figure 4.10 becomes visible. Click the Edit Data button to edit a range used to generate the Sparklines or instruct Excel how to graph hidden or empty cells in the data range. Use buttons in the Type group to change the chart type from line to column or win/loss. Click the check boxes in the Show group to show or hide data points in the chart or show markers. With options in the Style group you can change the line and/or marker appearance. Click the Axis button in the last group to customize the horizontal or vertical axis in the charts. Sparklines can be grouped, ungrouped, or cleared with the last three buttons in the tab.

Quick Steps

Customize Sparklines
1. Click in any Sparklines cell.
2. Click Sparkline Tools Design tab.
3. Change chart type, show/hide points or markers, change chart style, color, or marker color.

Figure 4.10 Sparkline Tools Design Tab

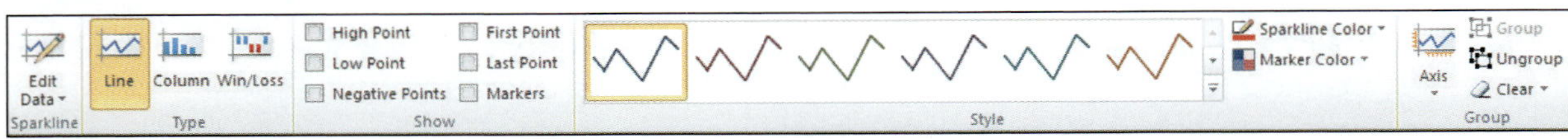

Project 4b Customizing Sparklines

Part 2 of 2

1. With **EL2-C4-P4-NewAgeDentalQ1Fees.xlsx** open, customize the Sparklines by completing the following steps:
   a. If necessary, click any Sparkline cell to activate the Sparkline Tools Design tab.
   b. Click the Sparkline Tools Design tab.
   c. Click the Sparkline Color button in the Style group and then click *Dark Red* (first option in the *Standard Colors* section) at the drop-down color palette.
   d. Click the *High Point* check box in the Show group to insert a check mark in the box. Excel adds a marker to each line graph at the highest point.
   e. Click the *Markers* check box in the Show group to insert a check mark. Excel adds a marker to each of the other data points on each line. Note that the color of the High Point marker is different from the color of the other markers.
   f. Click the Marker Color button in the Style group, point to *Markers*, and then click *Black, Text 1* (second option in first row of *Theme Colors* section) at the drop-down color palette.

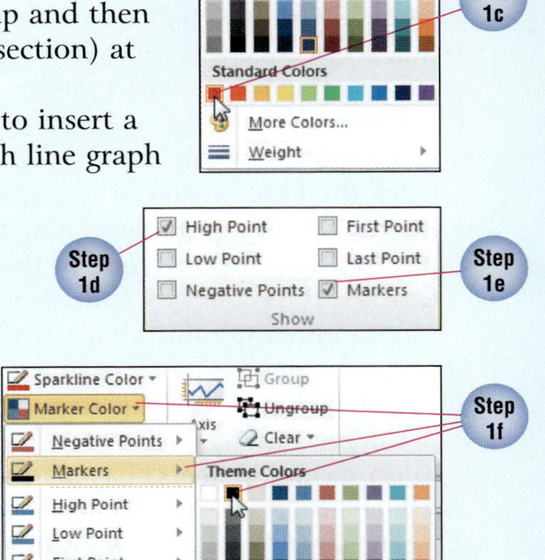

2. Improve the appearance of the Sparklines by widening the column and adding fill color by completing the following steps:
   a. Change the width of column G to 22.
   b. Select G6:G14, click the Home tab, and then apply *Blue, Accent 1, Lighter 80%* (fifth option in second row of *Theme Colors* section) fill color to the selected cells.
   c. Click in any cell to deselect the range.
3. Select G1:G4 and apply *White, Background 1* fill color (first option in *Theme Colors* section) at the drop-down color palette.
4. Make G5 the active cell, type **January to March trends**, and then format the cell so that it has the same formatting as the other titles in row 5.
5. Make G4 the active cell and apply a *Thick Bottom Border*.
6. Change the page orientation to landscape and then print the FeeSummary worksheet.
7. Save and then close **EL2-C4-P4-NewAgeDentalQ1Fees.xlsx**.

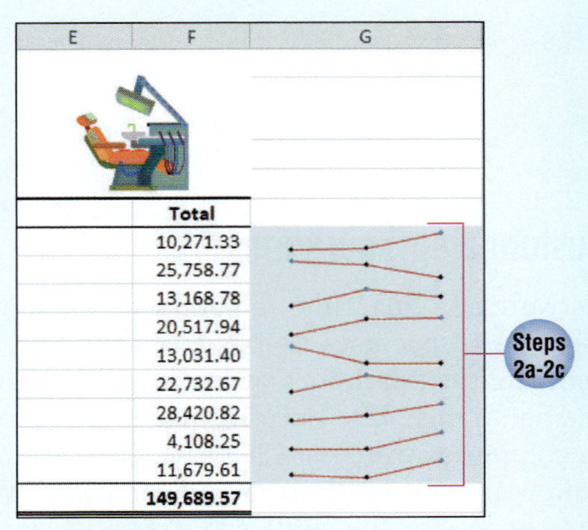

Chapter Summary

- A formula that references a cell in another worksheet within the same workbook contains a worksheet reference as well as a cell reference separated by an exclamation point.
- Range names can be used to simplify references to cells in another worksheet since the worksheet reference is automatically included in the range name definition.
- A disadvantage to using range names to reference other worksheets exists if there are several worksheets to be summarized since each name has to be defined before you can create the formula.
- A 3-D reference is used to summarize the same cell in a range that extends over two or more worksheets.
- A 3-D reference includes the starting worksheet name and the ending worksheet name separated by a colon similar to the method used to define a range of cells.
- A formula that references another worksheet is linked so that a change made in the source cell is automatically changed in the other worksheet to which the source cell has been linked.
- Formulas that reference a cell in another workbook must include a workbook reference in front of the worksheet and cell reference. Workbook references are enclosed in square brackets.
- When you create a formula that links to an external reference, Excel includes the drive and folder name in the path to the source workbook. If you move the location of the source workbook or change the source workbook file name, you have to edit the linked reference.
- Open the Edit Links dialog box to edit or remove a linked external reference.
- The Consolidate feature is another method that can be used to summarize data in multiple worksheets or workbooks.
- The Consolidate button is located in the Data Tools group in the Data tab.
- At the Consolidate dialog box, choose the summary function you want to use for the data that will be aggregated, add the references containing the data you want to summarize, specify the location of the labels to duplicate, and indicate whether to create a link to the source data.
- PivotTables are interactive tables that organize and summarize data based on categories in rows or columns.
- Create a PivotTable using the PivotTable button in the Tables group in the Insert tab.
- Add fields to the PivotTable using the field name check boxes in the PivotTable Field List pane.
- Once created, a PivotTable can be used to view a variety of scenarios by filtering the row, column, or report headings.
- Use buttons in the contextual PivotTable Tools Options and Design tabs to format the PivotTable and/or edit the features used in the table.
- Slicers are used to filter data in a PivotTable without having to open a filter drop-down list.

- A Slicer pane contains all of the items in the designated field so that the report can be filtered with one mouse click.
- Click the Insert Slicer button in the Sort & Filter group of the PivotTable Tools Options tab to add a Slicer pane to a PivotTable.
- A PivotChart displays the data in a PivotTable in a specified chart type.
- Filter a PivotChart using buttons in the PivotChart Filter pane.
- Sparklines are miniature charts inserted into a cell.
- Add Sparklines to a worksheet to show trends or high or low values in a range next to the source data.
- To add Sparklines, select an empty range next to the source data, click the Insert tab and then click the desired chart type in the Sparklines group. At the Create Sparklines dialog box, type the range containing the values you want to graph, or drag to select the range and then click OK.
- Sparklines can be customized using options in the Sparkline Tools Design tab.

Commands Review

FEATURE	RIBBON TAB, GROUP	BUTTON	KEYBOARD SHORTCUT
Consolidate	Data, Data Tools		
Edit Links	Data, Connections		
Manage range names	Formulas, Defined Names		Ctrl + F3
PivotChart	Insert, Tables OR PivotTable Tools Options, Tools		
PivotTable	Insert, Tables		
Sparklines	Insert, Sparklines		

Concepts Check Test Your Knowledge

Completion: In the space provided at the right, indicate the correct term, command, or number.

1. This symbol separates a worksheet reference from a cell reference. ____________
2. This term describes a formula that references the same cell in a range that spans two or more worksheets. ____________
3. Assume a workbook contains the following defined range names that reference cells in four worksheets: Qtr1, Qtr2, Qtr3, and Qtr4. Provide the Sum formula to add the data in the four ranges. ____________
4. This would be the formula entry to link to an external reference C12 in a worksheet named Summary in a workbook named QtrlySales. ____________
5. Open this dialog box to change the source of a linked external reference if you moved the source workbook to another folder. ____________
6. Click this button to permanently remove a linked external reference and convert the linked cells to their existing values. ____________
7. This is the default function active when you open the Consolidate dialog box. ____________
8. Add fields to a PivotTable report by clicking the field check box in this pane. ____________
9. The PivotTable Styles gallery is accessible from this tab. ____________
10. Insert this type of pane to filter a PivotTable with one mouse click. ____________
11. Change the summary function for a PivotTable numeric field by clicking this button in the PivotTable Tools Options tab. ____________
12. A PivotChart visually displays the data from this source. ____________
13. Buttons to filter a PivotChart are found here. ____________
14. This is the first step to complete to add Sparklines in a worksheet. ____________
15. Click this tab to customize Sparklines. ____________

Skills Check Assess Your Performance

Note: Check with your instructor before completing these Assessments if you submit your work in hard copy to see if you need to print two copies of worksheets in which you have created formulas with one copy showing the cell formulas.

Assessment 1

SUMMARIZE DATA IN MULTIPLE WORKSHEETS USING RANGE NAMES

1. Open **NewAgeDentalQ1Fees.xlsx**.
2. Save the workbook with Save As and name it **EL2-C4-A1-NewAgeDentalQ1Fees**.
3. The workbook contains three worksheets with dental fees earned in January, February, and March for three dentists at the dental clinic. Create a range name in F13 of each worksheet to reference the total fees earned by the dentist for the quarter as follows:
   a. Name F13 in the Popovich worksheet *PopovichTotal*.
   b. Name F13 in the Vanket worksheet *VanketTotal*.
   c. Name F13 in the Jovanovic worksheet *JovanovicTotal*.
4. Make FeeSummary the active worksheet and then type the following label in A6:

   Quarter 1 fees for Popovich, Vanket, and Jovanovic
5. Make F6 the active cell and create the Sum formula to add the total fees earned by each dentist using the range names created in Step 3.
6. Format F6 to the Accounting Number Format style and then adjust the column width to AutoFit.
7. Print the FeeSummary worksheet.
8. Save and then close **EL2-C4-A1-NewAgeDentalQ1Fees.xlsx**.

Assessment 2

SUMMARIZE DATA USING LINKED EXTERNAL REFERENCES

1. Open **PremiumFitnessSalesSummary.xlsx**.
2. Save the workbook with Save As and name it **EL2-C4-A2-PremiumFitnessSalesSummary**.
3. Open **PremiumFitnessQ1.xlsx**, **PremiumFitnessQ2.xlsx**, **PremiumFitnessQ3.xlsx**, and **PremiumFitnessQ4.xlsx**.
4. Tile all of the open workbooks.
5. Starting in cell B5 in **EL2-C4-A2-PremiumFitnessSalesSummary.xlsx**, create formulas to populate the cells in column B by linking to the appropriate source cell in **PremiumFitnessQ1.xlsx**. ***Hint: After creating the first formula, edit the entry in B5 to use a relative reference to the source cell (instead of an absolute) so you can copy and paste the formula in B5 to B6:B9.***
6. Create formulas to link to the appropriate source cells for the second, third, and fourth quarter sales.
7. Close the four quarterly sales workbooks. Click Don't Save when prompted to save changes.

8. Maximize **EL2-C4-A2-PremiumFitnessSalesSummary.xlsx**.
9. Print the worksheet.
10. Save and then close **EL2-C4-A2-PremiumFitnessSalesSummary.xlsx**.

Assessment 3

BREAK LINKED REFERENCES

1. Open **EL2-C4-A2-PremiumFitnessSalesSummary.xlsx**. Click the Enable Content button in the Message bar if the Security Warning appears saying that Automatic update of links has been disabled.
2. Convert the formulas to their existing values by breaking the links to the external references in the four quarterly sales workbooks.
3. Save, print, and then close **EL2-C4-A2-PremiumFitnessSalesSummary.xlsx**.

Assessment 4

SUMMARIZE DATA USING 3-D REFERENCES

1. Open **MayParkEntries.xlsx**.
2. Save the workbook with Save As and name it **EL2-C4-A4-MayParkEntries**.
3. With AttendanceSummary the active worksheet, summarize the data in the three park worksheets using 3-D references as follows:
   a. Delete the label in A7.
   b. Copy A6:A22 from any of the park worksheets and paste to A6:A22 in the AttendanceSummary worksheet.
   c. Copy D6:D21 from any of the park worksheets and paste to D6:D21 in the AttendanceSummary worksheet.
   d. Type the label **Entries** right-aligned in B6 and E6.
   e. Make B7 the active cell and then create a 3-D formula to sum the attendance values in the three park worksheets for Day 1. Copy and paste the formula to the remaining cells in column B to complete the summary to Day 16.
   f. Make E7 the active cell and then create a 3-D formula to sum the attendance values in the three park worksheets for Day 17. Copy and paste the formula to the remaining cells in column E to complete the summary to Day 31.
   g. Type the label **Total Vehicle and Individual Entrances** in A24.
   h. Create a Sum formula in E24 to compute the grand total.
   i. Apply formatting options to the grand total as desired to make the total stand out.
4. Print the AttendanceSummary worksheet.
5. Save and then close **EL2-C4-A4-MayParkEntries.xlsx**.

Assessment 5

SUMMARIZE DATA IN A PIVOTTABLE AND PIVOTCHART

1. Open **NewAgeDental2012Fees.xlsx**.
2. Save the workbook with Save As and name it **EL2-C4-A5-NewAgeDental2012Fees**.
3. Create a PivotTable report in a new worksheet as follows:
   a. Display the range named *FeeSummary* and then insert a PivotTable in a new worksheet.
   b. Add the *Service Provided* field as row labels.

c. Add the *Dentist* field as column labels.
d. Sum the *FeesBilled* field.

4. Apply *Pivot Style Medium 20* to the PivotTable (sixth option in third row in *Medium* section).
5. Format the values to the Comma Style number format with zero decimals and right-align the dentist names.
6. Name the worksheet *PivotTable*. In rows 1 and 2 above the table enter an appropriate title and subtitle merged and centered across the PivotTable report and then print the PivotTable report.
7. Create a PivotChart from the PivotTable using the Clustered Column chart type and move the chart to its own sheet named *PivotChart*.
8. Filter the PivotChart by the dentist named *Jovanovic*.
9. Print the PivotChart.
10. Save and then close **EL2-C4-A5-NewAgeDental2012Fees.xlsx**.

Assessment 6

FILTERING A PIVOTTABLE USING SLICERS

1. Open **EL2-C4-A5-NewAgeDental2012Fees.xlsx**.
2. Save the workbook with Save As and name it **EL2-C4-A6-DentalFeesFiltered**.
3. Click the PivotTable sheet to view the PivotTable report.
4. Insert Slicer panes for the *Dentist* and *Service Provided* fields.
5. Move the Slicer panes below the PivotTable report.
6. Using the Dentist Slicer pane, filter the PivotTable by *Popovich*. Hold down the Shift key and then click the button for *Vanket* in the Dentist Slicer pane. Use the Shift key to filter by multiple fields in a Slicer pane when the two fields are adjacent in the pane.
7. Using the Service Provided Slicer pane, filter the PivotTable report by *Crowns and Bridges*. Hold down the Ctrl key and then click the button for *Root Canals*. Use the Ctrl key to filter by multiple fields in a Slicer pane when the fields are not adjacent in the pane.
8. Print the PivotTable report.
9. Save and then close **EL2-C4-A6-DentalFeesFiltered.xlsx**.

Assessment

CREATING AND CUSTOMIZING SPARKLINES

1. Open **EL2-C4-A2-PremiumFitnessSalesSummary.xlsx**.
2. Save the workbook with Save As and name it **EL2-C4-A7-PremiumFitnessSalesSummary**.
3. Select H5:H9 and insert Line Sparklines referencing the data range B5:E9.
4. Show the high point and markers on each line.
5. Change the Sparkline color to *Dark Blue* (in *Standard Colors* section).
6. Change the width of column H to 19.
7. Type the label **Region Sales by Quarter** in H4.
8. Change the page orientation to landscape and then print the worksheet.
9. Save and then close **EL2-C4-A7-PremiumFitnessSalesSummary.xlsx**.

Visual Benchmark Demonstrate Your Proficiency

SUMMARIZING REAL ESTATE SALES AND COMMISSION DATA

1. Open **HillsdaleOctSales.xlsx**.
2. Save the workbook with Save As and name it **EL2-C4-VB-HillsdaleOctSales**.
3. Create the PivotTable report shown in Figure 4.11 in a new worksheet named *PivotTable*. Use *Pivot Style Medium 11* and column widths set to 18.
4. Create the PivotChart report shown in Figure 4.12 in a new worksheet named *PivotChart*. Use the 3-D Clustered Column chart type and *Style 26*.
5. Print the PivotTable and PivotChart sheets.
6. Save and then close **EL2-C4-VB-HillsdaleOctSales.xlsx**.

Figure 4.11 Visual Benchmark PivotTable

	A	B	C	D	E
1	FOR SALE SOLD	Hillsdale Realtors			
2		October Sales			
3	Sum of Sale Price	Column Labels			
4	Row Labels	Condominium	Single family home	Townhome	Grand Total
5	Chandler	$ 610,900	$ 325,500	$ 952,100	$ 1,888,500
6	Glendale	640,400	881,375		1,521,775
7	Mesa	275,800	846,750	165,800	1,288,350
8	Phoenix	695,000	2,148,100	174,900	3,018,000
9	**Grand Total**	**$ 2,222,100**	**$ 4,201,725**	**$ 1,292,800**	**$ 7,716,625**

Figure 4.12 Visual Benchmark PivotChart

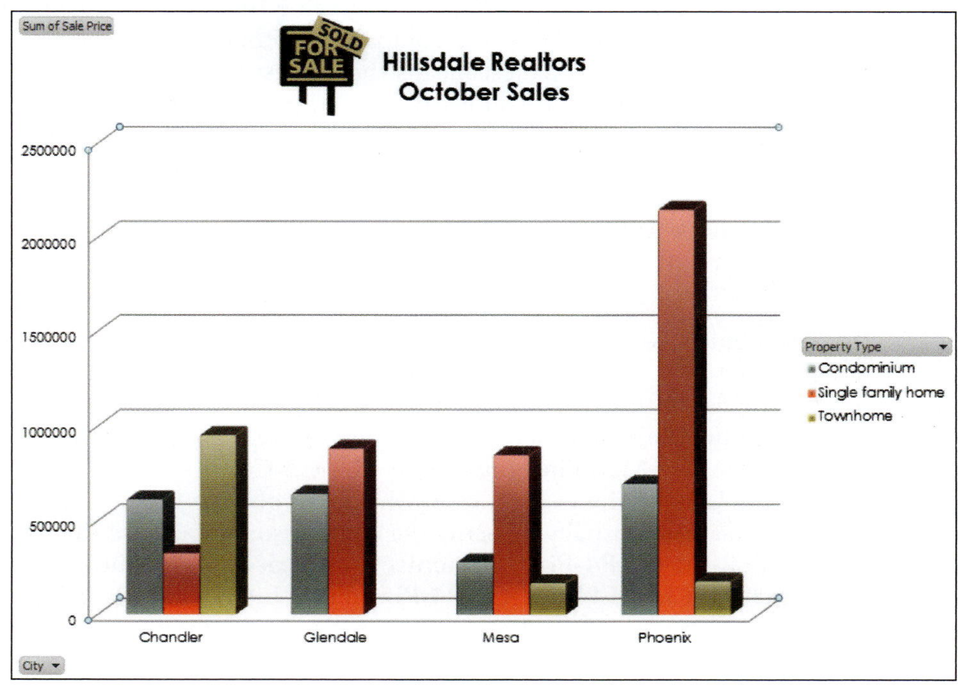

Case Study Apply Your Skills

Part 1

Yolanda Robertson of NuTrends Market Research is continuing to work on the franchise expansion plan for the owners of Pizza By Mario. Yolanda has received a new workbook from the owners with profit information by store. Yolanda would like the data summarized. Open the workbook named **PizzaByMarioSales&Profits.xlsx** and review the structure of the data. Yolanda would like a PivotTable report that provides the average gross sales and the average net income by city by state. You determine how to organize the layout of the report. ***Hint: You can add more than one numeric field to the*** **Values *list box***. Remove the grand totals at the right of the report so that a grand total row appears only at the bottom of the PivotTable. ***Hint: Use the Grand Totals button in the Layout group of the PivotTable Tools Design tab***. Apply formatting options to improve the report's appearance and make sure the report prints on one page in landscape orientation. Rename the worksheet containing the report *PivotTable*. Save the revised workbook and name it **EL2-C4-CS-P1-PizzaByMarioRpt**.

Part 2

Yolanda would like a chart that graphs the average net income data for the state of Michigan only. Create a PivotChart in a new sheet named *PivotChart* and filter the chart appropriately to meet Yolanda's request. You determine an appropriate chart style and elements to include in the chart. Yolanda will be using this chart at an upcoming meeting with the franchise owners and wants the chart to be of professional quality. Print the chart. Save the revised workbook and name it **EL2-C4-CS-P2-PizzaByMarioRpt** and then close the workbook.

Part 3

Help

Open **EL2-C4-CS-P1-PizzaByMarioRpt.xlsx**. Use the Help feature to find out how to modify a numeric field setting to show values as ranked numbers from largest to smallest. For example, instead of seeing the average value next to a city, you will see the city's ranking as it compares to other cities in the same state. Ranking from largest to smallest means the highest value in the state is ranked as 1. Using the information you learned in Help, change the display of the average sales to show the values ranked from largest to smallest using *City* as the base field. Remove the *Net Income* field from the PivotTable. Remove the grand total row at the bottom of the PivotTable. Make any other formatting changes to the report you think will improve the appearance. Print the PivotTable. Save the revised workbook and name it **EL2-C4-CS-P3-PizzaByMarioRpt**.

Part 4

Yolanda would like you to do some comparison research of another pizza franchise. Use the Internet to research the sales and net income information of a pizza franchise with which you are familiar. Create a new workbook that compares the total annual sales and net income values of the pizza franchise you researched with the Pizza By Mario information in **EL2-C4-CS-P1-PizzaByMarioRpt.xlsx**. Provide the URL of the website from which you obtained the competitive data. Create a chart that visually presents the comparison data. Save the workbook and name it **EL2-C4-CS-P4-PizzaFranchiseComparison**. Print the comparison data and the chart. Close **EL2-C4-CS-P4-PizzaFranchiseComparison.xlsx**.

UNIT 1

Performance Assessment

Note: Before beginning assessments, copy to your storage medium the Excel2010L2U1 subfolder from the Excel2010L2 folder on the CD that accompanies this textbook and then make Excel2010L2U1 the active folder.

Assessing Proficiency

In this unit, you have learned to apply advanced formatting options such as conditional formatting and custom number formats; perform advanced sort and filtering techniques; create functions that incorporate conditional logic, look up data, convert text, and calculate financial results; define a table and apply data management features to a table or list range; consolidate and summarize data and present summary information in PivotTables, PivotCharts, or Sparklines.

Assessment 1 Conditionally Format and Filter a Help Desk Worksheet

1. Open **RSRHelpDeskRpt.xlsx**.
2. Save the workbook using the name **EL2-U1-A1-RSRHelpDeskRpt**.
3. Apply conditional formatting to display the *3 Flags* icon set to the values in the *Priority* column. Calls with a priority code of 1 should display a red flag, priority 2 calls should display a yellow flag and priority 3 calls should display a green flag.
4. Create a custom format for the values in the *Time Spent* column. The format should display leading zeros, two decimal places, and the text *hrs* at the end of the entry separated by one space from the number.
5. Create two conditional formatting rules for the values in the *Time Spent* column as follows:
   a. For all entries where the time spent is less than 1 hour, apply bold and a pale green fill color.
   b. For all entries where the time spent is more than 2 hours, apply a bright yellow fill color.
6. Filter the worksheet by the bright yellow fill color applied in the *Time Spent* column. If necessary, delete the clip art image if the image overlaps the data.
7. Print the filtered worksheet.
8. Clear the filter and the filter arrow buttons and then print the worksheet.
9. Save and then close **EL2-U1-A1-RSRHelpDeskRpt.xlsx**.

Assessment 2 Use Conditional Logic Formulas in a Help Desk Worksheet

1. Open **EL2-U1-A1-RSRHelpDeskRpt.xlsx**.
2. Save the workbook using the name **EL2-U1-A2-RSRHelpDeskRpt.xlsx**.
3. Create range names for the following ranges. You determine appropriate names.
   a. Name the cells in A4:E6, which will be used in a lookup formula.
   b. Name the entries in the *Operator ID* column.
   c. Name the values in the *Time Spent* column.
   d. Name the cells in the *Status* column.
4. In I4, create a COUNTA formula to count the number of help desk calls in March using column A as the source range.
5. In I5 and I6, create COUNTIF formulas to count the number of active calls (I5) and the number of closed calls (I6). Use range names in the formulas.
6. Create COUNTIF formulas in K3 through K6 to count the calls assigned to Operator ID 1, 2, 3, and 4, respectively. Use range names in the formulas.
7. Create SUMIF formulas in L3 through L6 to calculate the total time spent on calls assigned to Operator ID 1, 2, 3, and 4, respectively. Use range names in the formulas. Format the results to display two decimal places.
8. Create AVERAGEIF formulas in M3 through M6 to find the average time spent on calls assigned to Operator ID 1, 2, 3, and 4, respectively. Use range names in the formulas. Format the results to display two decimal places.
9. Create the HLOOKUP formula with an exact match in F8 to return the last name for the operator assigned to the call. Use the range name for the lookup table in the formula.
10. Create the HLOOKUP formula with an exact match in G8 to return the first name for the operator assigned to the call. Use the range name for the lookup table in the formula.
11. Copy the HLOOKUP formulas in F8:G8 and paste to the remaining rows in the list.
12. Save, print, and then close **EL2-U1-A2-RSRHelpDeskRpt.xlsx**.

Assessment 3 Use Table and Data Management Features in a Help Desk Worksheet

1. Open **EL2-U1-A2-RSRHelpDeskRpt.xlsx**.
2. Save the workbook using the name **EL2-U1-A3-RSRHelpDeskRpt.xlsx**.
3. Format A7:I30 as a table using *Table Style Medium 20*.
4. Add a calculated column to the table in column J that multiplies the time spent times 15.00. Use the column heading *Cost* in J7. Format the results to display Comma Style number format.
5. Add a total row to the table. Display a sum total in columns H and J.
6. Add emphasis to the last column in the table and band the columns instead of the rows.
7. Create a drop-down list for the *Operator ID* column that displays the entries 1, 2, 3, 4.

8. RSR has a policy that help desk operators cannot spend more than three hours on a call. Calls that require more than three hours must be routed to the Help Desk manager and assigned to another group. Create a validation rule in the *Time Spent* column that ensures no value greater than 3 is entered. Create appropriate input and error messages.
9. Add the following two records to the table:

Date	3/30/2012	3/30/2012
Ticket No	14424	14425
Priority	2	2
Type of Call	Email	Password
Operator ID	3	4
Time Spent	.75	.25
Status	Active	Closed

10. Filter the table to display only those calls with a *Closed* status.
11. Print the filtered list.
12. Filter the worksheet to display only those calls with a *Closed* status where the type of call was *Password*.
13. Print the filtered list.
14. Clear both filters.
15. Save, print, and then close **EL2-U1-A3-RSRHelpDeskRpt.xlsx**.

Assessment 4 Add Subtotals and Outline a Help Desk Worksheet

1. Open **EL2-U1-A3-RSRHelpDeskRpt.xlsx**.
2. Save the workbook using the name **EL2-U1-A4-RSRHelpDeskRpt**.
3. Remove the Total row from the table.
4. Convert the table to a normal range.
5. Sort the list first by the operator's last name, then by the operator's first name, then by the call priority, and finally by the type of call, all in ascending order.
6. Add a subtotal to the list at each change in the operator last name to calculate the total cost of calls by operator.
7. Display the outlined worksheet at level 2 and then print the worksheet.
8. Display the outlined worksheet at level 3 and then print the worksheet.
9. Save and then close **EL2-U1-A4-RSRHelpDeskRpt.xlsx**.

Assessment 5 Use Financial and Text Functions to Analyze Data for a Project

1. Open **AllClaimsLoan.xlsx**.
2. Save the workbook using the name **EL2-U1-A5-AllClaimsLoan**.
3. Create formulas to analyze the cost of the loan from NEWFUNDS TRUST and DELTA CAPITAL as follows:
   a. In C10 and E10, calculate the monthly loan payments from each lender.
   b. In C12 and E12, calculate the principal portion of each payment for the first loan payment.
   c. In C14 and E14, calculate the total loan payments that will be made over the life of the loan from each lender.
4. In E20, use the text function =*PROPER* to return the loan company name for the loan that represents the lowest total cost to AllClaims Insurance Brokers. ***Hint: The argument for the function will reference either C4 or E4.***
5. In E21, use the text function =*LOWER* to return the loan application number for the loan company name you displayed in E20.
6. Save, print, and then close **EL2-U1-A5-AllClaimsLoan.xlsx**.

Assessment 6 Analyze Sales Using a PivotTable, a PivotChart, and Sparklines

1. Open **PrecisionBulkSales.xlsx**.
2. Save the workbook using the name **EL2-U1-A6-PrecisionBulkSales**.
3. Select A4:I22 and create a PivotTable in a new worksheet named *PivotTable* as follows:
   a. Add the *Category* field as the report filter field.
   b. Add the *Distributor* field as the row labels.
   c. Sum the North, South, East, and West sales values.
4. Apply formatting options to the PivotTable to make the data easier to read and interpret.
5. Print the PivotTable.
6. Create a PivotChart in a separate sheet named *PivotChart* that graphs the data from the PivotTable in a Clustered Cylinder chart.
7. Edit the chart fields to display only the sum of the North and the South values.
8. Move the legend to the bottom of the chart.
9. Print the chart.
10. Make Sheet1 the active sheet and then create Sparklines in J5:J22 that show the North, South, East, and West sales in a line chart. Set the width of column J to 18. Customize the Sparklines by changing the Sparkline color and adding data points. You determine which data point to show and the color of the points. Type an appropriate label in J4 and add other formatting you think would improve the appearance.
11. Save, print, and then close **EL2-U1-A6-PrecisionBulkSales.xlsx**.

Assessment 7 Link to an External Data Source and Calculate Distributor Payments

1. Open **PrecisionDistPymnt.xlsx**.
2. Save the workbook using the name **EL2-U1-A7-PrecisionDistPymnt**.
3. Open **EL2-U1-A6-PrecisionBulkSales.xlsx**.
4. Save the workbook using the name **EL2-U1-A7-PrecisionSource**.
5. Make the PivotTable worksheet active and then edit the PivotTable Field List so that *Sum of Total* is the only numeric field displayed in the table.
6. Save **EL2-U1-A7-PrecisionSource.xlsx**.
7. Arrange the display of the two workbooks vertically.
8. Create linked external references starting in D6 in **EL2-U1-A7-PrecisionDistPymnt.xlsx** to the appropriate source cells in the PivotTable in **EL2-U1-A7-PrecisionSource.xlsx** so that the distributor payment worksheet displays the total sales for each distributor. ***Note: Since you are linking to a PivotTable, Excel automatically generates a GETPIVOTDATA function formula in each linked cell.***
9. Close **EL2-U1-A7-PrecisionSource.xlsx**.
10. Maximize **EL2-U1-A7-PrecisionDistPymnt.xlsx**.
11. Format D6:D8 to the Accounting Number format style with zero decimals.

12. Precision Design and Packaging pays each distributor a percentage of sales depending on the total sales achieved. In the chart below is the percentage for each sales level.

Sales	**Percentage**
$600,000 or less	1%
Over $600,000 and up to $900,000	2%
Over $900,000	4%

Calculate the payment owed for the distributors in H6:H8. Perform the calculation using either one of the following two methods—choose the method that you find easier to understand.

- Create a nested IF statement; OR
- Create a lookup table in the worksheet that contains the sale ranges and the three percentage values. Next, add a column next to each distributor with a lookup formula to return the correct percentage and then calculate the payment using total sales times the percent value.

13. Format H6:H8 to the Comma Style number format.
14. Add the label *TOTALS* in B10 and then create formulas in D10 and H10 to calculate the total sales and total payments respectively. Format the totals and adjust column widths as necessary.
15. Print the worksheet. Write the GETPIVOTDATA formula for D6 at the bottom of the printout.
16. Break the link to the external references and convert the formulas to their existing values.
17. Save, print, and then close **EL2-U1-A7-PrecisionDistPymnt.xlsx**.

Writing Activities

The following activities give you the opportunity to practice your writing skills along with demonstrating an understanding of some of the important Excel features you have mastered in this unit. Use appropriate word choices and correct grammar, capitalization, and punctuation when setting up new worksheets. Labels should clearly describe the data that are presented.

Activity 1 Create a Worksheet to Track Video Rental Memberships

Vantage Video Rentals is offering a new membership program for their frequent customers. Customers will pay an annual membership fee that then entitles them to a discount on video rentals based on their membership category. Table U1.1 provides the three membership levels and discounts. The manager of Vantage

Table U1.1 Activity 1

Membership Category	Annual Fee	Discount on Video Rentals
Gold	$45.00	15%
Silver	$30.00	12%
Classic	$20.00	10%

Video Rentals has asked you to create a worksheet that will be used to provide a master list of customers who are participating in the membership program, the membership level for which they have paid, and the discount on video rentals they are entitled to receive. The worksheet will need to provide in list format the following information:

- Date annual membership needs to be renewed
- Customer name
- Customer telephone number
- Membership level
- Annual membership fee
- Discount on video rentals

Create a worksheet for the membership list. Use a lookup table to populate the cells containing the membership fee and the discount level. Create a drop-down list for the cell containing the membership level that restricts the data entered to the three membership categories. Use a special number format for the telephone number column so that all telephone numbers include the area code and are displayed in a consistent format. Enter a minimum of five sample records to test the worksheet with your settings. The manager anticipates approximately 35 regular customers will subscribe to the membership program. Format enough rows with the data features to include at least 35 memberships. Save the completed worksheet and name it **EL2-U1-Act01-VantageMemberships**. Print and then close the worksheet.

Activity 2 Create a Worksheet to Log Hours Walked in a Company Fitness Contest

The company at which you work is sponsoring a contest this year to encourage employees to participate in a walking fitness program during lunch hours. The company is offering to pay for a spa weekend at an exclusive luxury resort for participating employees in the department that logs the most miles or kilometers walked during the year. You work in Human Resources and are in charge of keeping track of each department's walking records. Create a worksheet that can be used to enter each department's totals by month and summarize the data to show the total distance walked for the entire company at the end of the year as follows:

- Four departments have signed up for the contest: Accounting, Human Resources, Purchasing, and Marketing. Create a separate worksheet for each department.
- Each department will send you a paper copy of their walking log each month. You will use this source document to enter the miles or kilometers walked by day. At the end of each month you want to calculate statistics by department to show the total distance walked, the average distance walked, and the number of days in the month in which employees walked during their lunch hour. When calculating the average and the number of days, include only those days in which employees logged a distance. In other words, exclude from the statistics those days in which employees did not log any distance. ***Hint: Consider adding a column that contains Yes or No to record whether or not employees participated in the walking program each day to use as the criteria range.***
- Create a summary worksheet that calculates the total of all miles or kilometers walked for all four departments.

Enter at least five days of sample data in each worksheet to test your settings. Save the completed workbook and name it **EL2-U1-Act02-FitnessProgram**. Print the entire workbook and then close the workbook.

Optional: Using the Internet or other sources, find information on the health benefits of walking. Prepare a summary of the information and include it in a memo announcing the contest. The memo is to be sent from Human Resources to all departments. Save the memo and name it **EL2-U2-Act02-FitnessMemo**. Print the memo and close the file.

Internet Research

Create a Worksheet to Compare Online Auction Listing Fees

You are assisting a friend who is interested in selling a few items by auction on the Internet. Research a minimum of two Internet auction sites for all selling and payment fees associated with selling online. For example, be sure to find out costs for the following activities involved in an auction sale:

- Listing fees (sometimes called insertion fees)
- Optional features that can be attached to an ad such as reserve bid fees, picture fees, listing upgrades, and so on
- Fees paid when the item is sold based on the sale value
- Fees paid to a third party to accept credit card payments (such as PayPal)

Create a worksheet in which you compare the fees for each auction site you researched. Include for each auction site two sample transactions and calculate the total fees that would be paid.

Sample transaction 1	Item sold at $24.99
Sample transaction 2	Item sold at $49.99

- Add optional features to the listing such as a picture and/or a reserve bid
- Assume in both sample transactions the buyer pays by credit card using a third party service

Based on your analysis, decide which auction site is the better choice from a cost perspective. Apply formatting options to make the worksheet easy to read and explain your recommendation for the lower cost auction site. Save the completed worksheet and name it **EL2-U1-Act03-AuctionAnalysis**. Print and then close the worksheet.

Level 2

Unit 2 ■ Managing and Integrating Data and the Excel Environment

Microsoft® Excel®

CHAPTER

Using Data Analysis Features

PERFORMANCE OBJECTIVES

Upon successful completion of Chapter 5, you will be able to:

- **Switch data arranged in columns to rows and vice versa**
- **Perform a mathematical operation during a paste routine**
- **Populate a cell using Goal Seek**
- **Save and display various worksheet models using Scenario Manager**
- **Create a scenario summary report**
- **Create a one-variable data table to analyze various outcomes**
- **Create a two-variable data table to analyze various outcomes**
- **View relationships between cells in formulas**
- **Identify Excel error codes and troubleshoot a formula using formula auditing tools**
- **Circle invalid data**
- **Use the Watch Window to track a value**

Tutorials

5.1 Pasting Data Using Paste Special Options

5.2 Using Goal Seek to Populate a Cell

5.3 Using Scenario Manager

5.4 Performing What-If Analysis Using Data Tables

5.5 Using Auditing Tools

5.6 Circling Invalid Data and Watching Formulas

Excel's Paste Special dialog box includes several options for pasting copied data. You can choose to paste attributes of a copied cell or alter the paste routine to perform a more complex operation. A variety of *what-if* analysis tools allow you to manage data to assist with decision-making or management tasks. Formula auditing tools can be used to troubleshoot a formula or view dependencies between cells. By working through the projects in this chapter, you will learn about these tools and features available in Excel to assist with accurate data analysis. Model answers for this chapter's projects appear on the following pages.

Excel2010L2C5

Note: Before beginning the projects, copy to your storage medium the Excel2010L2C5 subfolder from the Excel2010L2 folder on the CD that accompanies this textbook and then make Excel2010L2C5 the active folder.

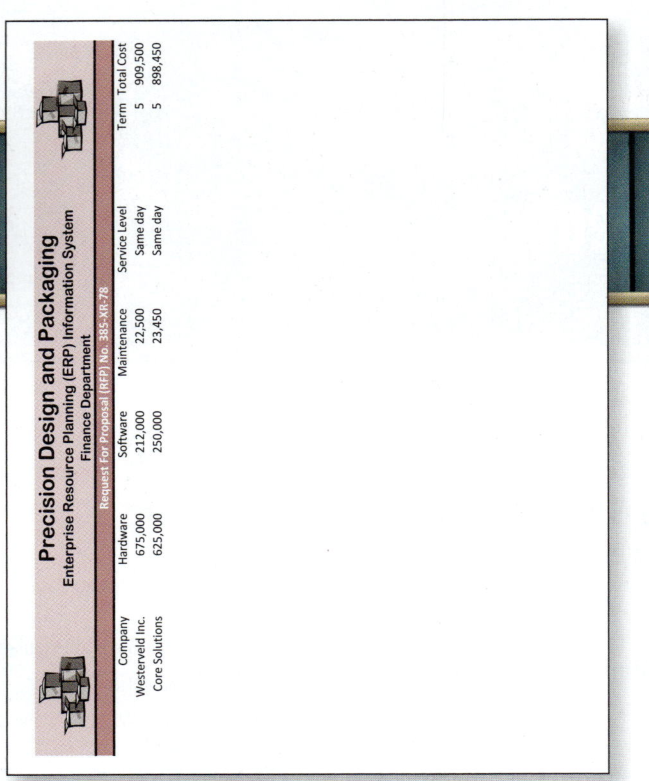

Precision Design and Packaging
Enterprise Resource Planning (ERP) Information System
Finance Department
Request For Proposal (RFP) No. 385-XR-78

Company	Hardware	Software	Maintenance	Service Level	Term	Total Cost
Westerveld Inc.	675,000	212,000	22,500	Same day	5	909,500
Core Solutions	625,000	250,000	23,450	Same day	5	898,450

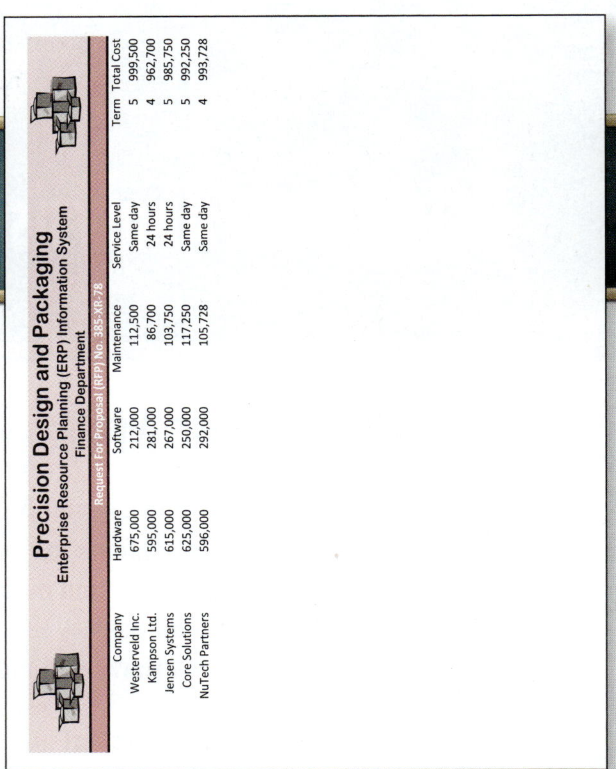

Precision Design and Packaging
Enterprise Resource Planning (ERP) Information System
Finance Department
Request For Proposal (RFP) No. 385-XR-78

Company	Hardware	Software	Maintenance	Service Level	Term	Total Cost
Westerveld Inc.	675,000	212,000	112,500	Same day	5	999,500
Kampson Ltd.	595,000	281,000	86,700	24 hours	4	962,700
Jensen Systems	615,000	267,000	103,750	24 hours	5	985,750
Core Solutions	625,000	250,000	117,250	Same day	5	992,250
NuTech Partners	596,000	292,000	105,728	Same day	4	993,728

Project 1 Analyze Data from a Request for Proposal
Project 1a, EL2-C5-P1-PrecisionERP.xlsx

Project 1b, EL2-C5-P1-PrecisionERP.xlsx

Math by Janelle Tutoring Service Student Assessment Report Whitney Orlowicz		
Assessments	**100**	**Session**
Objective test	64.5	1
Performance test	72.0	6
Problem-solving test	83.5	10
Comprehensive test	78.5	15
Final test	81.5	20
Average grade	76.0	

Project 2 Calculate a Target Test Score
EL2-C5-P2-JanelleTutorOrlowiczRpt.xlsx

Scenario Summary	Current Values:	LowInflation	HighInflation	OriginalForecast
Changing Cells:				
WageInc	13,016	12,010	15,224	13,016
SuppliesInc	2,255	2,150	2,765	2,255
TrainingInc	6,385	5,276	7,236	6,385
AdminIncrease	2,479	1,998	3,195	2,479
Result Cells:				
TotalNewCosts	659,786	657,085	664,071	659,786

Notes: Current Values column represents values of changing cells at time Scenario Summary Report was created. Changing cells for each scenario are highlighted in gray.

Project 3 Forecast a Budget Based on Various Inflation Rates
EL2-C5-P3-NationalCSDeptBdgt.xlsx

Precision Design and Packaging
Cost Price Analysis
"E" Container Bulk Cargo Box

Factory costs per shift			Variable unit production impact on cost	
Direct materials	$	580,000		3.21
Direct labor		880,552	425,000	3.78
Overhead		145,350	450,000	3.57
Total cost	$	1,605,902	475,000	3.38
			500,000	3.21
Standard production		500,000 units	525,000	3.06
			550,000	2.92
Cost per unit	$	3.21	575,000	2.79

Project 4 Compare Impact of Various Inputs Related to Cost and Sales Pricing
EL2-C5-P4-PrecisionEBoxCost.xlsx

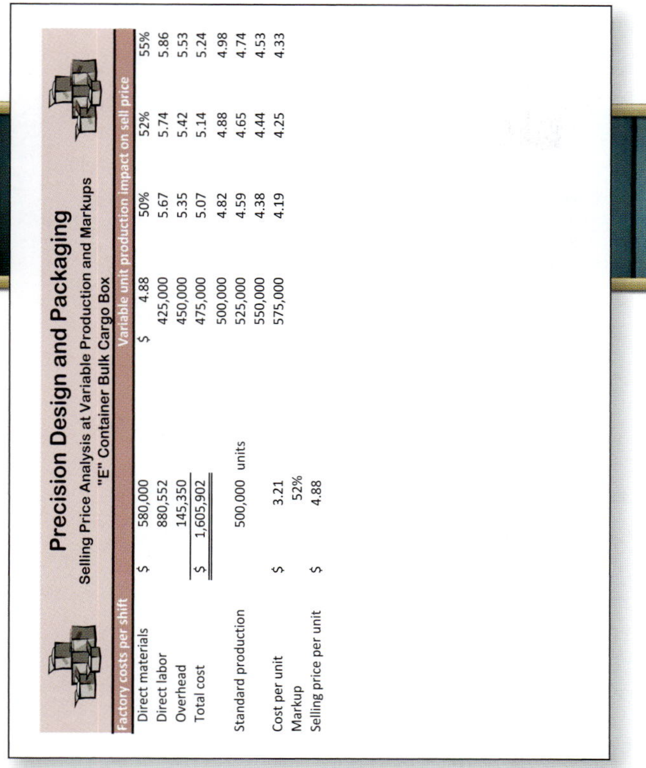

Precision Design and Packaging
Selling Price Analysis at Variable Production and Markups
"E" Container Bulk Cargo Box

Factory costs per shift			Variable unit production impact on sell price			
Direct materials	$	580,000	$ 4.88	50%	52%	55%
Direct labor		880,552	425,000	5.67	5.74	5.86
Overhead		145,350	450,000	5.35	5.42	5.53
Total cost	$	1,605,902	475,000	5.07	5.14	5.24
			500,000	4.82	4.88	4.98
Standard production		500,000 units	525,000	4.59	4.65	4.74
			550,000	4.38	4.44	4.53
Cost per unit	$	3.21	575,000	4.19	4.25	4.33
Markup		52%				
Selling price per unit	$	4.88				

EL2-C5-P4-PrecisionEBoxSell.xlsx

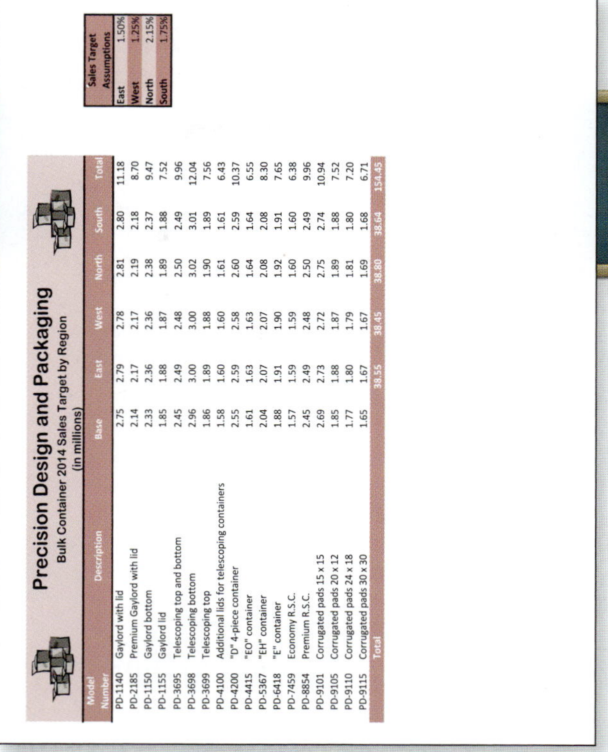

Precision Design and Packaging
Bulk Container 2014 Sales Target by Region
(in millions)

Model Number	Description	Base	East	West	North	South	Total
PD-1140	Gaylord with lid	2.75	2.79	2.78	2.81	2.80	11.18
PD-2185	Premium Gaylord with lid	2.14	2.17	2.17	2.19	2.18	8.70
PD-1150	Gaylord bottom	2.33	2.36	2.36	2.38	2.37	9.47
PD-1155	Gaylord lid	1.85	1.88	1.87	1.89	1.88	7.52
PD-3695	Telescoping top and bottom	2.45	2.49	2.48	2.50	2.49	9.96
PD-3698	Telescoping bottom	2.96	3.00	3.00	3.02	3.01	12.04
PD-3699	Telescoping top	1.86	1.89	1.88	1.90	1.89	7.56
PD-4100	Additional lids for telescoping containers	1.58	1.60	1.60	1.61	1.61	6.43
PD-4200	"D" 4-piece container	2.55	2.59	2.58	2.60	2.59	10.37
PD-4415	"EO" container	1.61	1.63	1.63	1.64	1.64	6.55
PD-5367	"EH" container	2.04	2.07	2.07	2.08	2.08	8.30
PD-6418	"E" container	1.88	1.91	1.90	1.92	1.91	7.65
PD-7459	Economy R.S.C.	1.57	1.59	1.59	1.60	1.60	6.38
PD-8854	Premium R.S.C.	2.45	2.49	2.48	2.50	2.49	9.96
PD-9101	Corrugated pads 15 x 15	2.69	2.73	2.72	2.75	2.74	10.94
PD-9105	Corrugated pads 20 x 12	1.85	1.88	1.87	1.89	1.88	7.52
PD-9110	Corrugated pads 24 x 18	1.77	1.80	1.79	1.81	1.80	7.20
PD-9115	Corrugated pads 30 x 30	1.65	1.67	1.67	1.69	1.68	6.71
	Total		38.55	38.45	38.80	38.64	154.45

Sales Target Assumptions	
East	1.50%
West	1.25%
North	2.15%
South	1.75%

Project 5 Audit a Worksheet to View and Troubleshoot Formulas

EL2-C5-P5-PrecisionSalesTrgt.xlsx

Project 1 Analyze Data from a Request for Proposal — 2 Parts

You will manipulate a worksheet containing vendor quotations for an enterprise resource planning information system by copying and pasting using Paste Special options.

Pasting Data Using Paste Special Options

The Paste drop-down gallery contains many options for pasting copied data grouped into three sections: *Paste*, *Paste Values*, and *Other Paste Options*. In Excel 2010, the Paste gallery includes a live preview of how the data will be pasted to assist you with choosing the correct paste option. Click *Paste Special* at the bottom of the Paste gallery to open the Paste Special dialog box shown in Figure 5.1. Use options in this dialog box to paste specific attributes of the source data, perform a mathematical operation in the destination range based on values in the source range, or carry out a more complex paste sequence.

Several options in the Paste Special dialog box are also available by clicking a button at the Paste drop-down gallery. For example, if you copied a range of cells that has border formatting applied and you want to paste the range without the borders, click the Paste button arrow and then click the No Borders button (first button in second row of the *Paste* section) at the drop-down gallery. This produces the same result as clicking the Paste button arrow, clicking *Paste Special* at the drop-down gallery, clicking *All except borders* in the *Paste* section of the Paste Special dialog box, and then clicking OK.

Figure 5.1 Paste Special Dialog Box

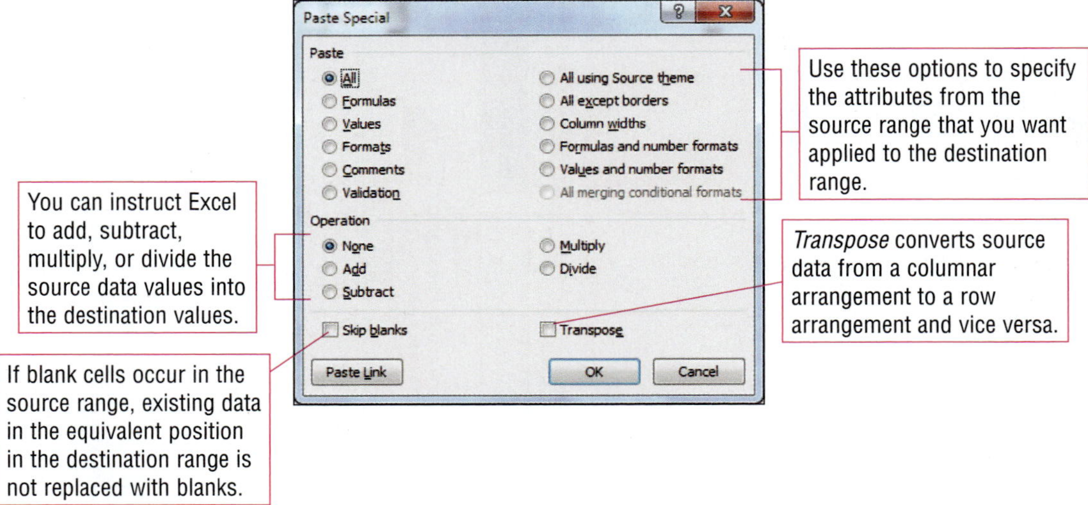
Paste Special
Paste
All
Formulas
Values
Formats
Comments
Validation
All using Source theme
All except borders
Column widths
Formulas and number formats
Values and number formats
All merging conditional formats
Operation
None
Add
Subtract
Multiply
Divide
Skip blanks
Transpose
Paste Link
OK
Cancel
Use these options to specify the attributes from the source range that you want applied to the destination range.
You can instruct Excel to add, subtract, multiply, or divide the source data values into the destination values.
Transpose converts source data from a columnar arrangement to a row arrangement and vice versa.
If blank cells occur in the source range, existing data in the equivalent position in the destination range is not replaced with blanks.

Transposing Data

Quick Steps

Transpose a Range
1. Select source range.
2. Click Copy button.
3. Click starting cell in destination range.
4. Click Paste button arrow.
5. Click *Transpose*.

A worksheet may have data arranged in a way that is not suitable for the analysis you want to perform. For example, examine the worksheet shown in Figure 5.2. This is the worksheet you will be working with in Project 1. Notice the layout of the information shows each company that submitted a proposal arranged in a separate column with the criteria for analysis, such as the cost of the hardware, arranged in rows. While at first glance this layout may seem appropriate, consider how you would analyze this data if you wanted to examine only those vendors that offer a five-year contract. To use the filter feature on this data, you need the contract term in a columnar format. Rearranging the data in this worksheet manually would be time-consuming and risky due to the possibility of errors made during the conversion process. The *Transpose* option in the Paste drop-down gallery or the Paste Special dialog box will convert columns to rows and rows to columns.

Figure 5.2 Project 1 Worksheet

	A	B	C	D	E	F
1	Precision Design and Packaging					
2	Enterprise Resource Planning (ERP) Information System					
3	Finance Department					
4	Request For Proposal (RFP) No. 385-XR-78					
5	Company	Westerveld Inc.	Kampson Ltd.	Jensen Systems	Core Solutions	NuTech Partners
6	Hardware	675,000	595,000	615,000	625,000	596,000
7	Software	212,000	281,000	267,000	250,000	292,000
8	Maintenance	22,500	21,675	20,750	23,450	26,432
9	Service Level	Same day	24 hours	24 hours	Same day	Same day
10	Term	5	4	5	5	4
11	Total Cost	909,500	897,675	902,750	898,450	914,432

Converting Data from Rows to Columns

Part 1 of 2

1. Open **PrecisionERP.xlsx**.
2. Save the workbook with Save As and name it **EL2-C5-P1-PrecisionERP**.
3. Convert the worksheet to arrange the company names in rows and the criteria data in columns by completing the following steps:
   a. Select A5:F11.
   b. Click the Copy button.
   c. Click in cell A13.
   d. Click the Paste button arrow and then click *Transpose* (last button in *Paste* section) at the drop-down gallery.

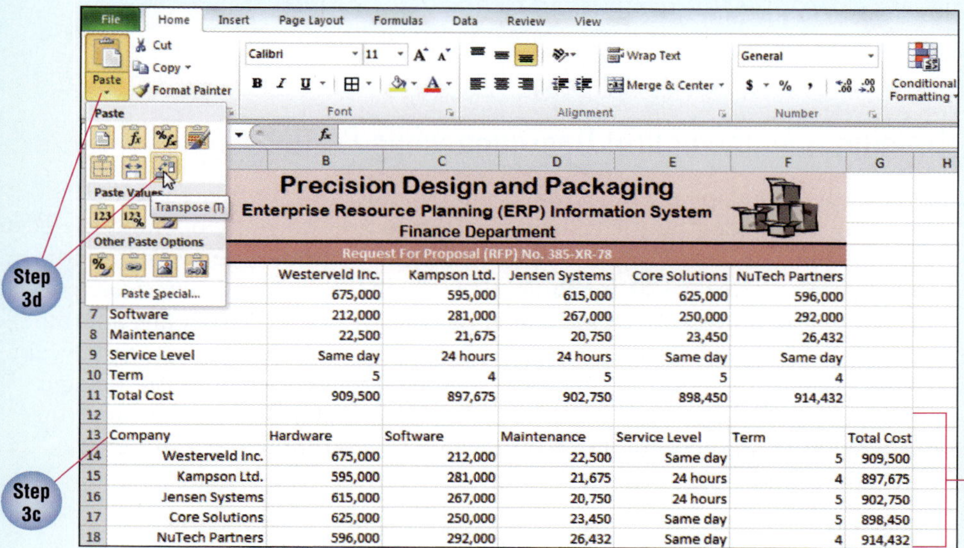

Live preview of how copied data will be pasted using *Transpose* option.

   e. Press the Esc key to remove the moving marquee from the source range and then click in any cell to deselect the range.
4. Delete rows 5–12.
5. Correct the merge and centering in rows 1–4 to extend the titles across columns A–G. If necessary, move or otherwise adjust the position of the clip art at the right side of the worksheet after merging and centering to column G.
6. Add a thick bottom border to A3 and A4.
7. Right-align the labels in A5:G5.
8. Select A5:G10, turn on the Filter feature, and then click in any cell to deselect the range.
9. Click the filter arrow button in F5 and then filter the worksheet to display only those vendors offering a 5-year contract.

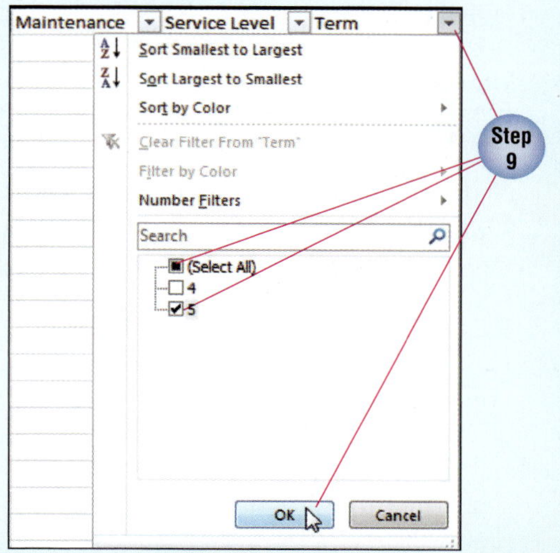

10. Click the filter arrow button in E5 and then filter the remaining rows to display only those vendors offering same day service.

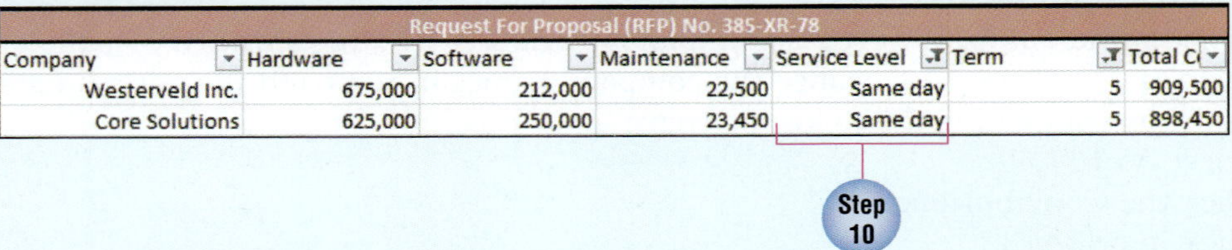
Request For Proposal (RFP) No. 385-XR-78

Company	Hardware	Software	Maintenance	Service Level	Term	Total C
Westerveld Inc.	675,000	212,000	22,500	Same day	5	909,500
Core Solutions	625,000	250,000	23,450	Same day	5	898,450

11. Print the filtered worksheet.
12. Turn off the Filter feature and then save **EL2-C5-P1-PrecisionERP.xlsx**.

Quick Steps

Perform Mathematical Operation during Paste

1. Select source range values.
2. Click Copy button.
3. Click starting cell in destination range.
4. Click Paste button arrow.
5. Click *Paste Special*.
6. Click desired mathematical operation.
7. Click OK.

Performing a Mathematical Operation while Pasting

A range of cells in a copied source range can be added to, subtracted from, multiplied by, or divided by the cells in the destination range by opening the Paste Special dialog box and selecting the mathematical operation you want to perform. For example, in the worksheet for Project 1a, the values in the *Maintenance* column relate to annual maintenance fees charged by each vendor. To compare the total cost of the system from all of the vendors, you want to see the maintenance value for the life cycle of the contract. In Project 1b, you will copy and paste using a multiply operation to perform the calculation for you. This method means you will not have to add a new column to the worksheet to show the maintenance fees for the entire term of the contract.

Project 1b Multiplying the Source Cells by the Destination Cells

Part 2 of 2

1. With **EL2-C5-P1-PrecisionERP.xlsx** open, select F6:F10. These are the cells that contain the term for each company's contract.
2. Click the Copy button.
3. Paste the source range and instruct Excel to multiply the values when pasting by completing the following steps:
   a. Click D6.
   b. Click the Paste button arrow and then click *Paste Special* at the drop-down gallery.

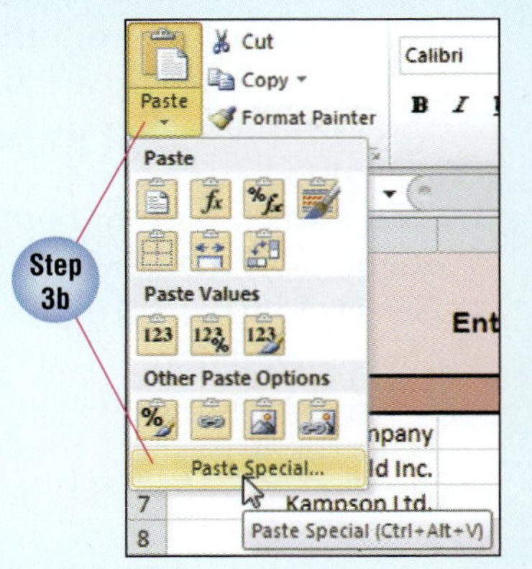

c. Click *Multiply* in the *Operation* section of the Paste Special dialog box and then click OK.
d. Press the *Esc* key to remove the moving marquee from the source range and then click in any cell to deselect the range.
4. Print the worksheet.
5. Save and then close **EL2-C5-P1-PrecisionERP.xlsx**.

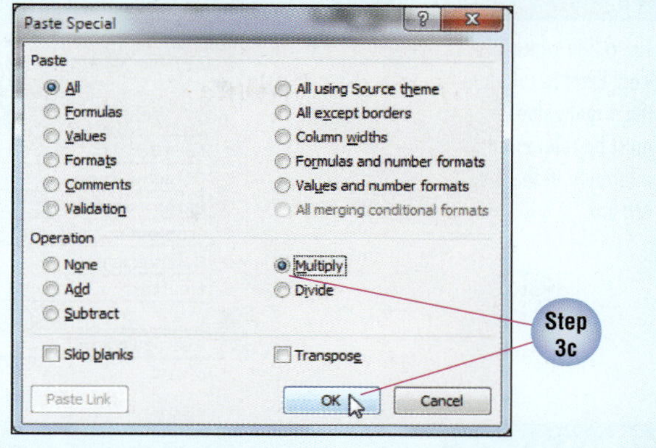

Selecting Other Paste Special Options

Other options at the Paste Special dialog box include *Formulas* or *Values* to paste the source formulas or displayed values only, *Formats* to paste only formatting options from the source, *Validation* to paste a validation rule, *All using Source theme* to apply the theme from the source, *All except borders* to paste everything except borders from the source, and *Column widths* to adjust the destination cells to the same column width as the source. To paste formulas or values including the number formats from the source click the *Formulas and number formats* or the *Values and number formats* option.

Project 2 Calculate a Target Test Score — 1 Part

Using a grades worksheet for a student, you will determine the score a student needs to earn on a final test in order to achieve a specified final average grade.

Using Goal Seek to Populate a Cell

Goal Seek calculates a value using a target that you want to achieve in another cell that is dependent on the cell you want Goal Seek to populate. For example, the worksheet shown in Figure 5.3 shows Whitney's grades on the first four tutoring assessments. The value in B11 (average grade) is calculated as the average of the five values in B5:B9. Note that the final test is showing a grade of zero although the test has not yet occurred. Once the final test grade is entered, the value in B11 will update to reflect the average of all five scores. Suppose Whitney wants to achieve a final average grade of 76% in her tutoring assessments. Using Goal Seek, you can determine the score she needs to earn on the final test in order to achieve the 76% average.

In Project 2 you will return a value in B9 that the Goal Seek feature will calculate based on the target value you will set in B11. Goal Seek causes Excel to calculate in reverse—you specify the ending value and Excel figures out the input numbers that will achieve the end result you want. Note that the cell in which you want Excel to calculate the target value must be referenced by a formula in the *Set cell* box. Goal Seek is useful for any situation where you know the result you want to achieve but are not sure what value will get you there.

Quick Steps

Use Goal Seek to Return a Value
1. Make desired cell active.
2. Click Data tab.
3. Click What-If Analysis button.
4. Click *Goal Seek*.
5. Enter desired cell address in *Set cell* text box.
6. Enter desired target value in *To value* text box.
7. Enter dependent cell address in *By changing cell* text box.
8. Click OK.
9. Click OK or Cancel to accept or reject results.

The cell in which you want Excel to calculate the target value must be referenced by a formula in the *Set cell* box.

Goal Seek

Figure 5.3 Project 2 Worksheet

	A	B	C
1	**Math by Janelle Tutoring Service**		
2	**Student Assessment Report**		
3	Whitney Orlowicz		
4	**Assessments**	**100**	**Session**
5	Objective test	64.5	1
6	Performance test	72.0	6
7	Problem-solving test	83.5	10
8	Comprehensive test	78.5	15
9	Final test	0.0	20
10			
11	Average grade	59.7	

Goal Seek can determine the value that needs to be entered for the final test in order to achieve an average grade that you specify in B11.

Project 2 Using Goal Seek to Return a Target Value

Part 1 of 1

1. Open **JanelleTutorOrlowiczRpt.xlsx**.
2. Save the workbook with Save As and name it **EL2-C5-P2-JanelleTutorOrlowiczRpt**.
3. Use Goal Seek to find the score Whitney needs to earn on the final test to achieve a 76% average grade by completing the following steps:
   a. Make B11 the active cell.
   b. Click the Data tab.
   c. Click the What-If Analysis button in the Data Tools group and then click *Goal Seek* at the drop-down list.
   d. If necessary, drag the Goal Seek dialog box to the right of the worksheet so that you can see all of the values in column B.
   e. With *B11* already entered in the *Set cell* text box, click in the *To value* text box and then type **76**.
   f. Press Tab and then type **b9** in the *By changing cell* text box.
   g. Click OK.
   h. Click OK at the Goal Seek Status dialog box that shows Excel found a solution.
4. Notice that Excel entered the value *81.5* in B9. This is the score Whitney must earn in order to achieve a final average grade of 76%.
5. Assume that Whitney wants to achieve a final average grade of 80%. Use Goal Seek to find the value that she will need to earn on the final test to accomplish the new target by completing the following steps:
   a. Click the What-If Analysis button in the Data Tools group and then click *Goal Seek* at the drop-down list.
   b. Click in the *To value* text box, type **80**, and then press Tab.
   c. Type **b9** in the *By changing cell* text box.
   d. Click OK.

What-If Analysis
Group
Ungroup
Scenario Manager...
Goal Seek...
Data Table...
Step 3c

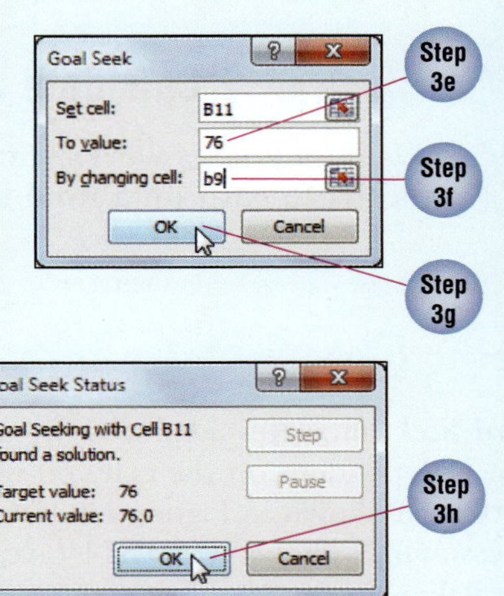

e. Notice that the value returned in B9 is 101.5. This is the new value Excel has calculated Whitney needs on the final test in order to earn an 80% final average grade.

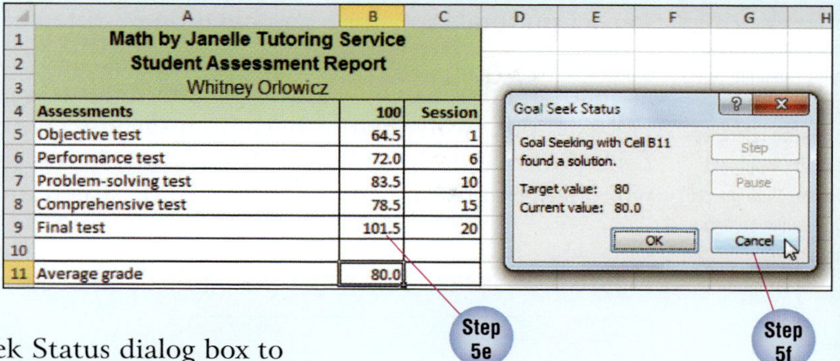

f. Click the Cancel button at the Goal Seek Status dialog box to restore the previous values since Whitney would not be able to score over 100 on the final test.

6. Save, print, and then close **EL2-C5-P2-JanelleTutorOrlowiczRpt.xlsx**.

Project 3 Forecast a Budget Based on Various Inflation Rates

3 Parts

You will determine the impact on a department's budget of various inflation rates to determine the funding request to present to management to maintain service.

Creating Assumptions for What-If Analysis Using Scenario Manager

The ***Scenario Manager*** allows you to store multiple sets of assumptions about data and then view the impact of those assumptions on your worksheet. You can switch the display between scenarios to test the various inputs on your worksheet model. You can save each scenario using a descriptive name such as *Best Case* or *Worst Case* to indicate the type of data assumptions you have stored. Examine the worksheet shown in Figure 5.4. In this worksheet, the Computing Services department budget for the next year has been calculated based on projected increases for various expense items. Assume that the department manager has more than one estimate for the percentages based on different inflation rates or vendor rate increases for

Quick Steps

Add a Scenario

1. Click Data tab.
2. Click What-If Analysis button.
3. Click *Scenario Manager*.
4. Click Add button.
5. Type name in *Scenario name* text box.
6. Type or select variable cells in *Changing cells* text box.
7. Click OK.
8. Enter values for each changing cell.
9. Click OK.
10. Click Close button.

Scenario Manager

Figure 5.4 Project 3 Worksheet

	A	B	C	D
1	National Online Marketing Inc.			
2	Computing Services Department			
3		Current budget	Projected increase	New budget
4	Wages and benefits	371,875	13,016	384,891
5	Computer supplies	150,350	2,255	152,605
6	Training and development	63,850	6,385	70,235
7	Other administrative costs	49,576	2,479	52,055
8	Total costs:	635,651		659,786

Create a range name for each changing cell. This allows you to see a descriptive reference next to the input text box rather than the cell address when adding a scenario.

next year. The manager can create and save various scenarios in order to view the impact on total costs for a combination of different forecasts.

Using the Scenario Manager dialog box shown in Figure 5.5 you can create as many models as you want to save in order to test various what-if conditions. For example, two scenarios have been saved in the example shown in Figure 5.5, *LowInflation* and *HighInflation*. When you add a scenario, you define which cells will change and then enter the data to be stored under the scenario name.

Figure 5.5 Scenario Manager Dialog Box and Scenario Values Dialog Box

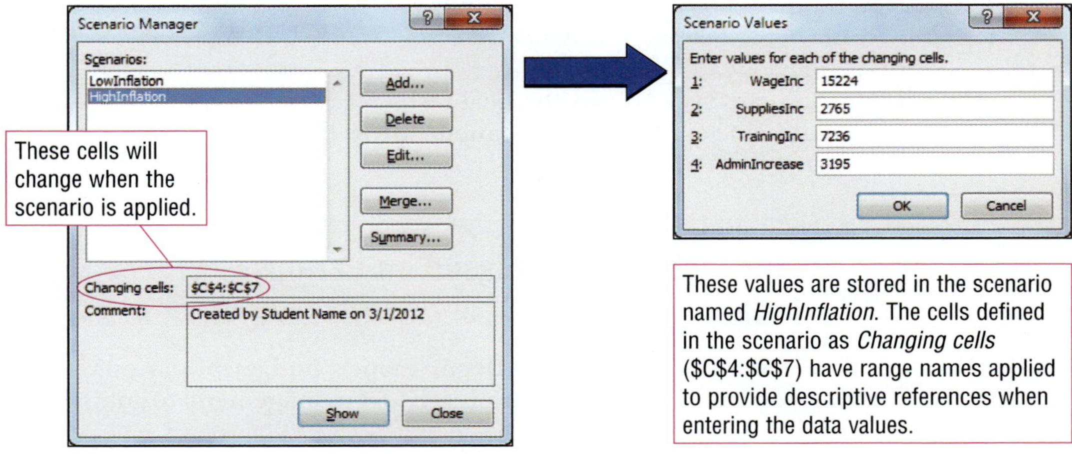

Project 3a Adding Scenarios to a Worksheet Model

Part 1 of 3

1. Open **NationalCSDeptBdgt.xlsx**.
2. Save the workbook with Save As and name it **EL2-C5-P3-NationalCSDeptBdgt**.
3. View the range names already created in the worksheet by clicking the down-pointing arrow at the right of the *Name* text box and then clicking *WageInc* at the drop-down list. The active cell moves to C4. A range name has been created for each data cell in column C to allow a descriptive label to show when you add scenarios in Steps 4 and 5.
4. Add a scenario with values assuming a low inflation rate for next year by completing the following steps:
   a. Click the Data tab.
   b. Click the What-If Analysis button in the Data Tools group and then click *Scenario Manager* at the drop-down list.
   c. Click the Add button at the Scenario Manager dialog box.
   d. At the Add Scenario dialog box with the insertion point positioned in the *Scenario name* text box, type **LowInflation** and then press Tab.
   e. Type **c4:c7** in the *Changing cells* text box and then press Enter or click OK. (As an alternative, you can move the dialog box out of the way and select the cells that will change in the worksheet.)

Add Scenario — Scenario name: LowInflation (Step 4d); Changing cells: c4:c7 (Step 4e); Ctrl+click cells to select non-adjacent changing cells.; Comment: Created by Student Name on 3/1/2012; Protection: Prevent, Hide; OK; Cancel

By default, Excel stores the user name and the date the scenario was created

f. With the insertion point positioned in the first text box labeled *1: WageInc*, type **12010** and press Tab.
g. Type **2150** and press Tab.
h. Type **5276** and press Tab.
i. Type **1998** and then press Enter or click OK.

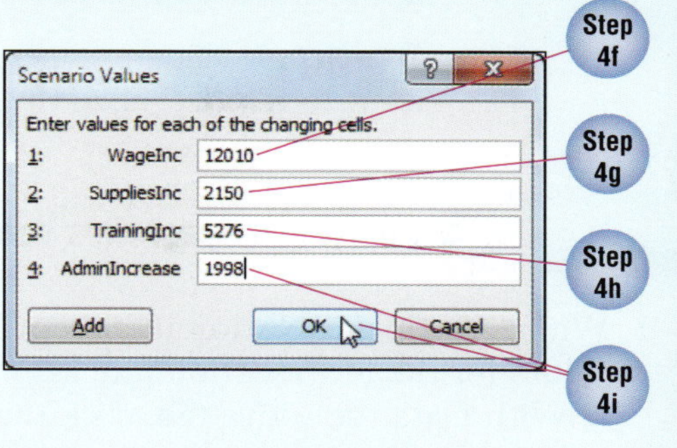

5. Add a second scenario to the worksheet assuming a high inflation rate by completing the following steps:
   a. Click the Add button at the Scenario Manager dialog box.
   b. Type **HighInflation** in the *Scenario name* text box and then click OK. Notice the *Changing cells* text box already contains the range C4:C7.
   c. At the Scenario Values dialog box, add the following values in the text boxes indicated:

1: WageInc	**15224**
2: SuppliesInc	**2765**
3: TrainingInc	**7236**
4: AdminIncrease	**3195**

   d. Click OK.

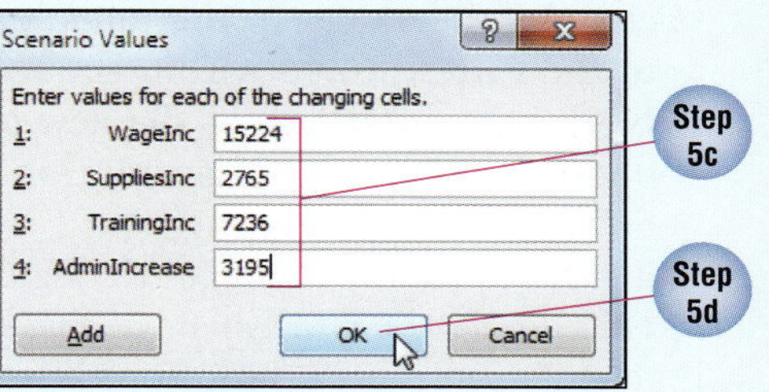

6. Add a third scenario named *OriginalForecast* that contains the original worksheet's values by completing the following steps:
   a. Click the Add button at the Scenario Manager dialog box.
   b. Type **OriginalForecast** in the *Scenario name* text box and then click OK.
   c. At the Scenario Values dialog box, notice the original values are already entered in each text box. Click OK.
7. Click the Close button to close the Scenario Manager dialog box.
8. Save **EL2-C5-P3-NationalCSDeptBdgt.xlsx**.

Applying a Scenario

After you have created the various scenarios you want to save with the worksheet, you can apply the values stored in a scenario to the variable cells to view the effects on your worksheet model. To do this, open the Scenario Manager dialog box, click the name of the scenario that contains the values you want to apply to the worksheet, and then click the Show button. Generally, you should create a scenario with the original values in the worksheet since Excel replaces the changing cell's contents when you show a scenario.

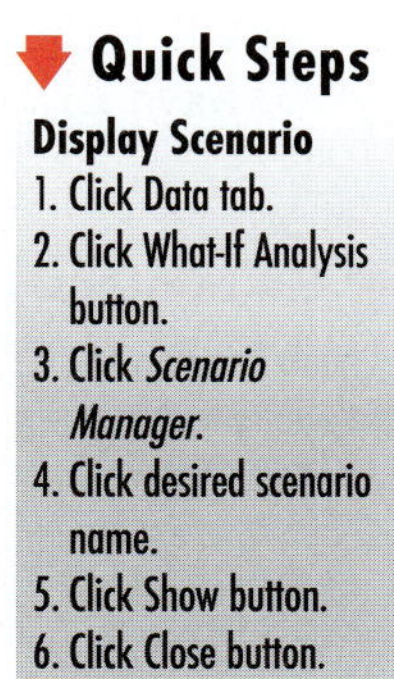

Quick Steps
Display Scenario
1. Click Data tab.
2. Click What-If Analysis button.
3. Click Scenario Manager.
4. Click desired scenario name.
5. Click Show button.
6. Click Close button.

Editing a Scenario

Change the values associated with a scenario by opening the Scenario Manager dialog box, clicking the name of the scenario that contains the values you want to change, and then clicking the Edit button. At the Edit Scenario dialog box, make any desired changes to the scenario name and/or changing cells and click OK to open the Scenario Values dialog box to edit the individual values associated with each changing cell. Click OK and then click Close when finished editing.

Deleting a Scenario

To delete a scenario, open the Scenario Manager dialog box, click the scenario you want to remove, click the Delete button, and then click the Close button.

Project 3b **Applying a Scenario's Values to the Worksheet** Part 2 of 3

1. With **EL2-C5-P3-NationalCSDeptBdgt.xlsx** open, apply the scenario containing the values for the low inflation rate assumptions by completing the following steps:
   a. With Data the active tab, click the What-If Analysis button and then click *Scenario Manager* at the drop-down list.
   b. Click *LowInflation* in the *Scenarios* list box and then click the Show button. Excel changes the values in the range C4:C7 to the values stored within the scenario. Notice the total cost of the new budget under a low inflation assumption is $657,085.

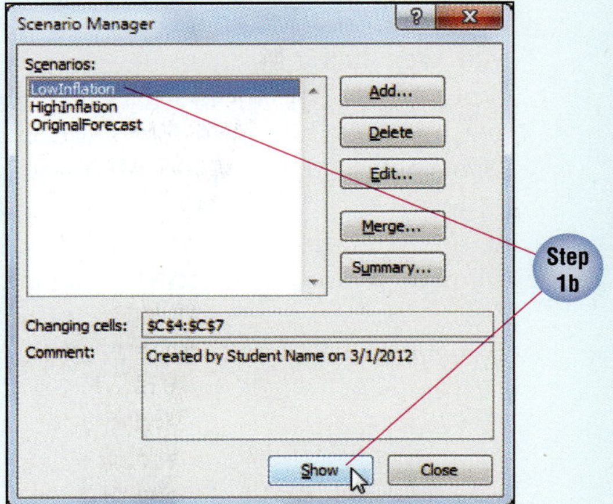

2. With the Scenario Manager dialog box still open, change the worksheet to display the high inflation rate assumptions by clicking *HighInflation* in the *Scenarios* list box and then clicking the Show button. Notice the total cost of the new budget under the high inflation assumption is $664,071.

	A	B	C	D
1	National Online Marketing Inc.			
2	Computing Services Department			
3		Current budget	Projected increase	New budget
4	Wages and benefits	371,875	15,224	387,099
5	Computer supplies	150,350	2,765	153,115
6	Training and development	63,850	7,236	71,086
7	Other administrative costs	49,576	3,195	52,771
8	Total costs:	635,651		664,071

worksheet with *HighInflation* values shown at Step 2

3. Show the worksheet with the *OriginalForecast* scenario's data values.
4. Click the Close button.

5. Save **EL2-C5-P3-NationalCSDeptBdgt.xlsx**.

Quick Steps

Create Scenario Summary Report
1. Click Data tab.
2. Click What-If Analysis button.
3. Click *Scenario Manager.*
4. Click Summary button.
5. If necessary, change cell address in *Result cells* text box.
6. Click OK.

Compiling a Scenario Summary Report

You can create a scenario summary report to compare scenarios side-by-side in a worksheet or a PivotTable. At the Scenario Summary dialog box shown in Figure 5.6 in the *Result cells* text box, enter the formula cell or cells that change by applying the data in the various scenarios. Enter multiple cell addresses in this text box separated by commas.

Figure 5.6 Scenario Summary Dialog Box

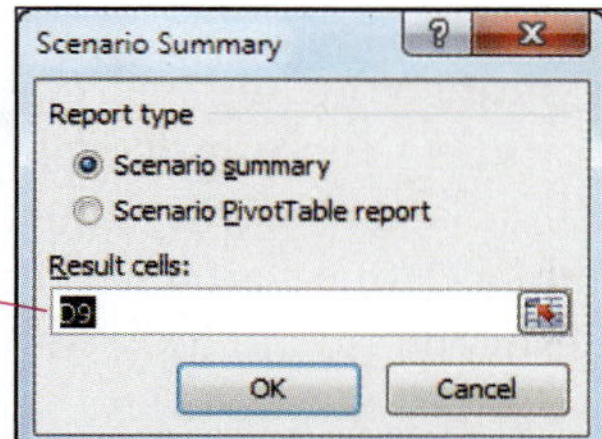

Project 3c Generating a Scenario Summary Report

Part 3 of 3

1. With **EL2-C5-P3-NationalCSDeptBdgt.xlsx** open, display a scenario summary report by completing the following steps:
   a. With Data the active tab, click the What-If Analysis button and then click *Scenario Manager* at the drop-down list.
   b. Click the Summary button at the Scenario Manager dialog box.
   c. At the Scenario Summary dialog box, with the *Report type* set to *Scenario summary* and the *Result cells* displaying the address *D8*, click OK.

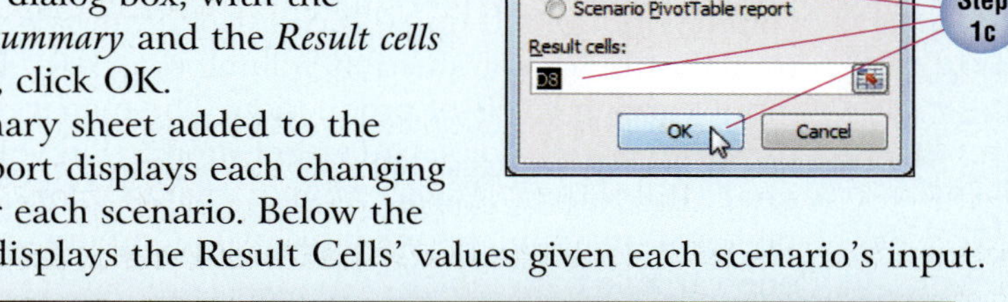

2. Examine the Scenario Summary sheet added to the workbook. The summary report displays each changing cell with the input values for each scenario. Below the Changing Cells table, Excel displays the Result Cells' values given each scenario's input.

Scenario Summary worksheet created at Step 1

Scenario Summary	Current Values:	LowInflation	HighInflation	OriginalForecast
Changing Cells:				
WageInc	13,016	12,010	15,224	13,016
SuppliesInc	2,255	2,150	2,765	2,255
TrainingInc	6,385	5,276	7,236	6,385
AdminIncrease	2,479	1,998	3,195	2,479
Result Cells:				
TotalNewCosts	659,786	657,085	664,071	659,786

Notes: Current Values column represents values of changing cells at time Scenario Summary Report was created. Changing cells for each scenario are highlighted in gray.

3. Print the Scenario Summary worksheet.
4. Save and then close **EL2-C5-P3-NationalCSDeptBdgt.xlsx**.

Project 4 Compare Impact of Various Inputs Related to Cost and Sales Pricing

2 Parts

Using a one-variable and a two-variable data table, you will analyze the impact on the cost per unit and selling price per unit of a manufactured container.

Performing What-If Analysis Using Data Tables

Data Table

Quick Steps

Create One-Variable Data Table

1. Create variable data in column at right of worksheet.
2. Enter formula one row above and one cell right of variable data.
3. Select data range including formula cell.
4. Click Data tab.
5. Click What-If Analysis button.
6. Click *Data Table*.
7. Type cell address for variable data in source formula in *Column input cell* text box.
8. Press Enter or click OK.

A ***data table*** is a range of cells that contains a series of input values. Excel calculates a formula substituting each input value in the data table range and places the result in the cell adjacent to the value. You can create a one-variable and a two-variable data table. A one-variable data table calculates a formula by modifying one input value in the formula. A two-variable data table calculates a formula substituting two input values. Data tables provide a means to analyze various outcomes in a calculation that occur as a result of changing a dependent value without creating multiple formulas.

Creating a One-Variable Data Table

Design a one-variable data table with the variable input data values either in a series down a column or across a row. Examine the worksheet shown in Figure 5.7. Assume that management wants to calculate the effects on the cost per unit for a variety of production volumes given a standard set of costs per factory shift. The worksheet includes the total costs for direct materials, direct labor, and overhead.

The formula in B8 sums the three cost categories. Based on a standard production volume of 500,000 units, the cost per unit is $3.21, calculated by dividing the total cost by the production volume (B8/B10). In E6:E12, the factory manager has input varying levels of production. The manager would like to see the change in the cost per unit for each level of production volume assuming the costs remain the same. In Project 4a, you will use a data table to show the various costs. This data table will manipulate one input value, production volume; therefore, the table is a one-variable data table.

Figure 5.7 Project 4a One-Variable Data Table

	A	B	C	D	E	F	G	H
1		Precision Design and Packaging						
2		Cost Price Analysis						
3		"E" Container Bulk Cargo Box						
4	Factory costs per shift				Variable unit production impact on cost			
5	Direct materials	$ 580,000						
6	Direct labor	880,552			425,000			
7	Overhead	145,350			450,000			
8	Total cost	$ 1,605,902			475,000			
9					500,000			
10	Standard production	500,000	units		525,000			
11					550,000			
12	Cost per unit	$ 3.21			575,000			

In this area of the worksheet, you can calculate the change in cost per unit based on varying the production volume using a data table.

Project 4a Creating a One-Variable Data Table

Part 1 of 2

1. Open **PrecisionEBoxCost.xlsx**.
2. Save the workbook with Save As and name it **EL2-C5-P4-PrecisionEBoxCost**.
3. Calculate the cost per unit for seven different production levels using a one-variable data table by completing the following steps:
   a. A data table requires that the formula for calculating the various outcomes be placed in the cell in the first row above and one column right of the table values. The data table's values have been entered in E6:E12; therefore, make F5 the active cell.
   b. The formula that calculates the cost per unit is =B8/B10. This formula has already been entered in B12. Link to the source formula by typing **=b12** and then pressing Enter.

			Variable unit production impact on cost		
$	580,000			=b12	
	880,552		425,000		
	145,350		450,000		
$	1,605,902		475,000		
			500,000		
	500,000	units	525,000		
			550,000		
$	3.21		575,000		

Step 3b

   c. Select E5:F12.
   d. Click the Data tab.
   e. Click the What-If Analysis button and then click *Data Table* at the drop-down list.

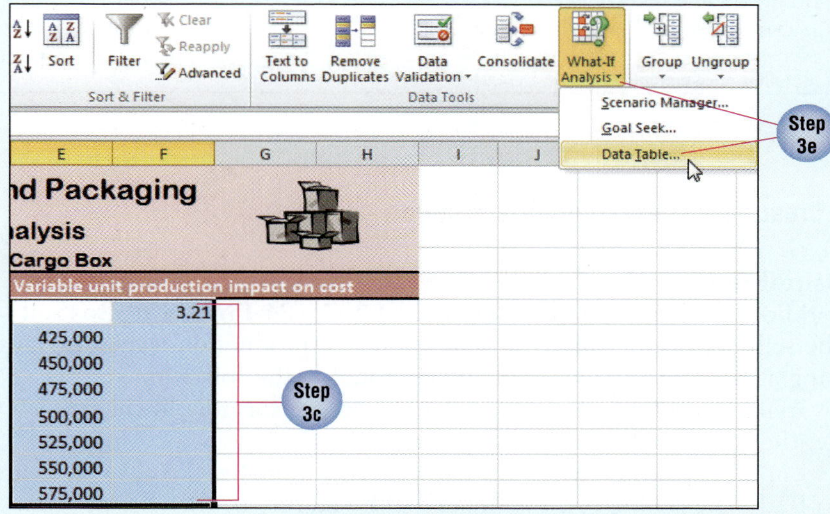

   f. At the Data Table dialog box, click in the *Column input cell* text box, type **b10**, and then press Enter or click OK. At the Data Table dialog box, Excel needs to know which reference in the source formula is the address for which the variable data is to be inserted. (The production volume is B10 in the source formula.)

Data Table
Row input cell:
Column input cell: b10
OK Cancel
Step 3f

   g. Click in any cell to deselect the range.
4. Print the worksheet.
5. Save and then close **EL2-C5-P4-PrecisionEBoxCost.xlsx**.

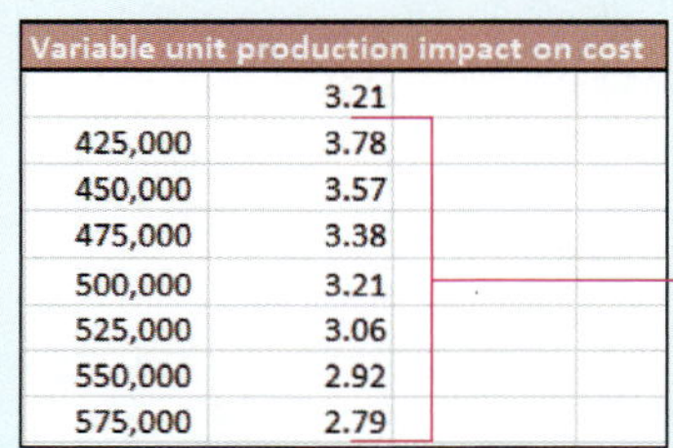

Variable unit production impact on cost		
	3.21	
425,000	3.78	
450,000	3.57	
475,000	3.38	
500,000	3.21	
525,000	3.06	
550,000	2.92	
575,000	2.79	

Costs are calculated by the data table at each production volume. Notice the costs are higher at lower volumes and decrease as production volume increases.

Quick Steps

Create Two-Variable Data Table

1. Create variable data at right of worksheet with one input series in a column and another in a row across the top of the table.
2. Enter formula in top left cell of table.
3. Select data table range.
4. Click Data tab.
5. Click What-If Analysis button.
6. Click *Data Table*.
7. Type cell address for variable data in source formula in *Row input cell* text box.
8. Press Tab.
9. Type cell address for variable data in source formula in *Column input cell* text box.
10. Press Enter or click OK.

Creating a Two-Variable Data Table

A data table can substitute two variables in a source formula. To modify two input cells, design the data table with a column along the left containing one set of variable input values and a row along the top of the table containing the second set of variable input values. In a two-variable data table, the source formula is placed at the top left cell in the table. In the worksheet shown in Figure 5.8, the source formula will be inserted in E5, which is the top left cell in the data table.

Figure 5.8 Project 4b Two-Variable Data Table

	A	B	C	D	E	F	G	H
1	Precision Design and Packaging							
2	Selling Price Analysis at Variable Production and Markups							
3	"E" Container Bulk Cargo Box							
4	Factory costs per shift				Variable unit production impact on sell price			
5	Direct materials	$ 580,000				50%	52%	55%
6	Direct labor	880,552			425,000			
7	Overhead	145,350			450,000			
8	Total cost	$ 1,605,902			475,000			
9					500,000			
10	Standard production	500,000	units		525,000			
11					550,000			
12	Cost per unit	$ 3.21			575,000			
13	Markup	52%						
14	Selling price per unit	$ 4.88						

This data table contains two input variables—production units and markup percentage. The data table will calculate a selling price at each production volume and at each markup percentage.

Project 4b **Creating a Two-Variable Data Table** Part 2 of 2

1. Open **PrecisionEBoxSell.xlsx**.
2. Save the workbook with Save As and name it **EL2-C5-P4-PrecisionEBoxSell**.
3. Calculate the selling price per unit for seven different production levels and three different markups using a two-variable data table by completing the following steps:
   a. In a two-variable data table, Excel requires the source formula in the top left cell in the data table; therefore, make E5 the active cell.
   b. Type **=b14** and press Enter. The formula that you want Excel to use to create the data table is in B14. The selling price is calculated by adding to the cost per unit (B12) an amount equal to the cost per unit times the markup percentage (B13).

			Variable unit
$ 580,000			=b14
880,552			425,000
145,350			450,000
$ 1,605,902			475,000
			500,000
500,000	units		525,000
			550,000
$ 3.21			575,000
52%			
$ 4.88			

Step 3b

   c. Select E5:H12.

d. Click the Data tab.
e. Click the What-If Analysis button and then click *Data Table* at the drop-down list.
f. At the Data Table dialog box with the insertion point positioned in the *Row input cell* text box, type **b13** and press Tab. Excel needs to know which reference in the source formula is the address relating to the variable data in the first row of the data table. (The markup value is in B13 in the source formula.)

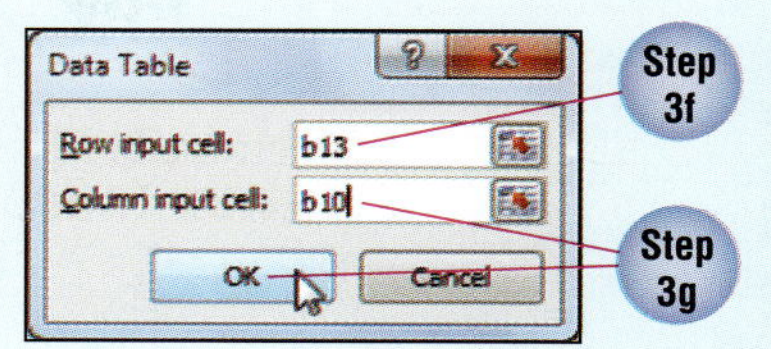

g. Type **b10** in the *Column input cell* text box and then press Enter or click OK. As in Project 4a, Excel needs to know which reference relates to the production volume in the source formula.
h. Click in any cell to deselect the range.

Variable unit production impact on sell price			
$ 4.88	50%	52%	55%
425,000	5.67	5.74	5.86
450,000	5.35	5.42	5.53
475,000	5.07	5.14	5.24
500,000	4.82	4.88	4.98
525,000	4.59	4.65	4.74
550,000	4.38	4.44	4.53
575,000	4.19	4.25	4.33

Selling prices are calculated by the data table at each production volume and at each percentage markup.

4. Print the worksheet.
5. Save and then close **EL2-C5-P4-PrecisionEBoxSell.xlsx**.

Project 5 Audit a Worksheet to View and Troubleshoot Formulas — 3 Parts

You will use buttons in the Formula Auditing group to view relationships between cells that comprise a formula, identify error codes in a worksheet, and troubleshoot errors using error checking tools.

Using Auditing Tools

The Formula Auditing group in the Formulas tab shown in Figure 5.9 contains buttons that are useful for viewing relationships between cells in formulas. Checking a formula for accuracy can be difficult when the formula is part of a complex sequence of operations. Opening a worksheet created by someone else can also present a challenge in understanding the relationships between sets of data. When Excel displays an error message in a cell, viewing the relationships between the dependencies of cells assists with finding the source of the error.

Quick Steps

Trace Precedent Cells
1. Open worksheet.
2. Make desired cell active.
3. Click Formulas tab.
4. Click Trace Precedents button.
5. Continue clicking until all relationships are visible.

Quick Steps

Trace Dependent Cells

1. Open worksheet.
2. Make desired cell active.
3. Click Formulas tab.
4. Click Trace Dependents button.
5. Continue clicking until all relationships are visible.

Figure 5.9 Formula Auditing Group in Formulas Tab

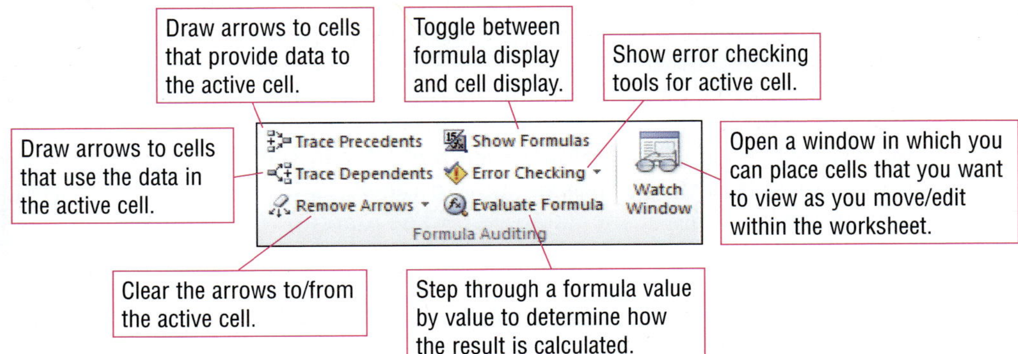

Draw arrows to cells that provide data to the active cell.
Toggle between formula display and cell display.
Show error checking tools for active cell.
Draw arrows to cells that use the data in the active cell.
Trace Precedents
Show Formulas
Trace Dependents
Error Checking
Remove Arrows
Evaluate Formula
Watch Window
Formula Auditing
Open a window in which you can place cells that you want to view as you move/edit within the worksheet.
Clear the arrows to/from the active cell.
Step through a formula value by value to determine how the result is calculated.

Trace Precedents and Trace Dependents

Trace Precedents

Trace Dependents

Remove Arrows

Show Formulas

Precedent cells are cells that provide data to a formula cell. For example, if cell B3 contains the formula =B1+B2, cell B1 and cell B2 are precedent cells. Dependent cells are cells that contain a formula that refers to other cells. In the previous example, cell B3 would be the dependent cell to cells B1 and B2 since B3 relies on the data from cells B1 and B2. Click a cell and click the Trace Precedents button to draw tracer arrows that show direct relationships to cell(s) that provide data to the active cell. Click the button a second time to show indirect relationships to cell(s) that provide data to the active cell at the next level. Continue clicking the button until no further arrows are drawn. Excel will sound a beep when you click the button if no more relationships exist.

Click a cell and click the Trace Dependents button to draw tracer arrows that show direct relationships to other cell(s) in the worksheet that use the active cell's contents. As with the Trace Precedents button, you can click a second time to show the next level of indirect relationships and continue clicking the button until no further tracer arrows are drawn.

Excel draws blue tracer arrows if no error is detected in the active cell and red tracer arrows if an error condition is detected within the active cell.

Project 5a Viewing Relationships between Cells and Formulas

Part 1 of 3

1. Open **EL2-C5-P4-PrecisionEBoxSell.xlsx**.
2. View relationships between cells and formulas by displaying tracer arrows between cells by completing the following steps:
   a. Make B8 the active cell.
   b. Click the Formulas tab.
   c. Click the Trace Precedents button in the Formula Auditing group. Excel draws a blue tracer arrow that shows the cells that provide data to B8.
   d. Click the Remove Arrows button in the Formula Auditing group. The blue tracer arrow leading to B8 is cleared.
   e. Make B14 the active cell.

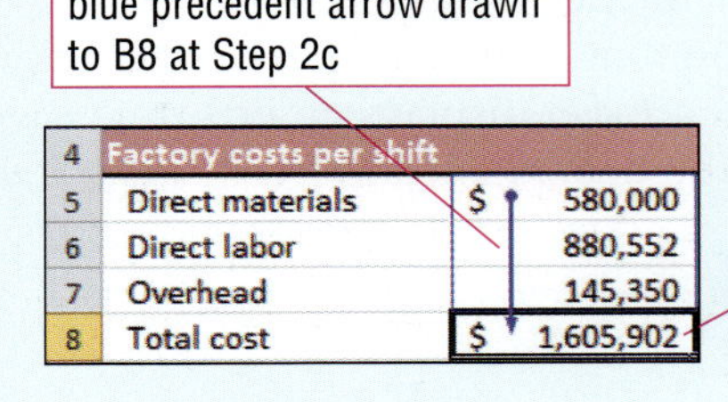

blue precedent arrow drawn to B8 at Step 2c
4 Factory costs per shift
5 Direct materials $ 580,000
6 Direct labor 880,552
7 Overhead 145,350
8 Total cost $ 1,605,902
Step 2a

f. Click the Trace Precedents button.
g. Click the Trace Precedents button a second time to show the next level of cells that provide data to B14.
h. Click the Trace Dependents button to view other cell(s) dependent on B14.

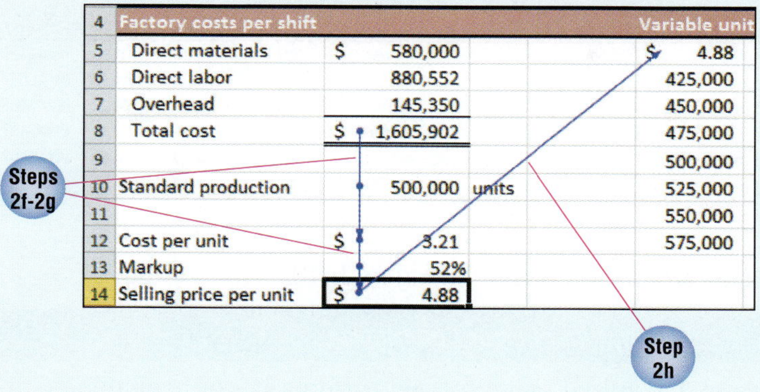

3. Click the Remove Arrows button to clear all of the arrows.
4. Click the Show Formulas button to display cell formulas. Click the Show Formulas button again to turn off the display of formulas.
5. Close **EL2-C5-P4-PrecisionEBoxSell.xlsx**. Click Don't Save when prompted to save changes.

Troubleshooting Formulas

Formulas in Excel can contain various types of errors. Some errors are obvious because Excel displays an error message such as *#VALUE!*. Other errors can occur that do not display error messages but are incorrect because the logic is flawed. For example, you could enter a formula in a cell which Excel does not flag as an error because the syntax is correct; however, the calculation could be incorrect for the data and the situation. Logic errors are difficult to find and require that you check a worksheet by entering proof formulas or by individually checking accuracy. A ***proof formula*** is a formula entered outside the main worksheet area that checks key figures within the worksheet. For example, in a payroll worksheet, a proof formula to check the total net pay column could add the total net pay to the totals of all of the deduction columns. The total displayed should be equal to the total gross pay amount in the worksheet.

Excel displays an error message code in a cell which is detected to have an error. Two types of error flags can occur. A green diagonal triangle in the upper left corner of a cell indicates an error condition. Activate the cell with the green triangle and an error checking button displays with which you can access error checking tools. Other cells indicate an error by displaying an entry such as *#NAME?*. Figure 5.10 displays a portion of the worksheet you will use in Project 5b to troubleshoot errors. Table 5.1 describes the three error codes that are displayed in Figure 5.10.

Reference errors can also occur—the formula uses correct syntax and logic but refers to the wrong data. These errors are difficult to find and only a thorough review and test of key figures reveal their existence.

Quick Steps

Trace Errors
1. Click cell containing error message.
2. Click Formulas tab.
3. Click down-pointing arrow on Error Checking button.
4. Click *Trace Error*.

Figure 5.10 Project 5b Partial Worksheet

	A	B	C	D	E	F	G	H	I	J	K
1	Precision Design and Packaging										
2	Bulk Container 2014 Sales Target by Region (in millions)										
3	Model Number	Description	Base	East	West	North	South	Total		Sales Target Assumptions	
4	PD-1140	Gaylord with lid	2.75	#NAME?	#N/A	2.81	2.80	#NAME?		East	1.50%
5	PD-2185	Premium Gaylord with lid	2.14	#VALUE!	#VALUE!	#VALUE!	#VALUE!	#VALUE!		West	#N/A
6	PD-1150	Gaylord bottom	2.33	#NAME?	#N/A	2.38	2.37	#NAME?		North	2.15%
7	PD-1155	Gaylord lid	1.85	#NAME?	#N/A	1.89	1.88	#NAME?		South	1.75%
8	PD-3695	Telescoping top and bottom	2.45	#NAME?	#N/A	2.50	2.49	#NAME?			
9	PD-3698	Telescoping bottom	2.96	#NAME?	#N/A	3.02	3.01	#NAME?			

Table 5.1 Error Codes in Worksheet Shown in Figure 5.10

Error Code	*Description of Error Condition*
#N/A	A required value for the formula is not available.
#NAME?	This error code indicates the formula contains an unrecognized entry.
#VALUE!	A value within the formula is of the wrong type or is otherwise invalid.

Error Checking

Evaluate Formula

The Error Checking button in the Formula Auditing group can be used to assist with finding the source of an error condition in a cell by displaying the Error Checking dialog box or by drawing a red tracer arrow to locate the source cell that is contributing to the error. The Evaluate Formula button can be used to step through a formula value by value to determine the position within the formula where an error exists.

Project 5b Troubleshooting Formulas

Part 2 of 3

1. Open **PrecisionSalesTrgt.xlsx**.
2. Save the workbook with Save As and name it **EL2-C5-P5-PrecisionSalesTrgt**.
3. Solve the #N/A error by completing the following steps:
   a. Make E4 the active cell.
   b. Point to the Trace Error button that displays next to the cell and read the ScreenTip that displays below the button.
   c. Look in the Formula bar at the formula that has been entered into the cell. Notice that the formula includes a reference to a named cell. You decide to use the tracer arrows to locate the source of the named cell.

d. Click the down-pointing arrow to the right of the Error Checking button in the Formula Auditing group of the Formulas tab and then click *Trace Error* at the drop-down list. Excel moves the active cell to K5 and draws a red tracer arrow from K5 to E4. Look in the Formula bar and notice that *#N/A* displays as the entry in K5. Also notice the cell name *West* displayed in the *Name* text box. Since a value does not exist in the cell named *West*, which is K5, the dependent cell E4 was not able to calculate its formula.

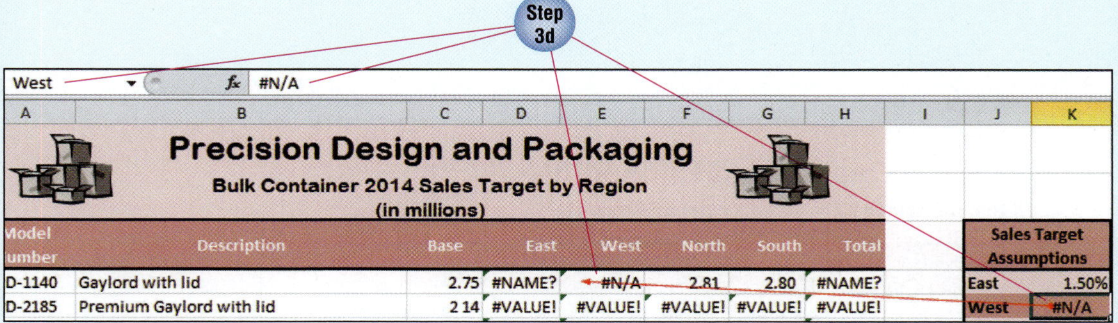

e. With K5 the active cell, type **1.25%** and press Enter. The red tracer arrow changes to blue now that the error is corrected and the #N/A error messages have disappeared.

f. Click the Remove Arrows button to clear the blue tracer arrow, and then right-align the entry in K5.

4. Solve the #NAME? error by completing the following steps:
   a. Make D4 the active cell, point to the Trace Error button that appears, and then read the ScreenTip that appears. The message indicates that the formula contains unrecognized text.
   b. Look at the entry in the Formula bar: *=C4+(C4*East)*. Notice the formula is the same as the formula you reviewed in Step 3c except that the named range is *East* instead of *West*. The formula appears to be valid.
   c. Click the down-pointing arrow to the right of the Name text box and view the range names in the drop-down list. Notice that a range named *East* is not in the list.
   d. Click *North* at the Name drop-down list. The active cell moves to K6. You know from this Step and from Step 3d that the named ranges should reference the percentage values within column K.
   e. Make K4 the active cell, type **East** in the Name text box, and press Enter. The #NAME? error is resolved.

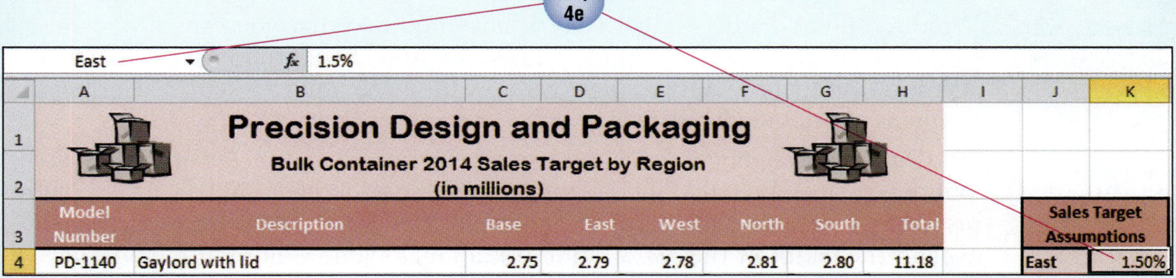

5. Solve the #VALUE! error by completing the following steps:
   a. Make D5 the active cell, point to the Trace Error button that appears, and then read the ScreenTip that appears. The message indicates that a value within the formula is of the wrong type.

b. Click the Trace Precedents button in the Formula Auditing group in the Formulas tab to display tracer arrows showing you the source cells that provide data to D5. Two blue arrows appear indicating two cells provide the source values: K4 and C5.
c. Make K4 the active cell and look at the entry in the Formula bar: *1.5%*. This value is valid.
d. Make C5 the active cell and look at the entry in the Formula bar: *2 14*. Notice there is a space instead of a decimal point between *2* and *1*.

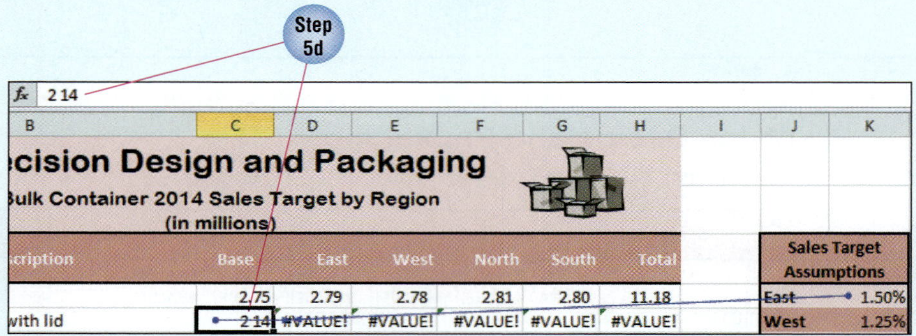

e. Click in the Formula bar and then edit the formula to delete the space between *2* and *1* and type a period to insert a decimal point. Press Enter. The #VALUE! error is resolved.
f. Click the Remove Arrows button to clear the blue tracer arrows.

6. Save **EL2-C5-P5-PrecisionSalesTrgt.xlsx**.

Quick Steps

Circle Invalid Data
1. Open worksheet containing validation rules.
2. Click Data tab.
3. Click down-pointing arrow on Data Validation button.
4. Click *Circle Invalid Data*.

Watch a Formula Cell
1. Click Formulas tab.
2. Click Watch Window button.
3. Click Add Watch button.
4. Click desired cell.
5. Click Add button.

Watch Window

Data Validation

Circling Invalid Data

Recall from Chapter 3 that Data Validation is a feature used to restrict entries entered into cells. If data validation rules have been set up after data has been entered, existing values are not tested against the new rules. In this situation, you can use the Circle Invalid Data feature to draw red circles around cells that do not conform to the new rule.

Watching a Formula

In a large worksheet, a dependent cell may not always be visible while you are making changes to other cells that affect a formula. You can open a Watch Window and add a dependent cell to the window so that you can view changes to the cell as you work within the worksheet. You can add multiple cells to the Watch Window providing a single window in which you can keep track of key formulas within a large worksheet.

Consider assigning a name to a cell that you want to track using the Watch Window. At the Watch Window, the cell's name will appear in the *Name* column providing you with a descriptive reference to the entry being watched. You can expand the width of the *Name* column if a range name is not entirely visible.

The Watch Window can be docked to the top, left, bottom, or right edge of the worksheet area by dragging the title bar of the window to the desired edge of the screen. Excel changes the window to a Watch Window task pane.

Circling Invalid Data and Watching a Formula Cell Part 3 of 3

1. With **EL2-C5-P5-PrecisionSalesTrgt.xlsx** open, view the Data Validation rule in effect for column C by completing the following steps:
   a. If necessary, make any cell containing a value in column C active.
   b. Click the Data tab.
   c. Click the top of the Data Validation button in the Data Tools group. (Do not click the down-pointing arrow on the button.) The Data Validation dialog box opens.
   d. Review the parameters for data entry in the Settings tab. Notice the restriction is that values should be greater than or equal to 1.57.
   e. Click OK.

2. Click the Data Validation button down-pointing arrow and then click *Circle Invalid Data* at the drop-down list. Three cells are circled in the worksheet: C11, C13, and C16.

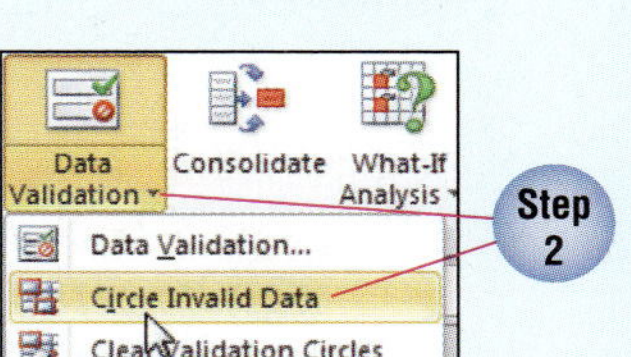

3. Watch the grand total cell update as you correct the invalid data by completing the following steps:
   a. Make H22 the active cell and then click the Formulas tab.
   b. Click the Watch Window button in the Formula Auditing group. A Watch Window opens.
   c. Click the Add Watch button in the Watch Window.
   d. At the Add Watch dialog box, move the dialog box out of the way if necessary to view cell H22. Notice H22 is entered by default as the watch cell. Click the Add button.

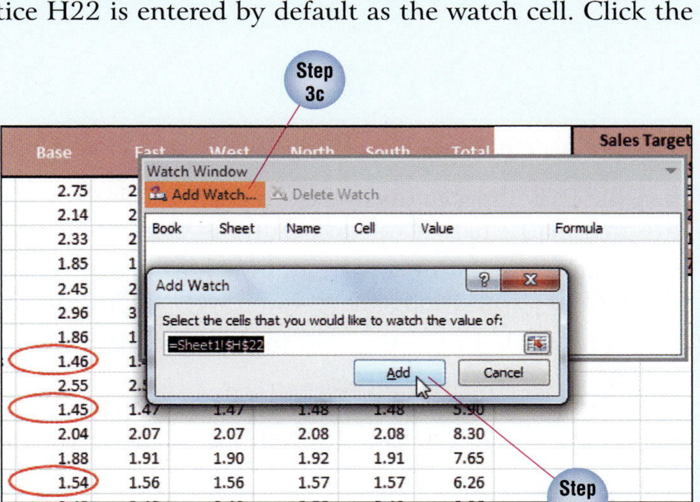

   e. Scroll up the worksheet if necessary until you can view C11. If necessary, drag the Watch Window to an out-of-the-way location in the worksheet.
   f. Make C11 the active cell, type 1.58, and press Enter. Notice the red circle disappears since you have now entered a value that conforms to the validation rule. Look at the value for H22 in the Watch Window. The new value is *153.67*.

g. Make C13 the active cell, type **1.61**, and press Enter. Look at the updated value for H22 in the Watch Window.

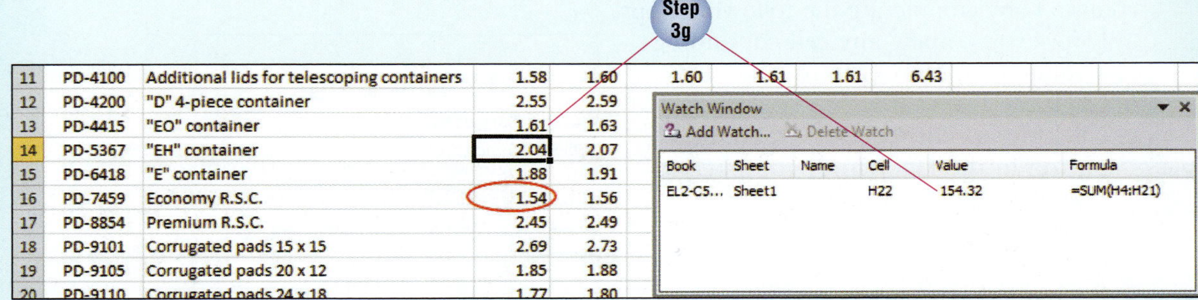

h. Make C16 the active cell, type **1.57**, and press Enter.
i. Click the Watch Window button to close the Watch Window.

4. Print the worksheet.
5. Save and then close **EL2-C5-P5-PrecisionSalesTrgt.xlsx**.

Checking a worksheet for accuracy using auditing and error checking tools is an important skill to develop. Worksheets provide critical information to decision-makers who rely on the validity of the data. After completing a worksheet, examine it carefully, looking for data entry mistakes, values that do not appear realistic, or other indications of potential errors that should be checked.

Chapter Summary

- Open the Paste Special dialog box to paste attributes of the source cell(s), or perform a mathematical operation during the paste.
- Transposing data during a paste routine means that data arranged in columns is converted to a row arrangement and rows are converted to columns.
- Click the Paste button arrow and then click *Paste Special* to access paste special options.
- The Goal Seek feature returns a value in a cell based on a target value you specify for another cell. The two cells must have a dependent relationship for Excel to calculate a value.
- Click the What-If Analysis button in the Data Tools group of the Data tab to locate the Goal Seek, the Scenario Manager, or the Data Table command.
- Scenario Manager allows you to save multiple sets of values for key cells in a worksheet. Switch between scenarios to view the impact of changing the input cells to one of the worksheet's saved data sets.

- A scenario summary report presents the input data for each key cell in a scenario in a tabular format with a results cell below each data set displaying the value if the data set is applied.
- A data table is a range of cells containing a series of input values with a calculated formula result adjacent to each input value.
- A one-variable data table modifies one input value within a formula.
- A two-variable data table modifies two input values within a formula.
- Design a one-variable data table with the input values in a columnar arrangement and the formula cell one row above and one column right of the input values.
- Design a two-variable data table with one set of input values in a columnar arrangement and the other set of input values starting in the first column right and first row above the first set of values. Add the formula cell to the top left cell within the input table.
- Buttons in the Formula Auditing group of the Formulas tab allow you to view relationships between cells and find and resolve errors.
- Use the Trace Precedents button to draw tracer arrows to cells that feed data into the active cell.
- Use the Trace Dependents button to draw tracer arrows to cells that use data from the active cell.
- Click the Trace Precedents or Trace Dependents button a second time to display an indirect set of relationship arrows at the next level.
- Logic errors occur when the formula is not correct for the data or the situation.
- Reference errors occur when a formula points to the wrong data cell.
- Use proof formulas to test the accuracy of key figures in a worksheet. A proof formula is entered outside the main worksheet area and double-checks data within the worksheet.
- Excel displays two types of error flags in a cell where an error has been detected.
- A green diagonal triangle in the upper left corner of the cell indicates an error is presumed. Click the active cell and use the Trace Error button to access error checking options.
- Error codes within a cell also indicate an error. For example, #NAME? means that the formula contains text that Excel cannot recognize.
- Other error codes include #VALUE?, which means a value within the formula is not valid, and #N/A, which means a value needed by the formula is not available.
- When a worksheet has data validation rules in force, data that was in existence before the rule was created is not tested. Use the Circle Invalid Data feature from the Data Validation button to place red circles around cells that do not test correct with the new rule.
- A Watch Window is a window that remains visible in the worksheet area while you scroll and edit other parts of a large worksheet. Add cells to the Watch Window that you want to keep an eye on while you make changes.
- After completing a worksheet, take time to examine the data carefully for data entry errors or logic errors that could impact the results.

Commands Review

FEATURE	RIBBON TAB, GROUP	BUTTON
Circle Invalid Data	Data, Data Tools	
Data Table	Data, Data Tools	
Goal Seek	Data, Data Tools	
Paste Special	Home, Clipboard	
Remove tracer arrows	Formulas, Formula Auditing	
Scenario Manager	Data, Data Tools	
Trace Dependents	Formulas, Formula Auditing	
Trace Error	Formulas, Formula Auditing	
Trace Precedents	Formulas, Formula Auditing	
Transpose	Home, Clipboard	
Watch Window	Formulas, Formula Auditing	

Concepts Check Test Your Knowledge

Completion: In the space provided at the right, indicate the correct term, command, or number.

1. This option from the Paste drop-down gallery will convert columns to rows and rows to columns. ____________________

2. Open this dialog box to perform a mathematical operation while pasting the copied range to the destination cells. ____________________

3. Use this feature if you know the end result you want to obtain but are not sure what input value you need to achieve the end value. ____________________

4. This feature allows you to store various sets of data for specified cells under a name. ____________________

5. This report compares various saved data sets side-by-side so you can view all of the results in one page. ____________________

6. A one-variable data table requires the formula to be entered at this location within the data table range. ____________________
7. In a two-variable data table, the source formula is entered at this location within the data table range. ____________________
8. The Data Table feature is accessed from this button. ____________________
9. Click this button to draw arrows to cells that feed data into the active cell. ____________________
10. Click this button to draw arrows to cells that use the data in the active cell. ____________________
11. This button in the Formula Auditing group can be used to assist with locating the source cell that is causing an error code. ____________________
12. This error code indicates that a value needed to calculate the formula result is not available. ____________________
13. This type of error occurs when the formula has correct syntax but is not correct for the data or the situation. ____________________
14. This type of formula is entered outside the main worksheet area and is used to check key figures within the worksheet. ____________________
15. Use this feature to test existing data in a worksheet that has had a new data validation rule created. ____________________

Skills Check Assess Your Performance

Assessment 1

CONVERT COLUMNS TO ROWS; ADD SOURCE CELLS TO DESTINATION CELLS; FILTER

1. Open **CutRateCars.xlsx**.
2. Save the workbook with Save As and name it **EL2-C5-A1-CutRateCars**.
3. Copy and paste A4:F12 below the worksheet, converting the data arrangement so that the columns become rows and vice versa.
4. Delete the original source data rows from the worksheet.
5. Adjust the merge and centering of the title rows across the top of the worksheet, adjust column widths as desired, and change any other formatting options you think would improve the appearance of the revised worksheet.
6. Copy the values in the *Shipping* column. Paste the values to the *Total Cost* values using an Add operation so that the Total Cost now includes the shipping fee.
7. Copy the values in the *Number of Cars* column. Paste the values to the *Total Cost* values using a Divide operation. Change the column heading from *Total Cost* to *Cost Per Car*. Adjust the column width as needed.

8. The values in the *Compact* column have a validation rule that you want to duplicate in the *Mid-Size* and *SUV* columns. Copy the *Compact* values and paste only the validation rule to the *Mid-Size* and *SUV* columns.
9. Save, print, and then close **EL2-C5-A1-CutRateCars.xlsx**.

Assessment 2

USE GOAL SEEK

1. Open **NationalCSDeptBdgt.xlsx**.
2. Save the workbook with Save As and name it **EL2-C5-A2-NationalCSDeptBdgt**.
3. Make D8 the active cell and open the Goal Seek dialog box.
4. Find the projected increase for *Wages and benefits* that will make the total cost of the new budget equal $655,000.
5. Accept the solution Goal Seek calculates.
6. Save, print, and then close **EL2-C5-A2-NationalCSDeptBdgt.xlsx**.

Assessment 3

USE SCENARIO MANAGER

1. Open **PrecisionCdnTarget.xlsx**.
2. Save the workbook with Save As and name it **EL2-C5-A3-PrecisionCdnTarget**.
3. Create scenarios to save various percentage data sets for the four regions using the following information:
   a. A scenario named *OriginalTarget* that stores the current values in K4:K7.
   b. A scenario named *LowSales* with the following values:
      East .20
      West .32
      Ontario .48
      Quebec .37
   c. A scenario named *HighSales* with the following values:
      East .36
      West .58
      Ontario .77
      Quebec .63
4. Apply the *LowSales* scenario and then print the worksheet.
5. Edit the *HighSales* scenario to change the Ontario value from *0.77* to *.73*. ***Hint: After selecting the scenario name and clicking the Edit button, click OK at the Edit Scenario dialog box to show the scenario values.***
6. Create a scenario summary report displaying H18 as the result cell.
7. Print the Scenario Summary sheet.
8. Save and then close **EL2-C5-A3-PrecisionCdnTarget.xlsx**.

Assessment

4 CREATE A TWO-VARIABLE DATA TABLE

1. Open **NationalCSDeptHlpDsk.xlsx**.
2. Save the workbook with Save As and name it **EL2-C5-A4-NationalCSDeptHlpDsk**.
3. Create a two-variable data table that will calculate the average cost per call in the data table for each level of total call minutes logged and at each average cost per minute.
4. Format the average costs to display two decimal places.
5. Save, print, and then close **EL2-C5-A4-NationalCSDeptHlpDsk.xlsx**.

Assessment

5 FIND AND CORRECT FORMULA ERRORS

1. Open **NationalCSDeptCapital.xlsx**.
2. Save the workbook with Save As and name it **EL2-C5-A5-NationalCSDeptCapital**.
3. Make D19 the active cell and use the Trace Error feature to draw red tracer arrows to find the source cell creating the #N/A error.
4. The CS department manager advises the cost of a Pix firewall is $4,720.00. Enter this data in the appropriate cell to correct the #N/A error.
5. Remove the tracer arrows.
6. The worksheet contains a logic error in one of the formulas. Find and correct the error.
7. Save, print, and then close **EL2-C5-A5-NationalCSDeptCapital.xlsx**.

Visual Benchmark Demonstrate Your Proficiency

1 FIND THE BASE HOURLY RATE FOR DRUM LESSONS

1. Open **DrumStudioLessons.xlsx**.
2. Save the workbook with Save As and name it **EL2-C5-VB1-DrumStudioLessons**.
3. The current worksheet is shown in Figure 5.11. The hourly rates in B5:B13 are linked to the cell named *BaseRate* which is located in B16. Intermediate-level and advanced-level lessons have $4 and $8 added to the hourly base rate.
4. The drum teacher wants to earn $2,645.50 per month from drum lessons (instead of the current total of $2,292.00). Use Goal Seek to change the base hourly rate to the required value needed to reach the drum teacher's target.
5. Save, print, and then close **EL2-C5-VB1-DrumStudioLessons.xlsx**.

Figure 5.11 Visual Benchmark

	A	B	C	D
1	THE DRUM STUDIO			
2	MONTHLY DRUM LESSON REVENUE			
3				
4	**Class**	**Hourly Rate**	**Registered Students**	**Monthly Revenue**
5	Basic Drum Theory	18.00	10	180.00
6	Beginner Rock Drumming	18.00	15	270.00
7	Intermediate Rock Drumming	22.00	8	176.00
8	Advanced Rock Drumming	26.00	4	104.00
9	Beginner Jazz Drumming	18.00	18	324.00
10	Developing Jazz Style	22.00	10	220.00
11	Single Pedal Drum Beats	18.00	22	396.00
12	Single Pedal Drum Fills	18.00	15	270.00
13	Bass Drum Doubles	22.00	16	352.00
14	**TOTAL**			**2,292.00**
15				
16	Base hourly rate for all lessons:	18.00		

2 CREATE SCENARIOS FOR DRUM LESSON REVENUE

1. Open **DrumStudioLessons.xlsx**.
2. Save the workbook with Save As and name it **EL2-C5-VB2-DrumStudioLessons**.
3. The drum teacher has decided to create three models for an increase in the base hourly rate charged for drum lessons before she decides which base rate to use for next year. Examine the Scenario Summary report shown in Figure 5.12. Create three scenarios to save the hourly base rates shown: Low Rate Increase, Mid Rate Increase, and High Rate Increase.
4. Generate the Scenario Summary report to show the monthly revenue for all classes at the three hourly base rates.
5. Format the report by changing fill color and font color and adding the descriptive text in row 7. Use your best judgment to match the colors shown in Figure 5.12.
6. Edit the Notes text in B20 so that the sentence correctly references the highlighted color for changing cells.
7. Print the Scenario Summary worksheet.
8. Save and then close **EL2-C5-VB2-DrumStudioLessons.xlsx**.

Figure 5.12 Visual Benchmark

	A	B	C	D	E	F	G
1							
2		**Scenario Summary**					
3				Current Values:	Low Rate Increase	Mid Rate Increase	High Rate Increase
5		Changing Cells:					
6			**BaseRate**	18.00	**20.00**	**22.00**	**24.00**
7		Result Cells:		***Monthly revenue for each lesson assuming no change in number of registered students***			
8			**BasicTheory**	180.00	200.00	220.00	240.00
9			**BegRock**	270.00	300.00	330.00	360.00
10			**IntRock**	176.00	192.00	208.00	224.00
11			**AdvRock**	104.00	112.00	120.00	128.00
12			**BegJazz**	324.00	360.00	396.00	432.00
13			**DevJazz**	220.00	240.00	260.00	280.00
14			**SinglePedalBeats**	396.00	440.00	484.00	528.00
15			**SinglePedalFills**	270.00	300.00	330.00	360.00
16			**BassDoubles**	352.00	384.00	416.00	448.00
17			**MonthlyRevTotal**	**2,292.00**	**2,528.00**	**2,764.00**	**3,000.00**
18		Notes: Current Values column represents values of changing cells at					
19		time Scenario Summary Report was created. Changing cells for each					
20		scenario are highlighted in green.					

Case Study Apply Your Skills

Part 1

Yolanda Robertson is continuing her work on the marketing information package for prospective new franchise owners. She has sent you a workbook named **PizzaByMarioStartup.xlsx**. The workbook contains information on the estimated capital investment required to start up a new franchise along with estimated sales and profits for the first year. The workbook calculates the number of months in which a new franchisee can expect to recoup his or her investment based on estimated sales and profits for the first year. Yolanda wants you to apply what-if analysis to find out the value that is needed for projected sales in Year 1 in order to pay back the initial investment in 12 months (instead of 17). Accept the proposed solution and use Save As to name the revised workbook **EL2-C5-CS-P1-PizzaByMarioStartup**. Print the worksheet.

Part 2

After reviewing the printout from Part 1, Yolanda is concerned that the revised sales figure is not attainable in the first year. Restore the sales for year 1 to the original value of $485,000. Yolanda has created the following three models for the startup investment worksheet.

Item	*Conservative*	*Optimistic*	*Aggressive*
Projected Sales	$450,000	$590,000	$615,000
Profit Percent	20%	22%	18%

Yolanda would like you to set up the worksheet to save each of these models. ***Hint: Use a comma to separate two cell references as the changing cells***. Create a report that shows Yolanda the input variables for each model and the impact of each on the number of months to recoup the initial investment. Save the revised workbook as **EL2-C5-CS-P2-PizzaByMarioStartup**. Print the summary report. Switch to the worksheet and show the model that reduces the number of months to recoup the initial investment to the lowest value. Print the worksheet. Save **EL2-C5-CS-P2-PizzaByMarioStartup**.

Part 3

Help

Yolanda would like you to check each formula in the worksheet to make sure the formulas are accurate before submitting this worksheet to the client. Since you did not create this worksheet, you decide to check if there is a feature in Excel that navigates to formula cells automatically so that you do not miss any calculated cells. Use the Help feature to find out how to select cells that contain formulas. Based on the information you learned in Help, select the cells within the worksheet that contain formulas and then review each formula cell in the Formula bar to ensure the formula is logically correct. ***Hint: When the formula cells are selected as a group, press the Enter key to move to the next formula cell without losing the selection***. When you are finished reviewing the formula cells, type the name of the feature you used in a blank cell below the worksheet and then print the worksheet. Save the revised workbook and name it **EL2-C5-CS-P3-PizzaByMarioStartup**.

Part 4

When meeting with a prospective franchise owner, Yolanda expects that the money required for the initial capital investment will present a challenge for some people that do not have an excellent credit rating. Assume that the owners of Pizza by Mario would be willing to finance the initial investment. Search the Internet for current lending rates for secured credit lines at the bank at which you have an account. In a new worksheet within the workbook, document the current loan rate that you found and the URL of the bank website from which you obtained the rate. Add two percentage points to the lending rate to compensate the owners for the higher risk associated with financing the startup. Create a linked cell in the new worksheet to the Total Estimated Initial Investment in Sheet1. Calculate the monthly loan payment for a term of five years. Add appropriate labels to describe the data and format the worksheet as desired to improve the worksheet appearance. Save the revised workbook and name it **EL2-C5-CS-P4-PizzaByMarioStartup**. Print the loan worksheet.

Microsoft® Excel

Protecting and Sharing Workbooks

CHAPTER

PERFORMANCE OBJECTIVES

Upon successful completion of Chapter 6, you will be able to:

- **Add information to a workbook's properties**
- **Add comments containing additional information or other notes to the reader**
- **Share a workbook with other people and view other users who have the shared workbook open at the same time**
- **Edit a shared workbook and resolve conflicts with changes**
- **Print a history of changes made to a shared workbook**
- **Stop sharing a workbook**
- **Protect cells within a worksheet to prevent changes**
- **Add a password to open a workbook**
- **Track changes made to a workbook**
- **Modify and resolve tracked changes**

Tutorials

6.1 Inserting and Editing Comments
6.2 Adding Workbook Properties
6.3 Printing and Editing Comments
6.4 Sharing a Workbook
6.5 Resolving Conflicts in a Shared Workbook
6.6 Protecting and Unprotecting Worksheets
6.7 Protecting and Unprotecting Workbook Structure
6.8 Adding Password Protection to a Workbook
6.9 Tracking Changes

In today's electronic business environment, collaborating with other people on an Excel workbook is becoming commonplace. Excel includes several features and tools which are useful for working in a collaborative environment. Adding information to a workbook's properties provides descriptive information about the nature and purpose of the workbook to other editors. Attaching a comment to a cell allows you to add explanatory information or ask questions when collaborating with others. Sharing a workbook, locking and unlocking worksheets and ranges, and tracking changes are all vital features for managing data accessed by multiple individuals. Through completing the projects in this chapter, you will learn how to use the collaborative tools in Excel. Model answers for this chapter's projects appear on the following page.

Excel2010L2C6

Note: Before beginning the projects, copy to your storage medium the Excel2010L2C6 subfolder from the Excel2010L2 folder on the CD that accompanies this textbook and then make Excel2010L2C6 the active folder.

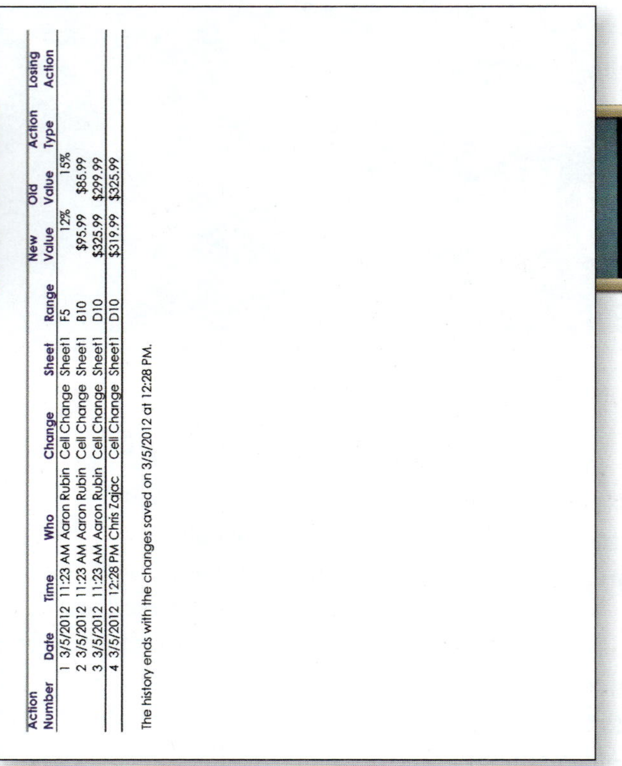

Action Number	Date	Time	Who	Change	Sheet	Range	New Value	Old Value	Action Type	Losing Action
1	3/5/2012	11:23 AM	Aaron Rubin	Cell Change	Sheet1	F5	12%	15%		
2	3/5/2012	11:23 AM	Aaron Rubin	Cell Change	Sheet1	B10	$95.99	$85.99		
3	3/5/2012	11:23 AM	Aaron Rubin	Cell Change	Sheet1	D10	$325.99	$299.99		
4	3/5/2012	12:28 PM	Chris Zajac	Cell Change	Sheet1	D10	$319.99	$325.99		

The history ends with the changes saved on 3/5/2012 at 12:28 PM.

Project 1 Add Workbook Properties, Insert Comments, and Share a Workbook Project 1g, EL2-C6-P1-CutRatePricing-Shared.xlsx History Sheet

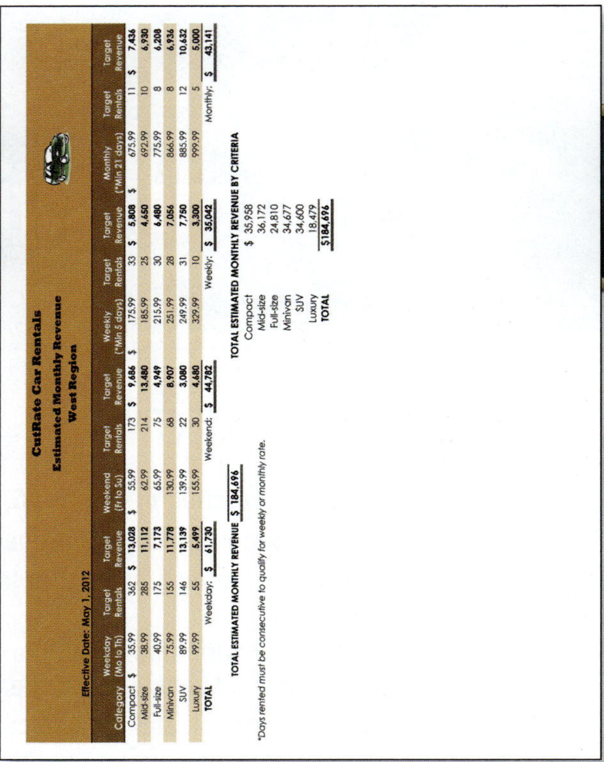

CutRate Car Rentals
Estimated Monthly Revenue
West Region

Effective Date: May 1, 2012

Category	Weekday (Mo to Th)	Target Rentals	Target Revenue	Weekend (Fr to Su)	Target Rentals	Target Revenue	Weekly (*Min 5 days)	Target Rentals	Target Revenue	Monthly (*Min 21 days)	Target Rentals	Target Revenue
Compact	$ 35.99	362	$ 13,028	$ 55.99	173	$ 9,686	$ 175.99	33	$ 5,808	$ 675.99	11	$ 7,436
Mid-size	38.99	285	11,112	62.99	214	13,480	185.99	25	4,650	692.99	10	6,930
Full-size	40.99	175	7,173	65.99	75	4,949	215.99	30	6,480	775.99	8	6,208
Minivan	75.99	155	11,778	130.99	68	8,907	251.99	28	7,056	866.99	8	6,936
SUV	89.99	146	13,139	139.99	22	3,080	249.99	31	7,750	885.99	12	10,632
Luxury	99.99	55	5,499	155.99	30	4,680	329.99	10	3,300	999.99	5	5,000
TOTAL		Weekday:	$ 61,730		Weekend:	$ 44,782		Weekly:	$ 35,042		Monthly:	$ 43,141

TOTAL ESTIMATED MONTHLY REVENUE $ 184,696

TOTAL ESTIMATED MONTHLY REVENUE BY CRITERIA

Compact	$ 35,958
Mid-size	36,172
Full-size	24,810
Minivan	34,677
SUV	34,600
Luxury	18,479
TOTAL	$184,696

*Days rented must be consecutive to qualify for weekly or monthly rate.

Project 3 Track and Resolve Changes Made to a Workbook Project 3c, EL2-C6-P3-CutRateWestRegion.xlsx

Project 1 Add Workbook Properties, Insert Comments, and Share a Workbook — 7 Parts

You will add the author's name and other descriptive information in a workbook's properties, insert comments with explanatory information, and then share the workbook with other users for editing purposes.

Adding Workbook Properties

Quick Steps

Add Information to Properties
1. Click File tab.
2. Click *Add a [property]* next to desired property name.
3. Type desired text.
4. Click outside property box.

Workbook properties include information about the workbook such as the author's name, a title, a subject, a category to which the workbook is related (such as *Finance*), and general comments about the workbook. This information can be added to the file at the Info tab Backstage view shown in Figure 6.1 or by using the Document Information Panel shown in Figure 6.2.

Some information is added to file properties automatically by Microsoft Excel. For example, workbook statistics such as the date the workbook was created, the date the workbook was last modified, and the name of the last person to save the workbook are maintained by Excel. Workbook properties are sometimes referred to as ***metadata***. Metadata is a term used to identify descriptive information about data.

Figure 6.1 Properties Pane in the Info Tab Backstage View

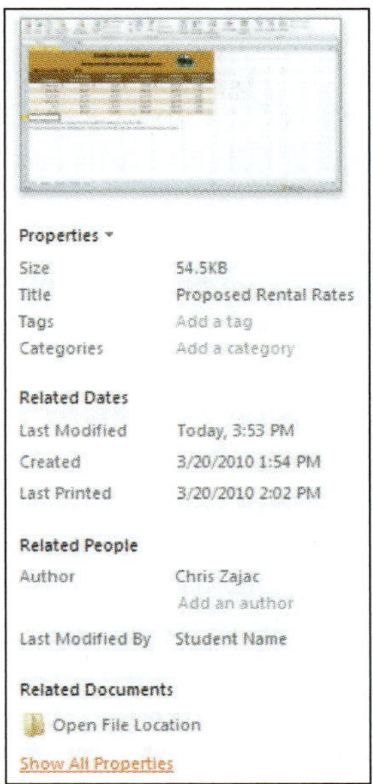

Figure 6.2 Document Information Panel

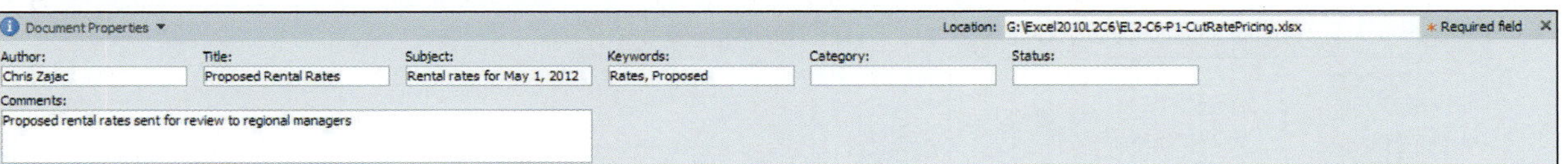

To add an author's name or other descriptive information about a workbook, click the File tab. By default, Excel displays the Info tab Backstage view with the workbook's properties displayed in the right pane. By default, Excel inserts in the *Author* property the name of the computer user (as defined when Microsoft Office is installed) when a new workbook is created. To add another author or make a change to a workbook property (such as Title), click the mouse to open the text box next to the property's name. For example, click over *Add a title* next to the Title property. A text box opens in which you can type the desired title. Click outside the text box to end the entry. Properties that do not display with a message *Add a [property]* cannot be edited. Click the hyperlink Show All Properties at the bottom of the right pane in the Info tab Backstage view to add more properties to the view.

The Document Information Panel shown in Figure 6.2 displays between the ribbon and the worksheet. If you prefer to add or edit properties while viewing the worksheet, open the panel by clicking the Properties button at the top of the right pane in the Info tab Backstage view and then click *Show Document Panel* at the drop-down list.

In Chapter 8, you will learn how to strip metadata including personal information from the file if you do not wish this information to be included when distributing a workbook outside your organization. Personal information can be useful, however, when you are browsing a list. The *Authors*, *Size*, and *Date Modified* appear in a ScreenTip when the mouse pointer rests on a workbook name in the Open dialog box. This information helps you select the correct file.

Quick Steps

Add or Edit Properties Using Document Information Panel

1. Click File tab.
2. Click Properties button.
3. Click *Show Document Panel*.
4. Add or edit properties as required.
5. Close Document Information Panel.

Project 1a Adding Information to Workbook Properties

1. Open **CutRatePricing.xlsx**.
2. Save the workbook with Save As and name it **EL2-C6-P1-CutRatePricing**.
3. Add an additional author's name, add a title, a subject, and comments to be associated with the workbook by completing the following steps:
   a. Click the File tab.
   b. At the Info tab Backstage view, click *Add an author* below the current author's name in the *Related People* section of the right pane to open an author property box.
   c. Type **Chris Zajac**.
   d. Click outside the author property box to close it.
   e. Click *Add a title* next to the *Title* property, type **Proposed Rental Rates**, and then click outside the title property box.
   f. Click the Show All Properties hyperlink at the bottom of the Properties pane to display additional properties.
   g. Click *Specify the subject* next to the *Subject* property, type **Rental rates for May 1, 2012**, and then click outside the subject property box.
   h. Click *Add comments* next to the *Comments* property, type **Proposed rental rates sent for review to regional managers**, and then click outside the comments property box.

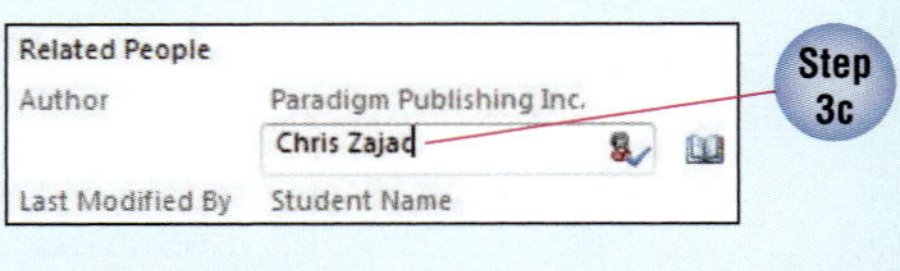

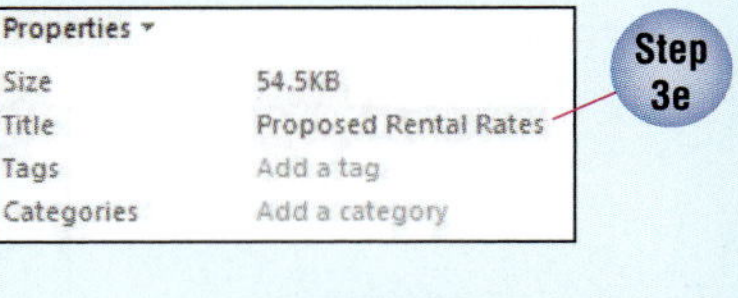

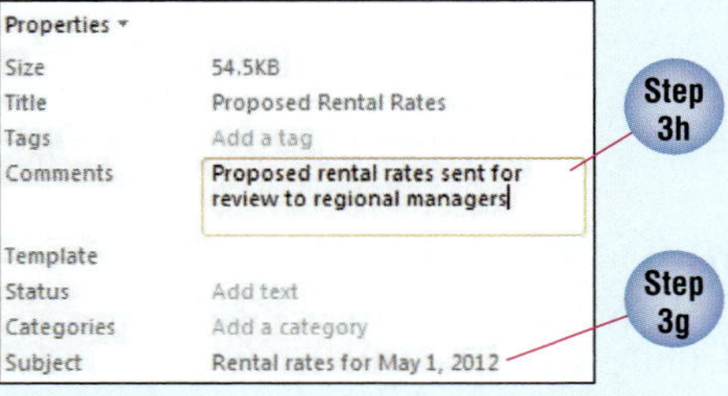

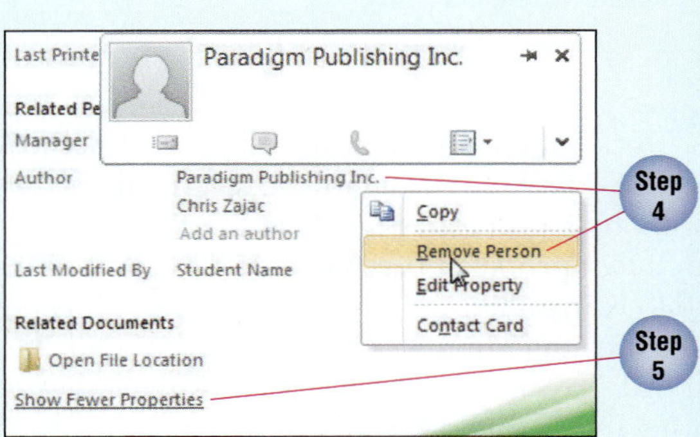

4. Right-click over *Paradigm Publishing Inc.* next to the *Author* property and then click *Remove Person* at the drop-down list.
5. Click the Show Fewer Properties hyperlink at the bottom of the Properties pane.
6. Compare your Properties pane with the one shown in Figure 6.1.
7. View the Document Information Panel and add text to a workbook property by completing the following steps:
   a. Click the Properties button at the top of the Properties pane (located below the miniature Excel worksheet) and then click *Show Document Panel* at the drop-down list. The Info tab Backstage view closes and the Document Information Panel displays between the ribbon and the worksheet. Using this panel you can view the worksheet while adding or modifying properties.
   b. Click in the *Keywords* property box, type **Rates, Proposed**, and then press Tab.
   c. Compare your Document Information Panel with the one shown in Figure 6.2.

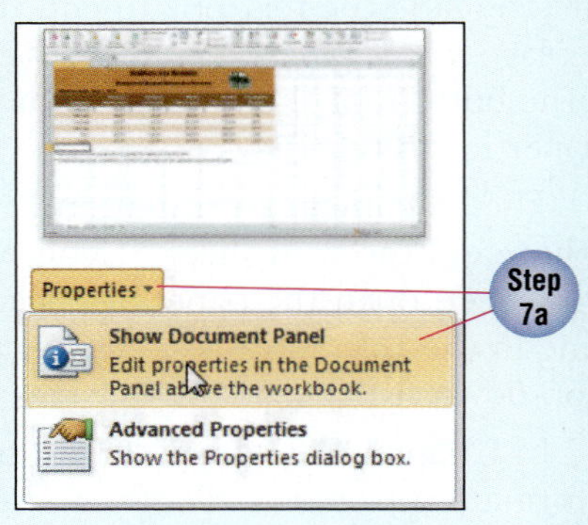

d. Click the Close button located at the top right corner of the Document Information Panel. Be careful to click the Close button within the Document Information Panel and not the Close button located at the top right of the ribbon.

Step 7d

8. Save **EL2-C6-P1-CutRatePricing.xlsx**.

Managing Comments

A ***comment*** is a pop-up box containing text that displays when the pointer is resting over a cell with an attached comment. Use a comment to provide instructions, identify critical information, or add other explanatory information about the cell entry. A comment is also useful when reviewing a worksheet with coworkers or other people with whom you are collaborating. Comments can be used by each reviewer to add his or her feedback or pose questions about a cell entry or layout.

Quick Steps

Insert Comment
1. Make desired cell active.
2. Click Review tab.
3. Click New Comment button.
4. Type comment text.
5. Click in worksheet area outside comment box.

Inserting a Comment

Insert a comment by clicking the Review tab and then clicking the New Comment button in the Comments group. This displays a shaded box with the user's name inside. Type the comment text and then click in the worksheet area outside the comment box. You can also insert a comment by right-clicking a cell and then clicking *Insert Comment* at the shortcut menu.

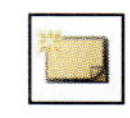

New Comment

Viewing a Comment

A small, red diagonal triangle appears in the upper right corner of a cell alerting the reader that a comment exists. Rest the mouse pointer over a cell containing a comment and the comment box displays. Turn on the display of all comments by clicking the Show All Comments button in the Comments group of the Review tab. Navigate to cells containing a comment by clicking the Next button or the Previous button in the Comments group of the Review tab.

Show All Comments

Next

Previous

Printing a Comment

By default, comments do not print. If you want comments printed with the worksheet, click the Page Layout tab, click the Page Setup group dialog box launcher, and then click the Sheet tab at the Page Setup dialog box. Click the *Comments* down-pointing arrow and then click either *At end of sheet* to print comments on the page after cell contents, or *As displayed on sheet* to print the comments as they appear within the worksheet area.

Editing and Deleting a Comment

Click a cell containing a comment and then click the Edit Comment button in the Comments group of the Review tab. (The New Comment button changes to the Edit Comment button when the active cell contains a comment.) You can also edit a comment by right-clicking the cell containing the comment and then clicking *Edit Comment* at the shortcut menu. Insert or delete text as desired and then click in the worksheet area outside the comment box.

Edit Comment

Delete

Quick Steps

Copy and Paste Comments

1. Select source cell containing comment.
2. Click Copy button.
3. Click destination cell(s).
4. Click Paste button arrow.
5. Click *Paste Special*.
6. Click *Comments*.
7. Click OK.

To delete a comment, click the cell containing the comment and then click the Delete button in the Comments group. You can also delete a comment by right-clicking the cell containing the comment and then clicking *Delete Comment* at the shortcut menu.

Copying and Pasting Comments

A comment that has been added to a cell can be copied and pasted to one or more cells. After copying the source cell, click the destination cell and then open the Paste Special dialog box. Click *Comments* in the *Paste* section and then click OK.

Project 1b **Inserting, Editing, Pasting, Viewing, and Deleting Comments** Part 2 of 7

1. With **EL2-C6-P1-CutRatePricing.xlsx** open, insert comments by completing the following steps:
   a. Make C10 the active cell.
   b. Click the Review tab and then click the New Comment button in the Comments group. A yellow shaded box with a black arrow pointing to C10 appears. The current user name is inserted in bold text at the top of the comment box followed by a colon and the insertion point is positioned at the left edge of the box on the second line.
   c. Type **Most competitors charge 175.00 for weekend rentals of luxury vehicles**.
   d. Click in the worksheet area outside the comment box. A small red diagonal triangle appears in the upper right corner of C10 indicating a comment exists for the cell.
   e. Right-click F8 and then click *Insert Comment* at the shortcut menu.
   f. Type **Consider reducing the discount for minivans to 18%** and then click in the worksheet area outside the comment box.
   g. Right-click F9, click *Insert Comment* at the shortcut menu, type **Last year this discount was 12%**, and then click in the worksheet area outside the comment box.
   h. Right-click F9, click *Copy* at the shortcut menu, right-click F10, point to *Paste Special*, and then click *Paste Special* at the shortcut menu.
   i. At the Paste Special dialog box, click *Comments* in the *Paste* section and then click OK.
   j. Press the Esc key to remove the moving marquee from F9.

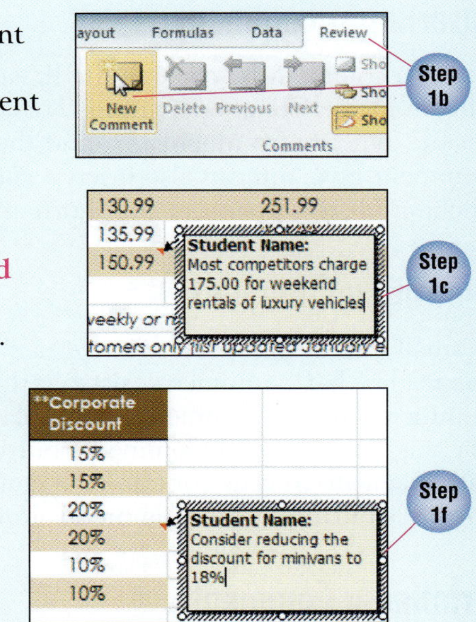

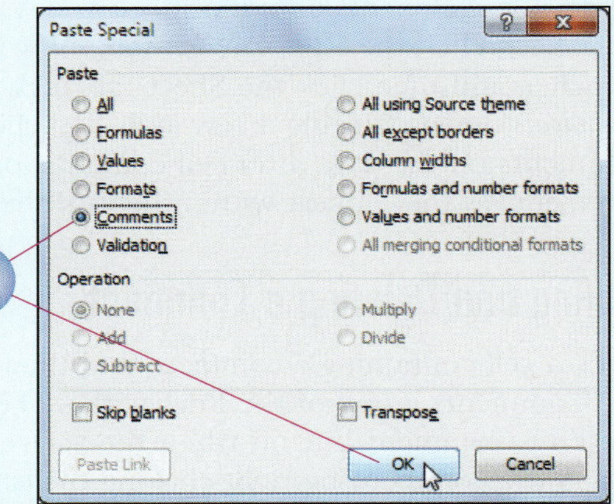

2. View comments by completing the following steps:
   a. Rest the mouse pointer on C10. The comment box pops up displaying the comment text.
   b. Rest the mouse pointer on F8 and then read the comment text that appears in the pop-up box.
   c. Rest the mouse pointer on F9, read the comment text that appears in the pop-up box, rest the mouse pointer on F10, and then read the pasted comment text in the pop-up box.
   d. Press Ctrl + Home to move the active cell to A1.
   e. Click the Next button in the Comments group of the Review tab. Excel displays the comment box in F8.
   f. Click the Next button in the Comments group of the Review tab. Excel displays the comment box in F9.
   g. Click the Next button to display the comment box in C10.
   h. Click Next to display the comment box in F10. Consider using the Next button to view comments in a large worksheet to ensure you do not miss any comment cells.
   i. Click the Show All Comments button in the Comments group of the Review tab. All comment boxes display in the worksheet area.

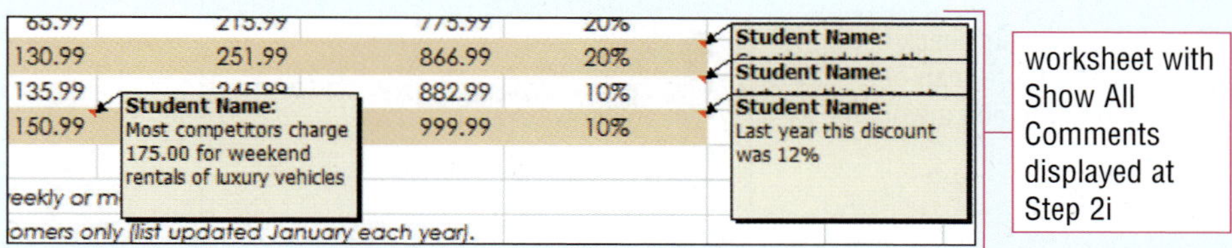

worksheet with Show All Comments displayed at Step 2i

   j. Click the Show All Comments button again to turn off the display of all comments.
3. Edit and delete a comment by completing the following steps:
   a. Right-click C10 and then click *Edit Comment* at the shortcut menu. The comment box pops up with an insertion point positioned at the end of the existing comment text.
   b. Change *175.00* to *168.99* by moving the insertion point and then inserting and deleting text as required.

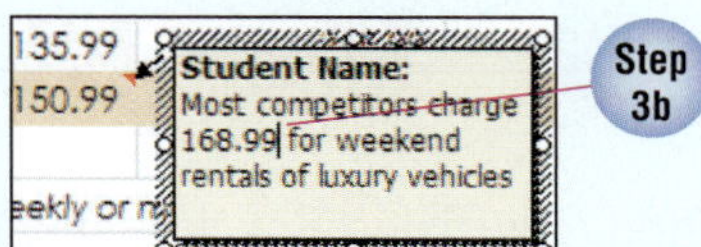

   c. Click in the worksheet area outside the comment box.
   d. Make F10 the active cell and then click the Edit Comment button in the Comments group of the Review tab.
   e. Change *12%* to *15%* and then click in the worksheet area outside the comment box.
   f. Right-click F8 and then click *Delete Comment* at the shortcut menu.
   g. Click F9 and then click the Delete Comment button in the Comments group in the Review tab.
4. Save **EL2-C6-P1-CutRatePricing.xlsx**.

Quick Steps

Share Workbook
1. Open workbook.
2. Click Review tab.
3. Click Share Workbook button.
4. Click *Allow changes by more than one user at the same time* check box.
5. Click OK to close Share Workbook dialog box.
6. Click OK to continue.

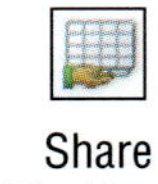

Share Workbook

Sharing a Workbook

A workbook may need to be circulated among several people so they can review, add, delete, or edit data. One method that is available for collaborating with other users is to share a workbook. A shared workbook is generally saved to a network folder that is accessible by the other individuals that need the file. Excel tracks each person's changes and displays a prompt when conflicts to a cell occur if two people have the file open at the same time and make changes to the same data.

To share a workbook, click the Review tab and then click the Share Workbook button in the Changes group. At the Share Workbook dialog box with the Editing tab active shown in Figure 6.3, click the *Allow changes by more than one user at the same time* check box.

Figure 6.3 Share Workbook Dialog Box with Editing Tab Selected

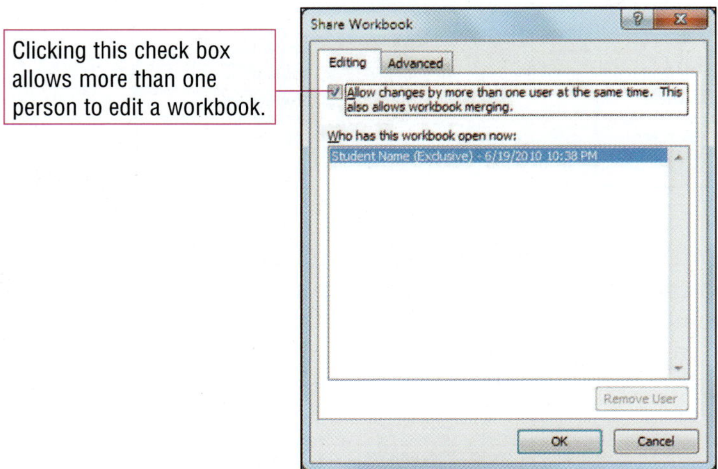

Figure 6.4 Share Workbook Dialog Box with Advanced Tab Selected

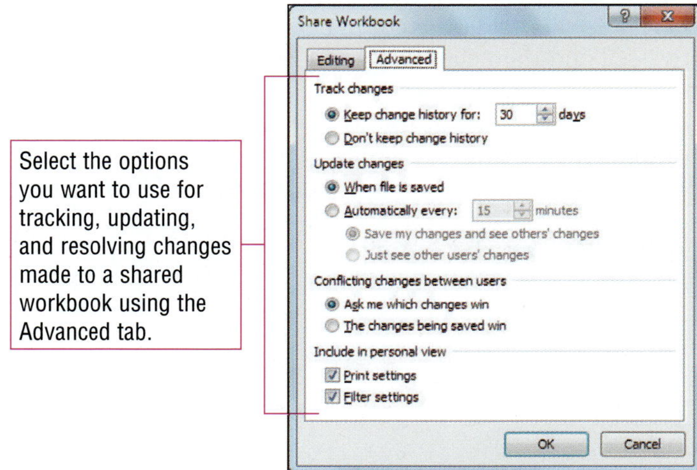

Click the Advanced tab in the Share Workbook dialog box to define the sharing options shown in Figure 6.4. A shared workbook should be saved to a network folder that is designated as a shared folder accessible by the other users. A network administrator is usually the person who creates a folder on a networked server designated with the read/write access rights for multiple accounts (referred to as a ***network share***) and can assist you with navigating to and saving to a network share. All individuals with access to the shared network folder have full access to the shared workbook. One drawback of a shared workbook is that it cannot support all Excel features. If you need to use a feature that is unavailable or make a change to a feature that is not allowed, you will first need to remove shared access. In a later section you will learn how to lock/unlock worksheets and cells for editing if you want to protect the worksheet or sections of the worksheet from change before you share the workbook.

Quick Steps

View Other Users of Shared Workbook
1. Open shared workbook.
2. Click Review tab.
3. Click Share Workbook button.
4. Review names in *Who has this workbook open now* list box.
5. Click OK.

Project 1c **Sharing a Workbook** Part 3 of 7

1. With **EL2-C6-P1-CutRatePricing.xlsx** open, use Save As to name the workbook **EL2-C6-P1-CutRatePricing-Shared**.
2. Assume that you are Chris Zajac, regional manager of CutRate Car Rentals. You want feedback on the proposed rental rates from another manager. Share the workbook so that the other manager can make changes directly within the file by completing the following steps:
   a. If necessary, click the Review tab.
   b. Click the Share Workbook button in the Changes group.
   c. At the Share Workbook dialog box with the Editing tab selected, click the *Allow changes by more than one user at the same time* check box to insert a check mark.
   d. Click OK.
   e. At the Microsoft Excel message box informing you that the workbook will now be saved and asking if you want to continue, click OK.
3. Notice that Excel adds *[Shared]* in the Title bar next to the workbook file name to indicate the workbook's status.
4. Close **EL2-C6-P1-CutRatePricing-Shared.xlsx**.

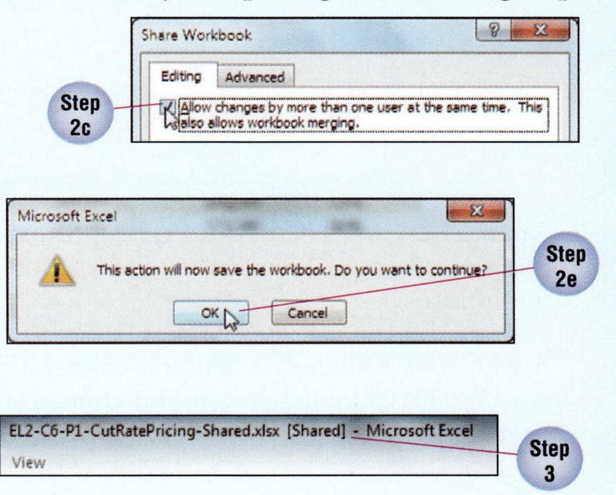

Changing the User Name

When a workbook is shared, Excel tracks the name of the user who edits a shared workbook. When Microsoft Office is installed, the user name information is entered by the person completing the installation. You can change the user name associated with the copy of Excel by opening the Excel Options dialog box.

Quick Steps

Change User Name
1. Click File tab.
2. Click Options button.
3. Select current entry in *User name* text box.
4. Type new user name.
5. Click OK.

Excel Options

Project 1d Changing the User Name and Editing a Shared Workbook Part 4 of 7

1. At a blank Excel screen, change the user name for the computer you are using to simulate an environment in which another manager is opening the shared workbook from a network share location by completing the following steps:
   a. Click the File tab.
   b. Click the Options button located near the bottom of the left pane at the Recent tab Backstage view.
   c. At the Excel Options dialog box with *General* selected in the left pane, make a note of the existing entry in the *User name* text box in the *Personalize your copy of Microsoft Office* section if the entry is a name other than your name. ***Note: You will be restoring the original user name in Project 1f. If necessary, write the user name down so you do not forget the correct entry.***
   d. Select the current entry in the *User name* text box, type **Aaron Rubin**, and then click OK.

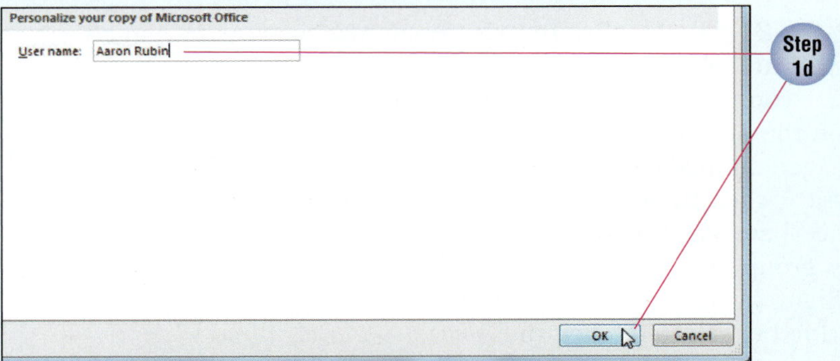

2. Open **EL2-C6-P1-CutRatePricing-Shared.xlsx**.
3. Assume you are Aaron Rubin and you decide to make a few changes to the proposed rental rates.
   a. Make F5 the active cell and change the entry from *15%* to *12%*.
   b. Make B10 the active cell and change the entry from *85.99* to *95.99*.
   c. Make D10 the active cell and change the entry from *299.99* to *325.99*.
4. Save **EL2-C6-P1-CutRatePricing-Shared.xlsx**.

Project 1e Viewing Other Users of a Shared Workbook Part 5 of 7

1. Start a new copy of Excel by clicking the Start button, clicking *All Programs*, clicking *Microsoft Office*, and then clicking *Microsoft Excel 2010*. ***Note: You are opening another copy of Excel to simulate an environment in which multiple copies of the shared workbook are open. You will also change the user name to continue the simulation using a different identity.***
2. Open the Excel Options dialog box and change the *User name* in the new copy of Excel to *Chris Zajac*. Refer to Project 1d, Steps 1a–1d if you need assistance with this step.
3. In the new copy of Excel, open **EL2-C6-P1-CutRatePricing-Shared.xlsx**.
4. Assume you are Chris Zajac and want to see who else is working on the shared workbook. View other users working on the shared workbook by completing the following steps:
   a. Click the Review tab.

b. Click the Share Workbook button in the Changes group.
c. At the Share Workbook dialog box with the Editing tab selected, look at the names in the *Who has this workbook open now* list box.
d. Click OK.

5. Leave both copies of Excel open for the next project.

Step 4c

Your dates will vary.

Resolving Conflicts in a Shared Workbook

When two users have a copy of a shared workbook open and each makes a change to the same cell, Excel prompts the second user to resolve the conflict by displaying the Resolve Conflicts dialog box shown in Figure 6.5. The cell address, original entry, and revised entry are shown for each user. You can choose to click the Accept Mine button to save your revision or the Accept Other button to remove your change and restore the cell to the entry made by the other user. Click the Accept All Mine button or the Accept All Others button to avoid being prompted at each individual cell that has a conflict.

Quick Steps

Resolving Conflict in Shared Workbook
1. Open shared workbook.
2. Make desired edits.
3. Click Save button.
4. Click Accept Mine or Accept Other button at each conflict.
5. Click OK.

HINT

Open the Share Workbook dialog box and click the Advanced tab to instruct Excel not to display the Resolve Conflicts dialog box by selecting *The changes being saved win* in the *Conflicting changes between users* section.

Figure 6.5 Resolve Conflicts Dialog Box

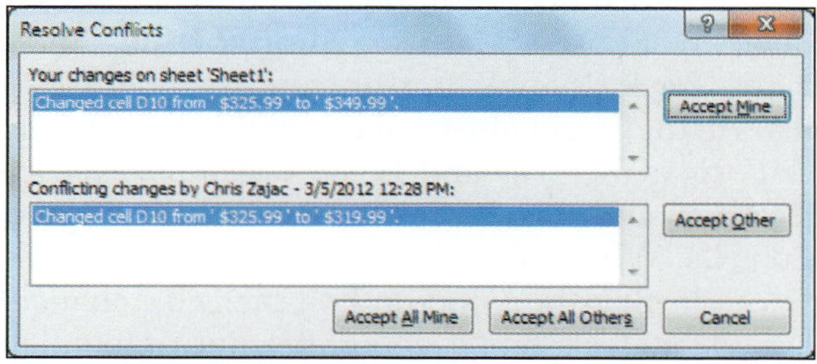

Project 1f **Resolving Conflicts in a Shared Workbook** Part 6 of 7

1. With **EL2-C6-P1-CutRatePricing-Shared.xlsx** open, assume that you are still Chris Zajac and that you decide to make a change to a proposed rental rate which will conflict with a change made by Aaron Rubin.
   a. Make sure the copy of Excel that is active is the second copy you opened for Project 1e in which you viewed the users with the shared workbook open using the identity Chris Zajac.
   b. Make D10 the active cell and change *325.99* to *319.99*.
   c. Save **EL2-C6-P1-CutRatePricing-Shared.xlsx**.
2. Switch to the other copy of Excel using the Taskbar. Assume that Aaron Rubin has decided to change the weekly luxury rate again. Edit the worksheet and resolve the conflict by completing the following steps:
   a. Make D10 the active cell and change the entry to *349.99*.
   b. Click the Save button. Since this change conflicts with the change made by Chris Zajac in Step 1b, Excel prompts the second user with the Resolve Conflicts dialog box.

c. Click the Accept Other button to restore the cell to the value entered by Chris Zajac.
d. At the Microsoft Excel message box informing you that the workbook has been updated with changes saved by other users, click OK.

3. Notice that a cell in which a conflict was resolved is displayed with a colored border. Rest the mouse over D10 to view the pop-up box with the name, date, and time the cell change was saved as well as the original and revised data entries.
4. Exit the active copy of Excel.
5. With the other copy of Excel active, close **EL2-C6-P1-CutRatePricing-Shared.xlsx**.
6. Change the user name back to the name you recorded in Project 1d, Step 1c.

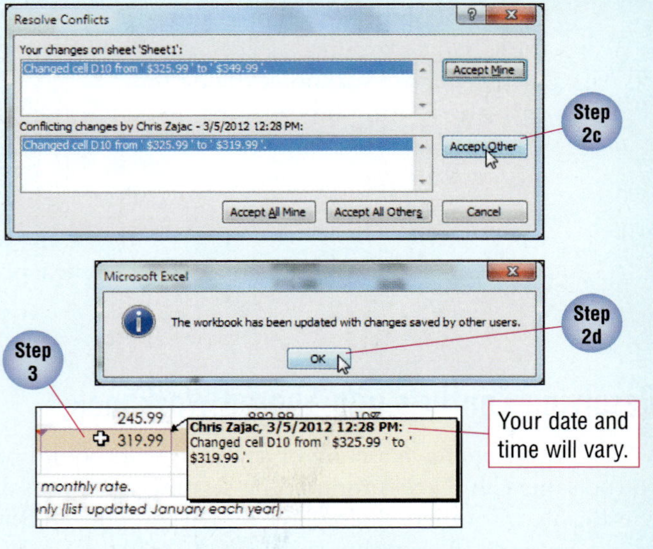

Printing History Sheet and Removing Shared Workbook Access

Quick Steps

Print History Sheet

1. Open shared workbook.
2. Click Review tab.
3. Click Track Changes button.
4. Click *Highlight Changes*.
5. Change *When* to *All*.
6. If necessary, clear *Who* check box.
7. If necessary, clear *Where* check box.
8. Click *List changes on a new sheet* check box.
9. Click OK.
10. Print History sheet.

Track Changes

Before changing the status of a shared workbook to an exclusive workbook, consider printing the change history in order to have a record of the workbook's editing actions made by all users who worked on the file. To do this, click the Review tab, click the Track Changes button, and then click *Highlight Changes* at the drop-down list. At the Highlight Changes dialog box shown in Figure 6.6, change *When* to *All*, clear the *Who* and *Where* check boxes, click the *List changes on a new sheet* check box, and then click OK. By default, Excel displays a colored border in changed cells. When you rest the mouse pointer over a cell with a colored border, Excel displays in a pop-up box the cell's change history. Clear the *Highlight changes on screen* check box if you prefer not to highlight changed cells in the worksheet.

To stop sharing a workbook, open the shared workbook, click the Review tab, and then click the Share Workbook button. At the Share Workbook dialog box with the Editing tab selected, clear the check box for *Allow changes by more than one user at the same time*. When you click OK, Excel displays a message box informing you that changing the workbook to exclusive status will erase all of the change history in the workbook and prevent users who might have the workbook open from saving their changes. Consider copying and pasting the cells in the History sheet to a new workbook and saving the history as a separate file since the History sheet is removed when the shared workbook is saved.

Figure 6.6 Highlight Changes Dialog Box

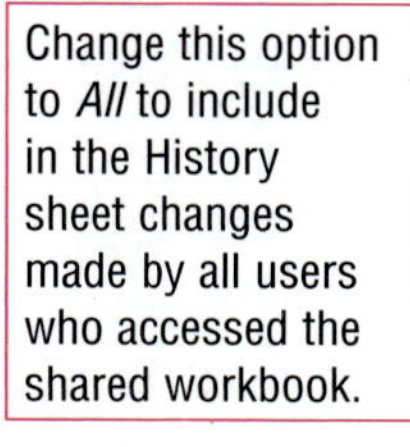

Change this option to *All* to include in the History sheet changes made by all users who accessed the shared workbook.

Click this check box to create a sheet named *History* in the workbook with a list of changes made by each user.

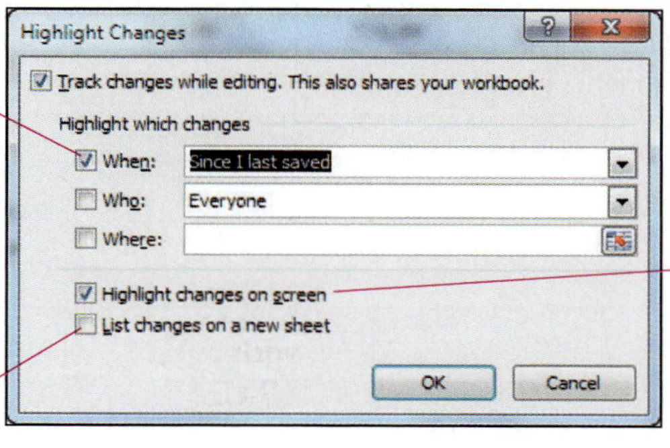

By default, this option is selected, which causes a colored border to display in changed cells. Resting the mouse pointer over a highlighted cell causes a pop-up box to display with the change history.

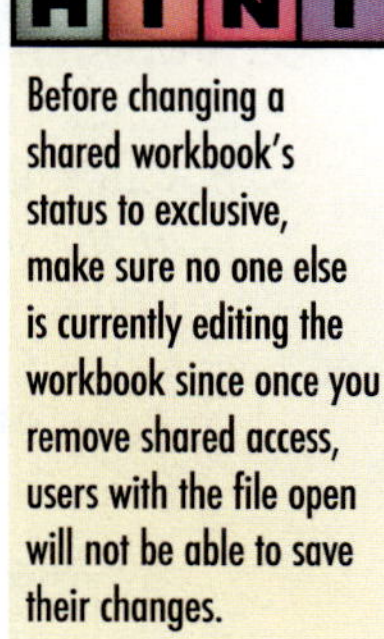

HINT

Before changing a shared workbook's status to exclusive, make sure no one else is currently editing the workbook since once you remove shared access, users with the file open will not be able to save their changes.

Quick Steps

Stop Sharing Workbook

1. Open shared workbook.
2. Click Review tab.
3. Click Share Workbook button.
4. Clear *Allow changes by more than one user at the same time* check box.
5. Click OK.
6. Click Yes.

Project 1g Printing the History Sheet and Removing Shared Access to a Workbook

Part 7 of 7

1. Open **EL2-C6-P1-CutRatePricing-Shared.xlsx**.
2. Create a new sheet named *History* and print the record of changes made to the shared workbook by completing the following steps:
   a. If necessary, click the Review tab.
   b. Click the Track Changes button in the Changes group and then click *Highlight Changes* at the drop-down list.
   c. At the Highlight Changes dialog box, click the down-pointing arrow at the right of the *When* list box and then click *All* at the drop-down list.
   d. If necessary, clear the *Who* check box if a check mark is displayed in the box.
   e. If necessary, clear the *Where* check box if a check mark is displayed in the box.
   f. Click the *List changes on a new sheet* check box to insert a check mark and then click OK.
   g. Print the History sheet.

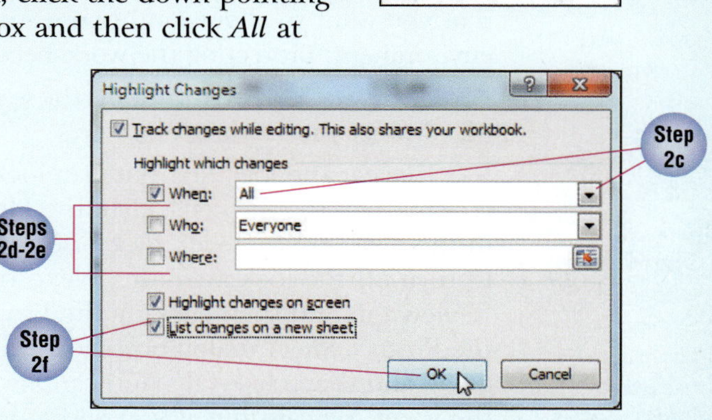

3. Stop sharing the workbook by completing the following steps:
   a. Click the Share Workbook button.
   b. Click the *Allow changes by more than one user at the same time* check box to clear the check mark.
   c. Click OK.
   d. At the Microsoft Excel message box informing you that the workbook will be removed from shared use, click Yes to make the workbook exclusive.

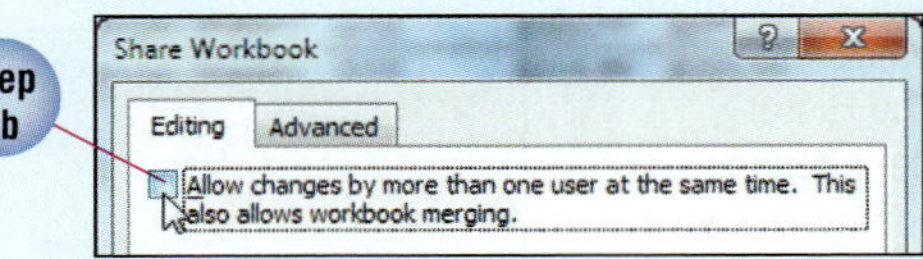

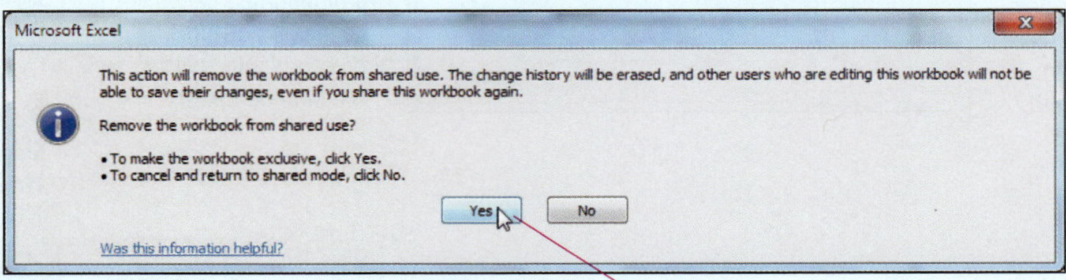

4. Close **EL2-C6-P1-CutRatePricing-Shared.xlsx**.

Lock and Unlock a Workbook, a Worksheet, and Ranges

4 Parts

You will protect a worksheet, unlock ranges, prevent changes to the structure of a workbook, and add a password to open a workbook.

Quick Steps

Protect Worksheet
1. Open workbook.
2. Activate desired sheet.
3. Click Review tab.
4. Click Protect Sheet button.
5. Type password to unprotect sheet.
6. Choose allowable actions.
7. Click OK.
8. Retype password.
9. Click OK.

Unlock Cells
1. Select cell(s) to be unlocked.
2. Click Home tab.
3. Click Format button.
4. Click *Lock Cell*.
5. Deselect cell(s).

Format

Protecting and Unprotecting Worksheets

Protecting a worksheet prevents another user from editing cells that you do not want accidentally deleted, modified, or otherwise changed. By default, when a worksheet is protected, each cell in the sheet is locked. This means no one can insert, delete, or modify the content. In most cases, some cells within the worksheet contain data that you want to allow another user to be able to change; therefore, in a collaborative environment, protecting the worksheet generally involves two actions:

1. Clear the lock attribute on those cells that will be allowed to be edited.
2. Protect the worksheet.

To clear the lock attribute (unlock) for the cells that will be allowed to be modified, select the cells, click the Home tab, and then click the Format button in the Cells group. Click *Lock Cell* in the *Protection* section at the drop-down list to turn off the lock attribute. Next, turn on worksheet protection by clicking the Review tab and then clicking the Protect Sheet button in the Changes group. At the Protect Sheet dialog box shown in Figure 6.7, select the actions you want to allow and then click OK. You can also choose to assign a password to unprotect the sheet. Be cautious if you add a password to remove protection since you will not be able to unprotect the worksheet if you forget the password. If necessary, write down the password and store it in a secure location.

Figure 6.7 Protect Sheet Dialog Box

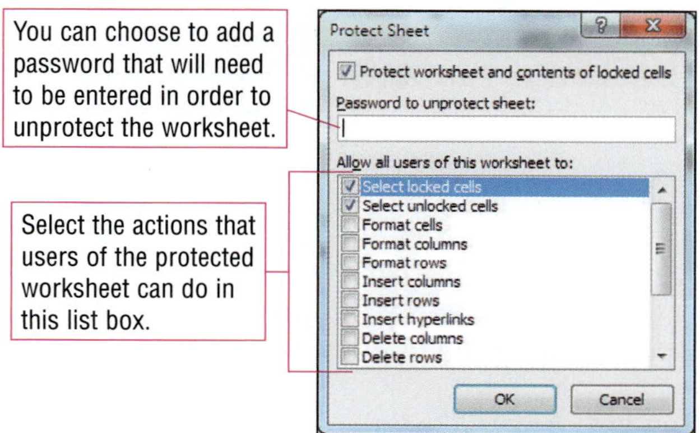

Project 2a Protecting an Entire Worksheet

Part 1 of 4

1. Open **CutRateFinalPrices.xlsx**.
2. Save the workbook with Save As and name it **EL2-C6-P2-CutRateFinalPrices**.
3. Protect the entire FinalPrices worksheet by completing the following steps:
   a. Make sure FinalPrices is the active sheet.
   b. Click the Review tab.
   c. Click the Protect Sheet button in the Changes group.
   d. At the Protect Sheet dialog box with the insertion point positioned in the *Password to unprotect sheet* text box, type **f4R$c** and then click OK.

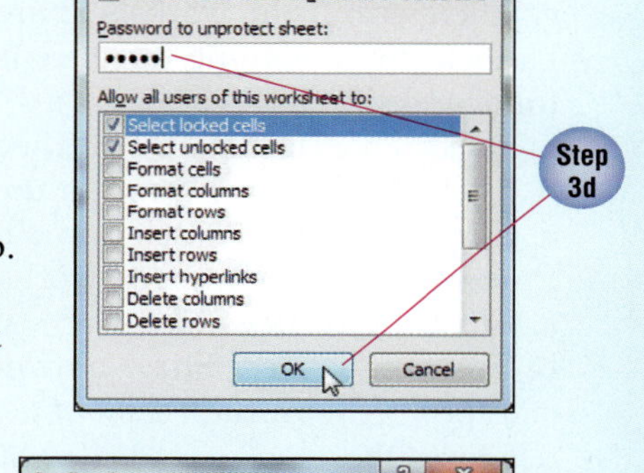

   e. At the Confirm Password dialog box with the insertion point positioned in the *Reenter password to proceed* text box, type **f4R$c** and then press Enter or click OK.

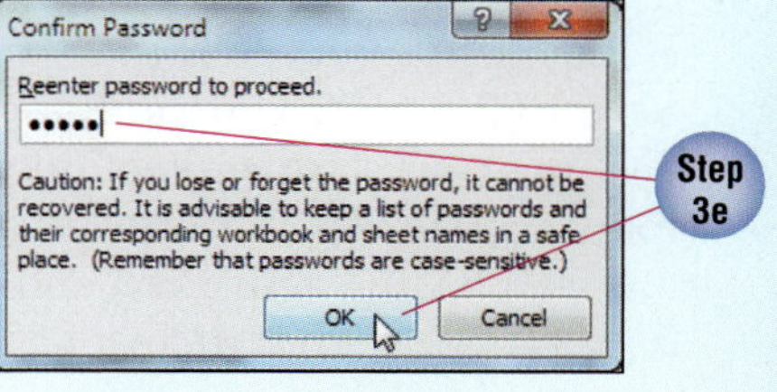

   f. Make any cell active in the FinalPrices sheet and attempt to delete the data or type new data. Since the entire worksheet is now protected, all cells are locked and Excel displays a message that the cell is read-only. Click OK at the Microsoft Excel message indicating that you need to unprotect the sheet to modify the protected cell.

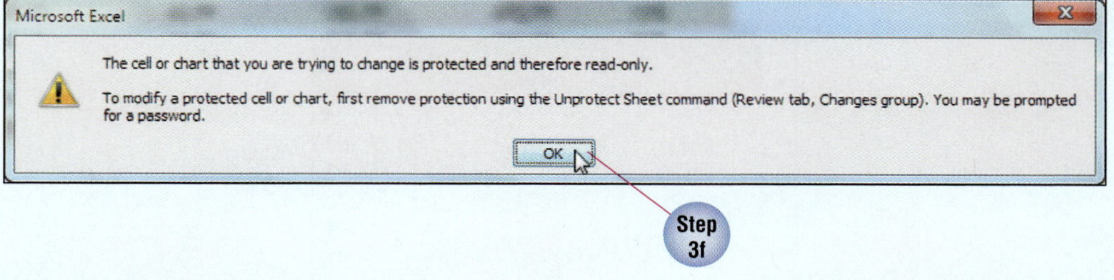

4. Notice the Protect Sheet button changes to the Unprotect Sheet button when a worksheet has been protected.
5. Save **EL2-C6-P2-CutRateFinalPrices.xlsx**.

Project 2b Unlocking Cells and Protecting a Worksheet

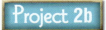

1. With **EL2-C6-P2-CutRateFinalPrices.xlsx** open, make TargetRevenue the active sheet.
2. Unlock the weekday target rental data cells that you want to allow to be edited by completing the following steps:
   a. Select C5:C10.
   b. Click the Home tab.
   c. Click the Format button in the Cells group.
   d. At the Format button drop-down list, look at the icon next to *Lock Cell* in the *Protection* section. The highlighted icon indicates the lock attribute is turned on.
   e. Click *Lock Cell* at the Format button drop-down list to turn the lock attribute off for the selected range.
   f. Click any cell within the range C5:C10 and click the Format button in the Cells group. Look at the icon next to *Lock Cell* in the drop-down list. The icon is no longer highlighted, indicating the cell is unlocked.
   g. Click within the worksheet area outside the drop-down list to close the menu.

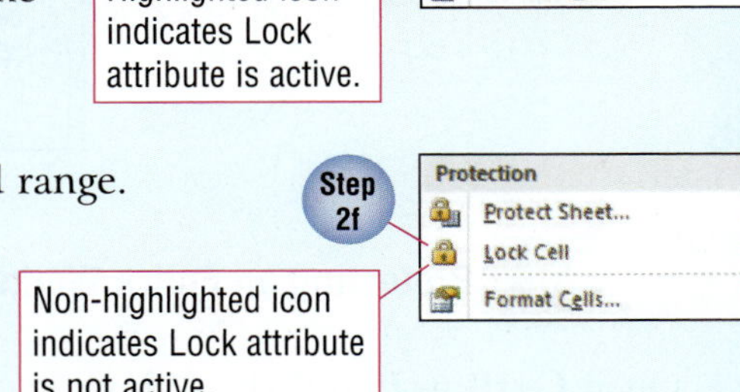

3. Unlock the remaining target rental ranges to allow the cells to be edited by completing the following steps:
   a. Select F5:F10, hold down the Ctrl key, select I5:I10 and L5:L10.
   b. Click the Format button in the Cells group and then click *Lock Cell* at the drop-down list.
   c. Click any cell to deselect the ranges.
4. Protect the TargetRevenue worksheet by completing the following steps:
   a. Click the Review tab.
   b. Click the Protect Sheet button in the Changes group.
   c. Type **f4R$c** in the *Password to unprotect sheet* text box.
   d. Click OK.
   e. Type **f4R$c** in the *Reenter password to proceed* text box and press Enter or click OK.
5. Save **EL2-C6-P2-CutRateFinalPrices.xlsx**.
6. Test the worksheet protection applied to the TargetRevenue sheet by completing the following steps:
   a. Make B8 the active cell and press the Delete key.
   b. Click OK at the Microsoft Office Excel message box indicating the protected cell is read-only.
   c. Make C8 the active cell and press the Delete key. Since C8 is unlocked, the contents of C8 are deleted and dependent cells are updated.

4	Category	Weekday (Mo to Th)	Target Rentals	Target Revenue
5	Compact	$ 36	675	$ 24,293
6	Mid-size	38.99	880	34,311
7	Full-size	40.99	425	17,421
8	Minivan	75.99		-
9	SUV	89.99	198	17,818
10	Luxury	99.99	86	8,599
11	TOTAL		Weekday:	$ 102,442

Step 6c

   d. Click the Undo button on the Quick Access toolbar to restore the contents of C8.
7. Save and then close **EL2-C6-P2-CutRateFinalPrices.xlsx**.

Figure 6.8 Unprotect Sheet Dialog Box

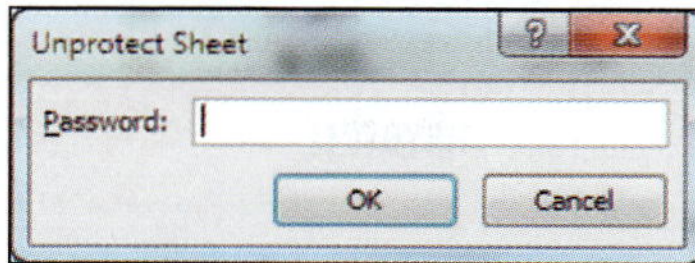

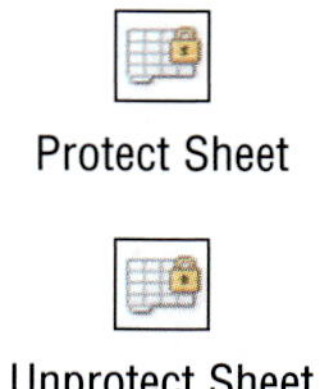

When a worksheet has protection turned on, the Protect Sheet button in the Changes group of the Review tab changes to the Unprotect Sheet button. To remove worksheet protection, click the Unprotect Sheet button. If a password was entered when the worksheet was protected, the Unprotect Sheet dialog box shown in Figure 6.8 appears. Type the password and press Enter or click OK.

Protecting and Unprotecting the Structure of a Workbook

The Protect Workbook button in the Changes group of the Review tab can be used to prevent changes to the structure of a workbook such as inserting a new sheet, deleting a sheet, or unhiding a hidden worksheet. At the Protect Structure and Windows dialog box shown in Figure 6.9 you can also turn on protection for the workbook's windows. Clicking the *Windows* check box prevents a user of the workbook from resizing or changing the position of the windows in the workbook.

As with protecting worksheets, an optional password can be entered that will be required to unprotect the workbook in the future.

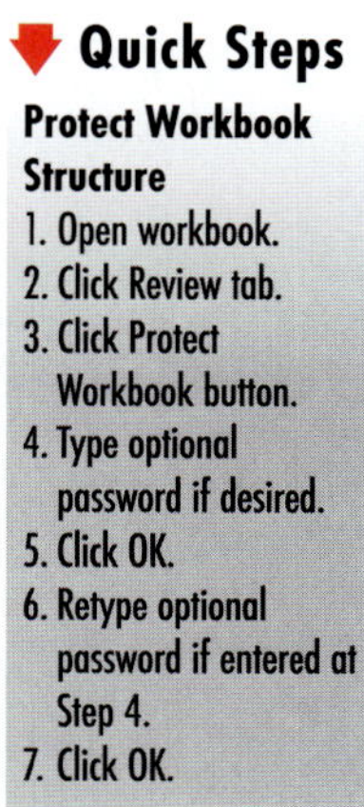
Quick Steps

Protect Workbook Structure
1. Open workbook.
2. Click Review tab.
3. Click Protect Workbook button.
4. Type optional password if desired.
5. Click OK.
6. Retype optional password if entered at Step 4.
7. Click OK.

Figure 6.9 Protect Structure and Windows Dialog Box

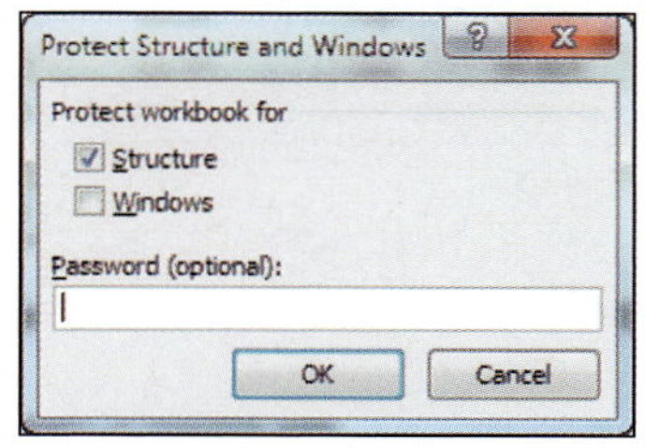

Project 2c **Protecting the Structure of a Workbook** Part 3 of 4

1. Open **EL2-C6-P2-CutRateFinalPrices.xlsx**.
2. Protect the workbook structure by completing the following steps:
   a. If necessary, click the Review tab.
   b. Click the Protect Workbook button in the Changes group.
   c. At the Protect Structure and Windows dialog box with the insertion point positioned in the *Password (optional)* text box, type w4R!c and press Enter or click OK.

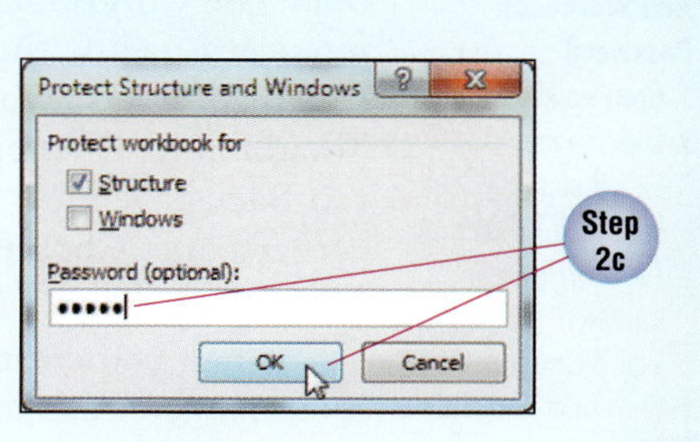

d. At the Confirm Password dialog box with the insertion point positioned in the *Reenter password to proceed* text box, type **w4R!c** and press Enter or click OK.

3. Test the workbook protection by attempting to insert a new worksheet by completing the following steps:
   a. Right-click the TargetRevenue sheet tab.
   b. Look at the shortcut menu. Notice that all of the options related to managing worksheets are dimmed, meaning the options are unavailable.
   c. Click within the worksheet area outside the pop-up list to close the menu.
4. Save **EL2-C6-P2-CutRateFinalPrices.xlsx**.

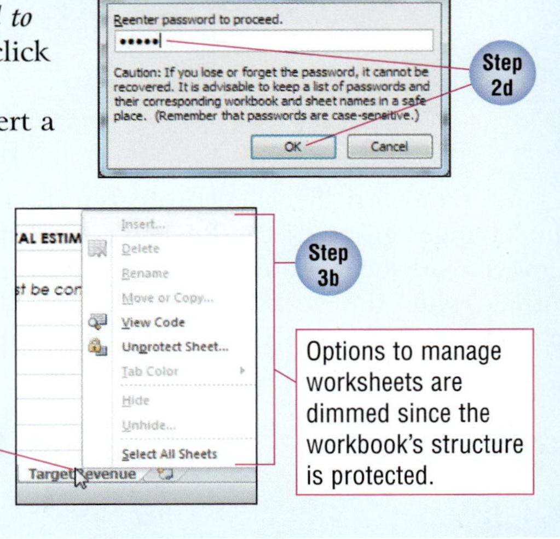

Unprotecting a Workbook

Protected Workbook

When the structure of a workbook has been protected, the Protect Workbook button in the Changes group of the Review tab displays with an orange shaded background to indicate protection is turned on. To remove workbook protection, click the Protect Workbook button. If a password was entered when the workbook was protected, the Unprotect Workbook dialog box shown in Figure 6.10 appears. Type the password and press Enter or click OK.

Figure 6.10 Unprotect Workbook Dialog Box

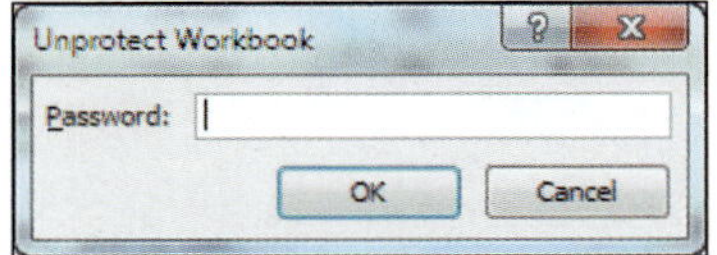

Adding and Removing a Password to a Workbook

Quick Steps

Add Workbook Password

1. Open workbook.
2. Click File tab.
3. Click Protect Workbook button.
4. Click *Encrypt with Password*.
5. Type password.
6. Press Enter or click OK.
7. Retype password.
8. Press Enter or click OK.
9. Save the workbook.

You can prevent unauthorized access to Excel data by requiring a password to open the workbook. Passwords to open the workbook are encrypted. An ***encrypted password*** means that the plain text you type is converted into a scrambled format called ***ciphertext*** which prevents unauthorized users from retrieving the password. To add an encrypted password to an open workbook, click the File tab. At the Info tab Backstage view shown in Figure 6.11, click the Protect Workbook button in the center pane. Click *Encrypt with Password* at the drop-down list to open the Encrypt Document dialog box shown in Figure 6.12.

When you create passwords, a guideline to follow is to include a combination of four character elements: uppercase letters, lowercase letters, symbols, and numbers. Passwords constructed according to this model are considered secure and more difficult to crack. Note that if you forget the password, you will not be able to open the workbook. If necessary, write down the password and store it in a secure location.

Figure 6.11 Info Tab Backstage View with Protect Workbook Drop-Down List

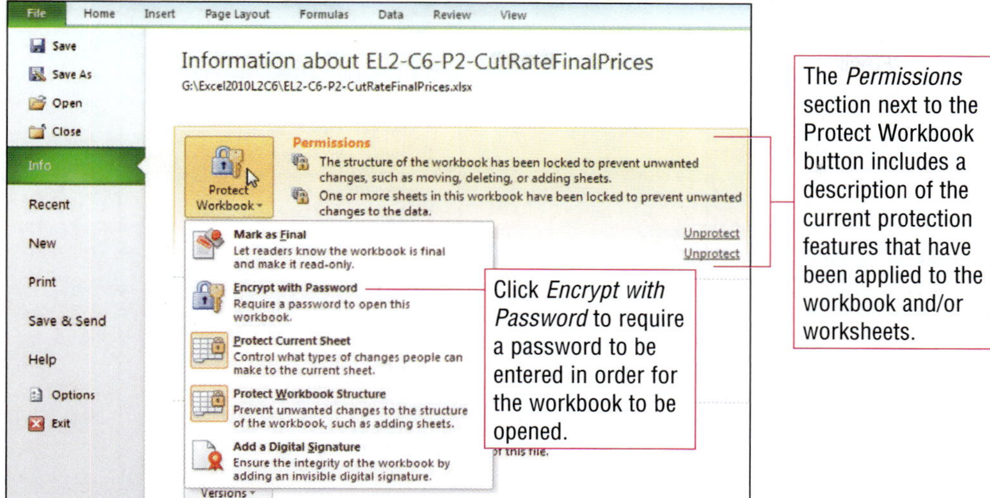

Figure 6.12 Encrypt Document Dialog Box

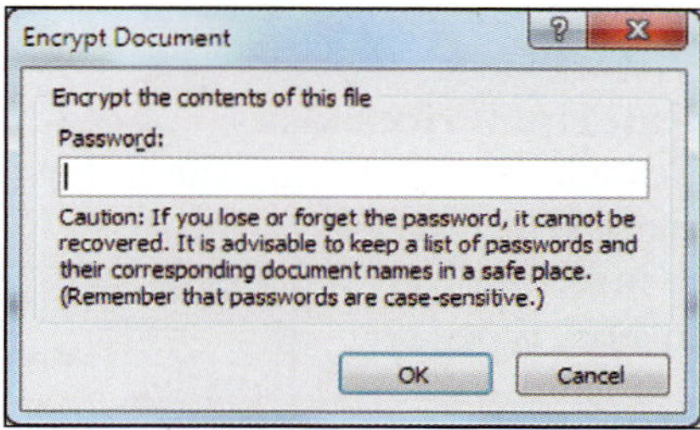

Project 2d Adding a Password to Open a Workbook

Part 4 of 4

1. With **EL2-C6-P2-CutRateFinalPrices.xlsx** open, add a password to open the workbook by completing the following steps:
   a. Click the File tab. The Backstage view opens with the Info tab selected.
   b. Read the information described in the *Permissions* section next to the Protect Workbook button. Since this workbook has protection features already applied, the existing features are described along with a hyperlink to unprotect each protected worksheet. In a workbook with no pre-existing protection, the *Permissions* section displays the text *Anyone can open, copy, and change any part of the workbook.*
   c. Click the Protect Workbook button.

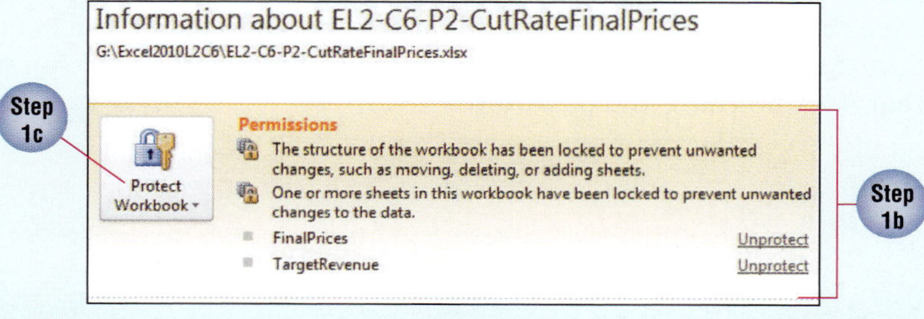

d. Click *Encrypt with Password* at the drop-down list.
e. At the Encrypt Document dialog box with the insertion point positioned in the *Password* text box, type p4E#c and then press Enter or click OK.

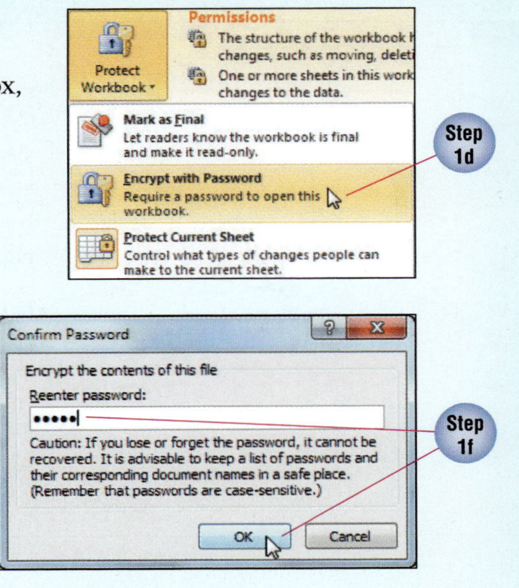

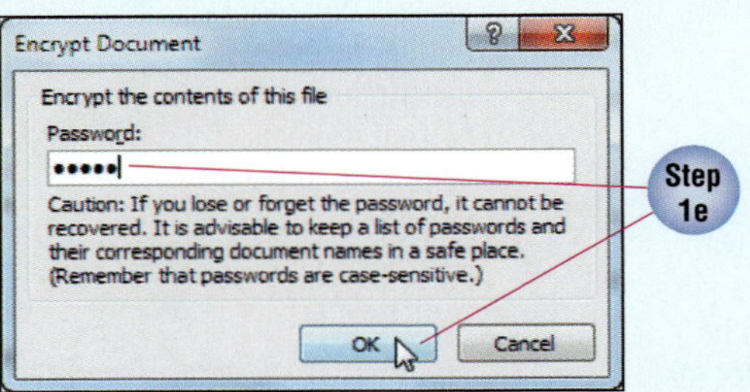

f. Type p4E#c at the Confirm Password dialog box with the insertion point positioned in the *Reenter password* text box and then press Enter or click OK.
g. Notice that Excel has added to the first line of the *Permissions* section next to the Protect Workbook button the text *A password is required to open this workbook.*
h. Click the Home tab to return to the worksheet.

2. Save and then close **EL2-C6-P2-CutRateFinalPrices.xlsx**.
3. Test the password security on the workbook by completing the following steps:
a. Open **EL2-C6-P2-CutRateFinalPrices.xlsx**.
b. At the Password dialog box with the insertion point positioned in the *Password* text box, type a password that is incorrect for the file and press Enter.
c. At the Microsoft Excel message box indicating that the password you supplied is not correct, click OK.
d. Open **EL2-C6-P2-CutRateFinalPrices.xlsx**.
e. Type p4E#c in the *Password* text box and then press Enter or click OK.
4. Close **EL2-C6-P2-CutRateFinalPrices.xlsx**.

To remove a password from a workbook, open the workbook using your password and then open the Save As dialog box. Click the Tools button located near the bottom right of the Save As dialog box (next to the Save button) and then click *General Options* at the drop-down list. At the General Options dialog box, select and then delete the password in the *Password to open* text box. Click OK to close the General Options dialog box and then click the Save button at the Save As dialog box to save the file using the same name. Click Yes at the Confirm Save As dialog box to replace the password-protected workbook with a new copy that does not have the password.

Project 3 Track and Resolve Changes Made to a Workbook — 3 Parts

You will begin tracking changes made to a workbook, view changes made by two users, and accept and reject changes.

Tracking Changes to a Workbook

As you learned in Project 1, Excel automatically tracks changes made to the workbook by each user when you share a workbook. As you saw with the History sheet in Project 1g, you can display and print a record of the changes. If a workbook is not shared, you can turn on the Track Changes feature and Excel will automatically share the workbook. To do this, click the Track Changes button in the Changes group of the Review tab and click *Highlight Changes* at the drop-down list. At the Highlight Changes dialog box, click the *Track changes while editing* check box and click OK.

As the owner of a shared workbook you might need to view the worksheet with all cells highlighted that have had changes made to the data. Figure 6.13 displays the worksheet you will edit in Project 3 with all changes highlighted. As you rest the mouse pointer over a highlighted cell, a pop-up box displays the name of the person who changed the cell along with the date, time, original entry, and revised entry.

Quick Steps

Track Changes
1. Open workbook.
2. Click Review tab.
3. Click Track Changes button.
4. Click *Highlight Changes.*
5. Click *Track changes while editing* check box.
6. Click OK twice.

Highlight Changes
1. Open tracked workbook.
2. Click Review tab.
3. Click Track Changes button.
4. Click *Highlight Changes.*
5. Change *When* to *Not yet reviewed.*
6. Make sure *Who* is *Everyone.*
7. Click OK.

Track Changes

Figure 6.13 Project 3 Worksheet with Changes Highlighted

	A	B	C	D	E	F	G	H	I	J	K	L	M
1	CutRate Car Rentals												
2	Estimated Monthly Revenue												
3	West Region												
4	Effective Date: May 1, 2012												
5	Category	Weekday (Mo to Th)	Target Rentals	Target Revenue	Weekend (Fr to Su)	Target Rentals	Target Revenue	Weekly (*Min 5 days)	Target Rentals	Target Revenue	Monthly (*Min 21 days)	Target Rentals	Target Revenue
6	Compact	$ 35.99	391	$			9,686	$ 175.99	46	$ 8,096	$ 675.99	11	$ 7,436
7	Mid-size	38.99	285				13,480	185.99	25	4,650	692.99	10	6,930
8	Full-size	40.99	175				4,949	215.99	30	6,480	775.99	8	6,208
9	Minivan	75.99	155	11,778	130.99	68	8,907	251.99	28	7,056	866.99	8	6,936
10	SUV	89.99	146	13,139	139.99	47	6,580	249.99	31	7,750	885.99	12	10,632
11	Luxury	99.99	55	5,499	155.99	30	4,680	329.99	10	3,300	999.99	5	5,000
12	TOTAL		Weekday:	$ 62,774		Weekend:	$ 48,282		Weekly:	$ 37,330		Monthly:	$ 43,141

Sam Forwell, 3/6/2012 2:47 PM:
Changed cell C6 from ' $362.00 ' to ' $391.00 '.

Changed cells in a shared workbook can be displayed with a colored border to identify which cells were revised. Each person's changes are identified with a different color.

Figure 6.14 Select Changes to Accept or Reject Dialog Box

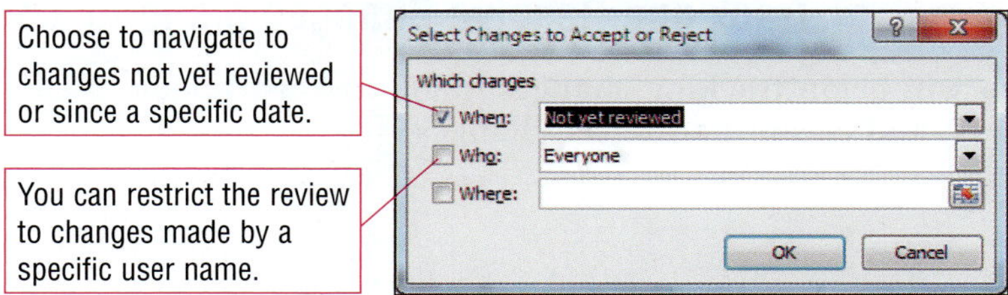

Accepting and Rejecting Tracked Changes

Quick Steps

Accept and Reject Changes

1. Open tracked workbook.
2. Click Review tab.
3. Click Track Changes button.
4. Click *Accept/Reject Changes.*
5. Make sure *When* is *Not yet reviewed.*
6. Make sure *Who* is *Everyone.*
7. Click OK.
8. Click Accept or Reject button at each change.

As well as displaying the worksheet with the changes highlighted, you can elect to navigate to each change and accept or reject the revision. To do this, click the Track Changes button in the Changes group of the Review tab and then click *Accept/Reject Changes* at the drop-down list. At the Select Changes to Accept or Reject dialog box shown in Figure 6.14, define which changes you want to review and then click OK.

Excel navigates to the first cell changed and displays the Accept or Reject Changes dialog box shown in Figure 6.15. Review the information in the dialog box and click either the Accept or Reject button. If you reject a change, the cell is restored to its original value. As you respond to each changed cell, the colored border is removed since the cell has been reviewed. The dialog box also includes an Accept All button and a Reject All button to do a global review if desired. Be cautious with accepting and rejecting changes since Undo is not available after you review the cells.

Figure 6.15 Accept or Reject Changes Dialog Box

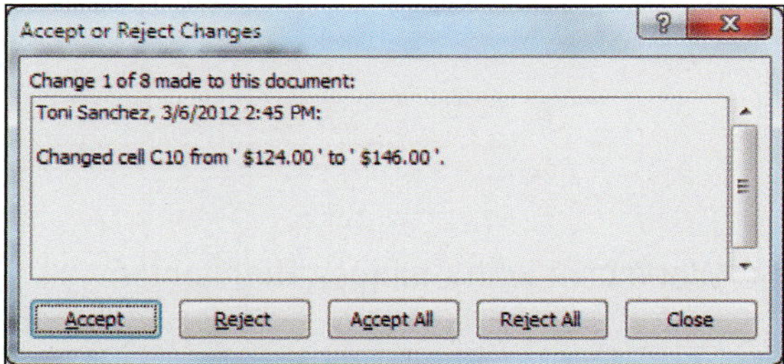

Project 3a **Tracking Changes Made to a Workbook** Part 1 of 3

1. Open **CutRateWestRegion.xlsx**.
2. Save the workbook with Save As and name it **EL2-C6-P3-CutRateWestRegion**.
3. Begin tracking changes made to the workbook by completing the following steps:
   a. If necessary, click the Review tab.
   b. Click the Track Changes button in the Changes group.
   c. Click *Highlight Changes* at the drop-down list.

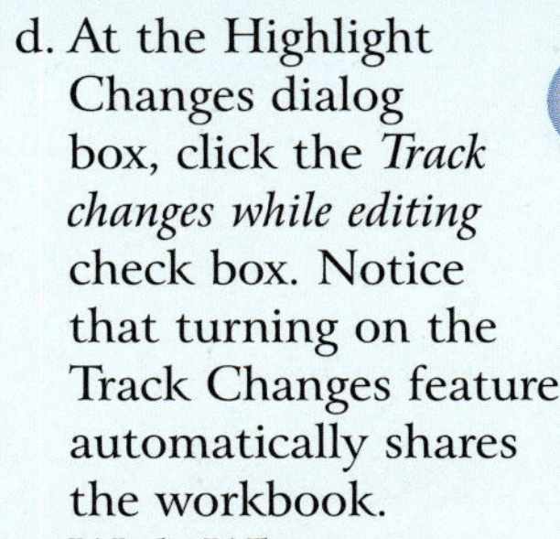

d. At the Highlight Changes dialog box, click the *Track changes while editing* check box. Notice that turning on the Track Changes feature automatically shares the workbook.

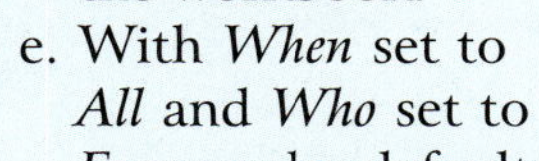

e. With *When* set to *All* and *Who* set to *Everyone* by default, click OK.

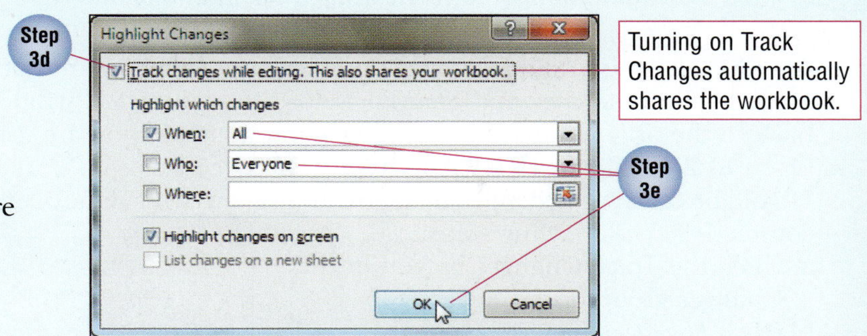

f. At the Microsoft Excel message box indicating that this action will now save the workbook, click OK to continue.

4. Close **EL2-C6-P3-CutRateWestRegion.xlsx**.

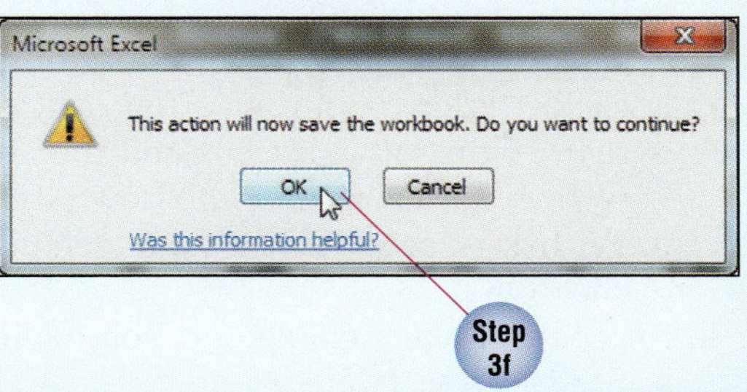

Project 3b Editing a Tracked Workbook

Part 2 of 3

1. Assume that you are Toni Sanchez, the SUV rental manager for the west region at CutRate Car Rentals. You have been asked to edit the target rental values for SUVs. At a blank Excel window, change the user name to *Toni Sanchez*. If necessary, refer to Project 1d, Step 1 if you need assistance with changing the user name. ***Note: Make sure you make a note of the original user name, which you will restore in Project 3c.***
2. Open **EL2-C6-P3-CutRateWestRegion.xlsx**.
3. Edit the SUV target data as follows:

C10 from	*124*	to	*146*
F10 from	*22*	to	*47*
I10 from	*22*	to	*31*
L10 from	*8*	to	*12*

4. Save and then close **EL2-C6-P3-CutRateWestRegion.xlsx**.
5. Assume that you are Sam Forwell, the compact rental manager for the west region at CutRate Car Rentals. You have been asked to edit the target rental values for compact cars. At a blank Excel window, change the user name to *Sam Forwell*.
6. Open **EL2-C6-P3-CutRateWestRegion.xlsx**.
7. Edit the compact target data as follows:

C6 from	*362*	to	*391*
F6 from	*165*	to	*173*
I6 from	*33*	to	*46*
L6 from	*15*	to	*11*

8. Save and then close **EL2-C6-P3-CutRateWestRegion.xlsx**.

Project 3c Highlighting and Reviewing Tracked Changes

1. Assume that you are the west region operations manager. You decide to review the changes made by Toni Sanchez and Sam Forwell. At a blank Excel window, change the user name back to the original user name for the computer that you are using.
2. Open **EL2-C6-P3-CutRateWestRegion.xlsx**.
3. Highlight cells with changes made by all users that have not yet been reviewed by completing the following steps:
   a. Click the Track Changes button in the Changes group of the Review tab.
   b. Click *Highlight Changes* at the drop-down list.
   c. At the Highlight Changes dialog box, click the down-pointing arrow at the right of the *When* list box and then click *Not yet reviewed* at the drop-down list.
   d. With *Who* set to *Everyone* by default, click OK.
4. Accept and reject changes as you navigate the worksheet by completing the following steps:
   a. Press Ctrl + Home to move the active cell to A1.
   b. Click the Track Changes button and then click *Accept/Reject Changes* at the drop-down list.
   c. At the Select Changes to Accept or Reject dialog box, with *When* set to *Not yet reviewed*, and *Who* set to *Everyone* by default, click OK.
   d. Excel moves the active cell to C10 where the first change was made and displays the Accept or Reject Changes dialog box. Click the Accept button to leave C10 at 146.

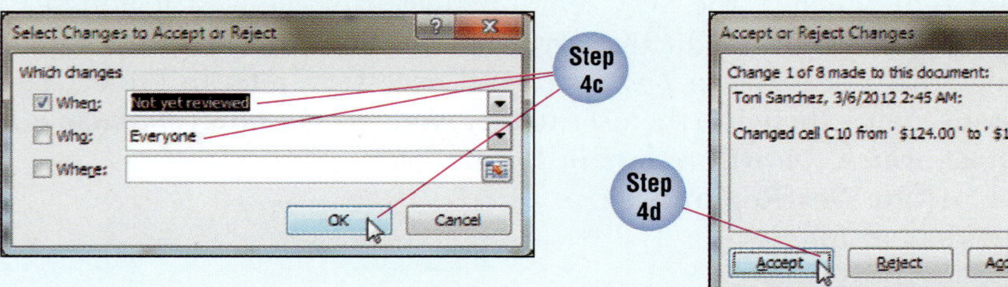

   e. Excel moves the active cell to F10. Click the Reject button to restore F10 to the original value of 22. ***Note: If necessary, drag the Accept or Reject Changes dialog box out of the way to see the cell being reviewed in the worksheet area.***

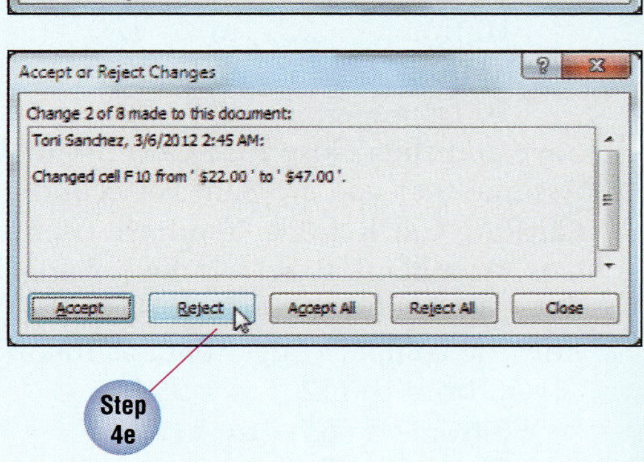

   f. Respond to the remaining changes as follows:

      Accept I10
      Accept L10
      Reject C6
      Accept F6
      Reject I6
      Accept L6

5. Print the worksheet.
6. Save and then close **EL2-C6-P3-CutRateWestRegion.xlsx**.

Stopping the Tracking of Changes in a Workbook

When you no longer need to track the changes made to a workbook, click the Track Changes button and click *Highlight Changes* at the drop-down list. At the Highlight Changes dialog box, clear the *Track changes while editing* check box and click OK. Excel displays the warning message that the workbook will no longer be shared and the change history will be erased. Click Yes to complete the action.

If you have not reviewed all changes made to the workbook, consider printing a copy of the History sheet before turning off the track changes feature. Refer to Project 1g, Step 2 for assistance with printing a history sheet.

Excel provides several methods to share and collaborate with other users of data in Excel. The method that you choose depends on factors such as the availability of a network share folder, the need to protect ranges or otherwise restrict access to sensitive data, and the resources available by the users who will receive the data. In Chapter 8 you will explore other features that are important to consider when you will be distributing a workbook which restrict access and remove personal information.

Chapter Summary

- Workbook properties include descriptive information about the workbook such as the author's name, title, subject, or comments.
- Workbook properties are sometimes referred to as *metadata*.
- Display the Info tab Backstage view or open the Document Information Panel to add information to a workbook's properties.
- Comments display text in a pop-up box when the cell pointer is resting on a cell to which a comment has been attached.
- Comments are useful to add explanatory notes, descriptions, or pose questions about a cell entry when a workbook is being created, edited, or shared with other reviewers.
- Insert, edit, view, or delete a comment using buttons in the Comments group of the Review tab. Comment text can be copied and pasted to another cell using the Paste Special dialog box.
- Sharing a workbook generally involves turning on the sharing feature and saving the workbook to a folder on a networked server that is accessible to the other users who need the file.
- Use the Share Workbook button in the Changes group of the Review tab to turn on the sharing feature.
- When Microsoft Office is installed, a user name is defined for the computer upon which the software has been copied. Excel automatically inserts this name in the *Author* workbook property as a new workbook is created.
- You can change the user name at the Excel Options dialog box.

- View other users who have a shared workbook open at the Share Workbook dialog box.
- When a workbook is shared, Excel automatically tracks the changes made by each person who accesses the file.
- If two users have a shared workbook open at the same time and each person makes a change to the same cell, a Resolve Conflicts dialog box appears when the second user saves the workbook.
- At the Resolve Conflicts dialog box, the second user can choose to accept the change made by him or her or restore the cell to the entry made by the last person to save the file.
- Print a History sheet that provides a detailed record of all changes made to a shared workbook before removing shared access to the workbook.
- When a shared workbook is changed to an exclusive workbook, all change history is removed from the file.
- An entire worksheet can be protected to prevent another person from accidentally inserting, deleting, or changing data that you do not want modified.
- Protect a worksheet using the Protect Sheet button in the Changes group of the Review tab.
- You can add a password that is required to unprotect a worksheet.
- Each cell in a worksheet has a lock attribute which activates when the worksheet is protected.
- To allow individual cells in a protected worksheet to be editable, select the cell(s) and turn off the lock attribute before protecting the worksheet.
- The Protect Workbook button in the Changes group of the Review tab is used to protect a workbook from a user inserting, deleting, renaming, or otherwise managing worksheets in the workbook.
- You can prevent unauthorized access to an Excel workbook by adding an encrypted password to open and/or modify the workbook.
- At the Info tab Backstage view, click the Protect Workbook button and then click *Encrypt with Password* to add a workbook password. Save the workbook after typing and confirming the password.
- Turn on or off the Track Changes feature or display changes in a shared workbook by opening the Highlight Changes dialog box.
- The Accept/Reject Changes feature is used to navigate to each changed cell in a worksheet and accept or reject the revision.

Commands Review

FEATURE	RIBBON TAB, GROUP	BUTTON	KEYBOARD SHORTCUT
Accept/Reject Changes	Review, Changes		
Add comment	Review, Comments		Shift + F2
Add password to a workbook	File, Info		
Change user name	File		
Delete comment	Review, Comments		
Document Information Panel	File, Info	Properties	
Edit comment	Review, Comments		
Highlight Changes	Review, Changes		
Paste Copied Comment	Home, Clipboard		Ctrl + Alt + V
Protect Workbook	Review, Changes		
Protect Worksheet	Review, Changes		
Share Workbook	Review, Changes		
Track Changes	Review, Changes		
Unlock cells	Home, Cells		

Concepts Check Test Your Knowledge

Completion: In the space provided at the right, indicate the correct term, command, or number.

1. Open this view to add descriptive information about a workbook such as a title or subject heading. ____________________

2. This panel displays the workbook's properties between the ribbon and the worksheet. ____________________

3. A diagonal red triangle in the upper right corner of a cell indicates this box will pop up when the mouse pointer rests on the cell. ____________________

4. Open this dialog box to turn on the feature that allows changes by more than one user at the same time. ________________

5. Change the user name for the computer that you are using by opening this dialog box. ________________

6. When two users have the same workbook open at the same time and each makes a change to the same cell, this dialog box appears when the second person saves the workbook. ________________

7. Open this dialog box to create a History sheet that includes a record of all changes made to a shared workbook. ________________

8. Add a password that is required to unprotect a worksheet at this dialog box. ________________

9. Select a cell that you want to allow changes to and then click this button and menu option to unlock the cell before protecting the worksheet. ________________

10. Prevent users from inserting or deleting worksheets in a workbook by opening this dialog box. ________________

11. Click this option from the Protect Workbook drop-down list at the Info tab Backstage view to assign a password to open a workbook. ________________

12. Turn this feature on and Excel automatically changes the workbook to a shared workbook if it is not already shared. ________________

13. Excel applies this formatting to cells in a shared workbook that have been modified in order to make the revised cells stand out. ________________

14. Use this feature to navigate to each changed cell in a shared workbook and decide whether to keep the change or restore the cell back to its previous value. ________________

15. This feature is not available to restore cells to their previous values after you have finished reviewing tracked changes. ________________

Skills Check Assess Your Performance

Assessment 1

ENTER AND DISPLAY WORKBOOK PROPERTIES; INSERT COMMENTS

1. Open **NationalCSDeptLicenses.xlsx**.
2. Save the workbook with Save As and name it **EL2-C6-A1-NationalCSDeptLicenses**.
3. Type the following text in the appropriate workbook properties:

Add an Author	**Student Name** (Substitute your name for *Student Name*.)
Title	**MSO 2010 License Chargeback**
Subject	**Journal entry by department**
Category	**JE supporting document**
Status	**Posted**
Comments	**Audit worksheet for Office 2010 site license with internal chargebacks**

4. Remove the existing author *Paradigm Publishing Inc.*
5. Display the Document Information Panel.
6. Insert a screen image of the worksheet showing the Document Information Panel in a new Microsoft Word document using either Print Screen with Paste, the Screenshot feature (Insert tab, Screenshot button in Illustrations group), or the Windows Snipping tool (Start button, All Programs, Accessories). Type your name a few lines below the screen image.
7. Save the Microsoft Word document and name it **EL2-C6-A1-NationalCSDeptLicenses.docx**.
8. Print **EL2-C6-A1-NationalCSDeptLicenses.docx** and then exit Word.
9. At the Microsoft Excel worksheet, close the Document Information Panel.
10. Make B8 the active cell and insert a new comment. Type **Check this quantity with Marty. The number seems high.** in the comment box.
11. Make B14 the active cell and insert a new comment. Type **Make a note in the budget file for next year. This quantity will increase by 5.** in the comment box.
12. Print the worksheet with the comments as displayed on the sheet.
13. Save and close **EL2-C6-A1-NationalCSDeptLicenses.xlsx**.

Assessment 2

SHARE A WORKBOOK; EDIT A SHARED WORKBOOK; PRINT A HISTORY SHEET

1. Open **PrecisionMfgTargets.xlsx**.
2. Save the workbook with Save As and name it **EL2-C6-A2-PrecisionMfgTargets**.
3. Share the workbook.
4. Change the user name to *Lorne Moir* and then edit the following cells:

C11	from	*4,352*	to	*5520*
C18	from	*15,241*	to	*15960*

5. Save the workbook.
6. Change the user name to *Gerri Gonzales* and then edit the following cells:

F4	from	*3,845*	to	*5126*
F9	from	*7,745*	to	*9320*

7. Save the workbook.
8. Create a History sheet with a record of the changes made to the data by all users.
9. Print the History sheet. ***Note: If you submit your assignment work electronically, create a copy of the History worksheet in a new workbook since the History worksheet is automatically deleted when the file is saved.***
10. Save and then close **EL2-C6-A2-PrecisionMfgTargets.xlsx**.
11. Change the user name back to the original user name for the computer you are using.

Assessment 3

REMOVE SHARED ACCESS

1. Open **EL2-C6-A2-PrecisionMfgTargets.xlsx**.
2. Save the workbook with Save As and name it **EL2-C6-A3-PrecisionMfgTargets**.
3. Remove the shared access to the workbook.
4. Close **EL2-C6-A3-PrecisionMfgTargets.xlsx**.

Assessment 4

PROTECT AN ENTIRE WORKSHEET; ADD A PASSWORD TO A WORKBOOK

1. Open **EL2-C6-A1-NationalCSDeptLicenses.xlsx**.
2. Save the workbook with Save As and name it **EL2-C6-A4-NationalCSDeptLicenses**.
3. Protect the entire worksheet using the password *L$07j* to unprotect.
4. Add the password *J07$e* to open the workbook.
5. Save and close **EL2-C6-A4-NationalCSDeptLicenses.xlsx**.
6. Open **EL2-C6-A4-NationalCSDeptLicenses.xlsx** and test the password to open the workbook.
7. Unprotect the worksheet to test the password to unprotect.
8. Close **EL2-C6-A4-NationalCSDeptLicenses.xlsx**. Click Don't Save when prompted to save changes.

Assessment 5

UNLOCK CELLS AND PROTECT A WORKSHEET; PROTECT WORKBOOK STRUCTURE

1. Open **PrecisionMfgTargets.xlsx**.
2. Save the workbook with Save As and name it **EL2-C6-A5-PrecisionMfgTargets**.
3. Select the range C4:F21 and unlock the cells.
4. Deselect the range and then protect the worksheet using the password *Mt14#* to unprotect.
5. Rename Sheet1 to *2014MfgTargets*.
6. Delete Sheet2 and Sheet3.
7. Protect the workbook structure to prevent users from inserting, deleting, or renaming sheets using the password *Mt14!shts* to unprotect.
8. Save and then close **EL2-C6-A5-PrecisionMfgTargets.xlsx**.

Assessment

6 TRACK CHANGES; ACCEPT/REJECT CHANGES; PRINT A HISTORY SHEET

1. Open **EL2-C6-A5-PrecisionMfgTargets.xlsx**.
2. Save the workbook with Save As and name it **EL2-C6-A6-PrecisionMfgTargets**.
3. Unprotect the workbook structure so that new sheets can added, deleted, renamed, or copied.
4. Turn on the Track Changes feature.
5. Change the user name to *Grant Antone* and then edit the following cells:

D4	from	*3,251*	to	*3755*
D17	from	*5,748*	to	*6176*

6. Save the workbook, change the user name to *Jean Kocsis*, and then edit the following cells:

E6	from	*6,145*	to	*5748*
E11	from	*2,214*	to	*3417*

7. Save the workbook and then change the user name back to the original user name for the computer you are using.
8. Accept and Reject changes as follows:

Accept	D4
Reject	D17
Reject	E6
Accept	E11

9. Create and print a History sheet of the changes made to the worksheet. ***Note: If you submit your assignment work electronically, create a copy of the History worksheet in a new workbook since the History worksheet is automatically deleted when the file is saved.***
10. Print the 2014MfgTargets worksheet.
11. Save and then close **EL2-C6-A6-PrecisionMfgTargets.xlsx**.

Visual Benchmark Demonstrate Your Proficiency

TRACK CHANGES; INSERT COMMENTS

1. Open **PawsParadise.xlsx**.
2. Save the workbook with Save As and name it **EL2-C6-VB-PawsParadise**.
3. Figure 6.16 illustrates the worksheet after the owner and operator reviewed the worksheet created by her kennel manager. While reviewing the service price list, the owner made comments and changed cells. Using Figure 6.16 and Figure 6.17 make the same changes to your copy of the worksheet making sure the changes are associated with the owner's name.
4. Create and print a History worksheet scaled to fit on one page. ***Note: If you submit your assignment work electronically, create a copy of the History worksheet in a new workbook since the History worksheet is automatically deleted when the file is saved.***
5. Print the worksheet with the changes highlighted and the comments as displayed on the worksheet.

6. Save and then close **EL2-C6-VB-PawsParadise.xlsx**.
7. Change the user name back to the original user name for the computer you are using.

Figure 6.16 Visual Benchmark Worksheet with Comments

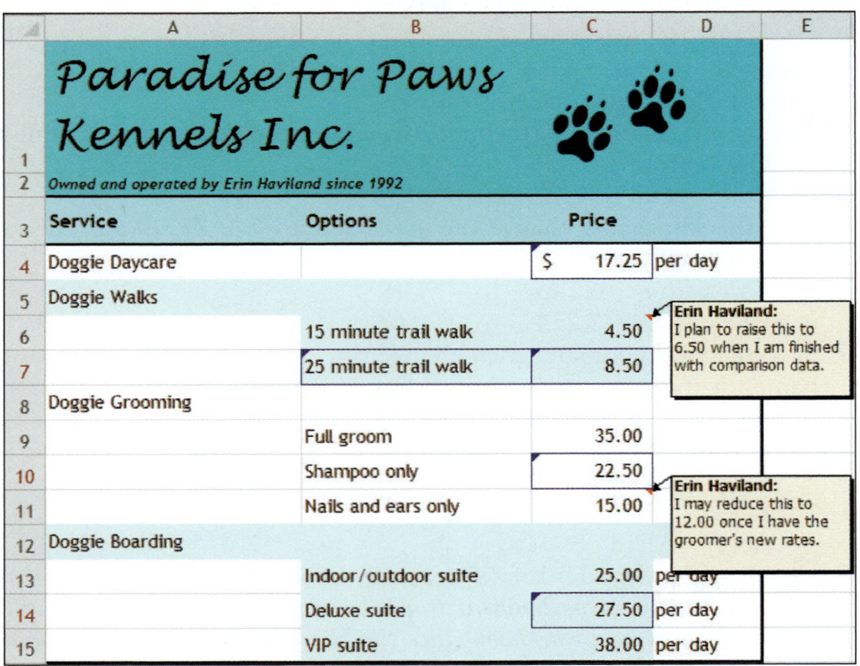

	A	B	C	D
1	Paradise for Paws Kennels Inc.			
2	*Owned and operated by Erin Haviland since 1992*			
3	**Service**	**Options**	**Price**	
4	Doggie Daycare		$ 17.25	per day
5	Doggie Walks			
6		15 minute trail walk	4.50	
7		25 minute trail walk	8.50	
8	Doggie Grooming			
9		Full groom	35.00	
10		Shampoo only	22.50	
11		Nails and ears only	15.00	
12	Doggie Boarding			
13		Indoor/outdoor suite	25.00	per day
14		Deluxe suite	27.50	per day
15		VIP suite	38.00	per day

Erin Haviland:
I plan to raise this to 6.50 when I am finished with comparison data.

Erin Haviland:
I may reduce this to 12.00 once I have the groomer's new rates.

Figure 6.17 Visual Benchmark History Worksheet

	A	B	C	D	E	F	G	H	I	J	K
1	Action Number	Date	Time	Who	Change	Sheet	Range	New Value	Old Value	Action Type	Losing Action
2	1	3/6/2012	10:46 AM	Erin Haviland	Cell Change	Sheet1	C4	$17.25	$16.50		
3	2	3/6/2012	10:46 AM	Erin Haviland	Cell Change	Sheet1	C7	$8.50	$8.25		
4	3	3/6/2012	10:46 AM	Erin Haviland	Cell Change	Sheet1	C10	$22.50	$20.00		
5	4	3/6/2012	10:46 AM	Erin Haviland	Cell Change	Sheet1	C14	$27.50	$28.50		
6	5	3/6/2012	10:46 AM	Erin Haviland	Cell Change	Sheet1	B7	25 minute trail walk	30 minute trail walk		
7											
8	The history ends with the changes saved on 3/6/2012 at 10:46 AM.										

Case Study Apply Your Skills

Part 1

Yolanda Robertson of NuTrends Market Research is working with Nicola Carlucci of Pizza by Mario on a workbook with projected franchise startups for 2014. The workbook is currently in draft format in a file named **PizzaByMarioNewFranchises.xlsx**. Open the workbook and use Save As to name the workbook **EL2-C6-CS-P1-PizzaByMarioNewFranchises**. Add an appropriate title and subject to the workbook's properties and include comment text to explain that the draft workbook was created in consultation with Nicola Carlucci. Yolanda has asked for your assistance with protecting the workbook to prevent accidental data modifications or erasure when the workbook is shared with others. Yolanda and Nicola have agreed that the city, state, and store numbers should be protected; however, the month a new store is planned to open and the names of prospective franchisees could change. Share the workbook. Yolanda and Nicola have agreed on the following passwords:

- Password to unprotect the worksheet is *U14@s*.
- Password to open the workbook is *SbM@14*.

Part 2

Use Save As to name the workbook **EL2-C6-CS-P2-PizzaByMarioNewFranchises**. Yolanda has reviewed her research files and meeting notes and has the following changes to make to the data. Make sure the user name is correct so that the following changes are associated with Yolanda:

Store 138 Franchisee is Jae-Dong Han
Store 149 Franchisee is Leslie Posno

Save the workbook. Nicola is in charge of logistics planning and has two changes to make to the months that stores are scheduled to open. Make sure the user name is correct so that the following changes are associated with Nicola:

Store 135 Open in February
Store 141 Open in December

Save the workbook and then display the worksheet with all of the changes made by Yolanda and Nicola highlighted. Create a History sheet. Print the worksheet with the cells highlighted and also print the History sheet. ***Note: If you submit your assignment work electronically, create a copy of the History worksheet in a new workbook since the History worksheet is automatically deleted when the file is saved.*** Restore the worksheet to exclusive use. Close **EL2-C6-CS-P2-PizzaByMarioNewFranchises.xlsx**. Change the user name back to the original user name for the computer you are using.

Part 3

Yolanda will be sending the shared workbook from Part 1 to Leonard Scriver, a colleague at the Michigan office of NuTrends Market Research. Yolanda wants Leonard to review the data and add his recommendations; however, Yolanda would prefer that Leonard save his copy using a different name so that the original shared version is not disrupted. Open **EL2-C6-CS-P1-PizzaByMarioNewFranchises.xlsx**. Unprotect the worksheet, remove the password to open the workbook, and then save the workbook using the name **EL2-C6-CS-P3-PizzabyMario-LScriver**. Based on Leonard's experience with franchise startups, he has the following recommendations which he prefers to show in comments within the worksheet.

Make sure the user name is correct so that the comment boxes display Leonard's name:

Store 136	Opening a second store in Chicago is more likely to occur in April
Store 144	Move this opening to June as resources at head office will be stretched in May
Store 152	Try to open this franchise at the same time as store 151

Show all comments within the worksheet and then print the worksheet making sure the comments print as displayed. Save and then close **EL2-C6-CS-P3-PizzabyMario-LScriver.xlsx**. Change the user name back to the original user name for the computer that you are using.

Part 4

Mario Carlucci has commented that the password to open the workbook is not intuitive for him and he has had trouble remembering the password. He wants to change the workbook password to something more user-friendly such as *Target14*. Yolanda and Nicola chose the passwords they have used in the workbook carefully based on their understanding of strong passwords that are more difficult to crack by unauthorized users. Yolanda has asked you to assist with a training package for Mario that will educate him on strong passwords. Research on the Internet the guidelines for creating strong passwords. Based on what you have learned from your research, create a document in Microsoft Word that highlights the components of a strong password. Include a table of dos and don'ts for creating strong passwords in a user-friendly easy-to-understand format for Mario. Finally, create a minimum of three examples that show a weak password improved by a stronger password. Include a suggestion for how to use the phrasing technique to create strong passwords so that they are easier to remember. Save the document and name it **EL2-C6-CS-P4-PizzaByMarioPasswords**. Print and then close **EL2-C6-CS-P4-PizzaByMarioPasswords.docx**.

Microsoft® Excel®

Automating Repetitive Tasks and Customizing Excel

PERFORMANCE OBJECTIVES

Upon successful completion of Chapter 7, you will be able to:

- **Record, run, and edit a macro**
- **Save a workbook containing macros as a macro-enabled workbook**
- **Create a macro that is run using a shortcut key combination**
- **Pin and unpin a frequently used file to the Recent Workbooks list**
- **Add and remove buttons for frequently used commands to the Quick Access toolbar**
- **Hide the ribbon to increase space in the work area**
- **Customize the display options for Excel**
- **Customize the ribbon by creating a custom tab and adding buttons**
- **Create and apply custom views**
- **Create and use a template**
- **Customize save options for AutoRecover files**

Tutorials

7.1 Using Macros
7.2 Managing Macros
7.3 Editing a Macro
7.4 Pinning Workbooks to the Recent Workbooks List
7.5 Customizing the Quick Access Toolbar
7.6 Customizing the Work Area
7.7 Customizing the Ribbon
7.8 Using Custom Templates

Automating and customizing the Excel environment can increase your efficiency and allow you to change the environment to accommodate your preferences. Create a macro when you find yourself repeating the same task frequently to save time and ensure consistency. Customize the Excel environment by adding a button for a frequently used command to the Quick Access toolbar to provide single-click access to the feature. Other ways to customize can involve tasks such as pinning frequently used files to the Recent Workbooks list, creating a custom template, ribbon tab, or custom view, or by modifying display and save options. Through completing the projects in this chapter, you will learn how to effectively automate and customize the Excel environment. Model answers for this chapter's projects appear on the following page.

Excel2010L2C7

Note: Before beginning the projects, copy to your storage medium the Excel2010L2C7 subfolder from the Excel2010L2 folder on the CD that accompanies this textbook and then make Excel2010L2C7 the active folder.

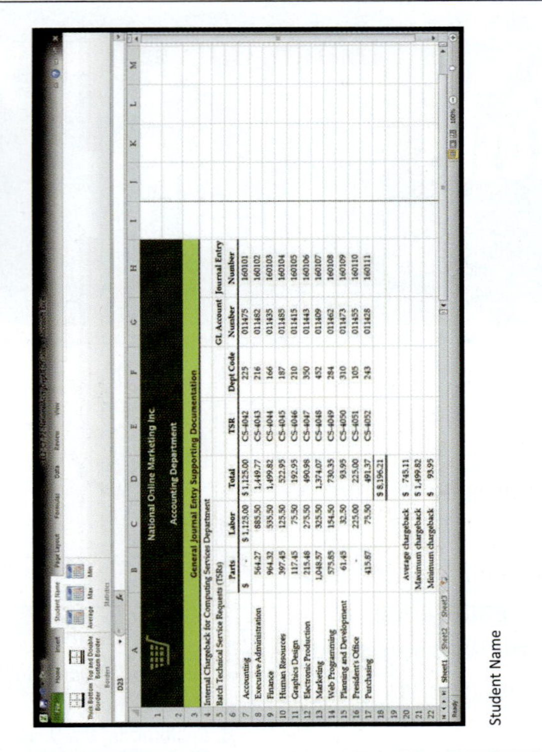

Student Name

Project 2 Customize the Excel Work Environment

Project 2f, EL2-C7-P2-NationalAcctgDeptJE.docx

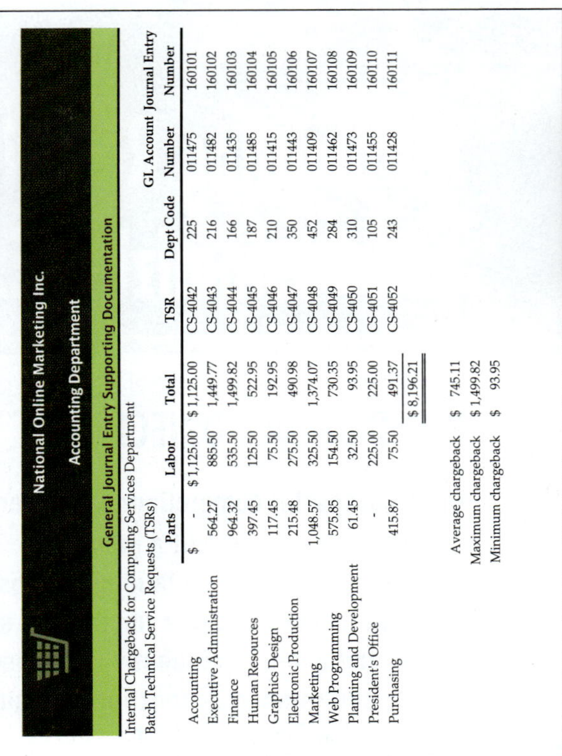

National Online Marketing Inc.

Accounting Department

General Journal Entry Supporting Documentation

Internal Chargeback for Computing Services Department

Batch Technical Service Requests (TSRs)

	Parts	Labor	Total	TSR	Dept Code	GL Account Number	Journal Entry Number
Accounting	$ -	$ 1,125.00	$ 1,125.00	CS-4042	225	011475	160101
Executive Administration	564.27	885.50	1,449.77	CS-4043	216	011482	160102
Finance	964.32	535.50	1,499.82	CS-4044	166	011435	160103
Human Resources	397.45	125.50	522.95	CS-4045	187	011485	160104
Graphics Design	117.45	75.50	192.95	CS-4046	210	011415	160105
Electronic Production	215.48	275.50	490.98	CS-4047	350	011443	160106
Marketing	1,048.57	325.50	1,374.07	CS-4048	452	011409	160107
Web Programming	575.85	154.50	730.35	CS-4049	284	011462	160108
Planning and Development	61.45	32.50	93.95	CS-4050	310	011473	160109
President's Office	-	225.00	225.00	CS-4051	105	011455	160110
Purchasing	415.87	75.50	491.37	CS-4052	243	011428	160111
			$ 8,196.21				
		Average chargeback	$ 745.11				
		Maximum chargeback	$ 1,499.82				
		Minimum chargeback	$ 93.95				

Project 2f, EL2-C7-P2-NationalAcctgDeptJE.xlsx

Noranda Sportsplex

Swimming Schedule

Winter 2012

Day	Start time	End time	Pool	Activity
MORNINGS				
Monday, Wednesday	6:30	7:50	Red pool	Aquafit
Tuesday, Thursday, Friday	6:30	7:50	Blue pool	Moms and tots
Monday, Wednesday	8:00	8:45		
Tuesday, Thursday, Friday	8:00	8:45		
Monday, Wednesday	8:00	8:45		
Tuesday, Thursday, Friday	8:00	8:45		
Monday, Wednesday	9:00	9:45		
Tuesday, Thursday, Friday	9:00	9:45		
Monday, Wednesday	9:00	9:45		
Tuesday, Thursday, Friday	9:00	9:45		
Monday, Wednesday	10:00	11:45		
Tuesday, Thursday, Friday	10:00	11:45		
Tuesday, Thursday, Friday	10:00	11:45		
Saturday, Sunday	9:00	11:45		
AFTERNOONS				
Monday, Wednesday	1:00	1:45		
Tuesday, Thursday, Friday	1:00	1:45		
Monday, Wednesday	1:00	1:45		
Tuesday, Thursday, Friday	1:00	1:45		
Monday, Wednesday	2:00	3:45		
Tuesday, Thursday, Friday	2:00	3:45		
Tuesday, Thursday, Friday	2:00	3:45		
Monday, Wednesday	2:00	3:45		
Tuesday, Thursday, Friday	2:00	3:45		
Monday, Wednesday	4:00	4:45		
Tuesday, Thursday, Friday	4:00	4:45		
Saturday, Sunday	2:00	4:45		
EVENINGS				
Monday, Wednesday	5:00	5:45		
Tuesday, Thursday, Friday	5:00	5:45		
Monday, Wednesday	5:00	5:45		
Tuesday, Thursday, Friday	5:00	5:45		
Monday, Wednesday	6:00	6:45		
Tuesday, Thursday, Friday	6:00	6:45		
Monday, Wednesday	7:00	7:45		
Tuesday, Thursday, Friday	7:00	7:45		
Monday, Wednesday	8:00	9:45		
Tuesday, Thursday, Friday	8:00	9:45		
Monday, Wednesday	8:00	9:45		
Tuesday, Thursday	8:00	9:45		
Friday	8:00	8:45		

Project 3 Save a Workbook as a Template

Project 3b, EL2-C7-P3-SwimSchWinter2012.xlsx

Model Answers

Create Macros

4 Parts

You will create, edit, run, and delete macros to automate tasks including assigning a macro to a shortcut key and storing frequently used macros in a macro workbook.

Automating Tasks Using Macros

A ***macro*** is a series of instructions stored in sequence that can be recalled and carried out whenever the need arises. Macros are generally created when a task that is never varied is repeated frequently. Saving the instructions in the macro not only saves time but ensures that the steps are consistently reapplied, which can avoid errors in data entry, formatting, or other worksheet options.

Take a few moments before you record a new macro to plan the steps you will need to perform. Also consider if the active cell location at the time the macro is run will be a factor. For example, will the first step in the macro involve positioning the cell at a specific location? If yes, during recording, you can position the active cell using a shortcut key or Go To command.

To create a macro, you begin by turning on the macro recorder. A macro is identified by assigning a unique name to the steps that will be saved. Macro names must begin with a letter and can be a combination of letters, numbers, and underscore characters. A macro name cannot include spaces—use the underscore character if you want to separate words in a macro name. At the Record Macro dialog box shown in Figure 7.1, you also choose the location in which to save the macro. By default, Excel saves the macro within the current workbook.

Macros can be assigned to a Ctrl shortcut key combination, which allows the macro to be run more quickly by pressing Ctrl plus the chosen lowercase or uppercase letter. Entering a description of the macro's purpose provides information to other users who might use or edit the macro. In a macro workbook that will be shared, also consider entering the creator's name and date into the description box for reference purposes. Do not be concerned if you make a typing mistake or have to cancel a dialog box while recording—correct your mistakes as you go

Quick Steps

Record Macro

1. Click View tab.
2. Click down-pointing arrow on Macros button.
3. Click *Record Macro.*
4. Type macro name.
5. Click in *Description* text box.
6. Type description text.
7. Click OK.
8. Perform desired actions.
9. Click Stop Recording button.

While creating the macro, mouse clicks to select tabs within the ribbon are not saved.

Macros

Figure 7.1 Record Macro Dialog Box

Macro names begin with a letter and can include a combination of letters, numbers, and underscore characters.

Assigning a macro to a Ctrl key combination enables the macro to be run by pressing Ctrl plus the letter.

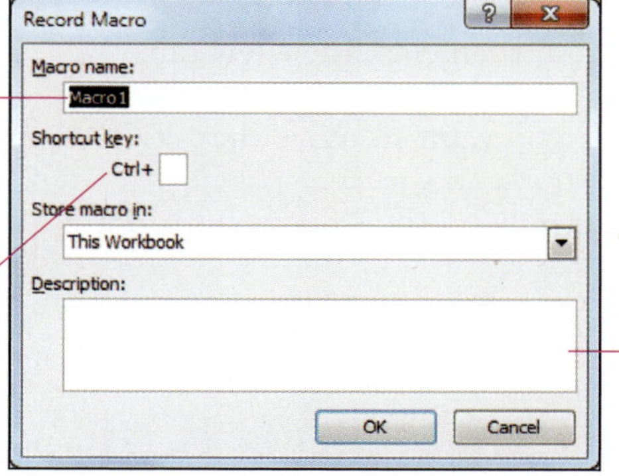

Including a description of the macro's purpose, the name of the person who created the macro, and the date recorded is useful for others who might need to run or edit the macro.

since only the end result is saved. Click OK when you are finished identifying the macro and the recorder begins saving the text and/or steps that you perform. Once you have completed the tasks you want saved, click the Stop Recording button in the Status bar to end recording.

Saving Workbooks Containing Macros

Quick Steps

Save Macro-Enabled Workbook

1. Click File tab.
2. Click Save As.
3. If necessary, navigate to desired drive and/or folder.
4. Type file name in *File name* text box.
5. Click *Save as type* list arrow.
6. Click *Excel Macro-Enabled Workbook (*.xlsm)*.
7. Click Save.

A workbook that contains a macro should be saved using the macro-enabled file format. The default XML-based file format (.xlsx) cannot store VBA macro code. (VBA stands for Visual Basic for Applications.) When a macro is created in Excel, the commands are written and saved in Microsoft Visual Basic. The macro recorder that you use when creating a macro converts your actions to Visual Basic statements for you behind the scenes. You can view and edit the Visual Basic code, or you can create macros from scratch by using the Visual Basic Editor in Microsoft Visual Basic. In Project 1e you will look at the Visual Basic statements created when the AcctgDocumentation macro was recorded and edit an instruction.

To save a workbook as a macro-enabled workbook, do one of the following actions:

- *New workbook*. Click the Save button on the Quick Access toolbar. Type the file name and change *Save as type* to *Excel Macro-Enabled Workbook (*.xlsm)*. Click the Save button.
- *Existing workbook*. Click the File tab and then click Save & Send. Click *Change File Type* in the File Types category in the center pane, click *Macro-Enabled Workbook (*.xlsm)* in the *Workbook File Types* section of the right pane, and then click the Save As button. At the Save As dialog box, type the file name and then click the Save button.

Project 1a **Creating a Macro and Saving a Workbook as a Macro-Enabled Workbook** Part 1 of 4

1. Assume that you work in the Accounting department at a large company. The company has a documentation standard for all Excel workbooks that requires each worksheet to show the department name, the author's name, the date the workbook was created, and a revision history. You decide to create a macro that will insert row labels for this data to standardize the documentation. Begin by starting a new blank workbook.
2. Create the documentation macro by completing the following steps:
   a. Make C4 the active cell and then click the View tab. (You are making a cell other than A1 the active cell because within the macro you want to move the active cell to the top left cell in the worksheet.)
   b. Click the down-pointing arrow on the Macros button in the Macros group.
   c. Click *Record Macro* at the drop-down list.

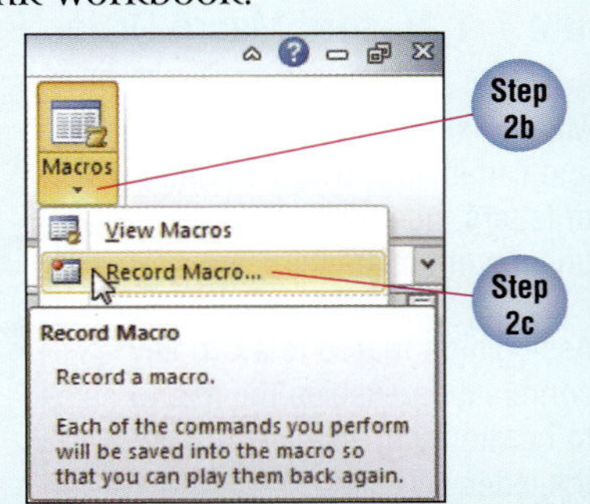

d. At the Record Macro dialog box with the insertion point positioned in the *Macro name* text box, type **AcctgDocumentation**.
e. Click in the *Description* text box and then type **Accounting department documentation macro. Created by [Student Name] on [Date].** where your name is substituted for *[Student Name]* and the current date is substituted for *[Date]*.

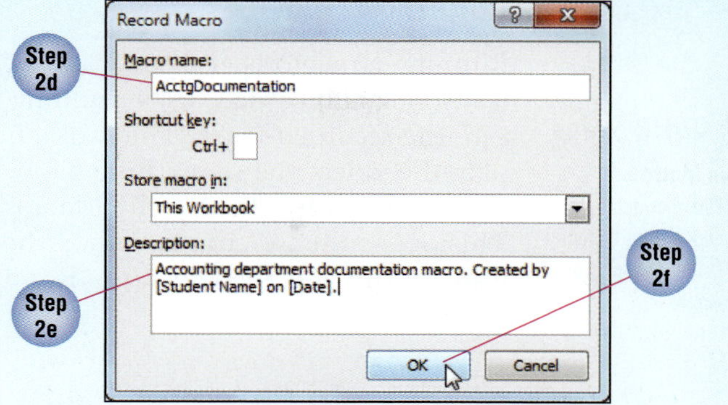

f. Click OK. The macro recorder is now turned on as indicated by the Stop Recording button in the Status bar (displays as a blue square next to *Ready*).
g. Press Ctrl + Home to move the active cell to A1. Including this command in the macro ensures that the documentation will always begin at A1 in all workbooks.
h. Type **Accounting department** and press Enter.
i. With the active cell in A2, type **Author** and press Enter.
j. With the active cell in A3, type **Date created** and press Enter.
k. With the active cell in A4, type **Revision history** and then press Enter three times to leave two blank rows before the worksheet will begin.

Steps 2h-2k

	A	B	C
1	Accounting department		
2	Author		
3	Date created		
4	Revision history		
5			
6			
7			
8			

l. Click the Stop Recording button located near the left side of the Status bar next to *Ready*.

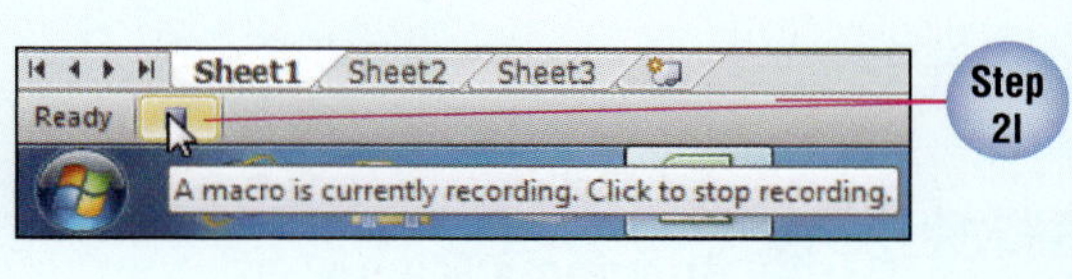

3. Save the workbook as a macro-enabled workbook by completing the following steps:
a. Click the File tab and then click Save As.
b. If necessary, navigate to the drive and/or folder for your student data files.
c. Click in the *File name* text box and type **EL2-C7-P1-Macros**.
d. Click the Save as type button, scroll up or down the pop-up list, and then click *Excel Macro-Enabled Workbook (*.xlsm)*.
e. Click the Save button.

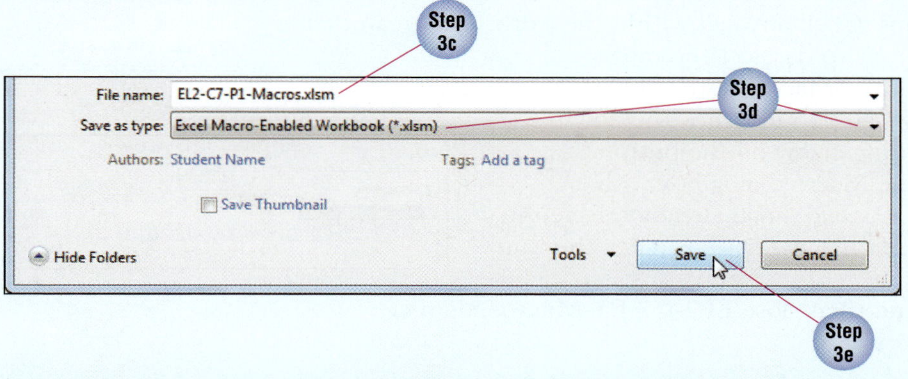

Running a Macro

Quick Steps

Run Macro
1. Click View tab.
2. Click Macros button.
3. Double-click macro name.

Running a macro is also sometimes referred to as playing a macro. Since a macro is a series of recorded tasks, running the macro involves instructing Excel to *play back* the recorded tasks. Think of a macro as a video you have made. When you play the video, the same thing happens every time. To run (play) a macro, view a list of macros by clicking the Macros button in the Macros group of the View tab. This opens the Macro dialog box shown in Figure 7.2. Click the macro name you want to run and then click the Run button, or double-click the macro in the *Macro name* list box.

Figure 7.2 Macro Dialog Box

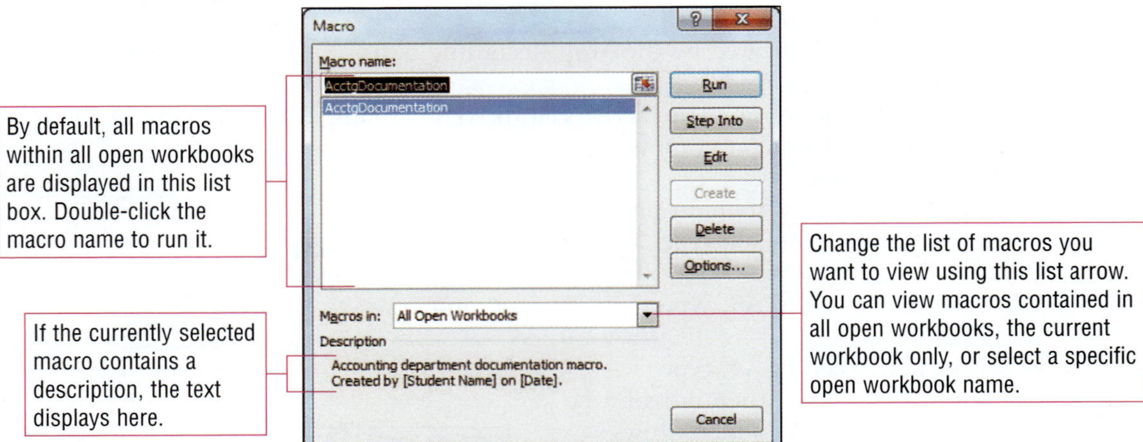

Macro
Macro name:
AcctgDocumentation
AcctgDocumentation
Run
Step Into
Edit
Create
Delete
Options...
Macros in:
All Open Workbooks
Description
Accounting department documentation macro.
Created by [Student Name] on [Date].
Cancel
By default, all macros within all open workbooks are displayed in this list box. Double-click the macro name to run it.
If the currently selected macro contains a description, the text displays here.
Change the list of macros you want to view using this list arrow. You can view macros contained in all open workbooks, the current workbook only, or select a specific open workbook name.

Project 1b **Running a Macro** Part 2 of 4

1. With **EL2-C7-P1-Macros.xlsm** open, run the AcctgDocumentation macro to test that the macro works correctly by completing the following steps:
   a. Select A1:A4 and press the Delete key to erase the cell contents.
   b. You want to test the Ctrl + Home command in the macro by making sure A1 is not active when the macro begins. Click any cell within the worksheet area other than A1 to deselect the range.
   c. Click the Macros button in the Macros group of the View tab. Do not click the down-pointing arrow on the button.
   d. At the Macro dialog box with *AcctgDocumentation* already selected in the *Macro name* list box, click the Run button.
2. Save and then close **EL2-C7-P1-Macros.xlsm**.

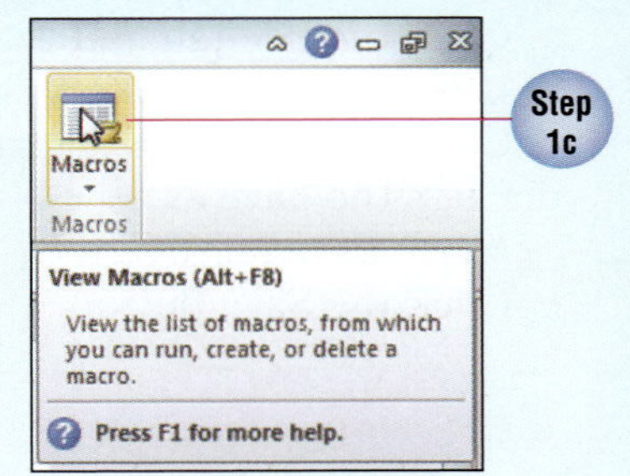

Macros
Macros
View Macros (Alt+F8)
View the list of macros, from which you can run, create, or delete a macro.
Press F1 for more help.
Step 1c

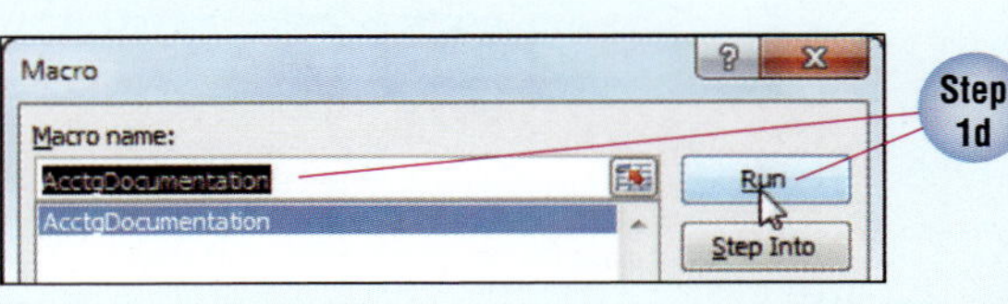

Macro
Macro name:
AcctgDocumentation
AcctgDocumentation
Run
Step Into
Step 1d

Assigning a Macro to a Shortcut Key

When you record a macro you have the option of assigning the macro to a Ctrl key combination. A macro that is assigned to a shortcut key can be run without displaying the Macro dialog box. You can choose any lowercase letter or uppercase letter for the macro. Excel distinguishes the case of the letter you choose when you type the letter at the *Shortcut key* text box at the Record Macro dialog box. For example, if you type an uppercase O, Excel defines the shortcut key as *Ctrl + Shift + O* as shown in Figure 7.3.

If an Excel feature is assigned to the key combination that you choose, your macro will override Excel's shortcut. For example, pressing Ctrl + p in Excel causes the Print dialog box to appear. If you create a macro and assign the macro to Ctrl + p, your macro's instructions are invoked instead of the Print dialog box. You can view a list of Excel-assigned keyboard shortcuts in Help by typing *keyboard shortcuts* in the Search text box of the Excel Help window. Select *Keyboard shortcuts in Excel 2010* in the Results list.

Quick Steps

Assign Macro to Shortcut Key

1. Click View tab.
2. Click down-pointing arrow on Macros button.
3. Click *Record Macro.*
4. Type macro name.
5. Click in *Shortcut key* text box.
6. Type desired letter.
7. Click in *Description* text box.
8. Type description text.
9. Click OK.
10. Perform desired actions.
11. Click Stop Recording button.

Record New Macro

Figure 7.3 Record Macro Dialog Box with Shortcut Key Assigned

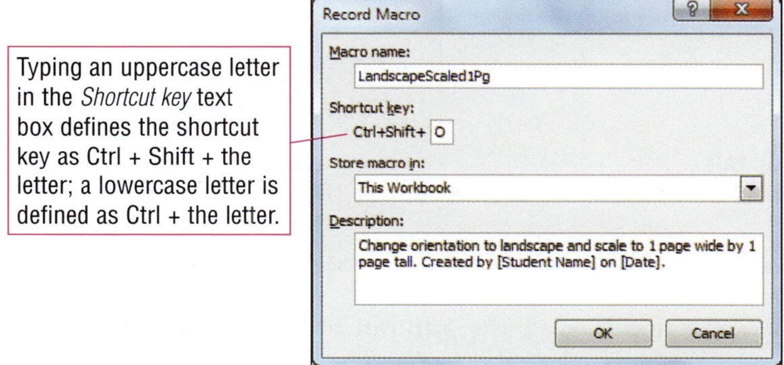

Project 1c Creating and Running a Macro Using a Shortcut Key

Part 3 of 4

1. Open **EL2-C7-P1-Macros.xlsm.**
2. The default security setting for any workbook that is opened containing a macro is *Disable all macros with notification*. This causes a security warning to appear in the message bar (between the ribbon and the formula bar) notifying you that macros have been disabled. Enable the macros in the workbook by clicking the Enable Content button in the Security Warning message bar.

Security Warning Macros have been disabled. Enable Content

Step 2

3. Create a macro assigned to a keyboard shortcut that changes print options for a worksheet by completing the following steps:

a. Once a macro has been recorded and stopped in an Excel session, the Stop Recording button in the Status bar changes to the Record New Macro button.

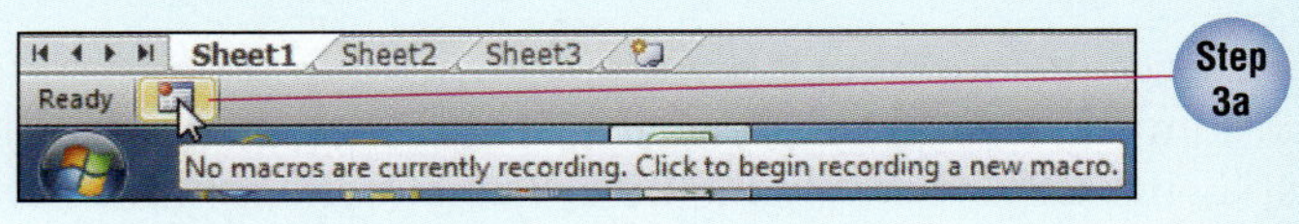

Click the Record New Macro button located at the left side of the Status bar next to *Ready*. If you exited Excel before starting this project, start a new macro by clicking the View tab, clicking the down-pointing arrow on the Macros button, and then clicking *Record Macro*.

b. Type **LandscapeScaled1Pg** in the *Macro name* text box.
c. Click in the *Shortcut key* text box, hold down the Shift key, and press the letter o.
d. Click in the *Description* text box and then type **Change orientation to landscape and scale to 1 page wide by 1 page tall. Created by [Student Name] on [Date].** Substitute your name for *[Student Name]* and the current date for *[Date]*.

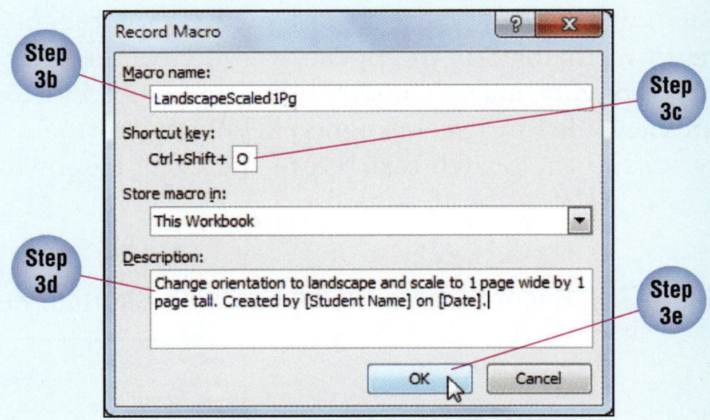

e. Click OK.
f. Click the Page Layout tab.
g. Click the Page Setup Dialog Box launcher located at the bottom right of the Page Setup group.
h. At the Page Setup dialog box with the Page tab selected, click *Landscape* in the *Orientation* section.
i. Click *Fit to* in the *Scaling* section to scale the printout to 1 page wide by 1 page tall.
j. Click OK.

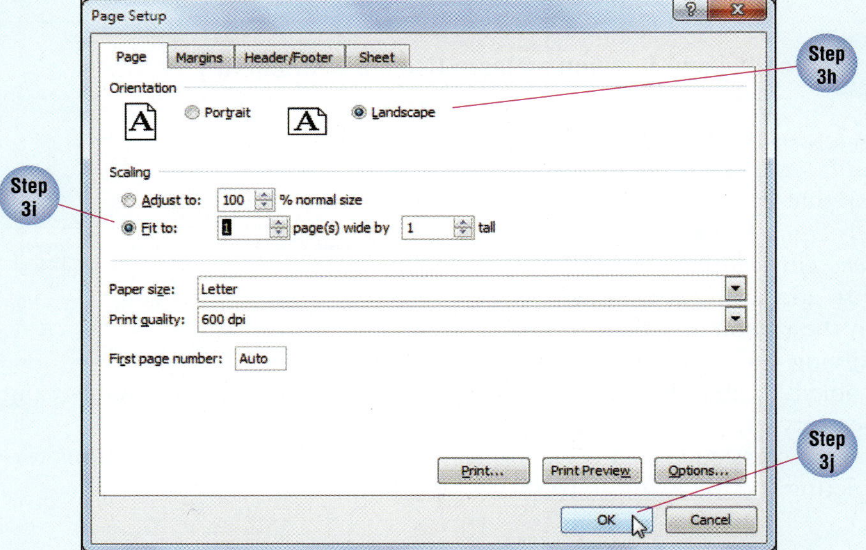

k. Click the Stop Recording button.

4. Press Ctrl + N to start a new blank workbook.
5. Press Ctrl + Shift + o to run the LandscapeScaled1Pg macro.
6. Type your name in A1, press Enter, and then press Ctrl + F2 to display the worksheet in the Print tab Backstage view. Notice in the Print Preview pane the page orientation is landscape. Review the options in the Settings category in the center pane. Notice that *Landscape Orientation* and *Fit Sheet on One Page* have been set by the macro.
7. Click the Home tab to return to the worksheet and then close the new workbook. Click Don't Save when prompted to save changes.
8. Save **EL2-C7-P1-Macros.xlsm**.

Editing a Macro

The actions that you performed while recording the macro are stored in Visual Basic for Applications program code. Each macro is saved as a separate module within a VBAProject for the workbook. A module can be described as a receptacle for the instructions. Each macro is contained within a separate module within the workbook. Figure 7.4 displays the Visual Basic macro code for the macro created in Project 1a.

Edit a macro if you need to make a change that is easy to decipher within the Visual Basic statements. If you need to make several changes to a macro or do not feel comfortable with the Visual Basic for Applications code window, you can re-record the macro. When you record a new macro that has the same name as an existing macro, Excel prompts you to replace the existing macro. You can then record the correct steps by overwriting the original macro.

Quick Steps

Edit Macro
1. Open workbook containing macro.
2. Click View tab.
3. Click Macros button.
4. Click desired macro name.
5. Click Edit button.
6. Make desired changes in Visual Basic code window.
7. Click Save button.
8. Click File.
9. Click *Close and Return to Microsoft Excel.*

Figure 7.4 Microsoft Visual Basic for Applications Window for Project 1a AcctgDocumentation Macro

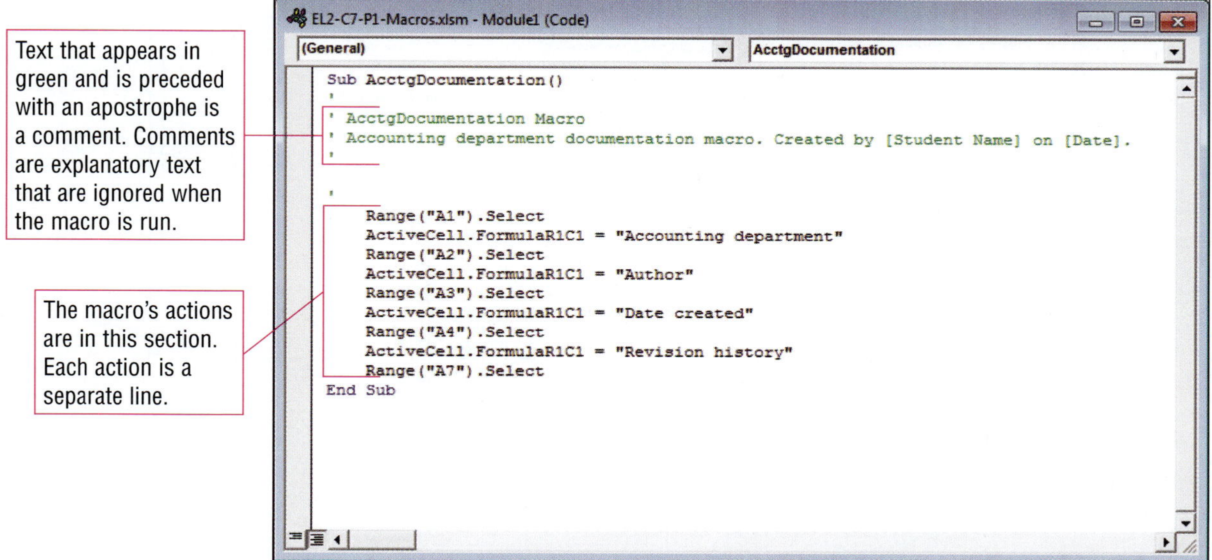

Project 1d Editing a Macro

1. With **EL2-C7-P1-Macros.xlsm** open, edit the AcctgDocumentation macro to leave only one blank row after the last entry by completing the following steps:
   a. If necessary, click the View tab.
   b. Click the Macros button in the Macros group.
   c. At the Macro dialog box with *AcctgDocumentation* already selected in the *Macro name* list box, click the Edit button. A Microsoft Visual Basic for Applications window opens with the program code displayed for EL2-C7-P1-Macros.xlsm Module1 (Code).

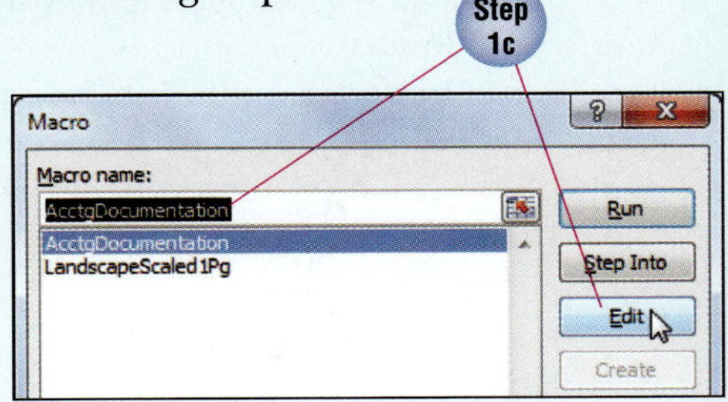

   d. Read the statements between the blue *Sub* and *End Sub* statements. *Sub* indicates the beginning of a procedure and *End Sub* indicates the end of the procedure. A procedure is a set of Visual Basic statements that perform actions. The name of the procedure is placed after the opening *Sub* statement and is the macro name. The lines beginning with a single apostrophe (') are comments. Comments are used in programming to insert explanatory text that describes the logic or purpose of a statement. Statements that begin with the apostrophe character are ignored when the macro is run. The commands that are executed when the macro is run are the indented lines of text below the comment lines.
   e. Position the insertion point at the beginning of the last statement before *End Sub* that reads *Range("A7").Select* and click the left mouse button. This is the last action in the macro that makes A7 the active cell. Notice the entry two lines above reads *Range("A4").Select*. To edit the macro and leave only one blank row you need to change the address from *A7* to *A6*.
   f. Use the Right Arrow key to move the insertion point, delete *7*, and type **6** so that the edited line reads *Range("A6").Select*.

EL2-C7-P1-Macros.xlsm - Module1 (Code)

(General) | AcctgDocumentation

```
Sub AcctgDocumentation()
'
' AcctgDocumentation Macro
' Accounting department documentation macro. Created by [Student Name] on [Date].
'

'
    Range("A1").Select
    ActiveCell.FormulaR1C1 = "Accounting department"
    Range("A2").Select
    ActiveCell.FormulaR1C1 = "Author"
    Range("A3").Select
    ActiveCell.FormulaR1C1 = "Date created"
    Range("A4").Select
    ActiveCell.FormulaR1C1 = "Revision history"
    Range("A6").Select
End Sub
```

Step 1f

   g. Click the Save button on the toolbar.

2. Click File and then click *Close and Return to Microsoft Excel*.
3. Test the edited macro to make sure only one blank row is left before the active cell by completing the following steps:
   a. Select A1:A4 and press the Delete key.
   b. Make any cell other than A1 the active cell.
   c. Click the Macros button in the Macros group of the View tab. Do not click the down-pointing arrow on the button.
   d. At the Macro dialog box, double-click *AcctgDocumentation* in the *Macro name* list box.
4. Save and close **EL2-C7-P1-Macros.xlsm**.

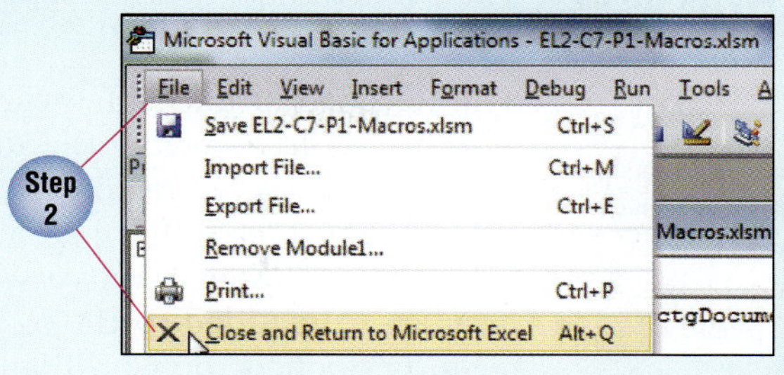

Deleting a Macro

If you no longer need a macro, the macro can be deleted at the Macro dialog box. Open the Macro dialog box, select the macro name in the *Macro name* list box, and then click the Delete button.

Quick Steps

Delete Macro
1. Open Macro dialog box.
2. Click macro name.
3. Click Delete button.
4. Click Yes.

Managing Macros

By default, macros are stored within the workbook that is active when the macro is recorded. When you close the workbook, the macros within the file are no longer available. For example, if you close the EL2-C7-P1-Macros.xlsm file, the AcctgDocumentation macro you created is not available to you in a new workbook. If you create macros that you want to use in other workbooks, one solution is to leave the workbook containing the macros open since the Macro dialog box, by default, displays macros in the *Macro name* list box from all open workbooks.

Consider creating a macros workbook with a set of standard macros that you wish to use in any file similar to the macros workbook you have created in Projects 1a through 1d. Open this workbook whenever you are working in Excel and the macros stored within the workbook will be available to you for all other files that you create or edit during an Excel session. Using this method, you can also copy the macros workbook to any other computer so that a set of standard macros can be distributed to others for their use.

Project 2 Customize the Excel Work Environment — 8 Parts

You will customize the Excel environment by pinning a frequently used workbook to the *Recent Workbooks* list, add buttons to the Quick Access toolbar to make features more accessible, minimize the ribbon to create more space in the work area, change display options, create a custom ribbon tab, and create custom views.

Quick Steps

Pin Workbook to *Recent Workbooks* List

1. Make sure workbook has been opened recently.
2. Click File tab.
3. If necessary, click Recent.
4. Click pin icon next to workbook name.

Unpin Workbook from *Recent Workbooks* List

1. Click File tab.
2. If necessary, click Recent.
3. Click blue pin icon next to workbook name.

Pinning Workbooks to the *Recent Workbooks* List

The Recent tab Backstage view displays by default the 20 most recently opened workbook file names in the *Recent Workbooks* section in the left pane. The right pane displays a list of folders to which you have recently navigated in a section titled *Recent Places*. To open a workbook you used recently, click the workbook name in the *Recent Workbooks* list. A workbook that you use frequently can be permanently added to the *Recent Workbooks* list. To do this, make sure you have recently opened the workbook, click the File tab, click Recent if the Recent tab is not already displayed, and then click the pin icon next to the workbook name. A workbook that is permanently pinned to the list displays with a blue push pin icon. Clicking the blue push pin icon unpins a workbook from the list.

To change the number of workbooks shown in the *Recent Workbooks* list, open the Excel Options dialog box and click *Advanced* in the left pane. Change the number in *Show this number of Recent Documents* text box in the *Display* section to the desired number of workbooks.

Pinned Workbook

Unpinned Workbook

Project 2a **Pinning a Frequently Used Workbook to the *Recent Workbooks* List** Part 1 of 8

1. Open **NorandaWinterSwimSch.xlsx**.
2. Scroll down the worksheet to review the winter swimming schedule and then close the workbook.
3. At a blank Excel screen, pin two workbooks to the *Recent Workbooks* list by completing the following steps:
   a. Click the File tab.
   b. By default the Recent tab Backstage view displays if no workbooks are currently open.
   c. Click the pin icon to the right of **NorandaWinterSwimSch.xlsx** in the *Recent Workbooks* list.
   d. Click the pin icon to the right of **EL2-C7-P1-Macros.xlsm.**

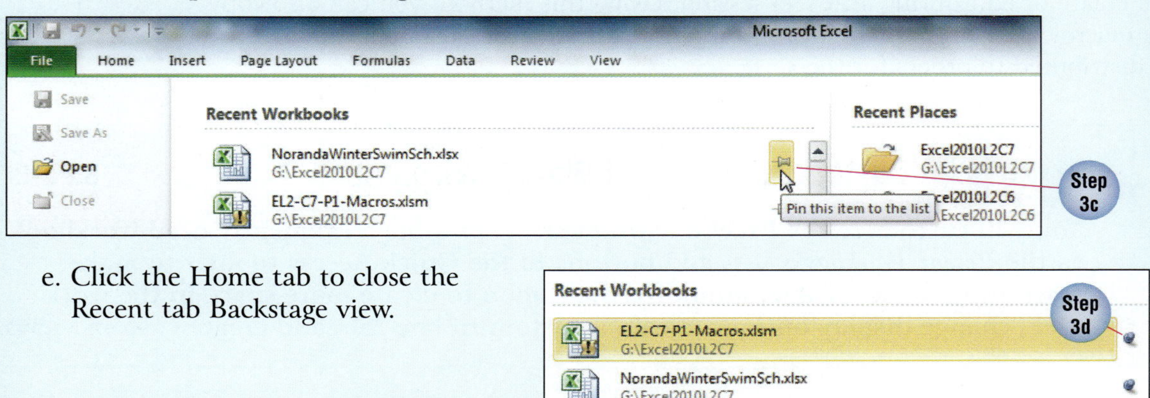

   e. Click the Home tab to close the Recent tab Backstage view.

4. Click the File tab and then click **EL2-C7-P1-Macros.xlsm** in the *Recent Workbooks* list to open the workbook.
5. Close **EL2-C7-P1-Macros.xlsm**.
6. Unpin the two workbooks by completing the following steps:
   a. Click the File tab.
   b. Click the blue push pin icon to the right of **EL2-C7-P1-Macros.xlsm**.
   c. Click the blue push pin icon to the right of **NorandaWinterSwimSch.xlsx**.
   d. Click the Home tab to close the Recent tab Backstage view.

Customizing the Quick Access Toolbar

As you work with Excel you may find that some features that you use frequently you would prefer to access from the Quick Access toolbar to save time and mouse clicks. Click the Customize Quick Access Toolbar button located at the right end of the toolbar to open the Customize Quick Access Toolbar drop-down list shown in Figure 7.5.

Customize Quick Access Toolbar

Click *More Commands* at the drop-down list to open the Excel Options dialog box with *Quick Access Toolbar* selected in the left pane as shown in Figure 7.6. Change the list of commands shown in the left list box by clicking the down-pointing arrow to the right of *Choose commands from* and then clicking the desired category. Scroll the list box to locate the command and then double-click the command name to add it to the Quick Access toolbar.

A few less popular features are only available by adding a button to the Quick Access toolbar. If a feature you are trying to locate is not available in any tab of the ribbon, search for the feature in the *All Commands* list.

Quick Steps

Add Button to Quick Access Toolbar
1. Click Customize Quick Access Toolbar button.
2. Click desired button.

OR
1. Click Customize Quick Access Toolbar button.
2. Click *More Commands*.
3. Click down-pointing arrow at right of *Choose commands from*.
4. Click desired category.
5. Double-click desired command in commands list box.
6. Click OK.

Remove Button from Quick Access Toolbar
1. Click Customize Quick Access Toolbar button.
2. Click desired button.

OR
1. Click Customize Quick Access Toolbar button.
2. Click *More Commands*.
3. Click desired command in right list box.
4. Click Remove button.
5. Click OK.

Figure 7.5 Customize Quick Access Toolbar Drop-down List

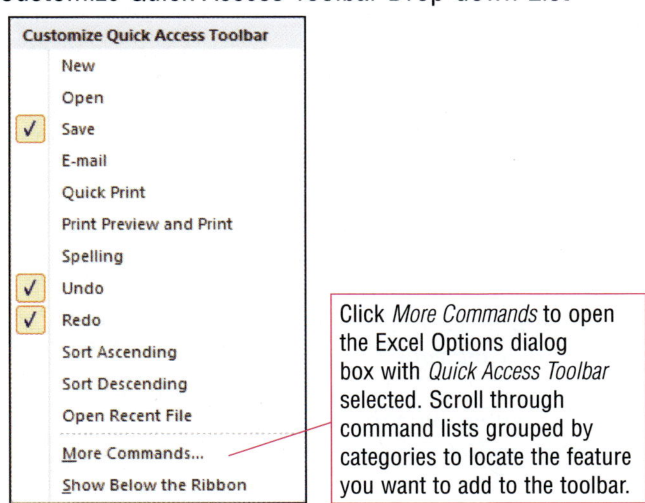
Customize Quick Access Toolbar
New
Open
Save
E-mail
Quick Print
Print Preview and Print
Spelling
Undo
Redo
Sort Ascending
Sort Descending
Open Recent File
More Commands...
Show Below the Ribbon
Click *More Commands* to open the Excel Options dialog box with *Quick Access Toolbar* selected. Scroll through command lists grouped by categories to locate the feature you want to add to the toolbar.

Figure 7.6 Excel Options Dialog Box with *Quick Access Toolbar* Selected

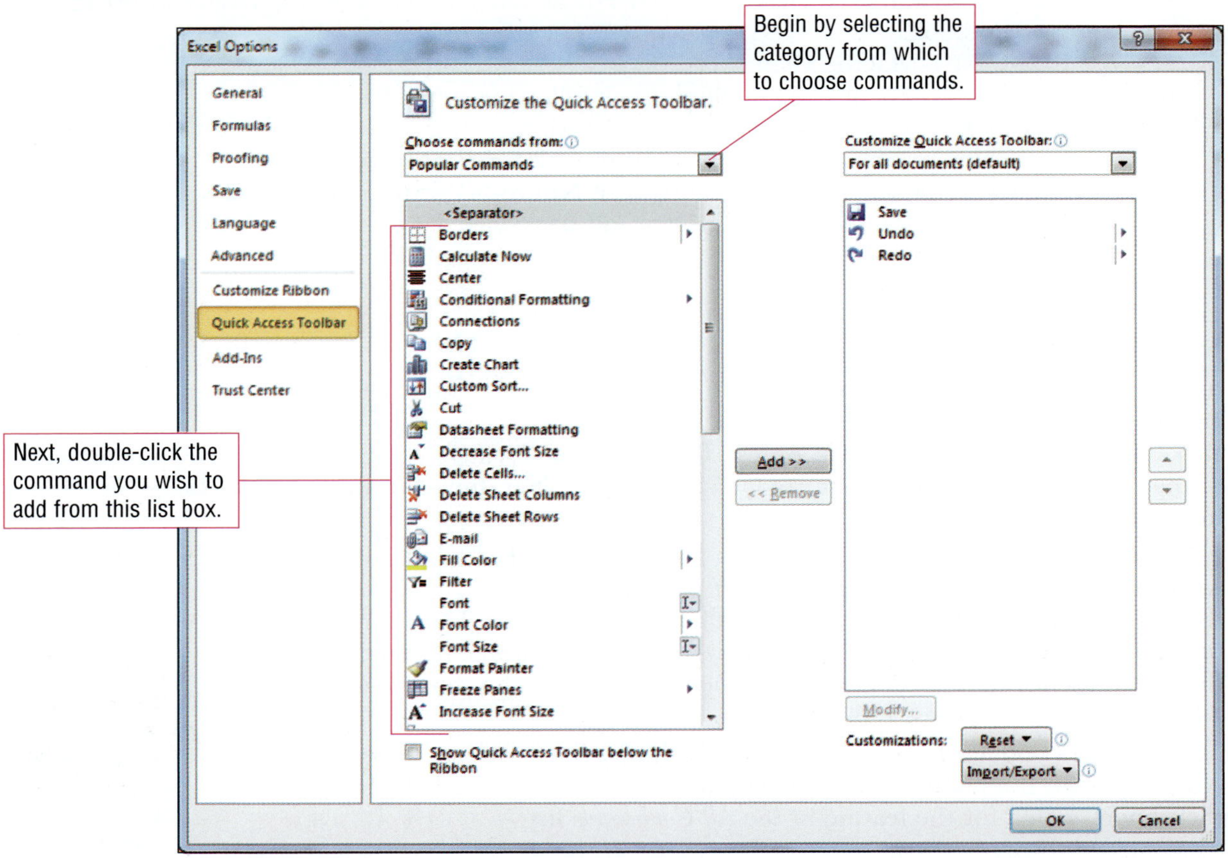

Begin by selecting the category from which to choose commands.

Next, double-click the command you wish to add from this list box.

Project 2b Adding Commands to the Quick Access Toolbar

Part 2 of 8

1. Press Ctrl + N to start a new blank workbook and then add the Print Preview and Print and Sort commands to the Quick Access toolbar by completing the following steps:
   a. Click the Customize Quick Access Toolbar button located at the right end of the Quick Access toolbar.
   b. Click *Print Preview and Print* at the drop-down list. Print Preview and Print is added to the end of the Quick Access toolbar. ***Note: Go to Step 1d if*** **Print Preview and Print** ***is already present on your Quick Access toolbar.***
   c. Click the Customize Quick Access Toolbar button.
   d. Click *More Commands* at the drop-down list.

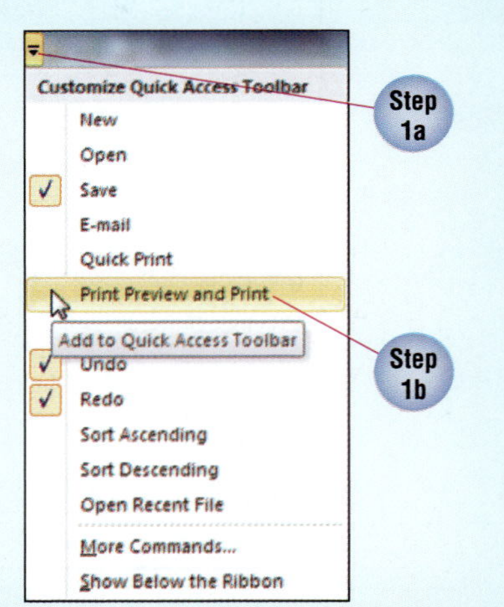

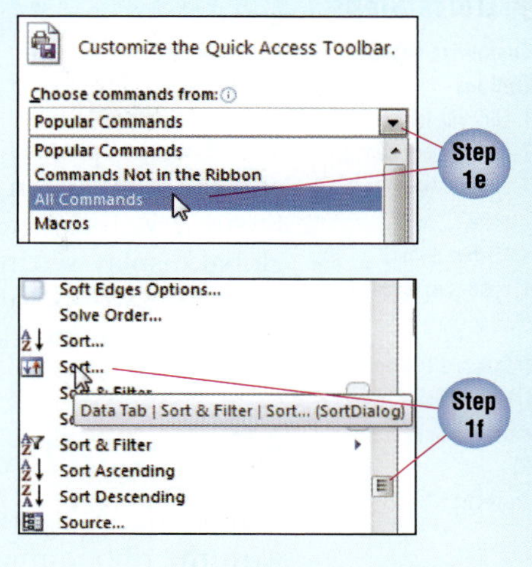

   e. At the Excel Options dialog box with *Quick Access Toolbar* selected in the left pane, click the down-pointing arrow next to *Choose commands from* and then click *All Commands*.
   f. Scroll down the *All Commands* list box and then double-click the *Sort* option that displays the ScreenTip *Data Tab | Sort & Filter | Sort.... (SortDialog)*. ***Note: The commands are organized in alphabetical order—you will need to scroll far down the list.***
   g. Click OK. The Sort button is added to the end of the Quick Access toolbar.
2. Type your name in A1, press Enter, and then click the Print Preview and Print button on the Quick Access toolbar to display the worksheet in Print Preview.
3. Click the Home tab to close the Print tab Backstage view.
4. Click the Sort button on the Quick Access toolbar to open the Sort dialog box.
5. Click the Cancel button at the Sort dialog box.

Project 2c Removing Buttons from the Quick Access Toolbar

Part 3 of 8

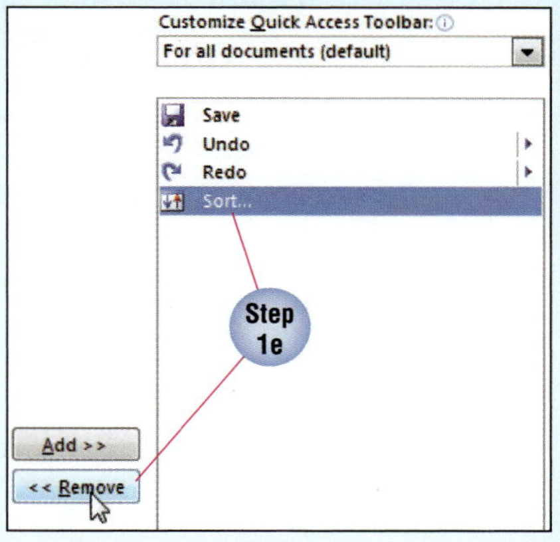

1. Remove the Print Preview and Print and Sort buttons from the Quick Access toolbar by completing the following steps:
   a. Click the Customize Quick Access Toolbar button.
   b. Click *Print Preview and Print* at the drop-down list. ***Note: Check with your instructor if* Print Preview and Print *was already present on the Quick Access toolbar before Project 2b. Your school may want the customized Quick Access toolbar to remain unchanged; go to Step 1d in this case.***
   c. Click the Customize Quick Access Toolbar button.
   d. Click *More Commands* at the drop-down list.
   e. At the Excel Options dialog box with *Quick Access Toolbar* selected in the left pane, click *Sort* in the right list box and then click the Remove button.
   f. Click OK.
2. Close the workbook. Click Don't Save when prompted to save changes.

Quick Steps

Customize Display Options

1. Click File tab.
2. Click Options button.
3. Click *Advanced* in left pane.
4. Change display options as required.
5. Click OK.

Minimize Ribbon

Click the Minimize the Ribbon button.

OR

Press Ctrl + F1.

Options

Minimize Ribbon

Changing Display Options to Customize the Work Area

The Excel Options dialog box contains many options for customizing the environment when the default options do not suit your needs. As shown in Figure 7.7, Excel groups options that affect the display of Excel by those that are global display settings, those that affect the entire workbook, and those that affect the active worksheet. Changes to workbook and/or worksheet display options are saved with the workbook.

Minimizing the Ribbon

When you are working with a large worksheet, you may find it easier to work with the ribbon minimized to provide more space within the work area. Figure 7.8 shows the worksheet you will use in Project 2d to customize the display options and minimize the ribbon. With the ribbon minimized, clicking a tab temporarily redisplays the ribbon to allow you to select a feature. As soon as you select the feature, the ribbon returns to the minimized state. Click the Minimize the Ribbon button located at the right end of the tab names (left of the Help button), or press Ctrl + F1, to toggle on or off the ribbon.

Figure 7.7 Excel Options Dialog Box with Display Options Shown

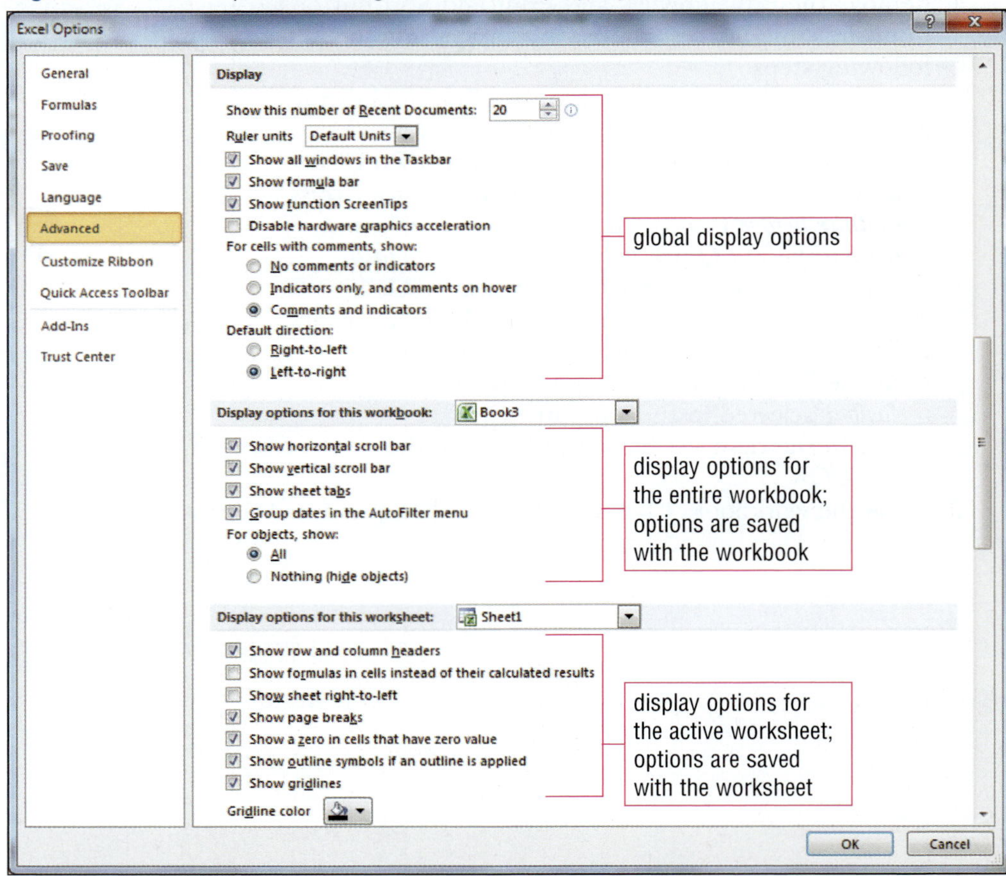

Figure 7.8 Project 2d Worksheet with Customized Display Options and Minimized Ribbon

Noranda Sportsplex

Winter Swimming Schedule

Day	Start time	End time	Pool	Activity
MORNINGS				
Monday, Wednesday	6:30	7:50	All	Adult swim
Tuesday, Thursday, Friday	6:30	7:50	All	Moms & tots swim
Monday, Wednesday	8:00	8:45	Blue, Green	Beginner aquafit
Tuesday, Thursday, Friday	8:00	8:45	Blue, Green	Adult swim
Monday, Wednesday	8:00	8:45	Red	Deep water aquafit
Tuesday, Thursday, Friday	8:00	8:45	Red	Deep water aquafit
Monday, Wednesday	9:00	9:45	Blue, Green	Intermediate aquafit
Tuesday, Thursday, Friday	9:00	9:45	Blue, Green	Leisure swim
Monday, Wednesday	9:00	9:45	Red	Senior aquafit
Tuesday, Thursday, Friday	9:00	9:45	Red	Beginner aquafit
Monday, Wednesday	10:00	11:45	All	Leisure swim
Tuesday, Thursday, Friday	10:00	11:45	Blue, Green	Senior aquafit
Tuesday, Thursday, Friday	10:00	11:45	Red	Deep water aquafit
Saturday, Sunday	9:00	11:45	All	Swimming lessons
AFTERNOONS				
Monday, Wednesday	1:00	1:45	Blue	Moms & tots swim
Tuesday, Thursday, Friday	1:00	1:45	Blue	Adult swim
Monday, Wednesday	1:00	1:45	Red, Green	Beginner aquafit
Tuesday, Thursday, Friday	1:00	1:45	Red, Green	Intermediate aquafit
Monday, Wednesday	2:00	3:45	All	Leisure swim
Tuesday, Thursday, Friday	2:00	3:45	Blue, Green	Private bookings
Tuesday, Thursday, Friday	2:00	3:45	Red	Diving club

Project 2d Customizing Display Options and Minimizing the Ribbon

Part 4 of 8

1. Open **NorandaWinterSwimSch.xlsx**.
2. Save the workbook with Save As and name it **EL2-C7-P2-NorandaWinterSwimSch**.
3. Turn off the display of the Formula bar since no formulas exist in the workbook, turn off the display of sheet tabs since only one sheet exists in the workbook, and turn off the display of row and column headers and gridlines by completing the following steps:
   a. Click the File tab.
   b. Click the Options button.
   c. Click *Advanced* in the left pane.
   d. Scroll down the Excel Options dialog box to the *Display* section and then click the *Show formula bar* check box to clear the check mark.
   e. Scroll down to the *Display options for this workbook* section and then click the *Show sheet tabs* check box to clear the check mark.

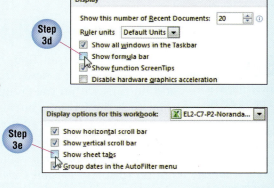

Step 3d

Display
Show this number of Recent Documents: 20
Ruler units Default Units
Show all windows in the Taskbar
Show formula bar
Show function ScreenTips
Disable hardware graphics acceleration

Step 3e

Display options for this workbook: EL2-C7-P2-Noranda...
Show horizontal scroll bar
Show vertical scroll bar
Show sheet tabs
Group dates in the AutoFilter menu

f. Scroll down to the *Display options for this worksheet* section and then click the *Show row and column headers* check box to clear the check mark.
g. Click the *Show gridlines* check box to clear the check mark.
h. Click OK.

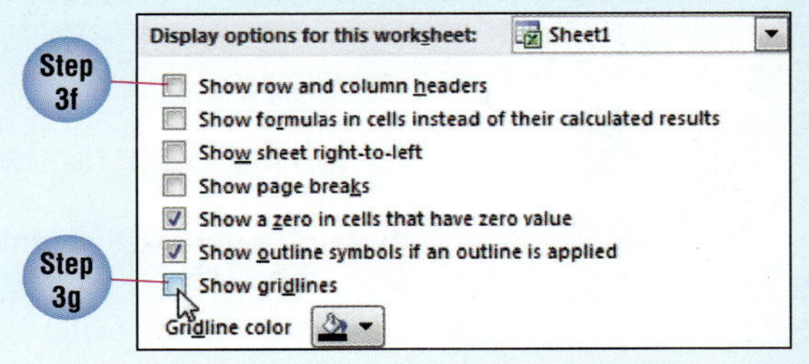

4. Click the Minimize the Ribbon button located at the right end of the ribbon tabs (next to the Help button) to hide the ribbon.
5. Compare your screen with the one shown in Figure 7.8 on page 231.
6. Save and then close **EL2-C7-P3-NorandaWinterSwimSch.xlsx**.

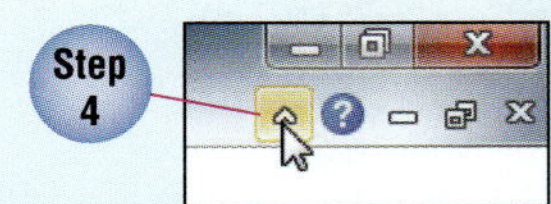

Project 2e Restoring Default Display Options

Part 5 of 8

1. Press Ctrl + N to start a new blank workbook.
2. Notice the display options that were changed in Project 2d that affect the workbook and the worksheet are restored to the default options. The Formula bar remains hidden since this option is a global display option. The ribbon remains minimized since the display of the ribbon is a toggle on/off option.
3. Open **EL2-C7-P2-NorandaWinterSwimSch.xlsx**.
4. Notice the sheet tabs, the row and column headers, and the gridlines remain hidden since these display option settings are saved with the workbook.
5. Close **EL2-C7-P3-NorandaWinterSwimSch.xlsx**.
6. Click the Expand the Ribbon button (previously the Minimize the Ribbon button) to redisplay the ribbon.
7. Redisplay the Formula bar by completing the following steps:
   a. Open the Excel Options dialog box.
   b. Click *Advanced* in the left pane.
   c. Scroll down the Excel Options dialog box to the *Display* section, click the *Show formula bar* check box to insert a check mark, and then click OK.
8. Close the workbook.

Customizing the Ribbon

HINT
Consider creating a custom tab with the buttons you use on a regular basis to save mouse clicks from frequently switching tabs and/or choosing options from drop-down lists (such as borders).

In addition to customizing the Quick Access toolbar, you can also customize the ribbon by creating a new tab. Within the new tab you can add groups and then add buttons within the groups. To customize the ribbon, click the File tab and then click the Options button. At the Excel Options dialog box, click *Customize Ribbon* in the left pane to open the dialog box shown in Figure 7.9.

The commands shown in the left list box are dependent on the current option for *Choose commands from*. Click the down-pointing arrow at the right of the current option (displays *Popular Commands*) to select from a variety of command lists such as *Commands Not In the Ribbon* or *All Commands*. The tabs shown in the right list box are dependent on the current option for *Customize the Ribbon*. Click the down-pointing arrow at the right of the current option (displays *Main Tabs*) to select *All Tabs*, *Main Tabs*, or *Tool Tabs*.

Figure 7.9 Excel Options Dialog Box with *Customize Ribbon* Selected

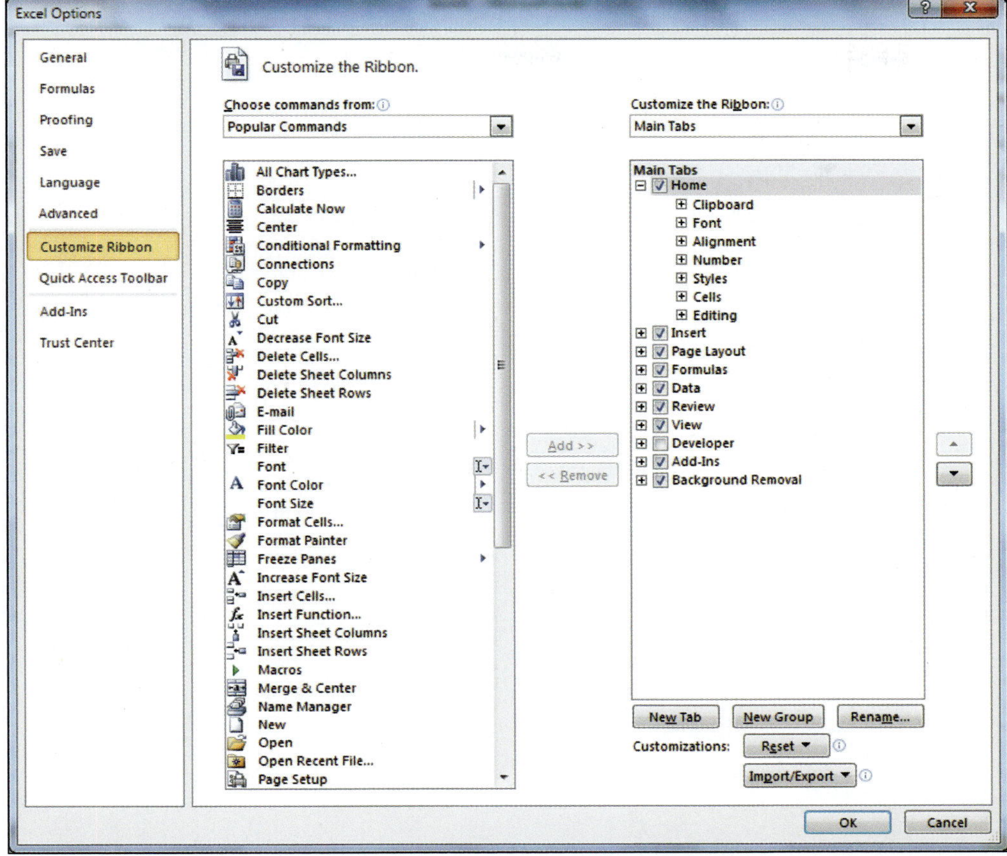

You can create a new group in an existing tab and add buttons within the new group, or you can create a new tab, create a new group within the tab, and then add buttons to the new group.

Creating a New Tab

To create a new tab, click the tab name in the *Main Tabs* list box that you want the new tab positioned after and then click the New Tab button located below the *Main Tabs* list box. This inserts a new tab in the list box along with a new group below the new tab as shown in Figure 7.10. If you selected the wrong tab name before clicking the New Tab button, you can move the new tab up or down the list box by clicking *New Tab (Custom)* and then clicking the Move Up or the Move Down buttons that display at the right side of the dialog box.

Renaming a Tab or Group

Rename a tab by clicking the tab name in the *Main Tabs* list box and then clicking the Rename button located below the *Main Tabs* list box. At the Rename dialog box, type the desired name for the tab and then press Enter or click OK. You can also display the Rename dialog box by right-clicking the tab name and then clicking *Rename* at the shortcut menu.

Quick Steps

Create a New Tab and Group

1. Click File tab.
2. Click Options.
3. Click *Customize Ribbon* in left pane.
4. Click tab name to precede new tab.
5. Click New Tab button.

Add New Group to Existing Tab

1. Click File tab.
2. Click Options.
3. Click *Customize Ribbon* in left pane.
4. Click tab name with which the new group is associated.
5. Click New Group button.

Rename a Tab or Group

1. Click File tab.
2. Click Options.
3. Click *Customize Ribbon* in left pane.
4. Click tab or group to be renamed.
5. Click Rename button.
6. Type new name.
7. Press Enter or click OK.

Add Buttons to Group

1. Click File tab.
2. Click Options.
3. Click *Customize Ribbon* in left pane.
4. Click group name in which to insert new button.
5. Change *Choose commands from* to desired command list.
6. Scroll down and click desired command.
7. Click Add button.

Figure 7.10 New Tab and Group Created in the Customize Ribbon Pane at the Excel Options Dialog Box

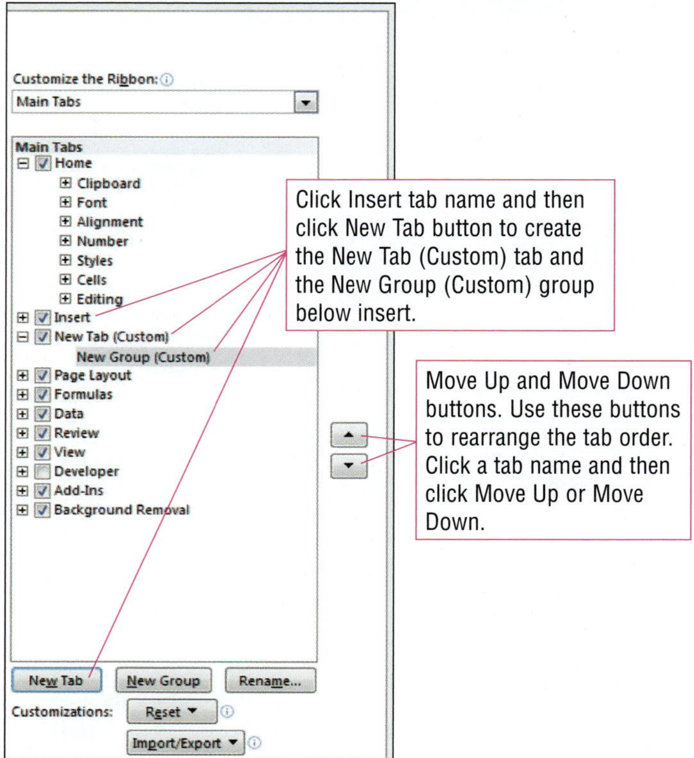
Customize the Ribbon:
Main Tabs
Main Tabs
Home
Clipboard
Font
Alignment
Number
Styles
Cells
Editing
Insert
New Tab (Custom)
New Group (Custom)
Page Layout
Formulas
Data
Review
View
Developer
Add-Ins
Background Removal
New Tab
New Group
Rename...
Customizations:
Reset
Import/Export
Click Insert tab name and then click New Tab button to create the New Tab (Custom) tab and the New Group (Custom) group below insert.
Move Up and Move Down buttons. Use these buttons to rearrange the tab order. Click a tab name and then click Move Up or Move Down.

Complete similar steps to rename a group. The Rename dialog box for a group name or a command name contains a *Symbol* list as well as the *Display name* text box. Type the new name for the group in the *Display name* text box and press Enter or click OK. The symbols are useful for identifying new buttons rather than the group name.

Adding Buttons to a Tab Group

Add commands to a tab by clicking the group name within the tab, clicking the desired command in the list box at the left, and then clicking the Add button that displays between the two list boxes. Remove commands in a similar manner. Click the command you want to remove from the tab group and then click the Remove button that displays between the two list boxes.

Project 2f **Customizing the Ribbon** Part 6 of 8

1. Open **NationalAcctgDeptJE.xlsx**.
2. Save the workbook with Save As and name it **EL2-C7-P2-NationalAcctgDeptJE.**
3. Customize the ribbon by adding a new tab and two new groups within the tab by completing the following steps:
   a. Click the File tab and then click the Options button.
   b. Click *Customize Ribbon* in the left pane of the Excel Options dialog box.

c. Click the Insert tab name in the *Main Tabs* list box located at the right of the dialog box.

d. Click the New Tab button located below the list box. (This inserts a new tab below the Insert tab and a new group below the new tab.)

e. With *New Group (Custom)* selected below *New Tab (Custom)*, click the New Group button that displays below the list box. (This inserts another new group below the new tab.)

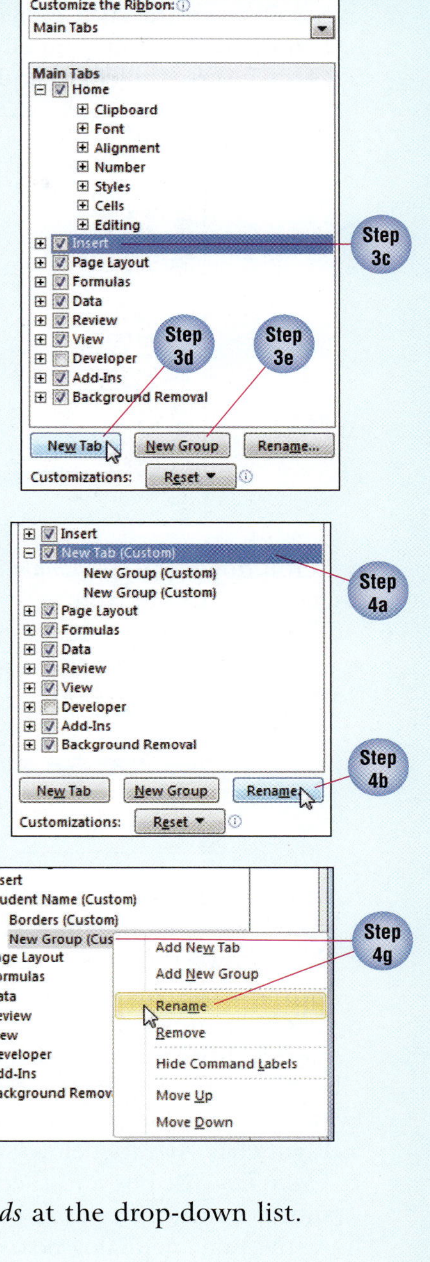

4. Rename the tab and the groups by completing the following steps:
   a. Click to select *New Tab (Custom)* in the *Main Tabs* list box.
   b. Click the Rename button that displays below the list box.
   c. At the Rename dialog box, type your first and last names and then press Enter or click OK.
   d. Click to select the first *New Group (Custom)* group name that displays below the new tab.
   e. Click the Rename button.
   f. At the Rename dialog box, type **Borders** in the *Display name* text box and then press Enter or click OK. The Rename dialog box for a group or button displays symbols in addition to the *Display name* text box. You will apply a symbol to a button in a later step.
   g. Right-click the New Group (Custom) group name below *Borders (Custom)* and then click *Rename* at the shortcut menu.
   h. Type **Statistics** in the *Display name* text box at the Rename dialog box and then press Enter or click OK.
5. Add buttons to the *Borders (Custom)* group by completing the following steps:
   a. Click to select *Borders (Custom)* in the *Main Tabs* list box.
   b. Click the down-pointing arrow at the right of the *Choose commands from* list box (currently displays *Popular Commands*) and then click *All Commands* at the drop-down list.

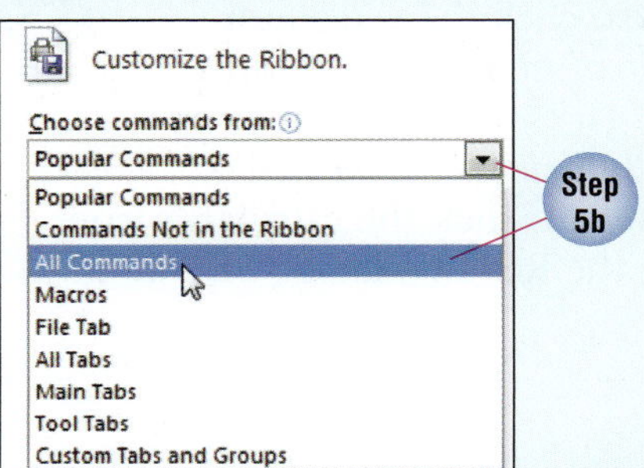

c. Scroll down the *All Commands* list box (the list displays alphabetically), click *Thick Bottom Border*, and then click the Add button located between the two list boxes. (This inserts the command below the Borders (Custom) group name.)

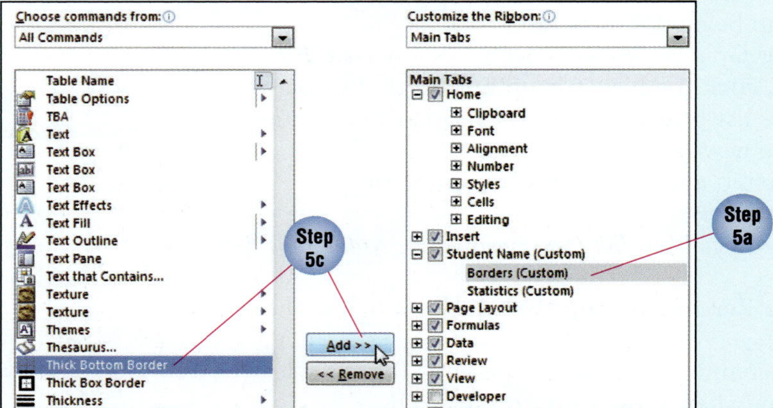

d. Scroll down the *All Commands* list box, click *Top and Double Bottom Border*, and then click the Add button.

6. Add buttons to the Statistics (Custom) group by completing the following steps:
   a. Click to select *Statistics (Custom)* in the *Main Tabs* list box.

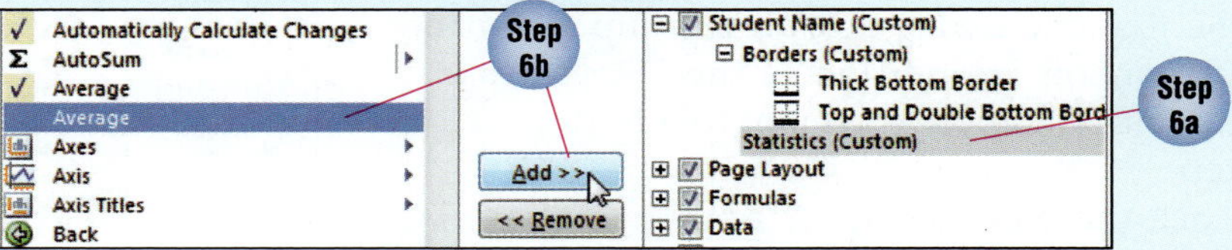

   b. Scroll up the *All Commands* list box, click *Average* (choose the *Average* option that does not have a check mark), and then click the Add button.
   c. Scroll down the *All Commands* list box, click *Max* (choose the *Max* option that does not have a check mark), and then click the Add button.
   d. Scroll down the *All Commands* list box, click *Min* (choose the *Min* option that does not have a check mark), and then click the Add button.

7. Change the symbol for the Average, Max, and Min buttons by completing the following steps:
   a. Right-click *Average* below *Statistics (Custom)* in the *Main Tabs* list box and then click *Rename* at the shortcut menu.
   b. At the Rename dialog box, click the calculator icon in the *Symbol* list box (second icon in fifth row) and then click OK.
   c. Right-click *Max* below *Statistics (Custom)*, click *Rename* at the shortcut menu, click the calculator icon in the *Symbol* list box at the Rename dialog box, and then click OK.

d. Change the symbol for *Min* to the calculator symbol by completing a step similar to Step 7c.

8. Click OK to close the Excel Options dialog box.
9. Use buttons in the custom tab to format and add formulas to the worksheet by completing the following steps:
   a. Make A3 the active cell, click the custom tab with your name, and then click the Thick Bottom Border button in the Borders group.

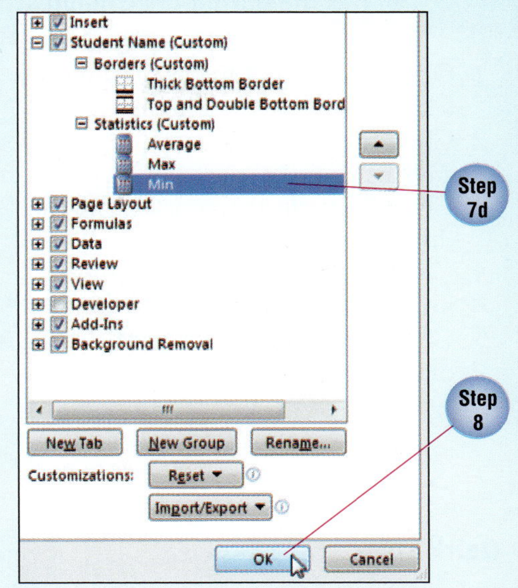

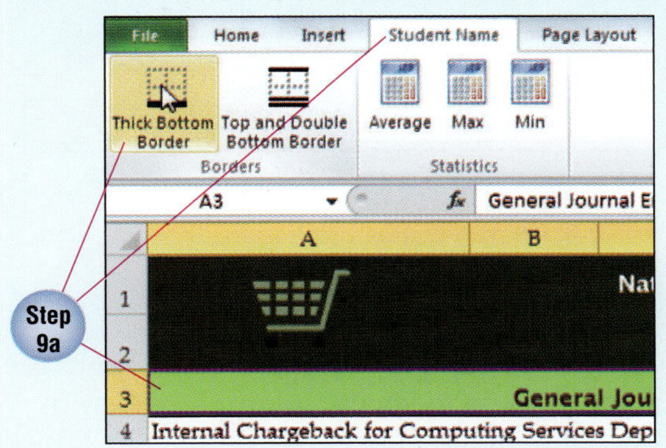

   b. Select B6:H6 and click the Thick Bottom Border button in the Borders group.
   c. Make D18 the active cell and then click the Top and Double Bottom Border button in the Borders group.
   d. Make D20 the active cell and then click the Average button in the Statistics group.
   e. With the range D7:D19 selected in the formula *=AVERAGE(D7:D19)*, drag to select D7:D17 and then press Enter.
   f. With D21 the active cell, click the Max button in the Statistics group, drag to select the range D7:D17, and then press Enter.
   g. With D22 the active cell, click the Min button in the Statistics group, drag to select the range D7:D17, and then press Enter.
10. Save **EL2-C7-P2-NationalAcctgDeptJE.xlsx.**
11. Insert a screen image of the worksheet showing the custom tab in a new Microsoft Word document using either Print Screen with Paste, the Screenshot feature (Insert tab, Screenshot button in Illustrations group), or the Windows Snipping tool (Start button, All Programs, Accessories). Type your name a few lines below the screen image.
12. Save the Microsoft Word document and name it **EL2-C7-P2-NationalAcctgDeptJE**.
13. Print **EL2-C7-P2-NationalAcctgDeptJE.docx** and then exit Word.
14. Print and then close **EL2-C7-P2-NationalAcctgDeptJE.xlsx**.

Resetting the Ribbon

Restore the original ribbon by clicking the Reset button that displays below the *Main Tabs* list box in the Excel Options dialog box with the Customize Ribbon pane selected. Clicking the Reset button displays two options—*Reset only selected Ribbon tab* and *Reset all customizations*. Click *Reset all customizations* to restore the ribbon to its original settings and then click Yes at the Microsoft Office message box that displays the message *Delete all Ribbon and Quick Access Toolbar customizations for this program?*

Project 2g Restoring the Ribbon

Part 7 of 8

1. Open the Excel Options dialog box and click *Customize Ribbon* in the left pane.
2. Click the Reset button located below the *Main Tabs* list box.
3. Click *Reset all customizations* at the drop-down list.
4. Click Yes at the Microsoft Office message box that appears.
5. Click OK to close the Excel Options dialog box.

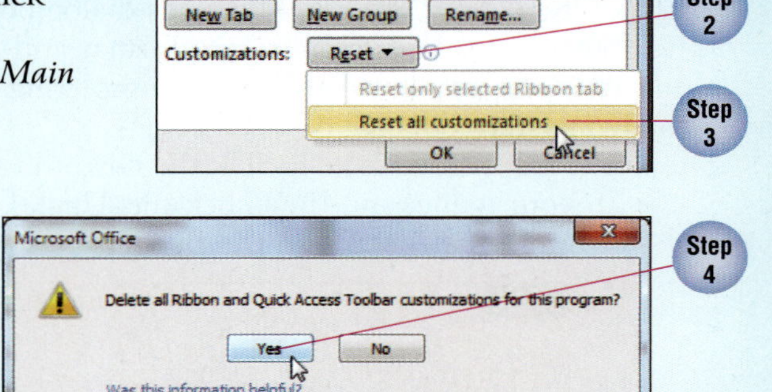

Quick Steps

Create Custom View
1. Change display and print settings as desired.
2. Click View tab.
3. Click Custom Views.
4. Click Add.
5. Type name for view.
6. Choose desired *Include in view* options.
7. Click OK.

Apply Custom View
1. Click View tab.
2. Click Custom Views.
3. Click desired view name.
4. Click Show.

HINT

You can only apply a custom view to the worksheet that was active when the view was created.

Custom views cannot be created for any worksheet in which a table resides.

Custom Views

Creating and Applying a Custom View

A ***custom view*** saves display and print settings for the active worksheet. You can create multiple custom views for the same worksheet and apply a view by selecting a stored view name at the Custom Views dialog box. For example, in Project 2h you will create four custom views that store display settings, hidden rows, and a row height for a swimming schedule. You will switch between views to show different portions of the worksheet such as showing the morning swimming activities only.

In a custom view you can save settings such as column widths, row heights, hidden rows and/or columns, filter settings, cell selections, windows settings, page layout options, and a print area. Begin a custom view by applying the desired settings to the active worksheet. When finished, click the View tab, click the Custom Views button in the Workbook Views group, click the Add button, type a name for the custom view, and then click OK.

Change a worksheet to display a custom view's settings by opening the Custom Views dialog box, selecting the desired view name in the *Views* list box and then clicking the Show button. You can also double-click the desired view name to apply the saved display and print settings to the worksheet. If a worksheet other than the one in which the view was created is active, you will be switched to the worksheet for which the view applies.

Creating and Applying Custom Views

Part 8 of 8

1. Open **NorandaWinterSwimSch.xlsx**.
2. Save the workbook with Save As and name it **EL2-C7-P2-NorandaWinterSwimSch-CustomViews**.
3. Create a custom view with display settings for all swimming sessions by completing the following steps:
   a. Click the File tab, click the Options button, and then click *Advanced* in the left pane at the Excel Options dialog box.
   b. Scroll down the dialog box to the section titled *Display options for this worksheet*, click the *Show gridlines* check box to clear the check mark, and then click OK.
   c. Select rows 4 to 45, click the Format button in the Cells group in the Home tab, click *Row Height* at the drop-down list, type 25 in the *Row height* text box at the Row Height dialog box, and then press Enter or click OK.
   d. Click in any cell to deselect the rows.
   e. Click the View tab.
   f. Click the Custom Views button in the Workbook Views group.
   g. Click the Add button at the Custom Views dialog box.
   h. With the insertion point positioned in the *Name* text box at the Add View dialog box, type AllSessions.
   i. With the *Print settings* and *Hidden rows, columns and filter settings* check boxes already selected, click OK.

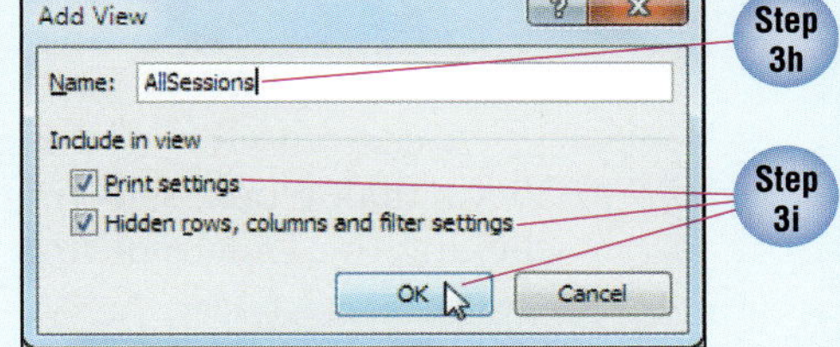

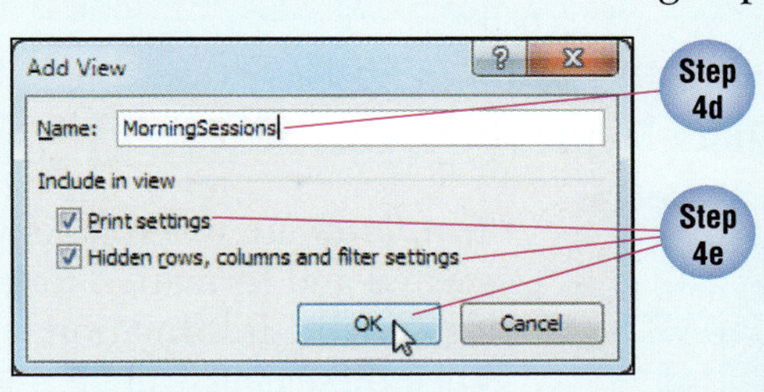

4. Create a second custom view to display only the morning swimming activities by hiding the rows containing the afternoon and evening activities by completing the following steps:
   a. Select rows 19 to 45, click the Home tab, click the Format button in the Cells group, point to *Hide & Unhide* in the *Visibility* section, and then click *Hide Rows*.
   b. Click the View tab and then click the Custom Views button in the Workbook Views group.
   c. At the Custom Views dialog box click the Add button.
   d. At the Add View dialog box, type MorningSessions in the *Name* text box.
   e. With the *Print settings* and *Hidden rows, columns and filter settings* check boxes already selected, click OK.
5. Click the Custom Views button in the Workbook Views group. With *AllSessions* currently selected in the *Views* list box, click the Show button to apply the custom view.

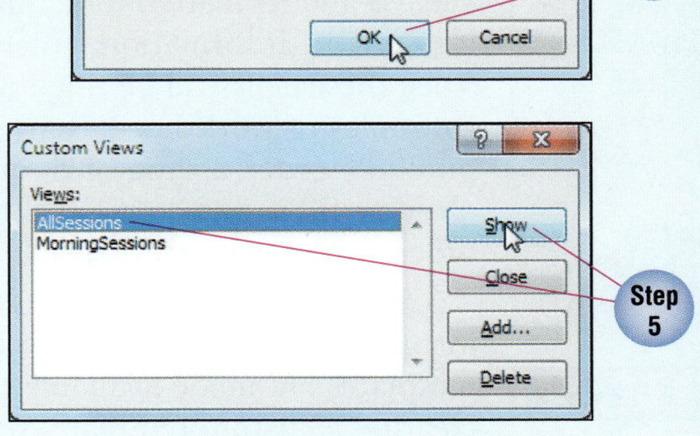

6. Create a third custom view to show only the afternoon swimming sessions by completing the following steps:
   a. Select rows 4 to 18 and hide the rows by completing a step similar to Step 4a.
   b. Hide rows 32 to 45.
   c. Create a custom view named *AfternoonSessions* by completing steps similar to Steps 4b through 4e.

7. Click the Custom Views button and then double-click *AllSessions* in the *Views* list box at the Custom Views dialog box.
8. Create a fourth custom view to show only the evening swimming sessions by completing the following steps:
   a. Hide rows 4 to 31.
   b. Create a custom view named *EveningSessions* by completing steps similar to Steps 4b through 4e.
9. Click the Custom Views button and then Show the *AllSessions* custom view.
10. Show the *MorningSessions* custom view.
11. Show the *AfternoonSessions* custom view.
12. Show the *EveningSessions* custom view.
13. Save and then close **EL2-C7-P2-NorandaWinterSwimSch-CustomViews.xlsx**.

A custom view that is no longer needed can be deleted by opening the Custom Views dialog box, selecting the custom view name in the *Views* list box and then clicking the Delete button.

Save a Workbook as a Template — 3 Parts

You will modify an existing workbook and save the revised version as a template.

Quick Steps

Save Workbook as Template
1. Open workbook.
2. Make desired changes.
3. Click File tab.
4. Click Save As.
5. Change *Save as type* to *Excel Template (*.xltx)*.
6. Type desired file name.
7. Click Save button.

If macros exist in the template workbook, change the *Save as type* to *Excel Macro-Enabled Template (*.xltm)*.

Saving a Workbook as a Template

Templates are workbooks with standard text, formulas, and formatting. Cells are created and formatted for all of the entries that do not change. Cells are also created for variable information which has formatting applied but which are left empty since these cells will be filled in when the template is used to generate a worksheet. Examples of worksheets that would be suited to a template include an invoice, a purchase order, a time card, or an expense form. These templates would be reused often to fill in information that is different for each individual invoice, purchase order, time card, or expense.

Several templates have already been created and are available to you either installed on the computer or by download from Microsoft Office Online. New templates are made available through Microsoft Office Online frequently. Before creating a custom template, search the Microsoft Office Online website to see if a template already exists that is suited to your purpose.

If no template exists that meets your needs, you can create your own custom template. To do this, create a workbook that contains all of the standard data, formulas, and formatting. Leave cells empty for any information that is variable;

however, format these cells as required. When you are ready to save the workbook as a template, use the Save As dialog box and change *Save as type* to *Excel Template (*.xltx)*.

Consider protecting the worksheet by locking all cells except those that will hold variable data before saving the workbook as a template.

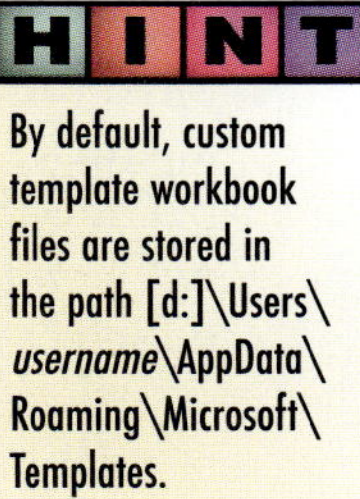

By default, custom template workbook files are stored in the path [d:]\Users\ *username*\AppData\ Roaming\Microsoft\ Templates.

Project 3a Saving a Workbook as a Template

Part 1 of 3

1. Open **EL2-C7-P2-NorandaWinterSwimSch.xlsx**.
2. Redisplay the row and column headers in the worksheet. Refer to Project 2d if you need assistance with this step.
3. Assume that you work at the Noranda Sportsplex and have to publish swimming schedules often. The sportsplex manager never changes the days or times the pool operates; however, the activities and assigned pools will often change. You decide to modify this workbook and then save it as a template to be reused whenever the schedule changes. To begin, make the following changes to the worksheet:
   a. Clear the cell contents for the ranges D5:E18, D20:E31, and D33:E45.
   b. Make A2 the active cell, delete *Winter* in *Winter Swimming Schedule* so that the subtitle reads *Swimming Schedule*.
   c. Insert a new row between row 2 and row 3 and merge and center the cells in the new row to match the subtitle. (This will be used later to enter the timeframe for the new schedule.)

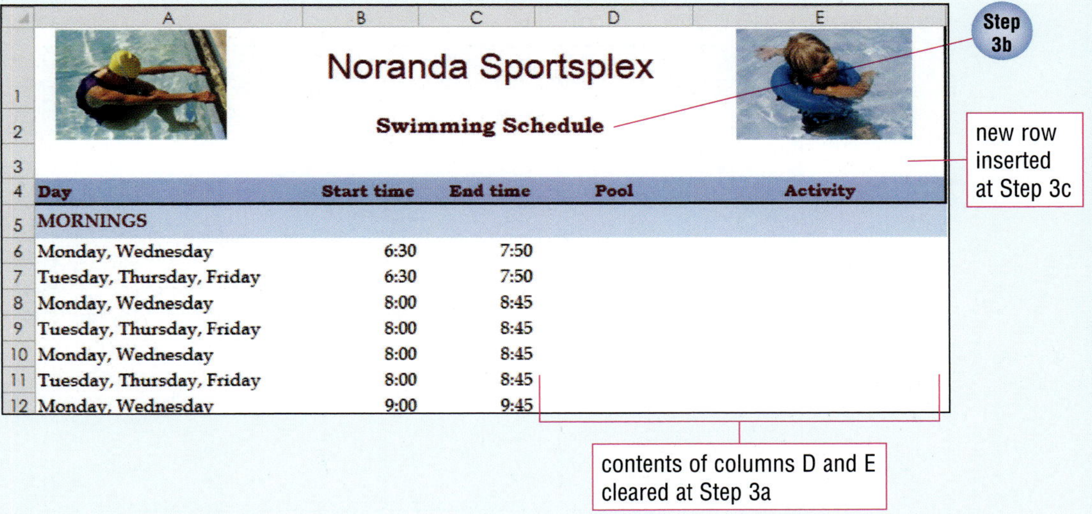

   d. Select and turn off the lock attribute for the following cells and ranges: A3, D6:E19, D21:E32, and D34:E46.
   e. Protect the worksheet. Do not assign a password to unprotect.

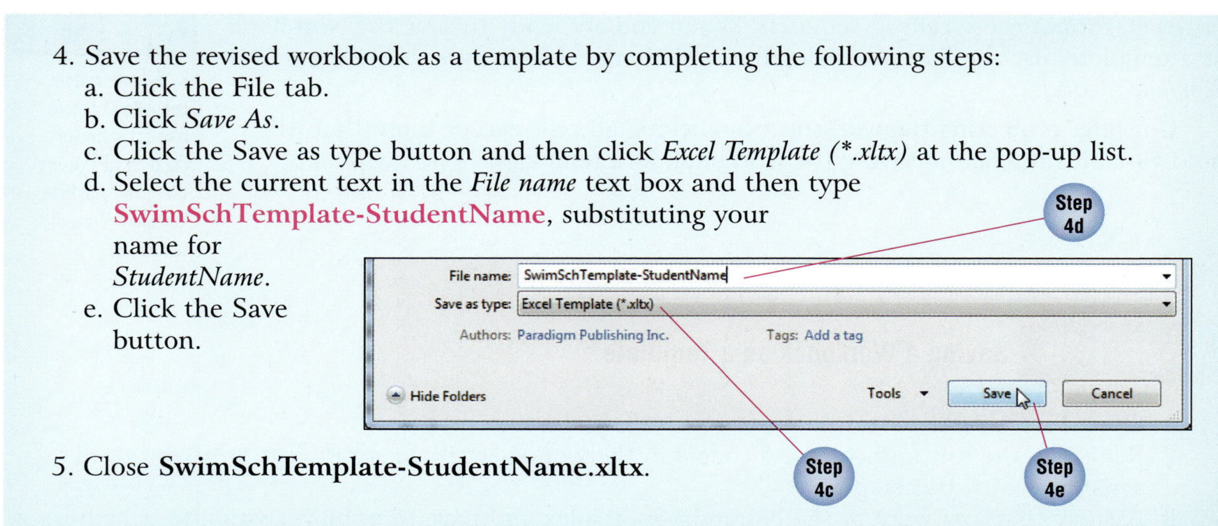

4. Save the revised workbook as a template by completing the following steps:
   a. Click the File tab.
   b. Click *Save As*.
   c. Click the Save as type button and then click *Excel Template (*.xltx)* at the pop-up list.
   d. Select the current text in the *File name* text box and then type **SwimSchTemplate-StudentName**, substituting your name for *StudentName*.
   e. Click the Save button.
5. Close **SwimSchTemplate-StudentName.xltx**.

Quick Steps

Use Custom Template
1. Click File tab.
2. Click New.
3. Click *My templates*.
4. Double-click desired template.

Using a Custom Template

To use a template that you created yourself, click the File tab and then click New. At the New tab Backstage view, click *My templates* in the Available Templates category at the top of the center pane. This opens the New dialog box shown in Figure 7.11. Double-click the desired template.

Figure 7.11 New Dialog Box

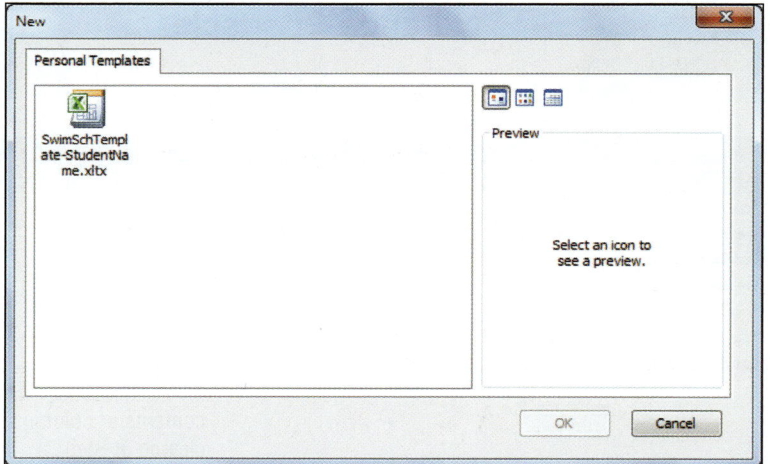

Project 3b Using a Custom Template

Part 2 of 3

1. At a blank Excel screen, open the template created in Project 3a by completing the following steps:
   a. Click the File tab.
   b. Click *New*.
   c. At the New tab Backstage view, click *My templates* in the Available Templates category of the center pane.

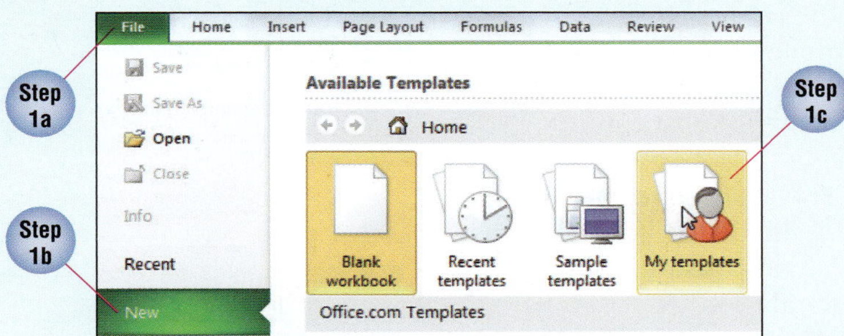

   d. At the New dialog box, double-click *SwimSchTemplate-StudentName.xltx,* where your name is substituted for *StudentName*.

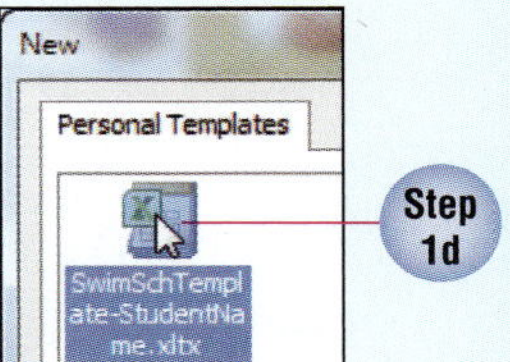

2. Look at the workbook name in the title bar. Notice that Excel has added *1* to the end of the name.
3. Make A3 the active cell and then type **Winter 2012**.
4. Enter data for the first two rows in the MORNINGS section by making up a pool name and activity for each row.
5. Click the Save button on the Quick Access toolbar.
6. Excel opens the Save As dialog box and automatically changes the *Save as type* option to *Excel Workbook (*.xlsx)*. Type **EL2-C7-P3-SwimSchWinter2012** in the *File name* text box, navigate to the Excel2010L2C7 folder on your storage medium, and then click the Save button.
7. Print and then close **EL2-C7-P3-SwimSchWinter2012.xlsx**.

Deleting a Custom Template

To delete a custom template, click the File tab and then click *New*. At the New tab Backstage view, click *My templates* in the Available Templates category of the center pane. At the New dialog box, right-click the template you want to delete and then click *Delete* at the shortcut menu. At the Delete File dialog box, click Yes.

Quick Steps

Delete Custom Template

1. Click File tab.
2. Click New.
3. Click *My templates*.
4. Right-click desired template name.
5. Click *Delete*.
6. Click Yes.
7. Close New dialog box.
8. Click Home tab.

Project 3c Deleting a Custom Template

Part 3 of 3

1. At a blank Excel screen, delete the template created in Project 3a by completing the following steps:
   a. Click the File tab.
   b. Click *New*.
   c. At the New tab Backstage view, click *My templates* in the Available Templates category of the center pane.
   d. At the New dialog box, right-click *SwimSchTemplate-StudentName.xltx,* where your name is substituted for *StudentName*.
   e. Click *Delete* at the shortcut menu.
   f. At the Delete File dialog box, click Yes.
2. Close the New dialog box.
3. Click the Home tab.

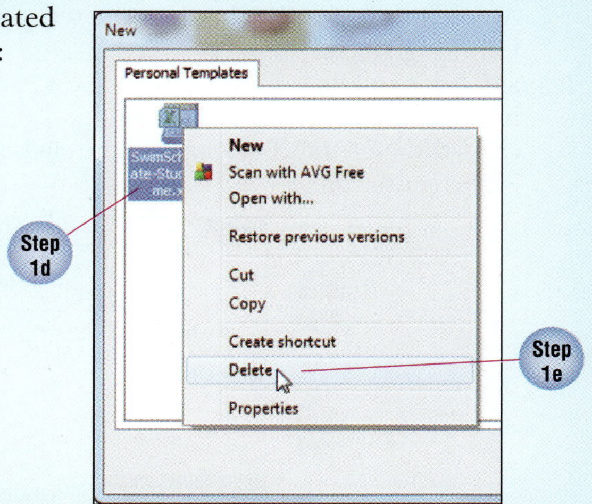

Project 4 Managing Excel's Save Options

2 Parts

You will review Excel's current save options, modify the AutoRecover options, and recover an unsaved workbook.

Quick Steps

Customize Save Options
1. Click File tab.
2. Click Options button.
3. Click *Save* in left pane.
4. Change save options as required.
5. Click OK.

Do not rely on AutoRecover and AutoSave as you work. Saving regularly to minimize data loss as protection against unforeseen events is a best practice.

Options

Customizing Save Options

AutoRecover saves versions of your work at the time interval specified so that you can restore all or part of your data should you forget to save or otherwise experience a situation that causes Excel to close unexpectedly (such as a power outage). When you restart Excel, the Document Recovery task pane opens with a list of workbooks that have an AutoRecover file. By default, Excel's AutoRecover feature is turned on and will automatically save AutoRecover information every 10 minutes. You can adjust the time interval to meet your needs. Keep in mind that data loss can still occur even with AutoRecover turned on. If, for example, the time interval is 20 minutes and a power outage occurrs, when you restart Excel the recovered file will not have the last 19 minutes of work if you did not save manually.

In conjunction with AutoRecover, Excel includes the ***AutoSave*** feature which will keep the last version of a workbook saved in a temporary file. You can recover the last version if you closed the workbook without saving or wish to return to the earlier version of the file. At the Recent tab Backstage view, you can view a listing of AutoSaved files.

Open the Excel Options dialog box with *Save* selected in the left pane to view and/or change the *AutoRecover* and *AutoSave* options.

Project 4a Customizing Save Options

Part 1 of 2

1. At a blank Excel screen, click the File tab and then click the Options button to open the Excel Options dialog box.
2. Click *Save* in the left pane of the Excel Options dialog box.
3. Take note of the current settings for *Save AutoRecover information every [ ] minutes* and *Keep the last autosaved version if I close without saving*. By default, both check boxes should be checked and the time interval is 10 minutes; however, the settings may have been changed on the computer you are using. In that case, write down the options so that you can restore the program to its original state.
4. If necessary, click the two check boxes to turn the AutoRecover and AutoSave features on.
5. Select the current value in the *Save AutoRecover information every [ ] minutes* text box and then type 2 to change the time interval to 2 minutes.
6. Click OK.

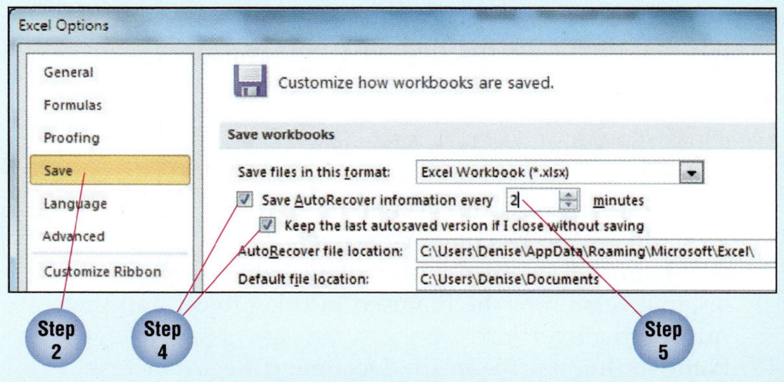

Project 4b Recovering a Workbook

Part 2 of 2

1. Open **EL2-C7-P2-NationalAcctgDeptJE.xlsx**.
2. Save the workbook with Save As and name it **EL2-C7-P4-NationalAcctgDeptJE**.
3. Note the system time at the bottom right corner of the screen. You want to make sure that more than two minutes elapses before you interrupt the Excel session.
4. Make the following changes to the worksheet:
   a. Select A7:A17 and change the font color to *Dark Red* (first color square in the *Standard Colors* section of the drop-down color palette).
   b. Select E7:E17 and change the font color to *Dark Red*.
   c. Delete rows 20 to 22 to remove the statistics from the workbook.

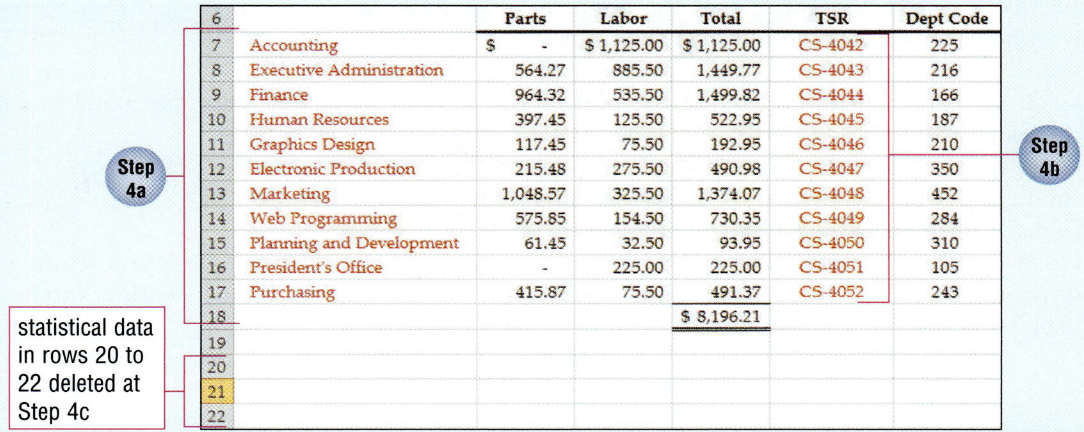

6		Parts	Labor	Total	TSR	Dept Code
7	Accounting	$ -	$ 1,125.00	$ 1,125.00	CS-4042	225
8	Executive Administration	564.27	885.50	1,449.77	CS-4043	216
9	Finance	964.32	535.50	1,499.82	CS-4044	166
10	Human Resources	397.45	125.50	522.95	CS-4045	187
11	Graphics Design	117.45	75.50	192.95	CS-4046	210
12	Electronic Production	215.48	275.50	490.98	CS-4047	350
13	Marketing	1,048.57	325.50	1,374.07	CS-4048	452
14	Web Programming	575.85	154.50	730.35	CS-4049	284
15	Planning and Development	61.45	32.50	93.95	CS-4050	310
16	President's Office	-	225.00	225.00	CS-4051	105
17	Purchasing	415.87	75.50	491.37	CS-4052	243
18				$ 8,196.21		
19						
20						
21						
22						

5. Make sure more than 2 minutes have elapsed since you checked the system time at Step 3. If necessary, wait until you are sure an AutoRecover file will have been saved.
6. Press Alt + Ctrl + Delete.
7. At the Windows screen, select *Start Task Manager*.
8. At the Windows Task Manager dialog box, click *Microsoft Excel - EL2-C7-P4-NationalAcctgDeptJE.xlsx* in the *Task* list box and then click the End Task button.
9. Click the End Now button at the End Program dialog box.
10. Close the Windows Task Manager dialog box.
11. Restart Microsoft Excel. When Excel opens the Document Recovery task pane will be open with two available files: the original version of the file used in this project and the AutoRecover version.
12. Point to the first file in the Document Recovery task pane. A ScreenTip displays informing you the first file is the AutoRecover version.
13. Point to the second file in the Document Recovery task pane. A ScreenTip displays informing you the second file is the original workbook.
14. Click the first file in the Document Recovery task pane. Notice the edited version of the file appears. Look at the additional information displayed next to the file name in the Title bar. Excel includes *(version 1)* and *[Autosaved]* in the file name. Notice also that an Autosaved file has the file extension *.xlsb*.
15. Click the second file in the Document Recovery task pane. Notice that the original workbook opens and the message *[Last saved by user]* is added to the file name in the Title bar.
16. Click the Close button located at the bottom of the Document Recovery task pane to close the pane.
17. Close both workbooks. Click Yes when prompted to save changes and then click *Save* at the Save As dialog box to accept the default name *EL2-C7-P4-NationalAcctgDeptJE (Autosaved).xlsx*.
18. Open the Excel Options dialog box. Restore the Save options to the settings you wrote down in Project 4a. If the Save options were the default options, change the time interval back to 10 minutes. Close the Excel Options dialog box.

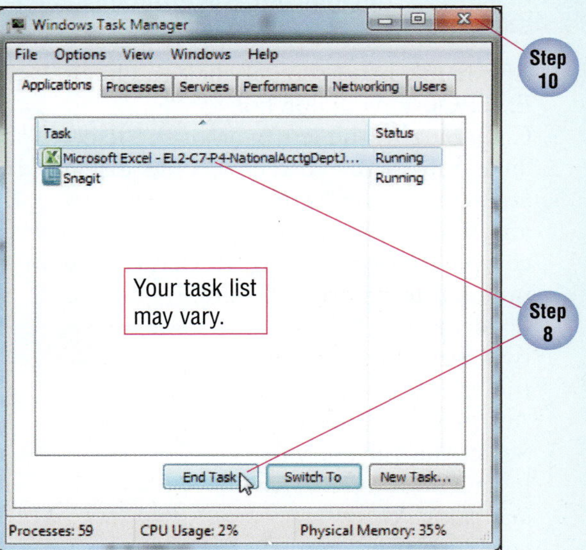

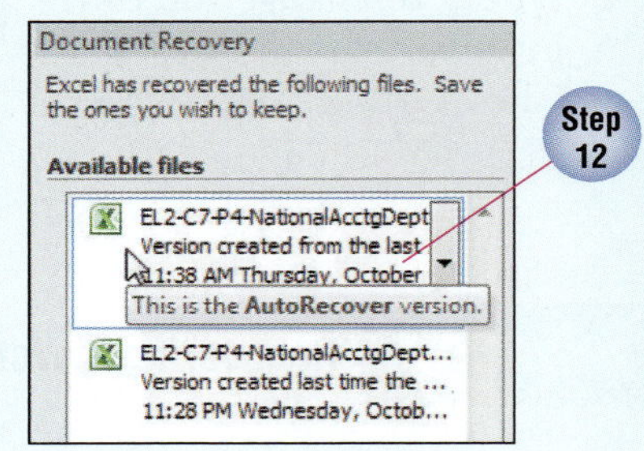

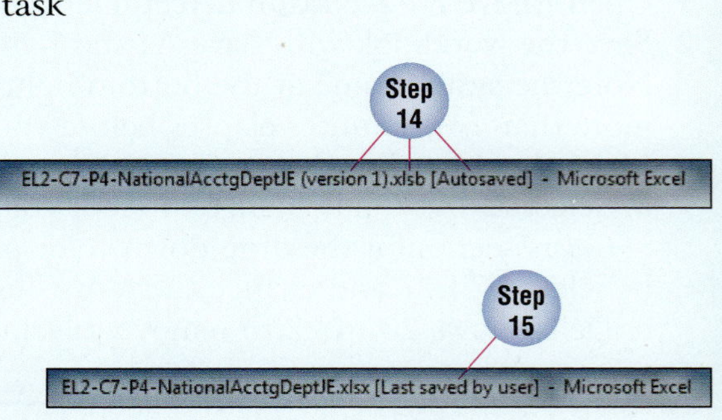

The Save options at the Excel Options dialog box also allow you to specify the drive and/or folder in which the AutoRecover file is stored as well as the default file location for all new workbooks.

At the Recent tab Backstage View, click *Recover Unsaved Workbooks* at the bottom of the *Recent Places* pane to view a list of Autosaved files.

Chapter Summary

- Create a macro for a set of tasks that you repeat frequently in which the steps do not vary.
- Start creating a new macro by clicking the View tab, the down-pointing arrow on the Macros button in the Macros group, and then *Record Macro*.
- At the Record Macro dialog box, assign a name to the macro, an optional shortcut key, and a description.
- The macro recorder is turned on after you click OK to close the Record Macro dialog box. All commands and keystrokes are recorded until you click the Stop Recording button.
- Workbooks that contain macros are saved in the *Excel Macro-Enabled Workbook (*.xlsm)* file format.
- Run a macro by opening the Macro dialog box and double-clicking the macro name.
- A macro assigned to a shortcut key is run by pressing Ctrl + the assigned letter.
- Excel differentiates the case of the letter typed in the *Shortcut key* text box at the Record Macro dialog box. An uppercase letter is assigned the shortcut key Ctrl + Shift + the assigned letter.
- If you assign a shortcut key to a macro that is the same as a shortcut key assigned to an Excel feature, the macro overrides the Excel shortcut.
- A macro's instructions are recorded in Visual Basic for Applications (VBA) program code. To edit a macro, open the Macro dialog box, click the macro name to be edited, and then click the Edit button. A Microsoft Visual Basic for Applications window opens with a code window in which you edit the macro's program code.
- After editing the macro, save the changes, click *File*, and then click *Close and Return to Microsoft Excel*.
- If you are not comfortable with editing a macro in Visual Basic for Applications, you can record a new macro to correct the steps using the same name to replace the existing macro.
- Delete a macro at the Macro dialog box.
- Macros are stored in the workbook in which they are created. When you open the Macro dialog box, all macros from all open workbooks are made accessible; therefore, to use a macro stored in another workbook you will need to open the other workbook first.
- Another option to make macros accessible to other workbooks is to create a macros workbook with all of your standard macros and open the macros workbook each time you start Excel.

- Pin a workbook that you want to make permanently available in the *Recent Workbooks* list at the Recent tab Backstage view.
- A pinned workbook displays with a blue push pin icon. Clicking the blue push pin icon unpins the workbook from the list.
- Add or delete a button to the Quick Access toolbar using the Customize Quick Access Toolbar button. Click *More Commands* from the drop-down list to open the Excel Options dialog box with *Quick Access Toolbar* selected to locate a feature you want to add in the commands list box.
- Display options in Excel are grouped by global display options, options that affect the current workbook, and options that affect the current worksheet.
- Customized workbook and worksheet display options are saved with the file.
- Minimize the ribbon to open more space in the work area when working with a large worksheet. The minimized ribbon displays only the tabs. Clicking a tab temporarily redisplays the ribbon to allow you to select a feature.
- You can customize the ribbon by creating a new tab, creating a new group within the new tab, and then adding buttons within the new group.
- To customize the ribbon, open the Excel Options dialog box and click *Customize Ribbon* in the left pane.
- Create a new ribbon tab by clicking the tab name that will precede the new tab and then clicking the New Tab button. A new group is automatically added with the new tab.
- Rename a custom tab by clicking to select the tab name, clicking the Rename button, typing a new name, and then pressing Enter or clicking OK. Rename a group using a similar process.
- Add buttons within a group by clicking the group name, selecting the desired command in the commands list box, and then clicking the Add button located between the two list boxes.
- Restore the ribbon to the default by clicking the Reset button located near the bottom right of the Excel Options dialog box with *Customize Ribbon* selected and then clicking *Reset all customizations* at the drop-down list.
- A custom view saves display settings so that you can apply the saved settings to a worksheet when needed. Multiple custom views can be created for the same worksheet at the Custom Views dialog box accessed by clicking the Custom Views button in the Workbook Views group of the View tab.
- Templates are workbooks with standard text, formatting, and formulas.
- A custom template is created from an existing workbook by saving the workbook as an *Excel template (*.xltx)* at the *Save as type* list at the Save As dialog box.
- To use a custom template, open the New tab Backstage view, click *My templates* to open the New dialog box and then double-click the custom template name.
- Delete a custom template at the New dialog box by right-clicking the template name and selecting *Delete* at the shortcut menu.
- By default, Excel saves your work every 10 minutes to an AutoRecover file. If your Excel session is unexpectedly terminated or you close the file without saving, you can recover the file when you restart Excel at the Document Recovery task pane.

Commands Review

FEATURE	RIBBON TAB, GROUP	BUTTON	KEYBOARD SHORTCUT
Custom Views	View, Workbook Views		
Customize Quick Access toolbar	File, Options		
Customize ribbon	File, Options		
Customize save options	File, Options		
Delete macro	View, Macros		Alt + F8
Display options	File, Options		
Edit macro	View, Macros		Alt + F8
Expand ribbon			
Minimize ribbon			Ctrl + F1
Record macro	View, Macros	OR	
Save as a macro-enabled workbook	File, Save As		F12
Use custom template	File, New		

Concepts Check Test Your Knowledge

Completion: In the space provided at the right, indicate the correct term, command, or number.

1. Macro names must begin with a letter and can contain a combination of letters, numbers, and this other character. ________________
2. Click this button to indicate you have finished the tasks or keystrokes you want saved in the macro. ________________
3. A workbook containing a macro is saved in this file format. ________________
4. A macro can be assigned to a shortcut key that is a combination of a lowercase or uppercase letter and this other key. ________________
5. Macro instructions are stored in this program code. ________________

6. A workbook that you use frequently can be permanently added to the *Recent Workbooks* list by clicking this icon next to the workbook name. ____________________

7. Click this option at the Customize Quick Access Toolbar drop-down list to locate a feature to add to the toolbar from a commands list box. ____________________

8. Display options are shown in the Excel Options dialog box with this option selected in the left pane. ____________________

9. Click this button to minimize the ribbon to provide more space in the work area. ____________________

10. Click this option in the left pane at the Excel Options dialog box to create a custom ribbon tab. ____________________

11. Click this button at the Custom Views dialog box to create a new custom view that will save the current display settings for the active worksheet. ____________________

12. Change *Save as type* to this option at the Save As dialog box to save the current workbook as a standard workbook that can be opened from the New dialog box. ____________________

13. This task pane opens when Excel is restarted after the previous session ended abnormally. ____________________

Skills Check Assess Your Performance

Assessment 1

CREATE MACROS

1. At a new blank workbook, create the following two macros:
   a. Create a macro named *Landscape* that changes the page orientation to landscape, sets custom margins at top = 1 inch; bottom, left, and right = 0.5 inch; and centers the worksheet horizontally. Assign the macro to the shortcut key Ctrl + Shift + Q. Enter an appropriate description that includes your name and the date the macro was created.
   b. Create a macro named *Technic* that applies the theme named *Technic* and turns off the display of gridlines in the active worksheet. Assign the macro to the shortcut key Ctrl + t. Enter an appropriate description that includes your name and the date the macro was created.
2. Save the workbook as a macro-enabled workbook named **MyMacros-StudentName**, with your name substituted for *StudentName*.
3. Leave the **MyMacros-StudentName.xlsm** workbook open for the next assessment.

Assessment 2

RUN MACROS

1. Open **NationalAcctgDeptCS.xlsx.**
2. Save the workbook with Save As and name it **EL2-C7-A2-NationalAcctgDeptCS.**
3. Press Ctrl + t to run the Technic macro.
4. Press Ctrl + Shift + Q to run the Landscape macro.
5. Save, print, and then close **EL2-C7-A2-NationalAcctgDeptCS.xlsx.**
6. Close **MyMacros-StudentName.xlsm.**

Assessment 3

CREATE MACROS; SAVE AS A MACRO-ENABLED WORKBOOK

1. Open **EL2-C7-A2-NationalAcctgDeptCS.xlsx.**
2. Create the following two macros within the current workbook:
   a. Create a macro named *FormulaBarOff* that turns off the display of the Formula bar and protects the worksheet. Do not enter a password to unprotect the sheet. Assign the macro to the shortcut key Ctrl + Shift + M. Enter an appropriate description that includes your name and the date the macro was created.
   b. Create a macro named *FormulaBarOn* that turns on the display of the Formula bar and unprotects the worksheet. Assign the macro to the shortcut key Ctrl + Shift + B. Enter an appropriate description that includes your name and the date the macro was created.
3. Test each macro to make sure the shortcut key runs the correct commands.
4. Save the revised workbook as a macro-enabled workbook and name it **EL2-C7-A3-NationalAcctgDeptCS.**
5. Close **EL2-C7-A3-NationalAcctgDeptCS.xlsm.**

Assessment 4

PRINT MACROS

1. Open **EL2-C7-A3-NationalAcctgDeptCS.xlsm** and enable content.
2. Open the Macro dialog box and edit the FormulaBarOff macro.
3. At the Microsoft Visual Basic for Applications window with the insertion point blinking in the code window, click File on the Menu bar and then click *Print*. At the Print - VBAProject dialog box, click OK. ***Note: The FormulaBarOn macro code will also print since both macros are stored within the VBA Project.***
4. Click File on the Menu bar and then click *Close and Return to Microsoft Excel.*
5. Close **EL2-C7-A3-NationalAcctgDeptCS.xlsm.**
6. Open **MyMacros-StudentName.xlsm** and enable content.
7. Open the Macro dialog box and edit the Landscape macro.
8. At the Microsoft Visual Basic for Applications window with the insertion point blinking in the code window, click File on the Menu bar and then click *Print*. At the Print - VBAProject dialog box, click OK. ***Note: The Technic macro code will also print since both macros are stored within the VBA Project.***
9. Click File on the Menu bar and then click *Close and Return to Microsoft Excel.*
10. Close **MyMacros-StudentName.xlsm.**

Assessment 5

CUSTOMIZE THE EXCEL ENVIRONMENT

1. Open **BillingsDec21.xlsx**.
2. Save the workbook with Save As and name it **EL2-C7-A5-BillingsDec21**.
3. Make the following changes to the Display options:
   a. Turn off the horizontal scroll bar.
   b. Turn off sheet tabs.
   c. Turn off row and column headers.
   d. Turn off gridlines.
4. Change the current theme to Origin.
5. Freeze the first four rows in the worksheet.
6. Create a screen image of the worksheet with the modified display options and paste the image into a new Word document. Type your name a few lines below the screen image.
7. Save the Word document and name it **EL2-C7-A5-BillingsDec21**.
8. Print **EL2-C7-A5-BillingsDec21.docx** and then exit Word.
9. Save and close **EL2-C7-A5-BillingsDec21.xlsx.**

Assessment 6

CREATE CUSTOM VIEWS

1. Open **BillingsDec21.xlsx**.
2. Save the workbook with Save As and name it **EL2-C7-A6-BillingsDec21**.
3. Select A4:I23 and custom sort in ascending order by *Attorney* and then by the client's *Last Name*.
4. With A4:I23 still selected turn on filter arrows.
5. Deselect the range and then filter the *Attorney* column to show only those rows with the attorney name *Kyle Williams*.
6. Create a custom view named *Williams* to save the filter settings.
7. Clear the filter in the *Attorney* column.
8. Filter the list by the *Attorney* named *Marty O'Donovan*.
9. Create a custom view named *O'Donovan* to save the filter settings.
10. Clear the filter in the *Attorney* column.
11. Create a custom view named *Martinez* by completing steps similar to those in Steps 8 and 9 and then clear the filter from the *Attorney* column.
12. Create a custom view named *Sullivan* by completing steps similar to those in Steps 8 and 9 and then clear the filter from the *Attorney* column.
13. Open the Custom Views dialog box. If necessary, drag the Custom Views dialog box Title bar to move the dialog box to the right of the worksheet. Create a screen image of the worksheet with the dialog box open and paste the image into a new Word document. Type your name a few lines below the screen image.
14. Save the Word document and name it **EL2-C7-A6-BillingsDec21**.
15. Print **EL2-C7-A6-BillingsDec21.docx** and then exit Word.
16. Close the Custom Views dialog box and then save and close **EL2-C7-A6-BillingsDec21.xlsx**.

Assessment 7

CREATE AND USE A TEMPLATE

1. Open **EL2-C7-A5-BillingsDec21.xlsx** and turn on the display of row and column headers.
2. Make the following changes to the workbook:
   a. Select and delete all of the data below the column headings in row 4.
   b. Delete the text in A3.
   c. Edit the subtitle in A2 to *Associate Weekly Billing Summary*.
3. Save the revised workbook as a template named **Billings-StudentName** with your name substituted for *StudentName*.
4. Close **Billings-StudentName.xltx**.
5. Start a new workbook based on the **Billings-StudentName.xltx** template.
6. Type the dates for Monday to Friday of the current week in A3 in the format *November 12 to 16, 2012*.
7. Enter the following two billings using Monday's date of the current week. Enter dates in the format mm/dd/yyyy. For example, *11/12/2012*.

IN-774	10665	[Monday's date]	Rankin	Jan	Maureen Myers	Insurance	4.50	100.00
EP-895	10996	[Monday's date]	Knox	Velma	Rosa Martinez	Estate	3.50	100.00

8. Save the worksheet as an Excel workbook named **EL2-C7-A7-Billings**.
9. Print and then close **EL2-C7-A7-Billings.xlsx**.
10. Display the New dialog box and right-click the template **Billings-StudentName.xltx**. Select *Copy* at the shortcut menu. Open a Computer window and navigate to the Excel2010L2C7 folder on your storage medium and then paste the template. Close the Computer window.
11. At the New dialog box, delete the custom template named **Billings-StudentName.xltx**.
12. Close the New dialog box and then click the Home tab.

Visual Benchmark Demonstrate Your Proficiency

1 CUSTOMIZE THE RIBBON

1. Create the custom tab including the groups and buttons shown in Figure 7.12. Substitute your name for *Student Name* in the tab. You can locate all of the buttons using the *All Commands* list.
2. Insert a screen image in a new Word document that shows the ribbon with the custom tab displayed in Microsoft Excel.
3. Save the Word document and name it **EL2-C7-VB1-MyRibbon**.
4. Print **EL2-C7-VB1-MyRibbon.docx** and then exit Word.
5. Restore the ribbon in Excel to its original settings.

Figure 7.12 Visual Benchmark 1

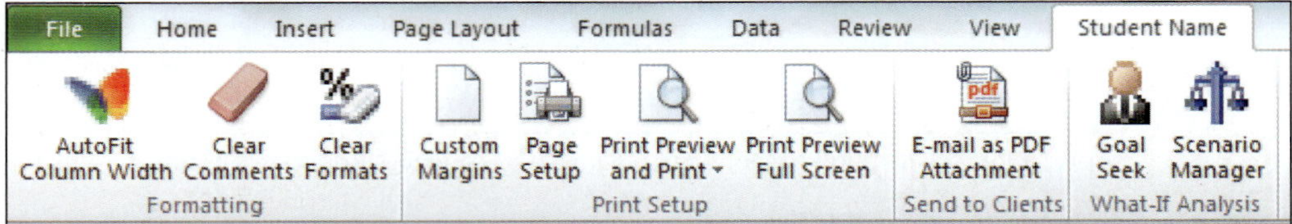

2 CREATE A CUSTOM TEMPLATE

1. Create a custom template that could be used to generate a sales invoice similar to the one shown in Figure 7.13. Use your best judgment to match the column widths, row heights, and color formatting. The font used in A1 is *Footlight MT Light 36-point* and *Garamond* for the remaining cells (18-point in A2 and 12-point elsewhere). Substitute an appropriate clip art image if the one shown is not available on the computer you are using. Recall that a template should only contain text, formulas, and formatting that is not variable from one invoice to another.
2. Save the workbook as a template and name it **EL2-C7-VB2-AudennitaSalesInv**.
3. Using the template, fill out a sales invoice using the data shown in Figure 7.13.
4. Save the completed invoice and name it **EL2-C7-VB2-AudennitaInvToVanderwyst**.
5. Print the invoice and then close **EL2-C7-VB2-AudennitaInvToVanderwyst.xlsx.**
6. Make a copy of the custom template at the New dialog box saving the copy to your storage medium in the Excel2010L2C7 folder.
7. Delete the custom template from the computer you are using at the New dialog box.

Figure 7.13 Visual Benchmark 2

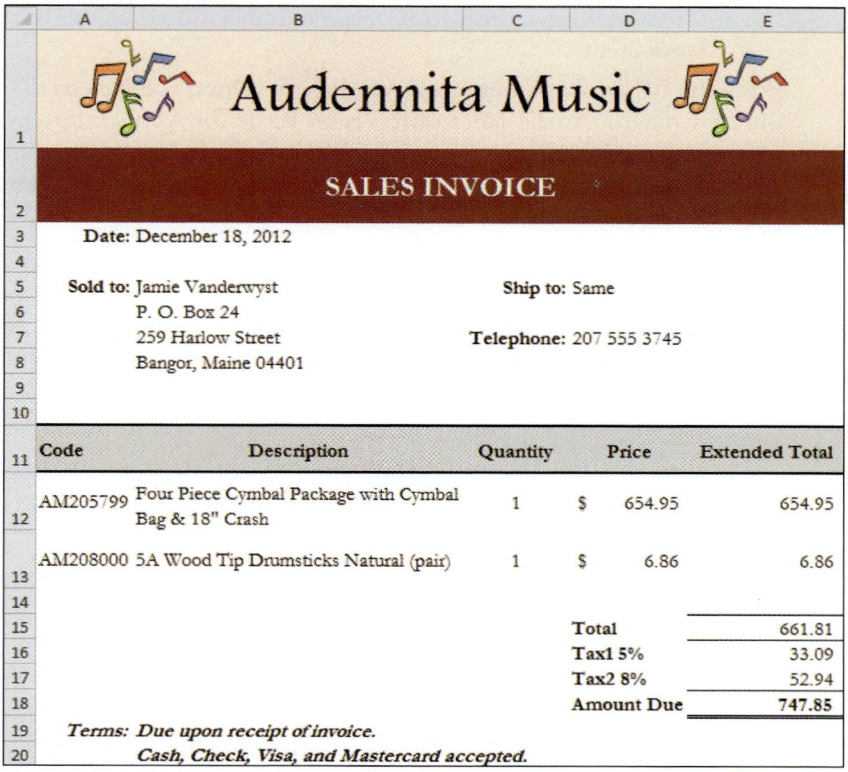

Audennita Music

SALES INVOICE

Date: December 18, 2012

Sold to: Jamie Vanderwyst
P. O. Box 24
259 Harlow Street
Bangor, Maine 04401

Ship to: Same

Telephone: 207 555 3745

Code	Description	Quantity	Price	Extended Total
AM205799	Four Piece Cymbal Package with Cymbal Bag & 18" Crash	1	$ 654.95	654.95
AM208000	5A Wood Tip Drumsticks Natural (pair)	1	$ 6.86	6.86
			Total	661.81
			Tax1 5%	33.09
			Tax2 8%	52.94
			Amount Due	**747.85**

Terms: ***Due upon receipt of invoice.***
Cash, Check, Visa, and Mastercard accepted.

Case Study Apply Your Skills

Part 1

Yolanda Robertson of NuTrends Market Research would like you to help her become more efficient by creating macros for the frequently performed tasks in the list below. In order to share the macros with colleagues in the office you decide to save all of the macros in a macro-enabled workbook named **EL2-C7-CS-P1-NuTrendMacros**. Delete Sheet2 and Sheet3 from the workbook. Rename Sheet1 to *MacroDocumentation*. Document the macros in the workbook by typing the macro names, the shortcut keys you assigned to each macro, and descriptions of the actions each macro performs. This documentation will assist your colleagues by informing them about the macros in the file. For example, in column A type the name of the macro, in column B type the macro's shortcut key, and in column C enter a description of the actions the macro performs.

Create a separate macro for each of the following tasks. At the Record Macro dialog box, type your name and the current date in the *Description* text box for each macro.

- Apply the theme named *Equity* and show all comments.
- Set the active column's width to 20.
- Apply conditional formatting to highlight the top 10 in a selected list. Accept the default formatting options.

- Apply the Accounting format with zero decimals.
- Create a footer that prints your name centered at the bottom of the worksheet.

Print the MacroDocumentation worksheet. Open the Macro dialog box and edit the first macro. At the Microsoft Visual Basic for Applications window, print the macros in the VBAProject. Close the Visual Basic for Applications window to return to the worksheet. Save **EL2-C7-CS-P1-NuTrendsMacros.xlsm**.

Part 2

Yolanda has received the file named **PizzaByMarioNewFranchiseRev.xlsx** from Nicola Carlucci. She wants you to format the workbook using the macros created in Part 1. Open the workbook and use Save As to name it **EL2-C7-CS-P2-PizzaByMarioNewFranchiseRev**. Run each macro created in Part 1 using the following information:

- Set all of the column widths to 20 except column C.
- Run the number formatting and the conditional formatting with the values in column E selected.
- Run the theme and footer macros.

Print the worksheet making sure the comments print as displayed. Save and then close **EL2-C7-CS-P2-PizzaByMarioNewFranchiseRev.xlsx**. Close **EL2-C7-CS-P1-NuTrendsMacros.xlsm**.

Part 3

Help

Yolanda would like to customize the Quick Access toolbar but finds the process cumbersome using the Excel Options dialog box to locate commands. Use Excel Help to learn how to add a button to the Quick Access toolbar directly from the ribbon. Test the information you learned by adding two buttons of your choosing to the Quick Access toolbar using the ribbon. For example, add the Orientation button from the Page Layout tab and the New Comment button from the Review tab. Using Microsoft Word, compose a memo to Yolanda that describes the steps to add a button to the Quick Access toolbar directly from the ribbon. Insert a screen image of the Quick Access toolbar in Excel that displays the buttons you added below the memo text. Save the Word memo and name it **EL2-C7-C3-P3-CustomizeQATMemo**. Print **EL2-C7-CS-P3-CustomizeQATMemo.docx** and then exit Word. Remove the two buttons you added to the Quick Access toolbar.

Part 4

Yolanda has mentioned that sometimes she sees a task pane named Document Recovery appear when she starts Excel. She has asked you to explain why the task pane appears and what she should do when she sees the task pane. Compose a memo to Yolanda using Microsoft Word in which you explain the AutoRecover and AutoSave features in your own words. Include an explanation that the Document Recovery task pane appears after Excel has not been properly closed and provide advice for Yolanda on how to review the files in the pane to make sure she has not lost data.

Microsoft® Excel®

CHAPTER

Importing, Exporting, and Distributing Data

PERFORMANCE OBJECTIVES

Upon successful completion of Chapter 8, you will be able to:

- **Import data from an Access table, a website, and a text file**
- **Append data from an Excel worksheet to an Access table**
- **Embed and link data in an Excel worksheet to a Word document**
- **Copy and paste data in an Excel worksheet to a PowerPoint presentation**
- **Export data as a text file**
- **Scan and remove private or confidential information from a workbook**
- **Mark a workbook as final**
- **Check a workbook for features incompatible with earlier versions of Excel**
- **Save an Excel worksheet as a PDF or XPS file**
- **Save an Excel worksheet as a web page**
- **Send an Excel worksheet via an email message**
- **Save an Excel worksheet to SkyDrive**

Tutorials

8.1 Importing Data from Access, a Text File, or a Website

8.2 Exporting Data from Excel

8.3 Copying and Pasting Worksheet Data between Programs

8.4 Copying and Pasting Worksheet Data to a Word Document

8.5 Exporting Data as a Text File

8.6 Preparing a Worksheet for Distribution

8.7 Converting a Workbook to a Different Format

8.8 Creating a PDF/XPS Copy of a Worksheet

8.9 Publishing a Worksheet as a Web Page

8.10 Sending a Workbook via Email; Saving a Workbook to Windows Live SkyDrive

Exchanging data contained in one program with another by importing or exporting eliminates duplication of effort and reduces the likelihood of data errors or missed entries that would arise if the data was retyped. One of the advantages of working with a suite of programs such as Word, Excel, Access, and PowerPoint is the ability to easily integrate data from one program to another. In this chapter you will learn how to bring data into an Excel worksheet from sources external to Excel and how to export data in a worksheet for use with other programs. You will also learn to use features that allow you to send Excel data using a variety of distribution methods. Model answers for this chapter's projects appear on the following pages.

Excel2010L2C8

Note: Before beginning the projects, copy to your storage medium the Excel2010L2C8 subfolder from the Excel2010L2 folder on the CD that accompanies this textbook and then make Excel2010L2C8 the active folder.

NuTrends Market Research
U.S. Population Estimates by State

Source: U.S. Census Bureau

ID	State	July2009	July2008	July2007	July2006
1	Alabama	4,708,708	4,677,464	4,637,904	4,597,688
2	Alaska	698,473	688,125	682,297	677,325
3	Arizona	6,595,778	6,499,377	6,362,241	6,192,100
4	Arkansas	2,889,450	2,867,764	2,842,194	2,815,097
5	California	36,961,664	36,580,371	36,226,122	35,979,208
6	Colorado	5,024,748	4,935,213	4,842,259	4,753,044
7	Connecticut	3,518,288	3,502,932	3,488,633	3,485,162
8	Delaware	885,122	876,211	864,896	853,022
9	District of Columbia	599,657	590,074	586,409	583,978
10	Florida	18,537,969	18,423,878	18,277,888	18,088,505
11	Georgia	9,829,211	9,697,838	9,533,761	9,330,086
12	Hawaii	1,295,178	1,287,481	1,276,832	1,275,599
13	Idaho	1,545,801	1,527,506	1,499,245	1,464,413
14	Illinois	12,910,409	12,842,954	12,779,417	12,718,011
15	Indiana	6,423,113	6,388,309	6,346,113	6,301,700
16	Iowa	3,007,856	2,993,987	2,978,719	2,964,391
17	Kansas	2,818,747	2,797,375	2,775,586	2,755,700
18	Kentucky	4,314,113	4,287,931	4,256,278	4,219,374
19	Louisiana	4,492,076	4,451,513	4,376,122	4,240,327
20	Maine	1,318,301	1,319,691	1,317,308	1,314,963
21	Maryland	5,699,478	5,658,655	5,634,242	5,612,196
22	Massachusetts	6,593,587	6,543,595	6,499,275	6,466,399
23	Michigan	9,969,727	10,002,486	10,050,847	10,082,438
24	Minnesota	5,266,214	5,230,567	5,191,206	5,148,346
25	Mississippi	2,951,996	2,940,212	2,921,723	2,897,150
26	Missouri	5,987,580	5,956,335	5,909,824	5,861,572
27	Montana	974,989	968,035	957,225	946,230
28	Nebraska	1,796,619	1,781,949	1,769,912	1,760,435
29	Nevada	2,643,085	2,615,772	2,567,752	2,493,405
30	New Hampshire	1,324,575	1,321,872	1,317,343	1,311,894
31	New Jersey	8,707,739	8,663,398	8,636,043	8,623,721
32	New Mexico	2,009,671	1,986,763	1,968,731	1,942,608
33	New York	19,541,453	19,467,789	19,422,777	19,356,564
34	North Carolina	9,380,884	9,247,134	9,064,074	8,866,977
35	North Dakota	646,844	641,421	638,202	636,771
36	Ohio	11,542,645	11,528,072	11,520,815	11,492,495
37	Oklahoma	3,687,050	3,644,025	3,612,186	3,574,334
38	Oregon	3,825,657	3,782,991	3,732,957	3,677,545
39	Pennsylvania	12,604,767	12,566,368	12,522,531	12,471,142
40	Rhode Island	1,053,209	1,053,502	1,055,009	1,060,196
41	South Carolina	4,561,242	4,503,280	4,424,232	4,339,399
42	South Dakota	812,383	804,532	797,035	788,519
43	Tennessee	6,296,254	6,240,456	6,172,862	6,089,453
44	Texas	24,782,302	24,304,290	23,837,701	23,369,024
45	Utah	2,784,572	2,727,343	2,663,796	2,583,724
46	Vermont	621,760	621,049	620,460	619,985
47	Virginia	7,882,590	7,795,424	7,719,749	7,646,996
48	Washington	6,664,195	6,566,073	6,464,979	6,372,243
49	West Virginia	1,819,777	1,814,873	1,811,198	1,807,237
50	Wisconsin	5,654,774	5,627,610	5,601,571	5,571,680
51	Wyoming	544,270	532,981	523,414	512,841
52	Puerto Rico	3,967,288	3,954,553	3,941,235	3,926,744

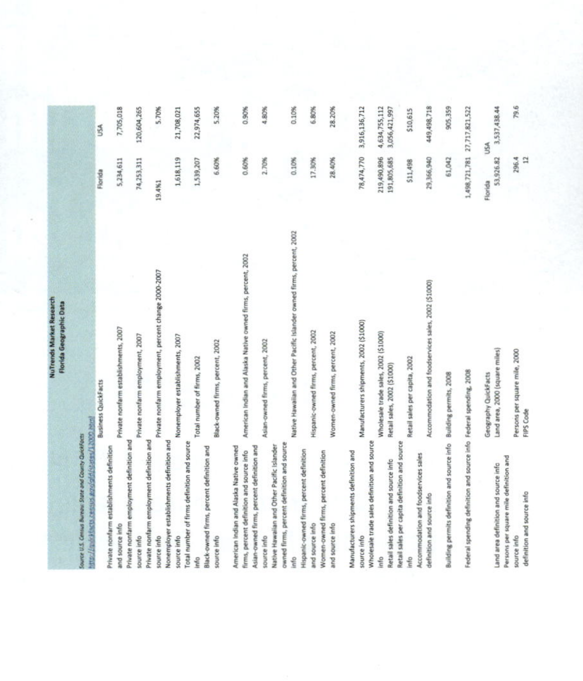

Project 1 Import Data from External Sources to Excel

Project 1a, EL2-C8-P1-NuTrendsCensusData.xlsx with PopulationEstimates Worksheet

Project 1b, EL2-C8-P1-NuTrendsCensusData.xlsx with FloridaGeographicData Worksheet

Housing Unit Estimates
100 Fastest Growing Counties
Change between July 1, 2008 and July 1, 2009

Source: Population Division, U.S. Census Bureau (HU-EST2005-06)

Rank	Geographic Area	Housing Unit Estimates		Change, 2008 to 2009	
		1-Jul-09	1-Jul-08	Number	Percent
1	Flagler County, FL	39,309	34,231	5,078	14.8
2	Sumter County, FL	35,786	31,715	4,071	12.8
3	Pinal County, AZ	108,777	98,666	10,111	10.2
4	Osceola County, FL	102,187	93,352	8,835	9.5
5	Franklin County, WA	20,433	18,681	1,752	9.4
6	Culpeper County, VA	16,154	14,775	1,379	9.3
7	Washington County, UT	48,777	44,908	3,869	8.6
8	Kendall County, IL	28,149	25,932	2,217	8.5
9	St. Lucie County, FL	117,020	108,130	8,890	8.2
10	Rockwall County, TX	22,103	20,528	1,575	7.7
11	Loudoun County, VA	93,374	86,915	6,459	7.4
12	Paulding County, GA	43,769	40,786	2,983	7.3
13	Walton County, FL	37,422	34,889	2,533	7.3
14	Yuba County, CA	25,437	23,749	1,688	7.1
15	Fannin County, GA	15,848	14,801	1,047	7.1
16	Jackson County, GA	21,072	19,690	1,382	7
17	St. Johns County, FL	74,850	69,964	4,886	7
18	Lee County, FL	312,724	292,830	19,894	6.8
19	Teton County, ID	3,693	3,460	233	6.7
20	Rutherford County, TN	90,147	84,753	5,394	6.4
21	Indian River County, FL	70,487	66,291	4,196	6.3
22	Henry County, GA	64,533	60,828	3,705	6.1
23	Forsyth County, GA	51,536	48,580	2,956	6.1
24	Barrow County, GA	23,141	21,841	1,300	6
25	Douglas County, CO	90,010	85,040	4,970	5.8
26	Newton County, GA	33,365	31,526	1,839	5.8
27	Cherokee County, GA	71,370	67,442	3,928	5.8
28	Brunswick County, NC	64,647	61,116	3,531	5.8
29	Iron County, UT	16,137	15,257	880	5.8
30	Deschutes County, OR	68,602	64,861	3,741	5.8
31	Lyon County, NV	16,647	15,750	897	5.7
32	Gallatin County, MT	34,097	32,266	1,831	5.7
33	Caroline County, VA	10,369	9,815	554	5.6
34	Nevada County, AR	5,600	5,305	295	5.6
35	Union County, NC	59,917	56,783	3,134	5.5
36	King George County, VA	8,283	7,859	424	5.4
37	Madison County, MS	34,109	32,388	1,721	5.3
38	Baldwin County, AL	89,900	85,380	4,520	5.3
39	Madison County, ID	10,412	9,890	522	5.3
40	Fayette County, TN	12,750	12,117	633	5.2

Page 1

11,860	11,272	588	5.2
29,896	28,427	1,469	5.2
18,358	683,244	35,114	5.1
15,248	14,515	733	5
12,475	11,877	598	5
27,656	121,564	6,092	5
40,596	133,916	6,680	5
52,979	50,465	2,514	5
26,591	25,335	1,256	5
44,427	42,331	2,096	5
65,570	62,501	3,069	4.9
44,673	42,591	2,082	4.9
42,578	40,624	1,954	4.8
7,189	6,860	329	4.8
14,871	14,194	677	4.8
2,529	2,415	114	4.7
17,108	16,337	771	4.7
42,277	40,373	1,904	4.7
50,452	239,179	11,273	4.7
03,449	194,333	9,116	4.7
47,207	140,628	6,579	4.7
91,613	87,521	4,092	4.7
40,220	38,427	1,793	4.7
25,667	120,072	5,595	4.7
17,505	16,734	771	4.6
17,369	16,606	763	4.6
60,524	57,874	2,650	4.6
39,522	37,802	1,720	4.6
15,082	14,427	655	4.5
12,005	11,484	521	4.5
10,162	9,722	440	4.5
10,743	10,278	465	4.5
76,074	72,788	3,286	4.5
4,175	3,995	180	4.5
29,050	27,801	1,249	4.5
40,240	38,513	1,727	4.5
99,474	669,785	29,689	4.4
31,140	29,823	1,317	4.4
5,759	5,516	243	4.4
46,574	44,611	1,963	4.4
94,768	90,778	3,990	4.4
6,293	6,029	264	4.4
44,733	42,859	1,874	4.4
56,686	54,314	2,372	4.4
30,294	29,028	1,266	4.4
89,761	86,013	3,748	4.4
86,749	83,141	3,608	4.3

Page 2

127,340	122,047	5,293	4.3
25,820	24,752	1,068	4.3
34,865	33,424	1,441	4.3
12,393	11,881	512	4.3
11,481	11,010	471	4.3
54,650	52,411	2,239	4.3
207,862	199,393	8,469	4.2
72,953	69,984	2,969	4.2
97,270	93,315	3,955	4.2
13,994	13,426	568	4.2
9,080	8,712	368	4.2
13,119	12,588	531	4.2
8,183	7,853	330	4.2

Page 3

Project 1c, EL2-C8-P1-NuTrendsCensusData.xlsx with HousingUnitData Worksheet

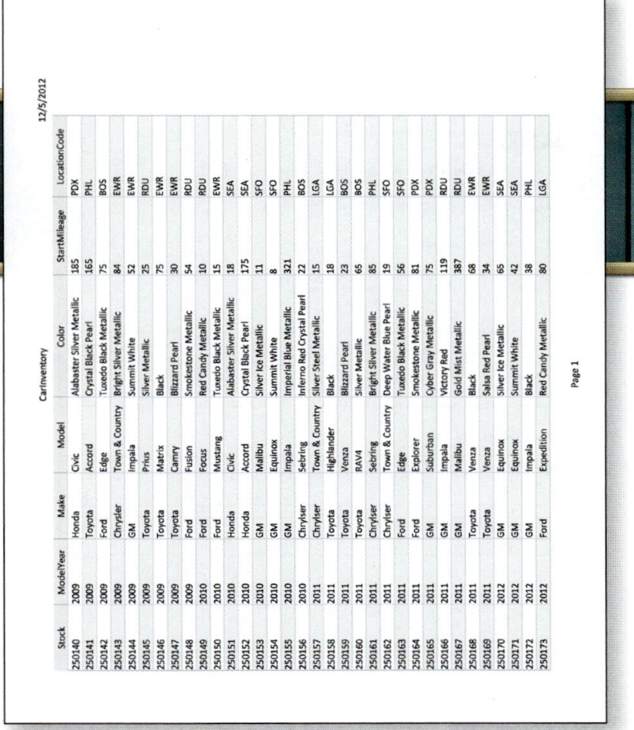
12/5/2012

CarInventory

Stock	ModelYear	Make	Model	Color	StartMileage	LocationCode
250140	2009	Honda	Civic	Alabaster Silver Metallic	185	PDX
250141	2009	Toyota	Accord	Crystal Black Pearl	165	PHL
250142	2009	Ford	Edge	Tuxedo Black Metallic	75	BOS
250143	2009	Chrysler	Town & Country	Bright Silver Metallic	84	EWR
250144	2009	GM	Impala	Summit White	52	EWR
250145	2009	Toyota	Prius	Silver Metallic	25	RDU
250146	2009	Toyota	Matrix	Black	75	EWR
250147	2009	Toyota	Camry	Blizzard Pearl	30	EWR
250148	2009	Ford	Fusion	Smokestone Metallic	54	RDU
250149	2010	Ford	Focus	Red Candy Metallic	10	RDU
250150	2010	Ford	Mustang	Tuxedo Black Metallic	15	EWR
250151	2010	Honda	Civic	Alabaster Silver Metallic	18	SEA
250152	2010	Honda	Accord	Crystal Black Pearl	175	SEA
250153	2010	GM	Malibu	Silver Ice Metallic	11	SFO
250154	2010	GM	Equinox	Summit White	8	SFO
250155	2010	GM	Impala	Imperial Blue Metallic	321	PHL
250156	2010	Chrysler	Sebring	Inferno Red Crystal Pearl	22	BOS
250157	2011	Chrysler	Town & Country	Silver Steel Metallic	15	LGA
250158	2011	Toyota	Highlander	Black	18	LGA
250159	2011	Toyota	Venza	Blizzard Pearl	23	BOS
250160	2011	Toyota	RAV4	Silver Metallic	65	BOS
250161	2011	Chrysler	Sebring	Bright Silver Metallic	85	PHL
250162	2011	Chrysler	Town & Country	Deep Water Blue Pearl	19	SFO
250163	2011	Ford	Edge	Tuxedo Black Metallic	56	SFO
250164	2011	Ford	Explorer	Smokestone Metallic	81	PDX
250165	2011	GM	Suburban	Cyber Gray Metallic	75	PDX
250166	2011	GM	Impala	Victory Red	119	RDU
250167	2011	GM	Malibu	Gold Mist Metallic	387	RDU
250168	2011	Toyota	Venza	Black	68	EWR
250169	2011	Toyota	Venza	Salsa Red Pearl	34	EWR
250170	2012	GM	Equinox	Silver Ice Metallic	65	SEA
250171	2012	GM	Equinox	Summit White	42	SEA
250172	2012	GM	Impala	Black	38	PHL
250173	2012	Ford	Expedition	Red Candy Metallic	80	LGA

Page 1

Project 2 Export Data in Excel

Project 2a, CarInventory Datasheet from CutRateInventory.accdb

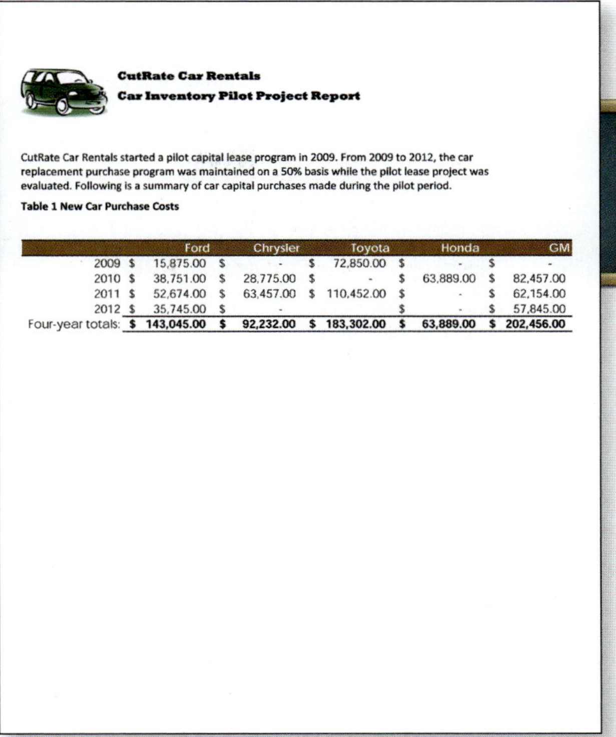
CutRate Car Rentals
Car Inventory Pilot Project Report

CutRate Car Rentals started a pilot capital lease program in 2009. From 2009 to 2012, the car replacement purchase program was maintained on a 50% basis while the pilot lease project was evaluated. Following is a summary of car capital purchases made during the pilot period.

Table 1 New Car Purchase Costs

	Ford	Chrysler	Toyota	Honda	GM
2009	$ 15,875.00	$ -	$ 72,850.00	$ -	$ -
2010	$ 38,751.00	$ 28,775.00	$ -	$ 63,889.00	$ 82,457.00
2011	$ 52,674.00	$ 63,457.00	$ 110,452.00	$ -	$ 62,154.00
2012	$ 35,745.00	$ -		$ -	$ 57,845.00
Four-year totals:	$ 143,045.00	$ 92,232.00	$ 183,302.00	$ 63,889.00	$ 202,456.00

Project 2b, EL2-C8-P2-CutRateCarRpt.docx

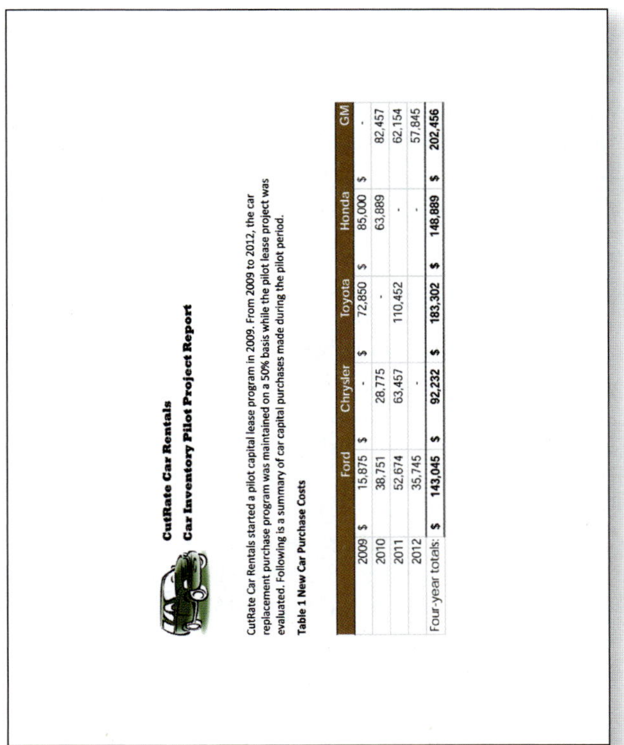
CutRate Car Rentals
Car Inventory Pilot Project Report

CutRate Car Rentals started a pilot capital lease program in 2009. From 2009 to 2012, the car replacement purchase program was maintained on a 50% basis while the pilot lease project was evaluated. Following is a summary of car capital purchases made during the pilot period.

Table 1 New Car Purchase Costs

	Ford	Chrysler	Toyota	Honda	GM
2009	$ 15,875	$ -	$ 72,850	$ 85,000	$ -
2010	38,751	28,775	-	63,889	82,457
2011	52,674	63,457	110,452	-	62,154
2012	35,745	-		-	57,845
Four-year totals:	$ 143,045	$ 92,232	$ 183,302	$ 148,889	$ 202,456

Project 2c, EL2-C8-P2-CutRateCarRptLinked.docx

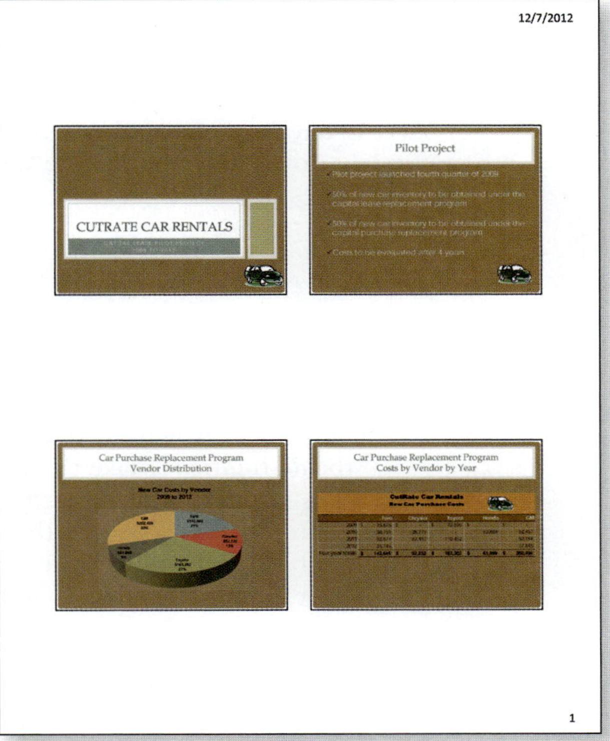

Project 2e, EL2-C8-P2-CutRateCarRpt.pptx

```
EL2-C8-P2-CutRateInventory.csv
CutRate Car Rentals,,,,,,
New Car Inventory,,,,,,
,,,,,,
Stock,ModelYear,Make,Model,Color,StartMileage,LocationCode
250145,2009,Toyota,Prius,Silver Metallic,25,RDU
250146,2009,Toyota,Matrix,Black,75,EWR
250147,2009,Toyota,Camry,Blizzard Pearl,30,EWR
250148,2009,Ford,Fusion,Smokestone Metallic,54,RDU
250149,2010,Ford,Focus,Red Candy Metallic,10,RDU
250150,2010,Ford,Mustang,Tuxedo Black Metallic,15,EWR
250151,2010,Honda,Civic,Alabaster Silver Metallic,18,SEA
250152,2010,Honda,Accord,Crystal Black Pearl,175,SEA
250153,2010,GM,Malibu,Silver Ice Metallic,11,SFO
250154,2010,GM,Equinox,Summit White,8,SFO
250155,2010,GM,Impala,Imperial Blue Metallic,321,PHL
250156,2010,Chrylser,Sebring,Inferno Red Crystal Pearl,22,BOS
250157,2011,Chrylser,Town & Country,Silver Steel Metallic,15,LGA
250158,2011,Toyota,Highlander,Black,18,LGA
250159,2011,Toyota,Venza,Blizzard Pearl,23,BOS
250160,2011,Toyota,RAV4,Silver Metallic,65,BOS
250161,2011,Chrylser,Sebring,Bright Silver Metallic,85,PHL
250162,2011,Chrylser,Town & Country,Deep Water Blue Pearl,19,SFO
250163,2011,Ford,Edge,Tuxedo Black Metallic,56,SFO
250164,2011,Ford,Explorer,Smokestone Metallic,81,PDX
250165,2011,GM,Suburban,Cyber Gray Metallic,75,PDX
250166,2011,GM,Impala,Victory Red,119,RDU
250167,2011,GM,Malibu,Gold Mist Metallic,387,RDU
250168,2011,Toyota,Venza,Black,68,EWR
250169,2011,Toyota,Venza,Salsa Red Pearl,34,EWR
250170,2012,GM,Equinox,Silver Ice Metallic,65,SEA
250171,2012,GM,Equinox,Summit White,42,SEA
250172,2012,GM,Impala,Black,38,PHL
250173,2012,Ford,Expedition,Red Candy Metallic,80,LGA

Page 1
```

Project 2f, EL2-C8-P2-CutRateInventory.csv

Compatibility Report for CutRateBuyLeaseAnalysis.xlsx
Run on 12/7/2012 11:15

The following features in this workbook are not supported by earlier versions of Excel. These features may be lost or degraded when opening this workbook in an earlier version of Excel or if you save this workbook in an earlier file format.

Significant loss of functionality	**# of occurrences**	**Version**
One or more cells in this workbook contain a conditional formatting type that is not supported in earlier versions of Excel, such as data bars, color scales, or icon sets.	1 Sheet1'!D13:D16	Excel 97-2003
Some cells contain conditional formatting with the 'Stop if True' option cleared. Earlier versions of Excel do not recognize this option and will stop after the first true condition.	1 Sheet1'!B5:K8	Excel 97-2003

Minor loss of fidelity		
A table style is applied to a table in this workbook. Table style formatting cannot be displayed in earlier versions of Excel.	1 Sheet1'!A4:K9	Excel 97-2003
Some cells or styles in this workbook contain formatting that is not supported by the selected file format. These formats will be converted to the closest format available.	16	Excel 97-2003

Project 3 Prepare a Workbook for Distribution

Project 3c, EL2-C8-P3-CutRateBuyLeaseAnalysisCompChk.xlsx

Project 1 Import Data from External Sources to Excel — 3 Parts

You will import U.S. Census Bureau data related to a market research project from an Access database, from the U.S. Census Bureau's website, and from a text file previously downloaded from the Census Bureau.

Importing Data into Excel

The Get External Data group in the Data tab contains buttons used to import data from external sources into an Excel worksheet. During an import or export routine, the program containing the original data is called the ***source***, and the program to which the data source is being copied, embedded, or linked is called the ***destination***. Make the cell active at which you want the import to begin and click the button representing the source application, or click the From Other Sources button to select the source from a drop-down list. A connection can be established to an external data source to avoid having to repeat the import process each time you need to analyze the data in Excel. Once a connection has been created, you can repeat the import in another worksheet by simply clicking the connection file in the Existing Connections dialog box.

Importing Data from Access

Exchanging data between Access and Excel is a seamless process since data in an Access datasheet is structured in the same row and column format as an Excel worksheet. You can import the Access data as an Excel table, a PivotTable Report, or as a PivotChart and a PivotTable report. The imported data can be placed in a cell you identify in the active worksheet or in a new worksheet. To import an Access table, click the Data tab and then click the From Access button in the Get External Data group. At the Select Data Source dialog box, navigate to the drive and/or folder in which the source database resides and then double-click the Access database file name in the file list. If the source database contains more than one table, the Select Table dialog box opens in which you choose the table containing the data you want to import. If the source database contains only one table you are not prompted to select a table name. Once the table is identified, the Import Data dialog box shown in Figure 8.1 appears. Choose how you want to view the data and the location to begin the import and click OK.

Quick Steps

Import Access Table
1. Make active cell at which to begin import.
2. Click Data tab.
3. Click From Access button.
4. Navigate to drive and/or folder.
5. Double-click source database file name.
6. If necessary, click desired table name and OK.
7. Select desired view format.
8. Click OK.

HINT

Only one table can be imported at a time. To import all of the tables in the source database, repeat the import process for each table.

From Access

Figure 8.1 Import Data Dialog Box

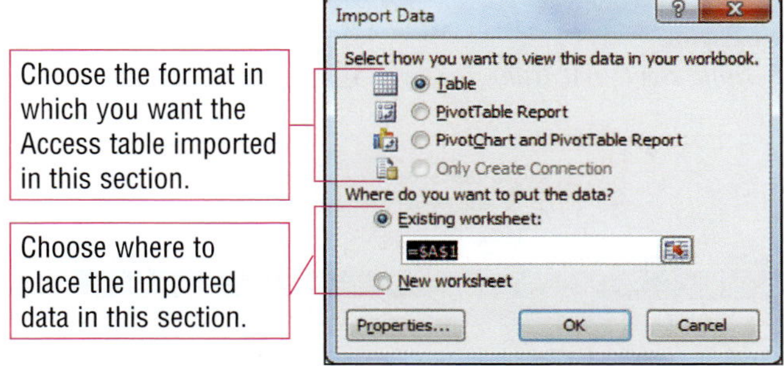

Project 1a **Importing Data from an Access Database** Part 1 of 3

1. Open **NuTrendsCensusData.xlsx**.
2. Save the workbook with Save As and name it **EL2-C8-P1-NuTrendsCensusData**.
3. Import four years of U.S. state population estimates compiled by the U.S. Census Bureau that are stored in an Access database by completing the following steps:
   a. With PopulationEstimates the active worksheet, make A5 the active cell if A5 is not currently active.
   b. Click the Data tab.
   c. Click the From Access button in the Get External Data group.
   d. At the Select Data Source dialog box, navigate to the Excel2010L2C8 folder on your storage medium and then double-click ***NuTrendsCensusData.accdb***.

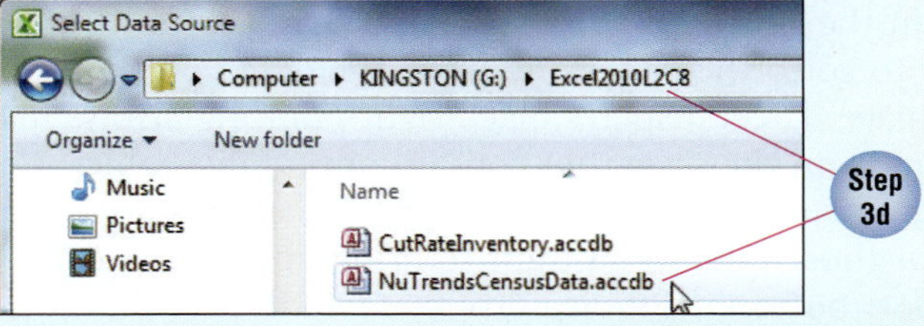

e. Since the source database contains more than one table, the Select Table dialog box appears. Click *PopByState* in the *Name* column and then click OK.

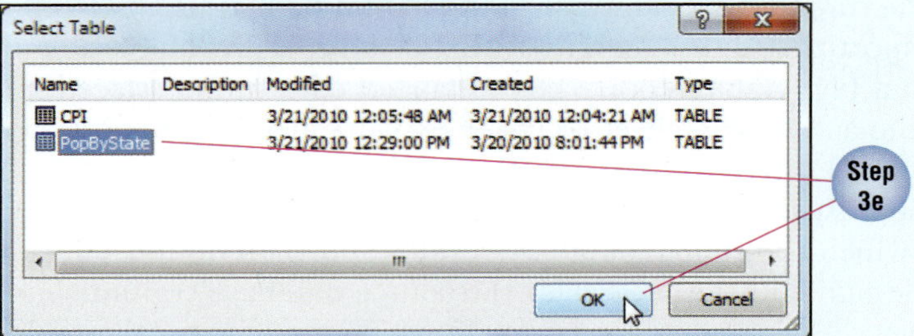

f. At the Import Data dialog box with *Table* selected in the *Select how you want to view this data in your workbook* section and with *=$A$5* in the *Existing worksheet* text box in the *Where do you want to put the data?* section, click OK.

4. Scroll down the imported table data. Notice the data is formatted as a table with filter arrow buttons.
5. Make the following changes to the worksheet:
   a. Remove the filter arrow buttons.
   b. Change the table style to *Table Style Medium 1* (first from left in *Medium* section) at the Format as Table drop-down gallery.
   c. Format all of the values to display a comma in the thousands and zero decimals.
   d. Adjust the column widths of columns C to F to 15.
   e. Center-align the labels in C5:F5.
6. Print the PopulationEstimates worksheet scaled to fit 1 page in width and height and centered horizontally between the left and right margins.
7. Save **EL2-C8-P1-NuTrendsCensusData.xlsx**.

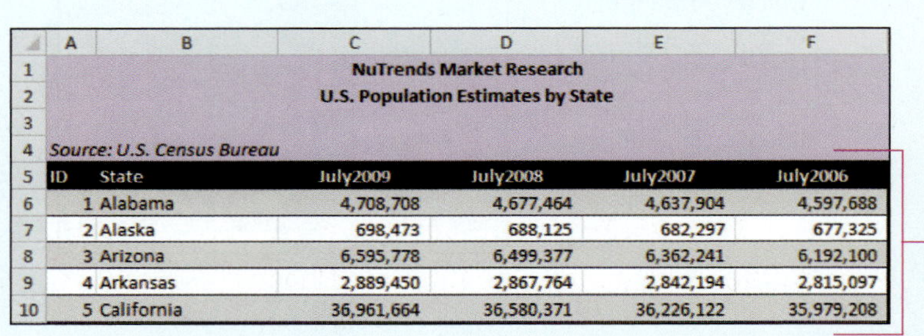

	A	B	C	D	E	F
1			NuTrends Market Research			
2			U.S. Population Estimates by State			
3						
4	*Source: U.S. Census Bureau*					
5	ID	State	July2009	July2008	July2007	July2006
6	1	Alabama	4,708,708	4,677,464	4,637,904	4,597,688
7	2	Alaska	698,473	688,125	682,297	677,325
8	3	Arizona	6,595,778	6,499,377	6,362,241	6,192,100
9	4	Arkansas	2,889,450	2,867,764	2,842,194	2,815,097
10	5	California	36,961,664	36,580,371	36,226,122	35,979,208

Quick Steps

Import Data from Web Page
1. Make active cell at which to begin import.
2. Click Data tab.
3. Click From Web button.
4. Navigate to desired web page.
5. Click arrows next to tables to import.
6. Click Import button.
7. Click OK.

Importing Data from a Website

Tables in a website can be downloaded directly from the web source using the New Web Query dialog box shown in Figure 8.2. Make active the cell at which you want to begin the import, click the Data tab, and then click the From Web button in the Get External Data group. Use the Address bar and web navigation buttons to go to the page containing the data you want to use in Excel. At the desired page, Excel displays black right-pointing arrows inside yellow boxes next to elements on the page that contain importable tables. Point to an arrow and a blue border surrounds the data Excel will capture if you click the arrow. Click the arrow for those tables you want to bring into your Excel worksheet and then click the Import button. In Project 1b, you will import multiple sections of data about Florida from the U.S. Census Bureau QuickFacts web page.

Figure 8.2 New Web Query Dialog Box

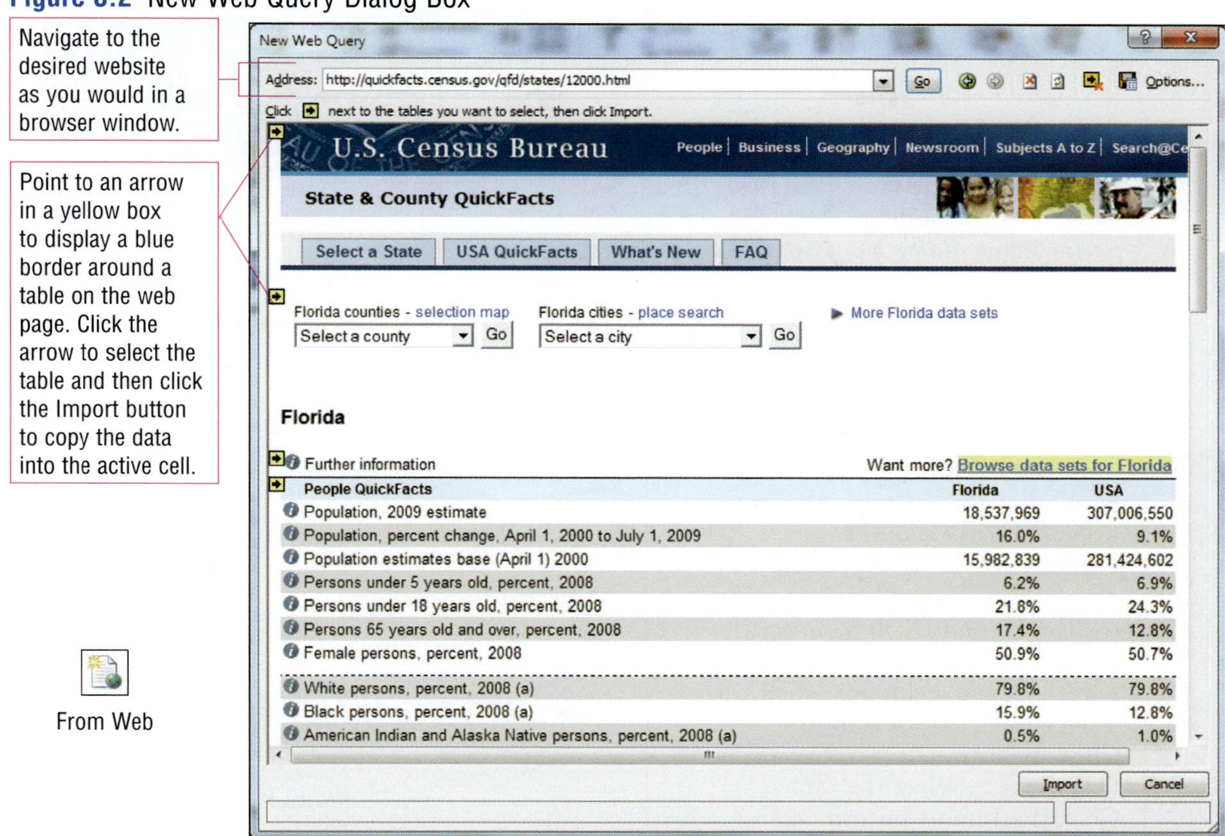

Project 1b Importing a Table from a Web Page Part 2 of 3

1. With **EL2-C8-P1-NuTrendsCensusData.xlsx** open, make FloridaGeographicData the active worksheet.
2. Import statistics related to Florida from the U.S. Census Bureau QuickFacts web page by completing the following steps:
   a. Make A6 the active cell if A6 is not currently active.
   b. Click the From Web button in the Get External Data group of the Data tab.
   c. At the New Web Query dialog box, select the current entry in the *Address* text box, type http://www.census.gov, and press Enter.
   d. Click the Data Tools link located near the top left of the web page.

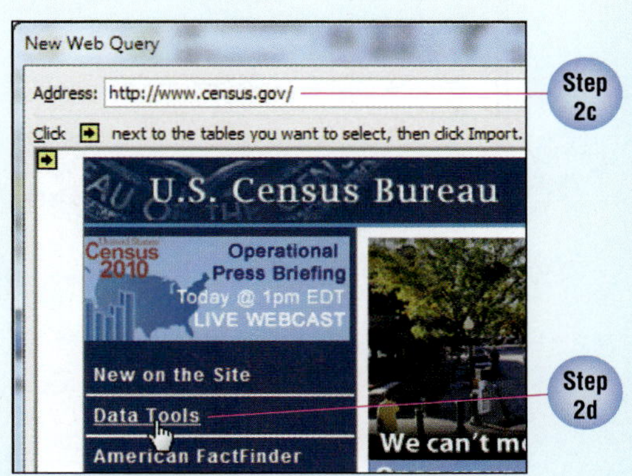

e. At the Data Access Tools page, scroll down the page if necessary and then click the QuickFacts link in the *Interactive Internet Tools* section.

f. At the State & County QuickFacts page, resize the New Web Query dialog box until you can see the entire map of the United States.

g. Click over the state of Florida in the map. ***Note: If a Script Error dialog box displays, click* Yes *to continue running scripts on the page*.**

h. At the Florida QuickFacts page, notice the black right-pointing arrows inside yellow boxes along the left edge of the page. Point to one of the arrows to see the blue border that surrounds a section of data; the border indicates the data that will be imported into Excel if you click the arrow.

i. Scroll down the page to the section titled *Business QuickFacts*.

j. Click the black right-pointing arrow inside the yellow box next to *Business QuickFacts* to select the table. The arrow changes to a check mark inside a green box when the table is selected for import.

k. Click the arrow next to *Geography QuickFacts* to select the table.

l. Click the Import button.

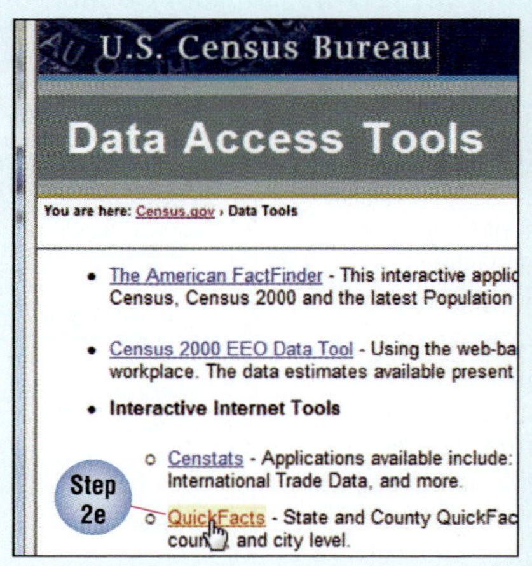

Business QuickFacts	Florida	USA
Private nonfarm establishments, 2007	523,461[1]	7,705,018
Private nonfarm employment, 2007	7,425,331[1]	120,604,265
Private nonfarm employment, percent change 2000-2007	19.4%[1]	5.7%
Nonemployer establishments, 2007	1,618,119	21,708,021
Total number of firms, 2002	1,539,207	22,974,655
Black-owned firms, percent, 2002	6.6%	5.2%
American Indian and Alaska Native owned firms, percent, 2002	0.6%	0.9%
Asian-owned firms, percent, 2002	2.7%	4.8%
Native Hawaiian and Other Pacific Islander owned firms, percent, 2002	0.1%	0.1%
Hispanic-owned firms, percent, 2002	17.3%	6.8%
Women-owned firms, percent, 2002	28.4%	28.2%
Manufacturers shipments, 2002 ($1000)	78,474,770	3,916,136,712
Wholesale trade sales, 2002 ($1000)	219,490,896	4,634,755,112
Retail sales, 2002 ($1000)	191,805,685	3,056,421,997
Retail sales per capita, 2002	$11,498	$10,615
Accommodation and foodservices sales, 2002 ($1000)	29,366,940	449,498,718
Building permits, 2008	61,042	905,359
Federal spending, 2008	149,872,178[1]	2,771,782,152[2]

Geography QuickFacts	Florida	USA
…are miles)	53,926.82	3,537,438..4
Persons per square mile, 2000	296.4	79.6

Click to select this table.

Import Cancel

Done

Step 2j

Step 2k

Step 2l

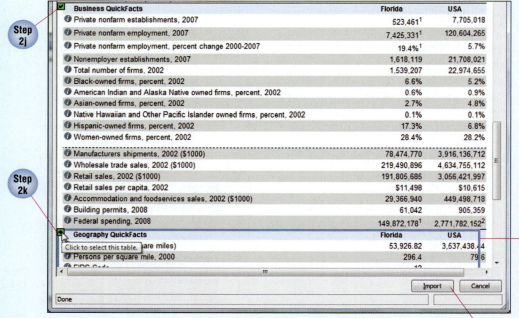

A blue border displays around the data that will be imported to Excel if the table is selected.

m. At the Import Data dialog box with *=$A$6* in the *Existing worksheet* text box in the *Where do you want to put the data?* section, click OK. Excel imports the data from the web page into the Excel worksheet starting in A6.

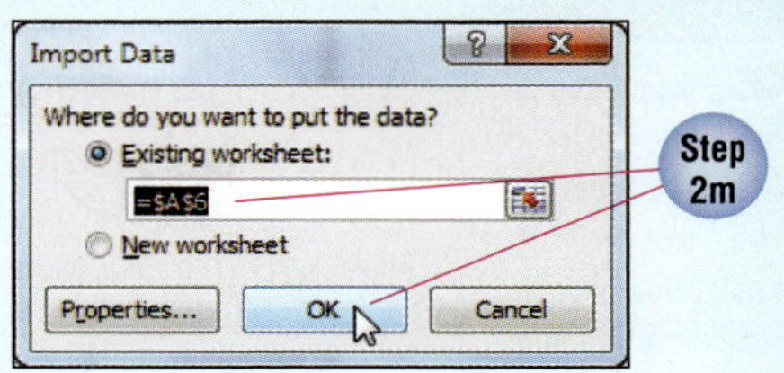

3. Make the following changes to the worksheet:
   a. Select the cells in Column A that contain imported text, click the Home tab, and then click the Wrap Text button in the Alignment group.
   b. Decrease the width of column A to 35.00 (250 pixels).
   c. Select the cells in Column A that contain imported text, click the Format button in the Cells group of the Home tab, and then click *AutoFit Row Height* at the drop-down list.
   d. Align the text in C6:D6 at the center.
   e. Change the page orientation to landscape.
4. Print the FloridaGeographicData worksheet scaled to fit 1 page width by 1 page height and centered between the left and right margins.
5. Save **EL2-C8-P1-NuTrendsCensusData.xlsx**.

Importing Data from a Text File

A text file is often used to exchange data between dissimilar programs since the file format is recognized by nearly all applications. Text files contain no formatting and consist of letters, numbers, punctuation symbols, and a few control characters only. Two commonly used text file formats separate fields with either a tab character (delimited file format) or a comma (comma separated file format). The text file you will use in Project 1c is shown in a Notepad window in Figure 8.3. If necessary, you can view and edit a text file in Notepad prior to importing.

Quick Steps

Import Data from Comma Separated Text File

1. Make active cell at which to begin import.
2. Click Data tab.
3. Click From Text button.
4. Double-click .csv file name.
5. Click Next.
6. Click *Comma* check box.
7. Click Next.
8. Click Finish.
9. Click OK.

From Text

Figure 8.3 Project 1c Text File Contents

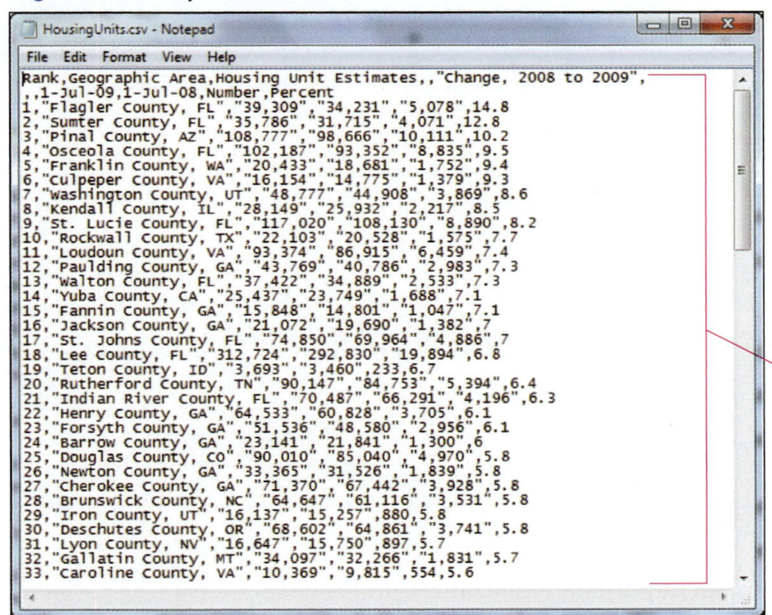

HousingUnits.csv - Notepad

File Edit Format View Help

```
Rank,Geographic Area,Housing Unit Estimates,,"Change, 2008 to 2009",
,,1-Jul-09,1-Jul-08,Number,Percent
1,"Flagler County, FL","39,309","34,231","5,078",14.8
2,"Sumter County, FL","35,786","31,715","4,071",12.8
3,"Pinal County, AZ","108,777","98,666","10,111",10.2
4,"Osceola County, FL","102,187","93,352","8,835",9.5
5,"Franklin County, WA","20,433","18,681","1,752",9.4
6,"Culpeper County, VA","16,154","14,775","1,379",9.3
7,"Washington County, UT","48,777","44,908","3,869",8.6
8,"Kendall County, IL","28,149","25,932","2,217",8.5
9,"St. Lucie County, FL","117,020","108,130","8,890",8.2
10,"Rockwall County, TX","22,103","20,528","1,575",7.7
11,"Loudoun County, VA","93,374","86,915","6,459",7.4
12,"Paulding County, GA","43,769","40,786","2,983",7.3
13,"Walton County, FL","37,422","34,889","2,533",7.3
14,"Yuba County, CA","25,437","23,749","1,688",7.1
15,"Fannin County, GA","15,848","14,801","1,047",7.1
16,"Jackson County, GA","21,072","19,690","1,382",7
17,"St. Johns County, FL","74,850","69,964","4,886",7
18,"Lee County, FL","312,724","292,830","19,894",6.8
19,"Teton County, ID","3,693","3,460",233,6.7
20,"Rutherford County, TN","90,147","84,753","5,394",6.4
21,"Indian River County, FL","70,487","66,291","4,196",6.3
22,"Henry County, GA","64,533","60,828","3,705",6.1
23,"Forsyth County, GA","51,536","48,580","2,956",6.1
24,"Barrow County, GA","23,141","21,841","1,300",6
25,"Douglas County, CO","90,010","85,040","4,970",5.8
26,"Newton County, GA","33,365","31,526","1,839",5.8
27,"Cherokee County, GA","71,370","67,442","3,928",5.8
28,"Brunswick County, NC","64,647","61,116","3,531",5.8
29,"Iron County, UT","16,137","15,257",880,5.8
30,"Deschutes County, OR","68,602","64,861","3,741",5.8
31,"Lyon County, NV","16,647","15,750",897,5.7
32,"Gallatin County, MT","34,097","32,266","1,831",5.7
33,"Caroline County, VA","10,369","9,815",554,5.6
```

Text files contain no formatting codes. A comma separated file (.csv) contains a comma separating each field. During the import, Excel starts a new column at each comma. Notice also that quotes surround text data. Excel strips the quotes from the data upon importing.

Most programs can export data in a text file. If you need to use data from a program that is not compatible with Excel, check the source program's export options for a text file format.

To import a text file into Excel, use the From Text button in the Get External Data group of the Data tab and then select the source file at the Import Text File dialog box. Excel displays in the file list any file in the active folder that ends with a text file extension *.prn, .txt,* or *.csv*. Once the source file is selected, Excel begins the Text Import Wizard, which guides you through the import process through three dialog boxes.

Project 1c Importing Data from a Comma Separated Text File Part 3 of 3

1. With **EL2-C8-P1-NuTrendsCensusData.xlsx** open, make HousingUnitData the active worksheet.
2. Import statistics related to the top-growing U.S. counties based on changes in housing units downloaded from the U.S. Census Bureau website in a text file by completing the following steps:
   a. Make A6 the active cell if A6 is not currently active.
   b. Click the Data tab.
   c. Click the From Text button in the Get External Data group.
   d. At the Import Text File dialog box, double-click the file named ***HousingUnits.csv*** in the file list.
   e. At the Text Import Wizard - Step 1 of 3 dialog box, with *Delimited* selected in the *Original data type* section, click Next. Notice the preview window in the lower half of the dialog box displays a sample of the data in the source text file. Delimited files use commas or tabs as separators, while fixed-width files use spaces.
   f. At the Text Import Wizard - Step 2 of 3 dialog box, click the *Comma* check box in the *Delimiters* section to insert a check mark and then click Next. Notice after you select the comma as the delimiter character, the data in the *Data preview* section updates to show the imported data arranged in Excel columns.

Step 2e

Step 2f

g. Click Finish at the Text Import Wizard - Step 3 of 3 dialog box to import all of the columns using the default *General* format. Formatting can be applied after the data has been imported into the worksheet.

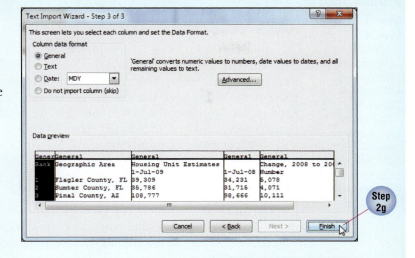

h. At the Import Data dialog box with *=$A$6* in the *Existing worksheet* text box in the *Where do you want to put the data?* section, click OK.

3. Scroll down the worksheet and view the imported data. The text file contained the top 100 counties in the United States ranked by change in housing units from 2008 to 2009. The number of housing units and the percent change are included.

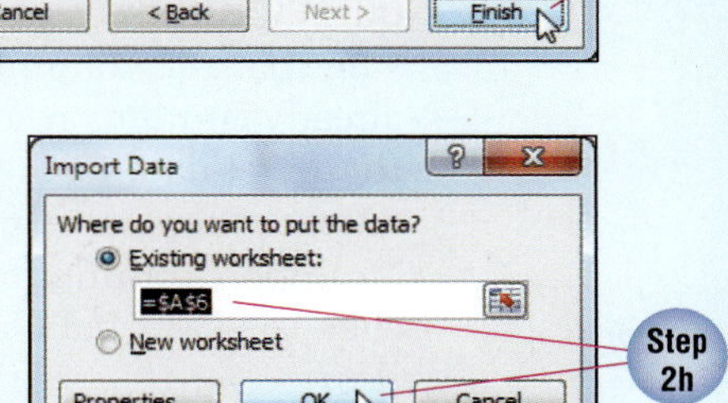

4. Make the following changes to the data:
   a. Select C6:D6, click the Home tab, and then click the Merge & Center button in the Alignment group.
   b. Merge and center E6:F6.
   c. Right-align E7.
   d. Change the width of columns C, D, and E to 14.00 (103 pixels).
5. Print the HousingUnitData worksheet centered between the left and right margins.
6. Save and then close **EL2-C8-P1-NuTrendsCensusData.xlsx**.

Export Data in Excel — 6 Parts

You will copy and paste data related to car inventory from an Excel worksheet to integrate with an Access database, a Word report, and a PowerPoint presentation. You will also save a worksheet as a comma separated text file for use in a non-Microsoft program.

Exporting Data from Excel

Excel data can be exported for use in other programs by copying the cells to the clipboard and pasting into the destination document or by saving the worksheet as a separate file in another file format. To use Excel data in Word, PowerPoint, or Access, use the copy and paste routine since the programs within the Microsoft Office Suite are designed for integration. To export the Excel data for use in other programs, open the Save As dialog box and change the *Save as type* option to the desired file format. If the file format for the destination program that you want

Quick Steps

Append Excel Data to Access Table

1. Select cells.
2. Click Copy button.
3. Start Access.
4. Open database.
5. Open table in Datasheet view.
6. Click Paste button arrow.
7. Click *Paste Append*.
8. Click Yes.
9. Deselect pasted range.

to use does not appear in the *Save as type* list, you can try copying and pasting the data or go to the Microsoft Office Online website and search for a file format converter that you can download and install.

Another way to save the current worksheet in another file format is to click the File tab and then click the Save & Send tab. At the Save & Send tab Backstage view, click *Change File Type* in the center pane. In the Change File Type pane at the right, click the desired file format in the *Workbook File Types* or *Other File Types* section and then click the Save As button. If necessary, navigate to the desired drive and/or folder in the Save As dialog box. Type the desired file name and then click the Save button.

Copying and Pasting Worksheet Data to an Access Table

Data in an Excel worksheet can be copied and pasted to an Access table datasheet, query, or form using the clipboard. To paste data into a table datasheet, make sure that the column structure in the two programs match. If the Access datasheet already contains records, you can choose to replace the existing records or append the Excel data to the end of the table. If you want to export Excel data to an Access database that does not have an existing table in which to receive the data, perform an import routine from Access. To do this, start Access, open the desired database, click the External Data tab, and then click the Import Excel spreadsheet button.

Project 2a Copying and Pasting Excel Data to an Access Datasheet

Part 1 of 6

1. Open **CutRateInventory.xlsx**.
2. Copy and paste the rows in the Inventory worksheet to the bottom of an Access table by completing the following steps:
   a. Make sure Inventory is the active worksheet.
   b. Select A5:G33 and click the Copy button in the Clipboard group in the Home tab.
   c. Start Microsoft Access 2010.
   d. Click File, then click New. At the New tab Backstage view, click the Open button.
   e. At the Open dialog box, navigate to the Excel2010L2C8 folder on your storage medium and then double-click the database named ***CutRateInventory.accdb***. If a Security Warning message displays below the ribbon stating that active content has been disabled, click the Enable Content button.
   f. Double-click the object named *CarInventory* in the Tables group of the Navigation pane at the left side of the Access window. This opens the CarInventory table in Datasheet view. Notice the structure of the columns in the datasheet is the same as the source worksheet in Excel.
   g. With the table open in Datasheet view, click the down-pointing arrow on the Paste button in the Clipboard group and then click *Paste Append* at the drop-down list.

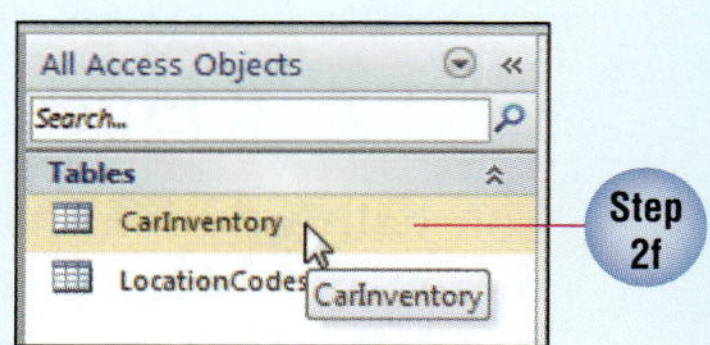

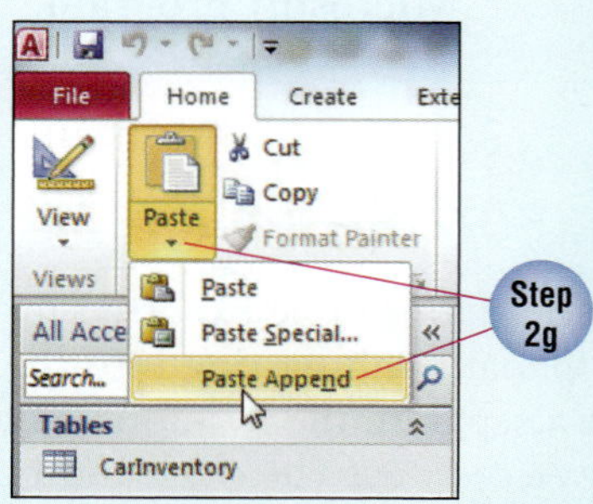

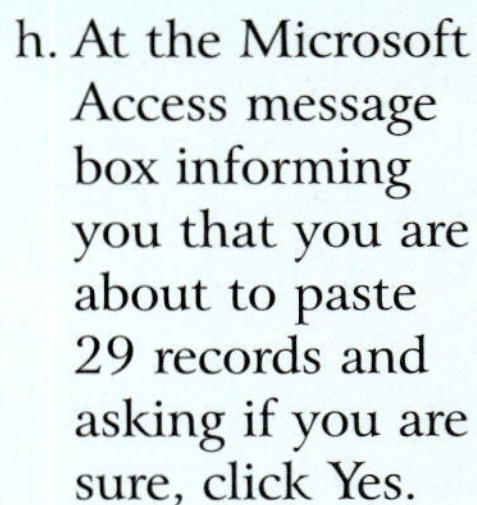
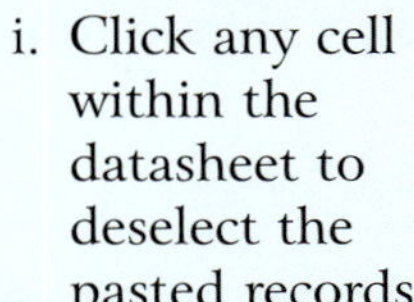

h. At the Microsoft Access message box informing you that you are about to paste 29 records and asking if you are sure, click Yes.

i. Click any cell within the datasheet to deselect the pasted records.

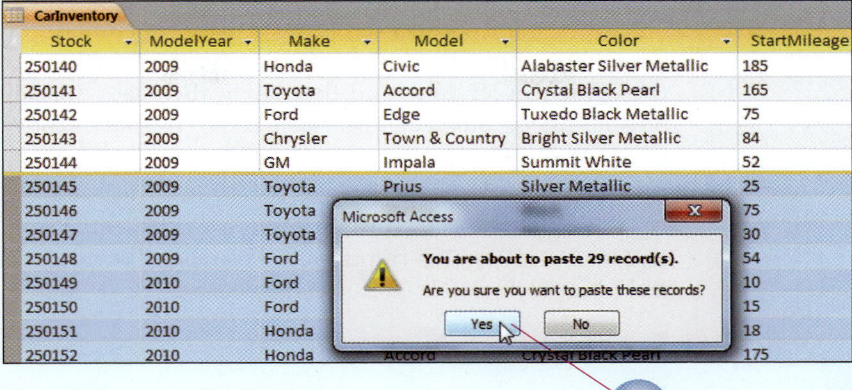

CarInventory

Stock	ModelYear	Make	Model	Color	StartMileage
250140	2009	Honda	Civic	Alabaster Silver Metallic	185
250141	2009	Toyota	Accord	Crystal Black Pearl	165
250142	2009	Ford	Edge	Tuxedo Black Metallic	75
250143	2009	Chrysler	Town & Country	Bright Silver Metallic	84
250144	2009	GM	Impala	Summit White	52
250145	2009	Toyota	Prius	Silver Metallic	25
250146	2009	Toyota			75
250147	2009	Toyota			30
250148	2009	Ford			54
250149	2010	Ford			10
250150	2010	Ford			15
250151	2010	Honda			18
250152	2010	Honda	Accord	Crystal Black Pearl	175

3. Print the datasheet in Access in landscape orientation by completing the following steps:
   a. Click the File tab, click the Print tab, and then click Print Preview at the Print tab Backstage view.
   b. Click the Landscape button in the Page Layout group in the Print Preview tab.
   c. Click the Page Setup button in the Page Layout group.
   d. At the Page Setup dialog box with the Print Options tab selected, change the Top and Bottom margins to 0.5 inch, the Left and Right margins to 1 inch, and then click OK.
   e. Click the Print button in the Print group and then click OK at the Print dialog box.
   f. Click the Close Print Preview button in the Close Preview group.

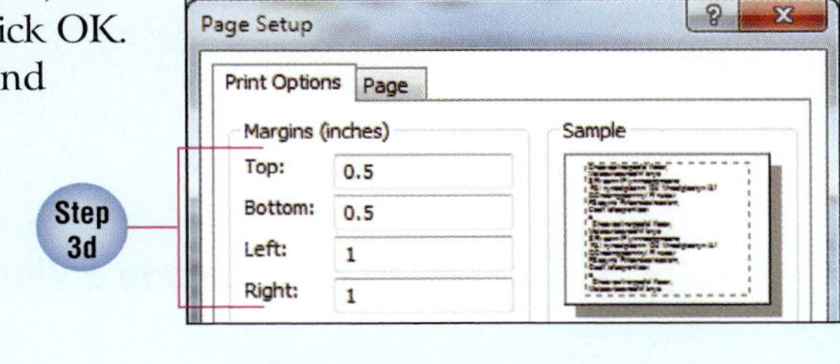

4. Click the File tab and then click the Exit button located at the bottom of the left pane in the Backstage view.
5. Click any cell to deselect the range in the Inventory worksheet and then press the Esc key to remove the moving marquee.
6. Leave the **CutRateInventory.xlsx** workbook open for the next project.

Copying and Pasting Worksheet Data to a Word Document

Using a process similar to the one in Project 2a, you can copy and paste Excel data, copy and embed Excel data as an object, or copy and link Excel data as an object in a Word document. Use the copy and paste method if the data being brought into Word is not likely to be updated or require editing once the source cells are pasted in the Word document. Copy and embed the data if you want to have the ability to edit the data once it is inserted in Word using Excel's editing tools and features. Copy and link the data if the information being pasted into Word is likely to be changed in the future and you want the document in Word updated if the data in the source file changes.

Quick Steps

Embed Excel Data in Word Document

1. Select cells.
2. Click Copy button.
3. Open Word document.
4. Position insertion point at desired location.
5. Click Paste button arrow.
6. Click *Paste Special*.
7. Click *Microsoft Excel Worksheet Object*.
8. Click OK.

Link Excel Data in Word Document

1. Select cells.
2. Click Copy button.
3. Open Word document.
4. Position insertion point at desired location.
5. Click Paste button arrow.
6. Click *Paste Special*.
7. Click *Microsoft Excel Worksheet Object*.
8. Click Paste link.
9. Click OK.

Embedding Excel Data into Word

To embed copied Excel data into a Word document, open the desired Word document, move the insertion point to the location at which you want to insert the copied Excel data, and then open the Paste Special dialog box. At the Paste Special dialog box, click *Microsoft Excel Worksheet Object* in the *As* list box and then click OK.

To edit an embedded Excel object in Word, double-click over the embedded cells to open the cells for editing in a worksheet. Word's ribbon is temporarily replaced with Excel's ribbon. Click outside the embedded object to restore Word's ribbon and close the worksheet object in Word.

Linking Excel Data into Word

Linking Excel data to a Word document means that the source data exists only in Excel. Word places a shortcut to the source data file name and range in the Word document. When you open a Word document containing a link, Word prompts you to update the links. Since the data resides in the Excel workbook only, be careful not to move or rename the original workbook from which you copied the cells or the link will no longer work.

To paste copied Excel data as a link in a Word document, open the desired Word document, move the insertion point to the location at which you want to link the cells, open the Paste Special dialog box, click *Microsoft Excel Worksheet Object* in the *As* list box, click *Paste link*, and then click OK.

Project 2b **Embedding Excel Data in a Word Document** Part 2 of 6

1. With **CutRateInventory.xlsx** open, copy and embed the data in the CarCosts worksheet to a Word document by completing the following steps:
   a. Make CarCosts the active worksheet.
   b. Select A4:F9.
   c. Click the Copy button in the Clipboard group.
   d. Start Microsoft Word 2010.
   e. Open **CutRateCarRpt.docx** from the Excel2010L2C8 folder on your storage medium.
   f. Save the document with Save As and name it **EL2-C8-P2-CutRateCarRpt**.
   g. Press Ctrl + End to move the insertion point to the end of the document.
   h. Click the down-pointing arrow on the Paste button in the Clipboard group and then click *Paste Special* at the drop-down list.

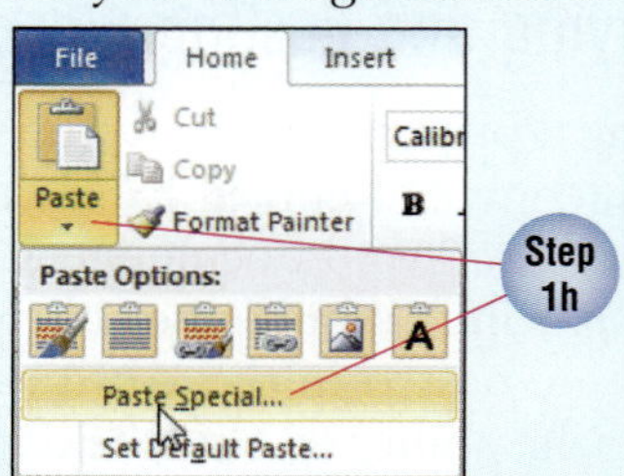

i. At the Paste Special dialog box, click *Microsoft Excel Worksheet Object* in the *As* list box and then click OK.

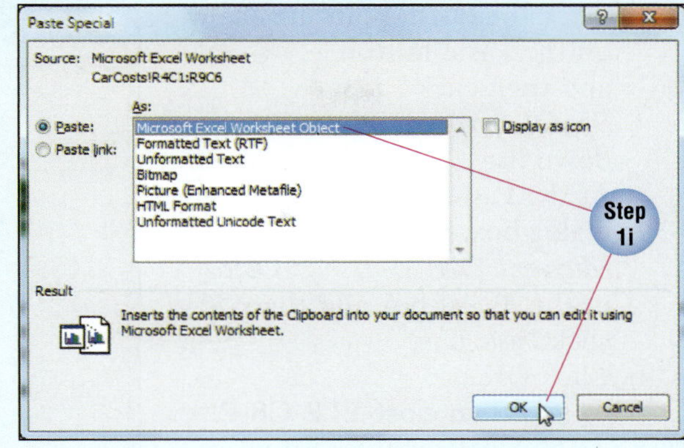

2. Save **EL2-C8-P2-CutRateCarRpt.docx**.
3. When you use Paste Special, the copied cells are embedded as an object in the Word document. Edit the embedded object using Excel's editing tools by completing the following steps:
   a. Double-click over any cell in the embedded worksheet object. The object is surrounded with a border and Excel's column and row headers appear with the cells. Word's ribbon is temporarily replaced with Excel's ribbon.
   b. Select B5:F9 and then click the Accounting Number Format button in the Number group.

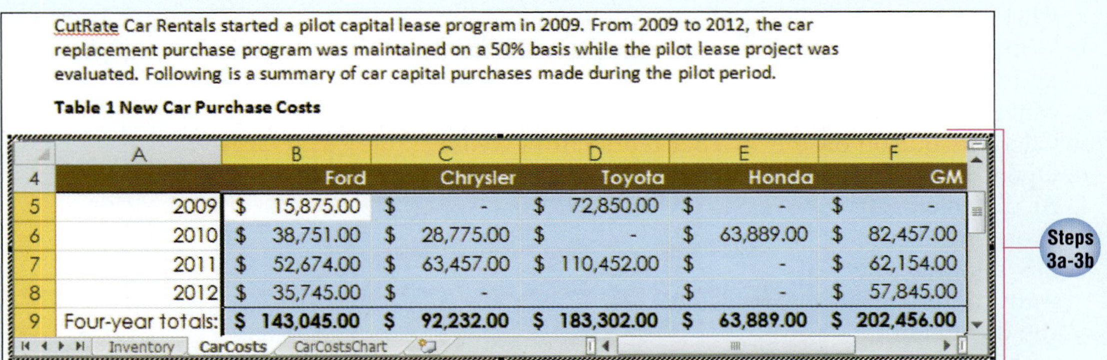

CutRate Car Rentals started a pilot capital lease program in 2009. From 2009 to 2012, the car replacement purchase program was maintained on a 50% basis while the pilot lease project was evaluated. Following is a summary of car capital purchases made during the pilot period.

Table 1 New Car Purchase Costs

	A	B	C	D	E	F
4		Ford	Chrysler	Toyota	Honda	GM
5	2009	$ 15,875.00	$ -	$ 72,850.00	$ -	$ -
6	2010	$ 38,751.00	$ 28,775.00	$ -	$ 63,889.00	$ 82,457.00
7	2011	$ 52,674.00	$ 63,457.00	$ 110,452.00	$ -	$ 62,154.00
8	2012	$ 35,745.00	$ -		$ -	$ 57,845.00
9	Four-year totals:	**$ 143,045.00**	**$ 92,232.00**	**$ 183,302.00**	**$ 63,889.00**	**$ 202,456.00**

   c. Click in the document outside the embedded object to close the object and restore Word's ribbon.
4. Save and then print **EL2-C8-P2-CutRateCarRpt.docx**.
5. Click the File tab and then click the Exit button located at the bottom of the left pane in the Backstage view.
6. Click any cell to deselect the range in the CarCosts worksheet and leave the **CutRateInventory.xlsx** workbook open for the next project.

Project 2c Linking Excel Data in a Word Document

Part 3 of 6

1. With **CutRateInventory.xlsx** open, copy and link the data in the CarCosts worksheet to a Word document by completing the following steps:
   a. With CarCosts the active worksheet, select A4:F9 and click the Copy button.
   b. Start Microsoft Word 2010.
   c. Open **CutRateCarRpt.docx**.
   d. Save the document with Save As and name it **EL2-C8-P2-CutRateCarRptLinked**.
   e. Press Ctrl + End to move the insertion point to the end of the document.

f. Click the down-pointing arrow on the Paste button and then click *Paste Special* at the drop-down list.
g. At the Paste Special dialog box, click *Microsoft Excel Worksheet Object* in the *As* list box and then click *Paste link*.
h. Click OK.

2. Save and then close **EL2-C8-P2-CutRateCarRptLinked.docx**. When data is linked, the data exists only in the source program. In the destination document, Word inserted a shortcut to the source range. Edit the source range and view the update to the Word document by completing the following steps:
   a. Click the button on the Taskbar representing the Excel file named **CutRateInventory.xlsx**.
   b. With CarCosts the active worksheet, press the Esc key to remove the moving marquee and then click any cell to deselect the copied range.
   c. Make E5 the active cell, type **85000**, and press Enter.
   d. Click the button on the Taskbar representing Word.
   e. Open **EL2-C8-P2-CutRateCarRptLinked.docx**.
   f. At the Microsoft Word message box asking if you want to update the document with data from the linked files, click Yes.

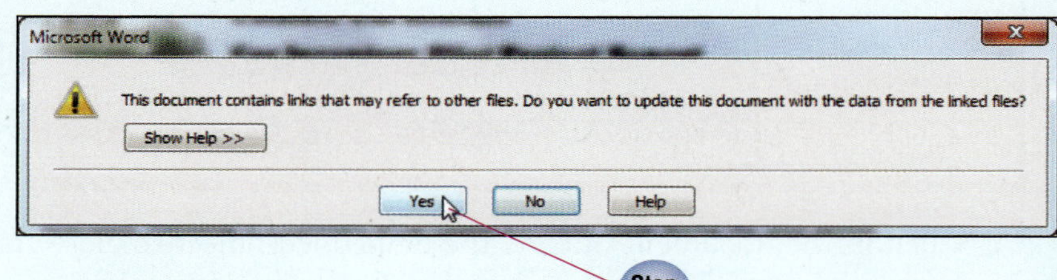

3. Notice the data inserted in the Excel worksheet is also shown in the linked Word document.
4. Save and then print **EL2-C8-P2-CutRateCarRptLinked.docx**.
5. Exit Word.
6. With CarCosts the active worksheet in **CutRateInventory.xlsx**, delete the contents of E5 and leave the workbook open for a later project.

Quick Steps

Break Link to Excel Object
1. Open document.
2. Right-click linked object.
3. Point to *Linked Worksheet Object*.
4. Click *Links*.
5. Click Break Link button.
6. Click Yes.
7. Save document.

Breaking a Link to an Excel Object

If you linked Excel data to a Word document and later decide you no longer need to maintain the link, you can break the connection between the source and destination files so that you are not prompted to update the object each time you open the document. Breaking the link means that the data in the Word document will no longer be connected to the data in the Excel workbook. If you make a change to the original source in Excel, the Word document will not reflect the updated information. To break a link, open the document, right-click over the linked object, point to *Linked Worksheet Object,* and click *Links* at the shortcut menu. This opens the Links dialog box. If more than one linked object exists in the document, click the source object for the link you want to break and then click the Break Link button. Click Yes to confirm you want to break the link at the message box that appears.

Breaking a Link Part 4 of 6

1. Start Word and open **EL2-C8-P2-CutRateCarRptLinked.docx**.
2. At the message asking if you want to update links, click No.
3. Break the link between the Excel workbook and the linked object by completing the following steps:
   a. Right-click over the linked Excel worksheet object.
   b. Point to *Linked Worksheet Object* and then click *Links* at the shortcut menu.
   c. At the Links dialog box, with the linked object file name selected in the *Source file* list box, click the Break Link button.
   d. At the Microsoft Word dialog box asking if you are sure you want to break the selected link, click Yes.
4. Save **EL2-C8-P2-CutRateCarRptLinked.docx** and then exit Word.

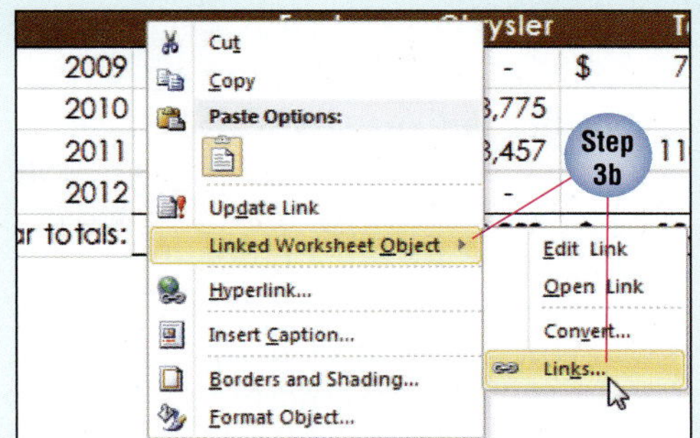

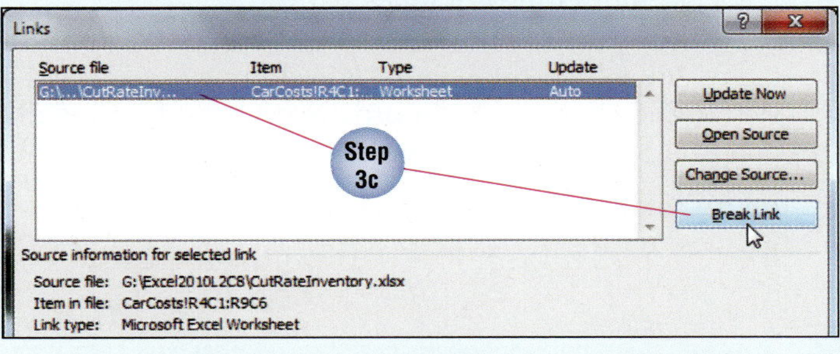

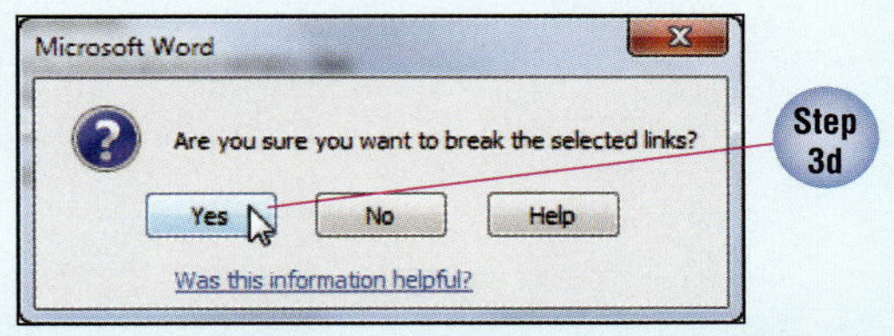

Copying and Pasting Worksheet Data to a PowerPoint Presentation

As with Word, you can copy and paste, copy and embed, or copy and link Excel data to slides in a PowerPoint presentation. Although you can create tables and charts in a PowerPoint slide, some people prefer to use Excel for these tasks and then copy and paste the data to PowerPoint. Presentations often incorporate charts to visually depict numerical data in a graph format that is easy to understand. In the Office 2010 suite, the charting system is fully integrated within Word, Excel, and PowerPoint. A chart inserted in a Word document or PowerPoint presentation is created as an embedded object with the source data used to generate the chart stored in an Excel worksheet; the Excel worksheet with the source data becomes part of the document or presentation file.

Quick Steps

Embed Excel Data in PowerPoint

1. Select cells.
2. Click Copy button.
3. Open PowerPoint presentation.
4. Make desired slide active.
5. Click Paste button arrow.
6. Click *Paste Special*.
7. Make sure *Microsoft Excel Worksheet Object* is selected in *As* list box.
8. Click OK.

Since the chart feature is fully integrated within Word, Excel, and PowerPoint, you can edit a chart in a PowerPoint presentation using the same techniques you learned to edit a chart in Excel. Clicking a chart on a PowerPoint slide causes the contextual Chart Tools Design, Chart Tools Layout, and Chart Tools Format tabs to become active with the same groups and buttons available in Excel.

Project 2e Embedding Excel Data in a PowerPoint Presentation

Part 5 of 6

1. With **CutRateInventory.xlsx** open, copy and embed the chart in the CarCostsChart worksheet to a slide in a PowerPoint presentation by completing the following steps:
   a. Make CarCostsChart the active worksheet.
   b. Click the Home tab and then click the Copy button.
   c. Start Microsoft PowerPoint 2010.
   d. Open **CutRateCarRpt.pptx**.
   e. Save the presentation with Save As and name it **EL2-C8-P2-CutRateCarRpt**.
   f. Click Slide 3 in the Slides pane.
   g. Click the Paste button in the Clipboard group. Since all charts are embedded by default, you do not need to use Paste Special.
2. Resize the chart to the approximate height and width shown and position the chart in the center of the slide horizontally.

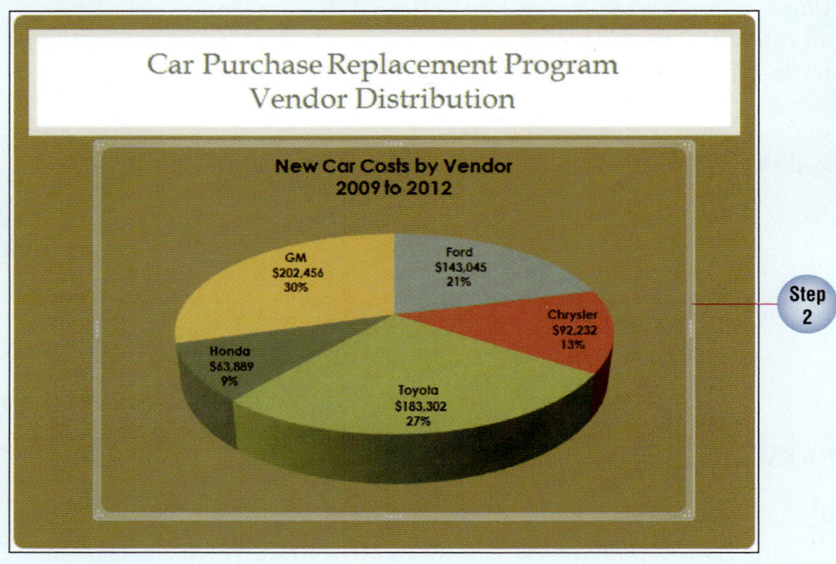

3. Copy and embed the table used to generate the chart in the CarCosts worksheet to the next slide in the PowerPoint presentation by completing the following steps:
   a. Click Slide 4 in the Slides pane.
   b. Click the button on the Taskbar representing the Excel workbook **CutRateInventory.xlsx**.
   c. Make CarCosts the active worksheet, select A1:F9, and click the Copy button.
   d. Click the button on the taskbar representing the PowerPoint presentation **EL2-C8-P2-CutRateCarRpt.pptx**.
   e. Click the down-pointing arrow on the Paste button and then click *Paste Special* at the drop-down list.

f. With *Microsoft Excel Worksheet Object* selected in the *As* list box, click OK.

4. Resize and position the embedded table to the approximate height, width, and position shown.

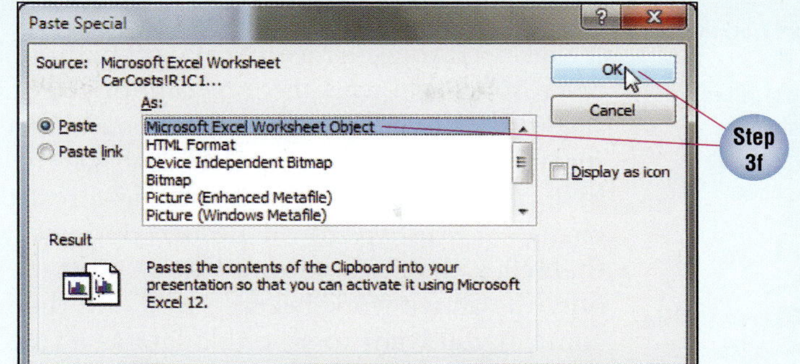

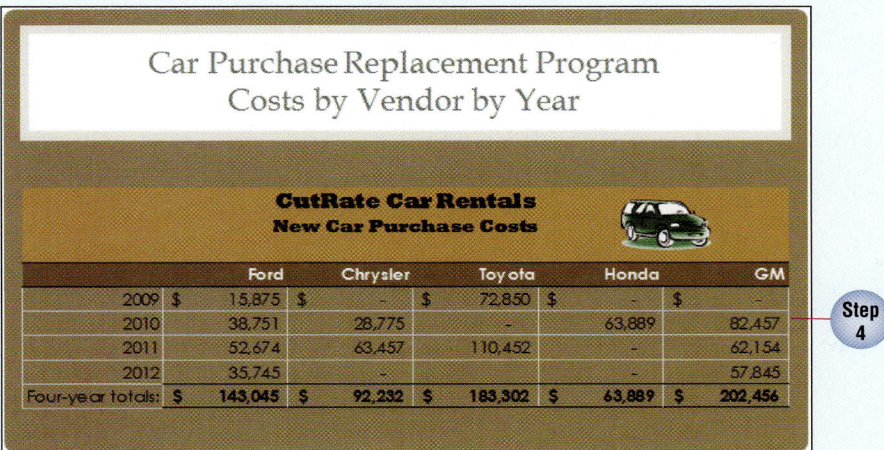

	Ford	Chrysler	Toyota	Honda	GM
2009	$ 15,875	$ -	$ 72,850	$ -	$ -
2010	38,751	28,775	-	63,889	82,457
2011	52,674	63,457	110,452	-	62,154
2012	35,745	-		-	57,845
Four-year totals:	$ 143,045	$ 92,232	$ 183,302	$ 63,889	$ 202,456

5. Click the File tab and then click the Print tab. At the Print tab Backstage view, click the button in the Settings category of the center pane that currently reads *Full Page Slides*, and then click *4 Slides Horizontal* at the drop-down list. Click the Print button.

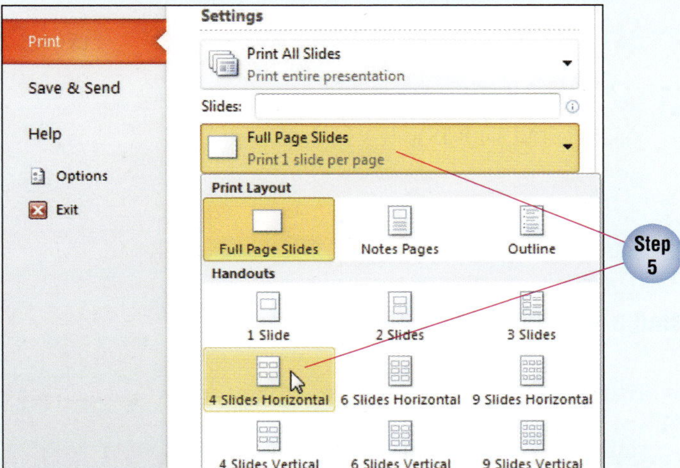

6. Save **EL2-C8-P2-CutRateCarRpt.pptx** and then exit PowerPoint.
7. Press the ESC key to remove the moving marquee and then click any cell to deselect the range in the CarCosts worksheet. Leave the **CutRateInventory.xlsx** workbook open for the next project.

Quick Steps

Export Worksheet as Text File

1. Make desired sheet active.
2. Click File tab.
3. Click Save & Send tab.
4. Click *Change File Type*.
5. Click desired text file type in *Other File Types* section.
6. Click Save As button.
7. If necessary, navigate to desired drive and/or folder.
8. Type file name.
9. Click Save button.
10. Click OK.
11. Click Yes.

Why so many text file formats? Although all systems support text files, differences occur across platforms. For example, a Macintosh computer denotes the end of a line in a text file with a carriage return character, Unix uses a linefeed character, and DOS inserts both a linefeed and a carriage return character code at the end of each line.

Exporting Excel Data as a Text File

If you need to exchange Excel data with a person who is not able to import a Microsoft Excel worksheet or cannot copy and paste using the clipboard, you can save the data as a text file. Excel provides several text file options including file formats suitable for computers that use the Macintosh operating system as shown in Table 8.1. To save a worksheet as a text file, open the Save As dialog box and change *Save as type* to the desired option. Type a file name for the text file and then click the Save button. Click OK at the message box that informs you that only the active worksheet is saved and then click Yes at the next message box to confirm you want to save the data as a text file.

Another way to save the current worksheet in a text file format is to click the File tab and then click the Save & Send tab. At the Save & Send tab Backstage view, click *Change File Type* in the center pane. In the Change File Type pane at the right, click *Text (Tab delimited) (*.txt)*, *CSV (Comma delimited) (*.csv)*, or *Formatted Text (Space delimited) (*.prn)* in the *Other File Types* section and then click the Save As button. If necessary, navigate to the desired drive and/or folder in the Save As dialog box. Type the desired file name and then click the Save button.

Table 8.1 Supported Text File Formats for Exporting

Text File Format Option	*File Extension*
Text (tab delimited)	.txt
Unicode text	.txt
CSV (Comma delimited)	.csv
Formatted text (Space delimited)	.prn
Text (Macintosh)	.txt
Text (MS-DOS)	.txt
CSV (Macintosh)	.csv
CSV (MS-DOS)	.csv

Project 2f **Exporting a Worksheet as a Text File** Part 6 of 6

1. With **CutRateInventory.xlsx** open, export the Inventory worksheet data as a text file by completing the following steps:
   a. Make Inventory the active worksheet.
   b. Click the File tab and then click the Save & Send tab.

c. Click *Change File Type* in the File Types category in the center pane in the Backstage view.
d. Click *CSV (Comma delimited) (*.csv)* in the *Other File Types* section in the right pane of the Backstage view.
e. Click the Save As button located below the *Other File Types* section in the right pane of the Backstage view.

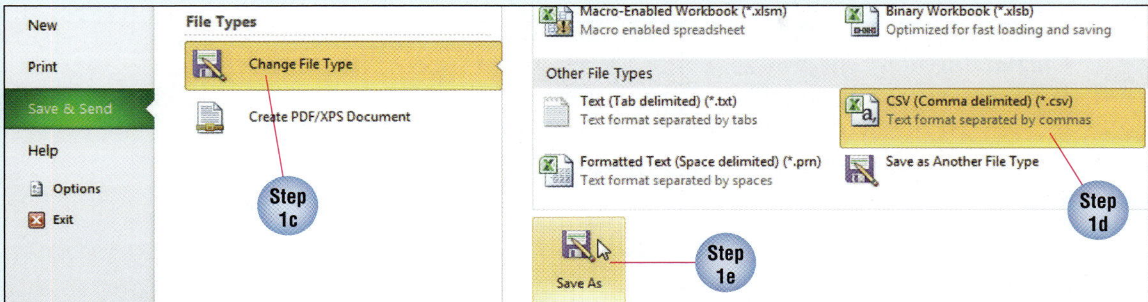

f. Type **EL2-C8-P2-CutRateInventory** in the *File name* text box.
g. Click the Save button.

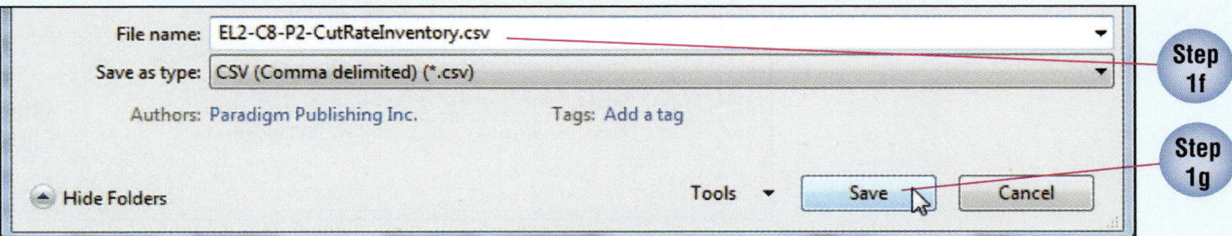

h. Click OK to save only the active sheet at the Microsoft Excel message box that informs you the selected file type does not support workbooks that contain multiple worksheets.

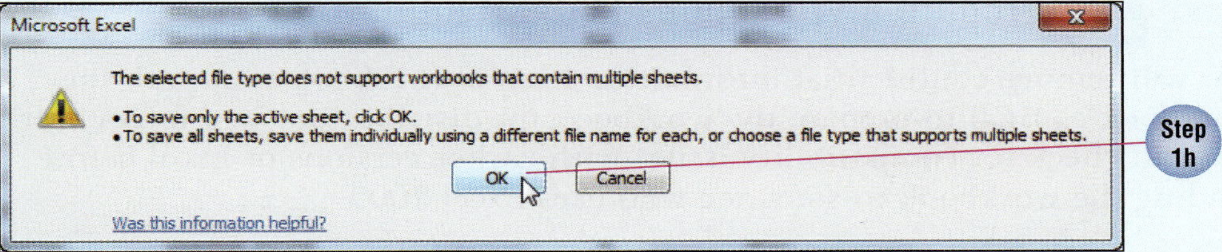

i. Click Yes to save the workbook in this format at the next message box that informs you **EL2-C8-P2-CutRateInventory.csv** may contain features that are not compatible with CSV (Comma delimited).

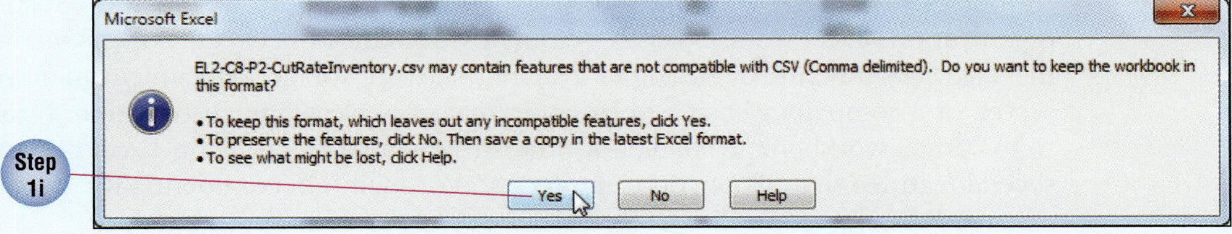

2. Close **EL2-C8-P2-CutRateInventory.csv**. Click Don't Save when prompted to save changes. (You do not need to save since no changes have been made since you changed the file type.)
3. Open Notepad and view the text file created in Step 1 by completing the following steps:
   a. Click the Start button, point to *All Programs*, click *Accessories*, and then click *Notepad*.
   b. Click File on the Notepad Menu bar and then click *Open*.
   c. Navigate to the Excel2010L2C8 folder on your storage medium.

d. Click the Text Documents (*.txt) button and then click *All Files (*.*)* at the drop-down list.

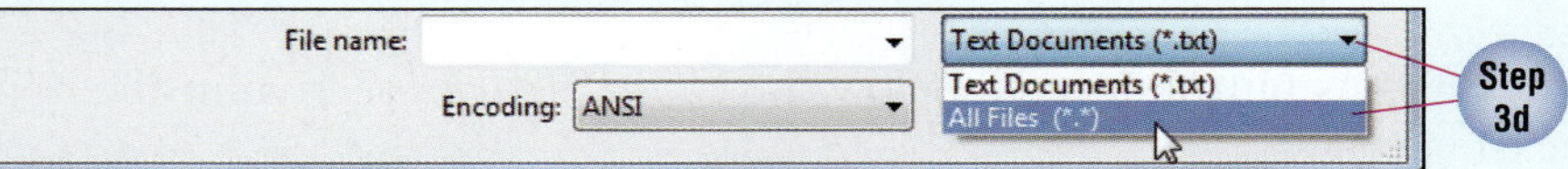

e. Double-click ***EL2-C8-P2-CutRateInventory.csv***.

f. If necessary, scroll down to view all of the data in the text file. Notice that a comma has been inserted between each column's data.

4. Click File on the Notepad Menu bar and then click *Print*. Click the Print button at the Print dialog box.
5. Exit Notepad.

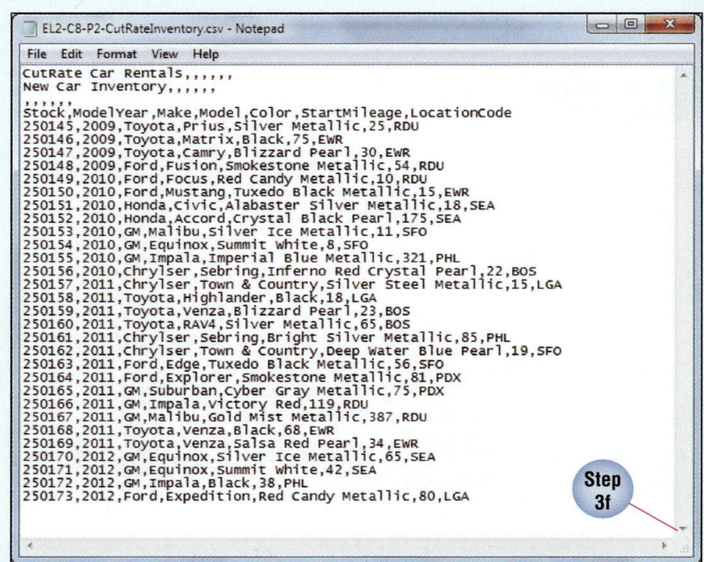


```
CutRate Car Rentals,,,,,,
New Car Inventory,,,,,,
,,,,,,
Stock,ModelYear,Make,Model,Color,StartMileage,LocationCode
250145,2009,Toyota,Prius,Silver Metallic,25,RDU
250146,2009,Toyota,Matrix,Black,75,EWR
250147,2009,Toyota,Camry,Blizzard Pearl,30,EWR
250148,2009,Ford,Fusion,Smokestone Metallic,54,RDU
250149,2010,Ford,Focus,Red Candy Metallic,10,RDU
250150,2010,Ford,Mustang,Tuxedo Black Metallic,15,EWR
250151,2010,Honda,Civic,Alabaster Silver Metallic,18,SEA
250152,2010,Honda,Accord,Crystal Black Pearl,175,SEA
250153,2010,GM,Malibu,Silver Ice Metallic,11,SFO
250154,2010,GM,Equinox,Summit White,8,SFO
250155,2010,GM,Impala,Imperial Blue Metallic,321,PHL
250156,2010,Chrylser,Sebring,Inferno Red Crystal Pearl,22,BOS
250157,2011,Chrylser,Town & Country,Silver Steel Metallic,15,LGA
250158,2011,Toyota,Highlander,Black,18,LGA
250159,2011,Toyota,Venza,Blizzard Pearl,23,BOS
250160,2011,Toyota,RAV4,Silver Metallic,65,BOS
250161,2011,Chrylser,Sebring,Bright Silver Metallic,85,PHL
250162,2011,Chrylser,Town & Country,Deep Water Blue Pearl,19,SFO
250163,2011,Ford,Edge,Tuxedo Black Metallic,56,SFO
250164,2011,Ford,Explorer,Smokestone Metallic,81,PDX
250165,2011,GM,Suburban,Cyber Gray Metallic,75,PDX
250166,2011,GM,Impala,Victory Red,119,RDU
250167,2011,GM,Malibu,Gold Mist Metallic,387,RDU
250168,2011,Toyota,Venza,Black,68,EWR
250169,2011,Toyota,Venza,Salsa Red Pearl,34,EWR
250170,2012,GM,Equinox,Silver Ice Metallic,65,SEA
250171,2012,GM,Equinox,Summit White,42,SEA
250172,2012,GM,Impala,Black,38,PHL
250173,2012,Ford,Expedition,Red Candy Metallic,80,LGA
```

Project 3 Prepare a Workbook for Distribution — 3 Parts

You will remove confidential information from a workbook and mark the workbook as final to prepare the workbook for distribution. In another workbook you will check for compatibility issues with earlier versions of Excel before sending the workbook to someone who uses Excel 2003.

Preparing a Workbook for Distribution

In today's workplace, you often work as part of a team both within and outside your organization. Excel workbooks are frequently exchanged between workers via email message attachments; by saving to a shared network folder, a document management server, or a company website; or by other means of electronic distribution. Prior to making a workbook available for others to open, view, and edit, Excel provides several features that allow you to protect and/or maintain confidentiality.

Removing Information from a Workbook before Distributing

Prior to distributing a workbook electronically to others, you should consider using the Document Inspector feature to scan the workbook for personal or other hidden information that you would not want others to be able to view. Recall from Chapter 6 that a workbook's properties, sometimes referred to as

metadata, include information that is tracked automatically by Excel such as the names of the individuals that accessed and edited a workbook. If a workbook will be sent electronically by email or made available on a document management server or other website, consider the implications of recipients of that workbook being able to look at some of this hidden information. Ask yourself if this information should remain confidential and if so, remove sensitive data and/or metadata before distributing the file. To do this, click the File tab. At the Info tab Backstage view, click the Check for Issues button located in the center pane and then click *Inspect Document* at the drop-down list. This opens the Document Inspector dialog box shown in Figure 8.4. By default, all check boxes are selected. Clear the check boxes for those items that you do not need or want to scan and remove and then click Inspect.

Note also that before removing sensitive data, you can save a copy of the original file that retains all content using password protection or other security measures to limit access. Another helpful use of the Document Inspector is as a tool to reveal the presence of headers, footers, hidden items, or other invisible items in a workbook for which you are not the original author.

The Document Inspector scans the workbook for the existence of any of the checked items. When completed, a dialog box similar to the one shown in Figure 8.5 appears. Excel displays a check mark in the sections for which no items were found and a red exclamation mark in the sections in which items were detected within the workbook. Click the Remove All button in the section that contains content you decide you want to remove. Click OK when finished and then distribute the workbook as needed.

Quick Steps

Use Document Inspector to Remove Private Information

1. Open workbook.
2. Click File tab.
3. Click Check for Issues button.
4. Click *Inspect Document.*
5. Clear check boxes for those items you do not want to scan and remove.
6. Click Inspect button.
7. Click Remove All button in those sections with items you want removed.
8. Click Close button.

Figure 8.4 Document Inspector Dialog Box

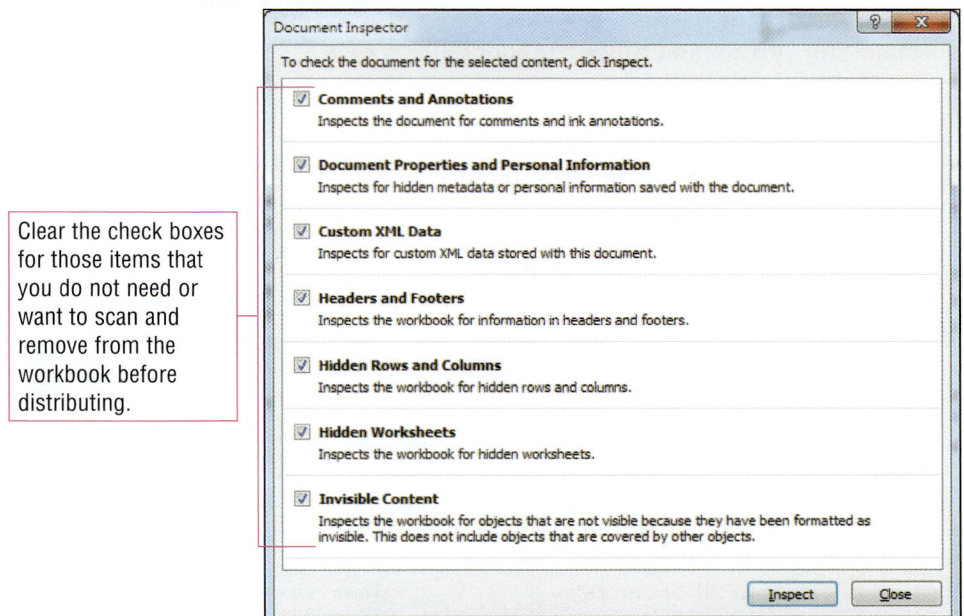

Figure 8.5 Document Inspector Dialog Box with Inspection Results Shown

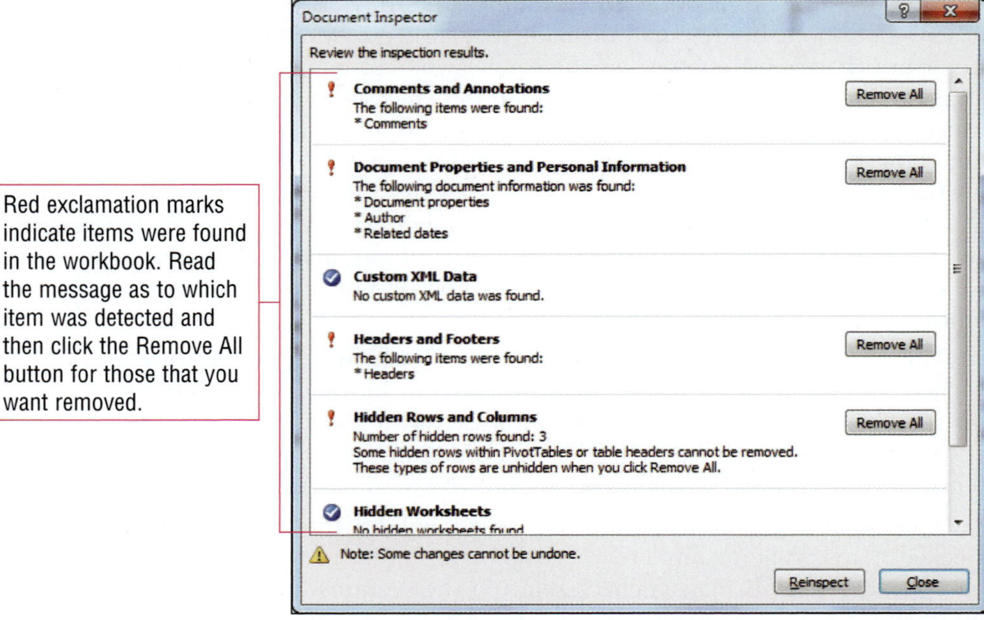

Red exclamation marks indicate items were found in the workbook. Read the message as to which item was detected and then click the Remove All button for those that you want removed.

Project 3a Removing Private and Confidential Data from a Workbook

Part 1 of 3

1. Open **CutRatePilotPrjRpt.xlsx**.
2. Save the workbook with Save As and name it **EL2-C8-P3-CutRatePilotPrjRpt**.
3. Examine the workbook for private and other confidential information by completing the following steps:
   a. Click the File tab.
   b. Read the property information in the fields in the Properties pane located at the right of the Info tab Backstage view.
   c. Click the Properties button at the top of the Properties pane (located below the miniature Excel worksheet) and then click *Advanced Properties* at the drop-down list.
   d. Click the Custom tab in the **EL2-C8-P3-CutRatePilotPrjRpt.xlsx** Properties dialog box.
   e. Position the mouse pointer on the right column boundary for the *Value* column in the *Properties* list box until the pointer changes to a vertical bar with left- and right-pointing arrows and then drag the column width right until you can read all of the text within the column.
   f. Notice that the extra information added to the workbook properties contains names and other data that you might not want widely circulated.

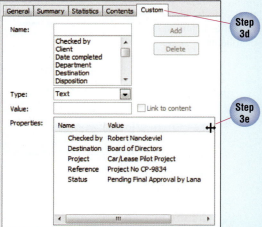

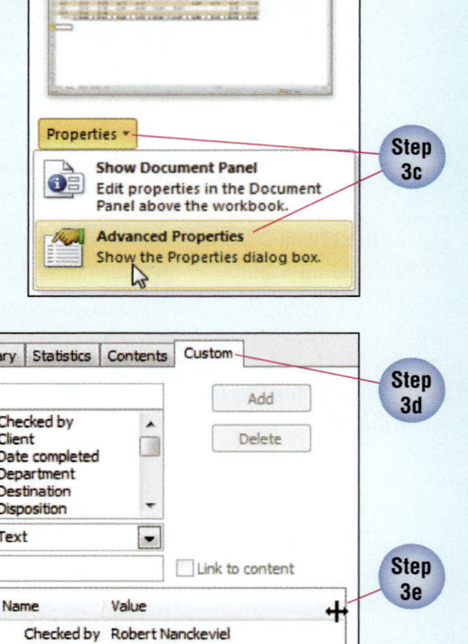

g. Click OK.
h. Click the Review tab and then click the Show All Comments button in the Comments group.
i. Read the two comments displayed in the worksheet area.

4. Scan the workbook for other confidential information using the Document Inspector by completing the following steps:
   a. Click the File tab, click the Check for Issues button in the *Prepare for Sharing* section at the Info tab Backstage view, and then click *Inspect Document* at the drop-down list.
   b. At the Microsoft Excel message box indicating the file contains changes that have not been saved, click Yes to save the file now.
   c. At the Document Inspector dialog box with all check boxes selected, click the Inspect button to check for all items.
   d. Read the messages in each section of the Document Inspector dialog box that display with a red exclamation mark.
   e. Click the Remove All button in the *Document Properties and Personal Information* section. Excel deletes the metadata and the section now displays with a check mark indicating the information has been removed.

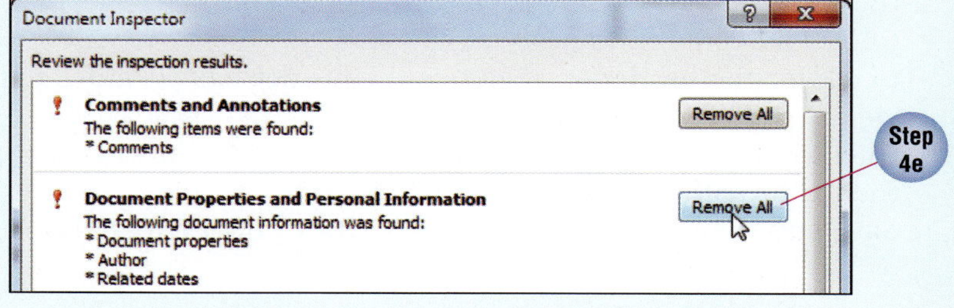

   f. Notice the inspection results indicate a header and three hidden rows were found. You decide to review these items before removing them. Click the Close button to close the Document Inspector dialog box.
5. Click the Home tab and then display the worksheet in Page Layout View and view the header.
6. Look at the row numbers in the worksheet area. Notice that after row 10, the next row number is 14. Select row numbers 10 and 14, right-click the selected rows, and then click *Unhide* at the shortcut menu to display rows 11 to 13.

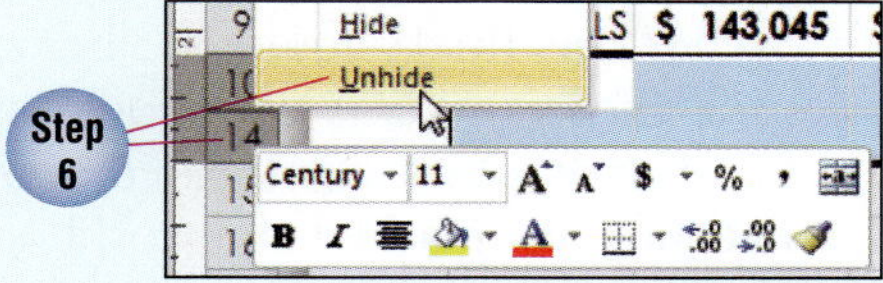

7. Change to Normal view and click any cell to deselect the range. Review the information that was in the hidden rows.
8. You decide the rows that were initially hidden should remain displayed but want to remove the header and the comments from reviewers of the workbook. Use the Document Inspector to remove these items by completing the following steps:
   a. Click the File tab, click the Check for Issues button, click *Inspect Document* at the drop-down list, and then click Yes to save the changes to the workbook.

b. Clear the check boxes for all items except *Comments and Annotations* and *Headers and Footers*.
c. Click the Inspect button.
d. Click the Remove All button in the *Comments and Annotations* section.
e. Click the Remove All button in the *Headers and Footers* section.
f. Click the Close button.

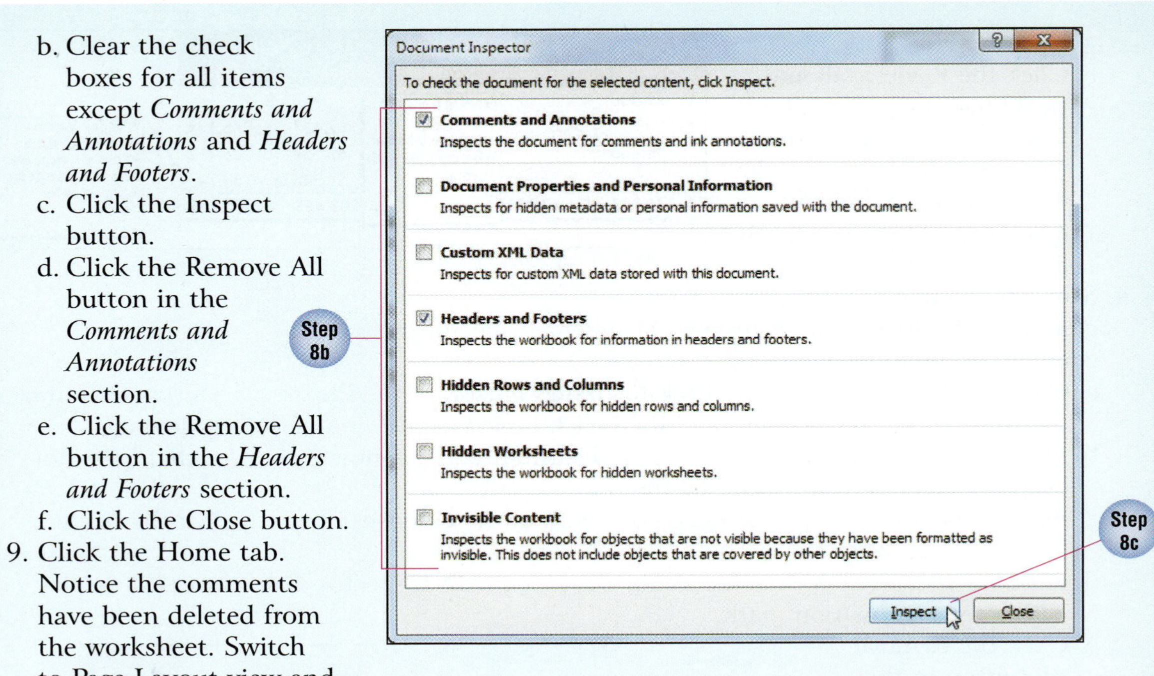

9. Click the Home tab. Notice the comments have been deleted from the worksheet. Switch to Page Layout view and check for the header text. Notice the header has been deleted. Switch back to Normal view.
10. Click the Show All Comments button in the Comments group of the Review tab to turn the feature off.
11. Save and then close **EL2-C8-P3-CutRatePilotPrjRpt.xlsx**.

Marking a Workbook as Final before Distributing

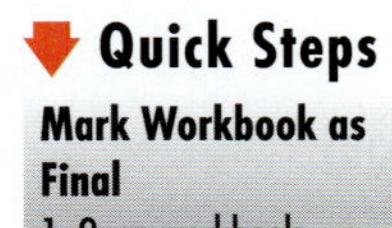

Quick Steps

Mark Workbook as Final

1. Open workbook.
2. Click File tab.
3. Click the Protect Workbook button.
4. Click *Mark as Final*.
5. Click OK twice.

Marked as Final

A workbook that will be distributed to others can be marked as final which means the workbook is prevented from having additions, deletions, or modifications made to cells. The workbook is changed to read-only and the status property is set to *Final*. In addition to protecting the workbook, marking a workbook as final also serves to indicate to the recipient(s) of the workbook that you consider the content complete. To mark a workbook as final, click the File tab. At the Info tab Backstage view, click the Protect Workbook button in the *Permissions* section located in the center pane and then click *Mark as Final* at the drop-down list. Note that marking a workbook as final should not be considered as secure as using password-protected, locked ranges. A workbook marked as final displays with the ribbon minimized and with a message located above the Formula bar that informs the reader that an author has marked the workbook as final to discourage editing. You can click the Edit Anyway button in the message bar to remove the Mark as Final feature, redisplay the ribbon, and make changes to the workbook.

As an alternative to *Mark as Final*, consider distributing a workbook published as a PDF or XPS document. In the PDF or XPS format, readers are not able to make changes to the workbook. You will learn how to publish a workbook in these formats in a later section.

Marking a Workbook as Final

Part 2 of 3

1. Open **EL2-C8-P3-CutRatePilotPrjRpt.xlsx**.
2. Save the workbook with Save As and name it **EL2-C8-P3-CutRatePilotPrjRptFinal**.
3. Mark the workbook as final to prevent changes and set the Status property to *Final* by completing the following steps:
   a. Click the File tab, click the Protect Workbook button in the *Permissions* section of the Info tab Backstage view, and then click *Mark as Final*.

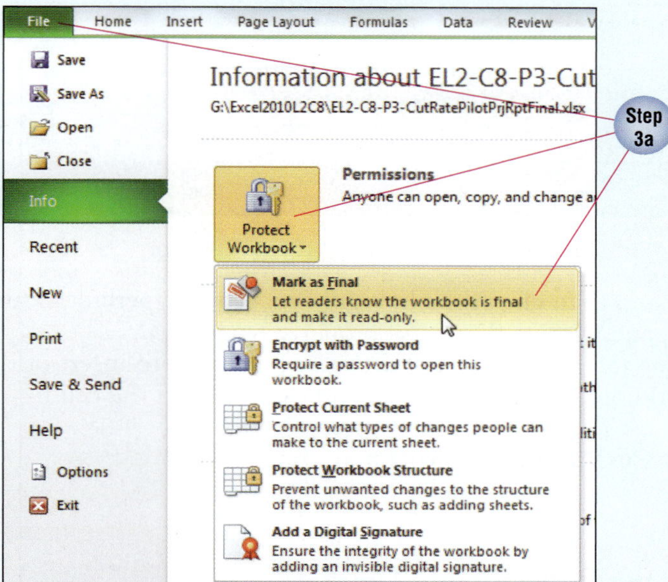

   b. Click OK at the message box that says the workbook will be marked as final and then saved.

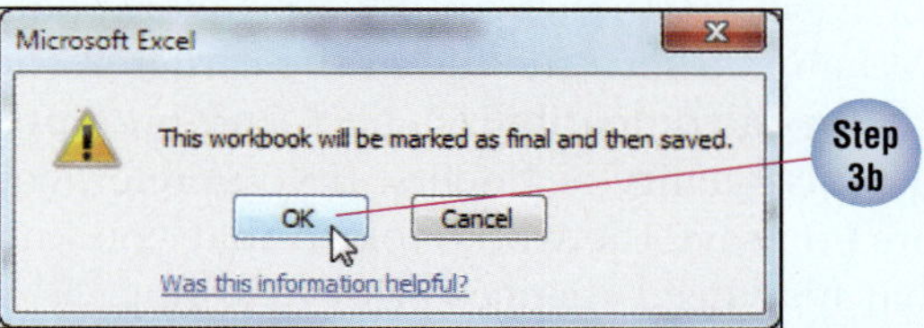

   c. Click OK at the second message box that says the workbook has been marked as final to indicate that editing is complete and that this is the final version of the document. ***Note: If this message box does not appear, it has been turned off by a previous user who clicked the*** **Don't show this message again** ***check box.***

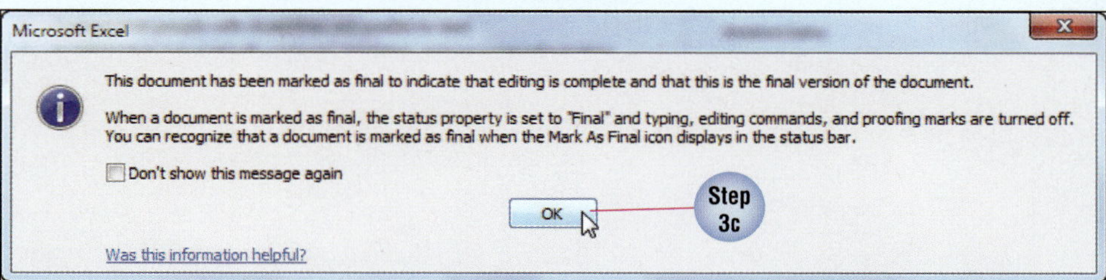

4. Notice the *Permissions* section of the Info tab Backstage view displays in orange and with a message indicating the workbook has been marked as final. Notice also the addition of *[Read-Only]* next to the file name in the Title bar.
5. Click the Home tab. The ribbon is minimized and a Marked as Final message displays above the Formula bar indicating that the workbook has been marked as final to discourage editing. Additionally, a *Marked as Final* icon displays in the Status bar next to *Ready*.

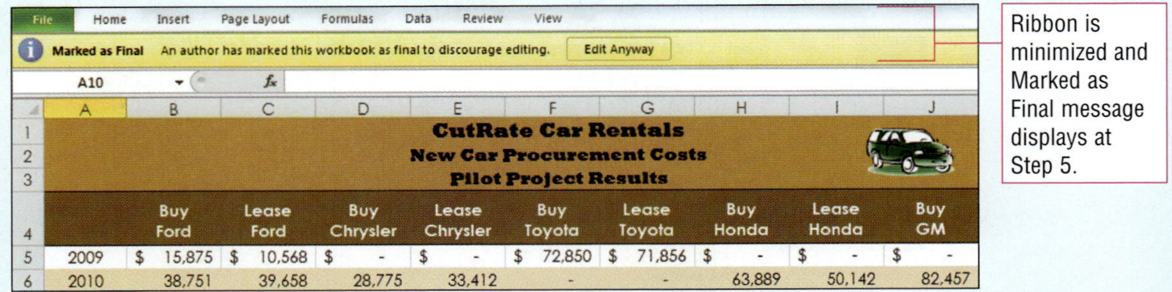

	A	B	C	D	E	F	G	H	I	J
4		Buy Ford	Lease Ford	Buy Chrysler	Lease Chrysler	Buy Toyota	Lease Toyota	Buy Honda	Lease Honda	Buy GM
5	2009	$ 15,875	$ 10,568	$ -	$ -	$ 72,850	$ 71,856	$ -	$ -	$ -
6	2010	38,751	39,658	28,775	33,412	-	-	63,889	50,142	82,457

Ribbon is minimized and Marked as Final message displays at Step 5.

6. Click the File tab and then click the Show All Properties hyperlink located at the bottom of the Properties pane. Notice the *Status* property reads *Final*.
7. Click the the Home tab. Make any cell active and attempt to insert or delete text in the cell. Since the workbook is now read-only, you cannot open the cell for editing or delete the contents.
8. Close **EL2-C8-P3-CutRatePilotPrjRptFinal.xlsx**.

Using the Compatibility Checker

Quick Steps

Check Workbook for Compatibility
1. Open workbook.
2. Click File tab.
3. Click Check for Issues button.
4. Click *Check Compatibility*.
5. Read information in *Summary* list box.
6. If desired, click *Copy to New Sheet* button.
OR
Click Close.

If you have a workbook that will be exchanged with other users that do not have Excel 2007 or Excel 2010, you can save the workbook in the Excel 97-2003 file format. When you save the file in the earlier version's file format, Excel automatically does a compatibility check and prompts you with information about loss of functionality or fidelity. If you prefer, you can run the compatibility checker before you save the workbook so that you know in advance areas of the worksheet that may need changes prior to saving.

In the Compatibility Checker Summary report, if an issue displays a Fix hyperlink, click Fix to resolve the problem. If you want more information about a loss of functionality or fidelity, click the Help hyperlink next to the issue. To return to the worksheet with the cells selected that are problematic for earlier Excel versions, click the Find hyperlink next to the issue.

Project 3c Checking a Workbook for Compatibility with Earlier Versions of Excel

Part 3 of 3

1. Open **CutRateBuyLeaseAnalysis.xlsx**.
2. Run the Compatibility Checker to check the workbook in advance of saving in an earlier Excel file format by completing the following steps:
   a. Click the File tab.
   b. Click the Check for Issues button in the *Prepare for Sharing* section at the Info tab Backstage view.
   c. Click *Check Compatibility* at the drop-down list.
   d. At the Microsoft Excel - Compatibility Checker dialog box, read the information in the *Summary* box in the *Significant loss of functionality* section.
   e. Scroll down and read the information displayed in the *Minor loss of fidelity* section.
   f. Scroll back up to the top of the *Summary* box.
   g. Click the Copy to New Sheet button.
3. At the Compatibility Report sheet, read the information in the box with the hyperlink Sheet1'!D13:D16 and then click the hyperlink. Sheet1 becomes active with the cells selected that have conditional formatting applied that is not supported in the earlier version of Excel (D13:D16).
4. Make the Compatibility Report sheet active and then print the worksheet with the worksheet scaled to *Fit Sheet on One Page*.
5. Use Save As to save the revised workbook and name it **EL2-C8-P3-CutRateBuyLeaseAnalysisCompChk**.
6. Make Sheet1 the active worksheet and deselect the range.
7. Click the File tab, click the Save & Send tab, click *Change File Type*, click *Excel 97-2003 Workbook (*.xls)* in the *Workbook File Types* section, and then click the Save As button located at the bottom of the Change File Type pane. Click the Save button at the Save As dialog box to accept the default file name. Click the Continue button at the Compatibility Checker dialog box.
8. Close **EL2-C8-P3-CutRateBuyLeaseAnalysisCompChk.xls**.

Step 2a

Step 2b

Step 2c

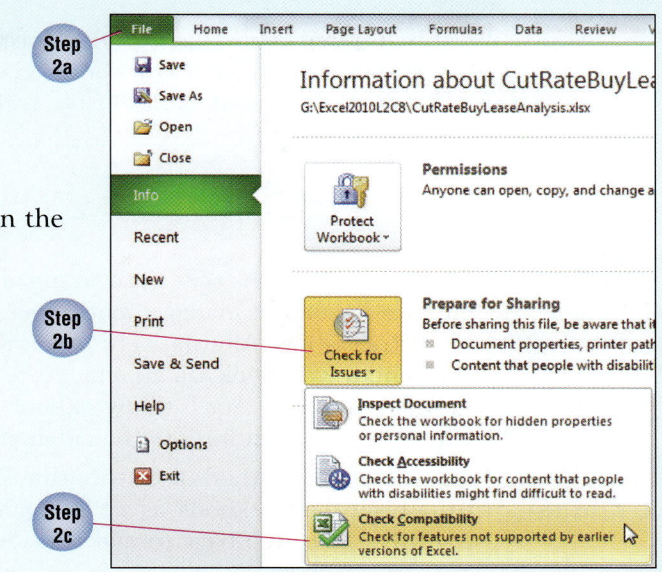

Step 2g

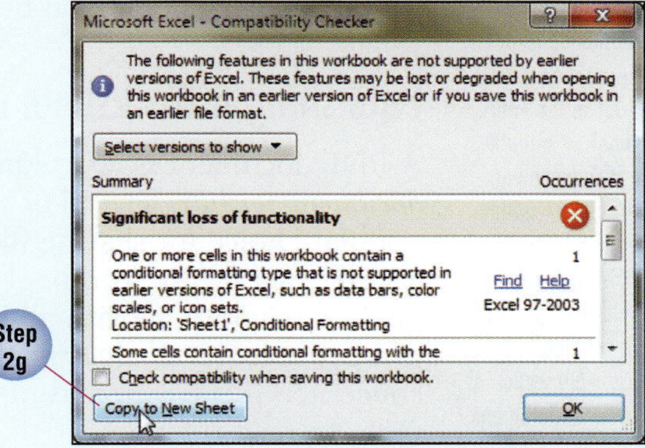

	Significant loss of functionality	# of occurrences	Version
6			
7			
8	One or more cells in this workbook contain a conditional formatting type that is not supported in earlier versions of Excel, such as data bars, color scales, or icon sets.	1	
9	Sheet1'!D13:D1		Excel 97-2003

Project  Distributing Workbooks

5 Parts

You will publish a worksheet as a PDF document, an XPS document, and as a web page. You will distribute a workbook via an email with a file attachment and save a workbook to Microsoft's SkyDrive website.

Quick Steps

Publish Worksheet as PDF
1. Open workbook.
2. Click File tab.
3. Click Save & Send tab.
4. Click *Create PDF/XPS Document.*
5. Click Create PDF/XPS button.
6. Click Publish button.

If a workbook contains multiple sheets, you can publish the entire workbook as a multi-page PDF document by clicking the Options button in the Publish as PDF or XPS dialog box and then clicking *Entire workbook* in the *Publish what* section of the Options dialog box.

Distributing Workbooks

Many organizations that need to make documents accessible by several users create a document management server or network share folder from which users can retrieve files. Alternatively, if you do not have access to these resources you can send a workbook via an email message by attaching the workbook file to the message. You can attach the workbook using your email program's file attachment feature, or you can initiate the email attachment feature directly from Excel.

A popular method of distributing documents that travel over the Internet is to publish the workbook as a PDF or XPS document. A workbook can also be published as a web page to make the content available on the Internet. Microsoft's SkyDrive web server allows you to store files on a web server that you can access from anywhere where you have an Internet connection.

Publishing a Worksheet as a PDF Document

A PDF document is a workbook saved in a fixed-layout format known as ***portable document format***. The PDF standard was developed by Adobe and has become a popular choice for sharing files with people outside an organization. By creating a PDF copy of the workbook, you ensure that the workbook will look the same on most computers with all fonts, formatting, and images preserved, no one can easily make changes to the workbook content, and you do not need to be concerned if the recipient of the file has Microsoft Excel on his or her computer in order to read the file.

To open and view a PDF file, the recipient of the file must have Adobe Reader installed on his or her computer. The reader is a free application available from Adobe if the computer being used does not currently have the reader installed. Go to www.adobe.com and click Get Adobe Reader to download and install the latest version of the reader software.

Project 4a **Publishing a Worksheet as a PDF Document** Part 1 of 5

1. Open **EL2-C8-P3-CutRatePilotPrjRpt.xlsx**.
2. Publish the worksheet as a PDF document by completing the following steps:
   a. Click the File tab.
   b. Click the Save & Send tab.
   c. Click *Create PDF/XPS Document* in the File Types category of the Save & Send tab Backstage view.

d. Click the Create PDF/XPS button located at the bottom of the Create a PDF/XPS Document category in the right pane.

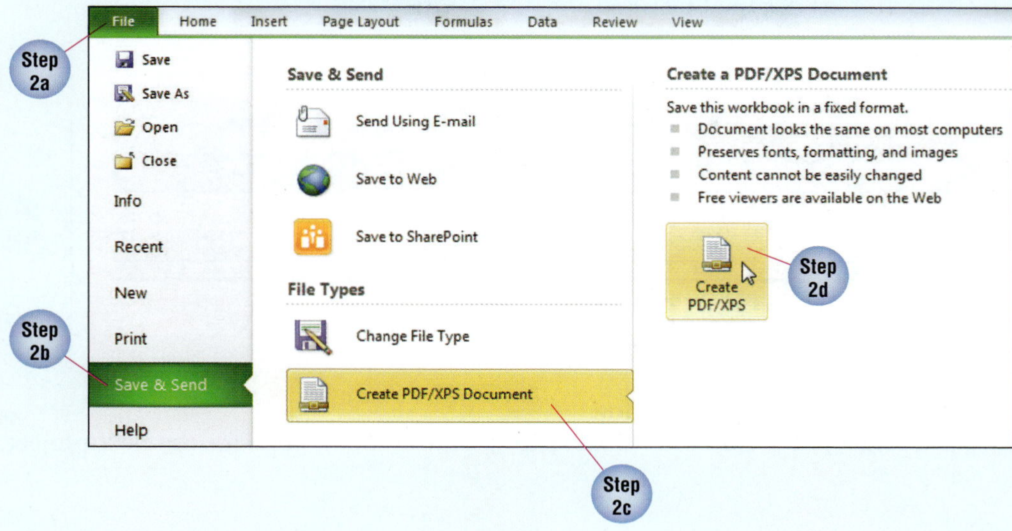

e. With *EL2-C8-P3-CutRatePilotPrjRpt.pdf* in the *File name* text box, click the Publish button in the Publish as PDF or XPS dialog box.

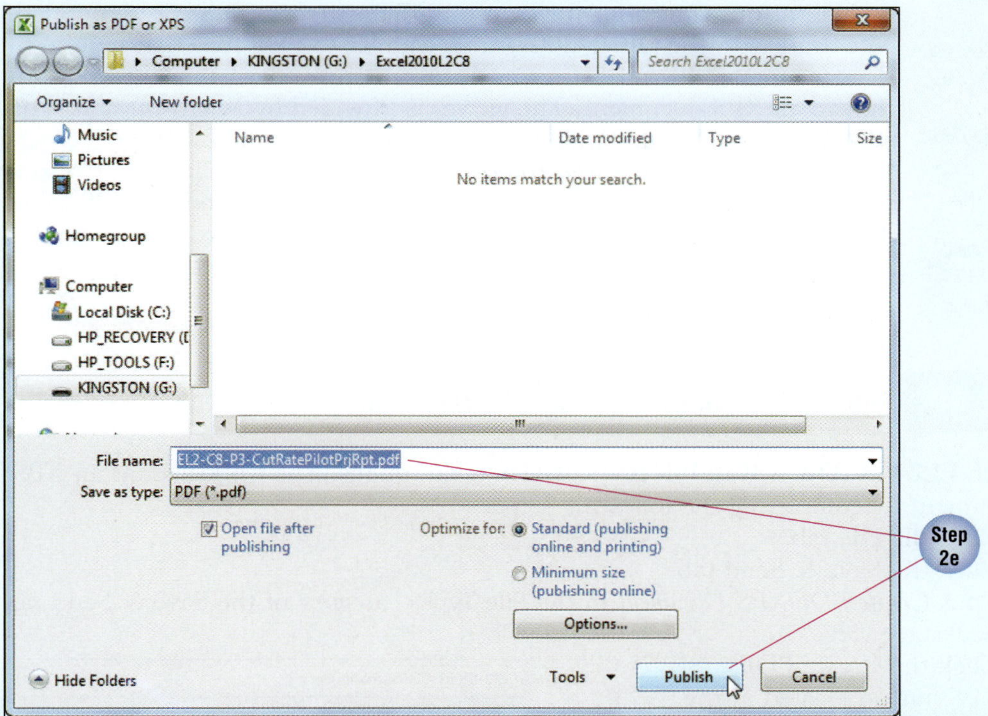

3. By default, an Adobe Reader (or an Adobe Acrobat) application window opens with the published worksheet displayed. Notice the worksheet has retained all of the Excel formatting and other visual features.

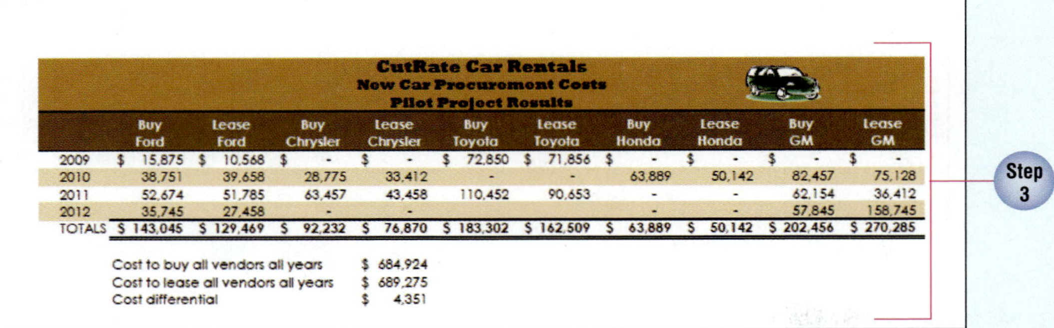

CutRate Car Rentals
New Car Procurement Costs
Pilot Project Results

	Buy Ford	Lease Ford	Buy Chrysler	Lease Chrysler	Buy Toyota	Lease Toyota	Buy Honda	Lease Honda	Buy GM	Lease GM
2009	$ 15,875	$ 10,568	$ -	$ -	$ 72,850	$ 71,856	$ -	$ -	$ -	$ -
2010	38,751	39,658	28,775	33,412	-	-	63,889	50,142	82,457	75,128
2011	52,674	51,785	63,457	43,458	110,452	90,653	-	-	62,154	36,412
2012	35,745	27,458	-	-			-	-	57,845	158,745
TOTALS	$ 143,045	$ 129,469	$ 92,232	$ 76,870	$ 183,302	$ 162,509	$ 63,889	$ 50,142	$ 202,456	$ 270,285

Cost to buy all vendors all years	$ 684,924
Cost to lease all vendors all years	$ 689,275
Cost differential	$ 4,351

4. Close the Adobe application window.
5. Leave the **EL2-C8-P3-CutRatePilotPrjRpt.xlsx** workbook open for the next project.

Quick Steps

Publish Worksheet as XPS
1. Open workbook.
2. Click File tab.
3. Click Save & Send tab.
4. Click *Create PDF/XPS Document.*
5. Click Create PDF/XPS button.
6. Click Save as type button.
7. Click *XPS Document (*.xps).*
8. Click Publish button.

Publishing a Worksheet as an XPS Document

XPS stands for ***XML Paper Specification***, which is another fixed-layout format with all of the same advantages as a PDF document. XPS was developed by Microsoft with the Office 2007 suite. Similar to PDF files that require the Adobe Reader program in which to view documents, you need the XPS viewer in order to read an XPS document. The viewer is provided by Microsoft and is packaged with Windows 7 and Windows Vista; however, to view an XPS document using Windows XP, you may need to download the viewer application. Go to www.microsoft.com and search using the phrase View and Generate XPS to locate the download page.

Project 4b Publishing a Worksheet as an XPS Document

Part 2 of 5

1. With **EL2-C8-P3-CutRatePilotPrjRpt.xlsx** open, publish the worksheet as an XPS document by completing the following steps:
   a. Click the File tab.
   b. Click the Save & Send tab.
   c. Click *Create PDF/XPS Document* in the File Types category of the Save & Send tab Backstage view.
   d. Click the Create PDF/XPS button located at the bottom of the Create a PDF/XPS Document category in the right pane.

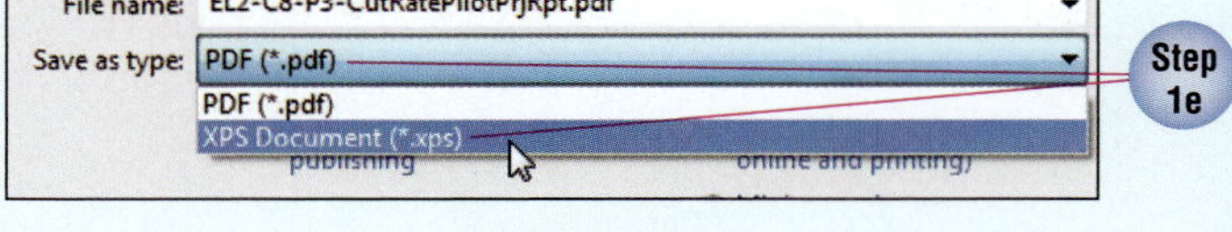

   e. At the Publish as PDF or XPS dialog box, click the Save as type button located below the *File name* text box and then click *XPS Document (*.xps)* at the drop-down list.

f. With *EL2-C8-P3-CutRatePilotPrjRpt.xps* in the *File name* text box, click the Publish button.

2. By default, an XPS Viewer application window opens with the published worksheet displayed. Notice that similar to the PDF document format, the XPS document format has retained all of the Excel formatting and other visual features.
3. Close the XPS Viewer application window.

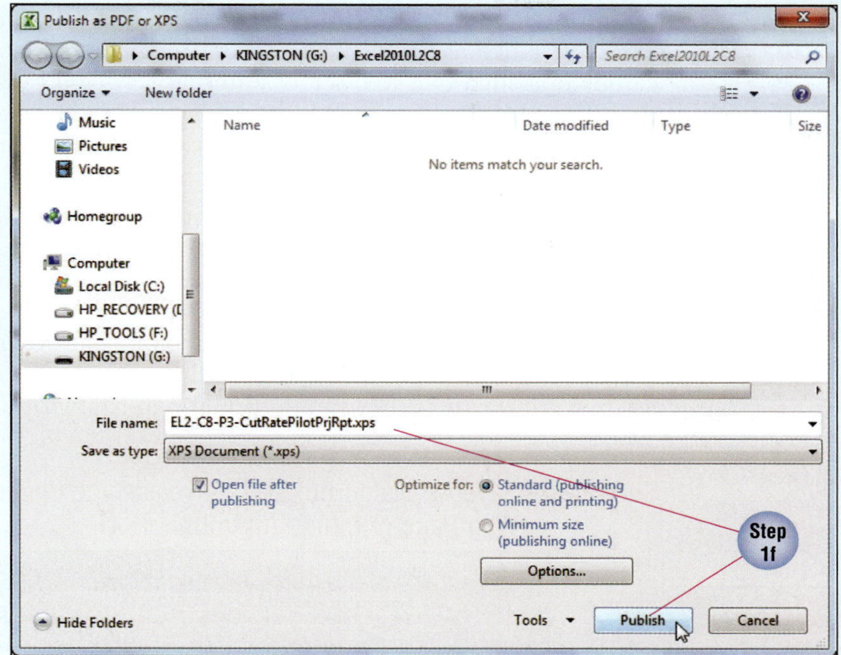

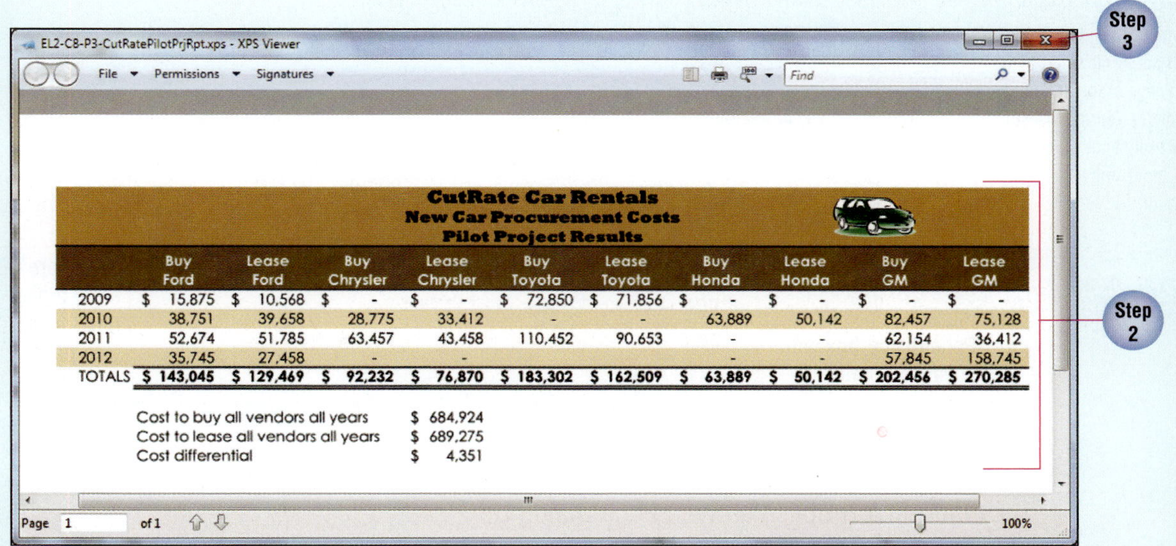

CutRate Car Rentals
New Car Procurement Costs
Pilot Project Results

	Buy Ford	Lease Ford	Buy Chrysler	Lease Chrysler	Buy Toyota	Lease Toyota	Buy Honda	Lease Honda	Buy GM	Lease GM
2009	$ 15,875	$ 10,568	$ -	$ -	$ 72,850	$ 71,856	$ -	$ -	$ -	$ -
2010	38,751	39,658	28,775	33,412	-	-	63,889	50,142	82,457	75,128
2011	52,674	51,785	63,457	43,458	110,452	90,653	-	-	62,154	36,412
2012	35,745	27,458	-	-			-	-	57,845	158,745
TOTALS	$ 143,045	$ 129,469	$ 92,232	$ 76,870	$ 183,302	$ 162,509	$ 63,889	$ 50,142	$ 202,456	$ 270,285

Cost to buy all vendors all years	$ 684,924
Cost to lease all vendors all years	$ 689,275
Cost differential	$ 4,351

4. Leave the **EL2-C8-P3-CutRatePilotPrjRpt.xlsx** workbook open for the next project.

Quick Steps

Publish Worksheet as Web Page

1. Open workbook.
2. Click File tab.
3. Click Save As.
4. Click Save as type button.
5. Click *Single File Web Page (*.mht; *.mhtml)*.
6. If necessary, change the drive and/or folder and/or file name.
7. Click Change Title button, type title, and click OK.
8. Click Publish button.
9. Set desired publishing options.
10. Click Publish.

HINT

Not all browsers support the single file (.mht) web page format. If you or others will not be viewing the page in Internet Explorer, consider using the traditional (.htm or .html) web page format.

Publishing a Worksheet as a Web Page

You can publish a worksheet as a single web page by changing the *Save as type* option to *Single File Web Page (*.mht; *.mhtml)*. In this format, all data in the worksheet such as graphics and other supplemental data is saved in a single file that can be uploaded to a web server. Alternatively, you can publish the worksheet in the traditional html (hypertext markup language) file format for web pages by changing the *Save as type* option to *Web Page (*.htm; *.html)*. In the *html* option, Excel creates additional files for supplemental data and saves the files in a subfolder.

When you choose a web page option at the *Save as type* list, the Save As dialog box changes as shown in Figure 8.6. At this dialog box, specify to publish the entire workbook or only the active sheet. Click the Change Title button if you want to add a title to the web page. The page title displays in the Title bar of the browser window and in the Internet Explorer tab when the page is viewed on the Internet. Click the Publish button and the Publish as Web Page dialog box appears as shown in Figure 8.7 with additional publishing options.

Figure 8.6 Save As Dialog Box with Save as Type Changed to Single File Web Page (*.mht; *.mhtml)

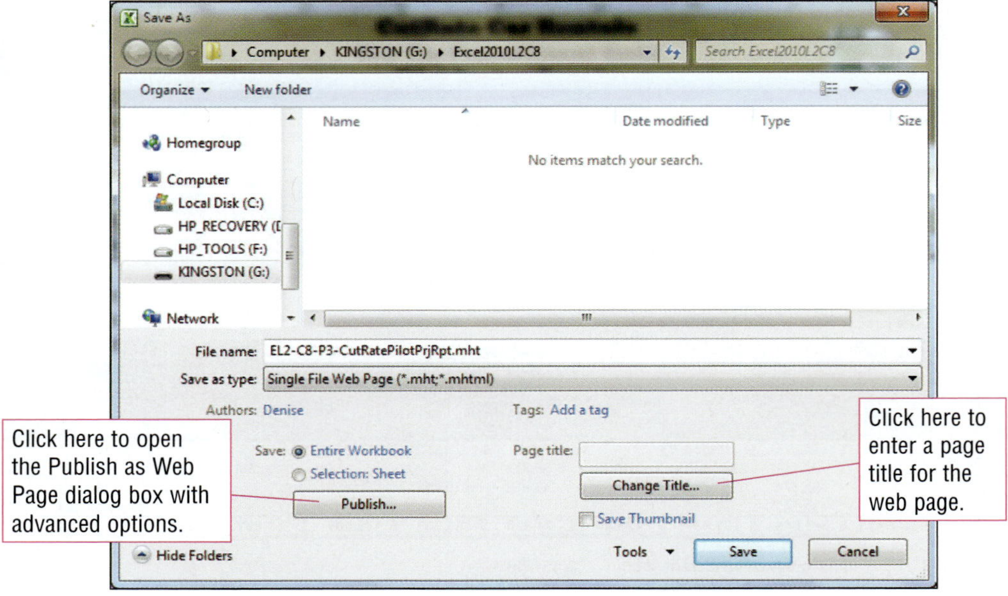

Figure 8.7 Publish as Web Page Dialog Box

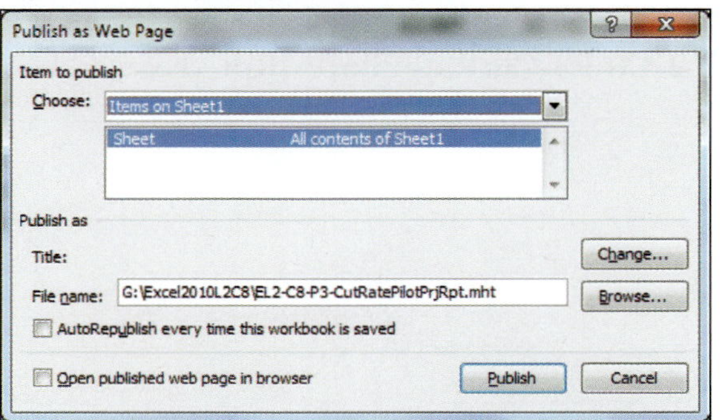

Project 4c Publishing a Worksheet as a Web Page

Part 3 of 5

1. With **EL2-C8-P3-CutRatePilotPrjRpt.xlsx** open, publish the worksheet as a single file web page by completing the following steps:
   a. Click the File tab.
   b. Click the Save As button.
   c. Click the Save as type button and then click *Single File Web Page (*.mht; *.mhtml)* at the pop-up list.
   d. Click the Change Title button.

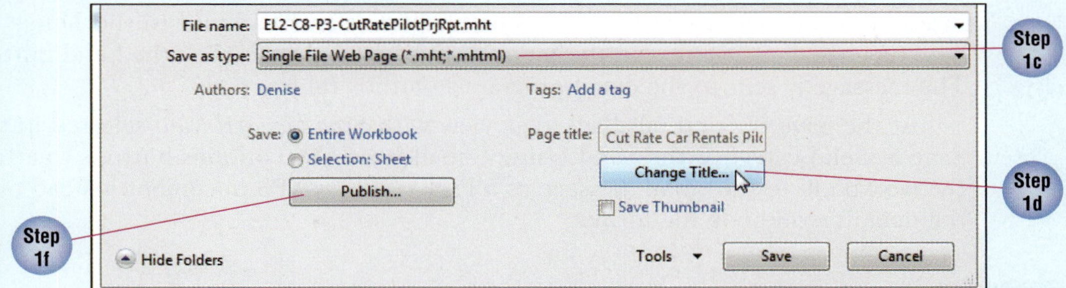

   e. At the Enter Text dialog box, type **CutRate Car Rentals Pilot Project Report** in the *Page title* text box and then click OK.

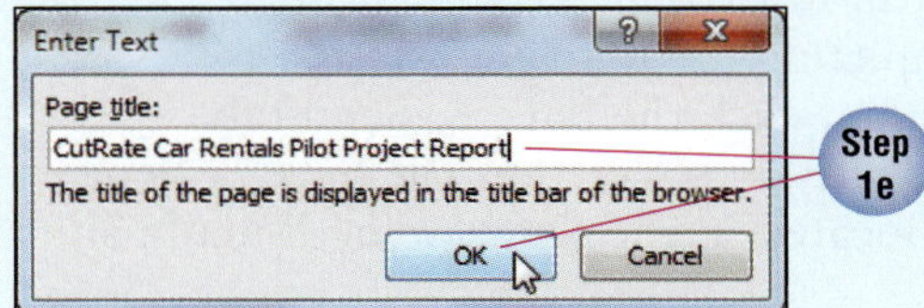

   f. Click the Publish button.
   g. At the Publish as Web Page dialog box, click the *Open published web page in browser* check box to insert a check mark and then click the Publish button. (This automatically displays the worksheet in your default web browser.)

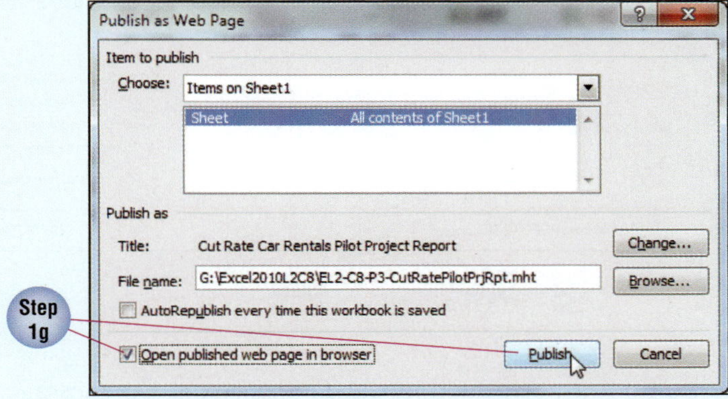

2. After viewing the web page, close the browser window.
3. Leave the **EL2-C8-P3-CutRatePilotPrjRpt.xlsx** workbook open for the next project.

Sending a Workbook via Email

Quick Steps

Send Workbook via Email

1. Open workbook.
2. Click File tab.
3. Click Save & Send tab.
4. Click Send as Attachment button.
5. Type recipient's email address in *To* text box.
6. If necessary, edit the *Subject* text.
7. Type message in message window.
8. Click Send.

A worksheet can be sent to others as a file attached to an email message. You can attach the workbook using your email program's file attachment feature, or you can choose to initiate the message from within Excel. To do this, click the File tab and then click the Save & Send tab. At the Save & Send tab Backstage view with *Send Using E-mail* already selected in the Save & Send category, click the Send as Attachment button located in the Send Using E-mail pane at the right side of the Backstage view. The default email program such as Microsoft Outlook launches an email message window with the workbook file already attached and the file name inserted in the *Subject* text box. Type the recipient's email address in the *To* text box, type the message text in the message window and then click the Send button. The message is sent to the email program's Outbox folder.

At the Save & Send tab Backstage view with *Send Using E-Mail* selected in the Save & Send category, the Send Using E-mail pane also contains buttons to attach the workbook to the email message as a PDF or as an XPS document instead of the default workbook file format.

Project 4d Sending a Workbook via Email

Part 4 of 5

1. With **EL2-C8-P3-CutRatePilotPrjRpt.xlsx** open, send the workbook as a file attached to an email message by completing the following steps:
   a. Click the File tab and then click the Save & Send tab.
   b. With *Send Using E-mail* already selected in the Save & Send category, click the Send as Attachment button located in the Send Using E-mail pane at the right side of the Backstage view.

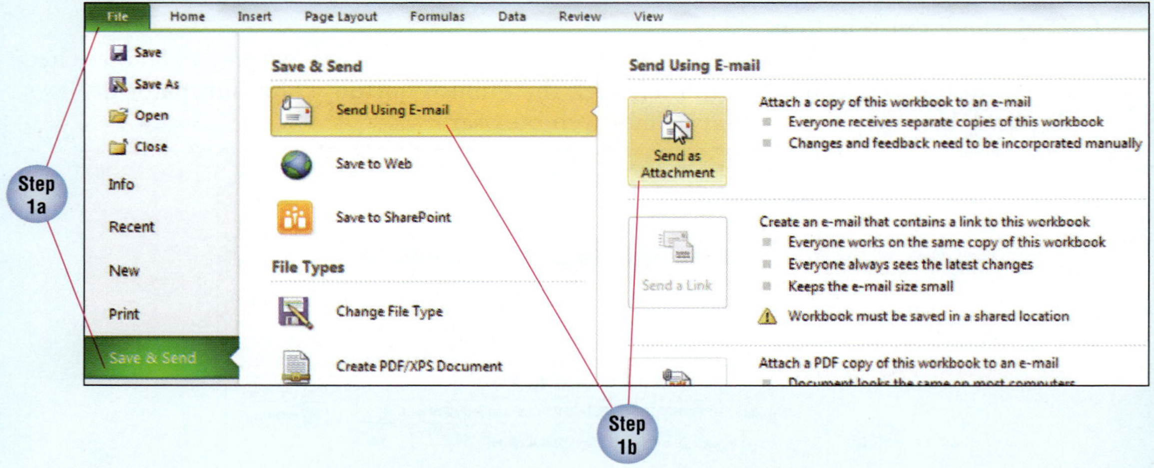

   c. With the insertion point positioned in the *To* text box at the message window, type your own email address.
   d. Click in the message window and type the following text:
      Here is the report on the new car procurement costs for the pilot project at CutRate Car Rentals. After four years, the cost differential between buying and leasing is $4,351 as shown in the attached worksheet.

e. Click the Send button. The message is sent and the message window closes.

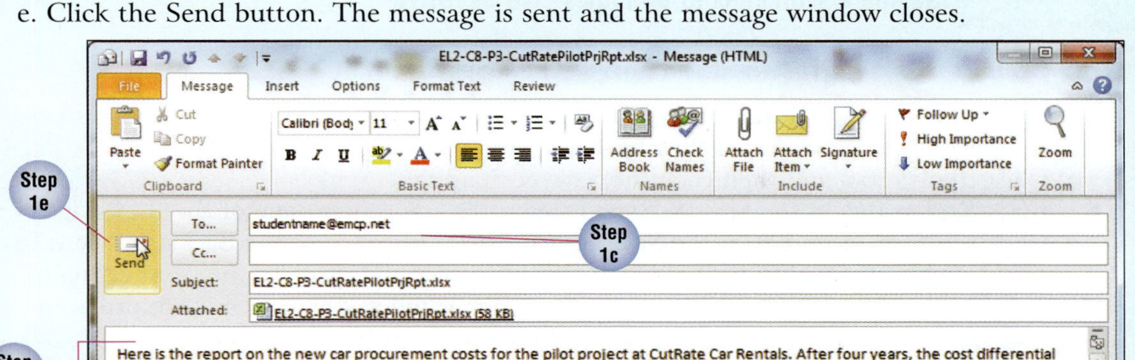

2. Open your email program (such as Microsoft Outlook).
3. Check your Inbox for the new message received and then open and view the message. ***Note: Depending on your mail server you may need to wait a few seconds for the message to be processed.***
4. Close the message and then exit the email program.
5. Leave the **EL2-C8-P3-CutRatePilotPrjRpt.xlsx** workbook open for the next project.

Saving a Workbook to Windows Live SkyDrive

Windows Live SkyDrive is a feature in Office 2010 that allows one to save and share documents to a storage location on the Internet. You can save a workbook to your SkyDrive location and then access the file from any other location with Internet access. This means you do not have to make a copy of the workbook on a USB drive or some other storage medium in order to work on the workbook at another location. You can also share the workbook with others by sending people a link to the SkyDrive location rather than sending the workbook as an email attachment. With multiple people editing the workbook on SkyDrive, you do not need to manage multiple versions of the same file.

In order to save the workbook to SkyDrive you need to have a Windows Live account. If you use hotmail or MSN messenger, the account with which you sign in to these applications is your Windows Live ID. If you do not already have a Windows Live user name and password, you can sign up for a free account at windowslive.com by clicking the Sign Up button. Windows Live SkyDrive is free and includes 25 GB of storage on the SkyDrive server.

Quick Steps

Save Workbook to SkyDrive

1. Open workbook.
2. Click File tab.
3. Click Save & Send tab.
4. Click Save to Web.
5. Click Sign In button.
6. Type Windows Live email address.
7. Press tab.
8. Type Windows Live password.
9. Click OK.
10. If necessary, select desired folder name.
11. Click Save As button.
12. Click Save button.

Saving a Workbook to Windows Live SkyDrive

Note: Complete this project only if you have a Windows Live ID.

1. With **EL2-C8-P3-CutRatePilotPrjRpt.xlsx** open, save the workbook to Windows Live SkyDrive by completing the following steps:
   a. Click the File tab and then click the Save & Send tab.
   b. Click *Save to Web* in the Save & Send category in the center pane of the Backstage view.
   c. Click the Sign In button in the Save to Windows Live pane of the Backstage view. Excel establishes a connection to the Windows Live server and displays the Connecting to docs.live.net dialog box in which you enter your Windows Live account information.

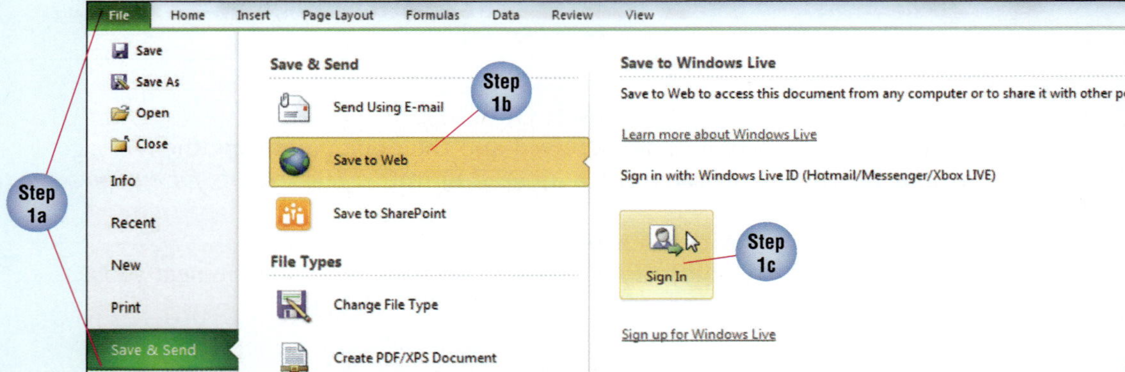

   d. With the insertion point positioned in the *E-mail address* text box, type the email address that you use for your Windows Live ID and then press tab.
   e. Type your Windows Live ID password and then click OK.
   f. With the *My Documents* folder name already selected in the *Personal Folders* list in the *Save to Windows Live SkyDrive* section of the Backstage view, click the Save As button.

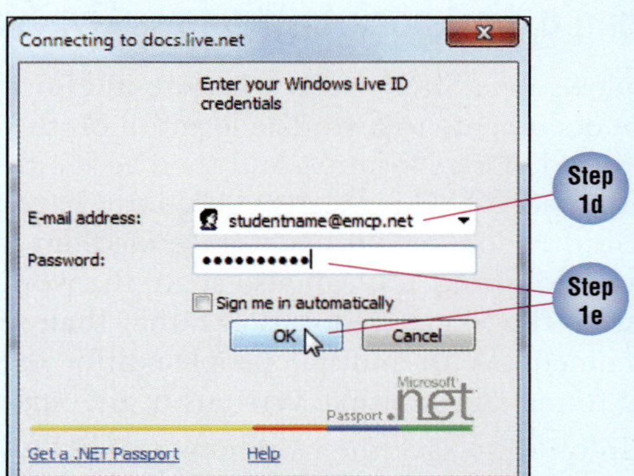

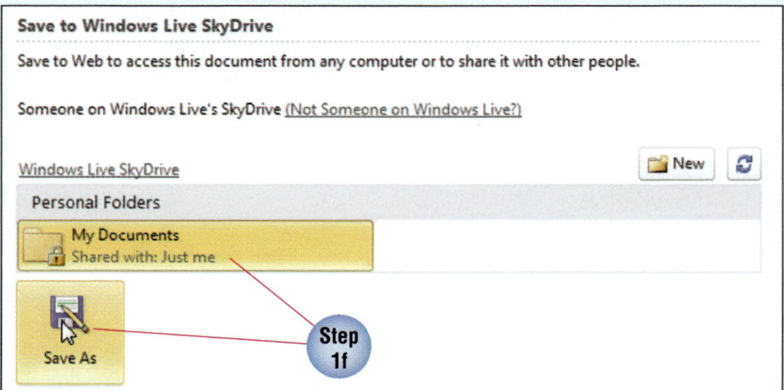

g. At the Save As dialog box with *EL2-C8-P3-CutRatePilotPrjRpt.xlsx* in the *File name* text box, click the Save button.

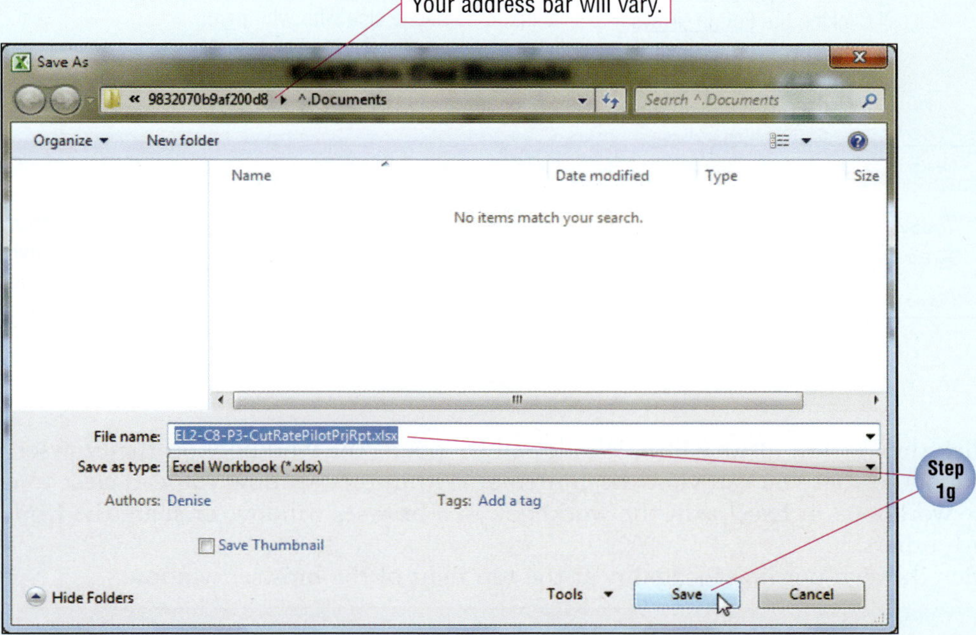

2. View the workbook stored on the Windows Live SkyDrive server by completing the following steps:
   a. Start Internet Explorer.
   b. Click in the Address bar and then type **http://live.com**.
   c. Sign in to Windows Live using your Windows Live ID email address and password.
   d. Point at the Office link located at the top of the Windows Live web page and then click *Your documents* at the drop-down list.

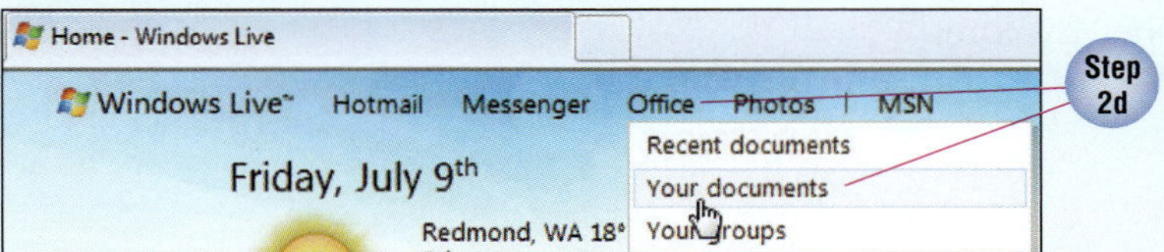

   e. Click the *My Documents* folder name in the *Personal* section.

f. Point at the Excel workbook name *EL2-C8-P3-CutRatePilotPrjRpt.xlsx* in the *Today* list to view the file options that display.

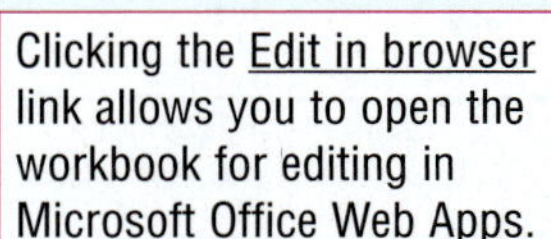

Clicking the Edit in browser link allows you to open the workbook for editing in Microsoft Office Web Apps.

Clicking the Share link allows you to send a link to someone else with whom you have given permission to view your My Documents folder in order to allow him or her access to the workbook.

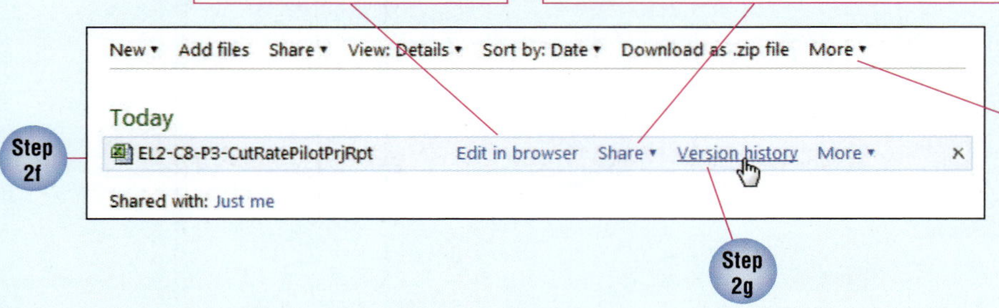

Clicking the More link displays a drop-down list from which you can move, copy, rename, or download the workbook.

g. Click the Version history link. Windows Live opens the workbook in the browser window so that you can view the contents. Within this window you can elect to open the workbook in Excel, edit the workbook in a browser window, or share the workbook with others.

h. Click the sign out link located near the top right of the browser window.

i. Close Internet Explorer.

3. Close **EL2-C8-P3-CutRatePilotPrjRpt.xlsx.**

Chapter Summary

- The Get External Data group in the Data tab contains buttons to use for importing data into an Excel worksheet from Access, from the Web, or from a text file.
- Only one Access table can be imported at a time.
- Tables in a website can be imported to Excel using the New Web Query dialog box.
- Text files are often used to exchange data between dissimilar programs since the file format is recognized by nearly all applications.
- Text files generally separate data between fields with either a tab character or a comma.

- The Text Import Wizard guides you through the process of importing a text file through three dialog boxes where you define the source file as delimited and select the delimiter character.
- Data in an Excel worksheet can be copied and pasted or copied and appended to an existing Access table.
- Worksheet data can be embedded or linked to a Word document. Embedding inserts a copy of the source data in the Word document and allows the object to be edited using Excel's tools within the Word environment, whereas linking the object inserts a shortcut to the Excel workbook from which the source data is retrieved.
- Breaking a link involves removing the connection between the source and destination programs so that the object is no longer updated in the destination document when the source data changes.
- You can embed and link objects to slides in a PowerPoint presentation using the same techniques as you would to embed or link cells to a Word document.
- In Office 2010, the charting tools are fully integrated. A chart copied and pasted from Excel to a PowerPoint presentation or a Word document is embedded by default.
- Save a worksheet as a text file by changing the file type at the Save & Send tab Backstage view.
- Excel includes several text file formats to accommodate differences that occur across operating system platforms that configure text files using various end of line character codes.
- The Document Inspector feature allows you to search for personal or hidden information and remove it before distributing a file.
- Once the workbook has been inspected, Excel displays a red exclamation mark in each section in which Excel detected the presence of the requested item. Clicking the Remove All button deletes the items from the workbook.
- Mark a Workbook as Final to change the workbook to a read-only file with the status property set to *Final*.
- Run the Compatibility Checker feature before saving a workbook in an earlier version of Excel to determine if a loss of functionality or fidelity will occur.
- The results of the compatibility check can be copied to a new worksheet for easy referencing and documentation purposes.
- A worksheet can be saved in PDF or XPS format, which are fixed-layout formats that preserve all of the Excel formatting and layout features.
- Adobe Reader is required in order to open and view a workbook saved as a PDF file.
- The XPS Viewer is included automatically with Windows Vista and Windows 7.
- If necessary, Adobe Reader or the XPS Viewer application can be downloaded from the Adobe or Microsoft websites. Both readers are free.
- Open the Save As dialog box and change the *Save as type* option to either *Single File Web Page* or *Web Page* to publish the current worksheet as a web page.
- An email message with the current workbook added as a file attachment can be generated from Excel using the Save & Send tab Backstage view. You can attach the workbook in the default .xlsx format, as a PDF, or as an XPS document.
- A workbook can be saved to a folder in your own personal storage location on Windows Live SkyDrive. From SkyDrive you can share, edit, or store the workbook from any location with Internet access.

Commands Review

FEATURE	RIBBON TAB, GROUP	BUTTON	KEYBOARD SHORTCUT
Compatibility checker	File, Info		
Copy	Home, Clipboard		Ctrl + C
Document Inspector	File, Info		
Import from Access table	Data, Get External Data		
Import from text file	Data, Get External Data		
Import from web page	Data, Get External Data		
Mark workbook as final	File, Info		
Paste Special	Home, Clipboard		
Save As	File		F12
Save as PDF/XPS	File, Save & Send		
Save as web page	File, Save As		
Send workbook via email	File, Save & Send		
Save workbook to Skydrive	File, Save & Send		

Concepts Check Test Your Knowledge

Completion: In the space provided at the right, indicate the correct term, command, or number.

1. This group in the Data tab contains buttons for importing data from Access. ____________________

2. If the source database used to import data contains more than one table, this dialog box appears after you select the data source to allow you to choose the desired table. ____________________

3. To import tables from a web page, open this dialog box to browse to the website and click arrows next to tables on the page that you want to import. ____________________

4. These are the two commonly used delimiter characters in delimited text file formats. ____________________

5. To add to the bottom of the active Access datasheet cells that have been copied to the clipboard, click this option at the Paste button drop-down list. ____________________

6. Choosing *Microsoft Excel Worksheet Object* at the Paste Special dialog box in a Word document and then clicking OK inserts the copied cells as this type of object. ____________________

7. If the Excel data you are pasting into a Word document is likely to be updated in the future and you want the Word document to reflect the updated values, paste the data as this type of object. ____________________

8. A chart copied from Excel and pasted to a slide in a PowerPoint presentation is pasted as this type of object by default. ____________________

9. Click this option in the *File Types* section of the Save & Send tab Backstage view to select the CSV file format in order to export the active worksheet as a text file. ____________________

10. This feature scans the open workbook for personal and hidden information and provides you with the opportunity to remove the items. ____________________

11. A workbook that has been marked as final is changed to this type of workbook to prevent additions, deletions, and modifications to cells. ____________________

12. Use this feature to check the current workbook for formatting or features used that are not available with versions of Excel prior to Excel 2007 and that could cause loss of functionality if saved in the earlier file format. ____________________

13. Save a worksheet in either of these fixed-layout formats that preserve Excel's formatting and layout features while allowing you to distribute the file to others who may not have Excel installed on their computer. ____________________

14. Click this button in the Save As dialog box once the *Save as type* option has been changed to a web page file format in order to type a page title. ____________________

15. This is the name of the free service from Microsoft which provides you with storage space on a Web server in order to save a workbook that you can share, edit, or download from any location with Internet access. ____________________

Skills Check Assess Your Performance

Assessment 1

IMPORT DATA FROM ACCESS AND A TEXT FILE

1. Open **HillsdaleResearchServices.xlsx**.
2. Save the workbook with Save As and name it **EL2-C8-A1-HillsdaleResearchServices**.
3. Make A6 of the CPIData worksheet the active cell if A6 is not currently active. Import the table named CPI from the Access database named **NuTrendsCensusData.accdb**.
4. Make the following changes to the worksheet:
   a. Apply *Table Style Medium 15* to the imported cells.
   b. Format the values in all columns *except* column A to one decimal place.
   c. Remove the filter arrow buttons and then center the column headings.
   d. If necessary, adjust column widths to accommodate the data.
5. Print the CPIData worksheet.
6. Make UIRateMI the active worksheet.
7. Make A6 the active cell if A6 is not currently active. Import the comma delimited text file named **UIRateMI.csv**.
8. Make the following changes to the data:
   a. Change the width of column B to 8.00 (61 pixels).
   b. Change the width of columns C to F to 15.00 (110 pixels).
   c. Change the width of column G to 5.00 (40 pixels).
   d. Center the months in column B.
9. Print the UIRate-MI worksheet.
10. Save and then close **EL2-C8-A1-HillsdaleResearchServices.xlsx**.

Assessment 2

LINK DATA TO A WORD DOCUMENT

1. Open **HillsdaleOctSalesByDateByRep.xlsx**.
2. Save the workbook with Save As and name it **EL2-C8-A2-HillsdaleOctSalesByDateByRep**.
3. With SalesByDate the active worksheet, link A3:G27 a double-space below the paragraph in the Word document named **HillsdaleOctRpt.docx**.
4. Change the margins in the Word document to *Narrow* (Top, Bottom, Left, and Right to 0.5 inch).
5. Use Save As to name the revised Word document **EL2-C8-A2-HillsdaleOctRpt.docx**.
6. Switch to Excel and then press the Esc key to remove the moving marquee and then deselect the range.
7. Change the value in F4 to *525000*.
8. Change the value in F5 to *212000*.
9. Save **EL2-C8-P2-HillsdaleOctSalesByDateByRep.xlsx**.
10. Switch to Word, right-click the linked object, and then click *Update Link* at the shortcut menu.

11. Print the Word document.
12. Break the link in the Word document.
13. Save **EL2-C8-P2-HillsdaleOctRpt.docx** and then exit Word.
14. Save and then close **EL2-C8-A2-HillsdaleOctSalesByDateByRep.xlsx**.

Assessment 3

EMBED DATA IN A POWERPOINT PRESENTATION

1. Open **HillsdaleOctSalesByDateByRep.xlsx**.
2. Save the workbook with Save As and name it **EL2-C8-A3-HillsdaleOctSalesByDateByRep**.
3. Make SalesByRep the active worksheet.
4. Display the worksheet at outline level 2 so that only the sales agent names, sale prices, and commissions display.
5. Create a column chart in a separate sheet to graph the sales commissions earned by each sales agent. You determine an appropriate chart style, title, and other chart elements.
6. Start PowerPoint and open **HillsdaleOctRpt.pptx**.
7. Save the presentation with Save As and name it **EL2-C8-A3-HillsdaleOctRpt**.
8. Embed the chart created in Step 5 on Slide 3 of the presentation.
9. Print the presentation as Handouts with three slides per page.
10. Save **EL2-C8-A3-HillsdaleOctRpt.pptx** and then exit PowerPoint.
11. Save and then close **EL2-C8-A3-HillsdaleOctSalesByDateByRep.xlsx**.

Assessment 4

EXPORT DATA AS A TEXT FILE

1. Open **HillsdaleOctSalesByDateByRep.xlsx**.
2. With SalesByDate the active worksheet, save the worksheet as a CSV (Comma delimited) (*.csv) text file named **EL2-C8-A4-HillsdaleOctSalesByDateByRep**.
3. Close **EL2-C8-A4-HillsdaleOctSalesByDateByRep.csv**. Click Don't Save when prompted to save changes.
4. Start Notepad and open **EL2-C8-A4-HillsdaleOctSalesByDateByRep.csv**.
5. Delete the first three rows at the beginning of the file that contain the title text from the top of the worksheet. The first words in the file should begin at the first row with the heading *Hillsdale Realtors*.
6. Delete the bottom row in the file that contains the total commission value and the ending commas.
7. Print the document.
8. Save **EL2-C8-A4-HillsdaleOctSalesByDateByRep.csv** and then exit Notepad.

Assessment

5 PREPARE A WORKBOOK FOR DISTRIBUTION

1. Open **Hillsdale2012Sales.xlsx**.
2. Save the workbook with Save As and name it **EL2-C8-A5-Hillsdale2012Sales**.
3. Display the Info tab Backstage view and show all properties. Read the information in the *Author, Title,* and *Subject* properties. Open the Properties dialog box (click *Advanced Properties* from the Properties button drop-down list) and read the information in the Statistics and Custom tabs. Close the Properties dialog box and click the Review tab.
4. Turn on the display of all comments and then read the comments that appear.
5. Change to Page Layout view and check for a header or footer in the workbook.
6. Use the Document Inspector feature to check the workbook for private and hidden information. Leave all options selected at the Document Inspector dialog box.
7. Remove all items that display with a red exclamation mark and then close the dialog box.
8. Click the Review tab, turn off the Show All Comments feature, and switch to Normal view.
9. Click the File tab. With the Info tab Backstage view displayed showing all properties, paste a screen image into a new Word document using the PrintScreen key, the Screenshot feature, or the Windows Snipping tool. Type your name a few lines below the screen image. Print the Word document and then exit Word without saving.
10. Run the Compatibility Feature to check for loss of functionality or fidelity in the workbook if saved in an earlier Excel version. Save the Summary report to a new sheet and then print the Compatibility Report sheet.
11. Mark the workbook as final.
12. Close **EL2-C8-A5-Hillsdale2012Sales.xlsx**.

Assessment

6 PREPARE AND DISTRIBUTE A WORKBOOK

1. Open **Hillsdale2012Sales.xlsx**.
2. Save the workbook with Save As and name it **EL2-C8-A6-Hillsdale2012Sales**.
3. Use the Document Inspector feature to remove comments and annotations only from the worksheet.
4. Publish the worksheet as a PDF file named **EL2-C8-A6-Hillsdale2012Sales.pdf**.
5. Publish the worksheet as a single file web page named **EL2-C8-A6-Hillsdale2012Sales.mht** with a page title *Hillsdale Realtors*.
6. Save and close **EL2-C8-A6-Hillsdale2012Sales.xlsx**.
7. Display the contents of the Excel2010L2C8 folder on your storage medium. Make sure the folder is displaying file extensions. Paste a screen image of the folder's contents into a new Word document using the PrintScreen key, the Screenshot feature, or the Windows Snipping tool. Type your name a few lines below the screen image. Print the Word document and then exit Word without saving. Close the Computer or Documents window.

Optional: With **EL2-C8-A6-Hillsdale2012Sales.xlsx** open, email the workbook to yourself. Compose an appropriate message within the message window as if you were an employee of Hillsdale Realtors sending the file to the office manager. Open the message window from the Inbox in your email program and print the message. Close the message window and exit your email program.

Optional: With **EL2-C8-A6-Hillsdale2012Sales.xlsx** open, display the Save & Send tab Backstage view with the *Save to Web* option active. Sign in to Windows Live and create a new folder in your SkyDrive folder space named *Excel2010L2C8*. ***Hint: A New Folder button displays above and right of the My Documents folder in Backstage view once you are signed in to Windows Live. When you click this button, you will be redirected to the Windows Live web page and once you sign in again you will be at the Create folder web page.*** Within Windows Live SkyDrive, upload the three files you created in this assessment into the Excel2010L2C8 folder. Paste a screen image that shows the three files in the Excel2010L2C8 folder in Windows Live into a new Word document using the PrintScreen key, the Screenshot feature, or the Windows Snipping tool. Type your name a few lines below the screen image. Print the Word document and then exit Word without saving. Sign out of Windows Live and close the Internet Explorer window. Click the Home tab and then close **EL2-C8-A6-Hillsdale2012Sales.xlsx**.

Visual Benchmark Demonstrate Your Proficiency

IMPORT, ANALYZE, AND EXPORT POPULATION DATA

1. Look at the data in the worksheet shown in Figure 8.8. Create this worksheet by importing the PopByState table from the Access database named ***NuTrendsCensusData.accdb*** into a new worksheet. Once imported, rows and columns not shown in the figure were deleted and the filter arrows removed. The worksheet has *Table Style Light 2* style and the Solstice theme applied. Add the title rows at the top of the imported data and change the title in B4 as shown. Use your best judgment to match other formatting characteristics such as column width, row height, number formatting, alignment, and fill color.
2. Rename the worksheet *PopulationTable* and then print the worksheet.
3. Select A4:B19 and create the chart shown in Figure 8.9 in a new sheet named *PopulationChart*. The chart has the *Style 36* style applied. Use your best judgment to match other chart options and formatting with the chart shown.
4. Save the workbook and name it **EL2-C8-VB-PizzaByMarioPopData**.
5. Start Microsoft Word and then open **PizzaByMarioReport.docx**. Use Save As to name the workbook **EL2-C8-VB-PizzaByMarioReport**. Change *Student Name* on page 1 to your name. Copy and paste the Excel chart, positioning the chart between the last two paragraphs on page 2 of the document. Make any formatting adjustments to the chart you think are necessary once the chart has been inserted. Save, print, and then close **EL2-C8-VB-PizzaByMarioReport.docx**.
6. Close **EL2-C8-VB-PizzaByMarioPopData.xlsx**.

Figure 8.8 Visual Benchmark *PopulationTable* Worksheet

	A	B
1	U.S. Population Estimates as of July 1, 2009	
2	U.S. Census Bureau	
3	States Selected for Franchise Expansion	
4	**State**	**Population**
5	Illinois	12,910,409
6	Indiana	6,423,113
7	Iowa	3,007,856
8	Kansas	2,818,747
9	Kentucky	4,314,113
10	Michigan	9,969,727
11	Minnesota	5,266,214
12	Missouri	5,987,580
13	Montana	974,989
14	Nebraska	1,796,619
15	North Dakota	646,844
16	Ohio	11,542,645
17	South Dakota	812,383
18	Wisconsin	5,654,774
19	Wyoming	544,270

Figure 8.9 Visual Benchmark *PopulationChart* Chart

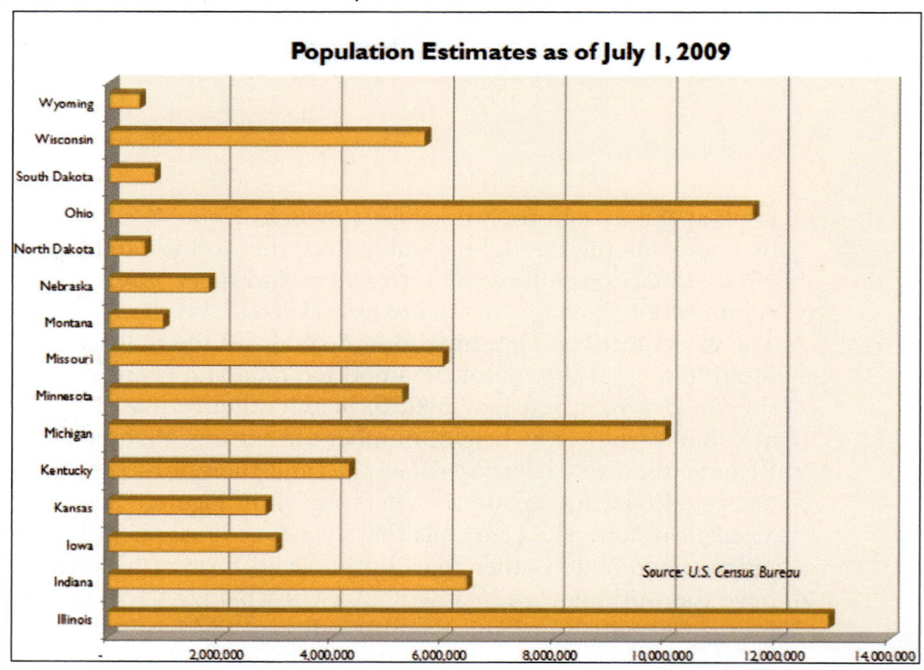

Case Study Apply Your Skills

Part 1

Yolanda Robertson of NuTrends Market Research would like new research data from the U.S. Census Bureau for her Pizza by Mario franchise expansion project. The franchise expansion is planned for the states of Illinois, Indiana, and Kentucky. Start a new workbook and set up three worksheets named using the state names. In each sheet, using the New Web Query feature, display the web page http://quickfacts.census.gov/qfd/, and import the People Quickfacts table for the state. Once the data is imported, delete column A, which is the definitions information. Add an appropriate title merged and centered above the imported data and apply formatting enhancements to improve the appearance of the column headings. Save the workbook and name it **EL2-C8-CS-P1-PizzaByMarioResearch**. Print all three worksheets.

Part 2

To prepare for an upcoming meeting with Mario and Nicola Carlucci of Pizza by Mario, Yolanda would like you to copy selected information from each state to a Word report. Open **PizzaByMarioExpansionResearch.docx**. Save the document using Save As and name it **EL2-C8-CS-P2-PizzaByMarioExpansionResearch**. From the Excel workbook you created in Part 1, copy and paste to the Word document the following data for each state (do not include the data in the *USA* column). Do not embed or link since the data will not be changed or updated.

Households
Persons per household
Median household income

If the data you imported does not contain these headings, locate and copy information closely related to number of households and income for the state.

At the bottom of the document, create a reference for the data from the U.S. Census Bureau. Check with your instructor for the preferred format for the reference. Save, print, and then close **EL2-C8-CS-P2-PizzaByMarioExpansionResearch.docx**. Close **EL2-C8-CS-P1-PizzaByMarioResearch.xlsx**.

Part 3

Yolanda has noticed that when she opens the workbook created in Part 1, a message appears in the message bar that says *Data connections have been disabled*. Yolanda has asked what this message means and wonders what circumstances are acceptable to click the Enable Content button. Research in Help how to manage connections to external data using the Workbook Connections dialog box. Since the data that was imported does not need to be refreshed in the future, you decide to remove the connections so that Yolanda does not see the security message in the future. Open **EL2-C8-CS-P1-PizzaByMarioResearch.xlsx** and click the Enable Content button that appears in the message bar. Open the Workbook Connections dialog box and, using the information you learned in Help, remove all of the connections. Save the revised workbook as **EL2-C8-CS-P3-PizzaByMarioResearch** and then close the workbook.

Compose a memo to Yolanda using Microsoft Word that provides a brief explanation of why the security warning message about data connections appears when a workbook is opened that contains external content. Base the memo on the information you learned in Help, making sure that you compose the explanation using your own words. Explain that you have created a new copy of the workbook with the connections removed. Save the Word memo and name it **EL2-C8-CS-P3-DataConnectionsMemo**. Print and then close **EL2-C8-CS-P3-DataConnectionsMemo.docx** and then exit Word.

Part

4

Yolanda noticed the *Send as Internet Fax* option in the Send Using E-Mail pane at the Save & Send tab Backstage view. Yolanda wants to know how to send a worksheet as an Internet fax since NuTrends Market Research may need to distribute information via fax in the future. Research in Excel Help how to use the Internet Fax feature. Next, search the Internet for at least two fax service providers. Using Microsoft Word, compose a memo to Yolanda that briefly explains how to use the Internet Fax feature in Excel, making sure you compose the explanation using your own words. Include in the memo the URL of the two fax service providers you visited and add your recommendation for the provider you want to use. Save the memo and name it **EL2-C8-CS-P4-InternetFaxMemo**. Print and then close **EL2-C8-CS-P4-InternetFaxMemo.docx** and exit Word.

UNIT 2

Performance Assessment

Excel2010L2U2

Note: Before beginning unit assessments, copy to your storage medium the Excel2010L2U2 subfolder from the Excel2010L2 folder on the CD that accompanies this textbook and then make Excel2010L2U2 the active folder.

Assessing Proficiency

In this unit, you have learned to use features in Excel that facilitate performing what-if analysis, identifying relationships between worksheet formulas, collaborating with others by sharing and protecting workbooks, and automating repetitive tasks using macros. You also learned how to customize the Excel environment to suit your preferences and integrate Excel data by importing from and exporting to external resources. Finally, you learned how to prepare and distribute a workbook to others by removing items that are private or confidential, by marking the workbook as final, by checking for features incompatible with earlier versions of Excel, and by saving and sending a worksheet in various formats.

Assessment 1 Use Goal Seek and Scenario Manager to Calculate Investment Proposals

1. Open **HillsdaleInvtPlan.xlsx**.
2. Save the workbook with Save As and name it **EL2-U2-A1-HillsdaleInvtPlan**.
3. Use Goal Seek to find the monthly contribution amount the client must make in order to increase the projected value of the plan to $65,000 at the end of the term. Accept the solution Goal Seek calculates.
4. Assign the range name *AvgReturn* to E8.
5. Create three scenarios for changing E8 as follows:

Scenario name	*Interest rate*
Moderate	5.5%
Conservative	4.0%
Aggressive	12.5%

6. Apply the *Aggressive* scenario and then print the worksheet.
7. Edit the *Moderate* scenario's interest rate to 8.0% and then apply the scenario.
8. Create and then print a Scenario Summary report.
9. Save and then close **EL2-U2-A1-HillsdaleInvtPlan.xlsx**.

Assessment 2 Calculate Investment Outcomes for a Portfolio Using a Two-Variable Data Table

1. Open **HillsdaleResearchInvtTbl.xlsx**.
2. Save the workbook with Save As and name it **EL2-U2-A2-HillsdaleResearchInvtTbl**.
3. Create a two-variable data table that calculates the projected value of the investment plan at the end of the term for each monthly contribution payment and at each interest rate in the range A11:G20.
4. Apply the Comma Style format to the projected values in the table and adjust column widths if necessary.
5. Make E8 the active cell and display precedent arrows.
6. Make A11 the active cell and display precedent arrows.
7. Remove the arrows.
8. Save, print, and then close **EL2-U2-A2-HillsdaleResearchInvtTbl.xlsx**.

Assessment 3 Solve an Error and Check for Accuracy in Investment Commission Formulas

1. Open **HillsdaleModeratePortfolio.xlsx**.
2. Save the workbook with Save As and name it **EL2-U2-A3-HillsdaleModeratePortfolio**.
3. Solve the #VALUE! error in E19. Use formula auditing tools to help find the source cell containing the invalid entry.
4. Check the logic accuracy of the formula in E19 by creating proof formulas below the worksheet as follows:
   a. In row 21, calculate the amount from the customer's deposit that would be deposited into each of the six funds based on the percentages in column B. For example, in B21 create a formula to multiply the customer's deposit in B19 ($5,000.00) times the percentage recommended for investment in the DW Bond fund in B5 (40%). Create a similar formula for the remaining funds in C21:G21.
   b. In row 22, multiply the amount deposited to each fund by the fund's commission rate. For example, in B22, create a formula to multiply the value in B21 ($2,000.00) times the commission rate paid by the DW Bond fund in B17 (1.15%). Create a similar formula for the remaining funds in C22:G22.
   c. In B23, create a SUM function to calculate the total of the commissions for the six funds in B22:G22.
   d. Add appropriate labels next to the values created in rows 21 to 23.
5. Save, print, and then close **EL2-U2-A3-HillsdaleModeratePortfolio.xlsx**.

Assessment 4 Document and Share a Workbook and Manage Changes in an Investment Portfolio Worksheet

1. Open **EL2-U2-A3-HillsdaleModeratePortfolio.xlsx**.
2. Save the workbook with Save As and name it **EL2-U2-A4-HillsdaleModeratePortfolio**.
3. Enter the following data into the workbook properties. ***Note: Remove an entry for those properties shown below in which text may already exist.***

Author	Logan Whitmore
Title	Recommended Moderate Portfolio
Comments	Proposed moderate fund
Subject	Moderate Investment Allocation

4. Paste a screen image of the Info tab Backstage view showing all properties into a new Word document. Type your name a few blank lines below the image, print the document, and then exit Word without saving.
5. Click the Review tab and then share the workbook.
6. Change the user name to *Carey Winters* and then edit the following cells:

B7	from	*10%*	to	*15%*
B8	from	*15%*	to	*10%*

7. Save **EL2-U2-A4-HillsdaleModeratePortfolio.xlsx**.
8. Change the user name to *Jodi VanKemenade* and then edit the following cells:

D17	from	*2.15%*	to	*2.32%*
E17	from	*2.35%*	to	*2.19%*

9. Save **EL2-U2-A4-HillsdaleModeratePortfolio.xlsx**.
10. Create and then print a History sheet. ***Note: If you submit your assignment work electronically, create a copy of the History worksheet in a new workbook named EL2-U2-A4-HillsdaleModeratePortfolioHistory.***
11. Change the user name back to the original name on the computer you are using.
12. Accept and reject changes made to the ModeratePortfolio worksheet as follows:

Reject	B7
Reject	B8
Accept	D17
Reject	E17

13. Save, print, and then close **EL2-U2-A4-HillsdaleModeratePortfolio.xlsx**.

Assessment 5 Insert Comments and Protect a Confidential Investment Portfolio Workbook

1. Open **EL2-U2-A4-HillsdaleModeratePortfolio.xlsx**.
2. Save the workbook with Save As and name it **EL2-U2-A5-HillsdaleModeratePortfolio.xlsx**.
3. Remove the shared access to the workbook.
4. Hide rows 20 to 23.
5. Make B17 the active cell and insert a comment. Type **Commission rate to be renegotiated in 2012** in the comment box.
6. Copy the comment in B17 and paste it to D17 and G17. Press the Esc key to remove the moving marquee from B17.
7. Edit the comment in G17 to change the year from *2012* to *2013*.
8. Protect the worksheet allowing editing to B19 only. Assign the password *hM$28* to unprotect the worksheet.
9. Encrypt the workbook with the password *Mod%82*.
10. Save and close **EL2-U2-A5-HillsdaleModeratePortfolio.xlsx**.
11. Test the security features added to the workbook by opening **EL2-U2-A5-HillsdaleModeratePortfolio.xlsx** using the password created in Step 9. Try to change one of the values in the range B5:B10 and B17:G17.
12. Make B19 the active cell and then change the value to *10000*.
13. Display all of the comments in the worksheet and then print the worksheet with the comments *As displayed on sheet* and with the worksheet scaled to fit on 1 page.
14. Save and then close **EL2-U2-A5-HillsdaleModeratePortfolio.xlsx**.

Assessment 6 Automate and Customize an Investment Portfolio Workbook

1. Open **EL2-U2-A5-HillsdaleModeratePortfolio.xlsx**.
2. Unprotect the worksheet, turn off the display of all comments, and then delete the comments in B17, D17, and G17.
3. Display the Custom Views dialog box. When a workbook has been shared, Excel automatically creates custom views (with the label *Personal View)* for each person who accessed the file as well as the original worksheet state before sharing was enabled. Delete all of the custom views in the dialog box and then add a new custom view named *ModeratePortfolioOriginalView*.
4. Create two macros to be stored in the active workbook as follows:
   a. A macro named *CustomDisplay* that applies the *Solstice* theme, and turns off the display of gridlines and row and column headers in the current worksheet. Assign the macro to the shortcut key Ctrl + Shift + T. Enter an appropriate description that includes your name and the date the macro was created.
   b. A macro named *CustomHeader* that prints the text *Private and Confidential* at the left margin. Assign the macro to the shortcut key Ctrl + Shift + H. Enter an appropriate description that includes your name and the date the macro was created.
5. Test the macros by opening **EL2-U2-A1-HillsdaleInvtPlan.xlsx**. Make InvestmentPlanProposal the active worksheet and then run the two macros created in Step 4. View the worksheet in Print Preview. Close Print Preview and then close **EL2-U2-A1-HillsdaleInvtPlan.xlsx** without saving the changes.
6. Print the Visual Basic program code for the two macros and then close the Microsoft Visual Basic window and return to Excel.
7. Create a custom view named *ModeratePortfolioTemplateView*.
8. Save the revised workbook as a macro-enabled workbook named **EL2-U2-A6-HillsdaleModeratePortfolio.xlsm** and remove the password to open the workbook.
9. Print the worksheet.
10. Display the Custom Views dialog box. Paste a screen image of the worksheet with the Custom Views dialog box open into a new Word document. Type your name a few blank lines below the image, print the document, and then exit Word without saving.
11. Close the Custom Views dialog box and then close **EL2-U2-A6-HillsdaleModeratePortfolio.xlsm**.

Assessment 7 Create and Use an Investment Planner Template

1. Open **EL2-U2-A2-HillsdaleResearchInvtTbl.xlsx**.
2. Make the following changes to the worksheet:
   a. Change the label in A3 to *Investment Planner*.
   b. Change the font color of A11 to white. This will make the cell appear to be empty. You want to disguise the entry in this cell because you think displaying the value at the top left of the data table will confuse Hillsdale customers.
   c. Clear the contents of E5:E7.
   d. Protect the worksheet allowing editing to E5:E7 only. Assign the password *H$pl@n* to unprotect the worksheet.
3. Save the revised workbook as a template named **HillsdaleInvPlan-StudentName** with your name substituted for *StudentName*.

4. Close **HillsdaleInvPlan-StudentName.xltx**.
5. Start a new workbook based on the **HillsdaleInvPlan-StudentName.xltx** template.
6. Enter the following information in the appropriate cells:
   a. *Monthly contribution* -475
   b. *Number of years to invest* 5
   c. *Forecasted annual interest rate* 4.75%
7. Save the workbook as an Excel workbook named **EL2-U2-A7-HillsdaleInvPlan**.
8. Print and then close **EL2-U2-A7-HillsdaleInvPlan.xlsx**.
9. Display the New dialog box. Copy the template created in this assessment to the Excel2010L2U2 folder on your storage medium.
10. Delete the custom template created in this assessment from the hard disk drive on the computer you are using.

Assessment 8 Export a Chart and Prepare and Distribute an Investment Portfolio Worksheet

1. Open **EL2-U2-A6-HillsdaleModeratePortfolio.xlsm** and enable the content if the security warning message bar appears.
2. Start Microsoft PowerPoint 2010 and then open **HillsdalePortfolios.pptx**.
3. Save the presentation with Save As and name it **EL2-U2-A8-HillsdalePortfolios**.
4. Copy the pie chart from the Excel worksheet to Slide 7 in the PowerPoint presentation.
5. Resize the chart on the slide and edit the legend if necessary to make the chart consistent with the other charts in the presentation.
6. Print the PowerPoint presentation as *9 Slides Horizontal Handouts*.
7. Save **EL2-U2-A8-HillsdalePortfolios.pptx** and then exit PowerPoint.
8. Deselect the chart in the Excel worksheet.
9. Inspect the document, leaving all items checked at the Document Inspector dialog box.
10. Remove all items that display with a red exclamation mark and then close the dialog box.
11. Change the file type to a workbook with an .xlsx file extension and name it **EL2-U2-A8-HillsdaleModeratePortfolio**. Click Yes when prompted that the file cannot be saved with the VBA Project. Click OK at the privacy warning message box.
12. Mark the workbook as final. Click OK if the privacy warning message box reappears.
13. Send the workbook as an XPS document to yourself in an email initiated from Excel. Include an appropriate message in the message window assuming you work for Hillsdale Financial Services and are sending the portfolio file to a potential client. Open the message window from the Inbox in your email program and print the message. Close the message window and exit your email program.
14. Display the Info tab Backstage view showing all properties. Paste a screen image into a new Word document. Type your name a few blank lines below the image, print the document, and then exit Word without saving.
15. Close **EL2-U2-A8-HillsdaleModeratePortfolio.xlsx**.

Writing Activities

The Writing, Internet Research, and Job Study activities give you the opportunity to practice your writing skills while demonstrating an understanding of some of the important Excel features you have mastered in this unit. Use appropriate word choices and correct grammar, capitalization, and punctuation when setting up new worksheets. Labels should clearly describe the data that is presented.

Create a Computer Maintenance Template

The Computing Services department of National Online Marketing Inc. wants to create a computer maintenance template for Help Desk employees to complete electronically and save to a document management server. This system will make it easy for a technician to check the status of any employee's computer from any location within the company. The Help Desk department performs the following computer maintenance tasks at each computer twice per year.

- Delete temporary Internet files
- Delete temporary document files that begin with a tilde (~)
- Update hardware drivers
- Reconfirm all serial numbers and asset records
- Have employee change password
- Check that automatic updates for the operating system is active
- Check that automatic updates for virus protection is active
- Confirm that automatic backup to the computing services server is active
- Confirm that employee is archiving all email messages
- Clean the computer's screen, keyboard, and system unit

In a new workbook, create a template that can be used to complete the maintenance form electronically. The template should include information that identifies the workstation by asset ID number, the department in which the computer is located, the name of the employee using the computer, the name of the technician that performs the maintenance, and the date the maintenance is performed. In addition, include a column next to each task with a drop-down list with the options: *Completed*, *Not Completed*, *Not Applicable*. Next to this column include a column in which the technician can type notes. At the bottom of the template include a text box with the following message text:

> **Save using the file naming standard CM-StationID##-yourinitials where ## is the asset ID. Example CM-StationID56-JW**

Protect the worksheet, leaving the cells unlocked that the technician will fill in as he or she completes a maintenance visit. Do not include a password for unprotecting the sheet. Save the template and name it **NationalCMForm-StudentName** with your name substituted for *StudentName*. Start a new workbook based on the custom template. Fill out a form as if you were a technician working on your own computer to test the template's organization and layout. Save the completed form as an Excel workbook named **EL2-U2-Act1-NationalCMForm**. Print the form scaled to fit one page in height and width. Copy the **NationalCMForm-StudentName.xltx** template file to your storage medium and then delete the template from the computer you are using.

Internet Research

Apply What-If Analysis to a Planned Move

Following graduation, you plan to move out of the state/province for a few years to gain experience living on your own. Create a new workbook to use as you plan this move to develop a budget for expenses in the first year. Research typical rents for apartments in the city in which you want to find your first job. Estimate other living costs in the city including transportation, food, entertainment, clothes, telephone, cable/satellite, cell phone, Internet, and so on. Calculate total living costs for an entire year. Next, research annual starting salaries for your chosen field of study in the same area. Estimate the take home pay at approximately 70% of the annual salary you decide to use. Using the take-home pay and the total living costs for the year, calculate if you will have money left over or have to borrow money to meet expenses.

Next, assume you want to save enough money to go on a vacation at the end of the year. Use Goal Seek to find the take-home pay you need to earn in order to have $2,000 left over at the end of the year. Accept the solution that Goal Seek provides and then create two scenarios in the worksheet as follows:

- A scenario named *LowestValues* in which you adjust each value down to the lowest amount you think is reasonable.
- A scenario named *HighestValues* in which you adjust each value up to the highest amount you think is reasonable.

Apply each scenario and watch the impact on the amount left over at the end of the year. Display the worksheet in the *HighestValues* scenario and then create a scenario summary report. Print the worksheet applying print options as necessary to minimize the pages required. Print the scenario summary report. Save the workbook as **EL2-U2-Act2-MyFirstYearBudget**. Close **EL2-U2-Act2-MyFirstYearBudget.xlsx**.

Research and Compare Smartphones

You work for an independent marketing consultant who travels frequently in North America and Europe for work. The consultant, Lindsay Somers, would like to purchase a smartphone. Lindsay will use the smartphone while traveling for conference calling, email, web browsing, text messaging, and making modifications to PowerPoint presentations, Word documents, or Excel worksheets. Using the Internet, research the latest smartphone from three different manufacturers. Prepare a worksheet that compares the three smartphones, organizing the worksheet so that the main features are shown along the left side of the page by category and each phone's specifications for those features are set in columns. At the bottom of each column, provide the hyperlink to the phone's specifications on the Web. Based on your perception of the best value, select one of the phones as your recommendation and note within the worksheet using a comment box in the price cell the phone you think Lindsay should select. Provide a brief explanation of why you selected the phone in the comment box. Make sure comments are displayed in the worksheet. Save the worksheet and name it **EL2-U2-Act3-Smartphones**. Publish the worksheet as a single file web page accepting the default file name and changing the page title to *Smartphone Feature and Price Comparison*. Print the web page from the Internet Explorer window. Close Internet Explorer and then close **EL2-U2-Act3-Smartphones.xlsx**.

Job Study

Prepare a Wages Budget and Link the Budget to a Word Document

You work at a small, independent, long-term care facility named Gardenview Place Long-Term Care. As assistant to the business manager, you are helping with the preparation of next year's hourly wages budget. Create a worksheet to estimate next year's hourly wages expense using the following information about hourly paid workers and the average wage costs in Table U2.1:

- The facility runs three 8-hour shifts, 7 days per week, 52 weeks per year.

  6 a.m. to 2 p.m.

  2 p.m. to 10 p.m.

  10 p.m. to 6 a.m.
- Each shift requires two registered nurses, four licensed practical nurses, and two health-care aid workers.
- At each shift, one of the registered nurses is designated as the charge nurse and is paid a premium of 15% of his or her regular hourly rate.
- The 6 a.m.-to-2 p.m. and 2 p.m.-to-10 p.m. shifts require one custodian; the 10 p.m.-to-6 a.m. shift requires two custodians.
- Each shift requires the services of an on-call physician and an on-call pharmacist. Budget for the physician and the pharmacist at 4 hours per shift.
- Add 14% to each shift's total wage costs to cover the estimated costs of benefits such as vacation pay, holiday pay, and medical care coverage plans for all workers *except* the on-call physician and on-call pharmacist, who do not receive these benefits.

Make use of colors, themes, or table features to make the budget calculations easy to read. Save the workbook and name it **EL2-U2-JS-GardenviewWageBdgt**. Print the worksheet, adjusting print options as necessary to minimize the pages required. Create a chart in a separate sheet to show the total hourly wages budget by worker category. You determine the chart type and chart options to present the information.

Start Word and open the document named **GardenviewOpBdgt.xlsx**. Edit the year on the title page to the current year. Edit the name and date at the bottom of the title page to your name and the current date. Link the chart created in the Excel worksheet to the end of the Word document. Save the revised document as **EL2-U2-JS-GardenviewOpBdgt**. Print and then close **EL2-U2-JS-GardenviewOpBdgt.docx**. Deselect the chart and close **EL2-U2-JS-GardenviewWageBdgt.xlsx**.

Table U2.1 Average Hourly Wage Rates

Wage Category	*Average Wage Rate*
Registered nurse	29.35
Licensed practical nurse	18.45
Health-care aid worker	13.91
Custodian	10.85
On-call physician	65.00
On-call pharmacist	47.00

D

E

F

N

O

P

Q

R

S

T

U

V

W

X

Excel 2010 Feature	Ribbon Tab, Group	Button	Shortcut
Accounting number format	Home, Number		
Align text left	Home, Alignment		
Align text right	Home, Alignment		
Bold	Home, Font		Ctrl + B
Borders	Home, Font		
Bottom align	Home, Alignment		
Cell styles	Home, Styles		
Center	Home, Alignment		
Change file type	File, Save & Send		
Clip Art	Insert, Illustrations		
Close workbook	File		Ctrl + F4
Comma style	Home, Number		
Comments	Review, Comments		
Conditional Formatting	Home, Styles		
Consolidate	Data, Consolidate		
Convert Text to Columns	Table Tools Design, Tools		
Copy	Home, Clipboard		Ctrl + C
Custom number format	Home, Number		
Cut	Home, Clipboard		Ctrl + X
Data Table	Data, Data Tools		
Data Validation	Data, Data Tools		

Excel 2010 Feature	Ribbon Tab, Group	Button	Shortcut
Decrease decimal	Home, Number		
Decrease indent	Home, Alignment		Ctrl + Alt + Shift + Tab
Delete cells	Home, Cells		
Document Inspector	File, Info		
Fill color	Home, Editing		
Financial functions	Formulas, Function Library		
Find & Select	Home, Editing		
Font color	Home, Font		
Format Painter	Home, Clipboard		
Goal Seek	Data, Data Tools		
Group and Ungroup	Data, Outline		Shift + Alt + Right Arrow key, Shift + Alt + Left Arrow key
Header & Footer	Insert, Text		
Help			F1
Hyperlink	Insert, Links		Ctrl + K
Import from Access, web page, or text file	Data, Get External Data		
Increase decimal	Home, Number		
Increase indent	Home, Alignment		Ctrl + Shift + Tab
Insert cells	Home, Cells		
Insert Chart dialog box	Insert, Charts		
Insert function dialog box	Formulas, Function Library		
Italic	Home, Font		Ctrl + I

Excel 2010 Feature	Ribbon Tab, Group	Button	Shortcut
Logical functions	Formulas, Function Library		
Lookup & Reference functions	Formulas, Function Library		
Macros	View, Macros		Alt + F8
Mark workbook as final	File, Info		
Math & Trigonometry functions	Formulas, Function Library		
Merge & Center	Home, Alignment		
Middle align	Home, Alignment		
Name Manager dialog box	Formulas, Defined Names		
New workbook	File, New		Ctrl + N
Number format	Home, Number	General	
Open dialog box	File	Open	Ctrl + O
Orientation	Home, Alignment		
Page orientation	Page Layout, Page Setup		
Paste	Home, Clipboard		Ctrl + V
Percent style	Home, Number	%	Ctrl + Shift + %
PivotTable or PivotChart	Insert, Tables or PivotTable Tools Options, Tools		
Print tab Backstage view	File, Print		Ctrl + P
Protect Worksheet	Review, Changes		
Remove Duplicates	Data, Data Tools or Table Tools Design, Tools		
Save or Save As	File	Save As	Ctrl + S, F12
Save as PDF/XPS	File, Save & Send		

Excel 2010 Feature	Ribbon Tab, Group	Button	Shortcut
Scenario Manager	Data, Data Tools		
Screenshot	Insert, Illustrations		
Share workbook	Review, Changes		
SmartArt	Insert, Illustrations		
Sort & Filter	Home, Editing		
Sparklines	Insert, Sparklines		
Spelling	Review, Proofing		
Statistical functions	Formulas, Function Library		
Subtotals	Data, Outline		
Sum	Home, Editing	Σ	Alt + =
Symbol dialog box	Insert, Symbols	Ω	
Text box	Insert, Text		
Text functions	Formulas, Function Library		
Themes	Page Layout, Themes		
Top align	Home, Alignment		
Trace Dependents or Trace Precedents	Formulas, Auditing		
Track Changes	Review, Changes		
Underline	Home, Font	U	Ctrl + U
Unlock cells	Home, Cells		
Wrap text	Home, Alignment		